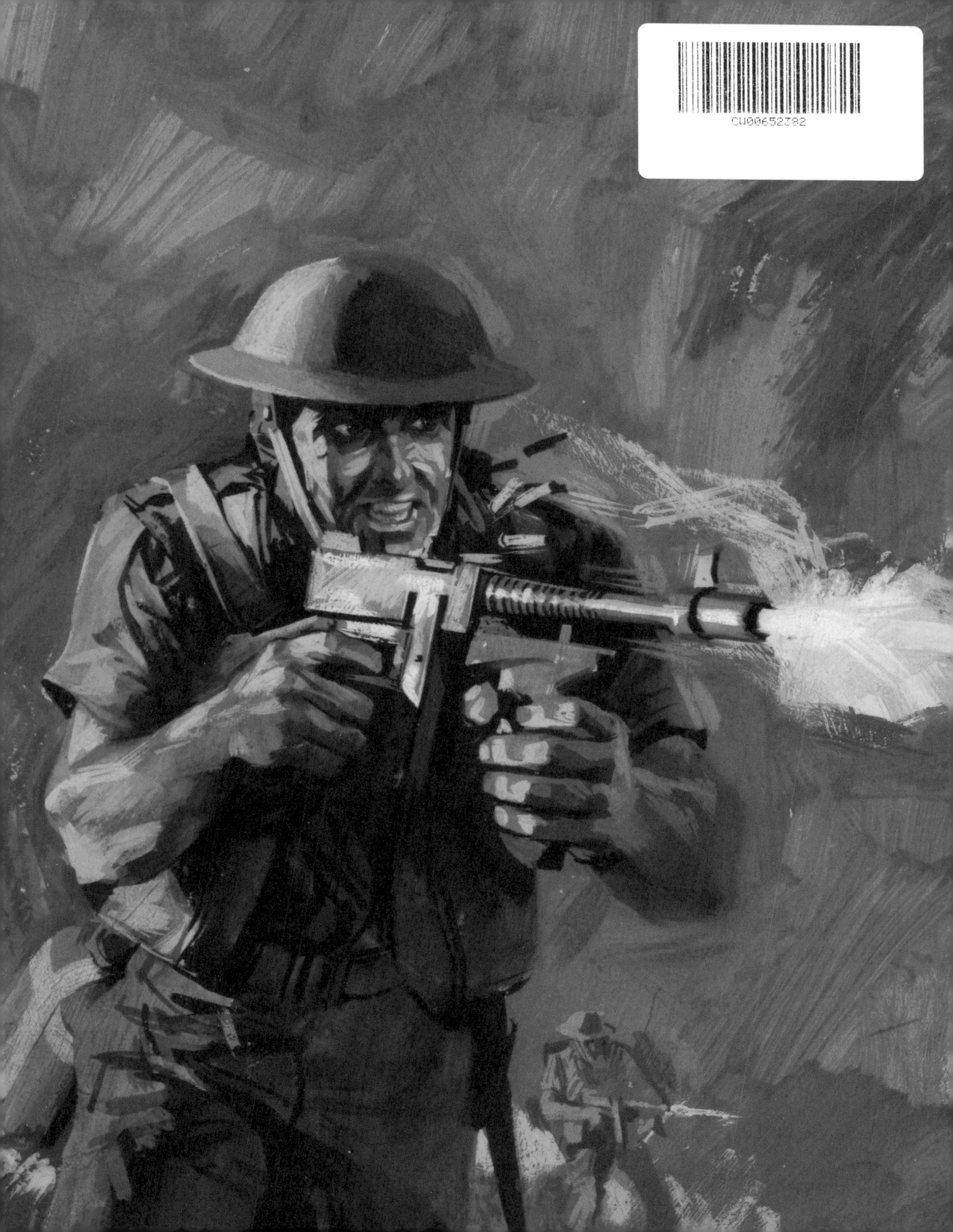

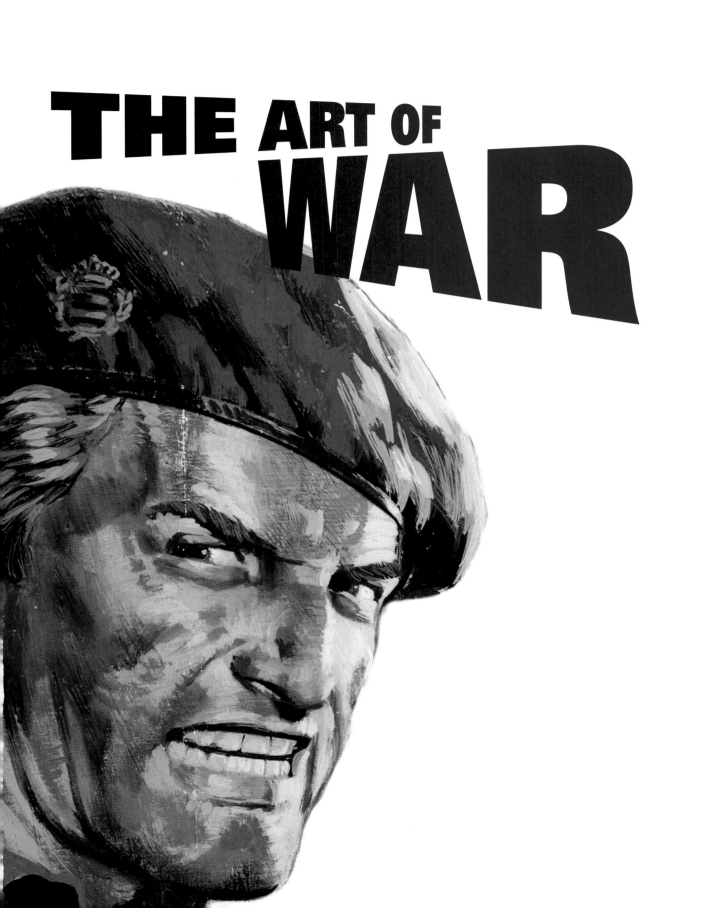

THE ART OF WAR

THIS IS A PRION BOOK

First published in Great Britain in 2008 by Prion
An imprint of the Carlton Publishing Group
20 Mortimer Street
London W1T 3JW

Introductions, text and book layout design © Carlton Books 2008.
Artworks © IPC Media 2008.

Published under licence from DC Comics.

Editorial Manager: Rod Green

Art Director: Lucy Coley
Design: Paul Heidenreich / Simon Mercer

Production: Claire Hayward

Scanning by Max Communications

Printed in Dubai

ISBN: 978-1-85375-662-7

ACKNOWLEDGEMENTS

The publishers would like to thank the team at
IPC Media Ltd and DC Comics for all their help
in compiling this book, particularly David Abbott
and Linda Lee.

David Roach would like to thank Paul
Heidenreich Steve Holland, Alberto Beccatini,
Oystein Sorensen, Oliver Frey, Jeff Slater, Richard
Parry, Roger Berry, Phil Clarke, Gino D'Achille,
Geoff West, David Abbott, Rod Green and Emily
and Isobel for constant inspiration. A very special
thanks to Peter Hansen for the loan of originals,
without which this book would not have been
possible

JAMES MAY

James May is a journalist and TV presenter who has dealt with subjects as
diverse as wine and the importance of the fibre-optic cable via motoring and
his regular appearances on *Top Gear*. He bought his first war comic – *Seek
and Strike* – for a shilling in 1968 from Chatwins Newsagents in Caerleon,
South Wales. He still has a collection of around 500 war comics close to his
downstairs lavatory, and 'came out' about them in his 2005 documentary
James May's Top Toys.

DAVID A. ROACH

David A. Roach is an artist, illustrator, writer and historian with
20 years experience in the comics industry. Among the comics he has
worked on are such iconic strips as *Batman*, *Judge Dredd*, *Dr Who*,
Star Wars and *Aliens*. As an author he is an editor and writer for
such books as *True Brit: The History of British Comics* and
The Super Hero Book, as well as the forthcoming
Fleetway Companion series and *Girls of the Comics*.
He is a regular writer for *Comic Book Artist* and
Comics International magazines.

THE ART OF WAR

DAVID ROACH

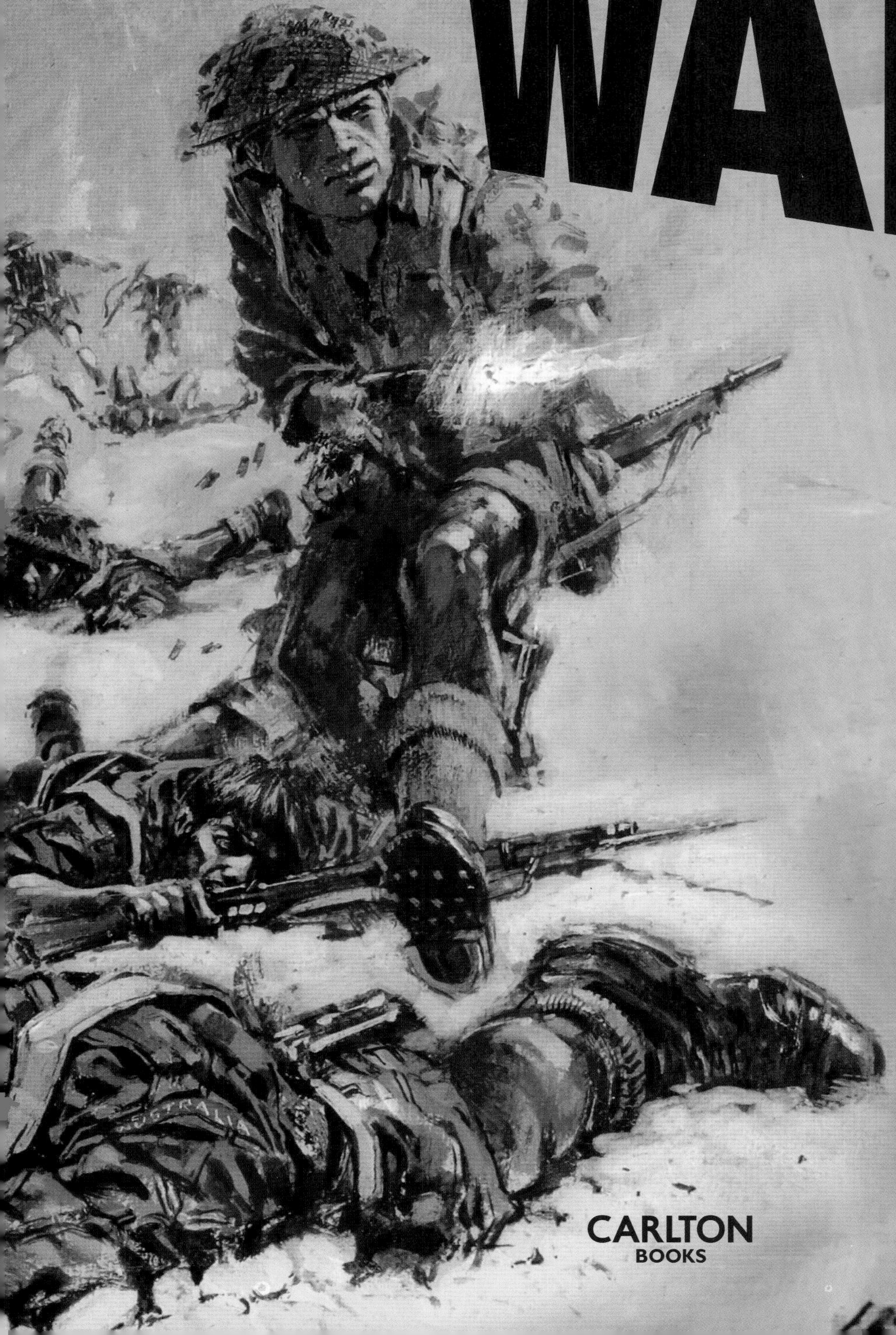

CARLTON
BOOKS

CONTENTS

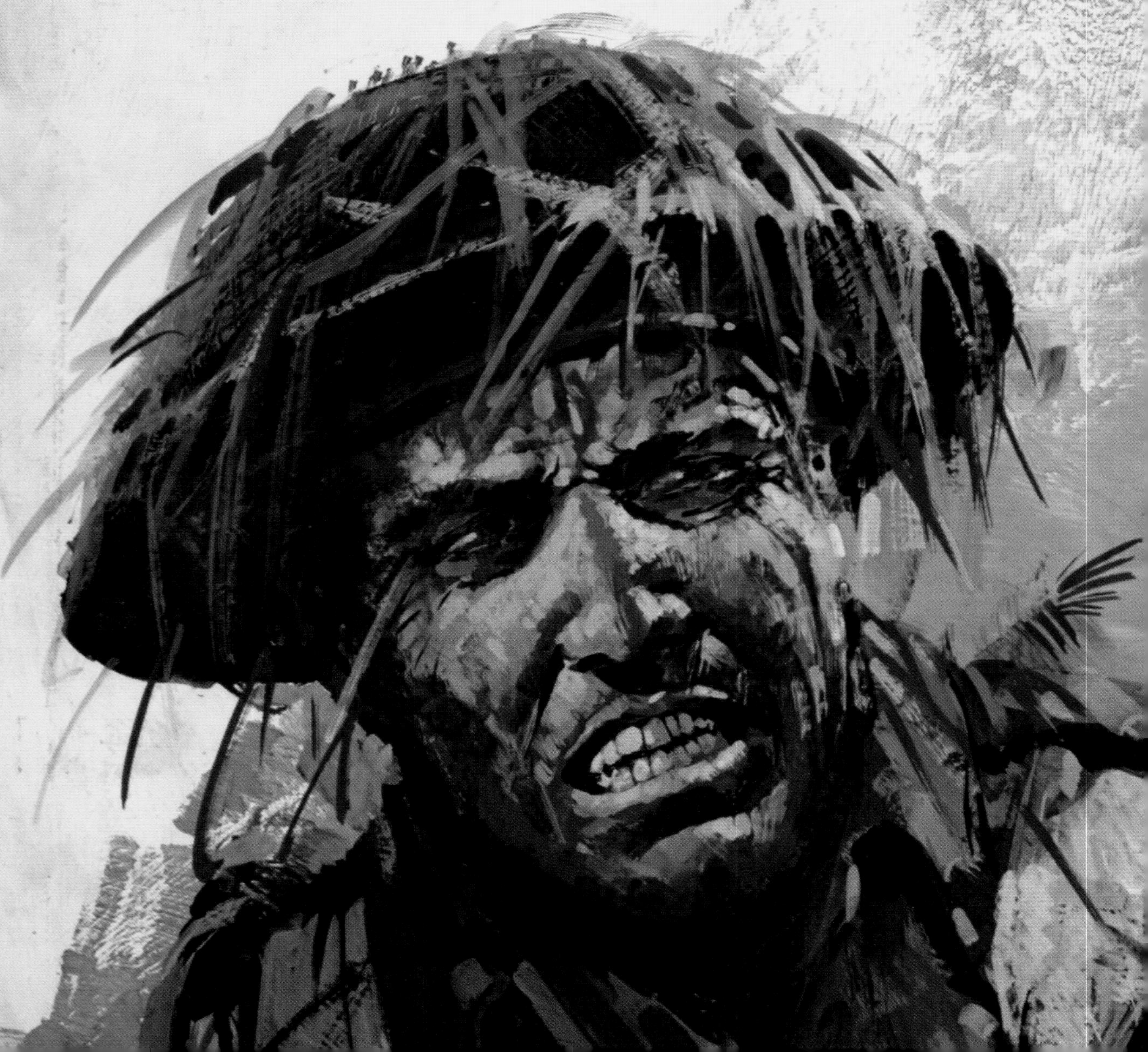

FOREWORD!

Since writing the introduction to *Aarrgghh!! It's War*, Prion's first collection of war-comic art, my life has plateaued. I am now the proud and lumpy-throated owner of an original, the cover artwork for *Wings of the Fleet*. Himmel!

For those of a list-making persuasion, it's No 157 from the *Air Ace Picture Library*, first published in 1963 (the year of my birth) and the work of Pino Dell'Orco, a war-comic great. During my youth, he helped to relieve me of quite a lot of my meagre pocket money.

I've had it mounted in an overtly ornate gold frame, as befitting a national treasure, and glazed on the back as well, so that the scribblings of editors and printers are still visible. On the front, too, the strips of peeling masking tape that were used to crop the picture before transfer to the printing plate have been left untouched, as a reminder to the onlooker that this old master was actually nothing more than a piece of consumable illustration.

I've spent hours looking at this thing. It shows a Fairey Swordfish on the final run-in to an attack on enemy shipping. The torpedo has just been released, livid tracers and bursts of flak surround the trusty old 'Stringbag', and the shadowy outline of a doomed cruiser can be glimpsed through a fog of battle rendered in broad strokes of orange paint. As usual, the aircraft has

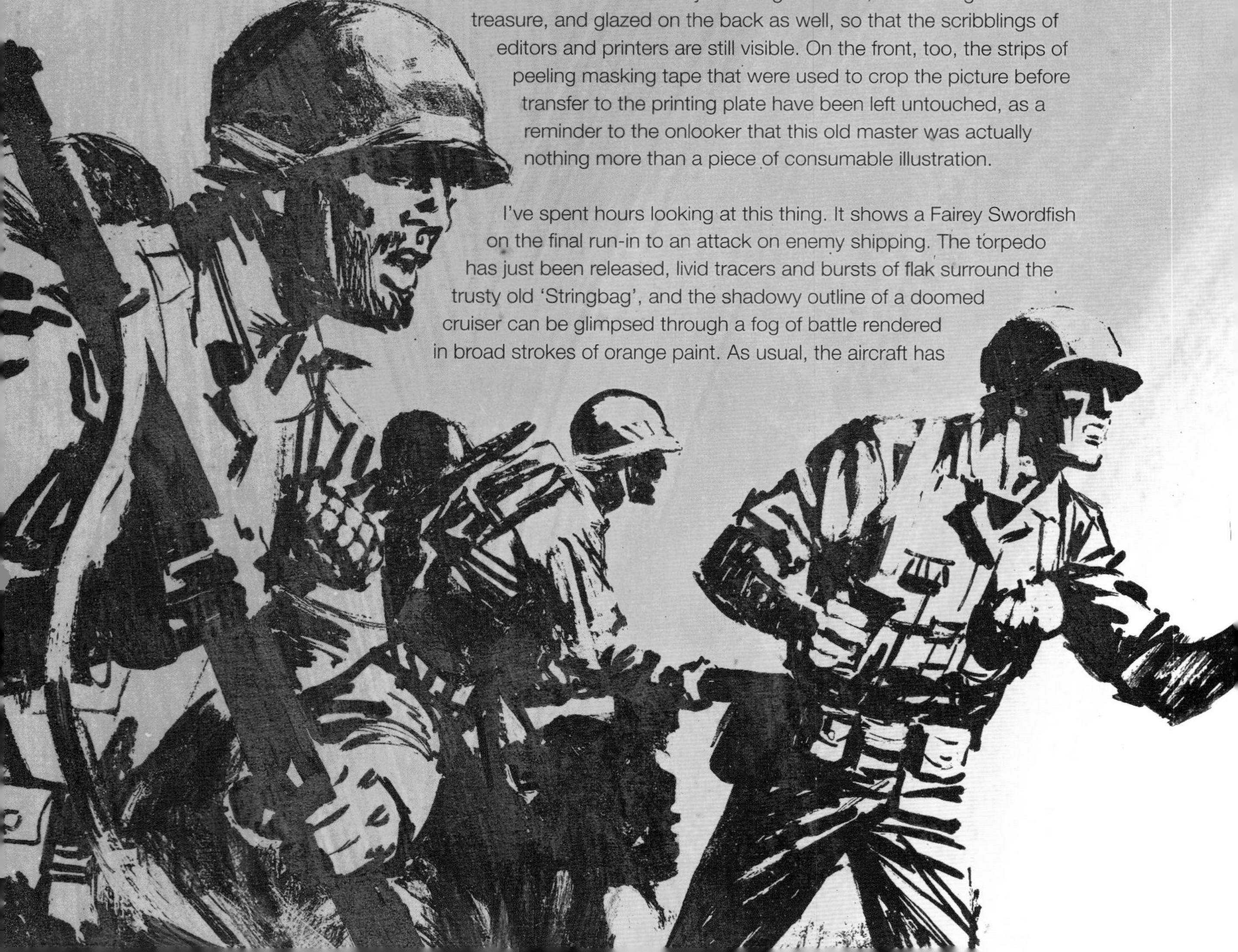

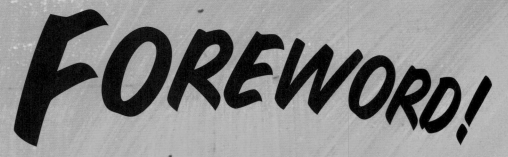

been depicted with a draughtsman's attention to accurate proportions and correct detailing. We wouldn't have tolerated anything less.

The grim-faced rear gunner blazes away at something off to the left of the frame. Although I can see only a part of the back of the pilot's head, I can sense his steely-eyed determination to hold her steady, to see the job through, to save the day and rid the world of tyranny. As regular readers, we pretty much knew that this was how the story would pan out, but that didn't put us off one bit. And just to make sure we knew what we were in for, the artist skillfully embodied the comic's robust themes in his picture. Dell'Orco was an artist, but was also a brilliant salesman.

That will be why, some time in 1984 when *Wings of the Fleet* was reprinted, I reached into my pocket for the money to buy it. Curiously, that reprint marked the demise of the *War Picture Library* after a run of 2103 issues.

This is the other thing that strikes me when I look at my prized original: the sheer industry of the war comics business. At one time IPC alone printed around 20 stories a month, and if we add to that the output of rivals Commando and the countless pretenders to the war-comic crown long since forgotten, it becomes apparent that works like mine were being produced at the staggering rate of more than one every working day.

I don't suppose Dell'Orco imagined, as he splashed out the angry red heart of another shellburst, that his daily grind would one day hang on the wall of a slightly nostalgic, middle-aged bloke. But he shouldn't have been surprised. Mere illustration it may have been, but it had artistry in it, and artistry endures.

So here's some more of the same. Crikey, Sarge – there's hundreds of 'em!

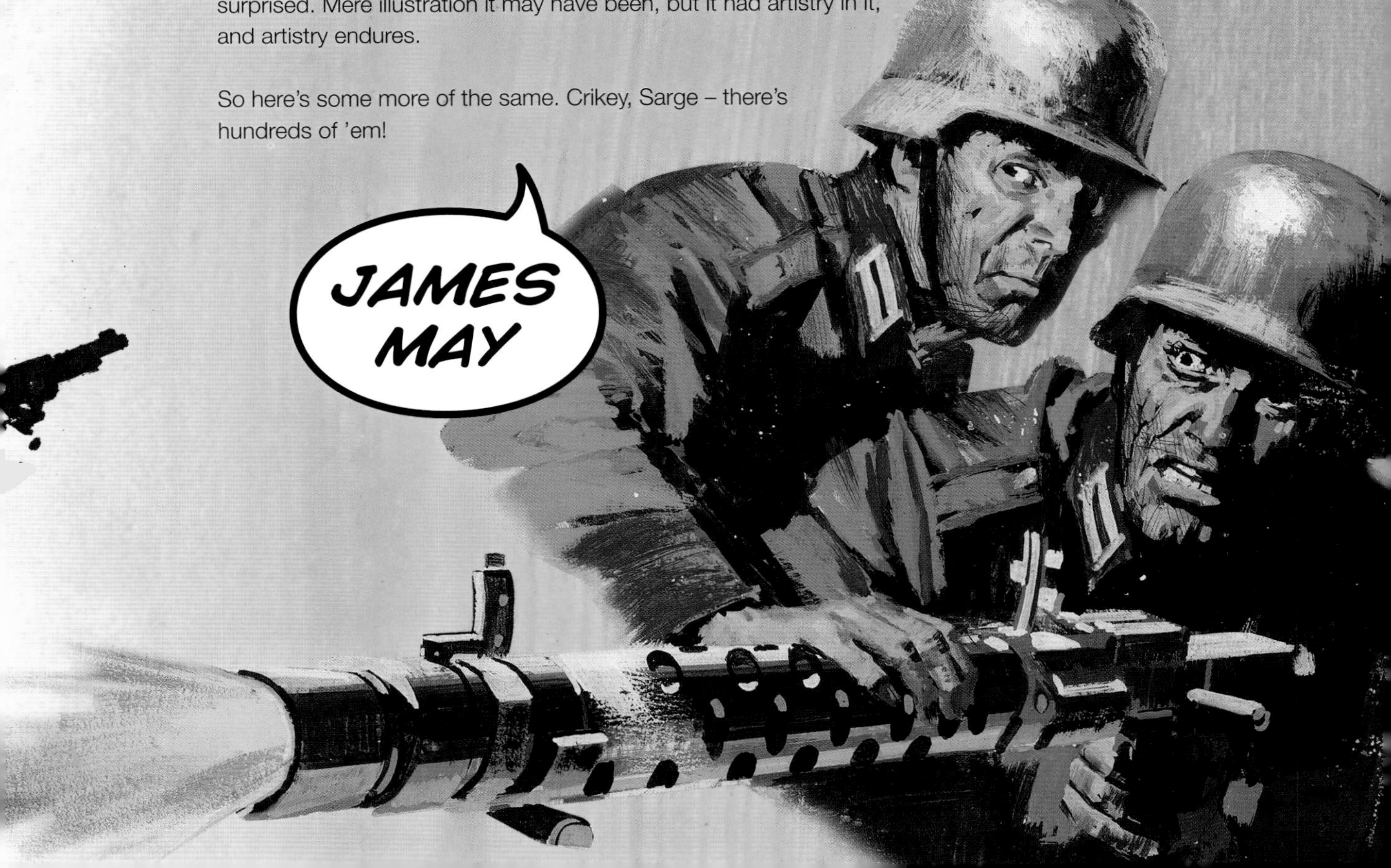
JAMES MAY

INTRODUCTION

When the first issue of the Amalgamated Press' *War Picture Library* appeared in September 1958, nobody could have predicted that decades later people would still be reading, collecting and buying coffee table art books devoted to this publishing phenomenon. Now, on the 50th anniversary of that momentous occasion, here is a second collection of the finest covers from *War*, its companion titles *Air Ace* and *Battle* as well as choice covers from *Thriller* and *Super Detective Library* amongst others. It is remarkable to think that what started life as just another of Amalgamated's line of small pocket-sized *Picture Library* comics would run for over 25 years, spawn several companion titles as well as a host of imitators, enjoy reprint editions all over Europe and inspire hordes of devoted collectors, but that is precisely what happened.

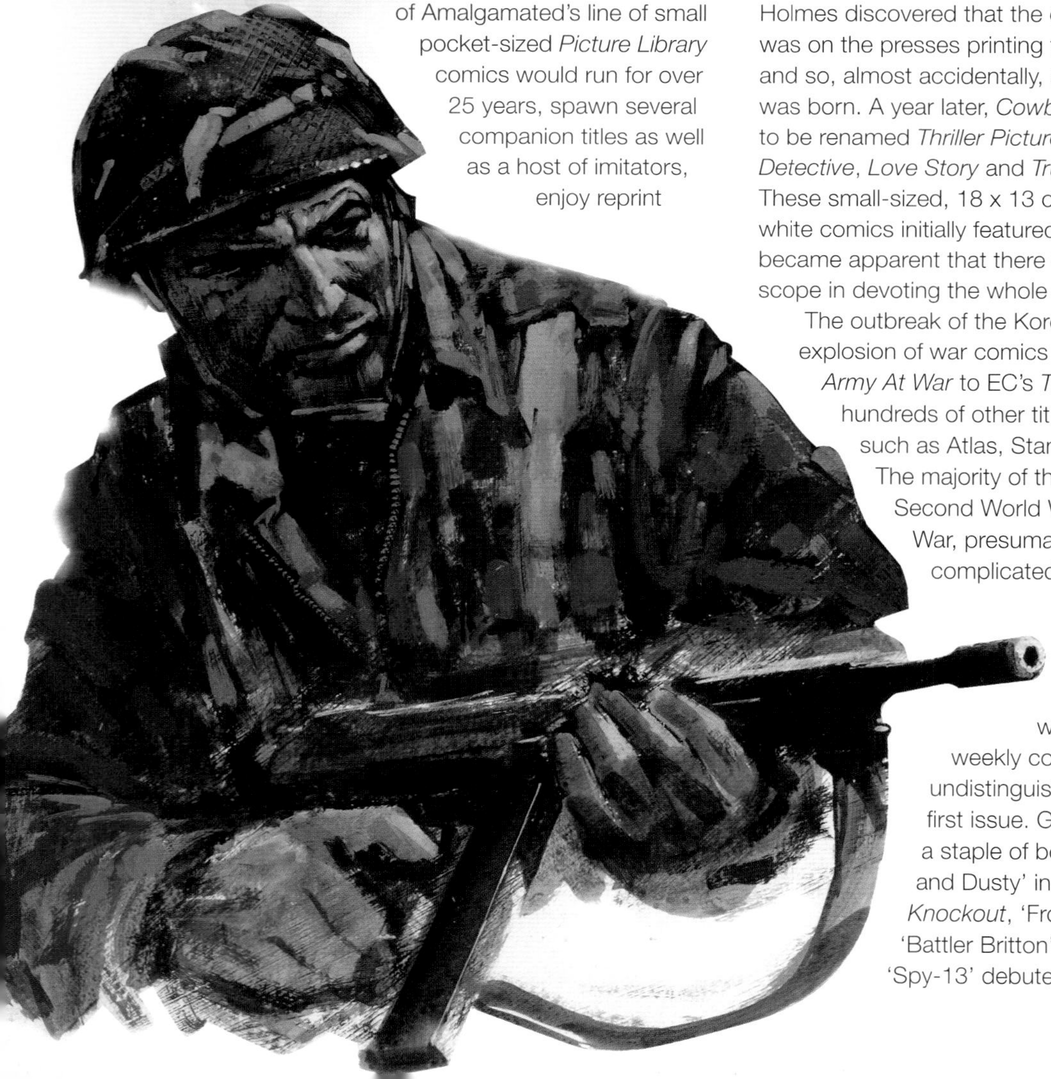

War Picture Library itself could trace its origins back to 1950 when Amalgamated Press Editor, Ted Holmes, noted the success of a line of comics the company had been packaging for Australia. The Australian *Cowboy Comics*, entirely written and drawn in the UK by British creators, were about the size of most American comics and slightly smaller than newsstand favourites like *The Beano* or *Knockout*. More *Cowboy* material was obviously required to meet demand but space at the printers was at a premium. Holmes discovered that the only spare capacity available was on the presses printing the small *Sexton Blake Library* and so, almost accidentally, a whole new comics format was born. A year later, *Cowboy* was joined by *Thriller* (later to be renamed *Thriller Picture Library*) and in time *Super Detective*, *Love Story* and *True Life* were added to the line. These small-sized, 18 x 13 cm (7 x 5 in), 64-page black and white comics initially featured several short strips but it soon became apparent that there was so much more creative scope in devoting the whole comic to one long tale.

The outbreak of the Korean War in 1950 inspired an explosion of war comics in the States from DC's *Our Army At War* to EC's *Two Fisted Tales* and literally hundreds of other titles from publishing houses such as Atlas, Standard, Fawcett and Quality. The majority of these concentrated on the Second World War rather than the Korean War, presumably preferring to explore a less complicated conflict with the guarantee of a victorious ending. Belatedly, Amalgamated realised that the time might be right for a realistically-drawn British war feature and in 1952 the new weekly comic *Lion* included the otherwise undistinguished 'Lone Commandos' in its first issue. Gradually, the war strip became a staple of boys' comics from 'Spike and Dusty' in *Tiger*, 'Johnny Wingco' in *Knockout*, 'Frogmen Are Tough' in *Lion* and 'Battler Britton' in *Sun*. Another war hero, 'Spy-13' debuted in *Thriller* in September 1958, the same month as *War's* first issue, but within a few years the *Thriller*, *Super Detective* and *Cowboy Picture* libraries had all been cancelled as *War* and its stablemates came to dominate the nation's spinner racks.

A strike in August of 1959 temporarily put a halt to all of Amalgamated's comics giving the Head of Juvenile Publications, Leonard Matthews, a chance to take stock of the company. He had become enthralled by the artists from Milan's Creazioni D'Ami studio whom he had recently begun to use in *Thriller* and was keen to employ them across a whole spectrum of comics. From its first issue, *War Picture Library* featured D'Ami studio artists and at Matthews' insistence they were to provide the lion's share of its art for at least the next five years.

Artists such as Ferdinando Tacconi, Nevio Zeccarra, Renzo Calegari and Gino D'Antonio had already appeared in *Thriller* and they were soon joined by Hugo Pratt, Kurt Caesar, Giorgio Trevisan and Renato Polese. Within a couple of years the talent pool had grown to include artists around the globe including creators from Barcelona's S.I. studio (Fernando Fernandez, Aldoma Puig and Jordi Longaron), The Solano Lopez Studio from Argentina (Jorge Moliterni and Solano Lopez himself), The Anglo-Spanish Bardon agency's group of Valencian artists (Jose Ortiz, Luis Bermejo, Alfredo Sanchis Cortes and Juan Gonzalez Alacreu) and Brussels' A.L.I. agency representing yet more Spaniards such as Victor De La Fuente and Jordi Penalva.

Rumours have persisted to this day that these armies of foreign artists were given so much work because they were cheaper than their British counterparts but this was simply not the case. Leonard Matthews had been aware that many of his British artists were somewhat pedestrian and while the best, such as Geoff Campion, Mike Western, Reg Bunn and Joe Colquhon, thrived, many more were simply not up to the job. Foreign Stars such as D'Antonio, Bermejo and Tacconi brought superb drawing and storytelling skills with a genuine sense of drama to their work that was perfect for the war comics. For a generation of British artists still trying to understand the possibilities of the comics medium, their work was a revelation. For a generation of British kids seeing this work for the first time, all they cared about was the fact that these were great comics.

When it came to commissioning covers, Matthews and *War* Editor, Alf Wallace, again turned to the D'Ami studio. In fact, the studio's first British covers had appeared as early as 1956 when Enrico DeSeta took over from Eric Parker to become the principal painter for the *Sexton Blake Library*. In 1958, DeSeta was joined by several other Milan-based artists including Giorgio De Gaspari, who soon moved over to the *Thriller* and *Cowboy* libraries.

De Gaspari was a revelation, an artist who was able to master that elusive combination of a wonderfully accomplished painting ability with a dynamic, exciting drawing style. His covers were at once believably realistic and truly exciting, full of explosions, straining muscles, gritted teeth and frenzied emotions. In *War's* first year of publication, De Gaspari painted 19 of the comic's 25

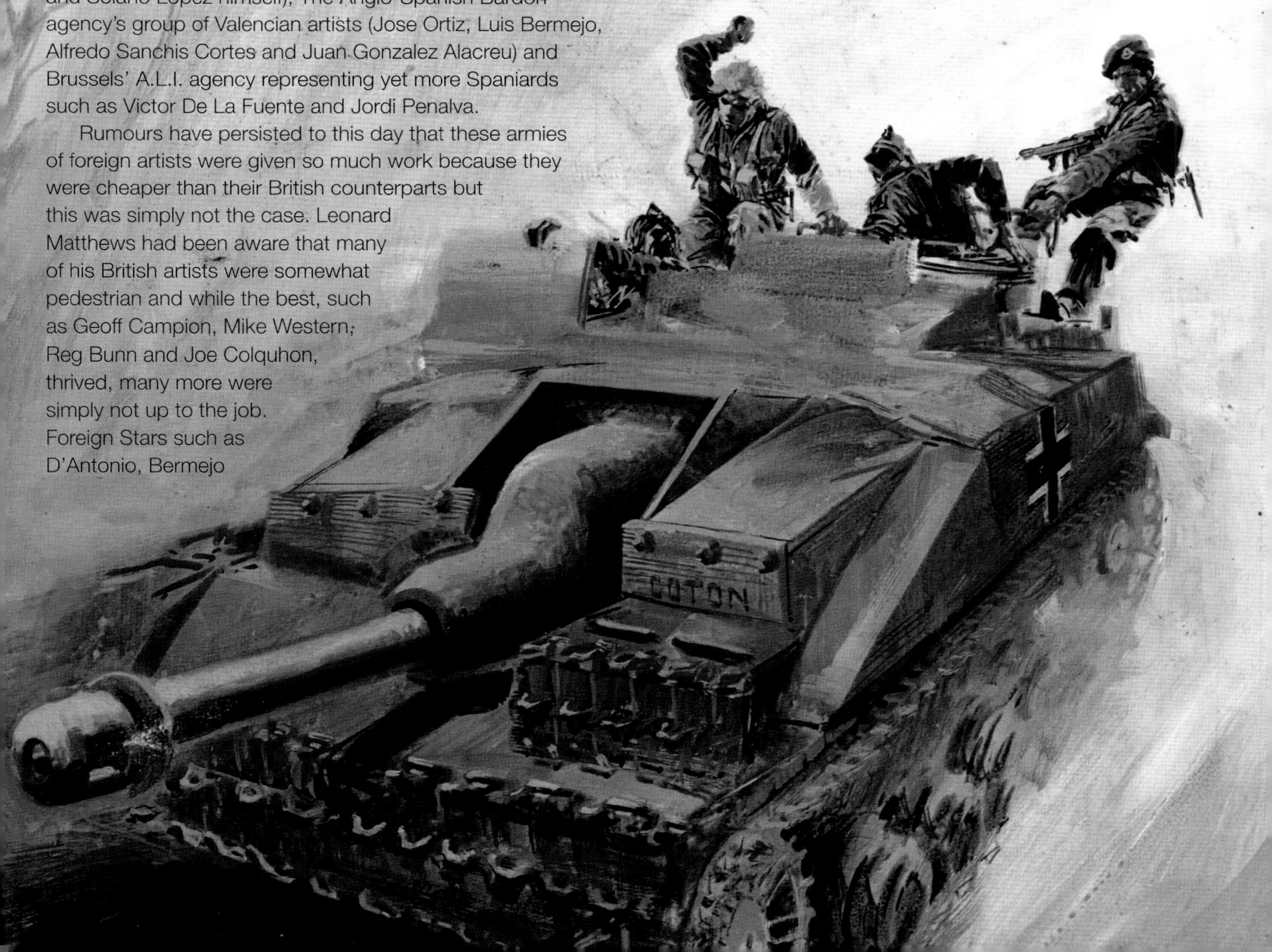
COTON

covers (with the venerable Septimus Scott providing most of the others). In 1960, however, the newly re-named Fleetway Publications (which it turn became IPC in 1969) launched a companion title called *Air Ace*, quickly followed by *Battle* and *War At Sea*, a line-up that was simply too much for one artist. To cope with this vast increase in demand, three more D'Ami studio artists were drafted in, beginning with Giovanni 'Nino' Caroselli. Like De Gaspari, Caroselli had appeared earlier in *Thriller* and *Sexton Blake* and would go on to paint almost 200 covers for the various war comics. While not as polished as DeGaspari, Caroseli certainly had it in him to come up with the occasional arresting cover design, and was a highly accomplished painter of aircraft, as evidenced by his stunning cover for *Air Ace* issue one. The third Italian painter to appear was Alessandro Biffignandi whose first British cover was published in early 1960 on *Air Ace* number four. Whereas Caroseli employed a somewhat restrained, almost pastel palette, Biffignandi's illustrations were vibrantly colourful and at times almost garish. Biffignandi would go on to paint over 400 war covers throughout the sixties, making him by far the most prolific foreign painter. While his early pictures were beautifully rendered and slick, very much in the De Gaspari style, he gradually developed a more individualistic approach. By the mid-sixties he had adopted a highly distinctive 'pointiliste' approach where his illustrations appeared to be built up from hundreds of tiny brush strokes, decorating scenes inspired by interior panels that were often drawn by his friend Gino D'Antonio.

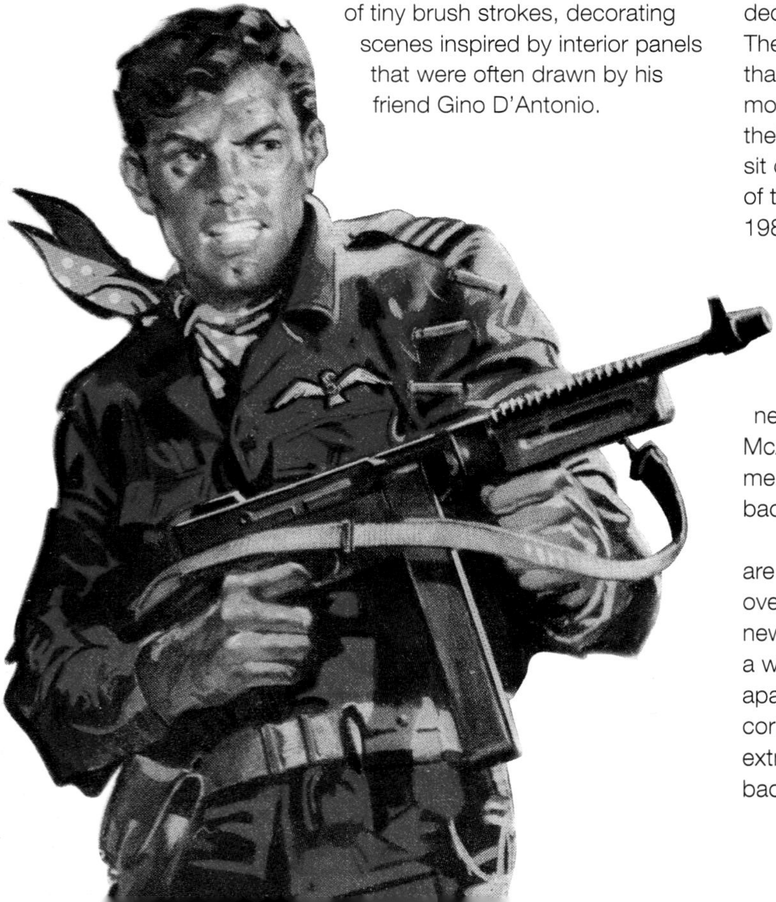

The last great Italian cover artist to appear in print was Pino Dell'Orco, another regular painter for *Thriller,* whose first war cover appeared on *Air Ace* 31. Dell'Orco had been an apprentice to Enrico De Seta in Rome and like Biffignandi and Caroselli had spent the 1950s working in the studio of Augusto Favalli, which produced countless movie posters for the Italian film industry. He would go on to paint over 300 covers for Fleetway, utilising several distinctive styles but always revealing a sure and wildly imaginative grasp of colour. While his fellow studio members created slick, beautifully rendered paintings, Dell'Orco was less concerned with polish, preferring to concentrate on the cover's design qualities and gut impact. His *Air Ace* covers in particular are a triumph of composition, all overlapping contrasting shapes, tones and colours. Stylistically he favoured broad, gestural washes of colour decorated with quick jabs of pencil or charcoal for detail. His more representational *War* and *Battle* covers usually featured large figures or machinery painted in vigorous, jabbing strokes and he would occasionally fill the entire illustration with just a simple close-up of a face. Ever the innovator, some later covers appeared to be bleached out black and white photos superimposed on a monotone background, but on closer inspection were found actually to be fully painted.

Dell'Orco would appear to have moved to the UK within a year of his first covers seeing print and for the rest of the decade he was represented by the Bryan Colmer agency. The remaining Italians stayed in Milan and, while it is known that DeGaspari occasionally flew over to London, for the most part their assignments were picked up by the head of their agency, Rinaldo 'Roy' D'Ami. Typically, D'Ami would sit down with Alf Wallace, Ted Bensberg (managing editor of the *Picture Library* line from 1961 until its dissolution in 1985), and other members of staff to plan out cover designs. An artist himself, D'Ami could quite easily sketch out cover concepts on the spot and send them back to Italy where his artists would paint them up. On some occasions, when the illustrations were delivered back to London it was felt that some alterations needed to be made, which is where art 'bodgers' like Roy McAdorey would come in. He would handle anything from merely changing the insignia on a badge to adding extra background figures or even redesigning the entire illustration.

Collectors seeing the original artwork for the first time are often shocked to see the covers plastered with paper overlays or completely cut up and re-pasted to make a new design altogether. Many early *Air Ace* covers featured a white border and this often entailed cutting the artwork apart and repositioning a figure or face in one of the bottom corners. For *Battle* the alterations could be even more extreme as many covers were printed with entirely white backgrounds. This might involve cutting out the principal

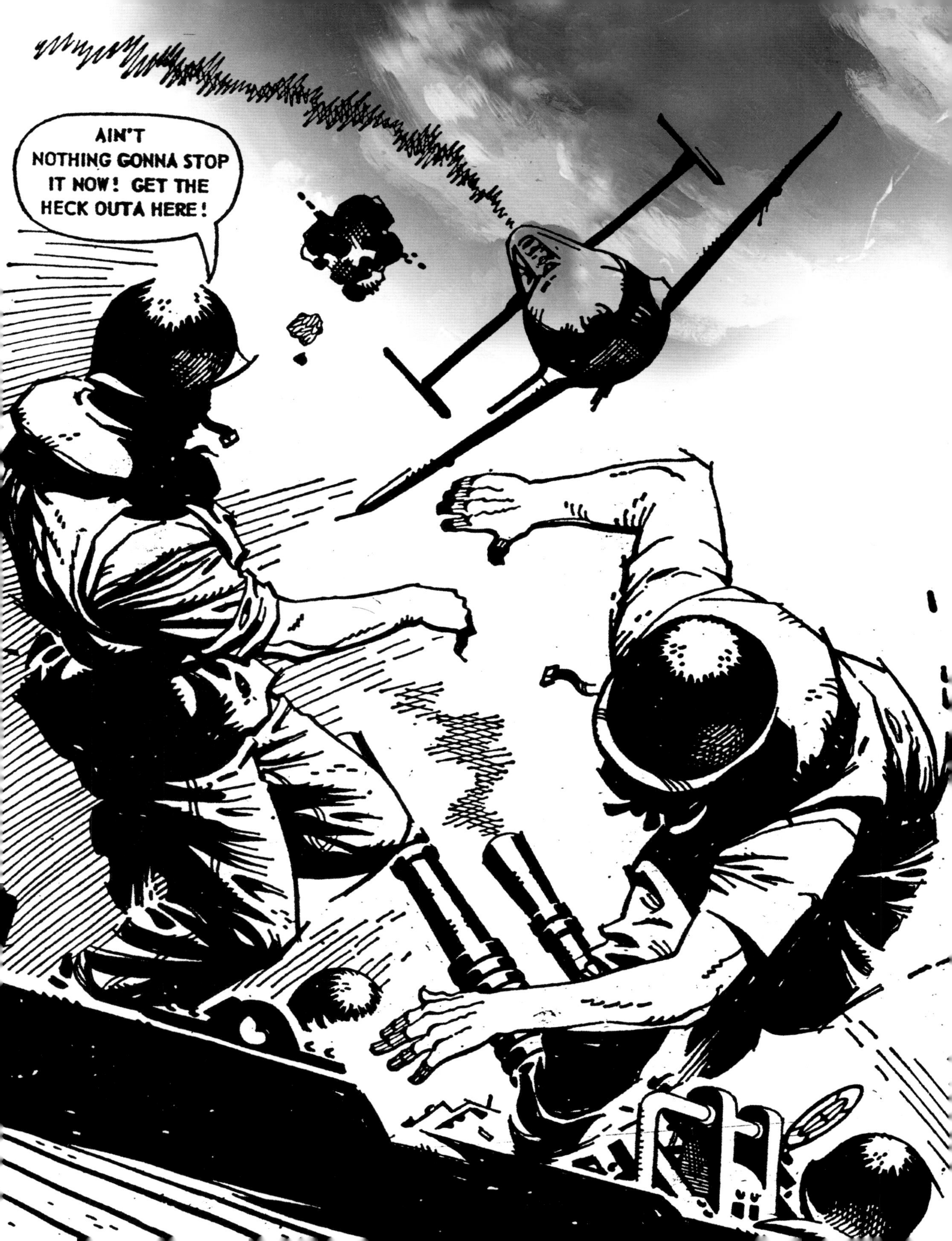
AIN'T NOTHING GONNA STOP IT NOW! GET THE HECK OUTA HERE!

figures and pasting them down on another board, consigning whatever background might have originally been painted to the bin. Biffignandi in particular would seem to have suffered at the hands of the production department and some of his butchered originals are quite heartbreakingly sliced and pasted. However, the sight of boldly painted soldiers superimposed on swastikas of dripping blood, swirling green vortexes or even pasted onto a real map certainly made a strong impression on the young comic fans of the day, so to some extent the ends justified the means.

It is surprising to realise quite how young these artists were. Even the great DeGaspari was only 31 when he painted the cover to *War* #1, while Biffignandi made his UK debut at 25. In retrospect, it would seem the Italian painters were enticed over to the British Market by both a strong exchange rate and the decline of the Italian cinema industry. While poster commissions were becoming ever harder to find, Fleetway was offering a seemingly limitless supply of commissions at a high page rate.

Despite being the company's highest-paid cover artist (at 30 guineas a cover, five guineas more than his nearest rival), DeGaspari moved out of comics entirely after 1962, finding lucrative illustration work from clients such as Readers Digest. Similarly, by the mid-sixties, Caroseli would appear to have largely abandoned comics as well, apparently finding success as a fine artist. Dell'Orco was the principal cover artist for *Air Ace* for a number of years and appeared sporadically throughout that title's run until its demise. Even while painting his earliest comic covers, he is known to have illustrated books and in the seventies he joined the London-based Artists Partners agency, leaving the comics industry behind.

As the Italians left, their places were filled primarily by Spanish artists led by Jordi Penalva, who had previously been the main cover artist for *Cowboy Picture Library*. Penalva combined a wonderful, gritty sense of the dramatic with a textural, highly accomplished painting ability. He was joined by several artists from Barcelona's S.I. agency, including Fernando Fernandez and Jordi Longaron, who had both served their apprenticeships on romance comics such as *Valentine* and *Marilyn*.

In many ways, the mid-sixties were a golden age for the picture libraries. Not only did they feature new painters such as Antonio Bernal, Carlo Jacono, Rafael Cortiella, Manuel Sanjulian and Jose Luis Macias, the cream of the world's strip artists and memorable stories from the best British writers, but the line itself began to expand. In 1963 the company brought out the chunky *War Holiday Special* repackaging four old strips for reading on holiday, which is where many fans, your author included, first discovered the war comics. *Battle Holiday Special* followed in 1964 as did *Air Ace* a few years later. *Giant War* debuted in 1964 and the *Super Library* series appeared in 1967.

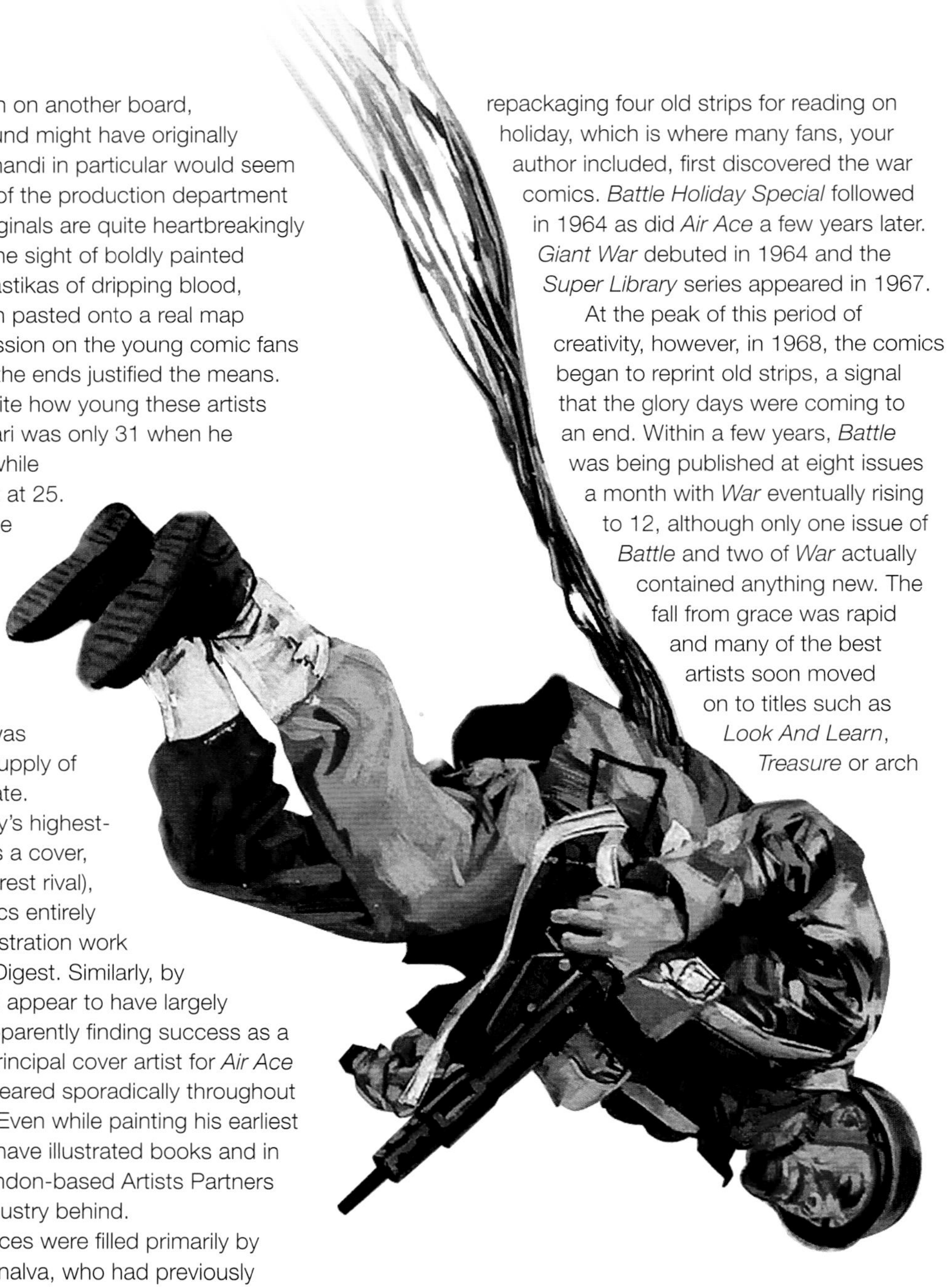

At the peak of this period of creativity, however, in 1968, the comics began to reprint old strips, a signal that the glory days were coming to an end. Within a few years, *Battle* was being published at eight issues a month with *War* eventually rising to 12, although only one issue of *Battle* and two of *War* actually contained anything new. The fall from grace was rapid and many of the best artists soon moved on to titles such as *Look And Learn*, *Treasure* or arch rival *Commando*, the longest-lasting of *War's* many clones. Some were even lured back to the resurgent Italian comics industry. It had also long been believed in the comics business that no reader stuck with any comic for more than seven years before outgrowing it and moving on to something new. Consequently, the companies felt they could regularly recycle the same few strips, safe in the knowledge that their original readers had long gone.

Perhaps nothing personified the decline of the war comics more than the departure of Allessandro Biffignandi. A stalwart of the line from almost its very beginning, he painted his last cover in 1969. It would seem that, having created over 400 covers, he was thoroughly sick of the war and was desperate for a change of direction. He certainly found it when Gino D'Antonio introduced him to the Italian publisher Renzo Barbieri who ran Edifumetto. He specialised in pocket-sized sexy horror comics. For the next decade Biffignandi created a mountain of covers for such titles as *Zora*, *Biancaneve* (a very adult *Snow White*), *Wallestein* and *Sukia*. These beautifully painted illustrations, invariably combining scantily dressed girls with grotesque scenes of horror, inspired a sizeable cult following who developed into avid collectors. In the 1980s, Biffignandi turned to romance book covers and became an enormous success there, too, emphasizing how lucky Fleetway was to have enjoyed his services for so long.

In 1970 the unthinkable happened when *Air Ace* was cancelled after issue 545 and, while the decade might have been a time of enormous output, little of it was actually new. The three new strips each month were occasionally well drawn but more often than not featured rather uninspiring fare from minor Spanish or Argentinian artisans. From the moment the reprint program commenced, the original covers were reprinted as well and quite a few old masters were hacked about even further to accommodate a new logo or cover design. The high points of these latter years were undoubtedly the energetic work of Oliver Frey, who drew many new strips and covers, and the prolific Graham Coton, whose prodigious cover output dwarfed even Biffignandi's.

In December 1984 IPC effectively closed down their entire *Picture Library* department, cancelling *Battle* with issue 1706 and *War*, which had lasted an extraordinary 2103 issues.

But that was not entirely the end of the story. A year later an ex-IPC editor by the name of Ron Phillips started reprinting these comics all over again. The series ran to almost 700 issues, lasting until 1992.

Across Europe various countries such as Italy, France and Norway had long translated these strips and these, too, often lasted well into the nineties.

In recent years, collectors here and abroad have begun to reassess the great comics of their childhoods and a new appreciation of just how terrific these publications really were has begun to grow. Volumes such as this and its predecessor, *AARRGGHH!! It's War*, along with Prion's other collections of vintage war strips, can only add to that ever-expanding fan base.

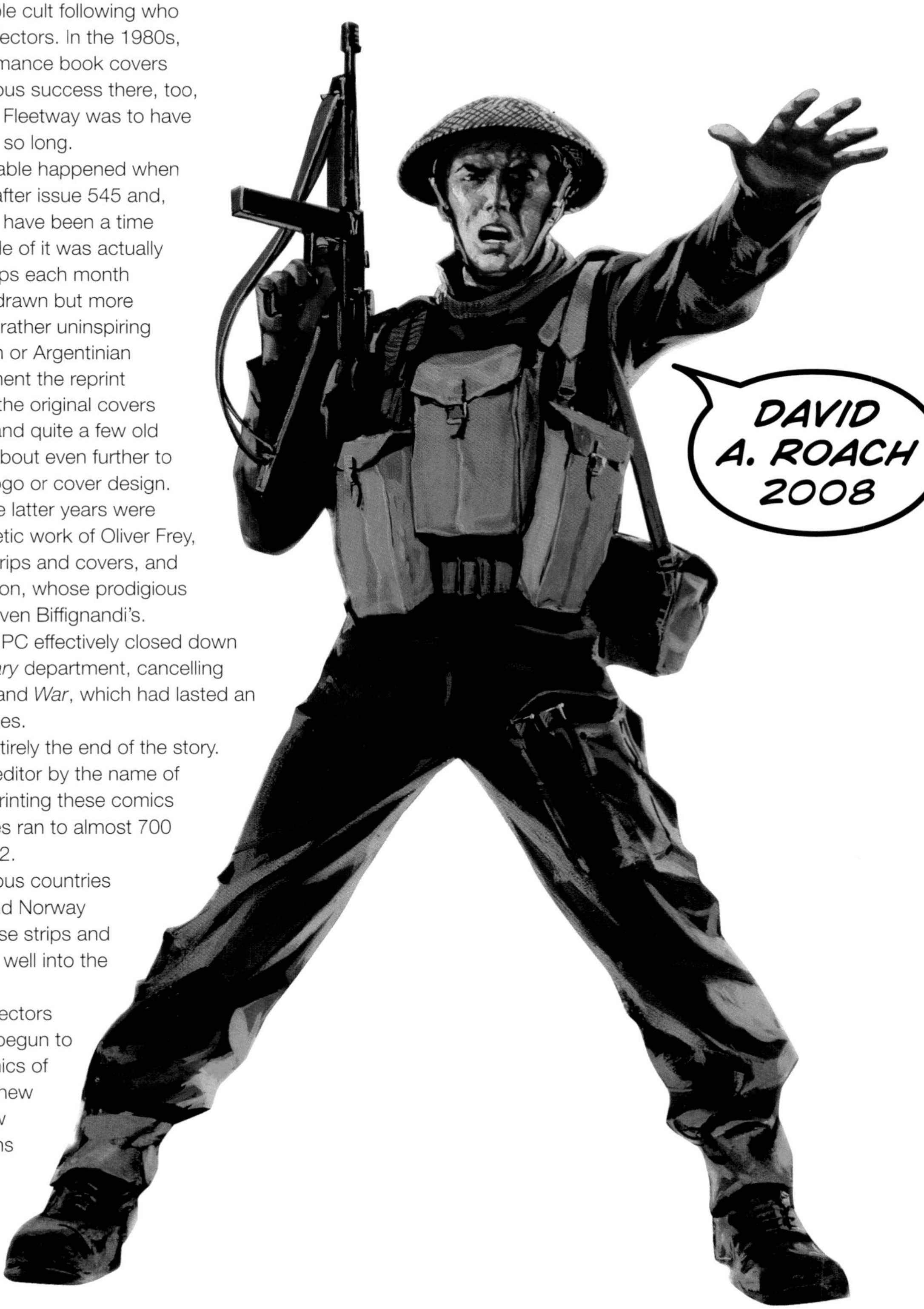
DAVID A. ROACH 2008

CHAPTER 1

ALLIED FORCES

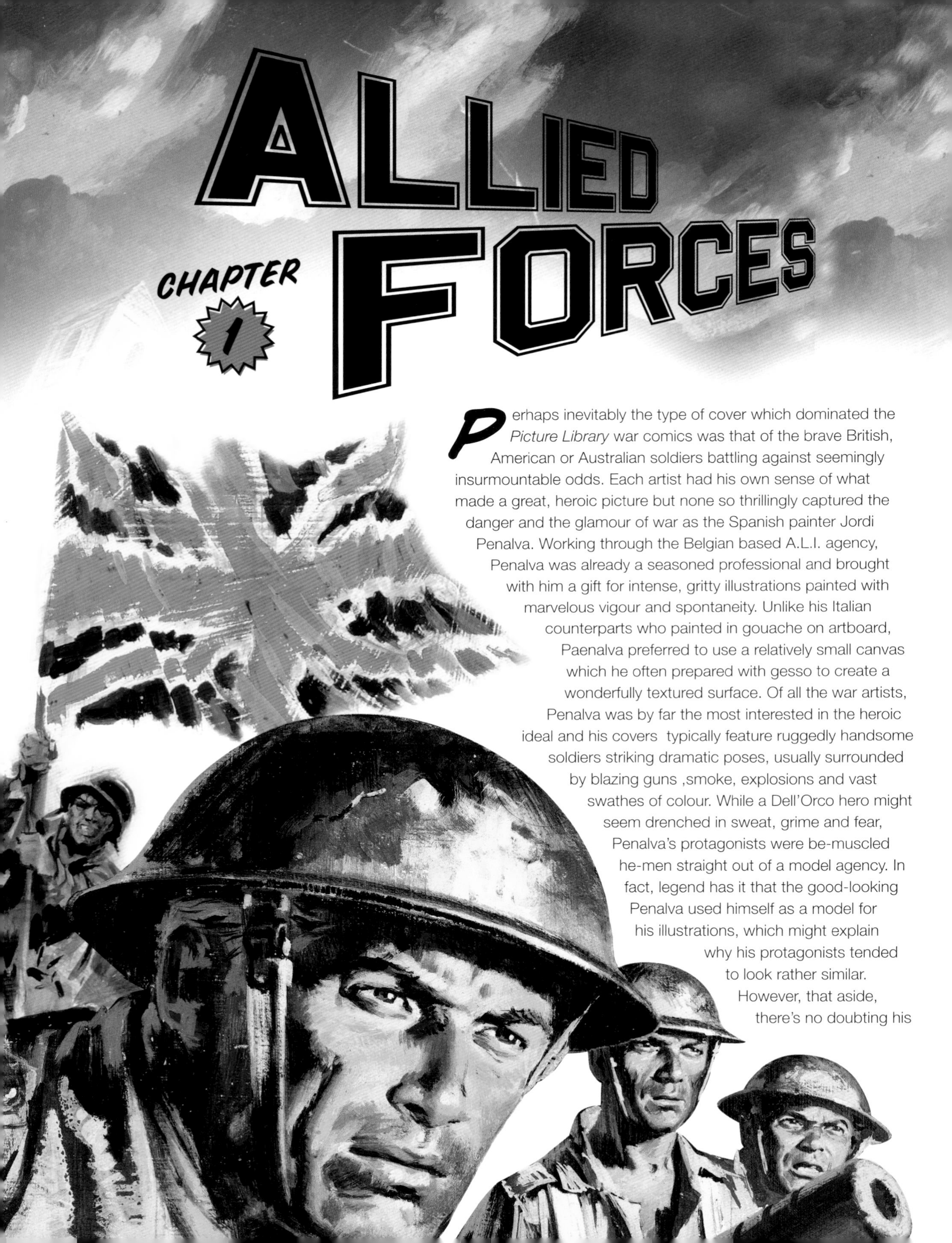

Perhaps inevitably the type of cover which dominated the *Picture Library* war comics was that of the brave British, American or Australian soldiers battling against seemingly insurmountable odds. Each artist had his own sense of what made a great, heroic picture but none so thrillingly captured the danger and the glamour of war as the Spanish painter Jordi Penalva. Working through the Belgian based A.L.I. agency, Penalva was already a seasoned professional and brought with him a gift for intense, gritty illustrations painted with marvelous vigour and spontaneity. Unlike his Italian counterparts who painted in gouache on artboard, Paenalva preferred to use a relatively small canvas which he often prepared with gesso to create a wonderfully textured surface. Of all the war artists, Penalva was by far the most interested in the heroic ideal and his covers typically feature ruggedly handsome soldiers striking dramatic poses, usually surrounded by blazing guns ,smoke, explosions and vast swathes of colour. While a Dell'Orco hero might seem drenched in sweat, grime and fear, Penalva's protagonists were be-muscled he-men straight out of a model agency. In fact, legend has it that the good-looking Penalva used himself as a model for his illustrations, which might explain why his protagonists tended to look rather similar. However, that aside, there's no doubting his considerable talent and many of the war libraries most striking and memorable covers sprang from his brush.

For sheer painting ability, probably only De Gaspari came close to matching him and when it came to visceral excitement he was without rivals. Take a cover like War 326 (on page 58) for instance ; here Penalva shows us a pair of ruggedly handsome Tommies emerging from an unidentified setting suffused with crimson smoke, literally parting the curtains symbolically to reveal an oncoming Nazi search party. The Brits appear to tower over the Germans and are armed with an axe-bladed pike and a vicious-looking mace. War was nothing like this, of course, but what the young readers of these comics were ultimately looking for was a ripping yarn, a vicarious thrill with the patina of truth but without the full horror of the reality of war. Many of the comics' best writers such as Norman Worker, Carney Allen, David Satherley and Bill Spence saw active service in the war and their scripts carried the ring of truth about them, while always remembering that they were catering for a predominantly young audience. That so many adults bought them and still collect them to this day is a testament to how successful these writers were at bridging the gap between fantasy and reality.

While most of the war cover artists worked overseas there were, nonetheless, a few British-based painters who worked successfully for these comics. None captured the heroic spirit of the Allied forces more effectively than Oliver Frey. Although he is now considered to be very much a part of the British comics scene, having enjoyed a long association with such comics as *Look and Learn*, *The Hotspur* and *Speed And Power* as well as *War* and *Battle*, Frey was actually born in Switzerland. As he recalls; "I'm a Swiss who was brought up on *Eagle*, following a three-year stay in Britain (1956-59) and, therefore, belong with the other talented European illustration crew who made the Fleetway Libraries what they were. I owe this privilege to E.J. Bensberg who was their editor when he first gave me a chance to be a *War Picture Library* artist after having seen some crude samples in 1969 [when Frey was only 21]. I was trying to earn some money to see me through two years at the London School of Film Technique, and ended up a full-time illustrator by just walking in off the street. When, after film school, I decided to settle in London, I had to have an agent, partly to satisfy the immigration authorities, who needed reassurance that as a freelance I would not be a burden to the state. Ted recommended Temple Art (now Temple Rogers) who represented me from 1973 until I gave up freelancing in 1984."

A couple of questions which have often puzzled collectors are – which came first, the cover or the story; and

who precisely came up with the cover designs themselves? Frey remembers that, "The script always came before the covers as they were part and parcel of producing the strip drawings. On the occasions where I was asked to produce the cover only, Ted Bensberg gave me photocopies of strip artist's pages that contained suitable starting off points for a cover composition. At first I had to produce a rough for approval, but as the relationship with Ted matured, he just let me get on with it. He was a very good editor for a rookie illustrator to work with; full of down-to-earth advice on composition, execution and colour usage."

Looking at these covers now, it is easy to see why Frey was eventually given a free hand to develop them with minimal editorial interference. If any word best sums up his covers that would be – explosive. Frey's covers invariably seemed to involve some sort of explosion or other, frequently with soldiers leaping out of the inferno, all guns blazing (typified by his cover to Battle 745 on page 36).

While Penalva's chiseled heroes personified an idealised image of the fighting man, Frey's were altogether earthier. His soldiers look like they've spent weeks or months in bitter, muddy, deadly combat and wear haunted, almost crazed expressions on their faces. At his best, as on the superb cover to Battle 705 (page 54) he was able to compose memorably iconic scenes and here his band of fighting men seem to emerge from the dirt lit up by an iridescent explosion behind them. It manages to be stirring while at the same time not overly glamourising the war; there is a sense that, yes, these soldiers are bravely taking on a deadly foe, but given the choice they would rather be anywhere else. For comics like these, there is always a fine line between celebrating the sacrifices made in the act of war and glorifying war itself. For the most part, the artists managed to draw that line with their usual style and accuracy.

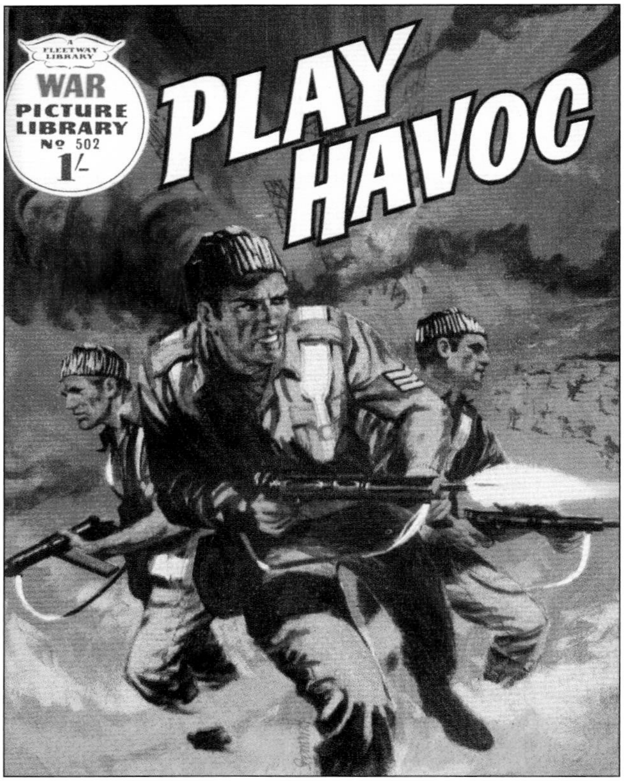
A FLEETWAY LIBRARY
WAR PICTURE LIBRARY
Nº 502
1/-
PLAY HAVOC

Fernando Fernandez, War 502, March 1969

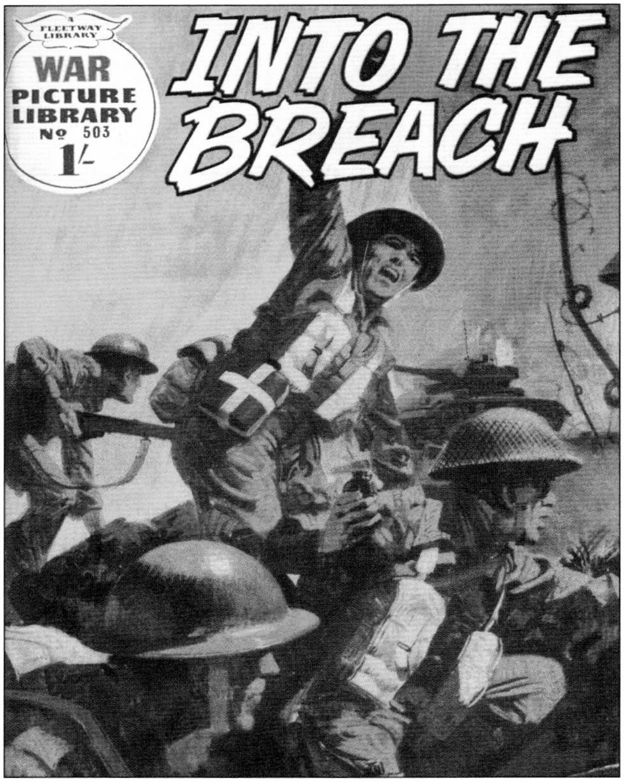
A FLEETWAY LIBRARY
WAR PICTURE LIBRARY
Nº 503
1/-
INTO THE BREACH

Allessandro Biffignandi, War 503, March, 1969

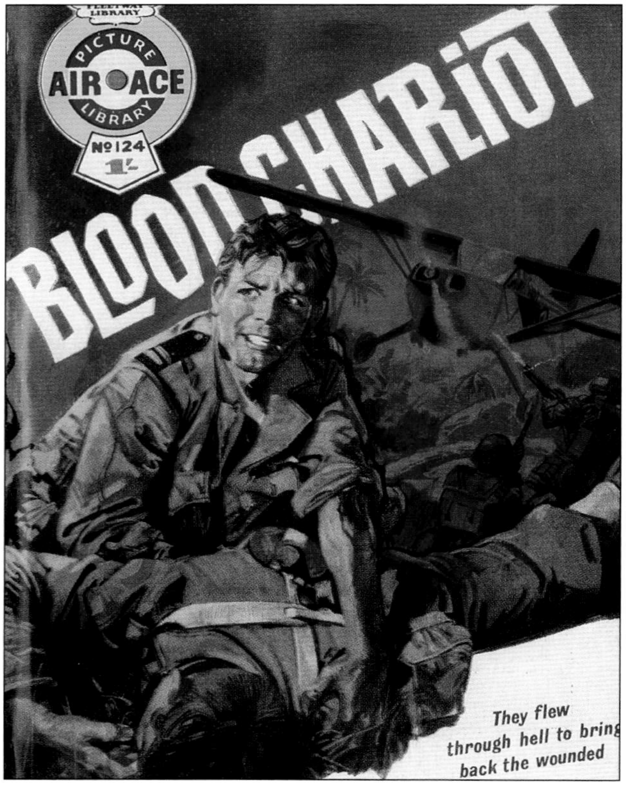
PICTURE AIR ACE LIBRARY
Nº 124
1/-
BLOOD CHARIOT
They flew through hell to bring back the wounded

Allessandro Biffignandi, Air Ace 124, November 1962

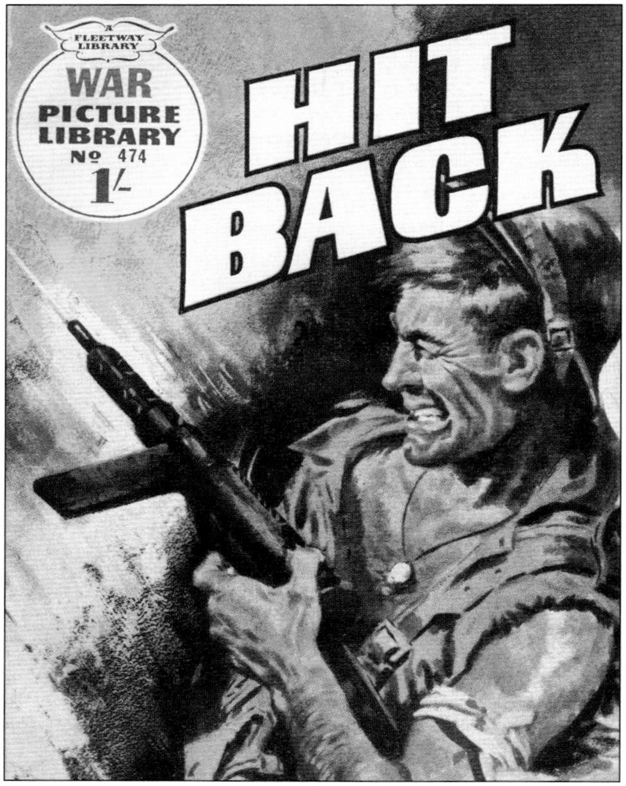
A FLEETWAY LIBRARY
WAR PICTURE LIBRARY
Nº 474
1/-
HIT BACK

Edwin Phillips, War 474, October 1968

Opposite: Allessandro Biffignandi, Battle 151, April 1964

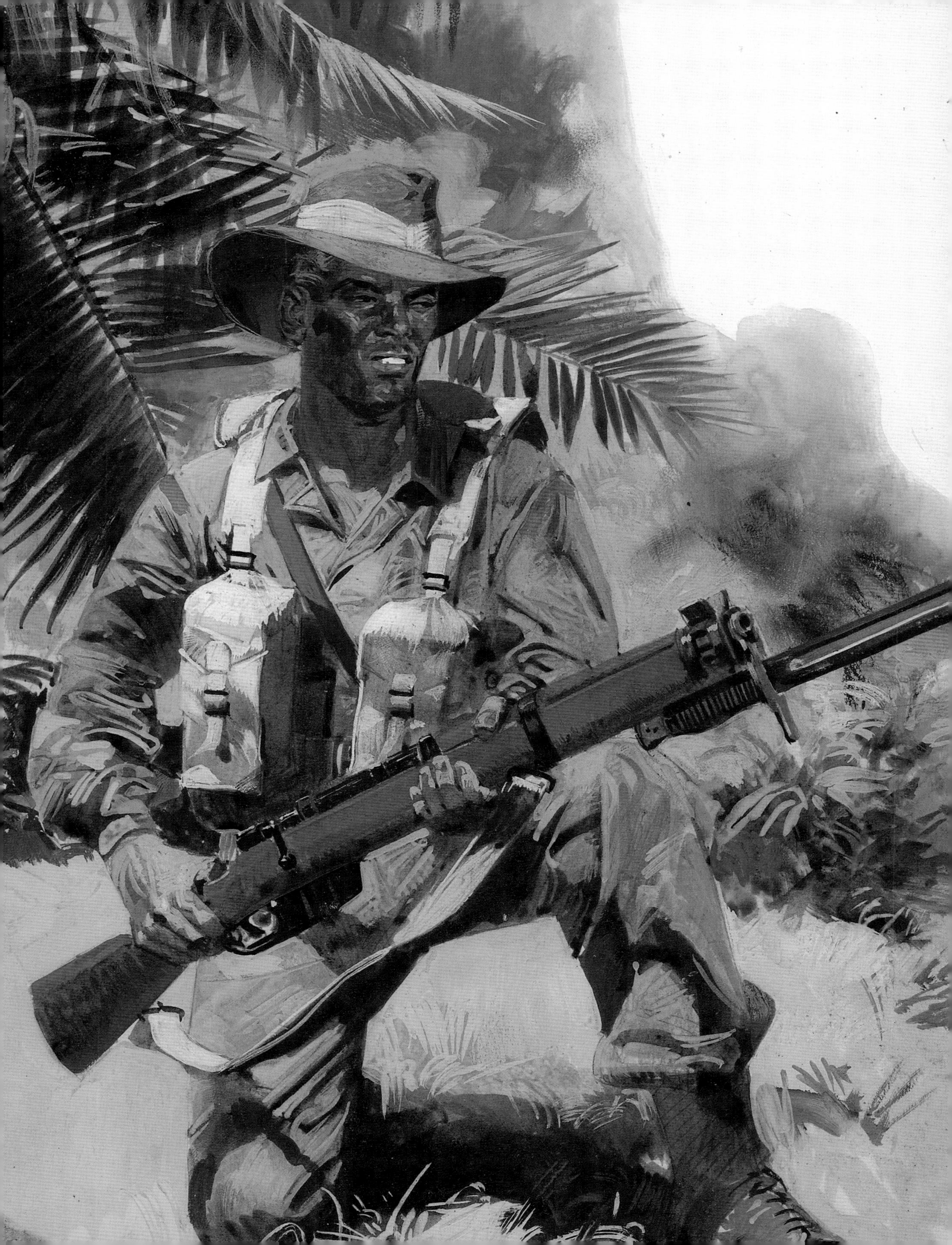

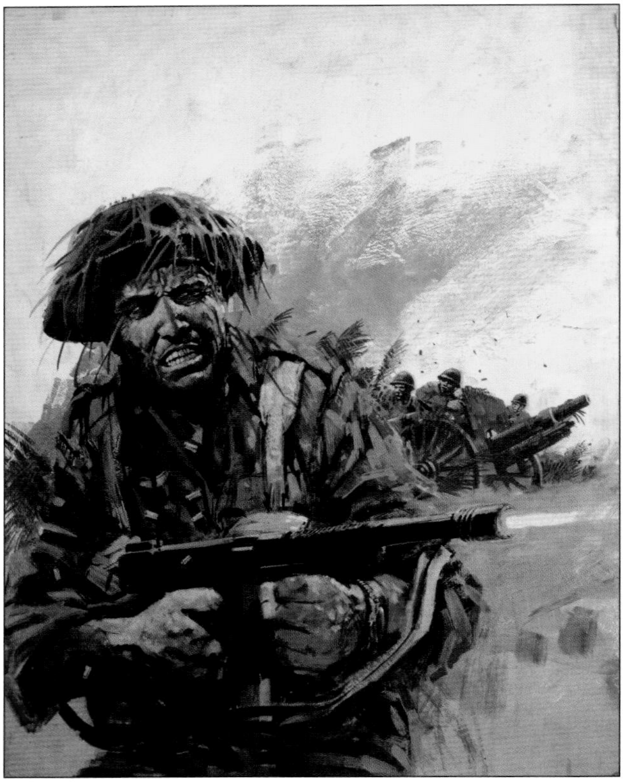

Graham Coton, War 1075, June 1975

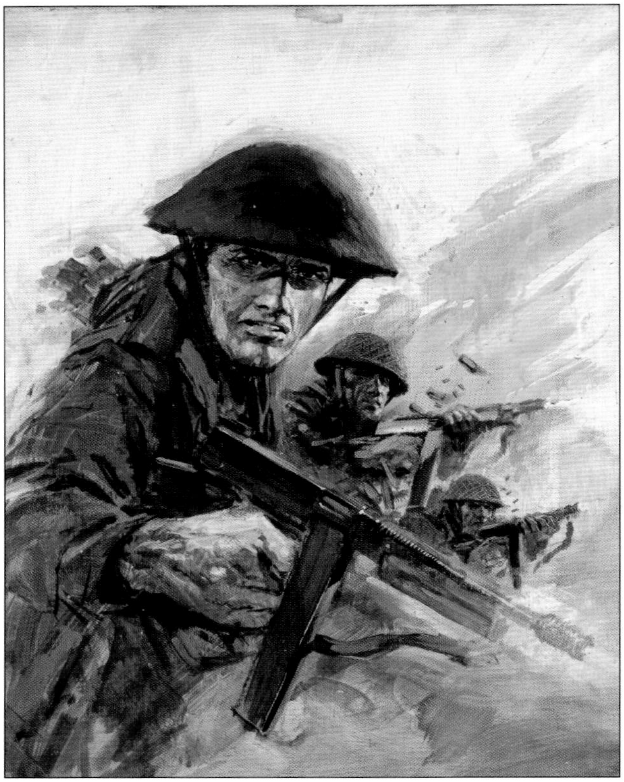

Graham Coton, War 2086, July 1984

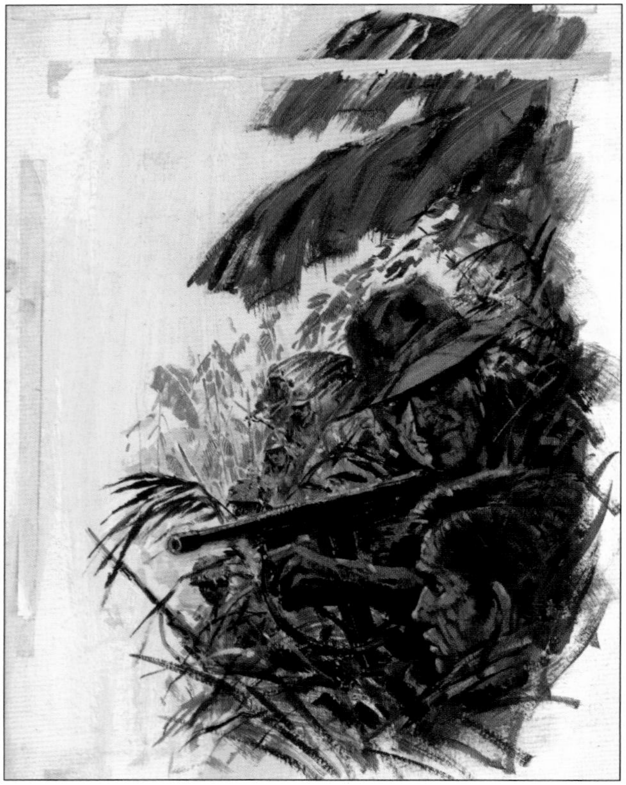

Graham Coton, War 1363, June 1977

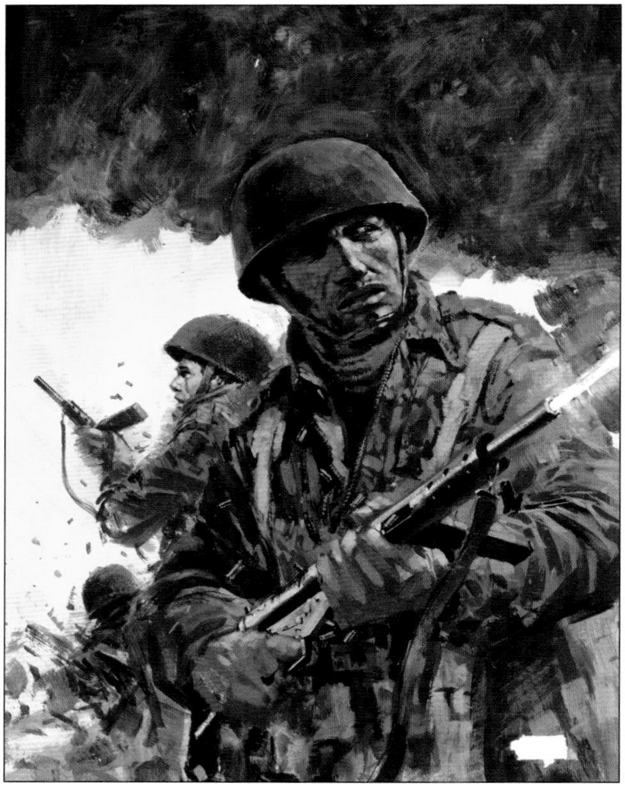

Graham Coton, War 1967, November 1982

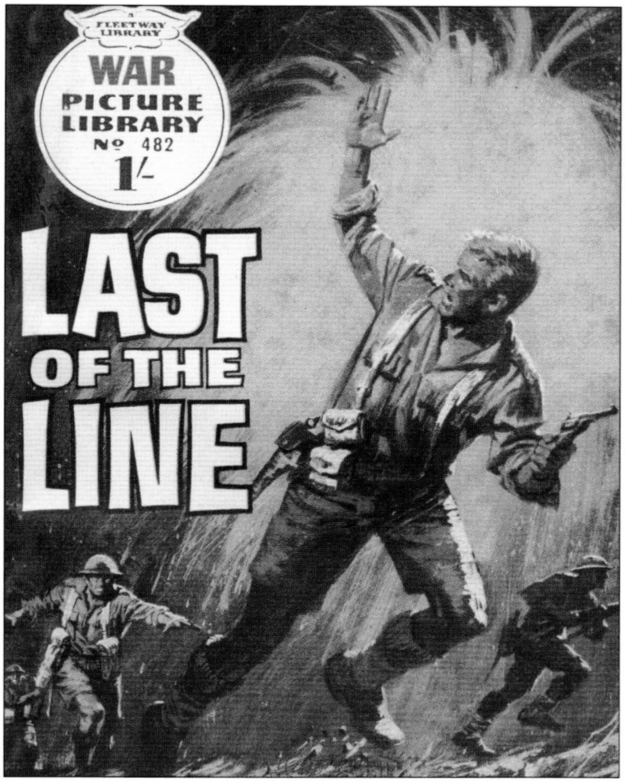
A FLEETWAY LIBRARY
WAR
PICTURE
LIBRARY
Nº 482
1/-
LAST OF THE LINE

Jordi Penalva, War 482, December 1968

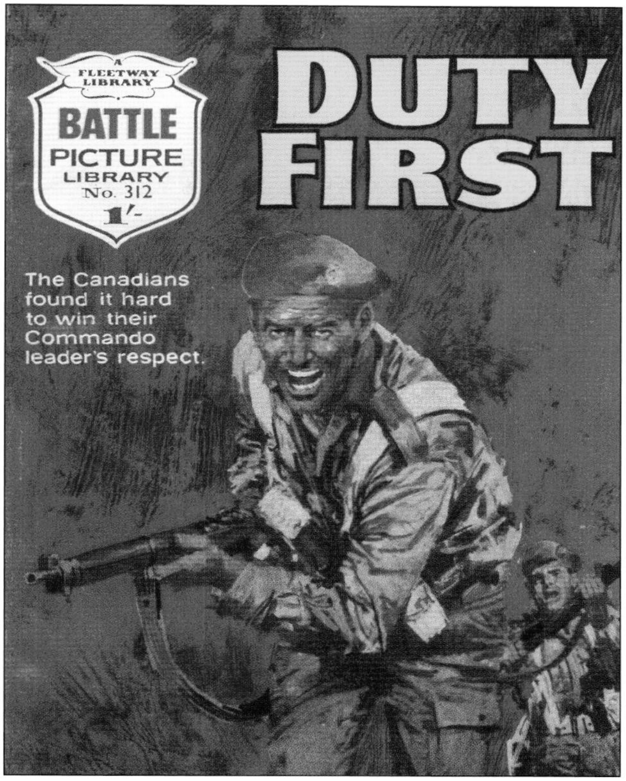
A FLEETWAY LIBRARY
BATTLE
PICTURE
LIBRARY
No. 312
1/-
DUTY FIRST
The Canadians found it hard to win their Commando leader's respect.

Jordi Longaron, Battle 312, August 1967

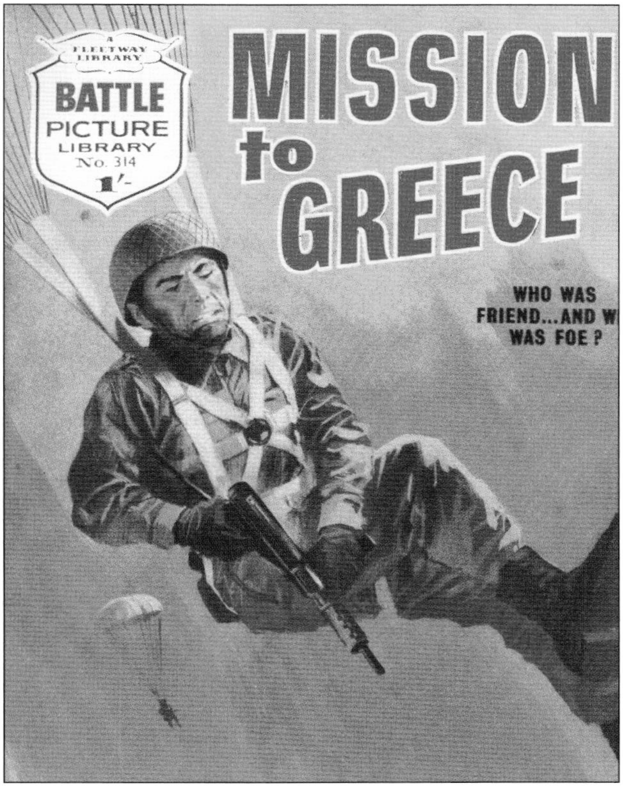
A FLEETWAY LIBRARY
BATTLE
PICTURE
LIBRARY
No. 314
1/-
MISSION to GREECE
WHO WAS FRIEND...AND W
WAS FOE ?

Carlo Jacono, Battle 314, September 1967

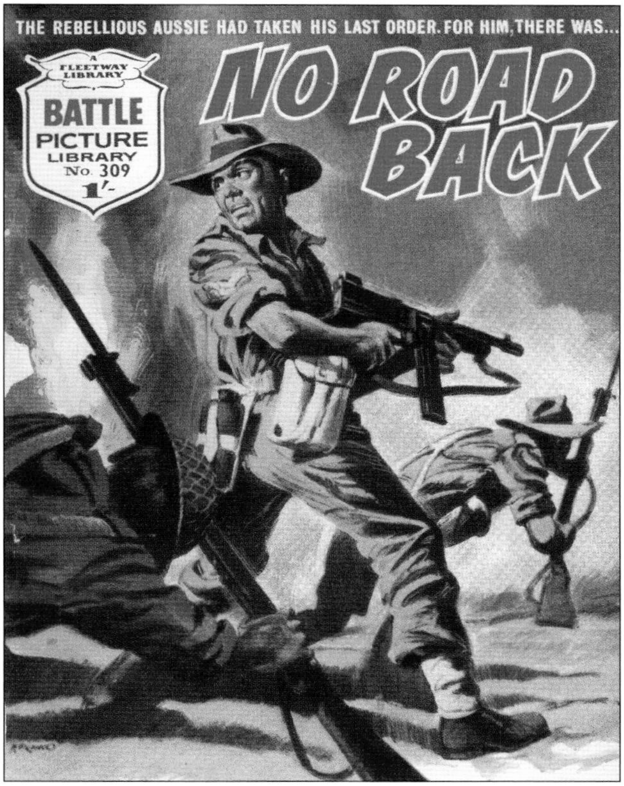
THE REBELLIOUS AUSSIE HAD TAKEN HIS LAST ORDER. FOR HIM, THERE WAS...
A FLEETWAY LIBRARY
BATTLE
PICTURE
LIBRARY
No. 309
1/-
NO ROAD BACK

Franco Picchioni, Battle 309, August 1967

Overleaf: Allessandro Biffignandi, Battle 141, February 1964

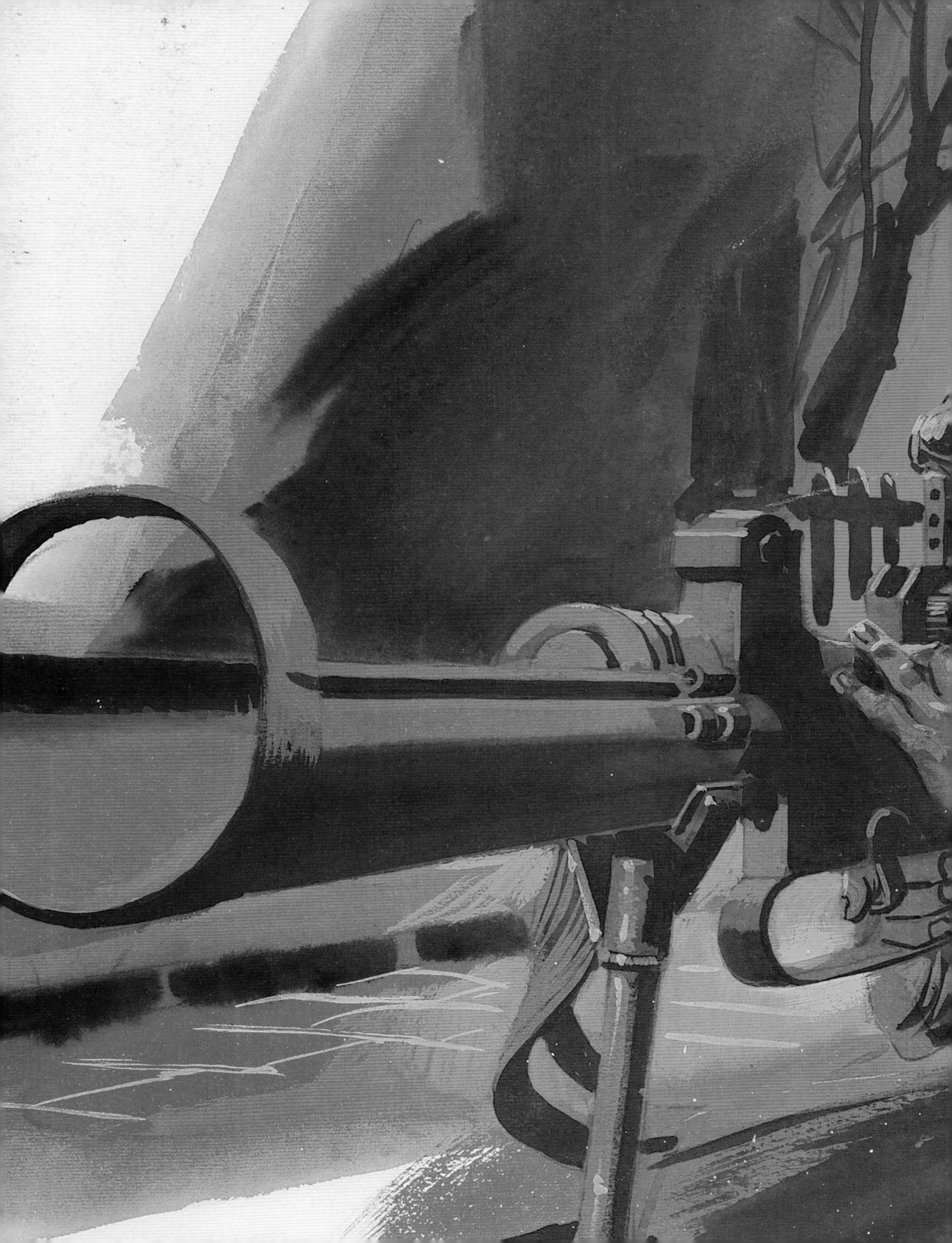

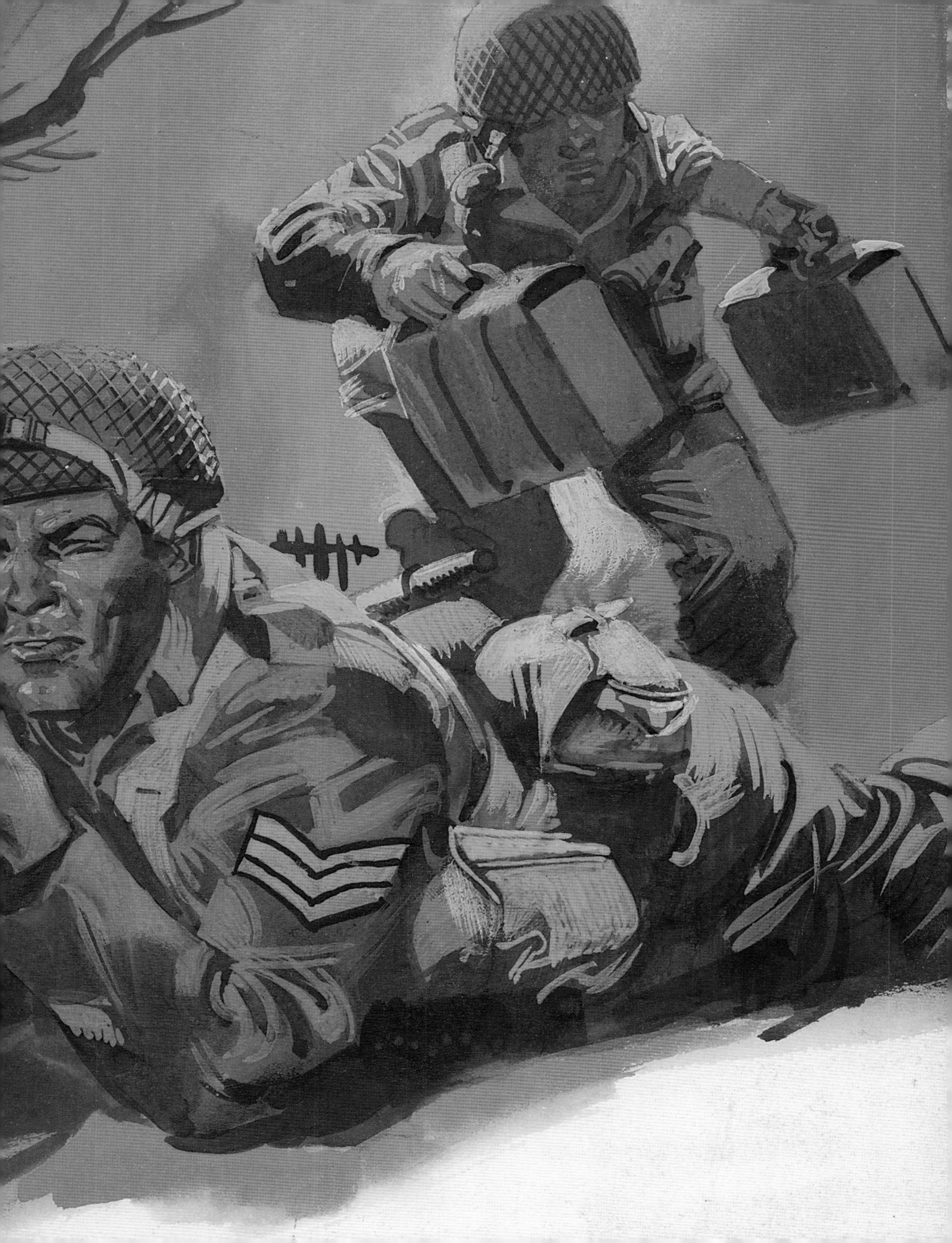

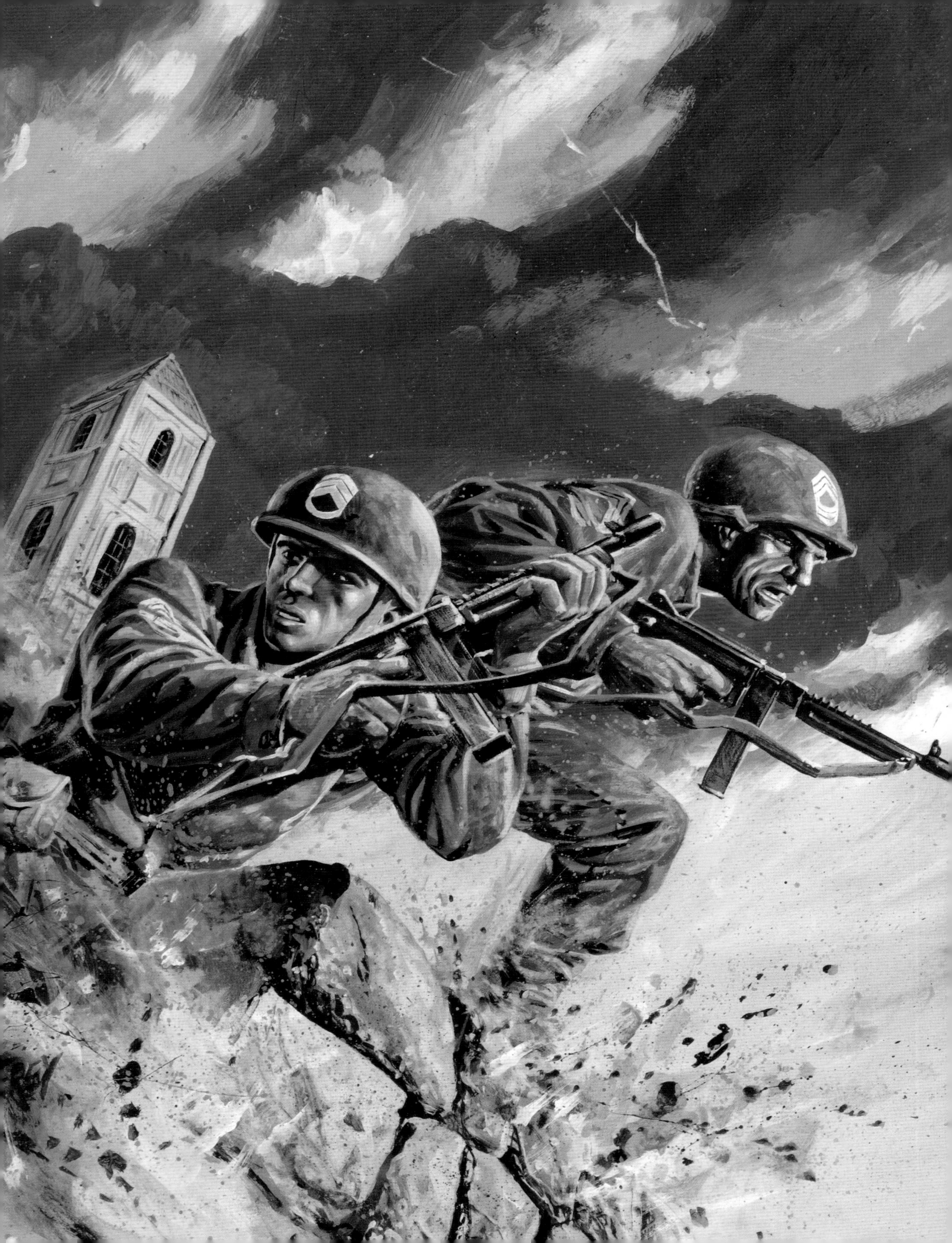

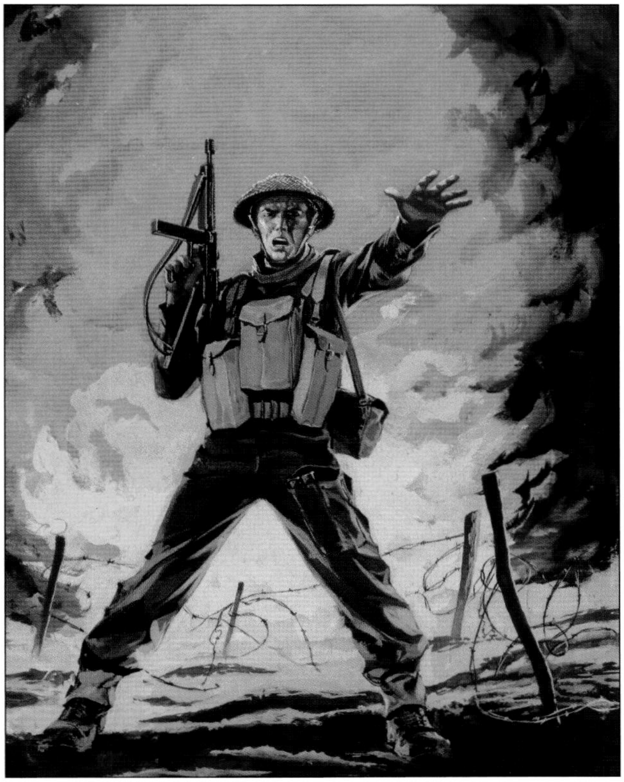

Nino Caroselli, War 126, December 1961

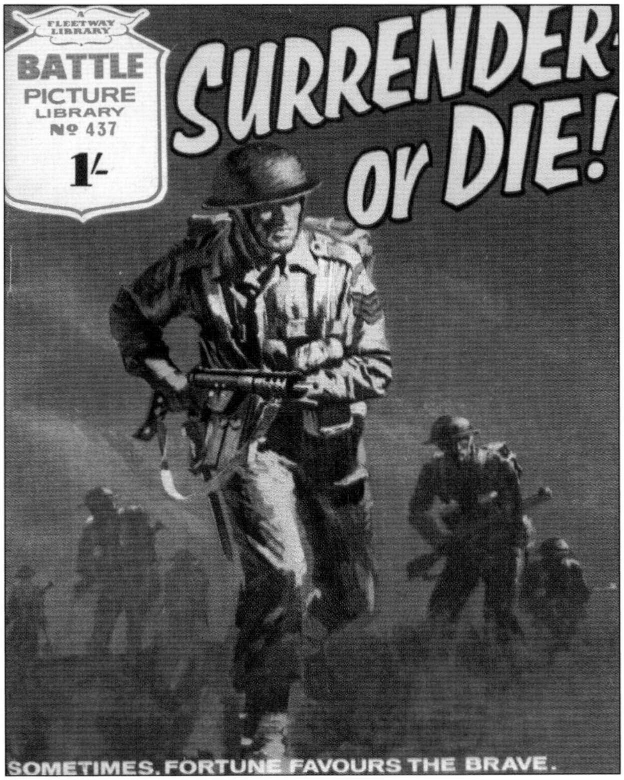
A FLEETWAY LIBRARY
BATTLE
PICTURE
LIBRARY
Nº 437
1/-
SURRENDER-
or DIE!
SOMETIMES, FORTUNE FAVOURS THE BRAVE.

Jordi Penalva, Battle 437, December 1969

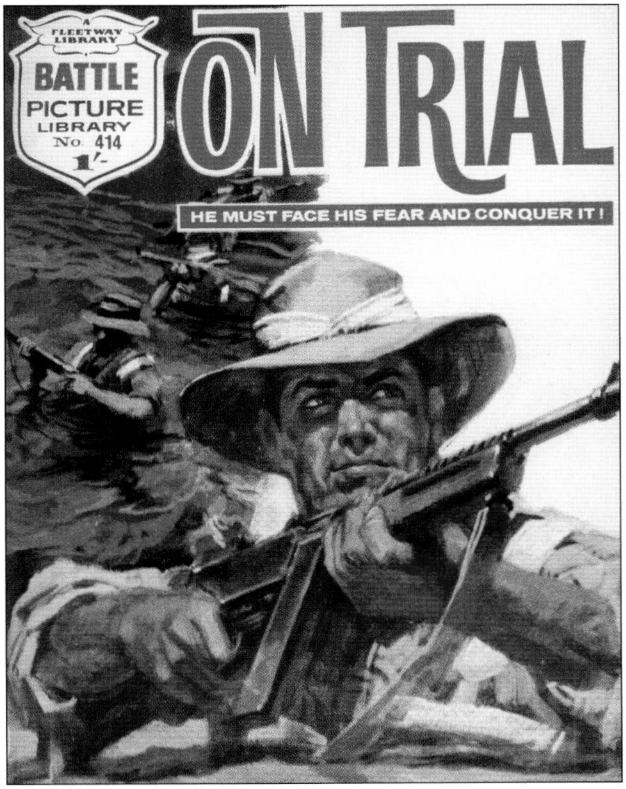
A FLEETWAY LIBRARY
BATTLE
PICTURE
LIBRARY
No. 414
1/-
ON TRIAL
HE MUST FACE HIS FEAR AND CONQUER IT!

Pino Dell'Orco, Battle 414, August 1969

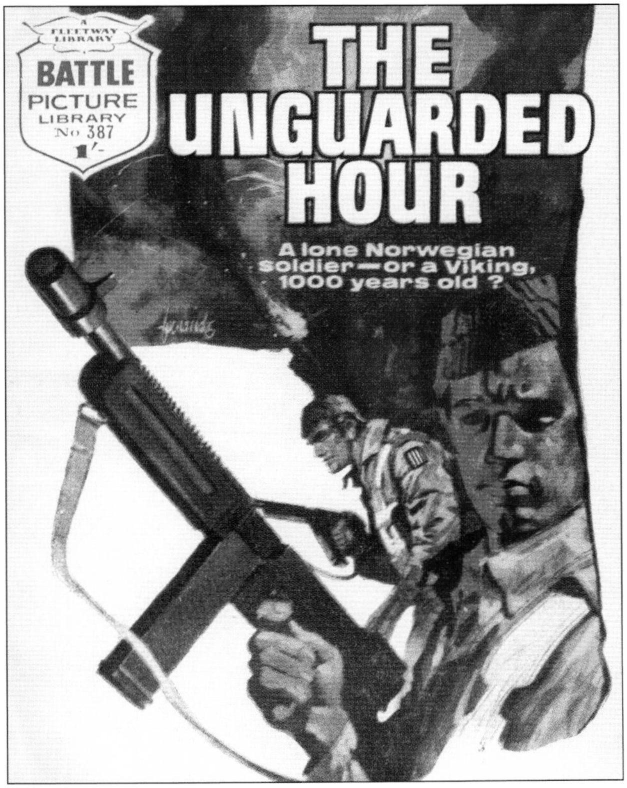
A FLEETWAY LIBRARY
BATTLE
PICTURE
LIBRARY
No 387
1/-
THE
UNGUARDED
HOUR
A lone Norwegian soldier—or a Viking, 1000 years old ?

Fernando Fernandez, Battle 387, March 1969

Opposite: Oliver Frey, Battle 986, March 1976

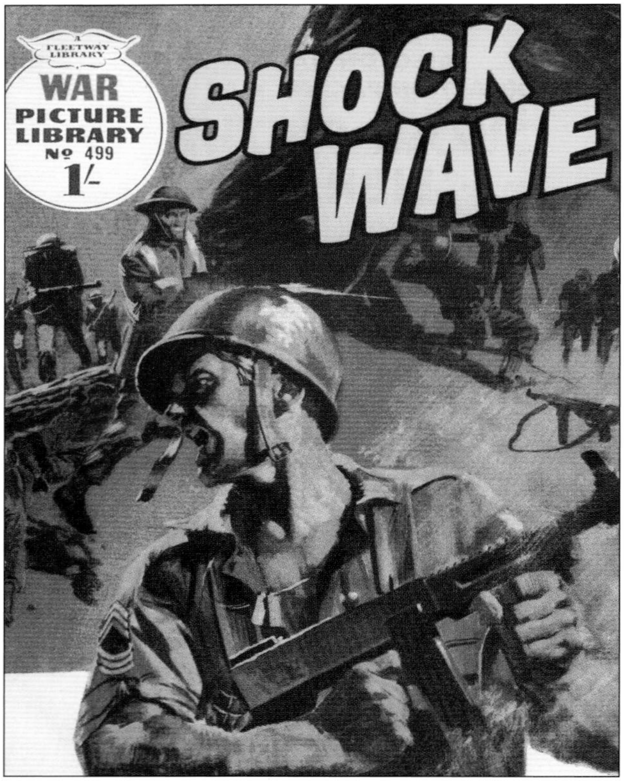
A FLEETWAY LIBRARY
WAR PICTURE LIBRARY Nº 499
1/-
SHOCK WAVE

Jordi Penalva, War 499, February 1969

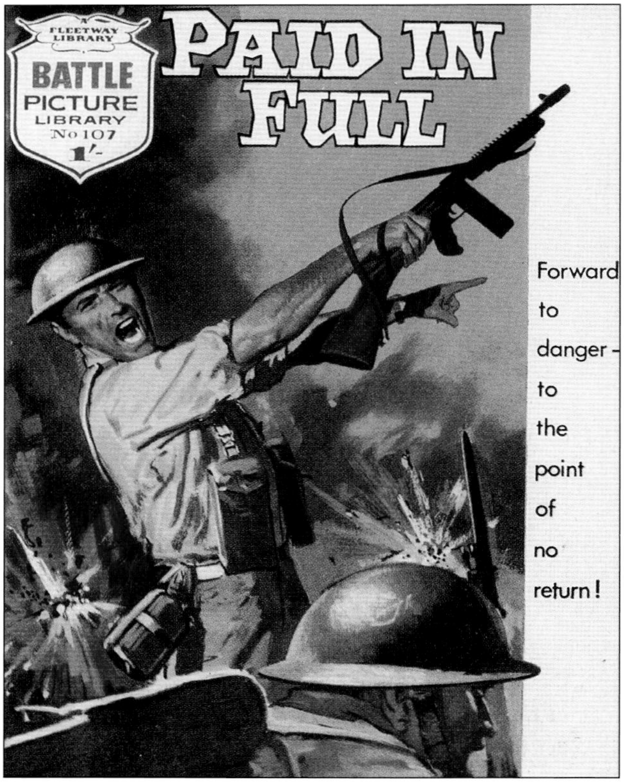
A FLEETWAY LIBRARY
BATTLE PICTURE LIBRARY No 107
1/-
PAID IN FULL
Forward to danger - to the point of no return!

Jordi Penalva, Battle 107, May 1963

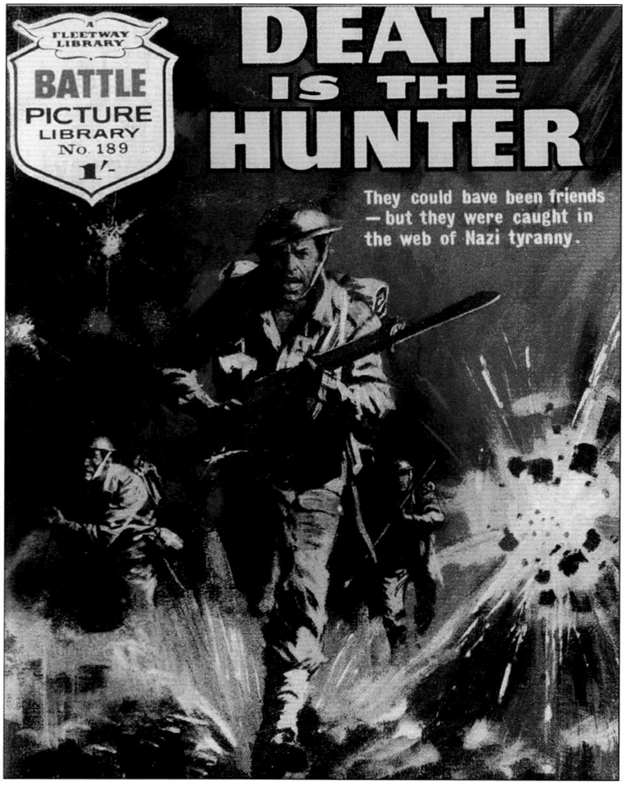
A FLEETWAY LIBRARY
BATTLE PICTURE LIBRARY No. 189
1/-
DEATH IS THE HUNTER
They could have been friends — but they were caught in the web of Nazi tyranny.

Jordi Penalva, Battle189, February 1965

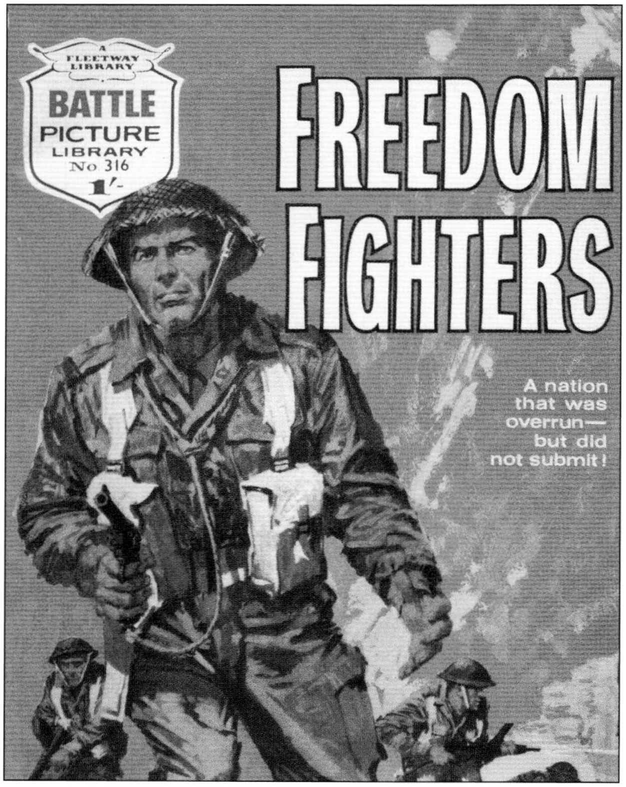
A FLEETWAY LIBRARY
BATTLE PICTURE LIBRARY No. 316
1/-
FREEDOM FIGHTERS
A nation that was overrun— but did not submit!

Jordi Longaron, Battle 316, September 1967

Opposite: Pino Dell'Orco, Battle15, June 1961

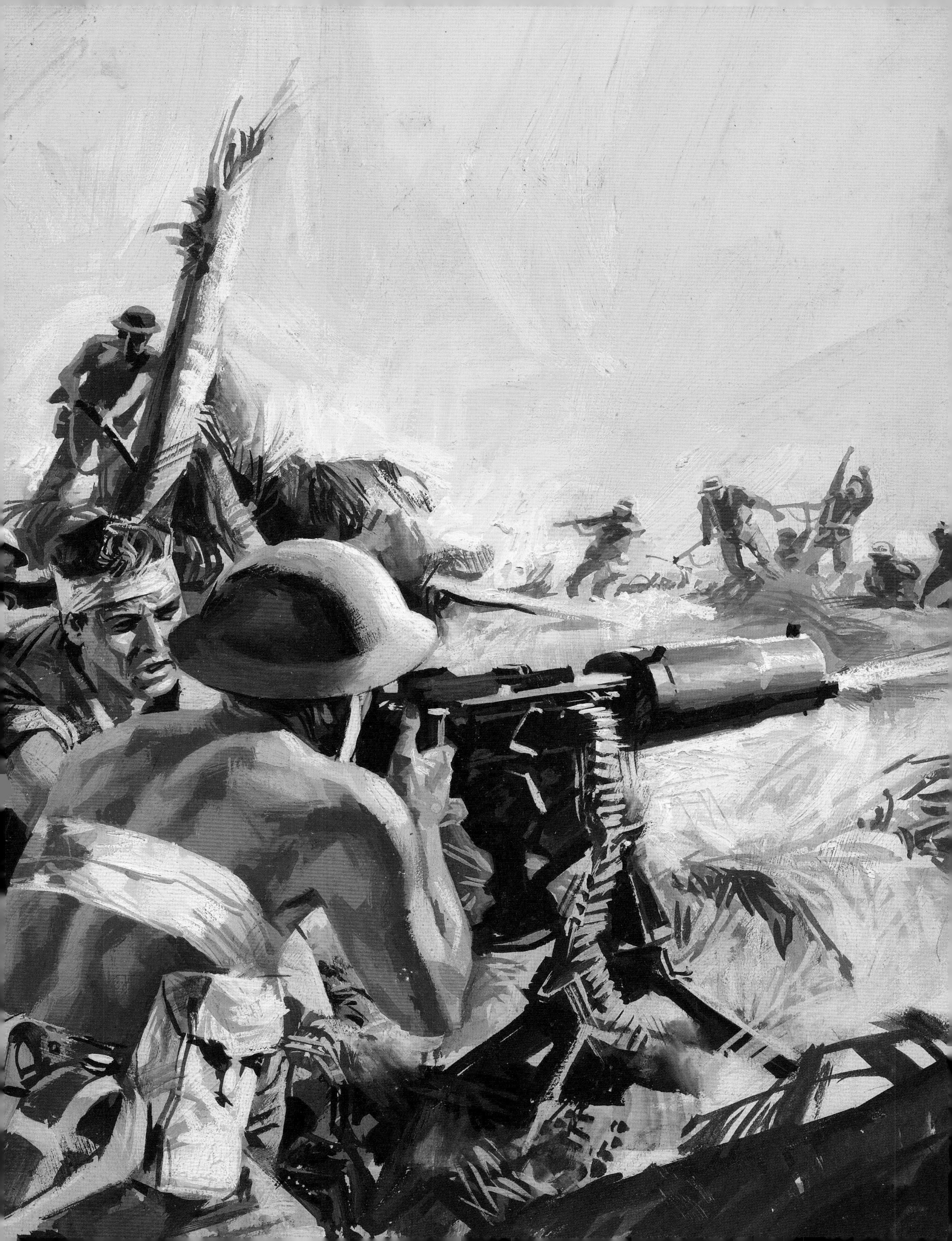

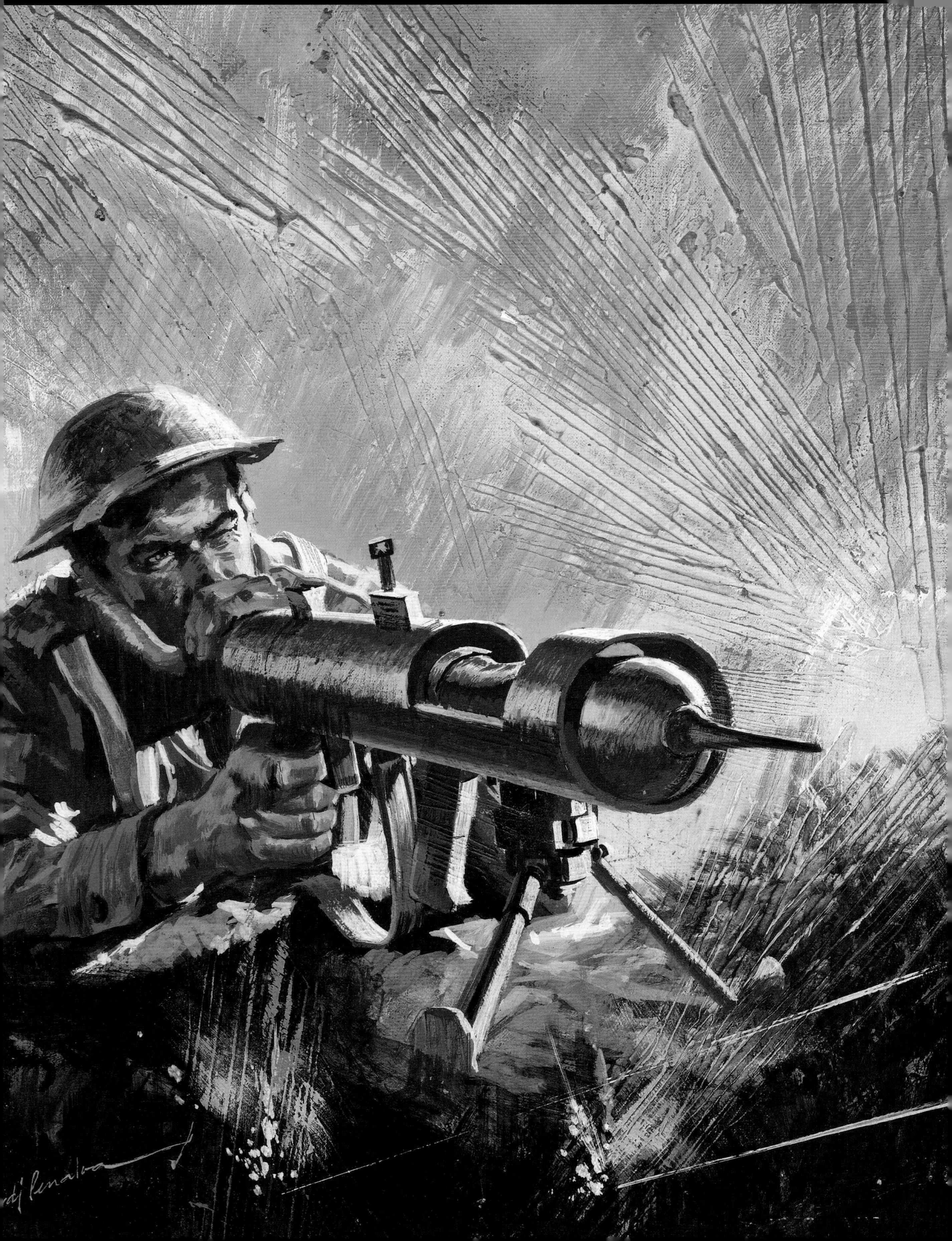

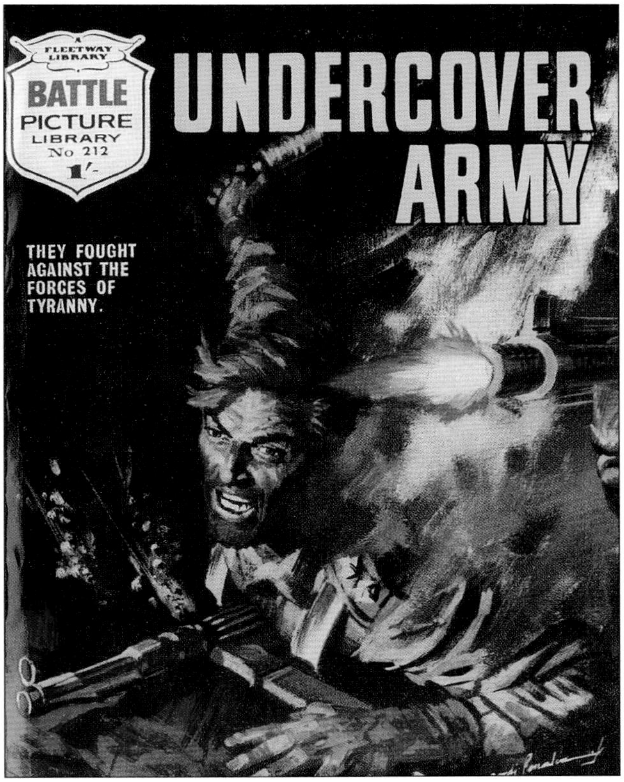
A FLEETWAY LIBRARY
BATTLE PICTURE LIBRARY No 212 1/-
UNDERCOVER ARMY
THEY FOUGHT AGAINST THE FORCES OF TYRANNY.
Jordi Penalva, Battle 212, July 1965

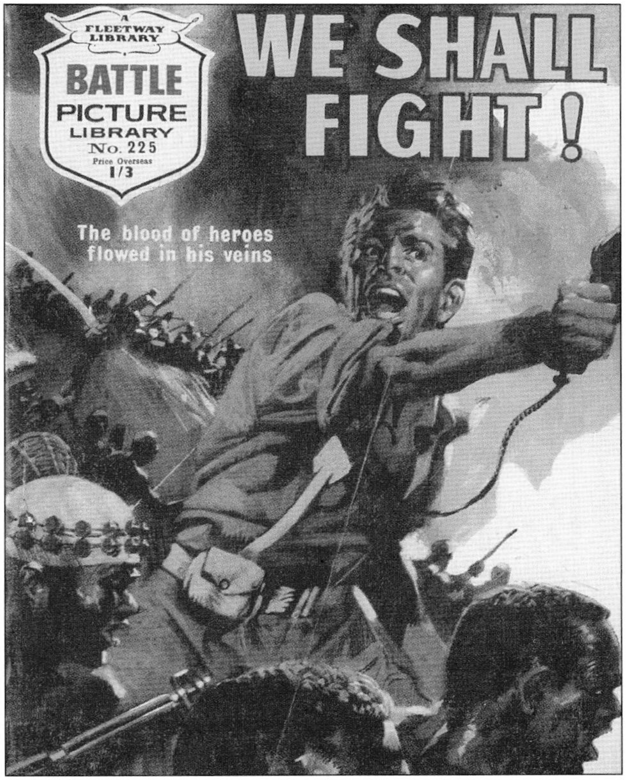
A FLEETWAY LIBRARY
BATTLE PICTURE LIBRARY No. 225 Price Overseas 1/3
WE SHALL FIGHT!
The blood of heroes flowed in his veins
Allessandro Biffignandi, Battle 225, November 1965

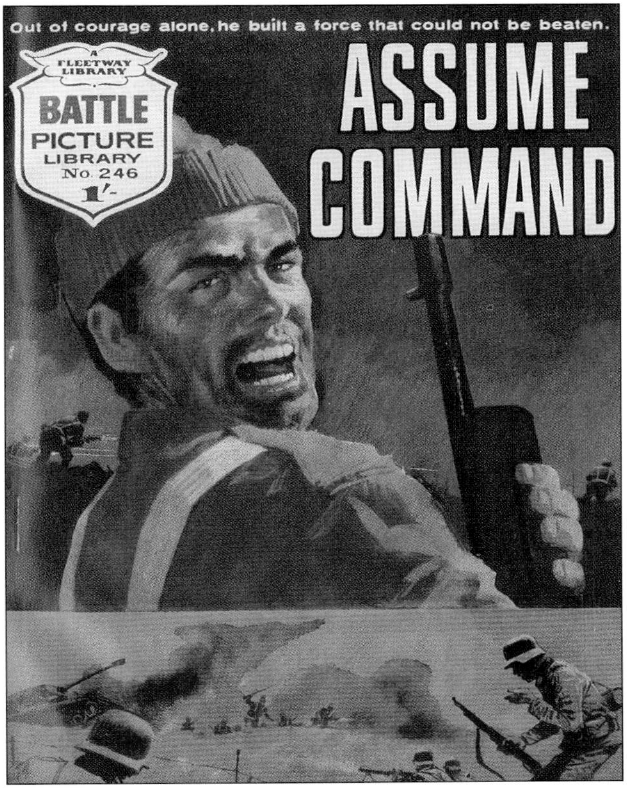
Out of courage alone, he built a force that could not be beaten.
A FLEETWAY LIBRARY
BATTLE PICTURE LIBRARY No. 246 1/-
ASSUME COMMAND
Carlo Jacono, Battle 246, April 1966

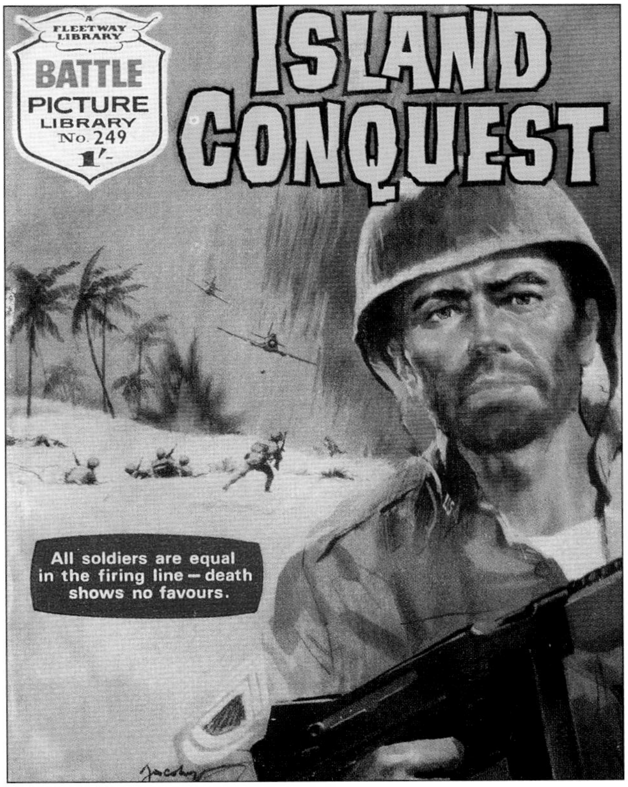
A FLEETWAY LIBRARY
BATTLE PICTURE LIBRARY No. 249 1/-
ISLAND CONQUEST
All soldiers are equal in the firing line – death shows no favours.
Carlo Jacono, Battle 249, May 1966

Opposite: Jordi Penalva, War 317, December 1965
Overleaf: Andrew Howat, Battle 433, December 1969

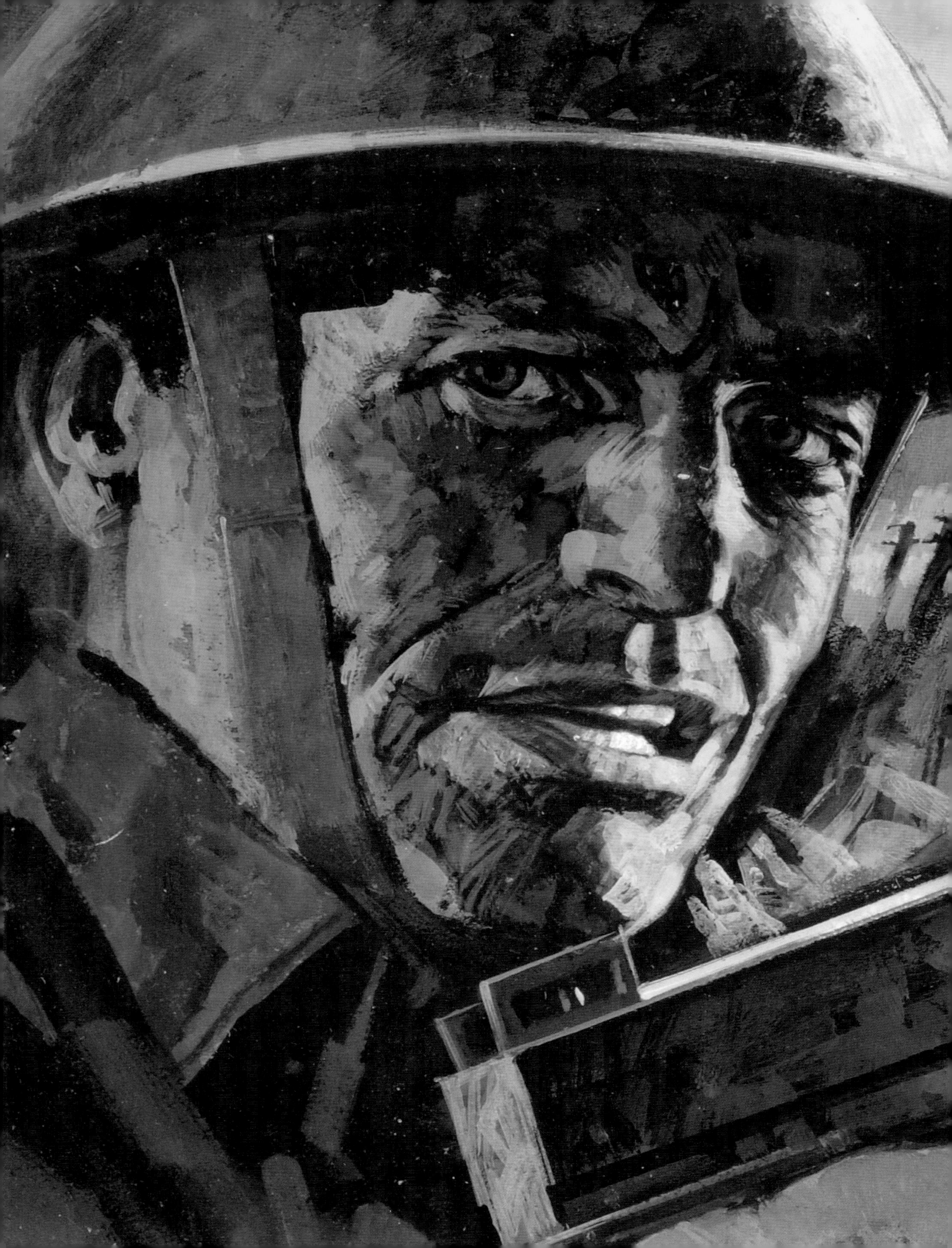

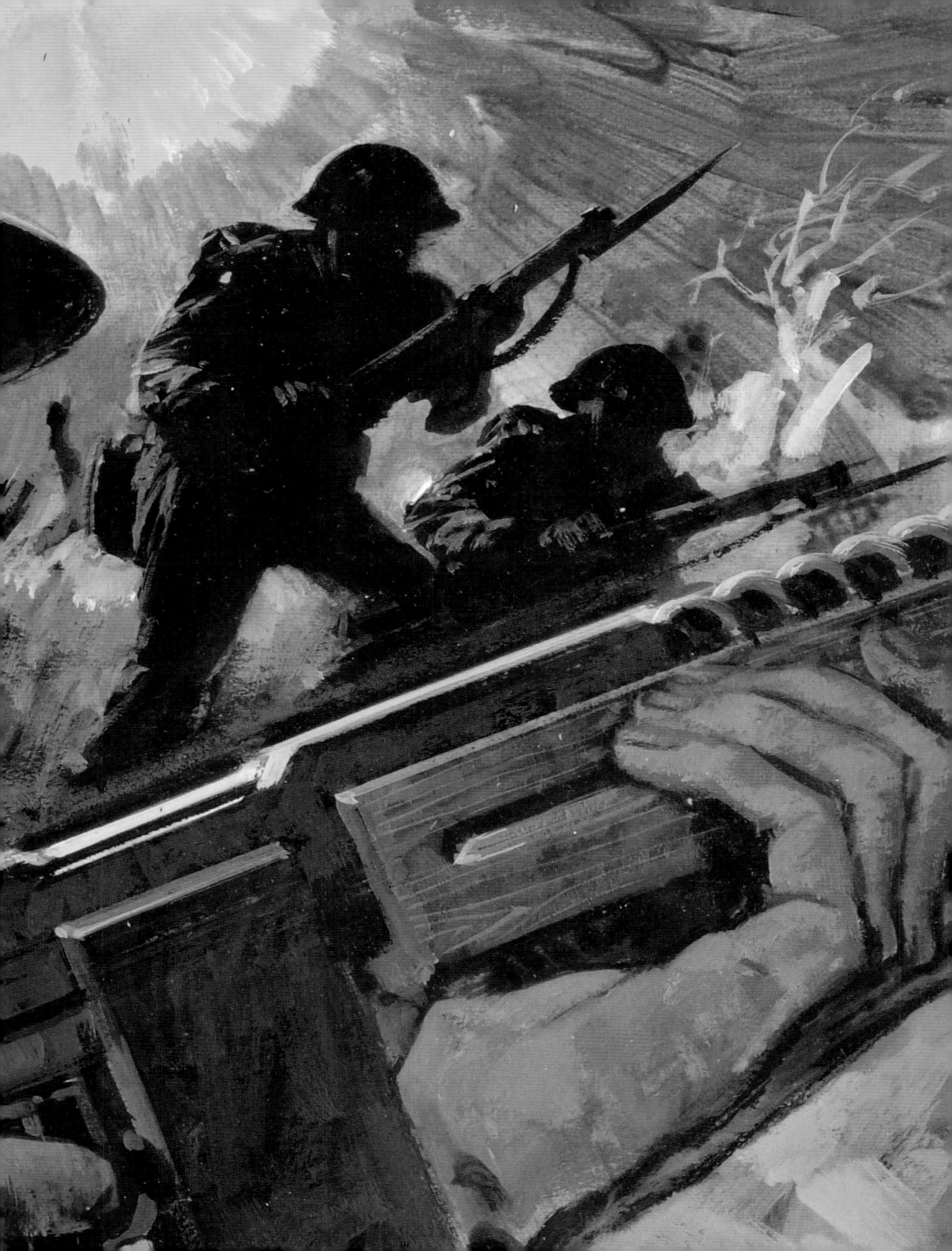

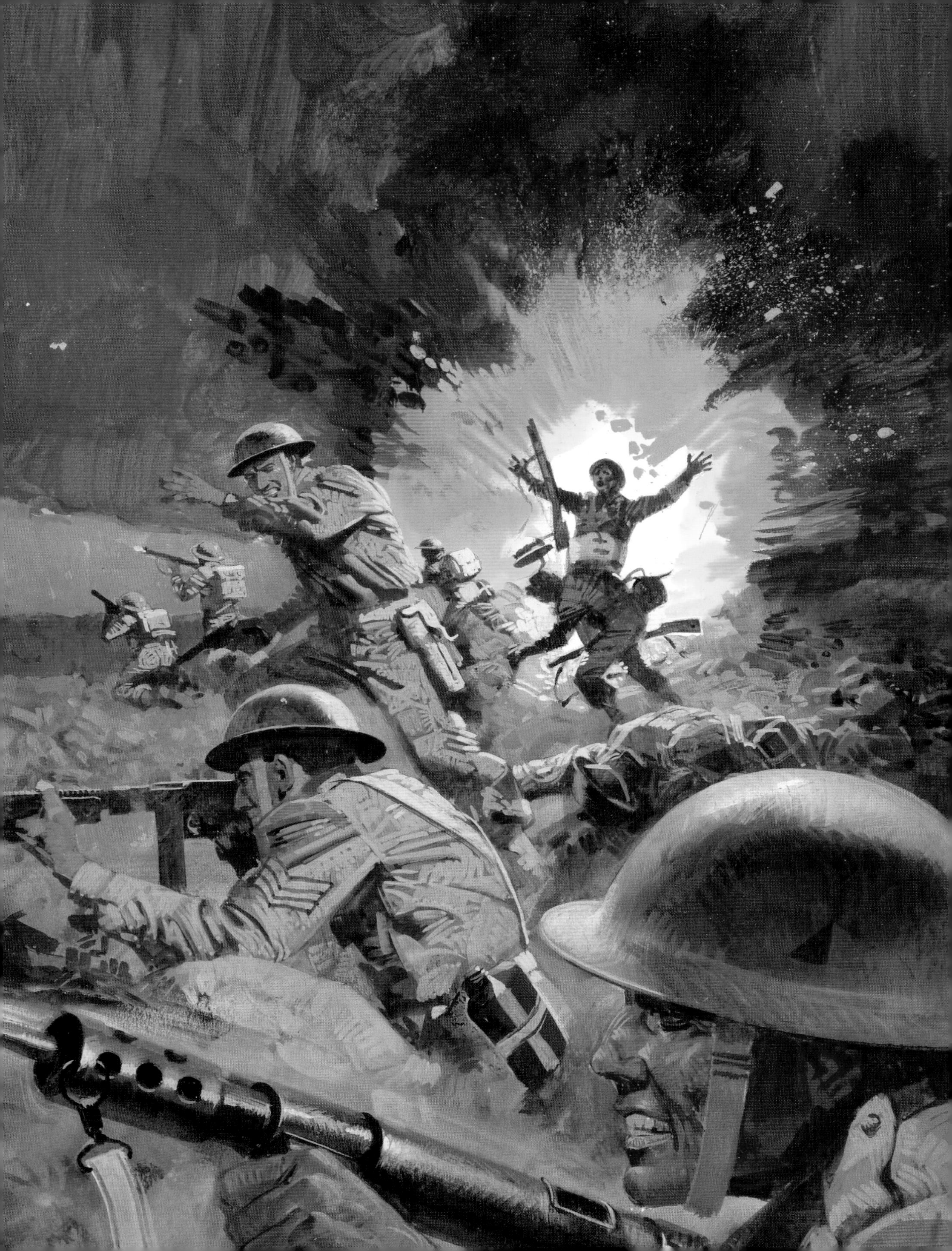

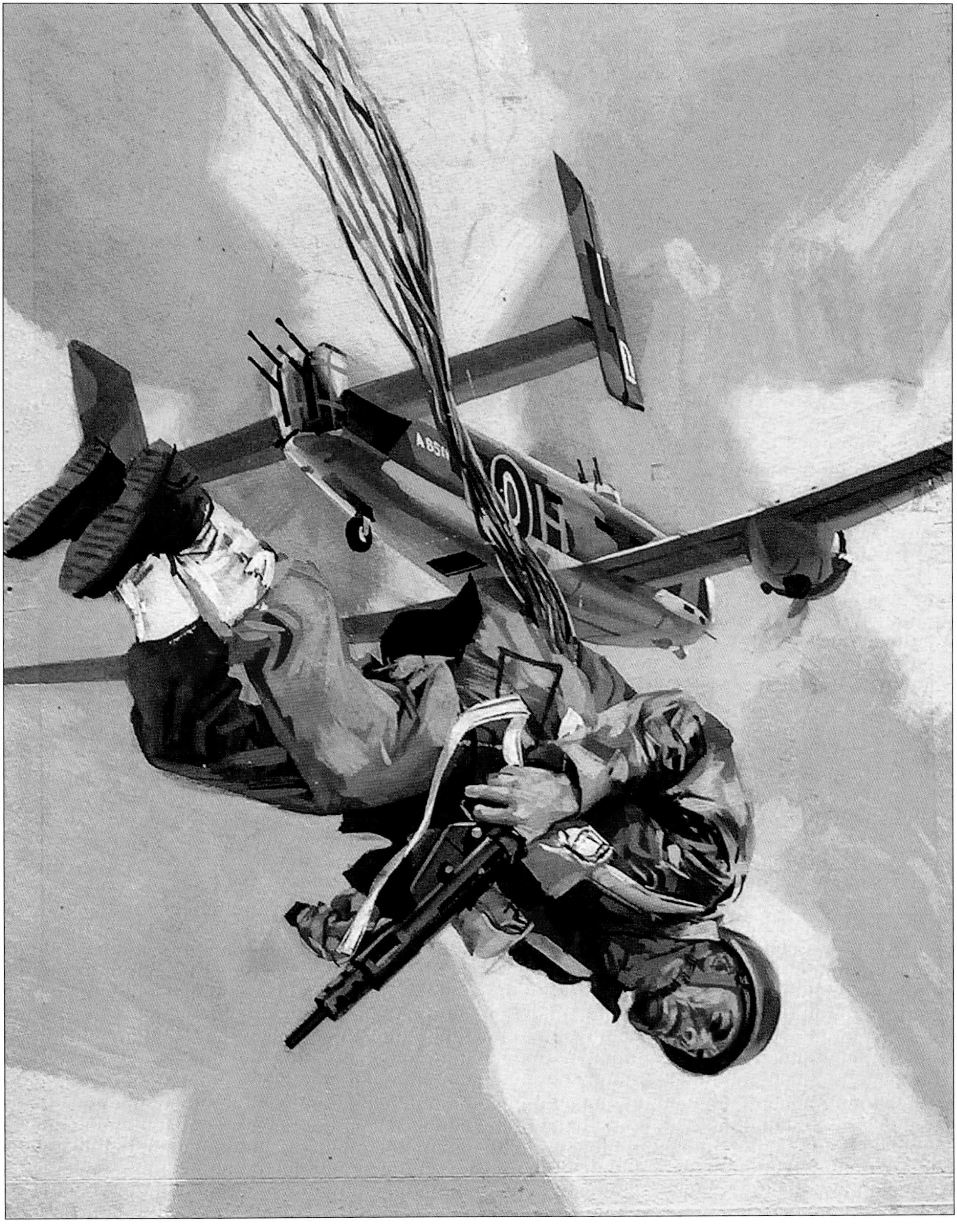
A 851

Pino Dell'Orco, War 158, August 1962
Opposite: Allessandro Biffignandi, Battle 357, August 1968

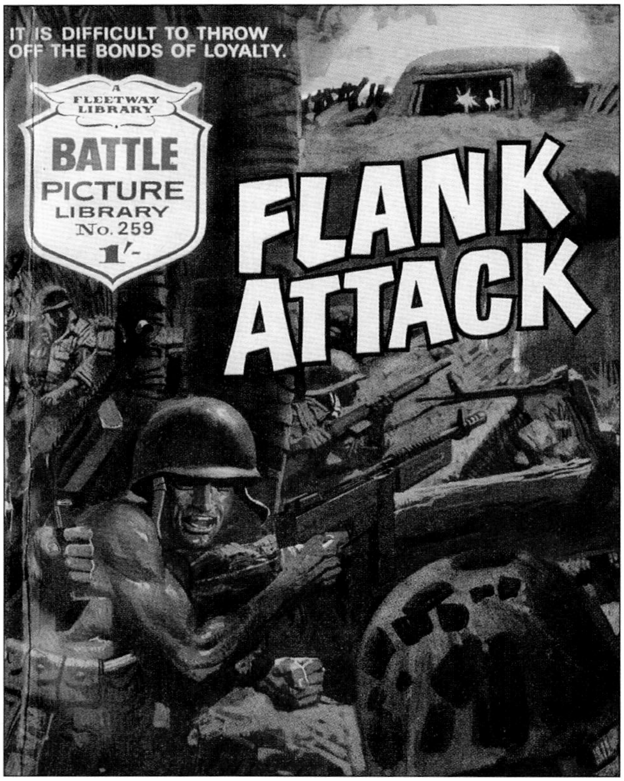
IT IS DIFFICULT TO THROW OFF THE BONDS OF LOYALTY.
A FLEETWAY LIBRARY
BATTLE PICTURE LIBRARY No. 259 1/-
FLANK ATTACK

Allessandro Biffignandi, Battle 259, July 1966

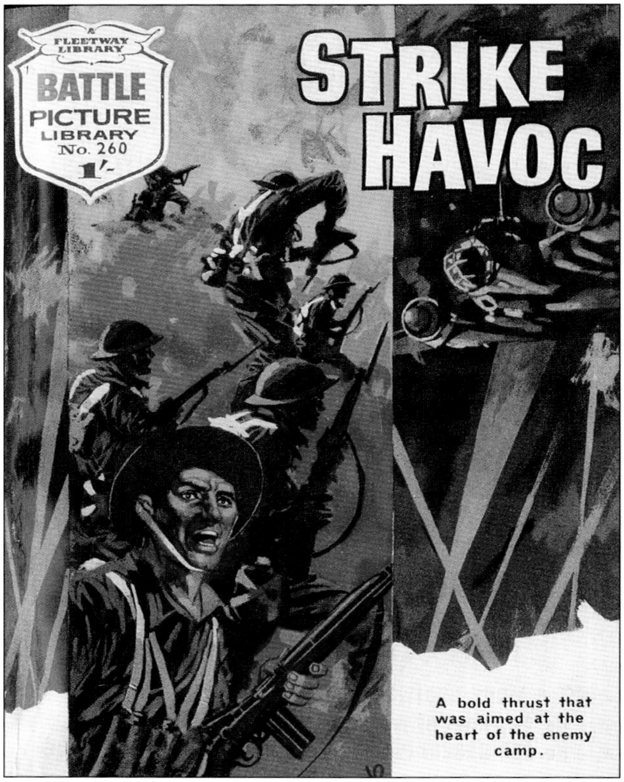
A FLEETWAY LIBRARY
BATTLE PICTURE LIBRARY No. 260 1/-
STRIKE HAVOC
A bold thrust that was aimed at the heart of the enemy camp.

Fernando Fernandez, Battle 260, July 1966

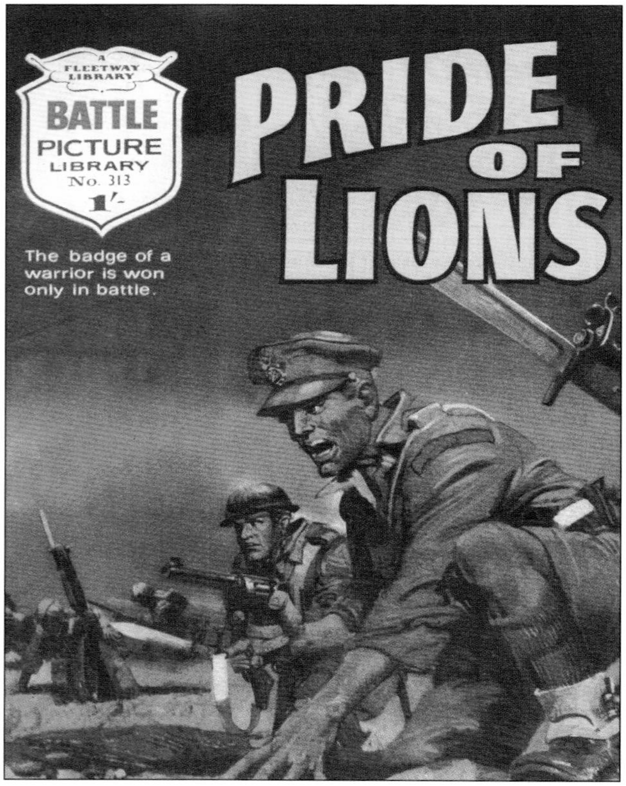
A FLEETWAY LIBRARY
BATTLE PICTURE LIBRARY No. 313 1/-
PRIDE OF LIONS
The badge of a warrior is won only in battle.

Allessandro Biffignandi, Battle 313, September 1967

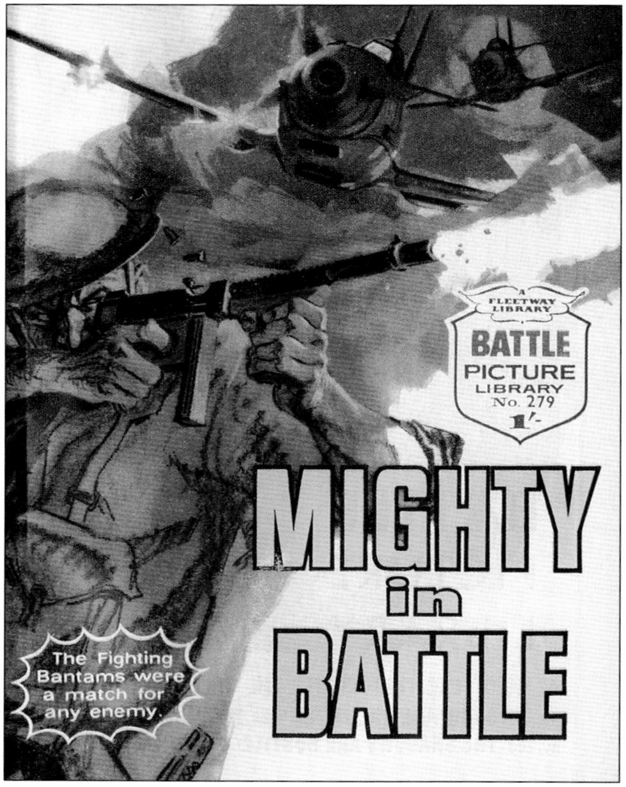
A FLEETWAY LIBRARY
BATTLE PICTURE LIBRARY No. 279 1/-
MIGHTY in BATTLE
The Fighting Bantams were a match for any enemy.

Artur Aldoma Puig, Battle 279, December 1966

Opposite: Jordi Penalva, Battle 197, April 1965

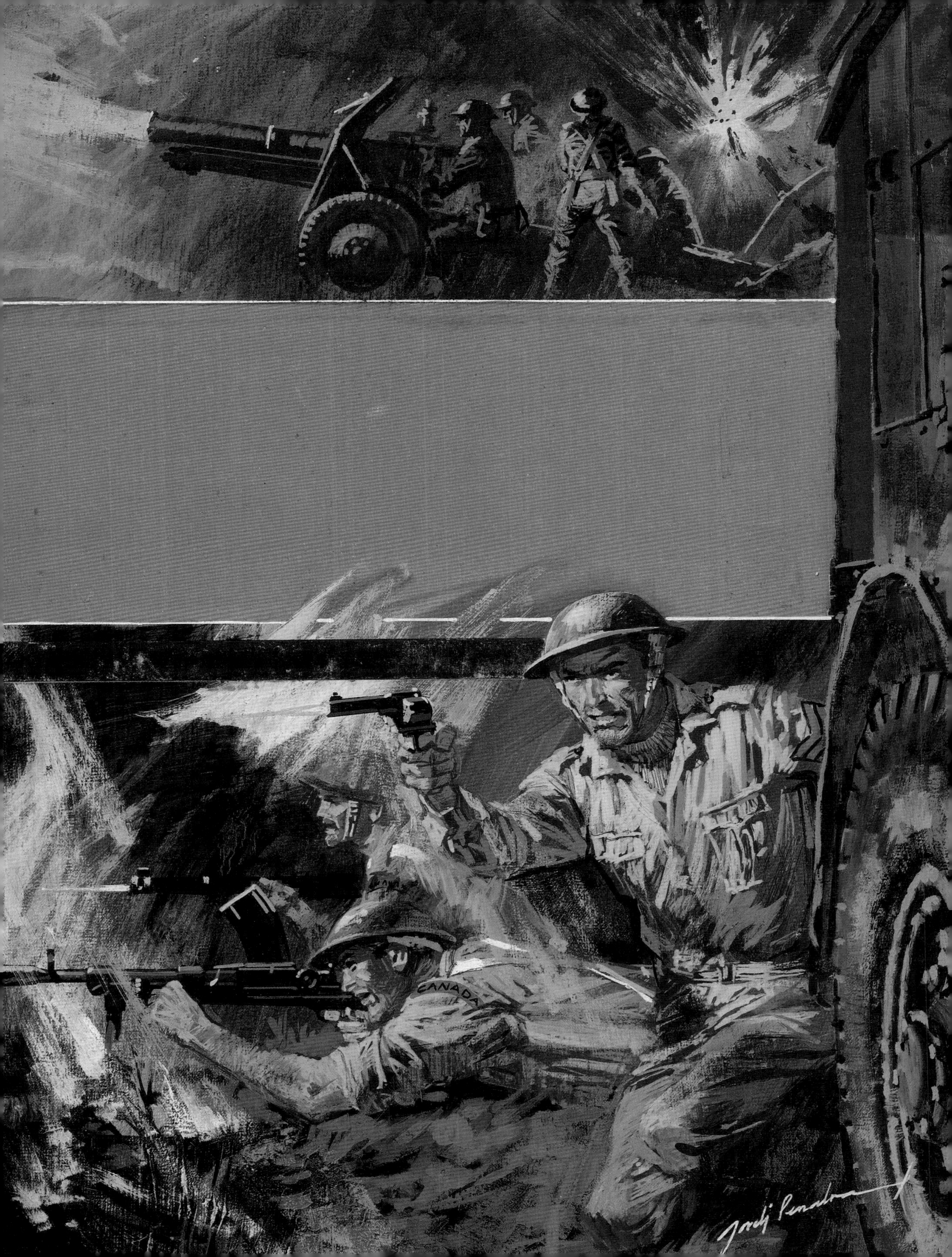
CANADA

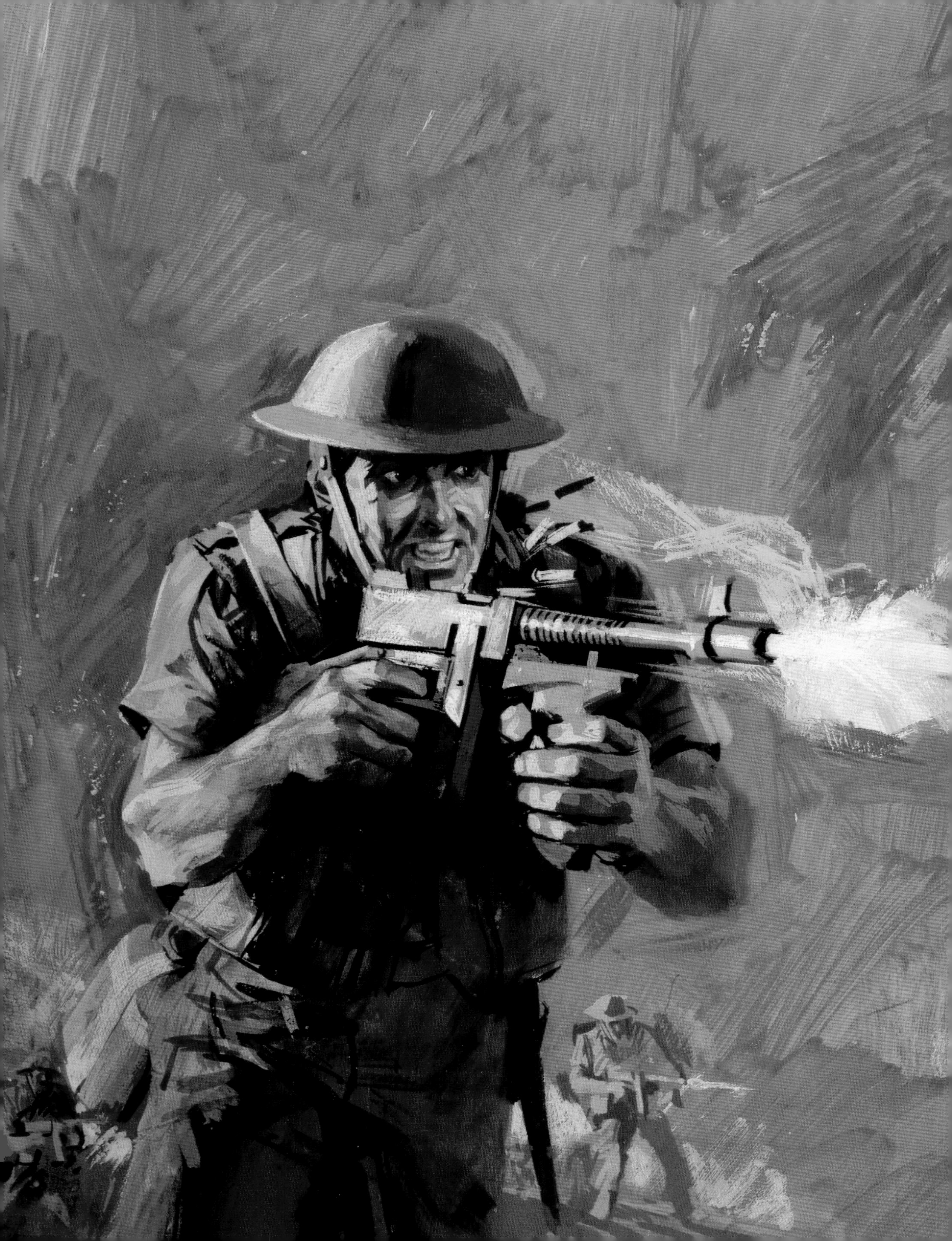

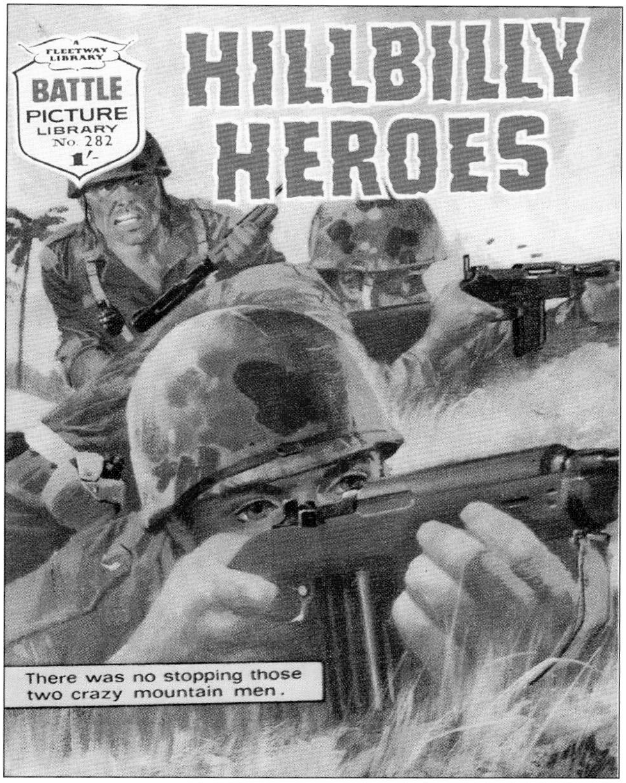
A FLEETWAY LIBRARY
BATTLE PICTURE LIBRARY No. 282 1/-
HILLBILLY HEROES
There was no stopping those two crazy mountain men.

Carlo Jacono, Battle 282, January 1967

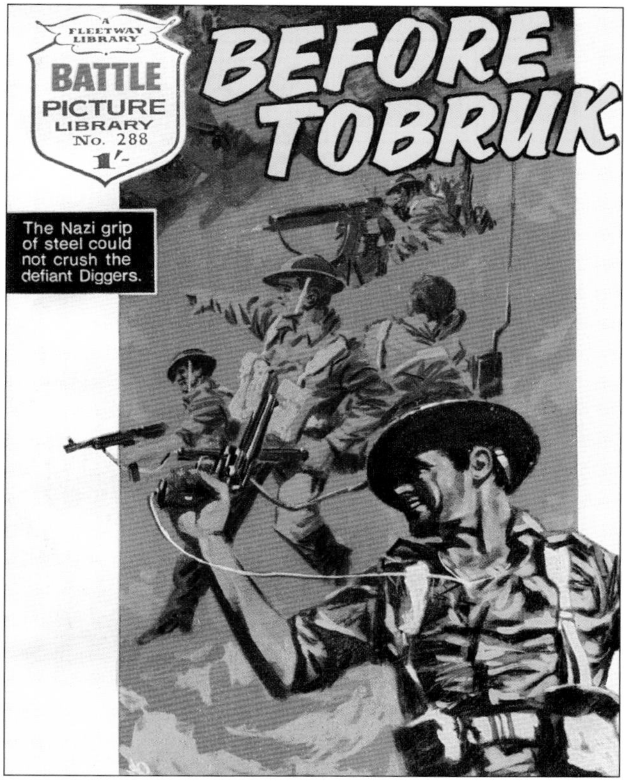
A FLEETWAY LIBRARY
BATTLE PICTURE LIBRARY No. 288 1/-
BEFORE TOBRUK
The Nazi grip of steel could not crush the defiant Diggers.

Fernando Fernandez, Battle 288, February 1967

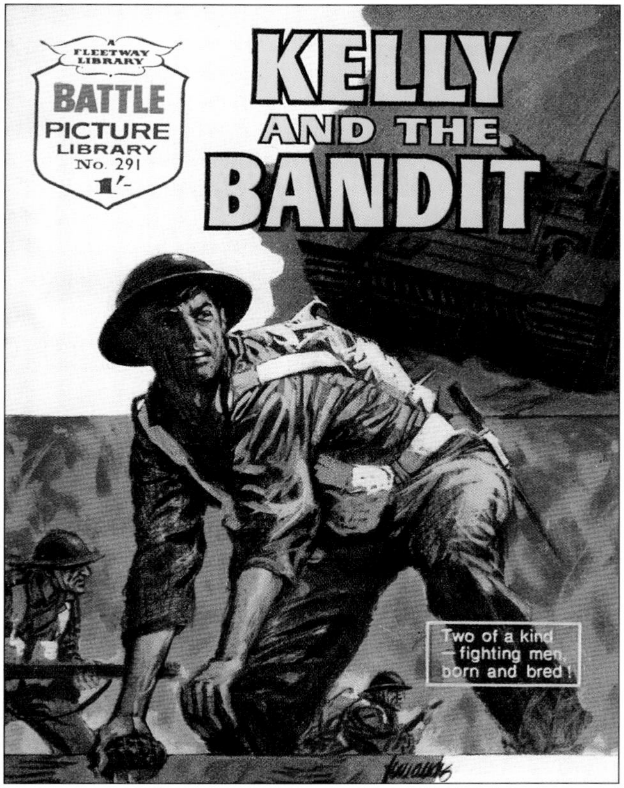
A FLEETWAY LIBRARY
BATTLE PICTURE LIBRARY No. 291 1/-
KELLY AND THE BANDIT
Two of a kind – fighting men born and bred!

Fernando Fernandez, Battle 291, March 1967

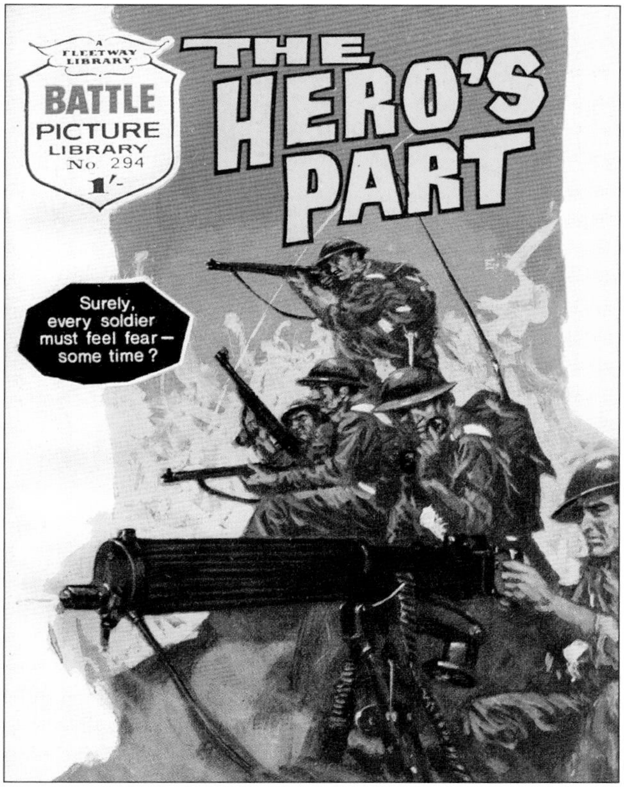
A FLEETWAY LIBRARY
BATTLE PICTURE LIBRARY No. 294 1/-
THE HERO'S PART
Surely, every soldier must feel fear – some time?

Fernando Fernandez, Battle 294, April 1967

Opposite: Pino Dell'Orco, War 128, January 1962
Overleaf: Oliver Frey, Battle 745, September 1973

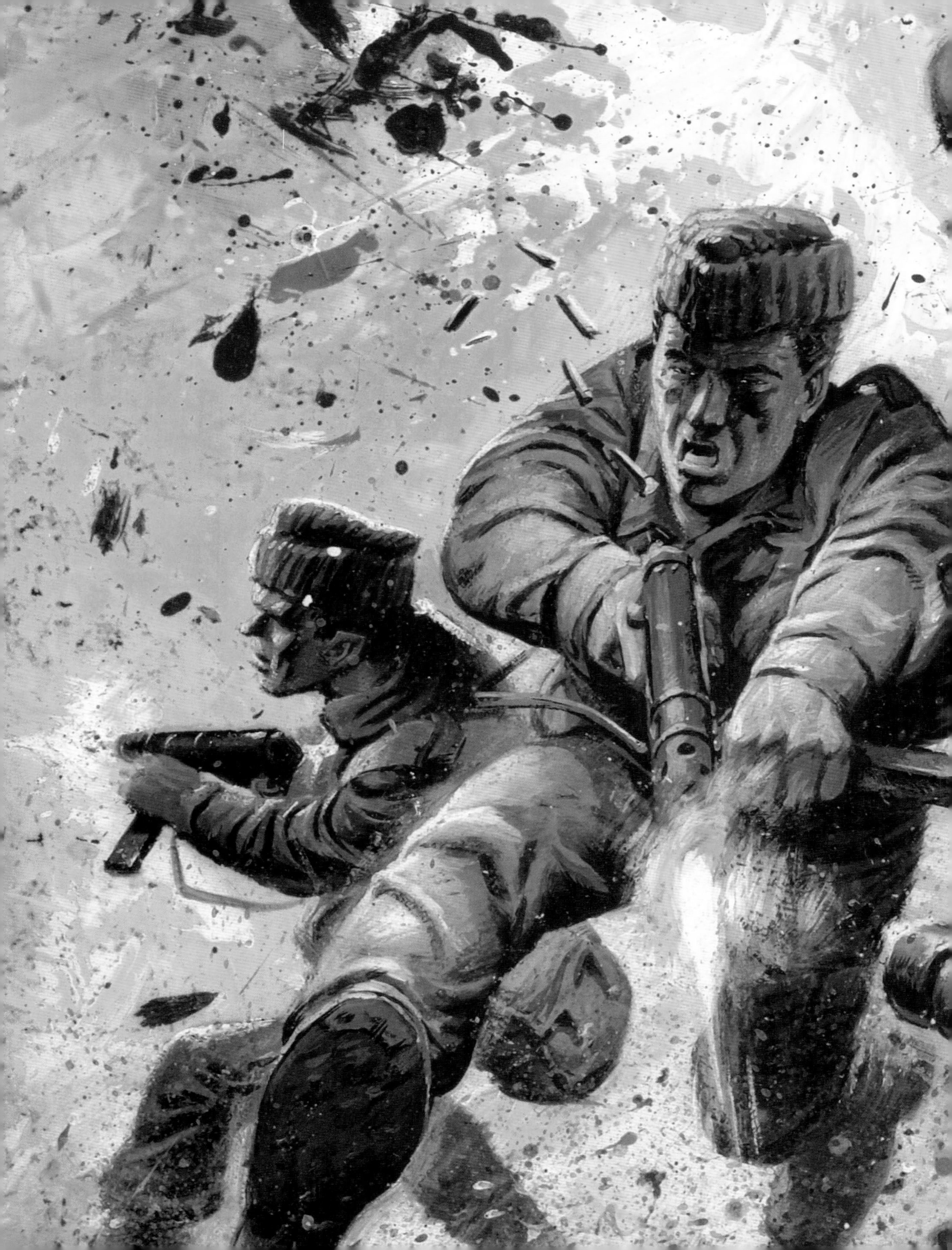

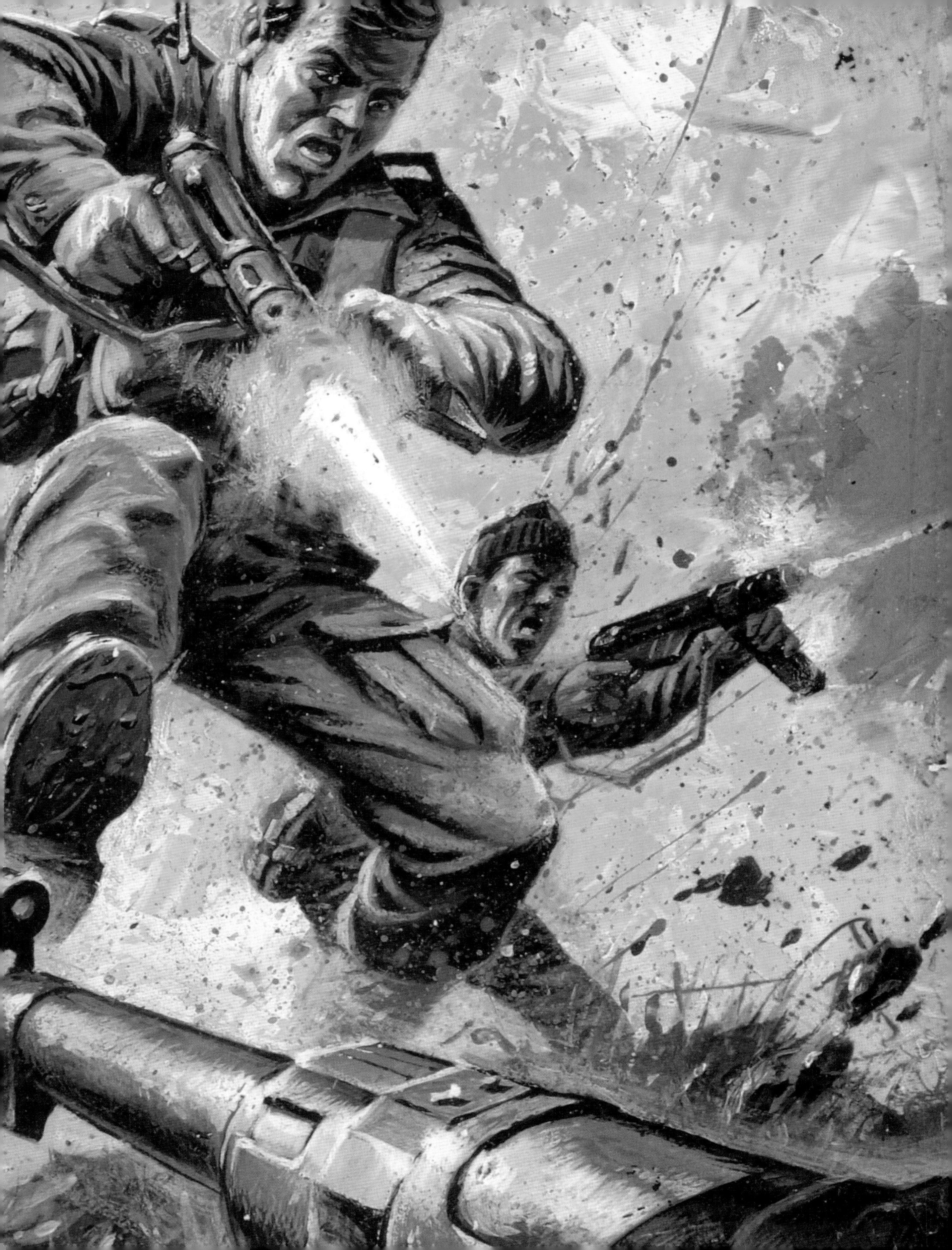

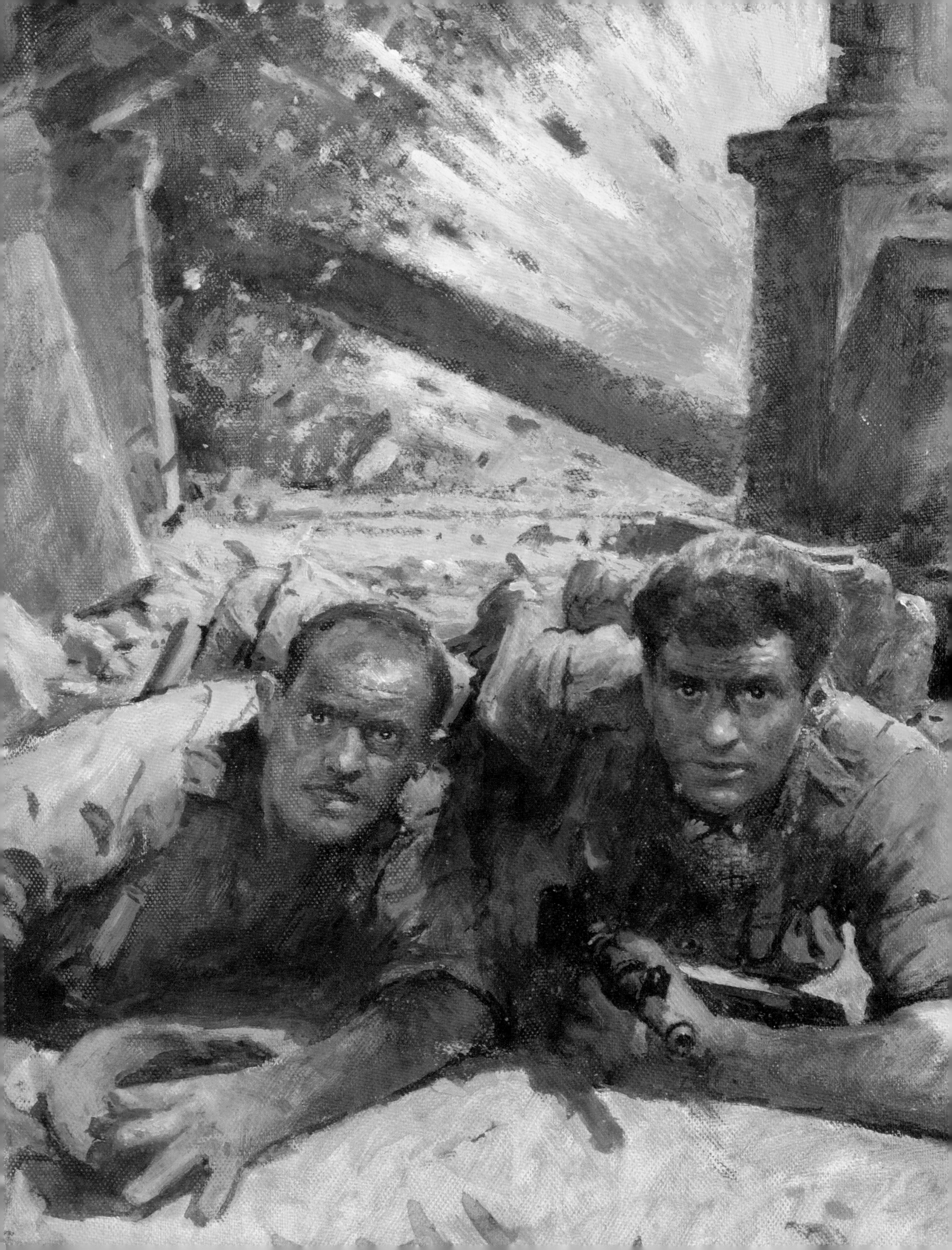

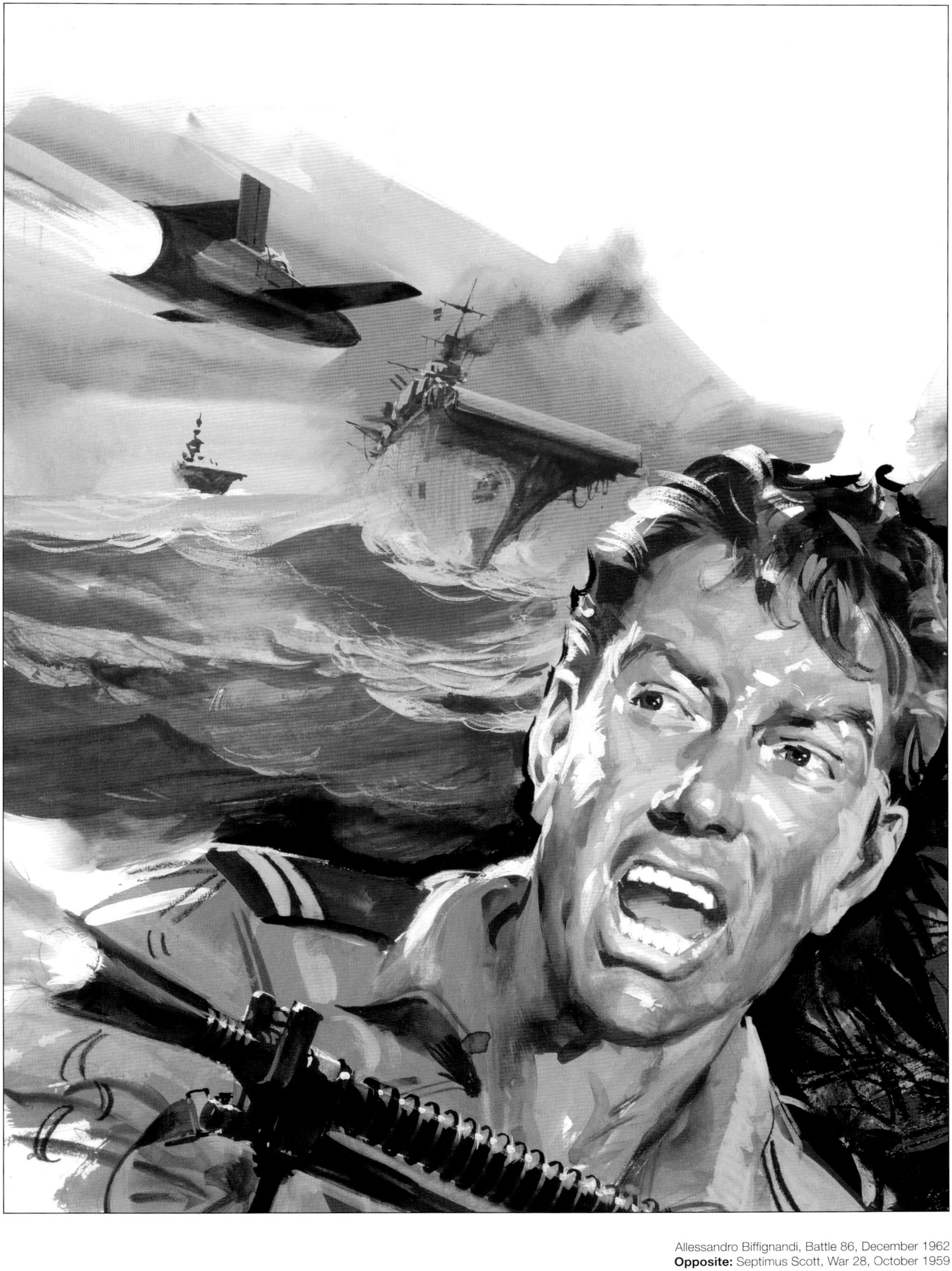

Allessandro Biffignandi, Battle 86, December 1962
Opposite: Septimus Scott, War 28, October 1959

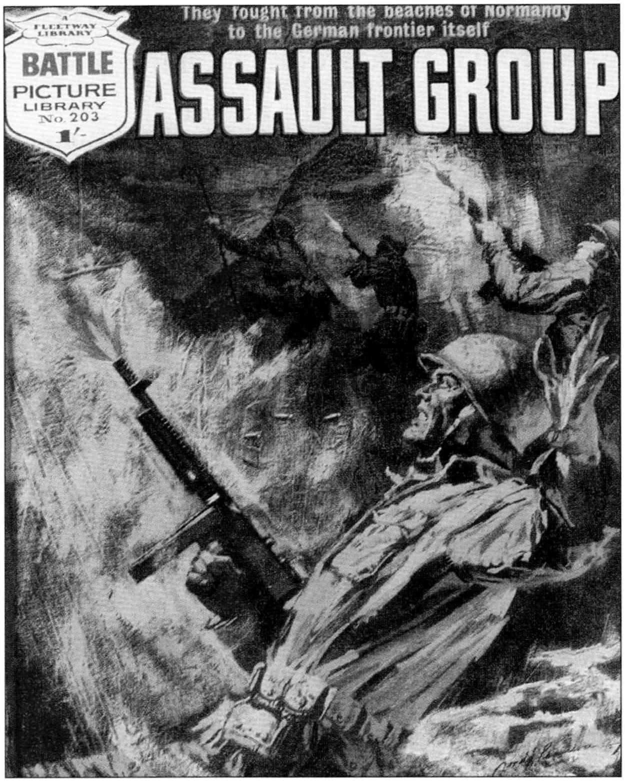
A FLEETWAY LIBRARY
BATTLE PICTURE LIBRARY No. 203
1/-
They fought from the beaches of Normandy
to the German frontier itself
ASSAULT GROUP

Jordi Penalva, Battle 203 May 190 65

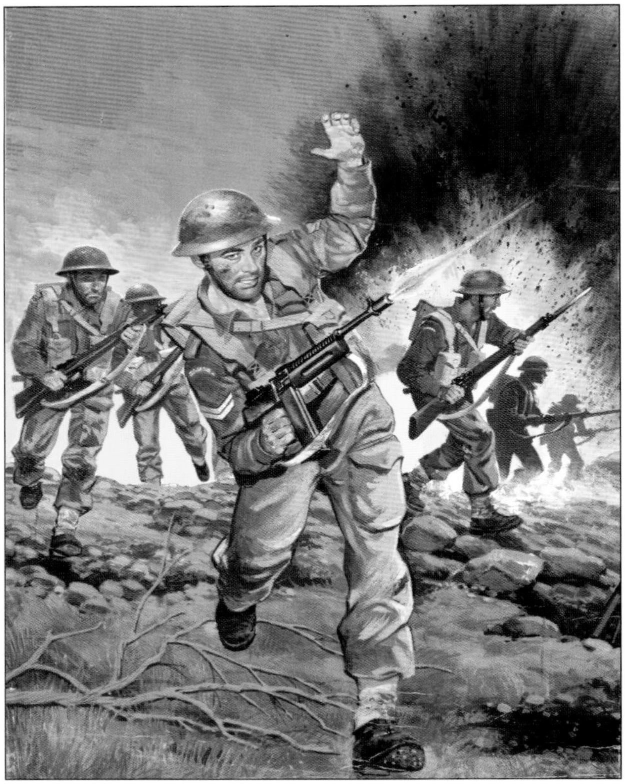

A.L.I. Agency, War 121, November 1961

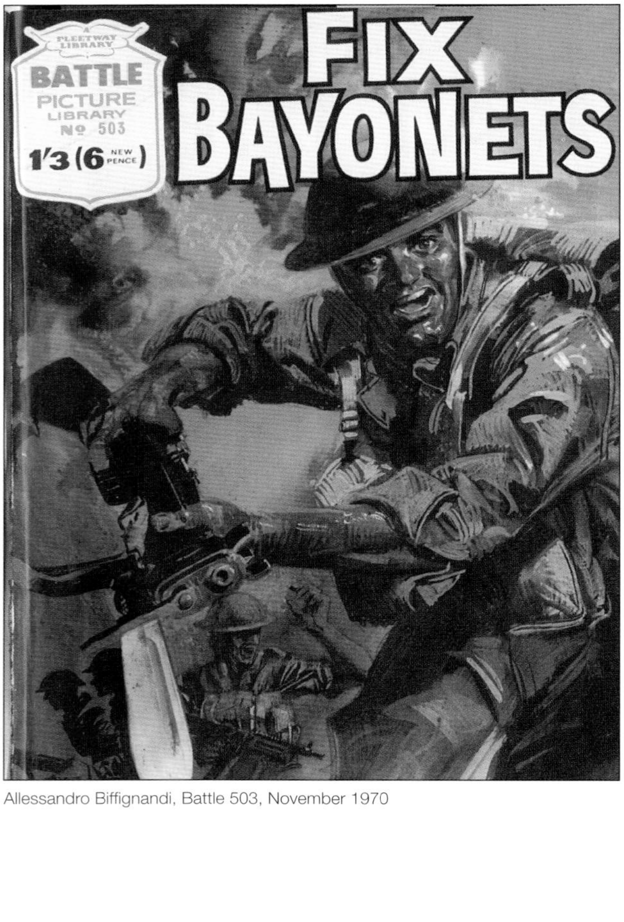
A FLEETWAY LIBRARY
BATTLE PICTURE LIBRARY Nº 503
1'3 (6 NEW PENCE)
FIX BAYONETS

Allessandro Biffignandi, Battle 503, November 1970

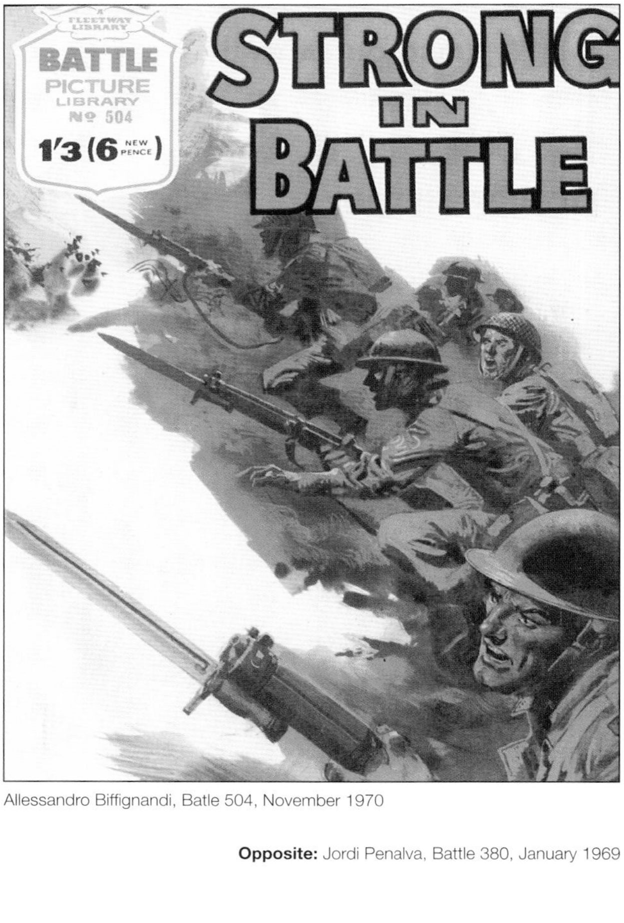
A FLEETWAY LIBRARY
BATTLE PICTURE LIBRARY Nº 504
1'3 (6 NEW PENCE)
STRONG IN BATTLE

Allessandro Biffignandi, Batle 504, November 1970

Opposite: Jordi Penalva, Battle 380, January 1969

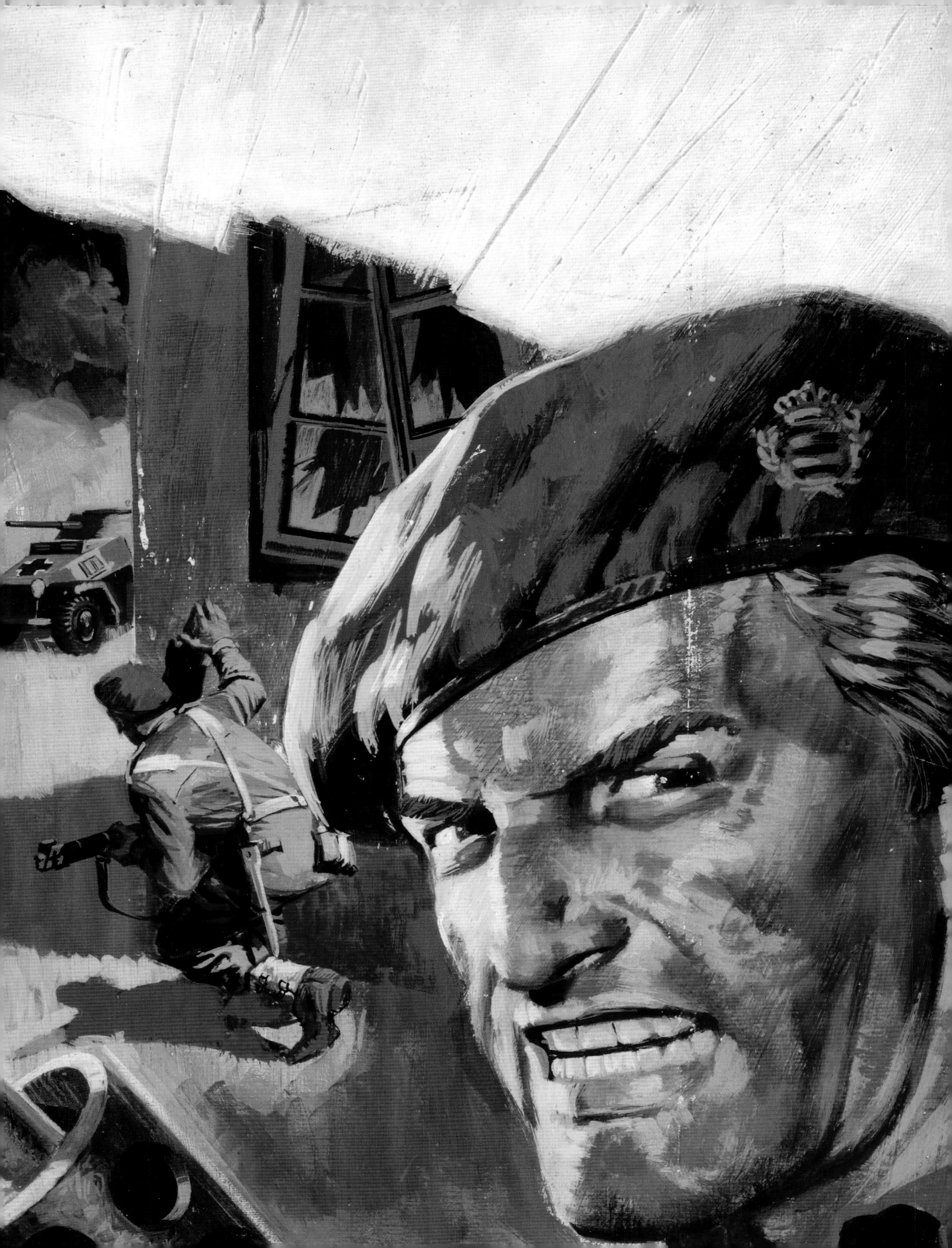

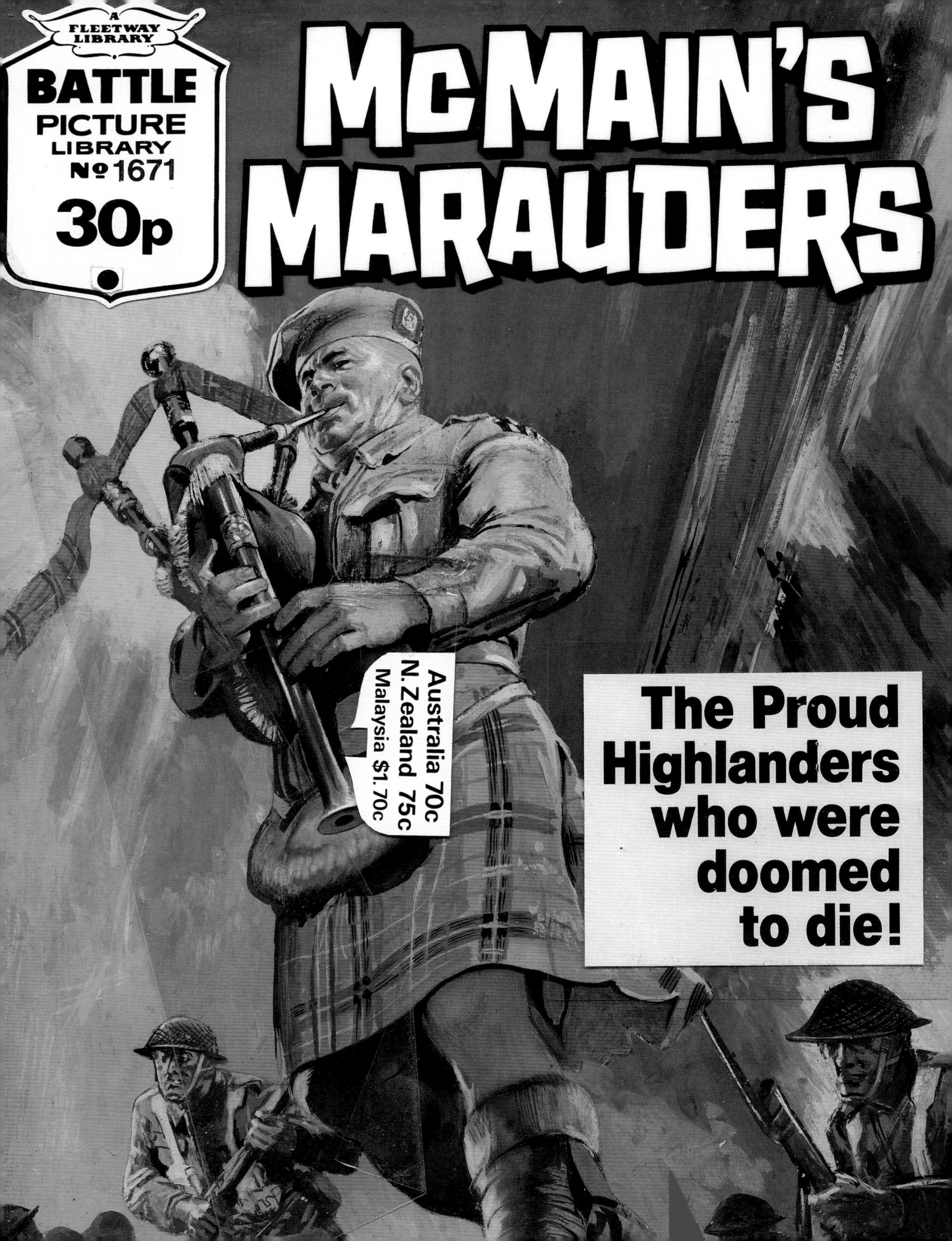
A FLEETWAY LIBRARY
BATTLE PICTURE LIBRARY
Nº 1671
30p
McMAIN'S MARAUDERS
Australia 70c
N. Zealand 75c
Malaysia $1.70c
The Proud Highlanders who were doomed to die!

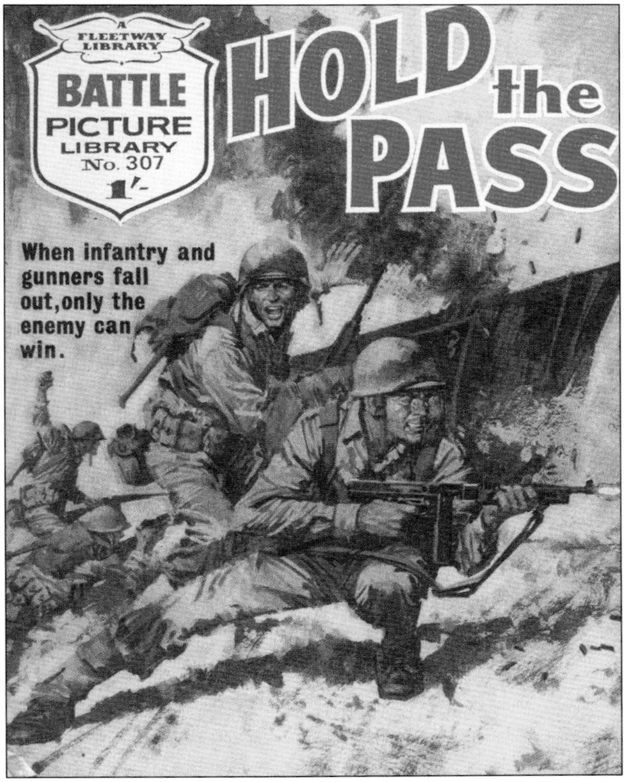
A FLEETWAY LIBRARY
BATTLE PICTURE LIBRARY No. 307
1/-
HOLD the PASS
When infantry and gunners fall out,only the enemy can win.

Jordi Longaron, Battle 307, July 1967

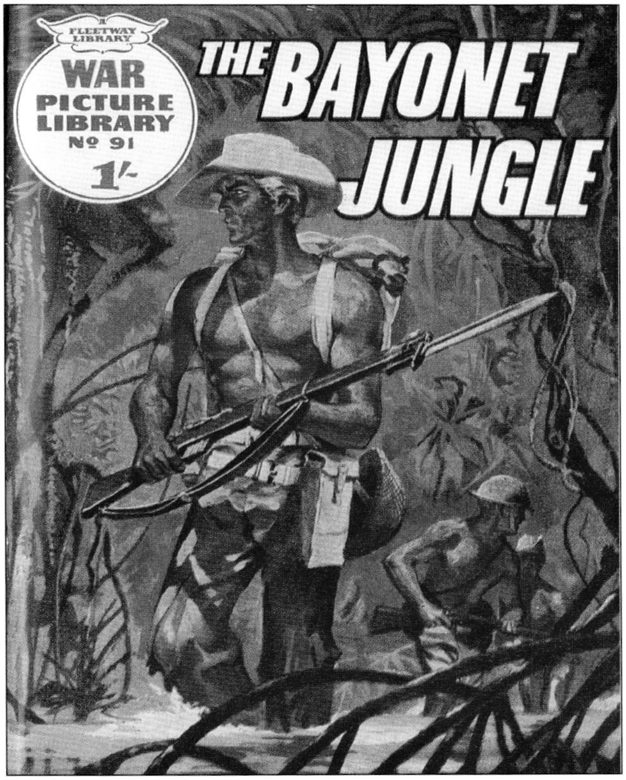
A FLEETWAY LIBRARY
WAR PICTURE LIBRARY Nº 91
1/-
THE BAYONET JUNGLE

Pino Dell'Orco, Battle 91, January 1963

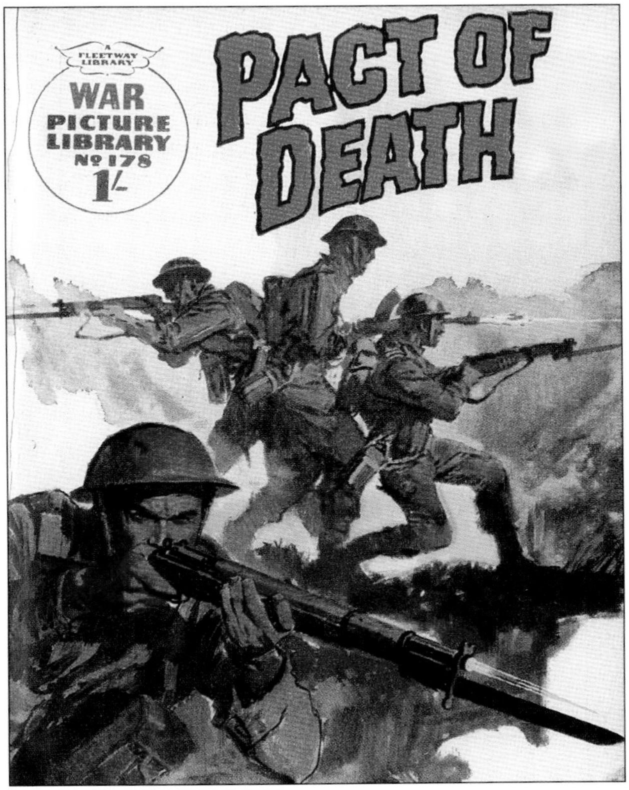
A FLEETWAY LIBRARY
WAR PICTURE LIBRARY Nº 178
1/-
PACT OF DEATH

Jordi Penalva, War 178, January 1963

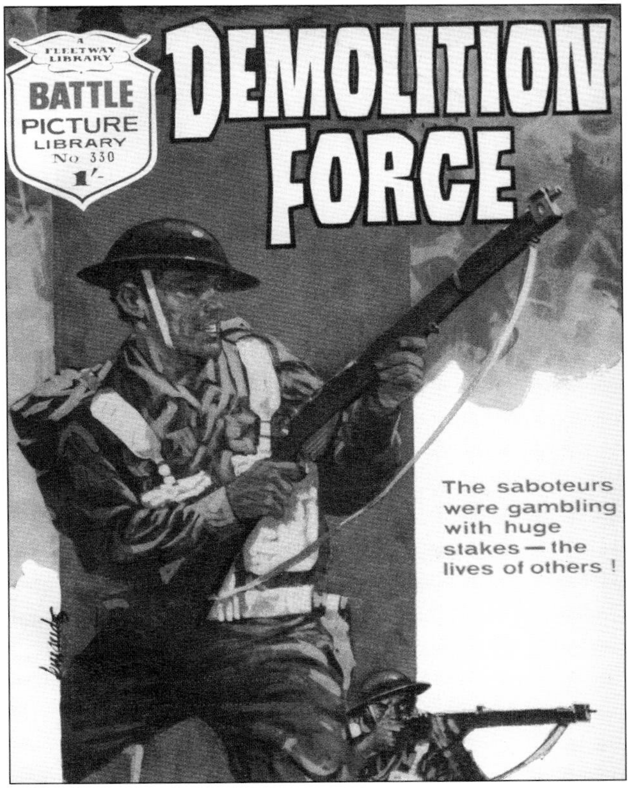
A FLEETWAY LIBRARY
BATTLE PICTURE LIBRARY No 330
1/-
DEMOLITION FORCE
The saboteurs were gambling with huge stakes — the lives of others !

Fernando Fernandez, Battle 330, January 1968

Opposite: Giorgio DeGaspari, originally War 83, January 1961

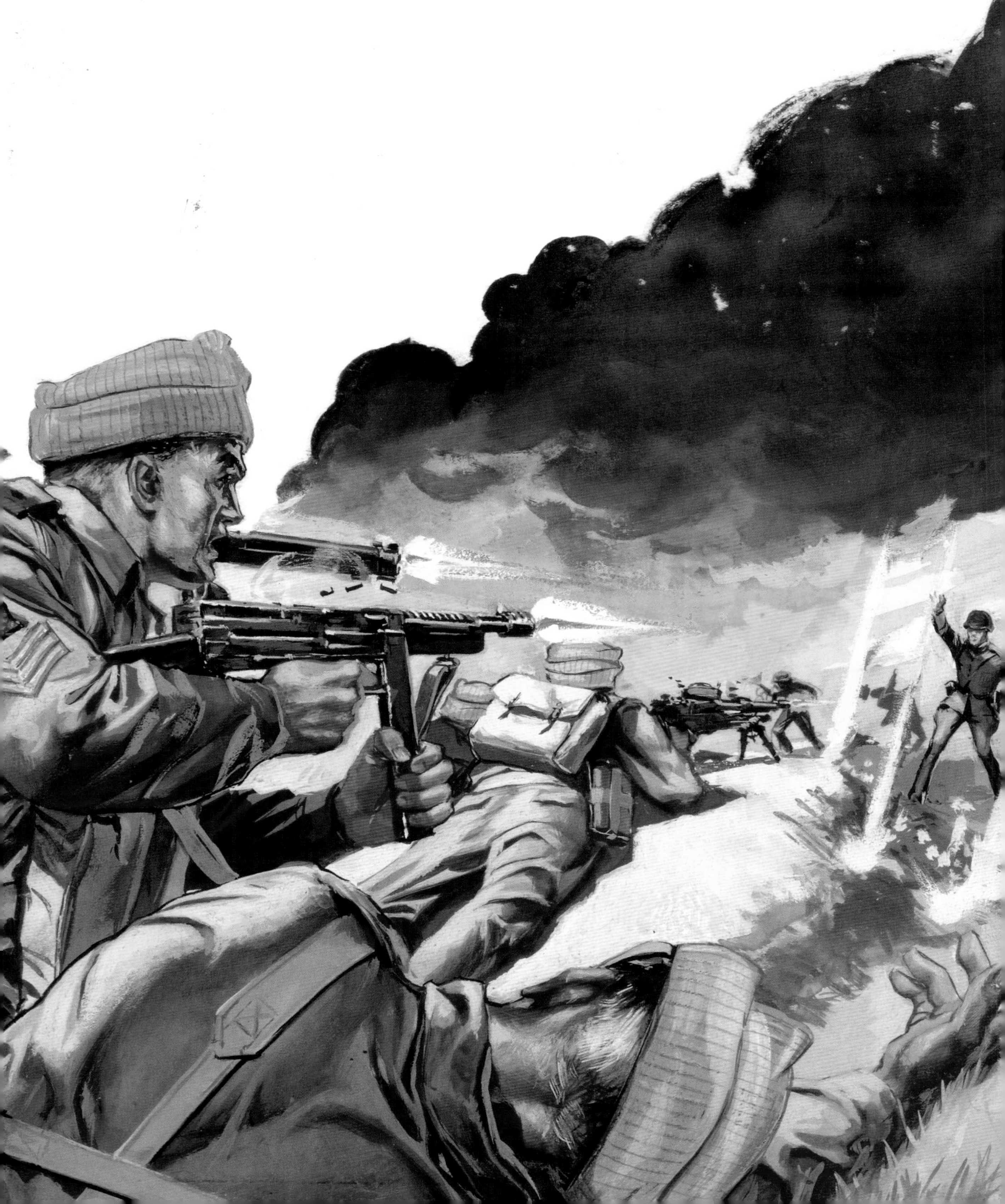

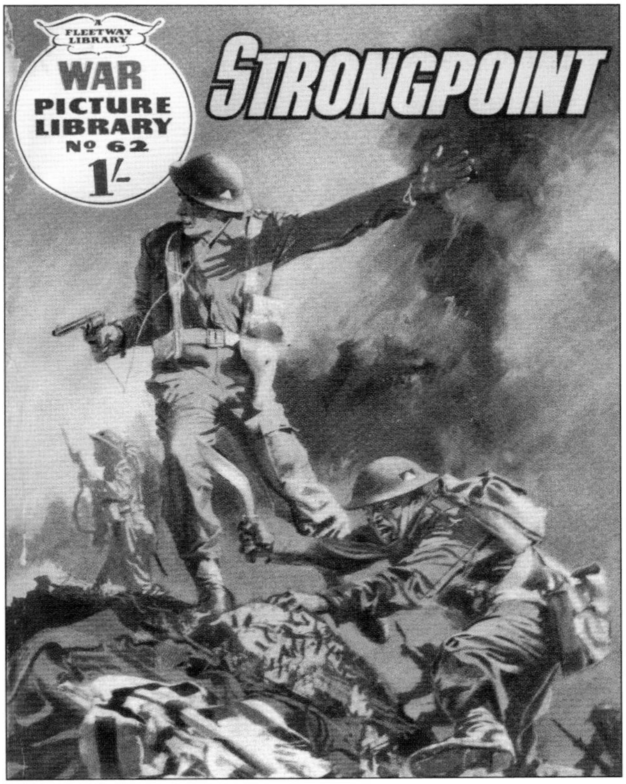
A FLEETWAY LIBRARY
WAR PICTURE LIBRARY Nº 62
1/-
STRONGPOINT

Giorgio DeGaspari, War 62, August 1960

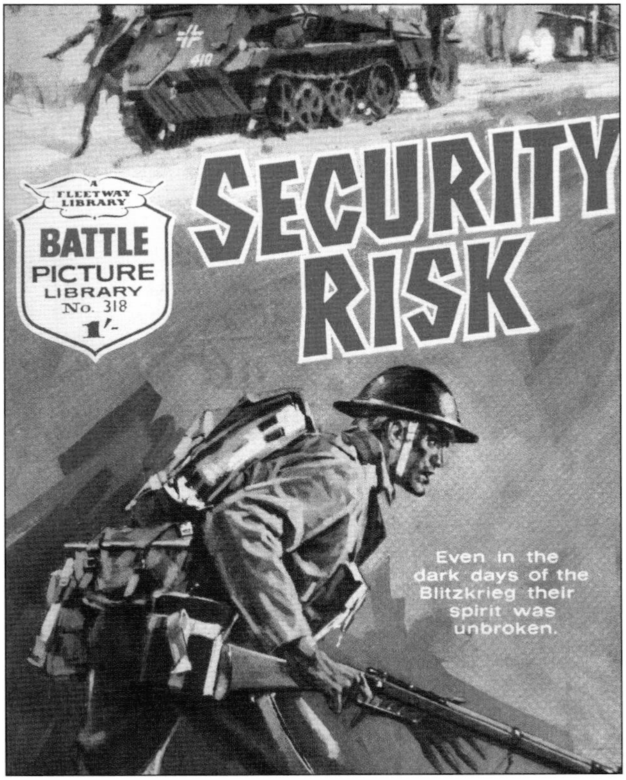
A FLEETWAY LIBRARY
BATTLE PICTURE LIBRARY No. 318
1/-
SECURITY RISK
Even in the dark days of the Blitzkrieg their spirit was unbroken.

Rafael, Lopez Espi Battle 318, October 1967

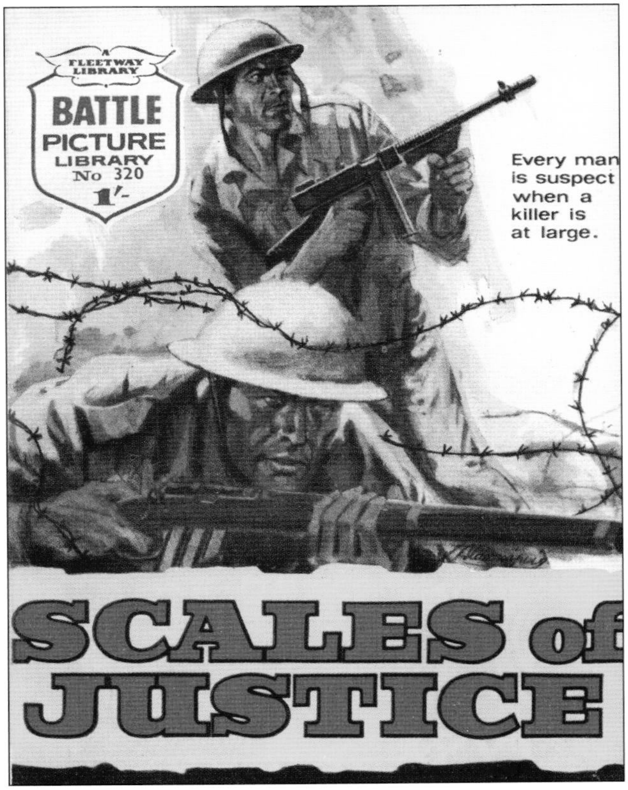
A FLEETWAY LIBRARY
BATTLE PICTURE LIBRARY No 320
1/-
Every man is suspect when a killer is at large.
SCALES of JUSTICE

Artur Aldoma Puig, Battle 320, October 1967

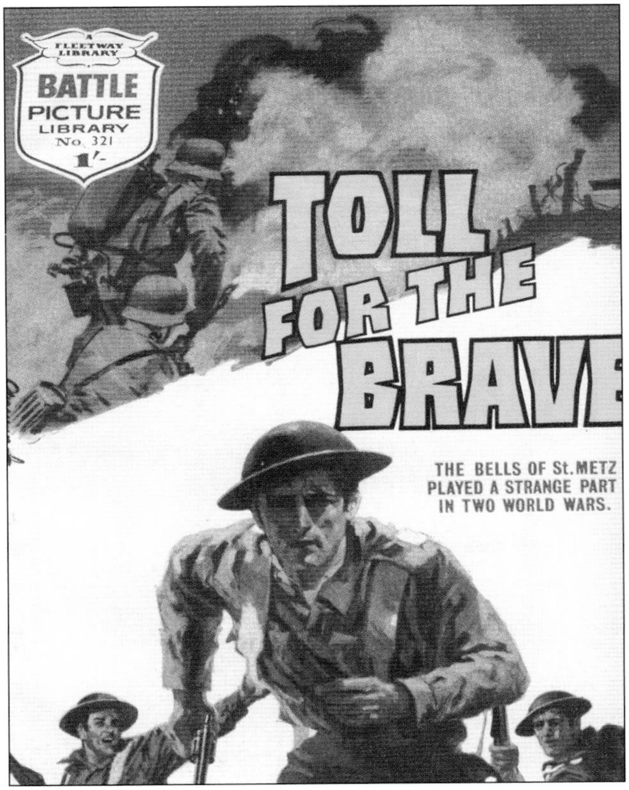
A FLEETWAY LIBRARY
BATTLE PICTURE LIBRARY No. 321
1/-
TOLL FOR THE BRAVE
THE BELLS OF St. METZ PLAYED A STRANGE PART IN TWO WORLD WARS.

Fernando Fernandez, Battle 321, November 1967

Opposite: Nino Caroselli, War 146, May 1962

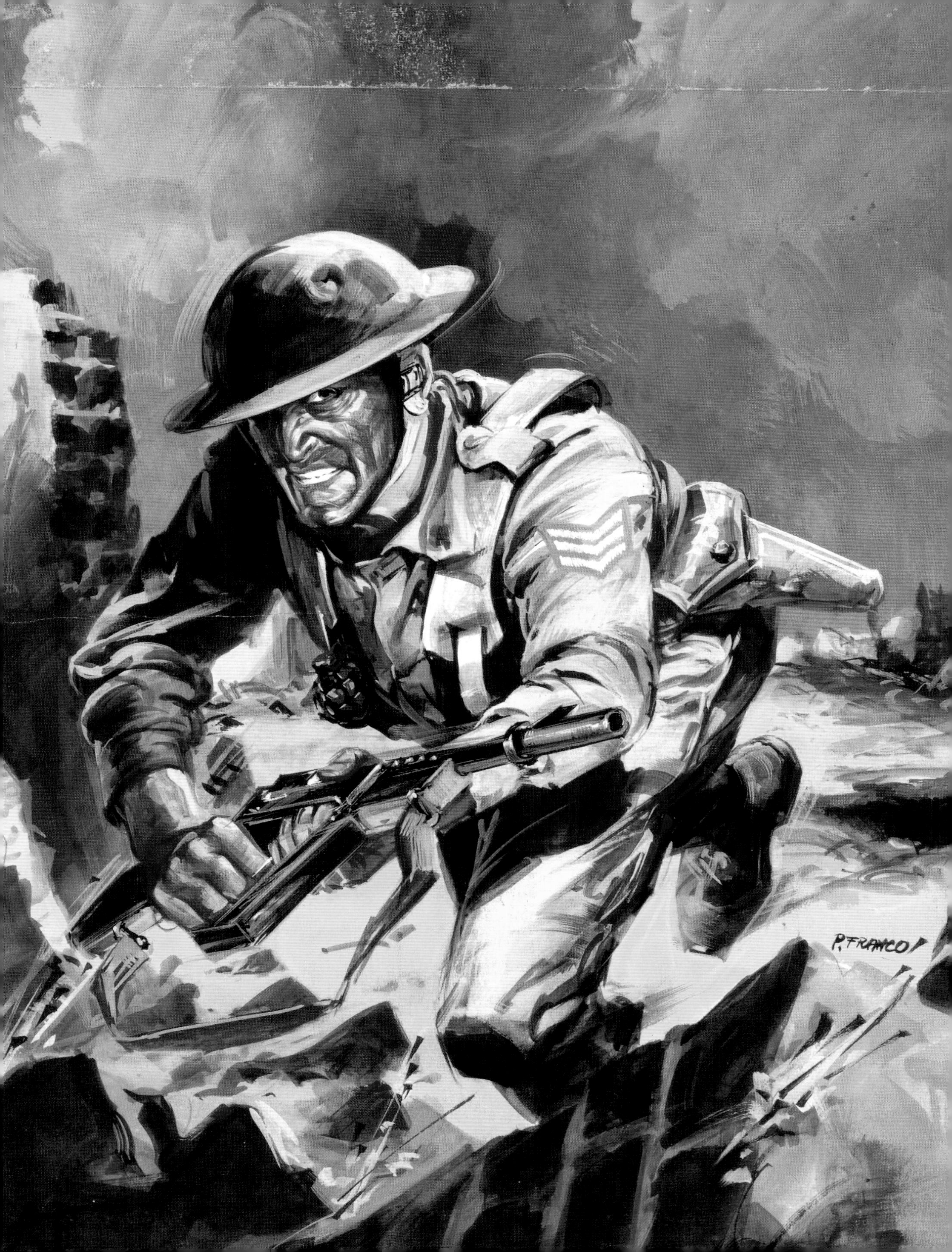
P. FRANCO

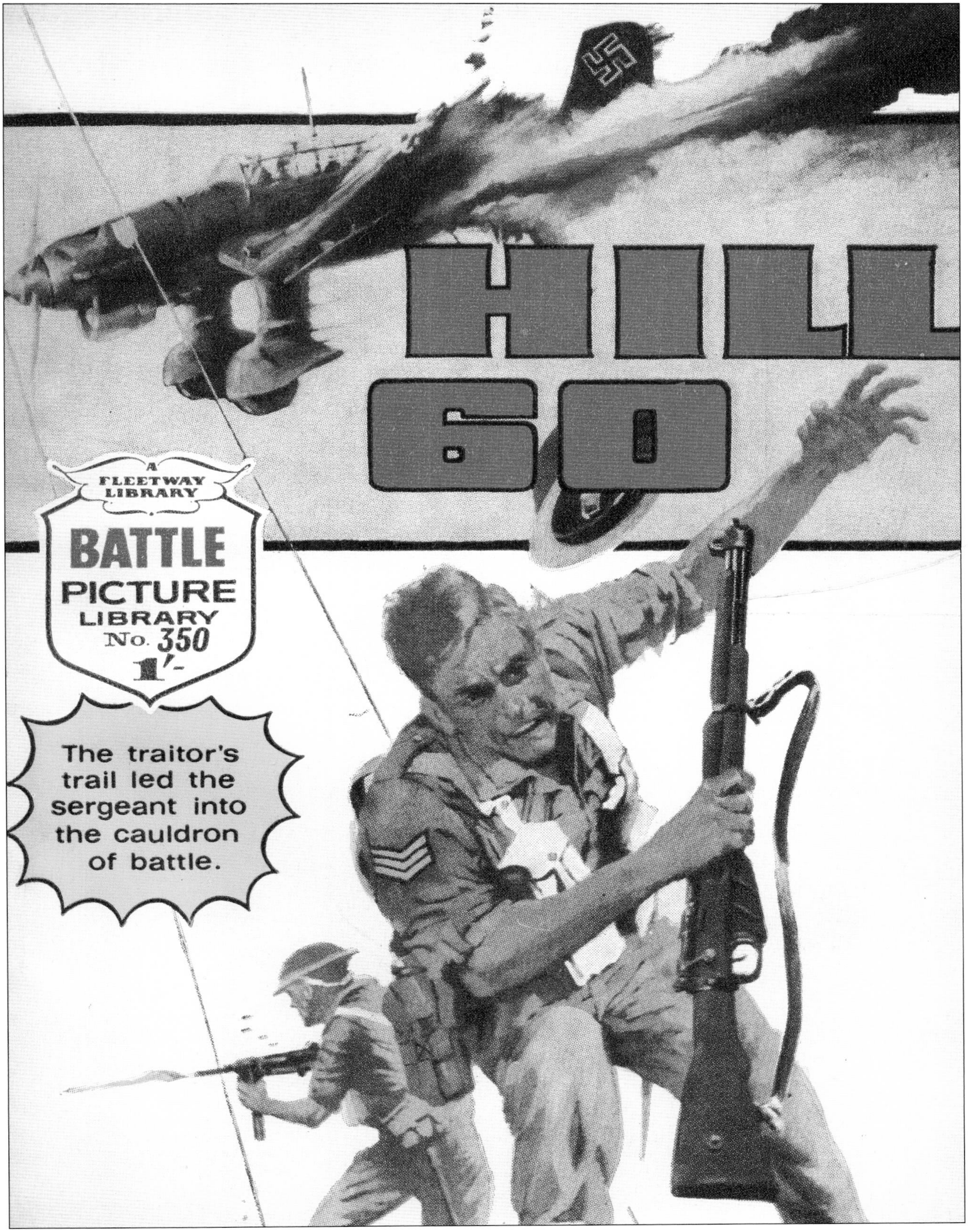
HILL 60
A FLEETWAY LIBRARY
BATTLE PICTURE LIBRARY
No. 350
1/-
The traitor's trail led the sergeant into the cauldron of battle.

Manuel Sanjulian, Battle 350, June 1968
Opposite: Franco Picchioni, War 622, November 1970

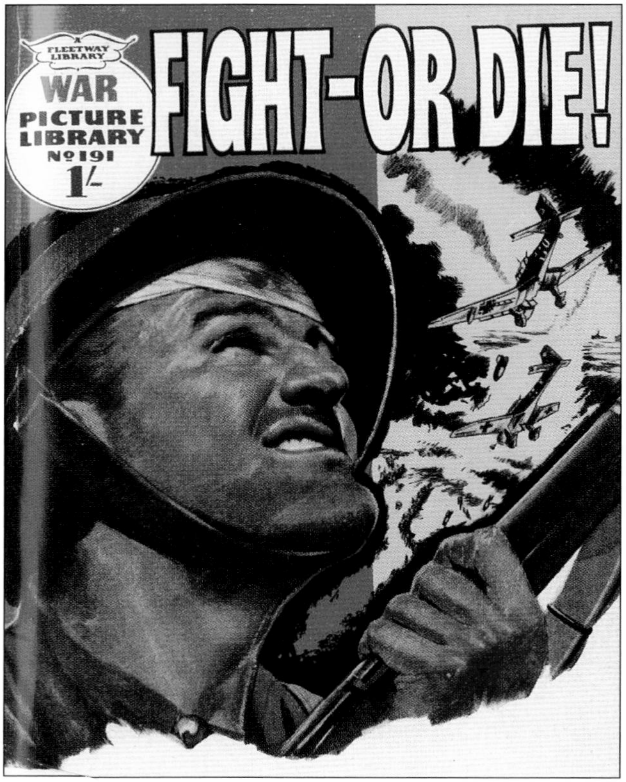
A FLEETWAY LIBRARY
WAR PICTURE LIBRARY
Nº 191
1/-
FIGHT-OR DIE!

Allessandro Biffignandi, War 191, April 1963

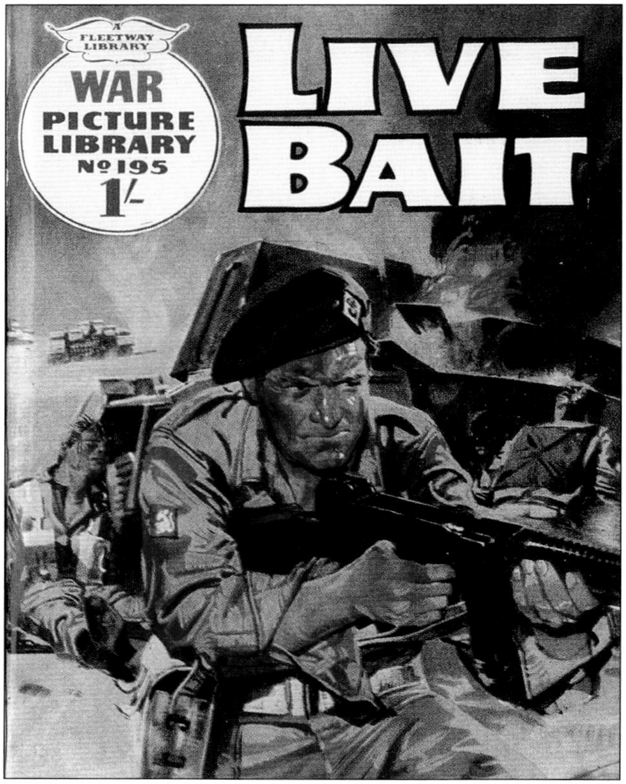
A FLEETWAY LIBRARY
WAR PICTURE LIBRARY
Nº 195
1/-
LIVE BAIT

Allessandro Biffignandi, War 195, May 1963

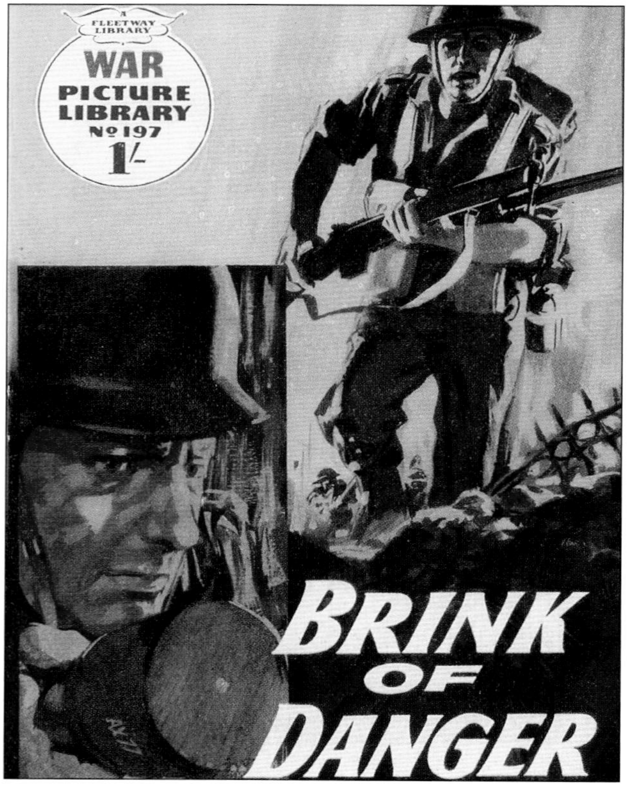
A FLEETWAY LIBRARY
WAR PICTURE LIBRARY
Nº 197
1/-
BRINK OF DANGER

Pino Dell'Orco, War 197, June 1963

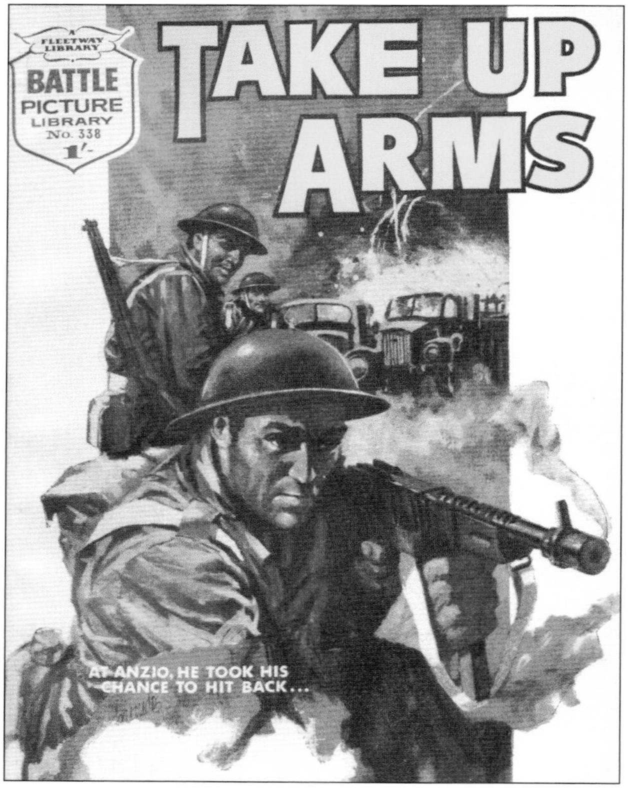
A FLEETWAY LIBRARY
BATTLE PICTURE LIBRARY
No. 338
1/-
TAKE UP ARMS
AT ANZIO, HE TOOK HIS CHANCE TO HIT BACK...

Fernando Fernandez, Battle 338, March 1968

Opposite: Allessandro Biffignandi, Battle 73, September 1962

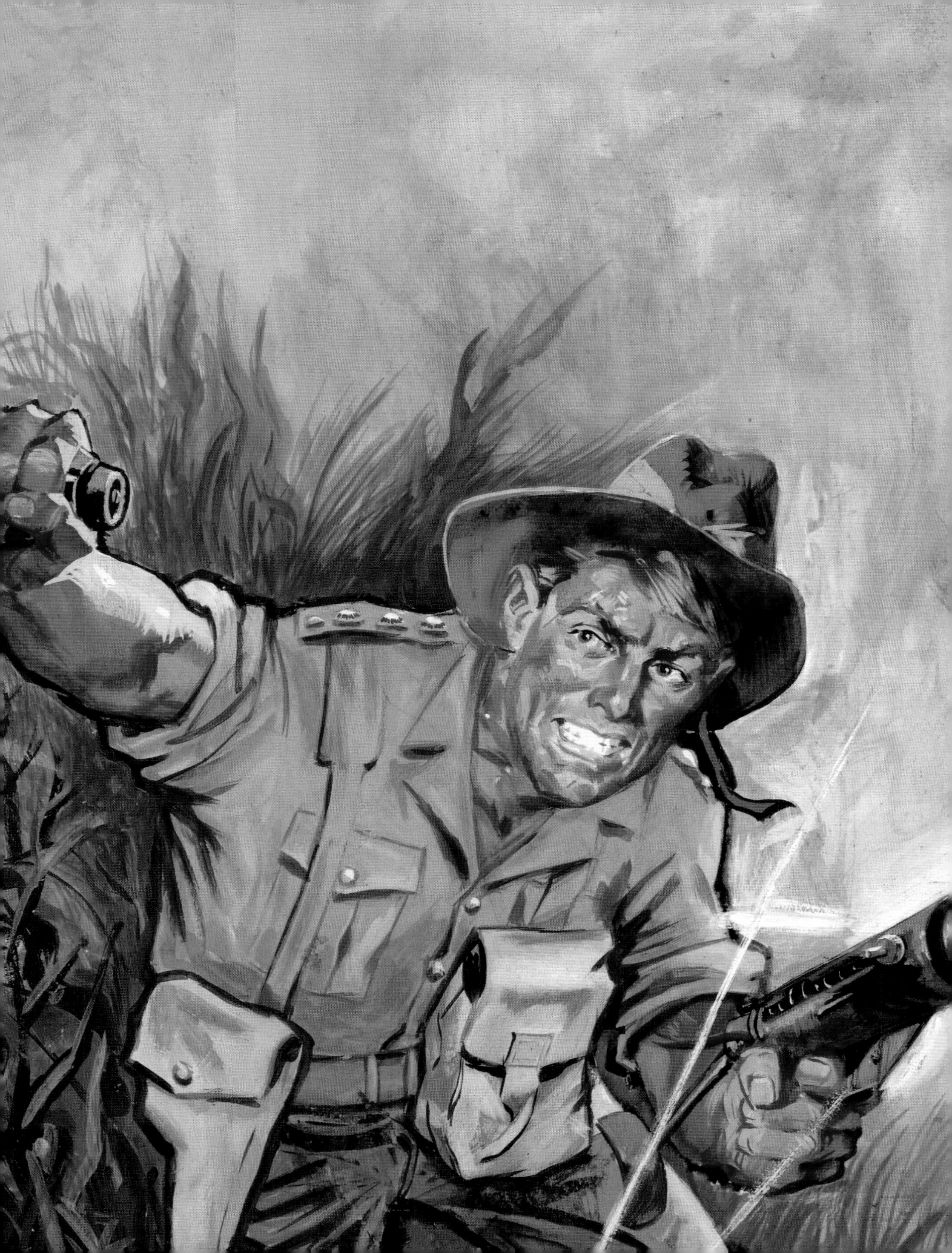

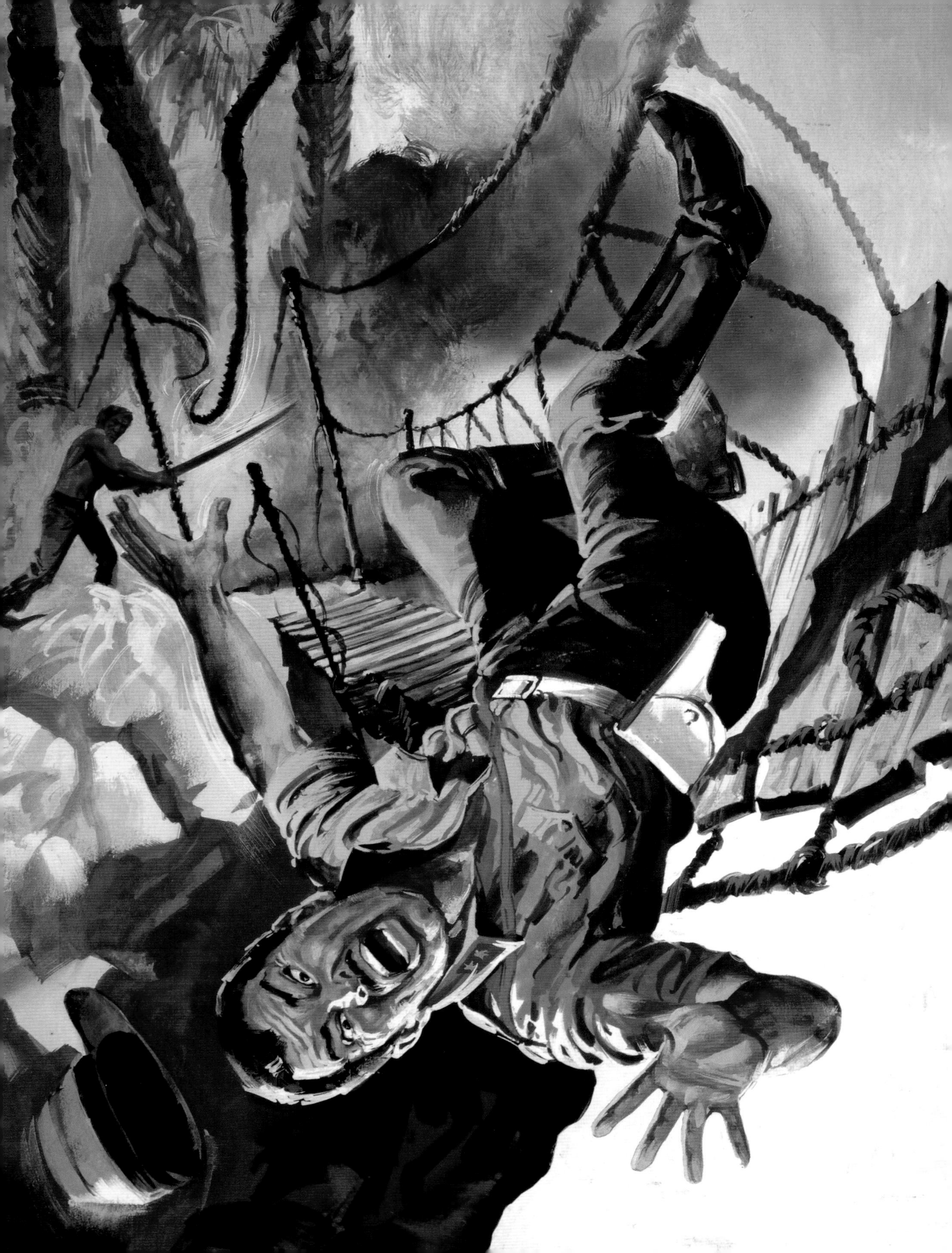

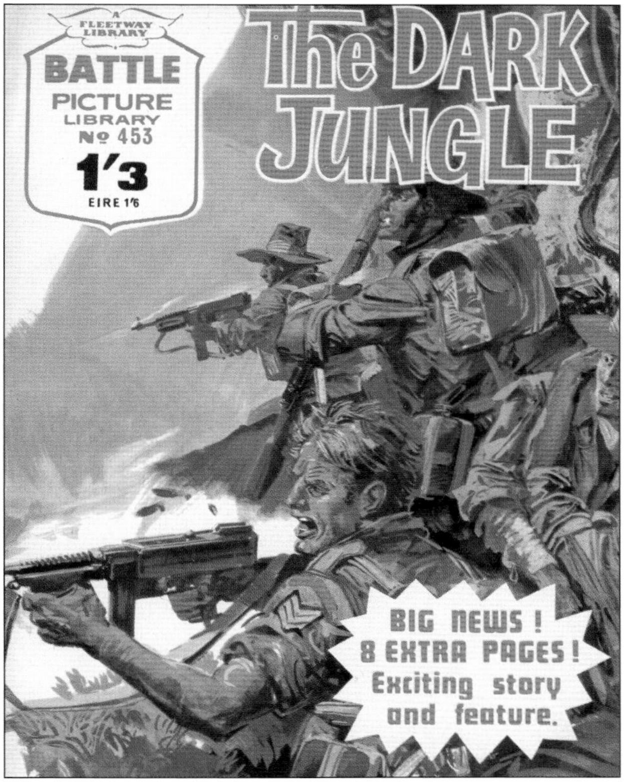
A FLEETWAY LIBRARY
BATTLE PICTURE LIBRARY Nº 453
1'3
EIRE 1'6
The DARK JUNGLE
BIG NEWS ! 8 EXTRA PAGES ! Exciting story and feature.

Allessandro Biffignandi, Battle 453, March 1970

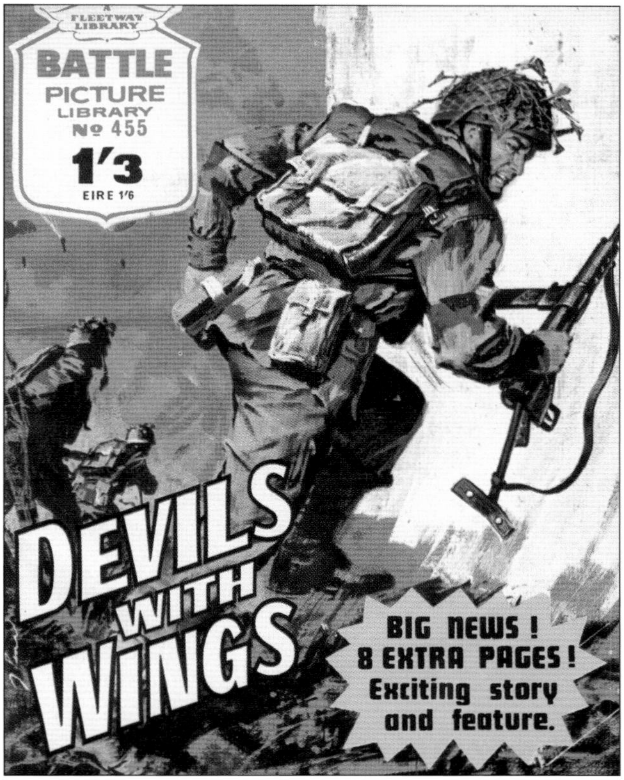
A FLEETWAY LIBRARY
BATTLE PICTURE LIBRARY Nº 455
1'3
EIRE 1'6
DEVILS WITH WINGS
BIG NEWS ! 8 EXTRA PAGES ! Exciting story and feature.

Jordi Penalva, Battle 455, March 1970

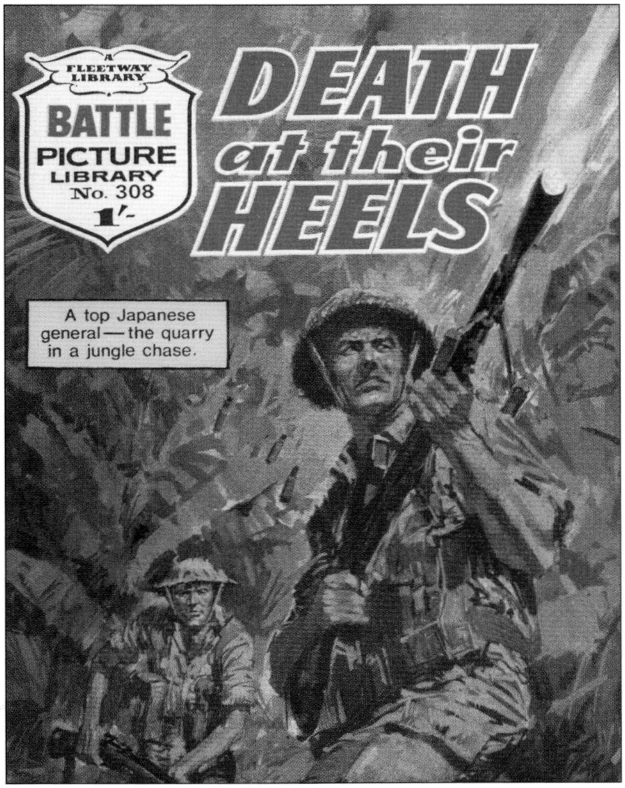
A FLEETWAY LIBRARY
BATTLE PICTURE LIBRARY No. 308
1/-
DEATH at their HEELS
A top Japanese general—the quarry in a jungle chase.

Jordi Longaron, Battle 308, July 1967

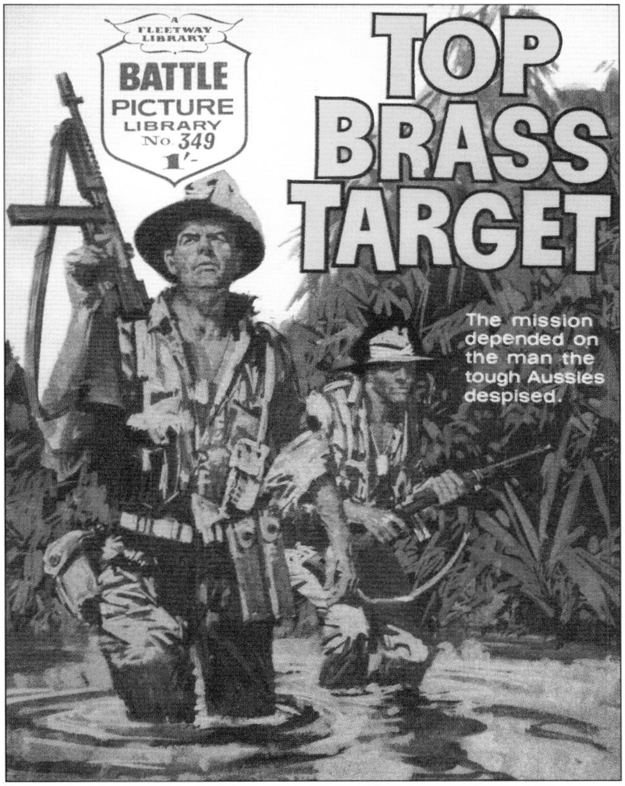
A FLEETWAY LIBRARY
BATTLE PICTURE LIBRARY No. 349
1/-
TOP BRASS TARGET
The mission depended on the man the tough Aussies despised.

Jordi Longaron, Battle 349, June 1968

Opposite: Franco Picchioni, Battle 412, August 1969
Overleaf: Graham Coton, Battle 1643, December 1983

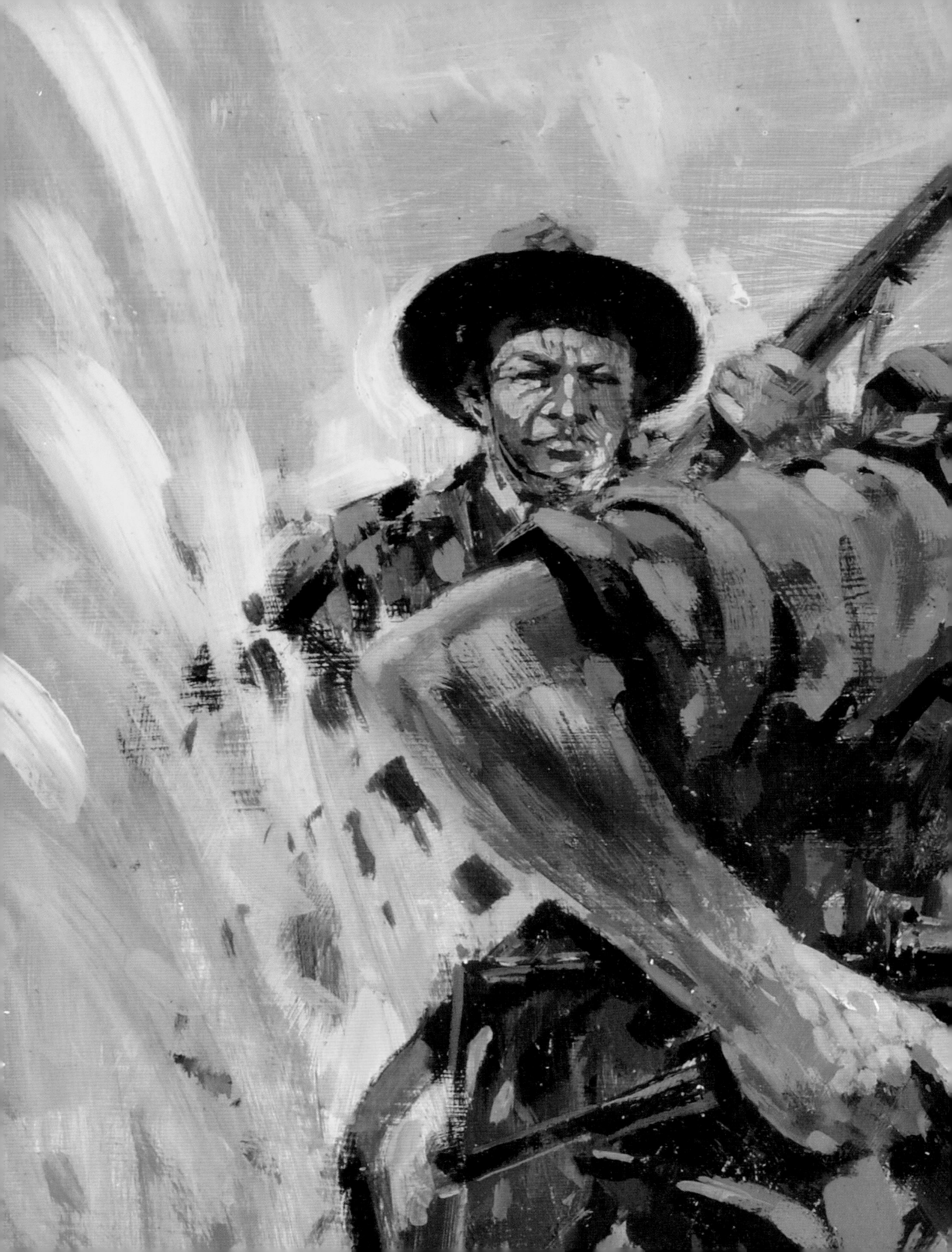

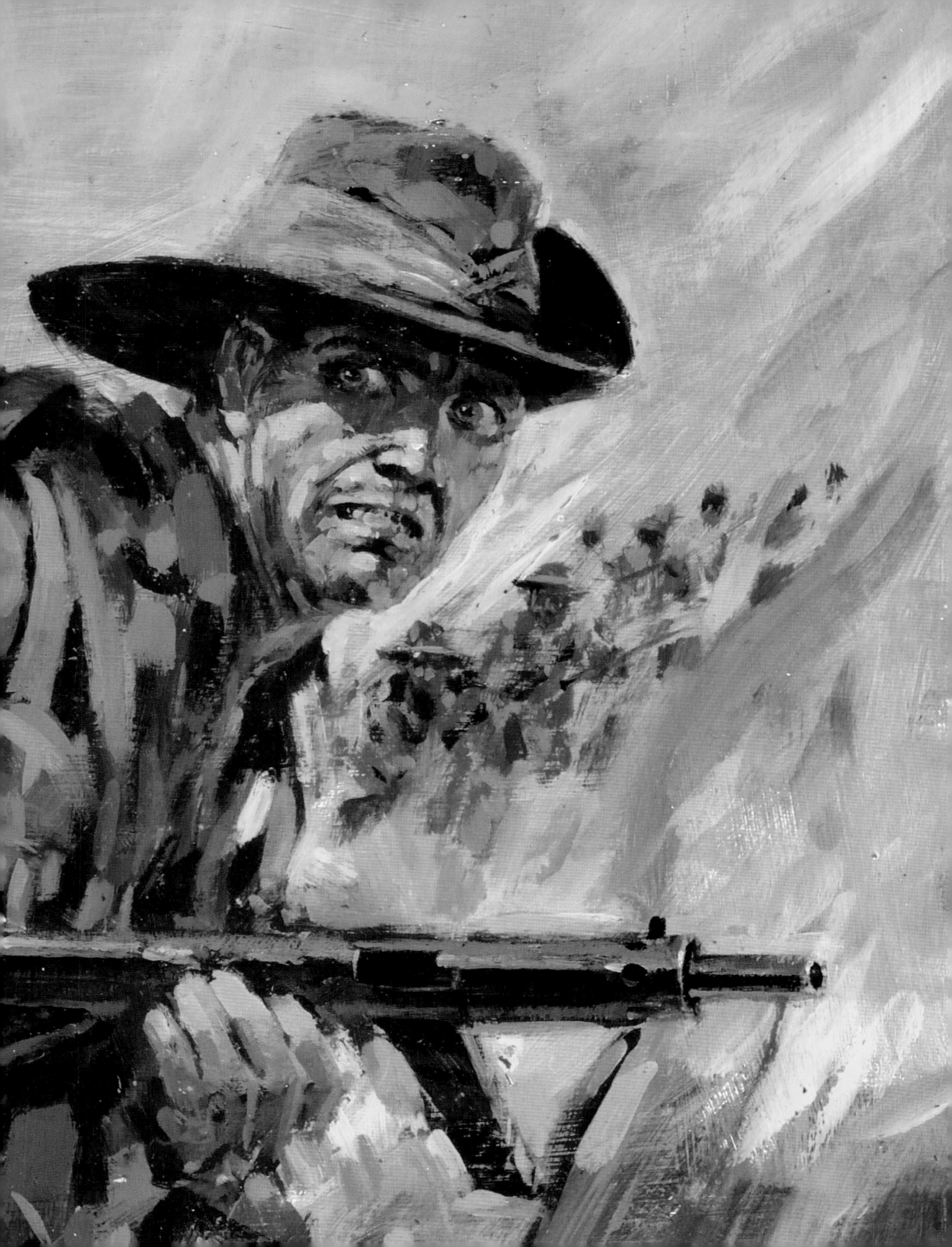

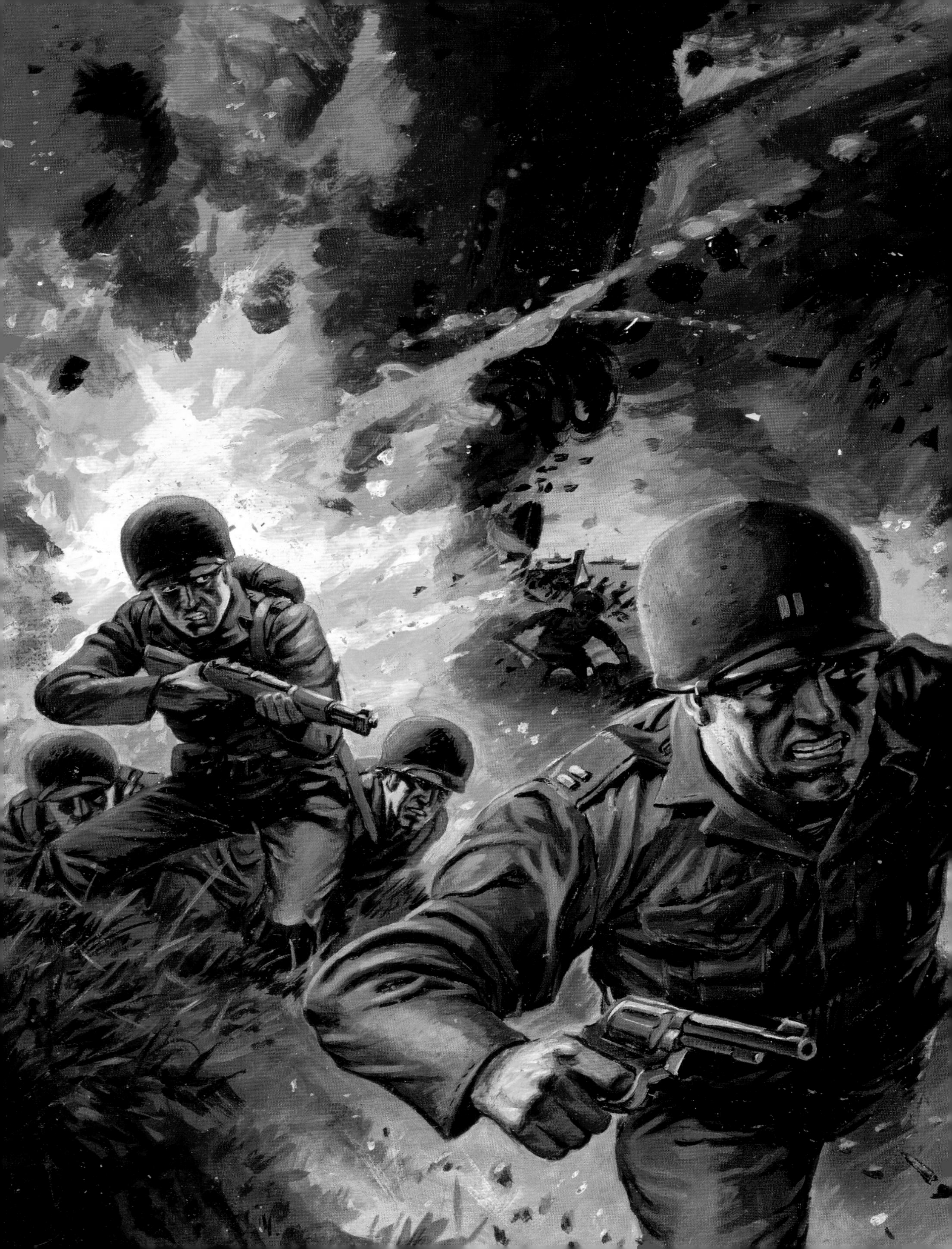

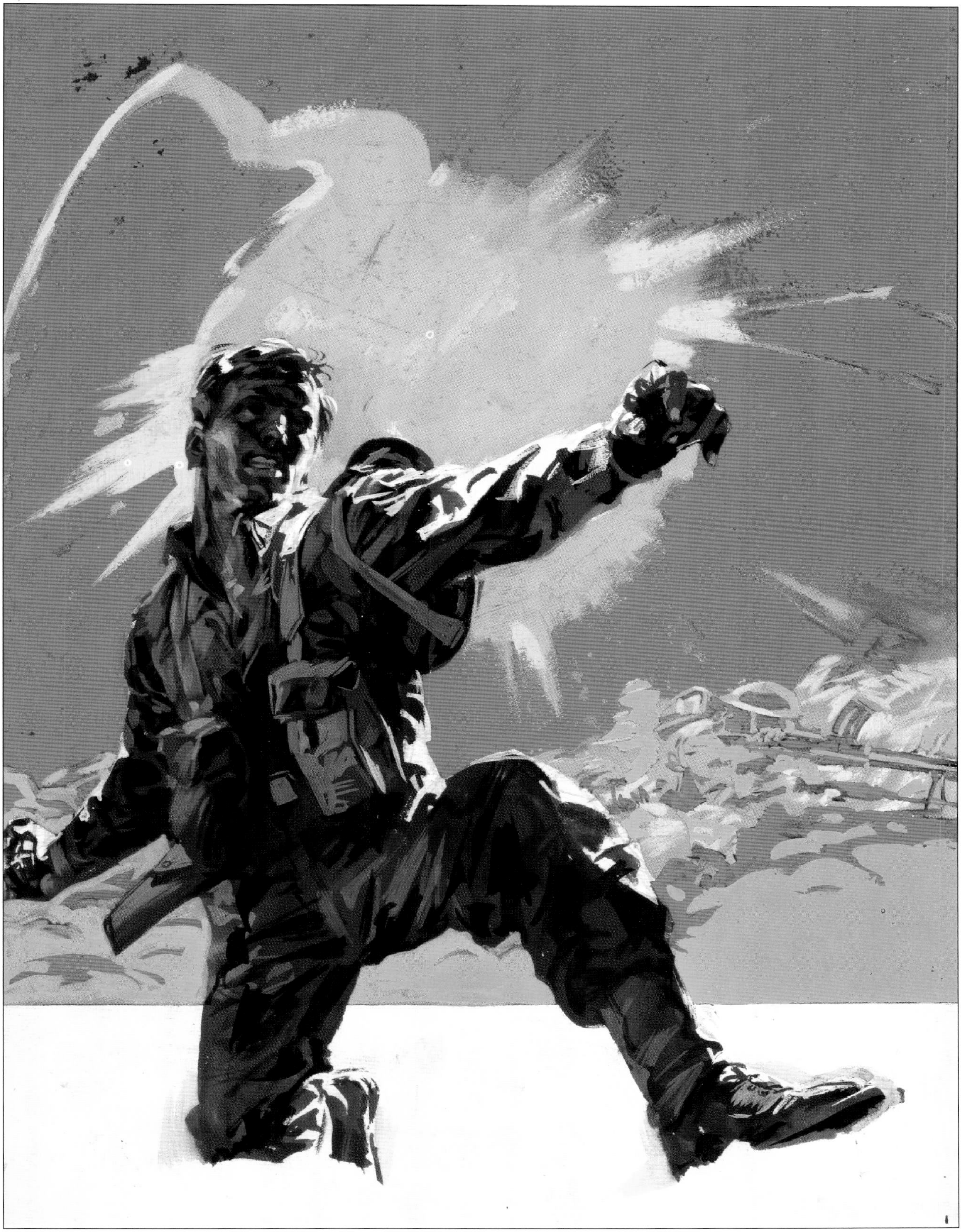

Pino Dell'Orco, Battle 66, July 1962
Opposite: Oliver Frey, Battle 705, April 1973

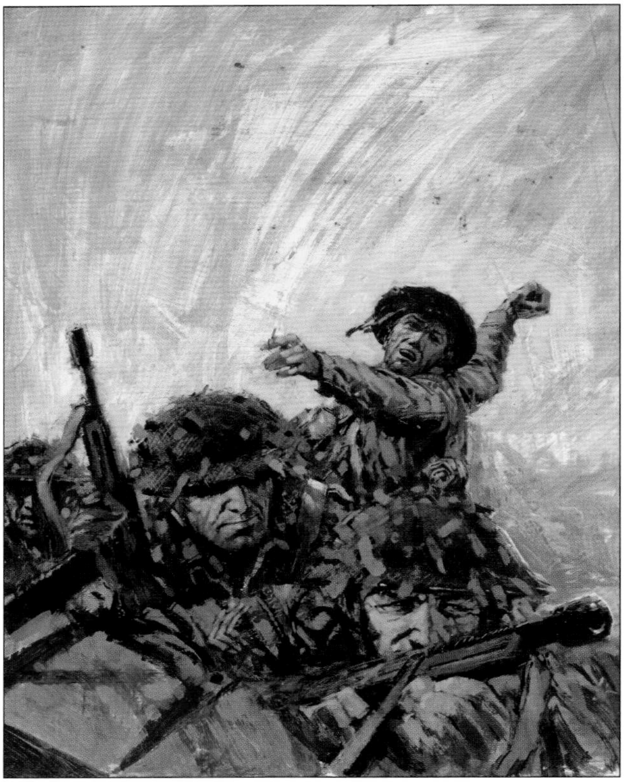

Graham Coton, War 1507, June 1978

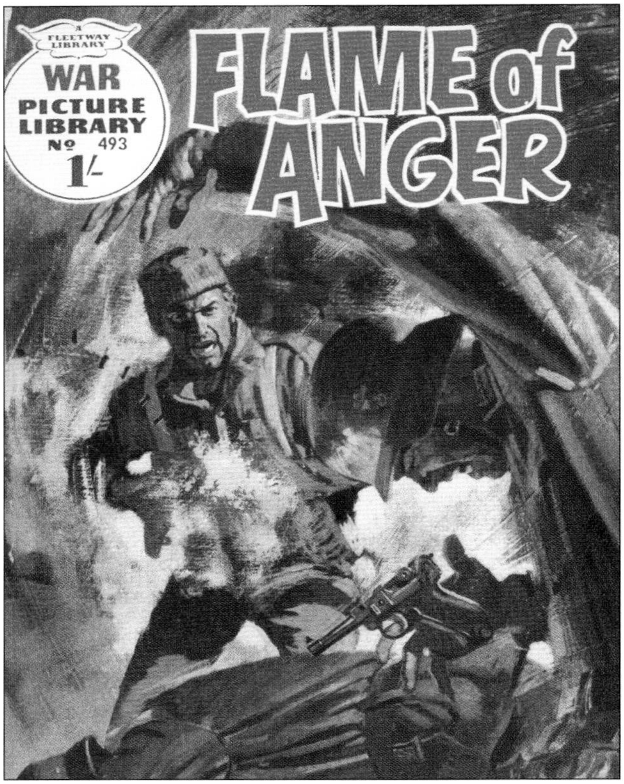
A FLEETWAY LIBRARY
WAR PICTURE LIBRARY
Nº 493
1/-
FLAME of ANGER

Jordi Penalva, War 493, January 1969

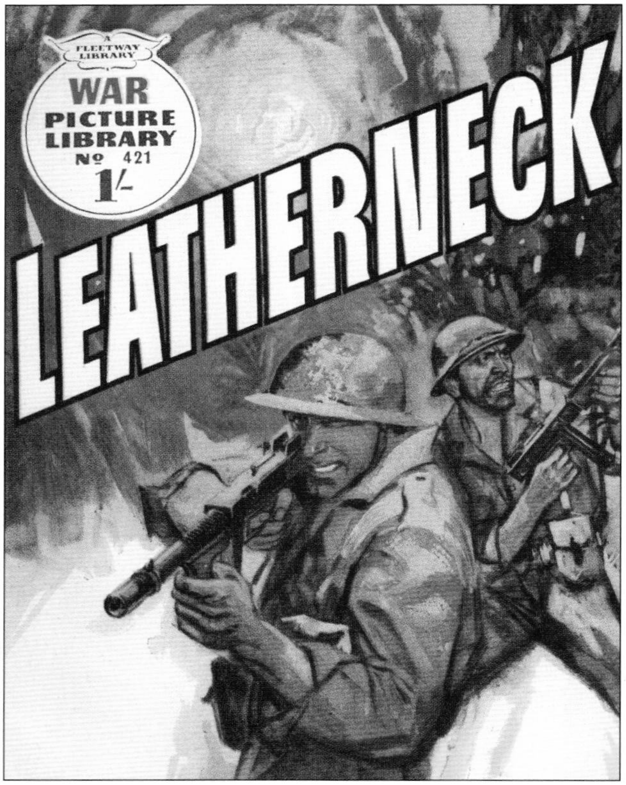
A FLEETWAY LIBRARY
WAR PICTURE LIBRARY
Nº 421
1/-
LEATHERNECK

Artur Aldoma Puig, War 421, January 1968

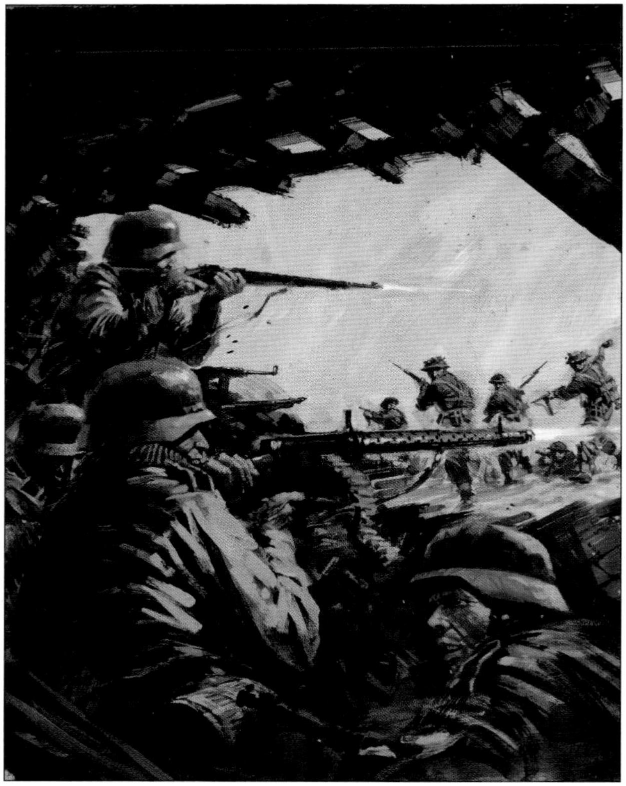

Graham Coton, War 1506, June 1978

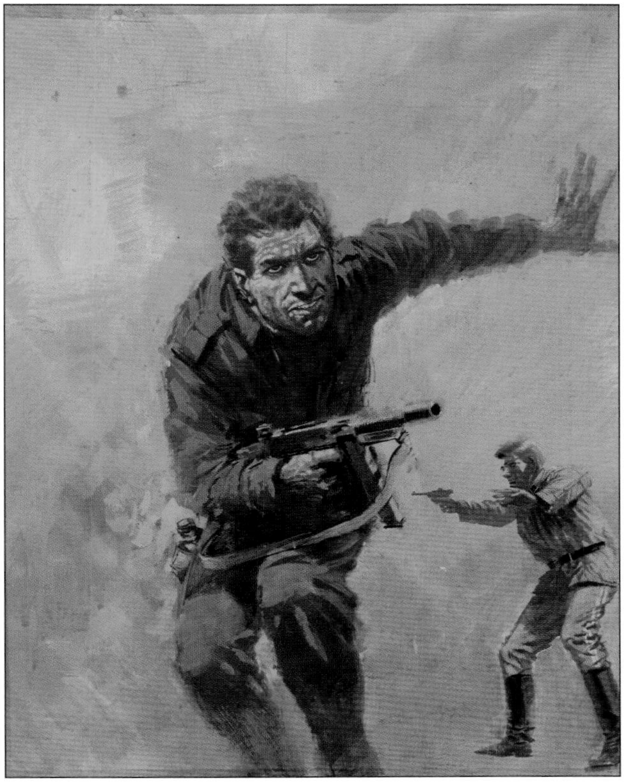

Graham Coton, War 785, September 1972

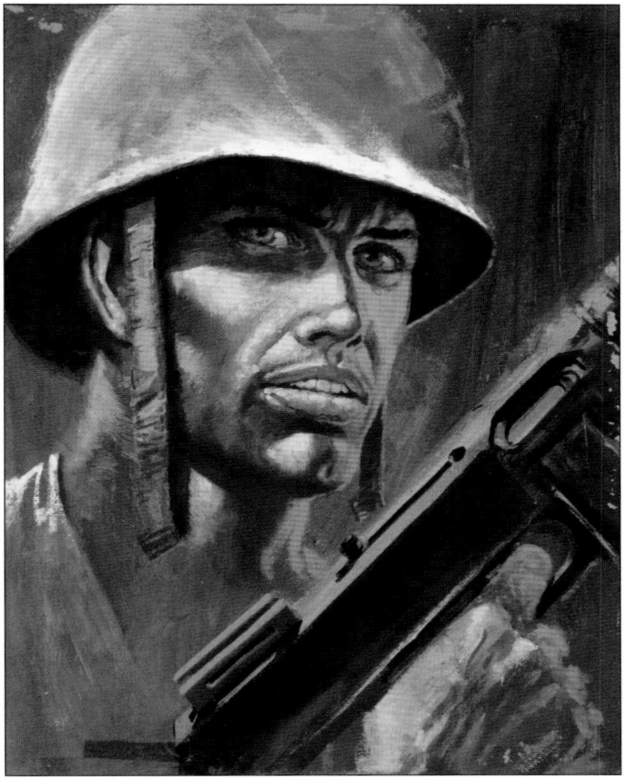

Graham Coton, War 688, September 1971

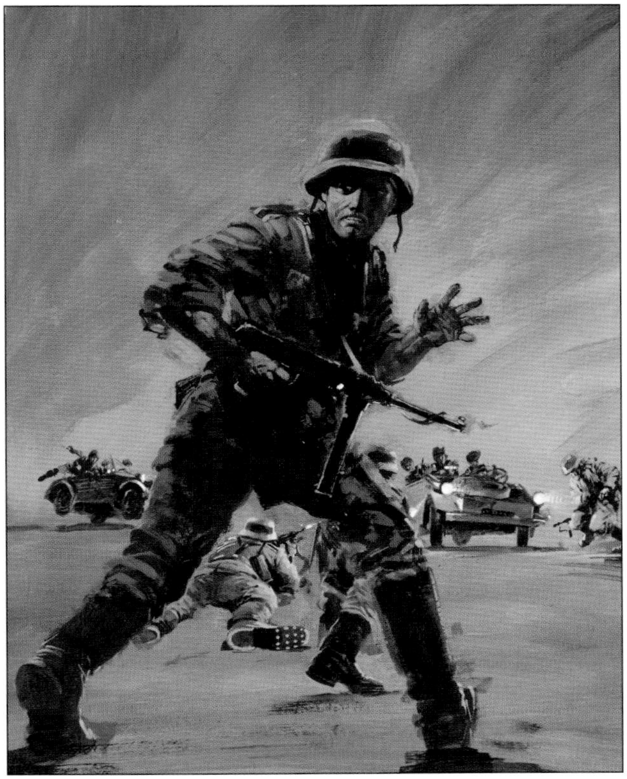

Graham Coton, War 1030, February 1975

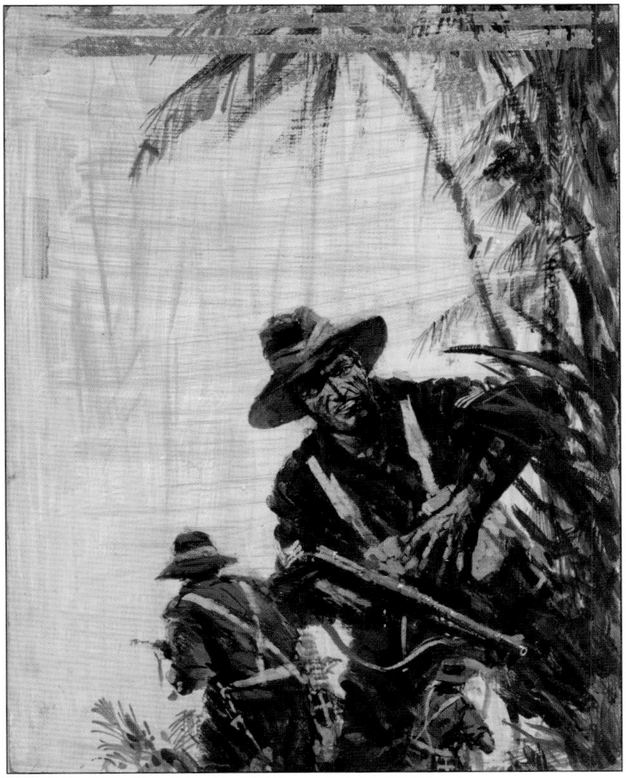

Graham Coton, War 1021, January 1975

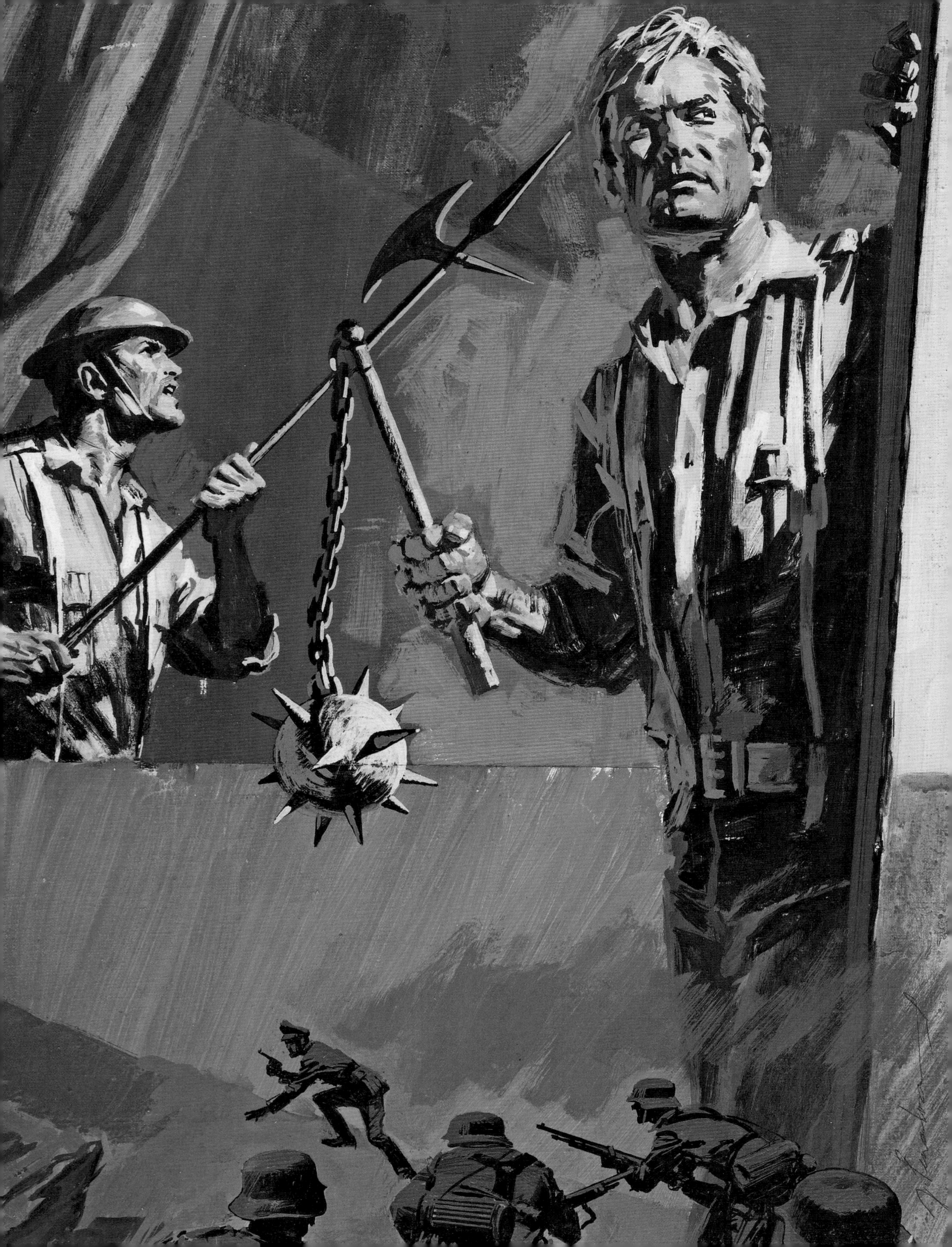

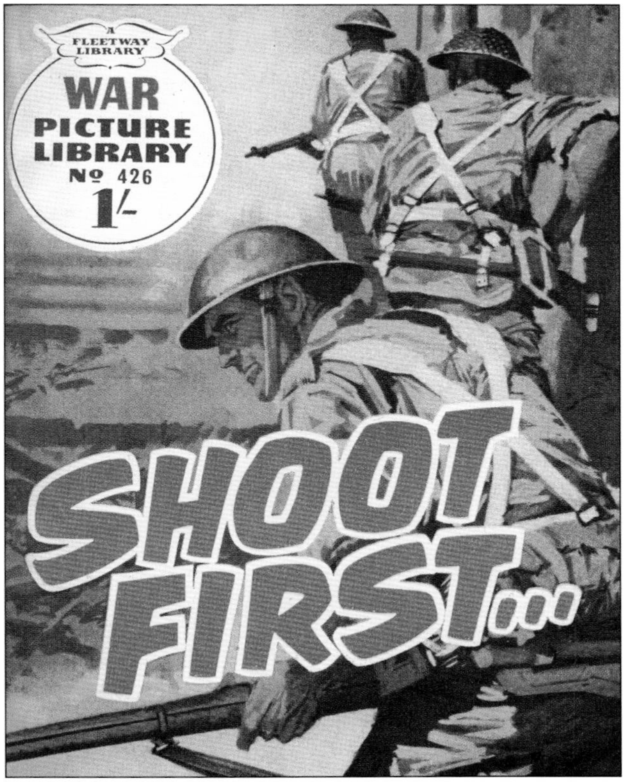
A FLEETWAY LIBRARY
WAR PICTURE LIBRARY
Nº 426
1/-
SHOOT FIRST...

Jordi Longaron, War 426, February 1968

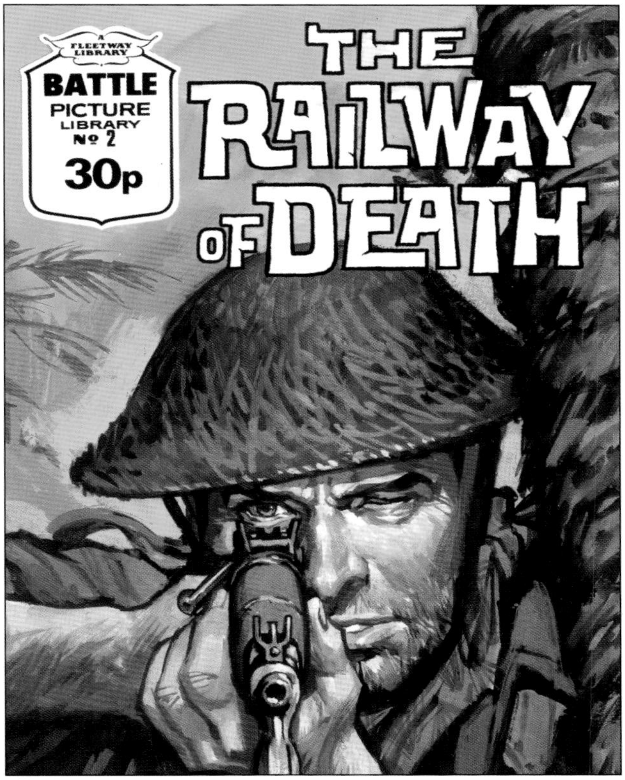
A FLEETWAY LIBRARY
BATTLE PICTURE LIBRARY
Nº 2
30p
THE RAILWAY OF DEATH

Nino Caroselli, Originally War 94, April 1961

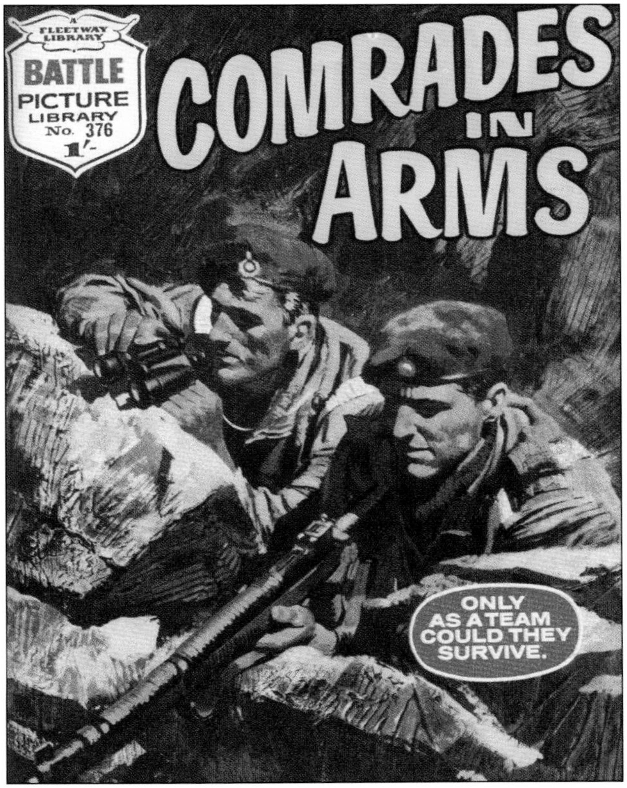
A FLEETWAY LIBRARY
BATTLE PICTURE LIBRARY
No. 376
1/-
COMRADES IN ARMS
ONLY AS A TEAM COULD THEY SURVIVE.

Jordi Penalva, Battle 376, December 1968

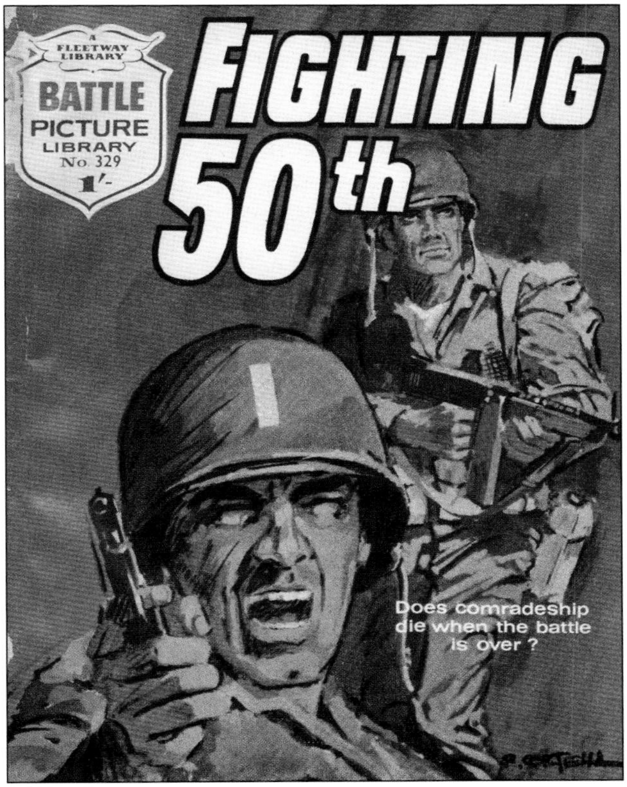
A FLEETWAY LIBRARY
BATTLE PICTURE LIBRARY
No. 329
1/-
FIGHTING 50th
Does comradeship die when the battle is over ?

Rafael Cortiella, Battle 329, January 1968

Opposite: Jordi Penalva, War 326, February 1966
Overleaf: Pino Dell'Orco, Battle148, March 1964

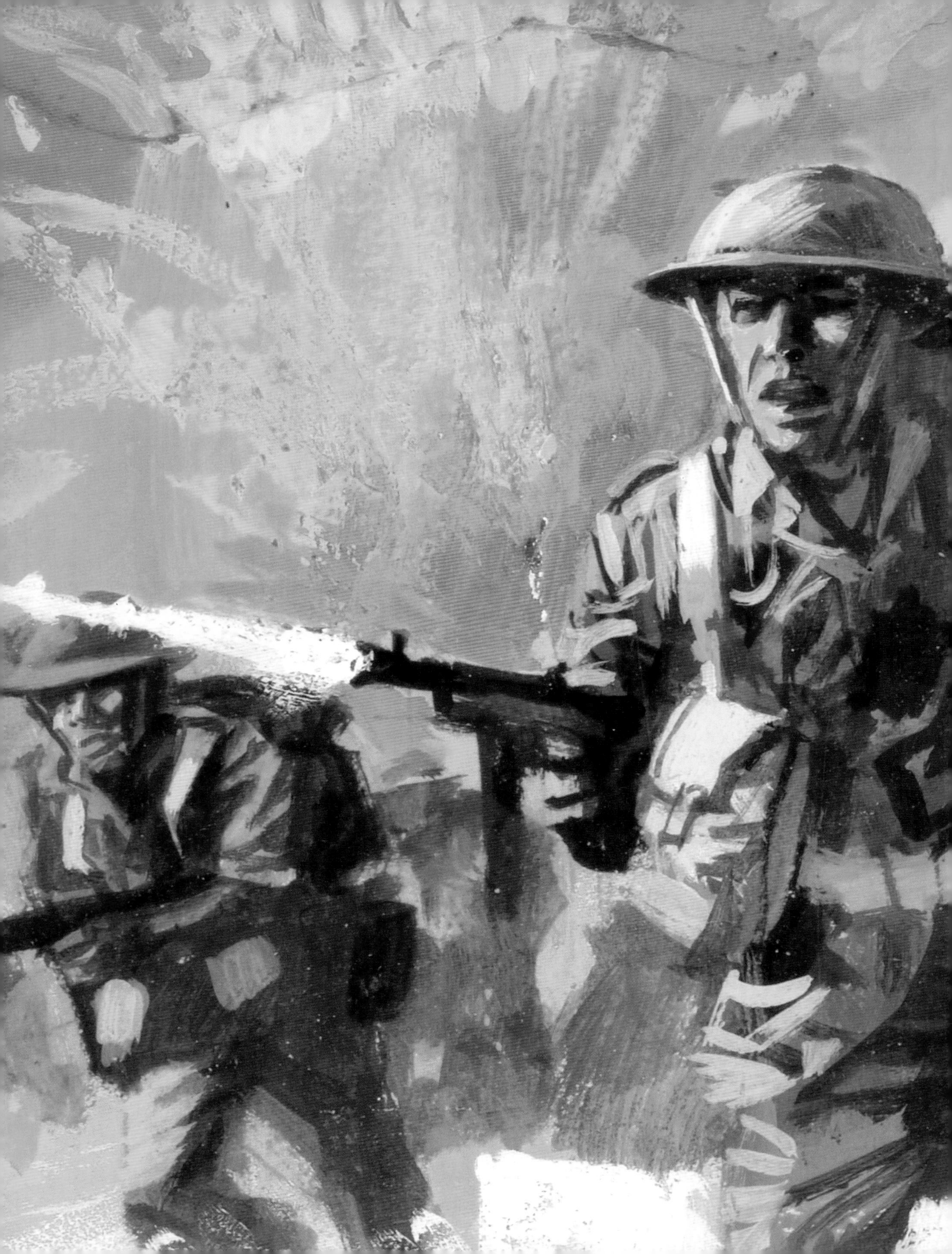

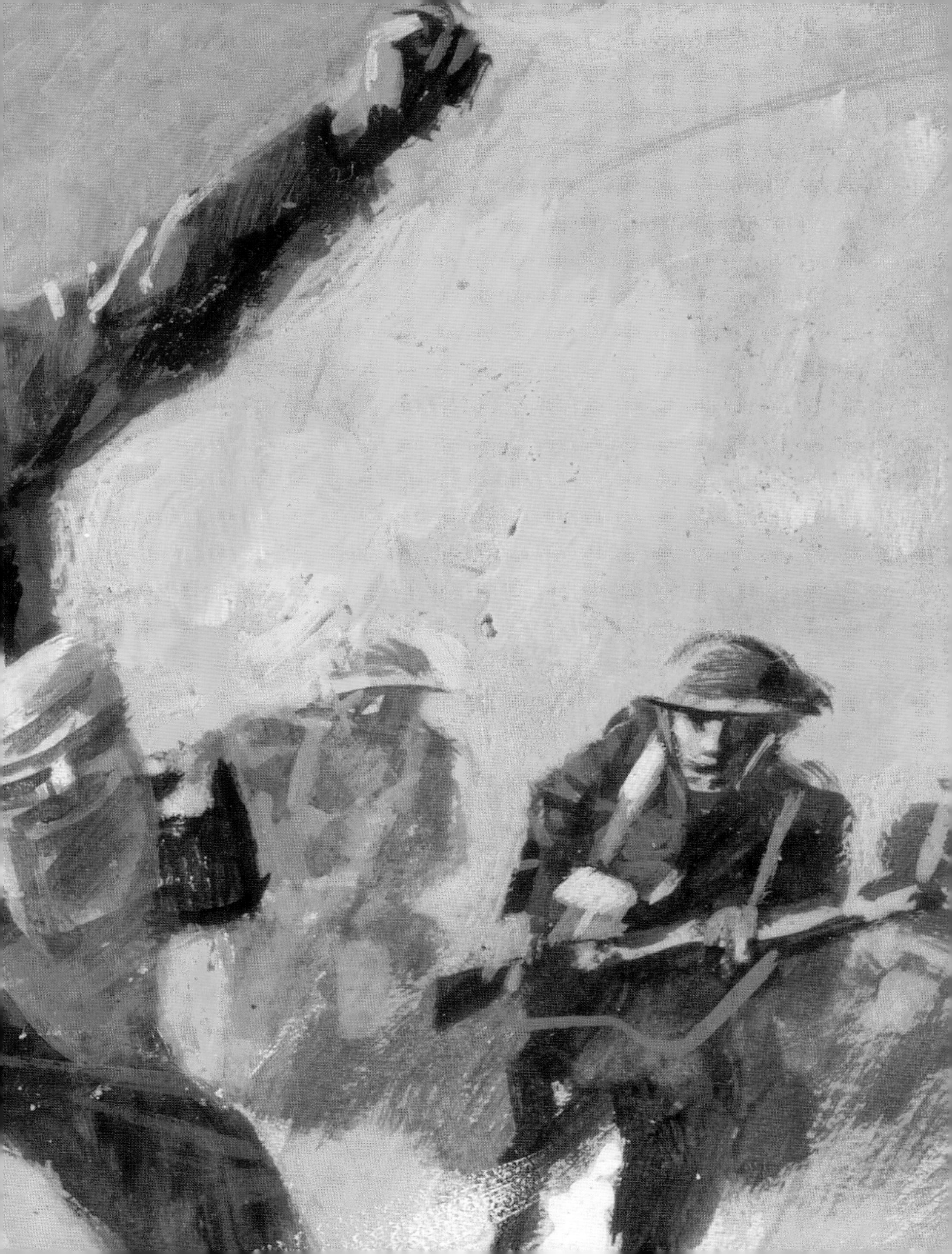

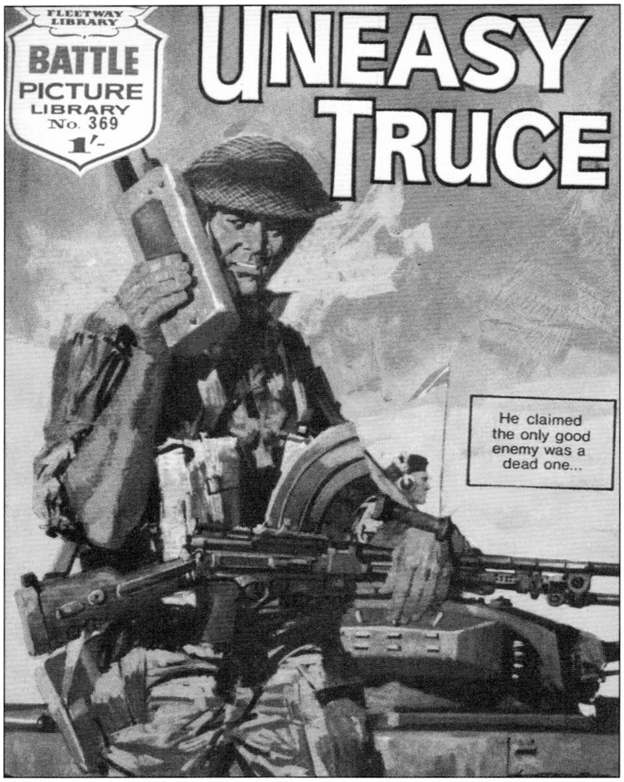
FLEETWAY LIBRARY
BATTLE PICTURE LIBRARY No. 369
1/-
UNEASY TRUCE
He claimed the only good enemy was a dead one...

Jordi Longaron, Battle 369, November 1968

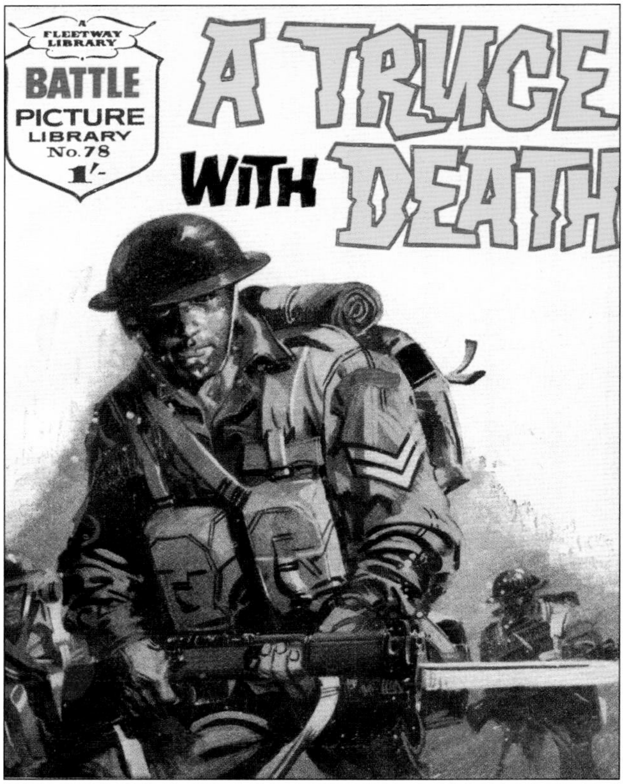
A FLEETWAY LIBRARY
BATTLE PICTURE LIBRARY No.78
1/-
A TRUCE WITH DEATH

Allessandro Biffignandi, Battle 78, October 1962

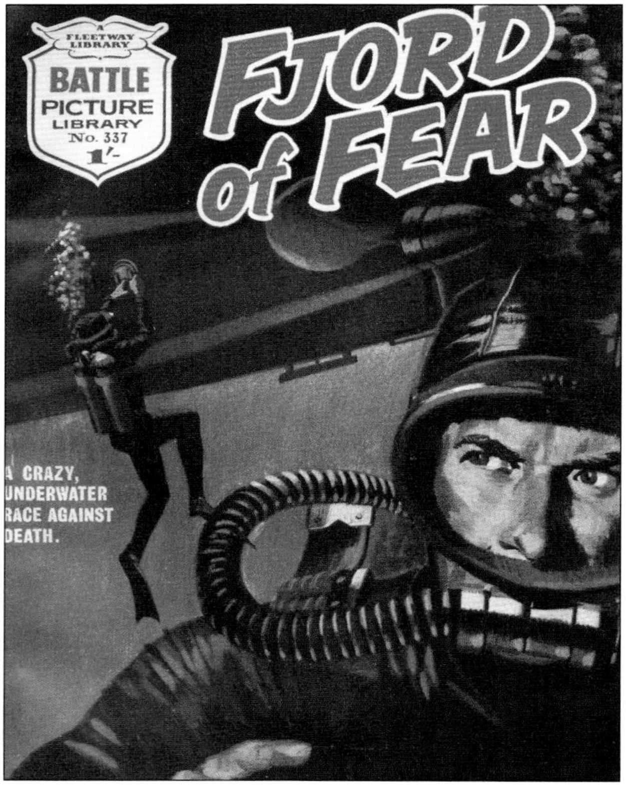
A FLEETWAY LIBRARY
BATTLE PICTURE LIBRARY No. 337
1/-
FJORD of FEAR
A CRAZY, UNDERWATER RACE AGAINST DEATH.

Carlo Jacono, Battle 337, March 1968

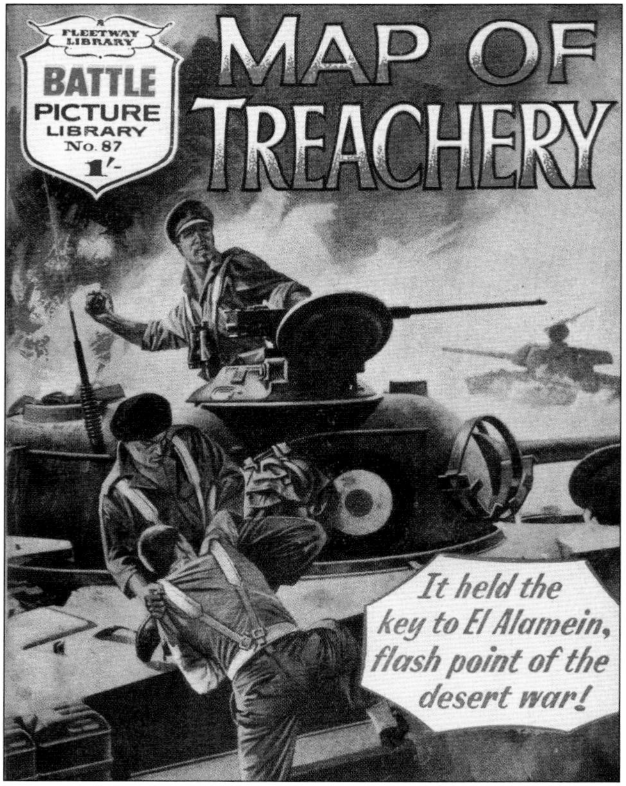
A FLEETWAY LIBRARY
BATTLE PICTURE LIBRARY No. 87
1/-
MAP OF TREACHERY
It held the key to El Alamein, flash point of the desert war!

D'Ami Studio, Battle 87, December 1962

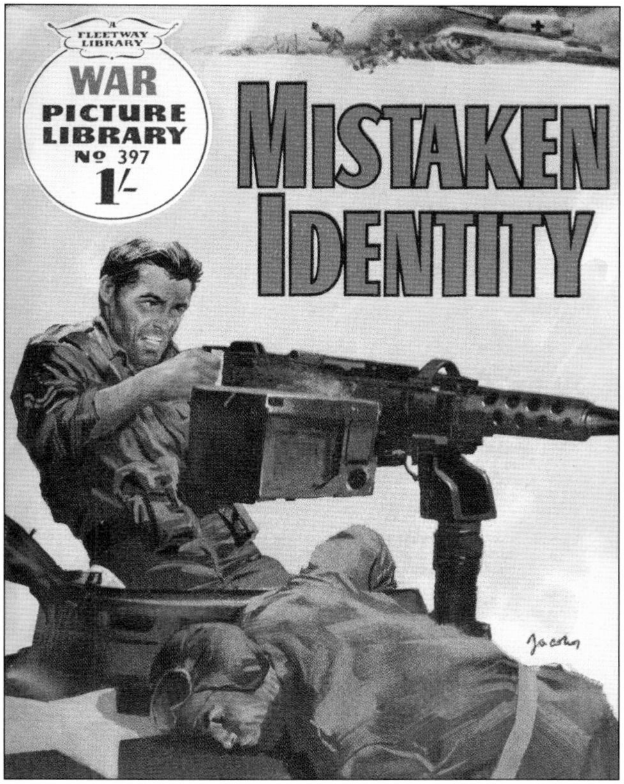
A FLEETWAY LIBRARY
WAR
PICTURE
LIBRARY
Nº 397
1/-
MISTAKEN
IDENTITY

Carlo Jacono, War 397, August 1967

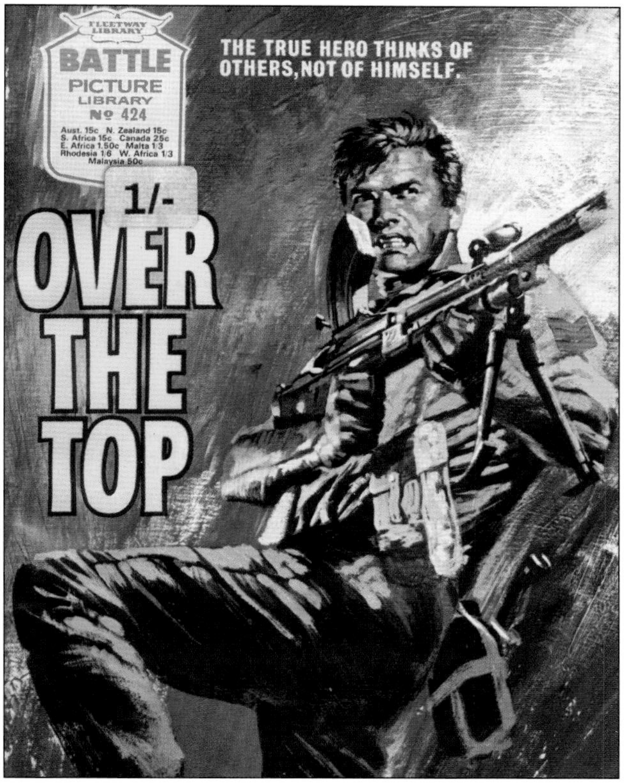
A FLEETWAY LIBRARY
BATTLE
PICTURE
LIBRARY
Nº 424
Aust. 15c N. Zealand 15c
S. Africa 15c Canada 25c
E. Africa 1.50c Malta 1/3
Rhodesia 1/6 W. Africa 1/3
Malaysia 50c
1/-
THE TRUE HERO THINKS OF
OTHERS, NOT OF HIMSELF.
OVER
THE
TOP

Jordi Penalva, Battle 424, October 1969

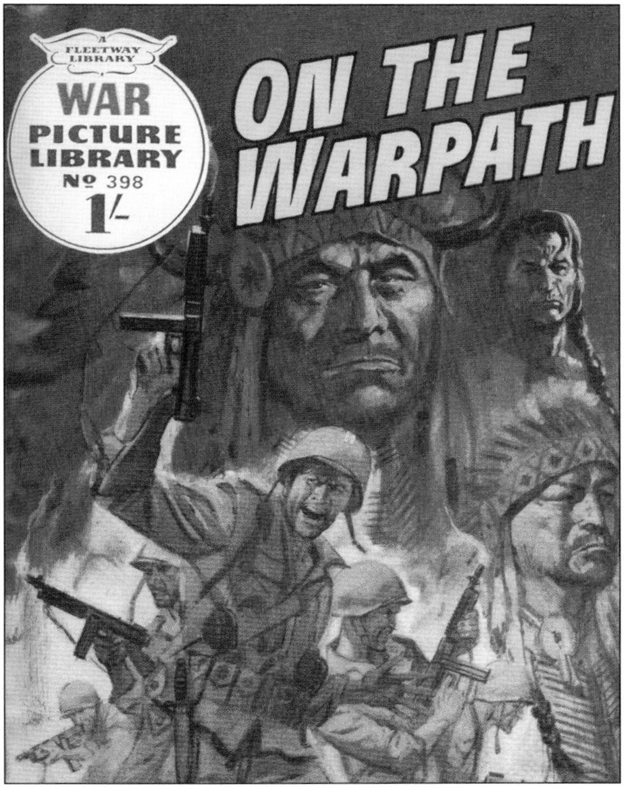
A FLEETWAY LIBRARY
WAR
PICTURE
LIBRARY
Nº 398
1/-
ON THE
WARPATH

Artur Aldoma, Puig War 398, August 1967

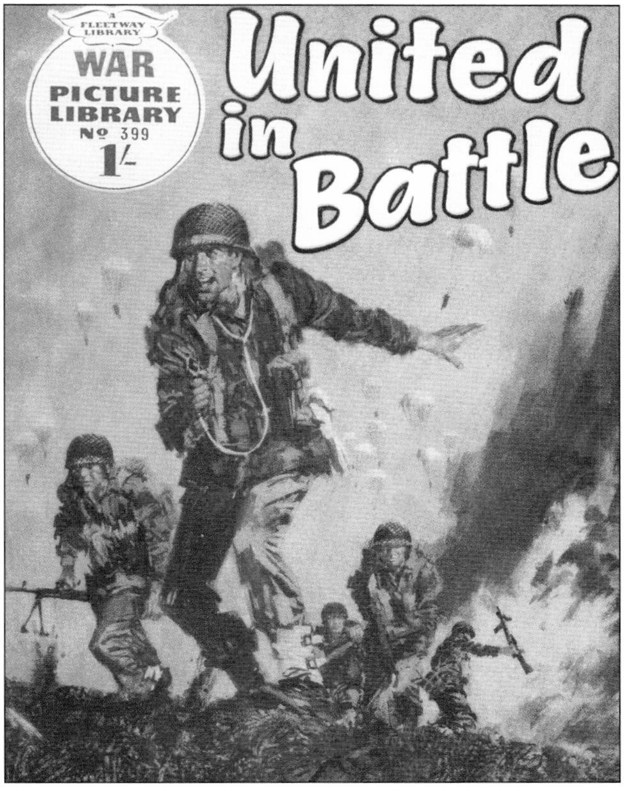
A FLEETWAY LIBRARY
WAR
PICTURE
LIBRARY
Nº 399
1/-
United
in
Battle

Jordi Longaron, War 399, August 1967

Overleaf: Jordi Penalva, Battle 286, February 1967

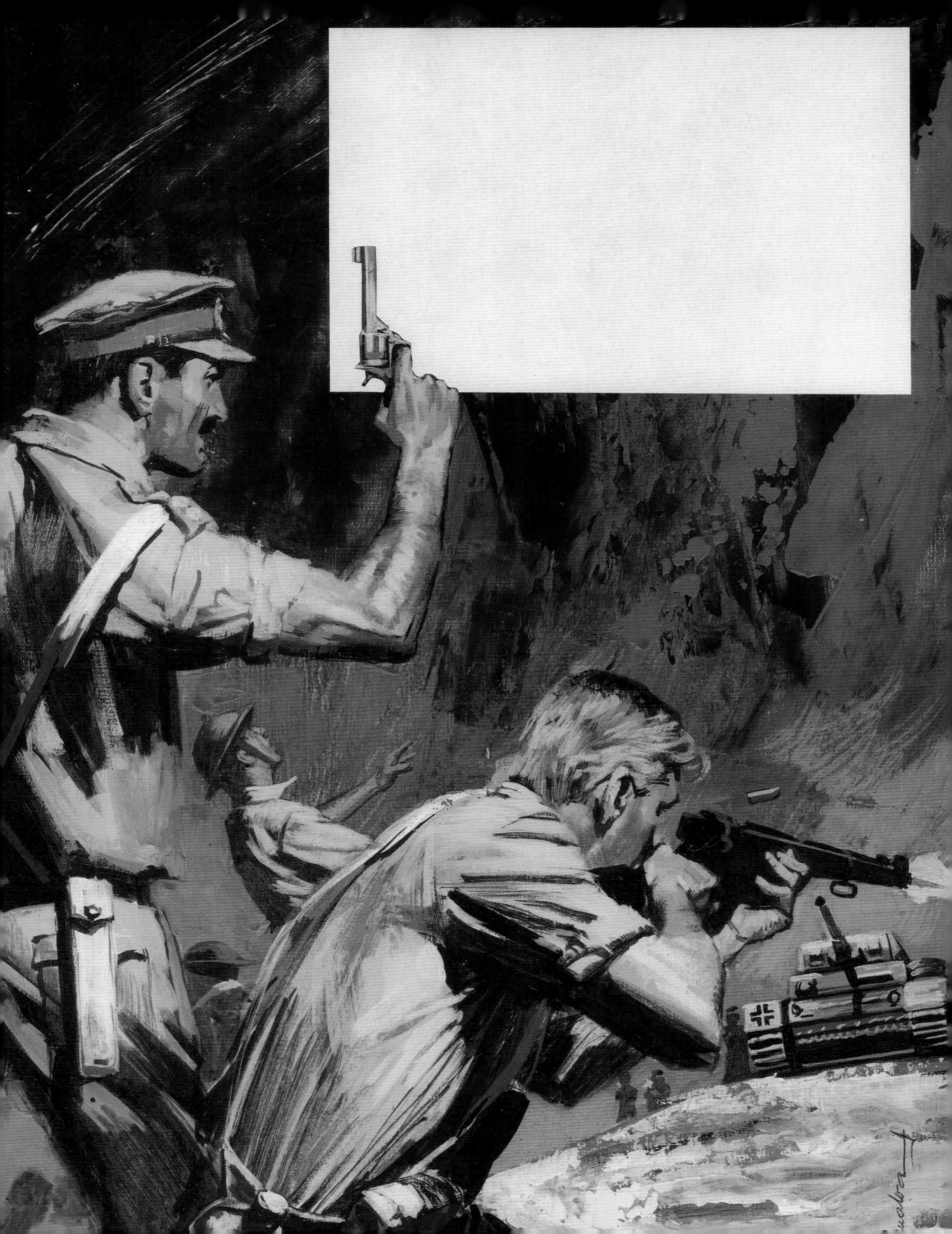

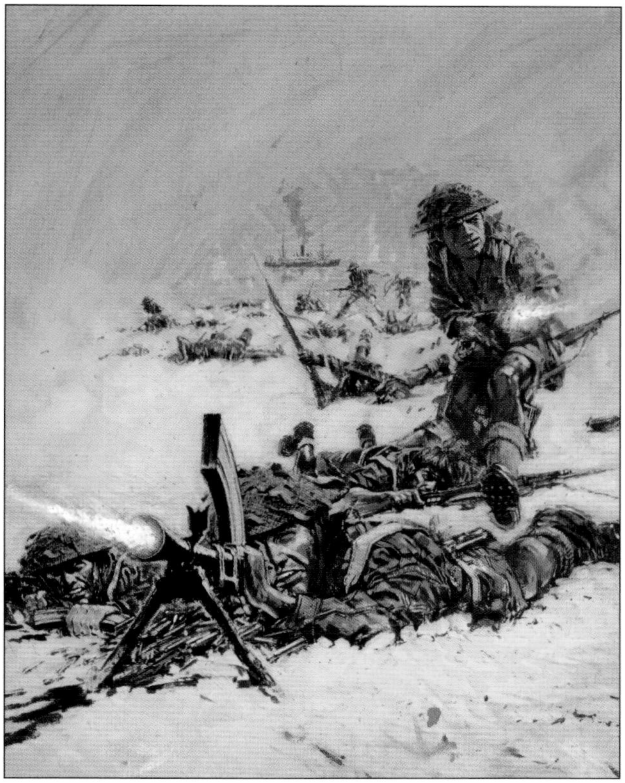

Graham Coton, War 1458, February 1978

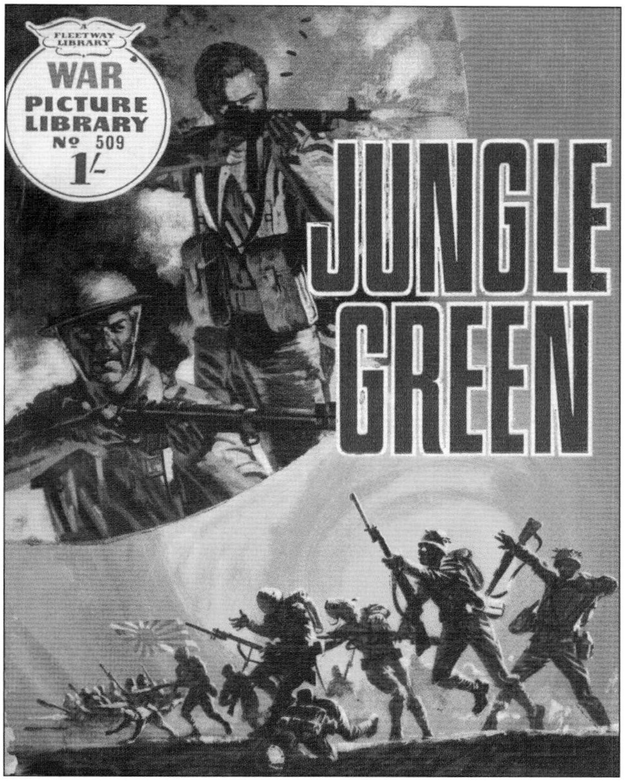
A FLEETWAY LIBRARY
WAR PICTURE LIBRARY
Nº 509
1/-
JUNGLE GREEN

Jordi Penalva, War 509, April 1969

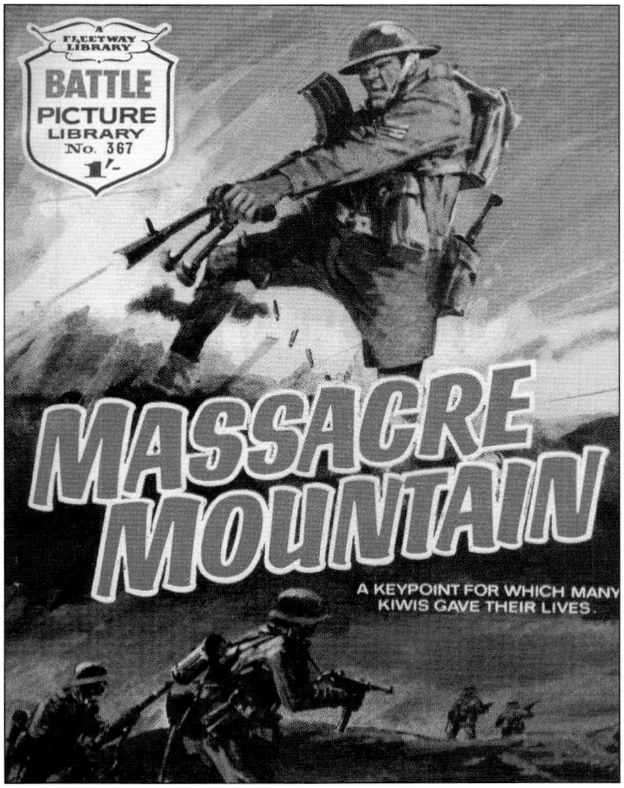
A FLEETWAY LIBRARY
BATTLE PICTURE LIBRARY
No. 367
1/-
MASSACRE MOUNTAIN
A KEYPOINT FOR WHICH MANY KIWIS GAVE THEIR LIVES.

Victor De La Fuente, War 367, October 1968

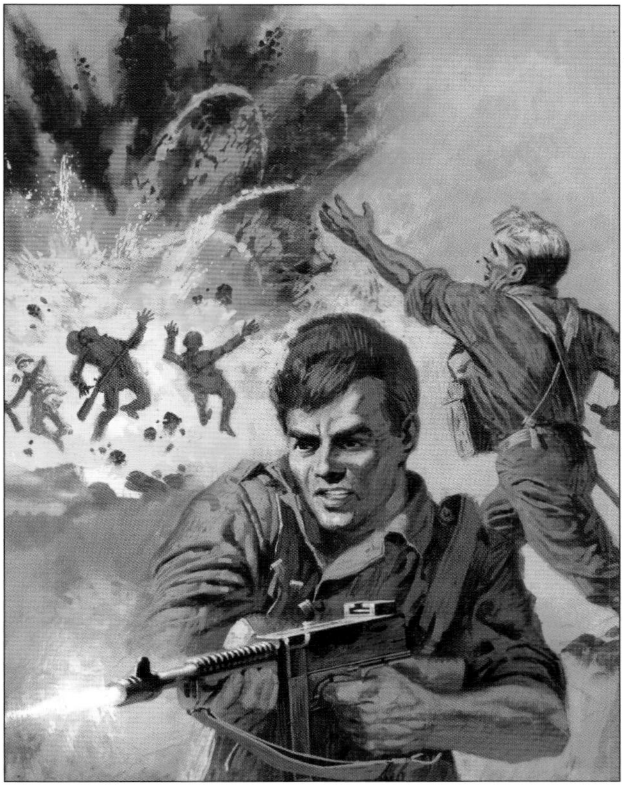

Gino D'Achille, War 874, August 1973

Opposite: Jordi Penalva, Battle 286, February 1967

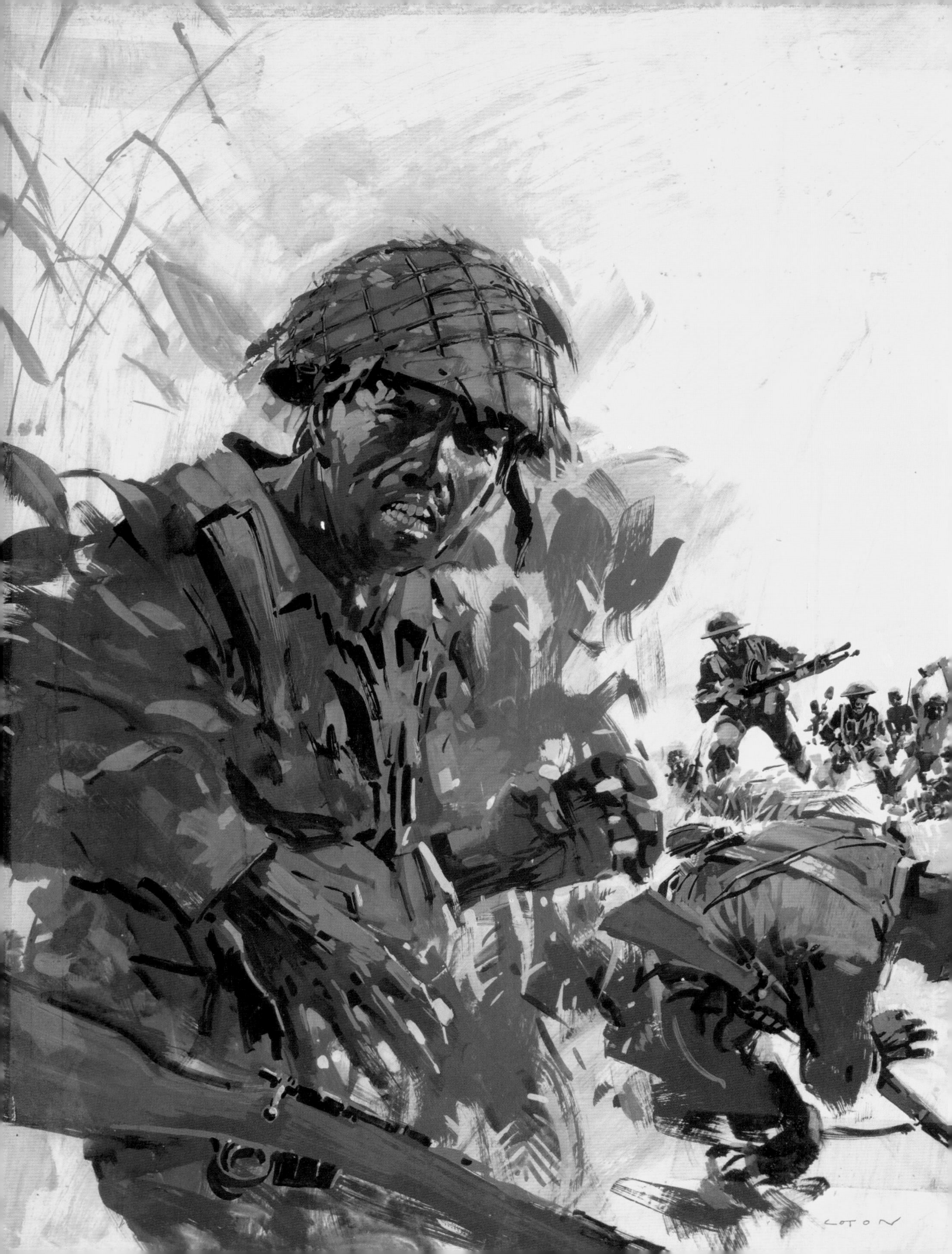
COTON

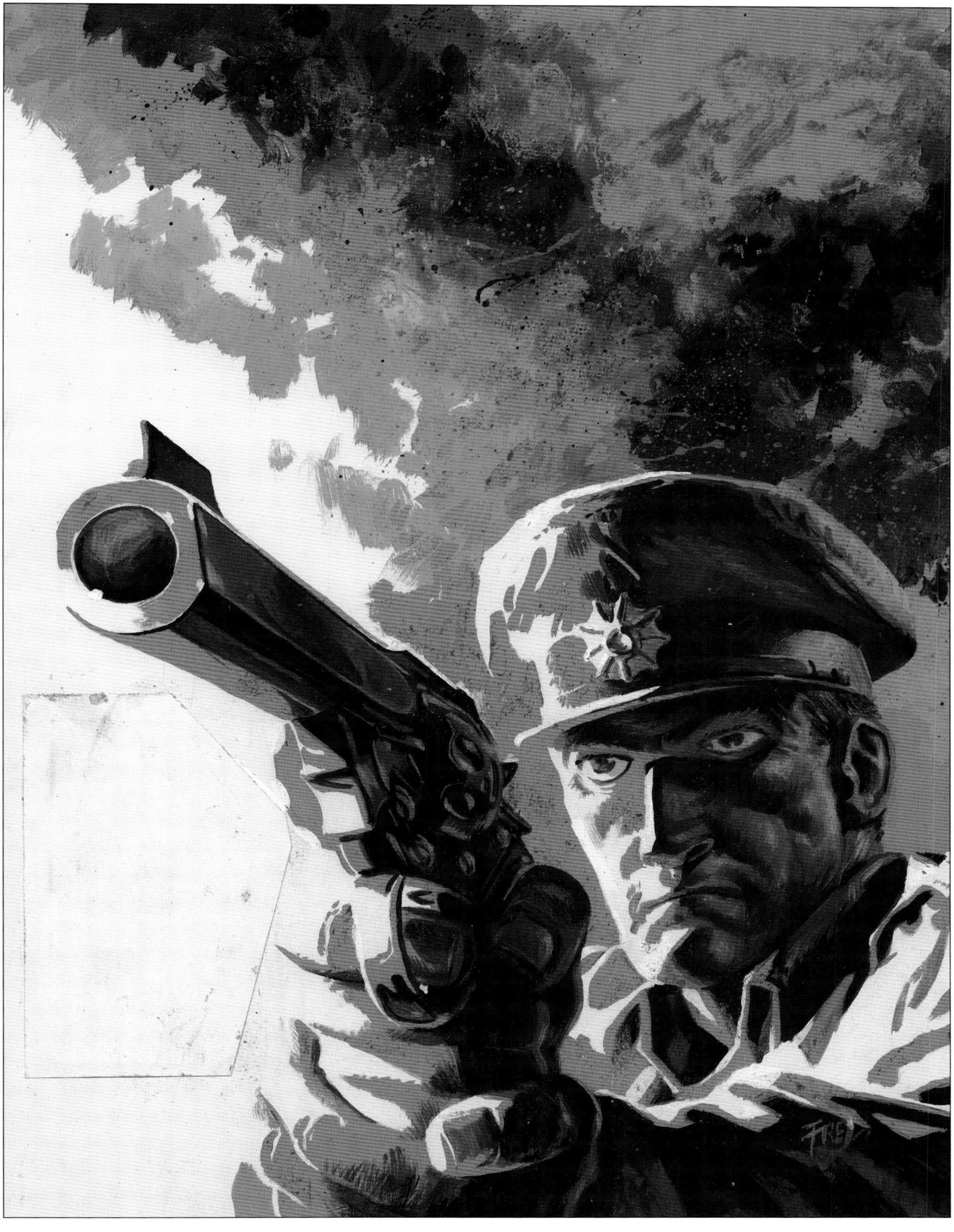
FREY

Oliver Frey, War 1147, December 1975
Opposite: Graham Coton, War 1546, September 1978

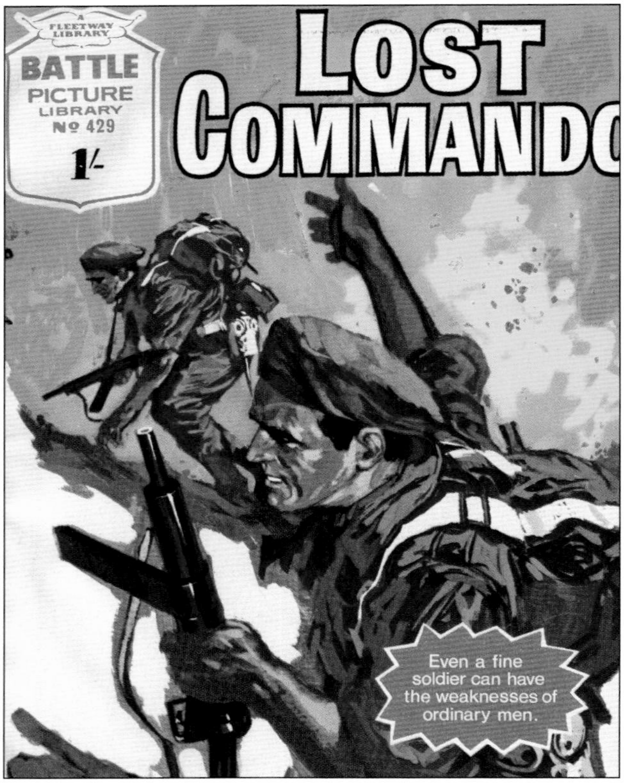
A FLEETWAY LIBRARY
BATTLE PICTURE LIBRARY Nº 429
1/-
LOST COMMANDO
Even a fine soldier can have the weaknesses of ordinary men.

Fernando Fernandez, Battle 429, November 1969

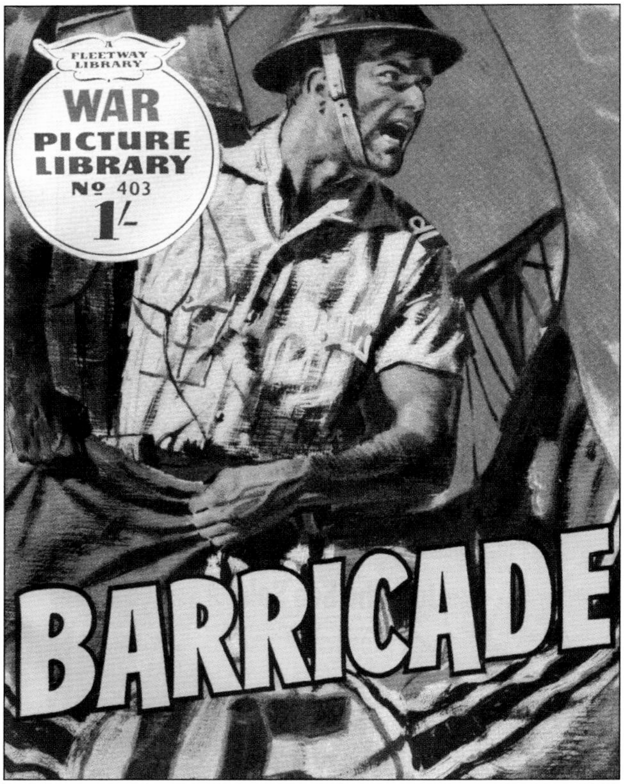
A FLEETWAY LIBRARY
WAR PICTURE LIBRARY Nº 403
1/-
BARRICADE

Jordi Penalva, War 403, September 1967

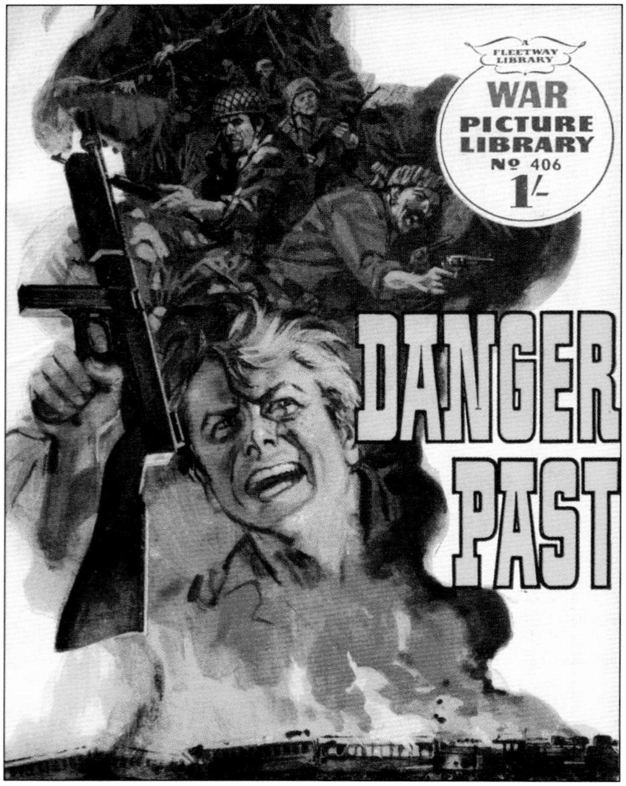
A FLEETWAY LIBRARY
WAR PICTURE LIBRARY Nº 406
1/-
DANGER PAST

Artur Aldoma Puig, War 406, October 1967

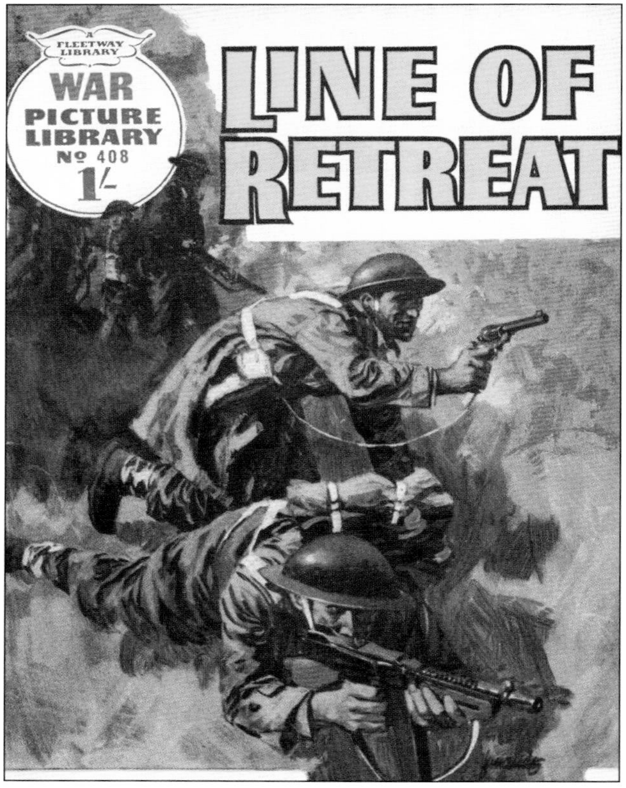
A FLEETWAY LIBRARY
WAR PICTURE LIBRARY Nº 408
1/-
LINE OF RETREAT

Fernando Fernandez, War 408, November 1967

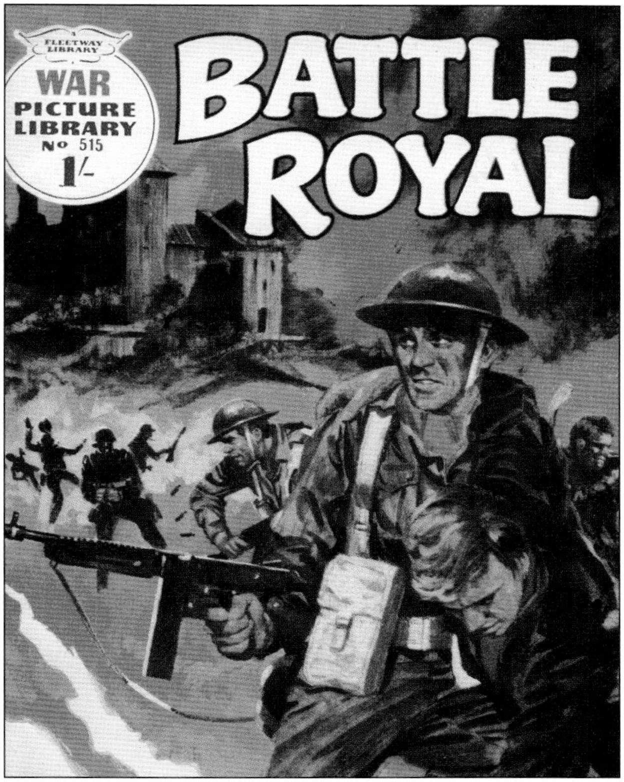
FLEETWAY LIBRARY
WAR
PICTURE
LIBRARY
No 515
1/-
BATTLE
ROYAL

Fernando Fernandez, War 515, May 1969

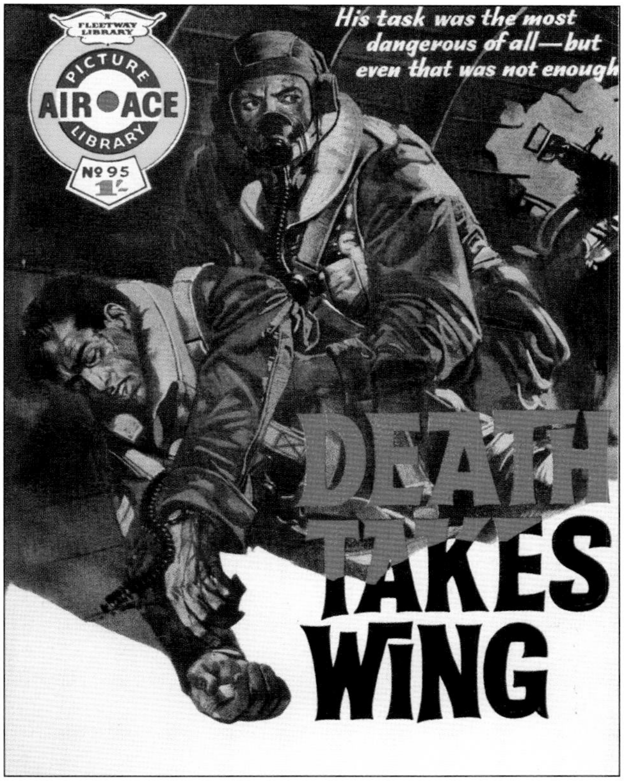
FLEETWAY LIBRARY
PICTURE
AIR ACE
LIBRARY
Nº 95
1/-
His task was the most dangerous of all—but even that was not enough
DEATH
TAKES
WING

Allessandro Biffignandi, Air Ace 95, April 1962

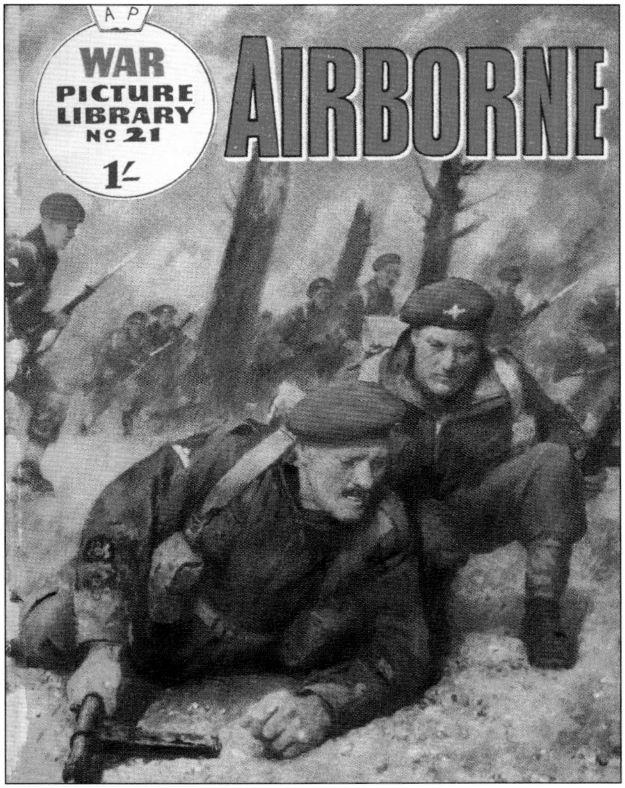
AP
WAR
PICTURE
LIBRARY
Nº 21
1/-
AIRBORNE

Septimus Scott, War 21, July 1959

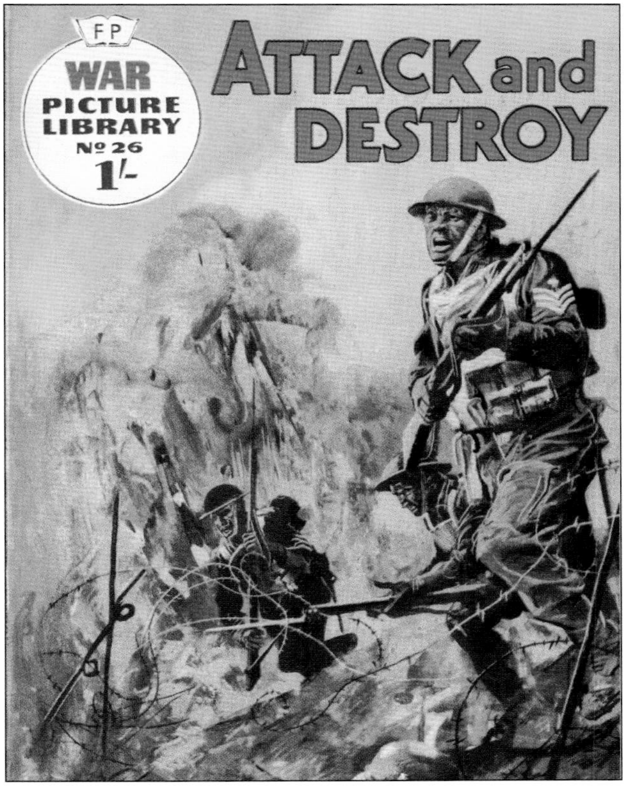
FP
WAR
PICTURE
LIBRARY
Nº 26
1/-
ATTACK and
DESTROY

Giorgio DeGaspari, War 26, October 1959

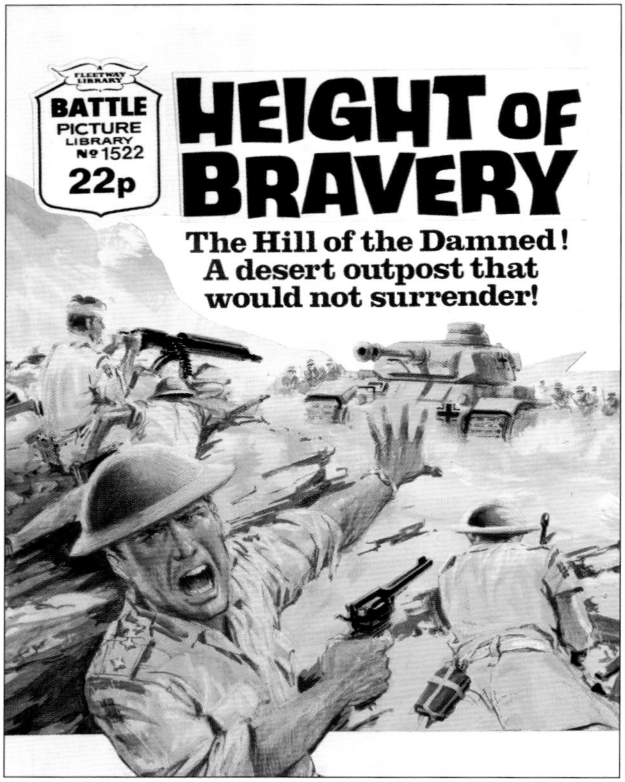
A FLEETWAY LIBRARY
BATTLE
PICTURE
LIBRARY
Nº 1522
22p
HEIGHT OF BRAVERY
The Hill of the Damned!
A desert outpost that
would not surrender!

Graham Coton, originally Battle 280, December 1966

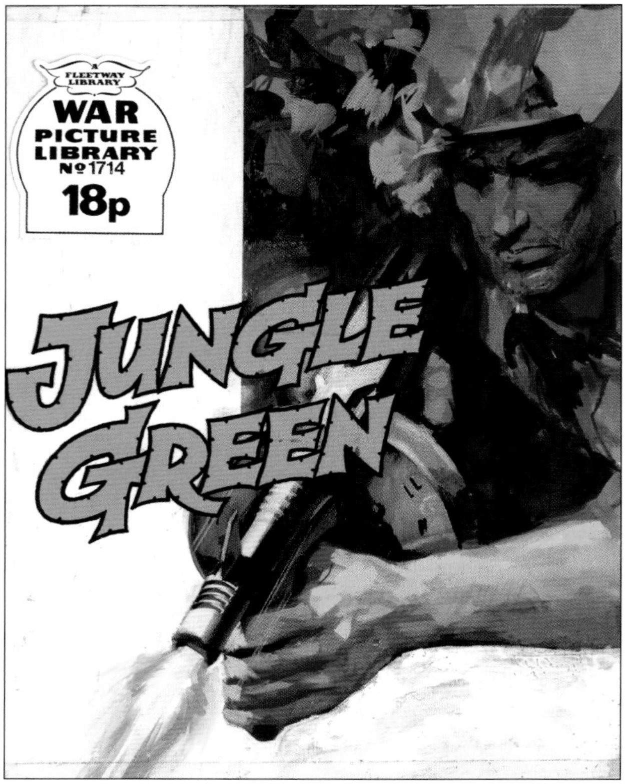
A FLEETWAY LIBRARY
WAR
PICTURE
LIBRARY
Nº 1714
18p
JUNGLE GREEN

Pino Dell'Orco, originally Battle 44, January 1962

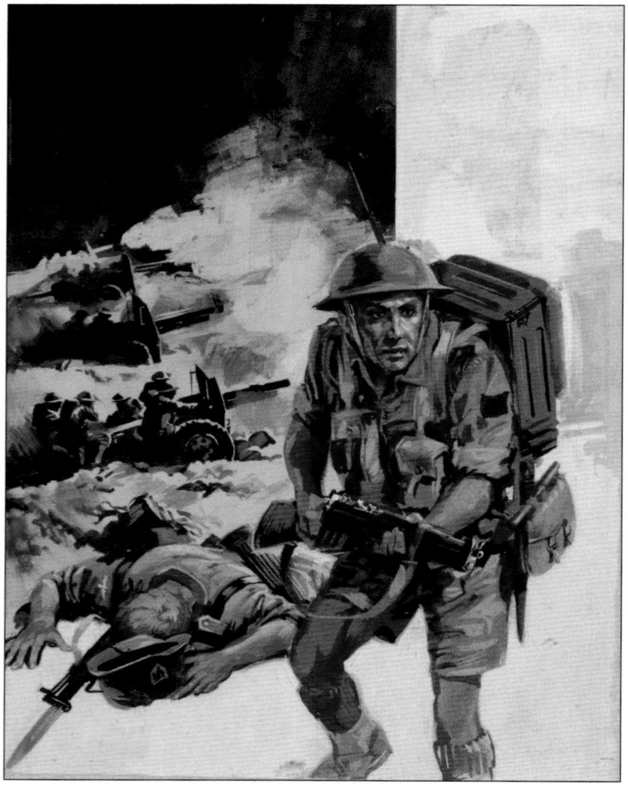

Pino Dell'Orco, War 157, August 1962

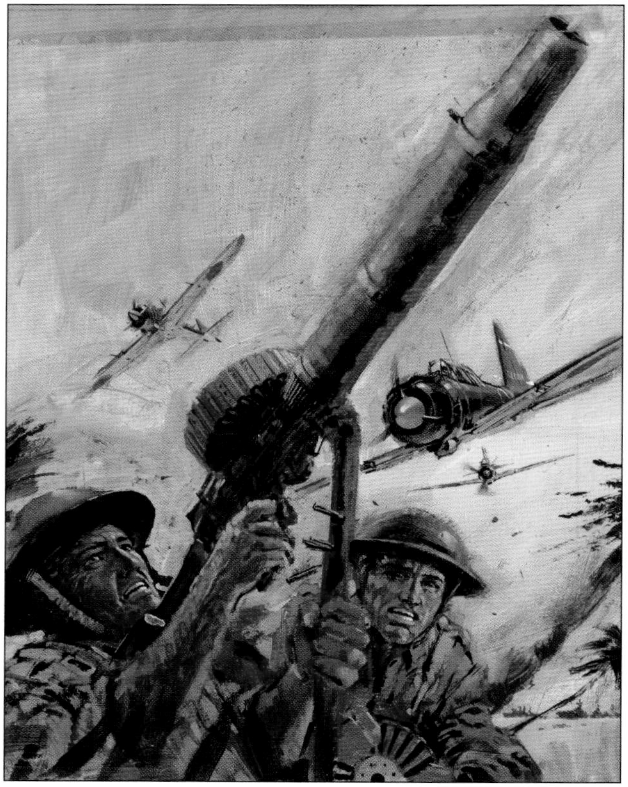

Graham Coton, War 1010, December 1974

Opposite: Jordi Penalva, Battle 156, May 1964

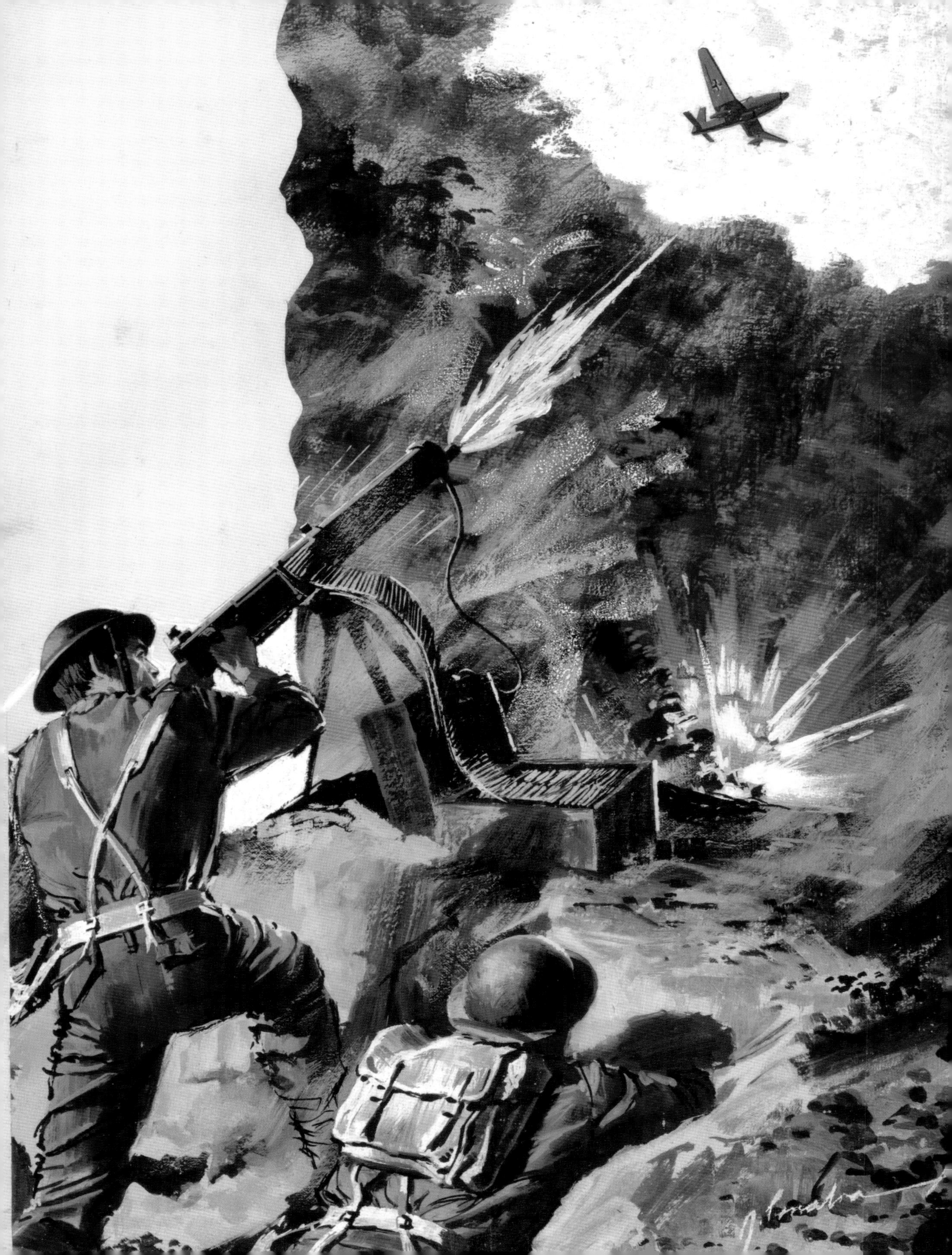

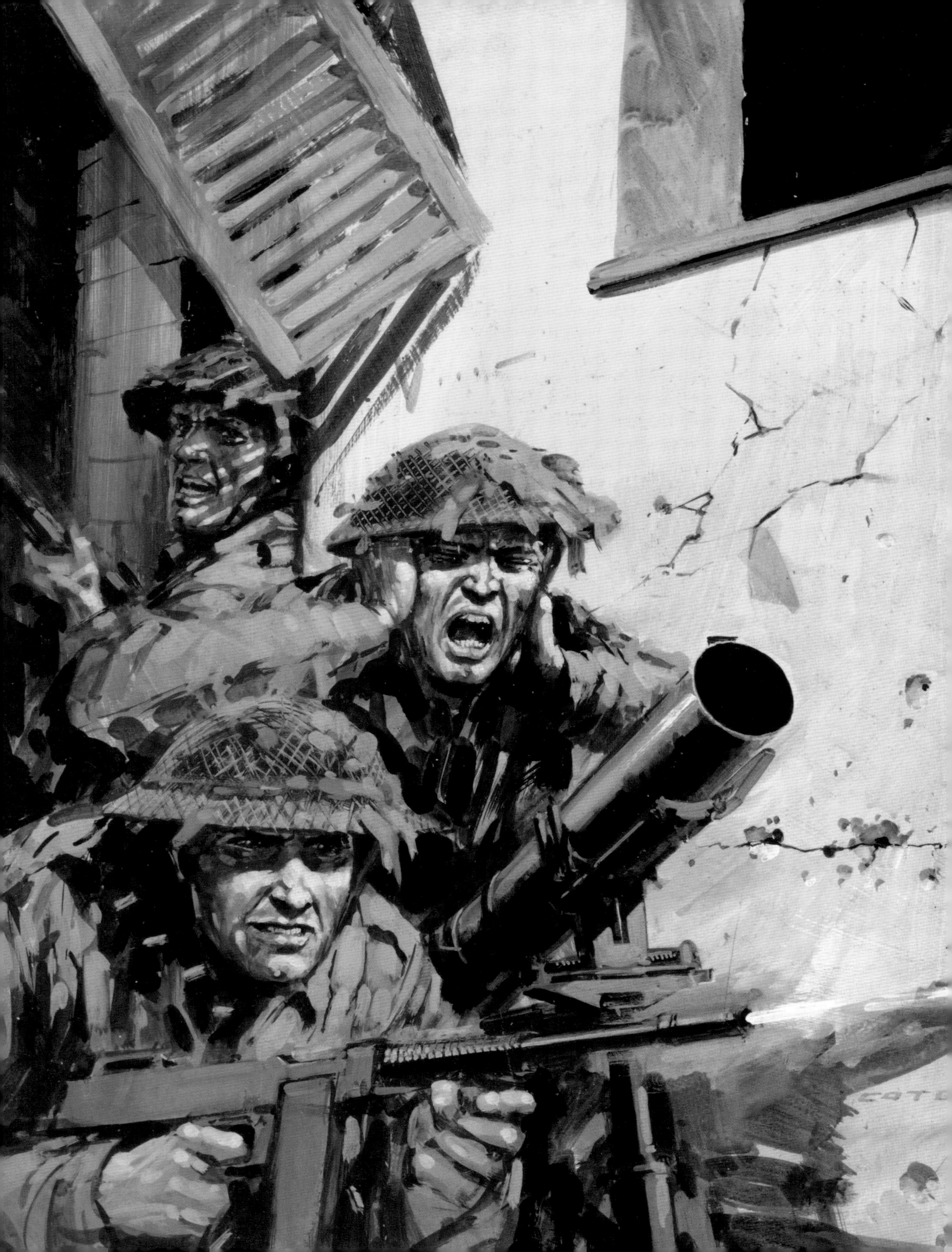

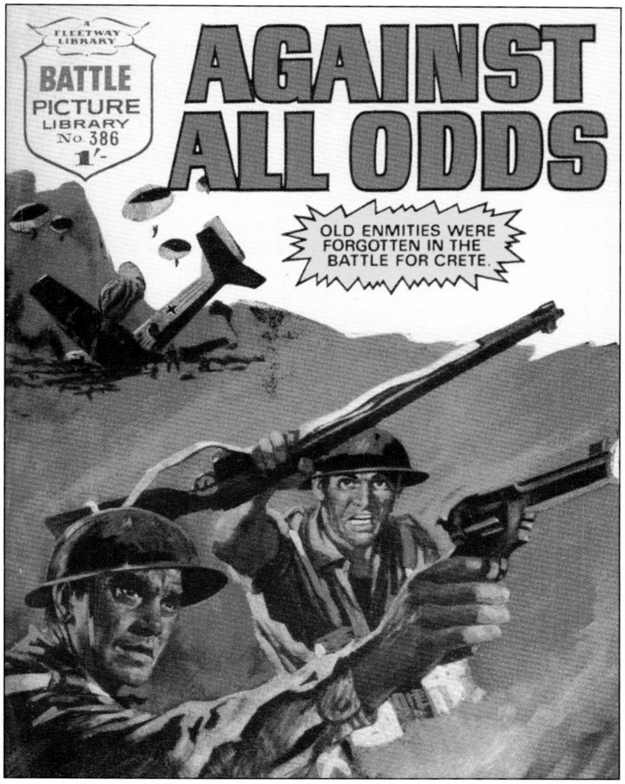
A FLEETWAY LIBRARY
BATTLE PICTURE LIBRARY No. 386 1/-
AGAINST ALL ODDS
OLD ENMITIES WERE FORGOTTEN IN THE BATTLE FOR CRETE.

Fernando Fernandez, Battle 386, March 1969

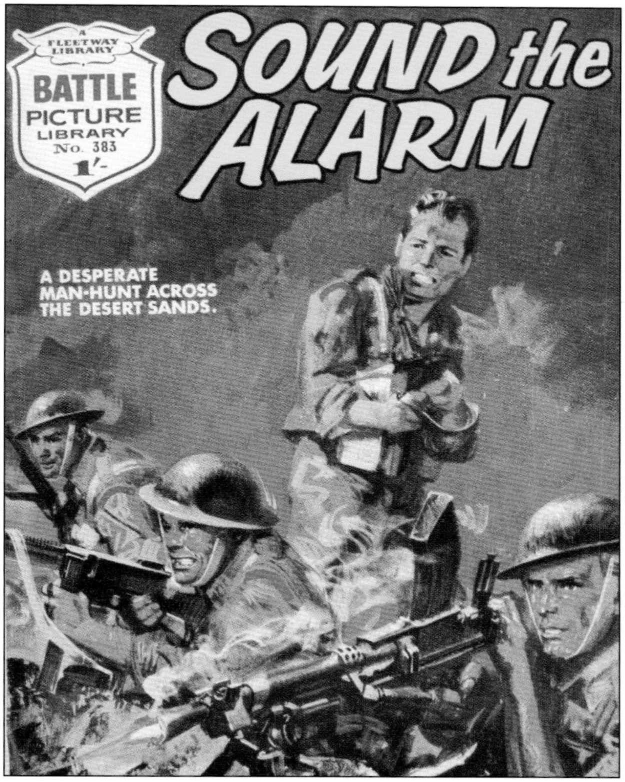
A FLEETWAY LIBRARY
BATTLE PICTURE LIBRARY No. 383 1/-
SOUND the ALARM
A DESPERATE MAN-HUNT ACROSS THE DESERT SANDS.

Allessandro Biffignandi, Battle 383, February 1969

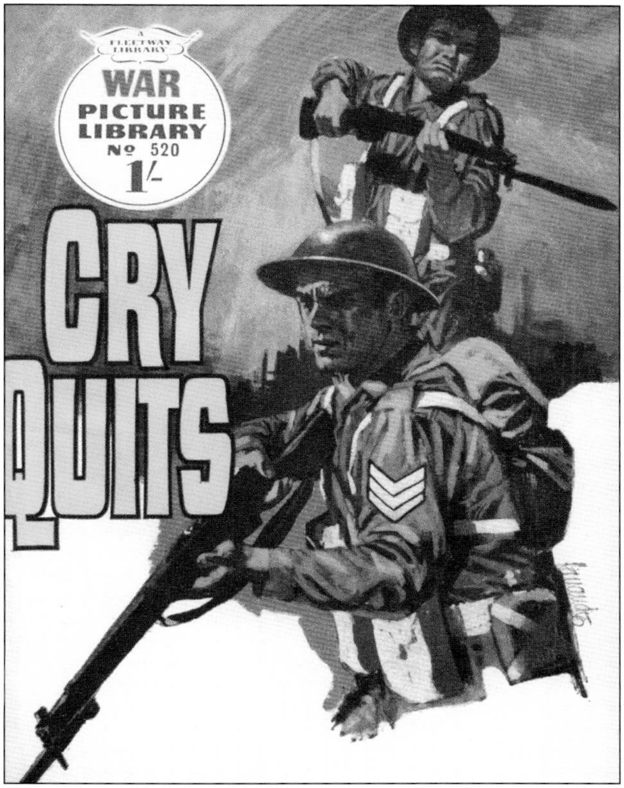
A FLEETWAY LIBRARY
WAR PICTURE LIBRARY Nº 520 1/-
CRY QUITS

Fernando Fernandez, War 520, June 1969

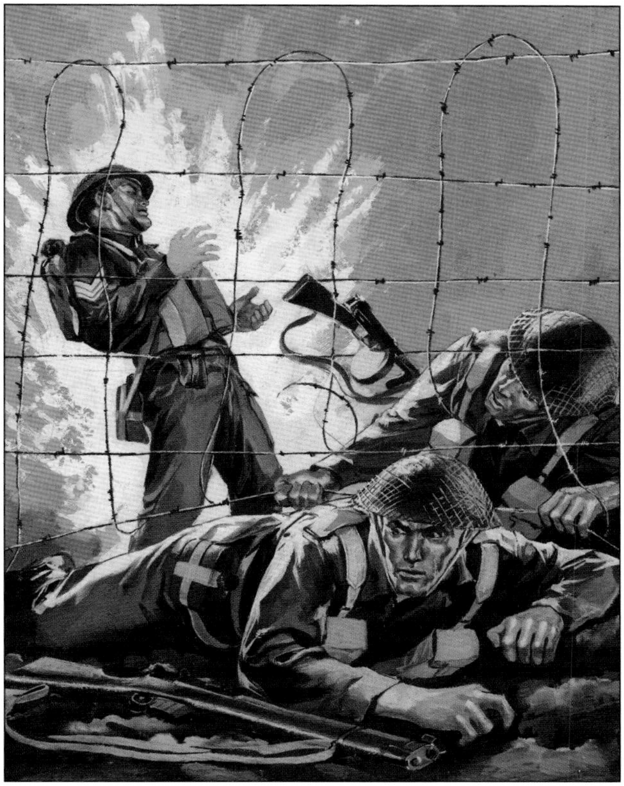

Nino Caroselli, War 134, February 1962

Opposite: Graham Coton, Battle 1321, September 1979

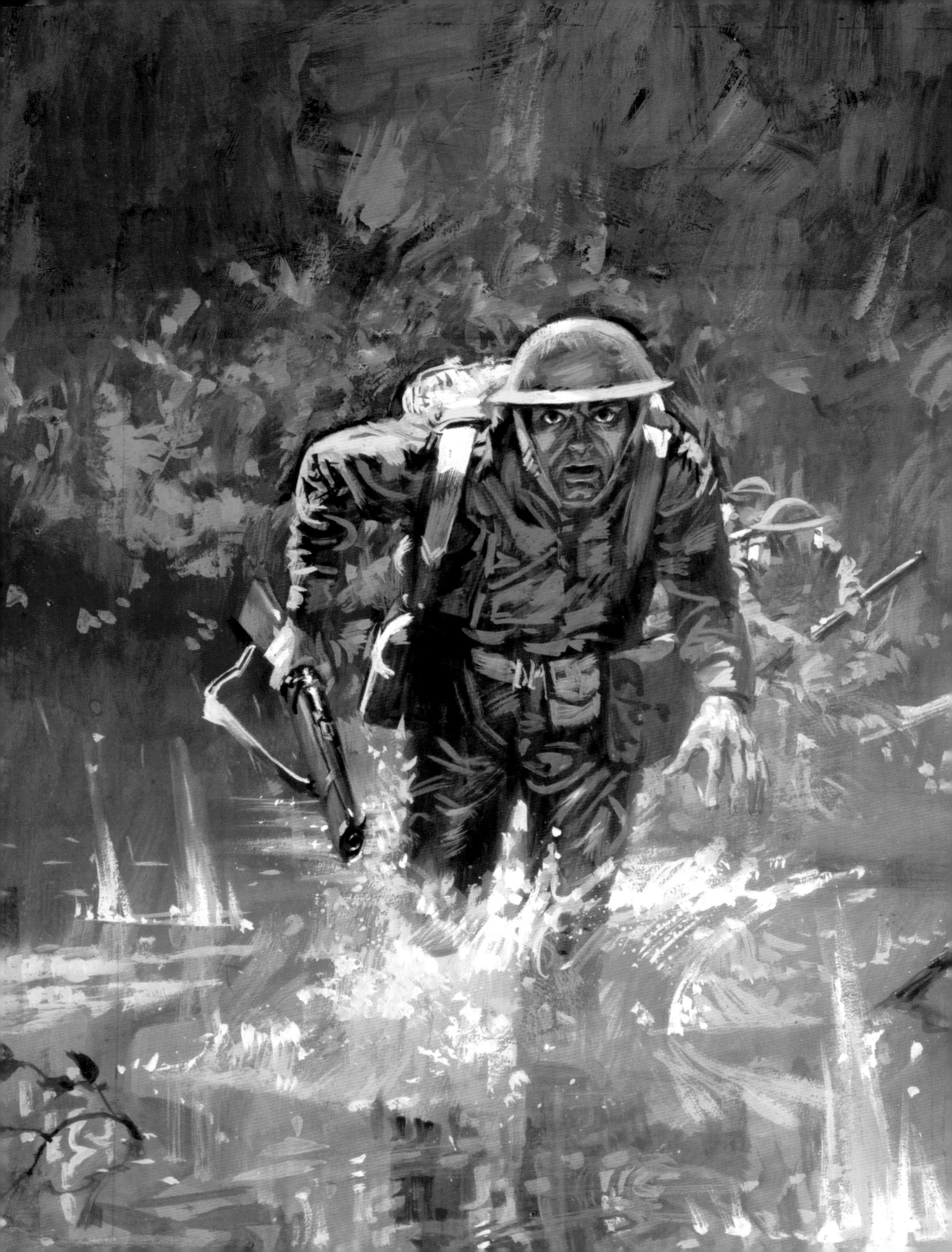

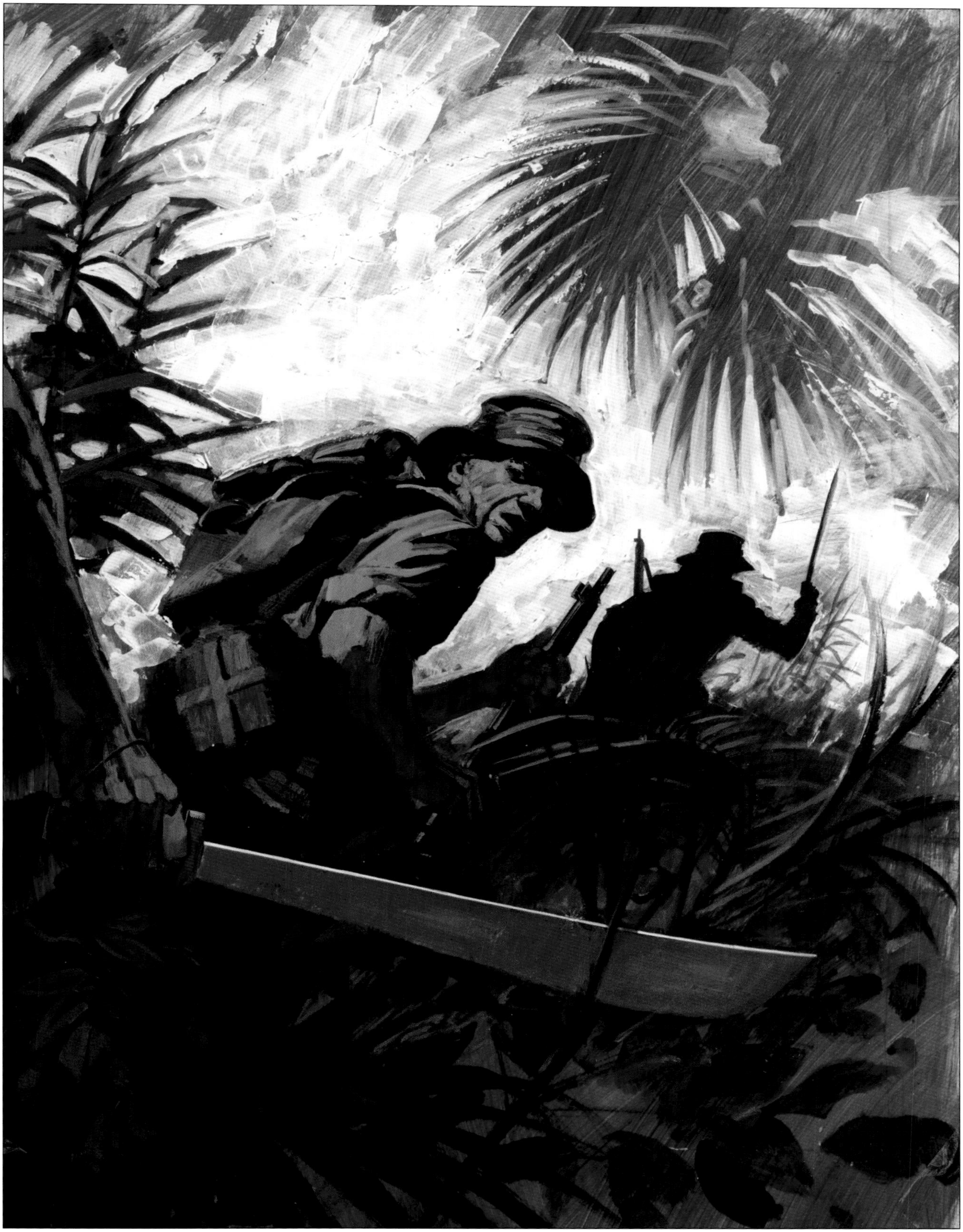

Andrew Howat, War 544, October 1969
Opposite: Pino Dell'Orco, War 198, June 1963

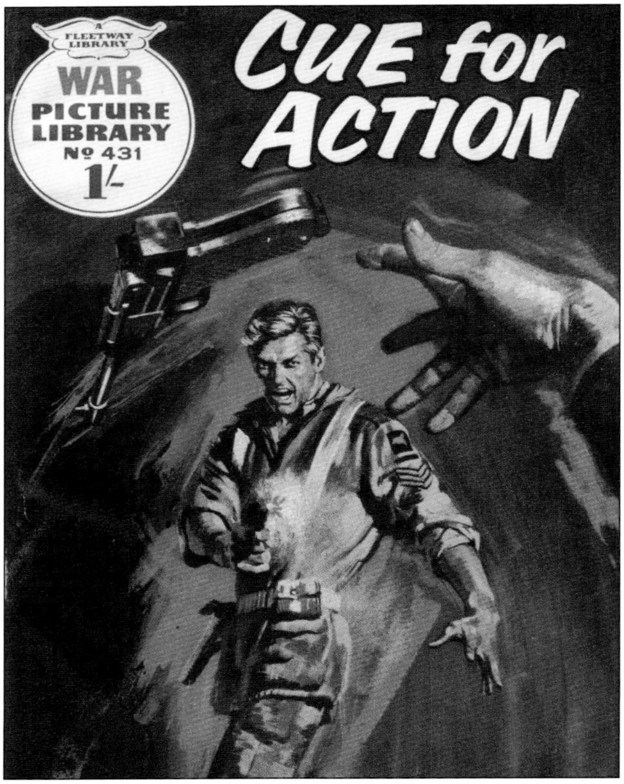
A
FLEETWAY
LIBRARY
WAR
PICTURE
LIBRARY
Nº 431
1/-
CUE for
ACTION

Jordi Penalva, War 431, March 1968

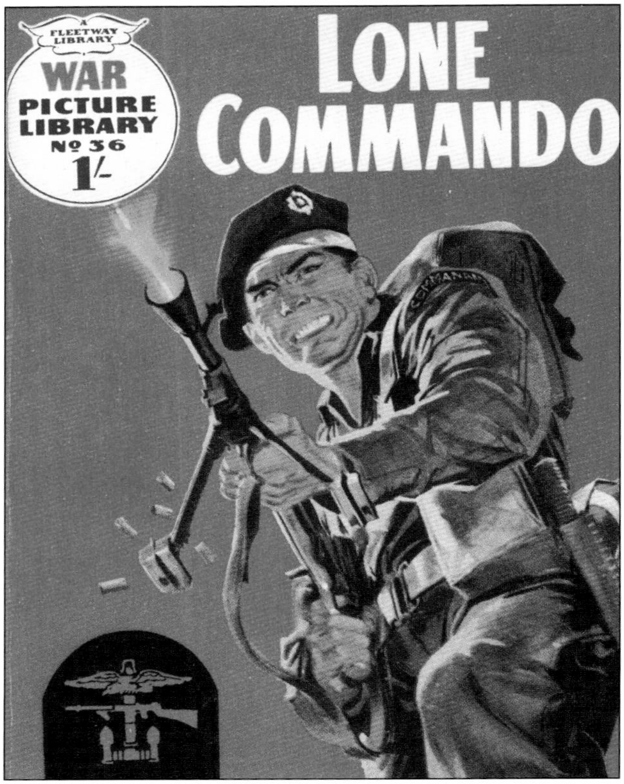
A
FLEETWAY
LIBRARY
WAR
PICTURE
LIBRARY
Nº 36
1/-
LONE
COMMANDO

Giorgio DeGaspari, War 36, February 1960

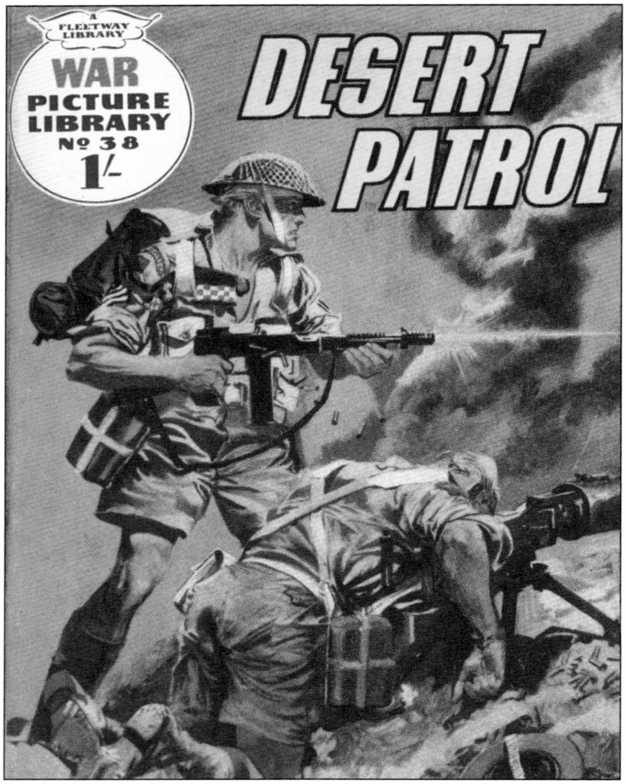
A
FLEETWAY
LIBRARY
WAR
PICTURE
LIBRARY
Nº 38
1/-
DESERT
PATROL

Giorgio DeGaspari, War 38, February 1960

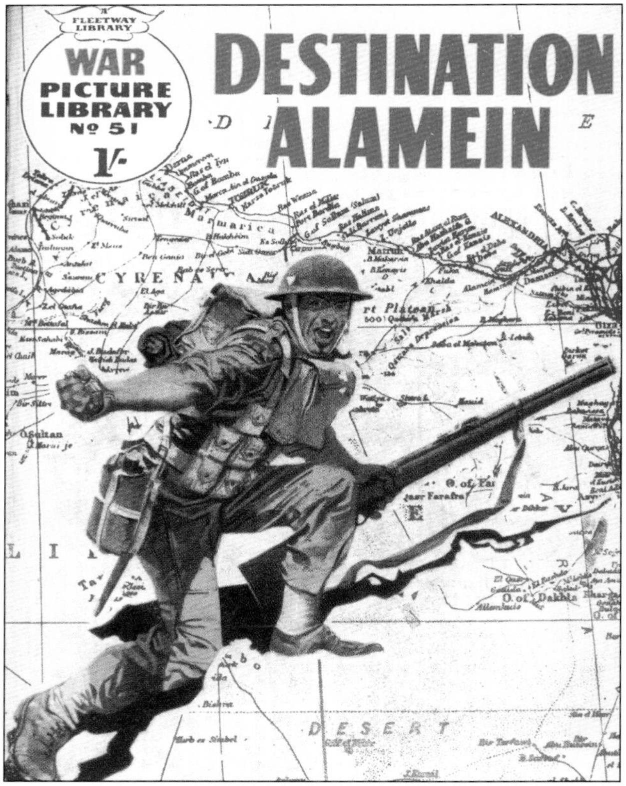
A
FLEETWAY
LIBRARY
WAR
PICTURE
LIBRARY
Nº 51
1/-
DESTINATION
ALAMEIN
CYRENAICA
ALEXANDRIA
DESERT

Allessandro Biffignandi, War 51, May 1960

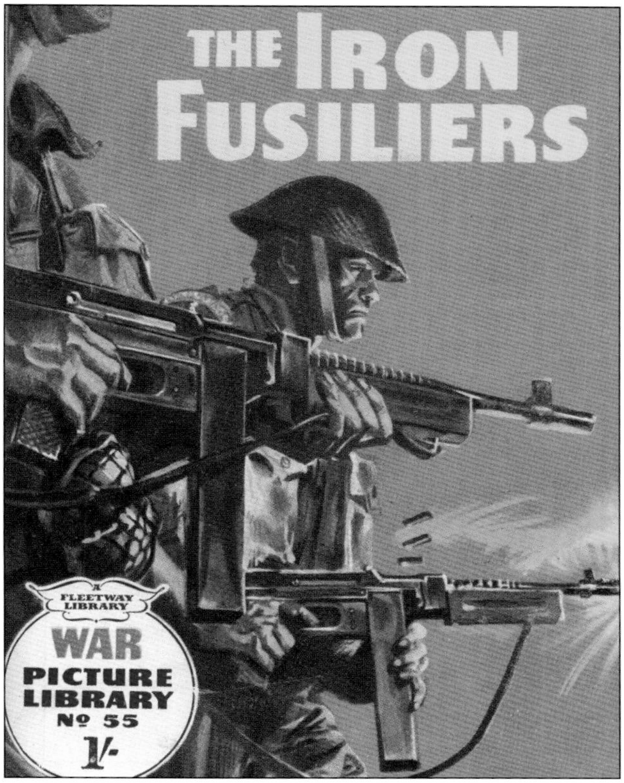
THE IRON FUSILIERS
A FLEETWAY LIBRARY
WAR PICTURE LIBRARY
Nº 55
1/-

Giorgio DeGaspari, War 55, June 1960

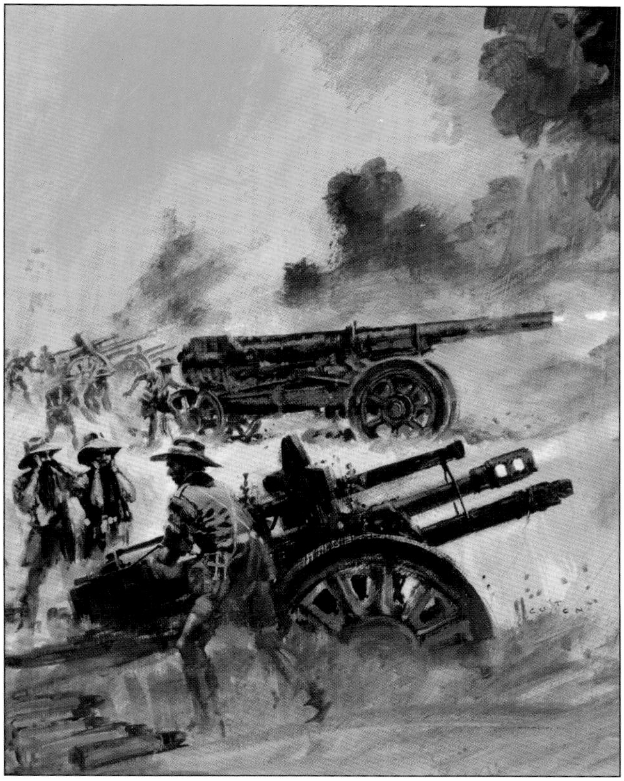

Graham Coton, War 1011, December 1974

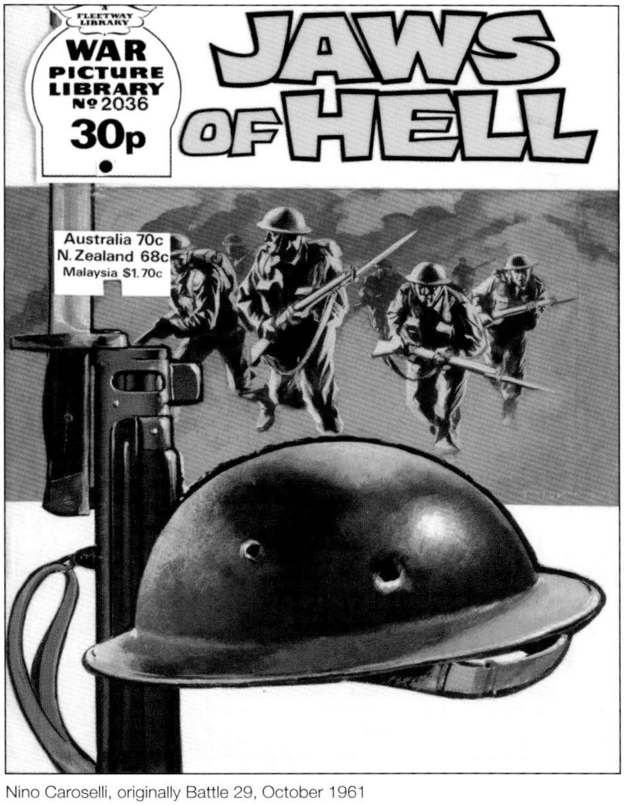
FLEETWAY LIBRARY
WAR PICTURE LIBRARY
Nº 2036
30p
JAWS OF HELL
Australia 70c
N. Zealand 68c
Malaysia $1.70c

Nino Caroselli, originally Battle 29, October 1961

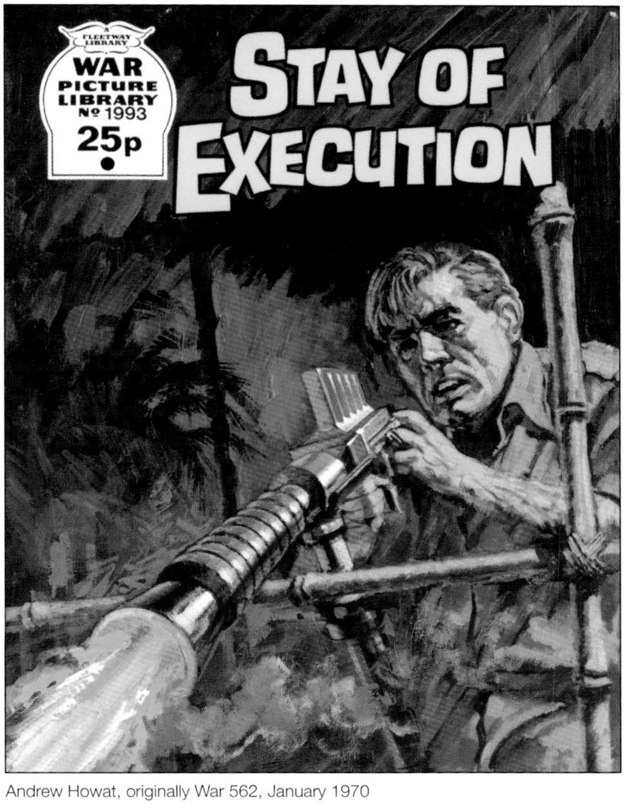
FLEETWAY LIBRARY
WAR PICTURE LIBRARY
Nº 1993
25p
STAY OF EXECUTION

Andrew Howat, originally War 562, January 1970

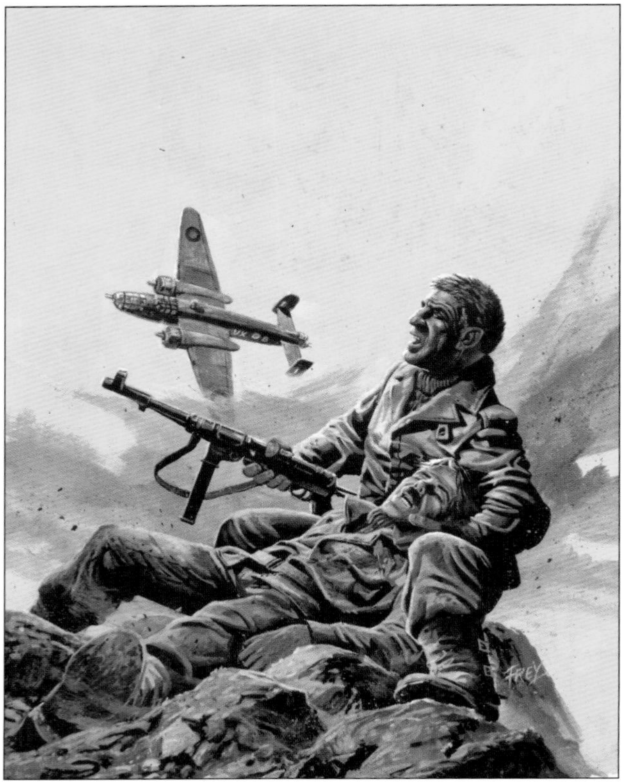

Oliver Frey, Battle 993, April 1976

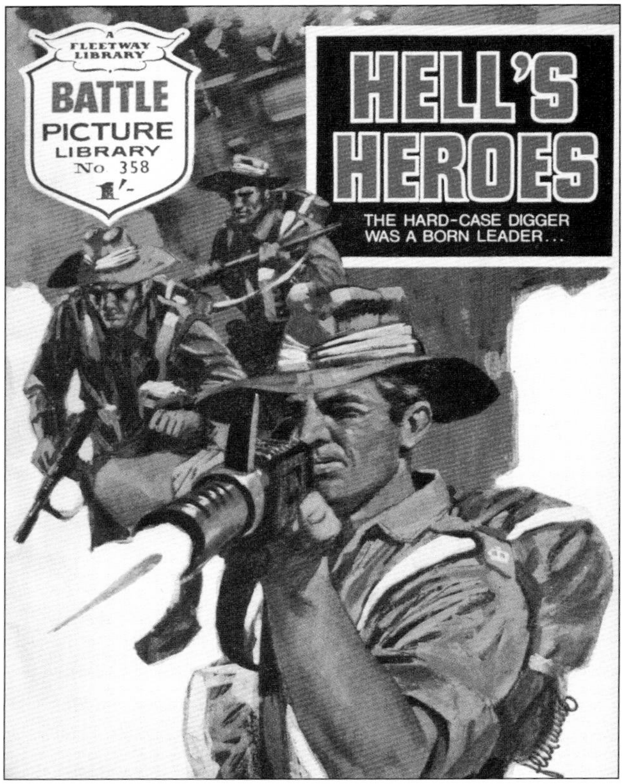
A FLEETWAY LIBRARY
BATTLE
PICTURE
LIBRARY
No 358
1/-
HELL'S HEROES
THE HARD-CASE DIGGER WAS A BORN LEADER...

Fernando Fernandez, Battle 358, August 1968

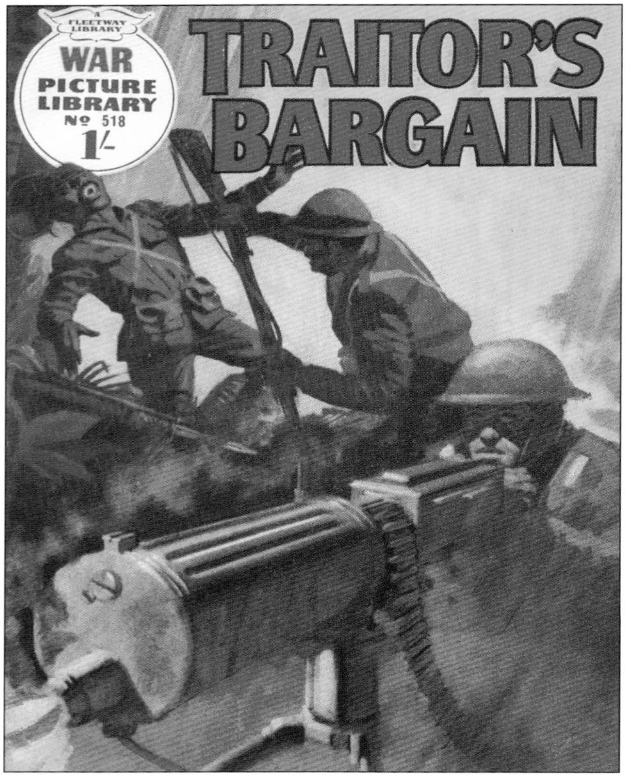
A FLEETWAY LIBRARY
WAR
PICTURE
LIBRARY
No 518
1/-
TRAITOR'S BARGAIN

Andrew Howat, War 518, June 1969

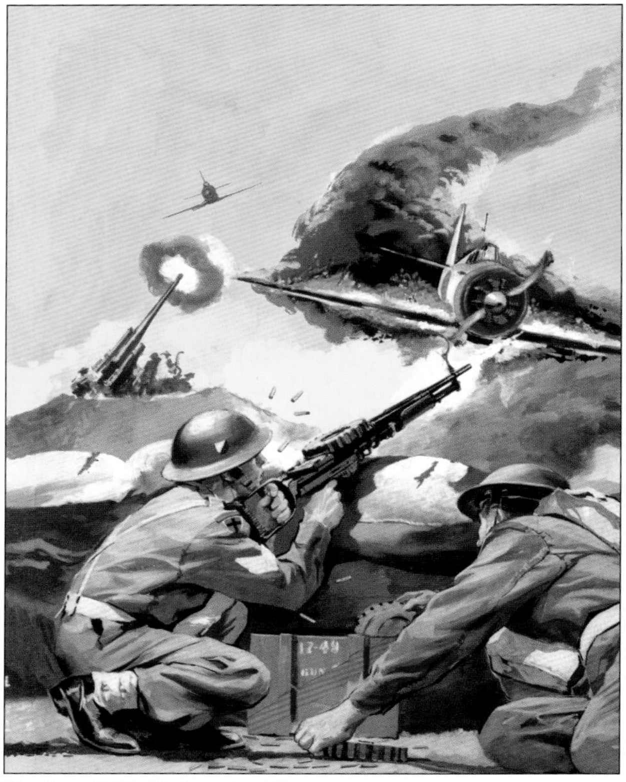

Nino Caroselli, War 75, November 1960

Opposite: Jordi Penalva, War 535, August 1969

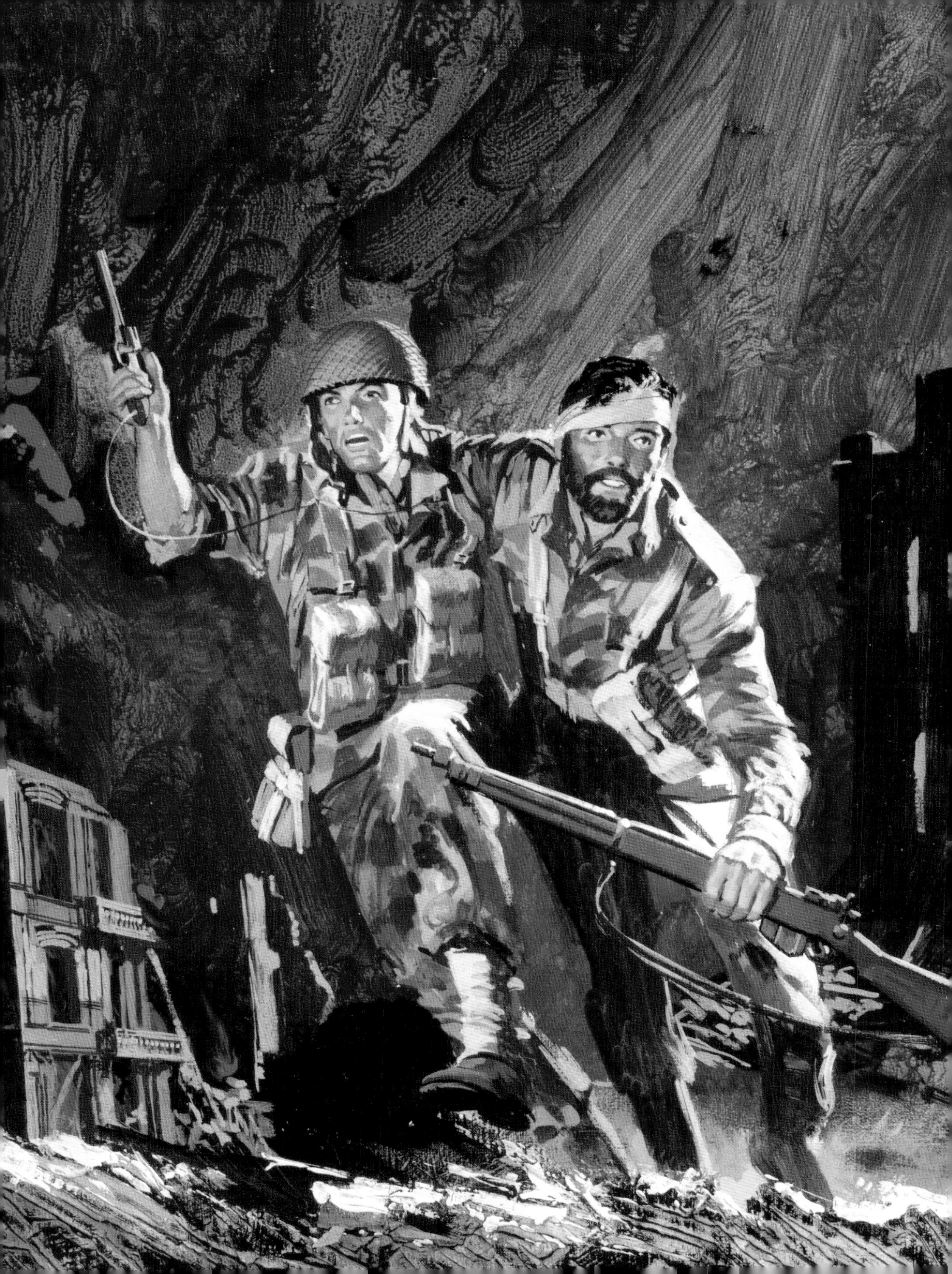

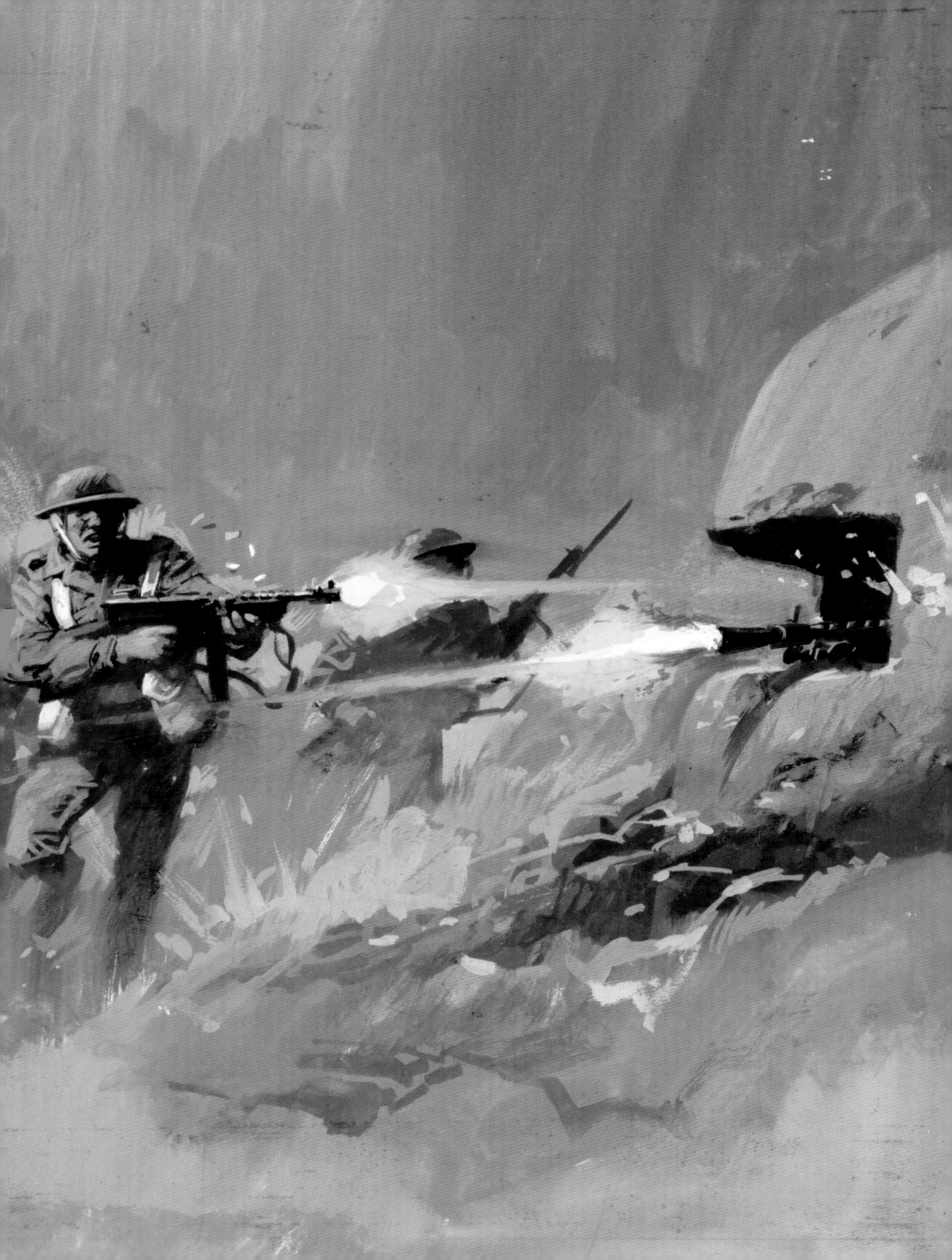

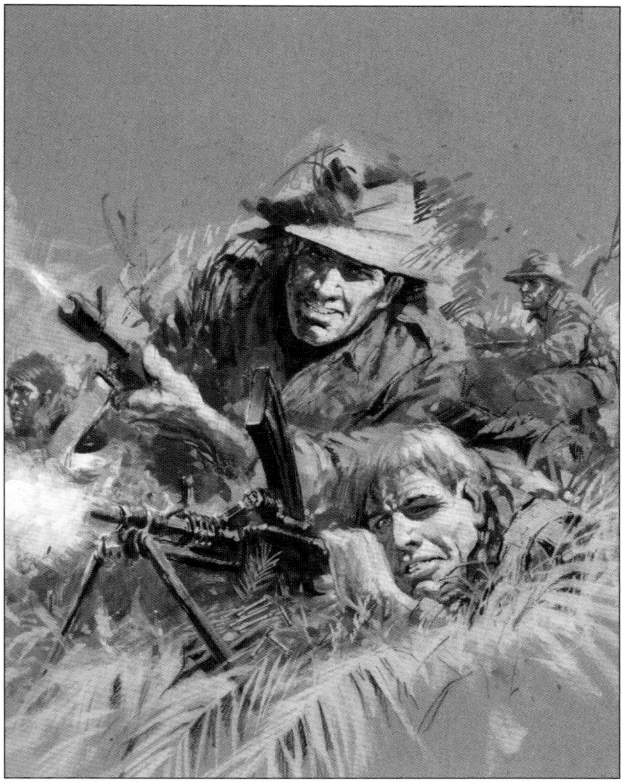

Graham Coton, Battle 540, July 1971

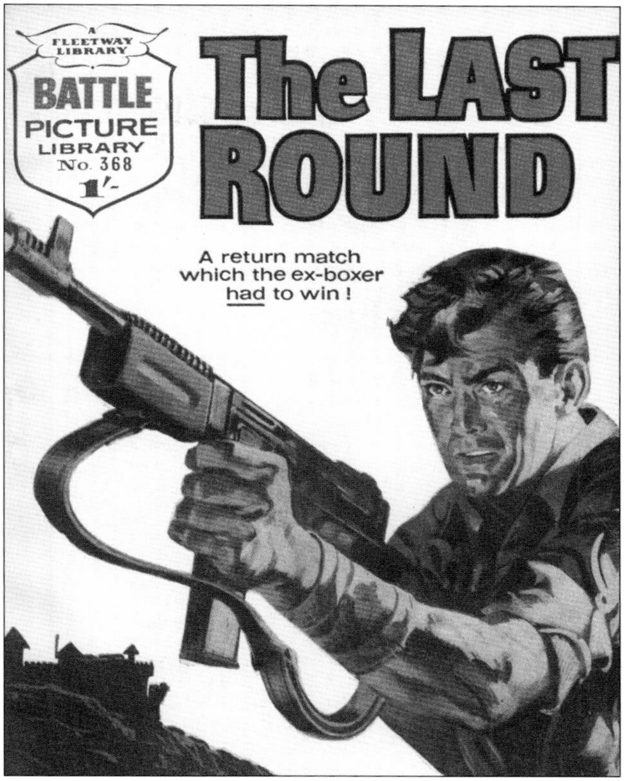
A FLEETWAY LIBRARY
BATTLE PICTURE LIBRARY No. 368 1/-
The LAST ROUND
A return match which the ex-boxer had to win !

Allessandro Biffignandi, Battle 368, October 1968

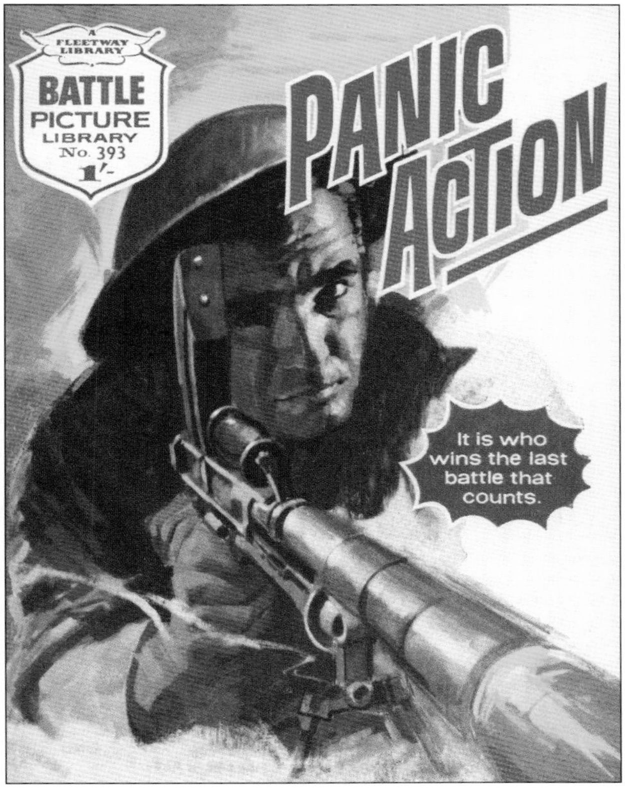
A FLEETWAY LIBRARY
BATTLE PICTURE LIBRARY No. 393 1/-
PANIC ACTION
It is who wins the last battle that counts.

Fernando Fernandez, Battle 393, July 1969

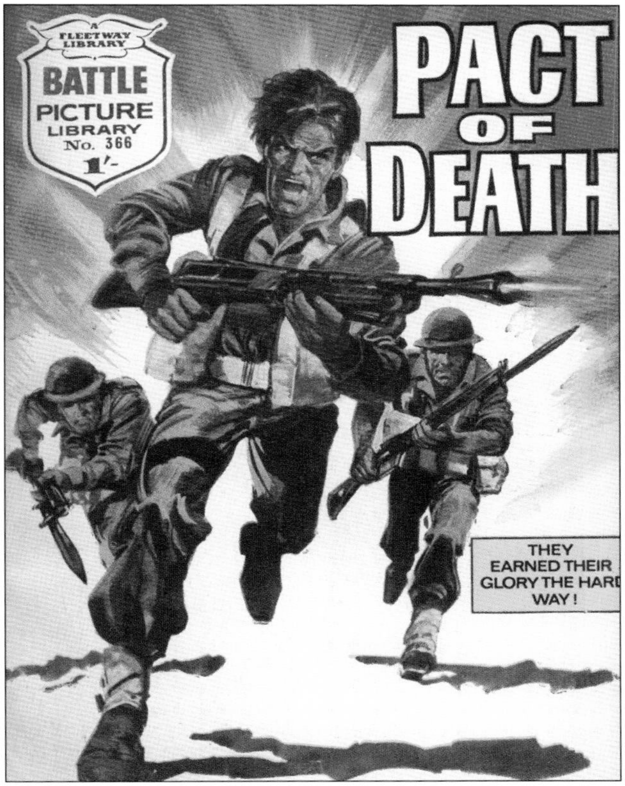
A FLEETWAY LIBRARY
BATTLE PICTURE LIBRARY No. 366 1/-
PACT OF DEATH

Allessandro Biffignandi, Battle 366, October 1968

Opposite: Pino Dell'Orco, War 296, July 1965
Overleaf: Nino Caroselli, War 71, December 1960

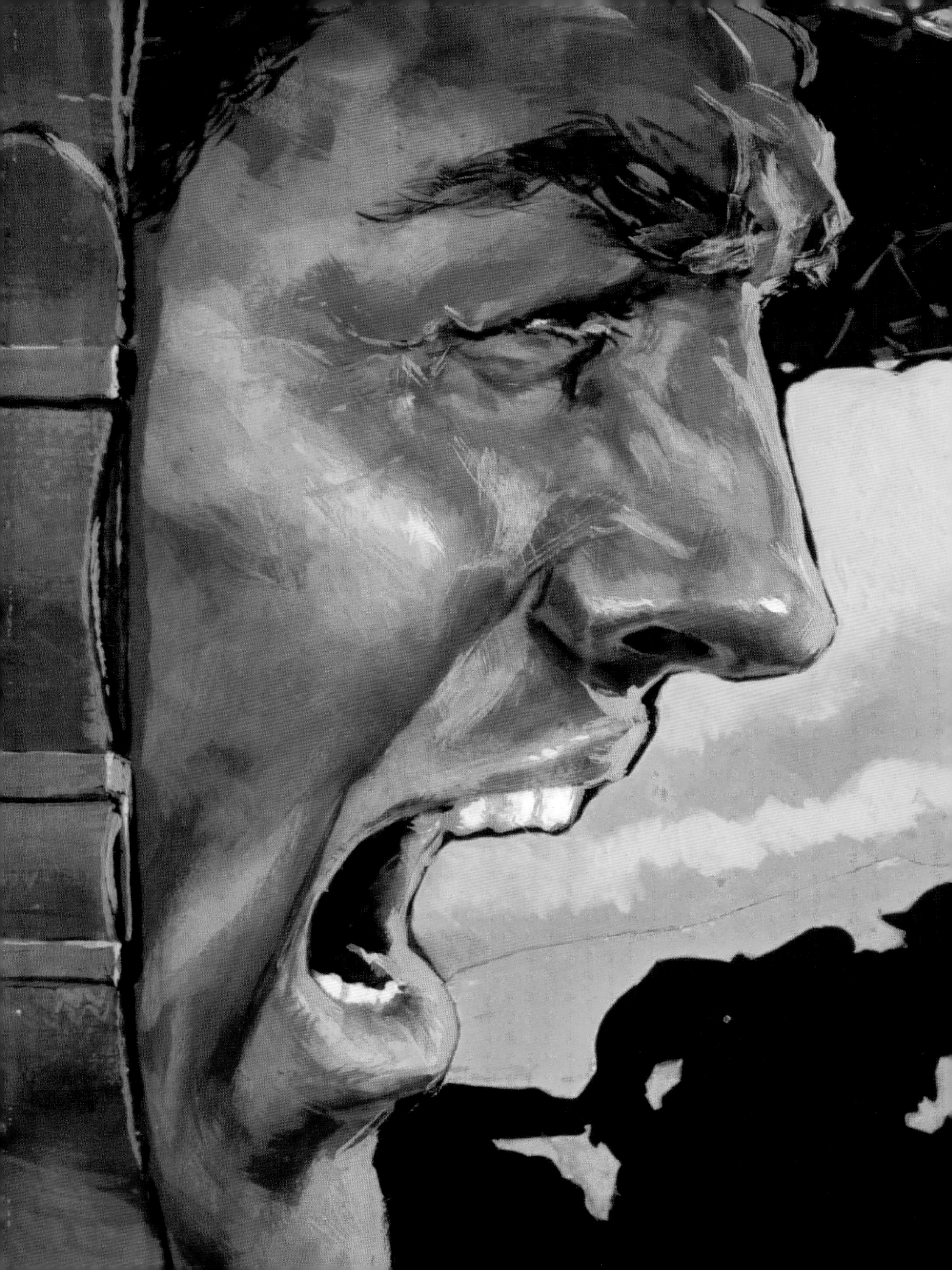

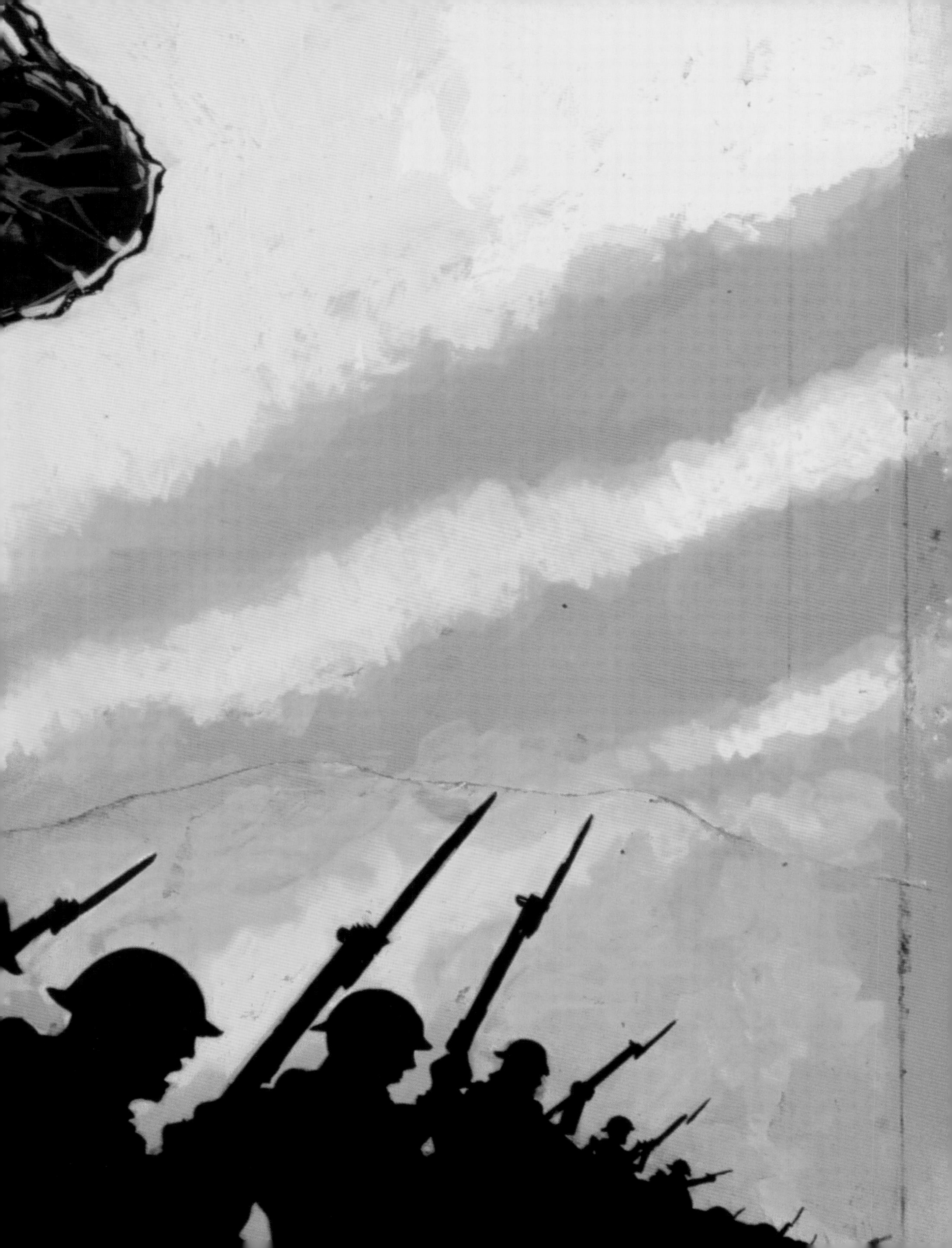

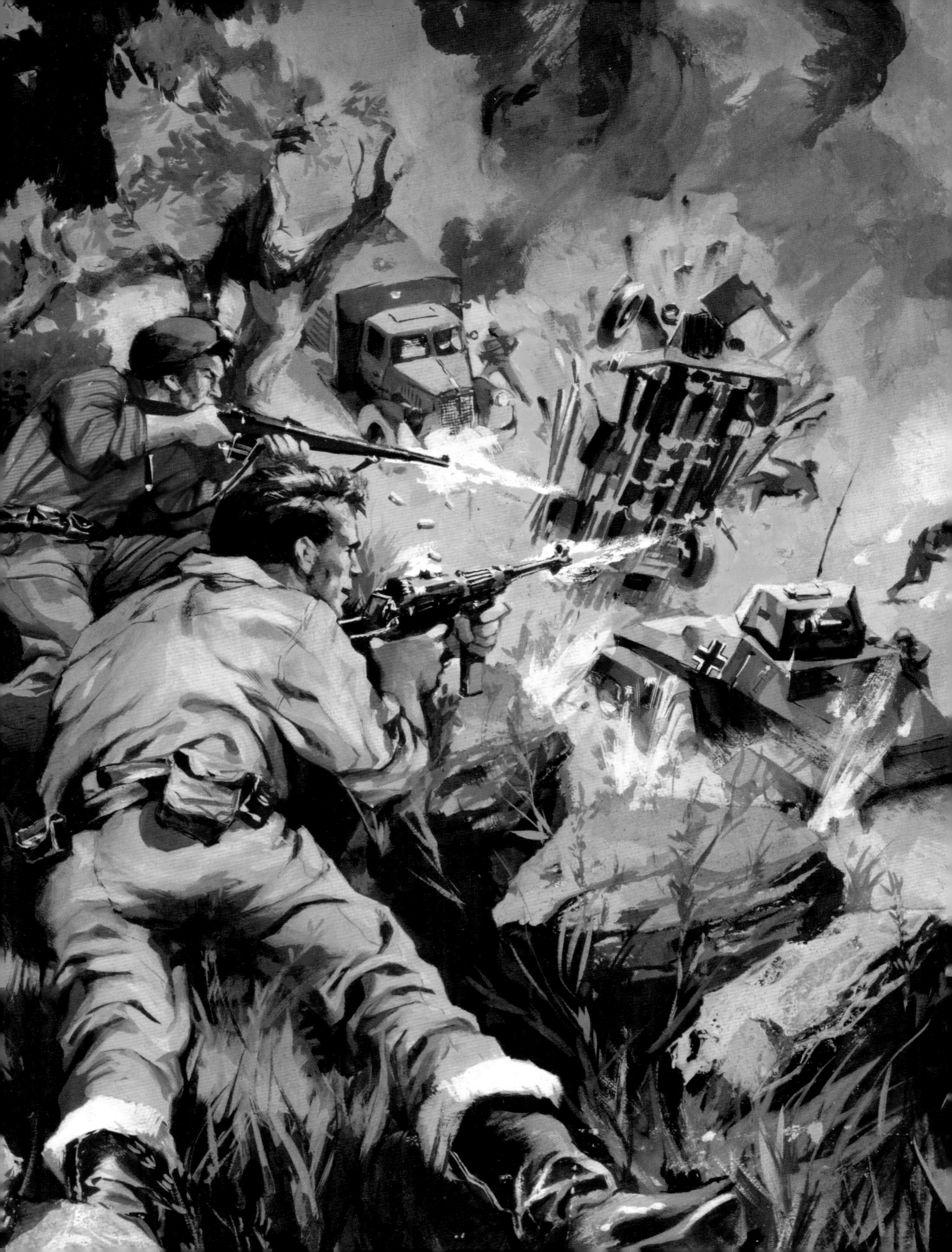

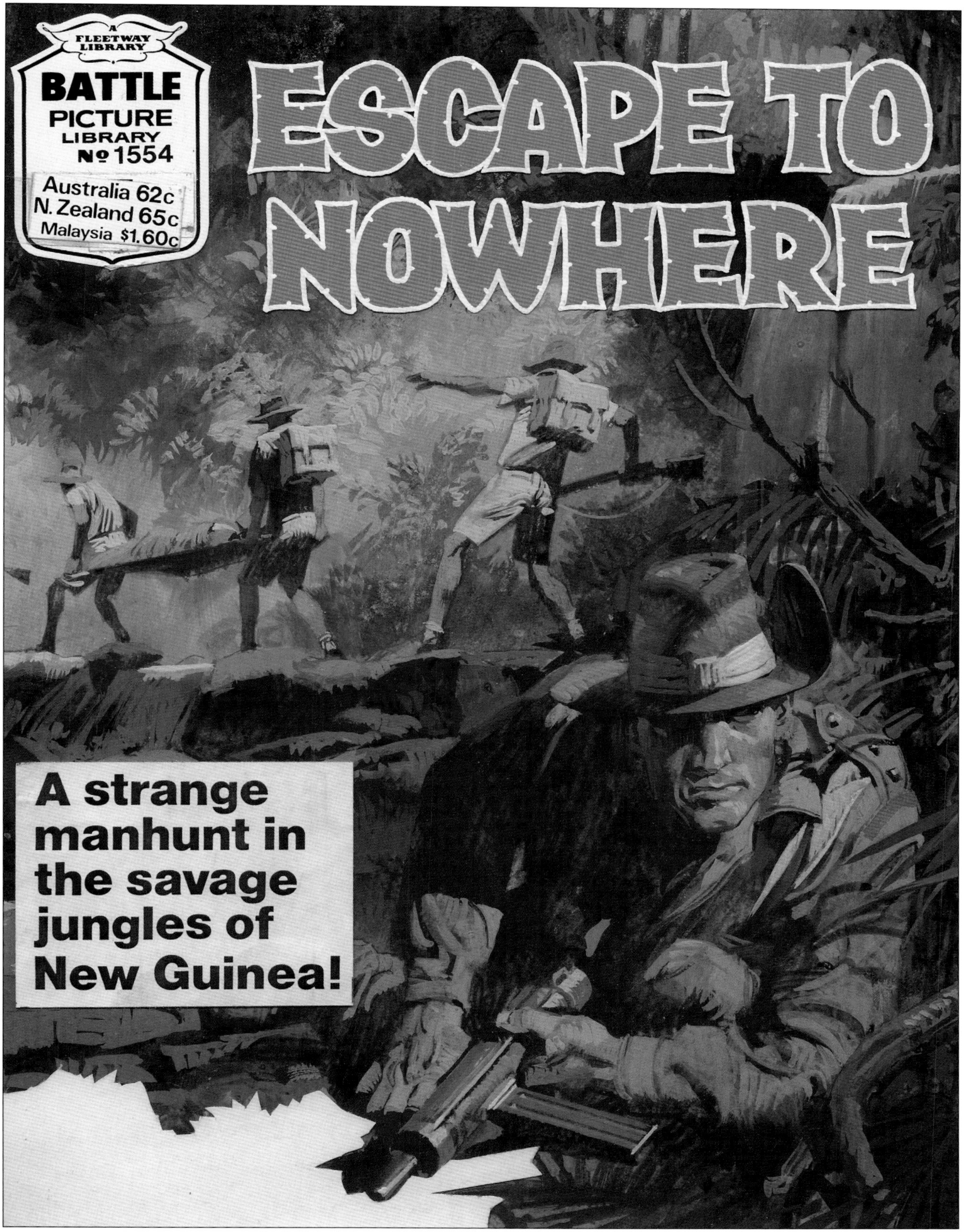
A FLEETWAY LIBRARY
BATTLE
PICTURE
LIBRARY
Nº 1554
Australia 62c
N. Zealand 65c
Malaysia $1.60c
ESCAPE TO NOWHERE
A strange manhunt in the savage jungles of New Guinea!

Allessandro Biffignandi, originally Battle 295, June 1965
Opposite: Nino Caroselli, War 33, January 1960

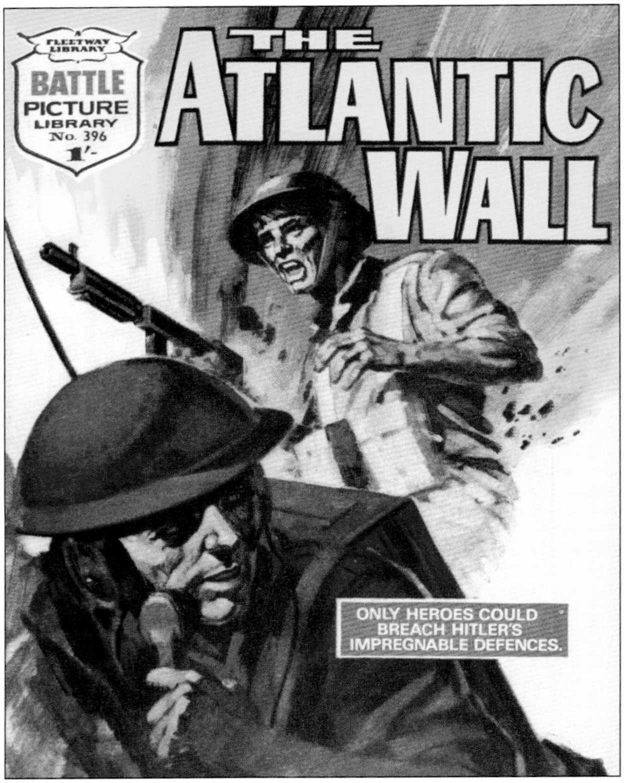
A FLEETWAY LIBRARY
BATTLE PICTURE LIBRARY
No. 396
1/-
THE ATLANTIC WALL
ONLY HEROES COULD BREACH HITLER'S IMPREGNABLE DEFENCES.

Andrew Howat, Battle 396, July 1969

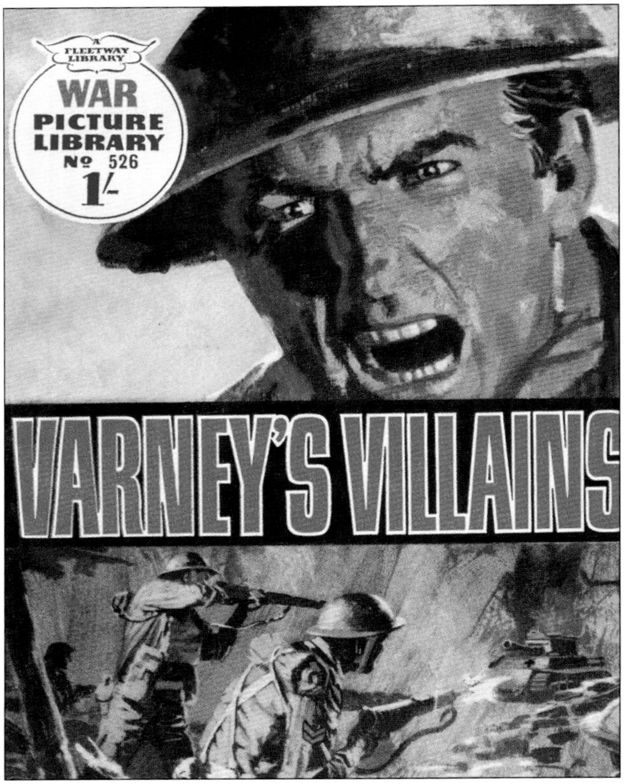
A FLEETWAY LIBRARY
WAR PICTURE LIBRARY
Nº 526
1/-
VARNEY'S VILLAINS

Jordi Penalva, War 526, July 1969

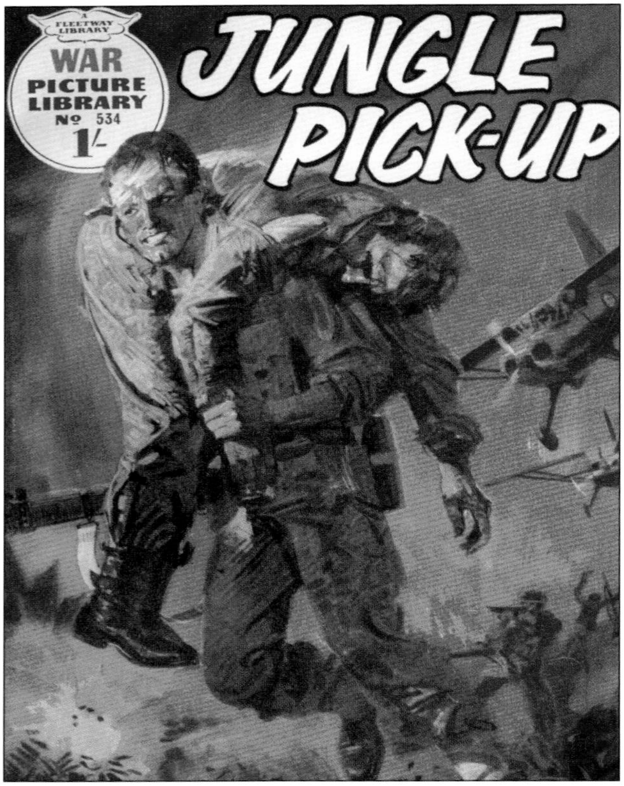
A FLEETWAY LIBRARY
WAR PICTURE LIBRARY
Nº 534
1/-
JUNGLE PICK-UP

Allessandro Biffignandi, War 534, August 1969

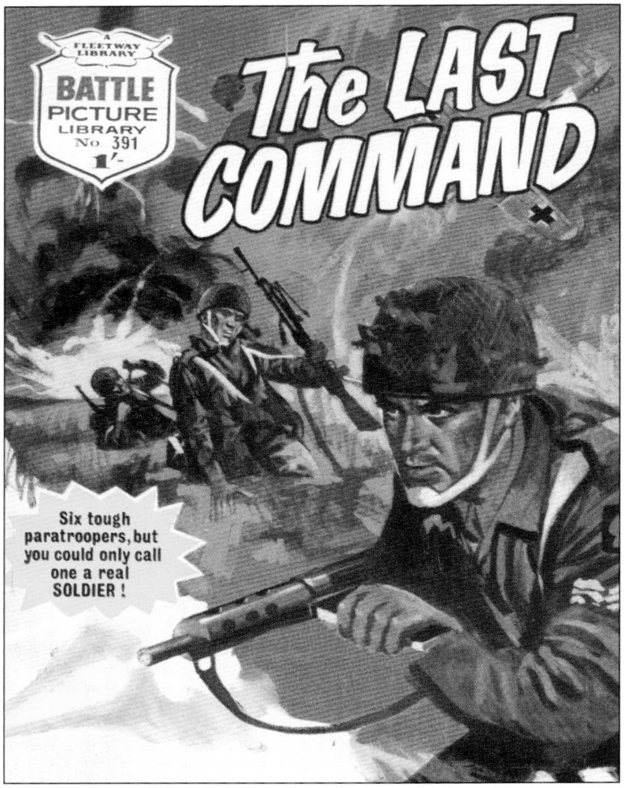
A FLEETWAY LIBRARY
BATTLE PICTURE LIBRARY
No. 391
1/-
The LAST COMMAND
Six tough paratroopers, but you could only call one a real SOLDIER !

Fernando Fernandez, Battle 391, April 1969

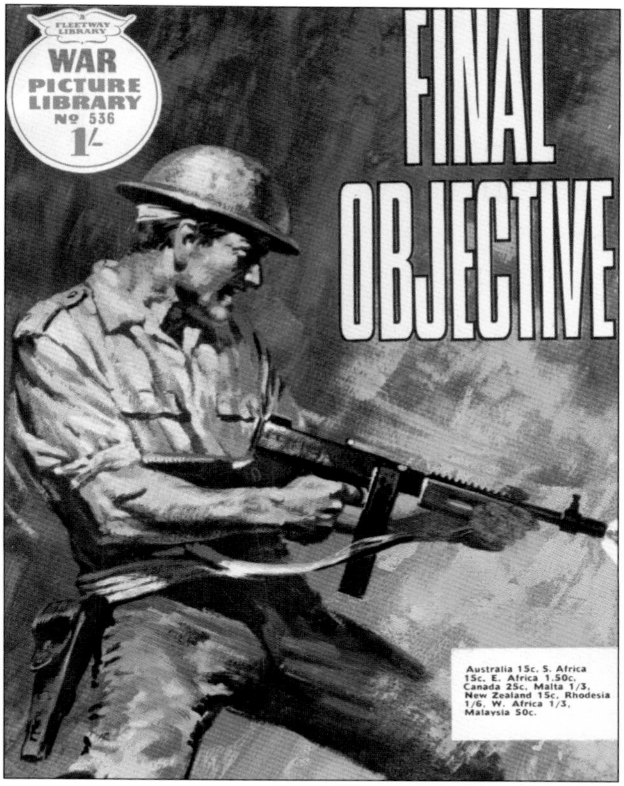
A FLEETWAY LIBRARY
WAR PICTURE LIBRARY
Nº 536
1/-
FINAL OBJECTIVE
Australia 15c. S. Africa 15c. E. Africa 1.50c. Canada 25c. Malta 1/3. New Zealand 15c. Rhodesia 1/6. W. Africa 1/3. Malaysia 50c.

Jordi Penalva, War 536, September 1969

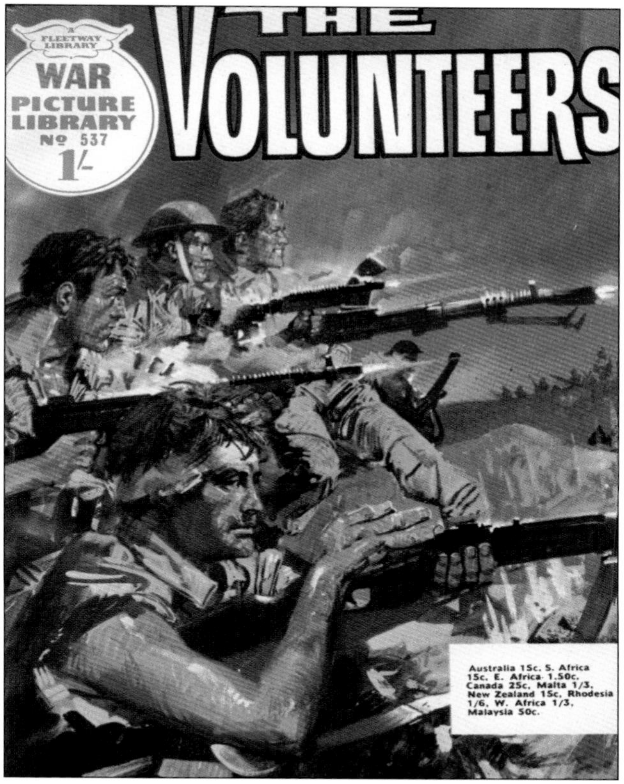
A FLEETWAY LIBRARY
WAR PICTURE LIBRARY
Nº 537
1/-
THE VOLUNTEERS
Australia 15c. S. Africa 15c. E. Africa 1.50c. Canada 25c. Malta 1/3. New Zealand 15c. Rhodesia 1/6. W. Africa 1/3. Malaysia 50c.

Allessandro Biffignandi, War 537, September 1969

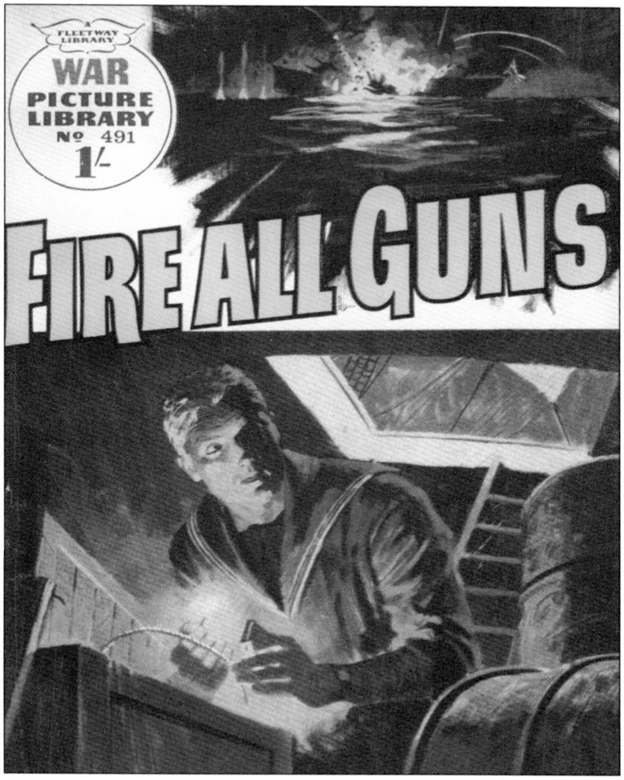
A FLEETWAY LIBRARY
WAR PICTURE LIBRARY
Nº 491
1/-
FIRE ALL GUNS

Jordi Penalva, War 491, January 1969

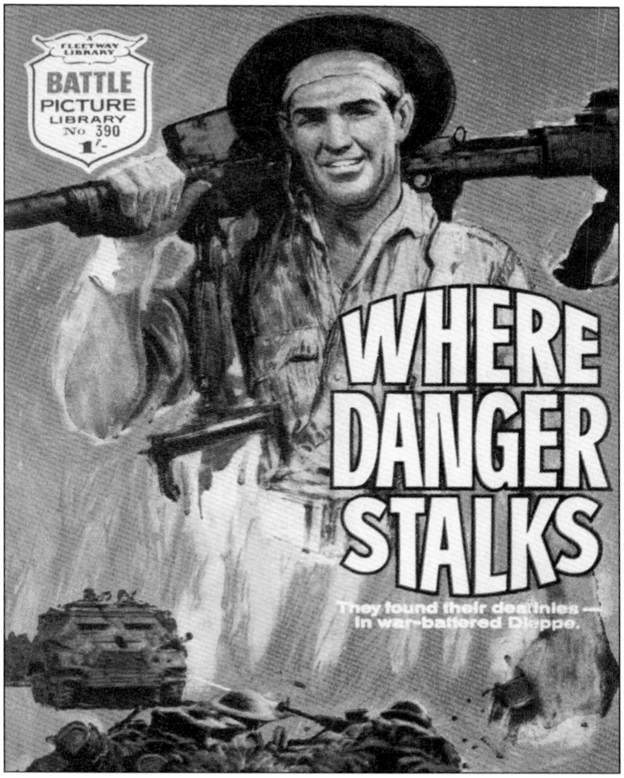
A FLEETWAY LIBRARY
BATTLE PICTURE LIBRARY
No 390
1/-
WHERE DANGER STALKS
They found their destinies — in war-battered Dieppe.

Graham Coton, Battle 390, April 1969

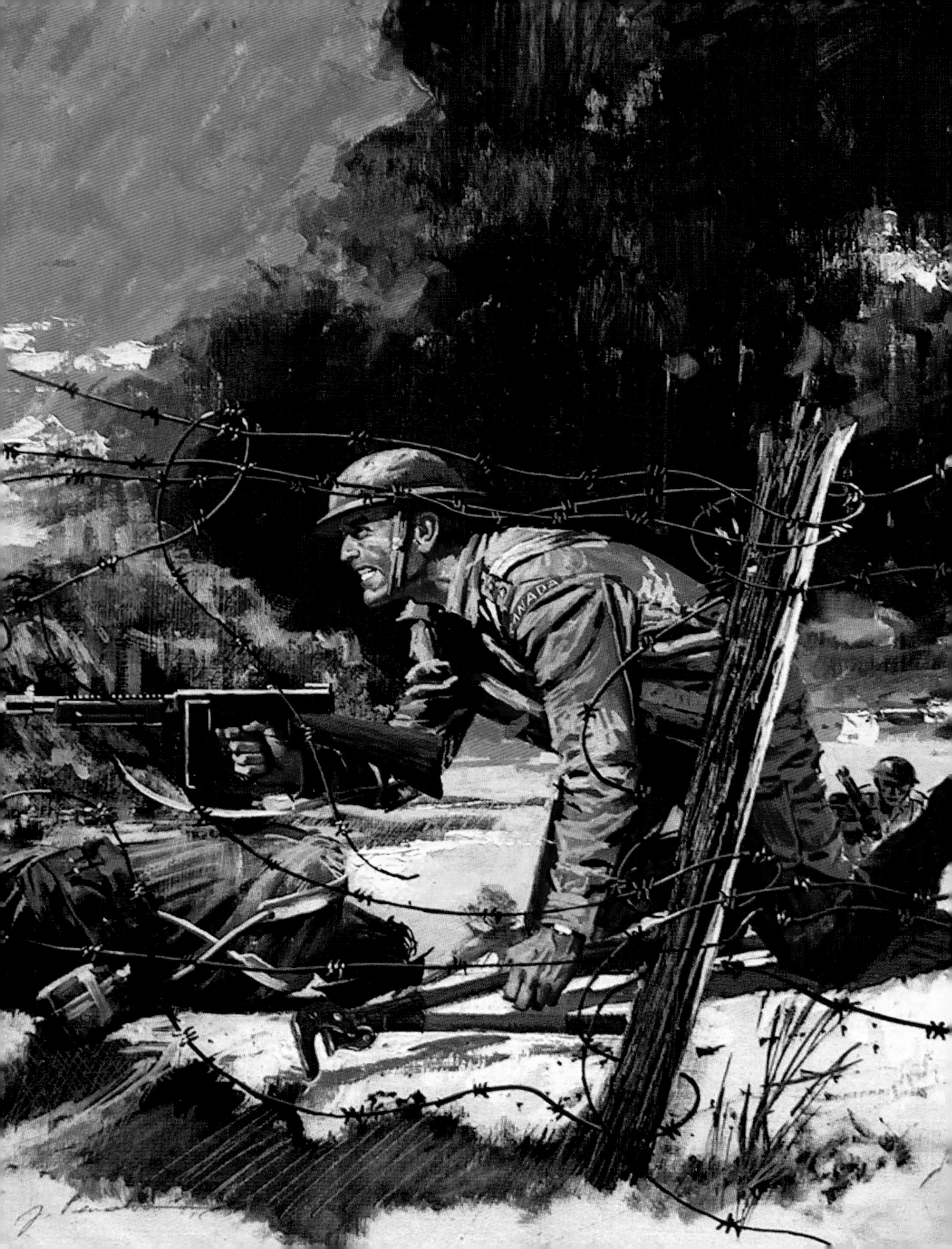
NADA

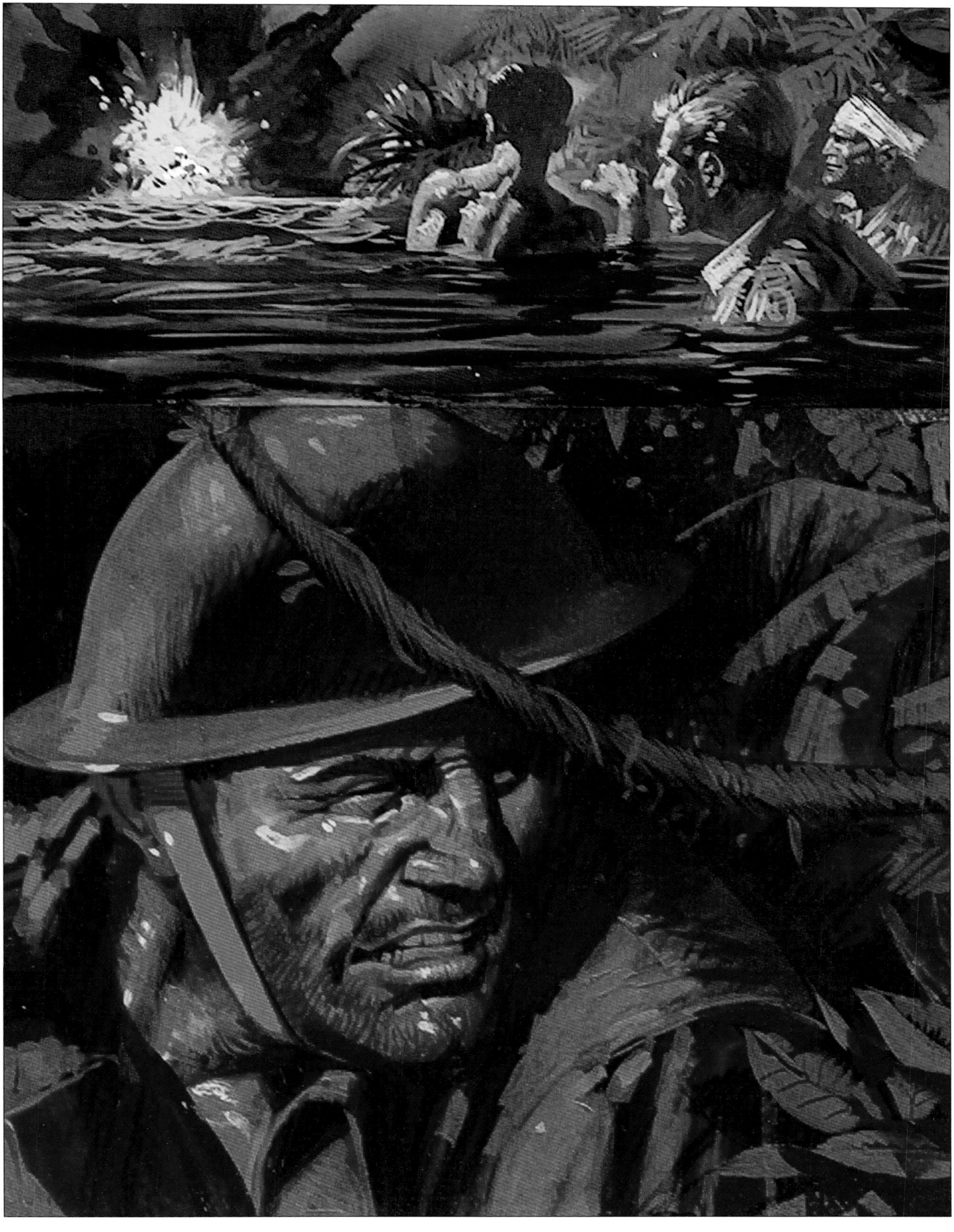

Allessandro Biffignandi, War 517, May 1969
Opposite: Jordi Penalva, Battle 126, October 1963

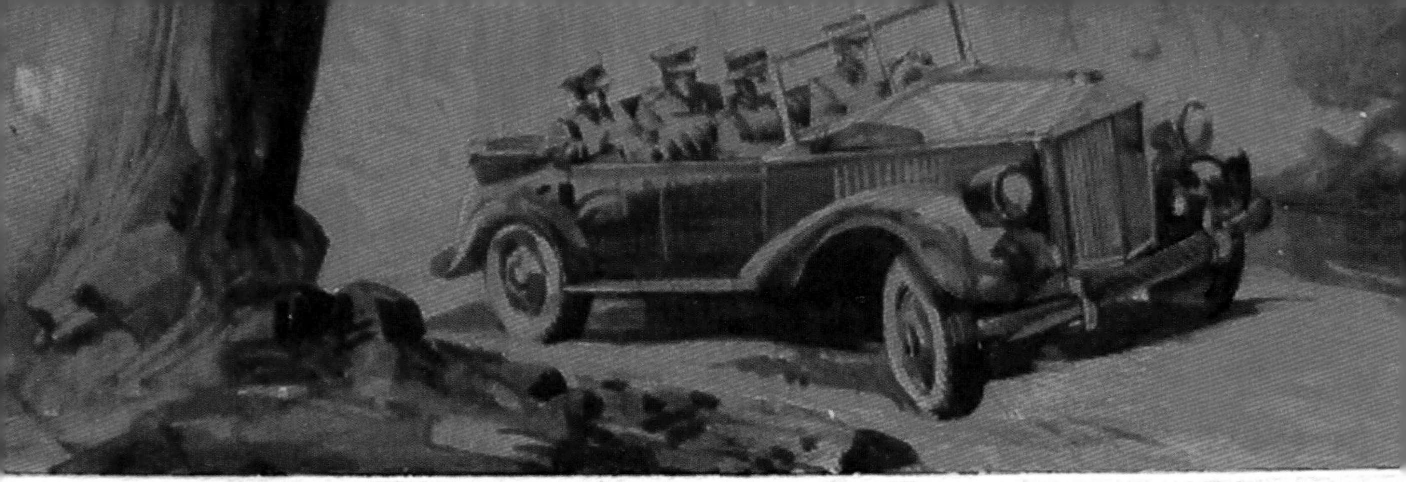

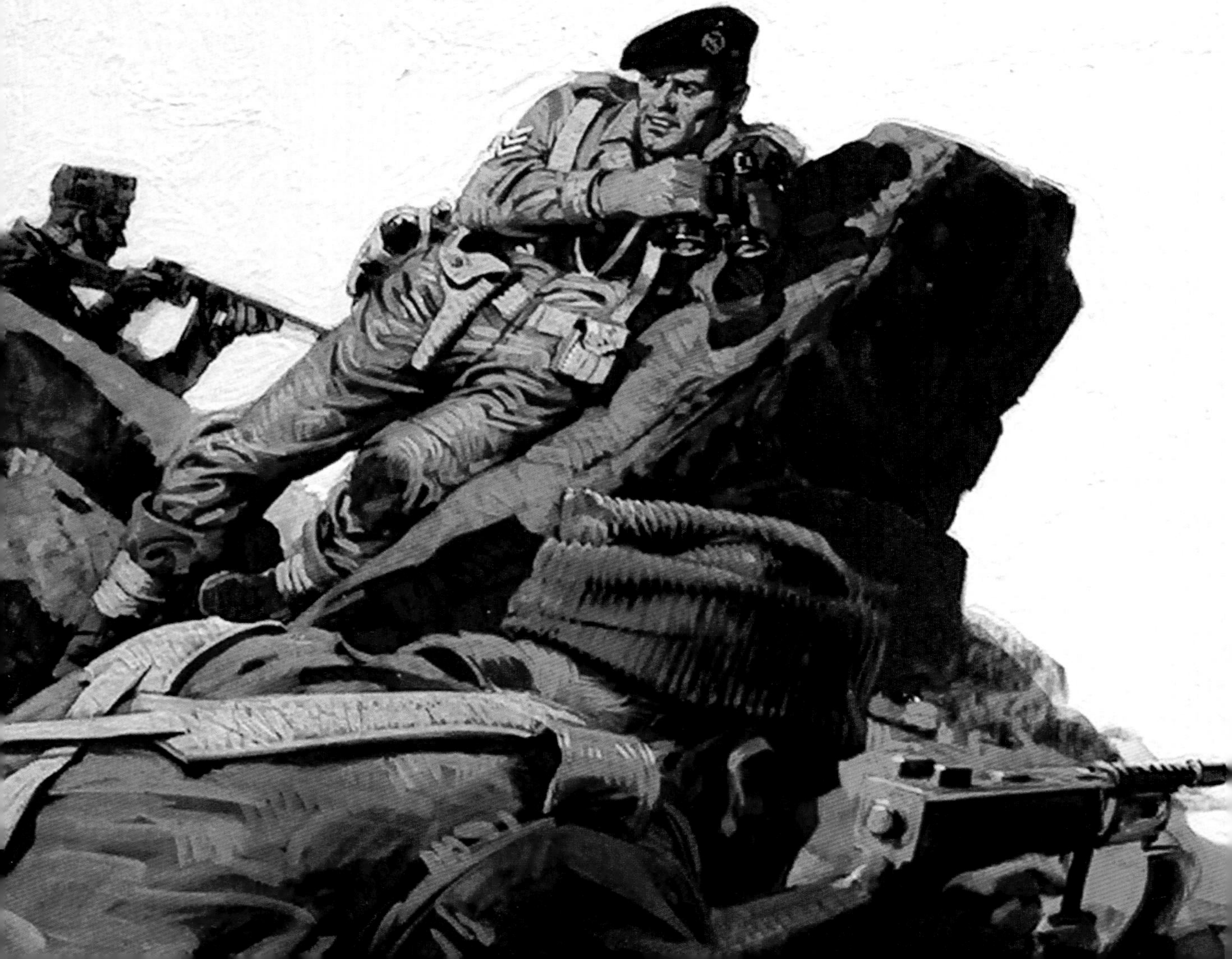

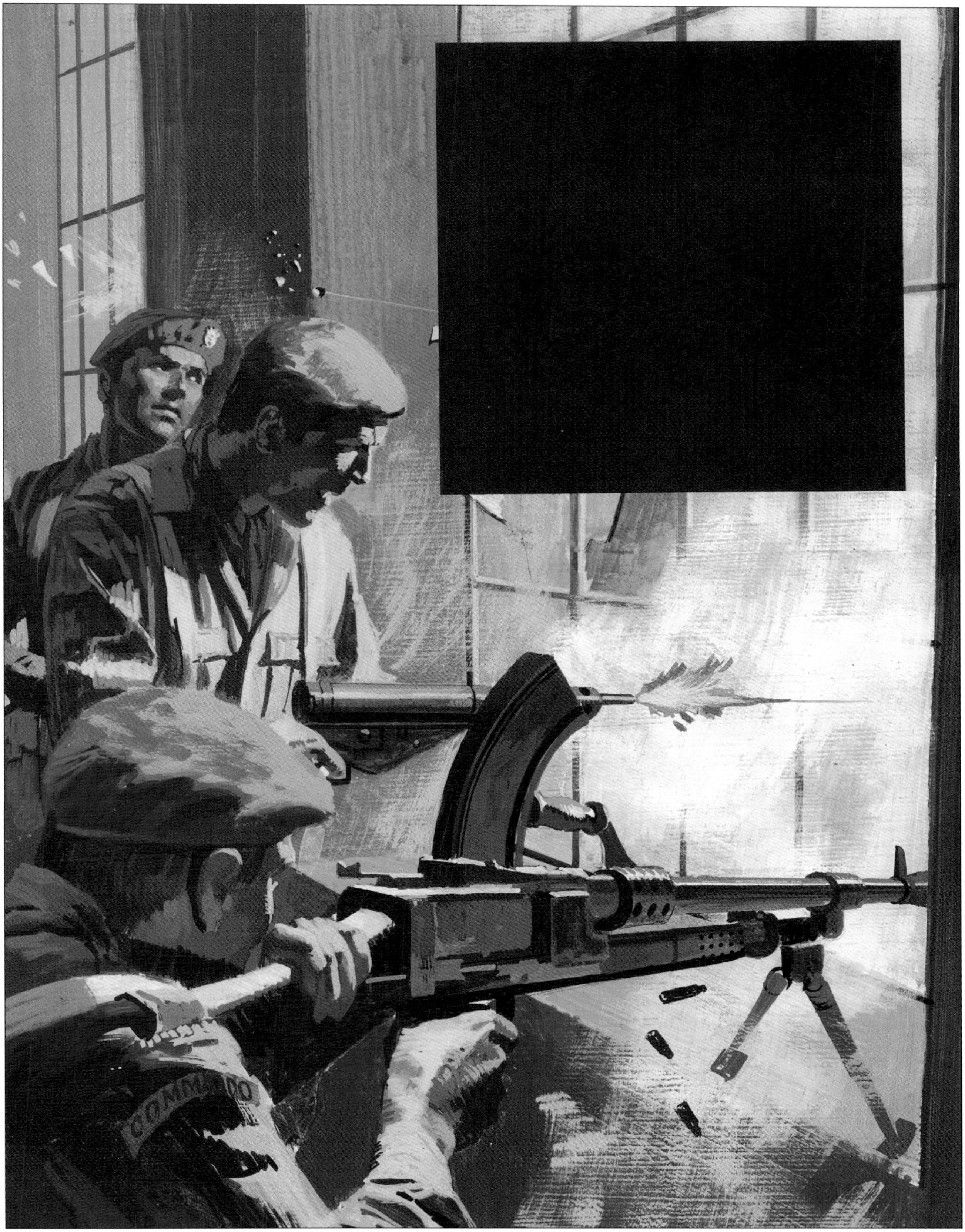
COMMANDO

Jordi Penalva, Battle 347, May 1968
Opposite: Allessandro Biffignandi, War 429, March 1968

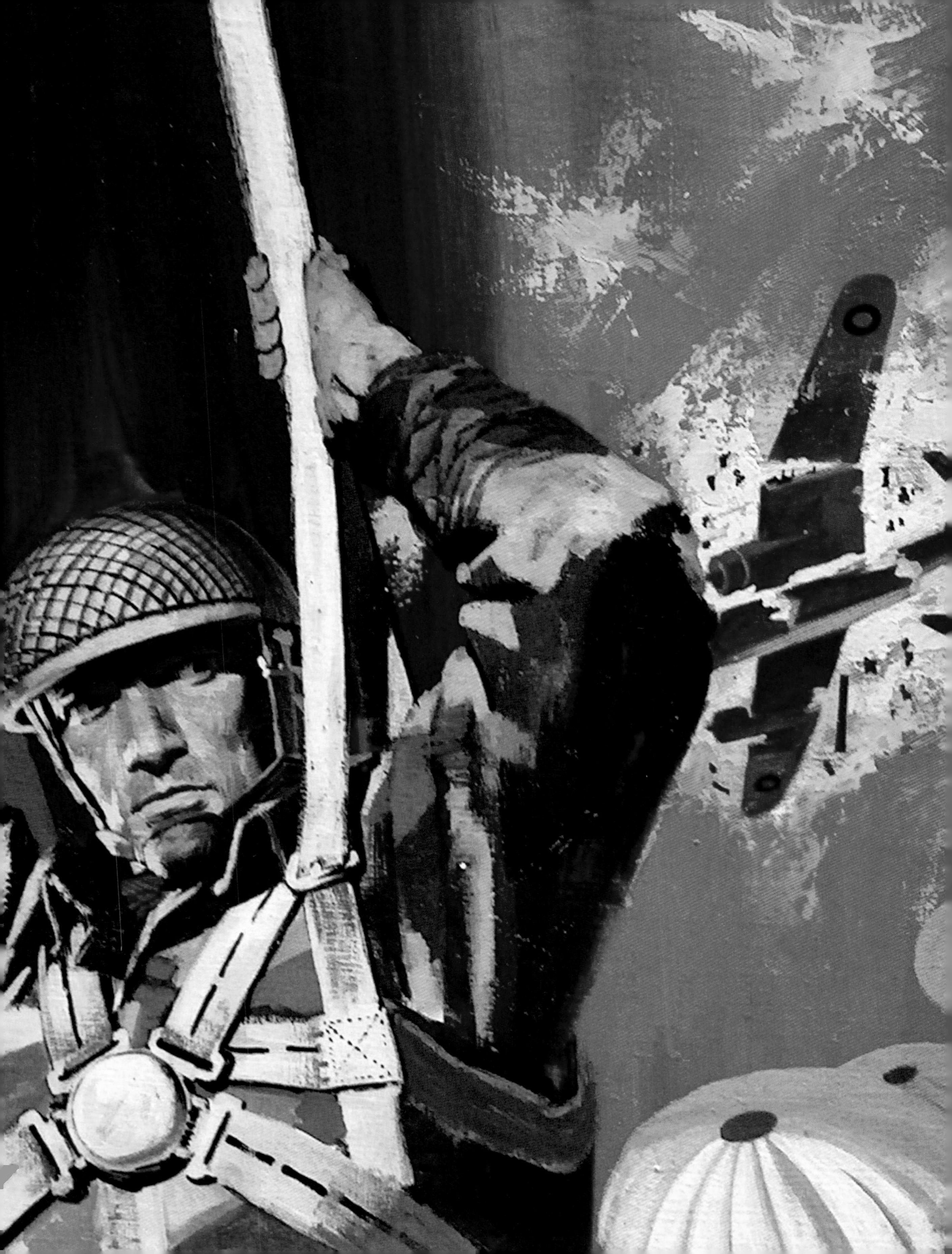

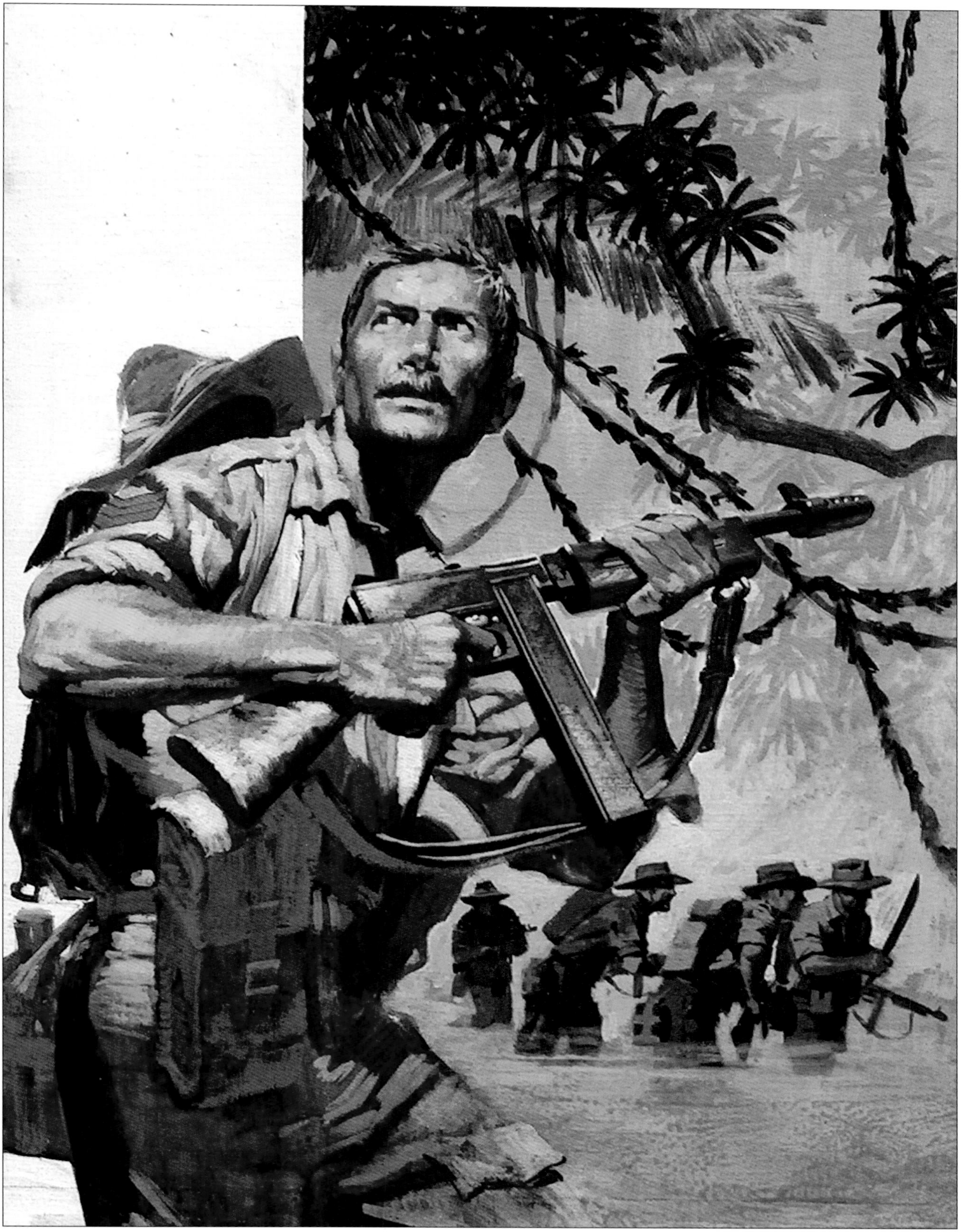

Jordi Penalva, unknown issue
Opposite: Jordi Penalva, Battle 451, March 1970
Overleaf: Nino Caroselli, War 63, August 1960

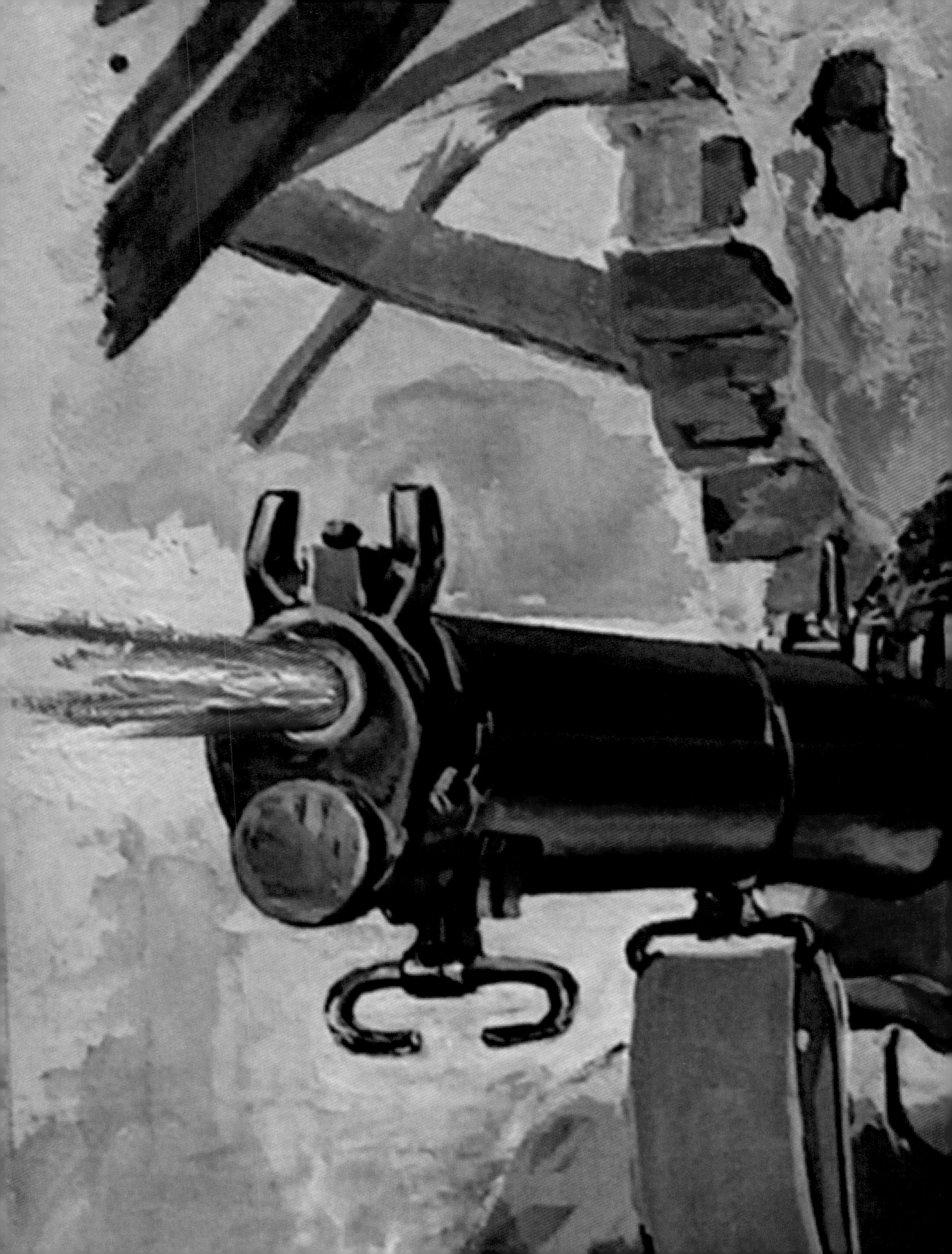

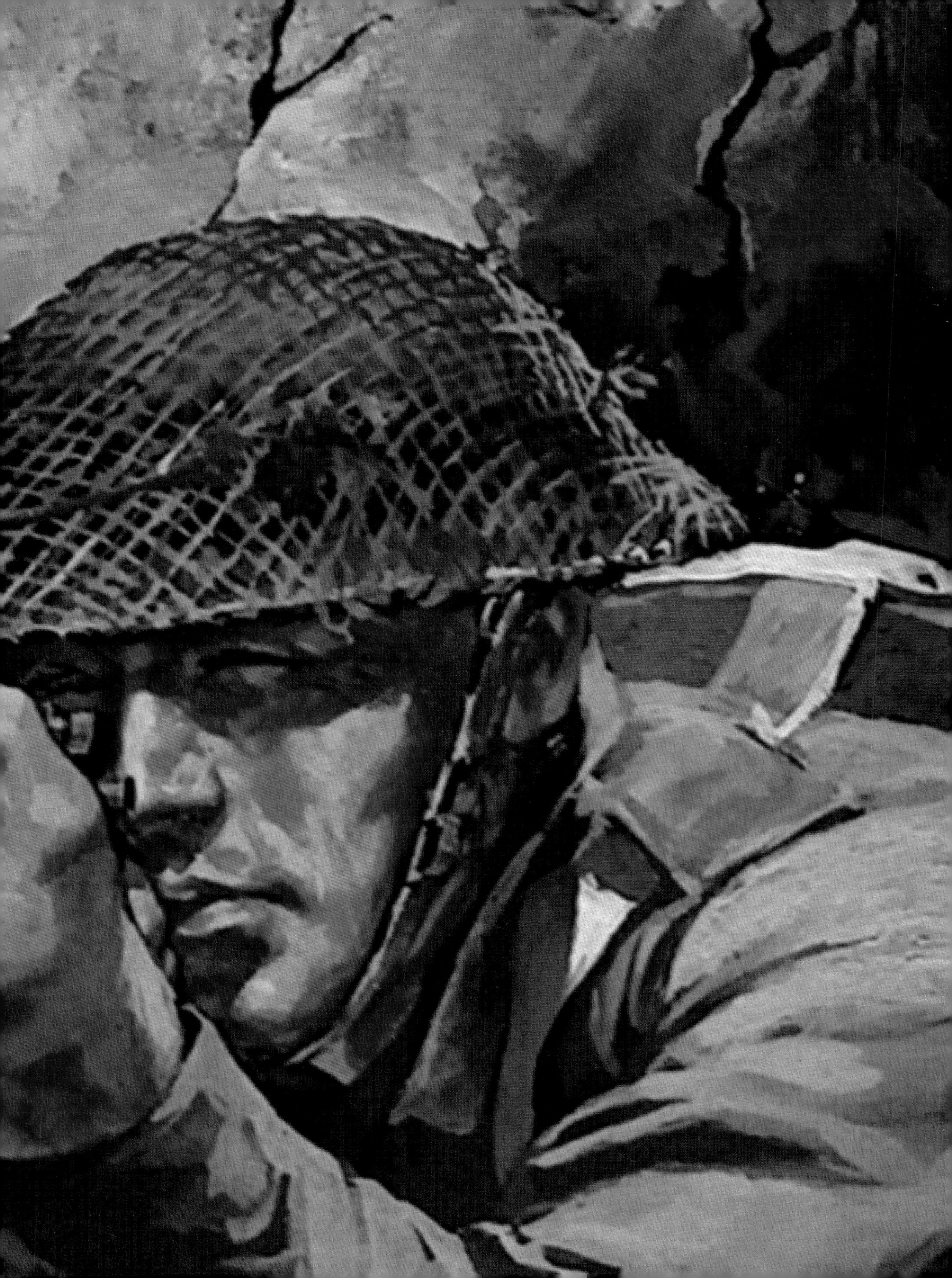

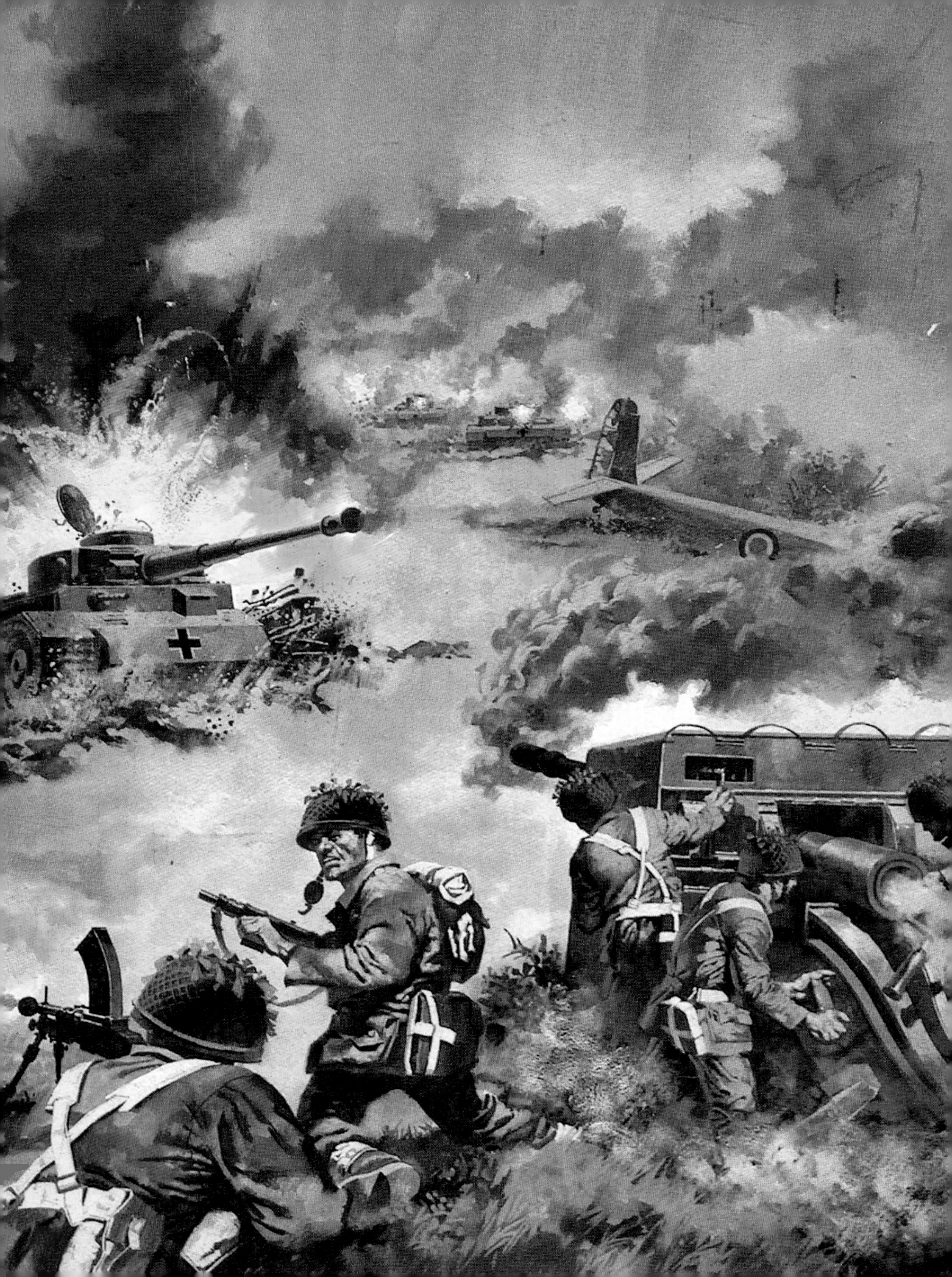

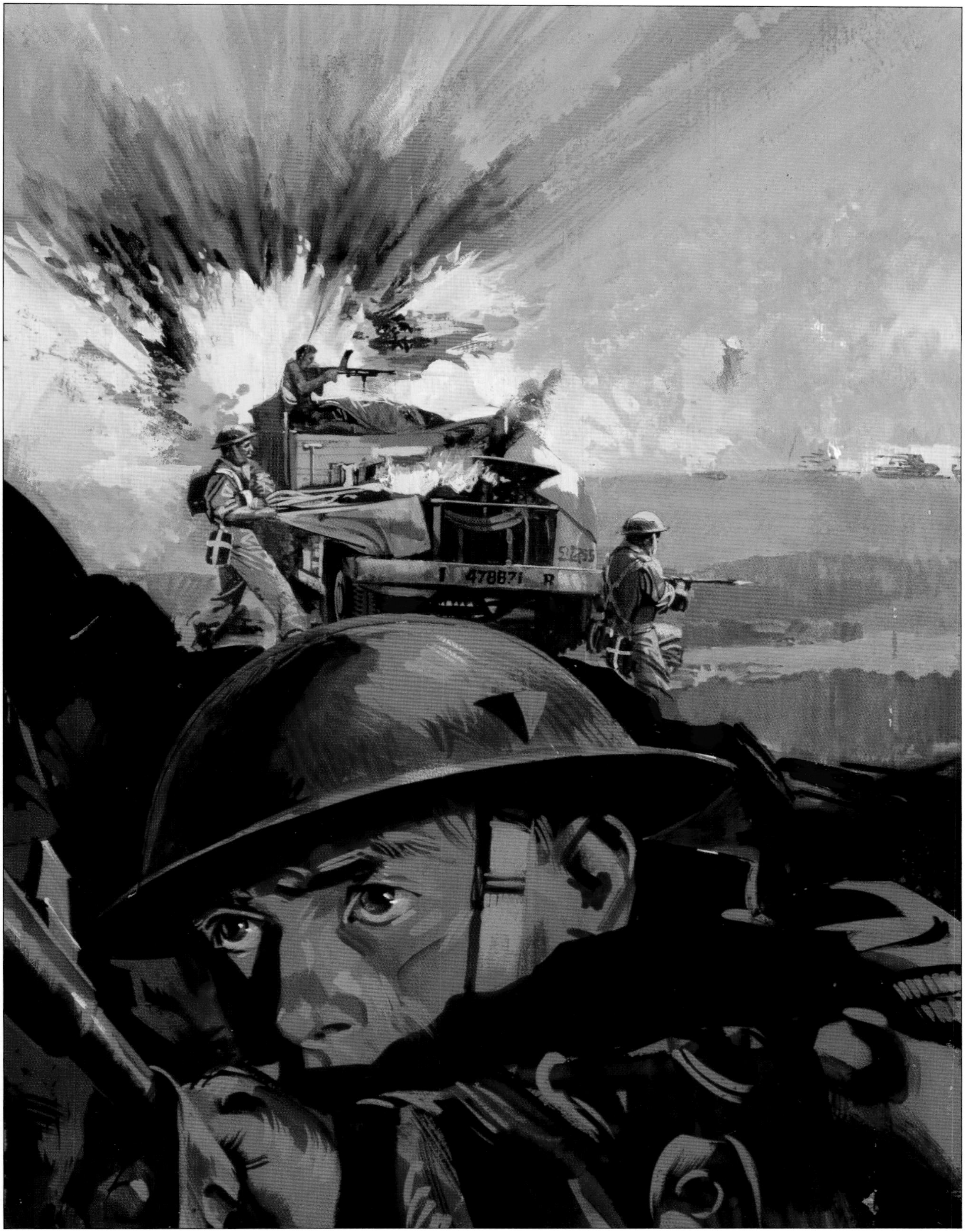

Allessandro Biffignandi, Battle 60, May 1962
Opposite: Gino D'Achille, Giant War, 1964

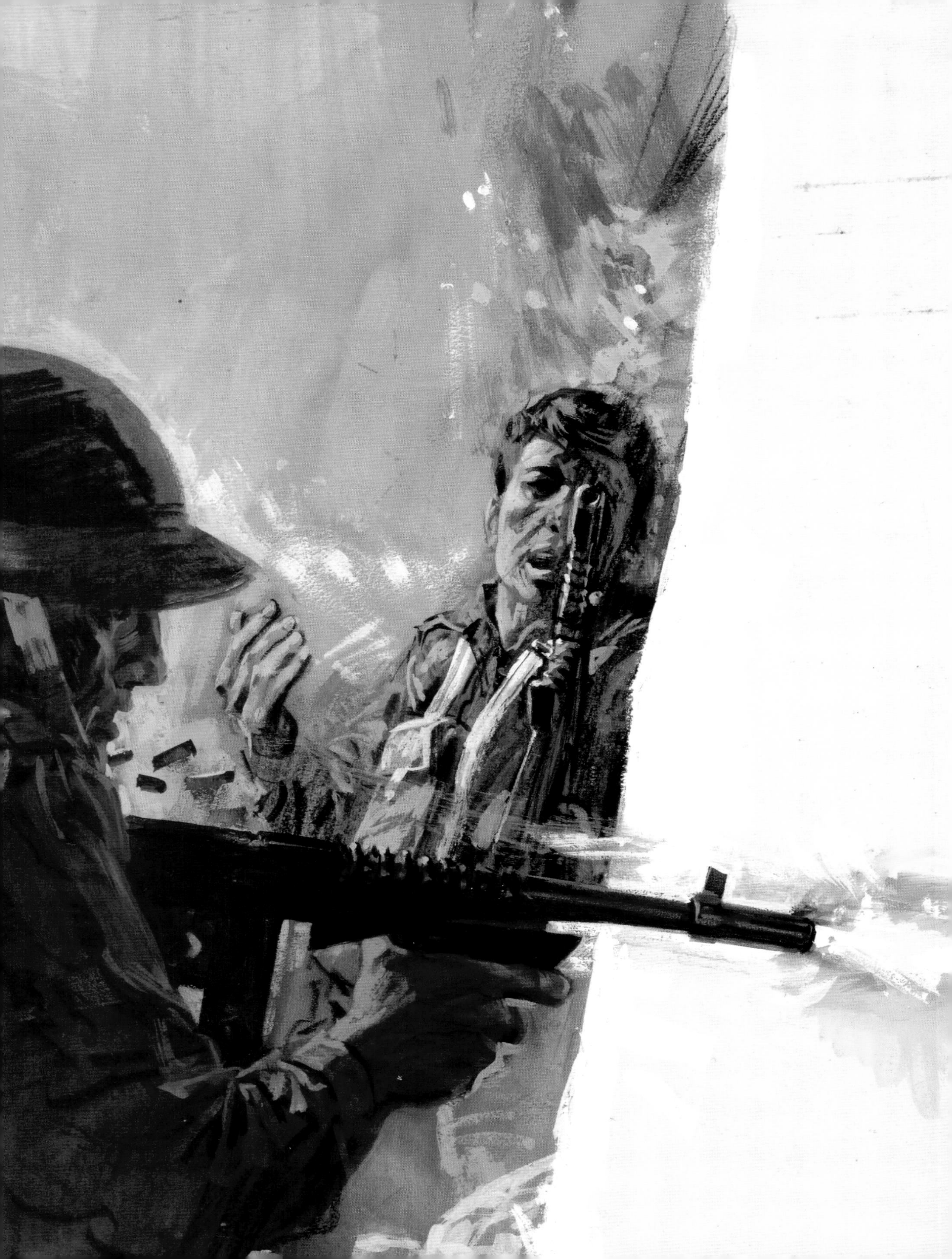

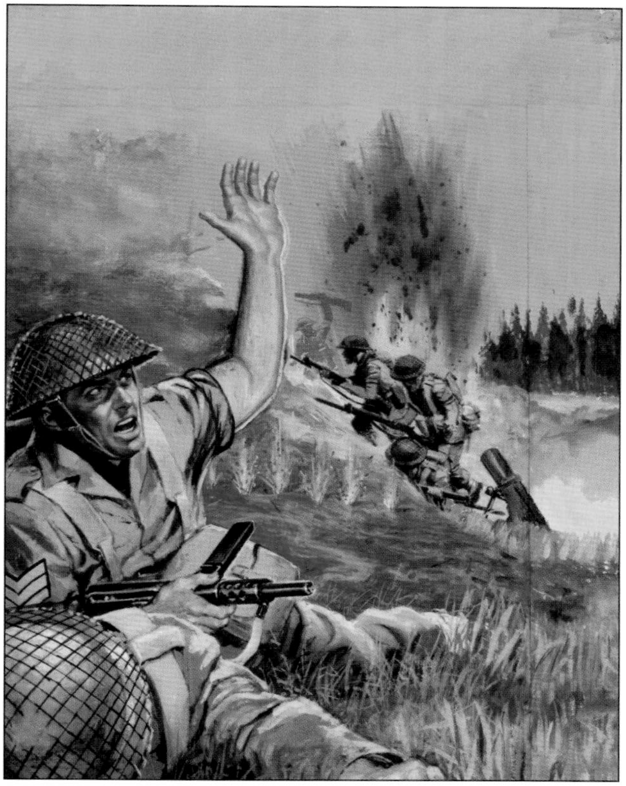

Nino Caroselli, Battle 694, February 1973

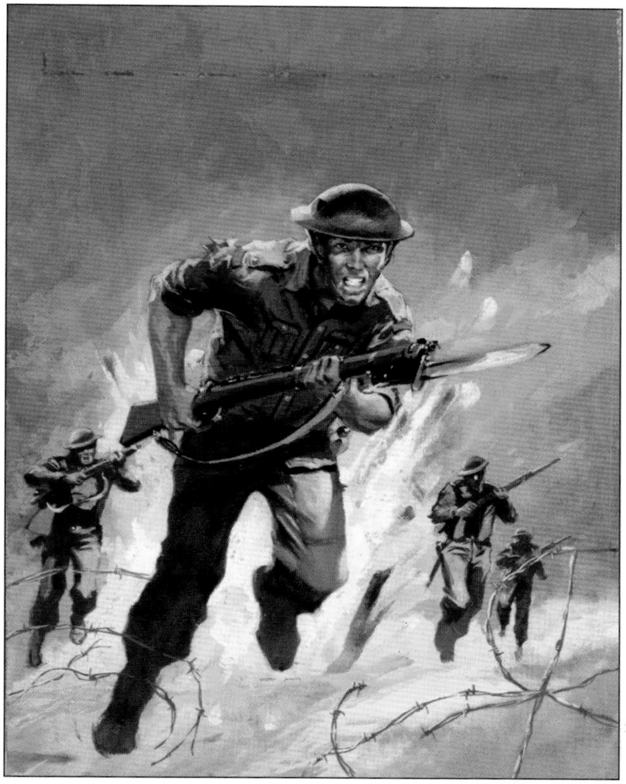

Nino Caroselli, War 34, January 1960

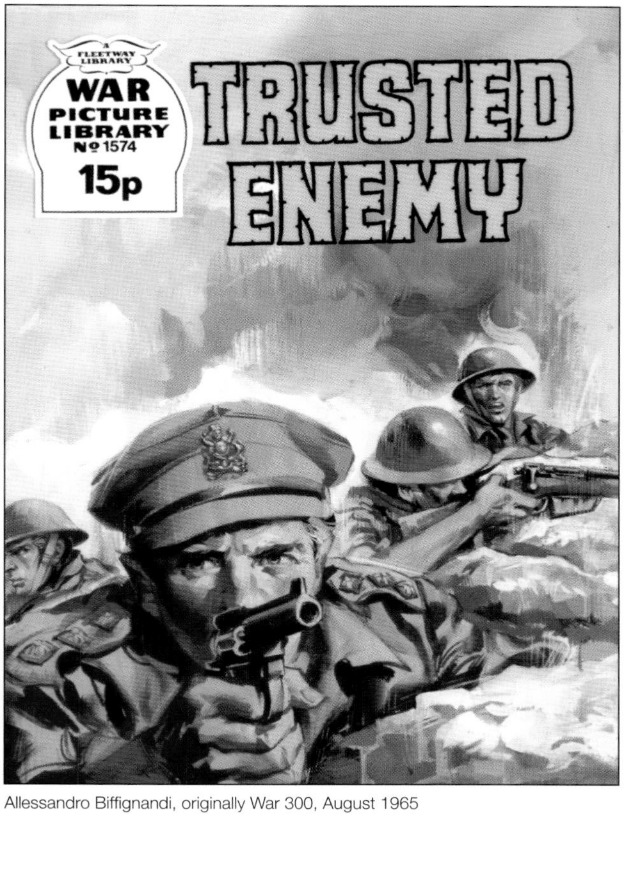
A FLEETWAY LIBRARY
WAR PICTURE LIBRARY
Nº 1574
15p
TRUSTED ENEMY

Allessandro Biffignandi, originally War 300, August 1965

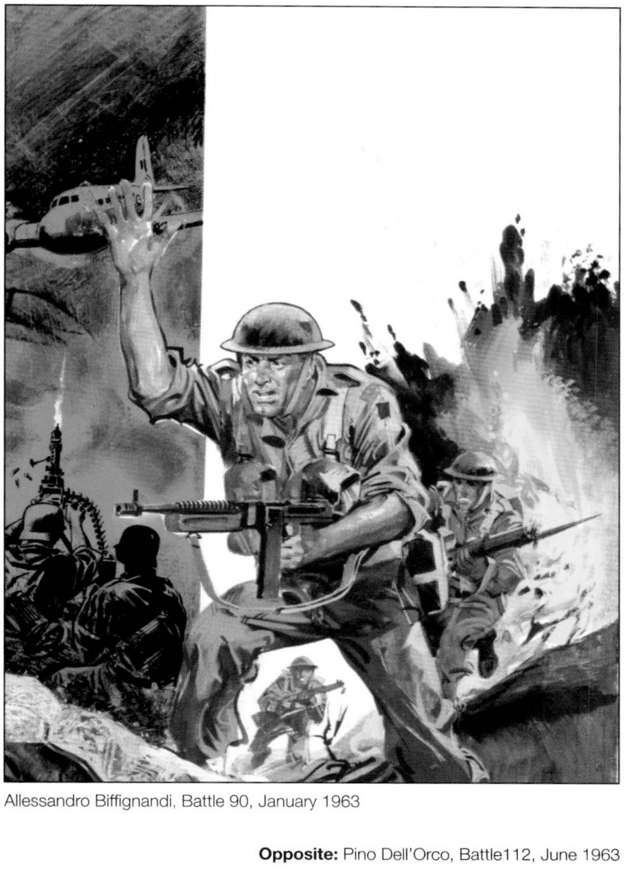

Allessandro Biffignandi, Battle 90, January 1963

Opposite: Pino Dell'Orco, Battle112, June 1963

AXIS POWERS

CHAPTER 2

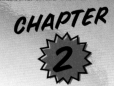

If the depiction of our own brave soldiers in war comics has almost always been straightforwardly heroic, then that of the various Axis forces is rather more complicated. In talking to one of the country's leading comic collectors, Richard Parry, it seems attitudes of children at the time were rather mixed when it came to "the enemy". Richard can remember his fellow kids having a sneaking admiration for the ruthless efficiency of the German soldiers and this may have been reflected in some of the *Picture Library* covers. When looking through the comics today, it is quite startling to see how many focus solely on German soldiers, from Graham Coton's cover for War 1386 (page 138) with it's onrushing battalion and Oliver Frey's sneering SS officer (*War* 585 on page 131), to Allessandro Biffignandi's U-Boat gunners for *Air Ace* 98 (page171). Giorgio De Gaspari's magnificent portrait of a U-boat commander from *War* 475 (on page 146) perhaps best illustrates this dichotomy for while there is a hint of cruelty in the commander's face, it is nonetheless a picture of a worthy foe. There is an aknowledgement that a few steps down from the inner circles of the Nazi party many German conscripts were simply doing their best to get through the war, much like our own boys were .

By contrast, the depiction of the Japanese was far less sympathetic. Parry remembers that, while swapping "War Books" (as children called the *Picture Library* comics back then) his friends would often have a sneaking admiration for the Germans but an utter hatred of the Japanese. It seems that memories of the Japanese treatment of the British in South East Asia were still vividly powerful in the fifties and sixties, and there are, perhaps, echoes of this in the war comics' covers .Graham Coton's cover to *War* 589 (on page 166) perfectly illustrates this, with his sword-wielding Japanese looking viciously savage as does another of his soldiers on the cover of issue 1782 (page 167). A third Coton cover (for *War* 769 on page 160), showing a startled, and startlingly young-looking, group of Japanese soldiers being showered by grenades, might be seen as some sort of wish fulfilment, however uncomfortable it might make us feel while seeing it today .

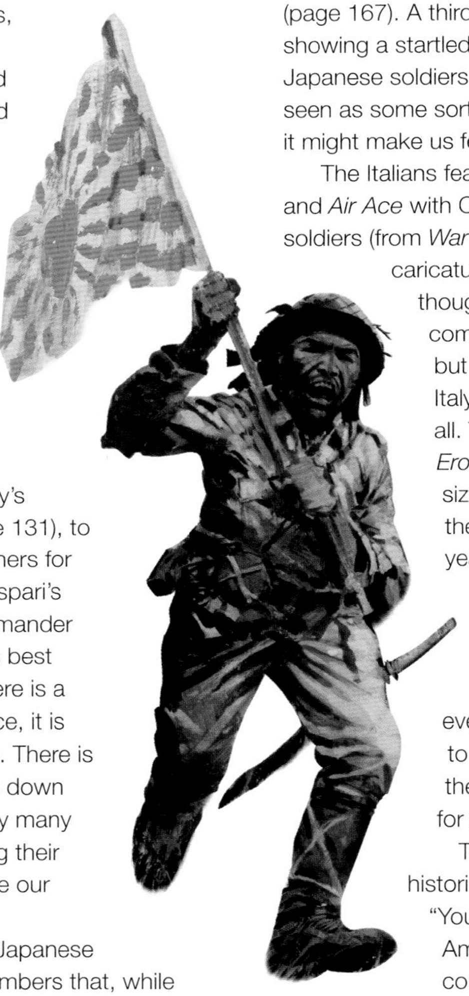

The Italians featured far less frequently in *War*, *Battle* and *Air Ace* with Coton's bedraggled bunch of surrendering soldiers (from *War* 2034 on page 140) summing up their caricature as the Axis' weakest link. Interestingly though, not only were a great number of these comics drawn and painted by Italian creators, but they were also extensively published in Italy itself – an astonishing 2219 issues in all. The first Italian printing; Dardo's *Collana Eroica*, started out as a 24-page magazine-sized comic in October 1962, but adopted the 68-page pocket format early the next year, lasting until 1971. A sister title, *Super Eroica*, lasted from 1965 until 1995 and other comics such as *Bazooka*, *RAF*, *Forza Joe* and *Pattuglia X* also collected the cream of IPC's war strips. The Italians even had a comic called *Hurricane* devoted to British aviation strips. All of this is made all the more surprising when one considers that for much of the war we were bitter enemies!

To explain this, the Italian academic and historian Alberto Beccatini has argued that, "You have to consider that Italy was very American-oriented during the 1960s, so it comes as no surprise that Italian readers appreciated those stories. Most Italians had all but forgotten that the Allies had been their enemies during the Second World War. Also, those who were reading these pocket comics were born in the late 1940s to the mid-1950s, so they had no direct experience or memory of the war, and were certainly more influenced by such American war films as *The Young Lions* or *The Longest Day*.

Another important thing to keep in mind about pocket-sized comics was that in Italy they were popular, up until the 1980s, among soldiers in barracks. Youngsters doing their compulsory year in the army would read them in their bunks (not to mention toilets). Although today these comics are looked after on the market – especially on account of the artists – at that time they were just considered easy reading and the average cultural level of those who read them was rather low. I'm sure that nobody in the sixties was aware that a good deal of them were drawn by Italian artists. In fact, when collectors knew that Pratt, Calegari, D'Antonio and others had been drawing them, that's when they began looking for those pocket comics – which were also reprinted through the 1980s and 1990s."

To understand the potentially uncomfortable position of the Italian D'Ami studio artists, Beccattini suggests that many had effectively to re-invent themselves after the war. "You see, there were 48 million fascists in this country in 1940, but just a few were left when Italy was freed by the Allies, who were, of course, welcomed as saviours." A particularly interesting example was Kurt Caesar who drew many of the best strips in the earliest *Air Aces* as well as several "Dogfight Dixon" episodes in *Thriller*. Born in France to German parents, Kurt Kaiser grew up in Germany before moving to Italy in the 1930s where he changed his surname to Caesar. In Italy, he drew several fascist-themed strips including the popular *Romano Il Legionario* about an Italian pilot in the Spanish civil war. Beccatini suggests that he might have "worked on those fascist stories mainly because it was a chance to draw a lot of aircraft, which he was good at. In fact, after the war and into the sixties he would continue drawing aircraft, warfare and spaceships." Whatever the exact nature of his political affiliations, it is known that during the war he followed Rommell on his African campaign where he drew numerous superb sketches on location in the desert. However, in 1944 he joined the resistance against the Nazis and was officially recognised for his activities. With such a varied and colourful wartime experience behind him, it is no surprise his strips had such a feeling of realism to them.

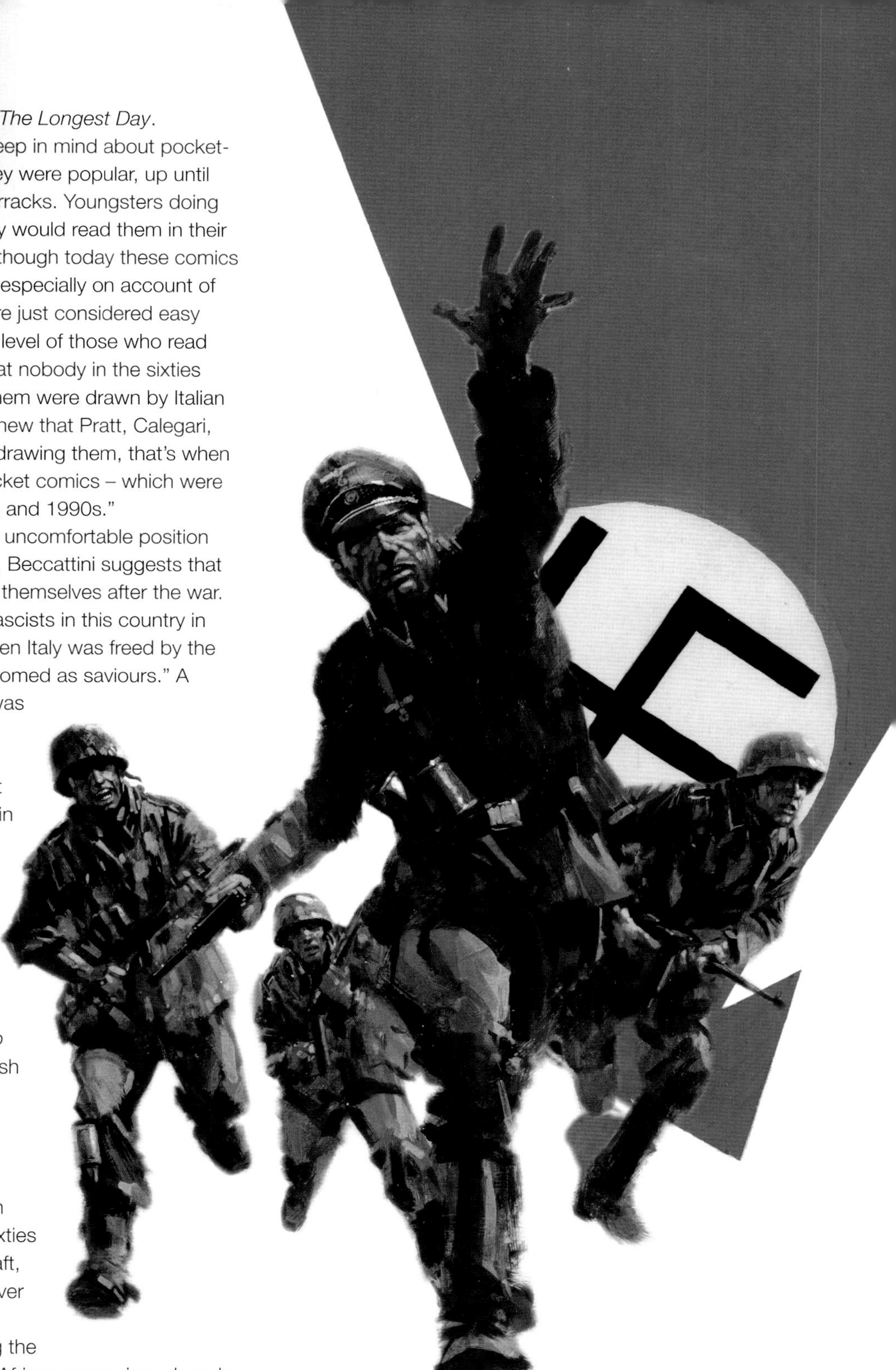

Whatever Caesars' feelings about drawing so many strips about brave British and American servicemen, he and his fellow Italian artists made an unforgettable contribution to war comics in this country.

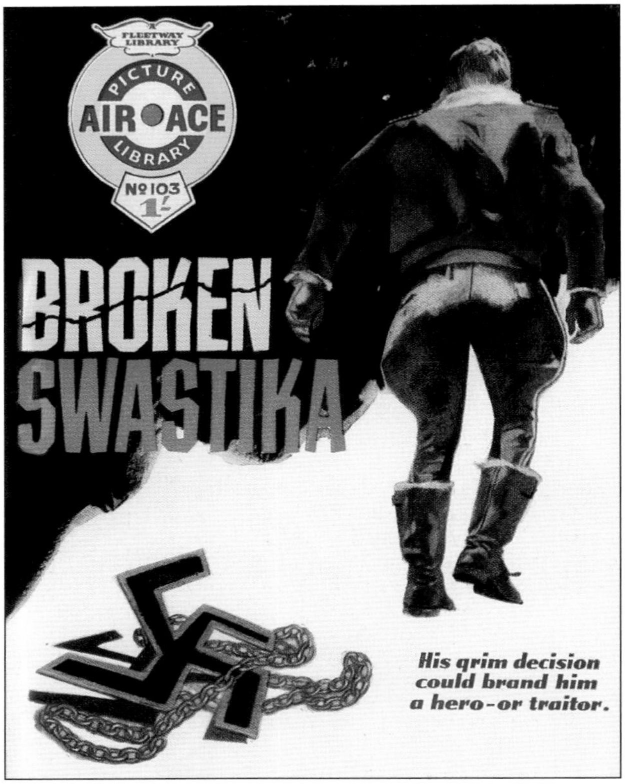
A FLEETWAY LIBRARY
PICTURE
AIR ACE
LIBRARY
No 103
1/-
BROKEN SWASTIKA
His grim decision could brand him a hero-or traitor.

Giorgio DeGaspari, Air Ace103, June 1962

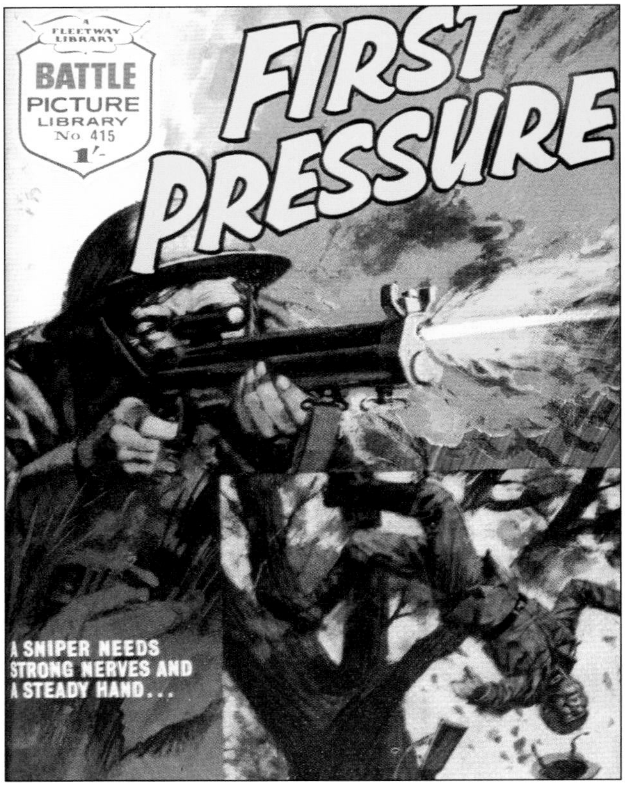
A FLEETWAY LIBRARY
BATTLE
PICTURE
LIBRARY
No. 415
1/-
FIRST PRESSURE
A SNIPER NEEDS STRONG NERVES AND A STEADY HAND...

Andrew Howat, Battle 415, September 1969

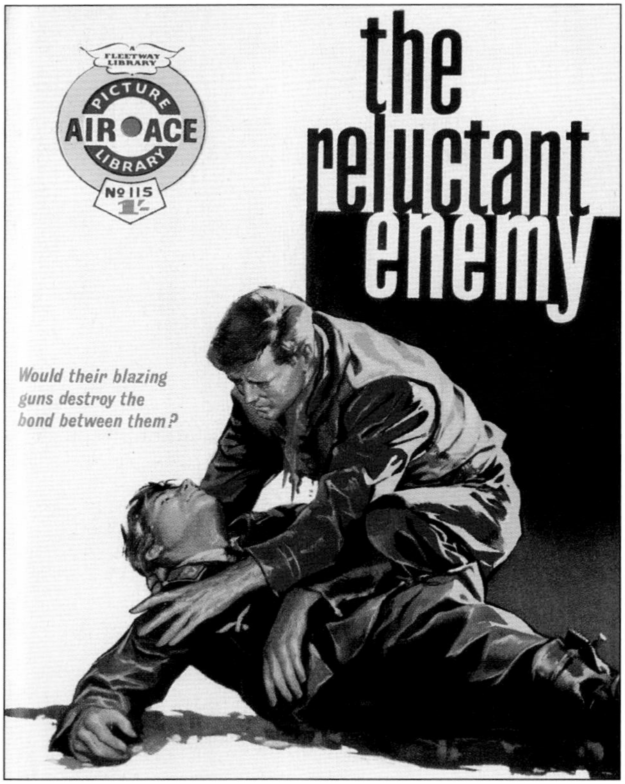
A FLEETWAY LIBRARY
PICTURE
AIR ACE
LIBRARY
No 115
1/-
the reluctant enemy
Would their blazing guns destroy the bond between them?

Allessandro Biffignandi, Air Ace 115, September 1962

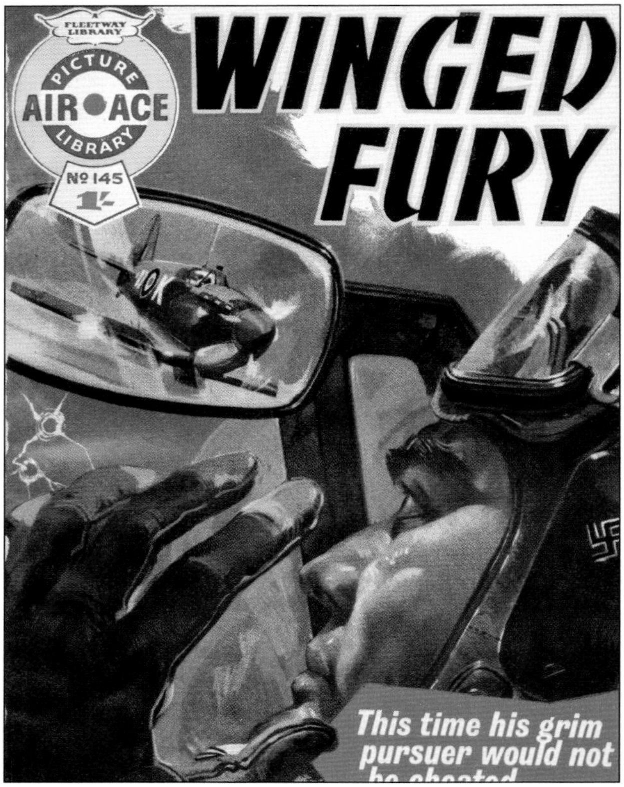
A FLEETWAY LIBRARY
PICTURE
AIR ACE
LIBRARY
No 145
1/-
WINGED FURY
This time his grim pursuer would not

Allessandro Biffignandi, Air Ace 145, April 1963

Opposite: 105 Giorgio DeGaspari, Air Ace 14, July 1960

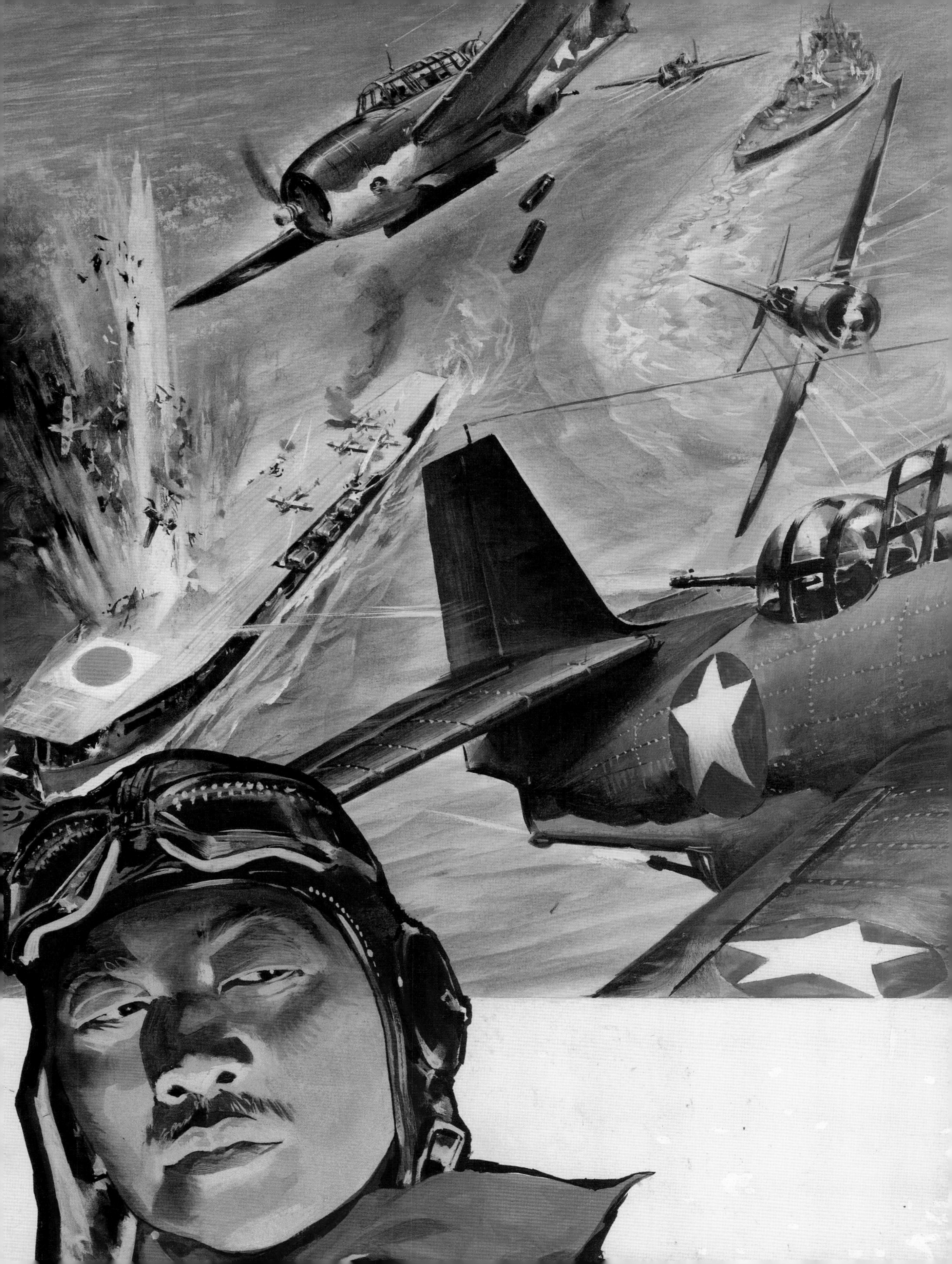

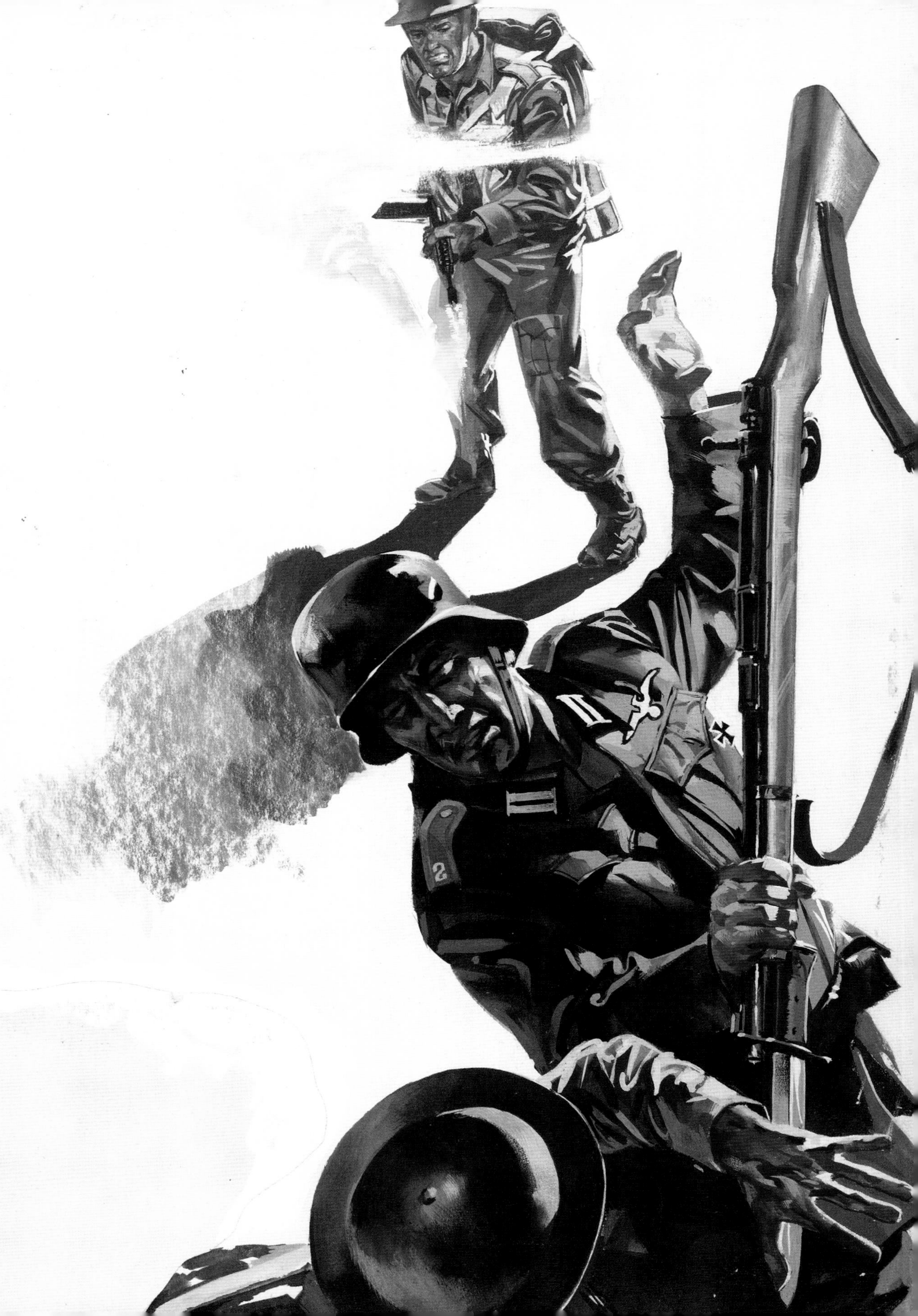

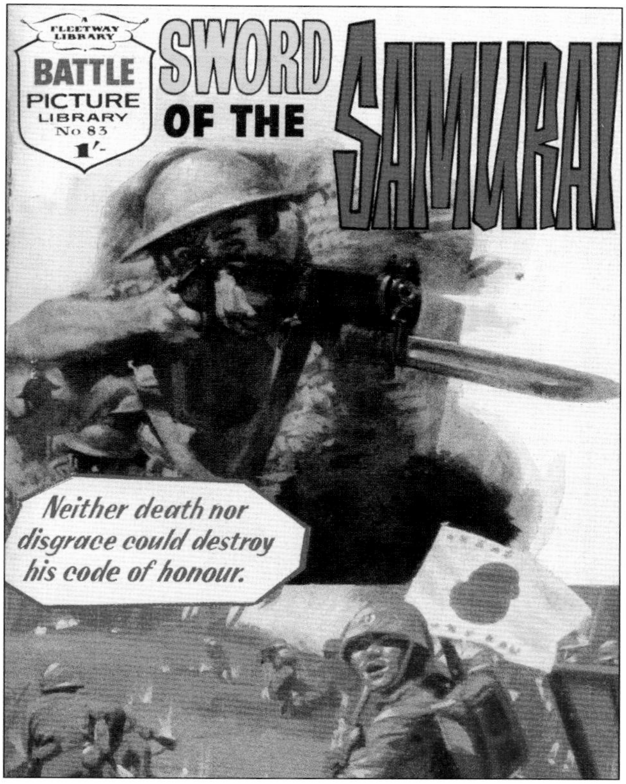
A FLEETWAY LIBRARY
BATTLE PICTURE LIBRARY No 83
1/-
SWORD OF THE SAMURAI
Neither death nor disgrace could destroy his code of honour.

Pino Dell'Orco, Battle 83, November 1962

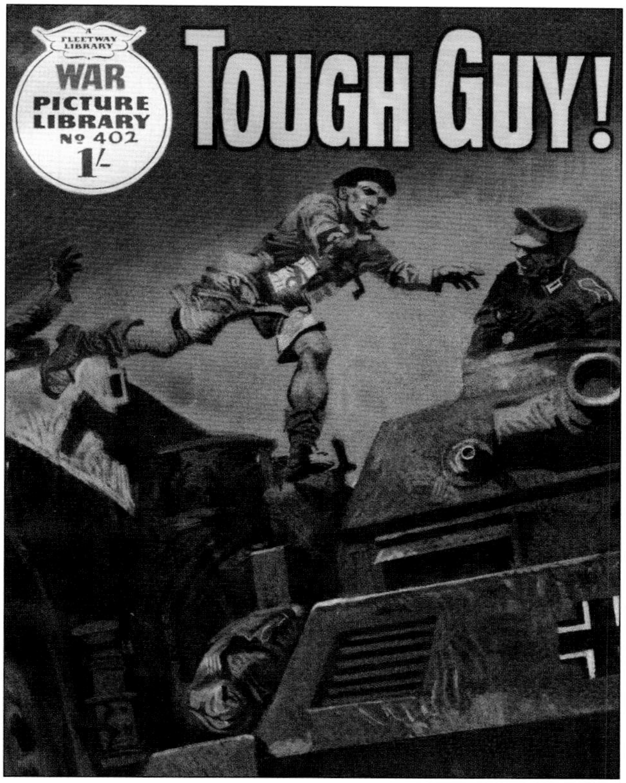
A FLEETWAY LIBRARY
WAR PICTURE LIBRARY Nº 402
1/-
TOUGH GUY!

Allessandro Biffignandi, War 402, September 1967

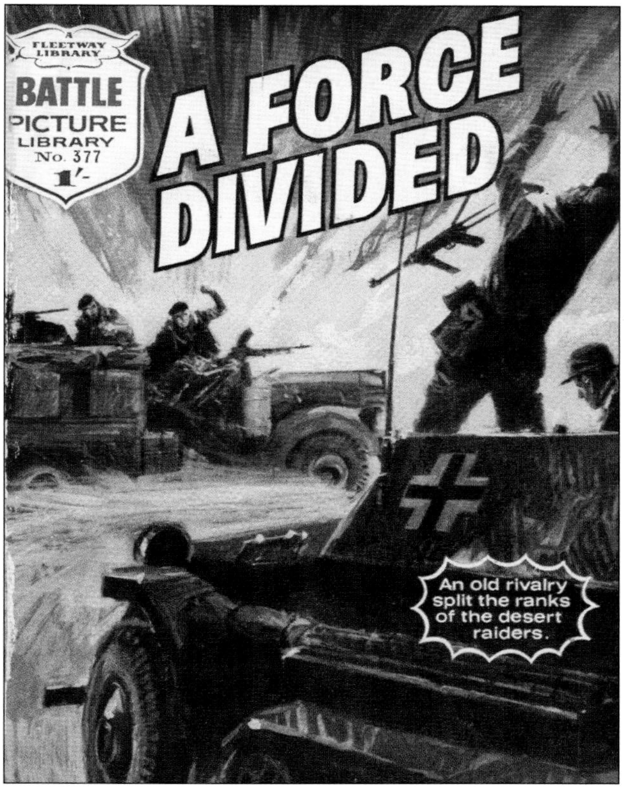
A FLEETWAY LIBRARY
BATTLE PICTURE LIBRARY No. 377
1/-
A FORCE DIVIDED
An old rivalry split the ranks of the desert raiders.

Jose Luis Macias, Battle 377, January 1969

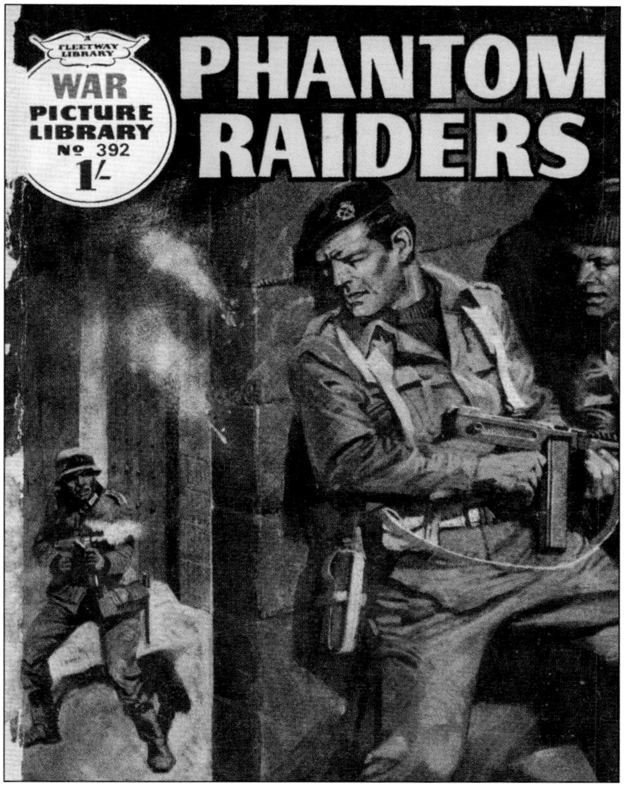
A FLEETWAY LIBRARY
WAR PICTURE LIBRARY Nº 392
1/-
PHANTOM RAIDERS

Allessandro Biffignandi, War 392, July 1967

Opposite: 106 Allessandro Biffignandi, Battle 23, August 1961
Overleaf: Graham Coton, War 1243, August 1976

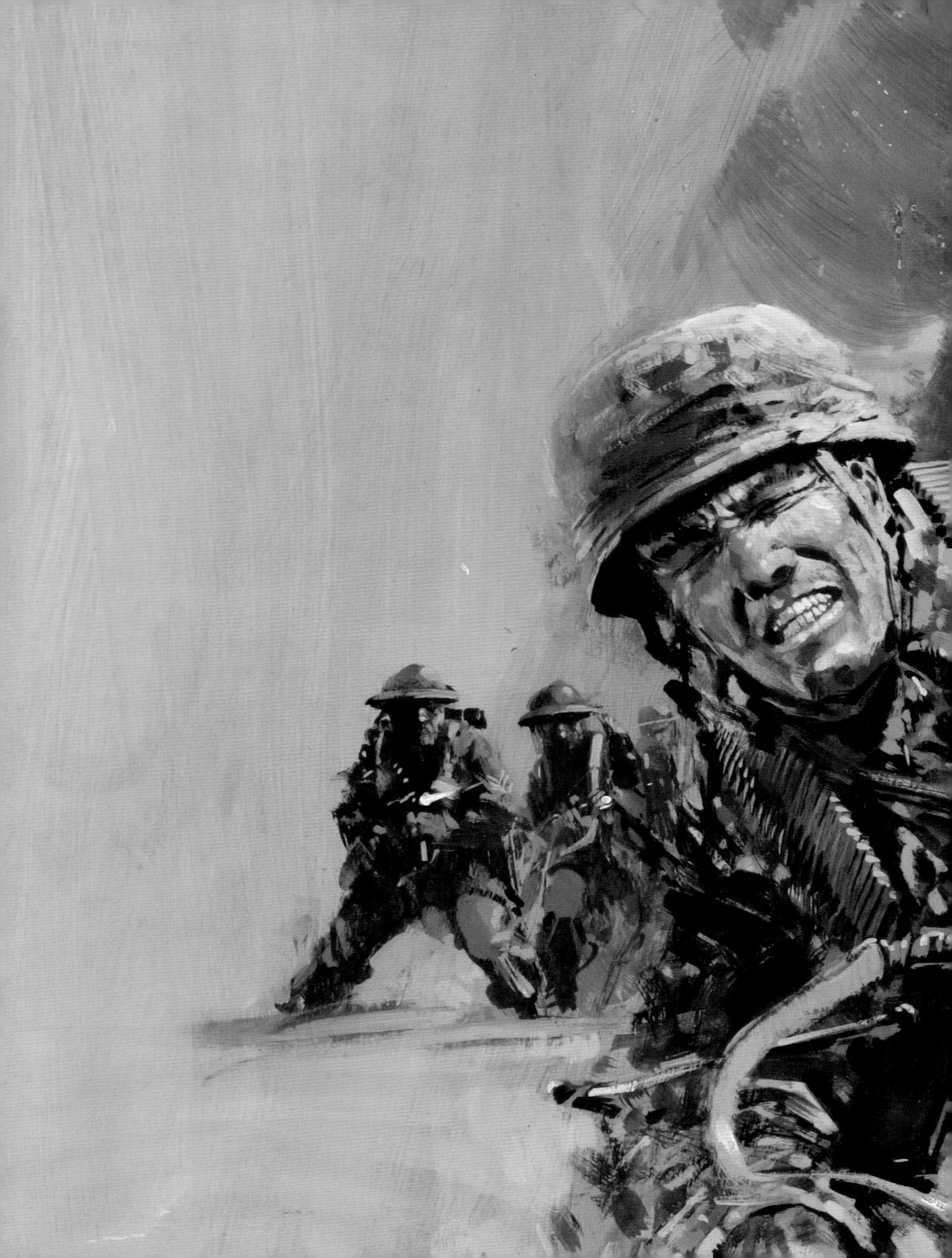

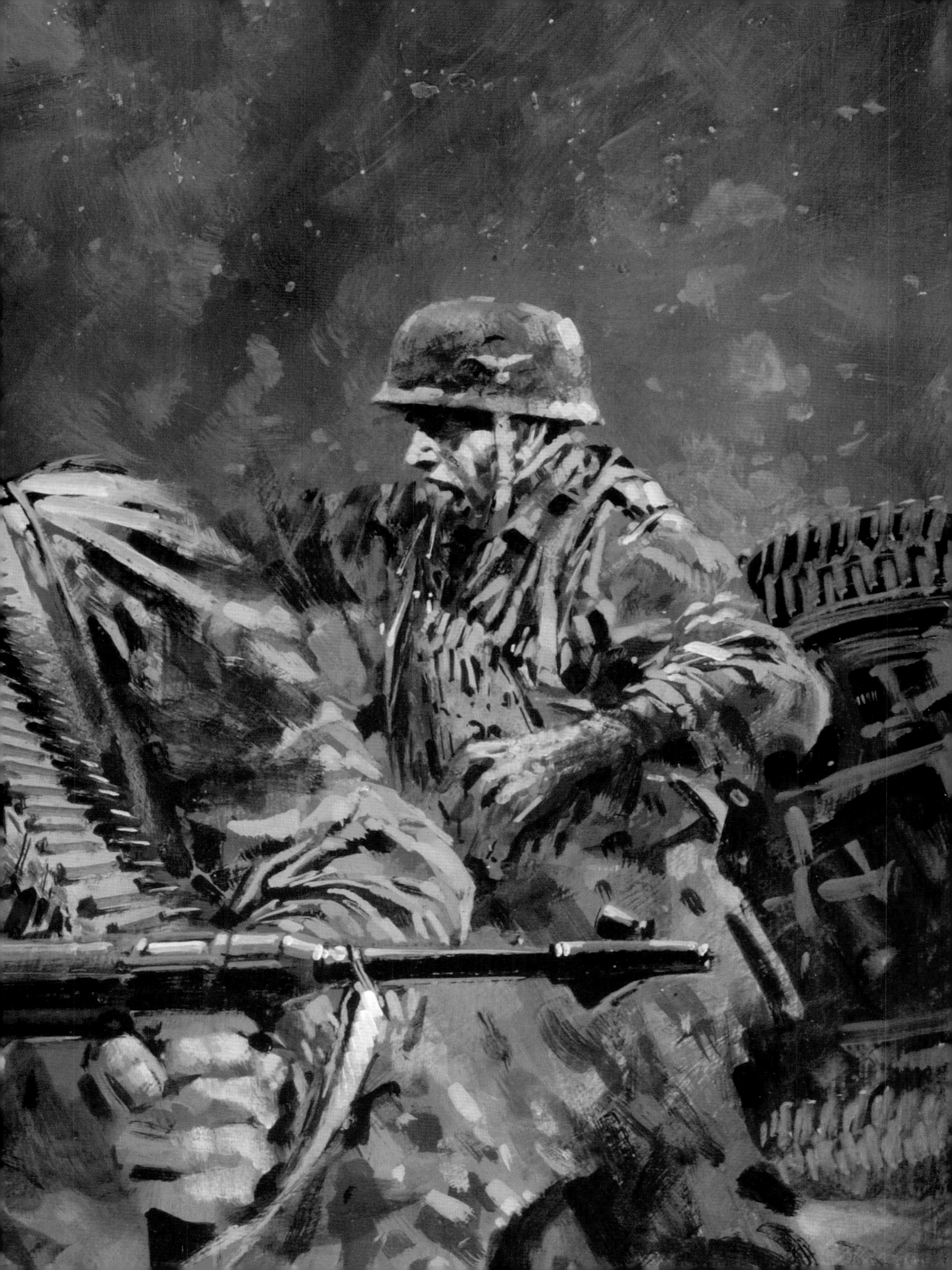

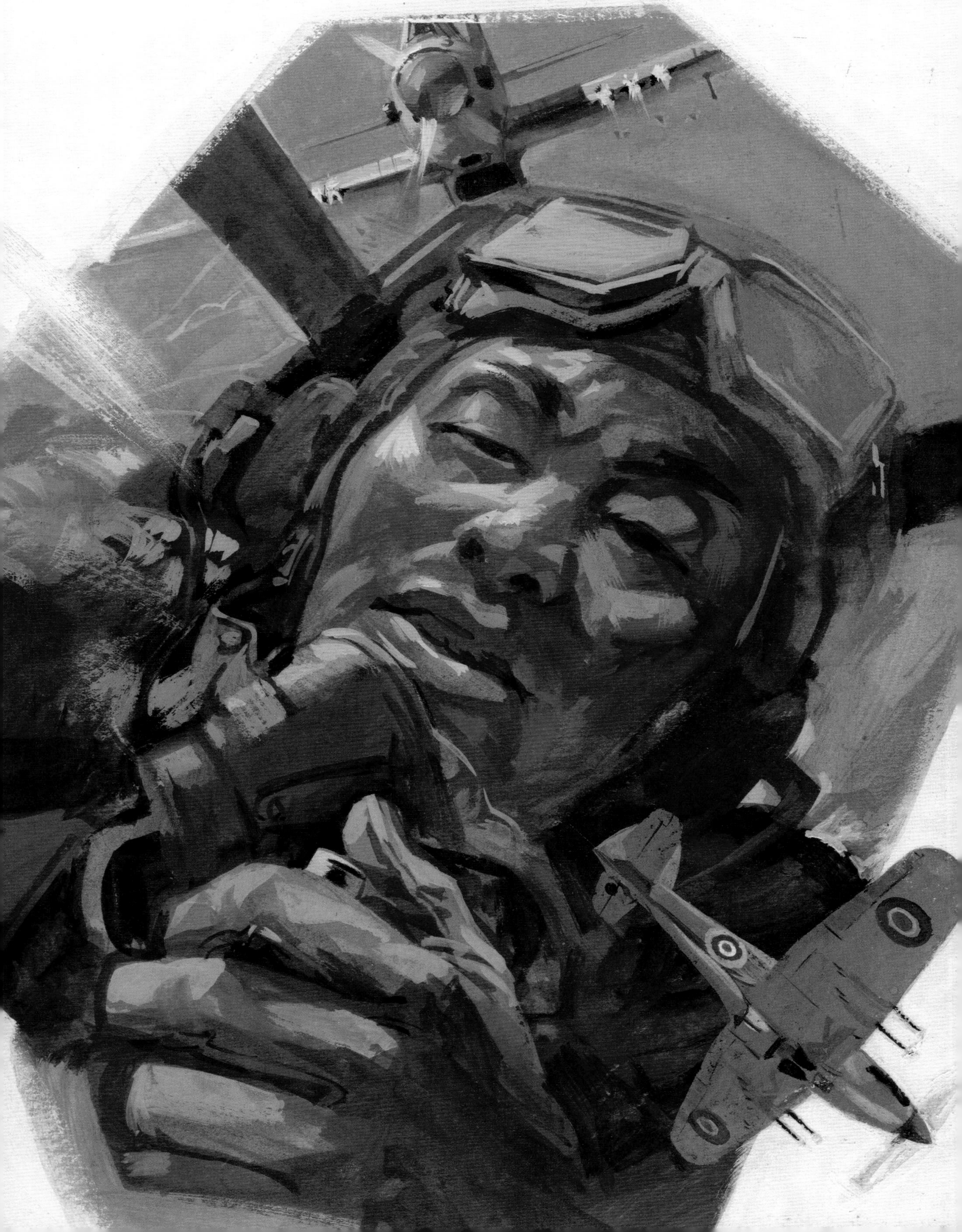

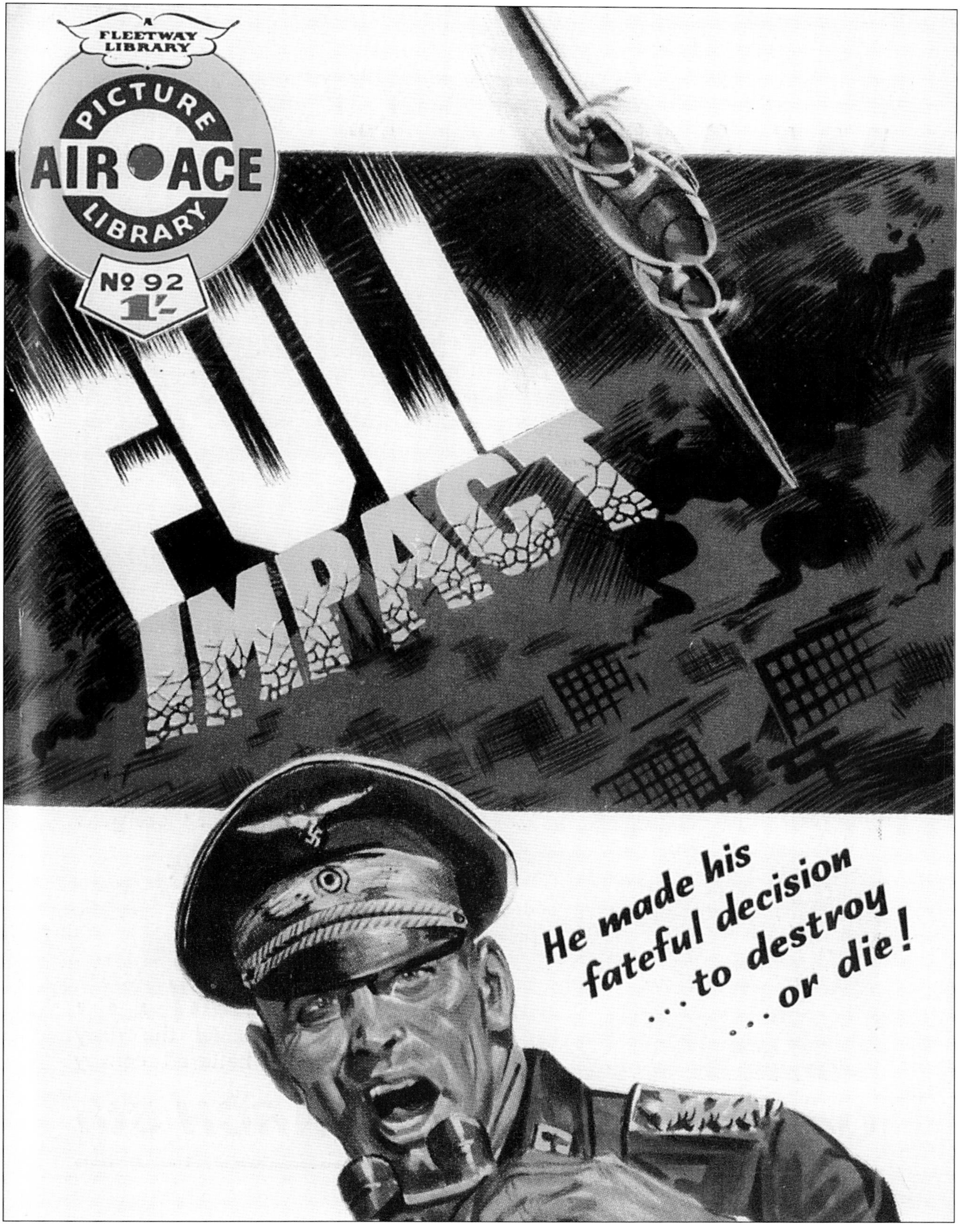
A FLEETWAY LIBRARY
PICTURE
AIR ACE
LIBRARY
Nº 92
1/-
FULL IMPACT
He made his
fateful decision
...to destroy
...or die!

Pino Dell'Orco, Air Ace 92, March 1962
Opposite: Pino Dell'Orco, Battle 75, September 1962

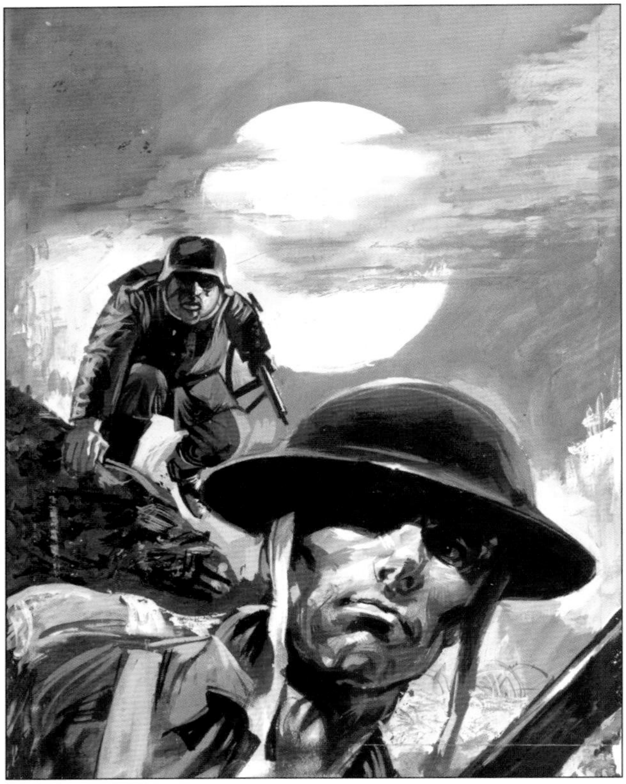

Pino Dell'Orco and Roy McAdorey, War 92, April 1961

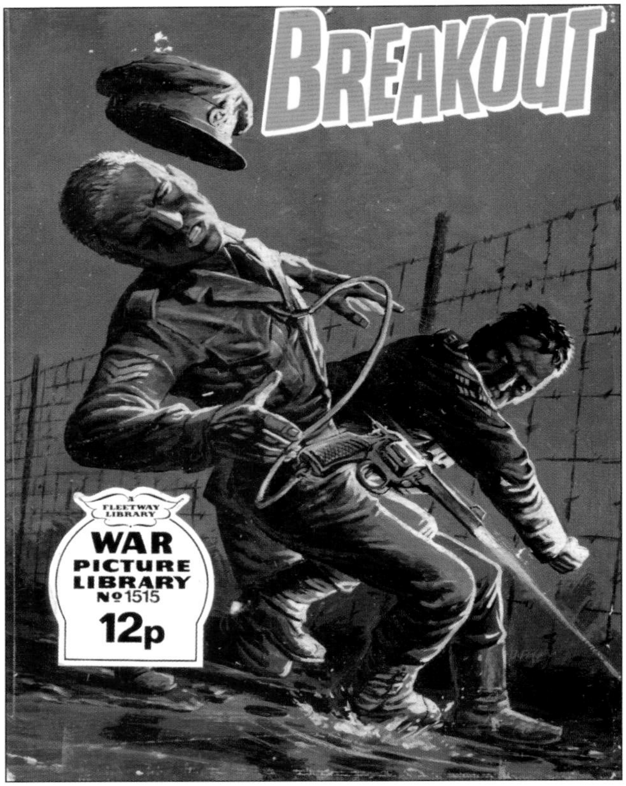
BREAKOUT
A FLEETWAY LIBRARY
WAR PICTURE LIBRARY
Nº 1515
12p

Oliver Frey, originally Battle 681, January 1973

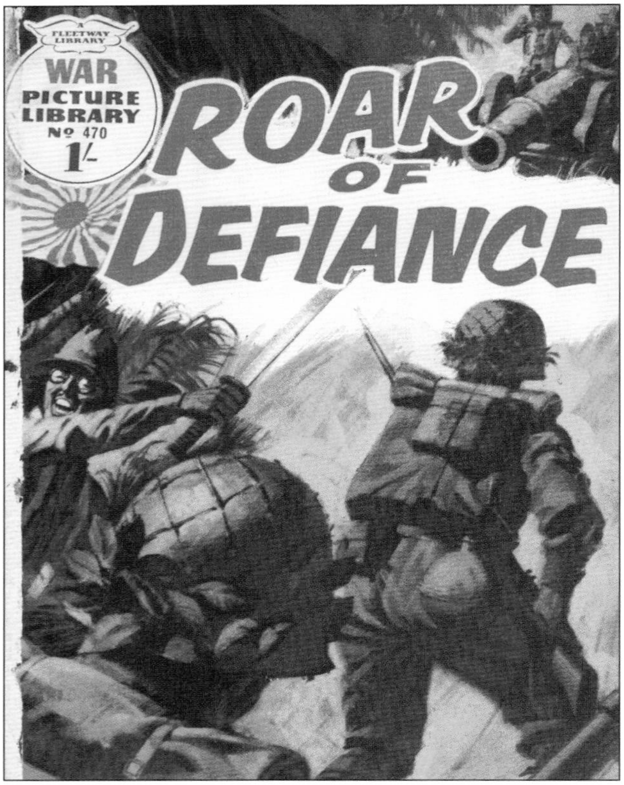
A FLEETWAY LIBRARY
WAR PICTURE LIBRARY
Nº 470
1/-
ROAR OF DEFIANCE

Andrew Howat, War 470, October 1968

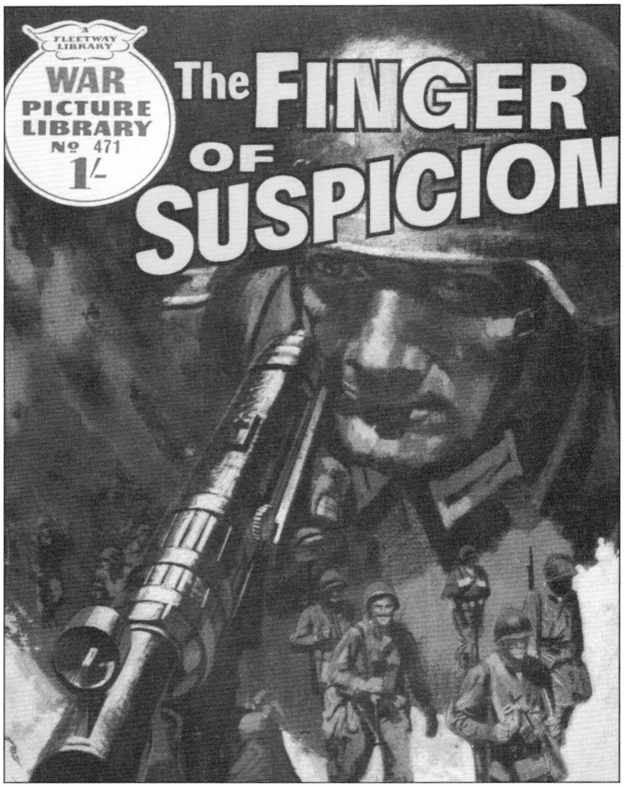
A FLEETWAY LIBRARY
WAR PICTURE LIBRARY
Nº 471
1/-
The FINGER OF SUSPICION

Jordi Penalva, War 471, October 1968

Opposite: Pino Dell'Orco, War 230, February 1964

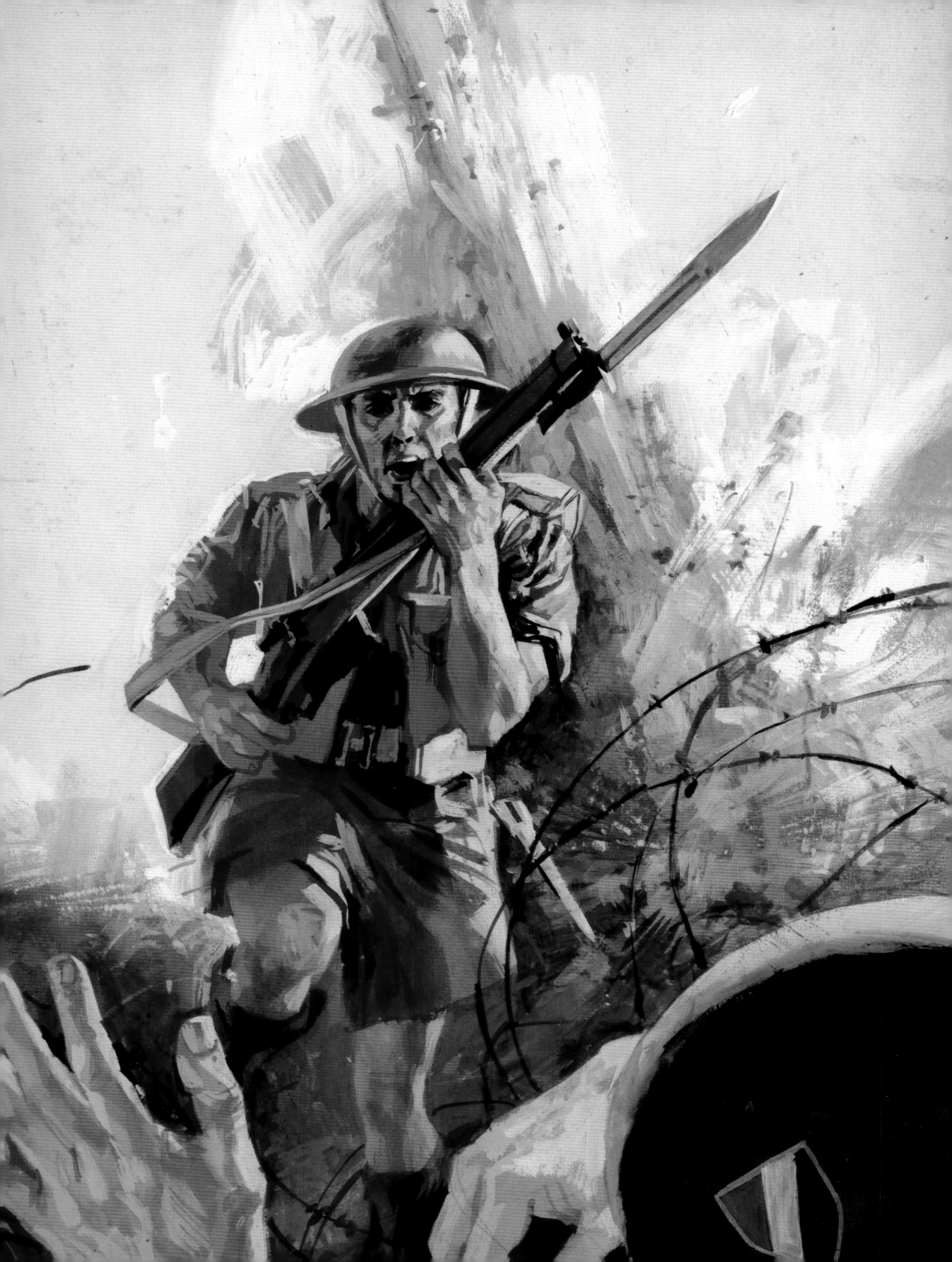

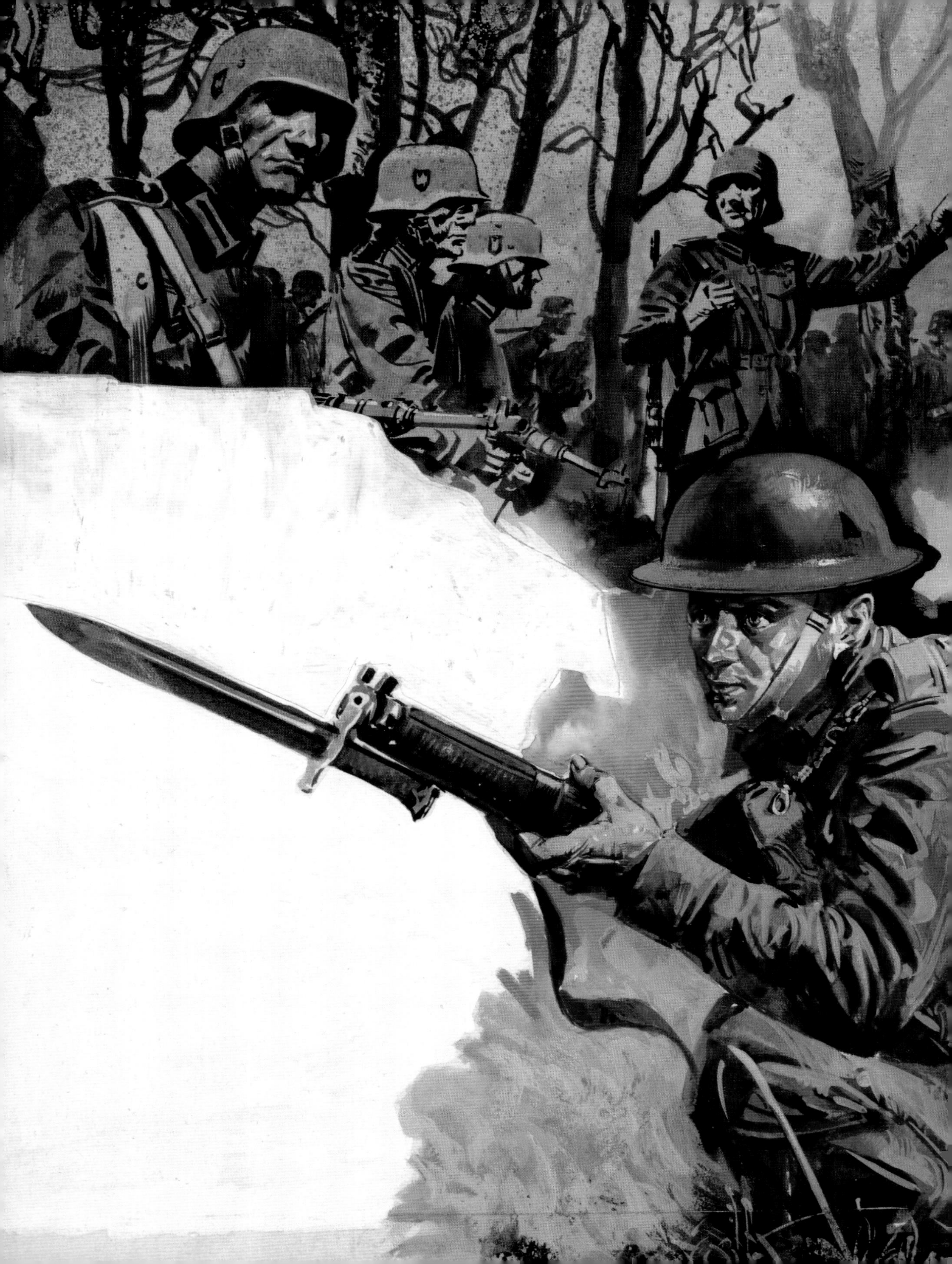

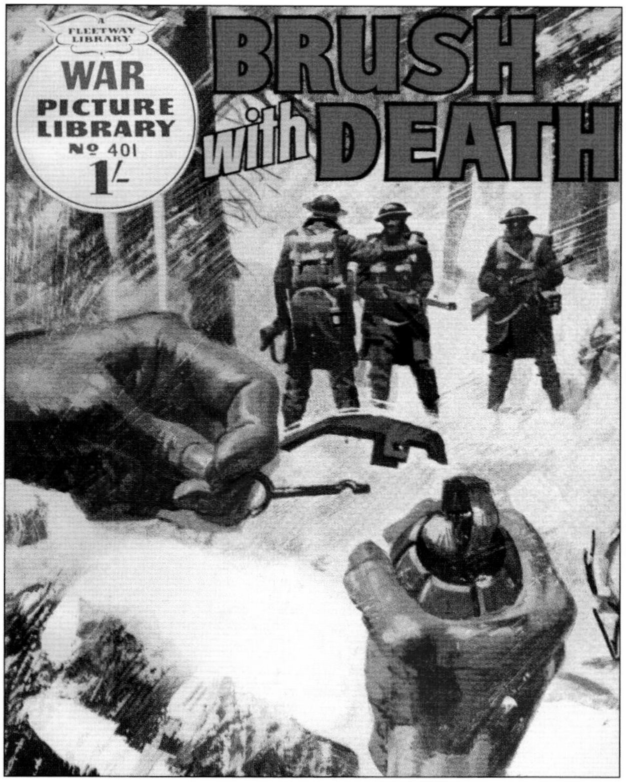
A FLEETWAY LIBRARY
WAR
PICTURE LIBRARY
Nº 401
1/-
BRUSH with DEATH

Jordi Penalva, War 401, September 1967

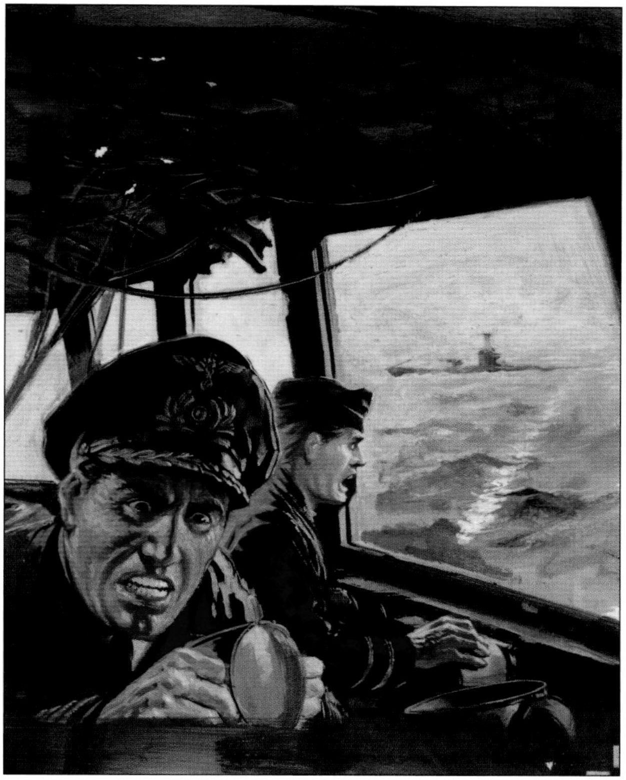

Graham Coton, Battle 413, August 1969

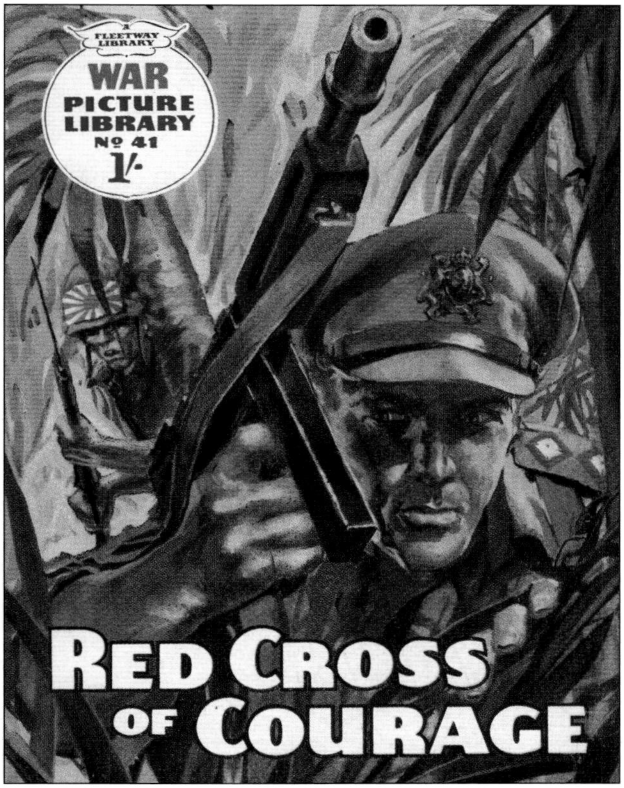
A FLEETWAY LIBRARY
WAR
PICTURE LIBRARY
Nº 41
1/-
RED CROSS OF COURAGE

Nino Caroselli, War 41, March 1960

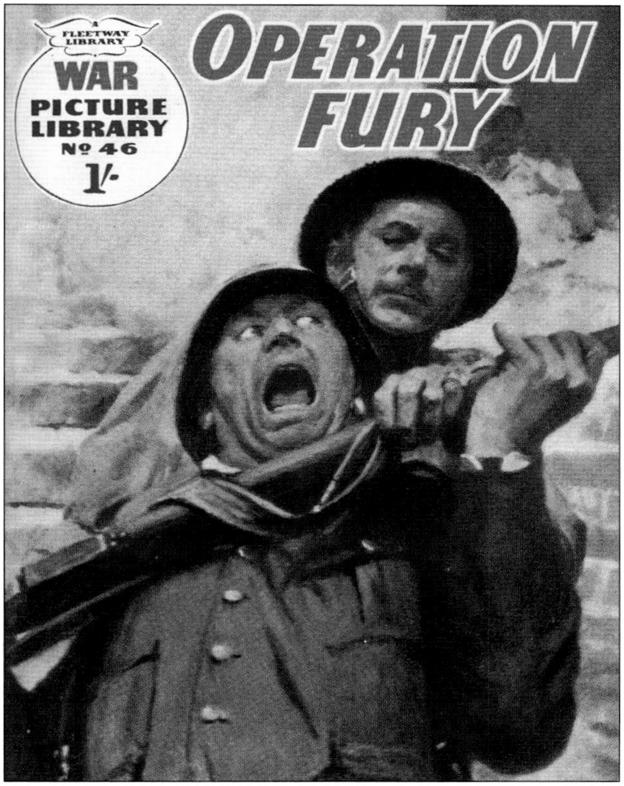
A FLEETWAY LIBRARY
WAR
PICTURE LIBRARY
Nº 46
1/-
OPERATION FURY

Septimus Scott, War 46, April 1960

Opposite: Allessandro Biffignandi, Battle 144, February 1964
Overleaf: Graham Coton, War 1303, January 1977

THE BI
ENI

TER

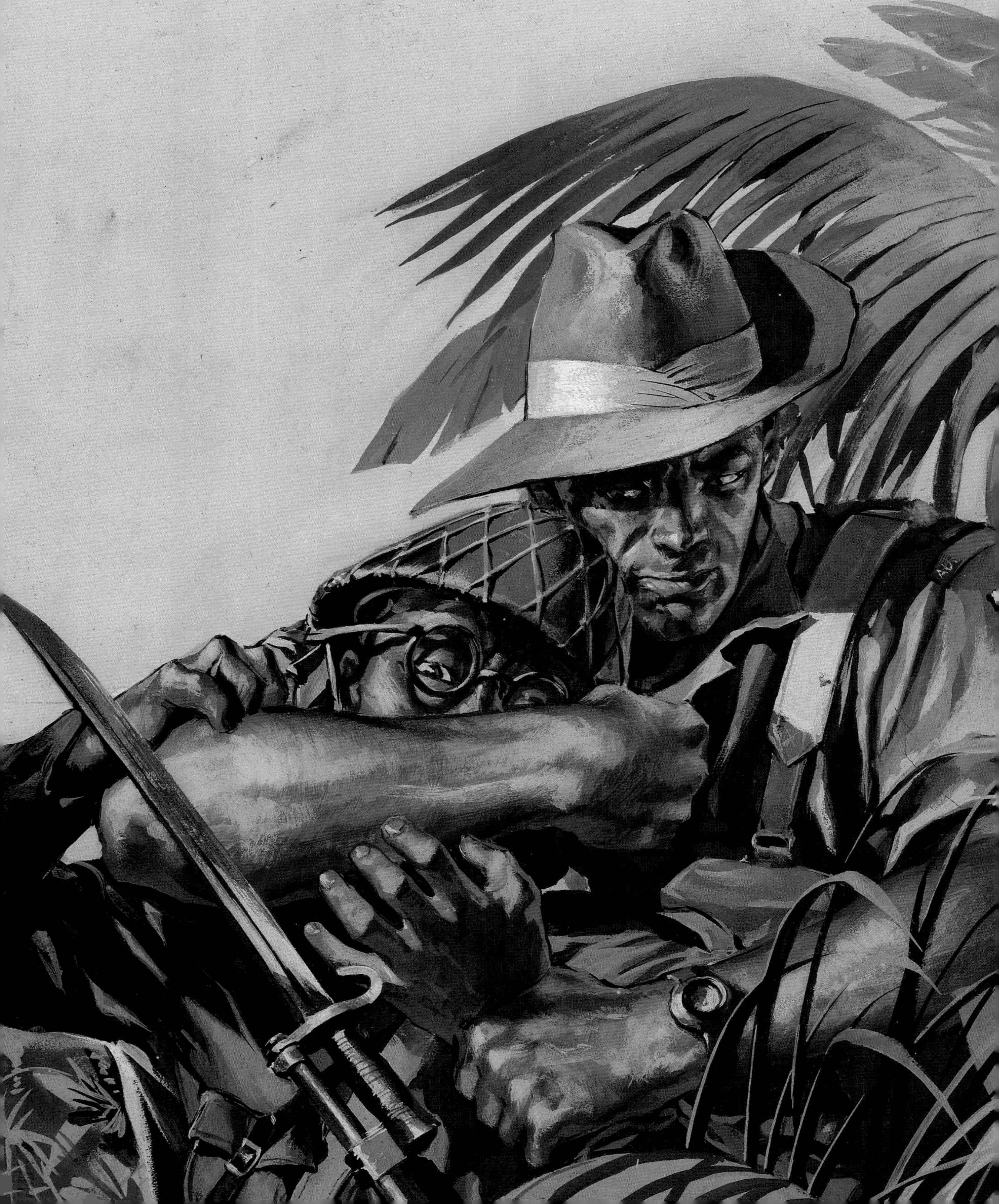

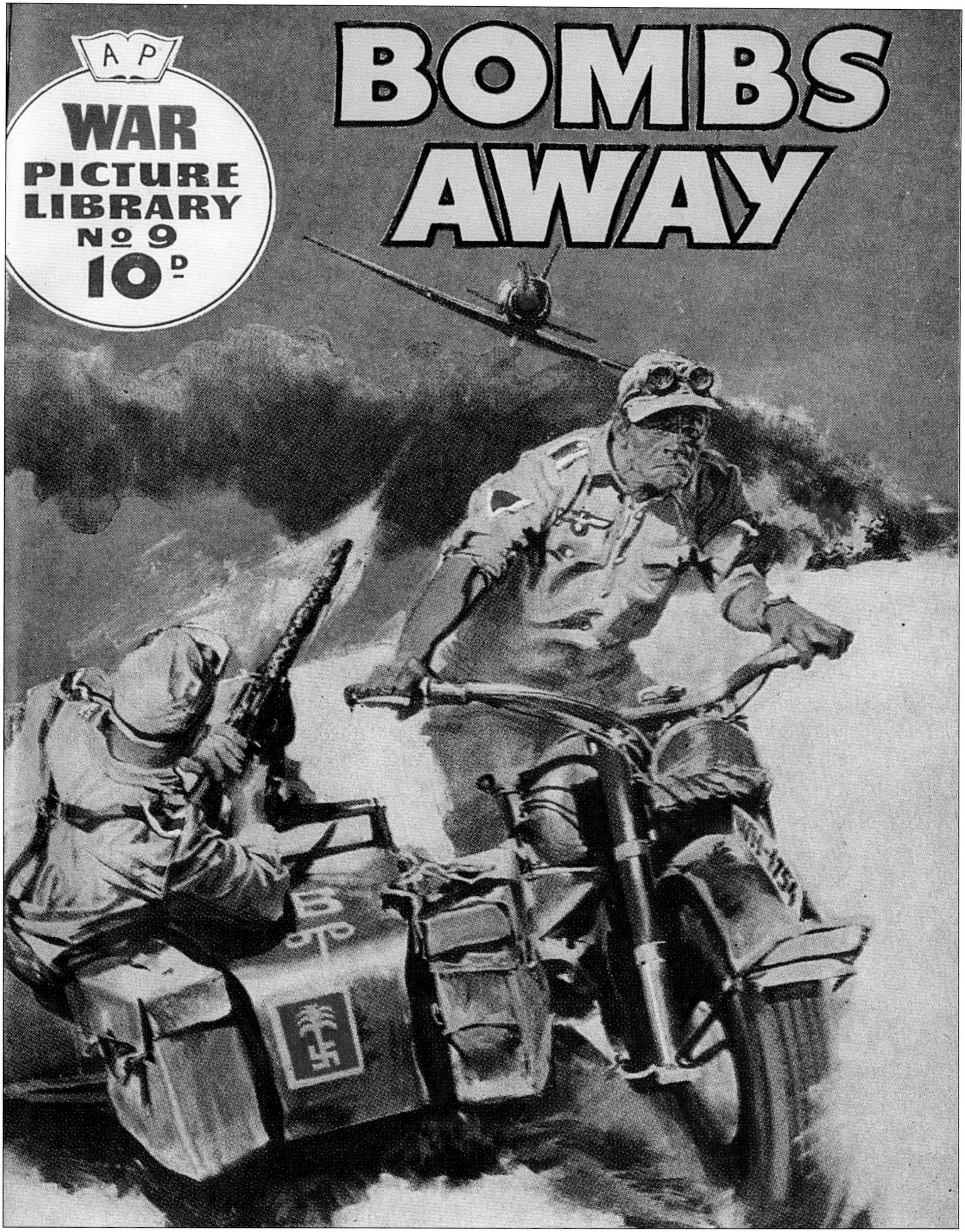
AP
WAR
PICTURE
LIBRARY
No 9
10D
BOMBS
AWAY

Giorgio DeGaspari, War 9, January 1959
Opposite: Nino Caroselli, War 101, June 1961

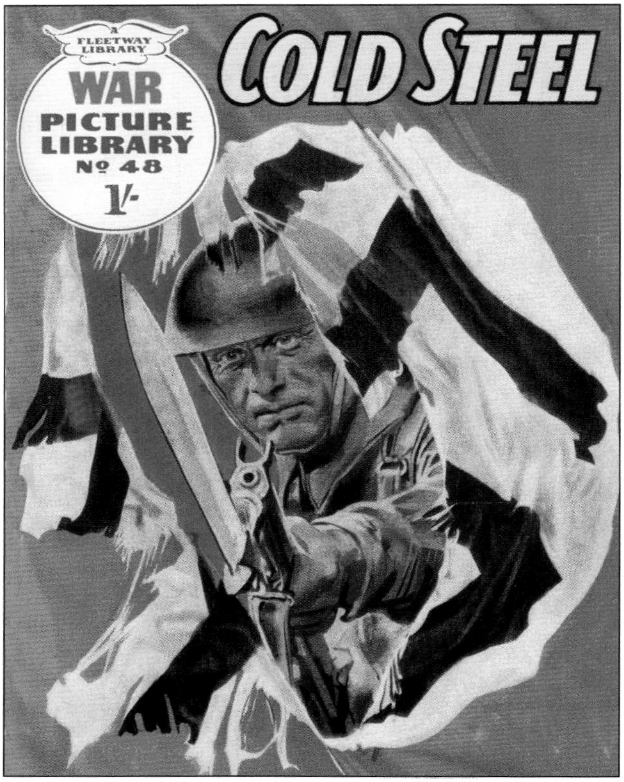
A FLEETWAY LIBRARY
WAR PICTURE LIBRARY
Nº 48
1/-
COLD STEEL

Giorgio DeGaspari, War 48, May 1960

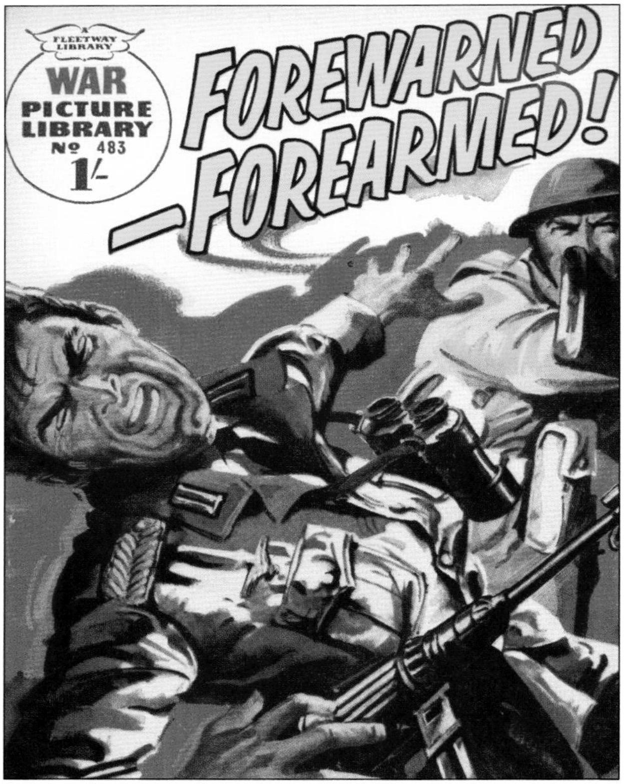
A FLEETWAY LIBRARY
WAR PICTURE LIBRARY
Nº 483
1/-
FOREWARNED —FOREARMED!

Allessandro Biffignandi, War483, December 1968

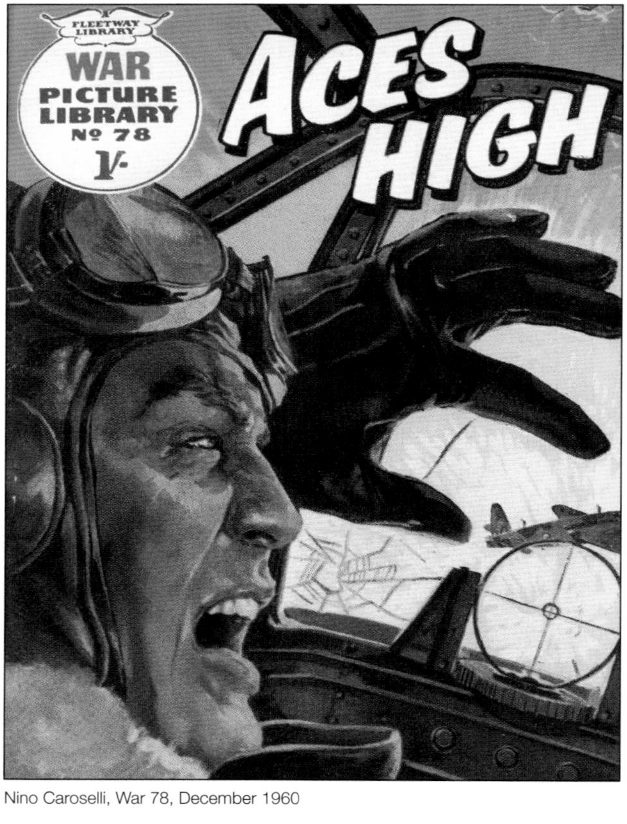
A FLEETWAY LIBRARY
WAR PICTURE LIBRARY
Nº 78
1/-
ACES HIGH

Nino Caroselli, War 78, December 1960

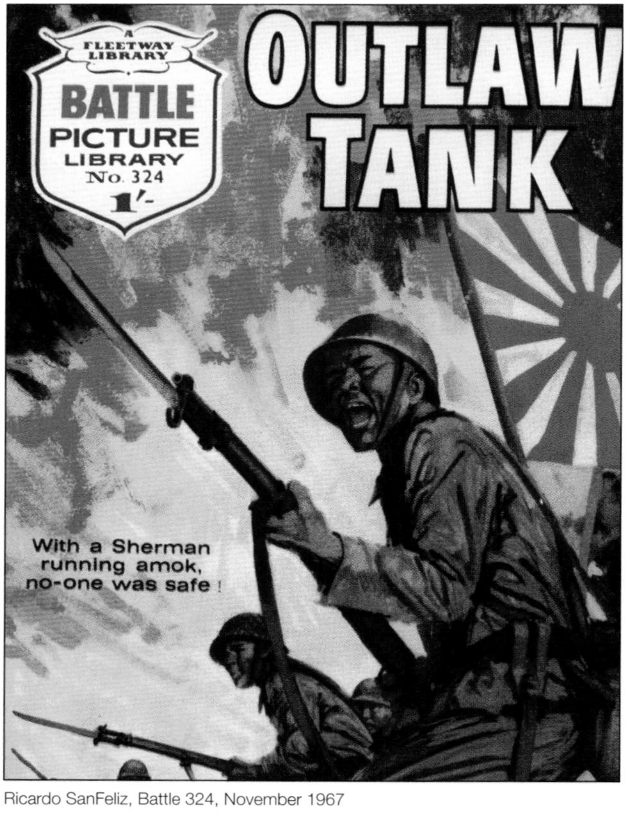
A FLEETWAY LIBRARY
BATTLE PICTURE LIBRARY
No. 324
1/-
OUTLAW TANK
With a Sherman running amok, no-one was safe !

Ricardo SanFeliz, Battle 324, November 1967

Opposite: Pino Dell'Orco, War 164, October 1962

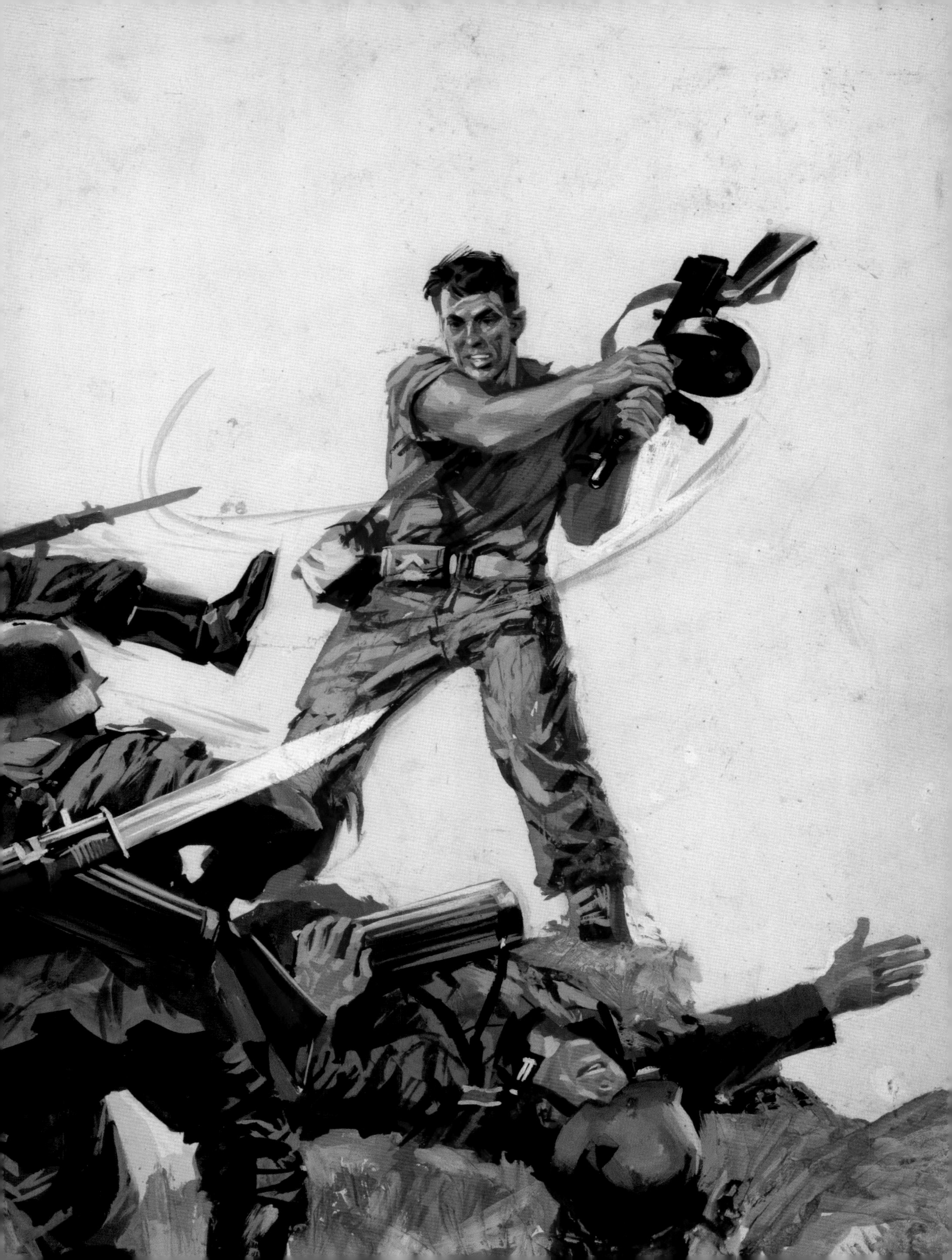

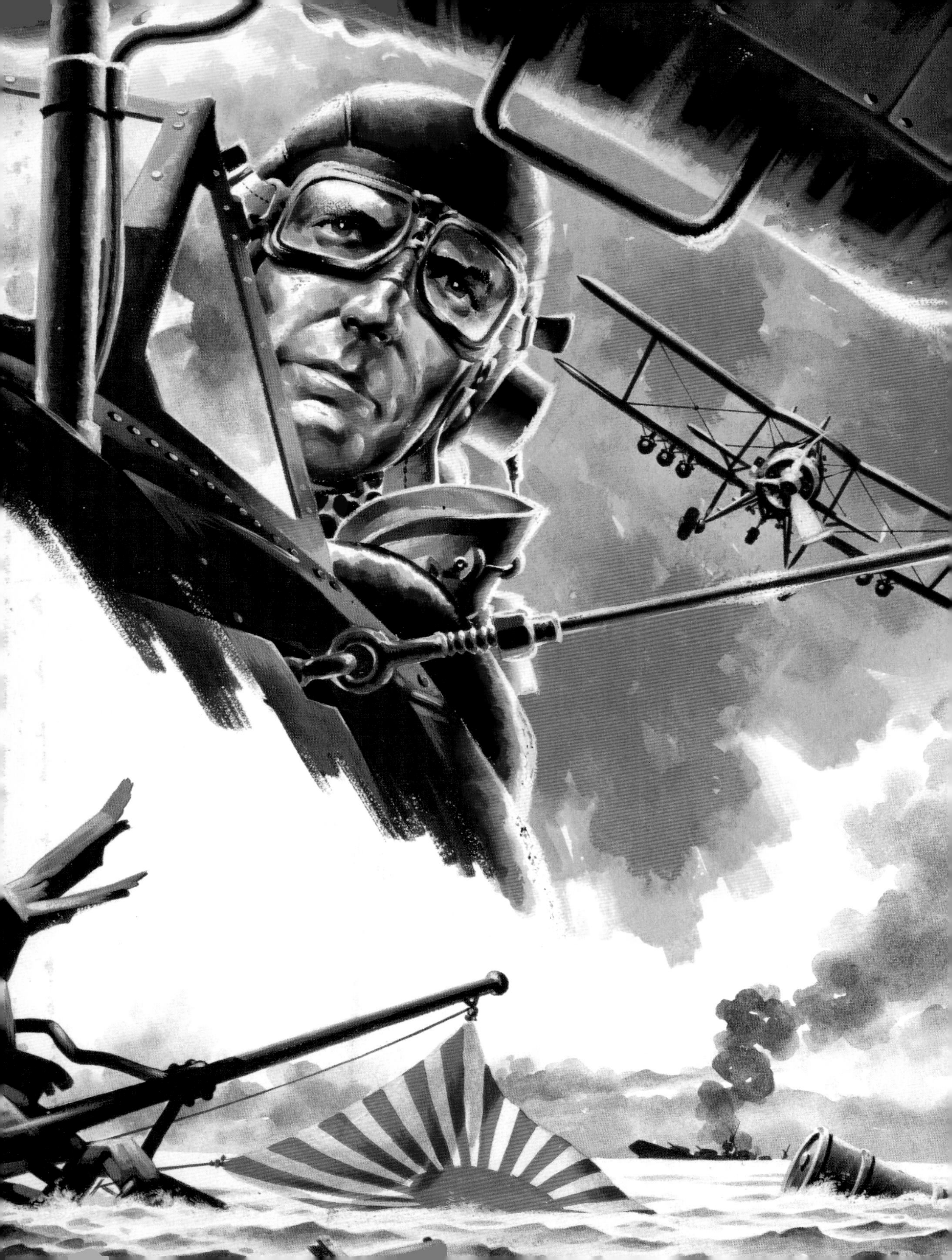

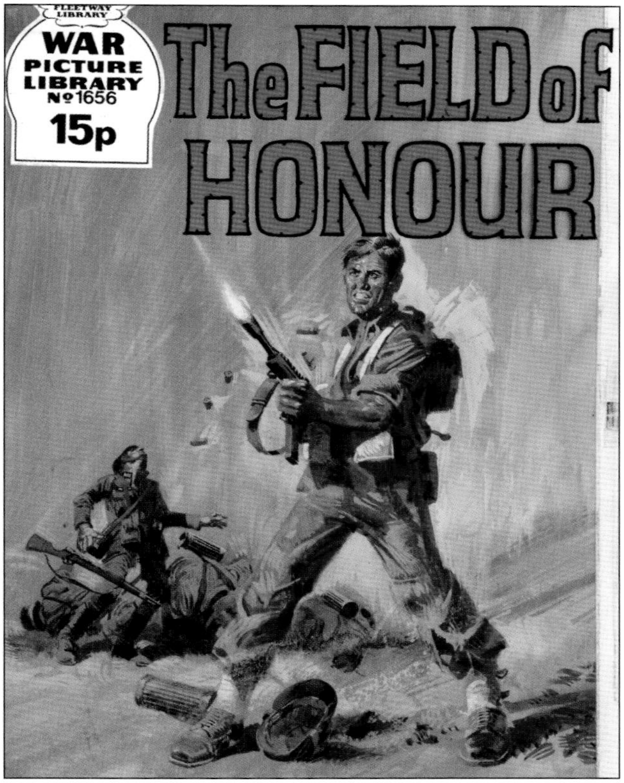
FLEETWAY LIBRARY
WAR PICTURE LIBRARY Nº1656
15p
The FIELD of HONOUR
Allessandro Biffignandi, Battle 185, January 1965

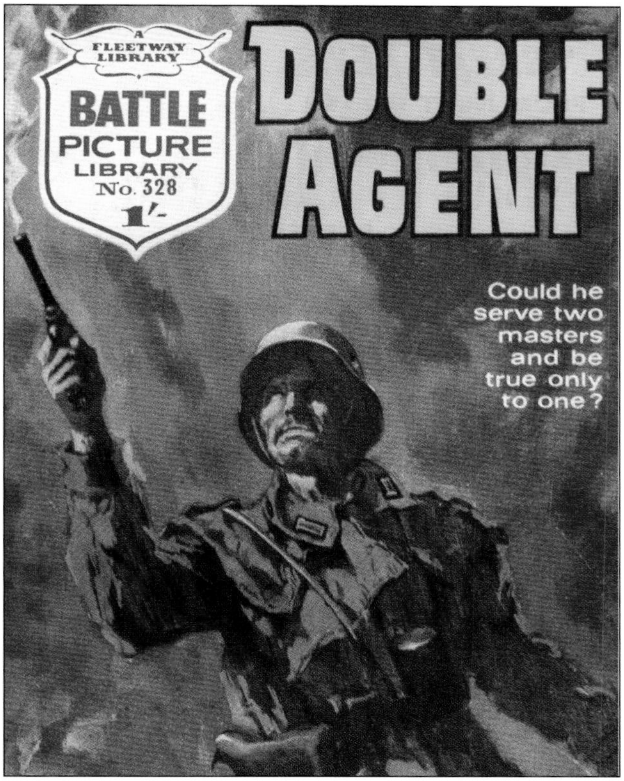
A FLEETWAY LIBRARY
BATTLE PICTURE LIBRARY No. 328
1/-
DOUBLE AGENT
Could he serve two masters and be true only to one?
Jordi Longaron, Battle 328, December 1967

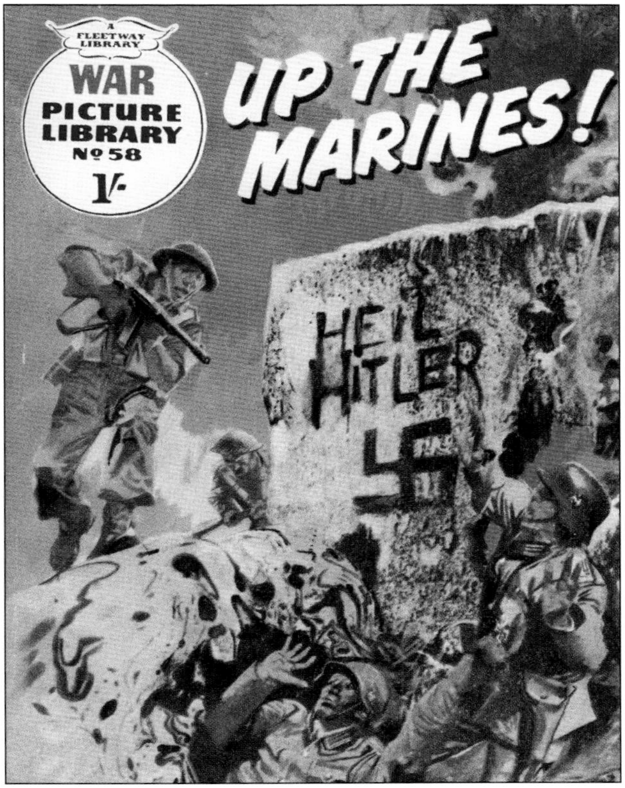
A FLEETWAY LIBRARY
WAR PICTURE LIBRARY Nº58
1/-
UP THE MARINES!
HEIL HITLER
Giorgio DeGaspari, War 58, July 1960

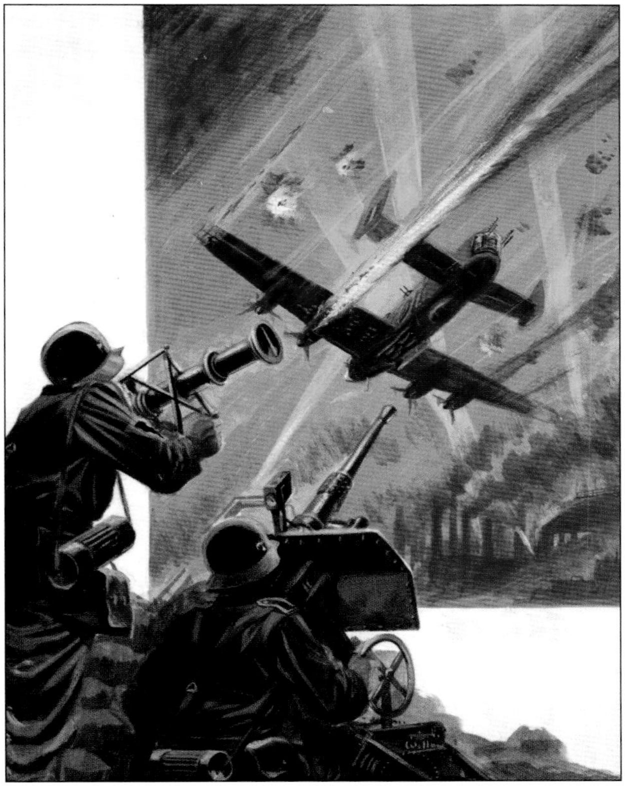
Alan Willow, Air Ace 397, July 1968

Opposite: Ian Kennedy, Air Ace 381, March 1968

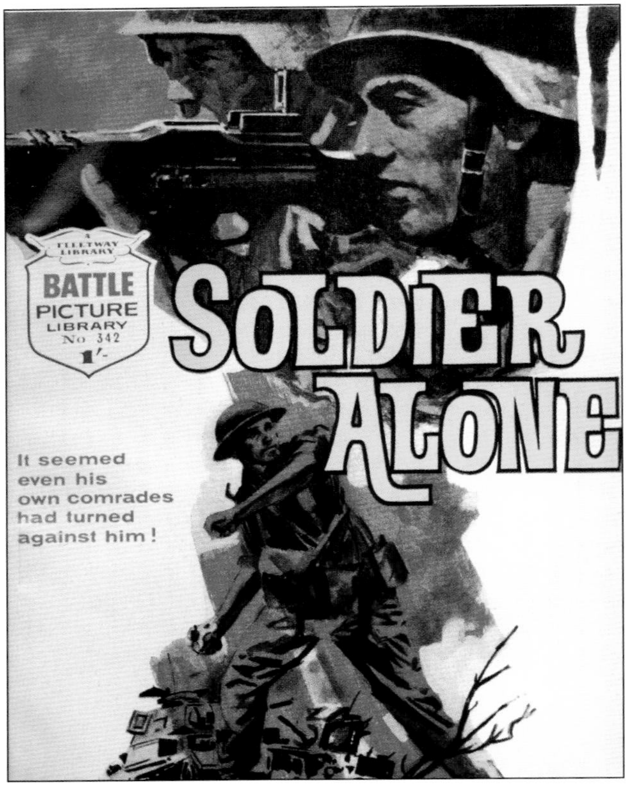
A FLEETWAY LIBRARY
BATTLE PICTURE LIBRARY No 342
1/-
SOLDIER ALONE
It seemed even his own comrades had turned against him!

Fernando Fernandez, Battle 342, April 1968

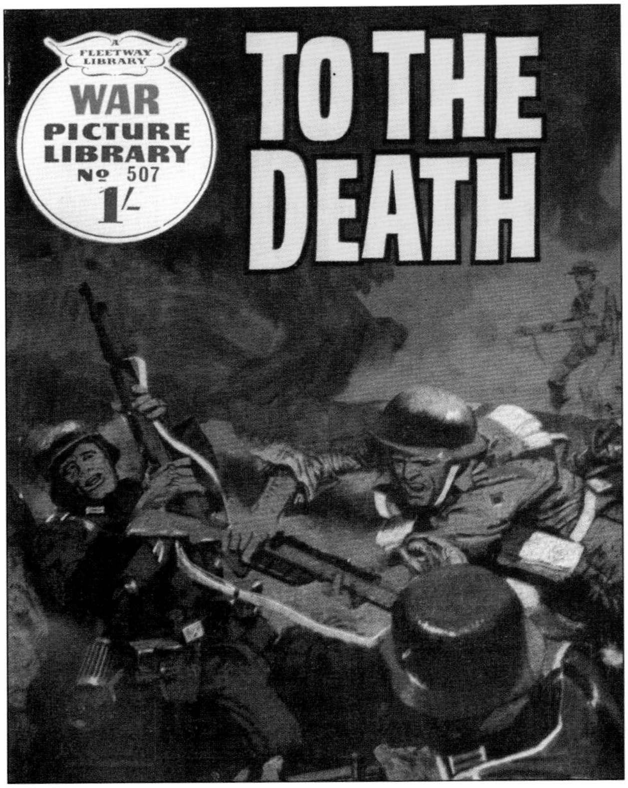
A FLEETWAY LIBRARY
WAR PICTURE LIBRARY Nº 507
1/-
TO THE DEATH

Allessandro Biffignandi, War 507, April 1969

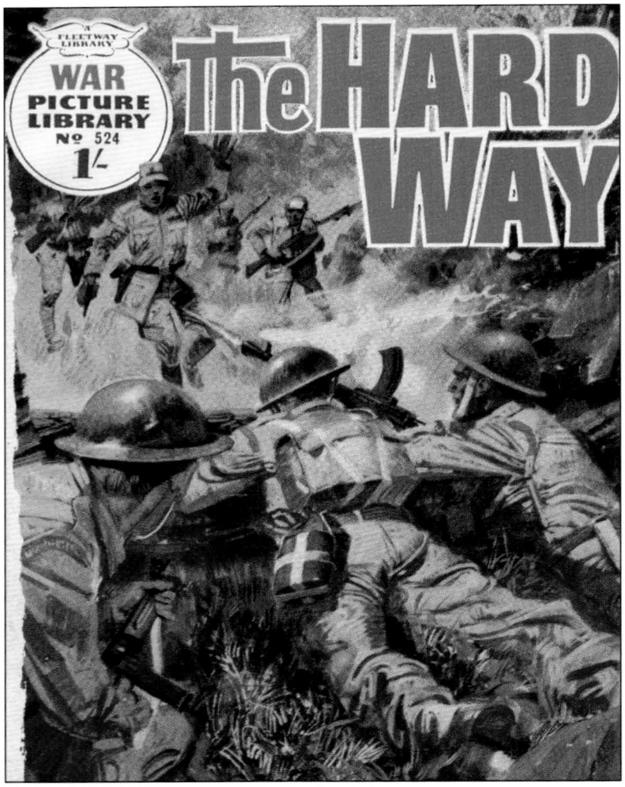
A FLEETWAY LIBRARY
WAR PICTURE LIBRARY Nº 524
1/-
The HARD WAY

Allessandro Biffignandi, War 524, July 1969

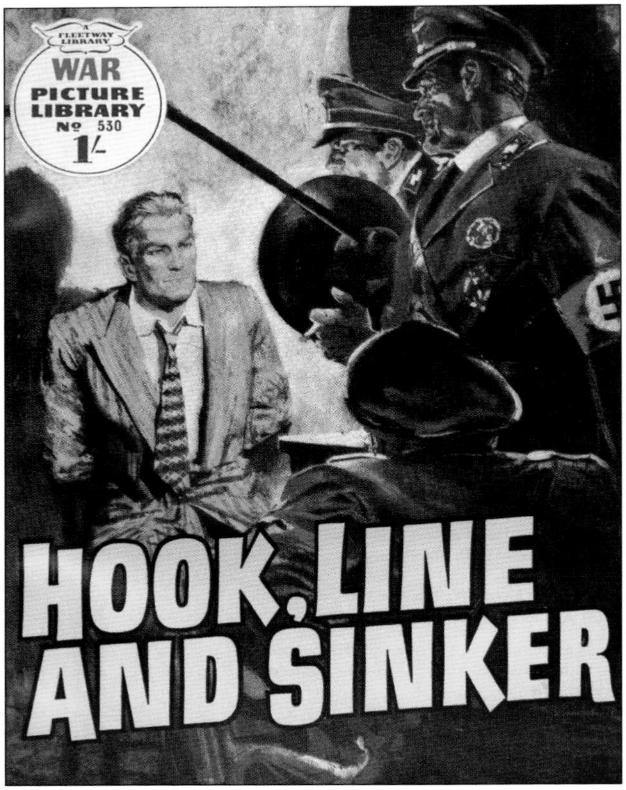
A FLEETWAY LIBRARY
WAR PICTURE LIBRARY Nº 530
1/-
HOOK, LINE AND SINKER

Giorgio DeGaspari, originally thriller 250, November 1958

Opposite: Allessandro Biffignandi, Battle 133, December 1963

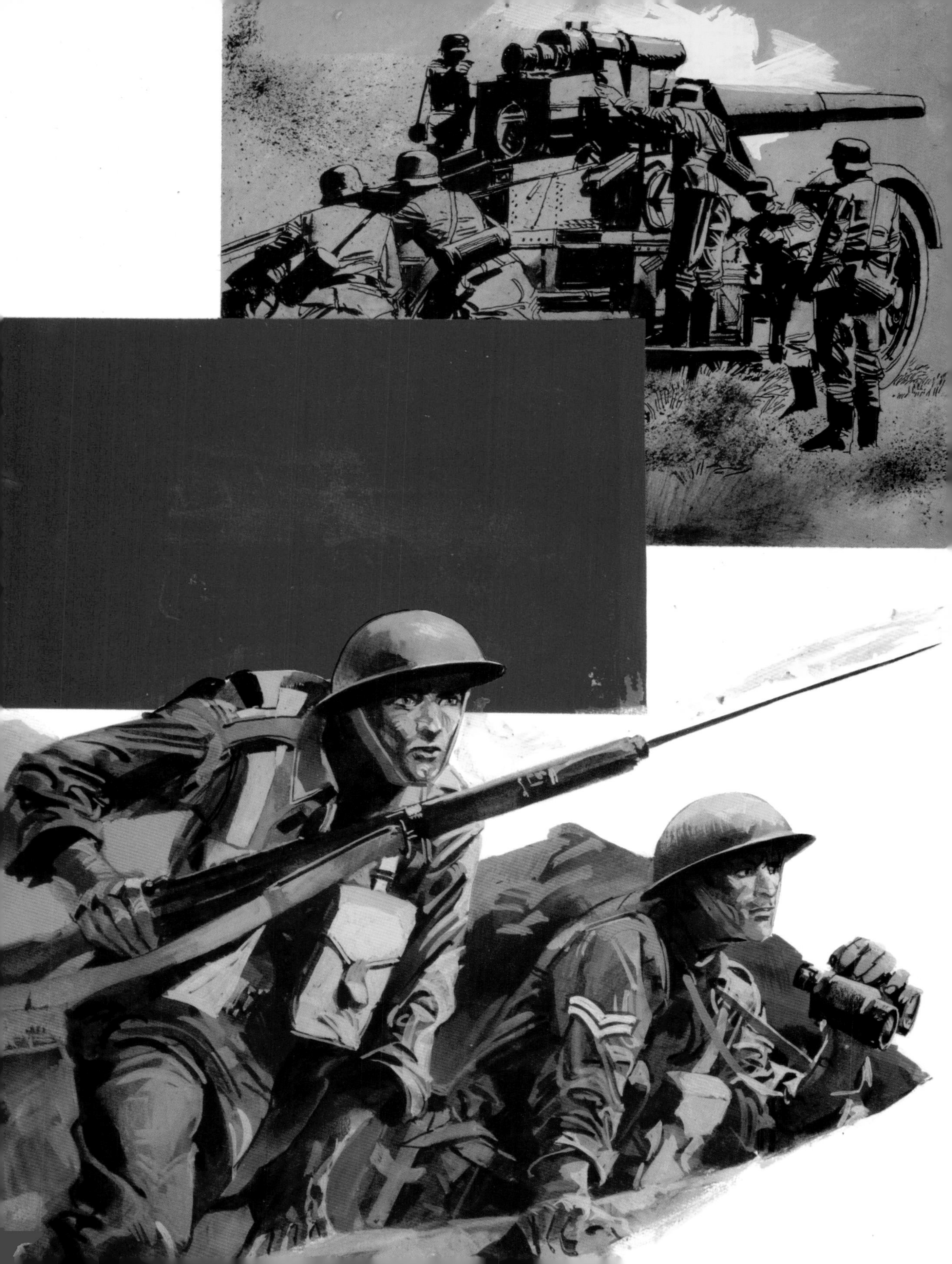

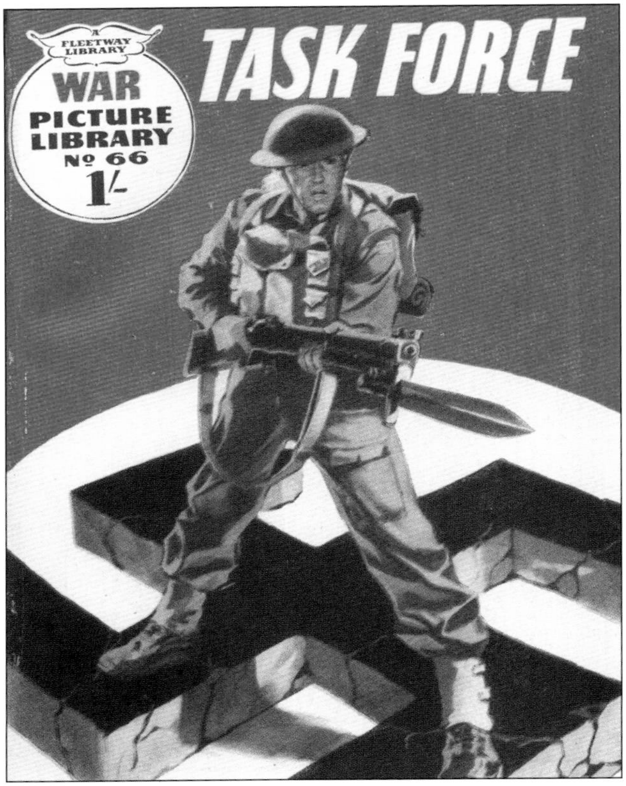
A FLEETWAY LIBRARY
WAR
PICTURE LIBRARY
Nº 66
1/-
TASK FORCE

Nino Caroselli, War 66, September 1960

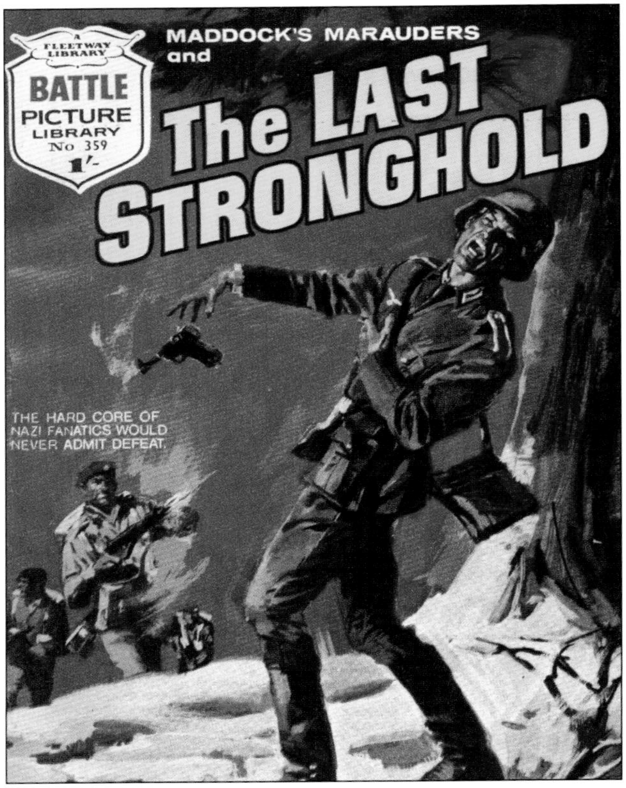
A FLEETWAY LIBRARY
BATTLE
PICTURE LIBRARY
No 359
1/-
MADDOCK'S MARAUDERS and
The LAST STRONGHOLD
THE HARD CORE OF NAZI FANATICS WOULD NEVER ADMIT DEFEAT.

Jordi Penalva, Battle 359, August 1968

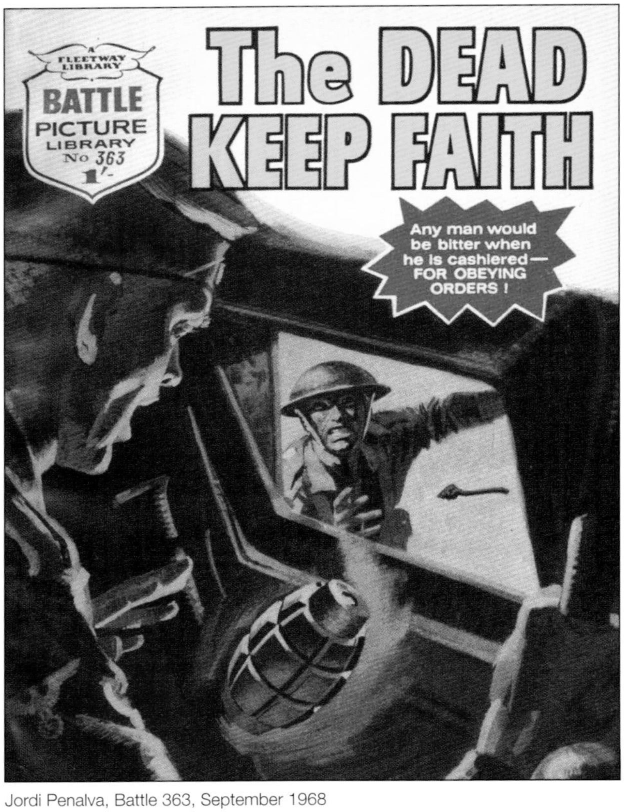
A FLEETWAY LIBRARY
BATTLE
PICTURE LIBRARY
No 363
1/-
The DEAD KEEP FAITH
Any man would be bitter when he is cashiered— FOR OBEYING ORDERS !

Jordi Penalva, Battle 363, September 1968

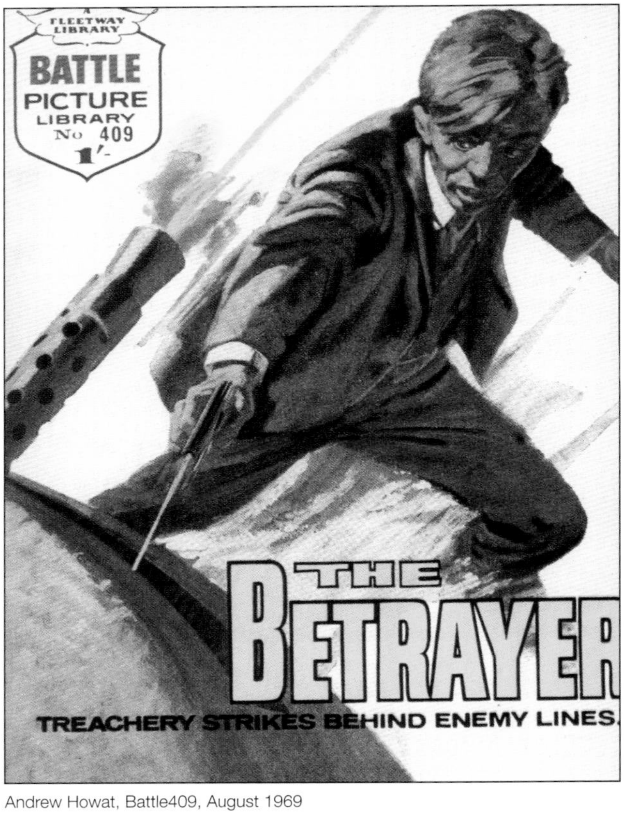
A FLEETWAY LIBRARY
BATTLE
PICTURE LIBRARY
No 409
1/-
THE BETRAYER
TREACHERY STRIKES BEHIND ENEMY LINES.

Andrew Howat, Battle409, August 1969

Opposite: 127 Nino Caroselli, War 378, March 1967

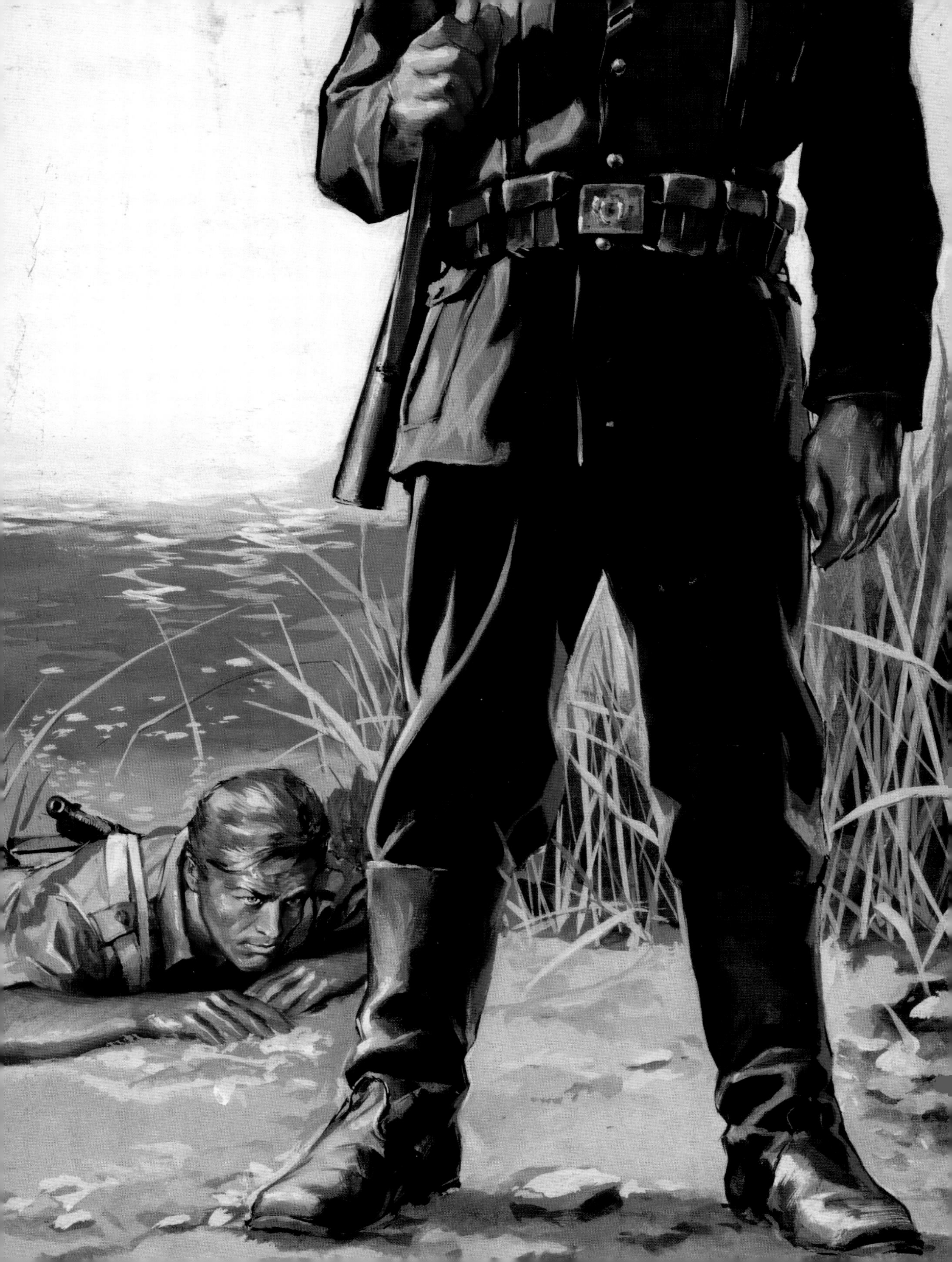

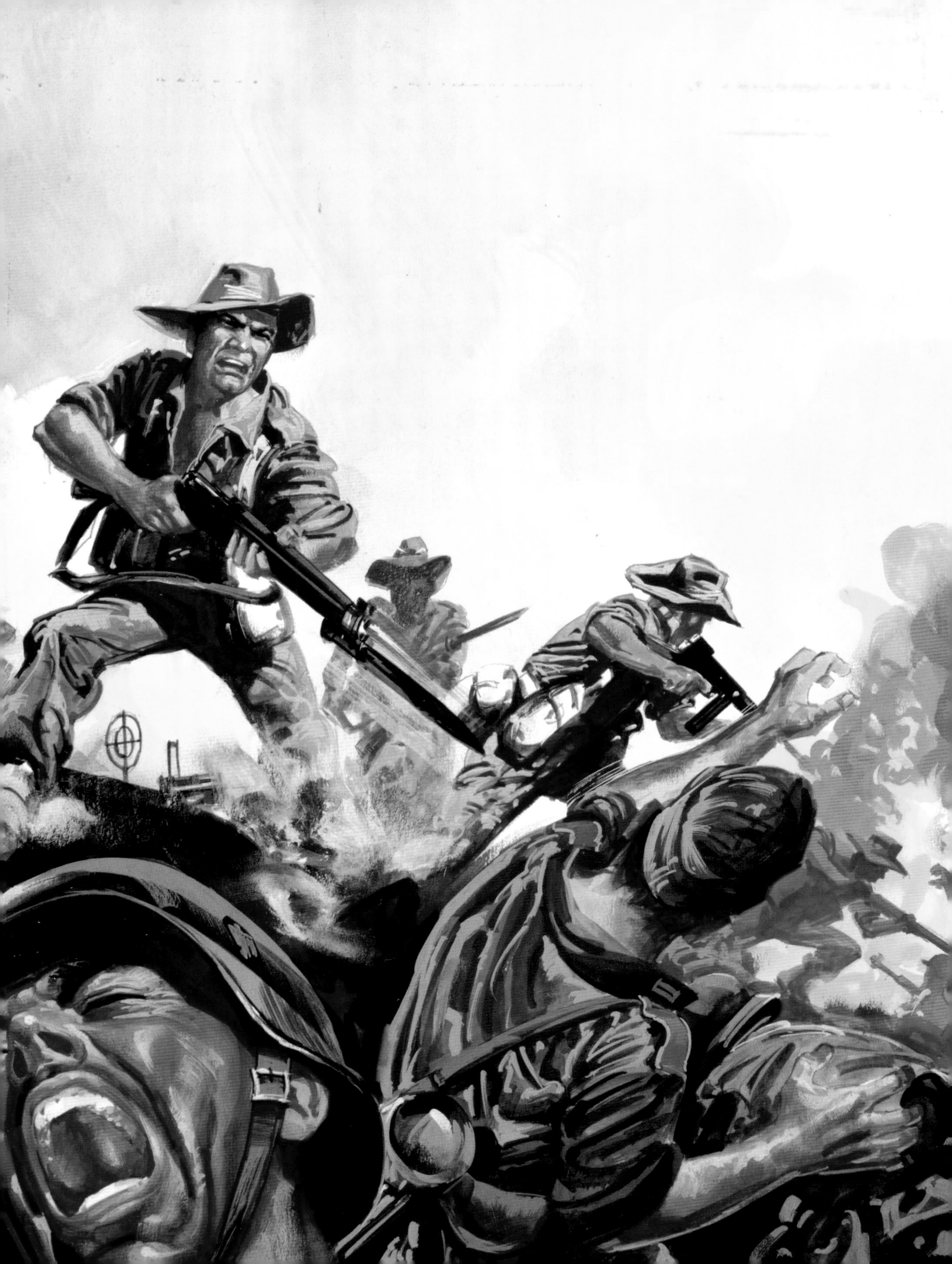

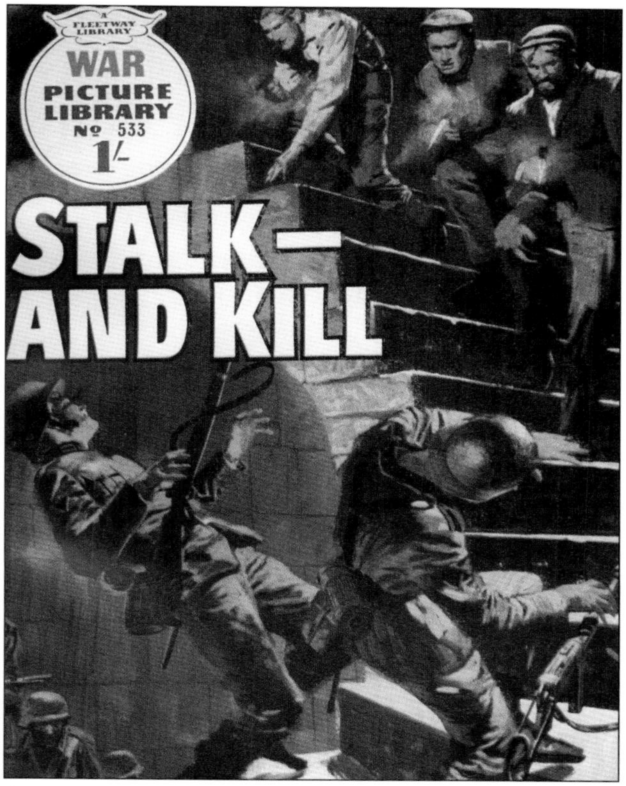
WAR
PICTURE
LIBRARY
Nº 533
1/-
STALK—
AND KILL

Jordi Penalva, War 533, August 1969

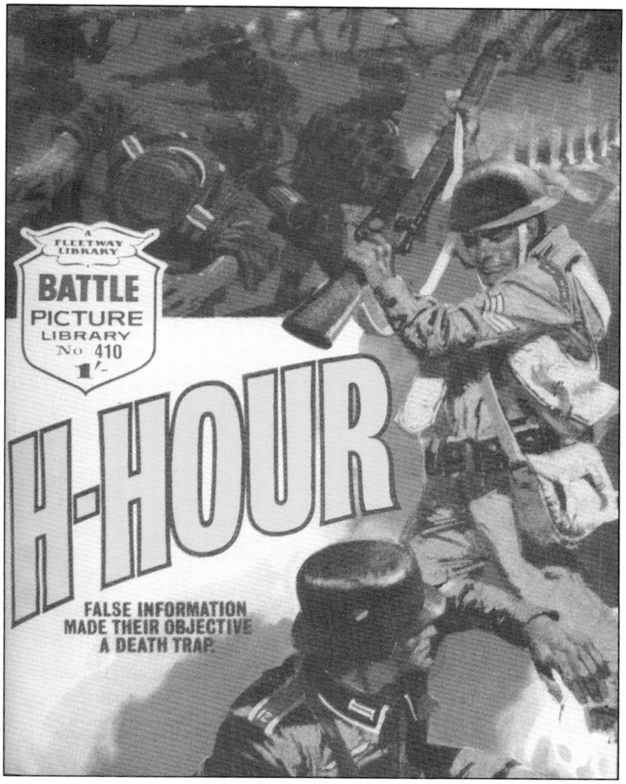
BATTLE
PICTURE
LIBRARY
No 410
1/-
H-HOUR
FALSE INFORMATION
MADE THEIR OBJECTIVE
A DEATH TRAP.

Allessandro Biffignandi, Battle 410, August 1969

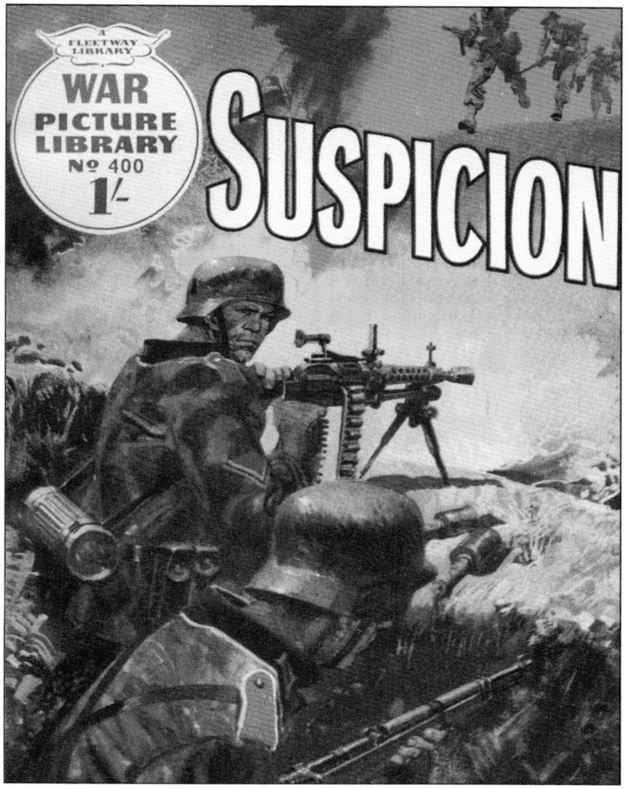
WAR
PICTURE
LIBRARY
Nº 400
1/-
SUSPICION

Allessandro Biffignandi, War 400, September 1967

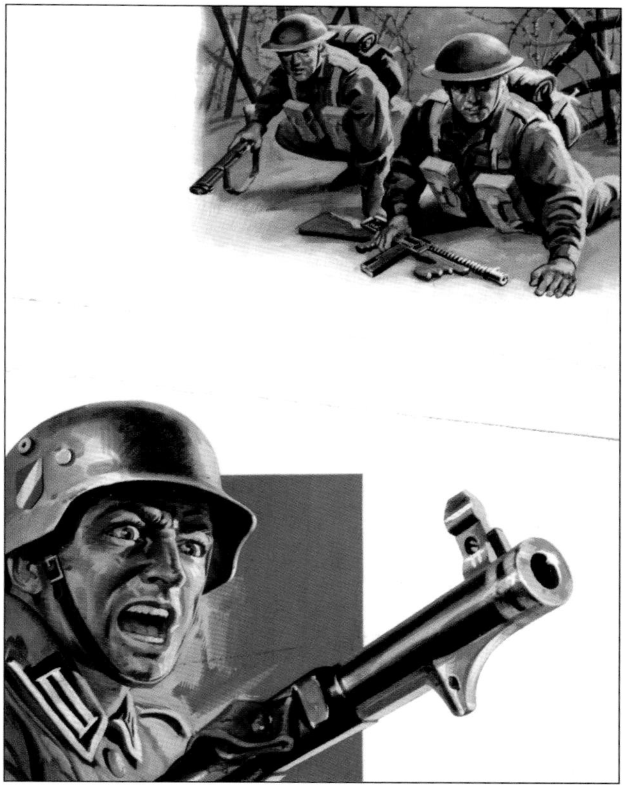

Nino Caroselli, Battle 137, January 1964

Opposite: Franco Picchioni, War481, November 1968

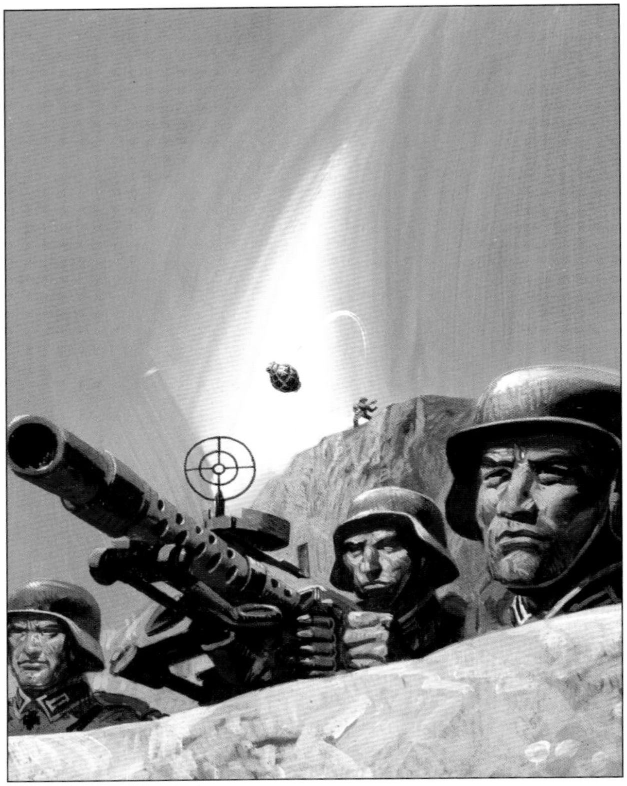

Allessandro Biffignandi, War 423, February 1968

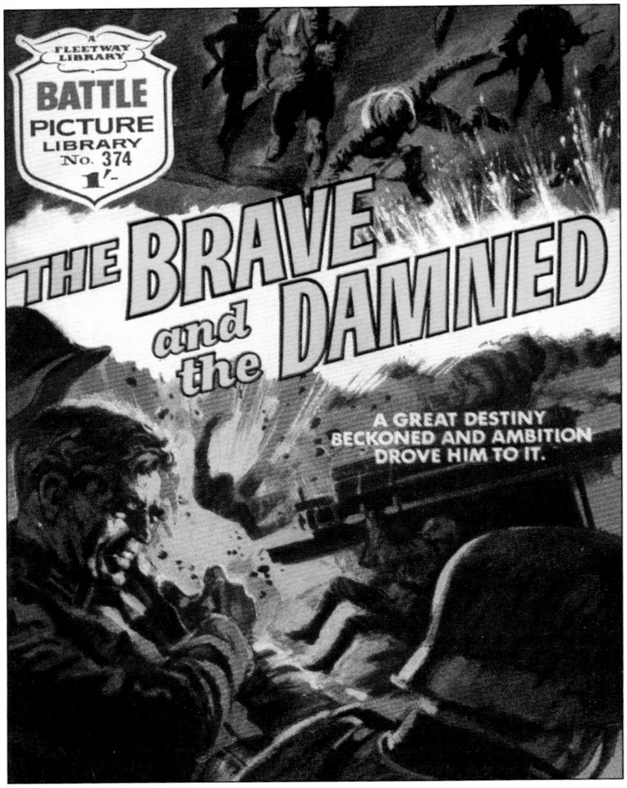
A FLEETWAY LIBRARY
BATTLE
PICTURE
LIBRARY
No. 374
1/-
THE BRAVE and the DAMNED
A GREAT DESTINY
BECKONED AND AMBITION
DROVE HIM TO IT.

Andrew Howat, War 374, December 1968

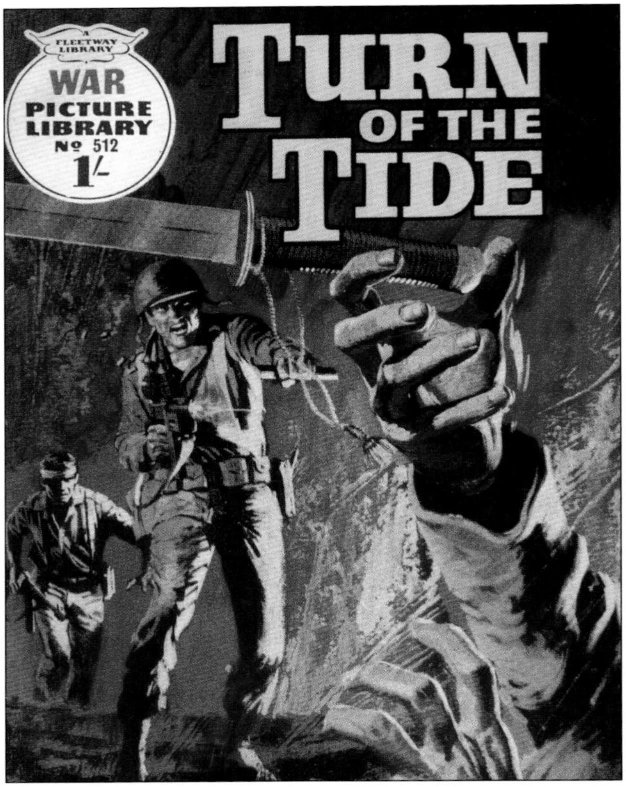
A FLEETWAY LIBRARY
WAR
PICTURE
LIBRARY
No 512
1/-
TURN
OF THE
TIDE

Jordi Penalva, War 512, May 1969

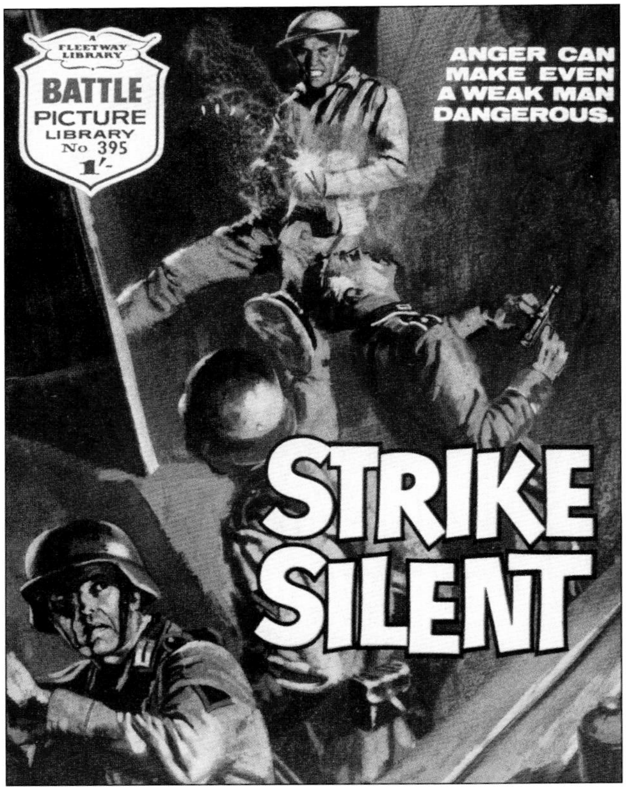
A FLEETWAY LIBRARY
BATTLE
PICTURE
LIBRARY
No 395
1/-
ANGER CAN
MAKE EVEN
A WEAK MAN
DANGEROUS.
STRIKE
SILENT

Jordi Penalva, War 395, May 1969

Opposite: Pino Dell'Orco, War 232, March 1964

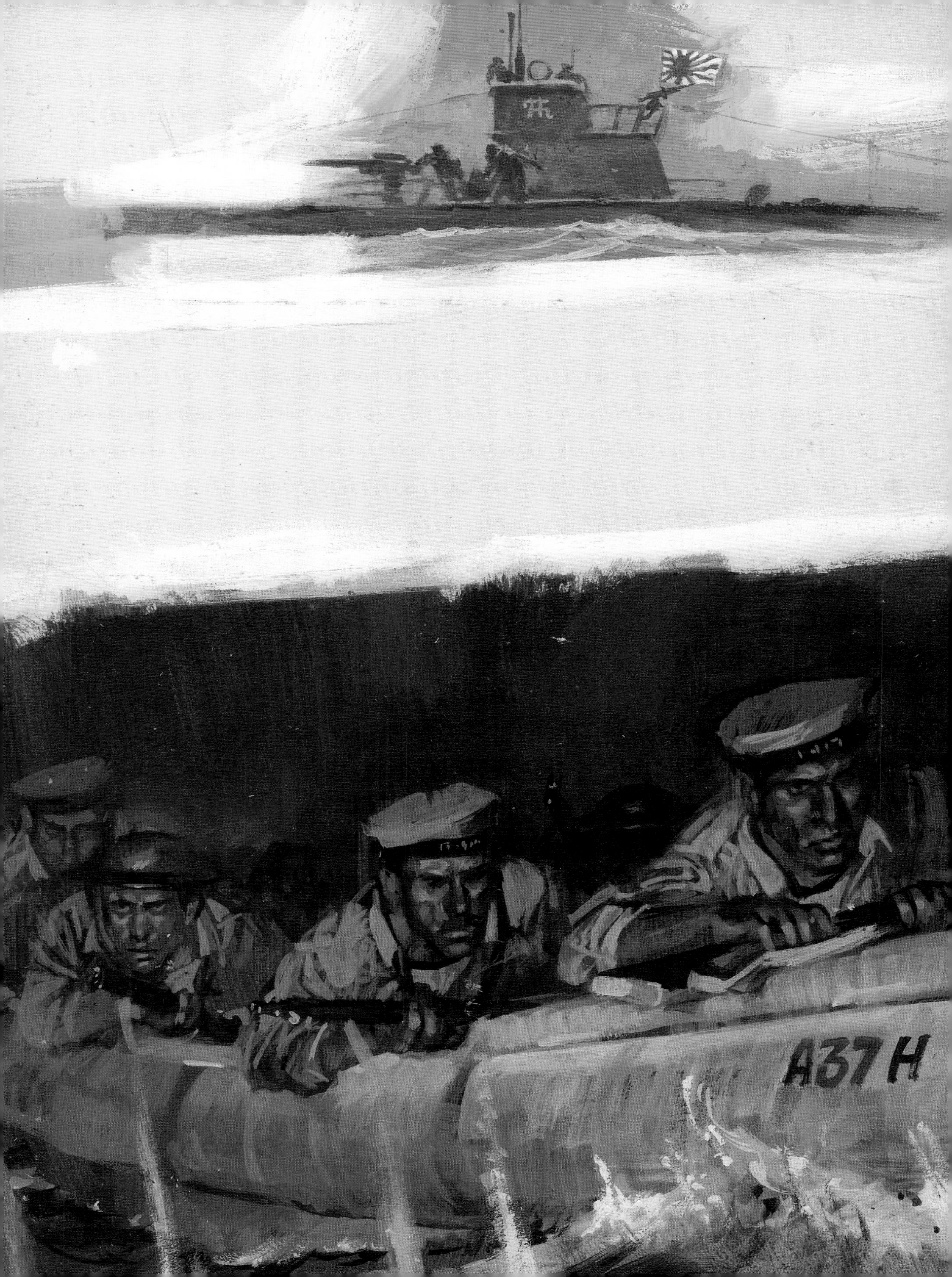
A37 H

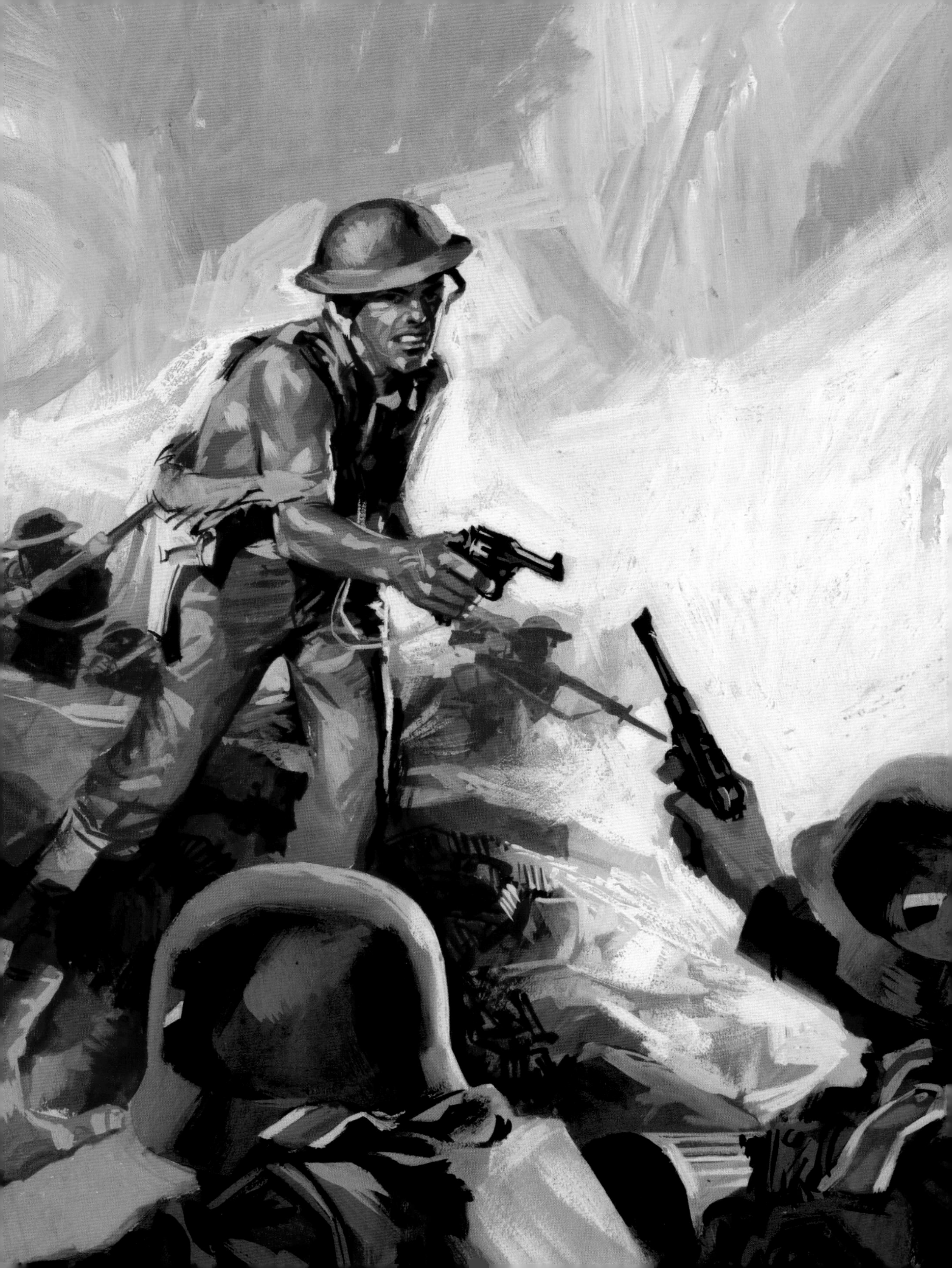

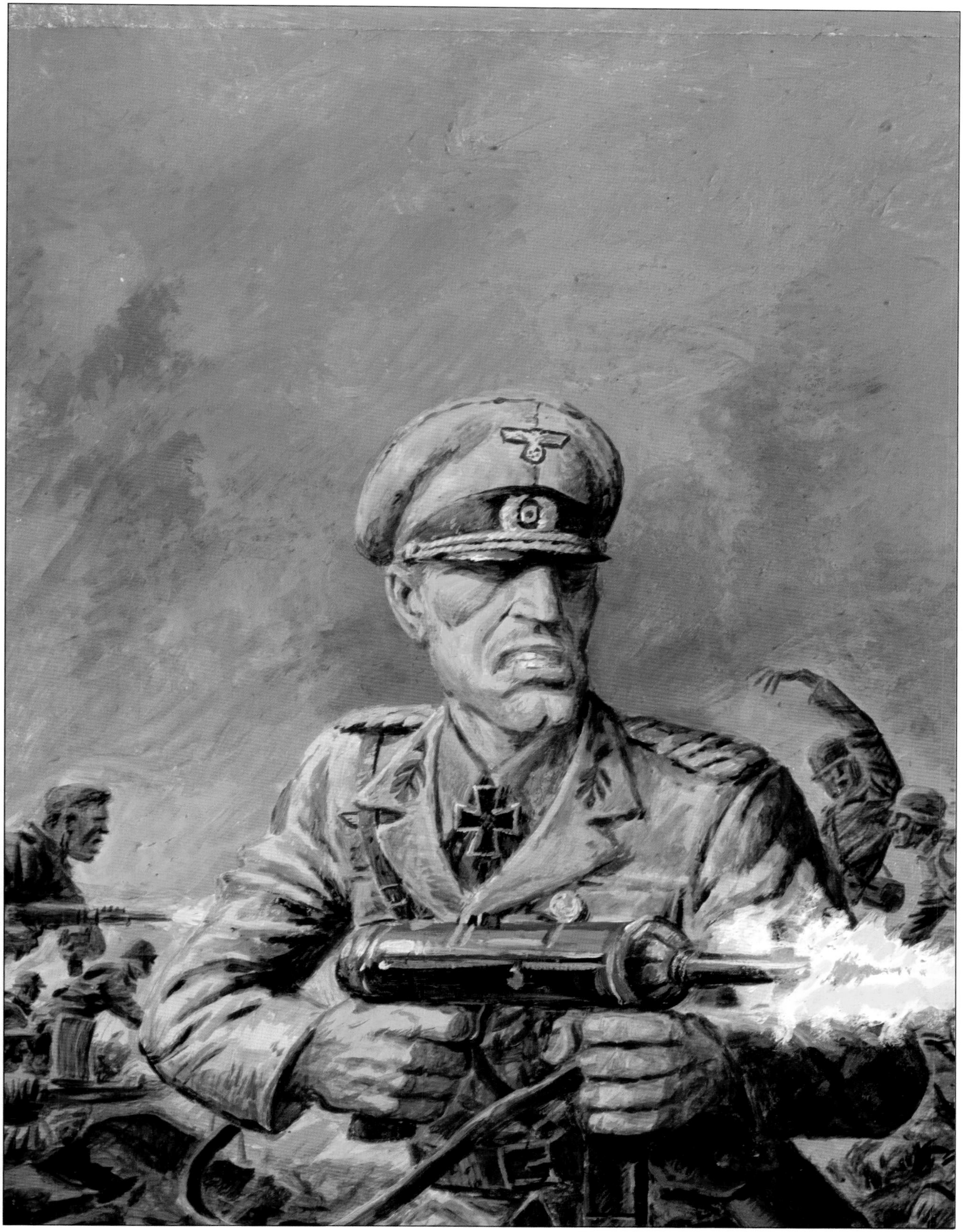

133 Oliver Frey, War 585, May 1970
Opposite: Pino Dell'Orco, War174, December 1962
Overleaf: Oliver Frey, War 745, April 1972

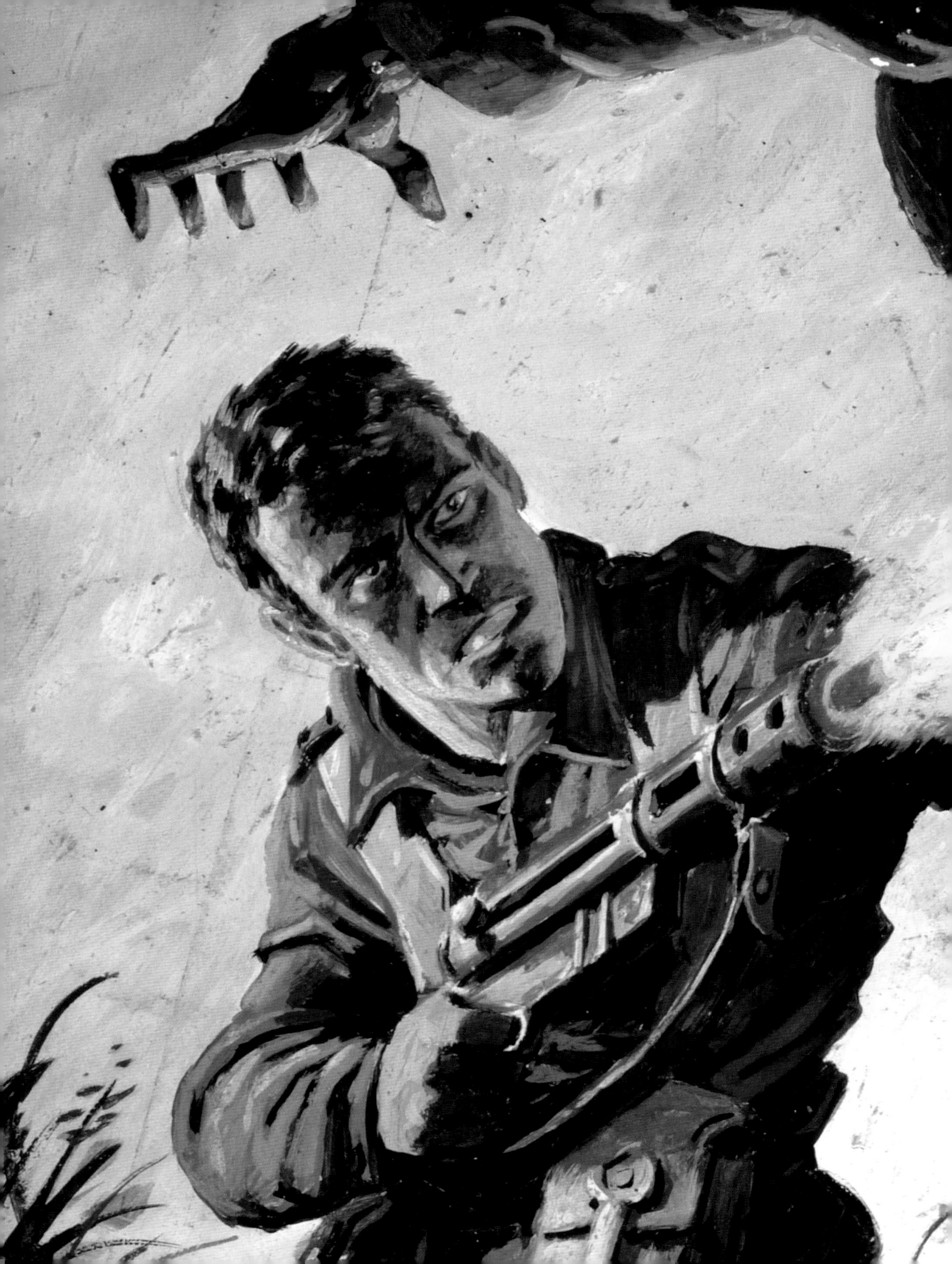

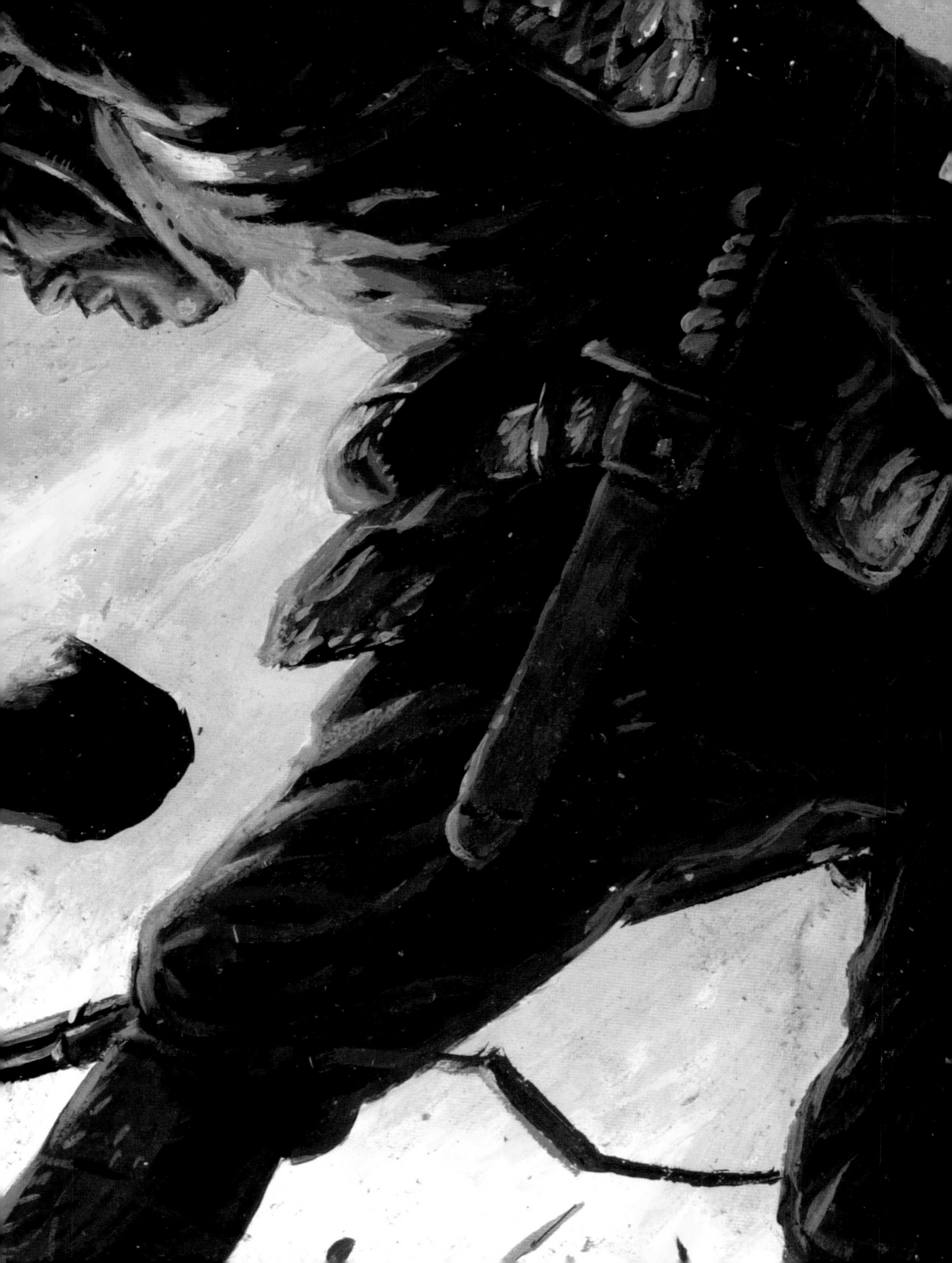

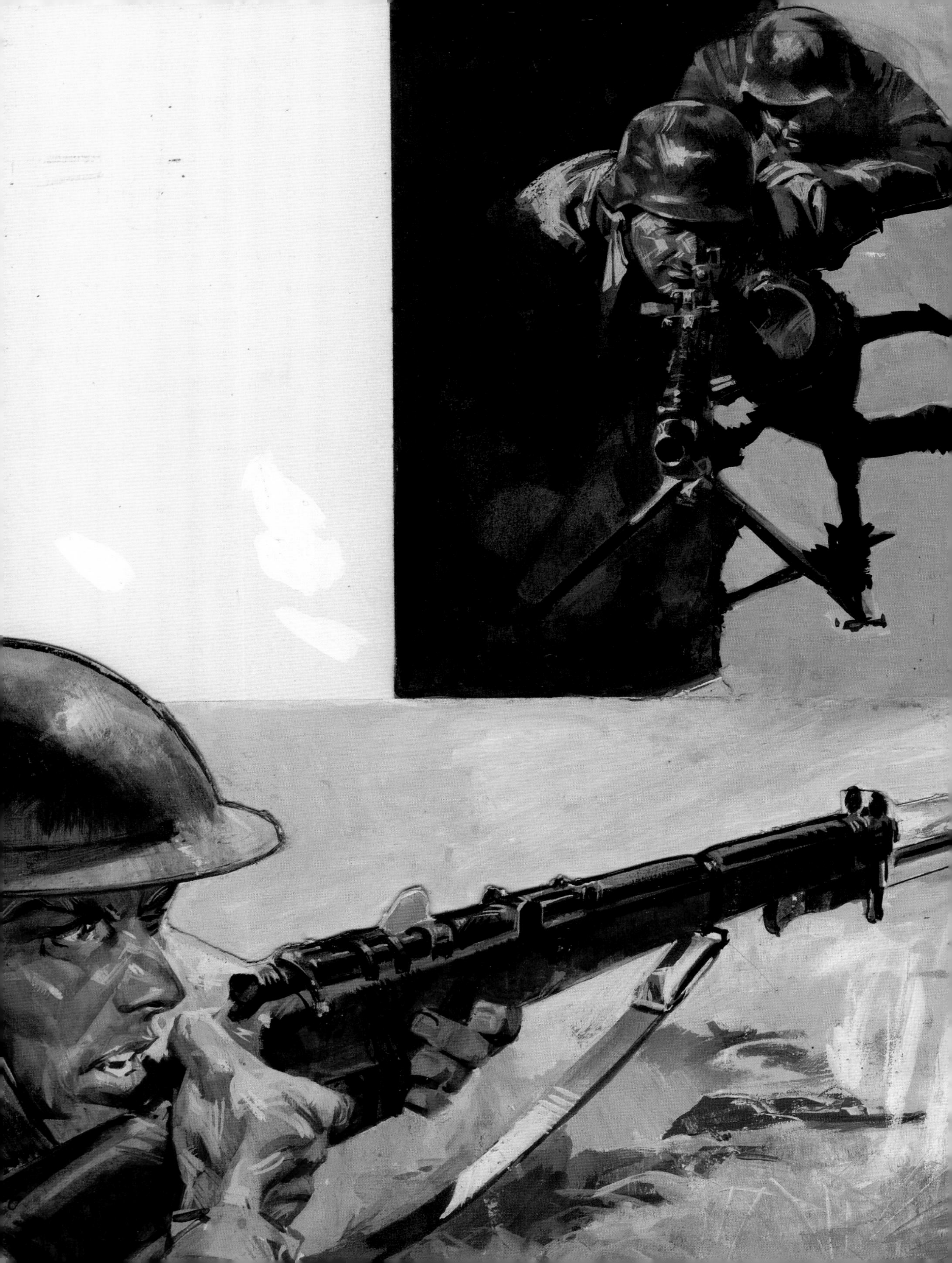

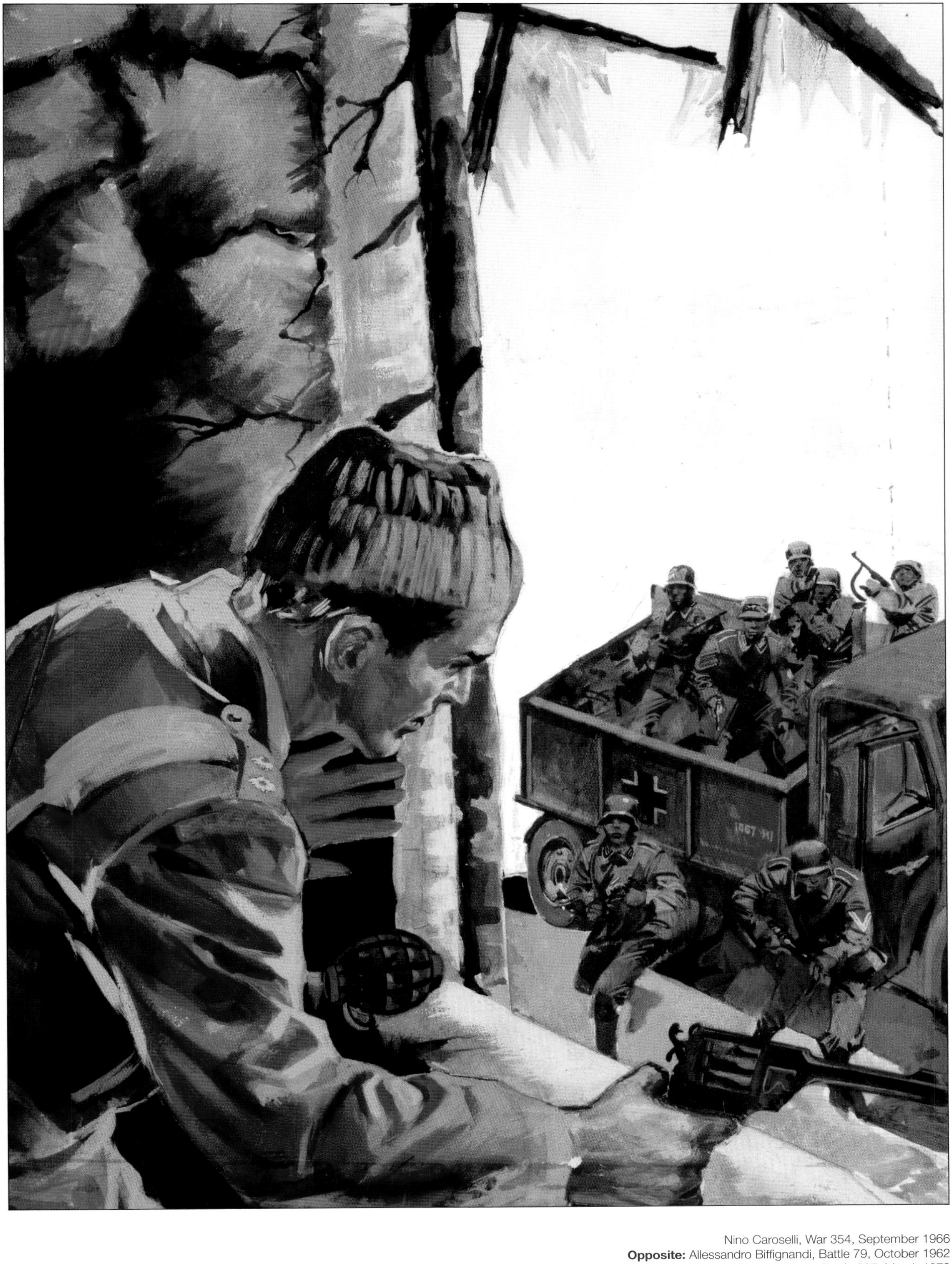

Nino Caroselli, War 354, September 1966
Opposite: Allessandro Biffignandi, Battle 79, October 1962
Overleaf: Graham Coton, Battle 697, March 1973

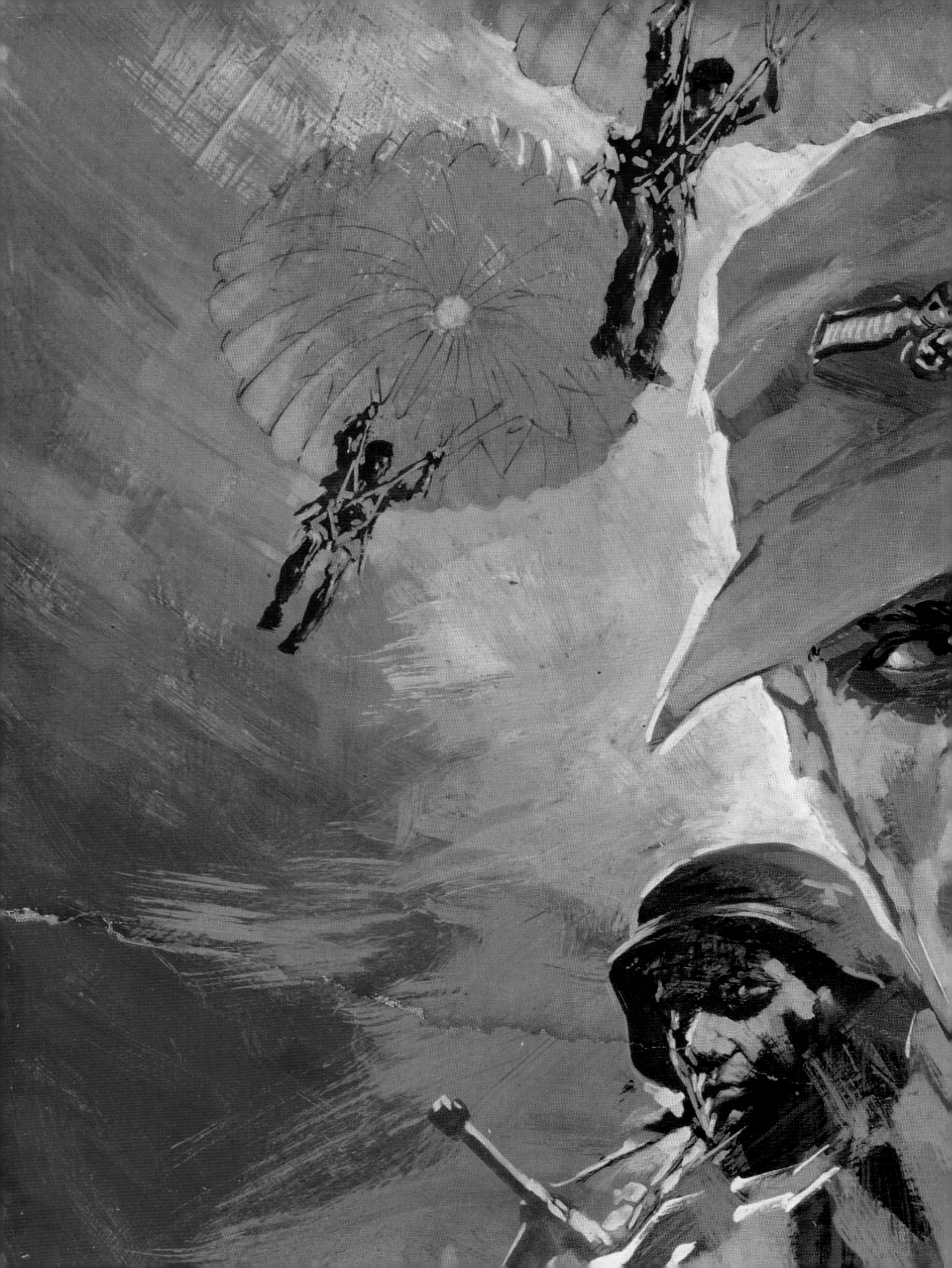

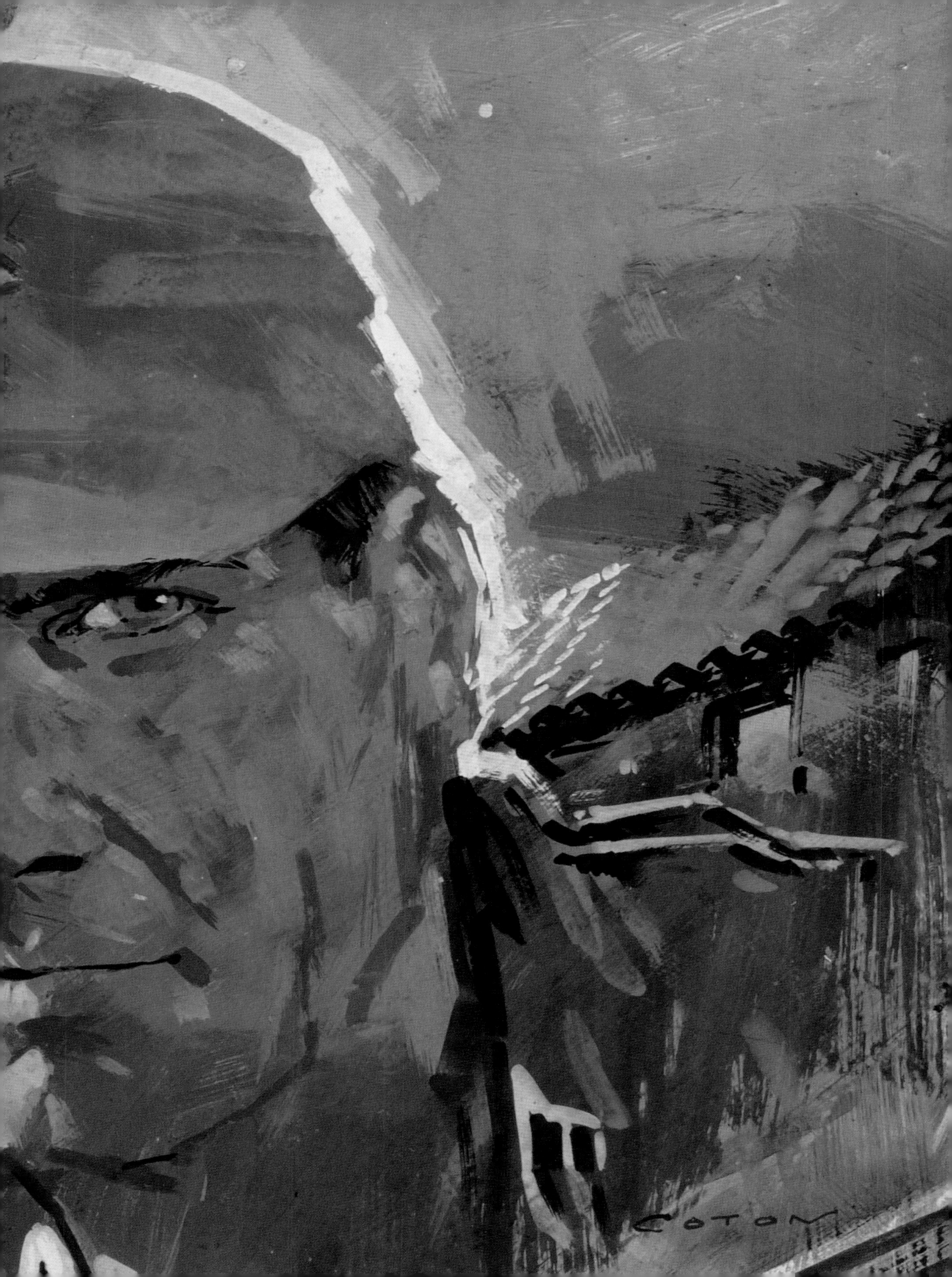

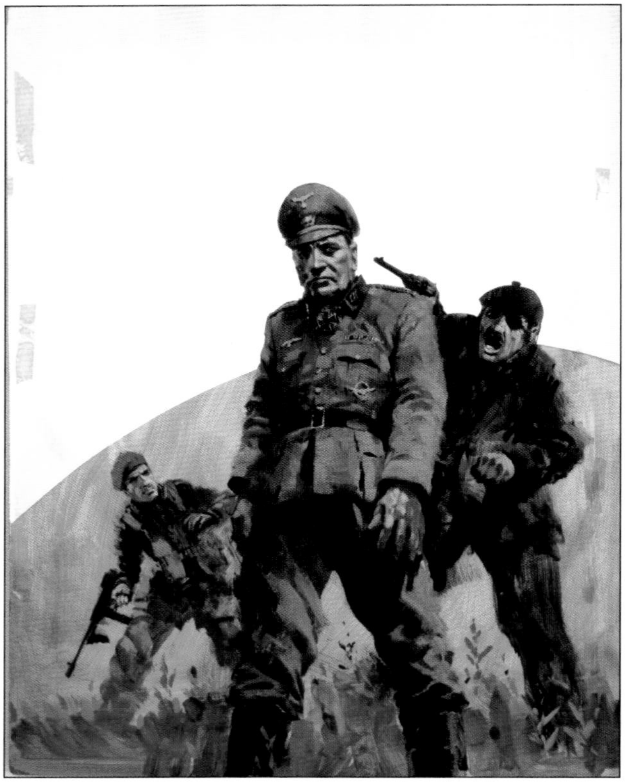

Graham Coton, War 1183, March 1976

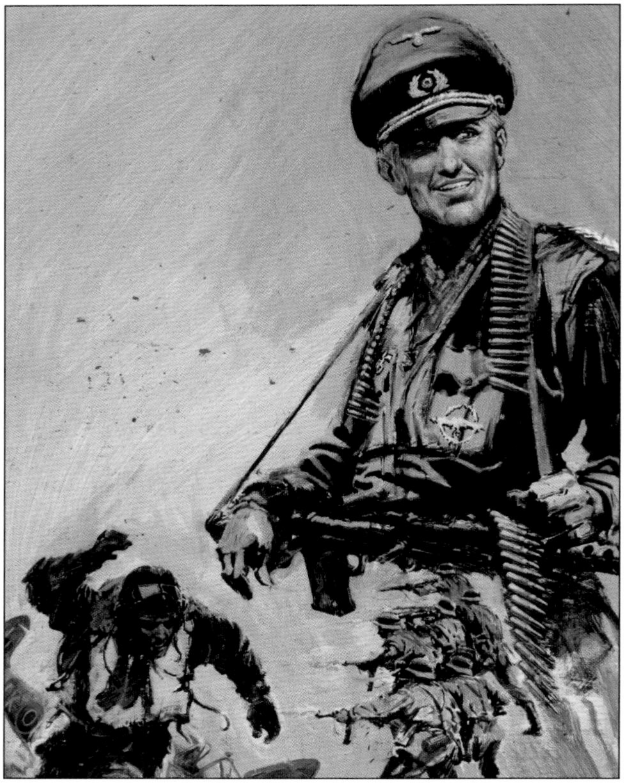

Graham Coton, Battle 425, October 1969

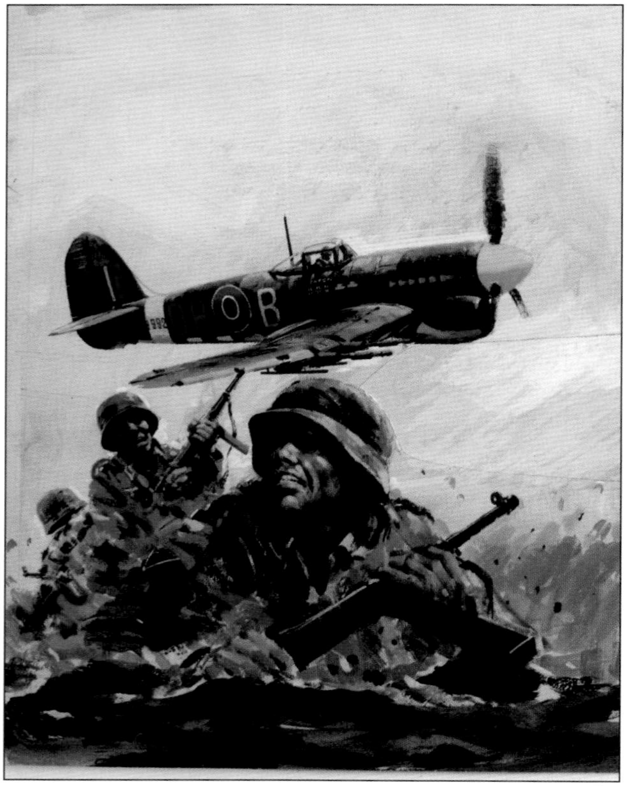

Graham Coton, War 1819, November 1980

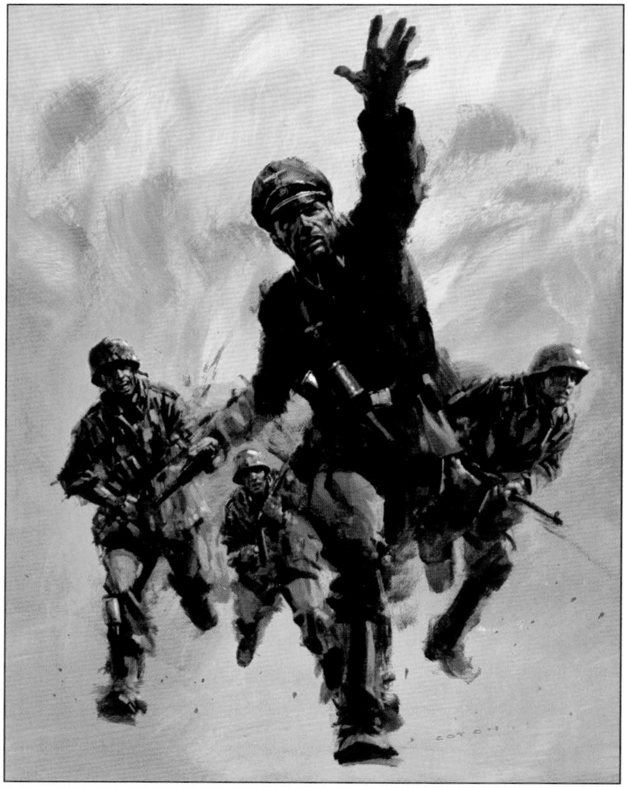

Graham Coton, War 1386, August 1977

Opposite: Oliver Frey, originally War 615, October 1970

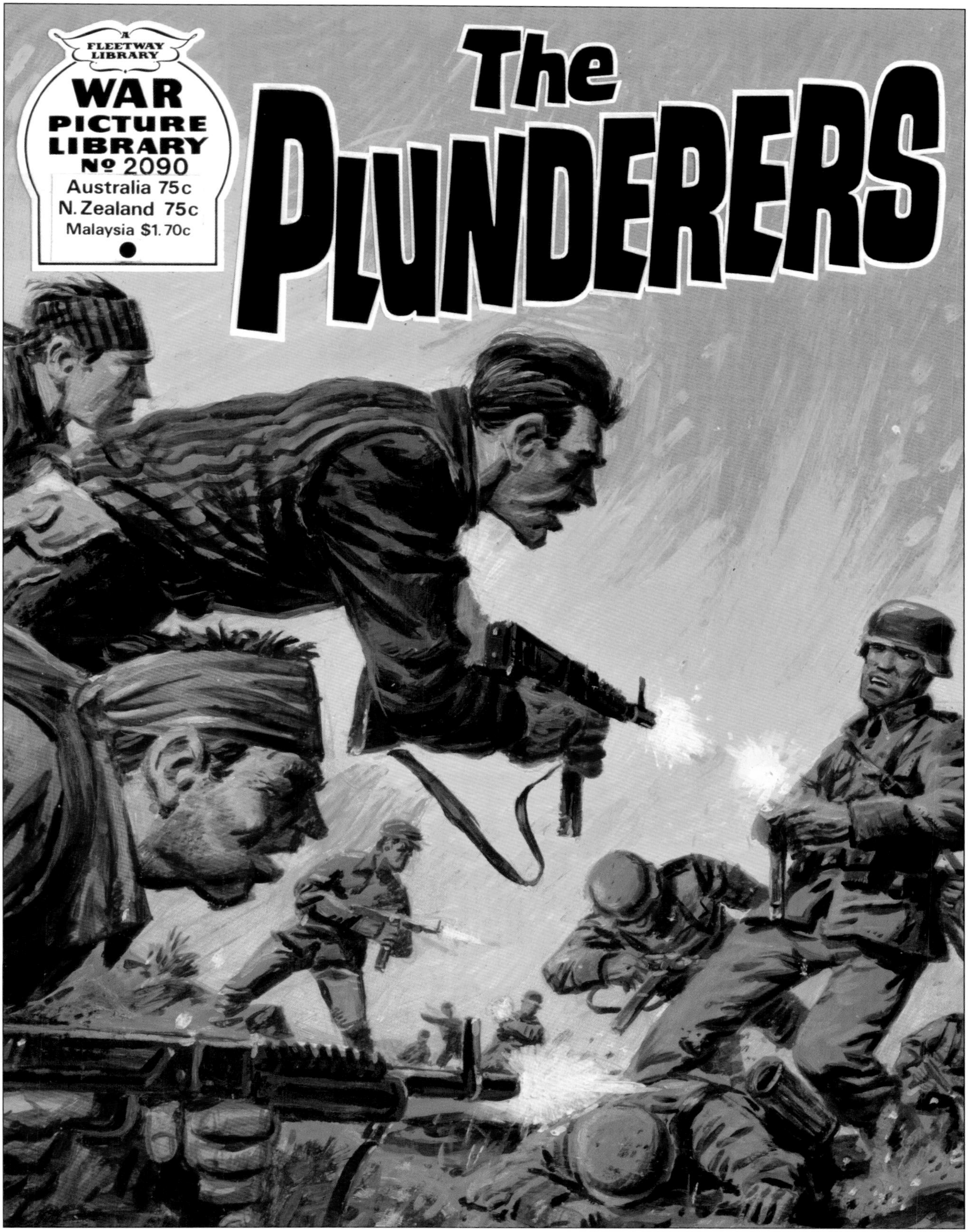
A FLEETWAY LIBRARY
WAR PICTURE LIBRARY
Nº 2090
Australia 75c
N. Zealand 75c
Malaysia $1.70c
The PLUNDERERS

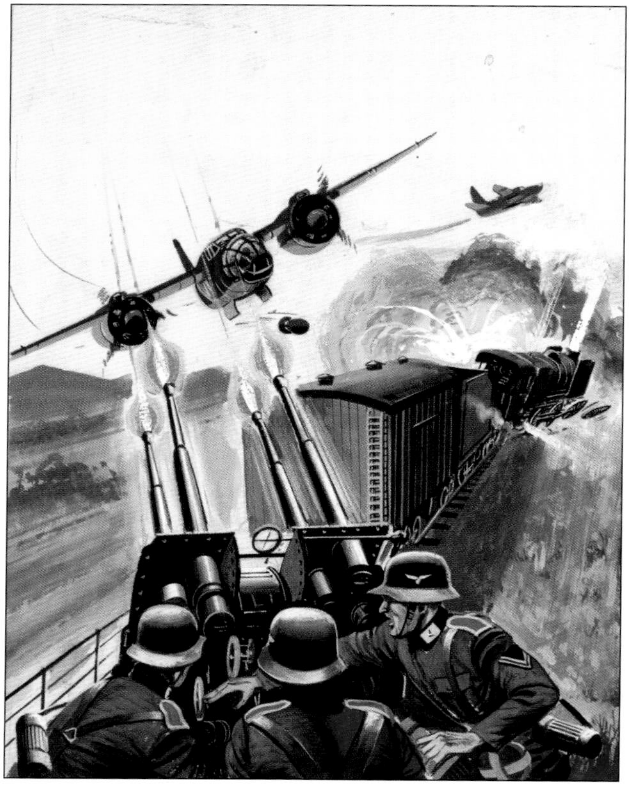

Alan Willow, Air Ace 255, August 1965

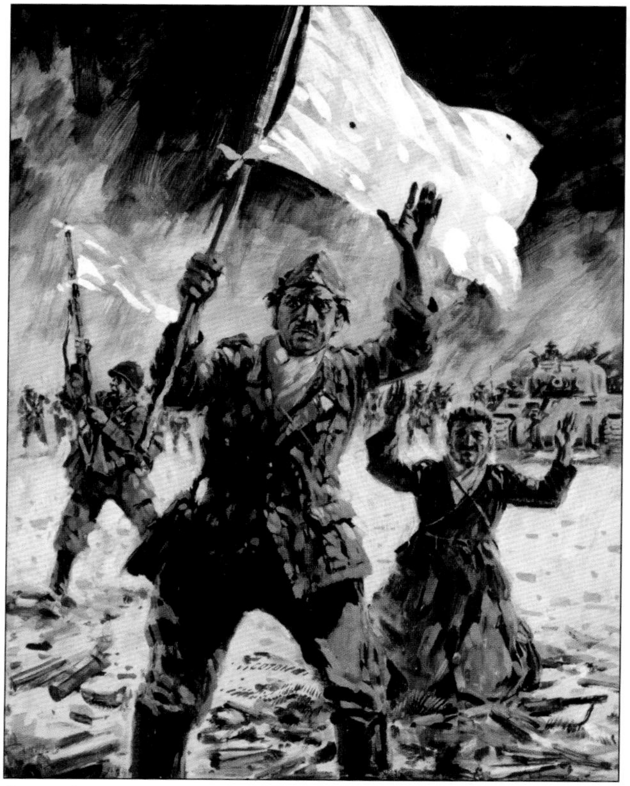

Graham Coton, War 2034, November 1983

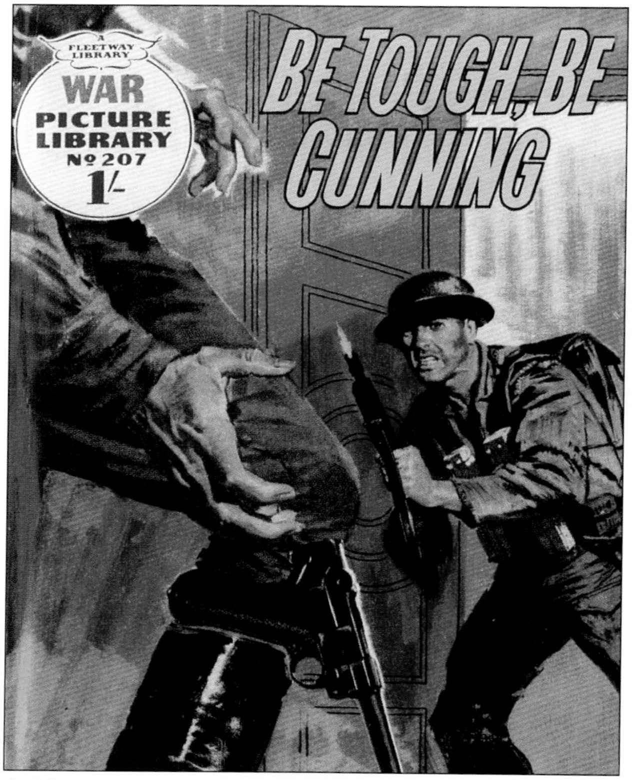
A FLEETWAY LIBRARY
WAR PICTURE LIBRARY
Nº 207
1/-
BE TOUGH, BE CUNNING

Jordi Penalva, War 207, August 1963

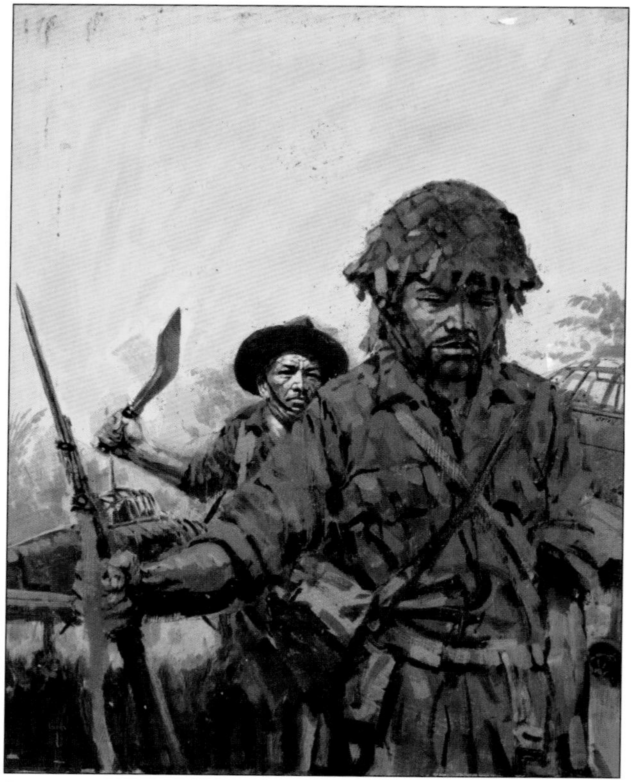

Graham Coton, War 2088, August 1984

Opposite: Graham Coton, War 1602, February 1979

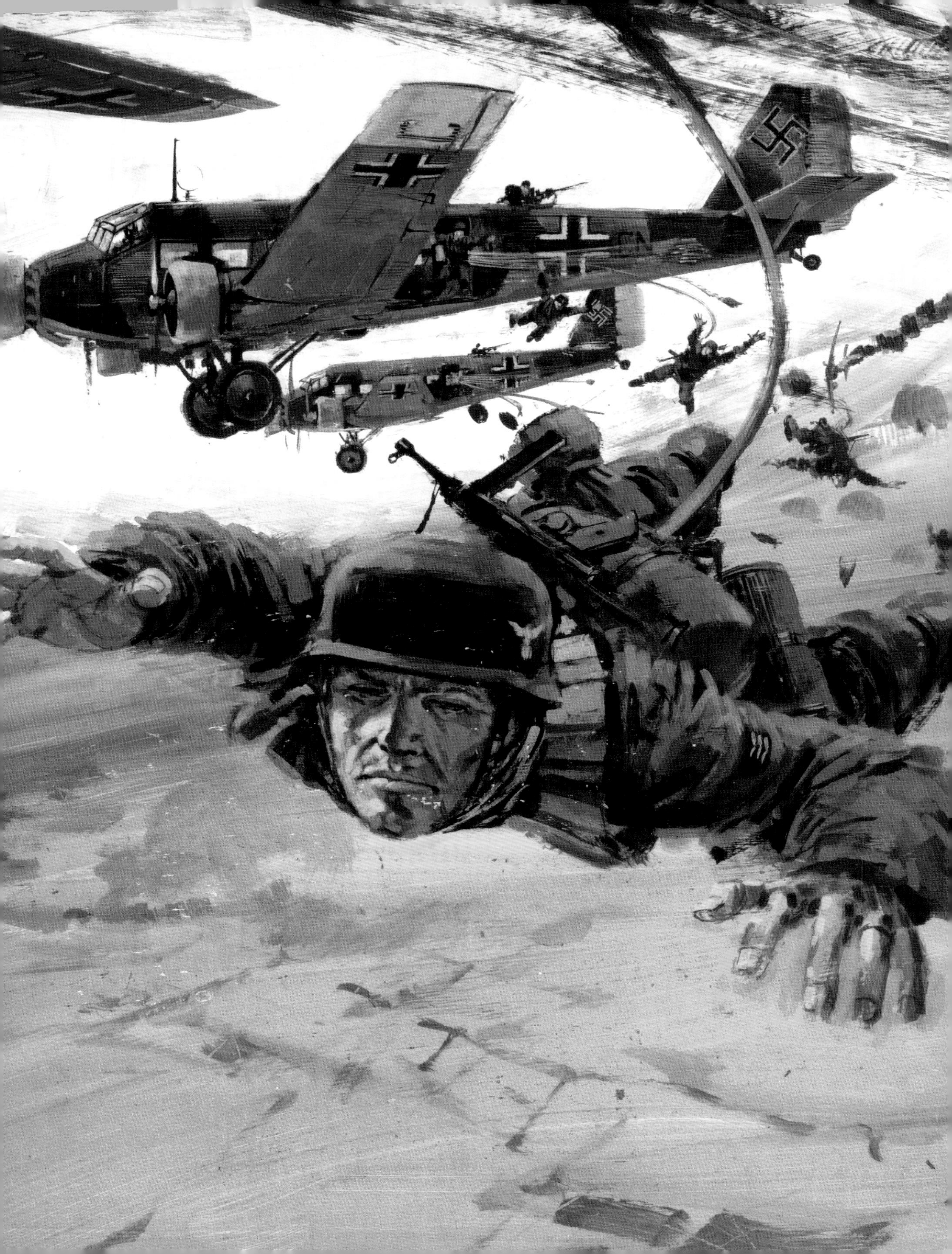

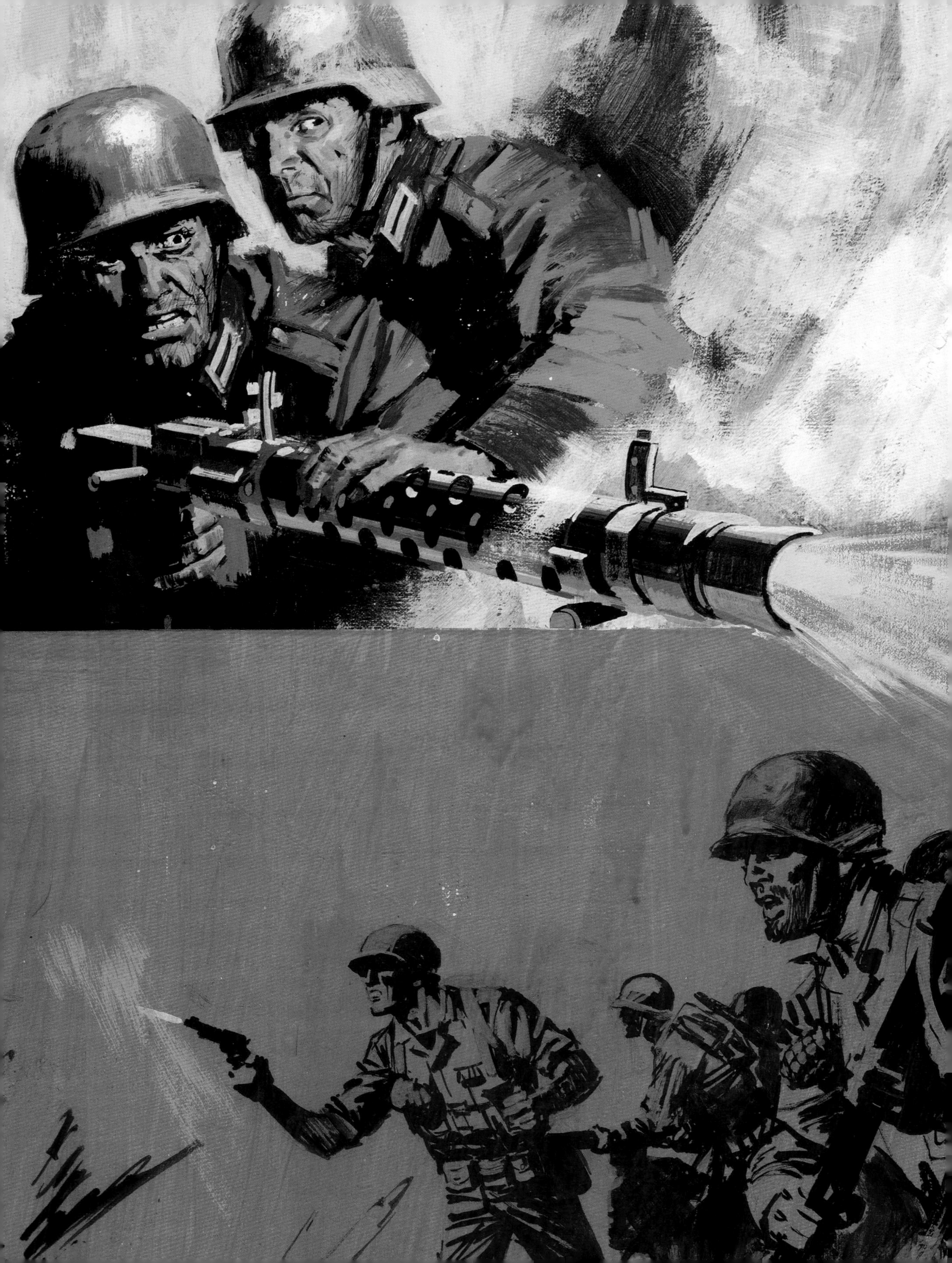

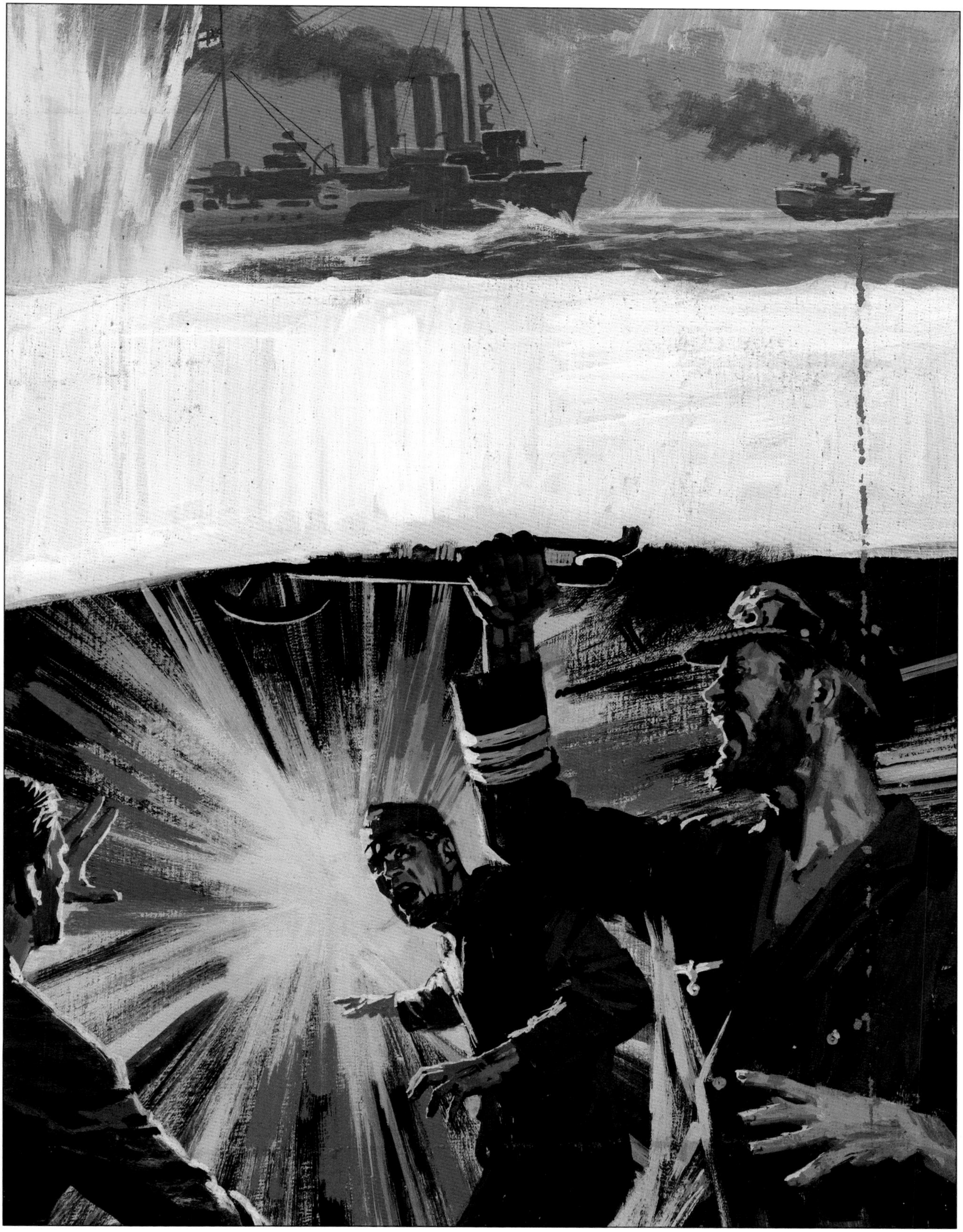

Jordi Penalva, War 318, December 1965
Opposite: Jordi Penalva, War 302, August 1965
Overleaf: Alan Willow, Air Ace 271, December 1965

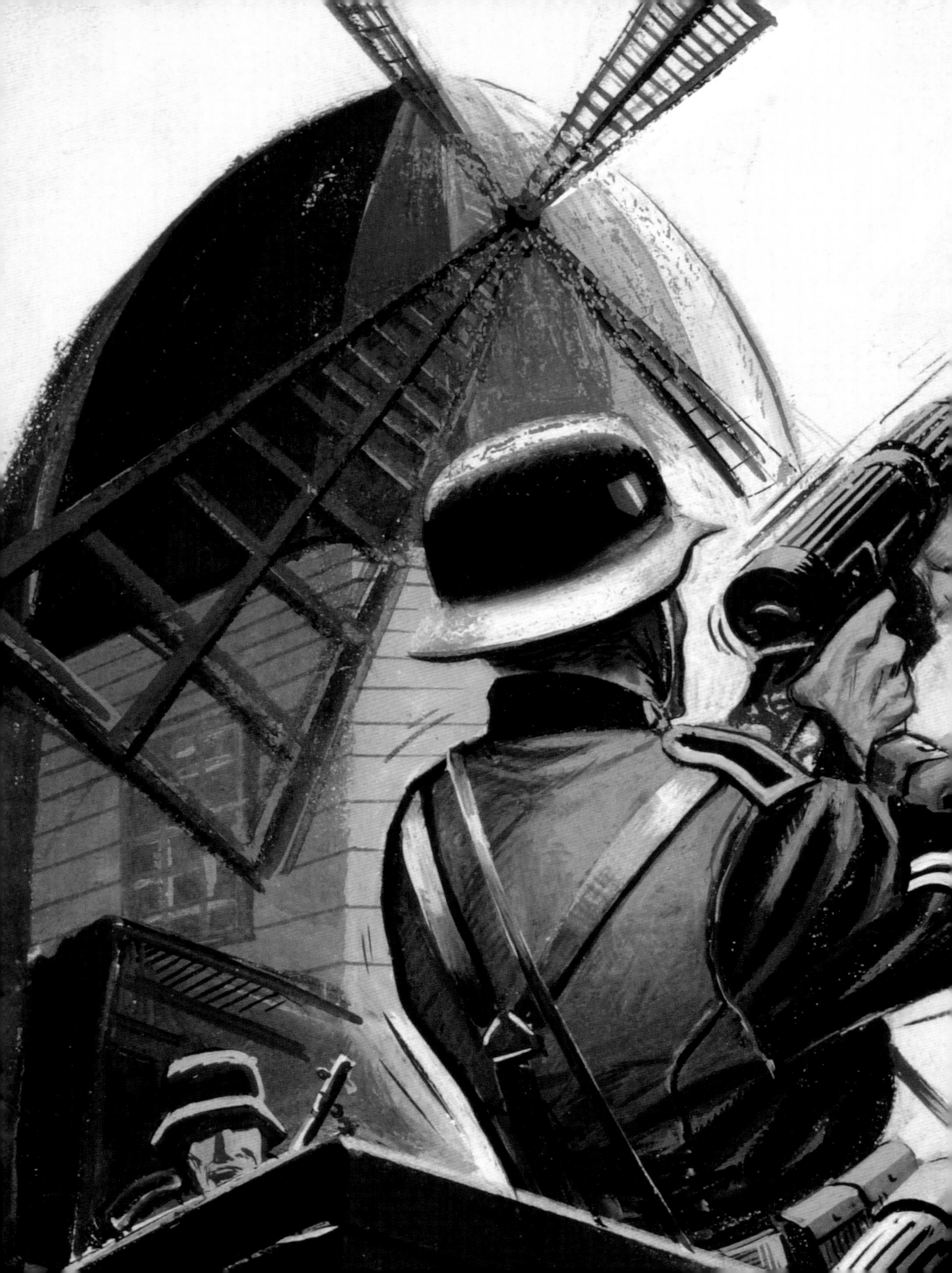

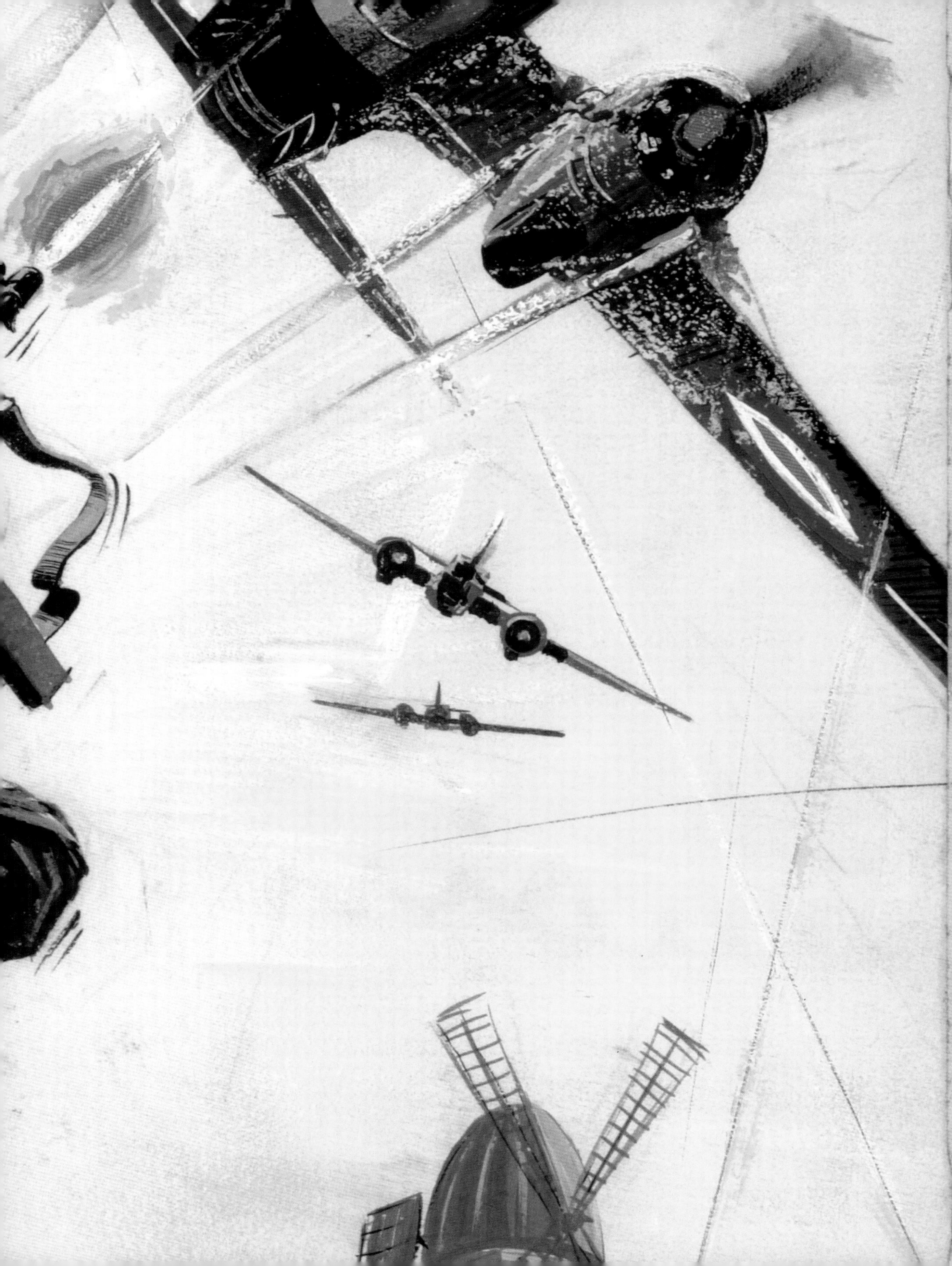

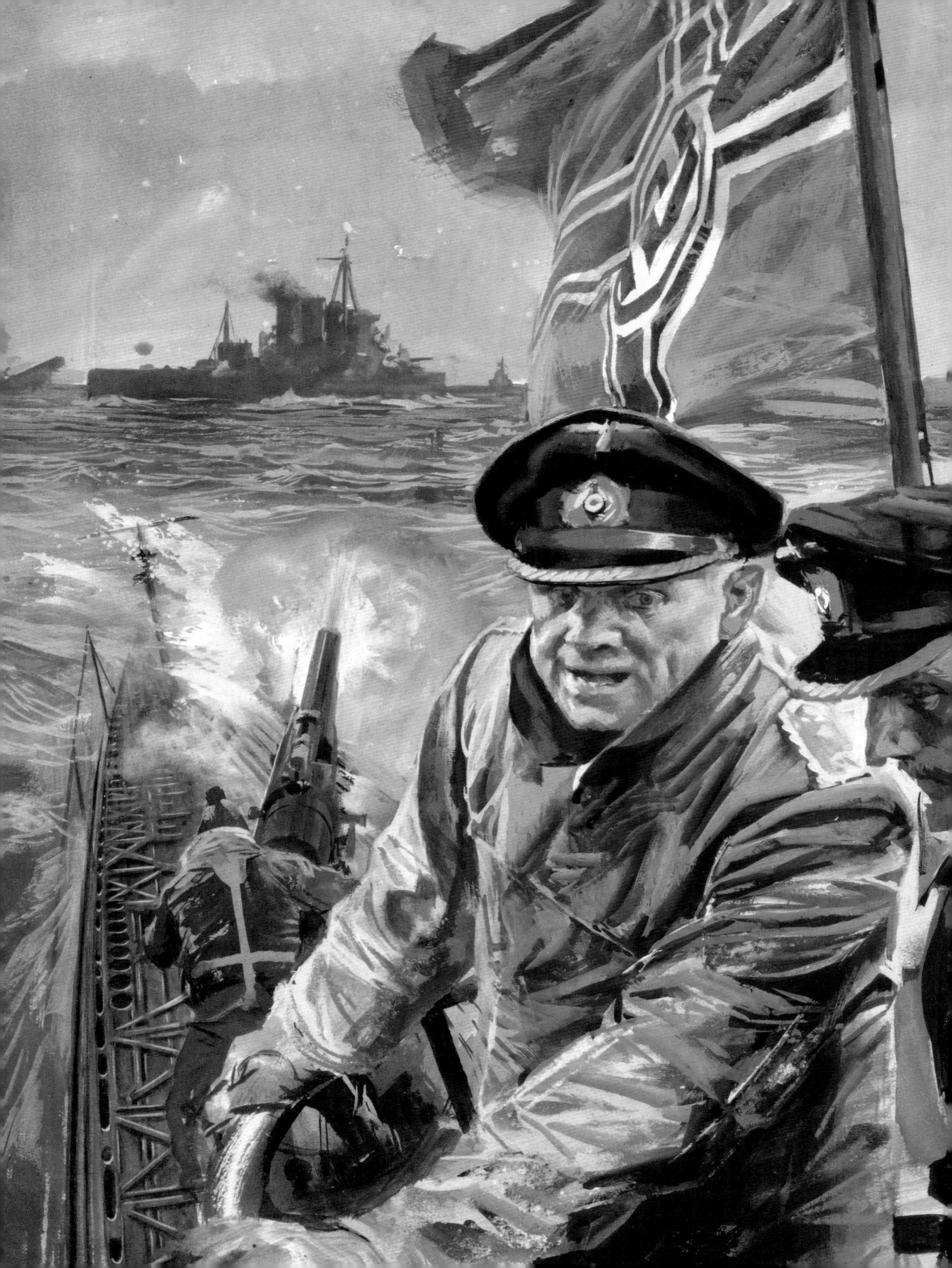

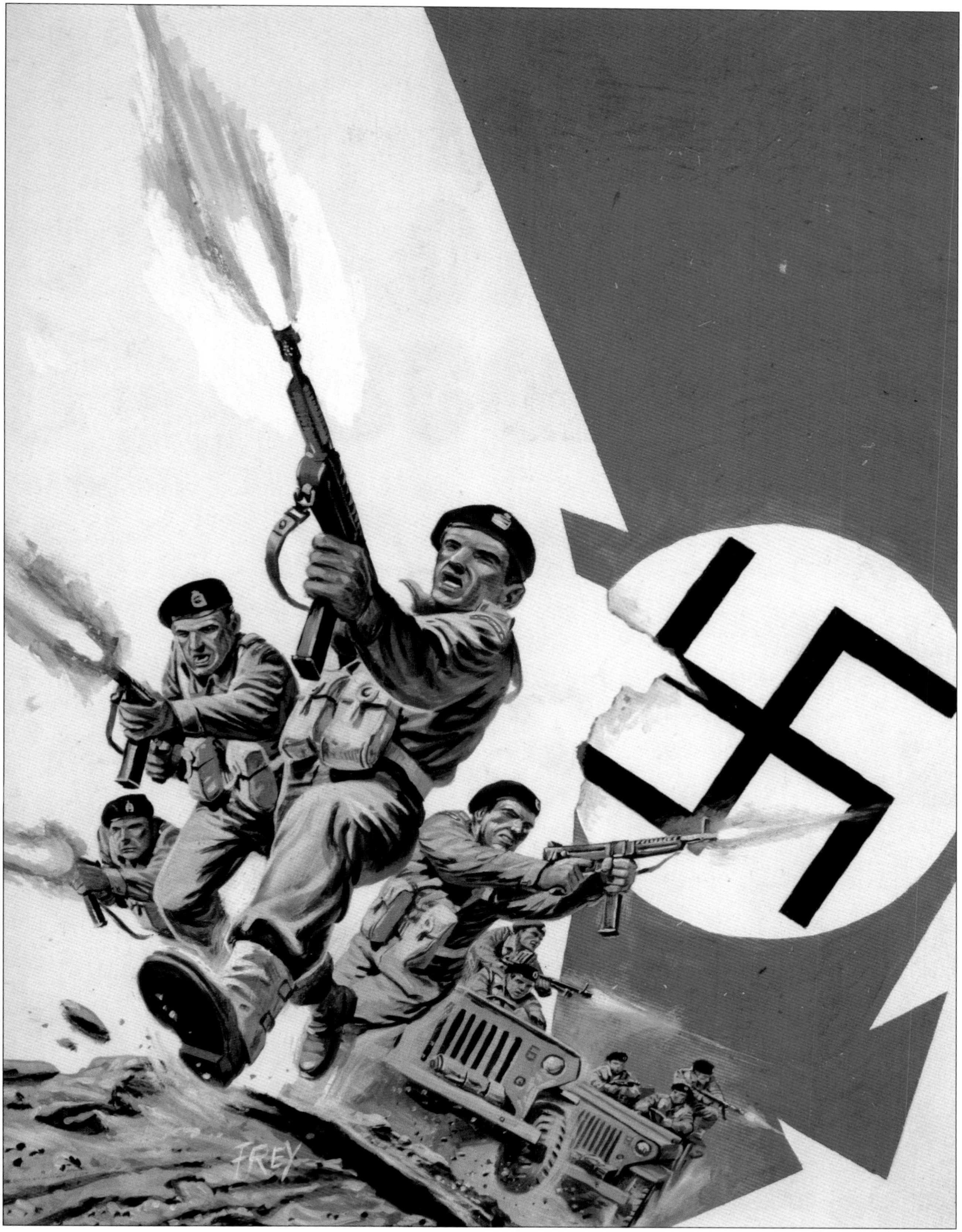
FREY

Oliver Frey, unknown
Opposite: Giorgio DeGaspari, War 475, December 1968

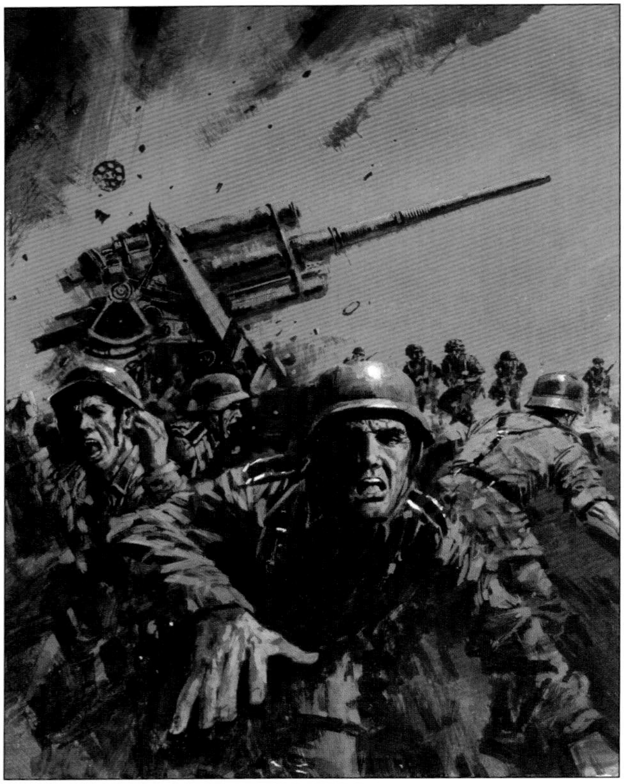

Graham Coton, Battle 1137, October 1977

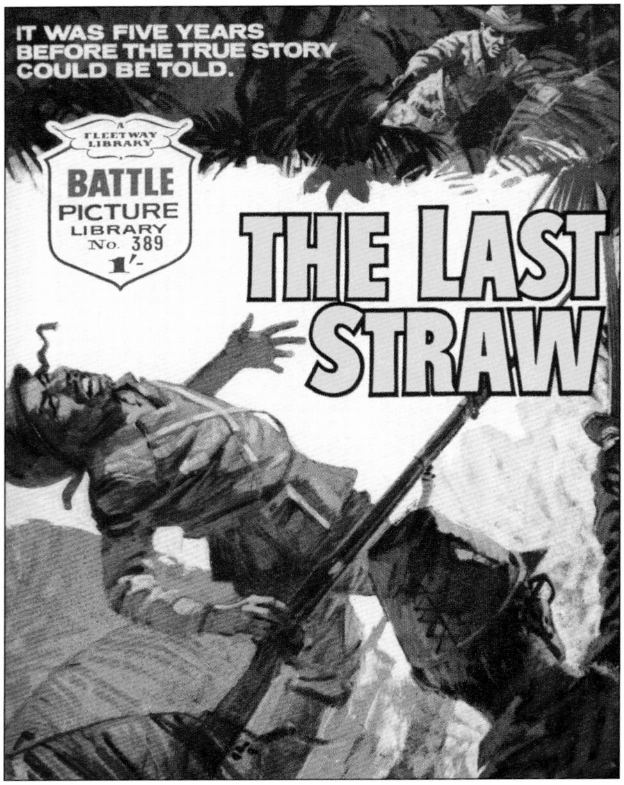
IT WAS FIVE YEARS BEFORE THE TRUE STORY COULD BE TOLD.
A FLEETWAY LIBRARY
BATTLE PICTURE LIBRARY No. 389 1/-
THE LAST STRAW

Alan Howat, Battle 389, April 1969

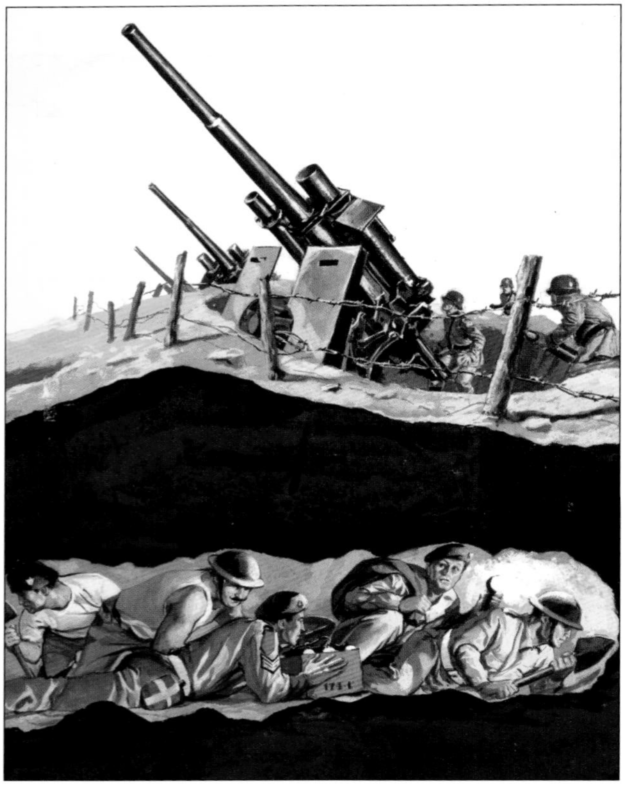

Nino Caroselli, War 371, January 1967

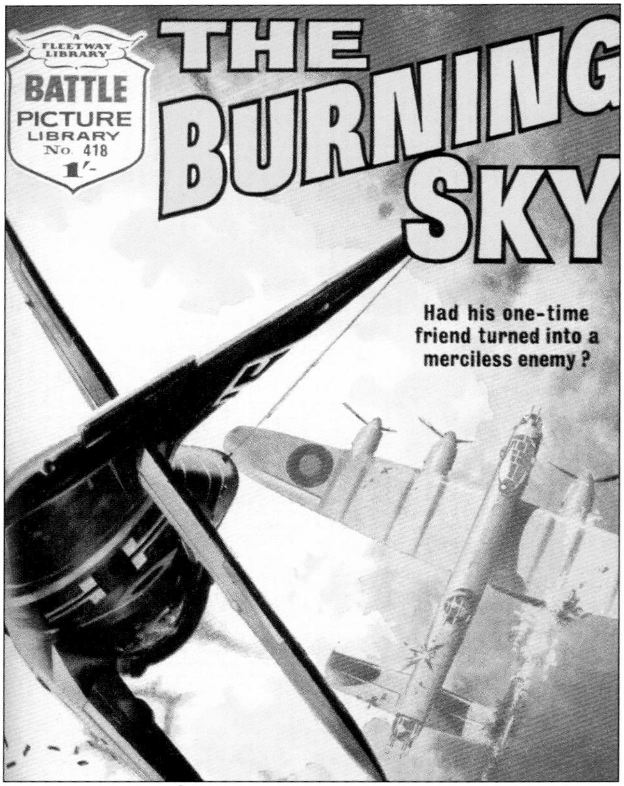
A FLEETWAY LIBRARY
BATTLE PICTURE LIBRARY No. 418 1/-
THE BURNING SKY
Had his one-time friend turned into a merciless enemy?

Ian Kennedy, Battle 418, September 1969

Opposite: Graham Coton, War 1848, April 1981
Overleaf: Graham Coton, War 970, August 1974

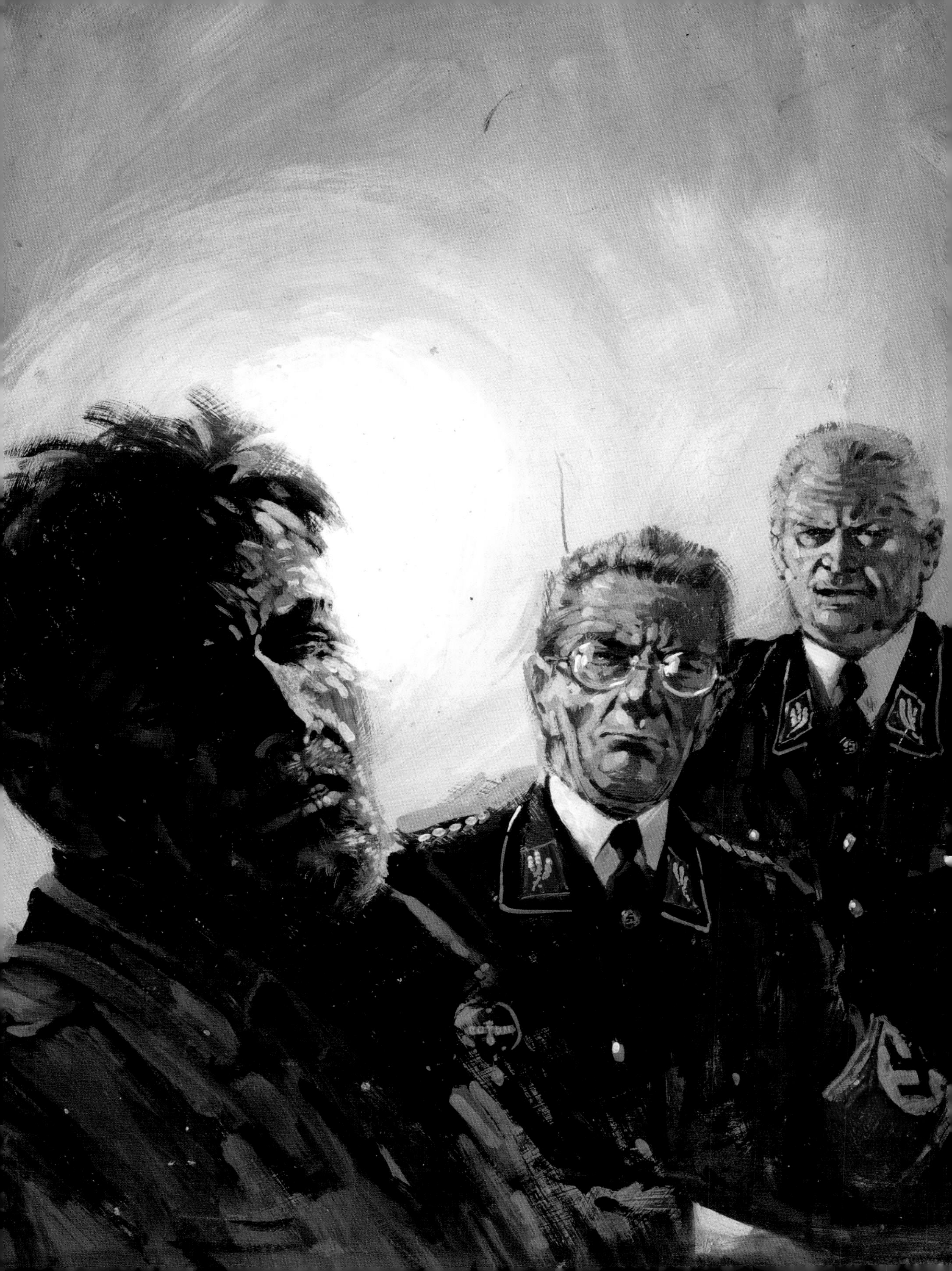

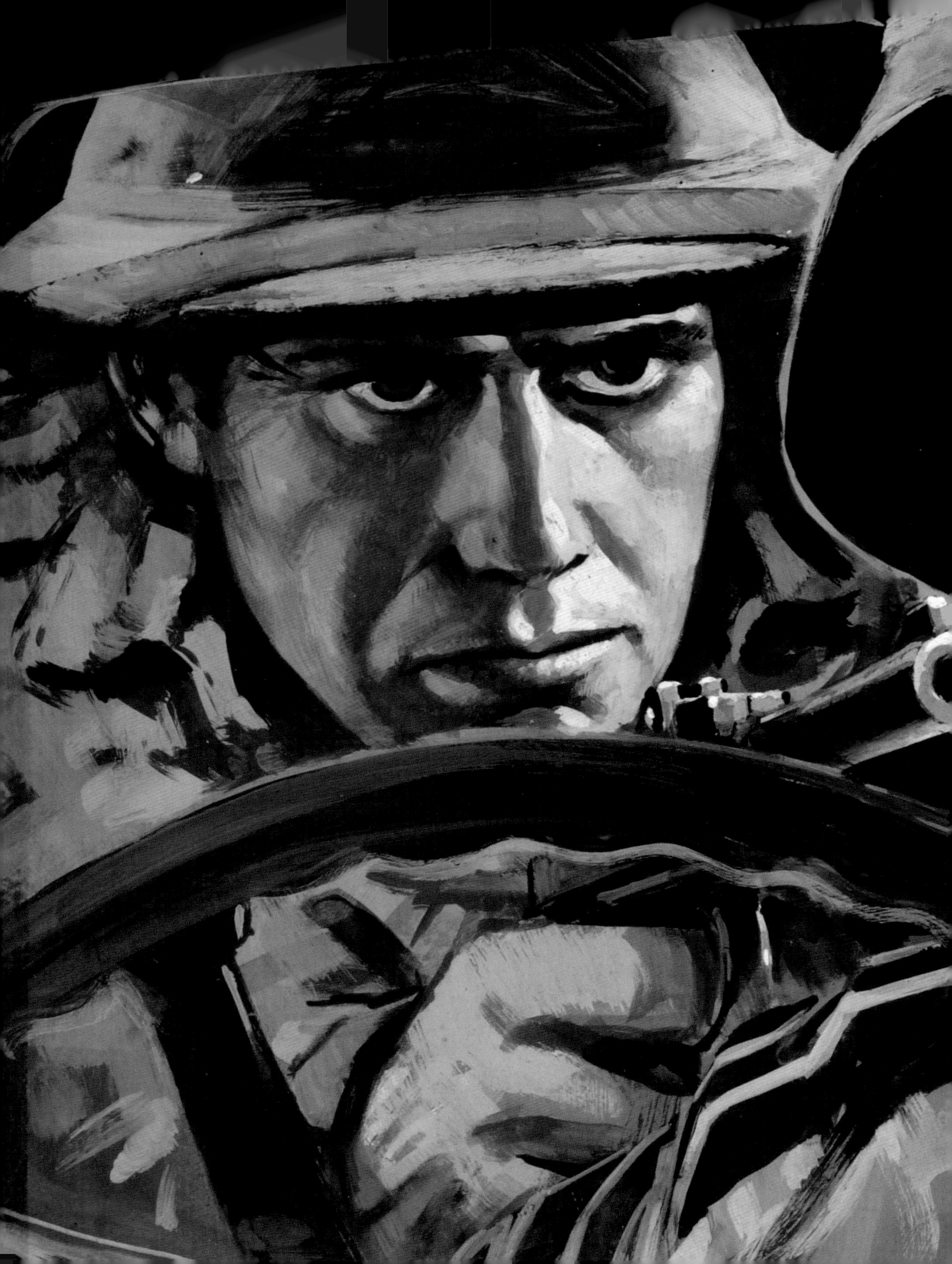

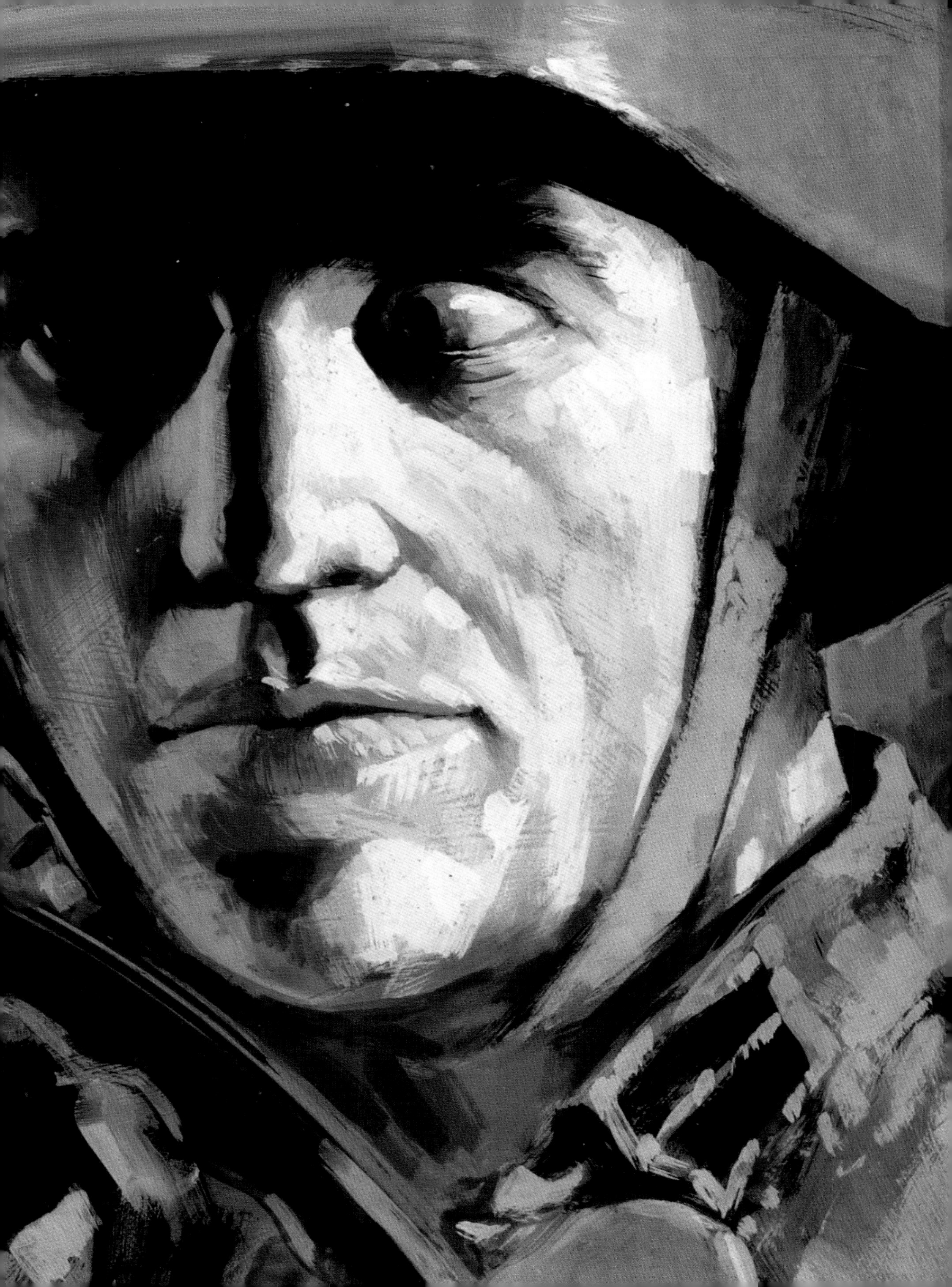

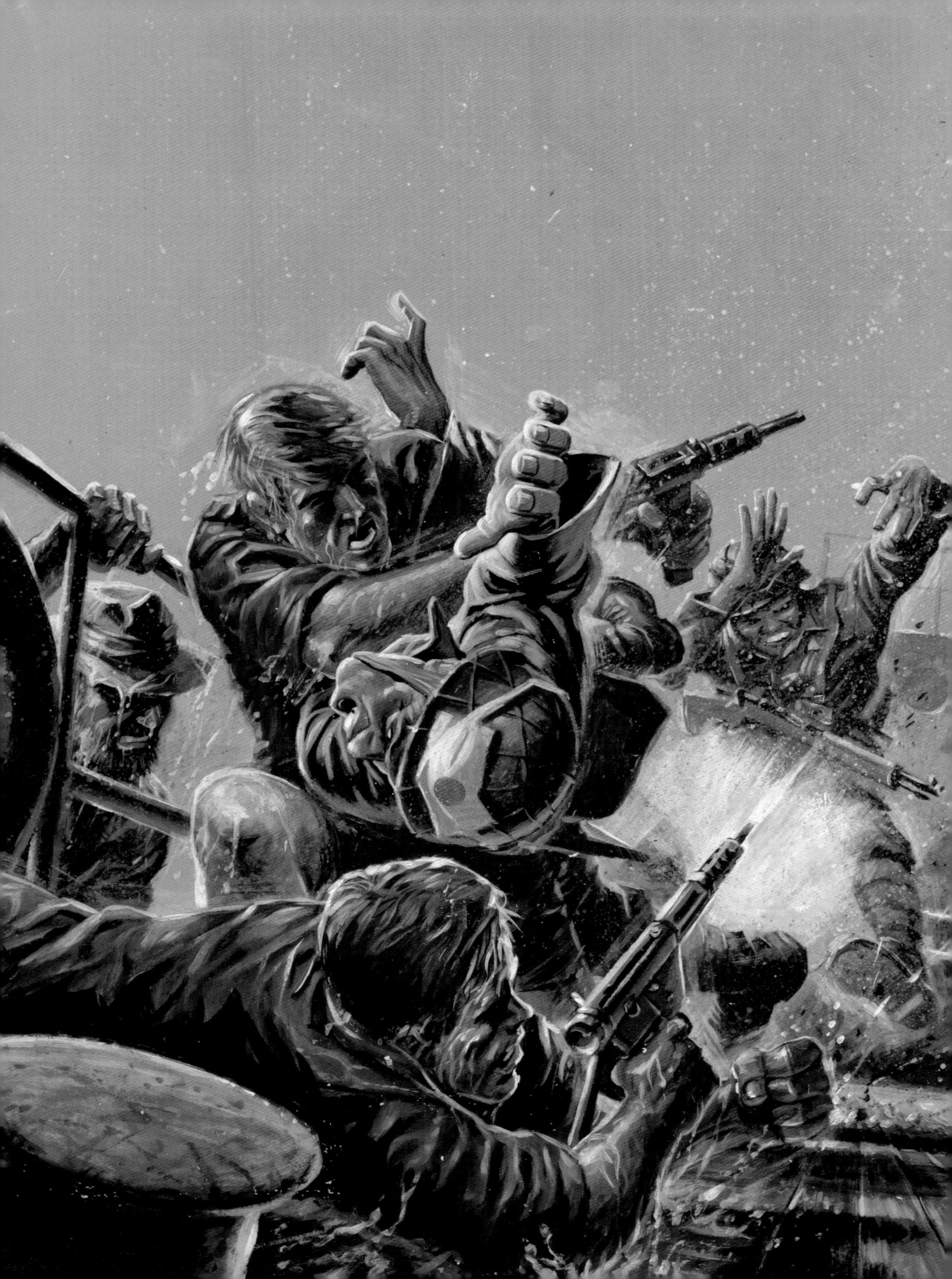

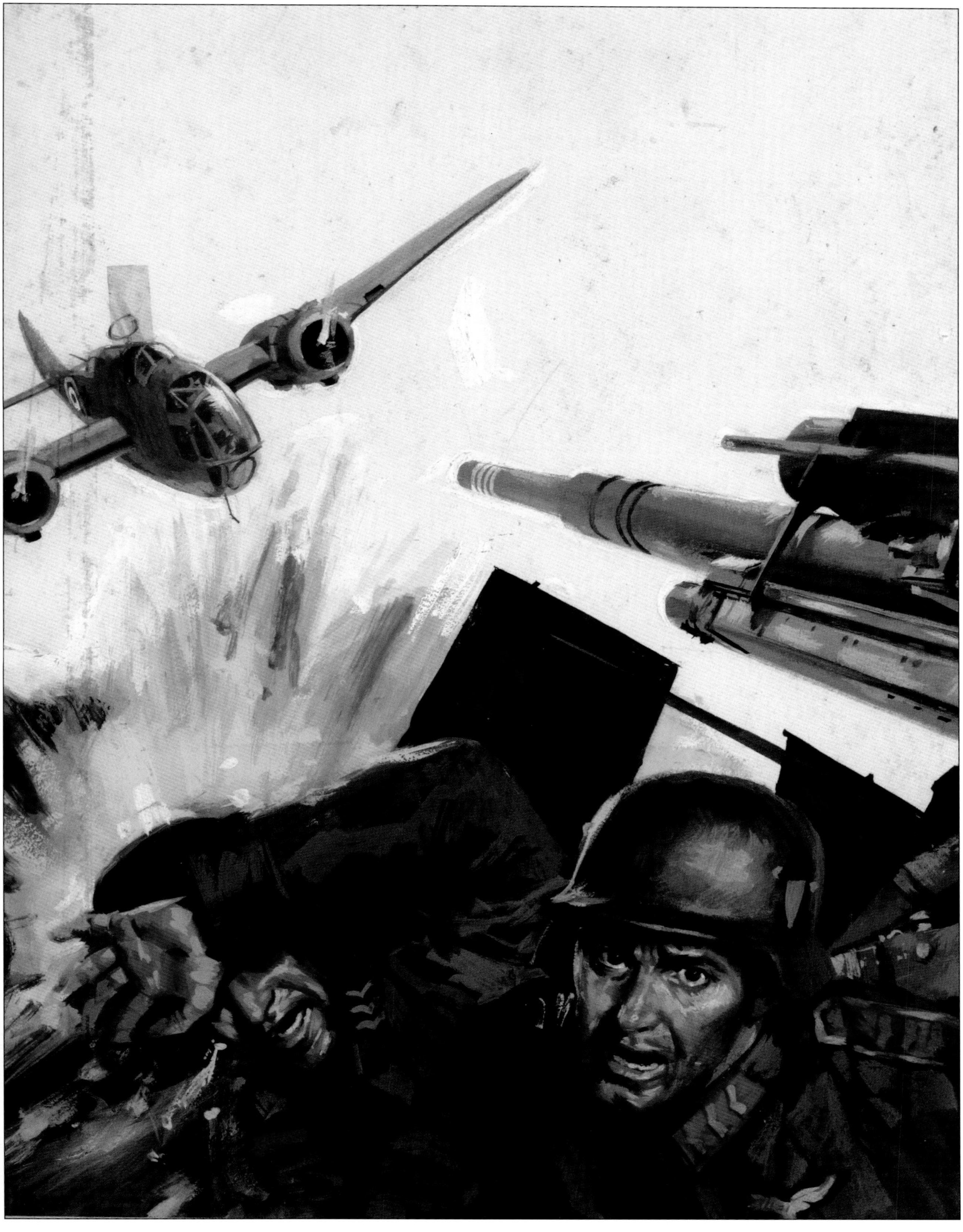

Pino Dell'Orco, War 187, March 1963
Opposite: Oliver Frey, War 945, May 1974

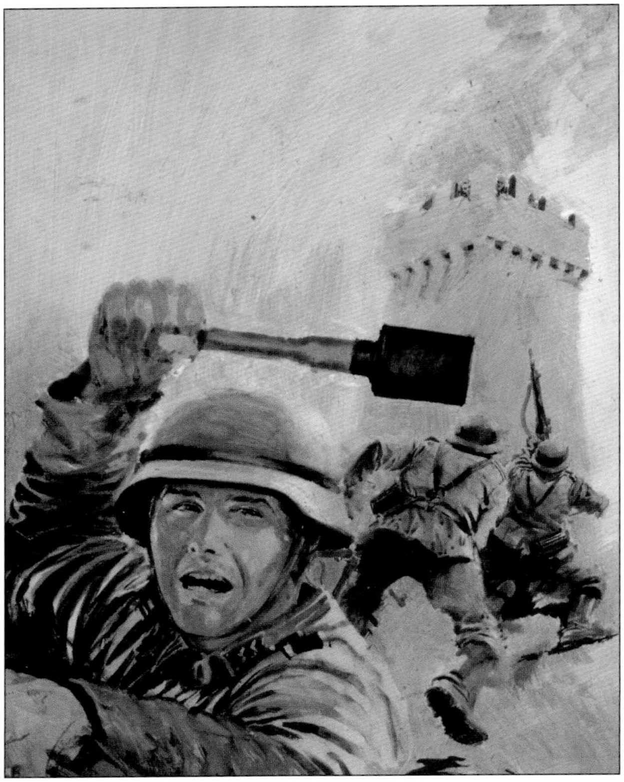

Graham Coton, War 768, July 1972

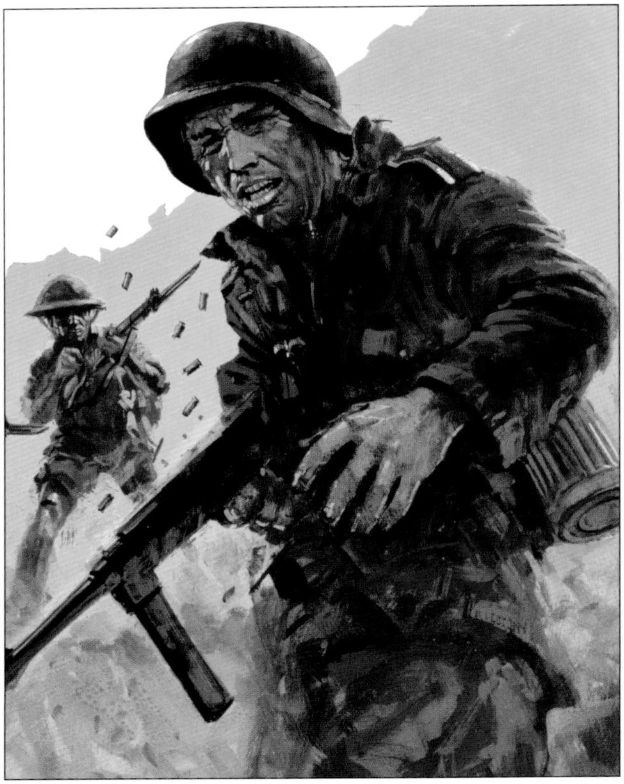

Graham Coton, War 1206, May 1976

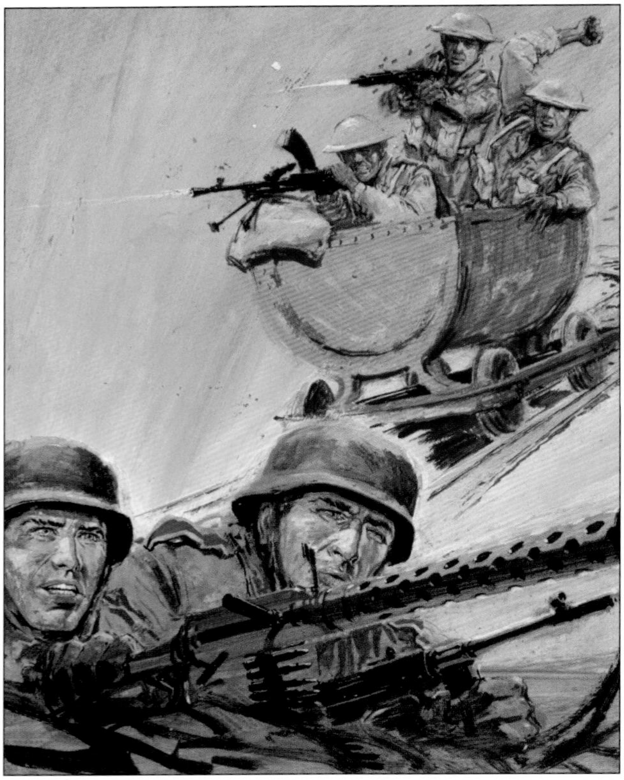

Graham Coton, War 555, December 1969

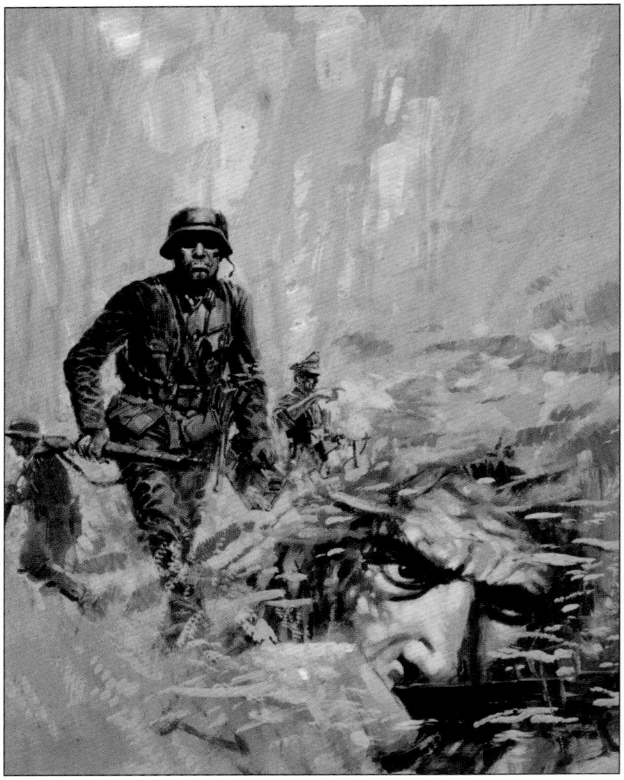

Graham Coton, War 721, January 1972

Opposite: Nino Caroselli, War 285, April 1965

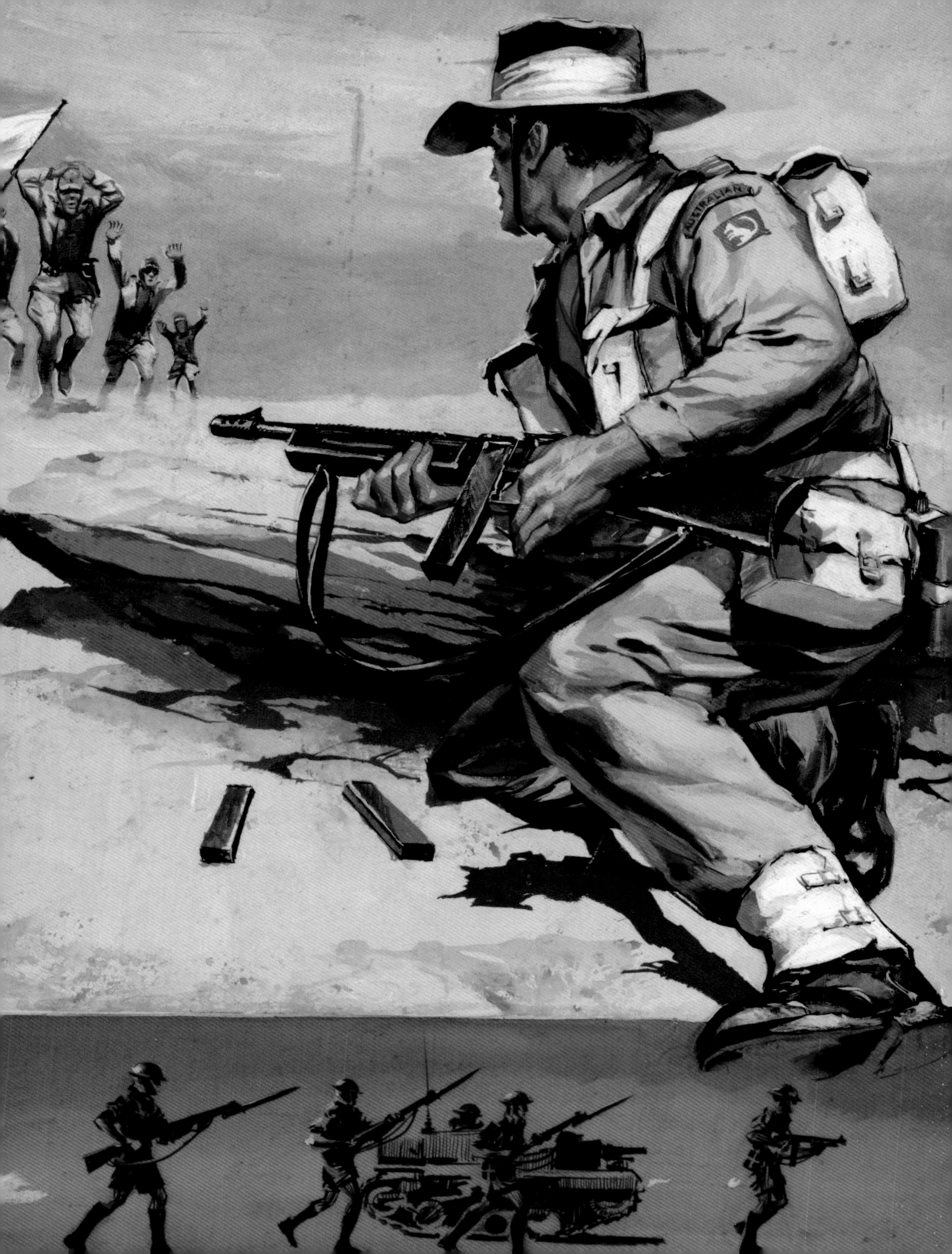
AUSTRALIAN

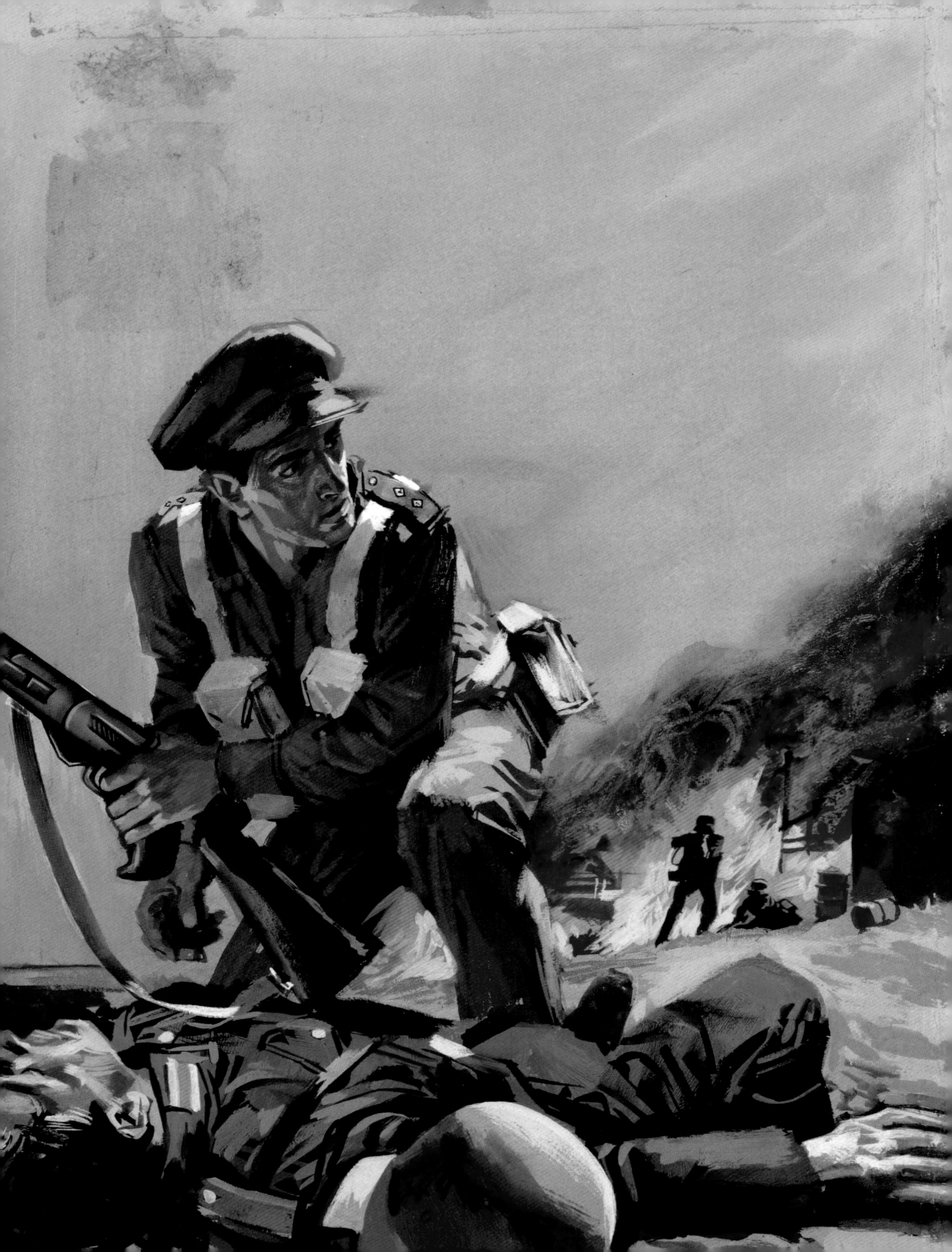

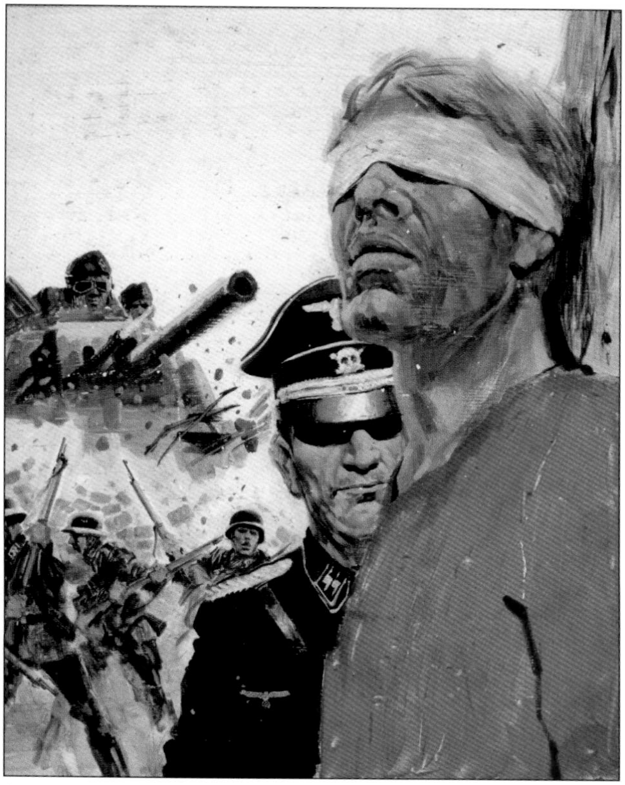
Graham Coton, War 620, November 1970

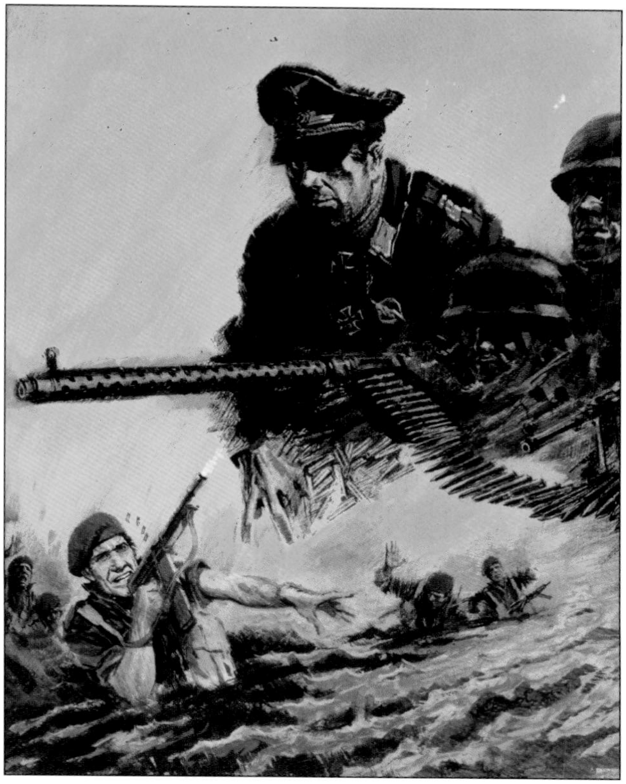
Graham Coton, War 599, July 1970

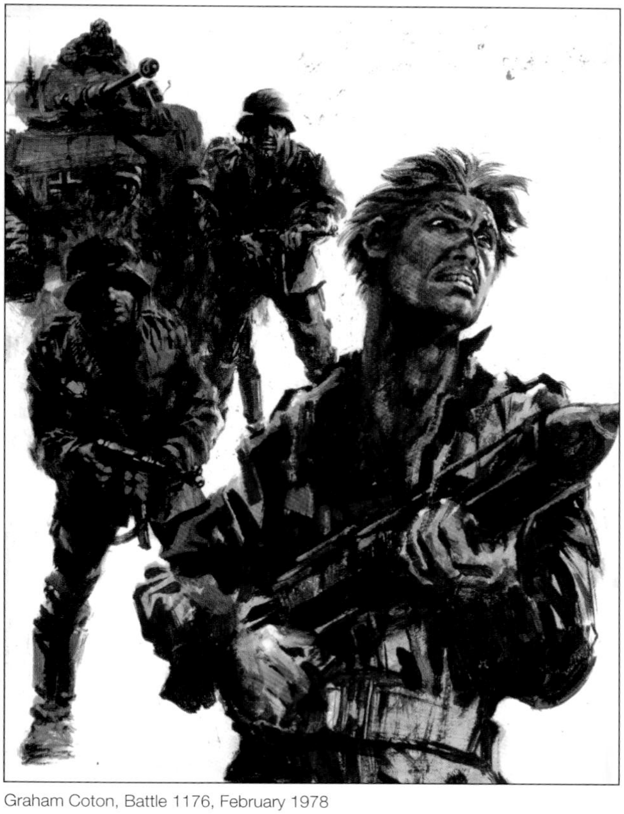
Graham Coton, Battle 1176, February 1978

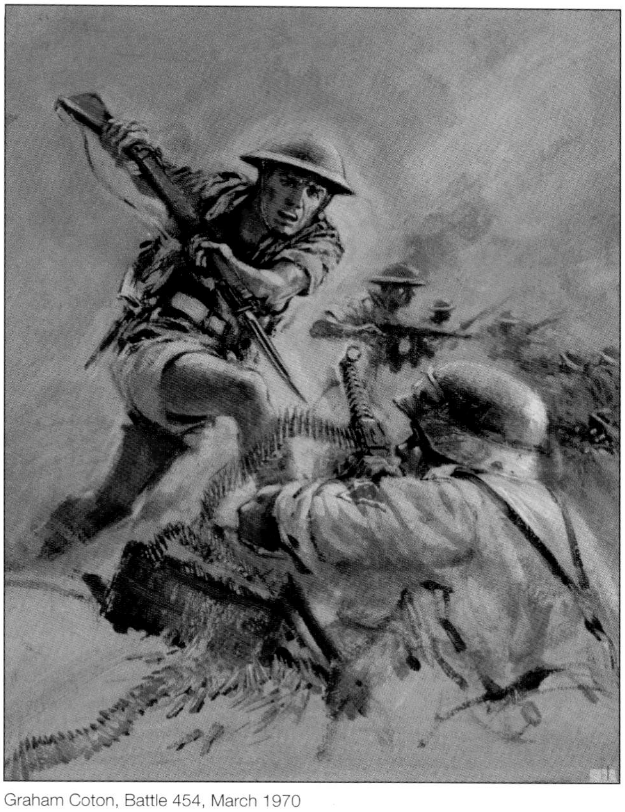
Graham Coton, Battle 454, March 1970

Opposite: Pino Dell'Orco, War 115, September 1961

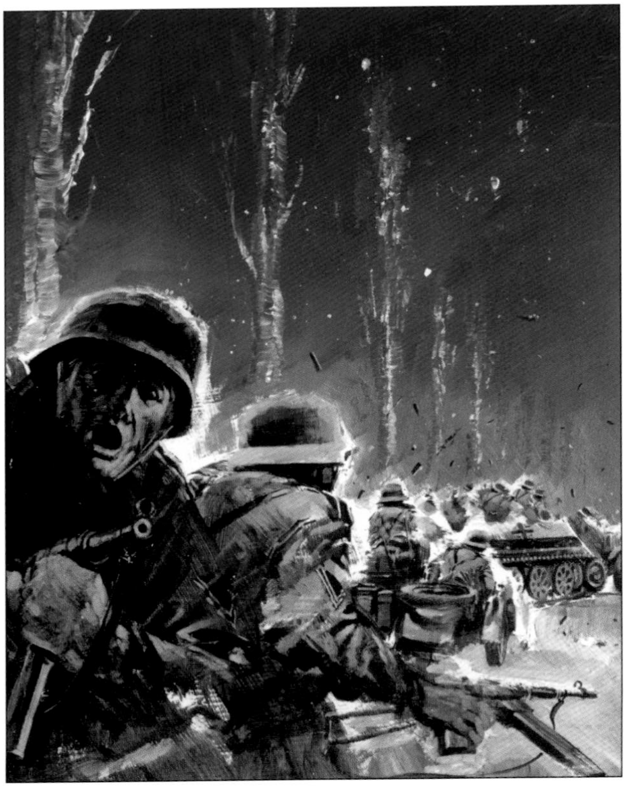

Graham Coton, Battle 563, October 1971

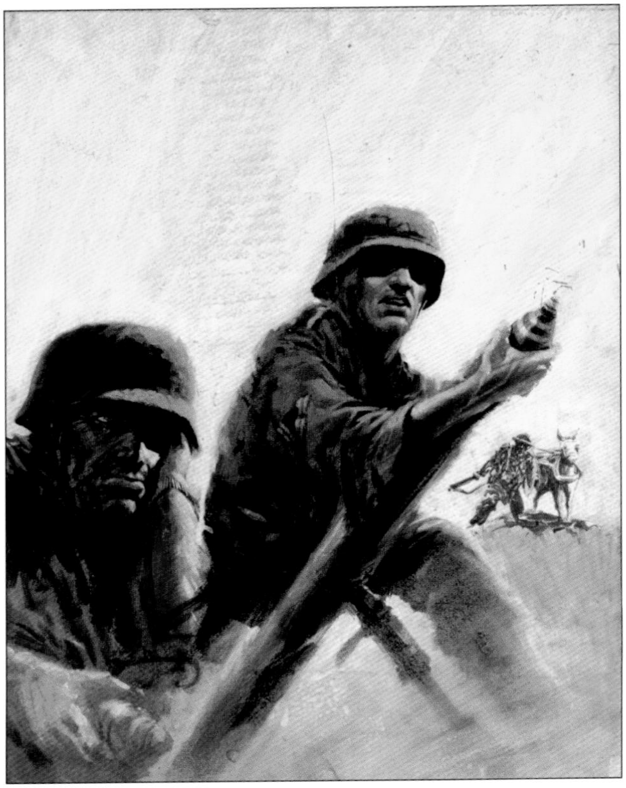

Graham Coton, War 604, August 1970

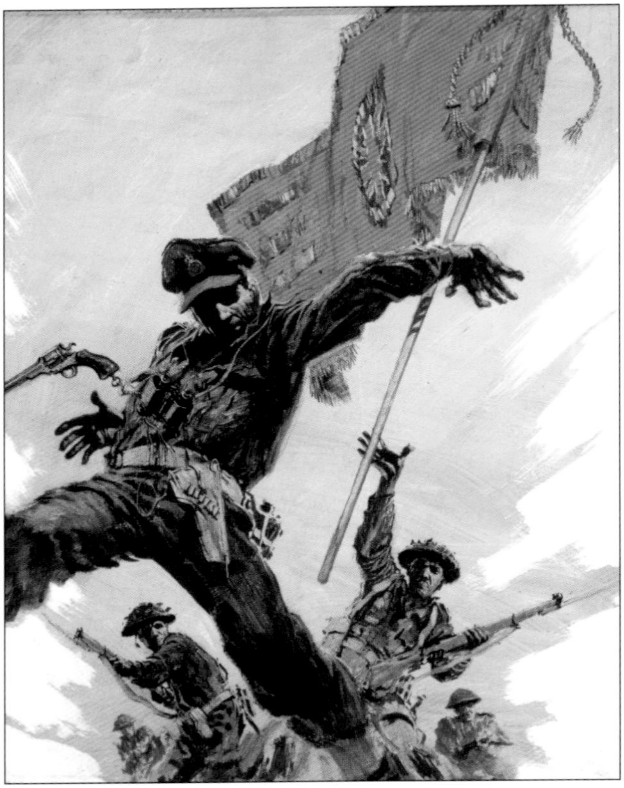

Graham Coton, War 560, January 1970

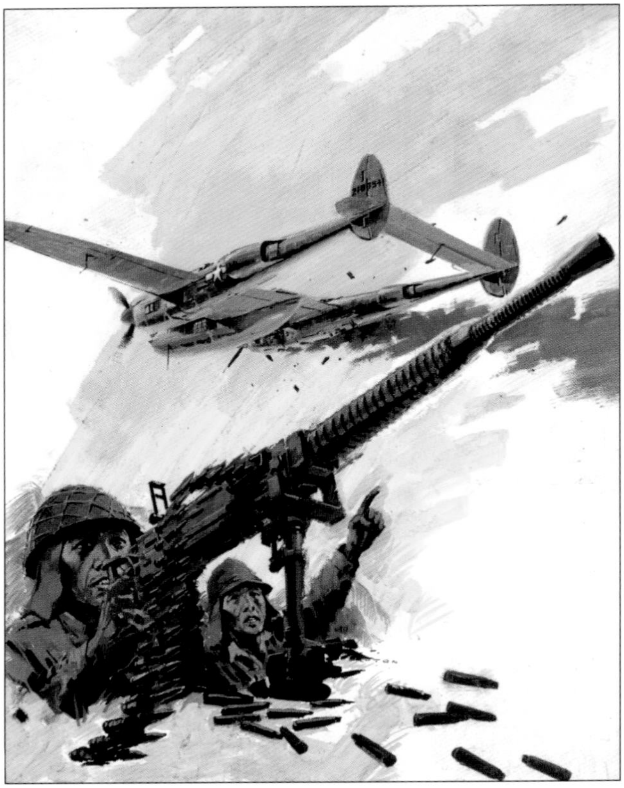

Graham Coton, War 824, February 1973

Opposite: Graham Coton, Battle 1523, April 1982
Overleaf: Graham Coton, War 769, July 1972

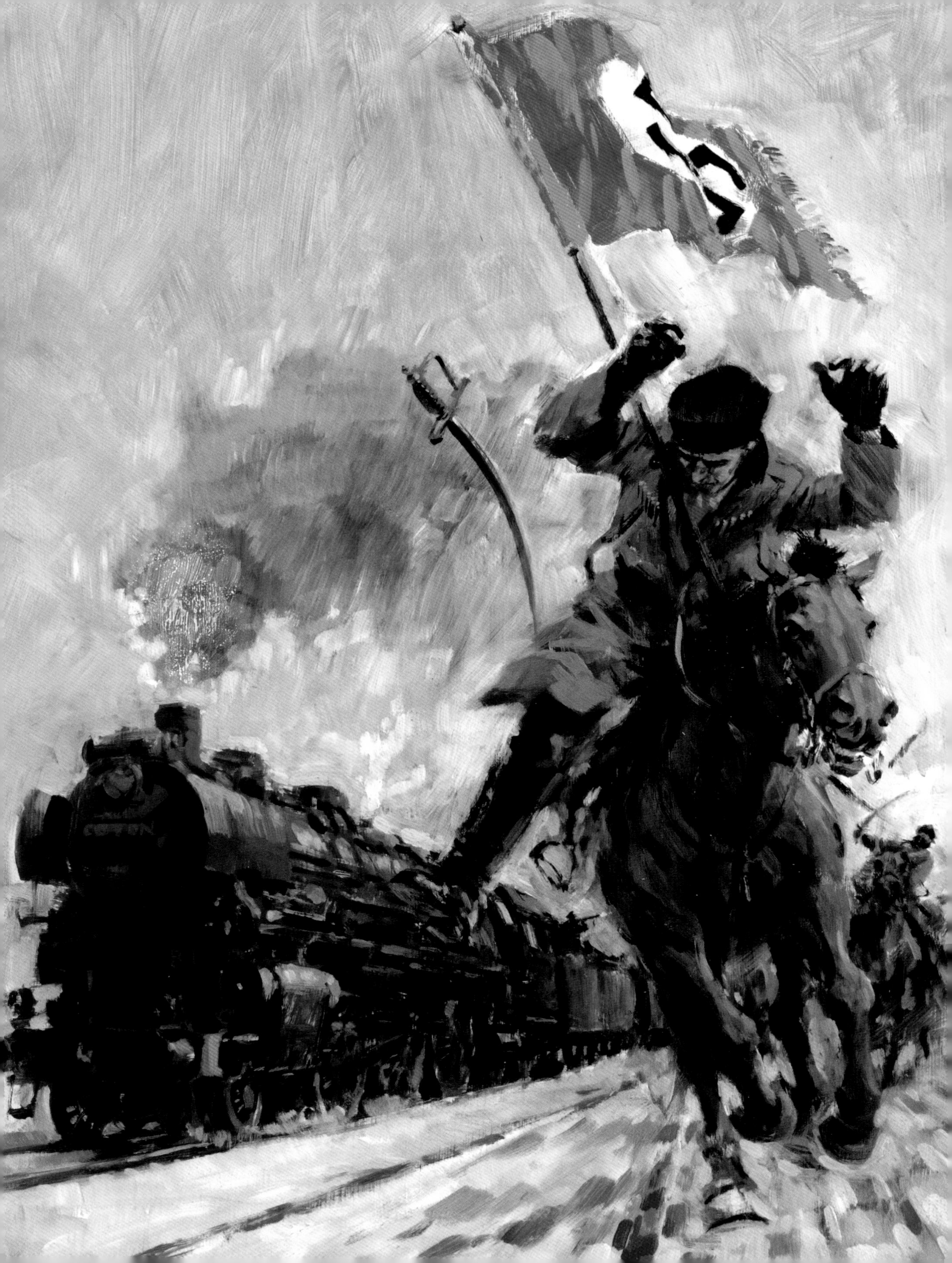

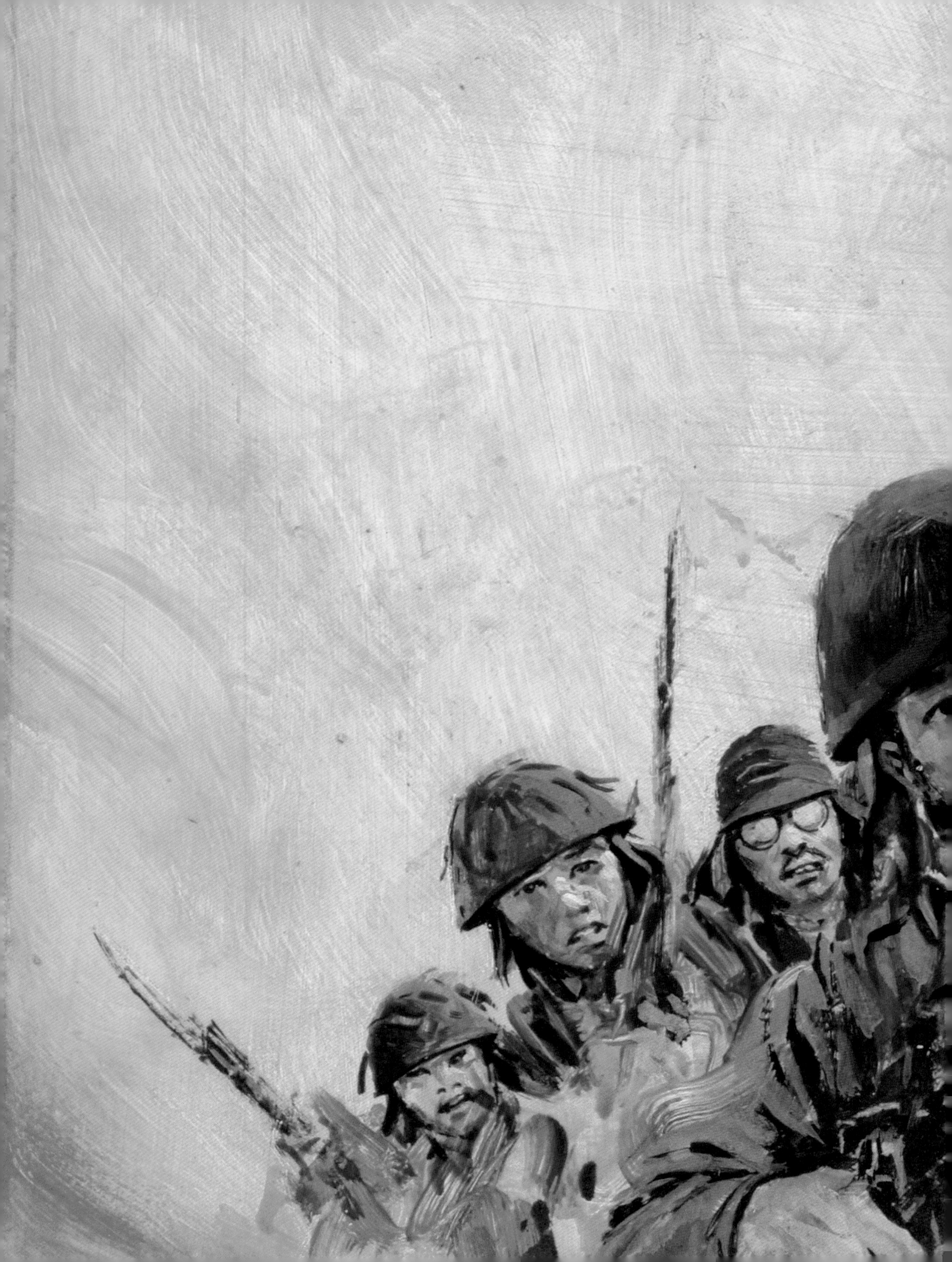

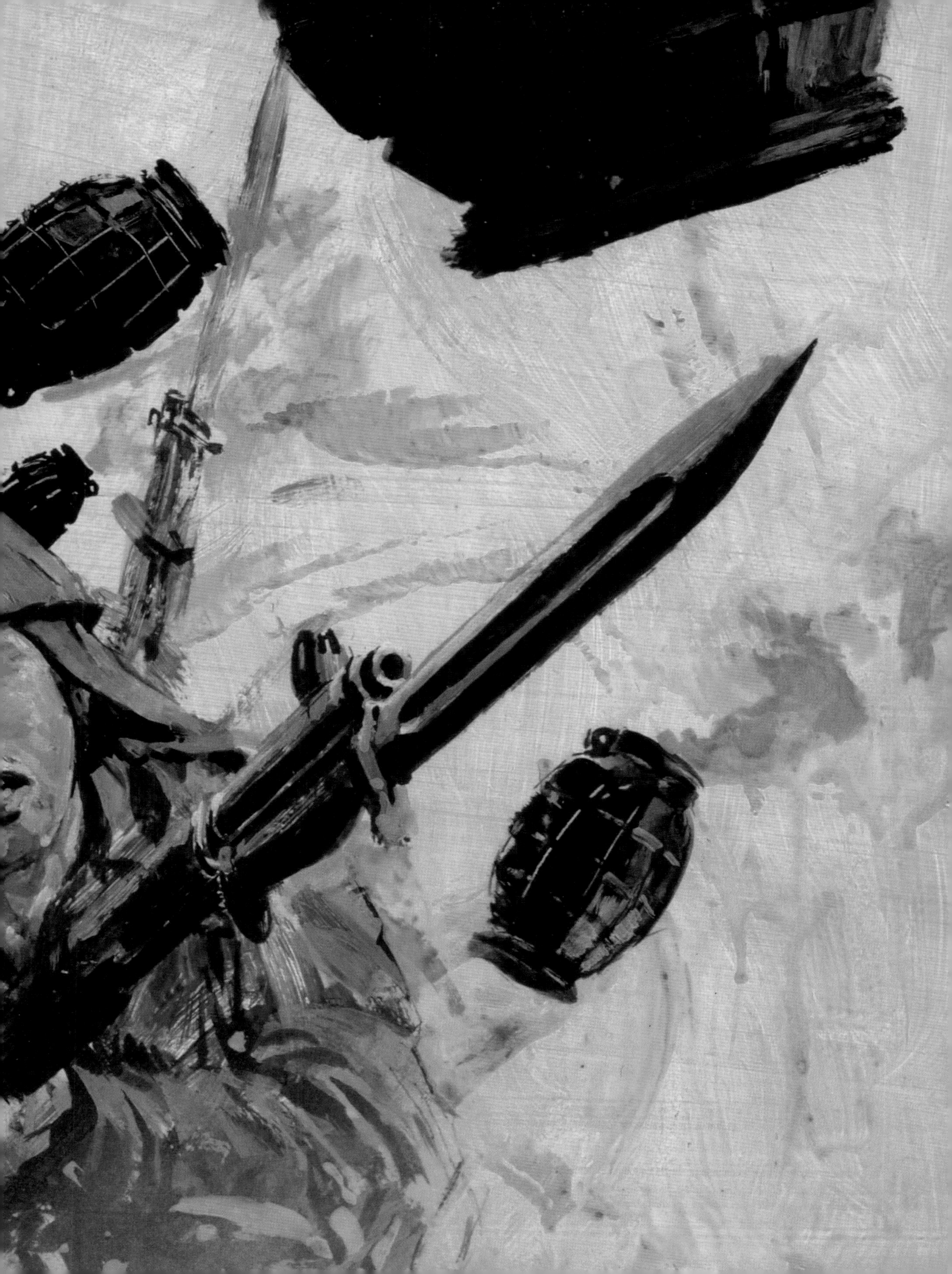

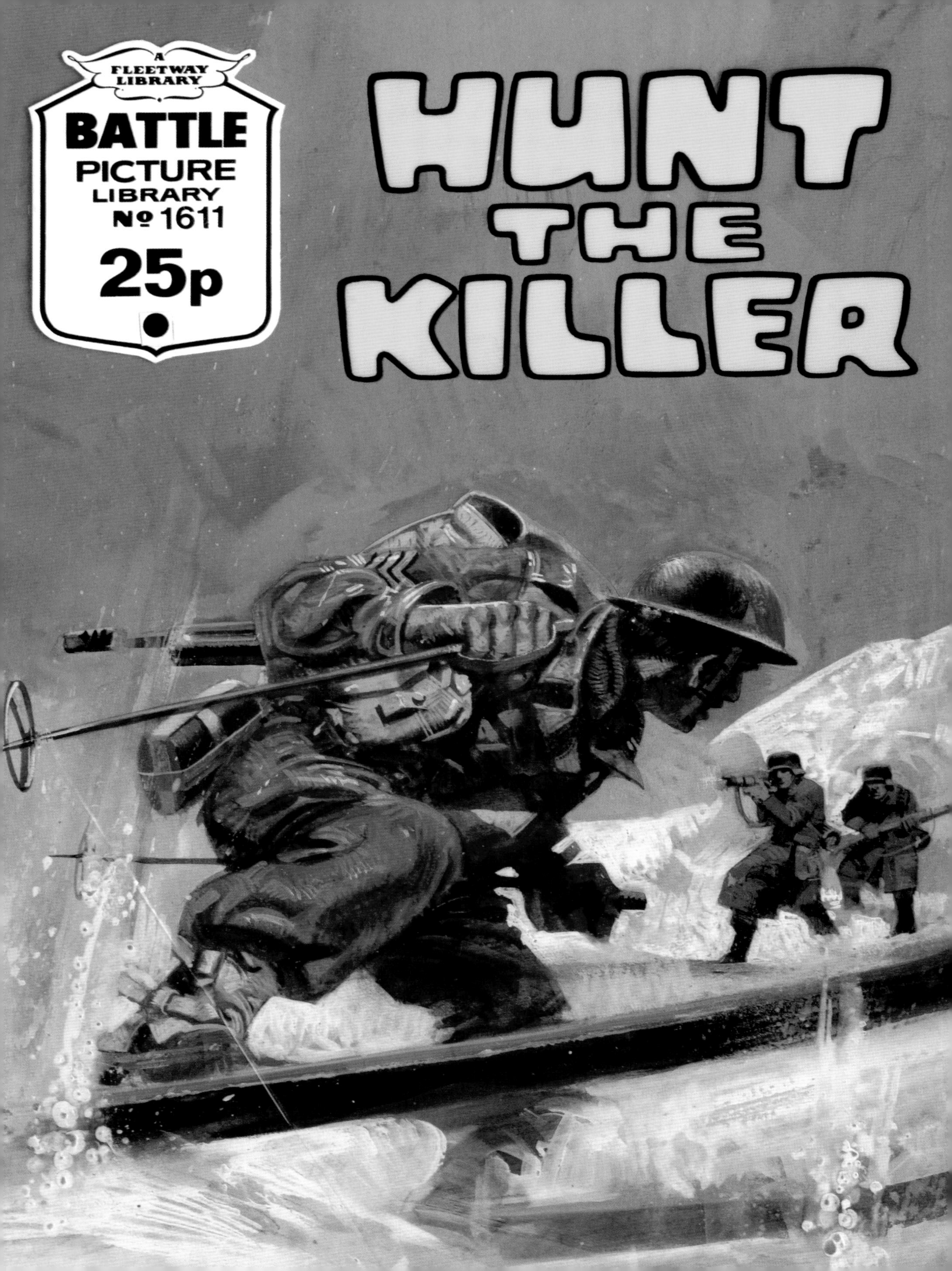
A
FLEETWAY
LIBRARY
BATTLE
PICTURE
LIBRARY
No 1611
25p
HUNT
THE
KILLER

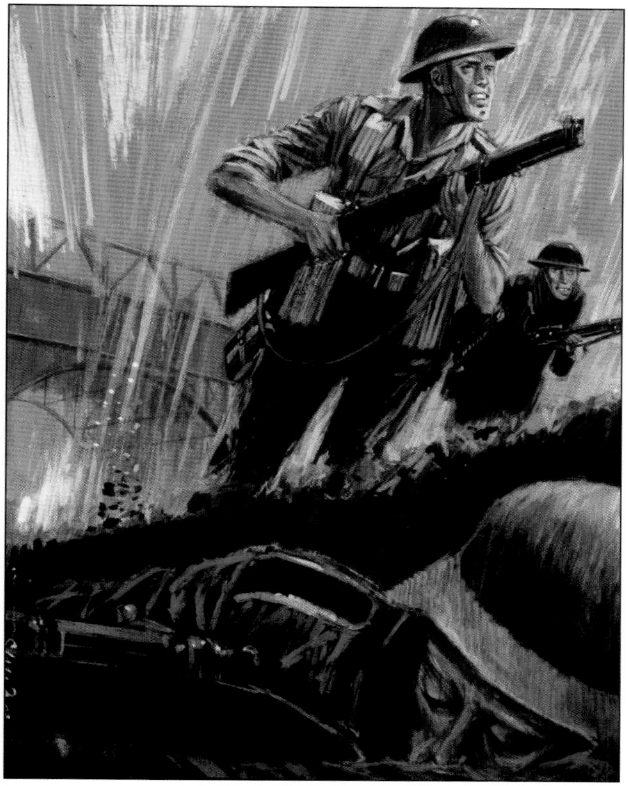

Jose Luis Macias, Battle 293, April 1967

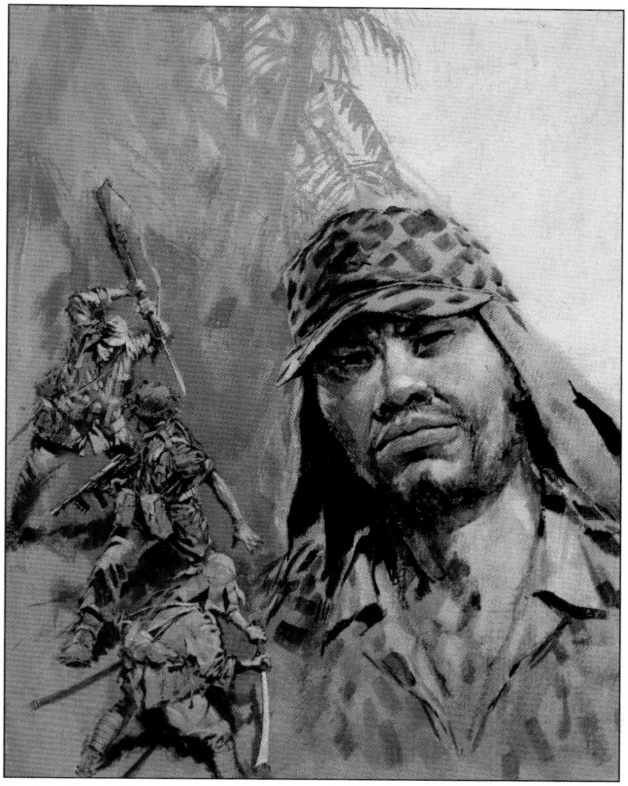

Graham Coton, Battle 475, July 1970

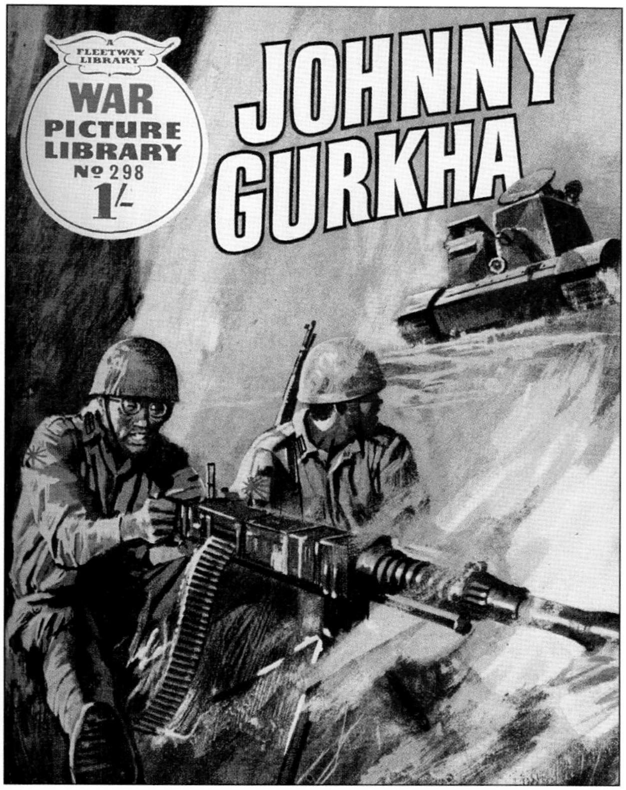
A FLEETWAY LIBRARY
WAR
PICTURE
LIBRARY
Nº 298
1/-
JOHNNY
GURKHA

Allessandro Biffignandi, War 298, July 1965

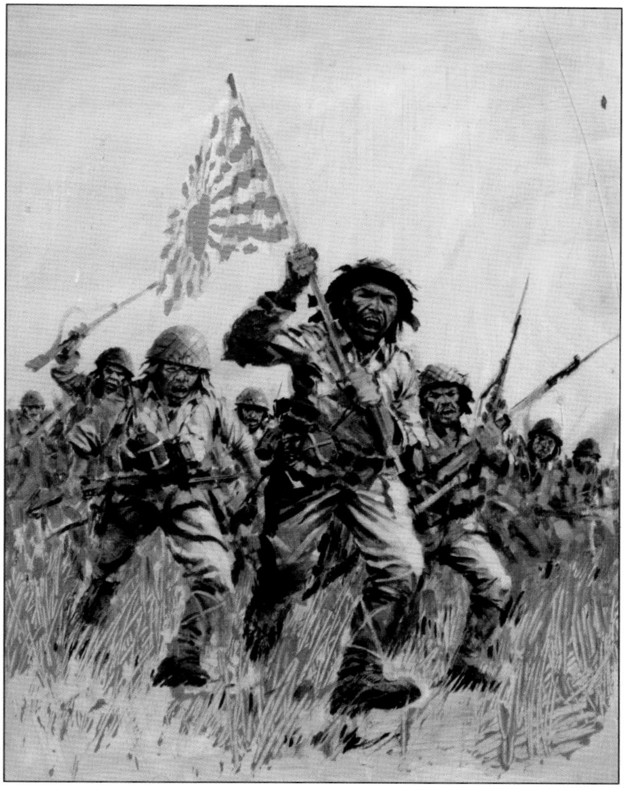

Graham Coton, War 1518, July 1978

Opposite: Allessandro Biffignandi, originally Battle 333, February 1968

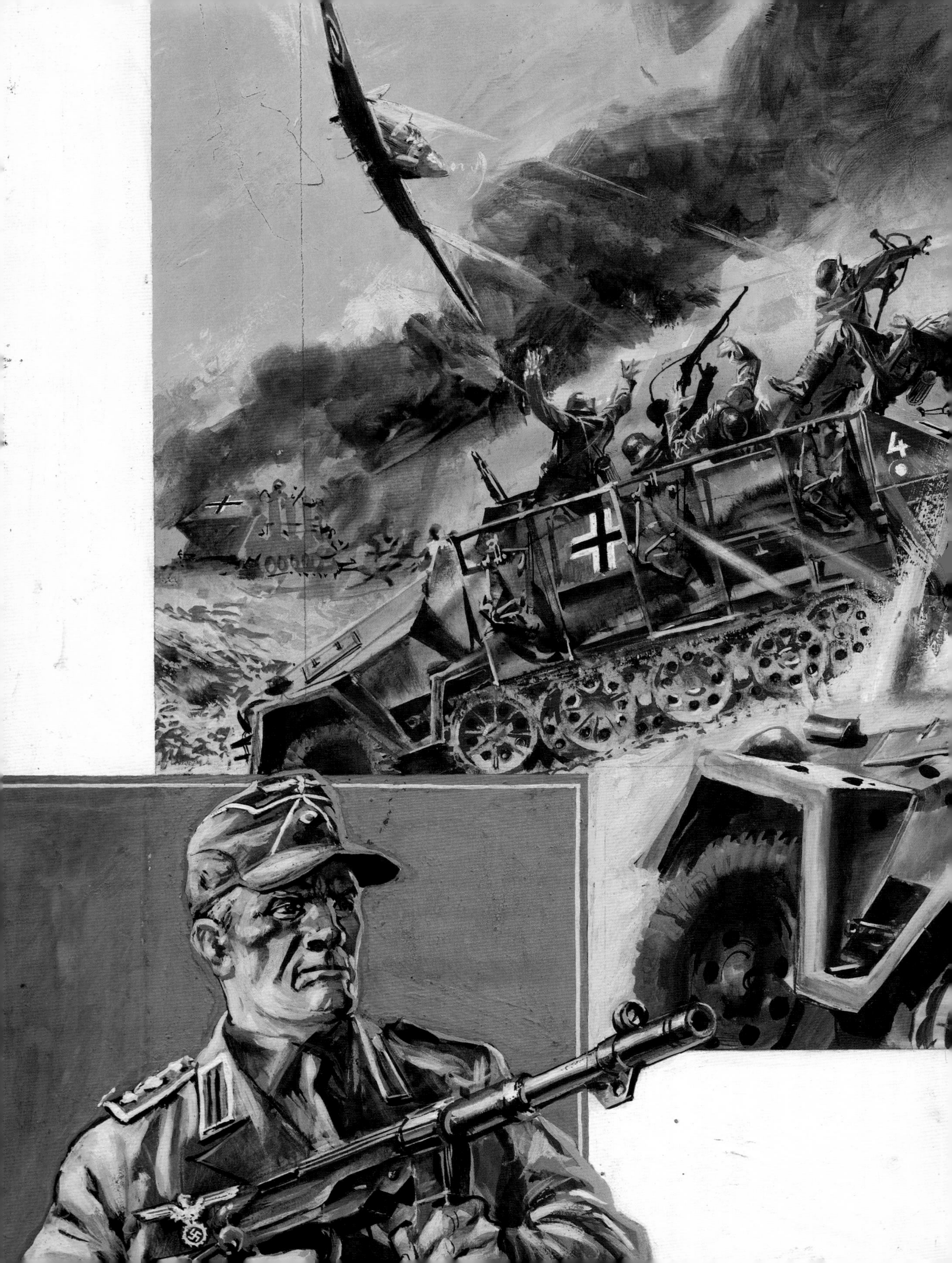

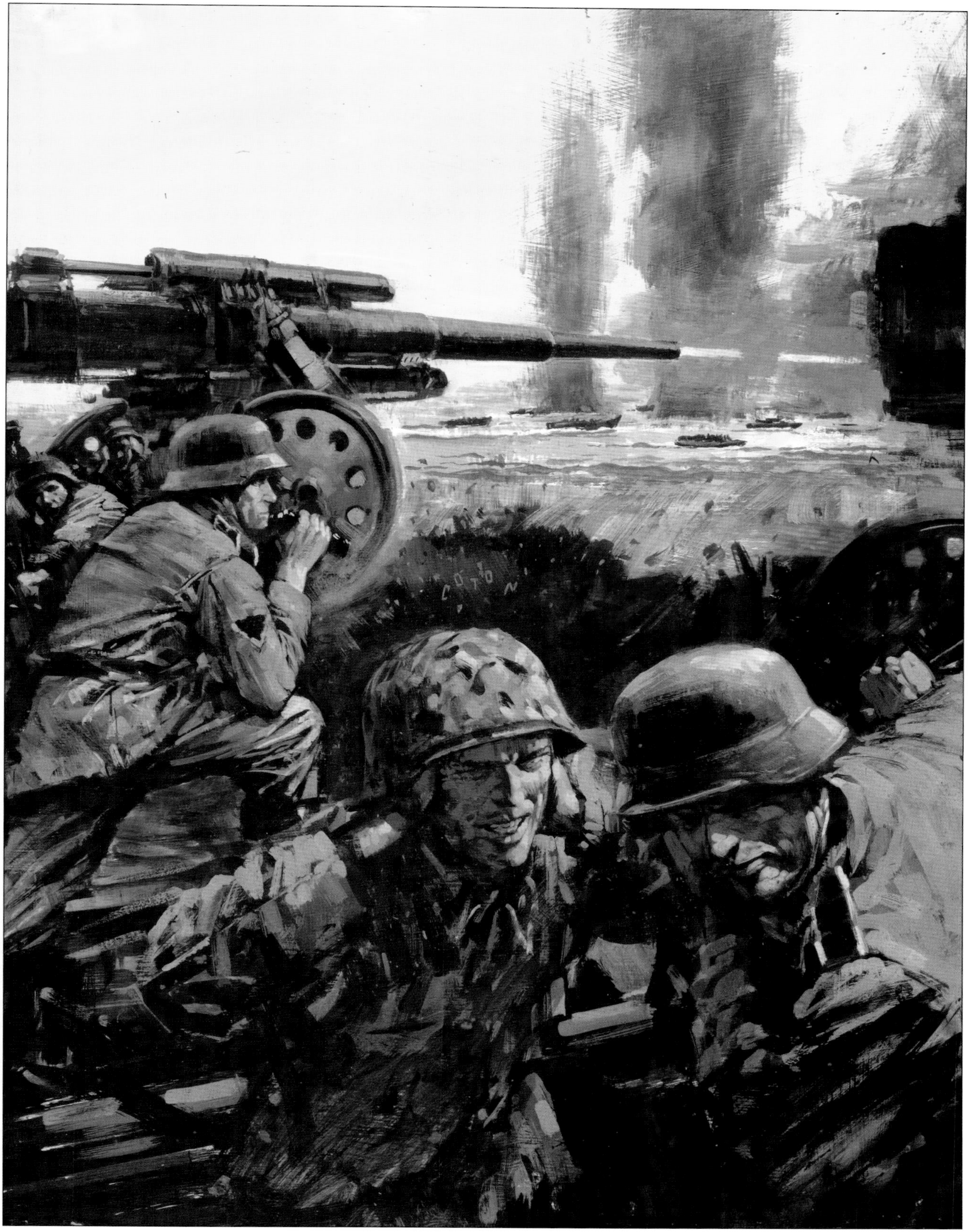
COTON

Graham Coton, War 1169, January 1976
Opposite: Giorgio DeGaspari, Air Ace 22, September 1960

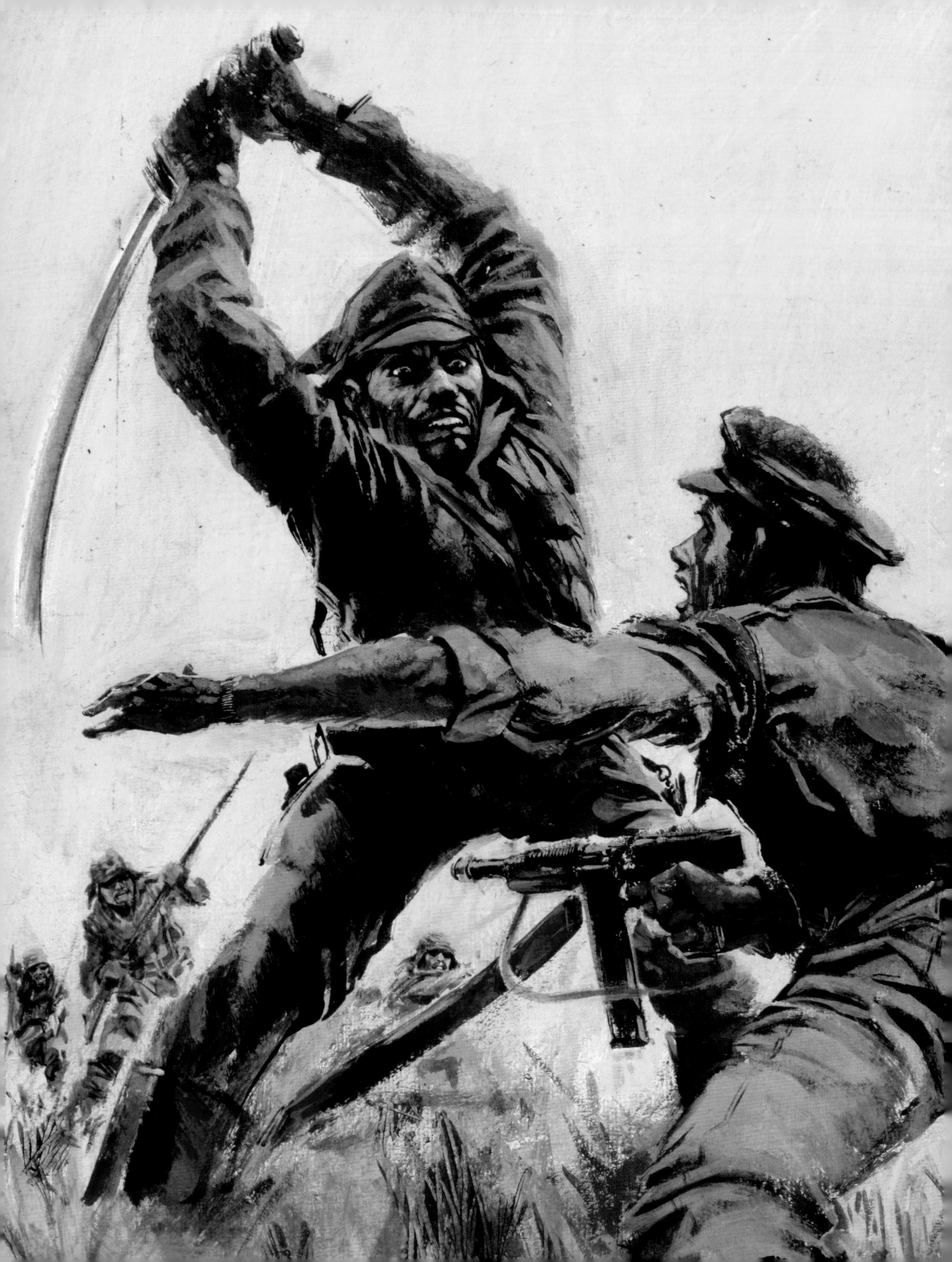

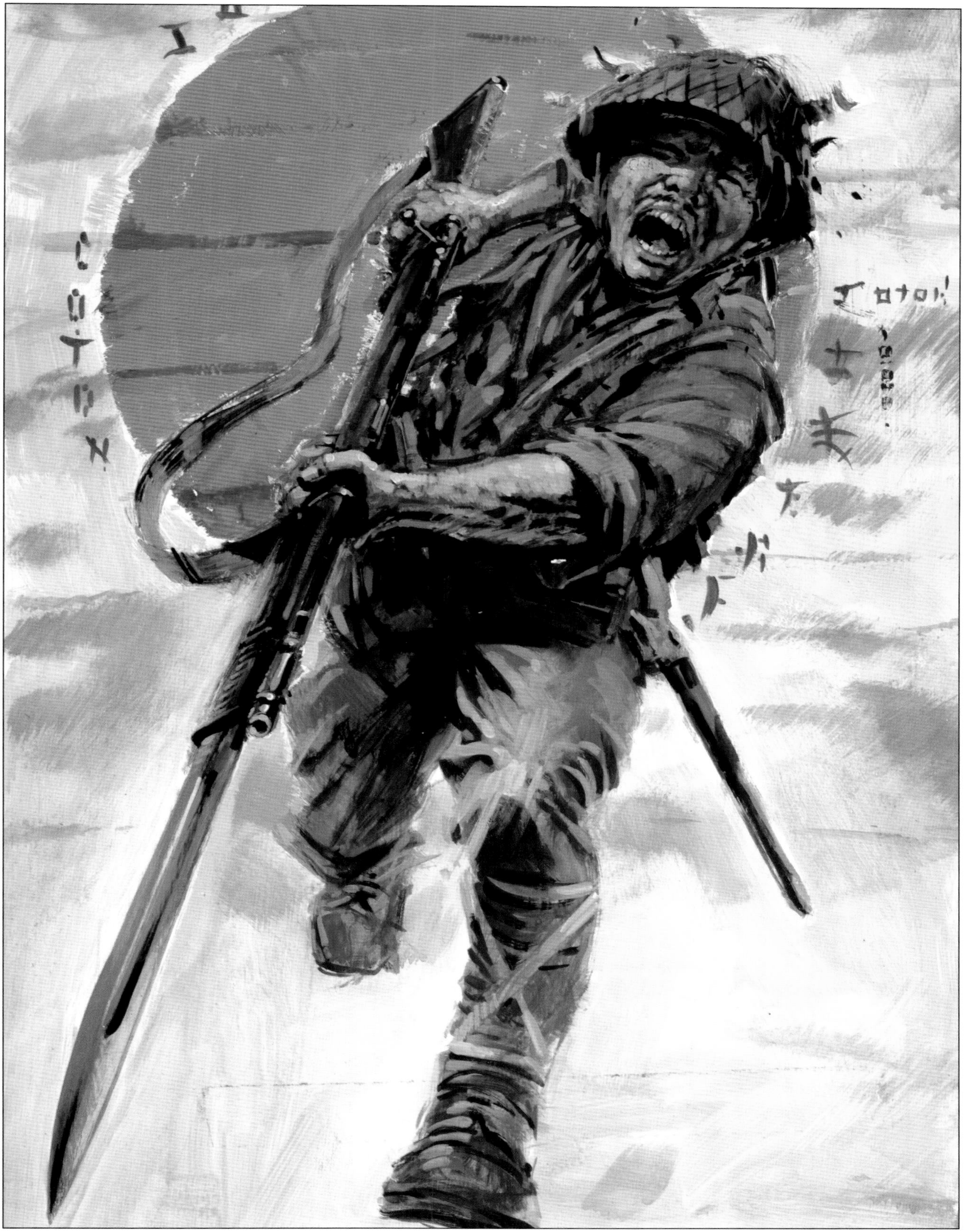

Graham Coton, War 1782, July 1980
Opposite: Graham Coton, War 589, May 1970

Air Aces

CHAPTER 3

The earliest issues of *War Picture Library* dealt equally with all theatres of combat on land, sea and in the air but reader reaction to the aviation strips was strong enough to warrant the launch of *Air Ace* in 1960 as a companion title. In fact, the first issue's strip "Target Top Secret" was originally intended for *War* but the new comic soon established its own personality. For much of its existence, *Air Ace* was to follow a slightly different path to the other picture libraries with its own, separate editorial team and often a different group of creators.

Regular *Air Ace* artists such as Juan Zanotto, Miguel Quesada, Juan Abellan, Victor Hugo Arias and Amador Garcia, for instance, drew little or no strips for the other titles. Similarly, its cover policy was different as, after the first few years where it broadly featured the same few Italian artists as *War* and *Battle*, it would go on to use first Pino Dell'Orco and then Allan Willow almost exclusively. Dell'Orco's reign as cover artist ran from 1963 to 1965 and marked the high point of his comics' output as he created a succession of startlingly imaginative illustrations. For Dell'Orco, these covers were always less about pretty pictures of planes, though he was a master of aviation art, but more a chance to play about with almost abstract compositions and avant garde colour theory.

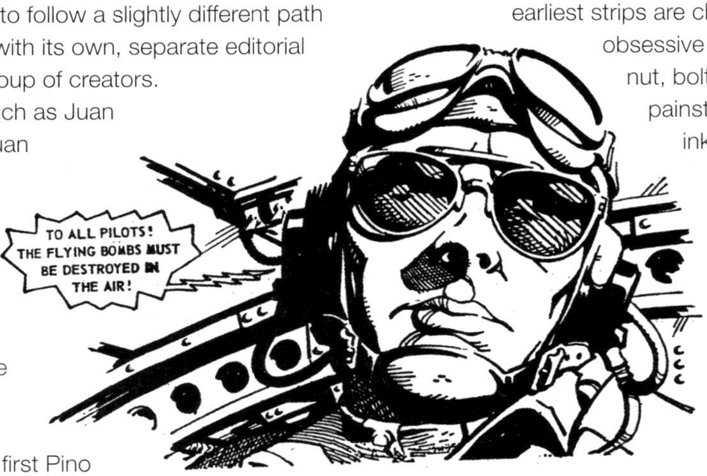
TO ALL PILOTS! THE FLYING BOMBS MUST BE DESTROYED IN THE AIR!

His successor, Alan Willow, painted most of the covers from mid 1965 to late 1966 and many more after that (96 in all) but was a much more conventional artist than his predecessor. Willow was a far less "painterly" artist than the Italians and appeared to be primarily a comic strip artist who had turned his hand to painting. Consequently, he perhaps lacked the finesse and verve of his European counterparts. However, there's no denying the poster-like impact of his best illustrations and, when reproduced in the larger format this book allows, his work carries a greater punch than was ever apparent in the comics themselves. Willow was one of several British artists courted by the editors of *Air Ace* (another contrast to the almost totally foreign talent pool used by *War* and *Battle*) and early issues contained welcome contributions from Mike Western, Joe Colquhon, Alan Philpott and George Stokes.

The best of the Brits, however, was Ian Kennedy whose polished, detailed artwork and genuine love of aeroplanes has made him one of the UK's most popular comic artists. All told, Kennedy drew 32 strips for the comic, which spanned a period of intense change for the artist. His earliest strips are characterised by an almost obsessive eye for detail with every nut, bolt, rivet and control dial painstakingly drawn in and inked with precise, rich brush strokes. Only the Italian artist, Kurt Caesar, another *Air Ace* regular, comes close to Kennedy's degree of accuracy. He was always a supremely versatile artist and, while aircraft may have been his favourite subject matter, he also drew strips for D C Thomson's *Hotspur* and *Judy* throughout his stint on *Air Ace*. For *Judy* he drew a succession of strips about gymnasts, horses and cavemen (really) all through the sixties and when that comic launched a companion title, *Judy Picture Library*, he painted a few covers for it, too, the first of his career.

By the mid-sixties his line work had become much finer, almost brittle, as he apparently swapped the warmth of his brush for the steely precision of a pen. From here on he established his mature style where he developed a stunning technique of delicate cross-hatching and minimal shadows.

Following on from his *Judy* covers he returned to *Air Ace* to become a regular cover artist there, too, crafting 23 covers altogether. These were typified by their detailed, feathered brush strokes, which were almost an attempt to duplicate his fine-lined inking technique in paint, and also by a love of extremely bright colours. Where some of his contemporaries might have shied away from the extremes of the palette, Kennedy was rarely afraid to use the brightest yellows, oranges or greens and his covers were by far the most vibrant the company ever published, outdoing even Dell'Orco at his boldest. Following *Air Ace*'s

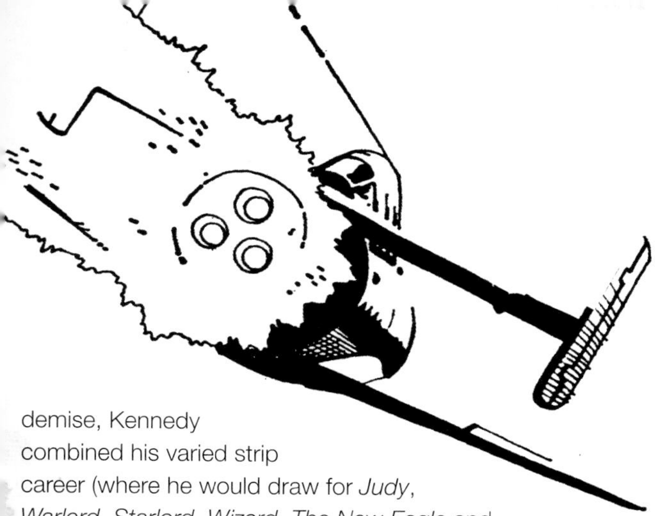

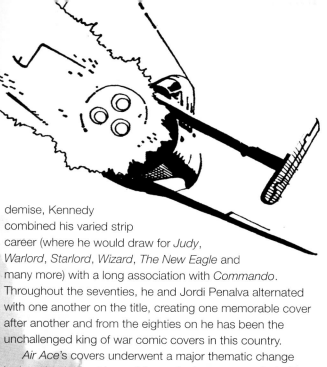

demise, Kennedy combined his varied strip career (where he would draw for *Judy*, *Warlord*, *Starlord*, *Wizard*, *The New Eagle* and many more) with a long association with *Commando*. Throughout the seventies, he and Jordi Penalva alternated with one another on the title, creating one memorable cover after another and from the eighties on he has been the unchallenged king of war comic covers in this country.

Air Ace's covers underwent a major thematic change in the mid-sixties. Many of the earliest covers, particularly those painted by Nino Caroselli, prominently featured pilots, either by sticking a head at the bottom of the cover or by showing a pilot in danger in his cockpit. Most of the earliest Second World War strips had focused on lone heroic pilots, be it "Battler Britton", "Paddy Payne" or D C Thomson's "Braddock") so perhaps *Air Ace*'s editors felt the need to humanise the comic somehow. Under Dell'Orco's tenure, however, the title largely abandoned people, preferring to focus on the hardware instead. It might well have been a policy that backfired as, in a move aimed at cost cutting, *Air Ace* began introducing reprints of "Dogfight Dixon" strips from *Thriller* in early 1966, predating the other picture libraries' reprint programs by a good two years.

This coincided with the departure of editor Bernard Smith and it was almost certainly his replacement, Ted Bensberg, who also brought back the doubty "Battler Britton" from his brief tenure in publishing limbo. For the rest of its existence, *Air Ace* featured one, or often two, new "Battler Britton" strips each month, mixed with the odd new traditional *Air Ace* strip, "Dogfight Dixon" and ever-increasing reprints from the comics' early days.

Among the many artists to draw "Battler Britton" here were Luis Martinez Mira (another *Commando* regular), Jaime Brocal Remohi, Amador Garcia, Carlos Pino and the young (at only 25) Enric Sio. Sio was soon to become feted in Spain as the artist on a series of highly experimental, colourful strips such as "Nus" and "Sorang" and as a regular on the groundbreaking *Dracula* magazine. His distinctive, solarised, high-contrast art style in his native country was clearly influenced by the surrealist photographer Man Ray… and how many comic artists can claim that? His *Air Ace* strips were rather more conventional, though still very attractive.

Air Ace was cancelled in December 1970 after 545 issues and, though "Battler Britton" transferred to *Battle Picture Library*, aeroplanes never again played such a significant role in British comics.

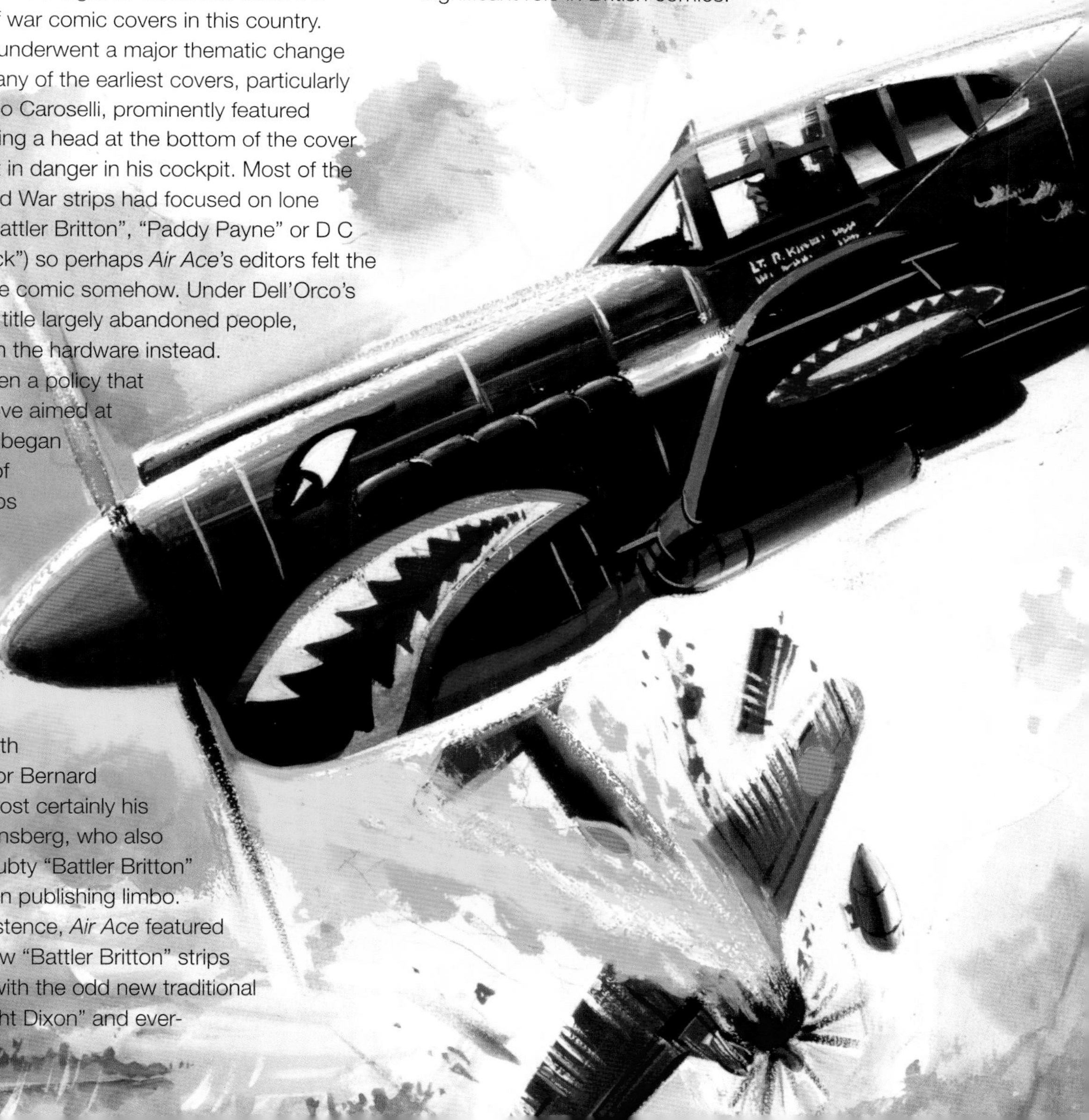

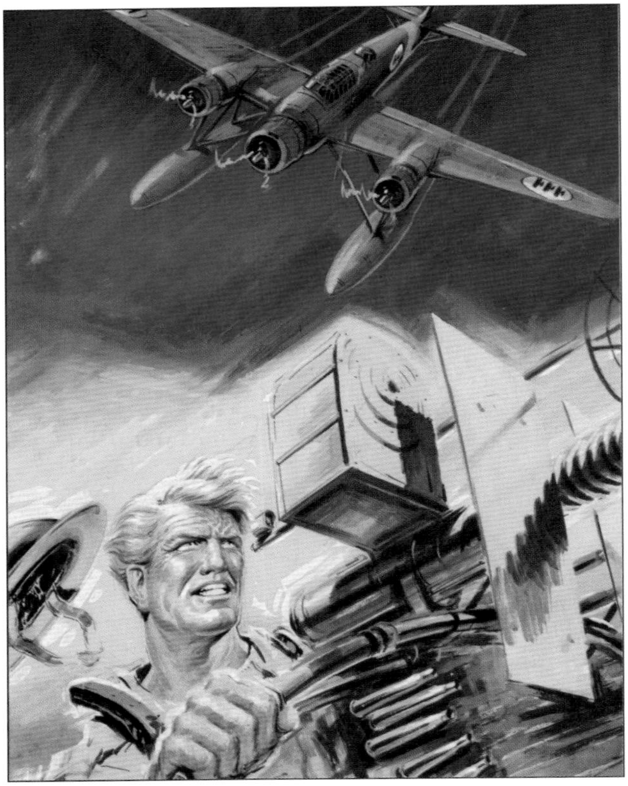

Graham Coton, Battle 230, December 1965

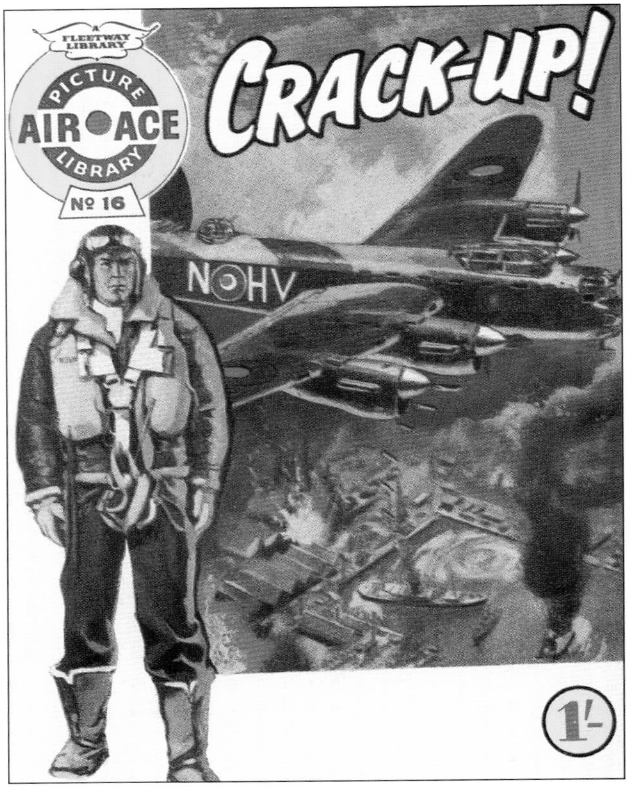
A FLEETWAY LIBRARY
PICTURE AIR ACE LIBRARY
Nº 16
CRACK-UP!
N HV
1/-

Nino Caroselli, Air Ace 16, July 1960

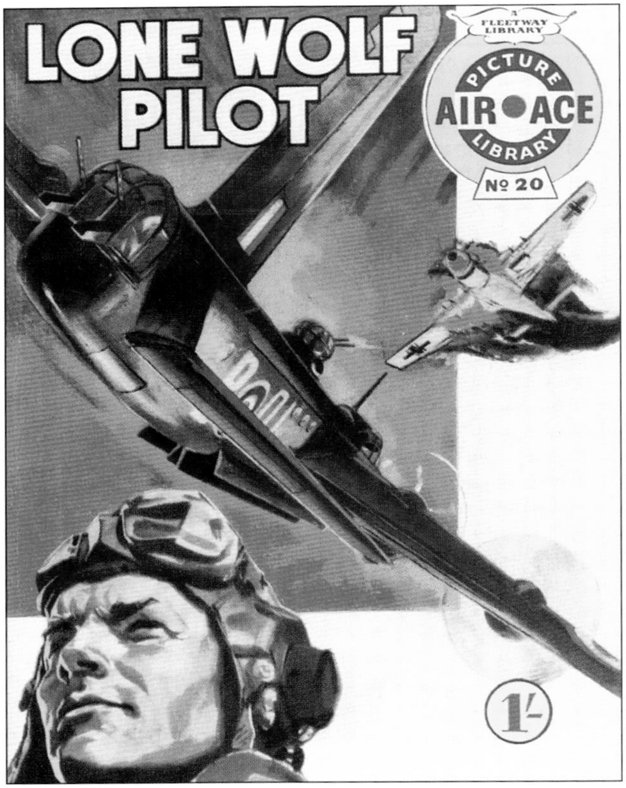
LONE WOLF PILOT
A FLEETWAY LIBRARY
PICTURE AIR ACE LIBRARY
Nº 20
1/-

Nino Caroselli, Air Ace 20, September 1960

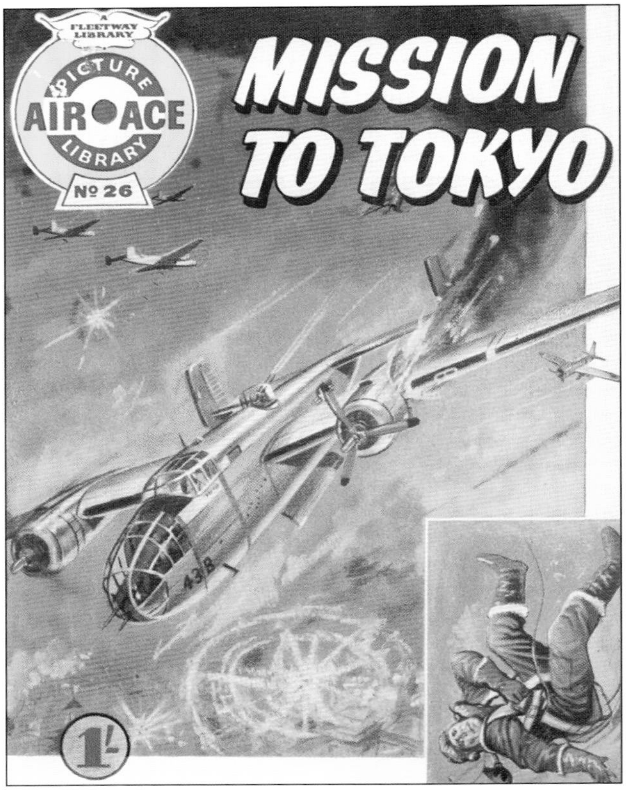
A FLEETWAY LIBRARY
PICTURE AIR ACE LIBRARY
Nº 26
MISSION TO TOKYO
1/-

Nino Caroselli, Air Ace 26, November 1960

Opposite: Alessandro Biffignandi, Air Ace 98, May 1962

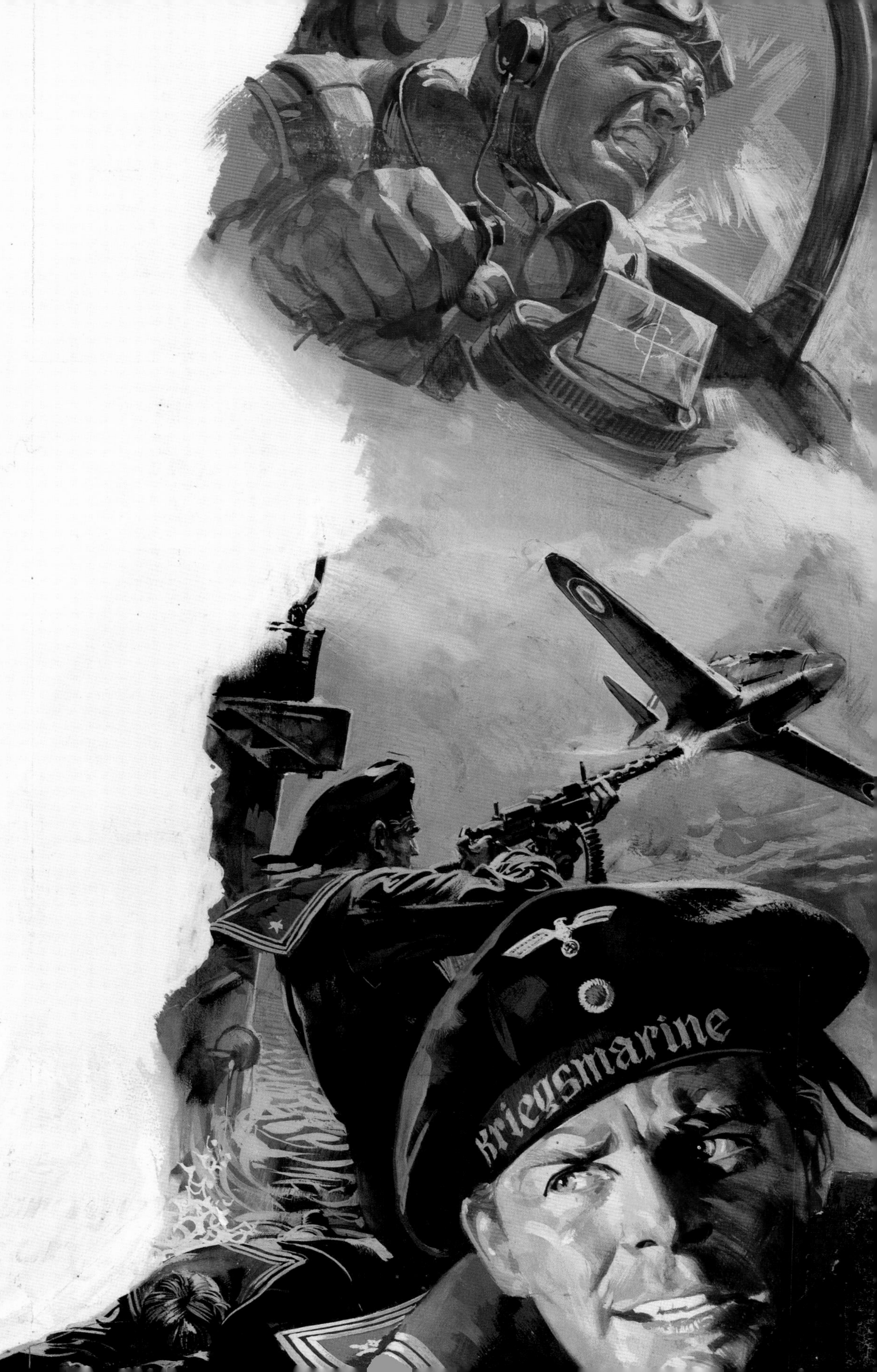
Kriegsmarine

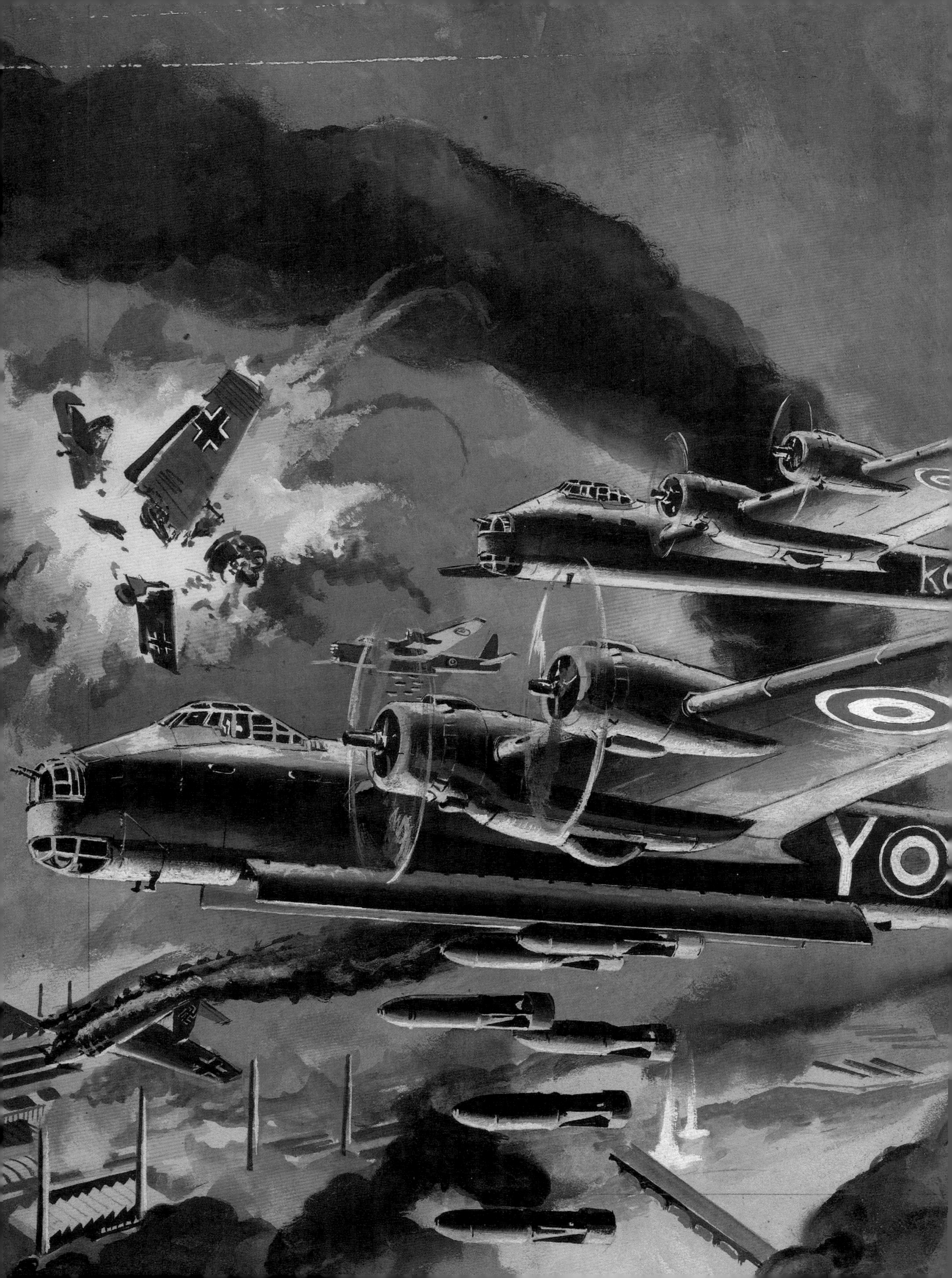
KO
YO

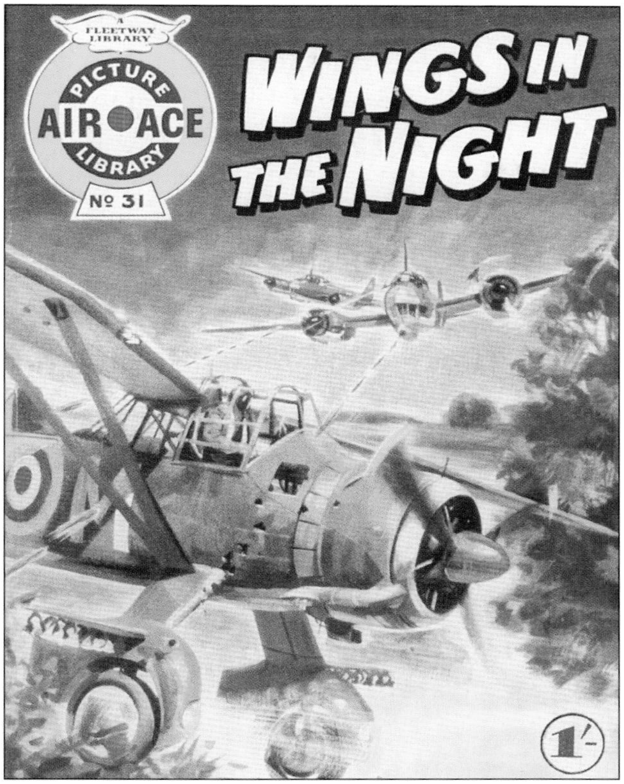
A FLEETWAY LIBRARY
PICTURE AIR ACE LIBRARY
Nº 31
WINGS IN THE NIGHT
1/-

Pino Dell'Orco, Air Ace 31, December 1960

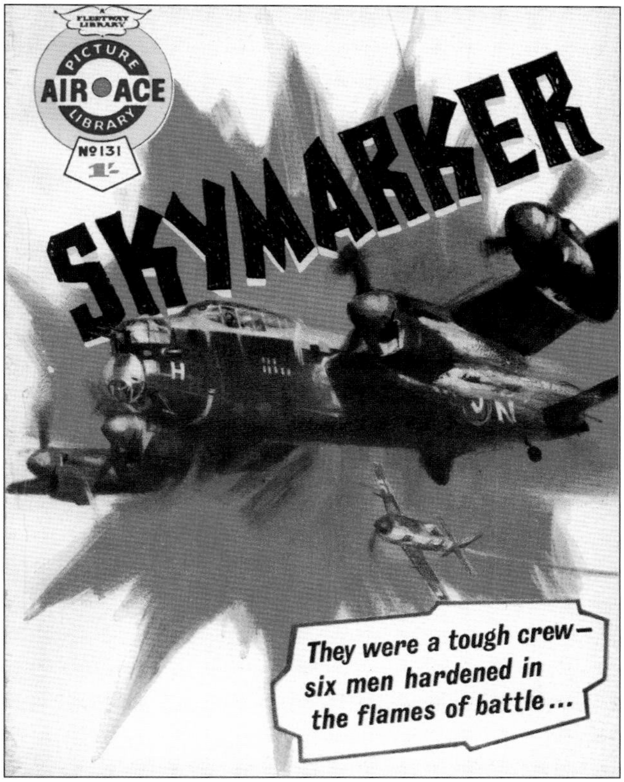
A FLEETWAY LIBRARY
PICTURE AIR ACE LIBRARY
Nº 131
1/-
SKYMARKER
They were a tough crew—six men hardened in the flames of battle...

Pino Dell'Orco, Air Ace 131, January 1963

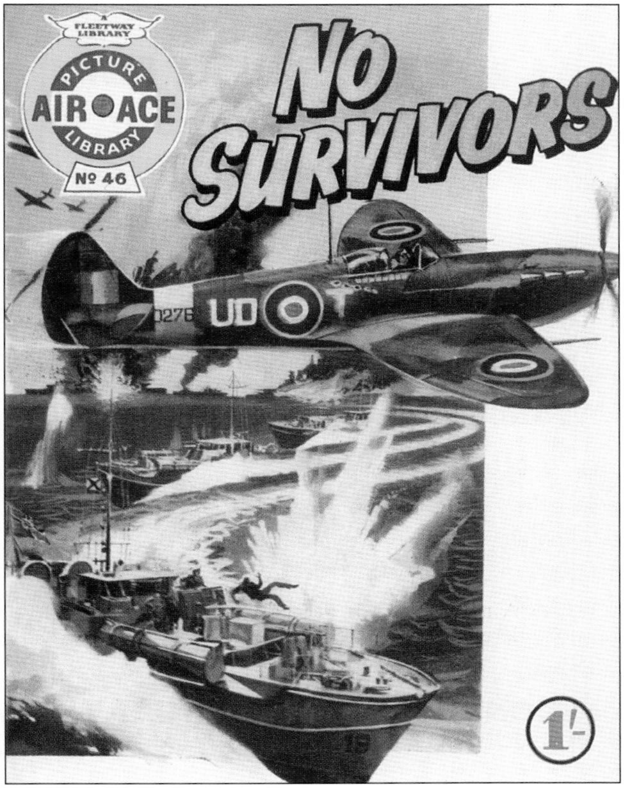
A FLEETWAY LIBRARY
PICTURE AIR ACE LIBRARY
Nº 46
NO SURVIVORS
UD
1/-

Allessandro Biffignandi, Air Ace 46, April 1961

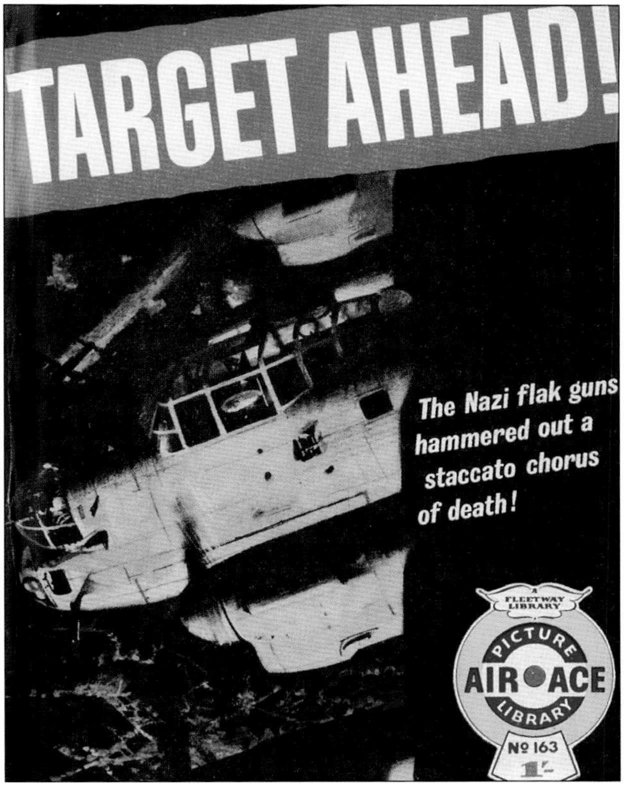
TARGET AHEAD!
The Nazi flak guns hammered out a staccato chorus of death!
A FLEETWAY LIBRARY
PICTURE AIR ACE LIBRARY
Nº 163
1/-

Pino Dell'Orco, Air Ace163, September 1963

Opposite: Nino Caroselli, Air Ace 1, January 1960
Overleaf: Allessandro Biffignandi, Air Ace 80, December 1961

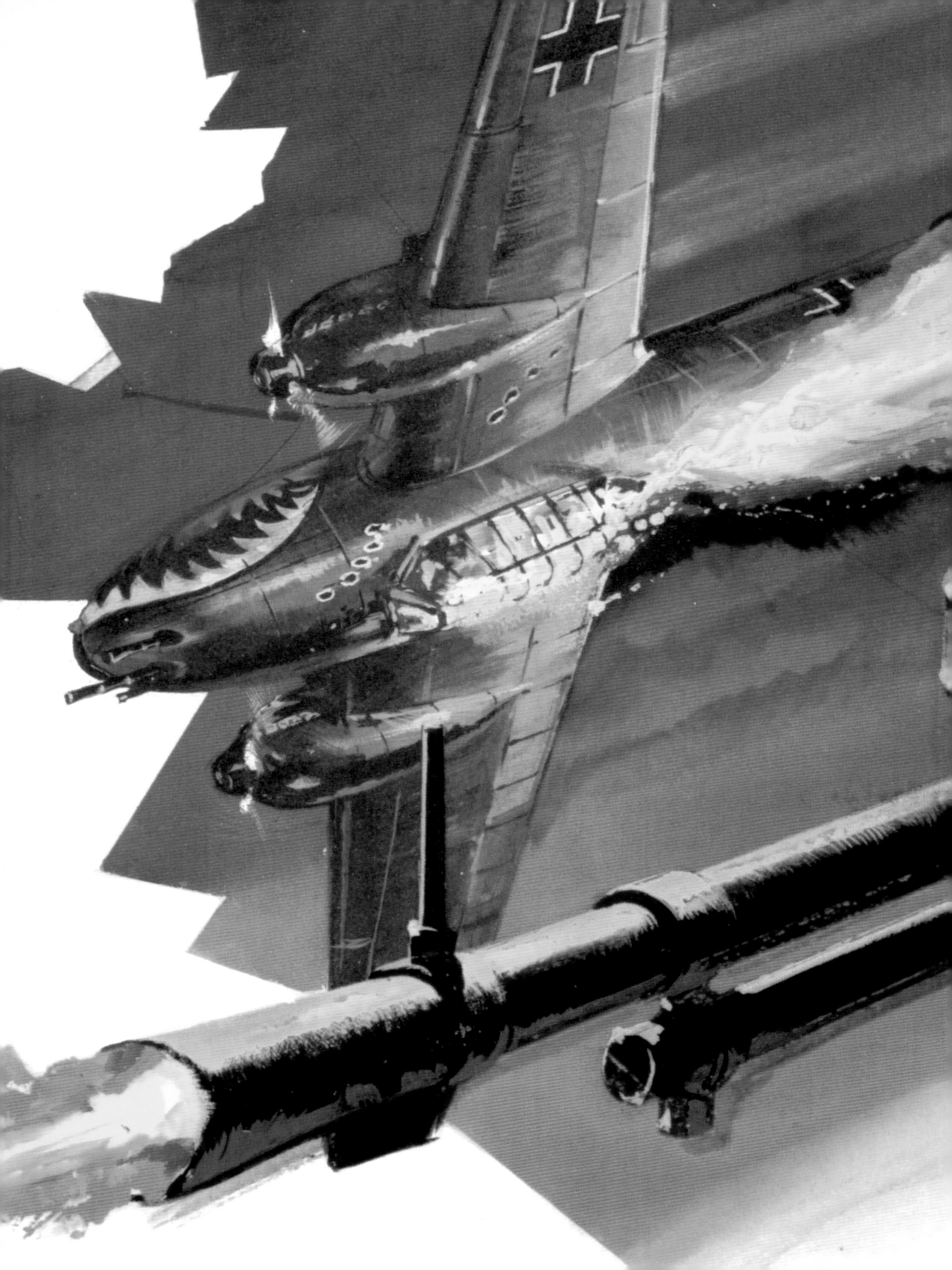

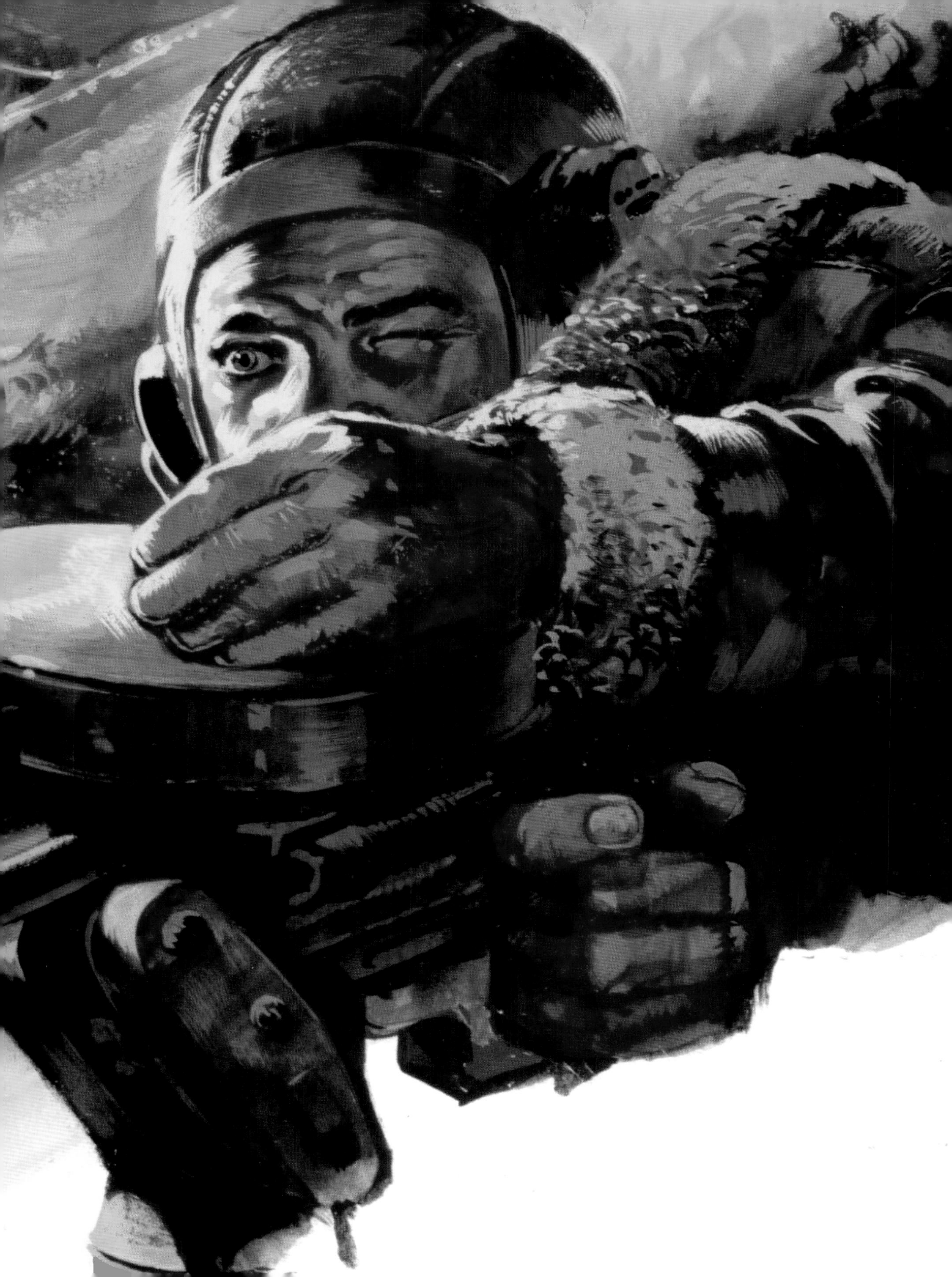

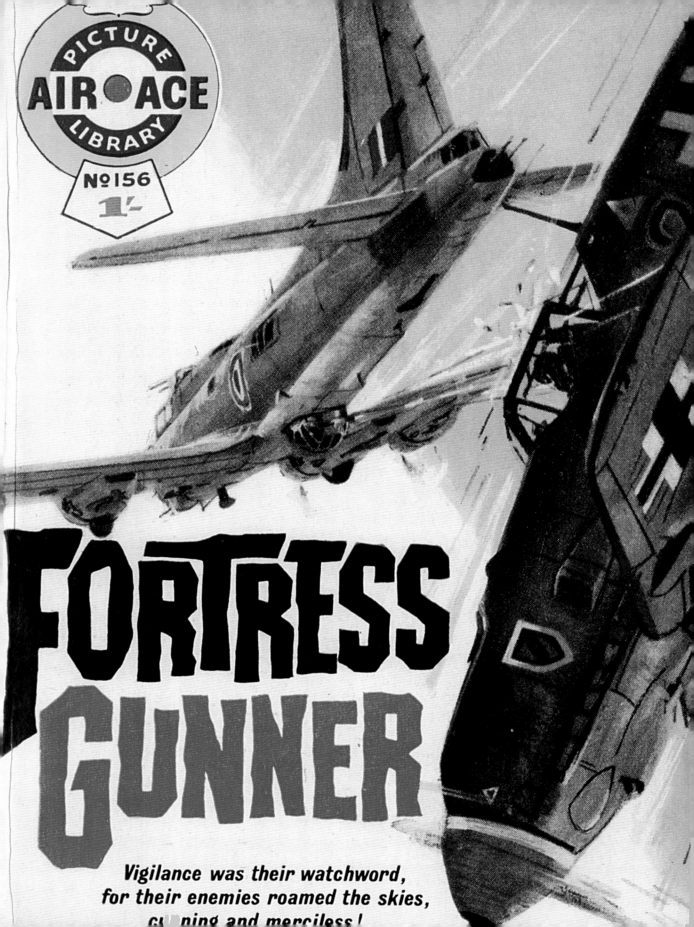

AIR ACE
PICTURE LIBRARY

Nº 156
1/-

FORTRESS GUNNER

*Vigilance was their watchword,
for their enemies roamed the skies,
cunning and merciless!*

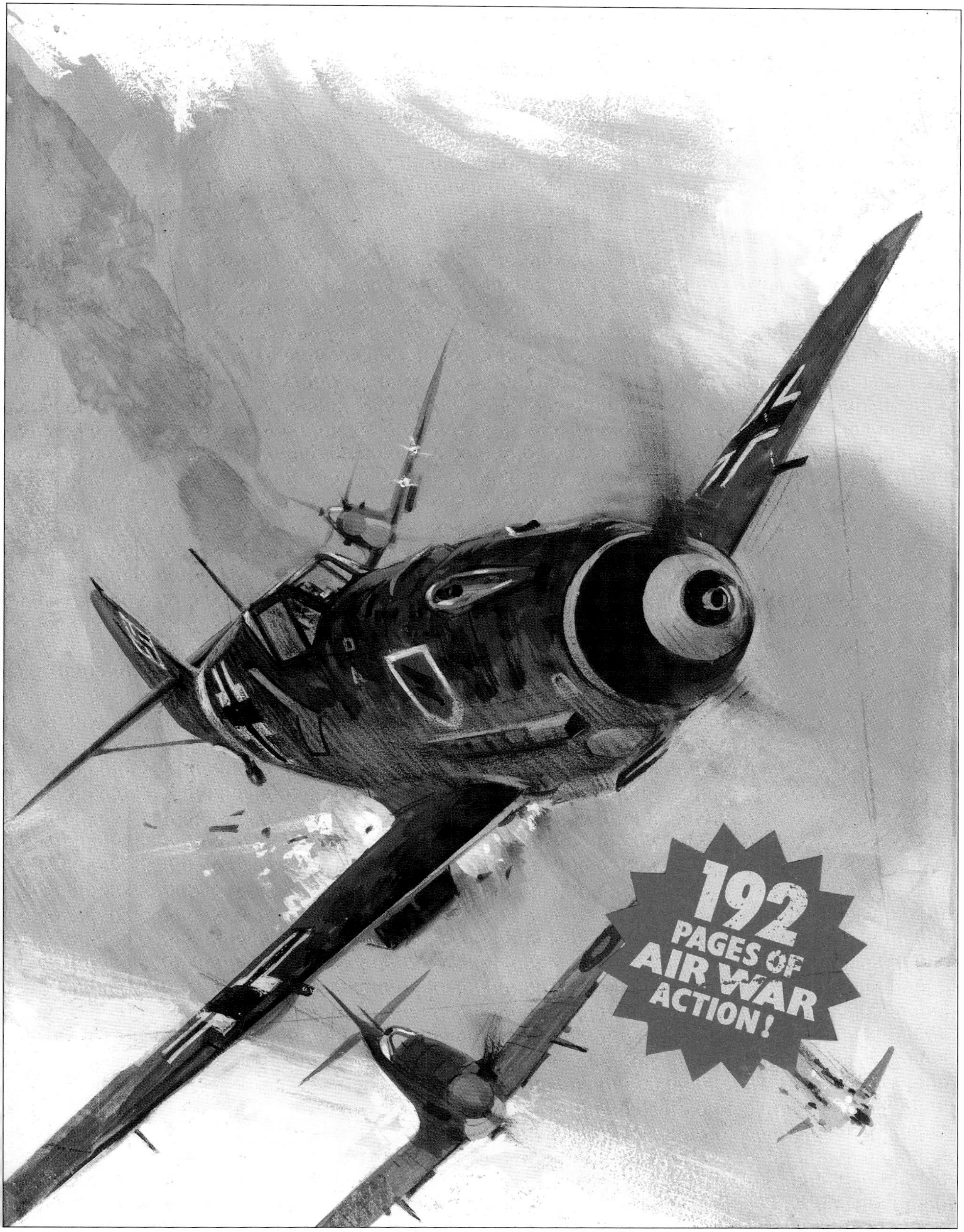
192
PAGES OF
AIR WAR
ACTION!

Pino Dell'Orco, Air Ace 169, October 1963
Opposite: Pino Dell'Orco, Air Ace 156, July 1963

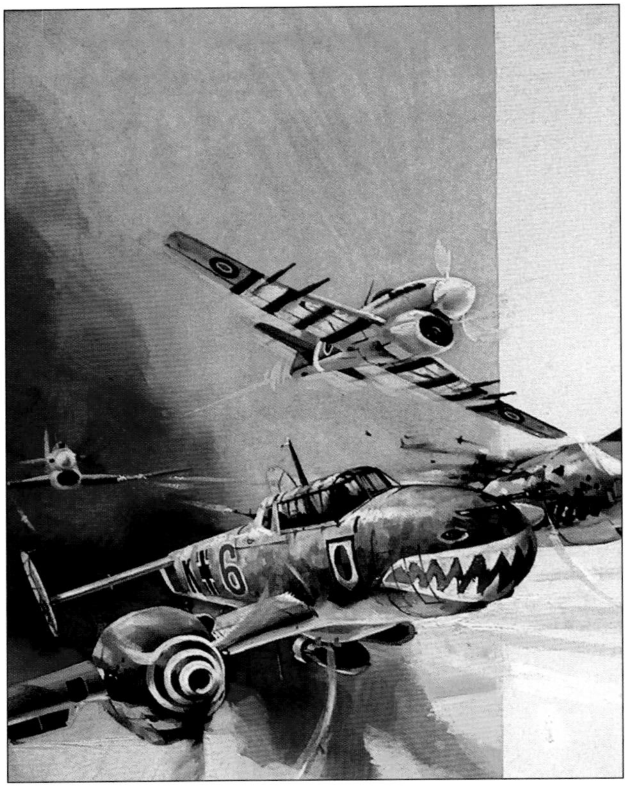

Pino Dell'Orco, Air Ace 171, November 1963

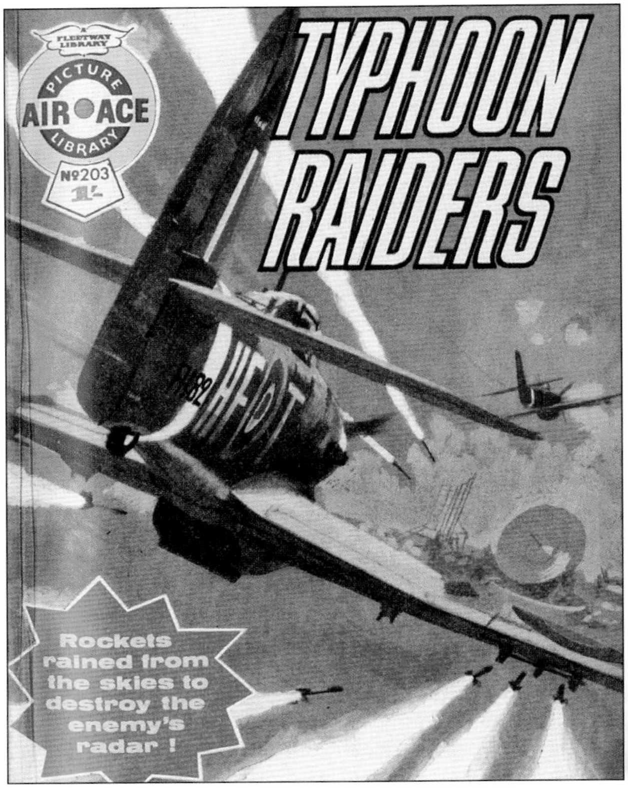
A FLEETWAY LIBRARY
PICTURE
AIR ACE
LIBRARY
Nº 203
1/-
TYPHOON RAIDERS
Rockets rained from the skies to destroy the enemy's radar !

Pino Dell'Orco, Air Ace 203, July 1964

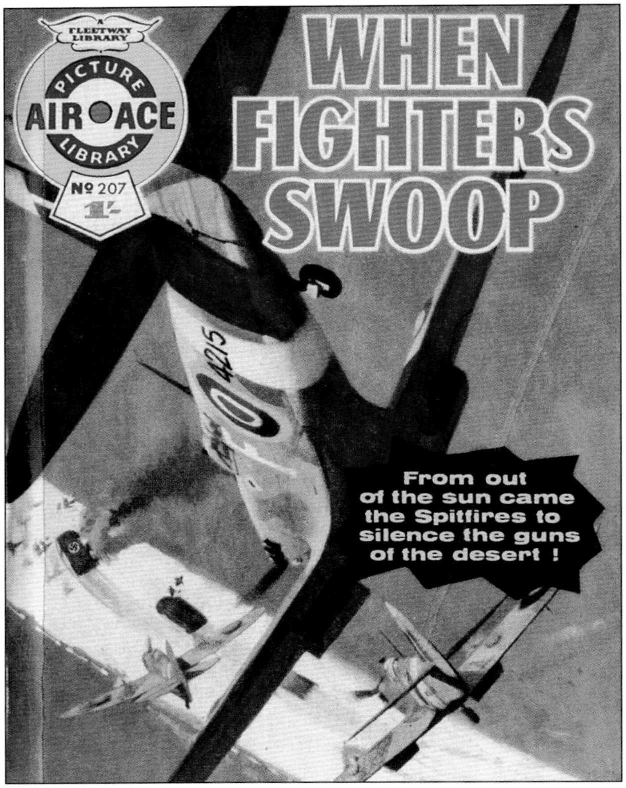
A FLEETWAY LIBRARY
PICTURE
AIR ACE
LIBRARY
Nº 207
1/-
WHEN FIGHTERS SWOOP
From out of the sun came the Spitfires to silence the guns of the desert !

Pino Dell'Orco, Air Ace 207, August 1964

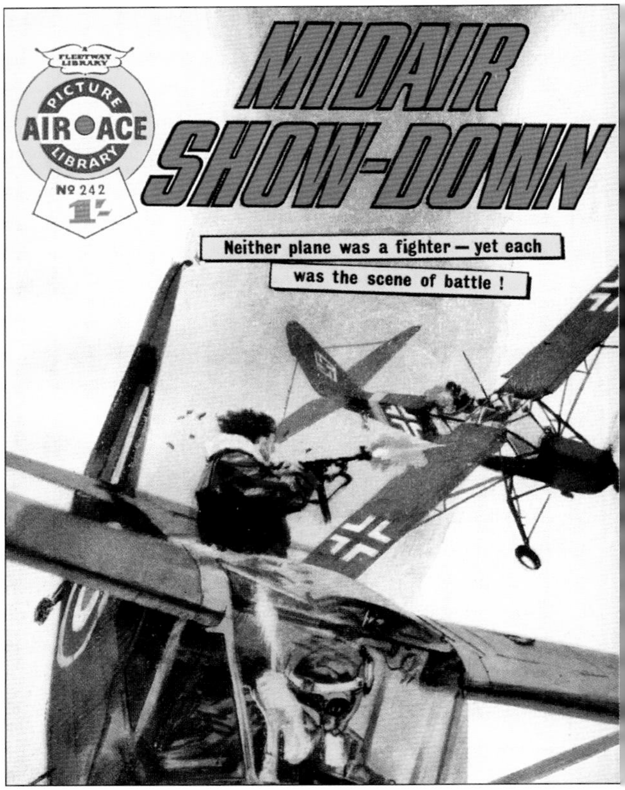
A FLEETWAY LIBRARY
PICTURE
AIR ACE
LIBRARY
Nº 242
1/-
MIDAIR SHOW-DOWN
Neither plane was a fighter — yet each
was the scene of battle !

Pino Dell'Orco, Air Ace 242, May 1965

Opposite: Alan Willow, Battle 206, June 1965

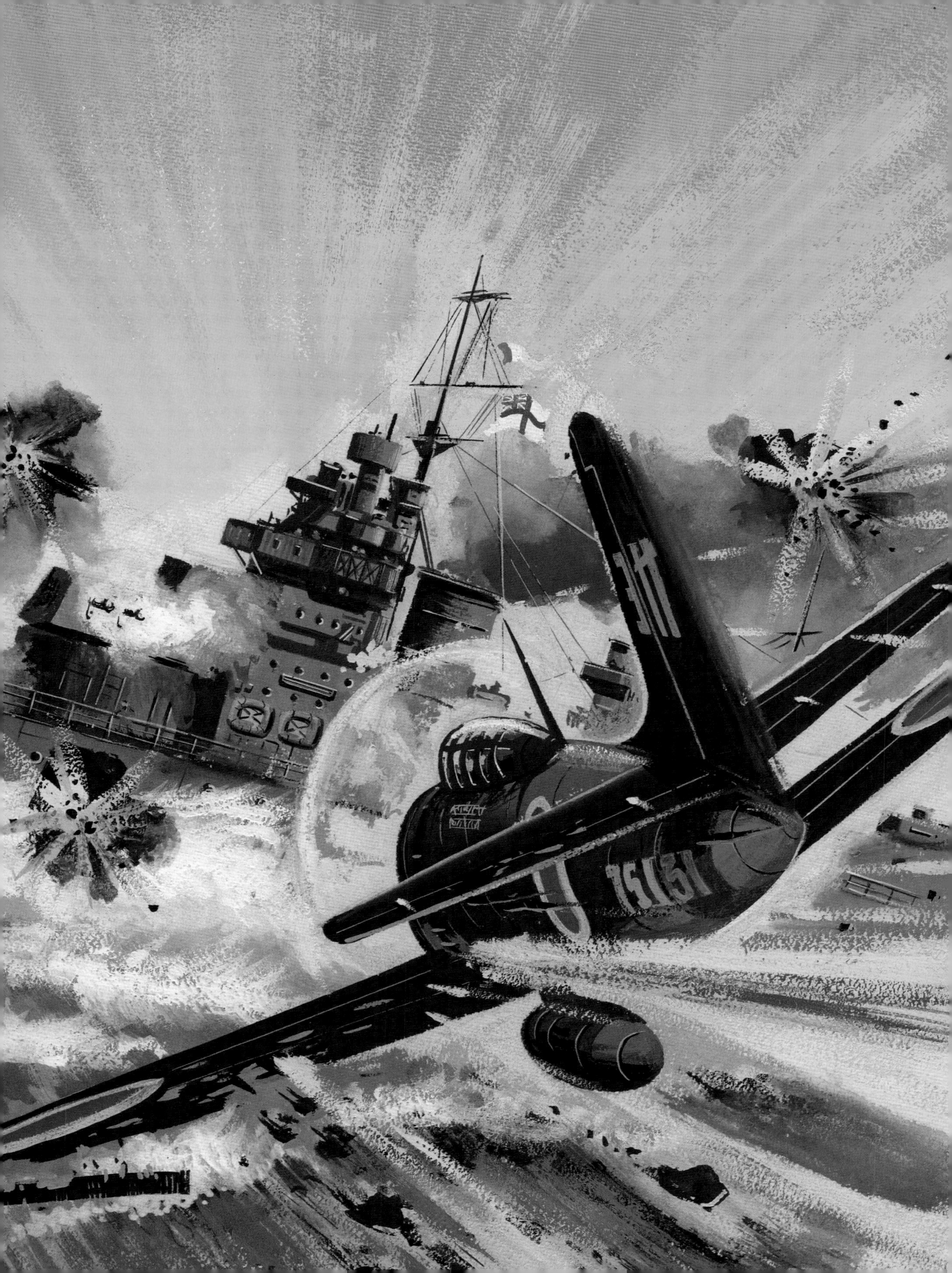

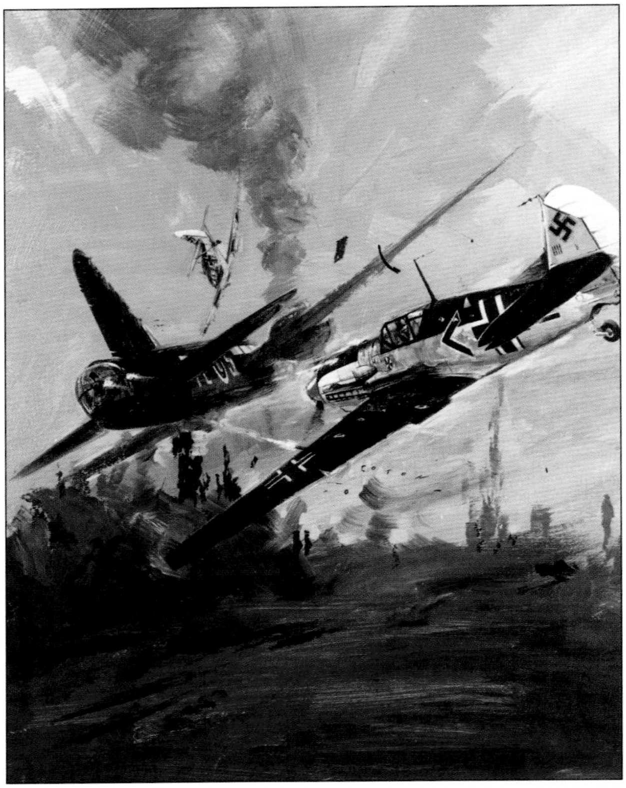

Graham Coton, Battle 753, October 1973

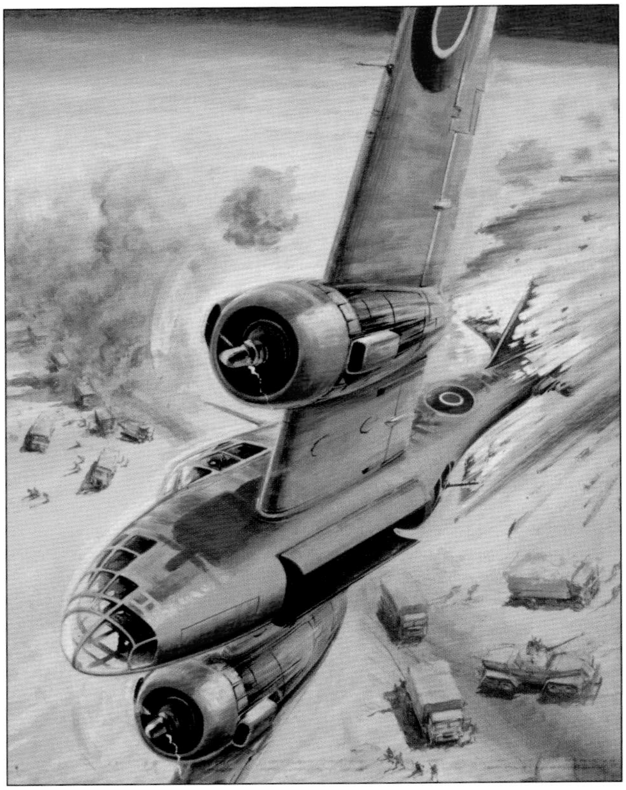

Graham Coton, Air Ace 278, February 1966

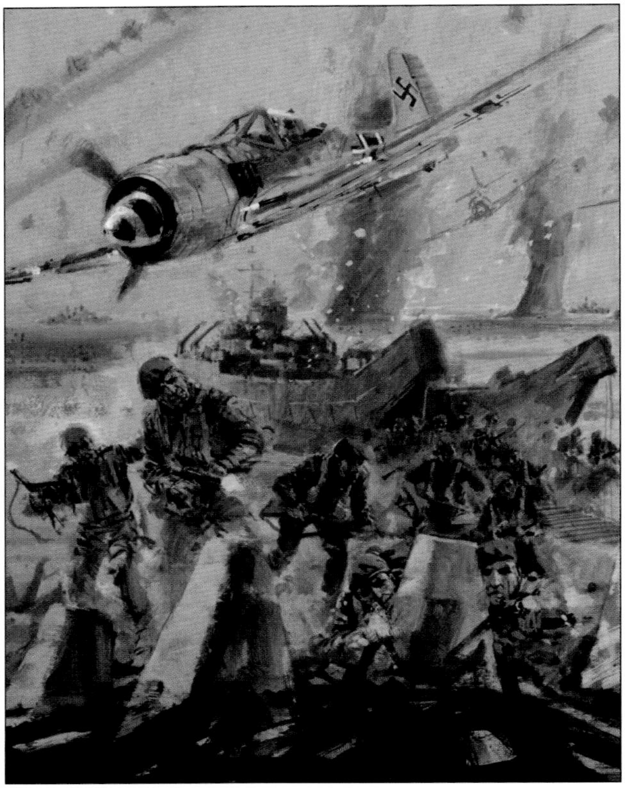

Graham Coton, War Holiday Special 1972

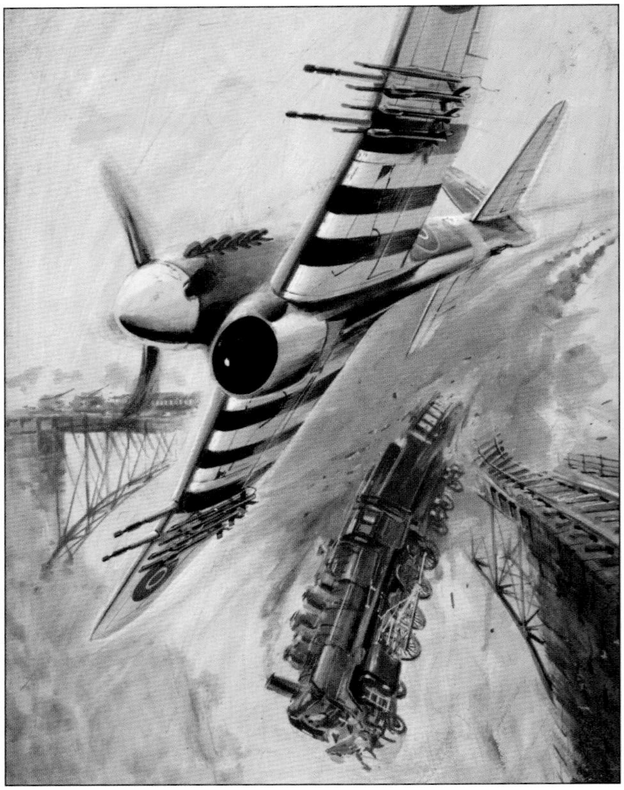

Graham Coton, Air Ace 327, February 1967

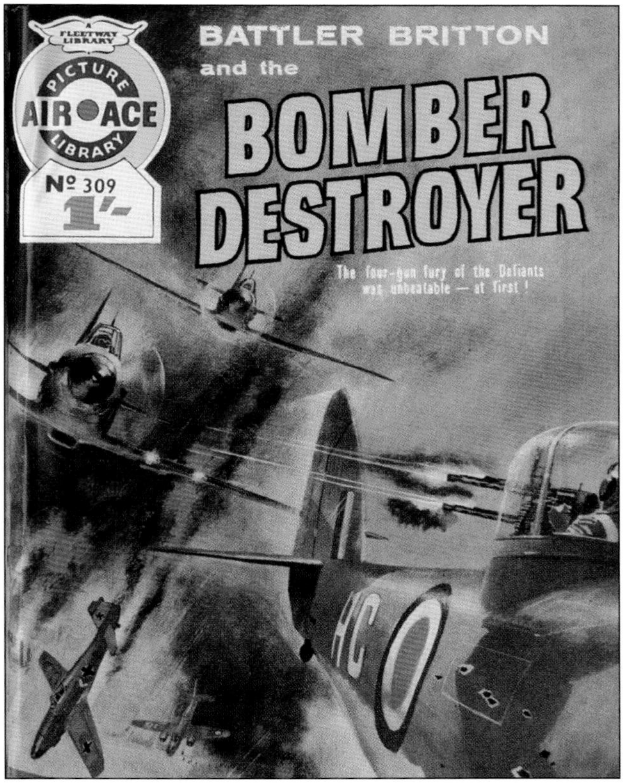
A FLEETWAY LIBRARY
PICTURE
AIR ACE
LIBRARY
Nº 309
1/-
BATTLER BRITTON
and the
BOMBER
DESTROYER
The four-gun fury of the Defiants was unbeatable — at first!
Carlo Jacono, Air Ace 309, September 1966

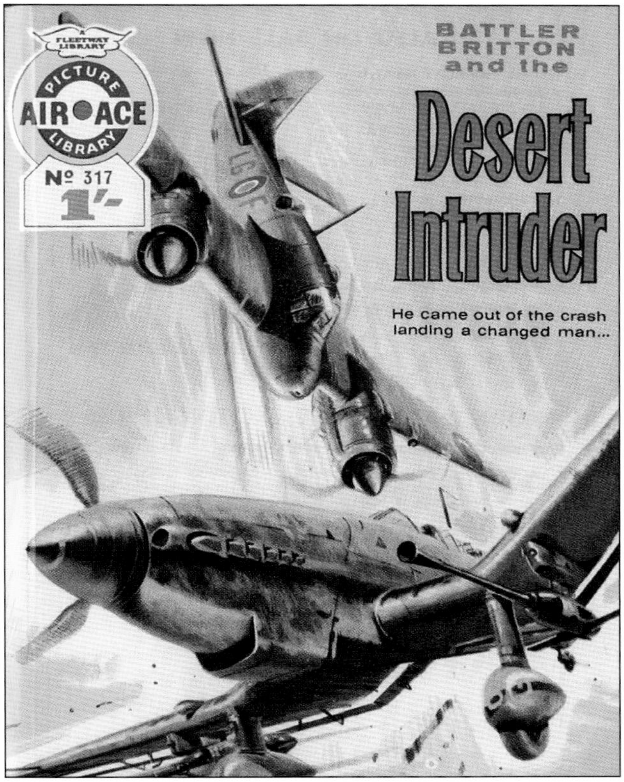
A FLEETWAY LIBRARY
PICTURE
AIR ACE
LIBRARY
Nº 317
1/-
BATTLER
BRITTON
and the
Desert
Intruder
He came out of the crash
landing a changed man...
Graham Coton, Air Ace 317, November 1966

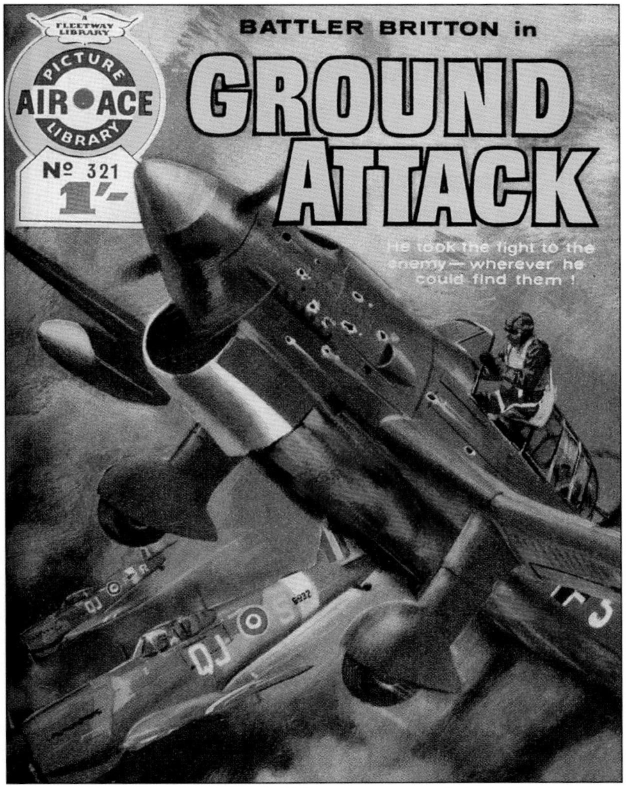
A FLEETWAY LIBRARY
PICTURE
AIR ACE
LIBRARY
Nº 321
1/-
BATTLER BRITTON in
GROUND
ATTACK
He took the fight to the
enemy — wherever he
could find them!
Carlo Jacono, Air Ace 321, December 1966

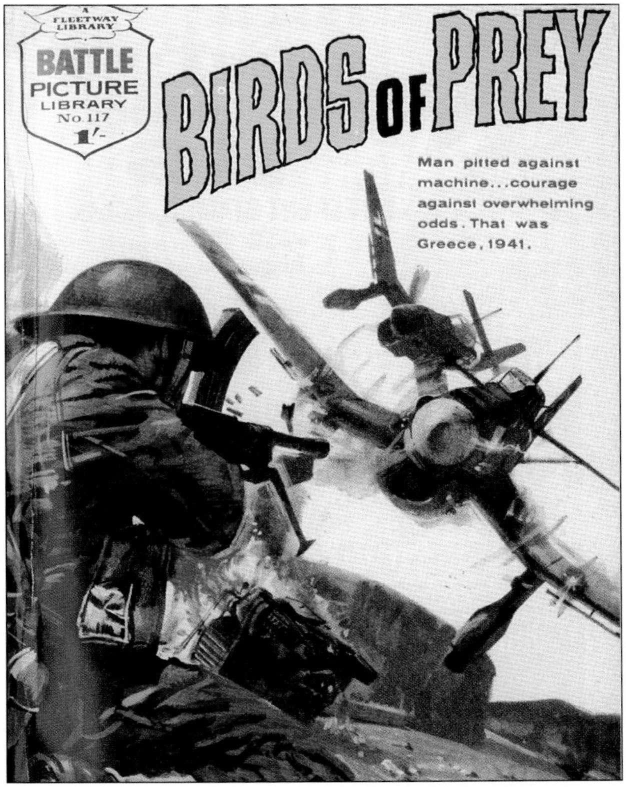
A FLEETWAY LIBRARY
BATTLE
PICTURE
LIBRARY
No. 117
1/-
BIRDS OF PREY
Man pitted against
machine...courage
against overwhelming
odds. That was
Greece, 1941.
Pino Dell'Orco, Batle 117, August 1963

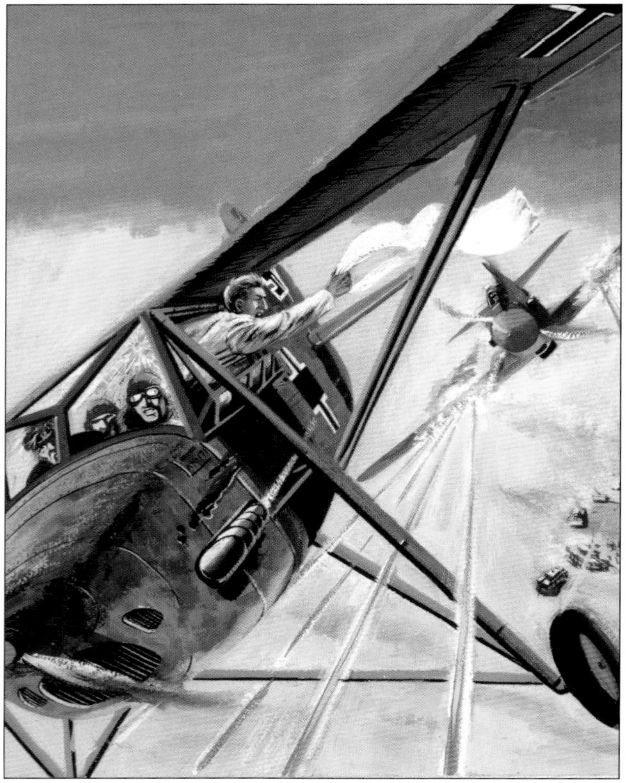

Alan Willow, Air Ace 237, March 1965

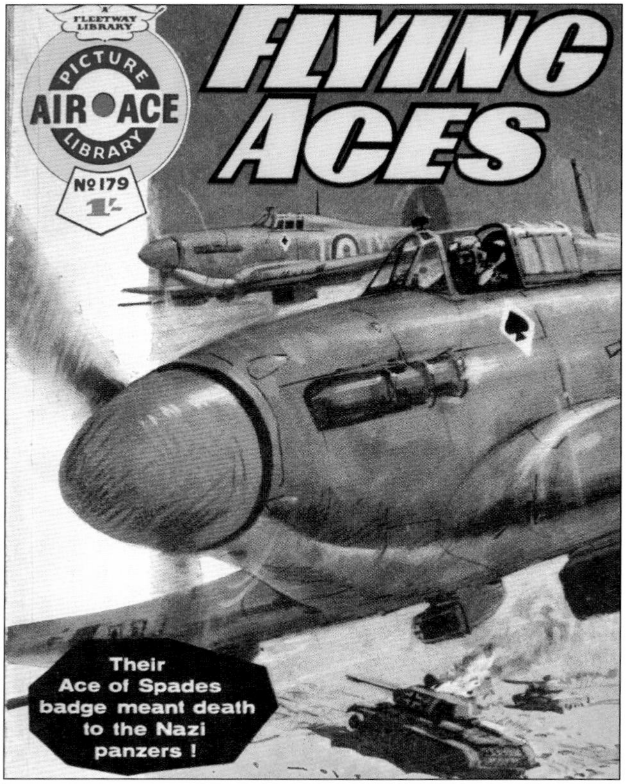
A FLEETWAY LIBRARY
PICTURE AIR ACE LIBRARY
Nº179
1/-
FLYING ACES
Their Ace of Spades badge meant death to the Nazi panzers !

Pino Dell'Orco, Air Ace 179, January 1964

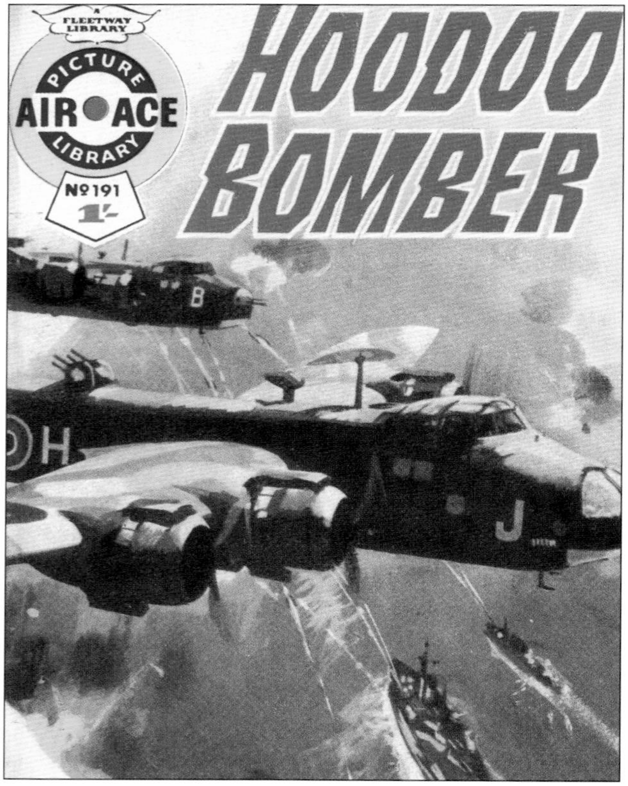
A FLEETWAY LIBRARY
PICTURE AIR ACE LIBRARY
Nº191
1/-
HOODOO BOMBER

Pino Dell'Orco, Air Ace 191, April 1964

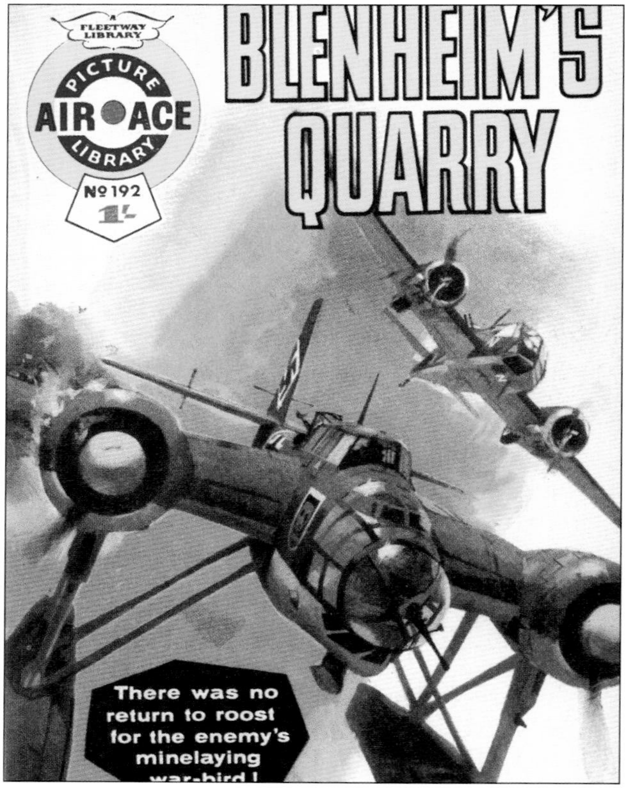
A FLEETWAY LIBRARY
PICTURE AIR ACE LIBRARY
Nº192
1/-
BLENHEIM'S QUARRY
There was no return to roost for the enemy's minelaying

Pino Dell'Orco, Air Ace192, April 1964

Opposite: Allessandro Biffignandi, Air Ace 84, January 1962

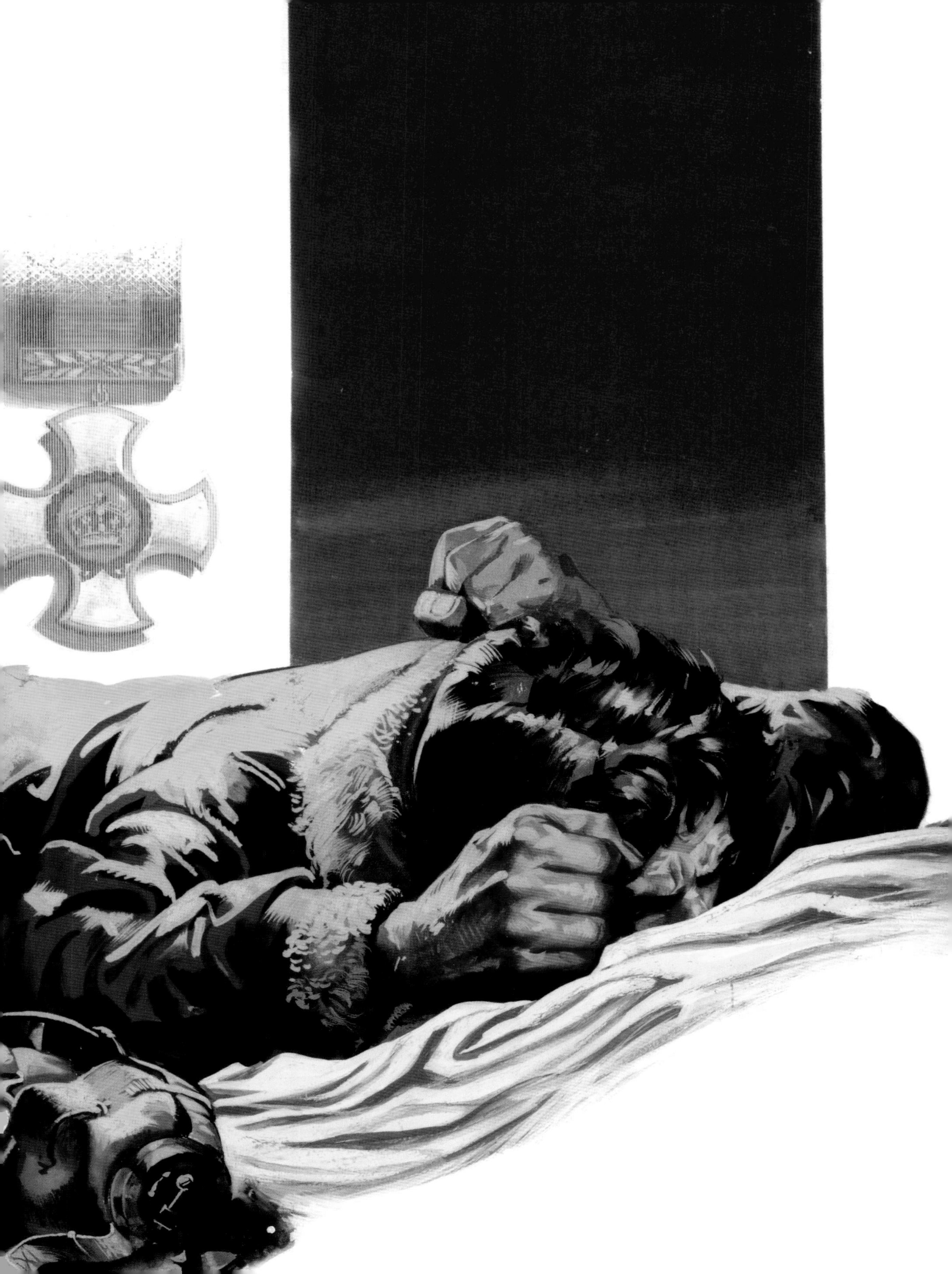

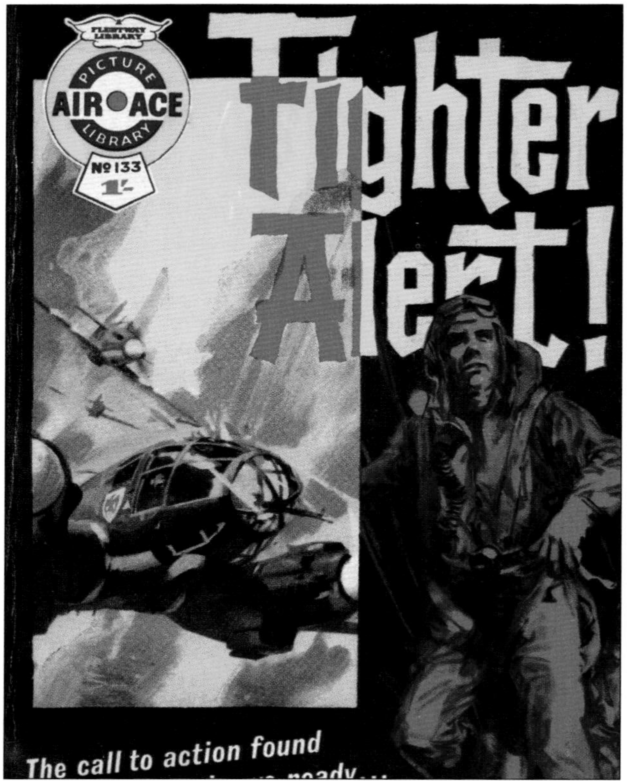
PICTURE
AIR ACE
LIBRARY
Nº133
Fighter Alert!
The call to action found

Pino Dell'Orco, Air Ace 133, January 1963

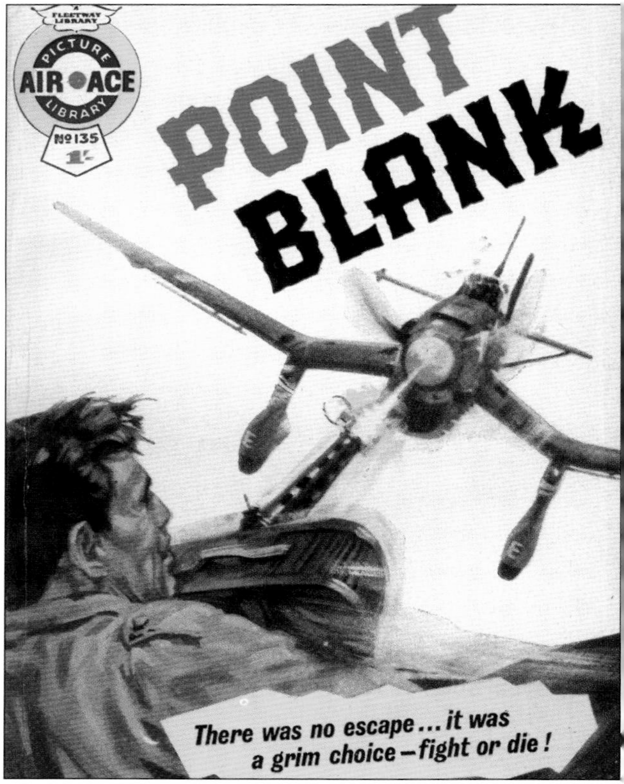
PICTURE
AIR ACE
LIBRARY
Nº135
POINT BLANK
There was no escape... it was a grim choice—fight or die!

Pino Dell'Orco, Air Ace 135, February 1963

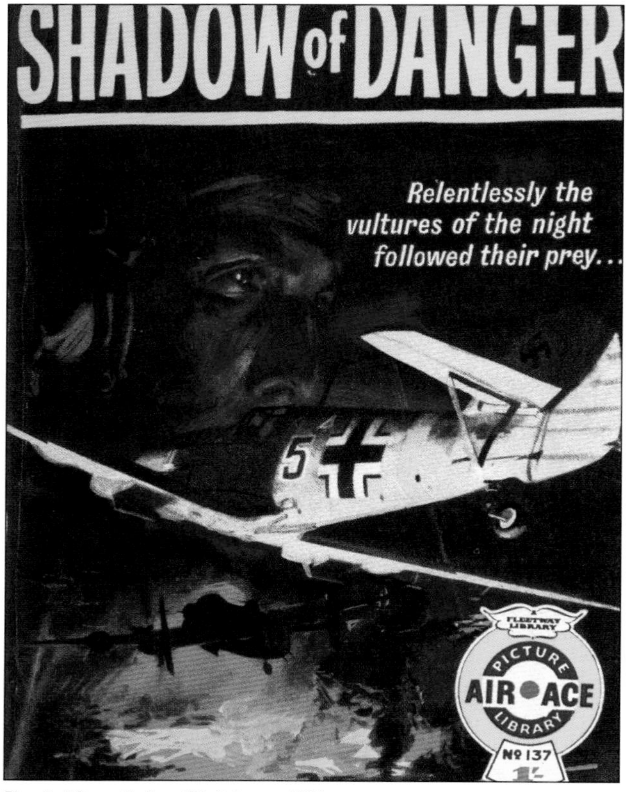
SHADOW of DANGER
Relentlessly the vultures of the night followed their prey...
PICTURE
AIR ACE
LIBRARY
Nº137

Pino Dell'Orco, Air Ace 137, February 1963

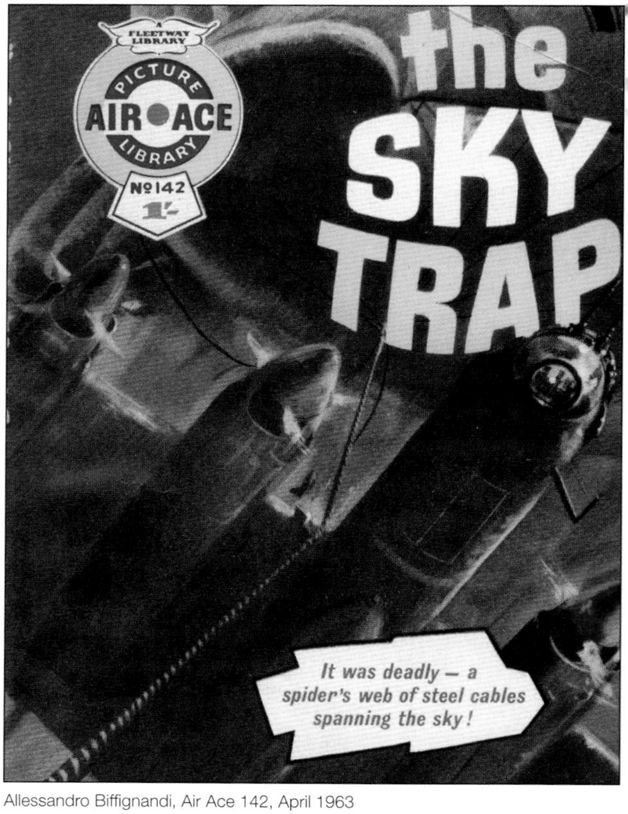
PICTURE
AIR ACE
LIBRARY
Nº142
the SKY TRAP
It was deadly — a spider's web of steel cables spanning the sky!

Allessandro Biffignandi, Air Ace 142, April 1963

Opposite: Pino Dell'Orco, Battle 1117, July 1977

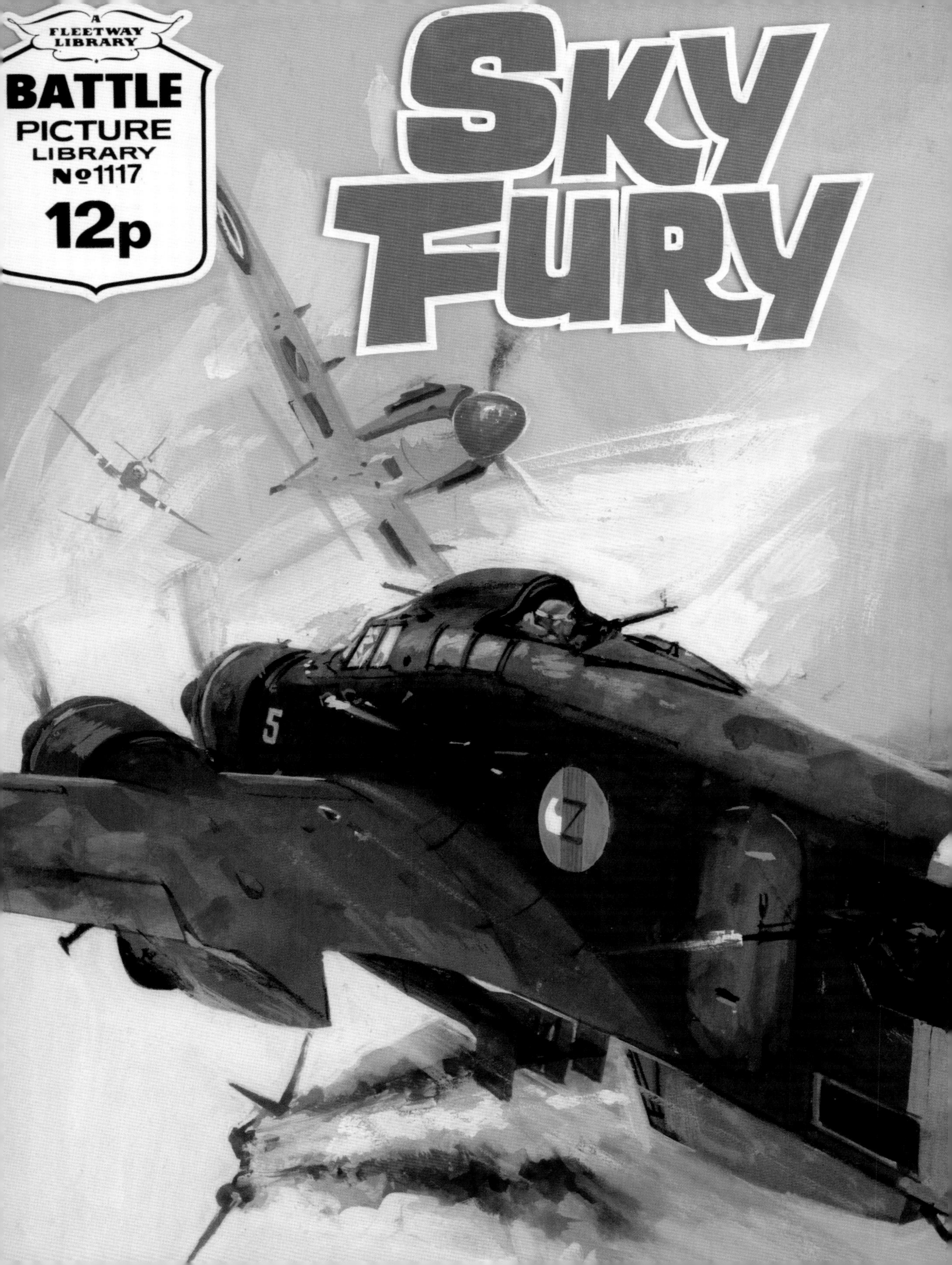
A FLEETWAY LIBRARY
BATTLE PICTURE LIBRARY
Nº1117
12p
SKY FURY

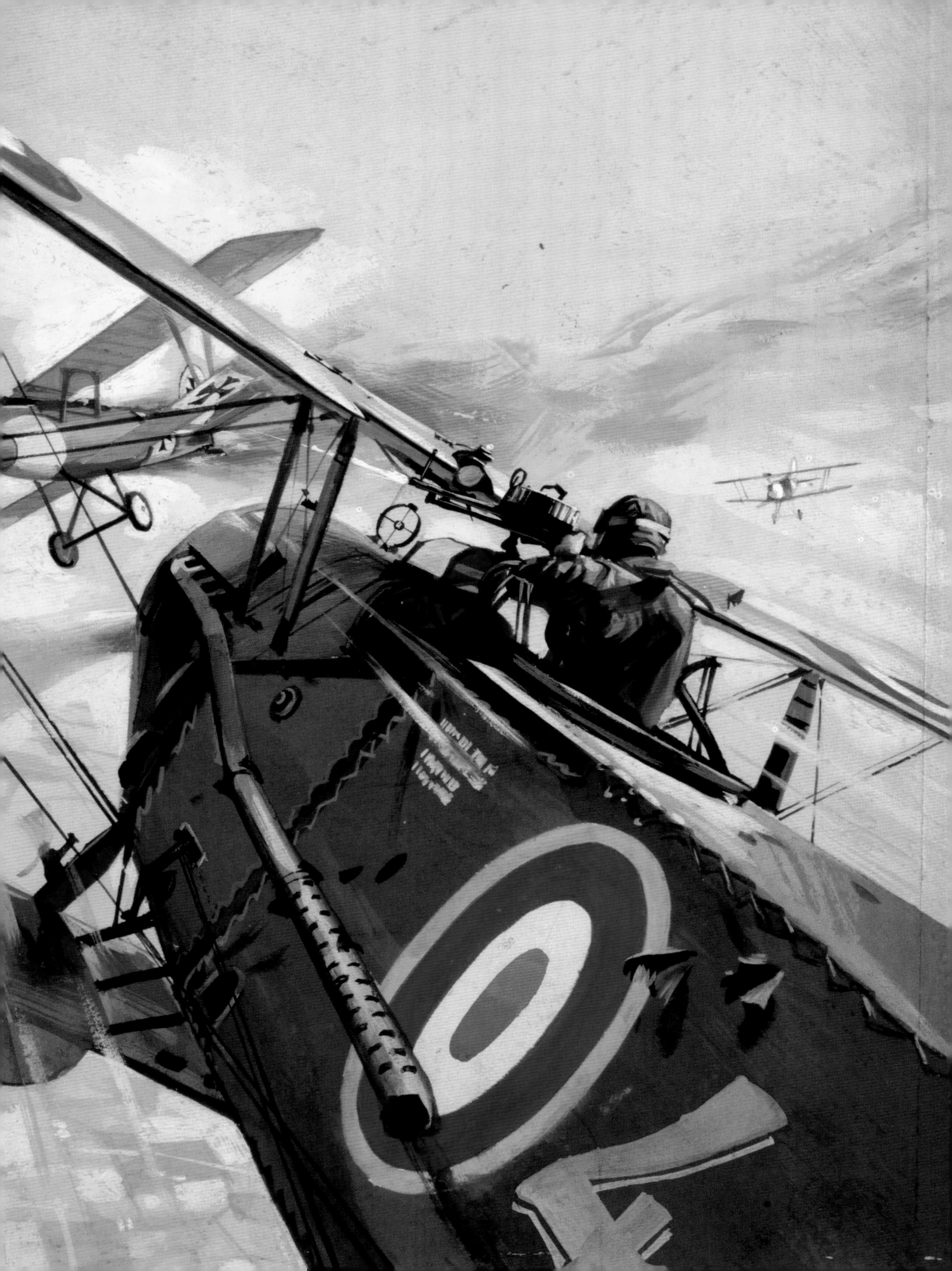

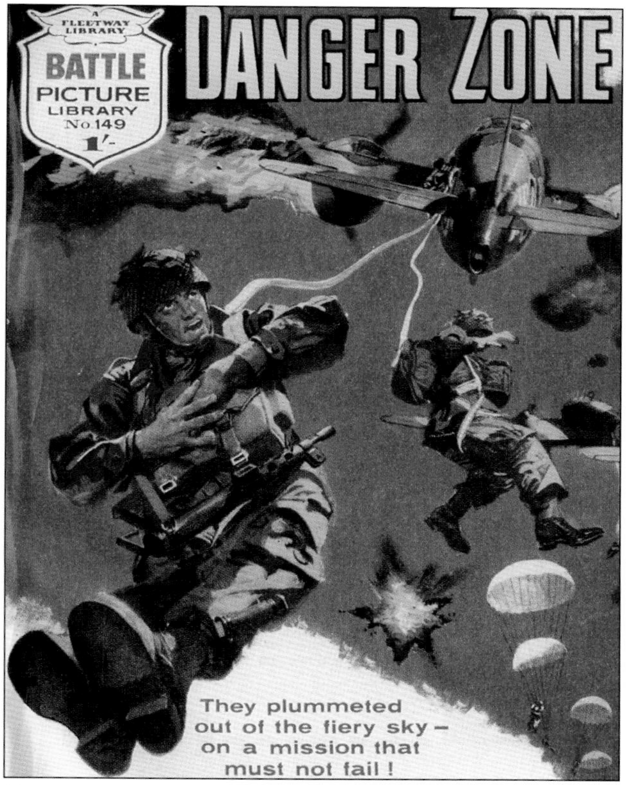
A FLEETWAY LIBRARY
BATTLE
PICTURE
LIBRARY
No 149
1/-
DANGER ZONE
They plummeted out of the fiery sky – on a mission that must not fail !
Allessandro Biffignandi, Battle 149, April 1964

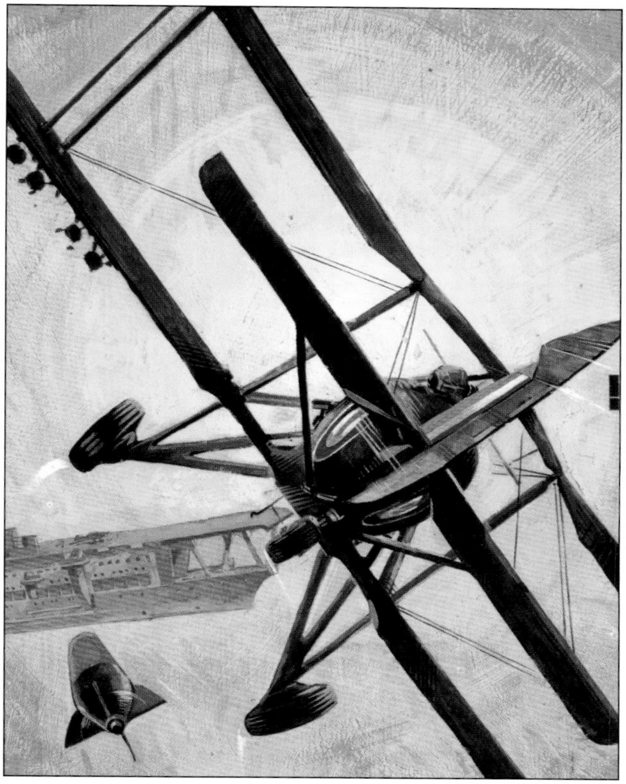
Graham Coton, Air Ace 371, January 1968

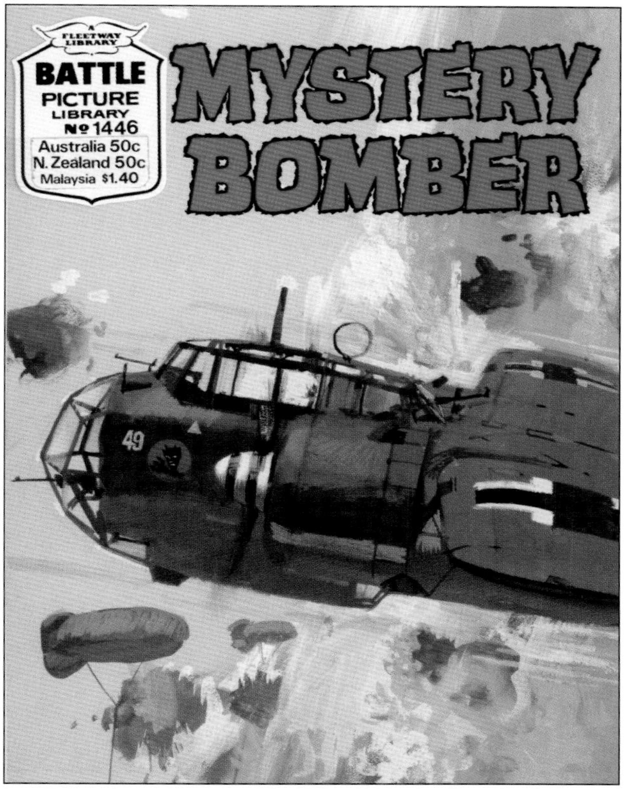
A FLEETWAY LIBRARY
BATTLE
PICTURE
LIBRARY
Nº 1446
Australia 50c
N. Zealand 50c
Malaysia $1.40
MYSTERY BOMBER
49
Pino Dell'Orco, originally Air Ace 217, October 1964

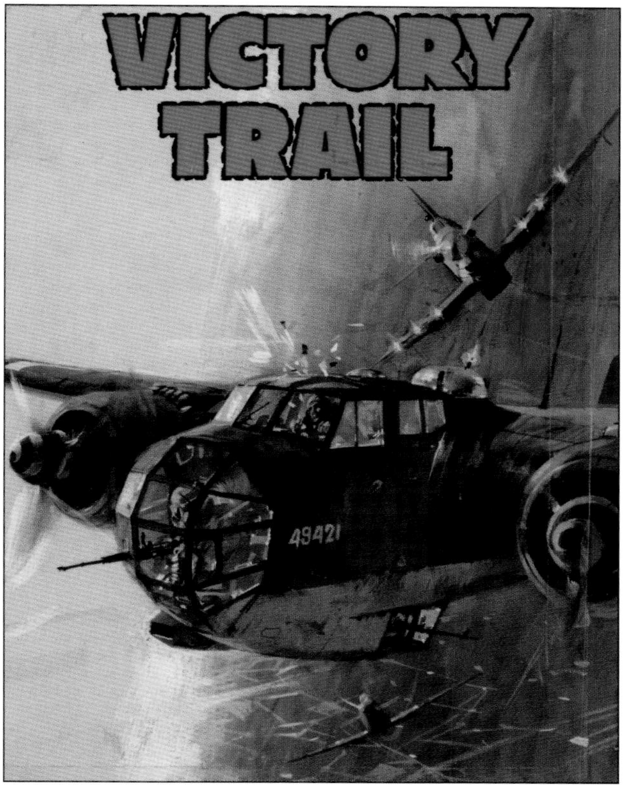
VICTORY TRAIL
49421
Pino Dell'Orco, originally Air Ace 190, April 64

Opposite: Pino Dell'Orco, Thriller 354, February 1961

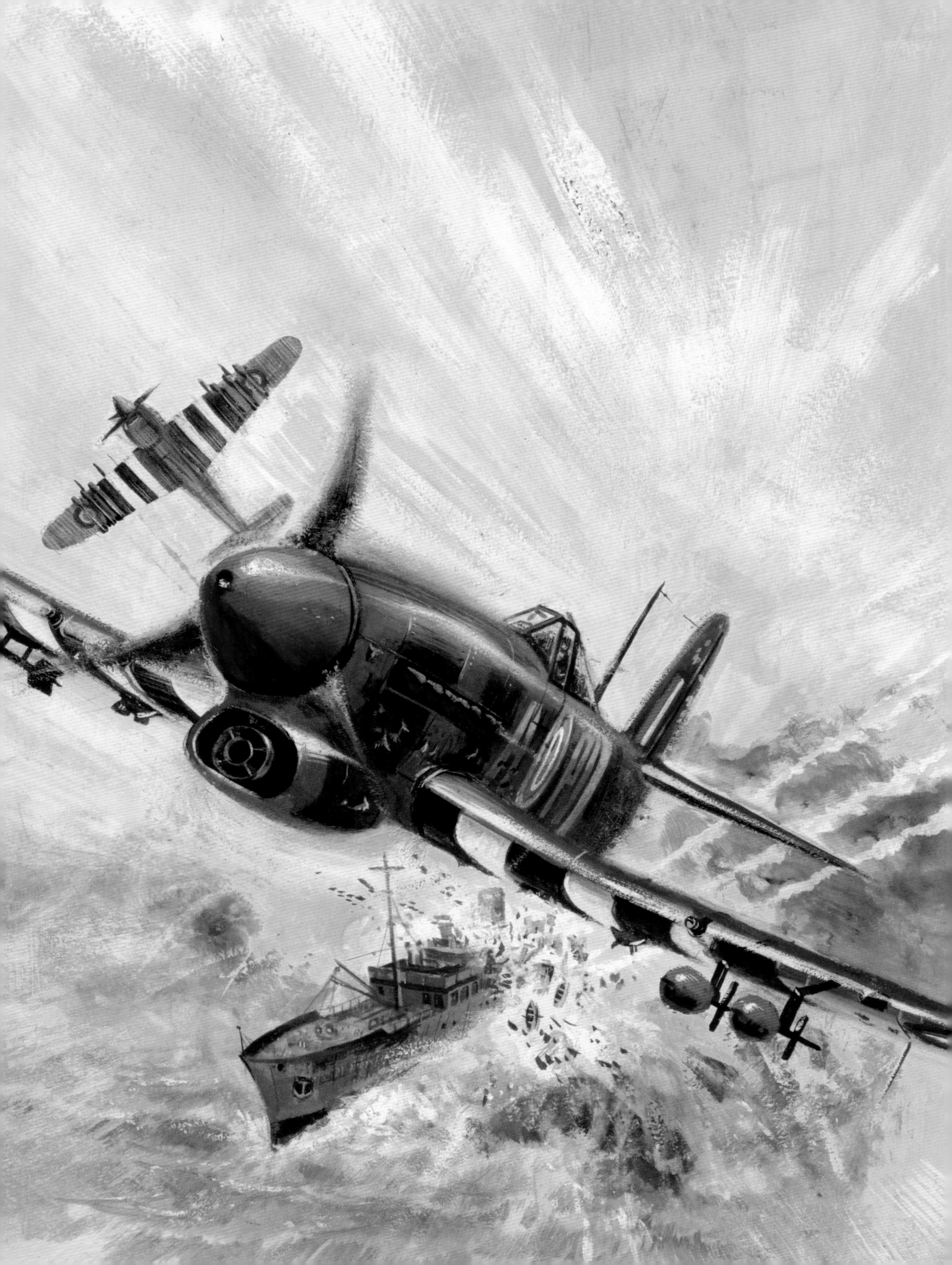

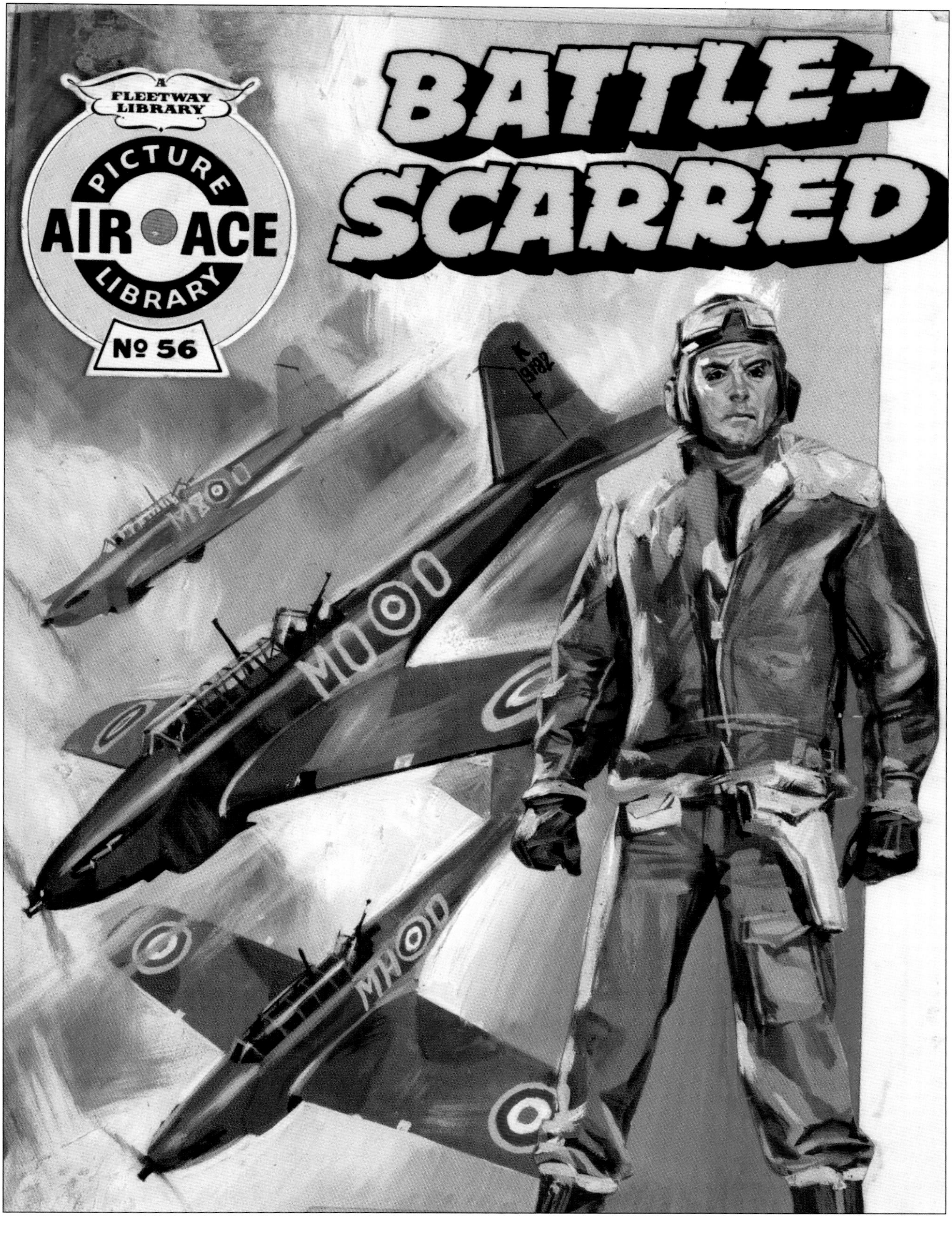
A
FLEETWAY
LIBRARY
PICTURE
AIR ACE
LIBRARY
Nº 56
BATTLE-
SCARRED

Pino Dell'Orco, Air Ace 56, June 1961
Opposite: Graham Coton, Air Ace 461, September 1969

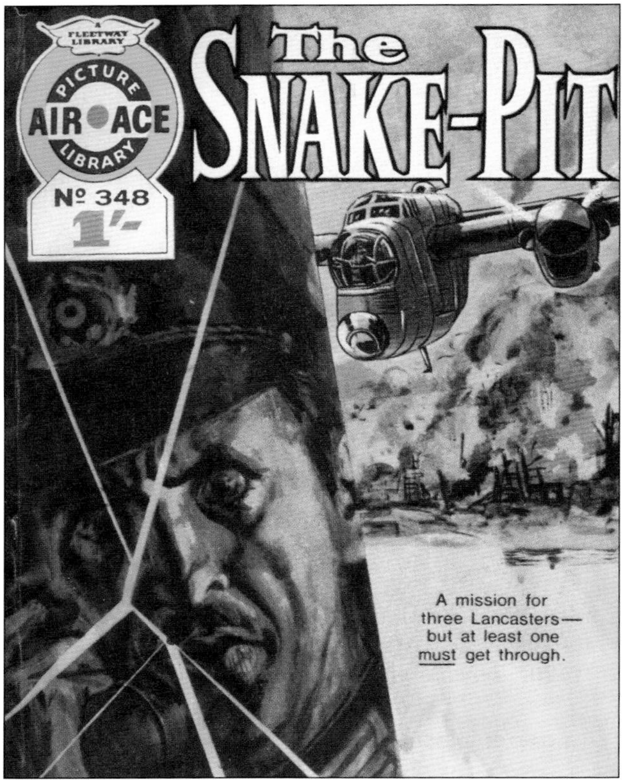
A FLEETWAY LIBRARY
PICTURE AIR ACE LIBRARY
Nº 348
1/-
The SNAKE-PIT
A mission for three Lancasters— but at least one must get through.

Rafael Lopez Espi, Air Ace 348, July 1967

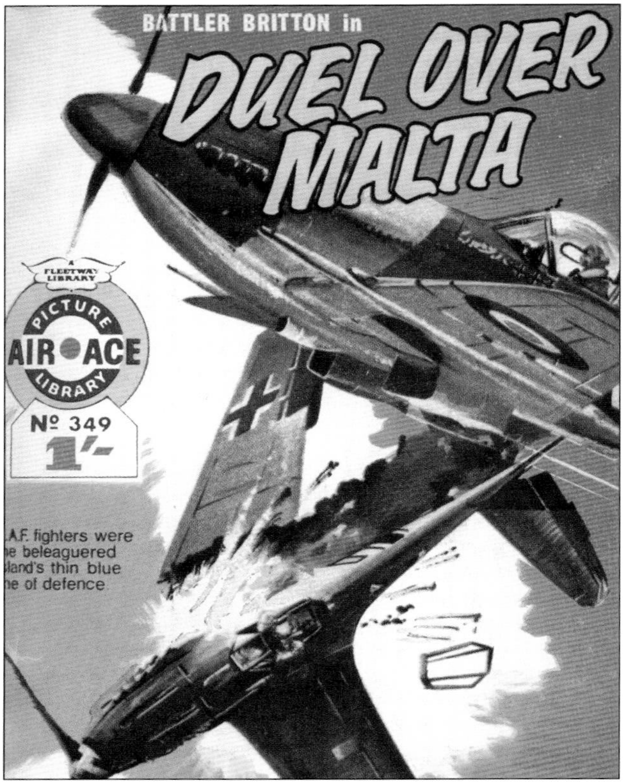
BATTLER BRITTON in
DUEL OVER MALTA
A FLEETWAY LIBRARY
PICTURE AIR ACE LIBRARY
Nº 349
1/-

Rafael Lopez Espi, Air Ace 349, July 1967

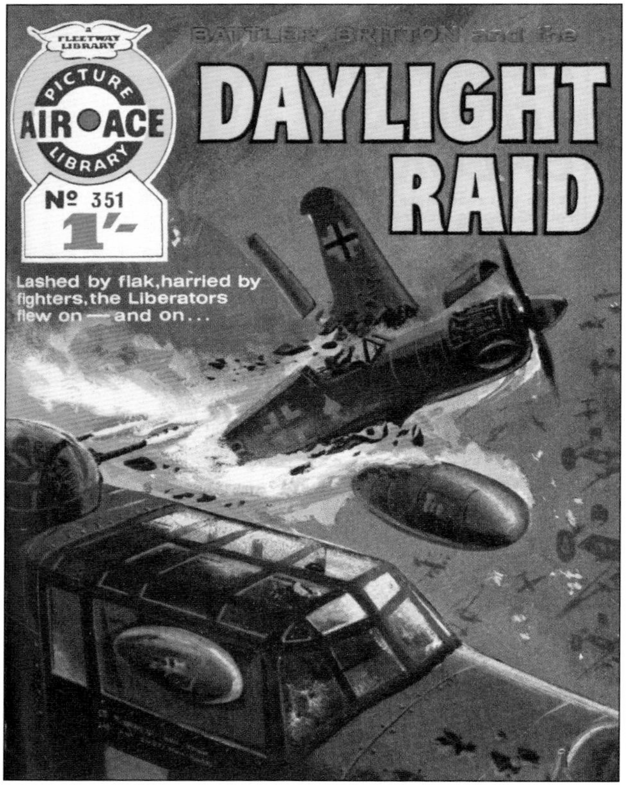
A FLEETWAY LIBRARY
PICTURE AIR ACE LIBRARY
Nº 351
1/-
BATTLER BRITTON and the
DAYLIGHT RAID
Lashed by flak, harried by fighters, the Liberators flew on—and on...

Alan Willow, Air Ace 351, August 1967

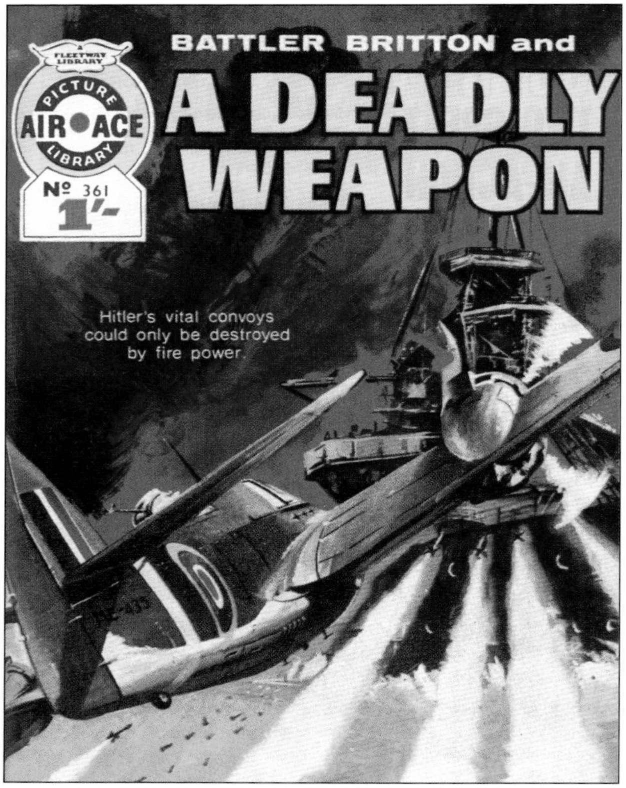
A FLEETWAY LIBRARY
PICTURE AIR ACE LIBRARY
Nº 361
1/-
BATTLER BRITTON and
A DEADLY WEAPON
Hitler's vital convoys could only be destroyed by fire power.

Giolitti Studio, Air Ace 361, October 1967

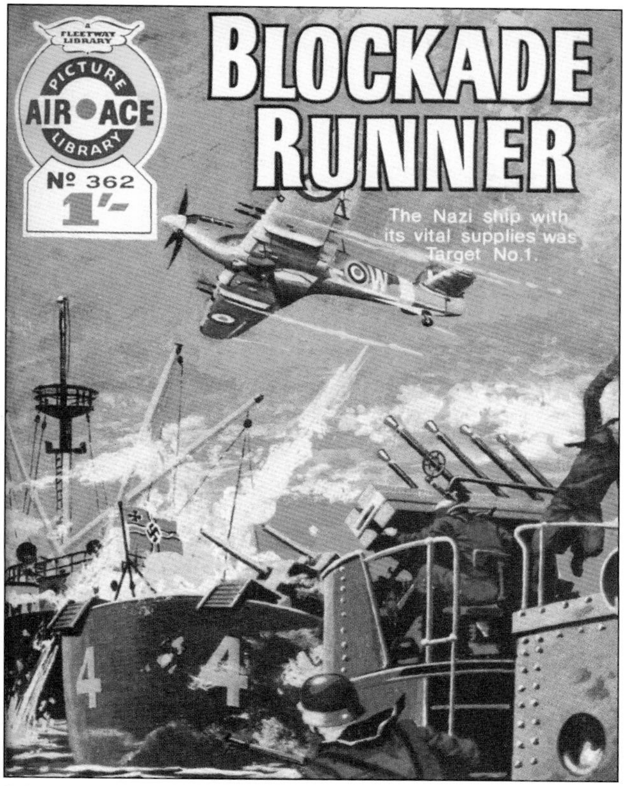
PICTURE AIR ACE LIBRARY
Nº 362
1/-
BLOCKADE RUNNER
The Nazi ship with its vital supplies was Target No.1.

Rafael Lopez Espi, Air Ace 362, November 1967

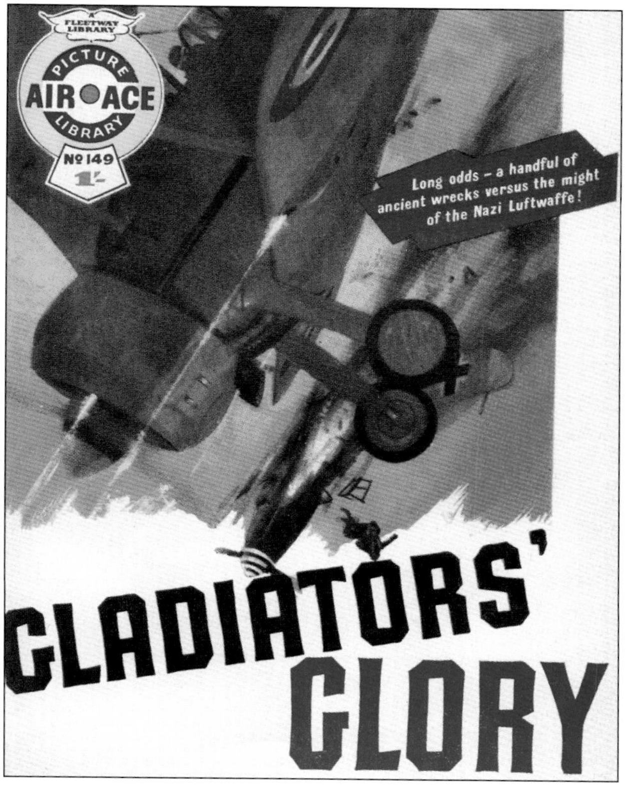
PICTURE AIR ACE LIBRARY
Nº 149
1/-
Long odds – a handful of ancient wrecks versus the might of the Nazi Luftwaffe!
GLADIATORS' GLORY

Pino Dell'Orco, Air Ace 149, May 1963

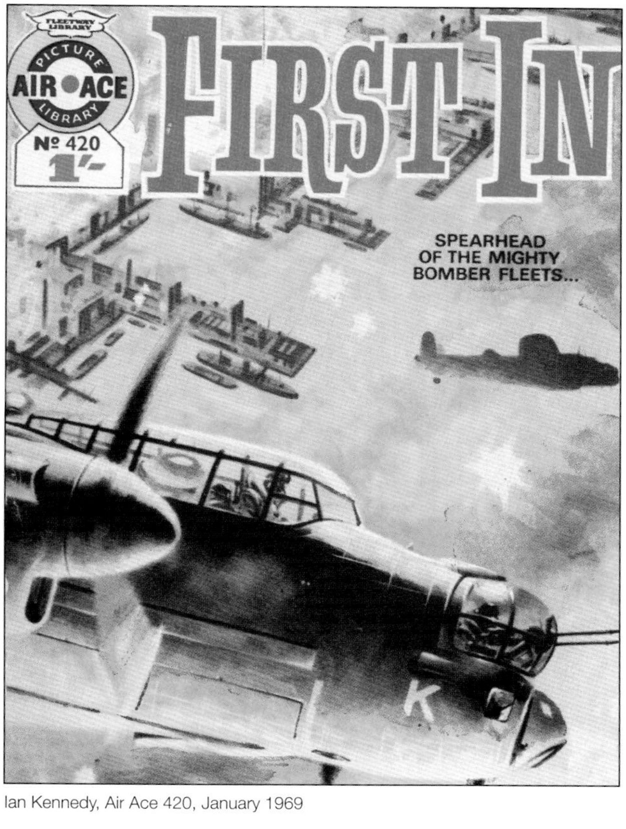
PICTURE AIR ACE LIBRARY
Nº 420
1/-
FIRST IN
SPEARHEAD OF THE MIGHTY BOMBER FLEETS...

Ian Kennedy, Air Ace 420, January 1969

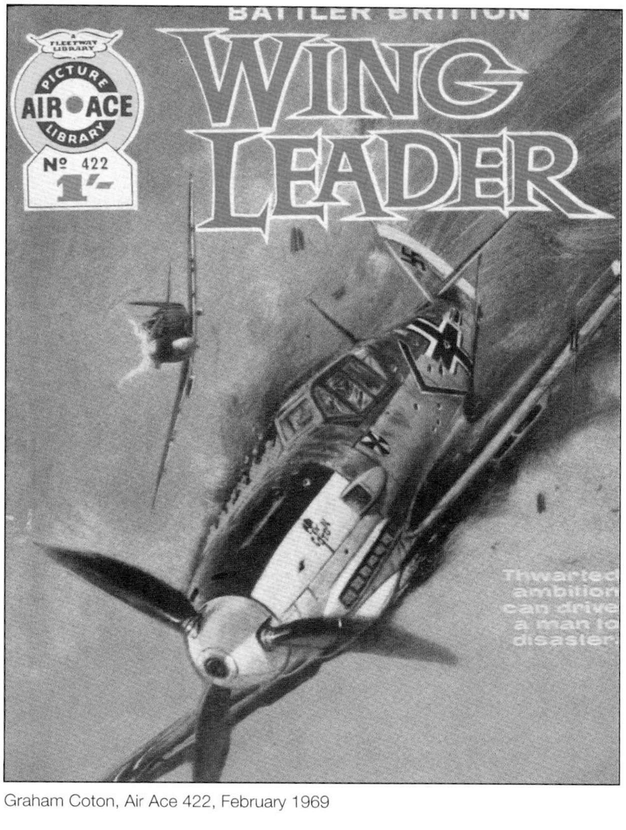
PICTURE AIR ACE LIBRARY
Nº 422
1/-
WING LEADER

Graham Coton, Air Ace 422, February 1969

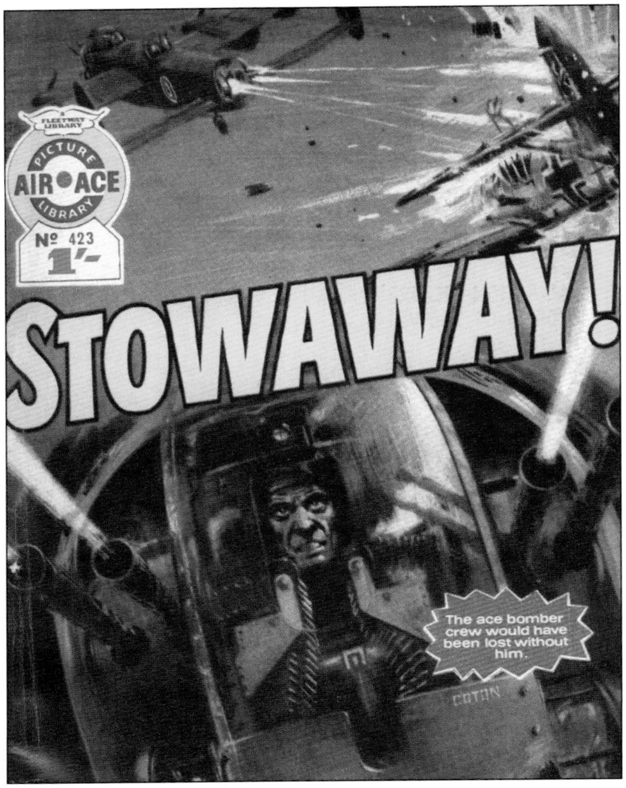
PICTURE
AIR ACE
LIBRARY
Nº 423
1/-
STOWAWAY!
The ace bomber crew would have been lost without him.
COTON

Graham Coton, Air Ace 423, February 1969

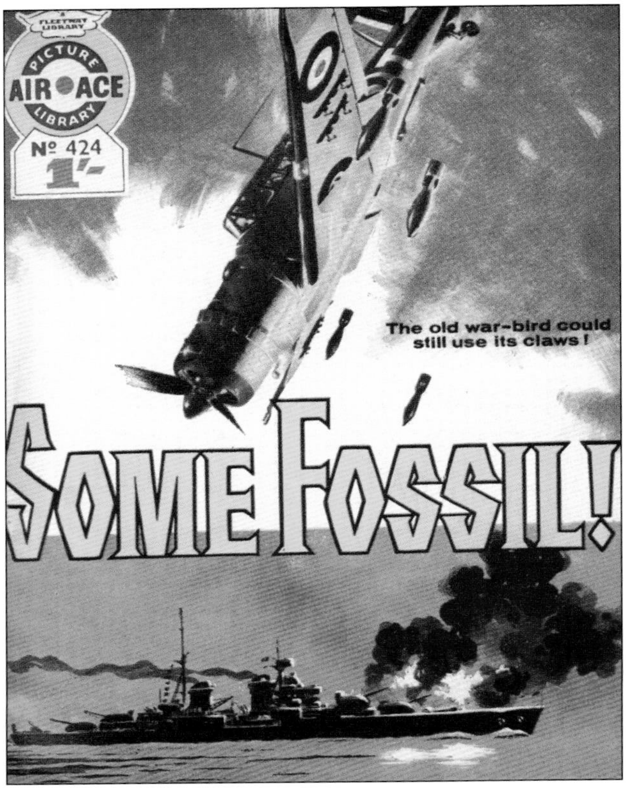
PICTURE
AIR ACE
LIBRARY
Nº 424
1/-
The old war-bird could still use its claws!
SOME FOSSIL!

Ian Kenedy, Air Ace 424, February 1969

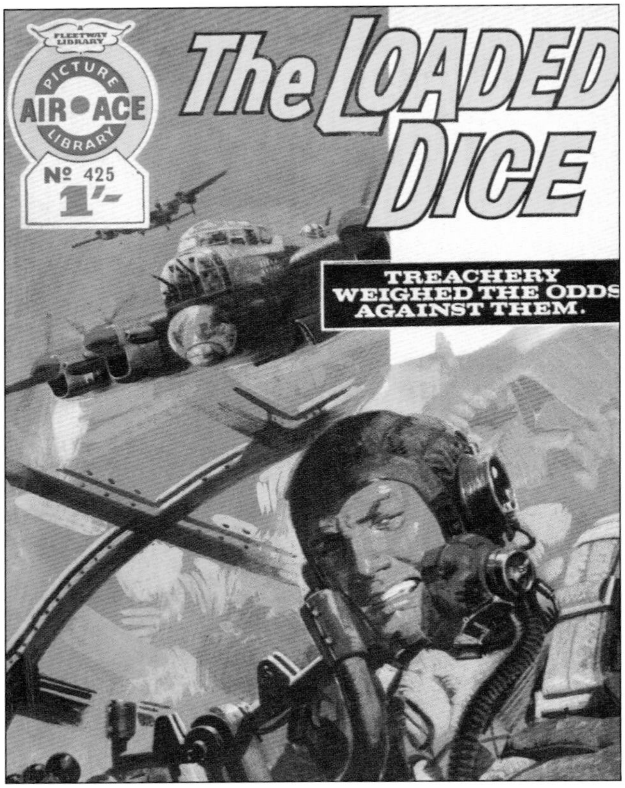
PICTURE
AIR ACE
LIBRARY
Nº 425
1/-
The LOADED DICE
TREACHERY WEIGHED THE ODDS AGAINST THEM.

Allessandro Biffignandi, Air Ace 425, February 1969

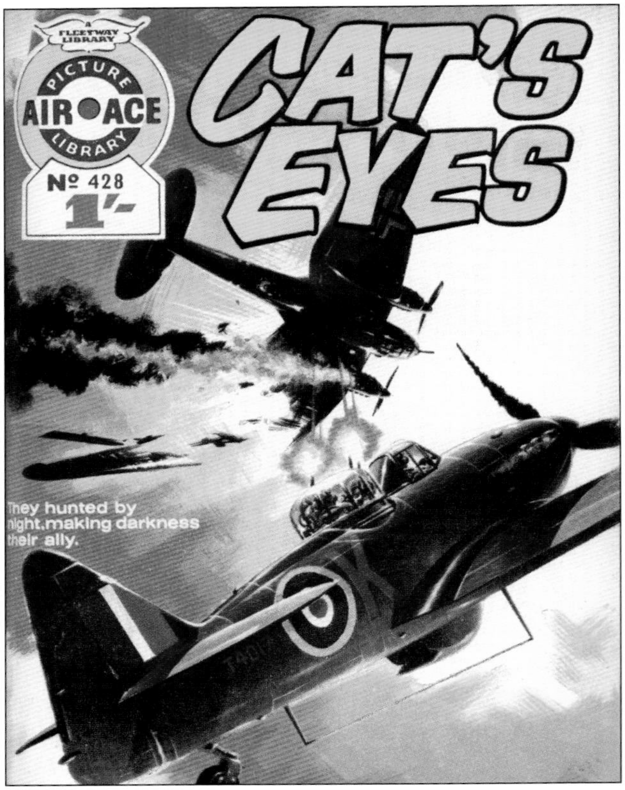
PICTURE
AIR ACE
LIBRARY
Nº 428
1/-
CAT'S EYES
They hunted by night, making darkness their ally.

Ian Kennedy, Air Ace 428, March 1969

Opposite: Giorgio DeGaspari, War 39, February 1960

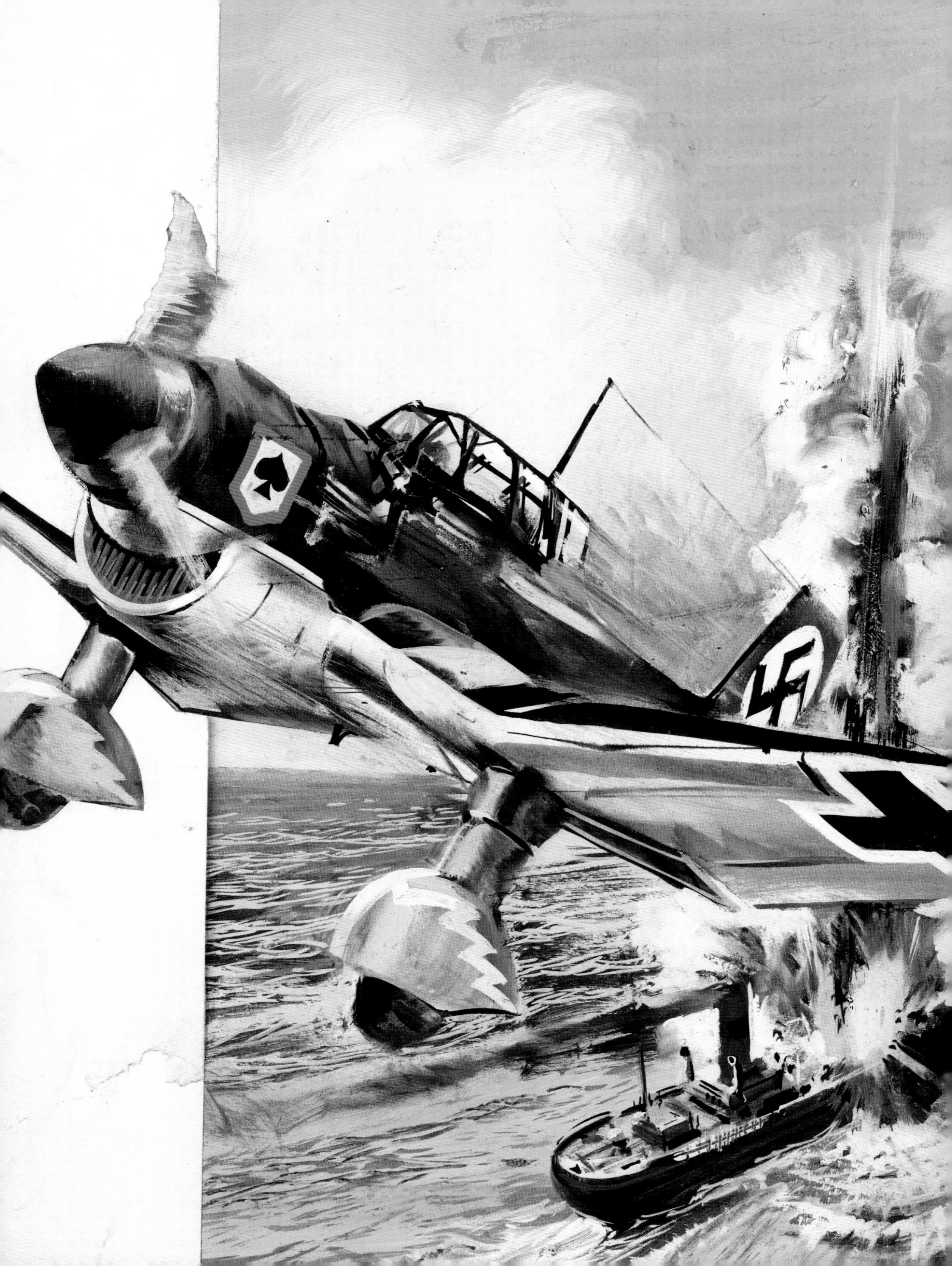

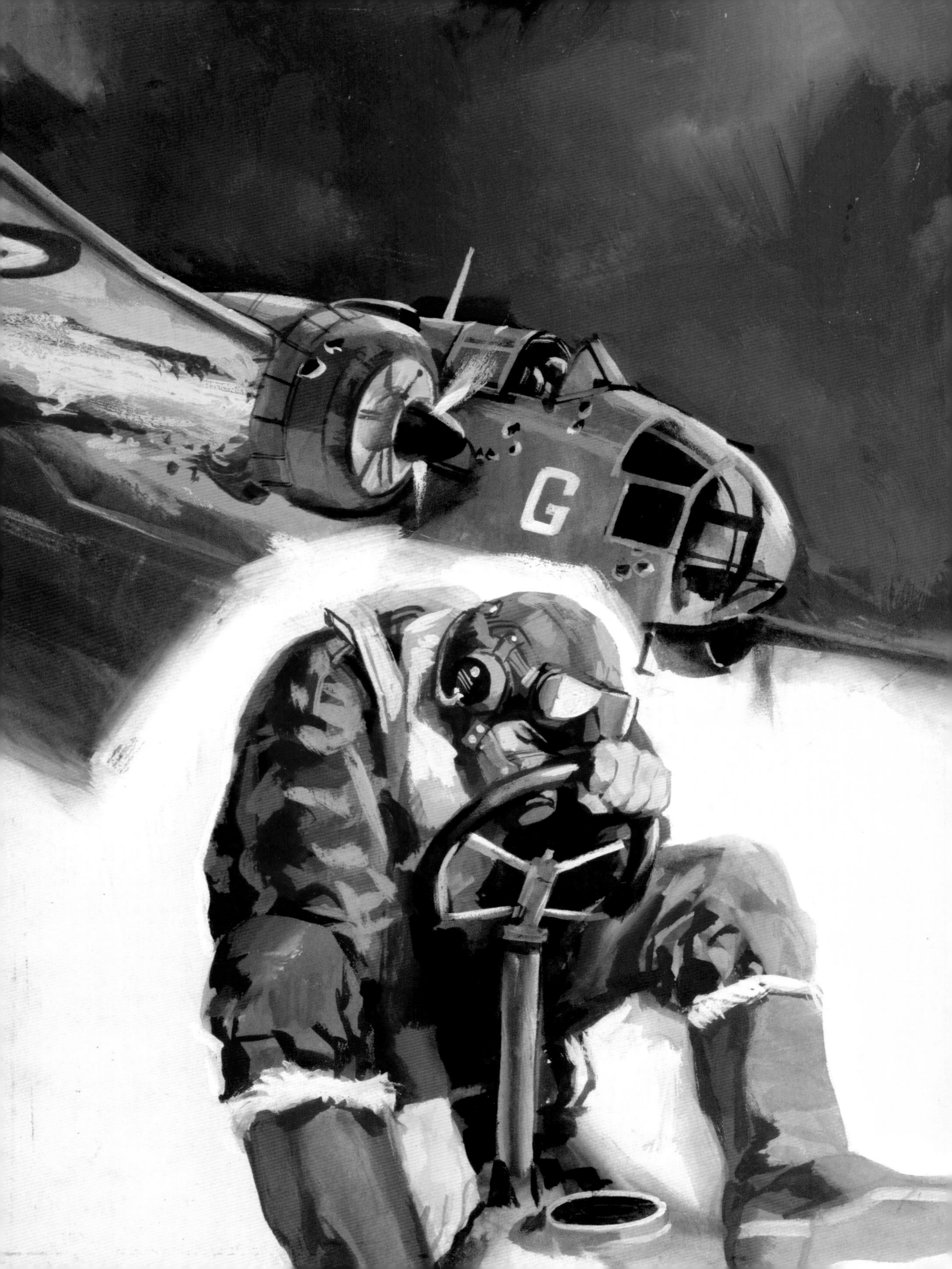

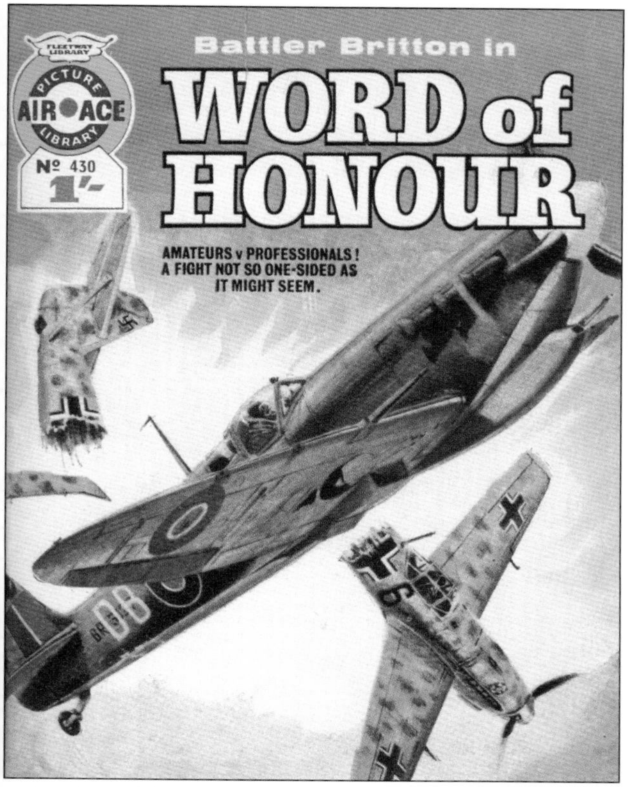
A FLEETWAY LIBRARY
PICTURE AIR ACE LIBRARY
Nº 430
1/-
Battler Britton in
WORD of HONOUR
AMATEURS v PROFESSIONALS! A FIGHT NOT SO ONE-SIDED AS IT MIGHT SEEM.
Graham Coton, Air Ace 430, April 1969

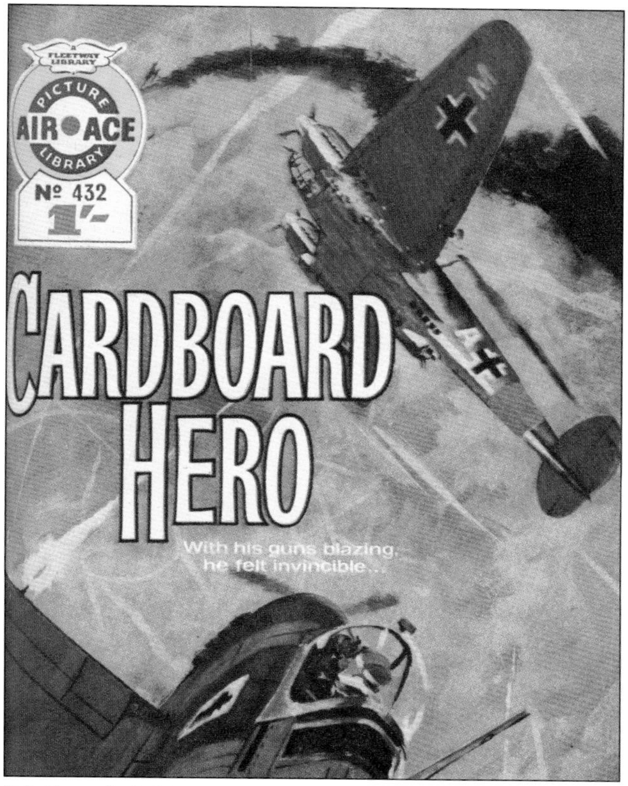
A FLEETWAY LIBRARY
PICTURE AIR ACE LIBRARY
Nº 432
1/-
CARDBOARD HERO
With his guns blazing, he felt invincible...
Rafael Lopez Espi, Air Ace 432, April 1969

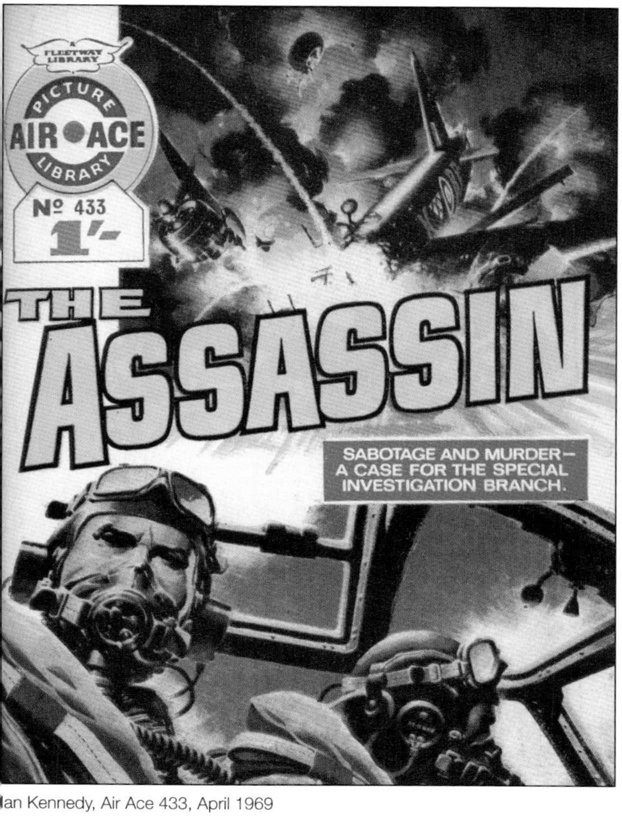
A FLEETWAY LIBRARY
PICTURE AIR ACE LIBRARY
Nº 433
1/-
THE ASSASSIN
SABOTAGE AND MURDER– A CASE FOR THE SPECIAL INVESTIGATION BRANCH.
Ian Kennedy, Air Ace 433, April 1969

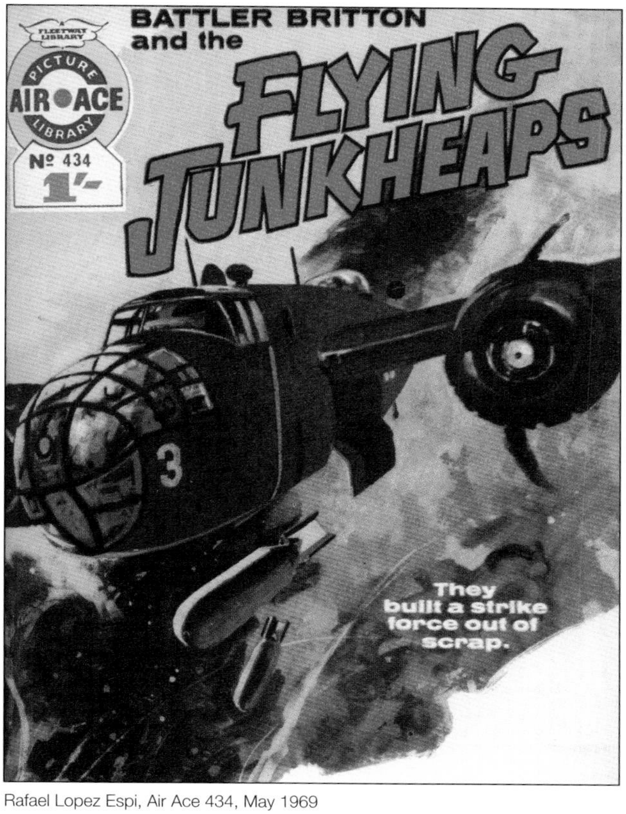
A FLEETWAY LIBRARY
PICTURE AIR ACE LIBRARY
Nº 434
1/-
BATTLER BRITTON and the
FLYING JUNKHEAPS
They built a strike force out of scrap.
Rafael Lopez Espi, Air Ace 434, May 1969

Opposite: Pino Dell'Orco, Air Ace 73, October 1961
Overleaf: Graham Coton, Battle 1613, July 1983

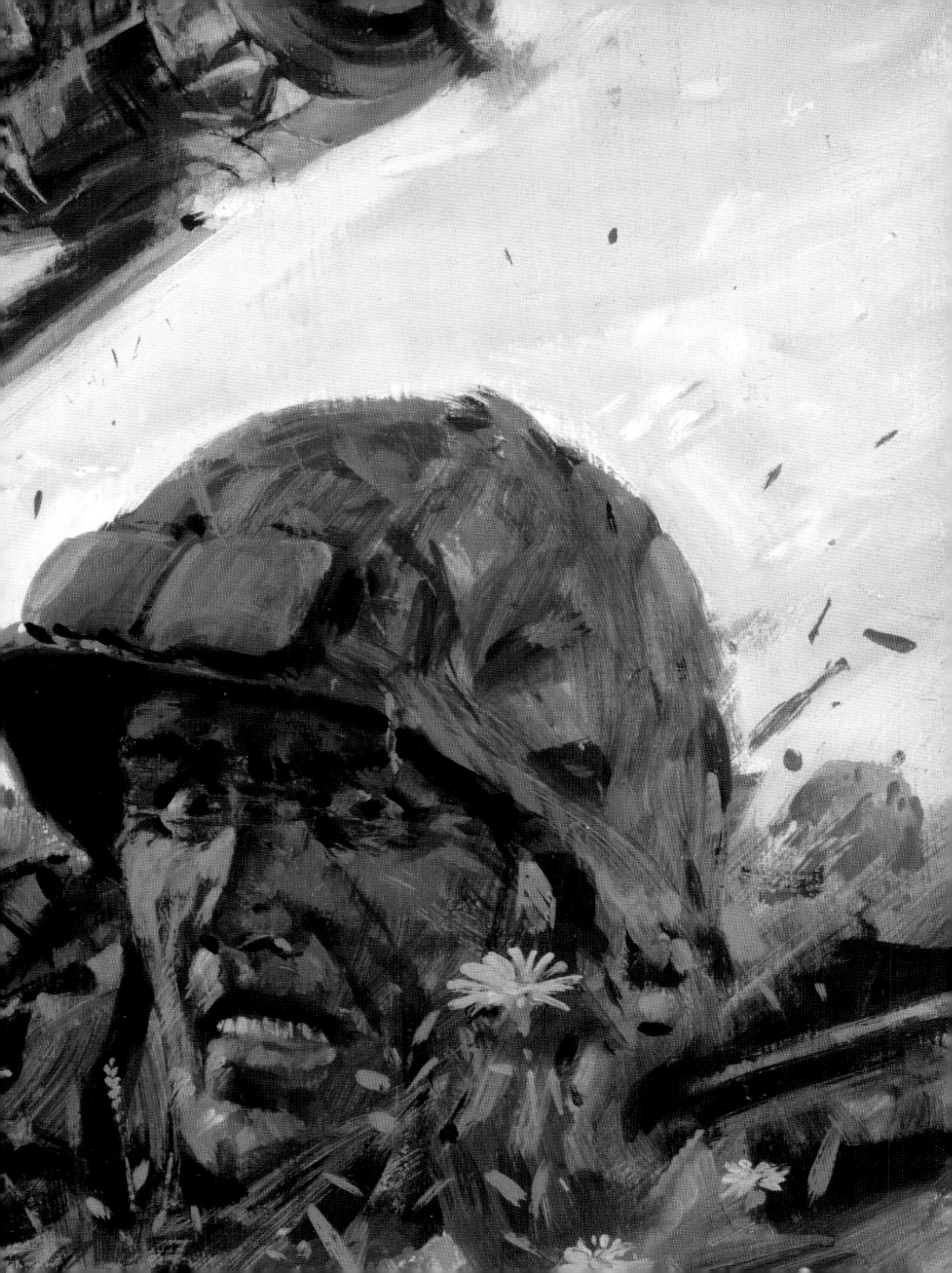

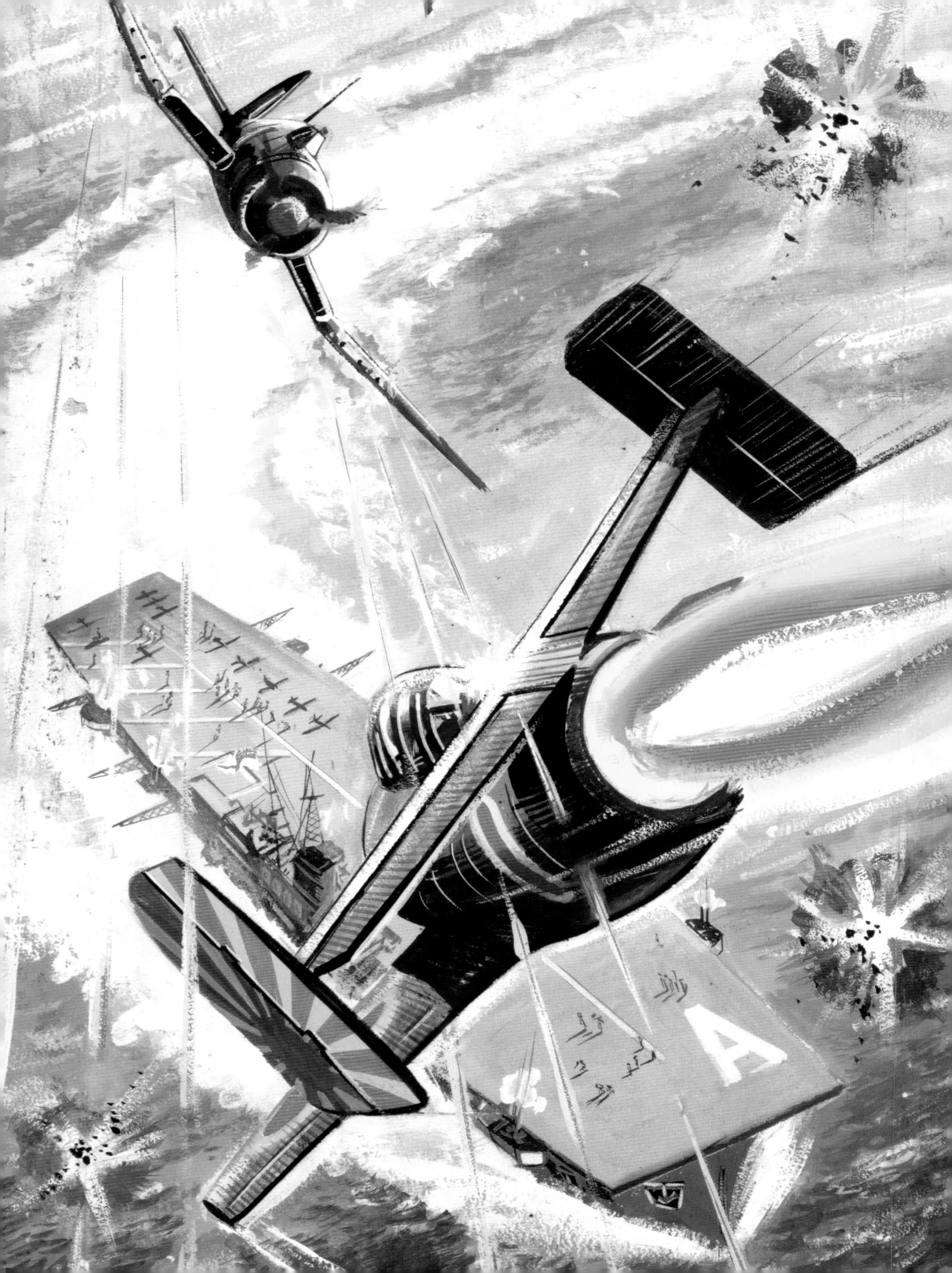
A

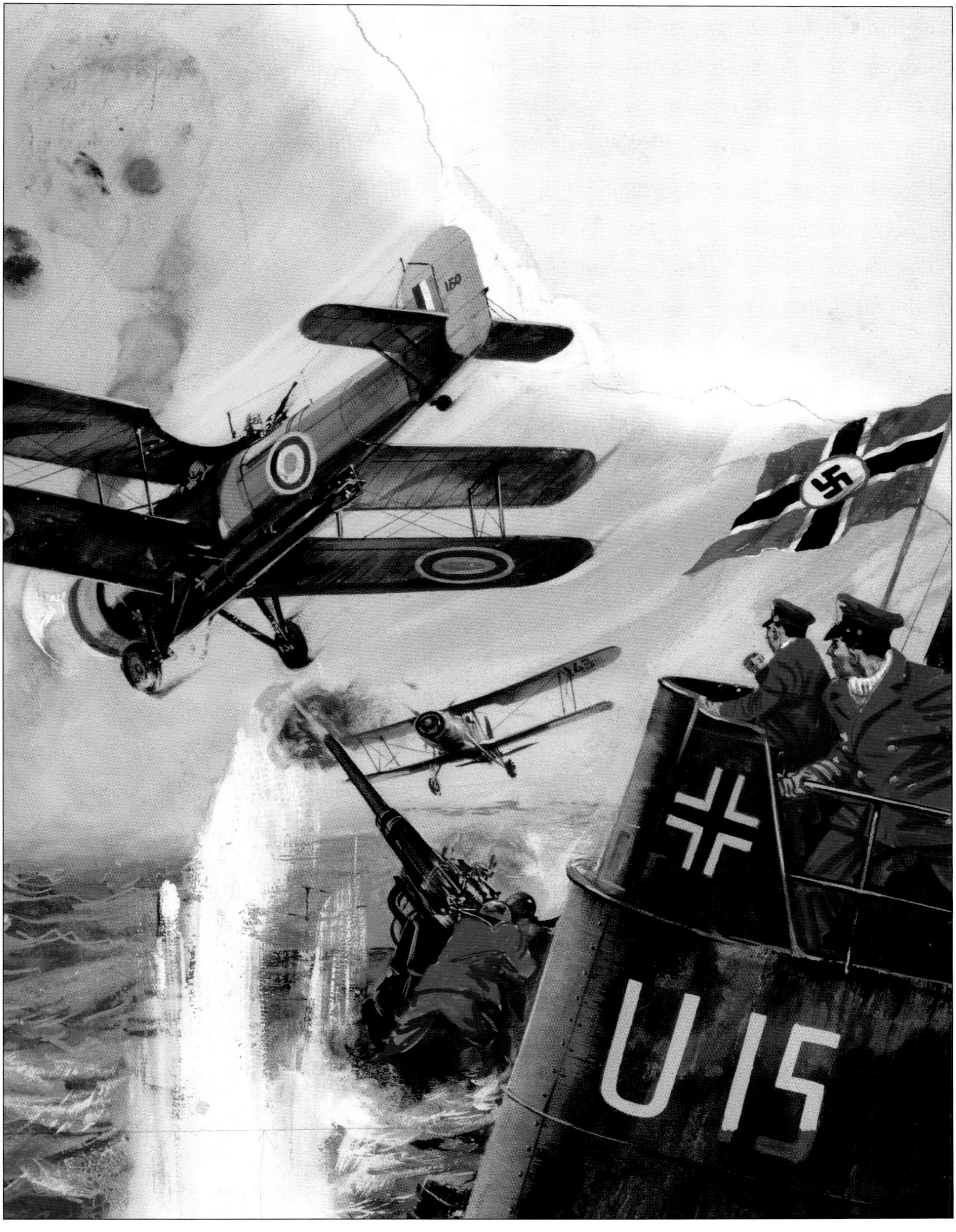
150
U15

Allessandro Biffignandi, War 84, February 1961
Opposite: Alan Willow, Battle 248, April 1966

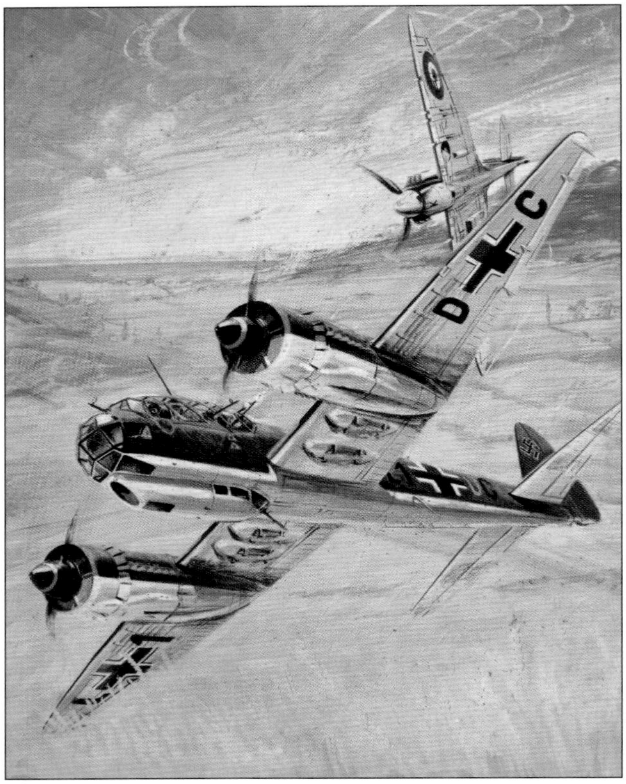

Graham Coton, Air Ace 360, October 1967

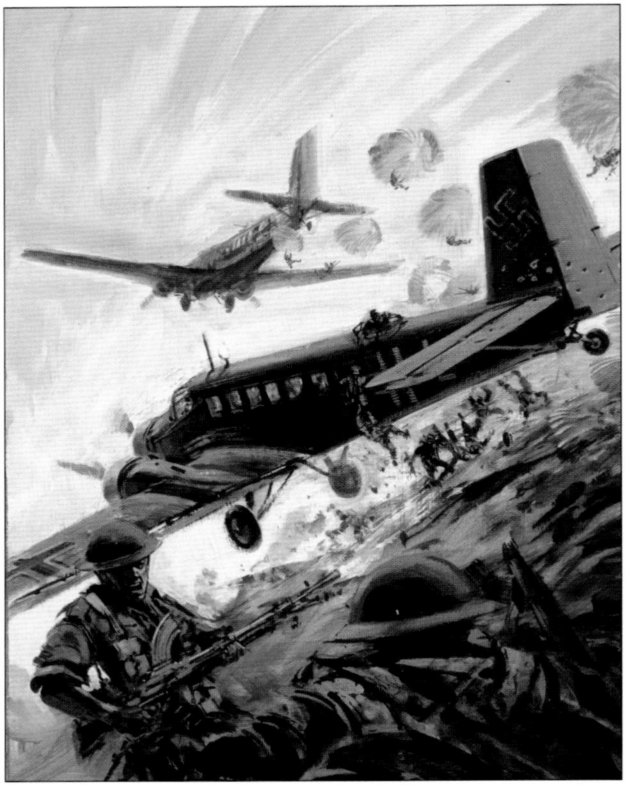

Graham Coton, Battle 1475, August 1981

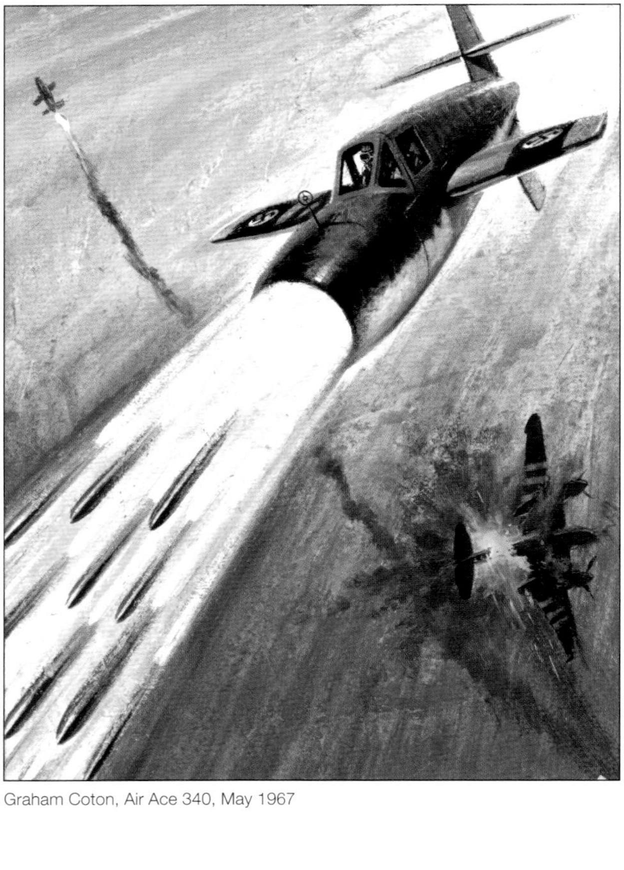

Graham Coton, Air Ace 340, May 1967

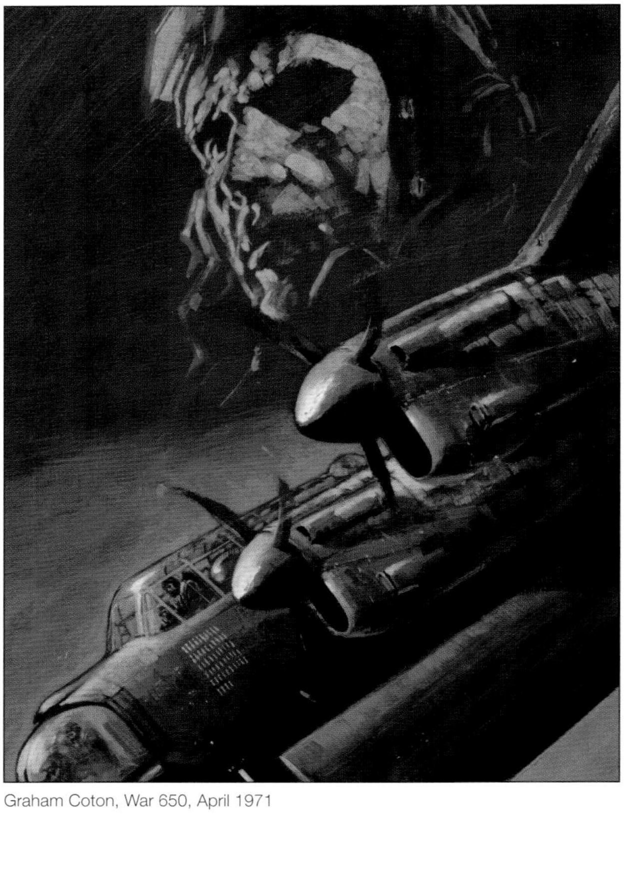

Graham Coton, War 650, April 1971

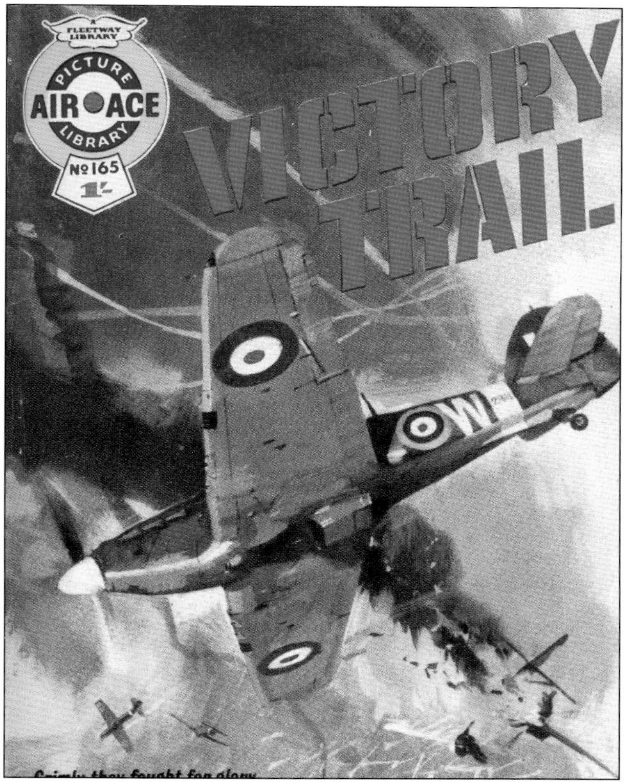
A FLEETWAY LIBRARY
PICTURE
AIR ACE
LIBRARY
Nº 165
1/-
VICTORY TRAIL.

Pino Dell'Orco, Air Ace 165, September 1963

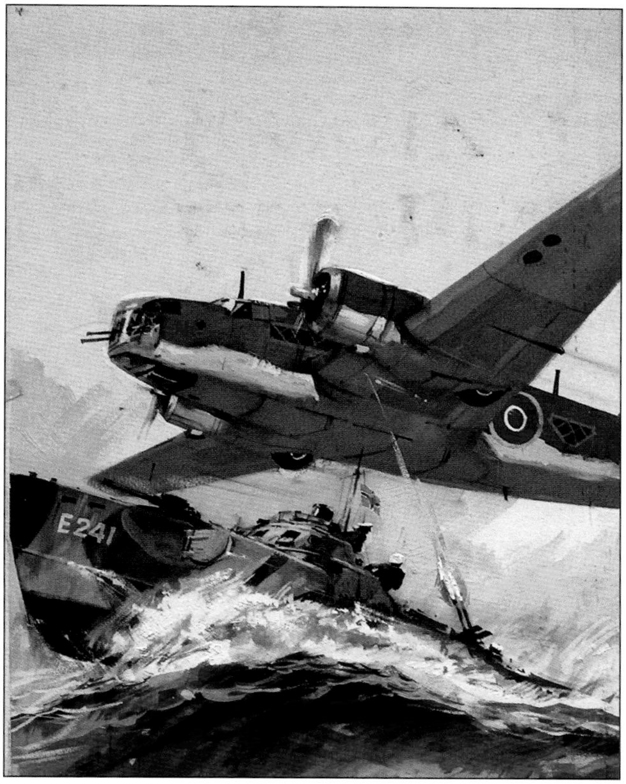
E241

Pino Dell'Orco, Air Ace 167, October 1963

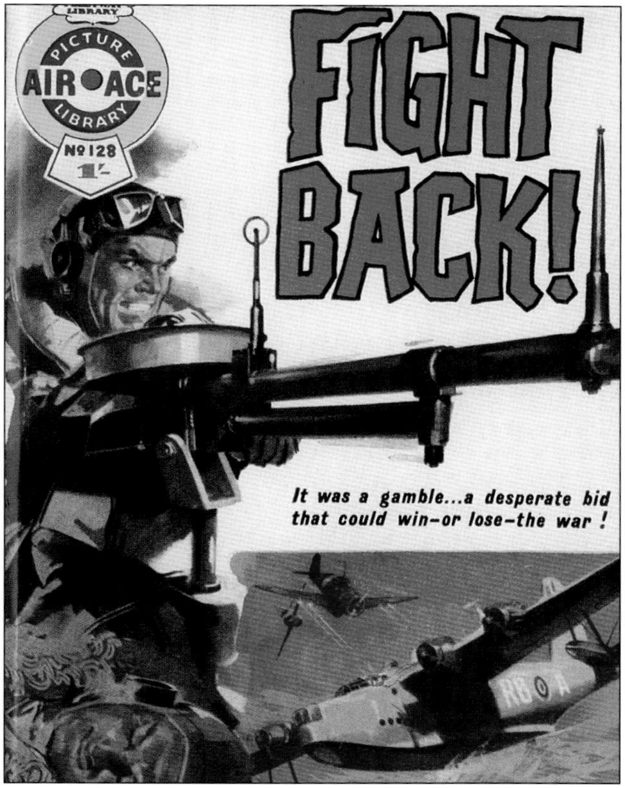
PICTURE
AIR ACE
LIBRARY
Nº 128
1/-
FIGHT BACK!
It was a gamble...a desperate bid that could win–or lose–the war !

Allessandro Biffignandi, Air Ace 128, December 1962

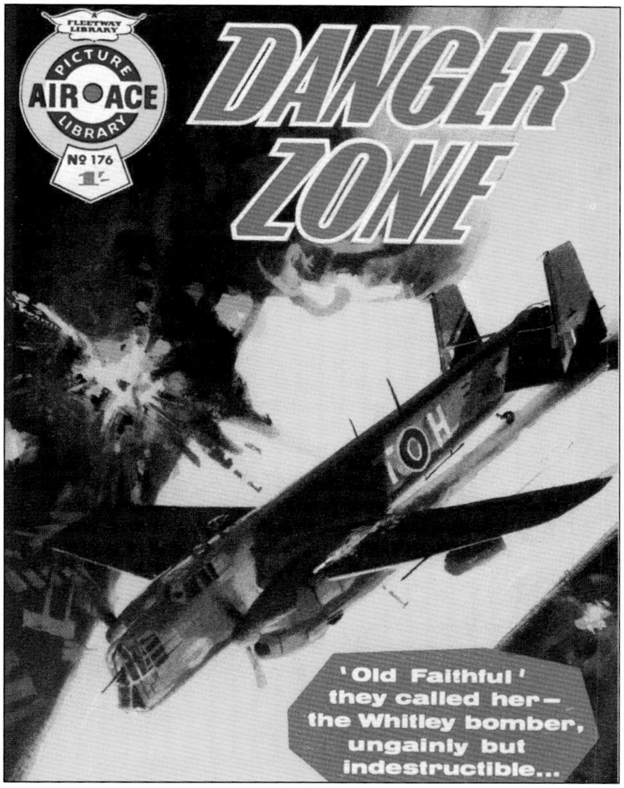
A FLEETWAY LIBRARY
PICTURE
AIR ACE
LIBRARY
Nº 176
1/-
DANGER ZONE
'Old Faithful' they called her– the Whitley bomber, ungainly but indestructible...

Pino Dell'Orco, Air Ace 176, December 1963

Overleaf: Graham Coton, War 1579, December 1978

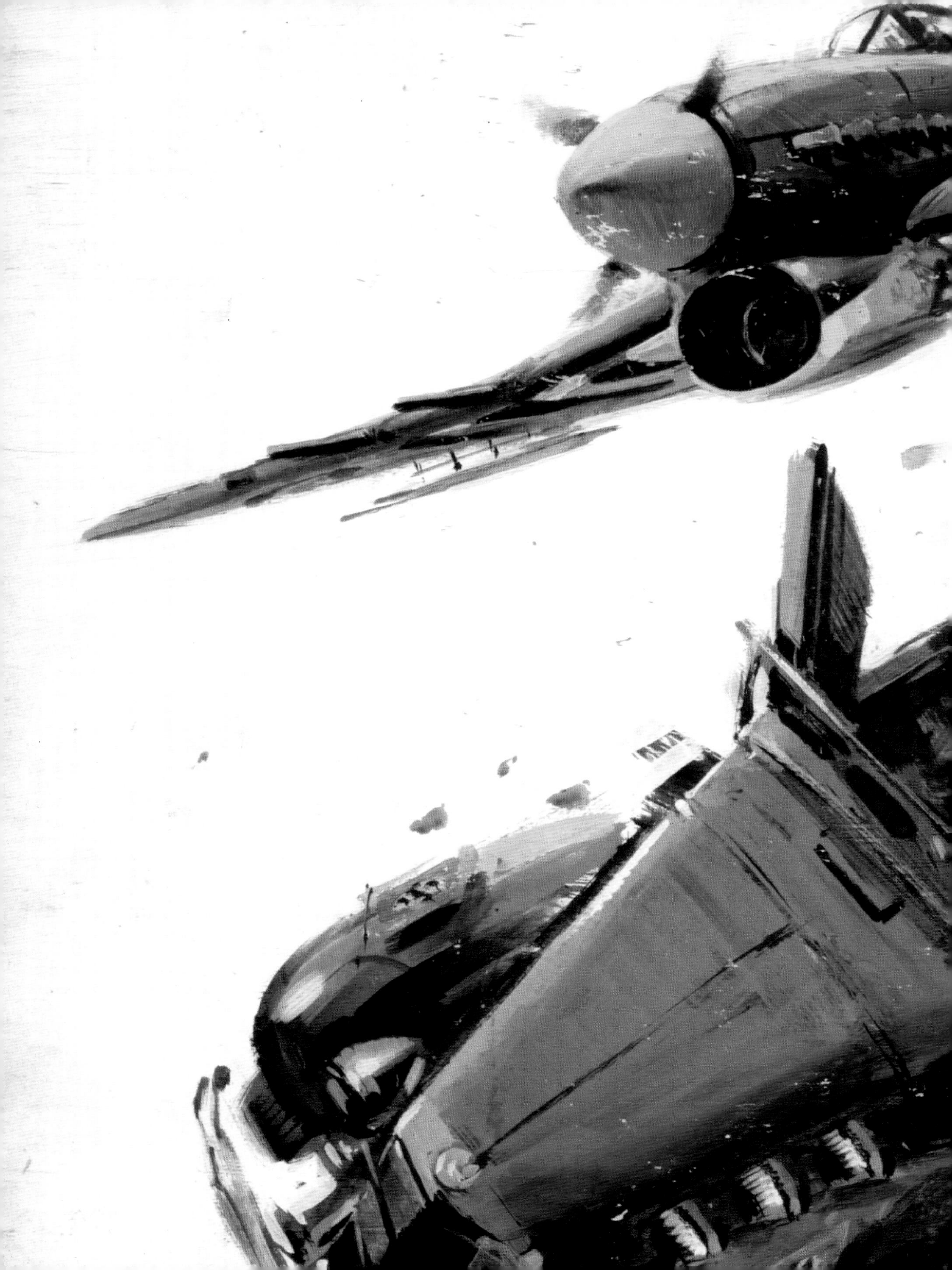

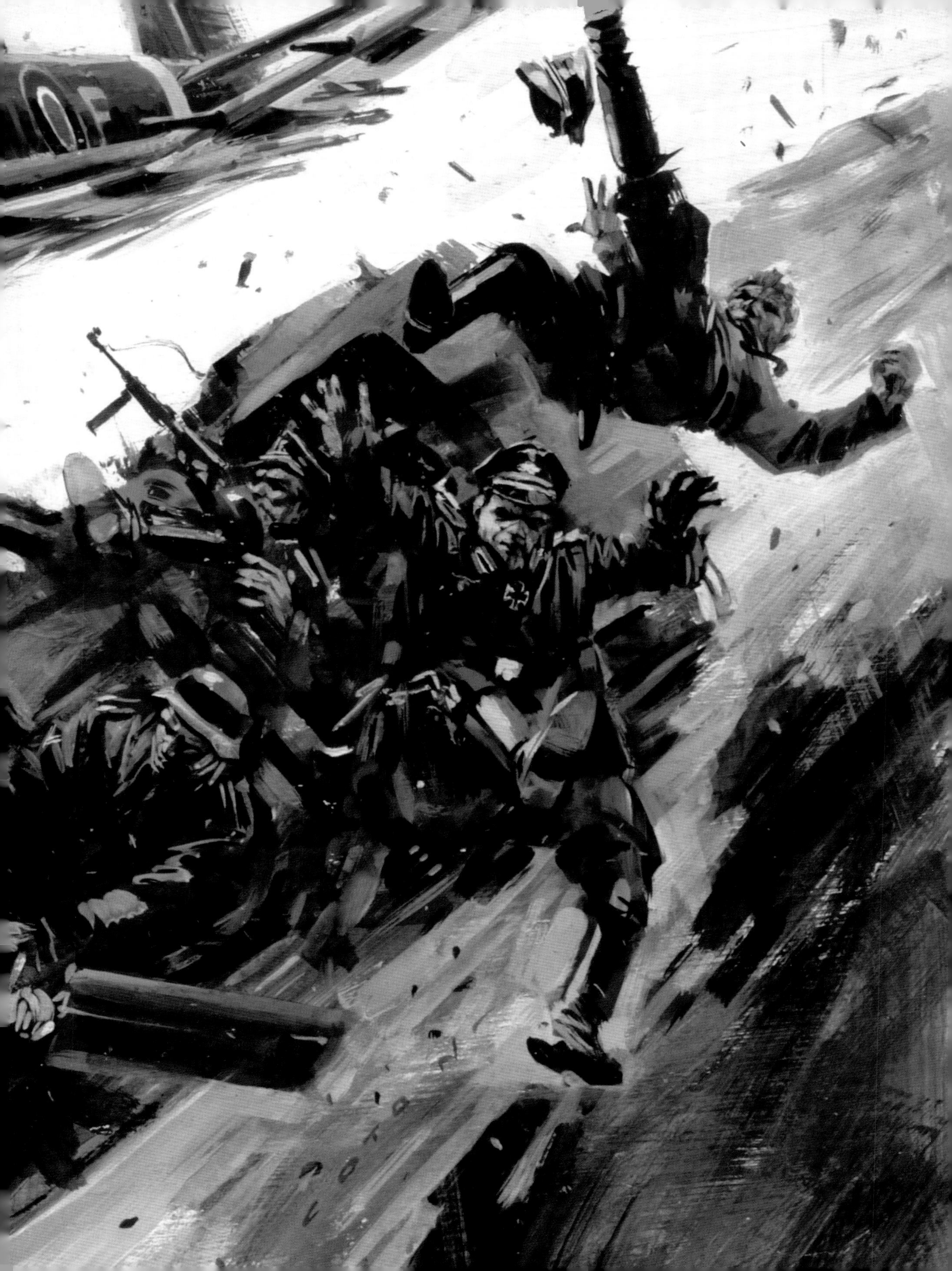

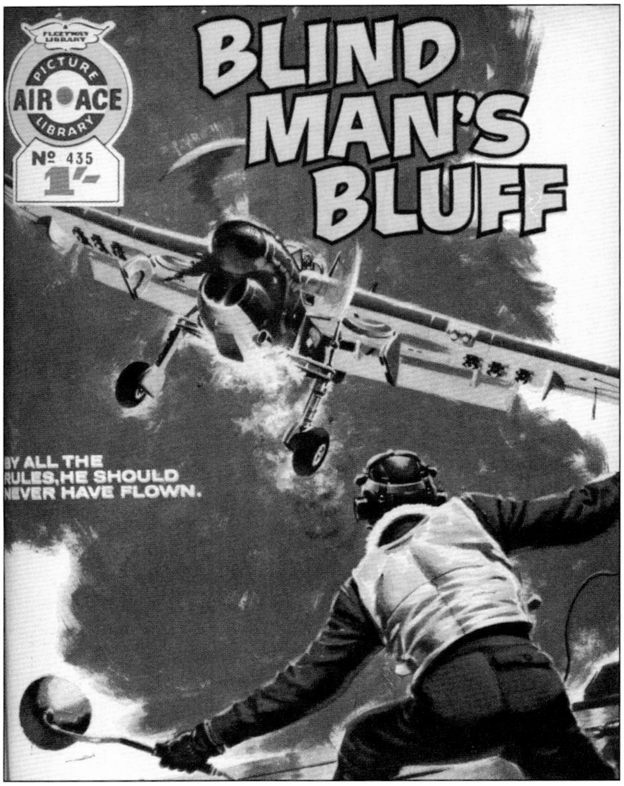
A FLEETWAY LIBRARY
PICTURE
AIR ACE
LIBRARY
Nº 435
1/-
BLIND MAN'S BLUFF
BY ALL THE RULES, HE SHOULD NEVER HAVE FLOWN.

Ian Kennedy, Air Ace 435, May 1969

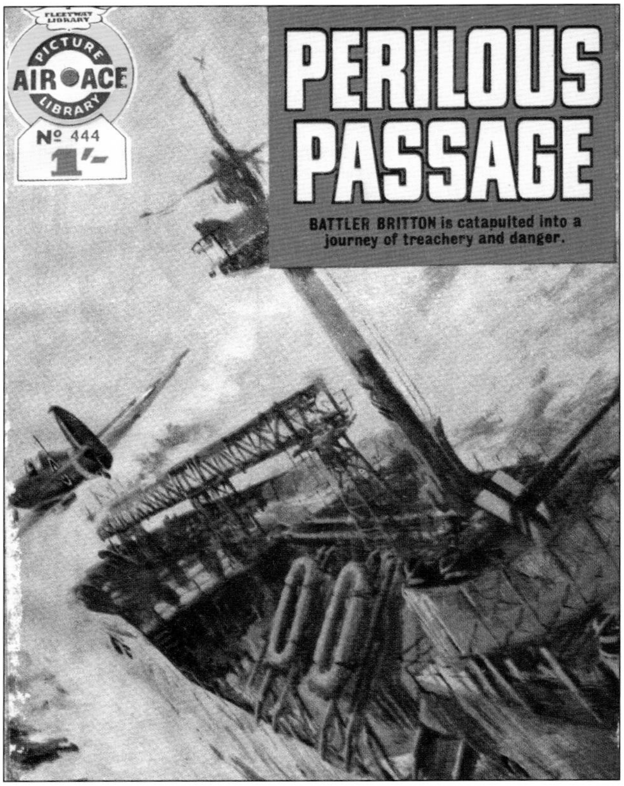
PICTURE
AIR ACE
LIBRARY
Nº 444
1/-
PERILOUS PASSAGE
BATTLER BRITTON is catapulted into a journey of treachery and danger.

Graham Coton, Air Ace 444, July 1969

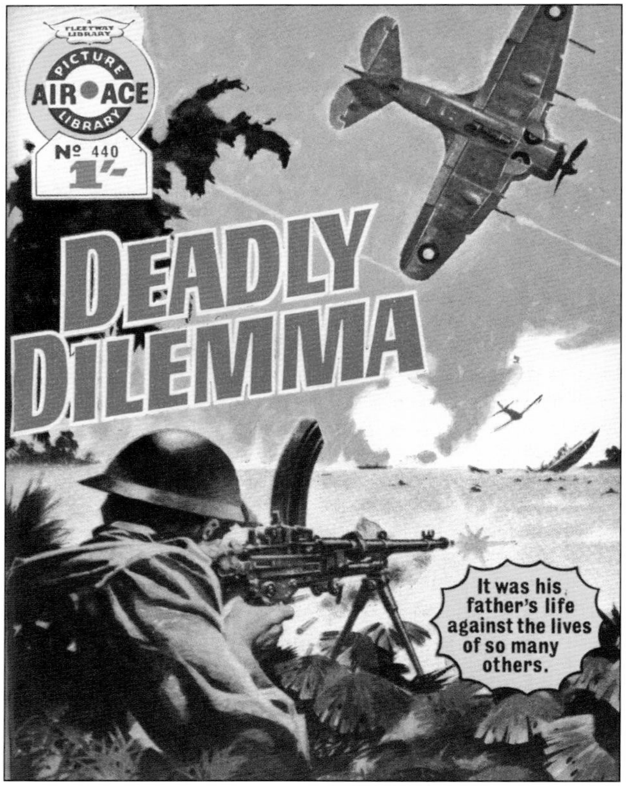
A FLEETWAY LIBRARY
PICTURE
AIR ACE
LIBRARY
Nº 440
1/-
DEADLY DILEMMA
It was his father's life against the lives of so many others.

Ian Kennedy, Air Ace 440, June 1969

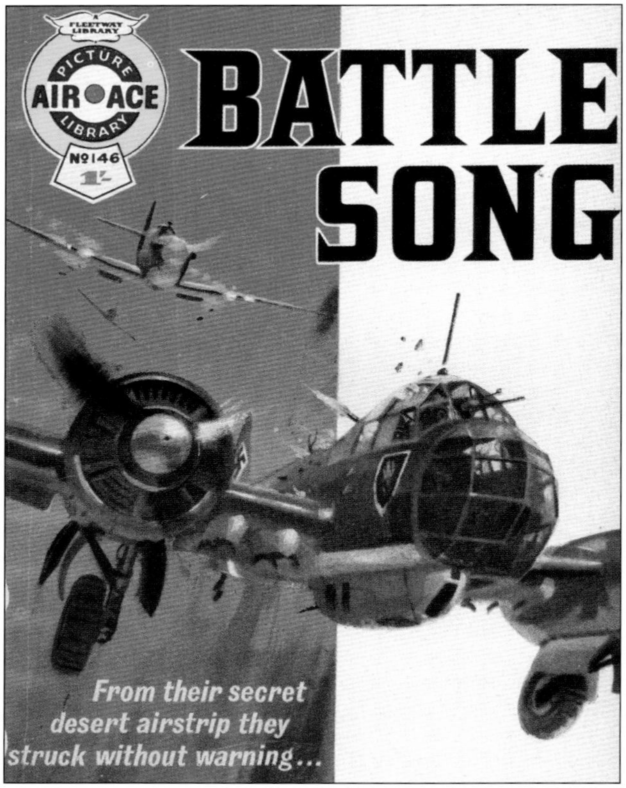
A FLEETWAY LIBRARY
PICTURE
AIR ACE
LIBRARY
Nº146
1/-
BATTLE SONG
From their secret desert airstrip they struck without warning...

Pino Dell'Orco, Air Ace 146, May 1963

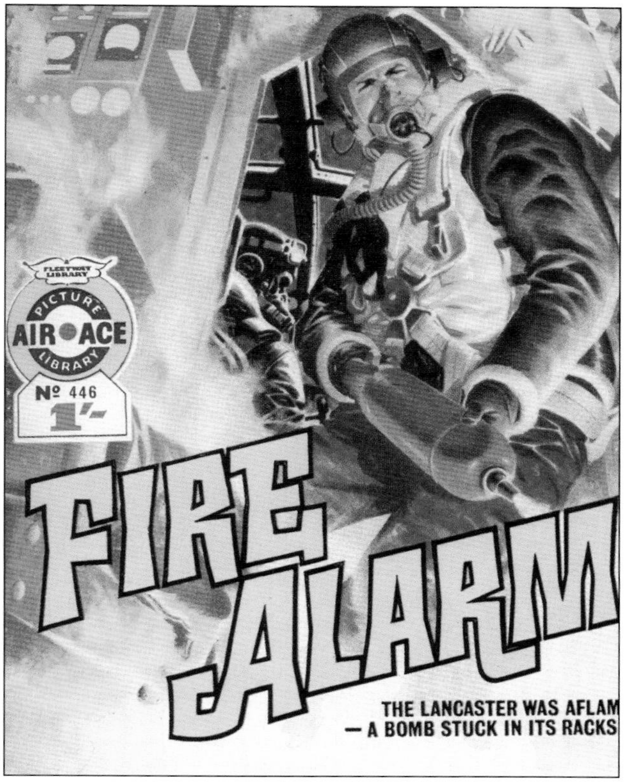
A FLEETWAY LIBRARY
PICTURE AIR ACE LIBRARY
Nº 446
1'-
FIRE ALARM
THE LANCASTER WAS AFLAM
— A BOMB STUCK IN ITS RACKS
Ian Kennedy, Air Ace 446, July 1969

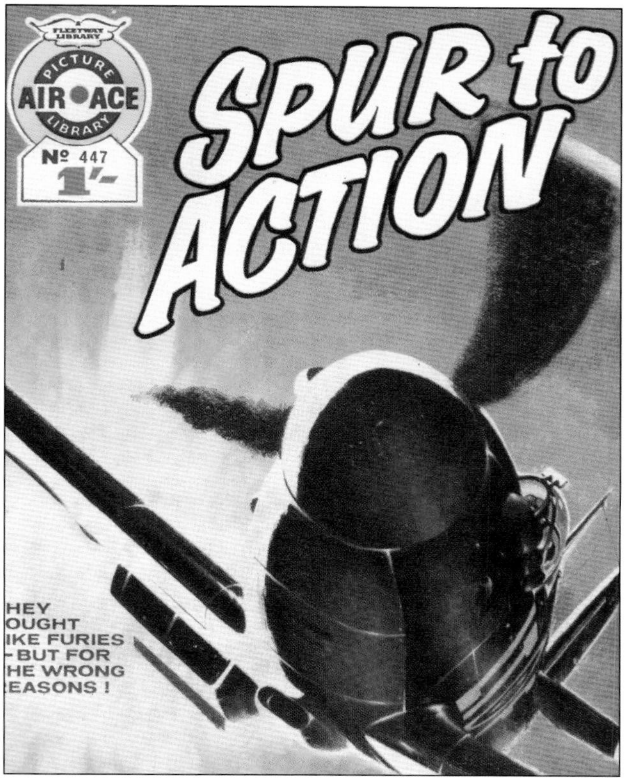
A FLEETWAY LIBRARY
PICTURE AIR ACE LIBRARY
Nº 447
1'-
SPUR to ACTION
HEY
OUGHT
IKE FURIES
- BUT FOR
HE WRONG
EASONS !
Ian Kennedy, Air Ace 447, July 1969

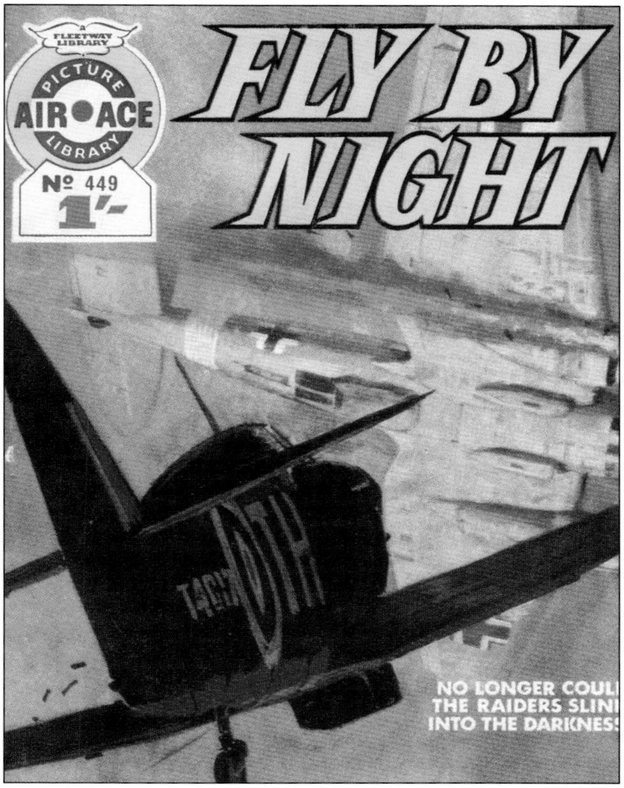
A FLEETWAY LIBRARY
PICTURE AIR ACE LIBRARY
Nº 449
1'-
FLY BY NIGHT
NO LONGER COUL
THE RAIDERS SLIN
INTO THE DARKNES
Graham Coton, Air Ace 449, July 1969

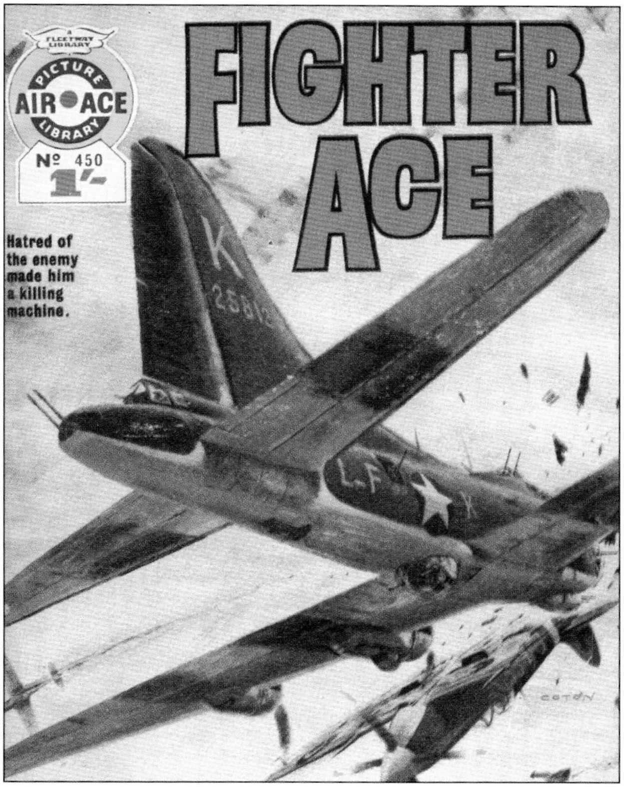
A FLEETWAY LIBRARY
PICTURE AIR ACE LIBRARY
Nº 450
1'-
FIGHTER ACE
Hatred of
the enemy
made him
a killing
machine.
COTON
Graham Coton, Air Ace 450, August 1969

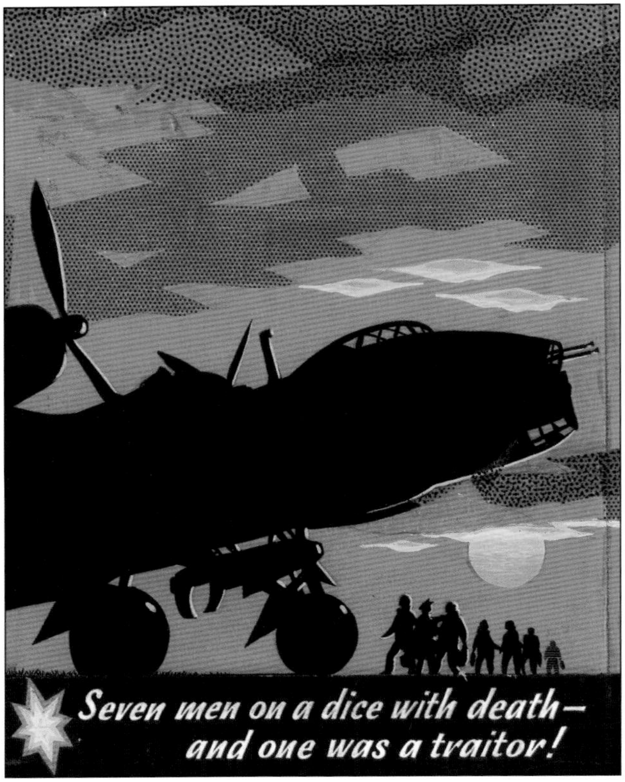
Seven men on a dice with death–
and one was a traitor!

Henry Fox, War 123, November 1961

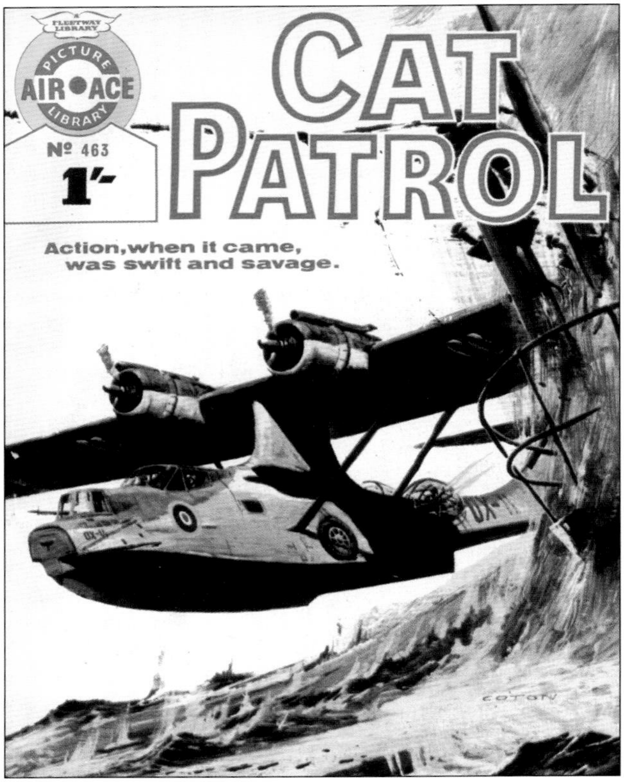
A FLEETWAY LIBRARY
PICTURE AIR ACE LIBRARY
Nº 463
1/-
CAT PATROL
Action, when it came,
was swift and savage.
COTON

Graham Coton, Air Ace 463, October 1969

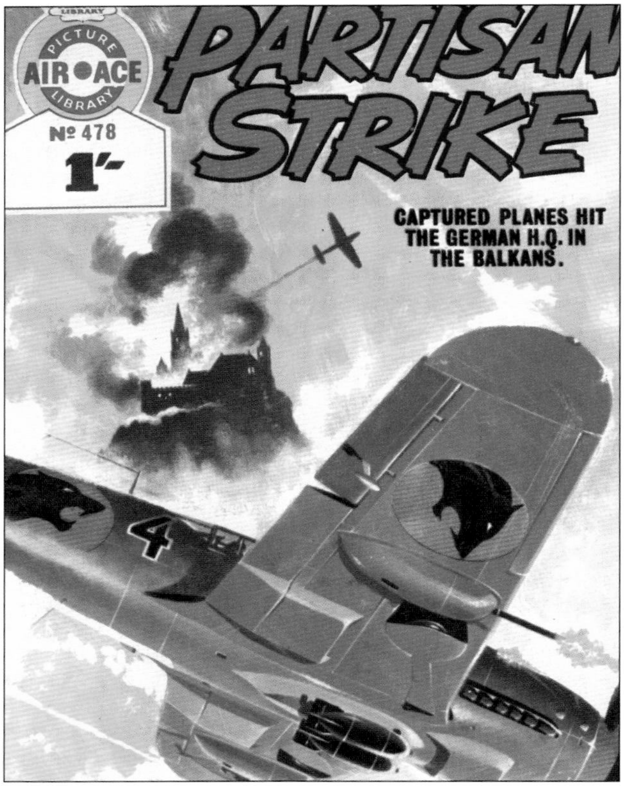
LIBRARY
PICTURE AIR ACE LIBRARY
Nº 478
1/-
PARTISAN STRIKE
CAPTURED PLANES HIT
THE GERMAN H.Q. IN
THE BALKANS.

Ian Kennedy, Air Ace 478, December 1969

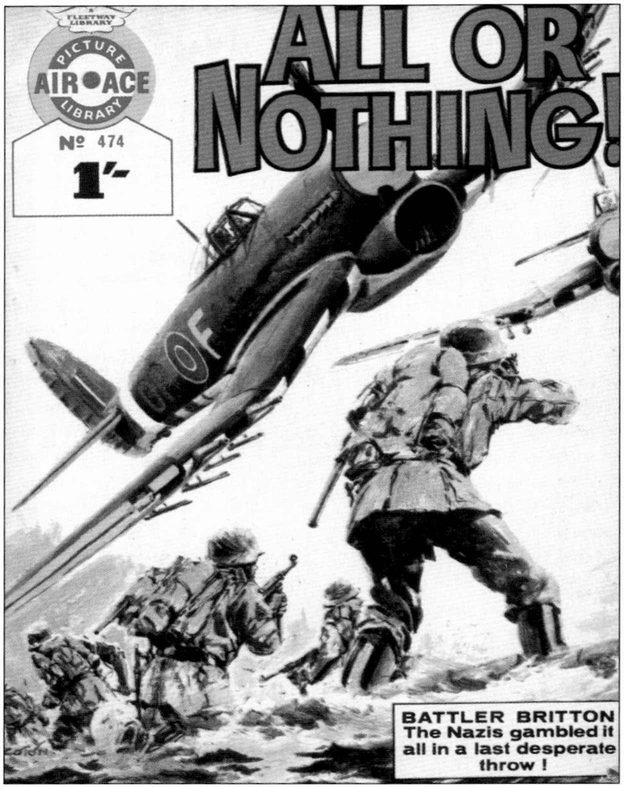
A FLEETWAY LIBRARY
PICTURE AIR ACE LIBRARY
Nº 474
1/-
ALL OR NOTHING!
BATTLER BRITTON
The Nazis gambled it
all in a last desperate
throw !

Graham Coton, Air Ace 474, December 1969

Opposite: Allessandro Biffignandi, Air Ace 104, June 1962
Overleaf: Alan Willow, Air Ace 252, July 1965

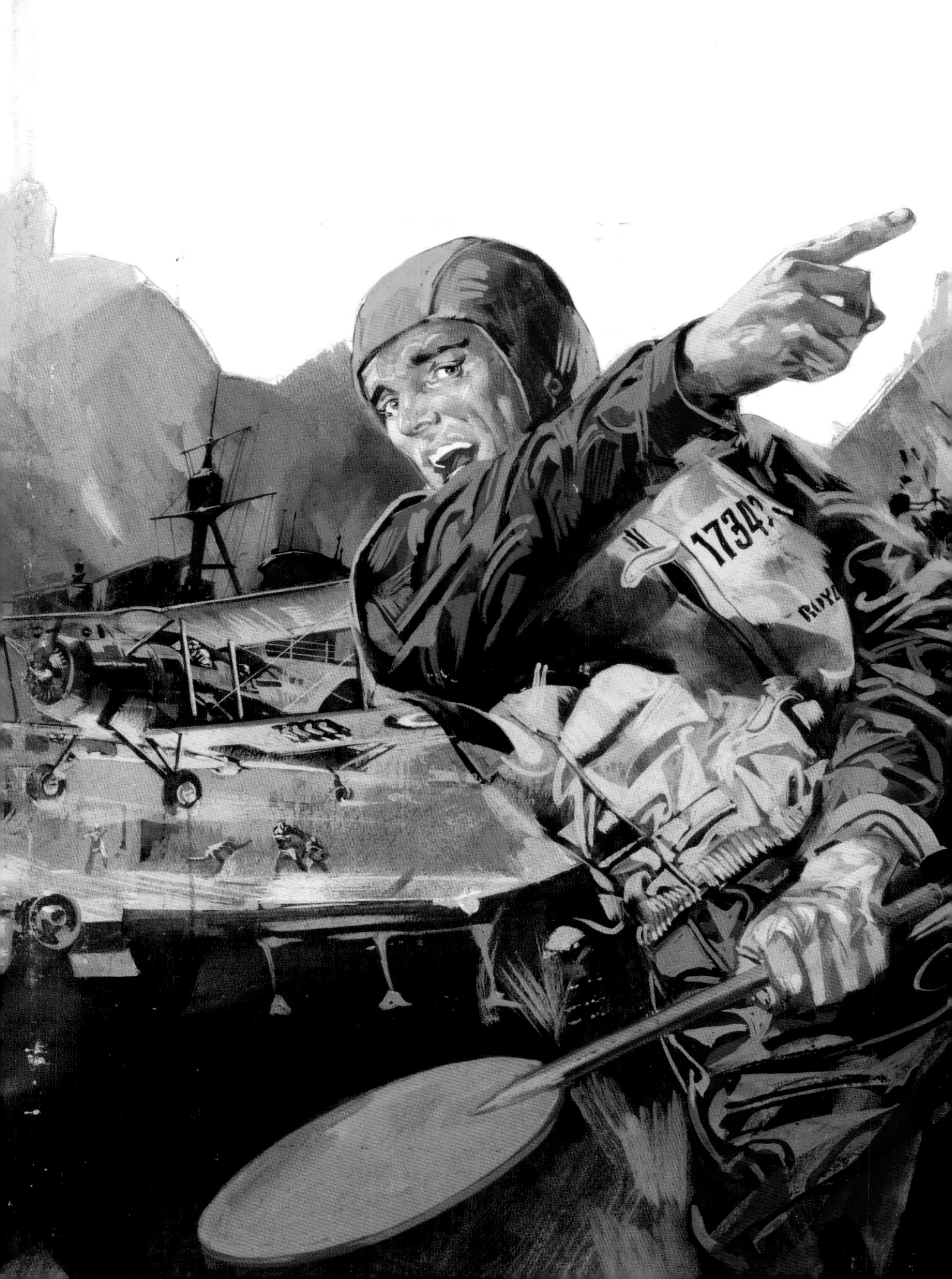

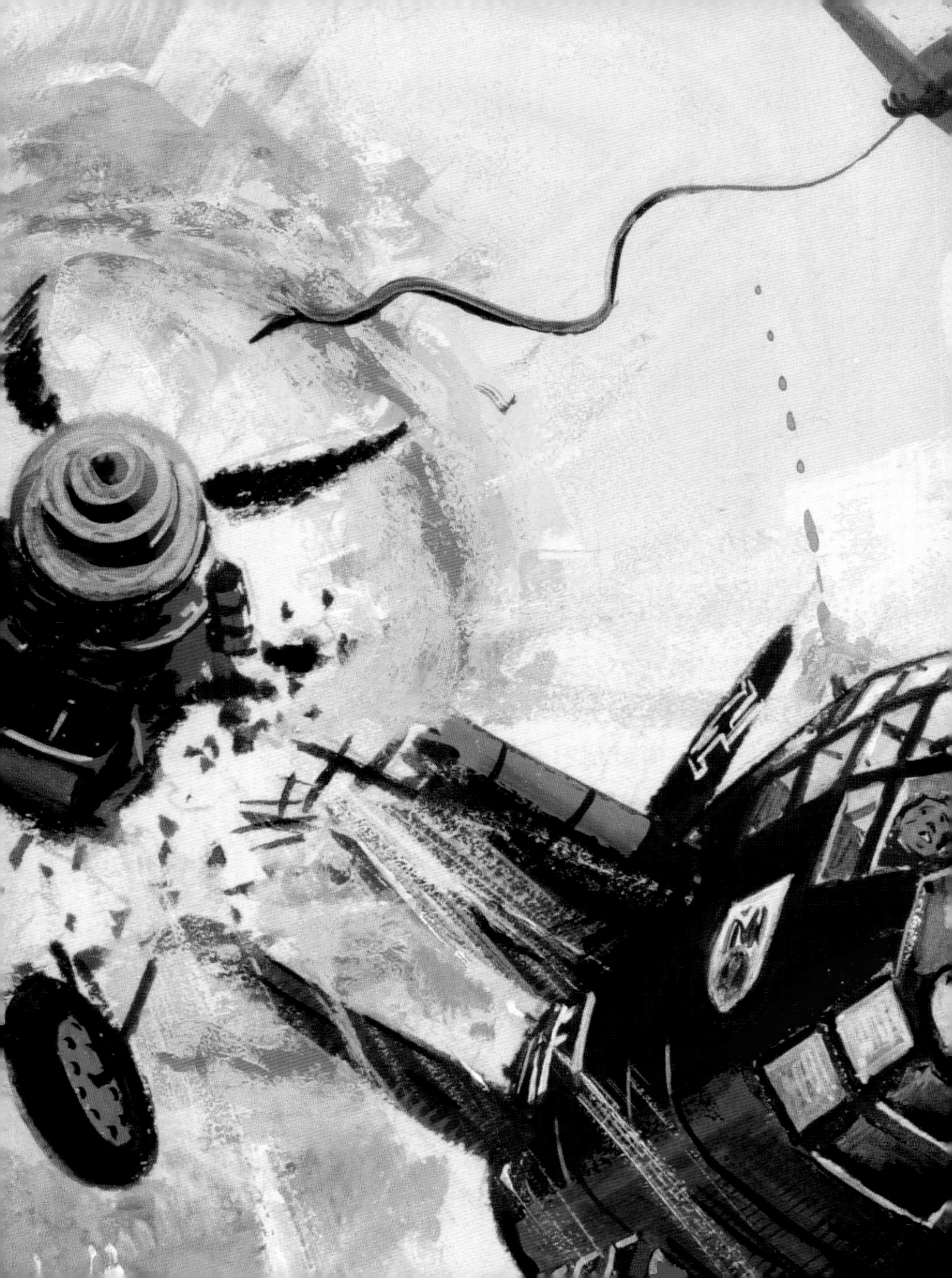

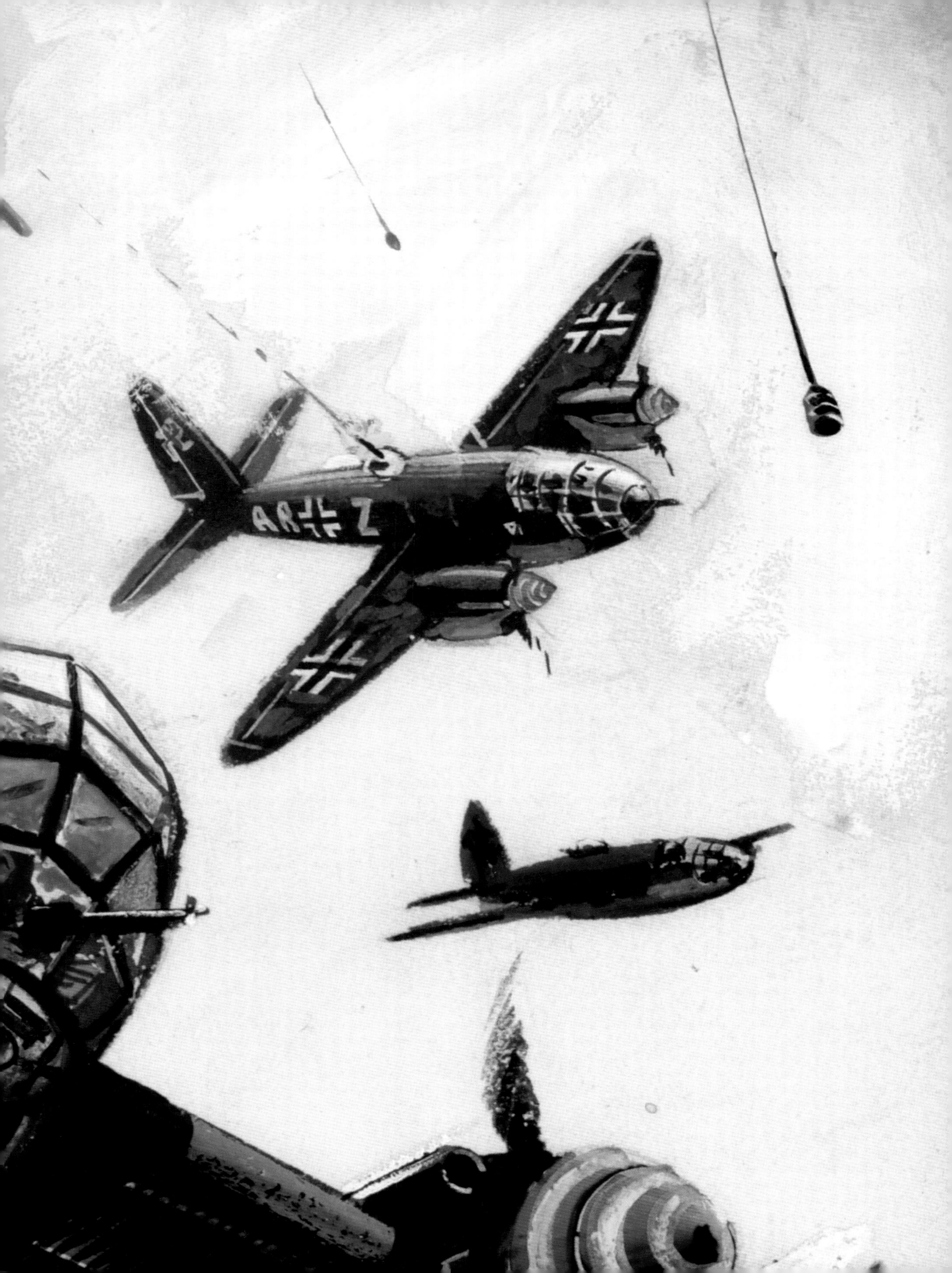
AR Z

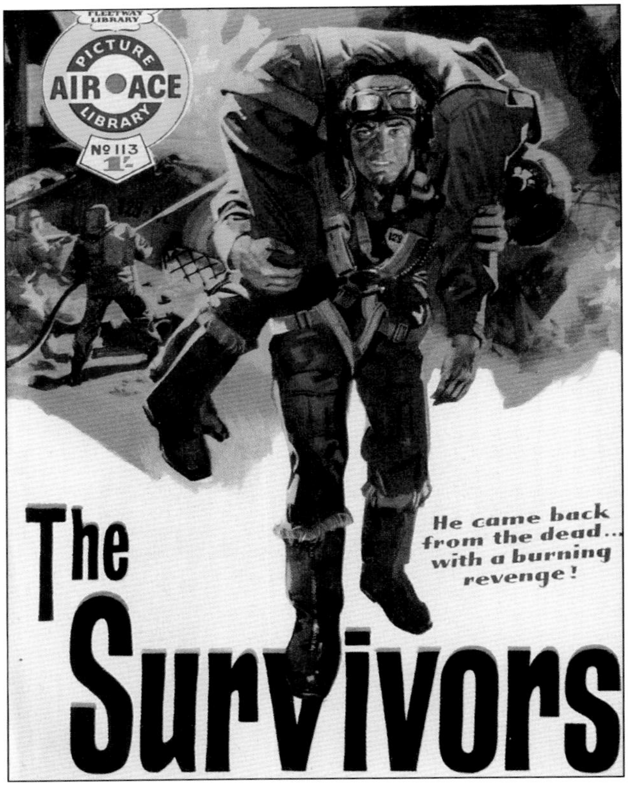
PICTURE
AIR ACE
LIBRARY
Nº 113
1/-
He came back from the dead... with a burning revenge!
The Survivors

Allessandro Biffignandi, Air Ace 113, August 1962

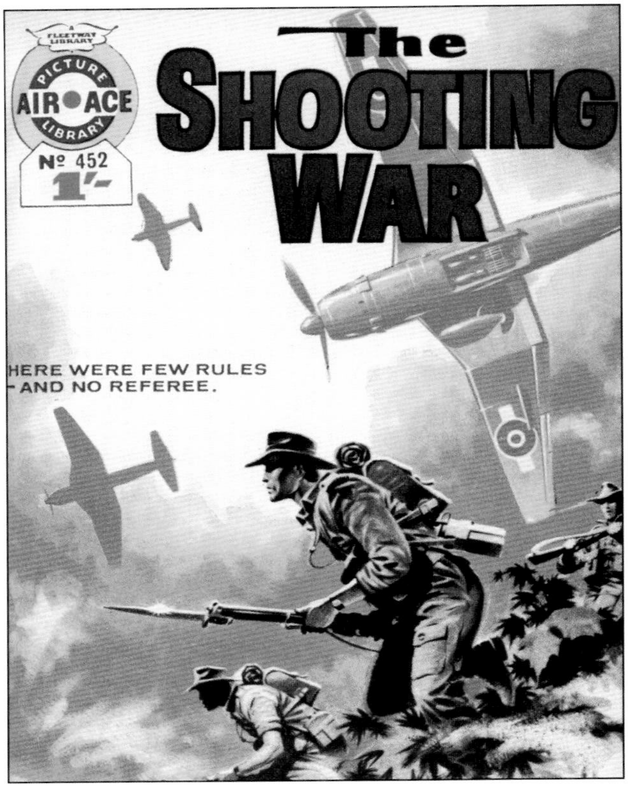
PICTURE
AIR ACE
LIBRARY
Nº 452
1/-
The SHOOTING WAR
HERE WERE FEW RULES
- AND NO REFEREE.

Ian Kennedy, Air Ace 452, August 1969

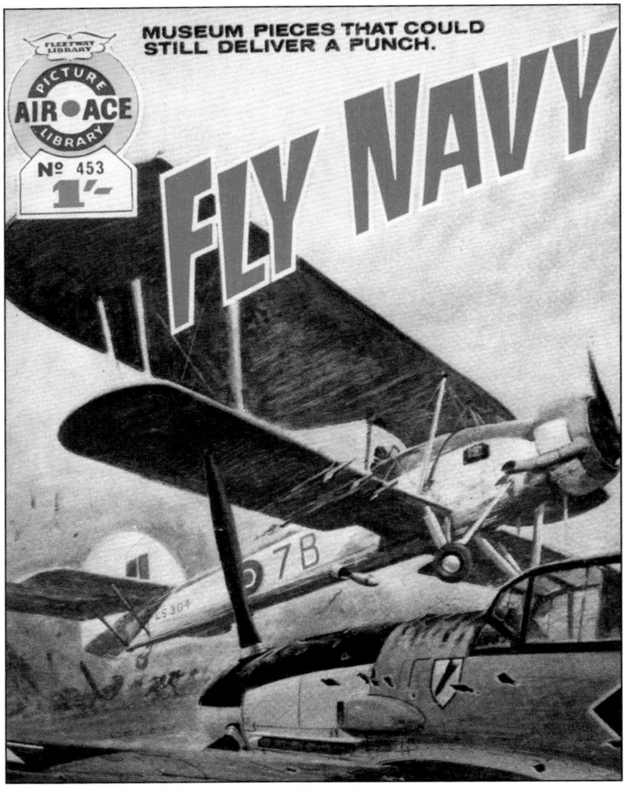
MUSEUM PIECES THAT COULD STILL DELIVER A PUNCH.
PICTURE
AIR ACE
LIBRARY
Nº 453
1/-
FLY NAVY
7B

Graham Coton, Air Ace 453, August 1969

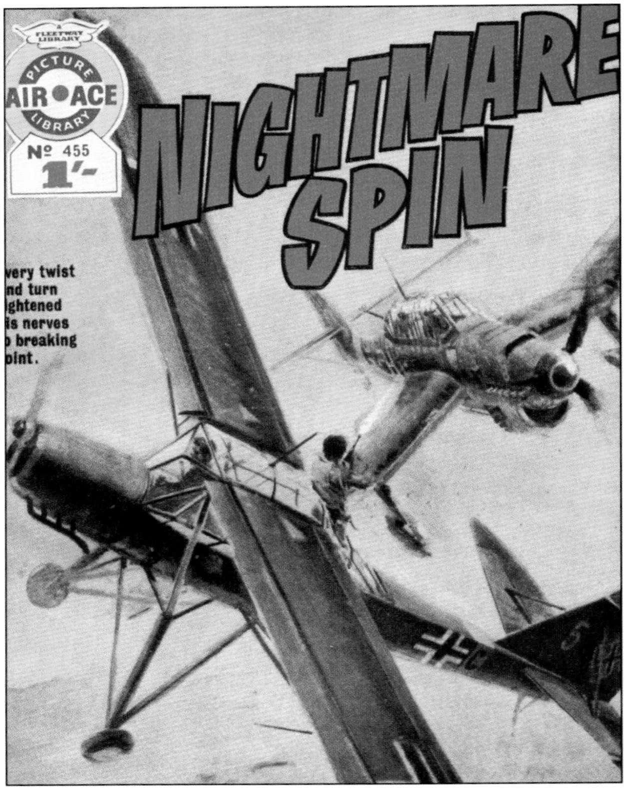
PICTURE
AIR ACE
LIBRARY
Nº 455
1/-
NIGHTMARE SPIN
very twist
nd turn
ightened
is nerves
breaking
oint.

Graham Coton, Air Ace 455, August 1969

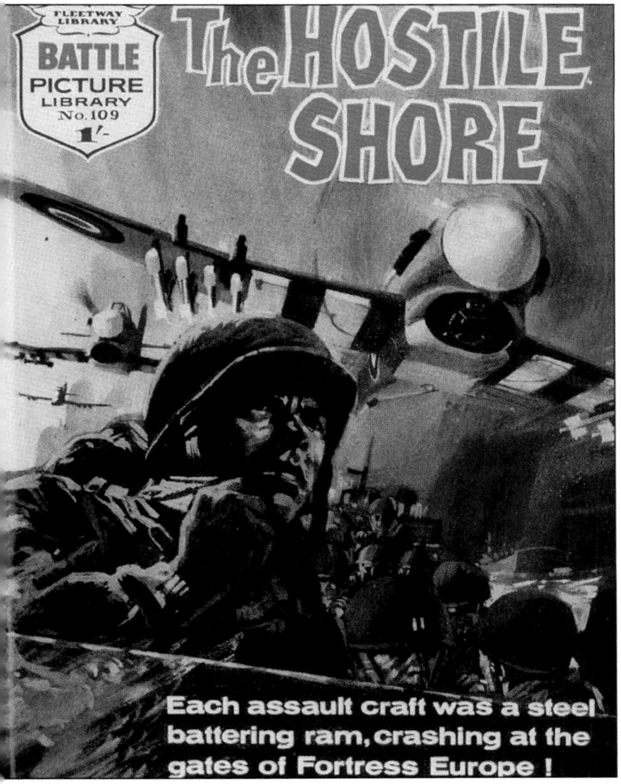
FLEETWAY LIBRARY
BATTLE PICTURE LIBRARY No. 109 1/-
The HOSTILE SHORE
Each assault craft was a steel battering ram, crashing at the gates of Fortress Europe !

Allessandro Biffignandi, Battle 109, June 1963

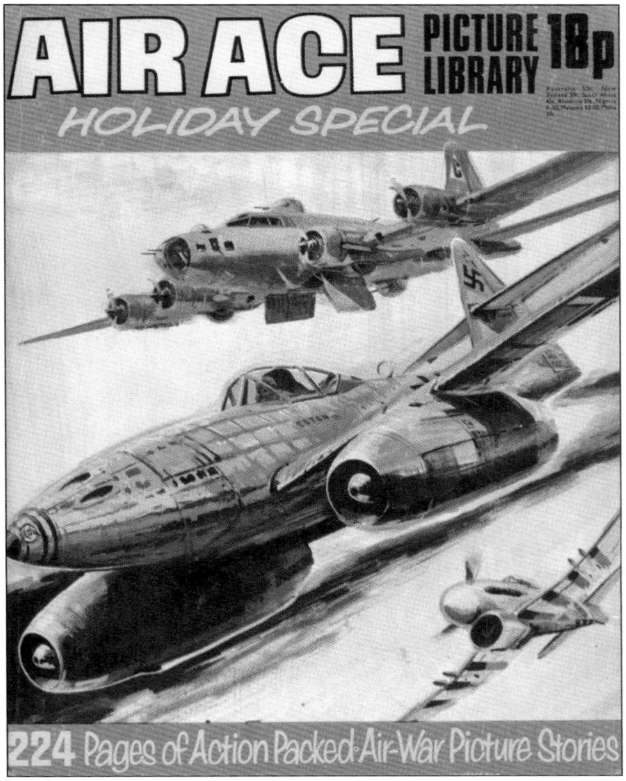
AIR ACE PICTURE LIBRARY 18p
HOLIDAY SPECIAL
224 Pages of Action Packed Air-War Picture Stories

Graham Coton, Air Ace holiday special 1973

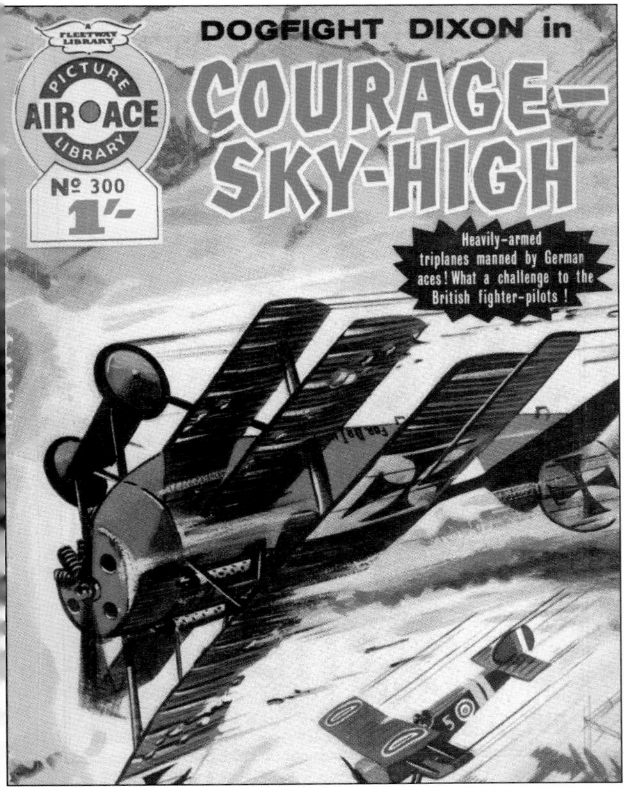
FLEETWAY LIBRARY
PICTURE AIR ACE LIBRARY
Nº 300 1/-
DOGFIGHT DIXON in
COURAGE-SKY-HIGH
Heavily-armed triplanes manned by German aces! What a challenge to the British fighter-pilots !

Alan Wlilow, Air Ace 300, July 1966

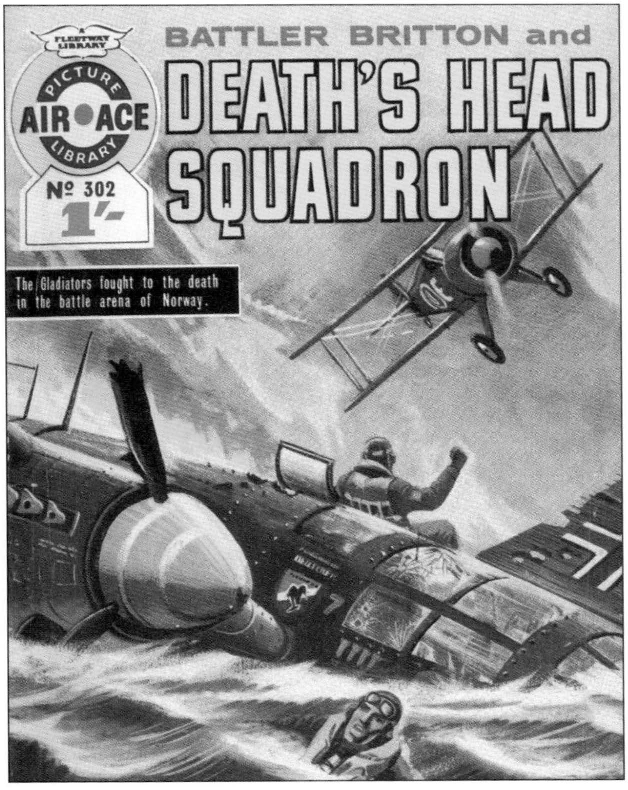
FLEETWAY LIBRARY
PICTURE AIR ACE LIBRARY
Nº 302 1/-
BATTLER BRITTON and
DEATH'S HEAD SQUADRON
The Gladiators fought to the death in the battle arena of Norway.

Alan Willow, Air Ace 302, August 1966

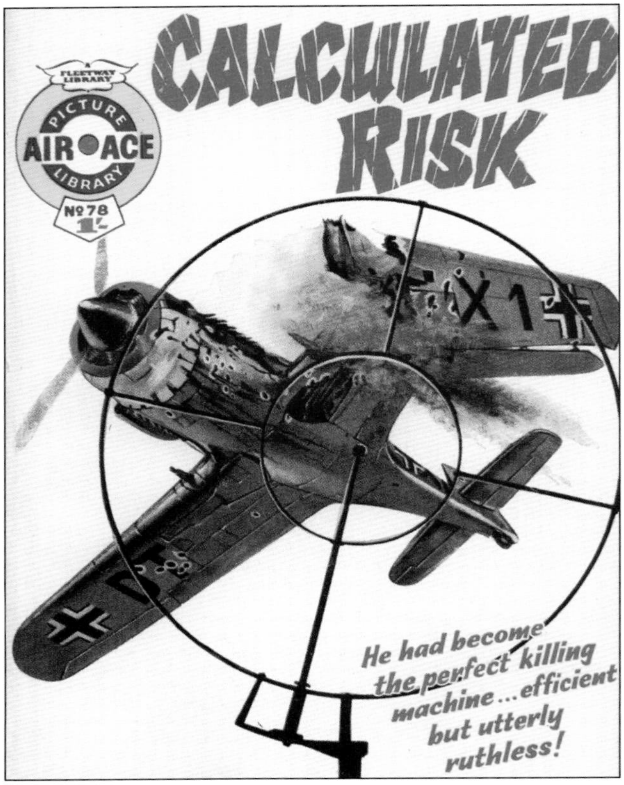
A FLEETWAY LIBRARY
PICTURE
AIR ACE
LIBRARY
Nº78
1/-
CALCULATED RISK
He had become the perfect killing machine ... efficient but utterly ruthless!

Nino Caroselli, Air Ace 78, December 1961

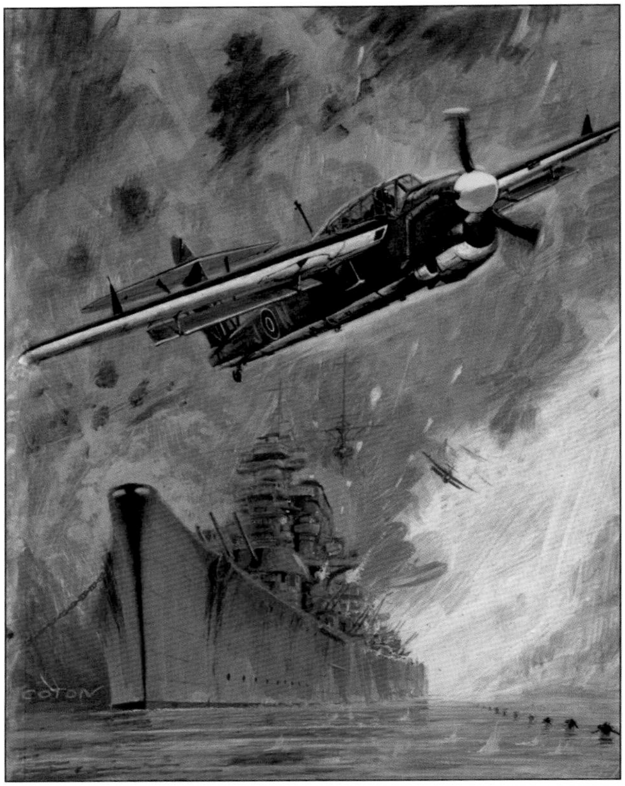
COTON

Graham Coton, Air Ace 366, December 1967

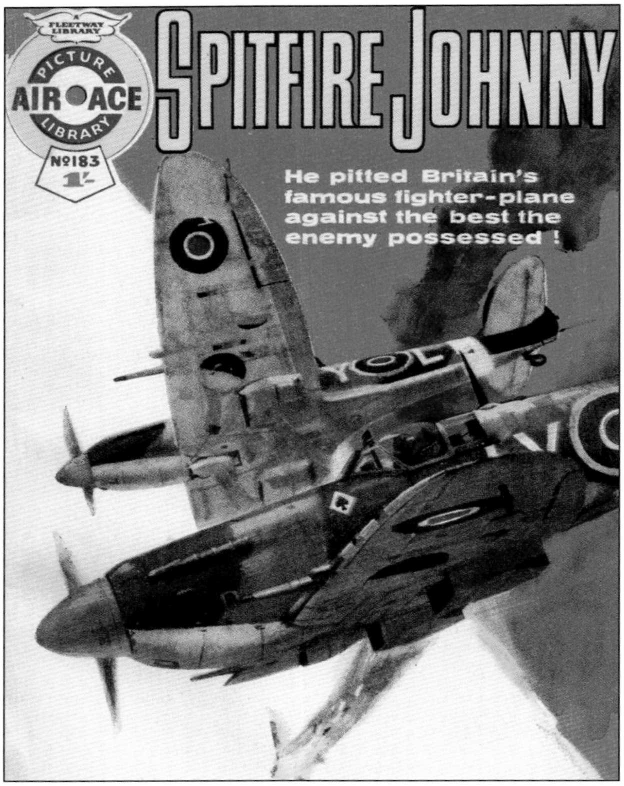
A FLEETWAY LIBRARY
PICTURE
AIR ACE
LIBRARY
Nº183
1/-
SPITFIRE JOHNNY
He pitted Britain's famous fighter-plane against the best the enemy possessed !

Pino Dell'Orco, Air Ace 183, February 1964

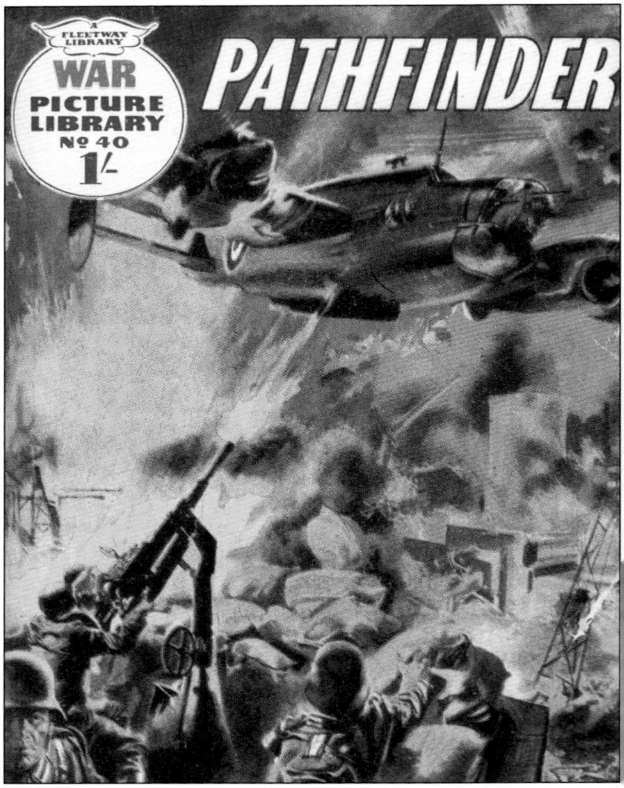
A FLEETWAY LIBRARY
WAR
PICTURE LIBRARY
Nº 40
1/-
PATHFINDER

Giorgio DeGaspari, War 40, March 1960

Opposite: Giorgio DeGaspari, War 24, September 1959

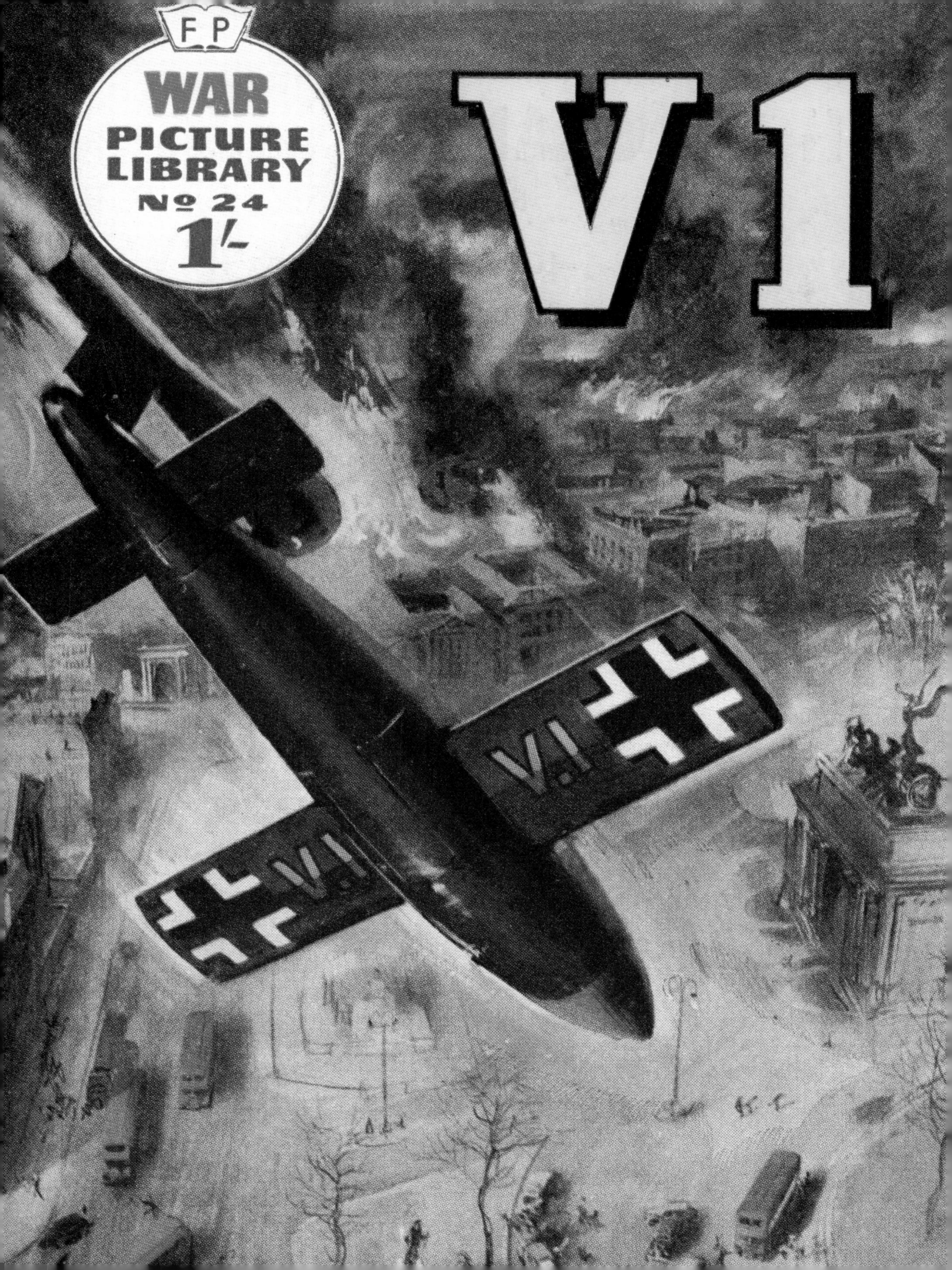
FP
WAR
PICTURE
LIBRARY
№ 24
1/-
V 1
V.I
V.I

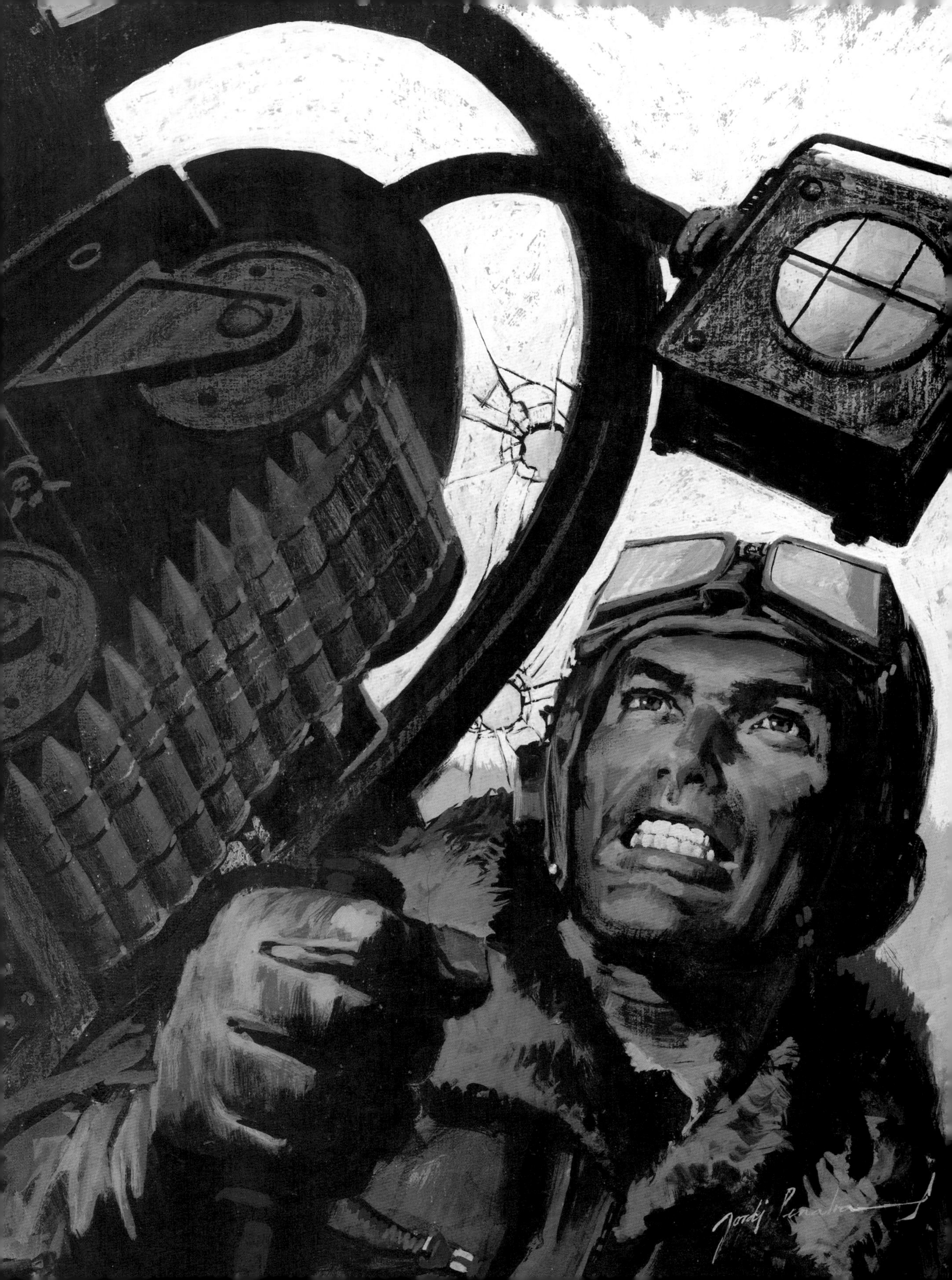

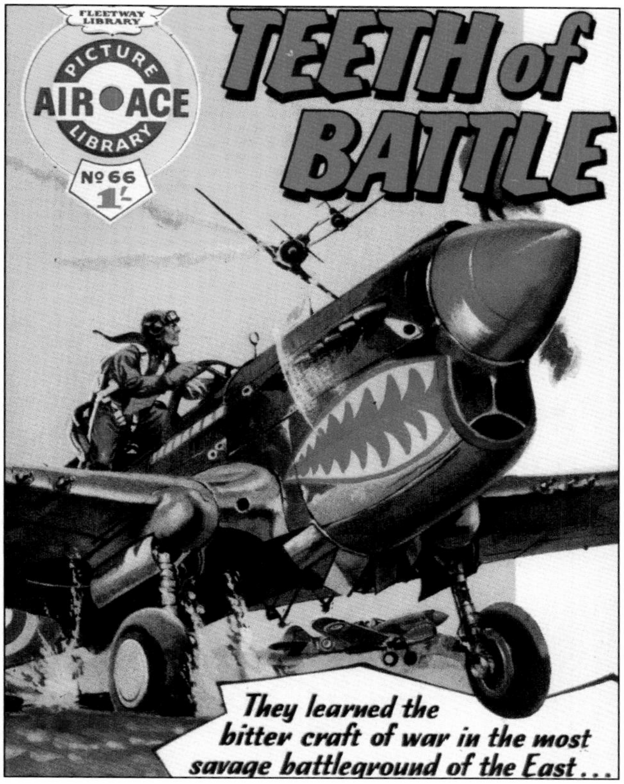
A FLEETWAY LIBRARY
PICTURE AIR ACE LIBRARY
Nº 66
1/-
TEETH of BATTLE
They learned the bitter craft of war in the most savage battleground of the East...
Nino Caroselli, Air Ace 66, September 1961

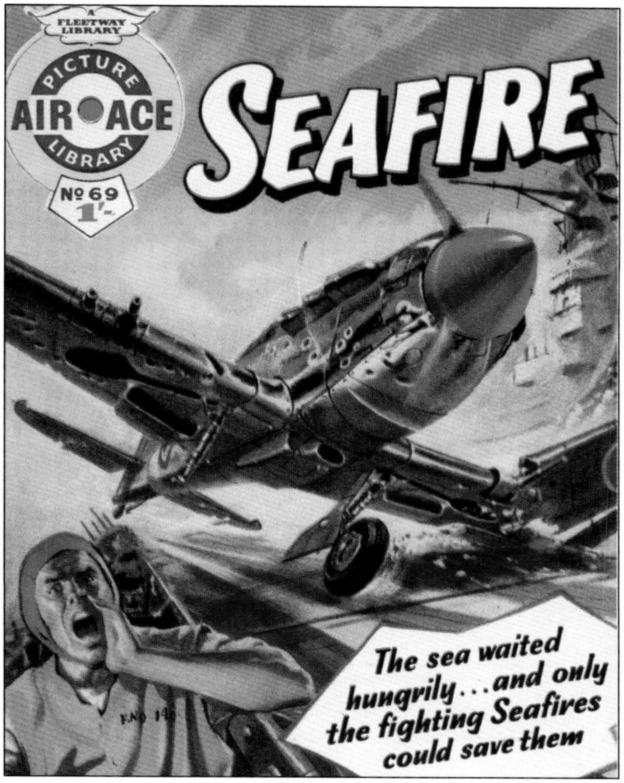
A FLEETWAY LIBRARY
PICTURE AIR ACE LIBRARY
Nº 69
1/-
SEAFIRE
The sea waited hungrily... and only the fighting Seafires could save them
Nino Caroselli, Air Ace 69, September 1961

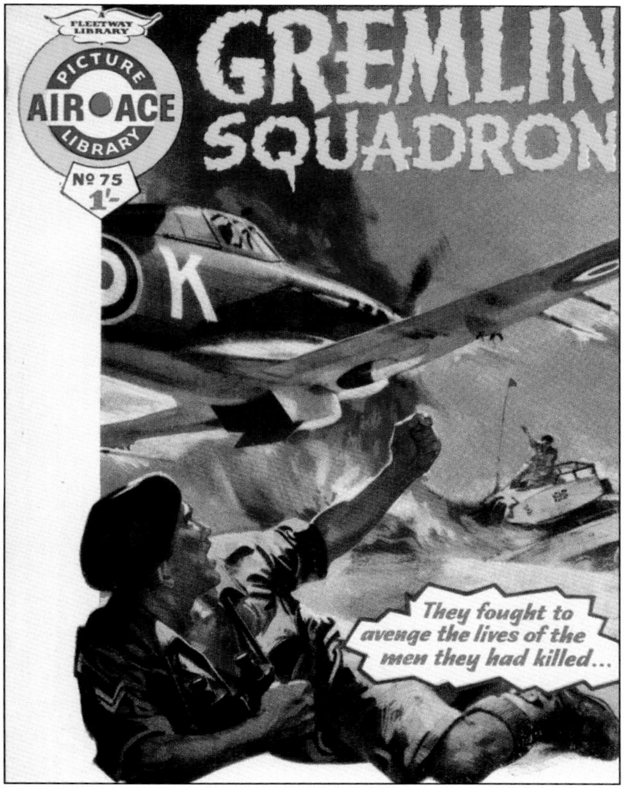
FLEETWAY LIBRARY
PICTURE AIR ACE LIBRARY
Nº 75
1/-
GREMLIN SQUADRON
They fought to avenge the lives of the men they had killed...
Allessandro Biffignandi, Air Ace 75, November 1961

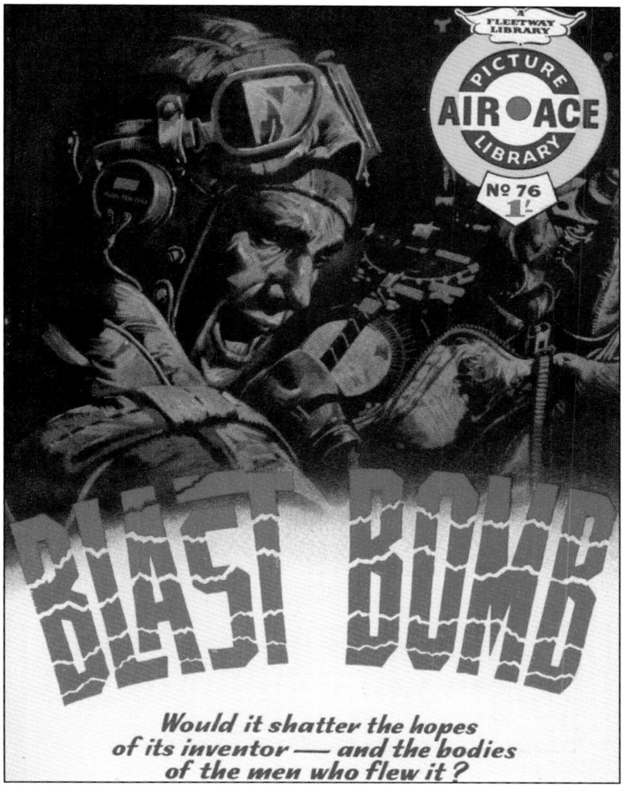
A FLEETWAY LIBRARY
PICTURE AIR ACE LIBRARY
Nº 76
1/-
BLAST BOMB
Would it shatter the hopes of its inventor — and the bodies of the men who flew it?
Allessandro Biffignandi, Air Ace 76, November 1961

Opposite: Jordi Penalva, Battle 228, November 1965
Overleaf: Nino Caroselli, Air Ace 12, June 1960

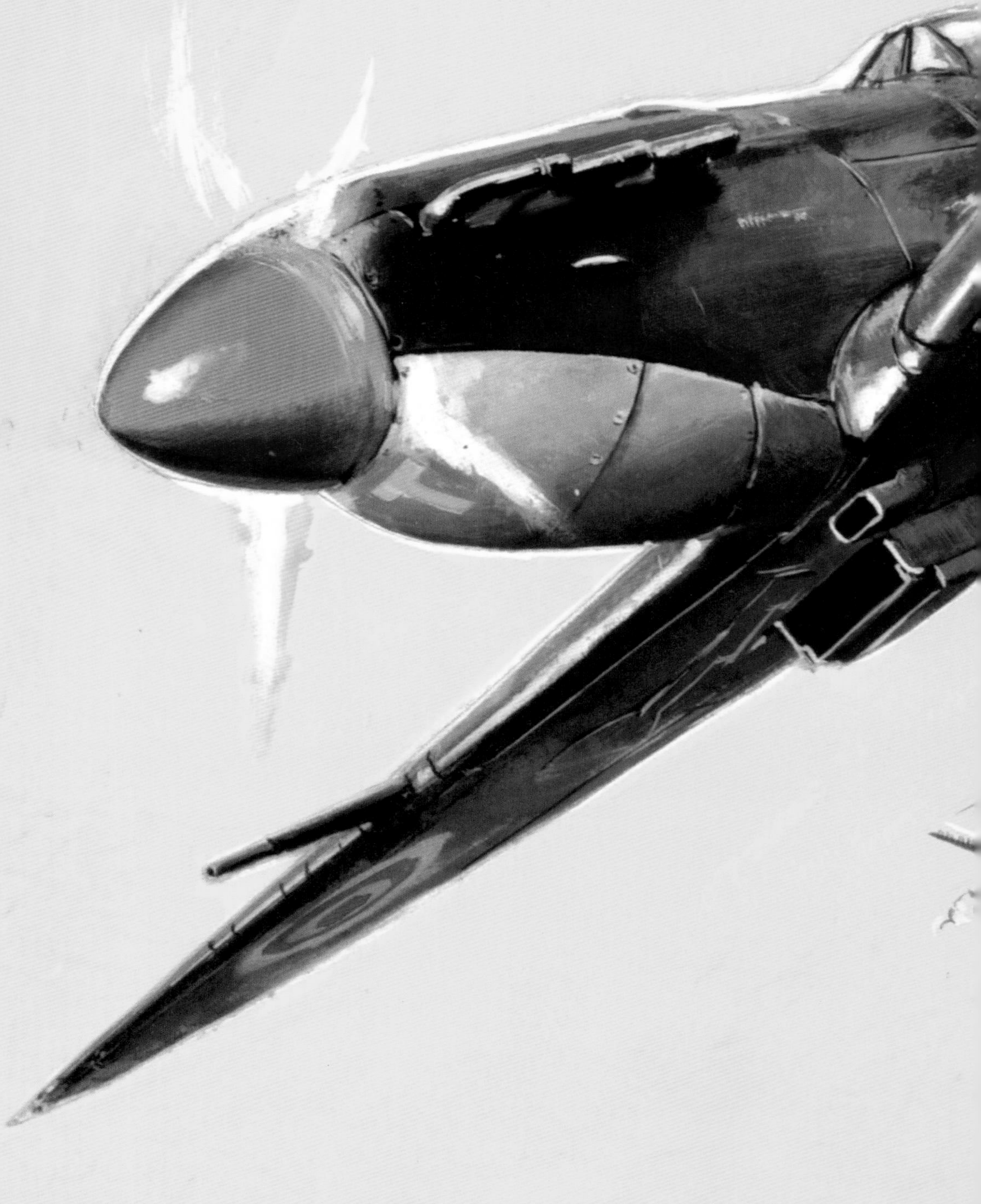

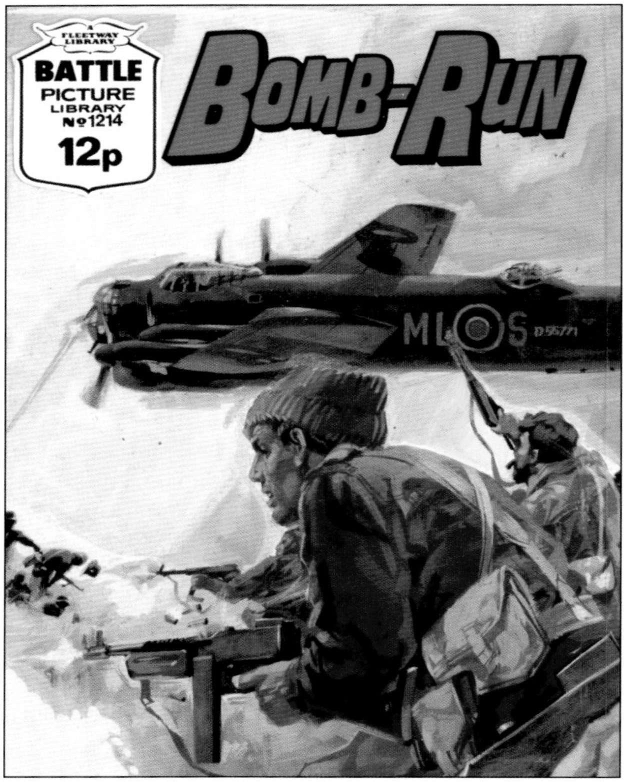
A FLEETWAY LIBRARY
BATTLE
PICTURE
LIBRARY
Nº1214
12p
BOMB-RUN
ML S
D5577

Pino Dell'Orco, originally Battle 77, October 1962

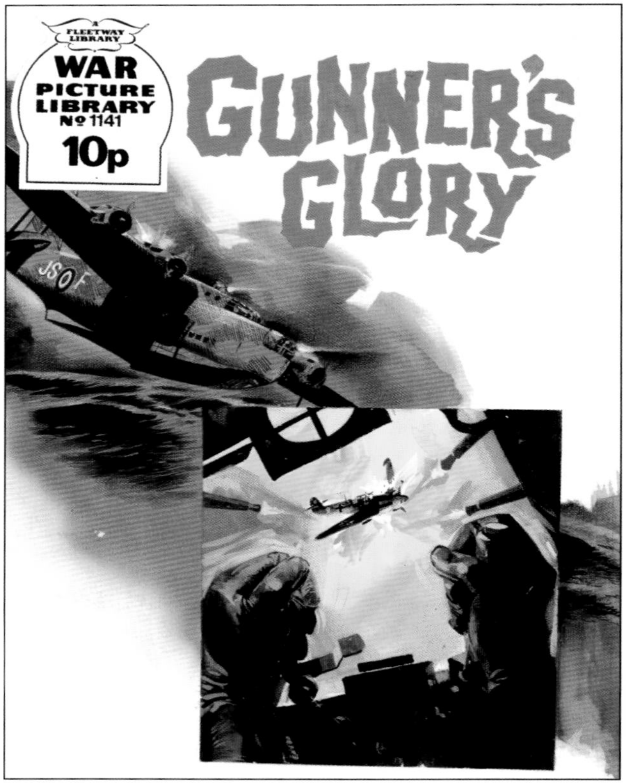
A FLEETWAY LIBRARY
WAR
PICTURE
LIBRARY
Nº 1141
10p
GUNNER'S
GLORY
JSOF

Pino Dell'Orco, originally Air Ace 136, February 1963

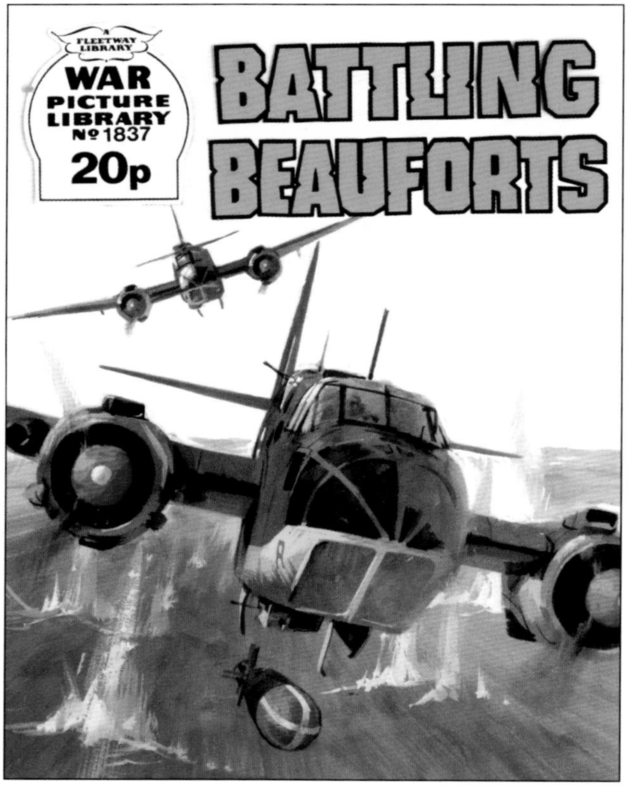
A FLEETWAY LIBRARY
WAR
PICTURE
LIBRARY
Nº 1837
20p
BATTLING
BEAUFORTS

Pino Dell'Orco, originally Air Ace 166, October 1963

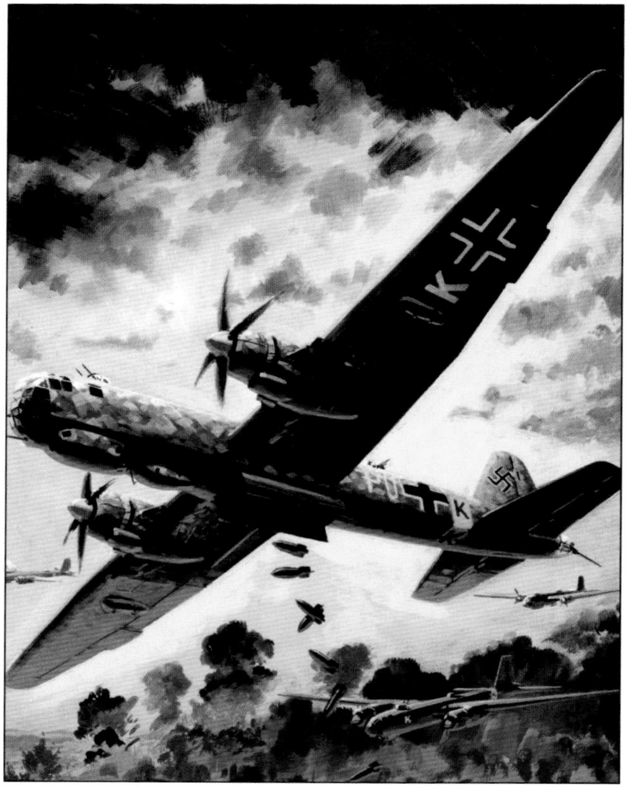

Graham Coton, Air Ace 265, October 1965

Opposite: Pino Dell'Orco, originally Battle 310, August 1967

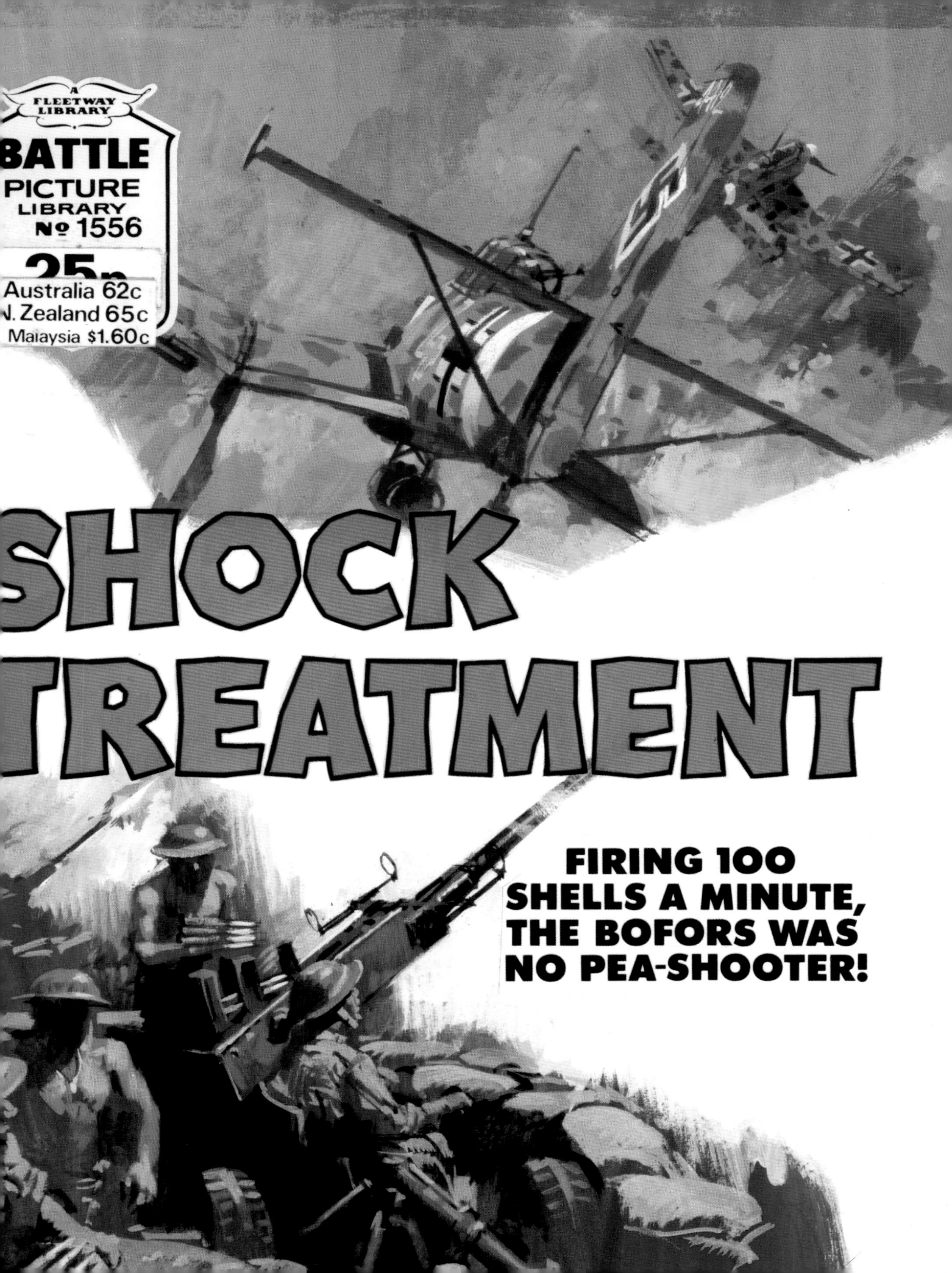
A FLEETWAY LIBRARY
BATTLE PICTURE LIBRARY
Nº 1556
25p
Australia 62c
Zealand 65c
Malaysia $1.60c
SHOCK TREATMENT
FIRING 100 SHELLS A MINUTE, THE BOFORS WAS NO PEA-SHOOTER!

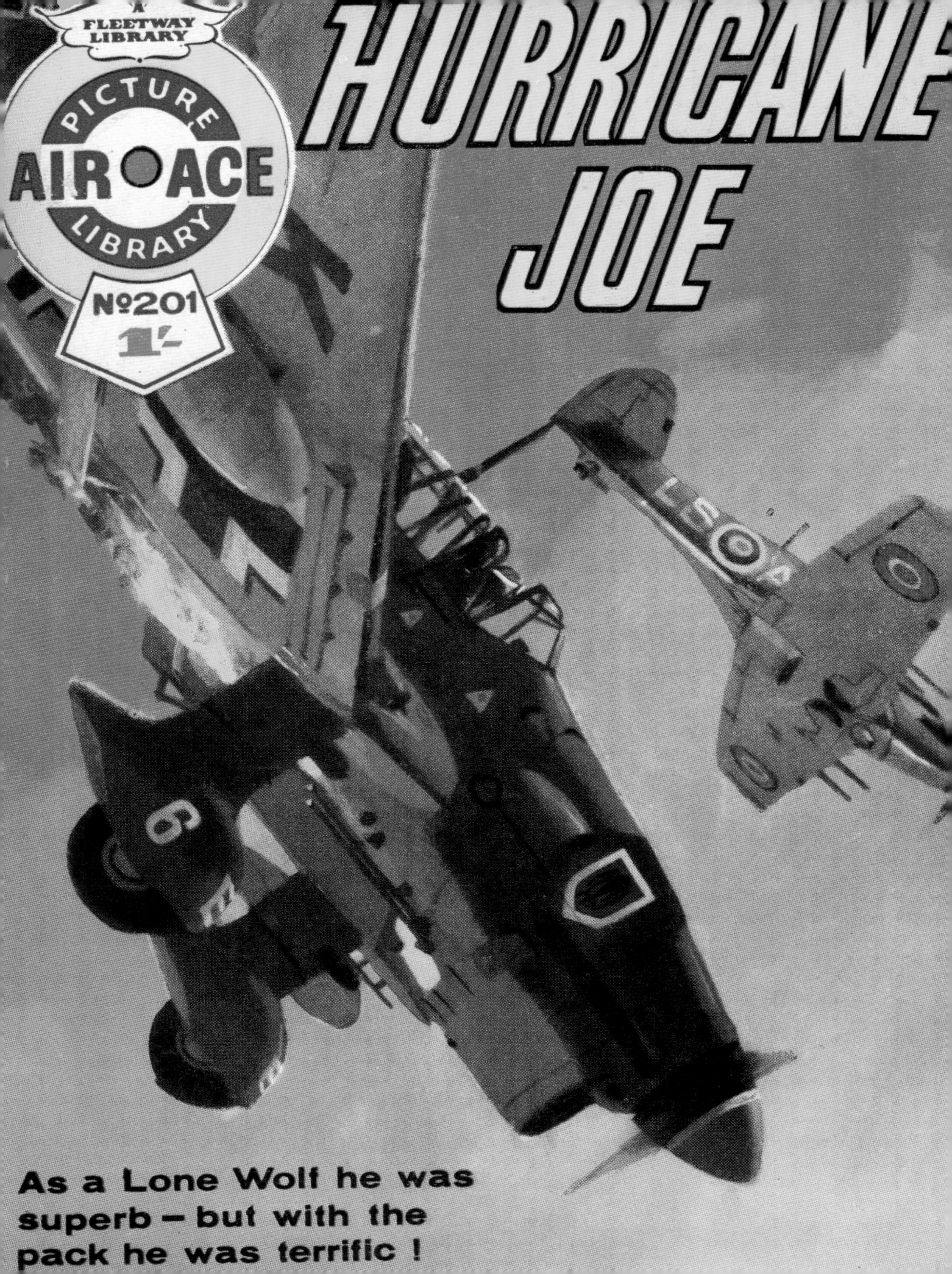
A FLEETWAY LIBRARY
PICTURE
AIR ACE
LIBRARY
№201
1/-
HURRICANE JOE
As a Lone Wolf he was superb – but with the pack he was terrific !

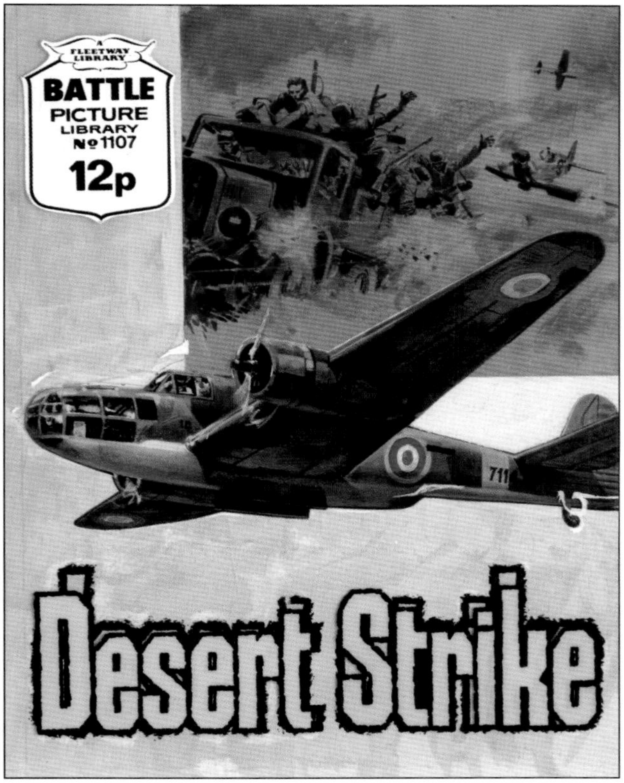
A FLEETWAY LIBRARY
BATTLE
PICTURE
LIBRARY
Nº1107
12p
Desert Strike

Allessandro Biffignandi, originally Air Ace 143, April 1963

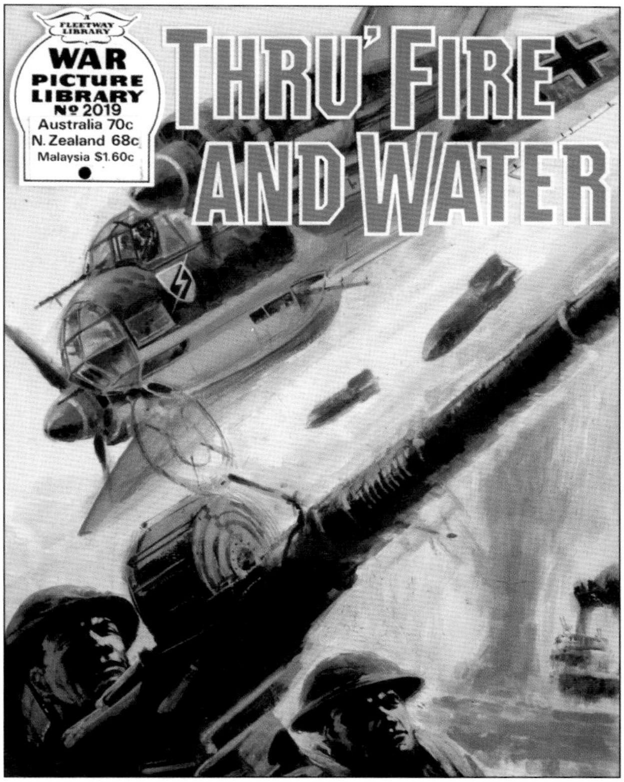
A FLEETWAY LIBRARY
WAR
PICTURE
LIBRARY
Nº2019
Australia 70c
N.Zealand 68c
Malaysia $1.60c
THRU' FIRE
AND WATER

Graham Coton, War 2019, August 1983

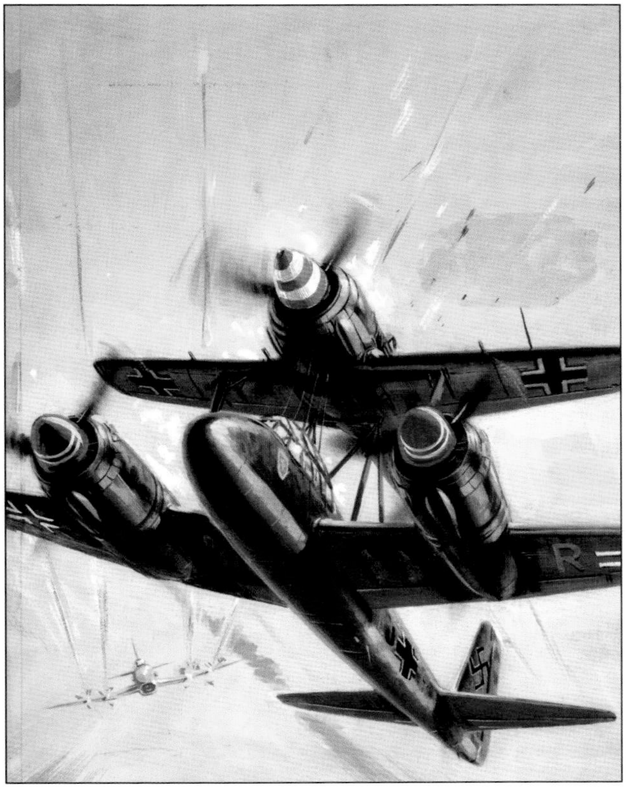

Alan Willow, Air Ace 293, May 1966

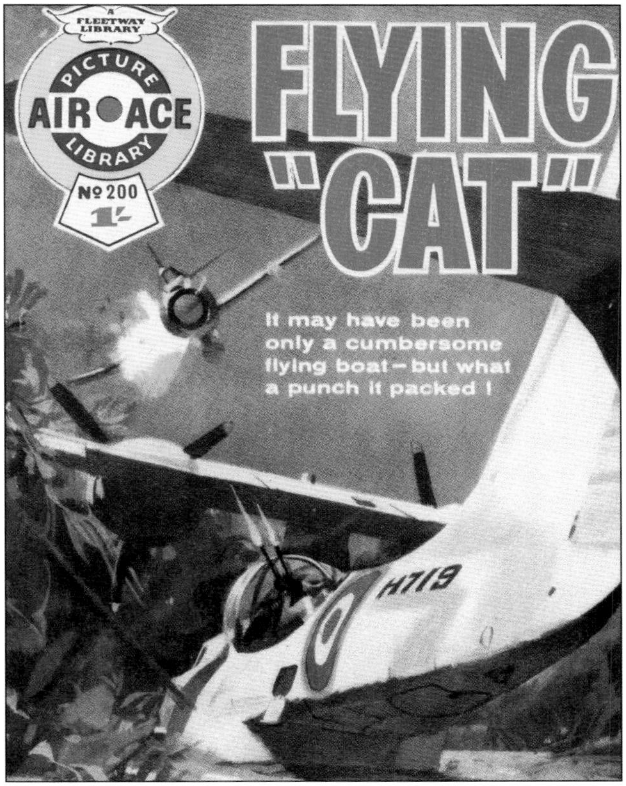
A FLEETWAY LIBRARY
PICTURE
AIR ACE
LIBRARY
Nº200
1/-
FLYING
"CAT"
It may have been only a cumbersome flying boat – but what a punch it packed !
H719

Pino Dell'Orco, Air Ace 200, June 1964

Opposite: Pino Dell'Orco, Air Ace 201, June 1964

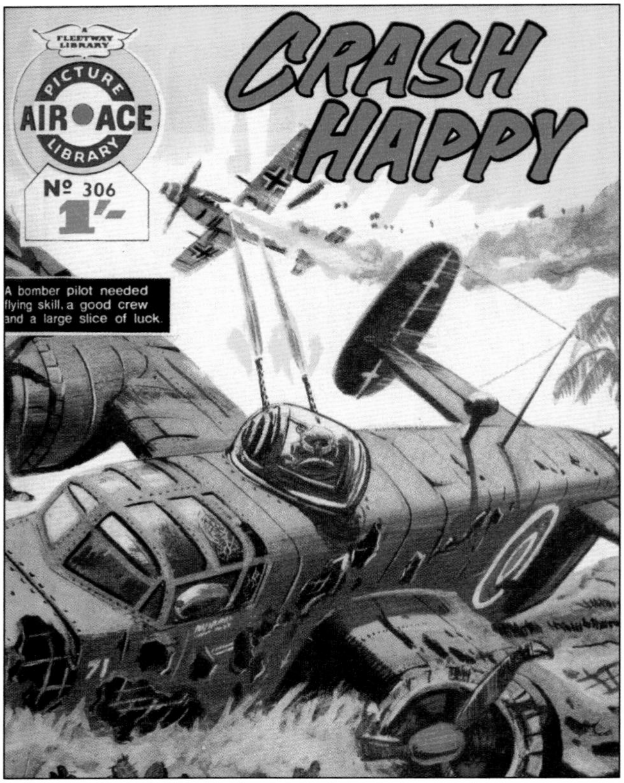
A FLEETWAY LIBRARY
PICTURE AIR ACE LIBRARY
Nº 306
1/-
CRASH HAPPY
A bomber pilot needed flying skill, a good crew and a large slice of luck.

Alan Willow, Air Ace 306, September 1966

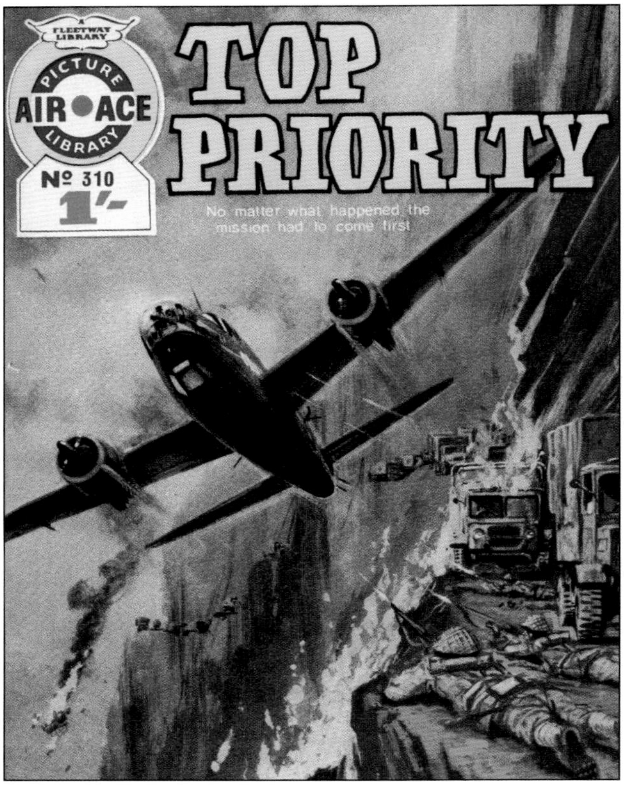
A FLEETWAY LIBRARY
PICTURE AIR ACE LIBRARY
Nº 310
1/-
TOP PRIORITY
No matter what happened the mission had to come first

Giorgio DeGaspari, Air Ace 310, October 1966

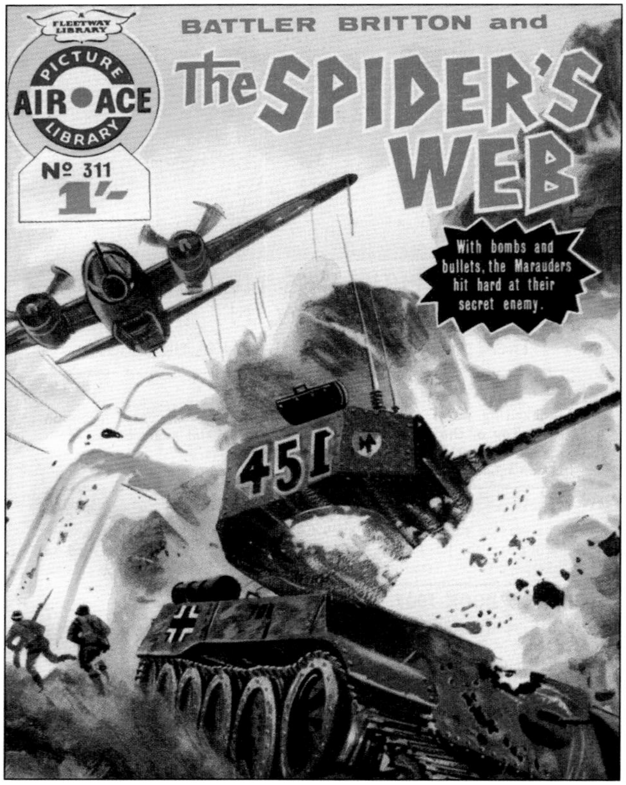
A FLEETWAY LIBRARY
PICTURE AIR ACE LIBRARY
Nº 311
1/-
BATTLER BRITTON and
The SPIDER'S WEB
With bombs and bullets, the Marauders hit hard at their secret enemy.
451

Alan Willow, Air Ace 311, October 1966

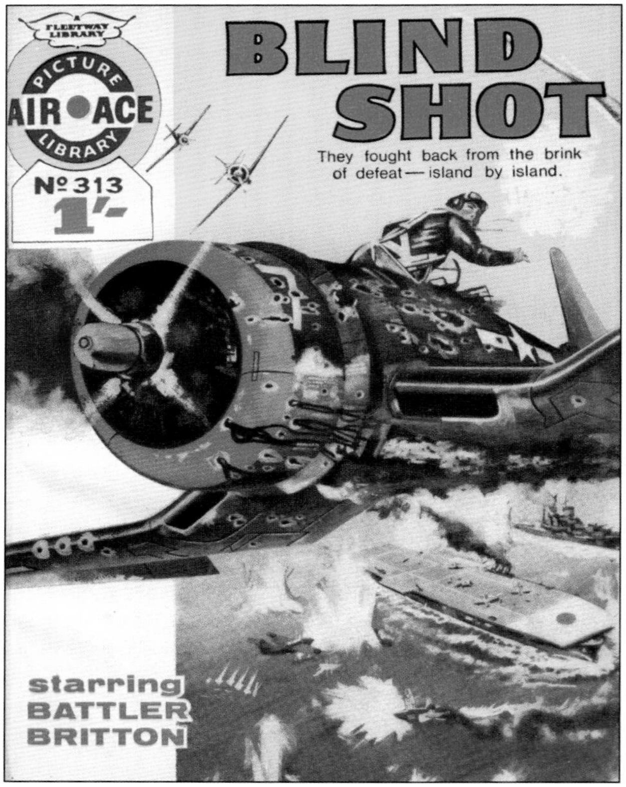
A FLEETWAY LIBRARY
PICTURE AIR ACE LIBRARY
Nº 313
1/-
BLIND SHOT
They fought back from the brink of defeat — island by island.
starring BATTLER BRITTON

Rafael Lopez Espi, Air Ace 313, October 1966

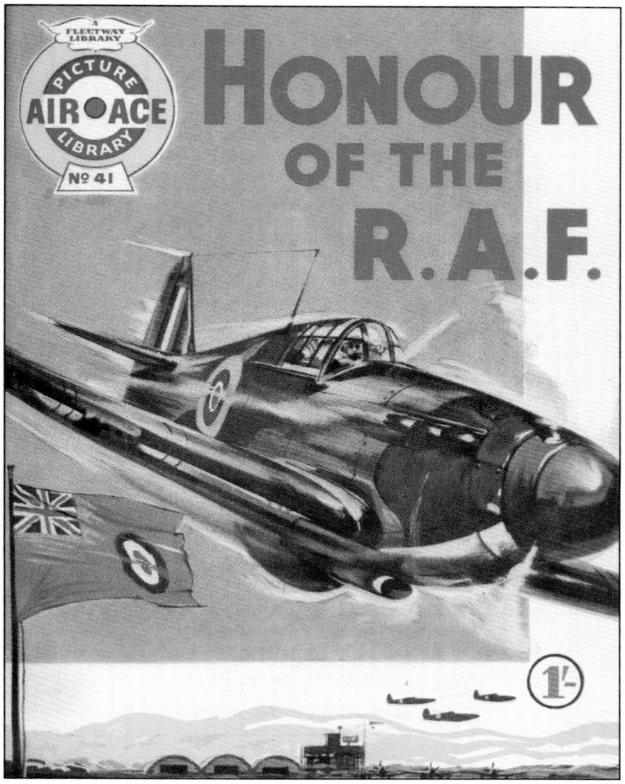
A FLEETWAY LIBRARY
PICTURE AIR ACE LIBRARY
Nº 41
HONOUR OF THE R.A.F.
1/-

Allessandro Biffignandi, Air Ace 41, February 1961

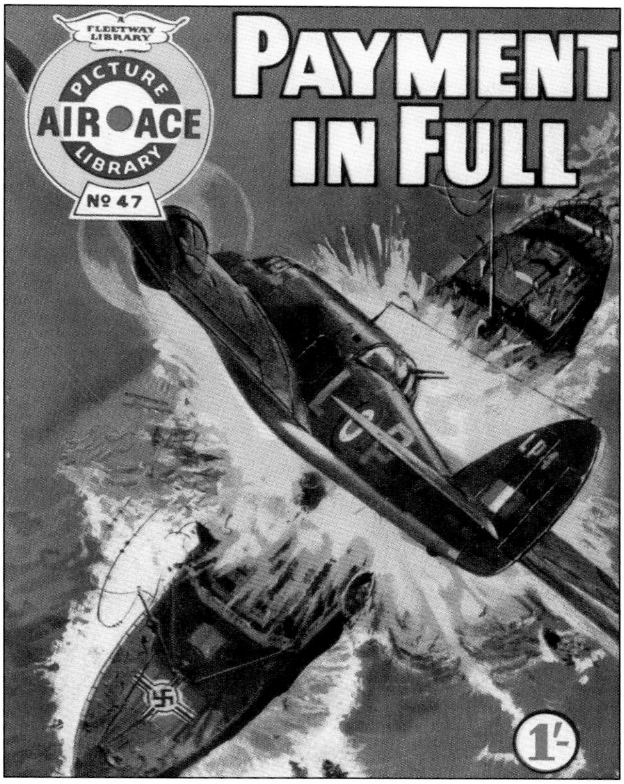
A FLEETWAY LIBRARY
PICTURE AIR ACE LIBRARY
Nº 47
PAYMENT IN FULL
1/-

Allessandro Biffignandi, Air Ace 47, April 1961

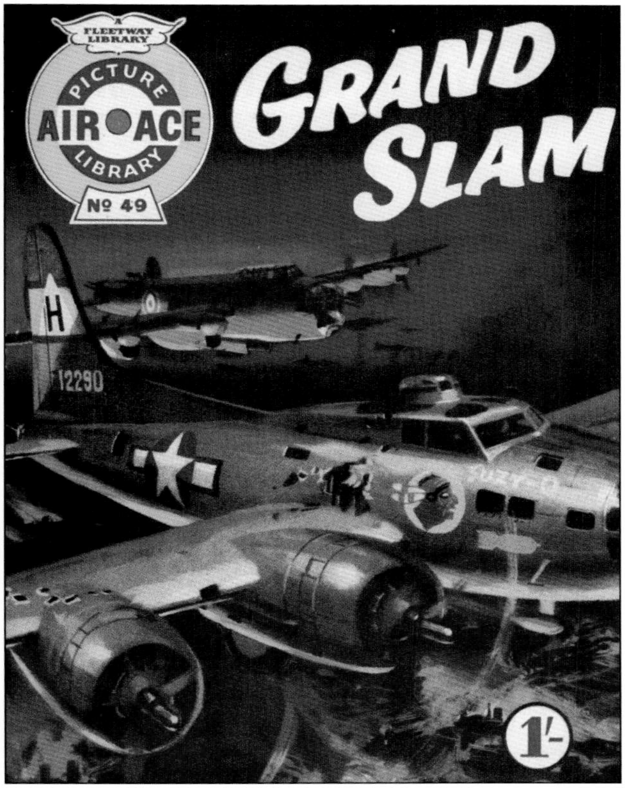
A FLEETWAY LIBRARY
PICTURE AIR ACE LIBRARY
Nº 49
GRAND SLAM
1/-

Pino Dell'Orco, Air Ace 49, April 1961

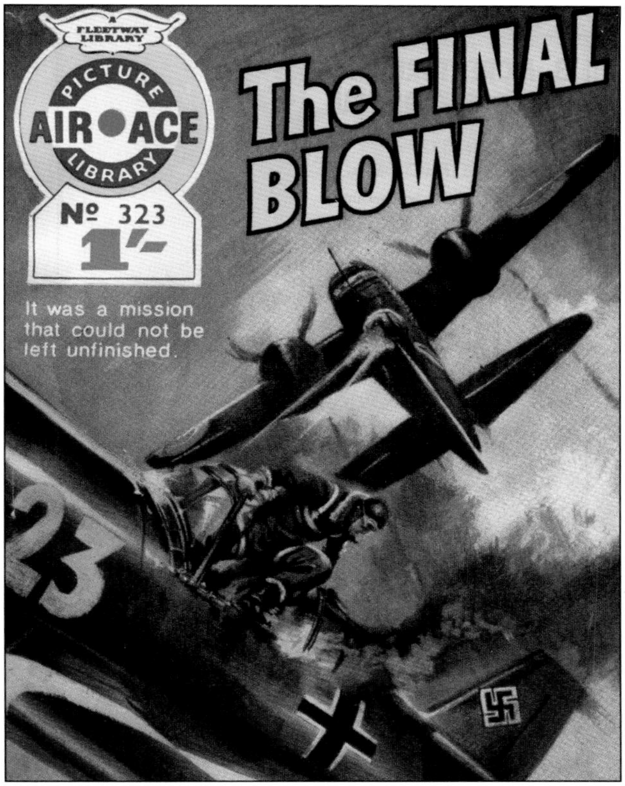
A FLEETWAY LIBRARY
PICTURE AIR ACE LIBRARY
Nº 323
1/-
The FINAL BLOW
It was a mission
that could not be
left unfinished.

Giolitti Studio, Air Ace 323, January 1967

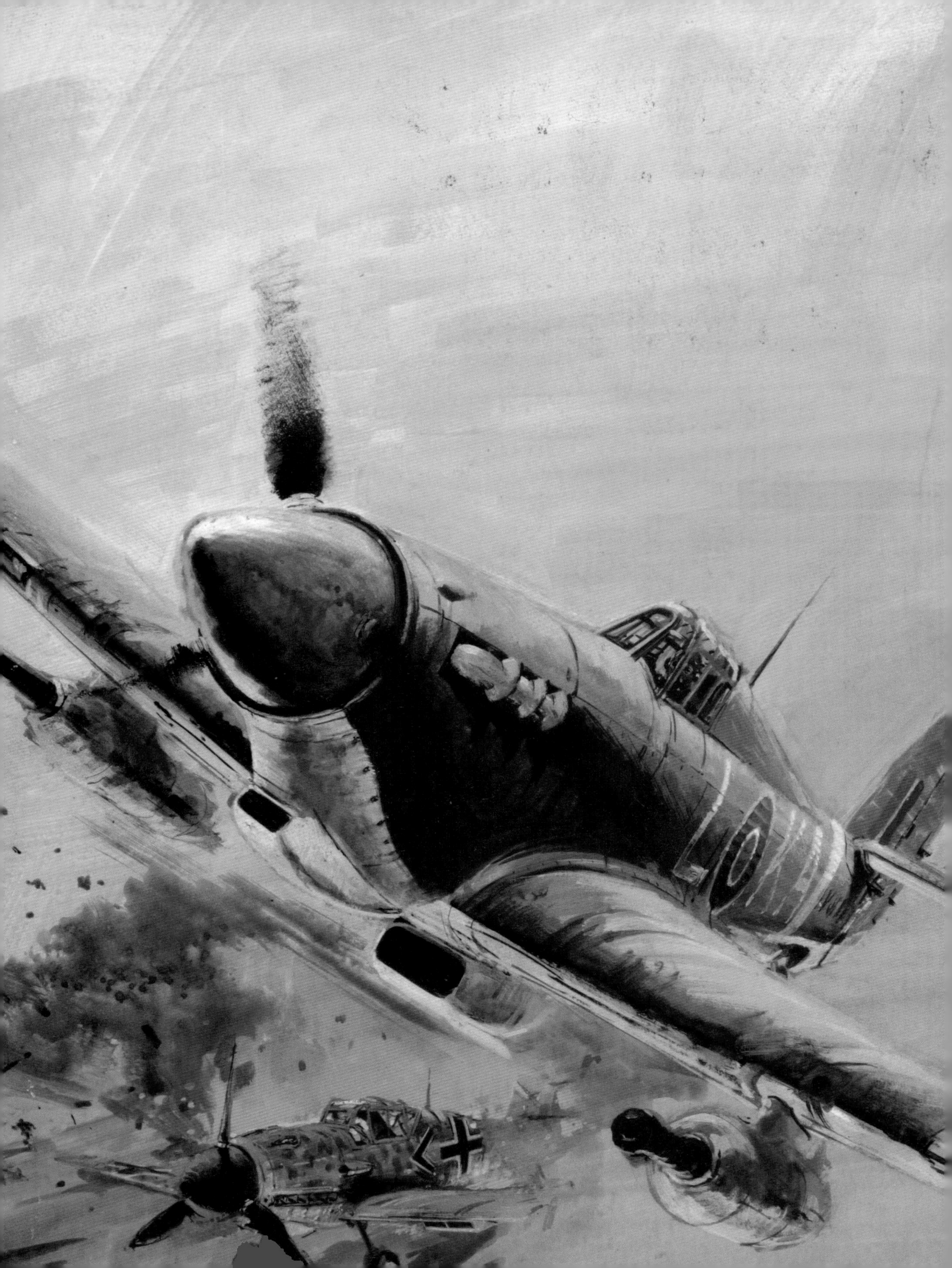

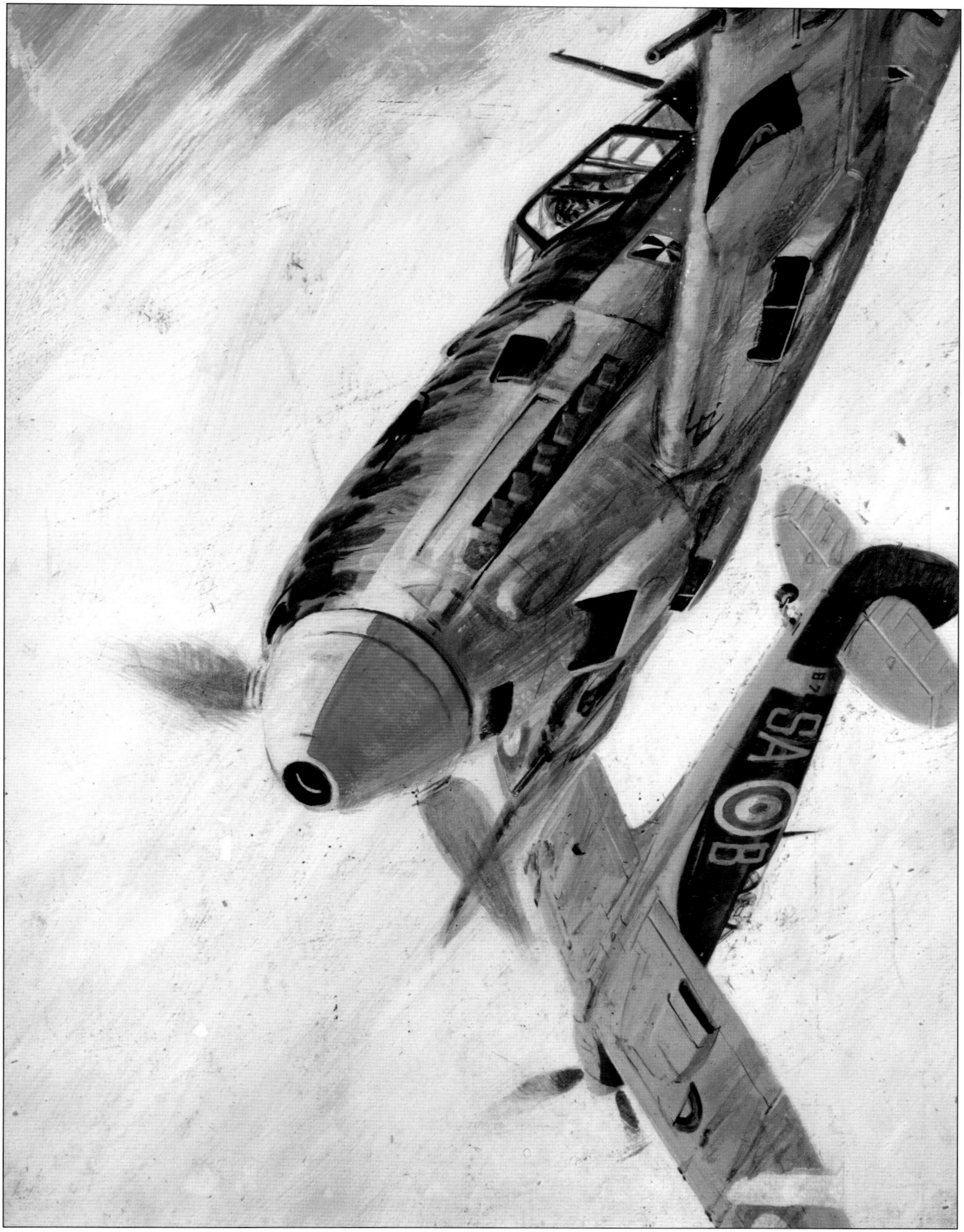
SA
B

Graham Coton, War 634, February 1971
Opposite: Graham Coton, Battle 641, August 1972

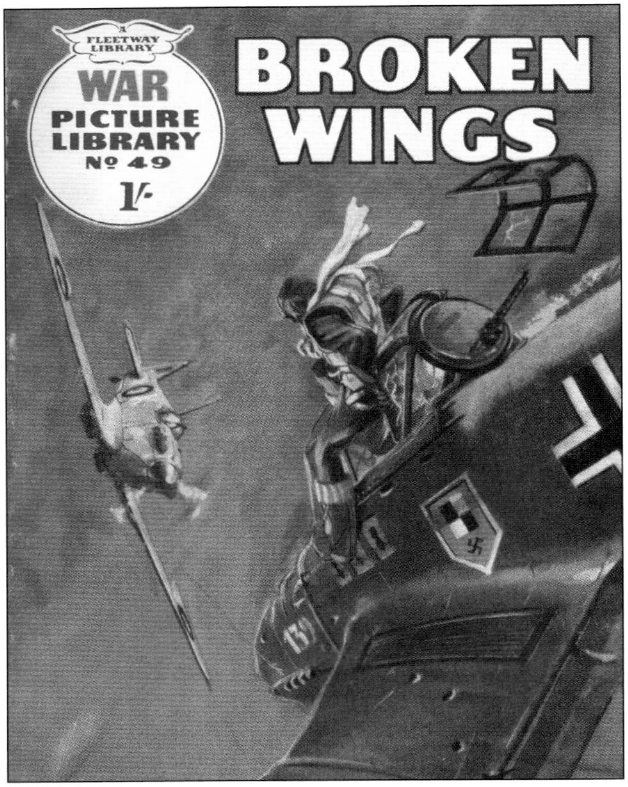

A FLEETWAY LIBRARY
WAR PICTURE LIBRARY Nº 49
1/-
BROKEN WINGS

Nino Caroselli, War 49, May 1960

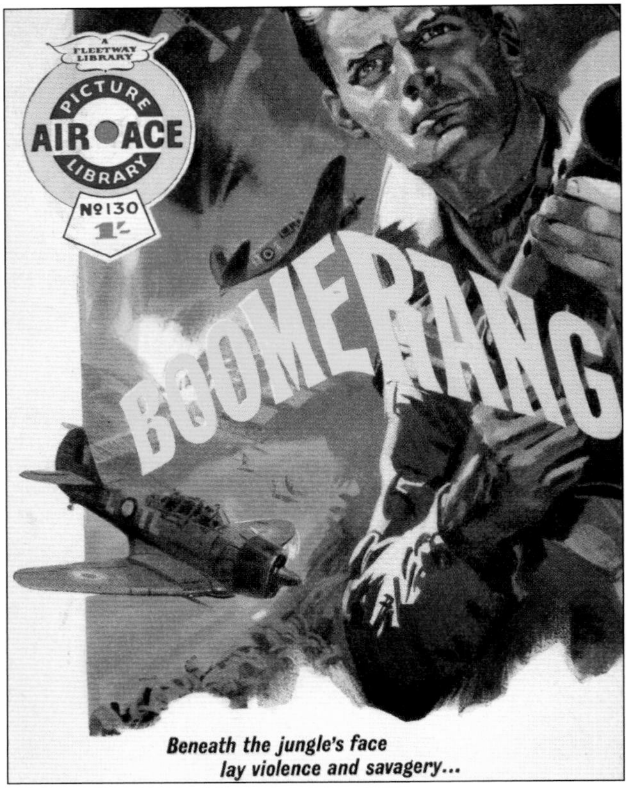

A FLEETWAY LIBRARY
PICTURE AIR ACE LIBRARY
Nº130
1/-
BOOMERANG
Beneath the jungle's face
lay violence and savagery...

Allessandro Biffignandi, Air Ace 130, January 1963

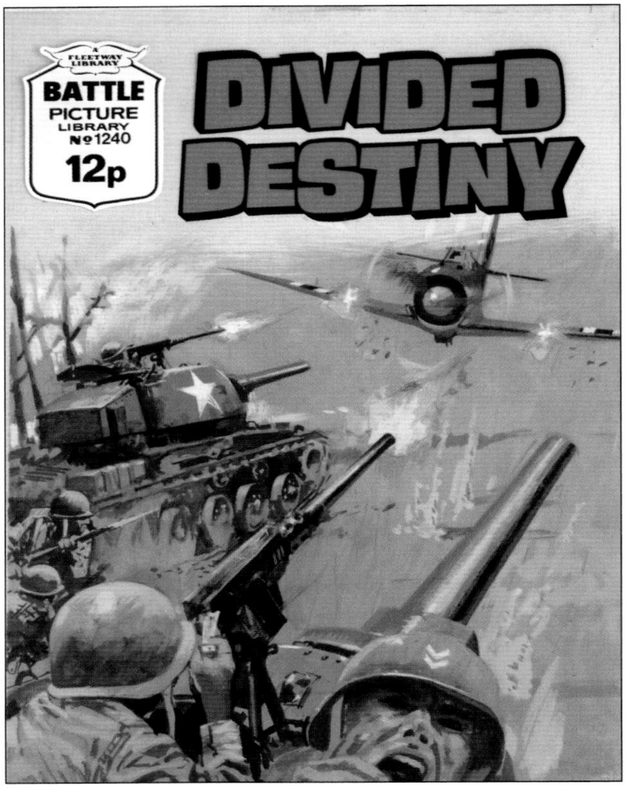

A FLEETWAY LIBRARY
BATTLE PICTURE LIBRARY Nº1240
12p
DIVIDED DESTINY

Pino Dell'Orco, originally Battle 208, June 1965

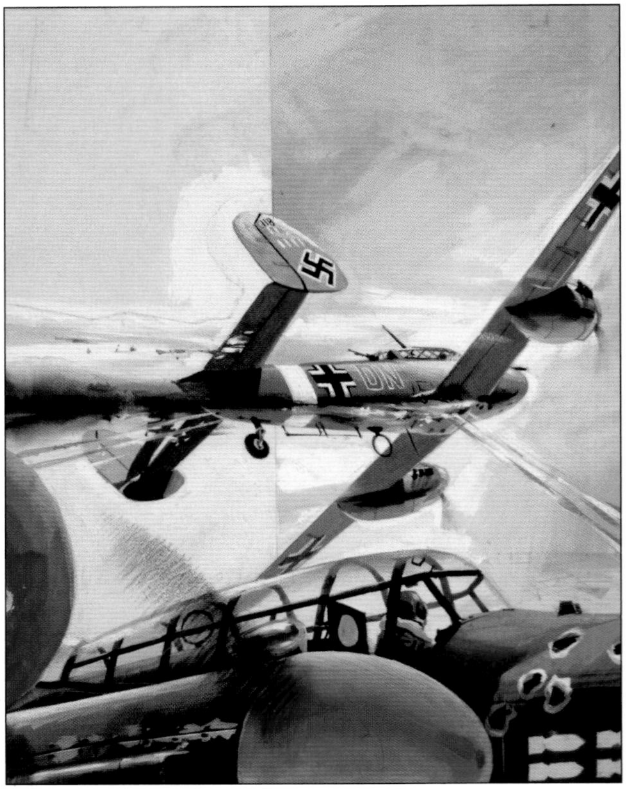

Pino Dell'Orco, originally Air Ace 187 March 1964

Opposite: Pino Dell'Orco, Air Ace 199, June 1964

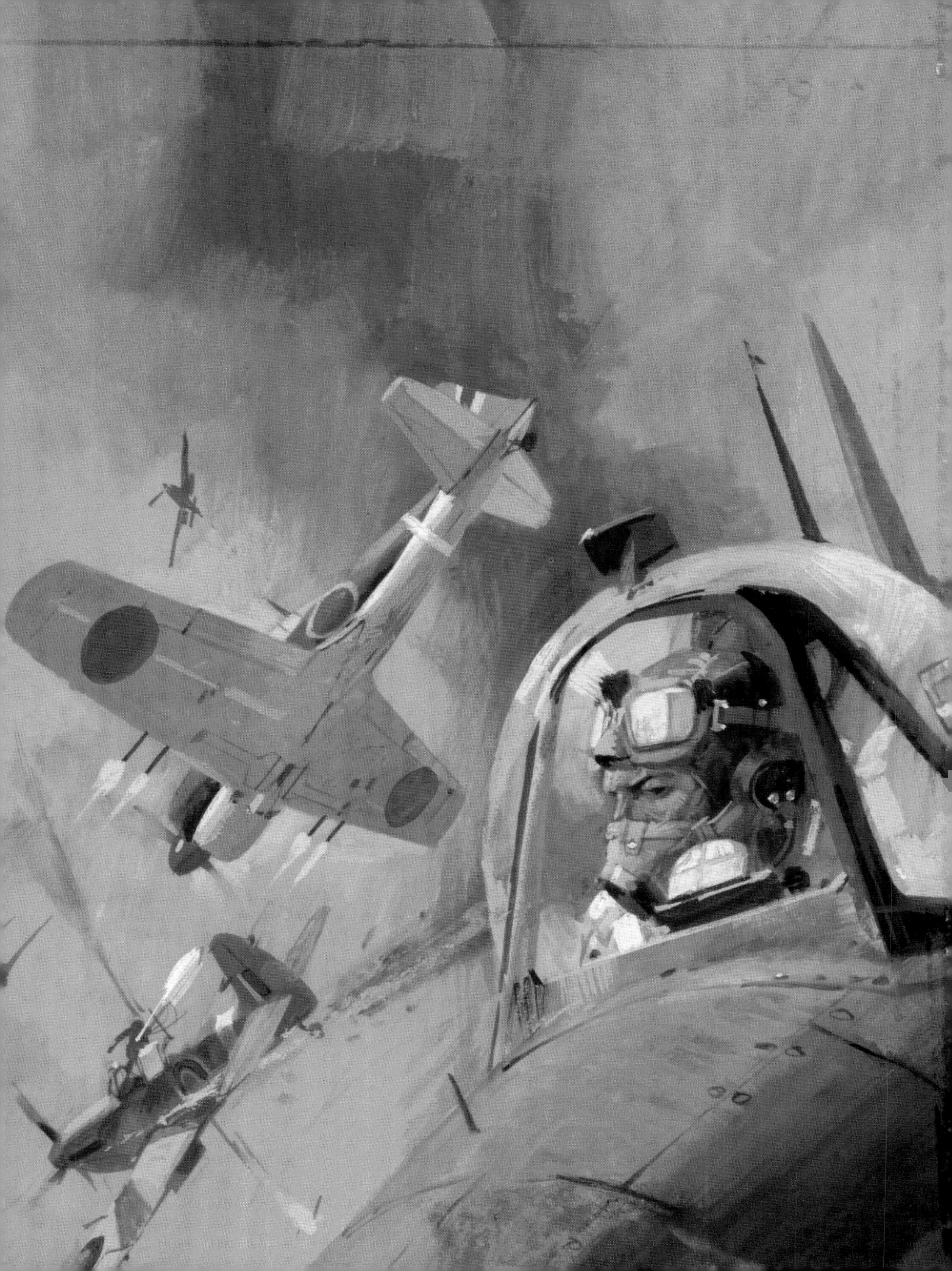

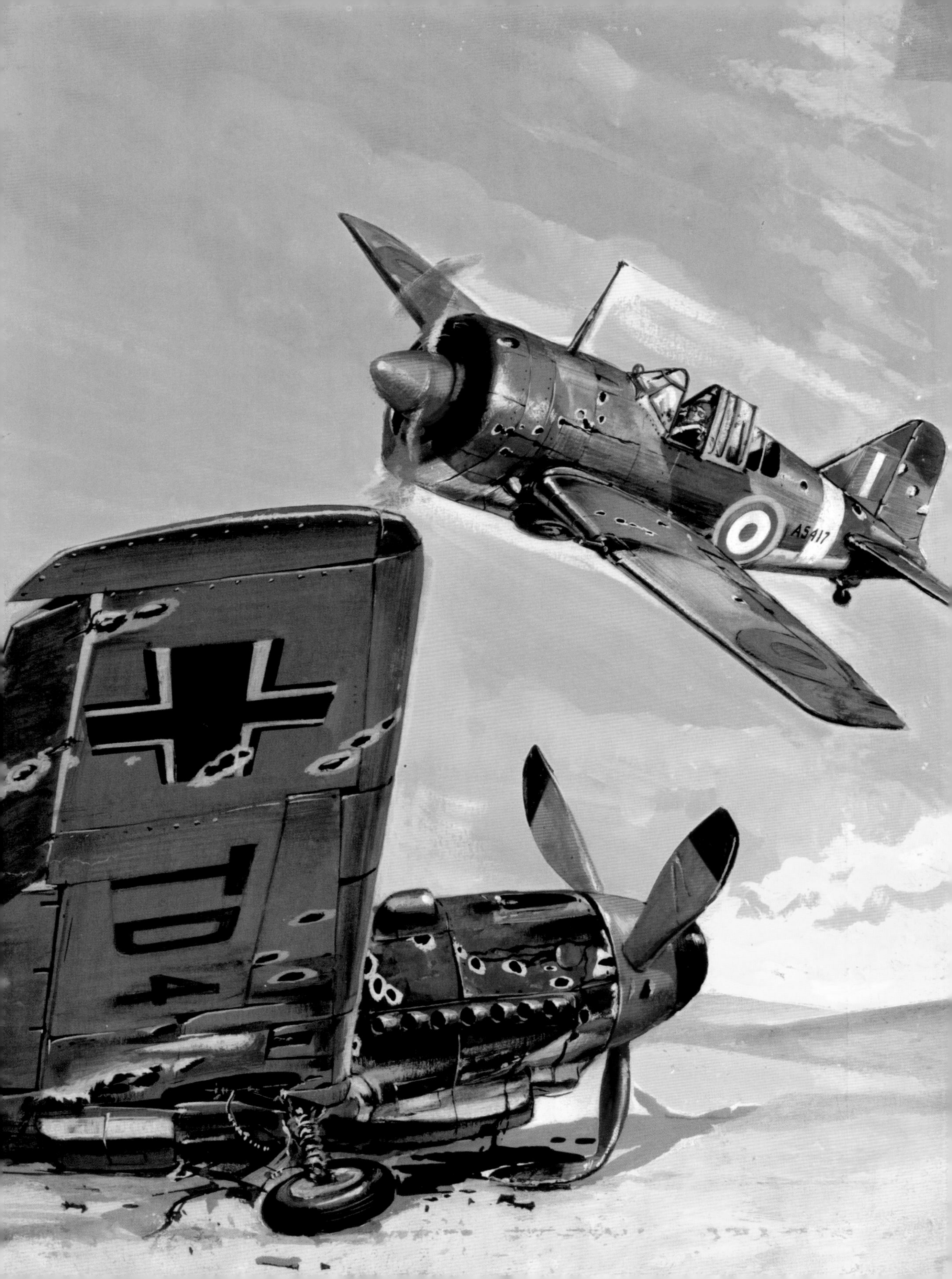
AS417

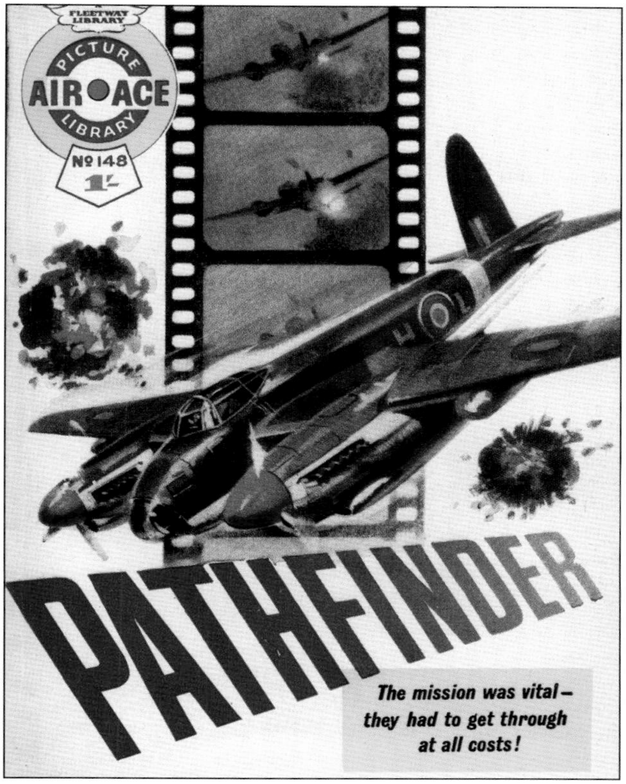
A FLEETWAY LIBRARY
PICTURE
AIR ACE
LIBRARY
Nº148
1/-
PATHFINDER
The mission was vital – they had to get through at all costs!

Allessandro Biffignandi, Air Ace 148, March 1963

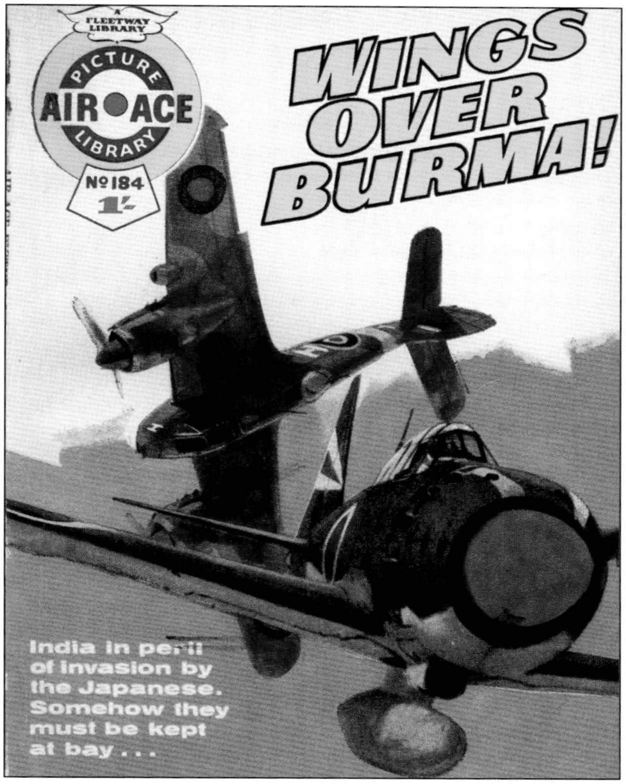
A FLEETWAY LIBRARY
PICTURE
AIR ACE
LIBRARY
Nº184
1/-
WINGS OVER BURMA!
India in peril of invasion by the Japanese. Somehow they must be kept at bay . . .

Pino Dell'Orco, Air Ace 184, February 1964

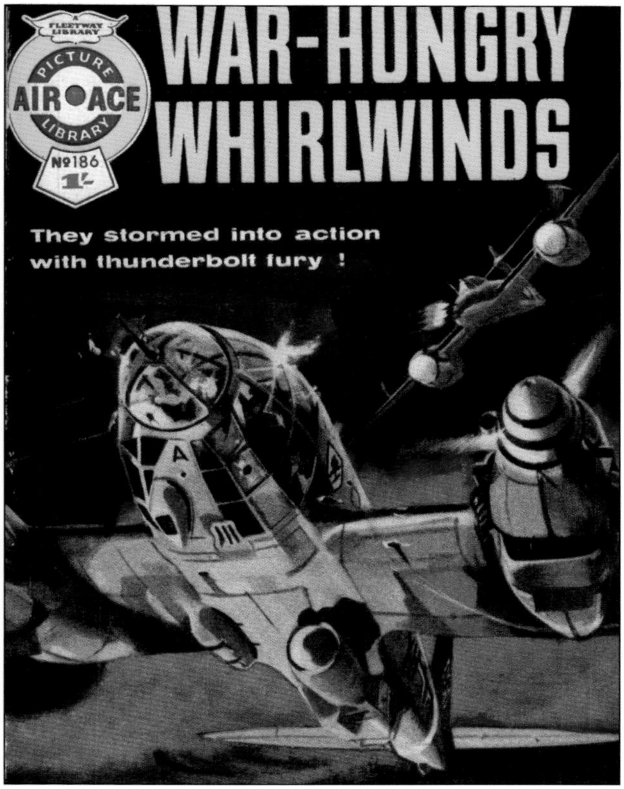
A FLEETWAY LIBRARY
PICTURE
AIR ACE
LIBRARY
Nº186
1/-
WAR-HUNGRY WHIRLWINDS
They stormed into action with thunderbolt fury !

Pino Dell'Orco, Air Ace 186, March 1964

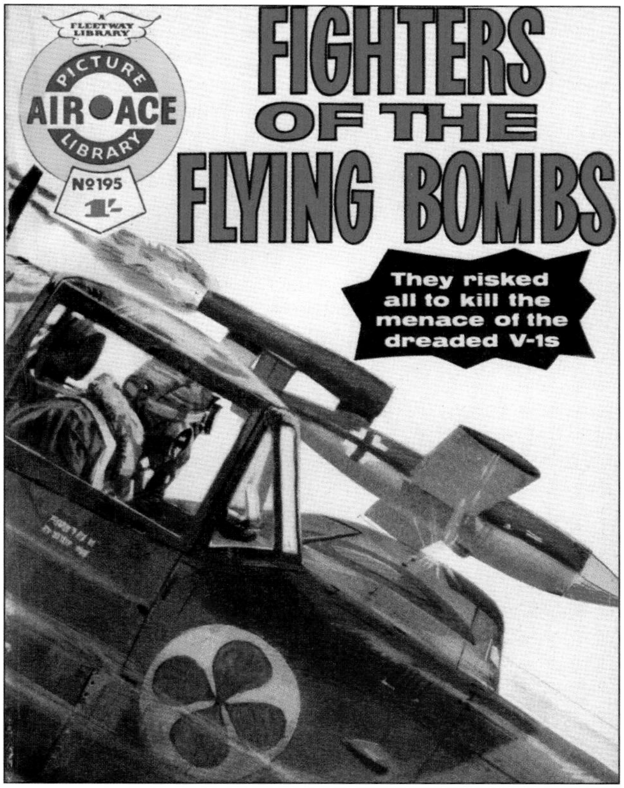
A FLEETWAY LIBRARY
PICTURE
AIR ACE
LIBRARY
Nº195
1/-
FIGHTERS OF THE FLYING BOMBS
They risked all to kill the menace of the dreaded V-1s

Pino Dell'Orco, Air Ace 195, May 1964

Opposite: Nino Caroselli, Air Ace 61, July 1961

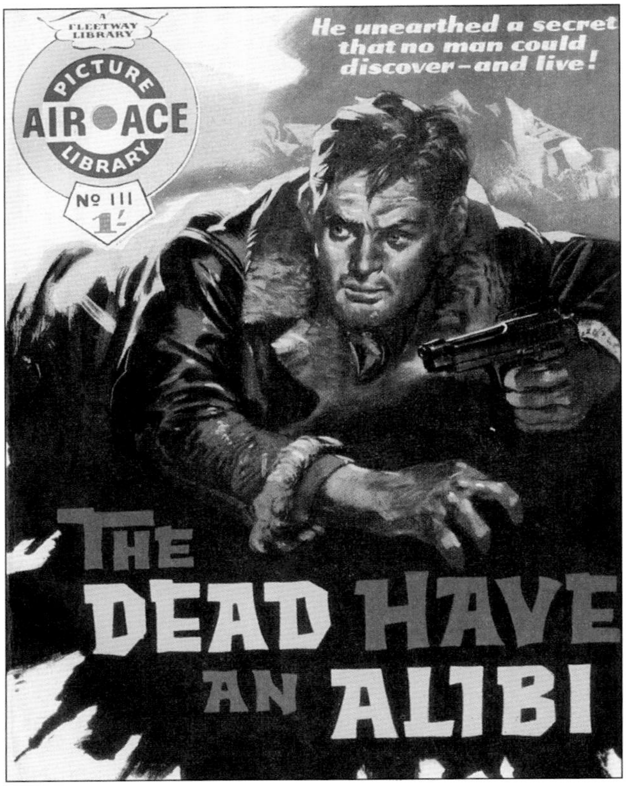
A FLEETWAY LIBRARY
PICTURE AIR ACE LIBRARY
Nº 111
1/-
He unearthed a secret that no man could discover – and live!
THE DEAD HAVE AN ALIBI

Allessandro Biffignandi, Air Ace 111, August 1962

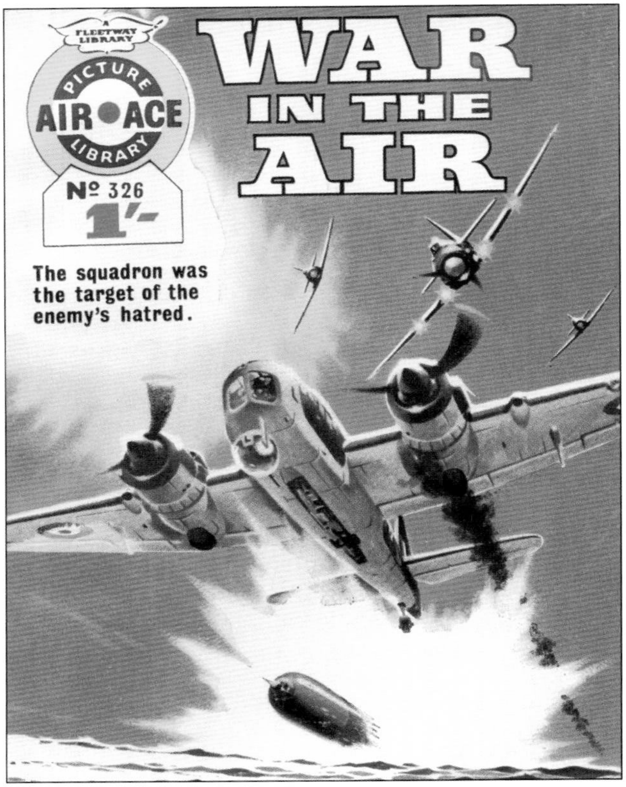
A FLEETWAY LIBRARY
PICTURE AIR ACE LIBRARY
Nº 326
1/-
WAR IN THE AIR
The squadron was the target of the enemy's hatred.

Ian Kennedy, Air Ace 326, February 1967

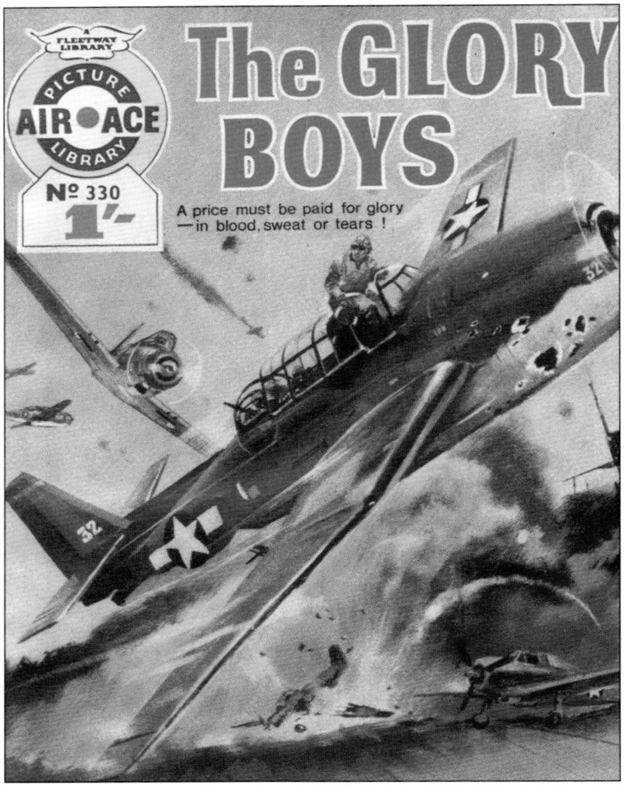
A FLEETWAY LIBRARY
PICTURE AIR ACE LIBRARY
Nº 330
1/-
The GLORY BOYS
A price must be paid for glory —in blood, sweat or tears !

Carlo Jacono, Air Ace 330, March 1967

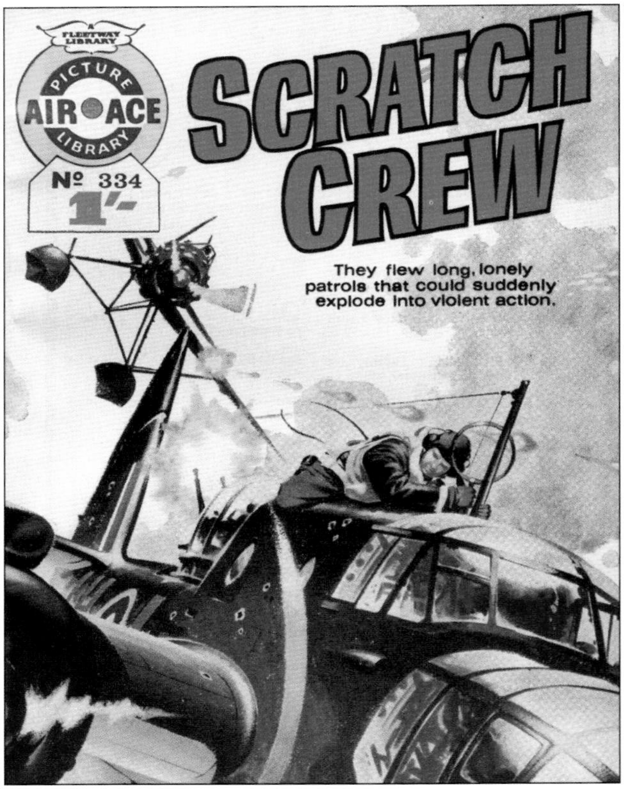
A FLEETWAY LIBRARY
PICTURE AIR ACE LIBRARY
Nº 334
1/-
SCRATCH CREW
They flew long, lonely patrols that could suddenly explode into violent action.

Ian Kennedy, Air Ace 334, April 1967

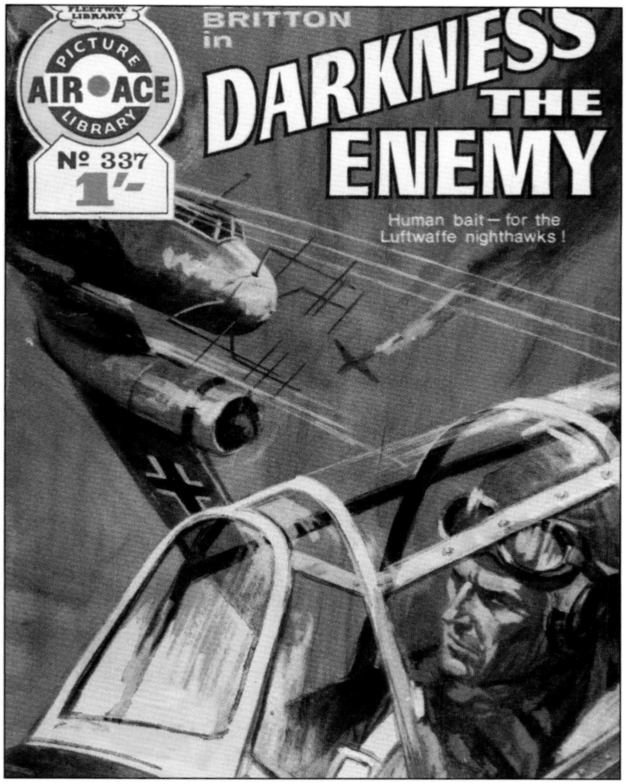
PICTURE
AIR ACE
LIBRARY
Nº 337
1/-
BRITTON in
DARKNESS THE ENEMY
Human bait—for the Luftwaffe nighthawks!

Rafael Lopez Espi, Air Ace 337, April 1967

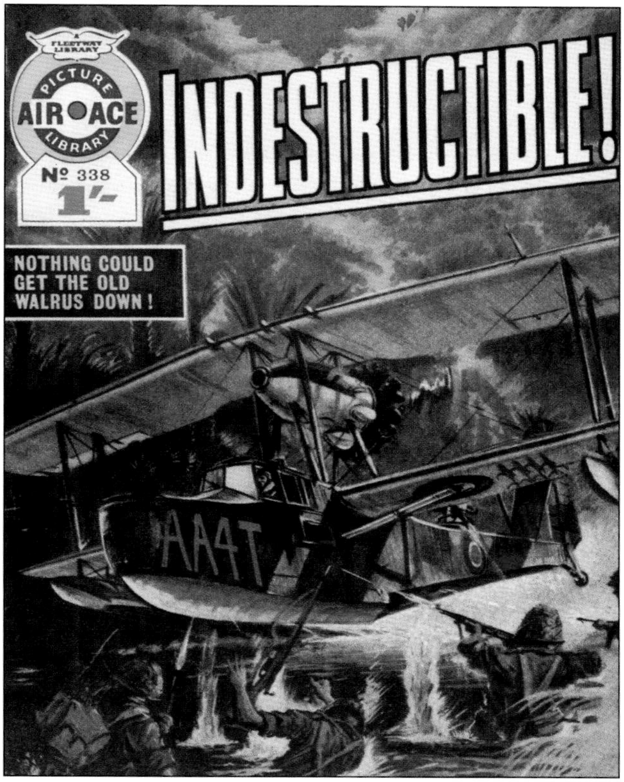
PICTURE
AIR ACE
LIBRARY
Nº 338
1/-
INDESTRUCTIBLE!
NOTHING COULD GET THE OLD WALRUS DOWN!

Alan Willow, Air Ace 338, May 1967

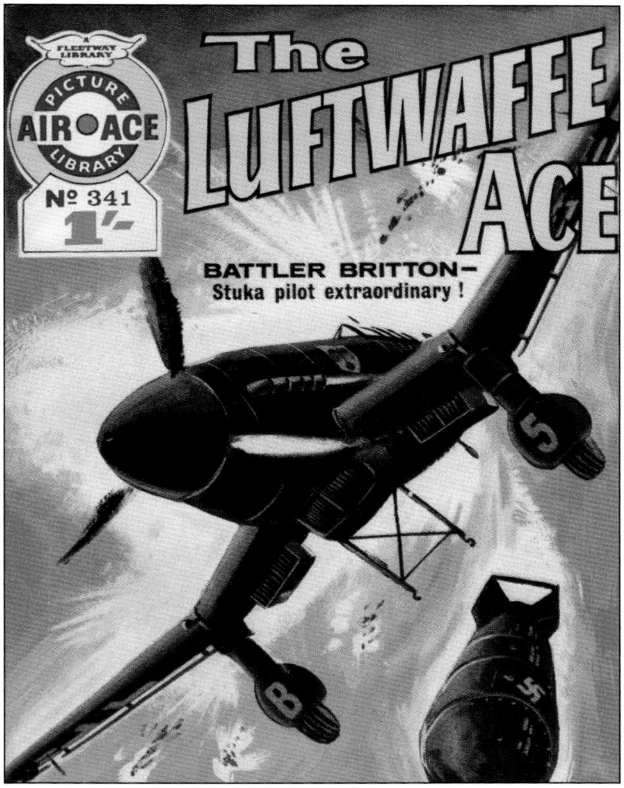
PICTURE
AIR ACE
LIBRARY
Nº 341
1/-
The LUFTWAFFE ACE
BATTLER BRITTON—
Stuka pilot extraordinary!

Alan Willow, Air Ace 341, May 1967

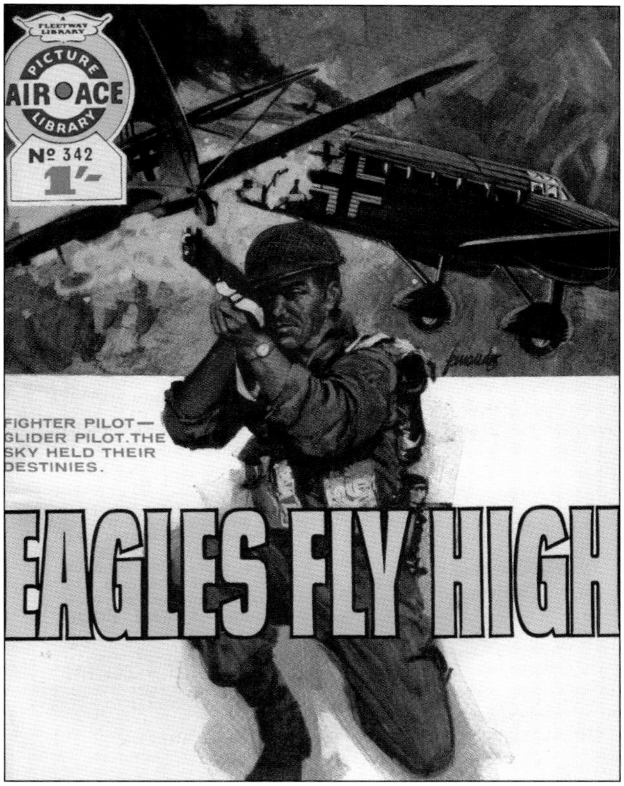
PICTURE
AIR ACE
LIBRARY
Nº 342
1/-
FIGHTER PILOT—GLIDER PILOT.THE SKY HELD THEIR DESTINIES.
EAGLES FLY HIGH

Fernando Fernandez, Air Ace 342, June 1967

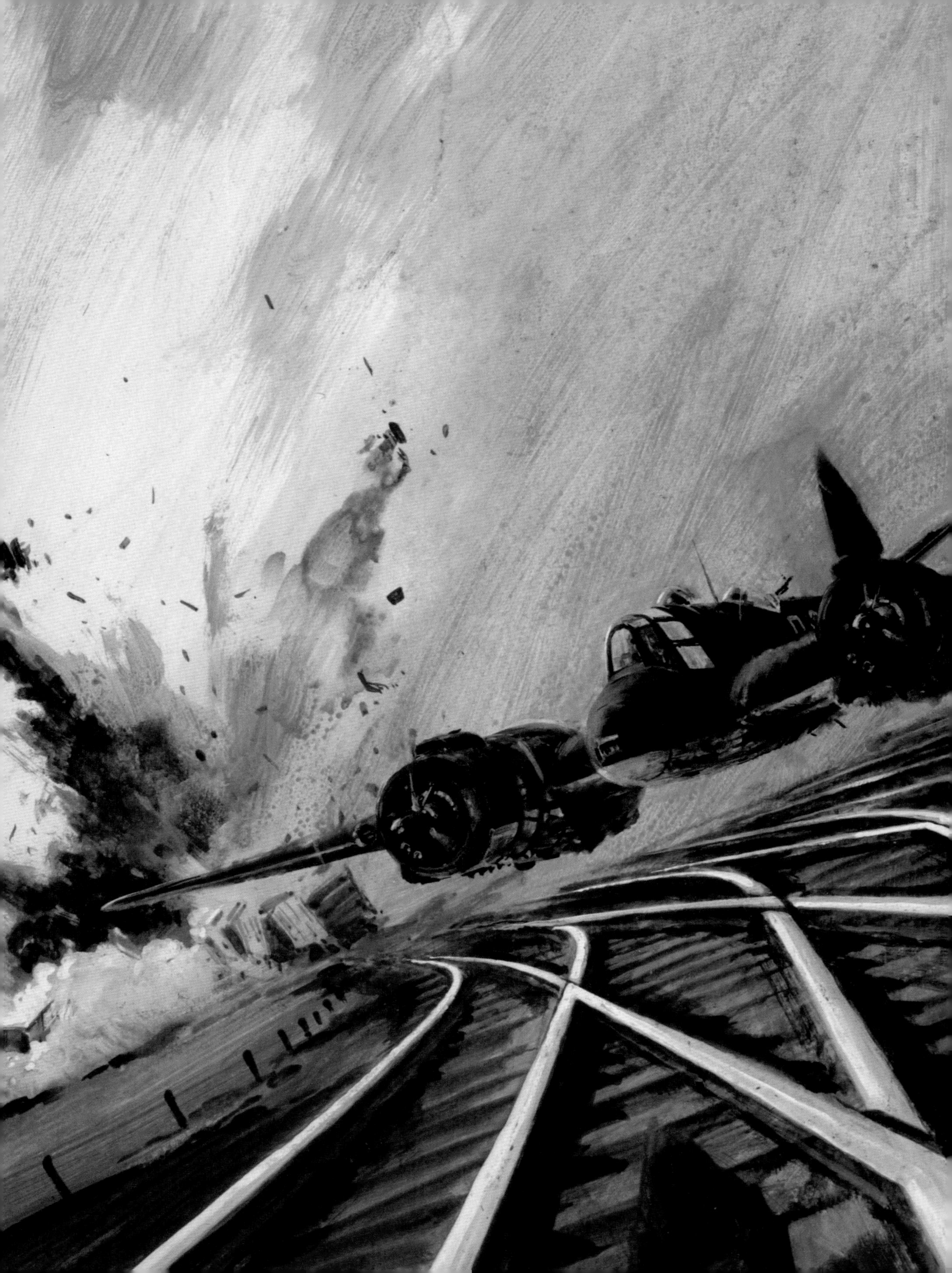

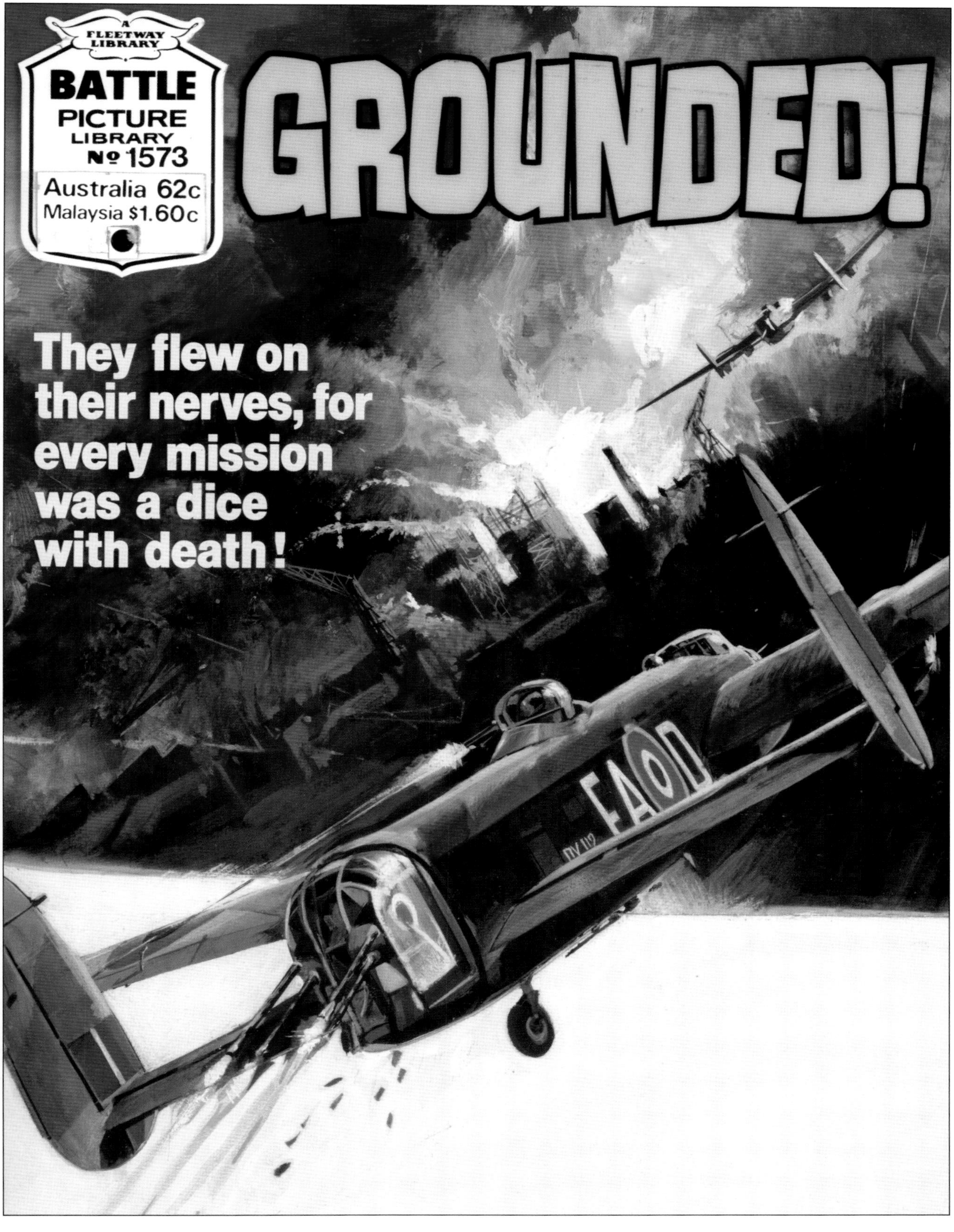
A FLEETWAY LIBRARY
BATTLE
PICTURE
LIBRARY
Nº 1573
Australia 62c
Malaysia $1.60c
GROUNDED!
They flew on their nerves, for every mission was a dice with death!
FA D

Marcello Ralli, originally Air Ace, 189 March 1964
Opposite: Graham Coton, War 1957, October 1982
Overleaf: Graham Coton, Battle 545, August 1971

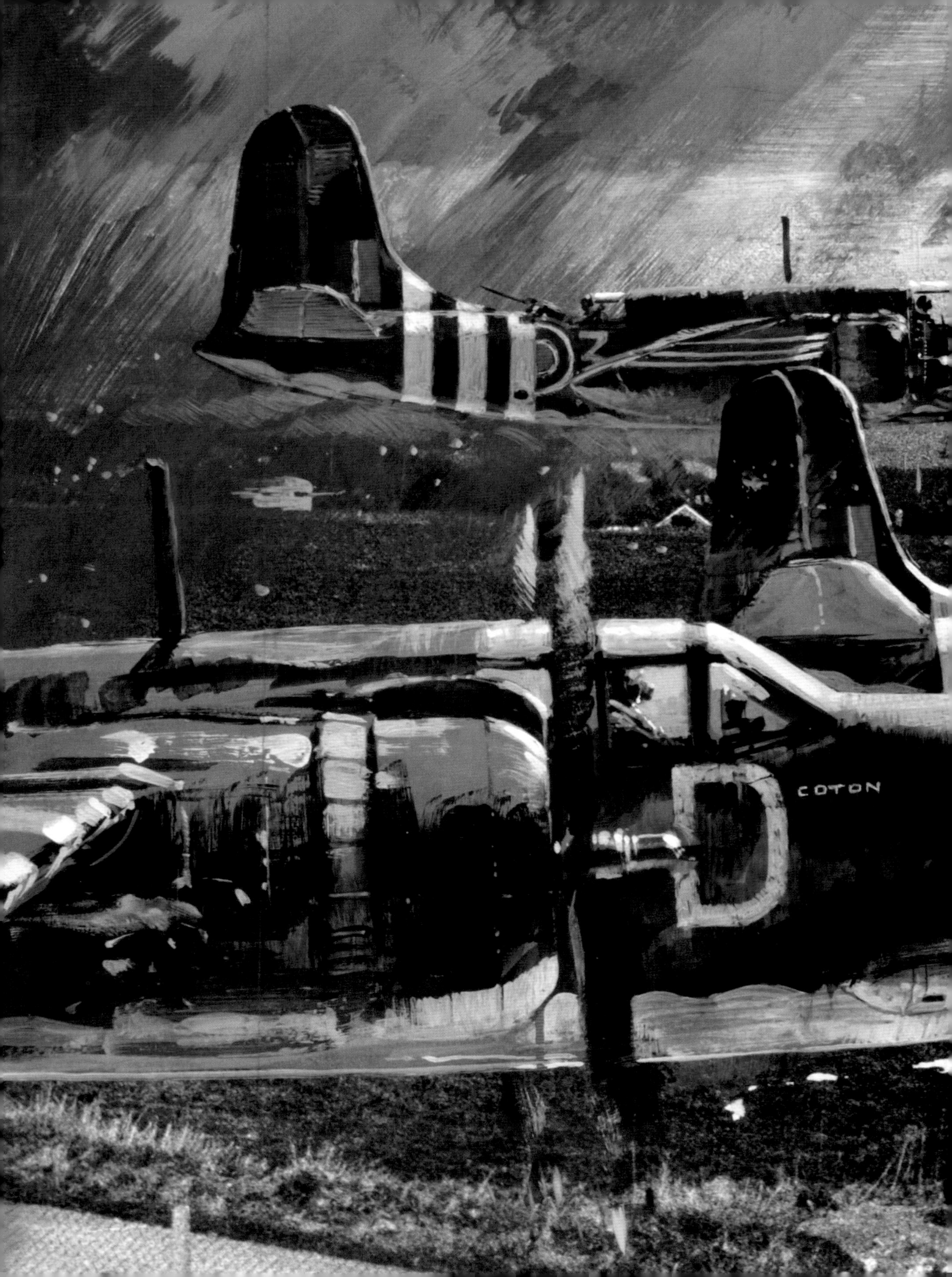
COTON

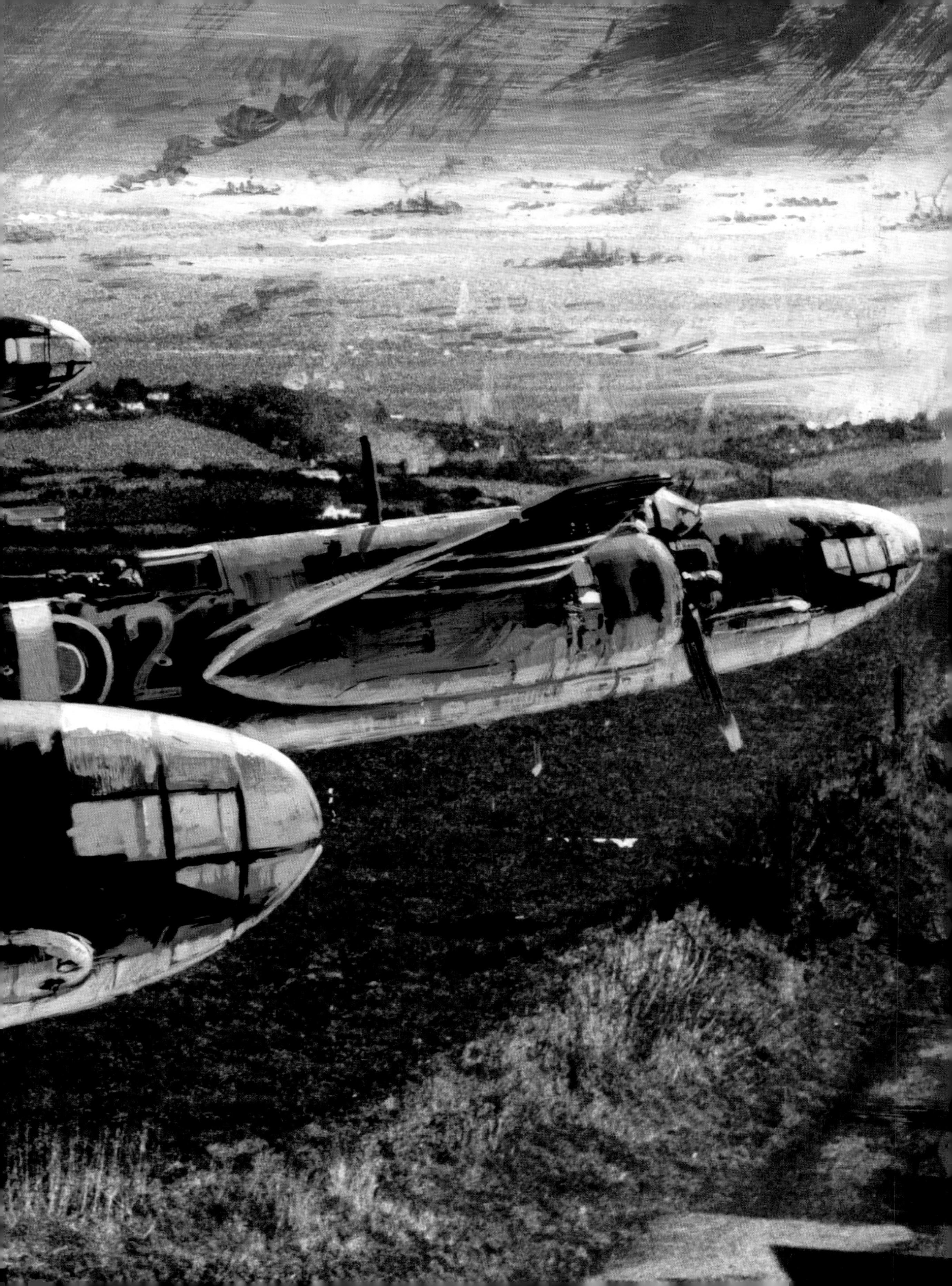

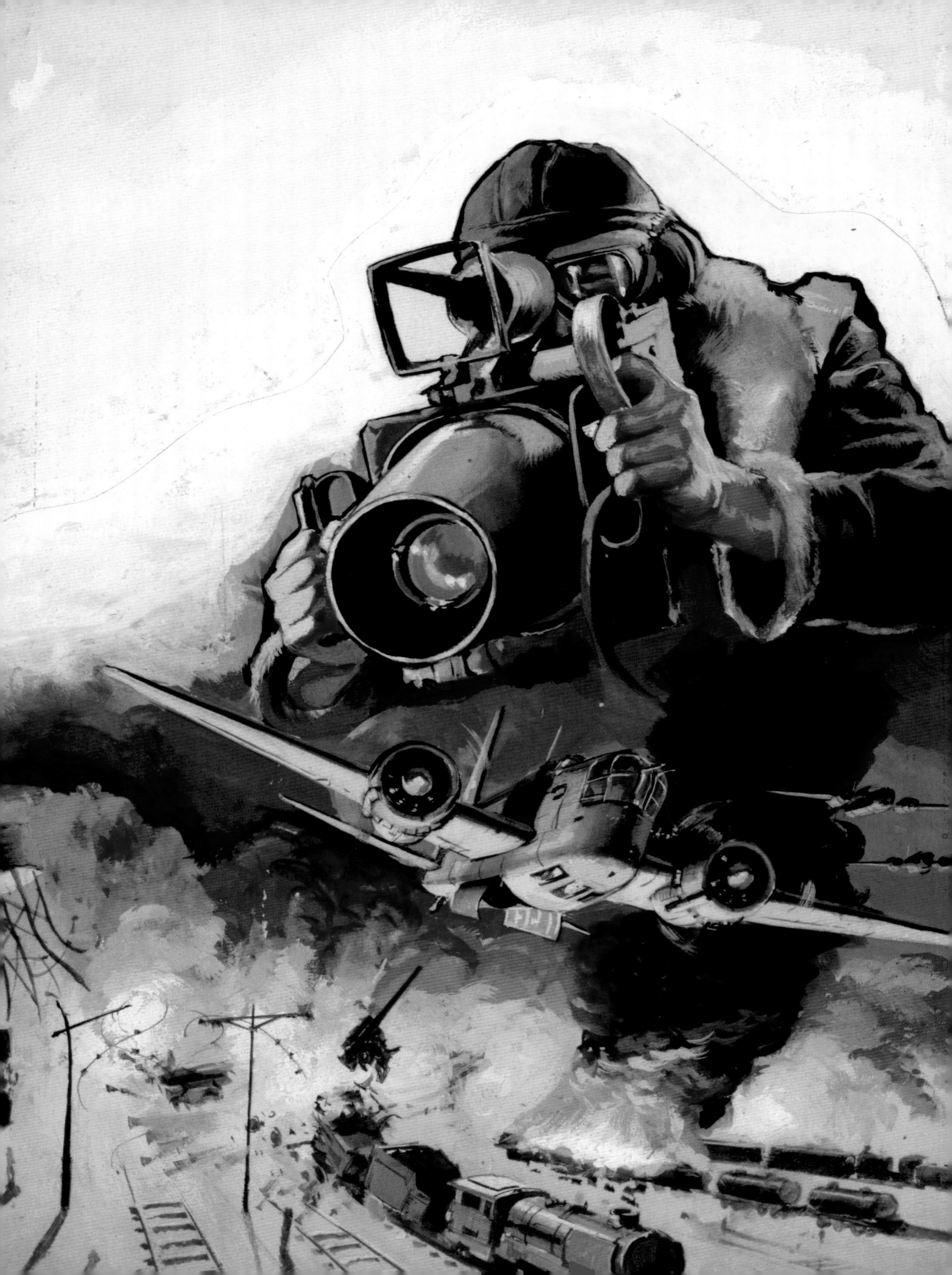

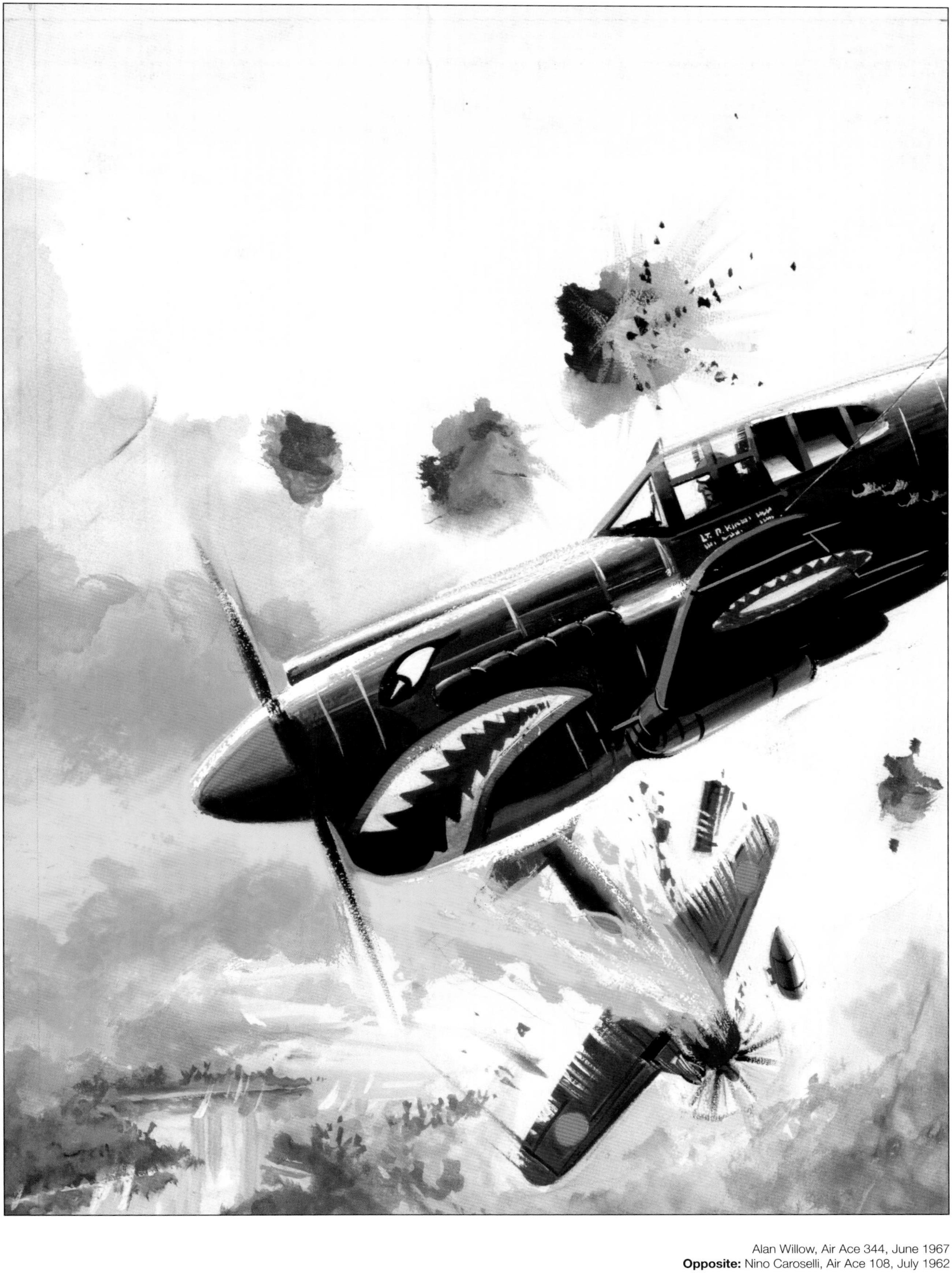

Alan Willow, Air Ace 344, June 1967
Opposite: Nino Caroselli, Air Ace 108, July 1962

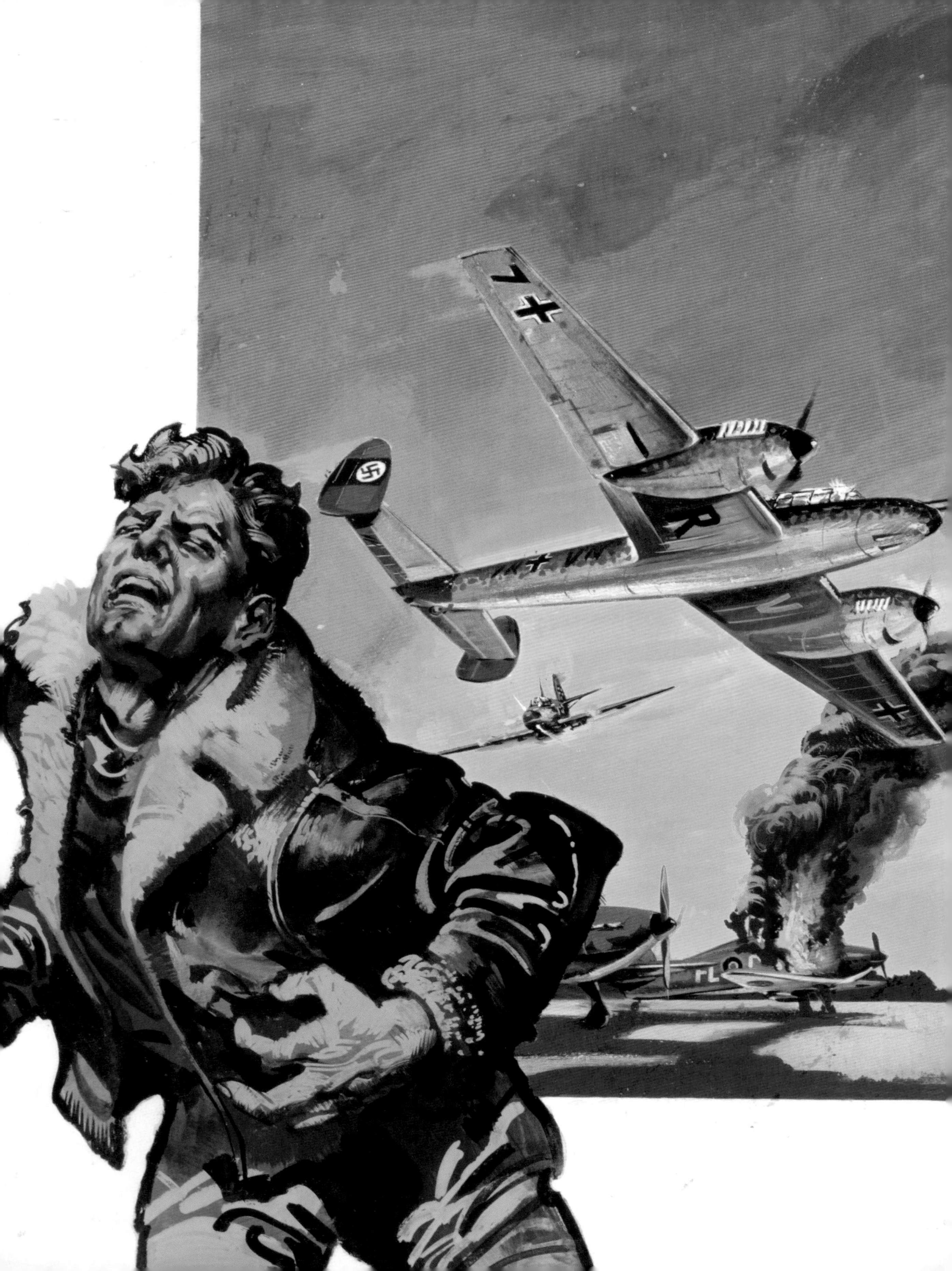

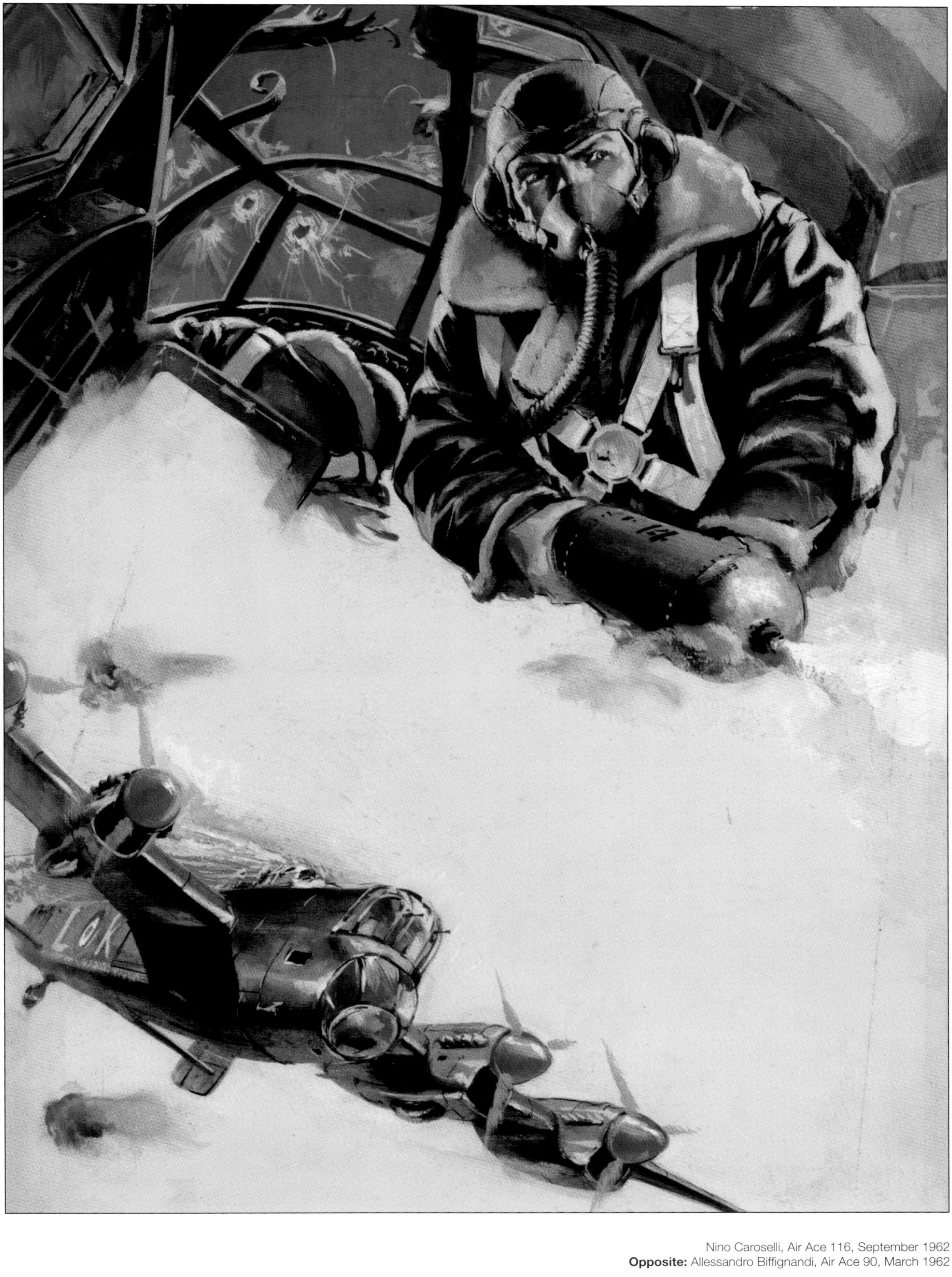

Nino Caroselli, Air Ace 116, September 1962
Opposite: Allessandro Biffignandi, Air Ace 90, March 1962

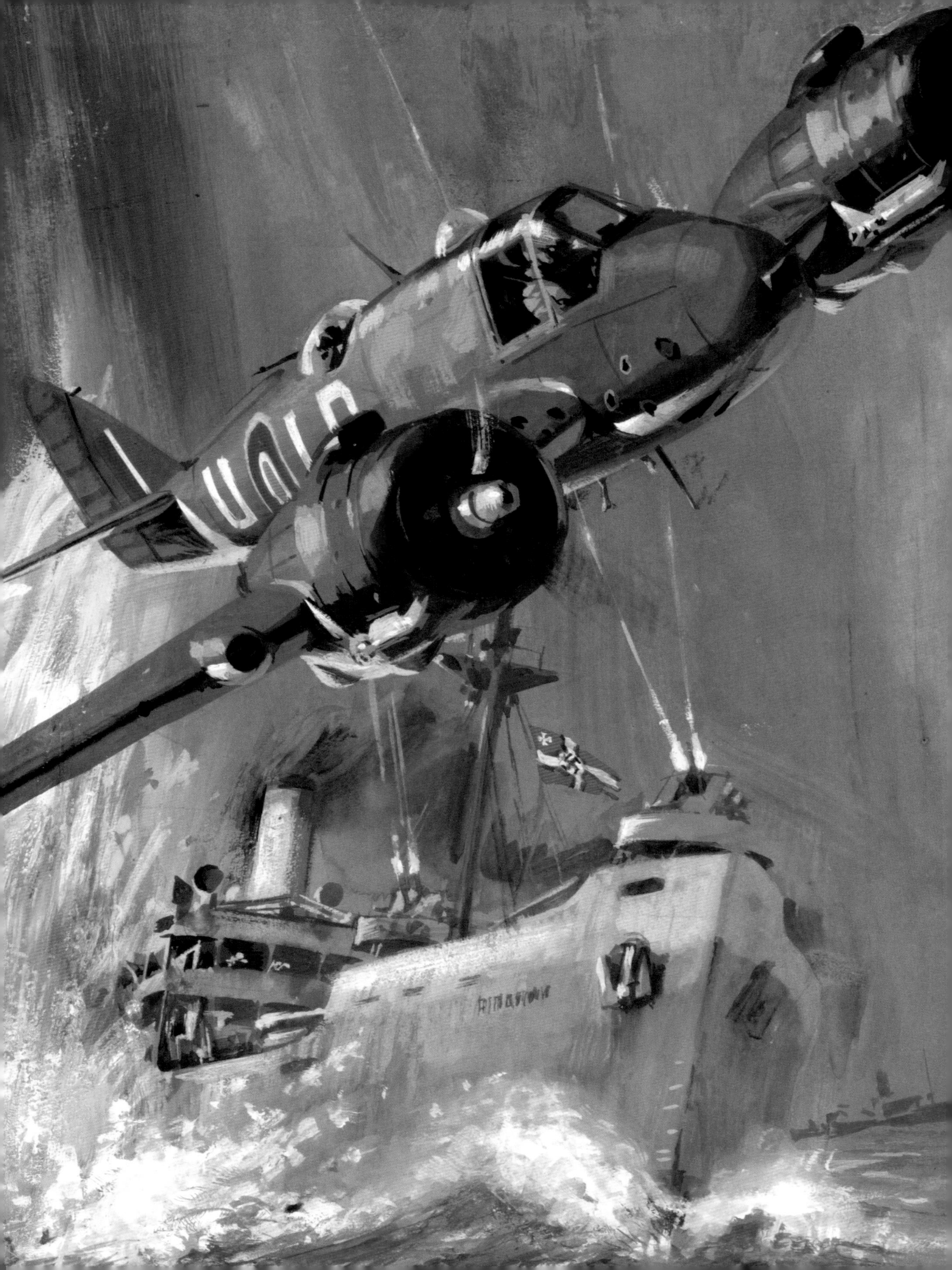

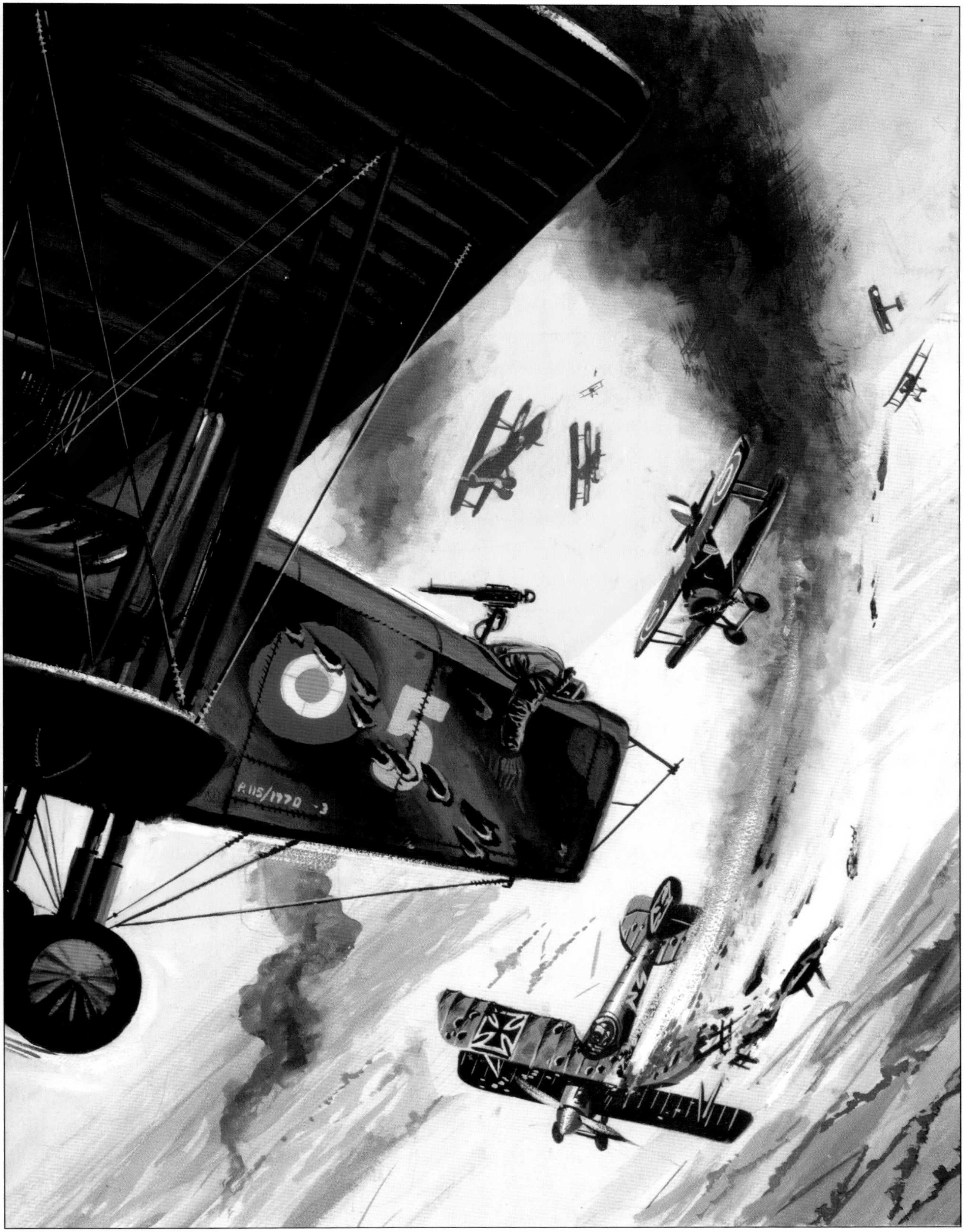
5
R 115/1770 -3

Alan Willow, Air Ace 322, January 1967
Opposite: Pino Dell'Orco, Air Ace 144, April 1963

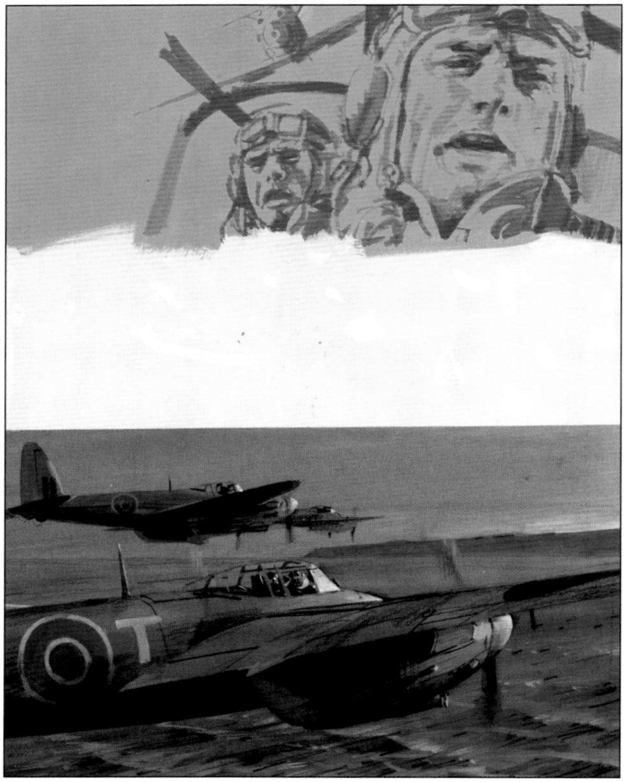

Pino Dell'Orco, Air Ace 520, July 1970

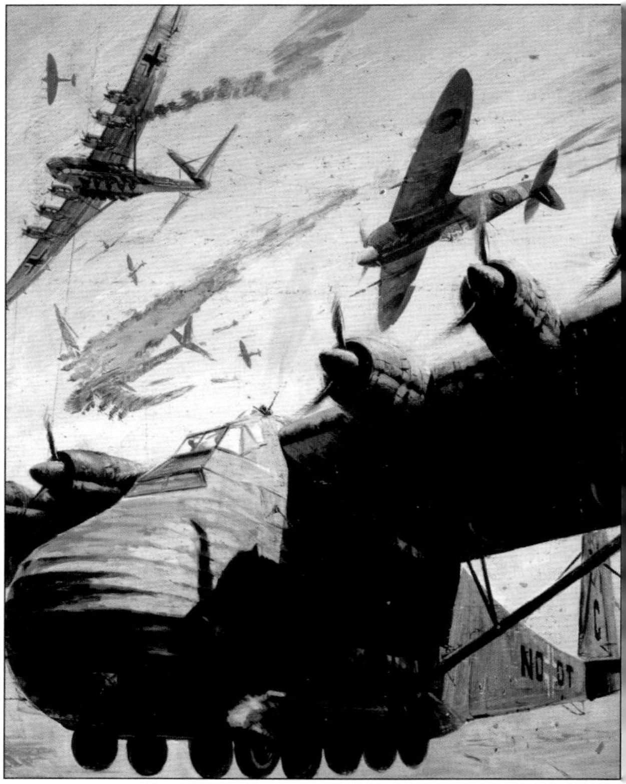

Graham Coton, Air Ace 408, October 1968

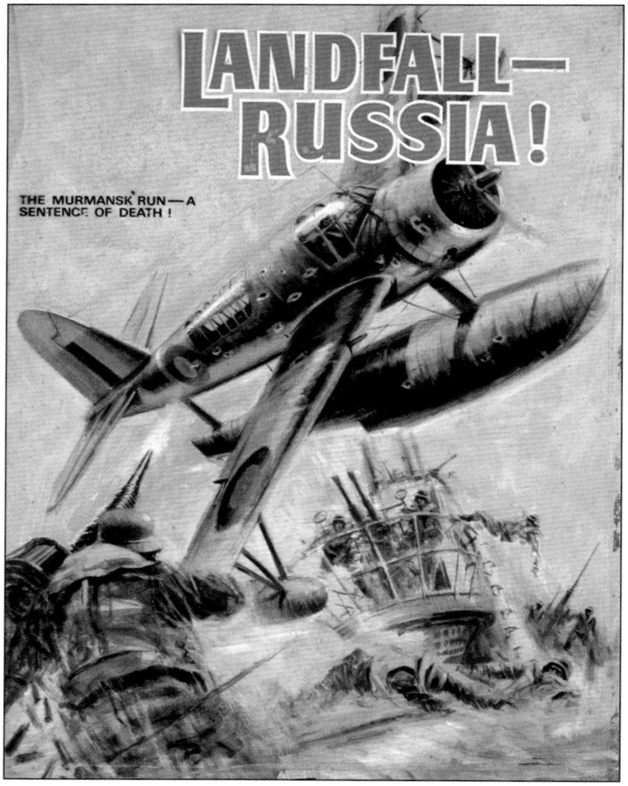
LANDFALL—
RUSSIA!
THE MURMANSK RUN—A SENTENCE OF DEATH!

Graham Coton, Air Ace 396, July 1968

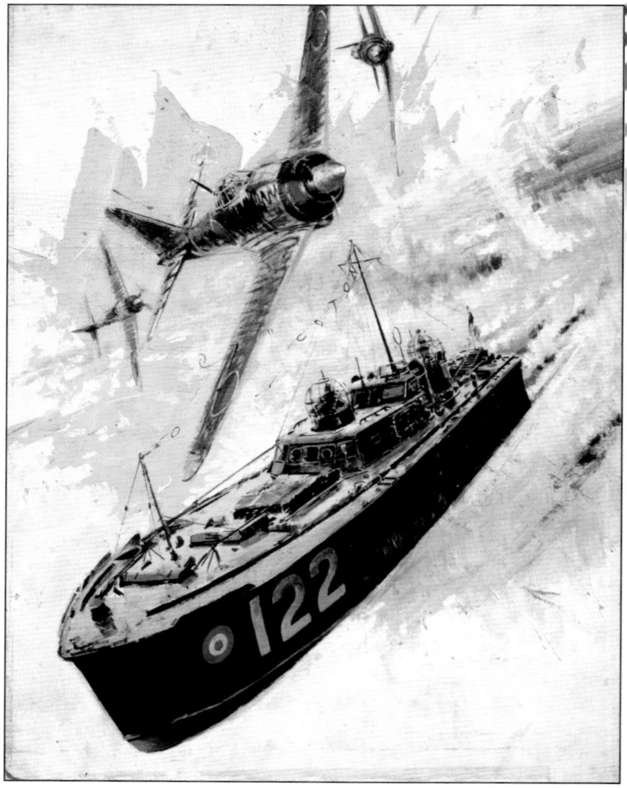

Graham Coton, War 921, February 1974

Opposite: Pino Dell'Orco, Air Ace 127, December 1962

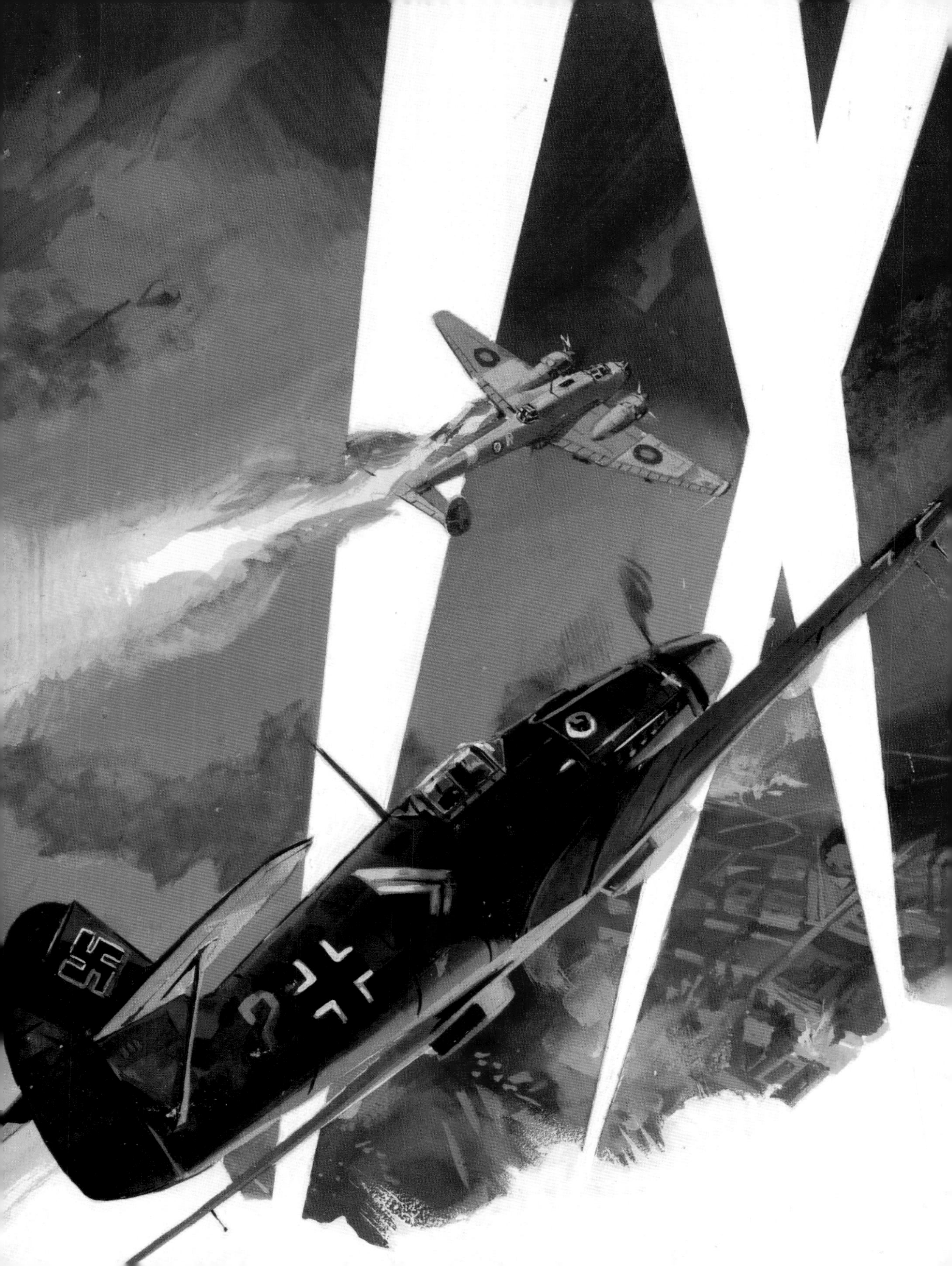

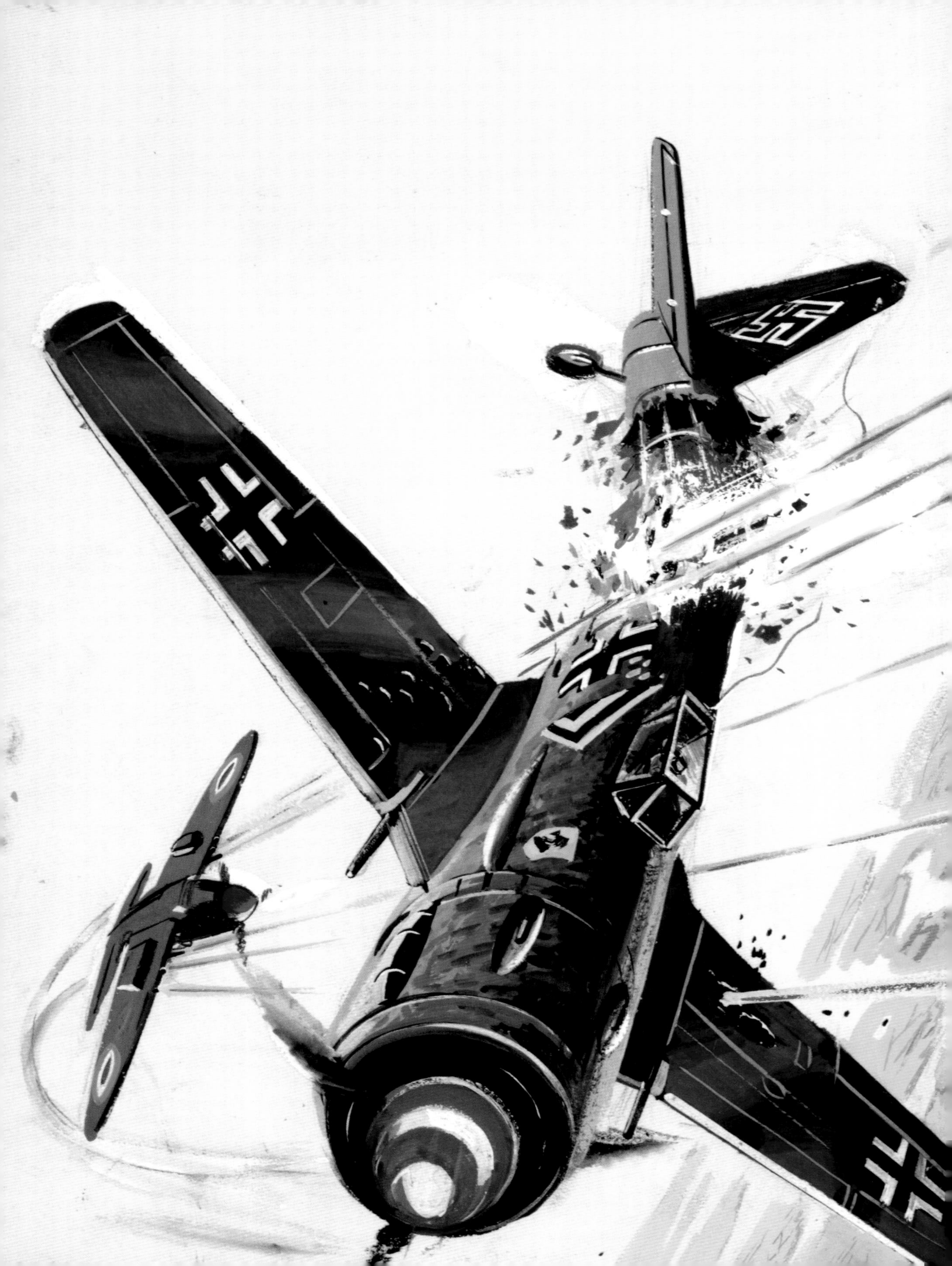

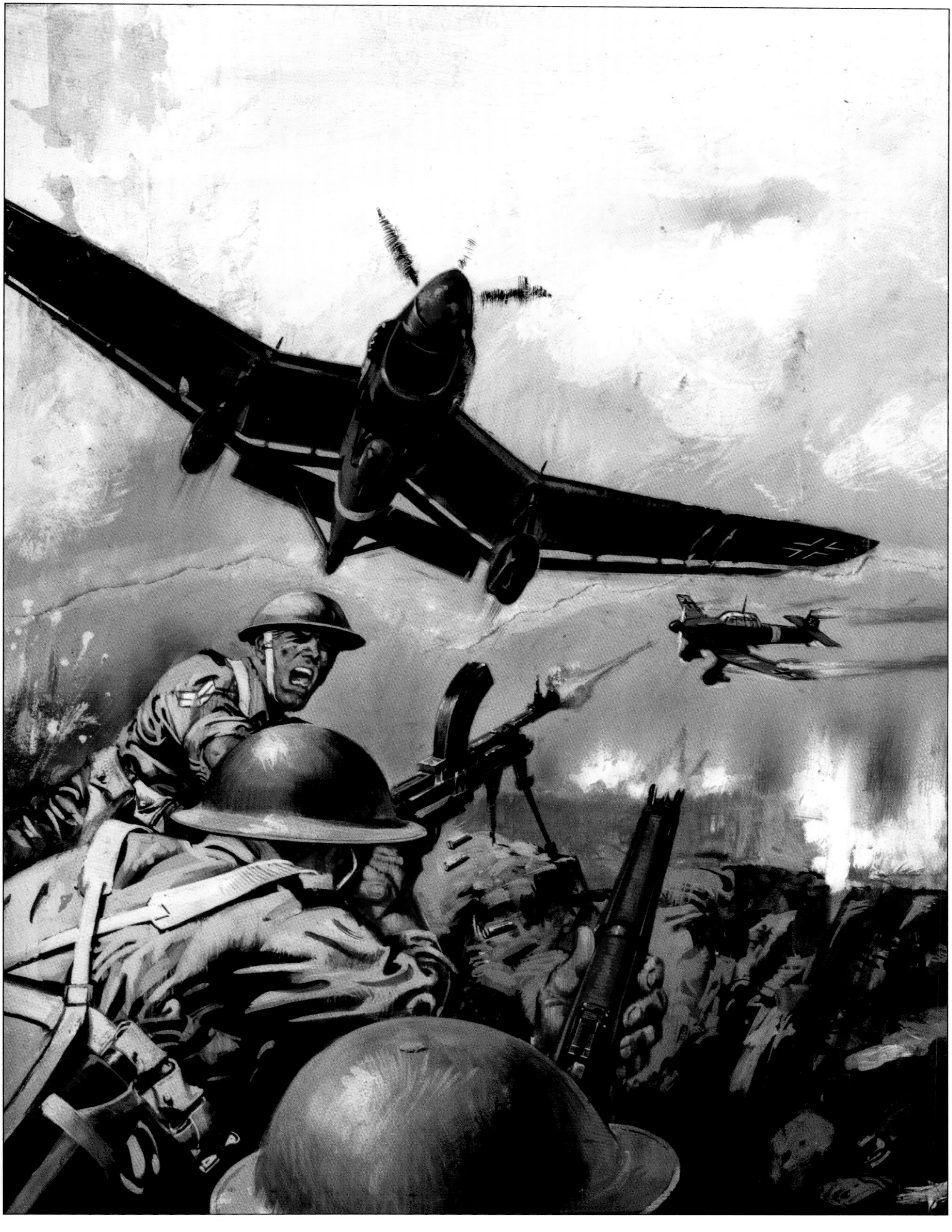

Allessandro Biffignandi, War 132, February 1962
Opposite: Alan Willow, Air Ace 254, August 1965

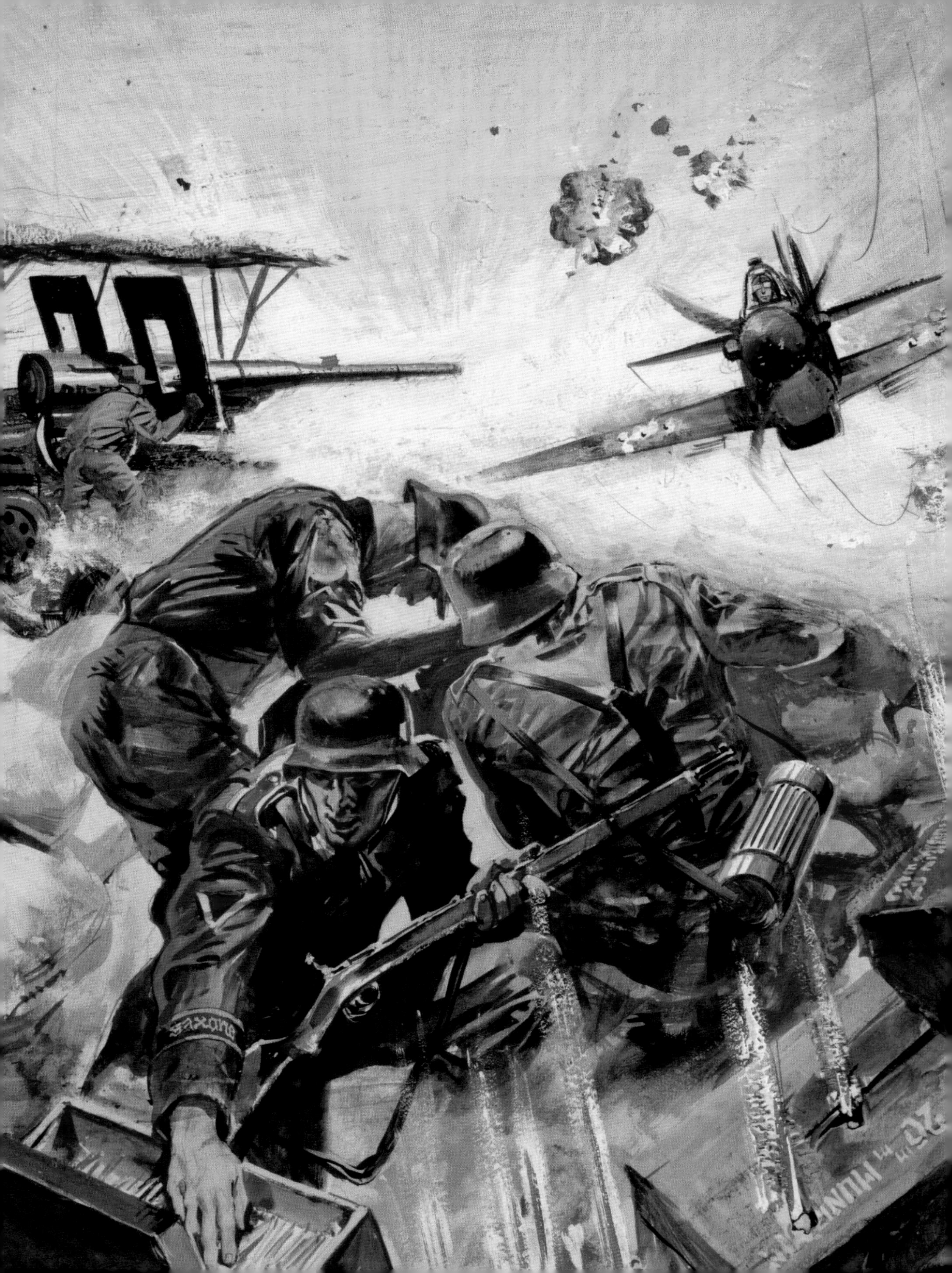

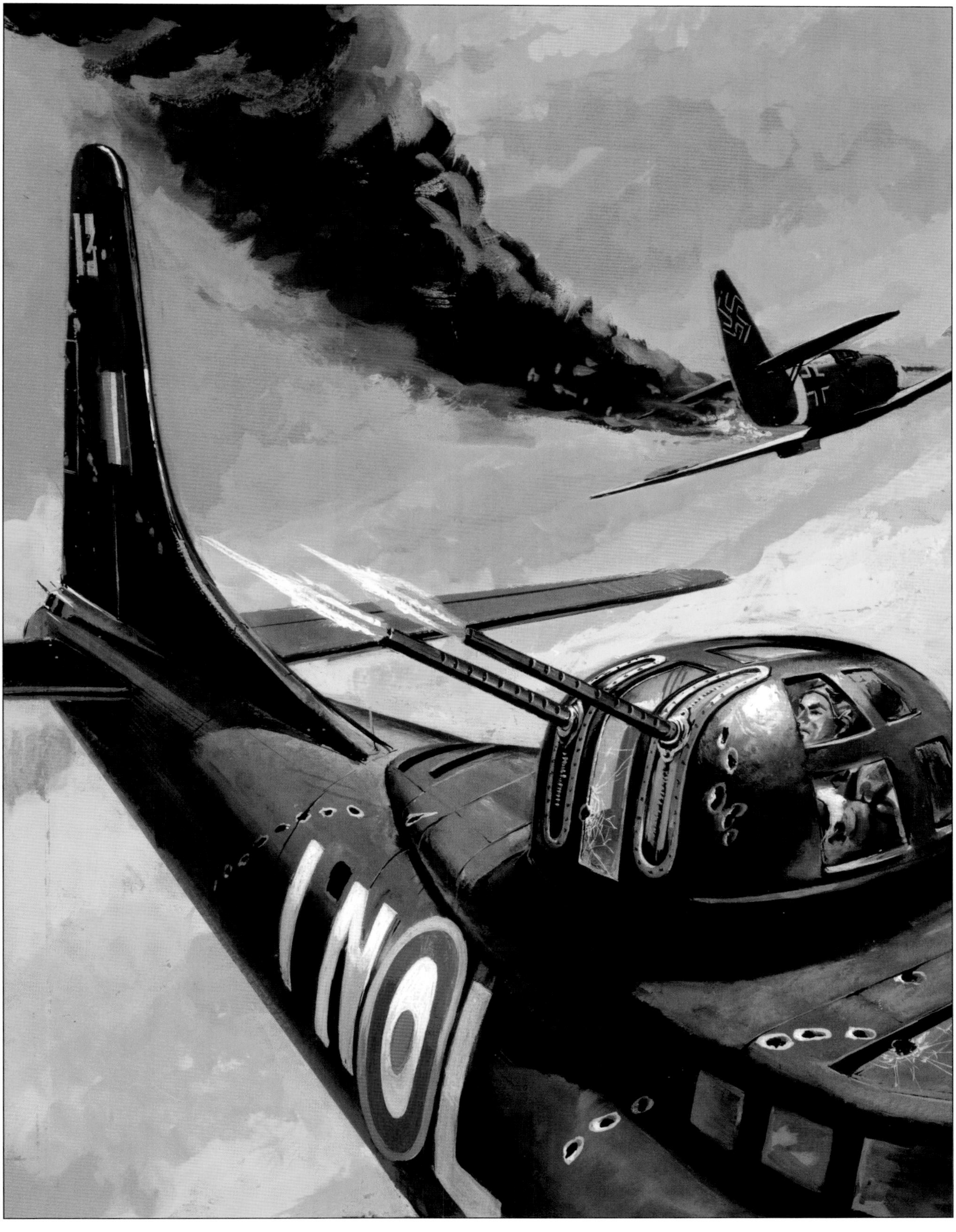

Nino Caroselli, Air Ace 25, October 1960
Opposite: Giorgio DeGaspari, Battle 263, August 1966

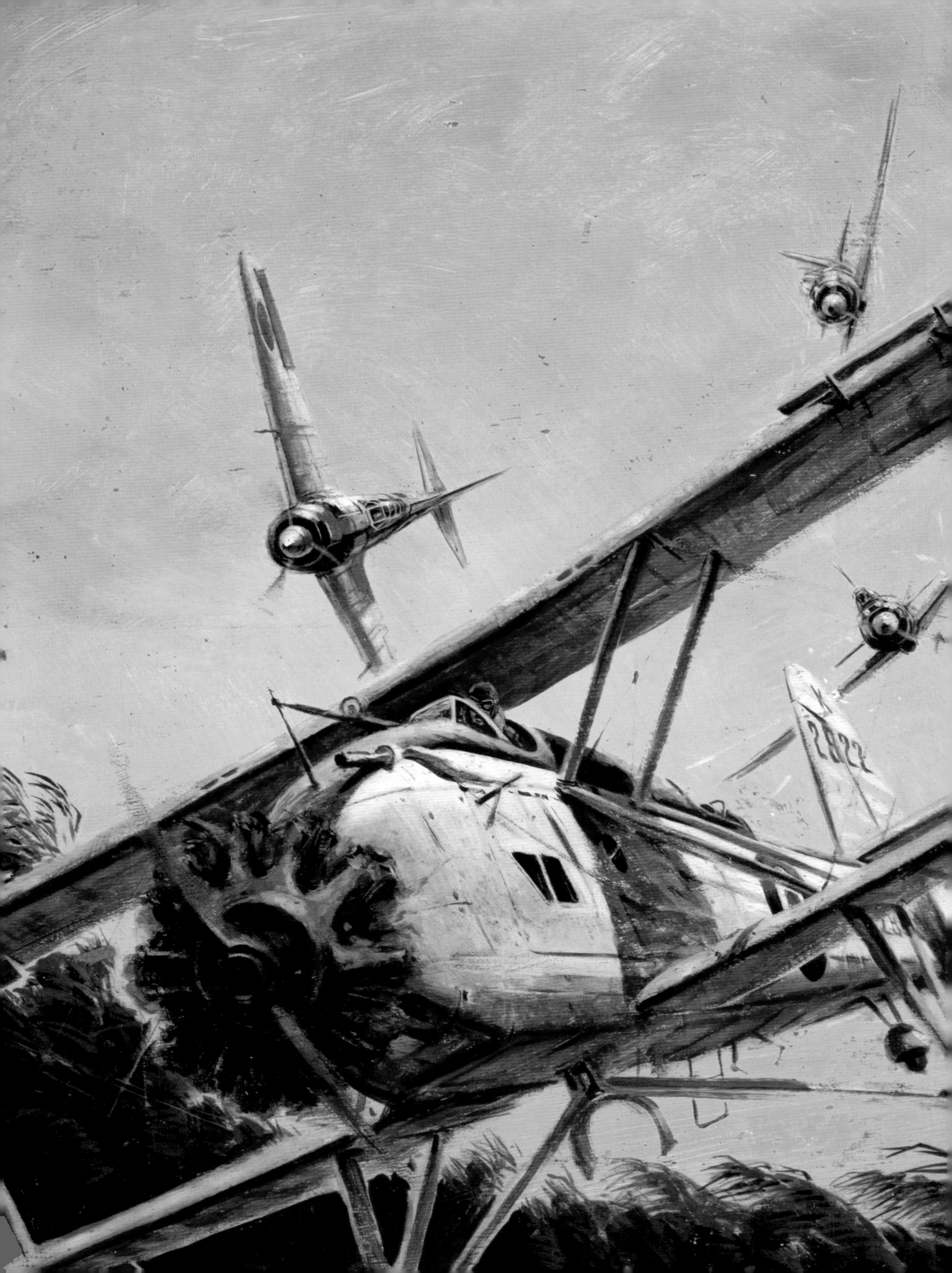
2822

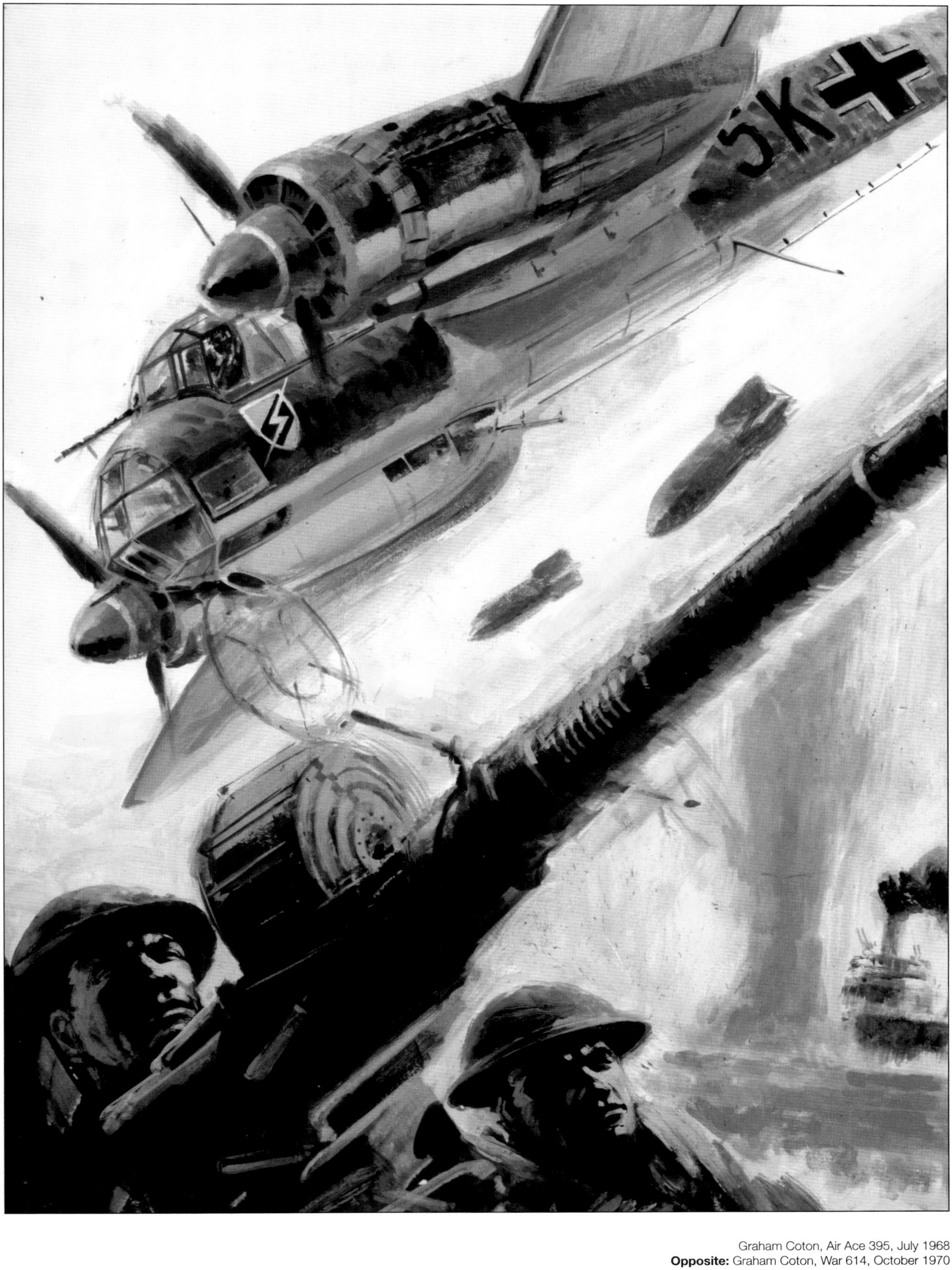
5K

Graham Coton, Air Ace 395, July 1968
Opposite: Graham Coton, War 614, October 1970

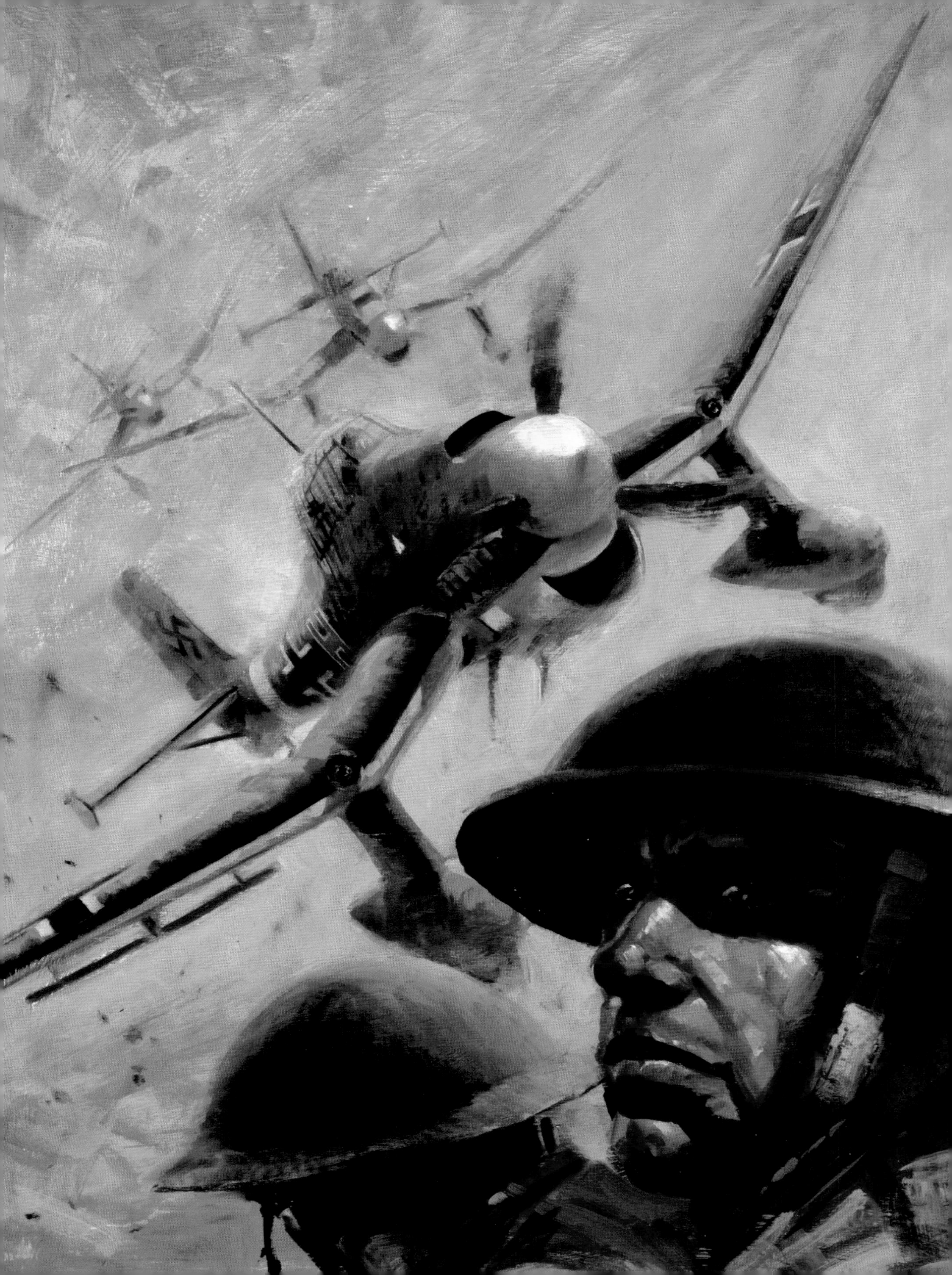

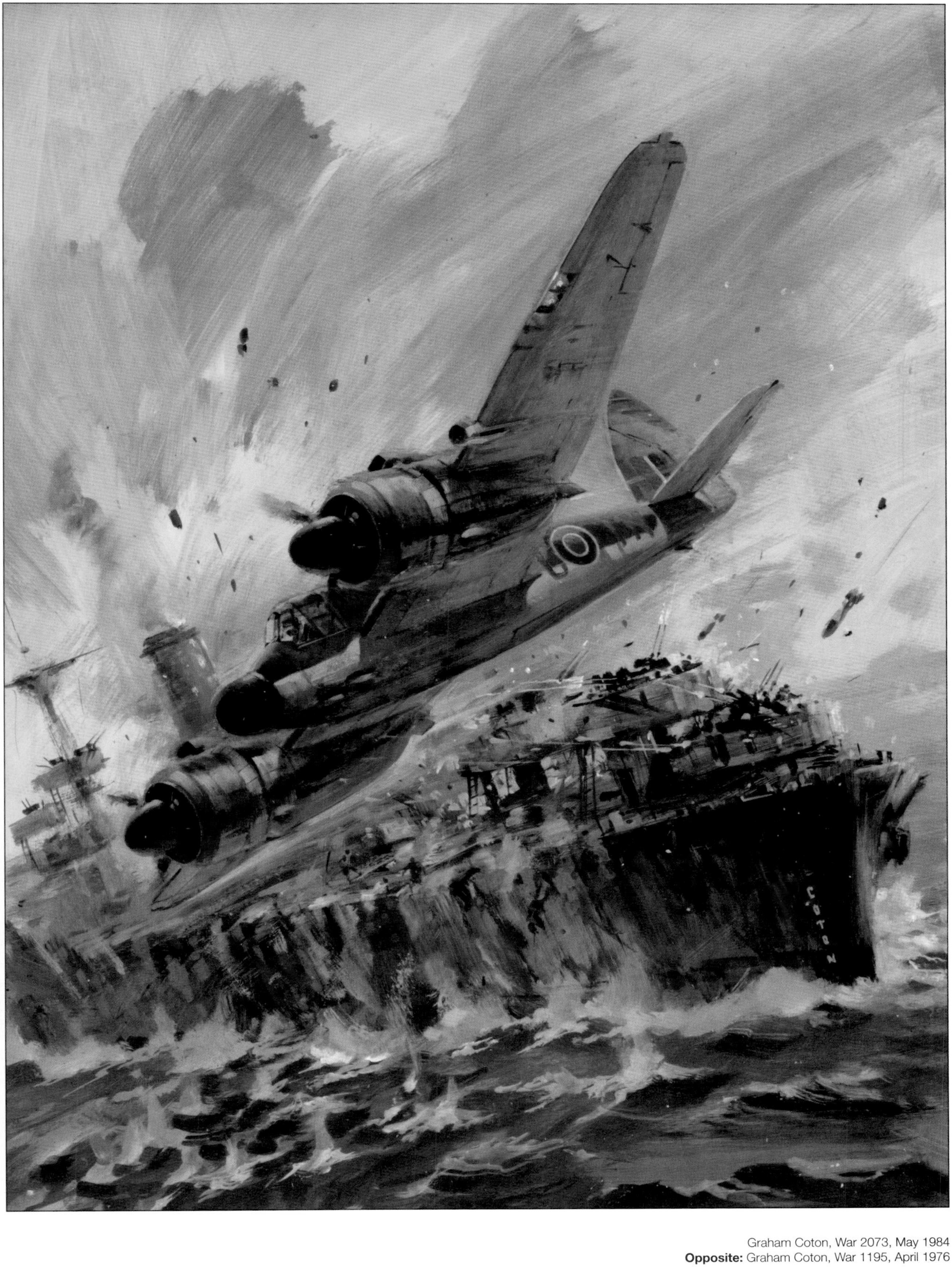
COTON

Graham Coton, War 2073, May 1984
Opposite: Graham Coton, War 1195, April 1976

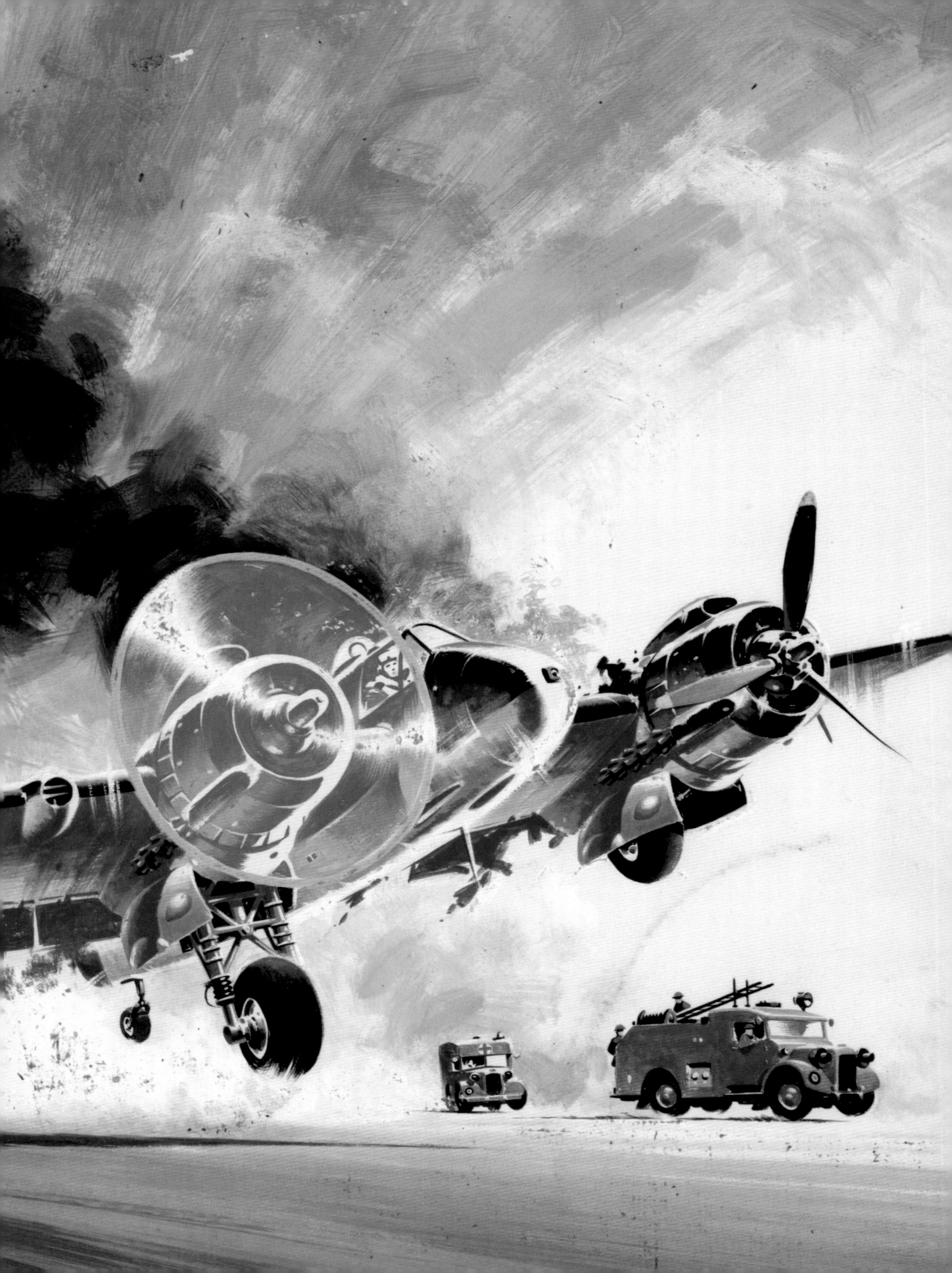

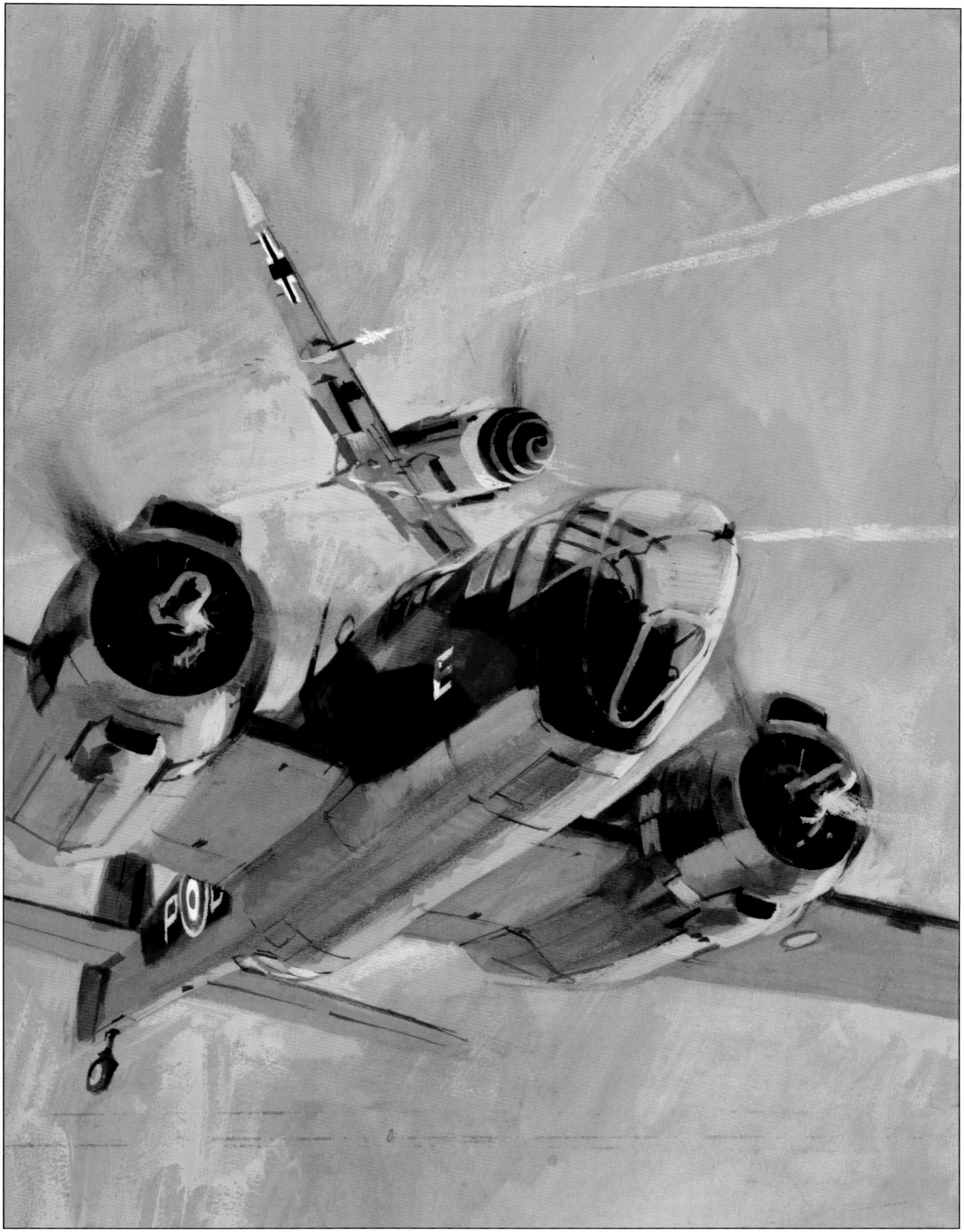

Pino Dell'Orco, Air Ace 174, December 1963
Opposite: Ian Kennedy, Air Ace 464, October 1969

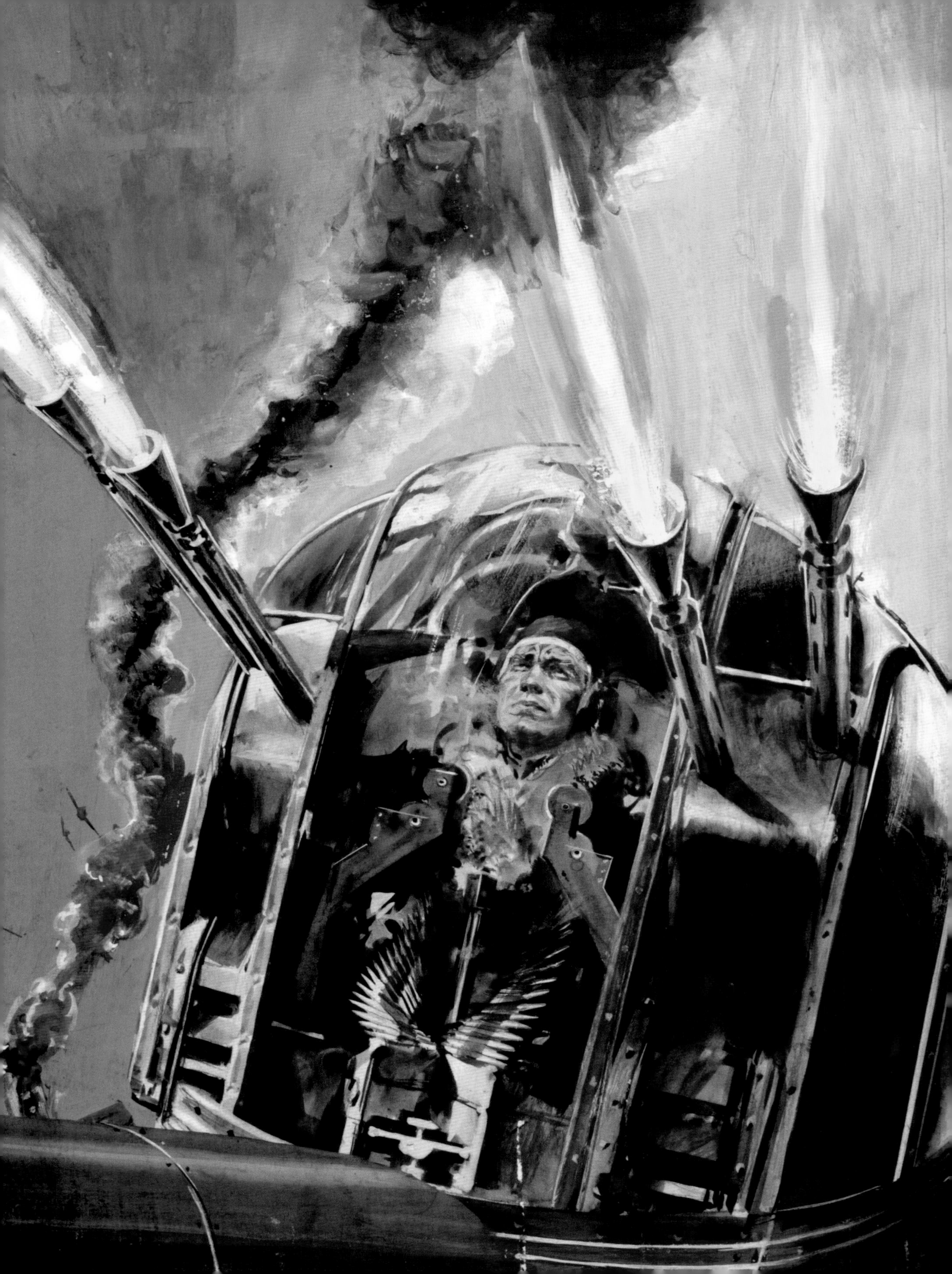

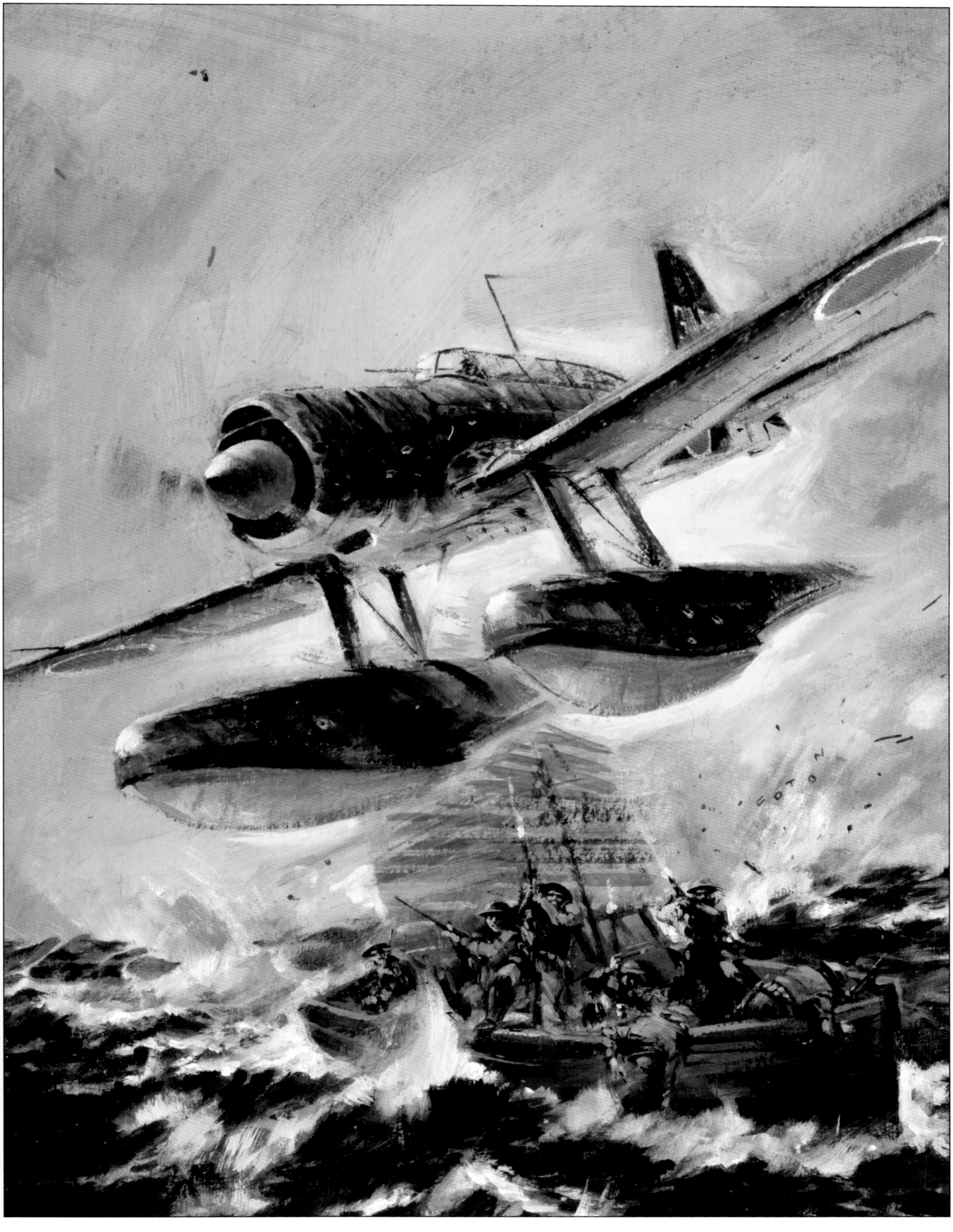

Graham Coton, War 1974, January 1983
Opposite: Giorgio DeGaspari, Air Ace 5, March 1960

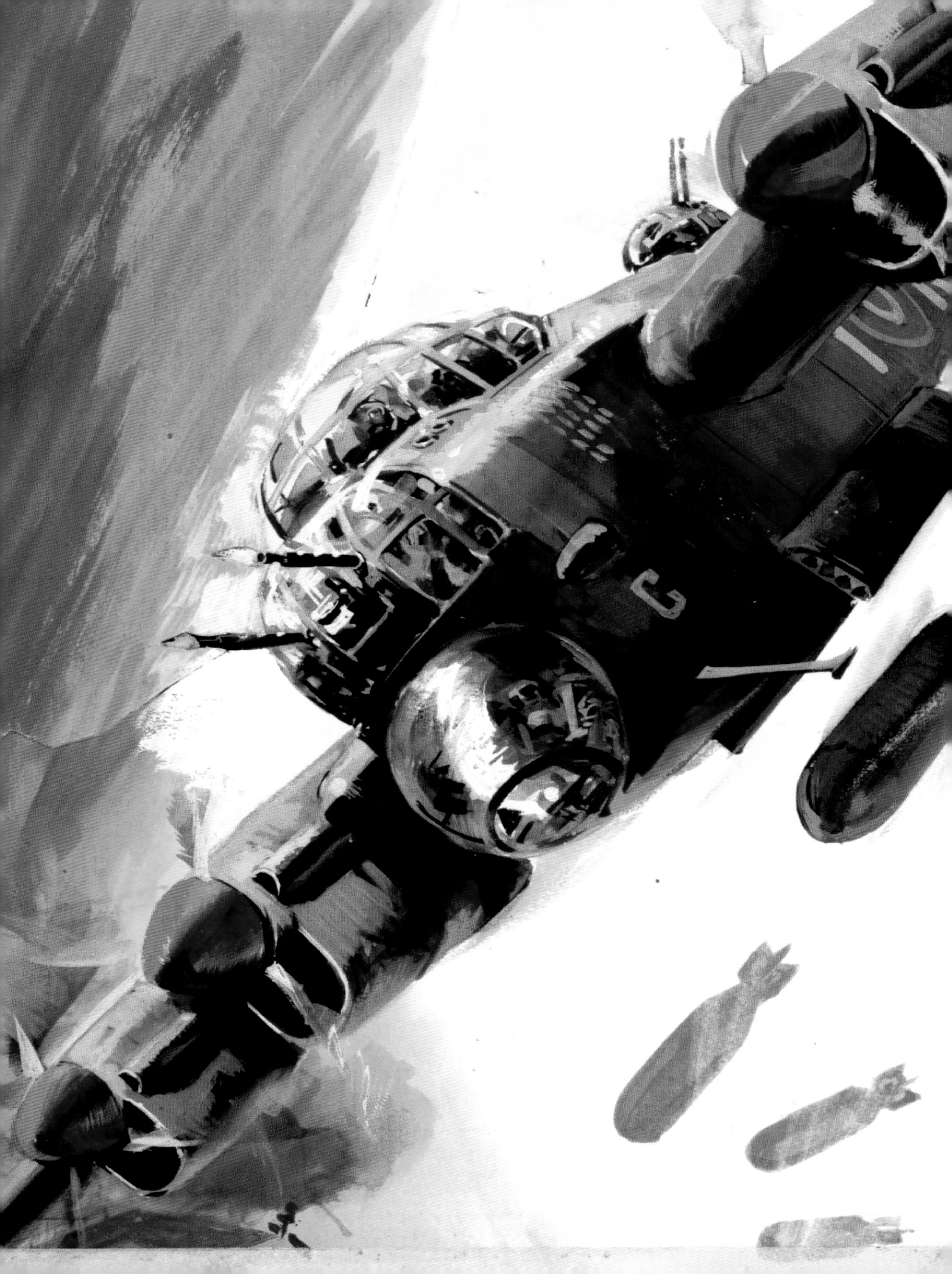

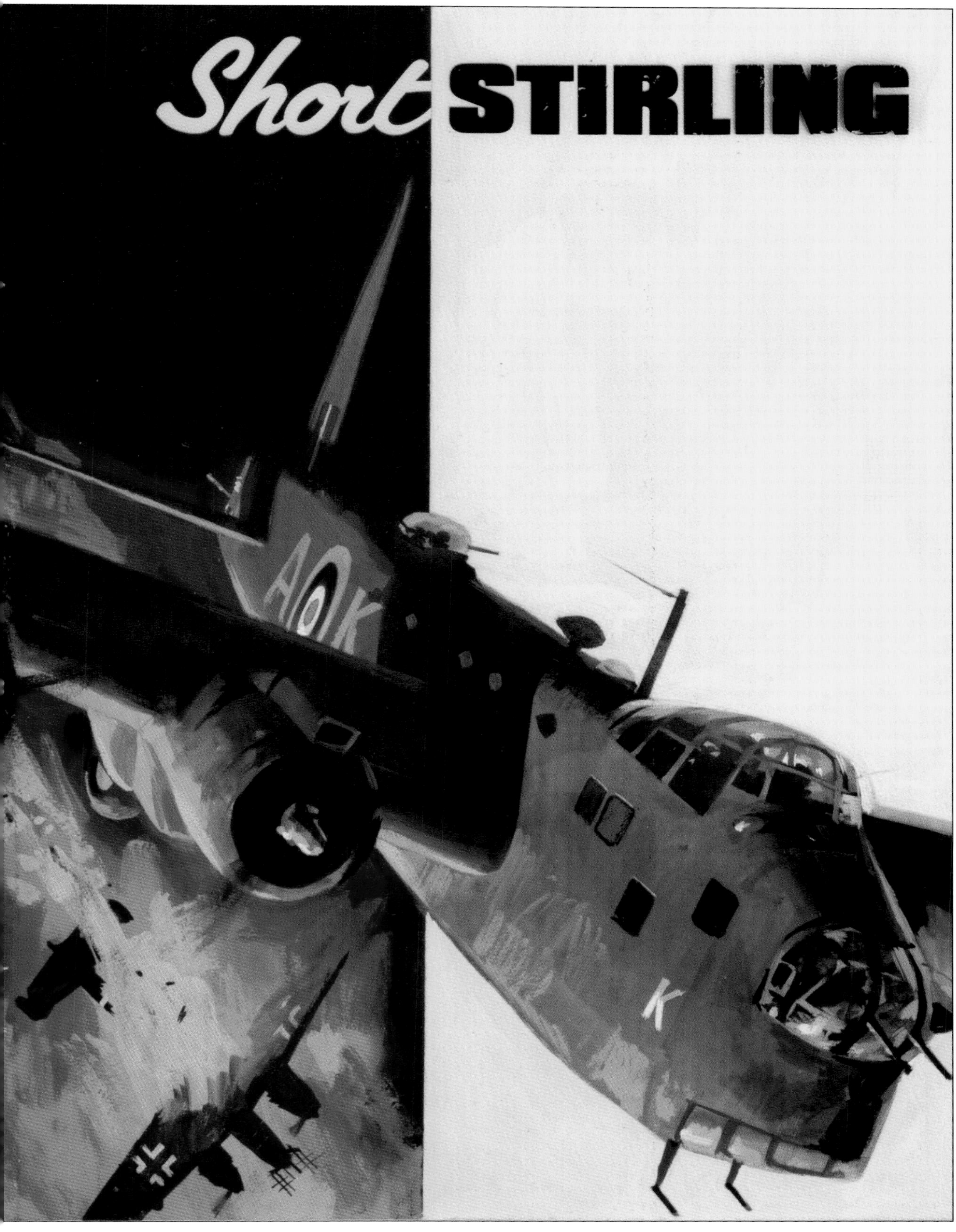
Short STIRLING

Pino Dell'Orco, Air Ace 180, January 1964
Opposite: Allessandro Biffignandi, Air Ace 140, 1963

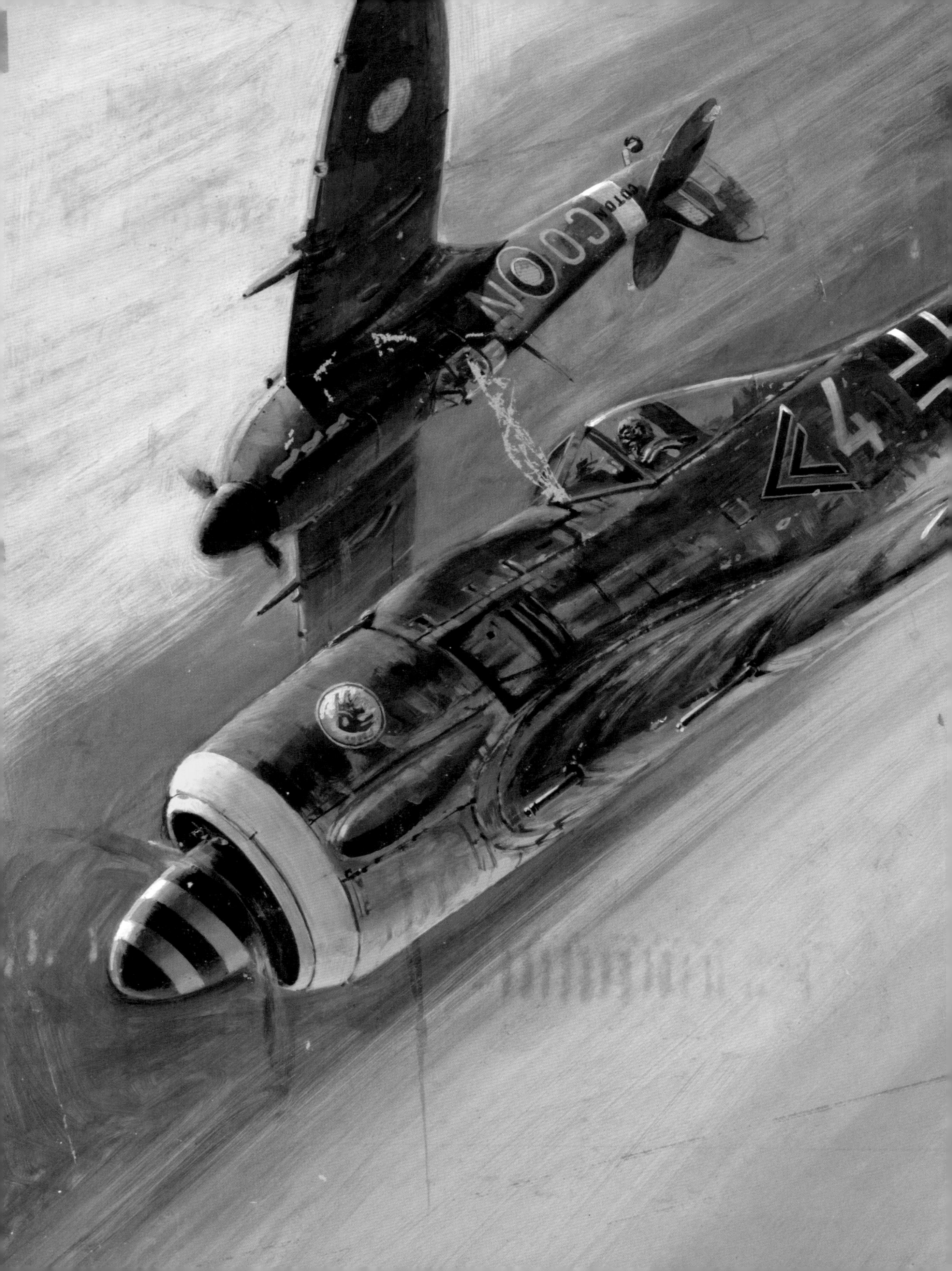

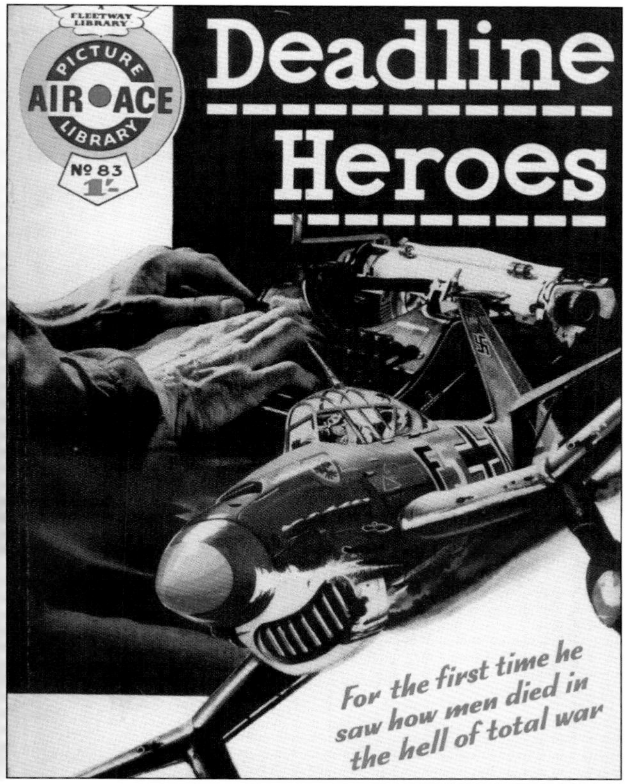
A FLEETWAY LIBRARY
PICTURE AIR ACE LIBRARY
Nº 83
1/-
Deadline Heroes
For the first time he saw how men died in the hell of total war

Nino Caroselli, Air Ace 83, January 1962

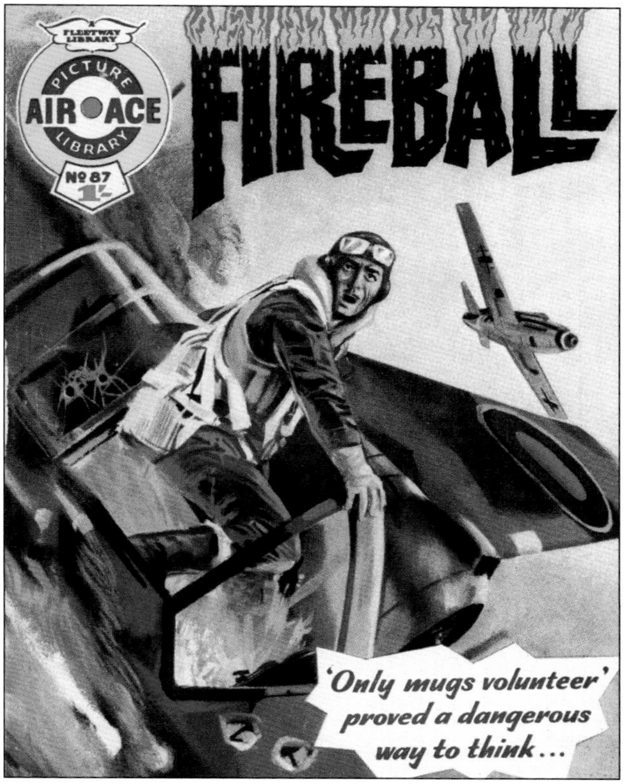
A FLEETWAY LIBRARY
PICTURE AIR ACE LIBRARY
Nº 87
1/-
FIREBALL
'Only mugs volunteer' proved a dangerous way to think...

Nino Caroselli, Air Ace 87, February 1962

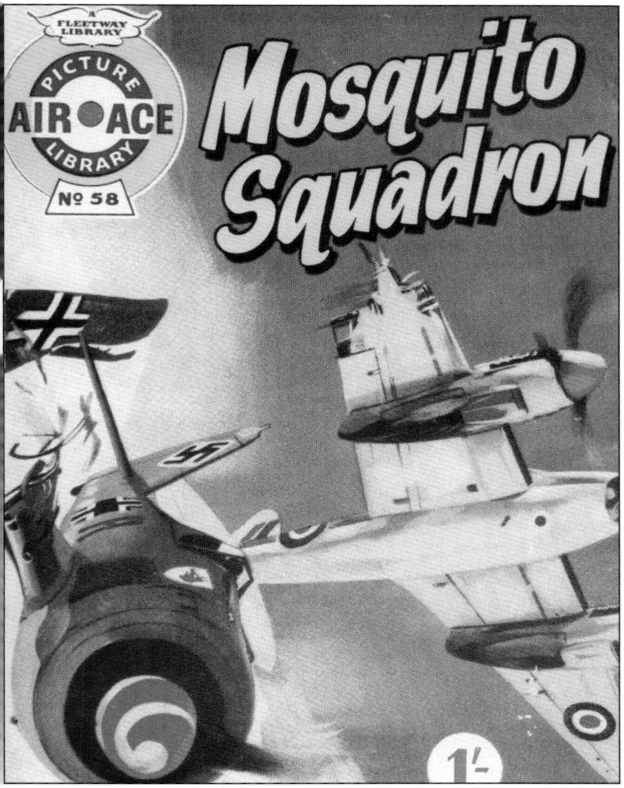
A FLEETWAY LIBRARY
PICTURE AIR ACE LIBRARY
Nº 58
Mosquito Squadron
1/-

Pino Dell'Orco, Air Ace 58, July 1961

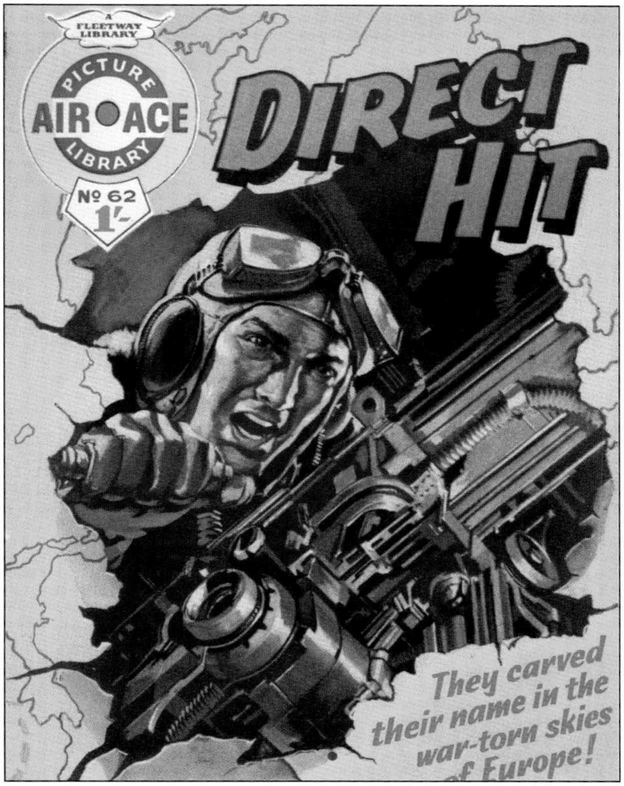
A FLEETWAY LIBRARY
PICTURE AIR ACE LIBRARY
Nº 62
1/-
DIRECT HIT
They carved their name in the war-torn skies of Europe!

Nino Caroselli, Air Ace 62, August 1961

Opposite: Graham Coton, Battle 1675, May 1984

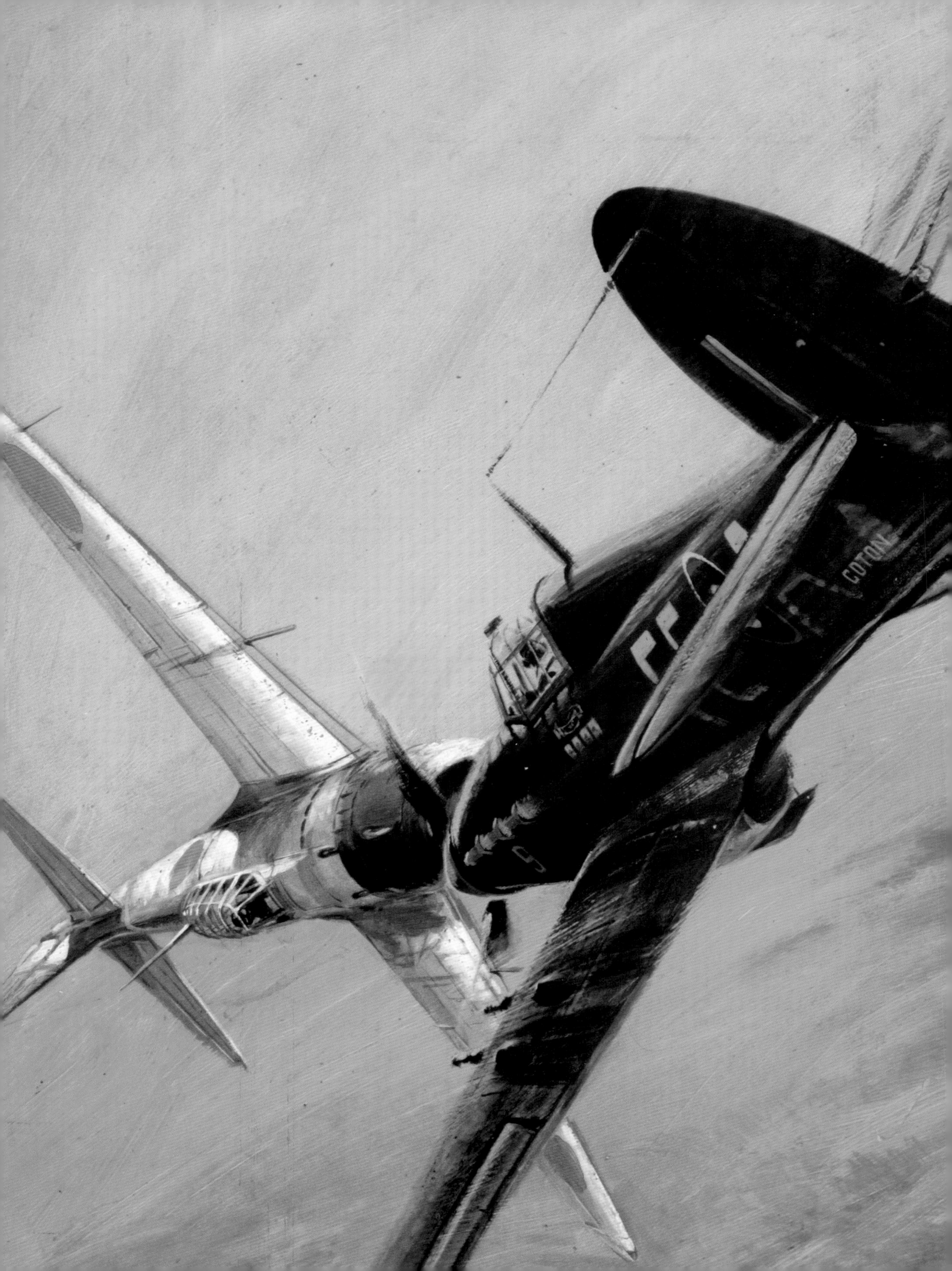
COTON

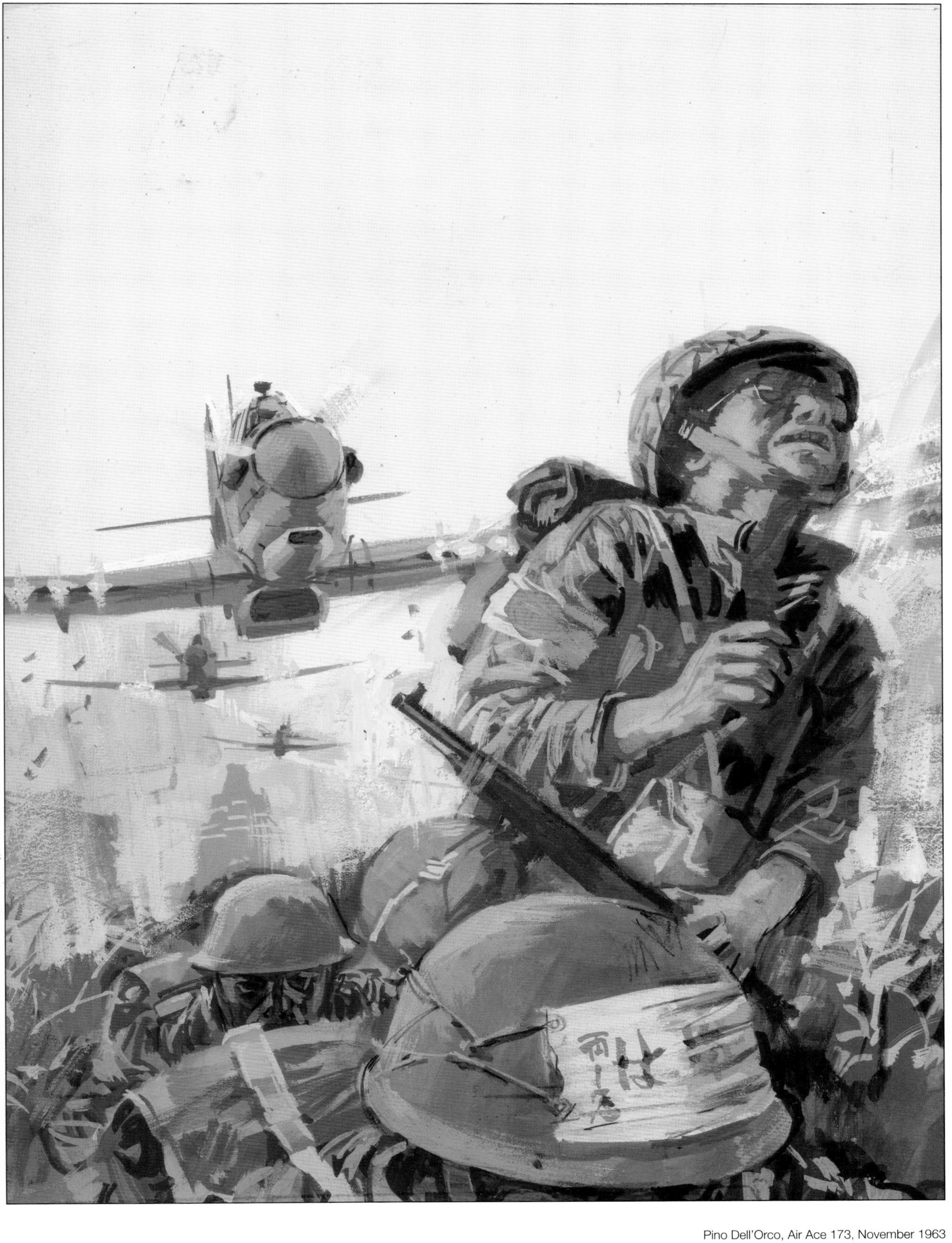

Pino Dell'Orco, Air Ace 173, November 1963
Opposite: Graham Coton, Battle 1431, December 1980

HEAVY ORDNANCE

CHAPTE[R] 4

From their very earliest issues the picture libraries celebrated the various machines and weapons of war. *War* featured all manner of aeroplanes, tanks, boats, armoured cars, V1 flying bombs, submarines, trucks, trains and blazing artillery before the success of the earliest spin-off title, *Air Ace*, seemed to suggest that their readership would embrace each of the various arenas of warfare. This theory that was soon disproved when the 1962 title *War At Sea* was less enthusiastically received. It might well have been that these naval stories were simply too harsh and unromantic to enthuse their young readership. There was a dangerous glamour to flying through the sky, protected by only the flimsiest of shells, while sailing in a vast, rusting old hulk, constantly on the look out for for invisible hunters beneath the waves was simply grim. That said, in the right hands there was always the possibility of transforming that humdrum reality into something altogether more exciting. Allessandro Biffignandi's stirring cover to *War* 282 (on page 284) doesn't stint on the doomed atmosphere of a ship under attack but still manages to come up with a dramatic image of sailors fighting to their last breath. His ship is little more than a collection of vast grey masses drawn at strange angles to each other which seem to suggest a ship breaking up even as its crew scurry down a rope ladder, silhouetted against a raging fire. In the foreground the indomitable sailors fight on to the last, a gunner blazing away at the unseen enemy while the captain barks his final orders through a megaphone to his doomed crew.

By contrast, Giorgio DeGaspari's cover to *Battle* 244 (page 273) adopts a more panoramic view of war on the waves as he shows the titanic battle between a German submarine and a monolithic tanker. Though using only a very limited palette of greys and blues, De Gaspari's sheer draughtsmanship and artistic skills create a scene of astonishing scale and realism. This is a multi-million dollar production for the price of a few pennies. Here DeGaspari orchestrates a mini epic with each figure given a distinct role, from the tiny allied sailors firing at the U-boat to the lone submariner hiding behind the coning tower. His great versatility as an artist is shown through the contrasts between the cold, grey, steel hulls of ship and sub, the choppy sea and the ominous smoke billowing from the stricken tanker. Even amongst an output as consistently excellent as DeGaspari's this cover is something special.

The king of vehicles, machines and weaponry, however, was undeniably Graham Coton, who was also by far the most prolific cover artist for *War* and *Battle*. Coton's earliest covers had been painted for *Air Ace* (the first appearing on issue 11) and altogether he created 104 illustrations for the comic. He would go on to paint many hundreds more for the remaining picture libraries right through to their cancellations in 1984. By all acounts Coton was something of an

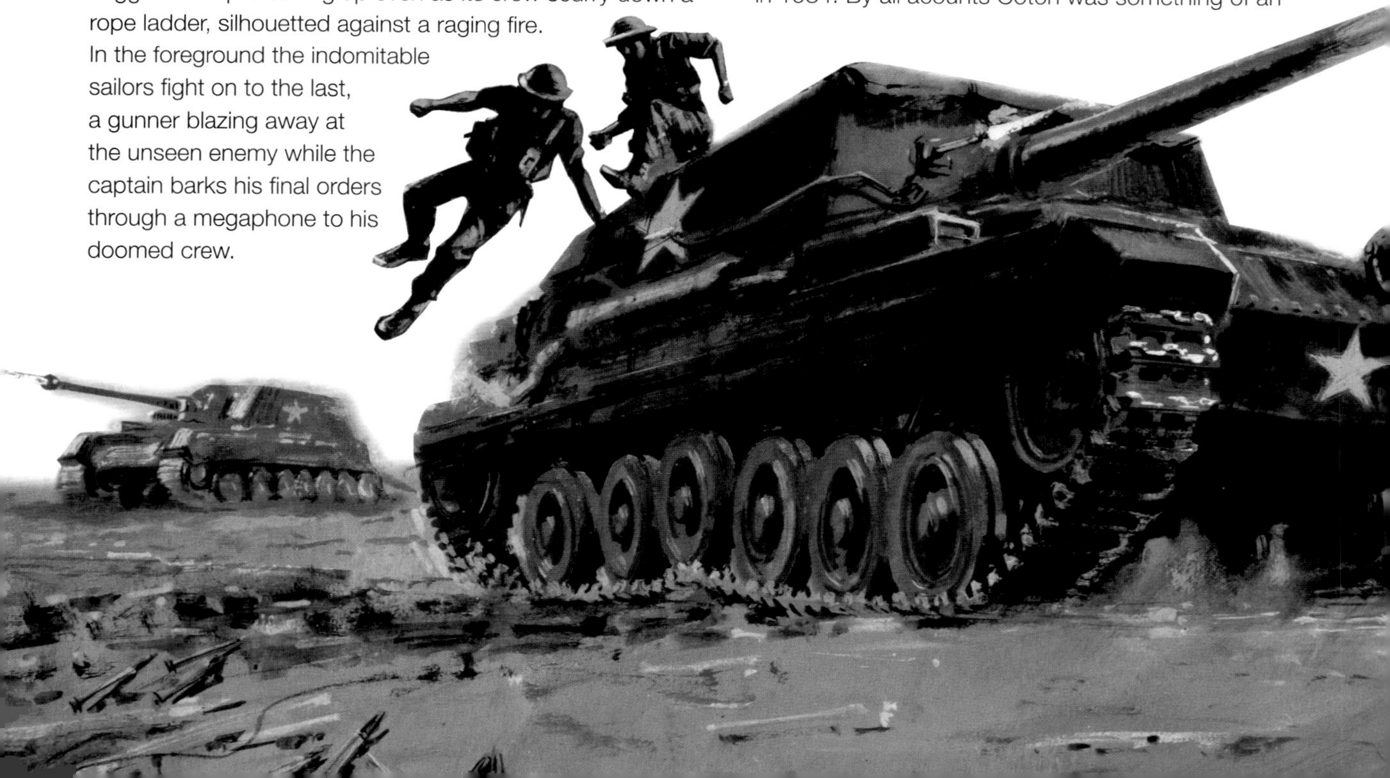

artistic prodigy, although a promising tenure at art school was cut short in 1944 when he volunteered for the RAF (definitely a portend of things to come). On de-mob, he abandoned education, spurred on by the necessity to earn a living, starting to work for the Amalgamated Press on the newly launched *Cowboy Comics*.Throughout the fifties and sixties he honed his skills as a comic strip artist on titles such as *Knockout*, *Tiger*, *Top Spot* and *Look and Learn*, gradually establishing an elaborately detailed pen and ink style .

His earliest war covers were seemingly crafted through delicate washes of watercolour paints but by the end of the sixties he had undergone a dramatic transformation and embraced oils with startling enthusiasm. The Coton that emerged here was unrecognisable from his intricately cross-hatched comic strips, choosing instead vast textured swathes of muted grey, green and brown oil paints apparently applied with a palette knife. Anyone seeing his originals for the first time is immediately struck by their sheer scale as he frequently chose to work on enormous slabs of masonite board measuring several feet wide. The covers of this mature period have nothing to do with precision and restraint, they are all about expression ,vigour, mood and texture. Not for Coton the handsome leading men of Penalva, instead his soldiers are often brutish and savage-looking, seemingly hewn out of rock or mud. Above all else, Coton was supremely an artist of machinery, of diving Messerschmitts and lumbering Blenheims, of Tigers, Panzers, U-boats and Jeeps. Oliver Frey can remember their editor, Ted Bensberg, complaining that Cotons' colours were perhaps a bit "muddy" but that he could live with it because his art was just so powerful. In a way that monotone palette was part of his appeal, his monumental, mechanical behemoths appearing to have been drained of their colour, reflecting the life-sapping warfare for which they were created. His aircraft carrier on the cover of *Battle* 615 (on page 325) has the shape, tone and texture of granite slicing through a sea of viscous tar. An aerial dogfight such as *War* 634 (page 225) shows how he constructed an image using tones of grey, spotted with a few derisive daubs of blue and red. This was a far cry from the jaunty heroism of "Battler Britton" and it is easy to caricature Coton as a one-note miserablist, but that would doing him a great disservice. Yes, war is hell and he lets you know it, but there is also a sense on wonder in his art, a celebration of these extraordinary instruments of destruction.

Look underneath the trowelled on paint, the edifices

of battleship grey and Somme-trench sienna, and there is revealed the sure hand of a born draughtsman. Uniquely amongst the cover artists, Coton manages to marry the gestural immediacy of his oils with the obsessive detail of the enthusiast. His Me 262 on the cover to the 1973 *Air Ace Holiday Special* (page 211) is both remarkably accurate in its drawing, while also thrillingly alive with movement and menace. He could also have a little fun from time to time. Who else could carry off such bizarre juxtapositions as a duel between a U-boat and a steam boat (*Battle* 1655 on page 264) and a game of "chicken" between a Nazi half-track and a thundering locomotive (*War* 673 on page 306)? For fans growing up in the seventies and eighties, Coton was very much the face of *War* and *Battle* and his covers came to personify the genre. But his very ubiquity has tended to obscure his quite considerable ability and it is significant that after the comics died he carried on painting as prolifically as before, both commercially (thriving with both advertising and book covers), and for his own enjoyment. He was very much a true artist and we, as readers, did not perhaps realise quite what we had until it was gone.

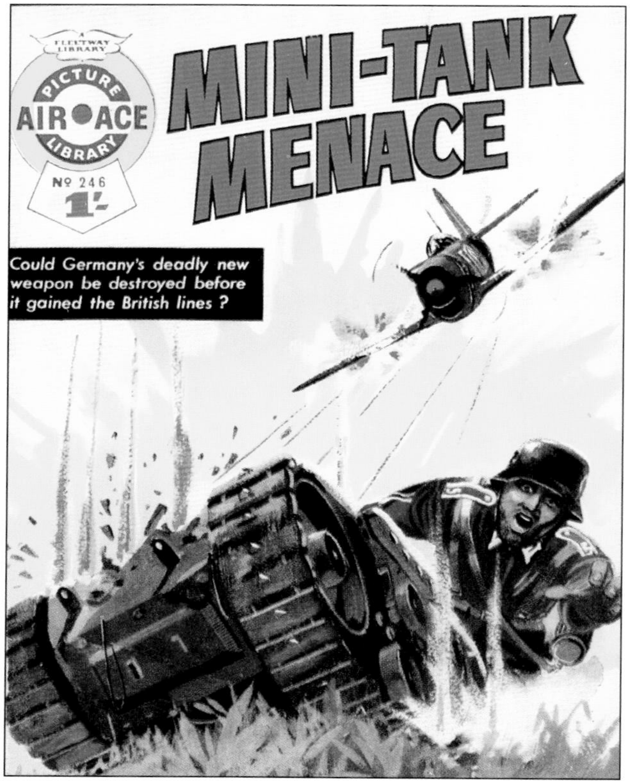
A FLEETWAY LIBRARY
PICTURE
AIR ACE
LIBRARY
Nº 246
1/-
MINI-TANK MENACE
Could Germany's deadly new weapon be destroyed before it gained the British lines ?

Alan Willow, Air Ace 246, June 1965

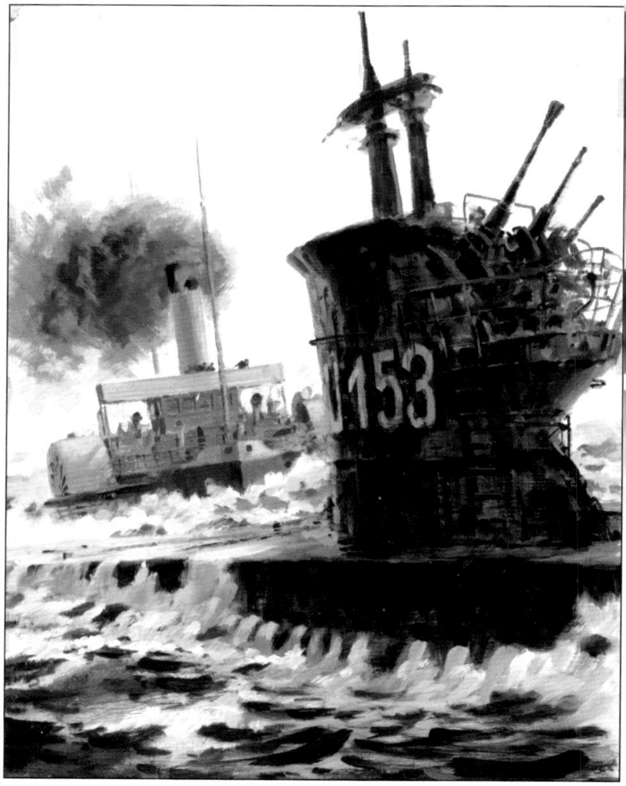
153

Graham Coton, Battle 1655, February 1984

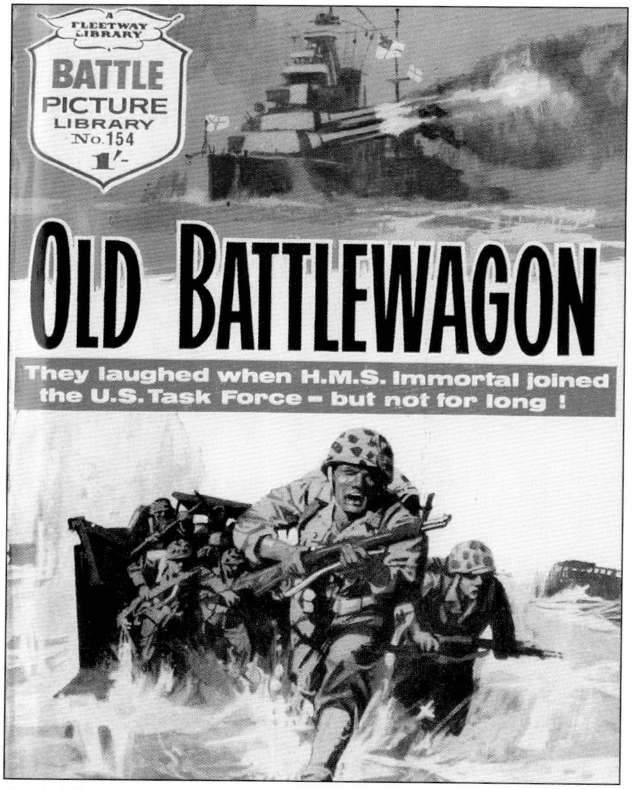
A FLEETWAY LIBRARY
BATTLE
PICTURE
LIBRARY
No. 154
1/-
OLD BATTLEWAGON
They laughed when H.M.S. Immortal joined the U.S. Task Force – but not for long !

Pino Dell'Orco, Battle 154, May 1964

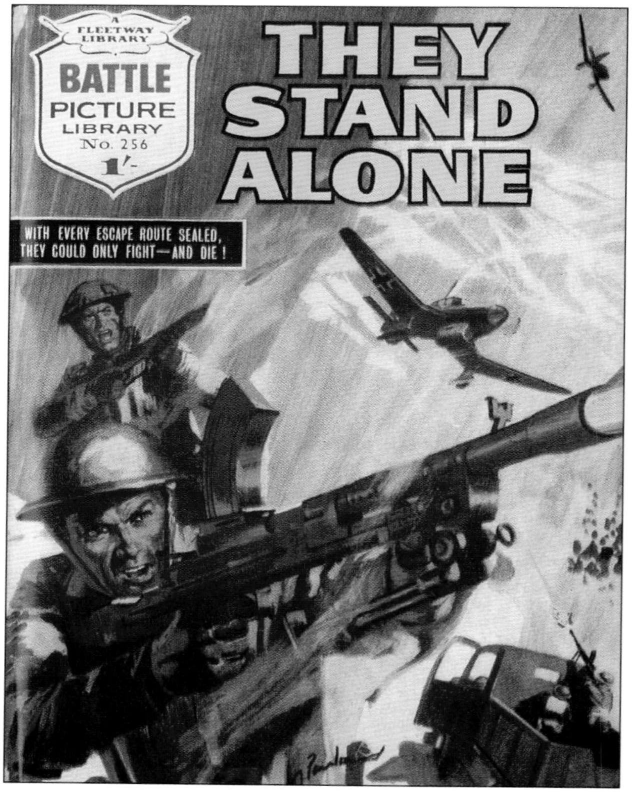
A FLEETWAY LIBRARY
BATTLE
PICTURE
LIBRARY
No. 256
1/-
THEY STAND ALONE
WITH EVERY ESCAPE ROUTE SEALED, THEY COULD ONLY FIGHT—AND DIE !

Jordi Penalva, Battle 256, June 1966

Opposite: Allessandro Biffignandi, Battle 222, October 1965

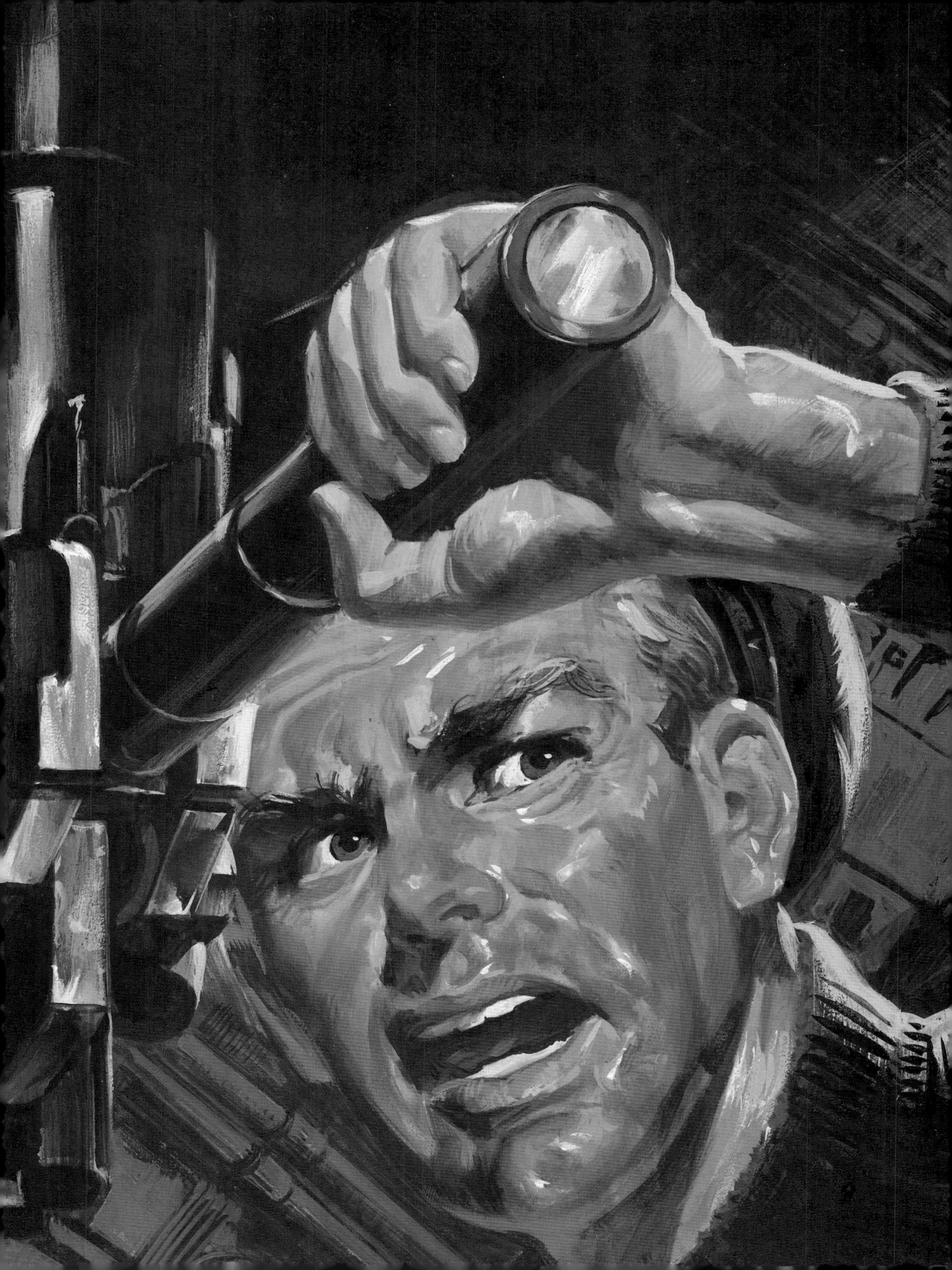

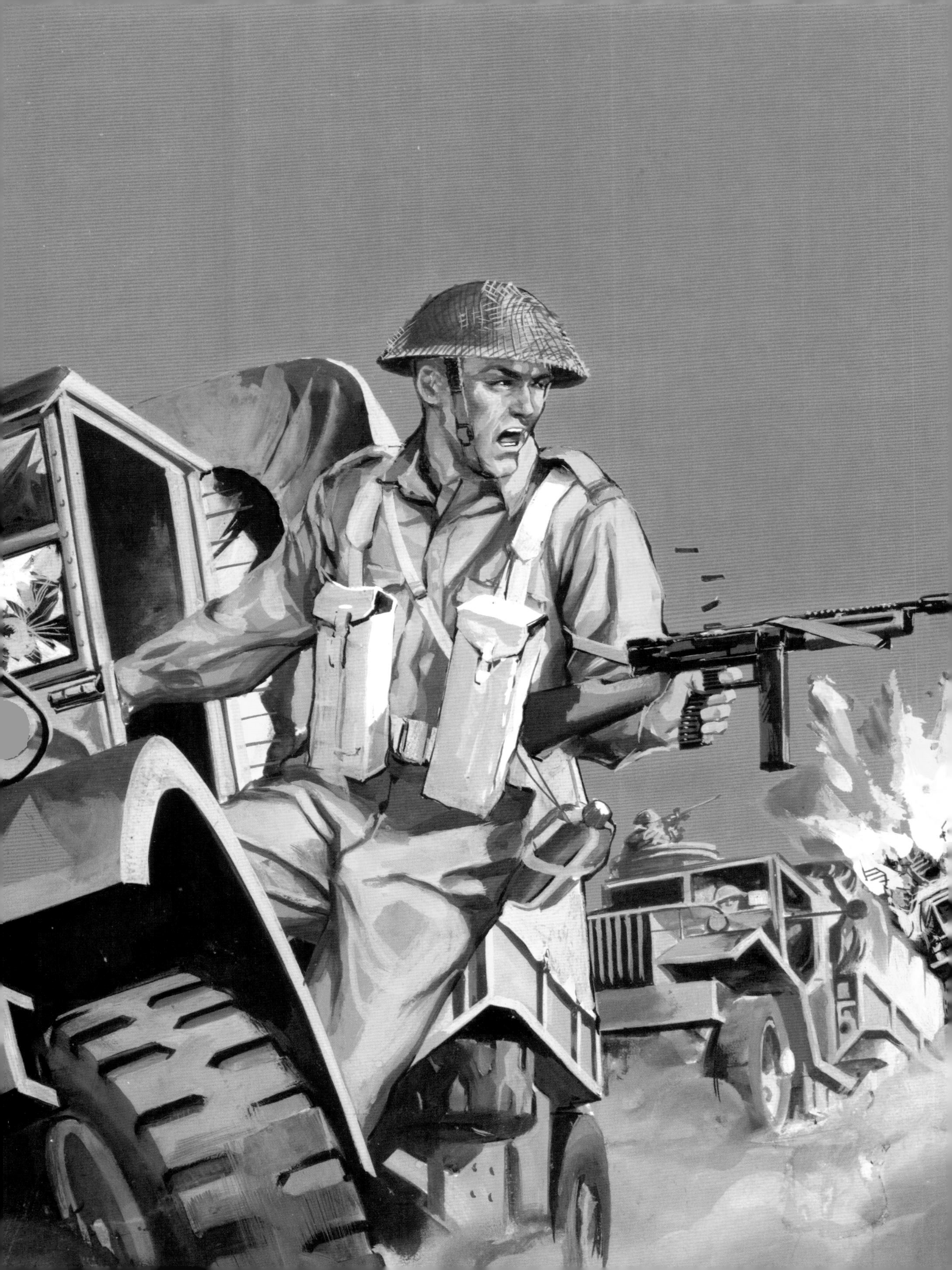

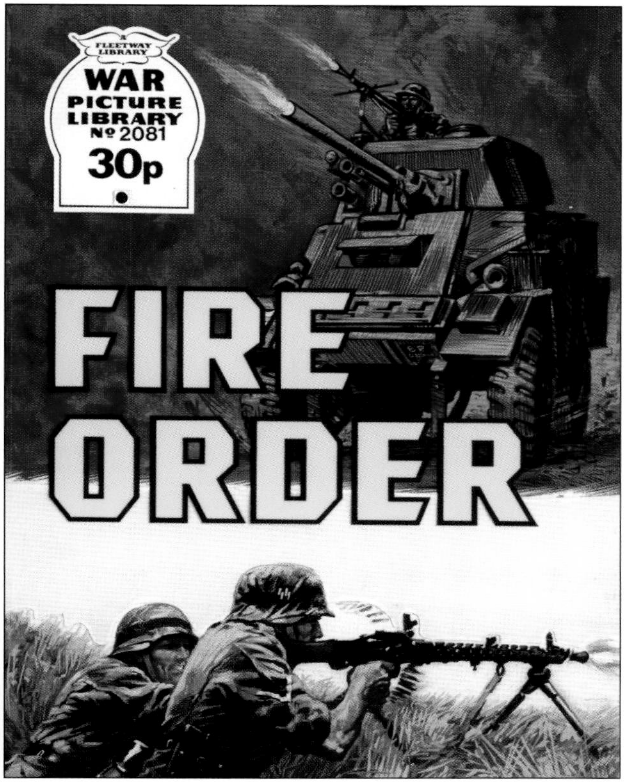
A FLEETWAY LIBRARY
WAR
PICTURE
LIBRARY
Nº 2081
30p
FIRE
ORDER

Giolitti studio, Battle 171, September 1964

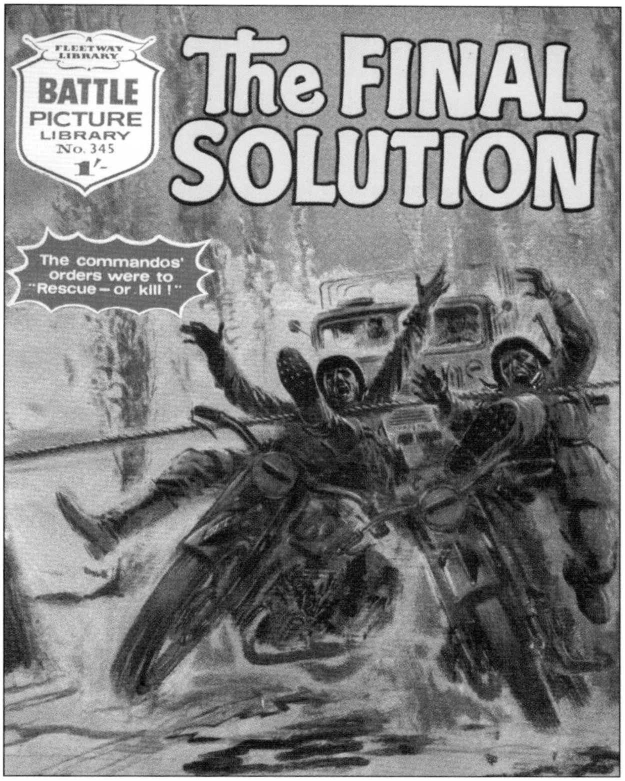
A FLEETWAY LIBRARY
BATTLE
PICTURE
LIBRARY
No. 345
1/-
The FINAL
SOLUTION
The commandos' orders were to "Rescue – or kill !"

Graham Coton, Battle 345, May 1968

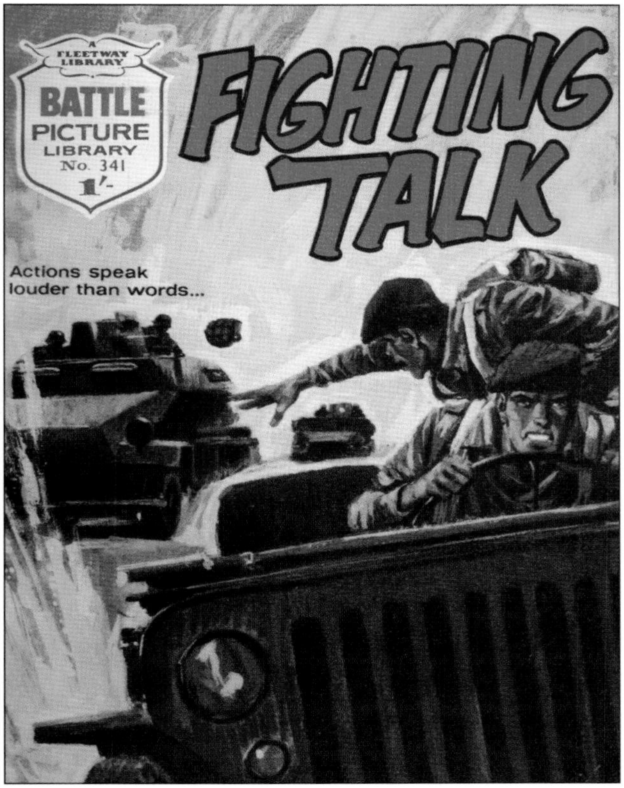
A FLEETWAY LIBRARY
BATTLE
PICTURE
LIBRARY
No. 341
1/-
FIGHTING
TALK
Actions speak louder than words...

Jose Luis Macias, Battle 341, April 1968

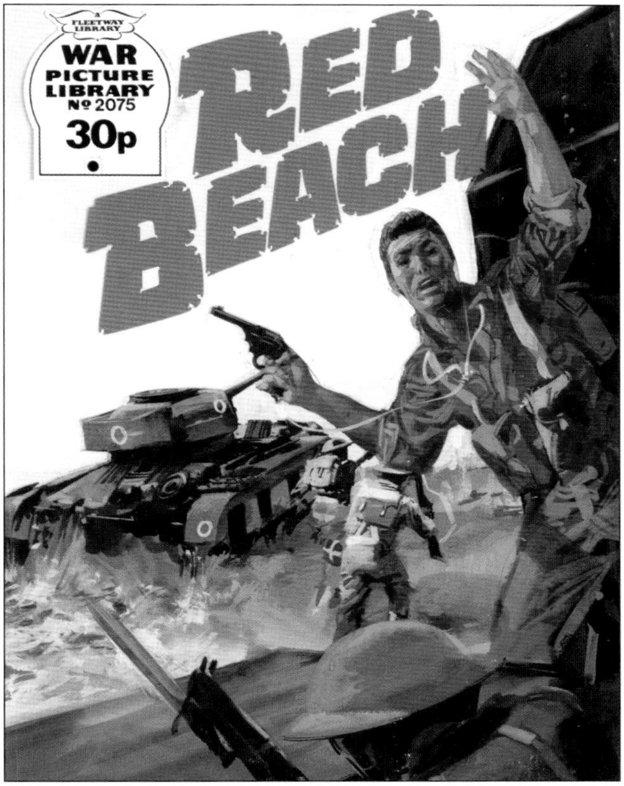
A FLEETWAY LIBRARY
WAR
PICTURE
LIBRARY
Nº 2075
30p
RED
BEACH

Pino Dell'Orco, Battle 54, April 1962

Opposite: Nino Caroselli, War 67, October 1960
Overleaf: Graham Coton, War 1421, October 1977

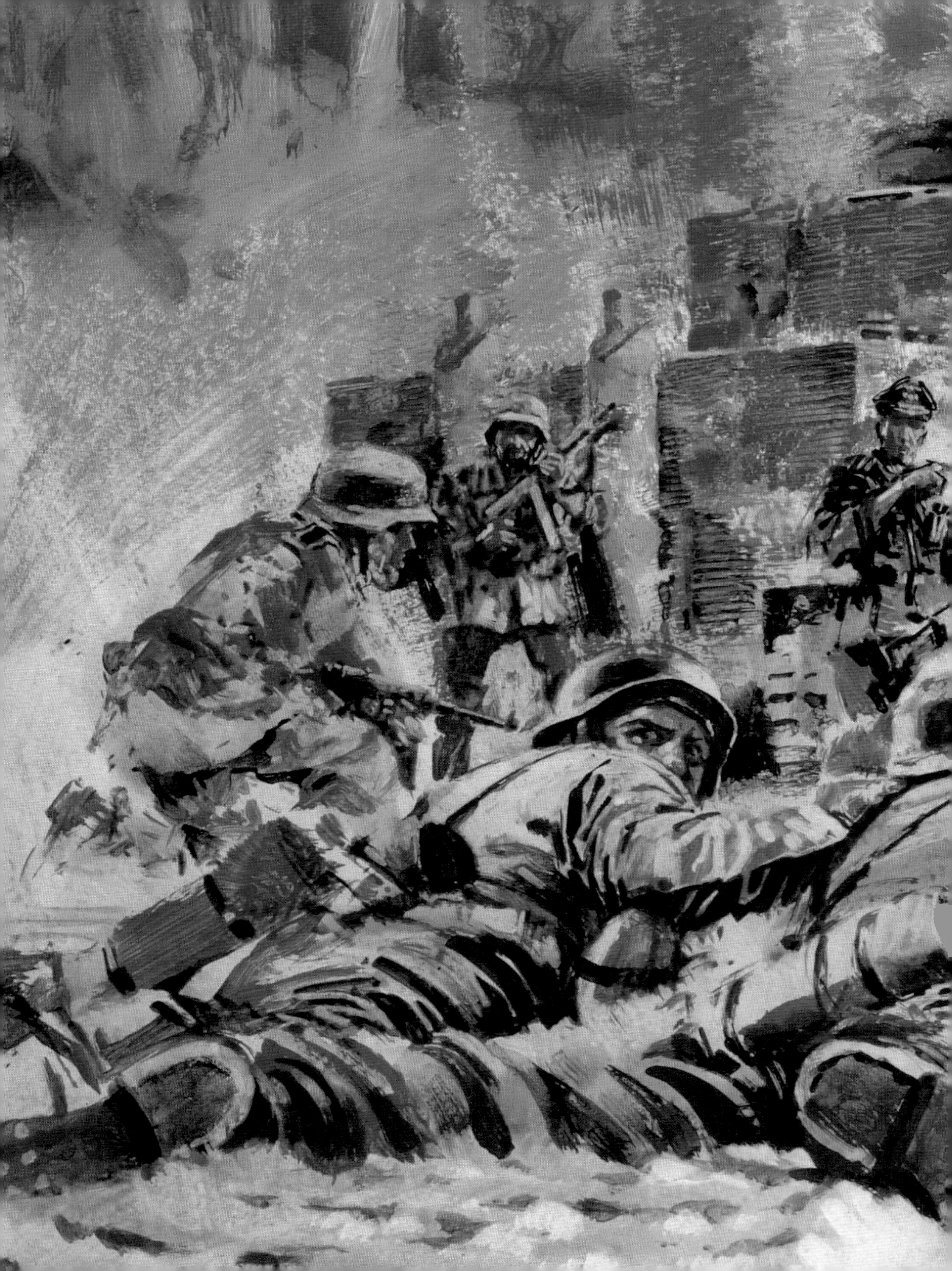

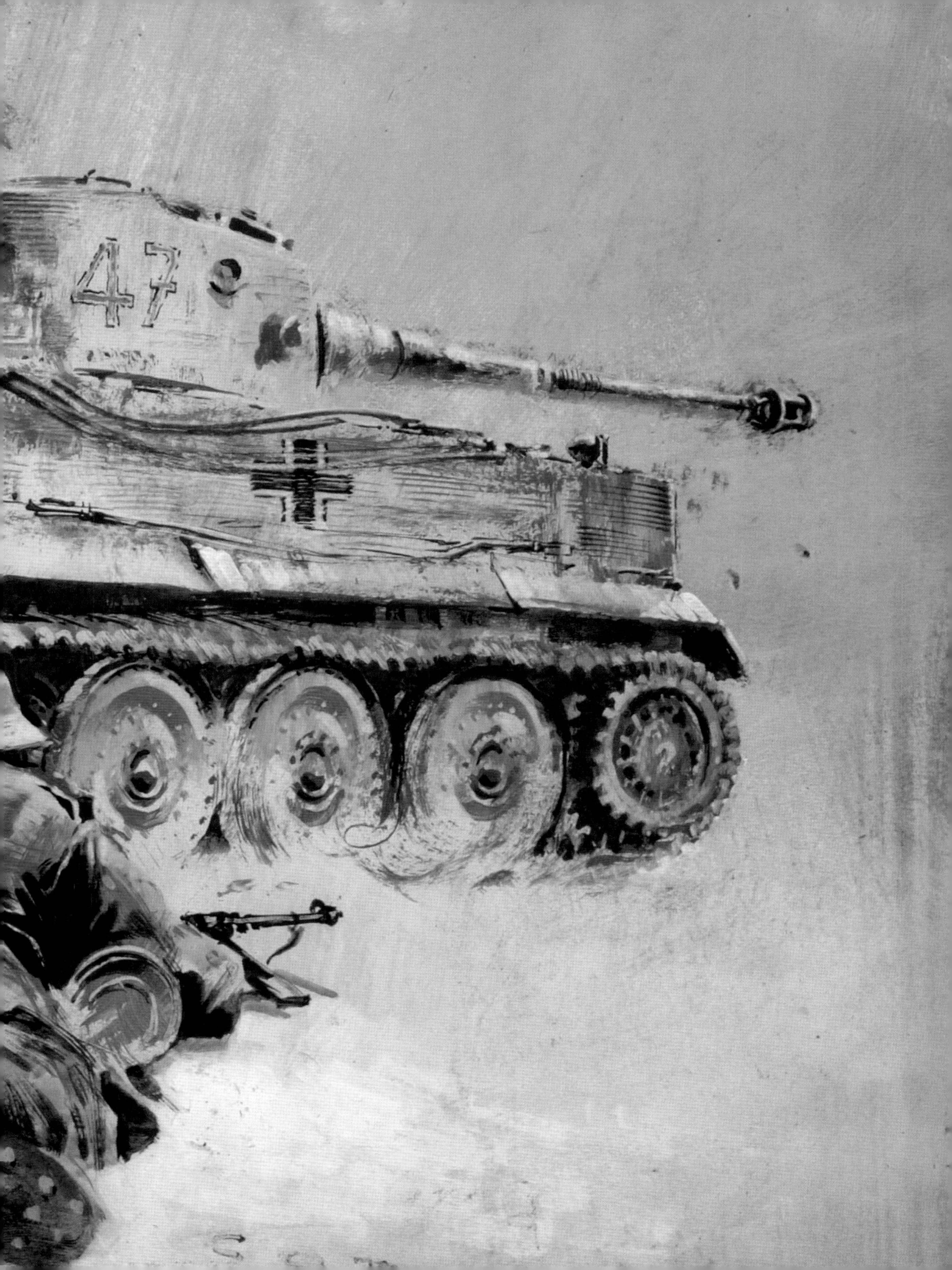

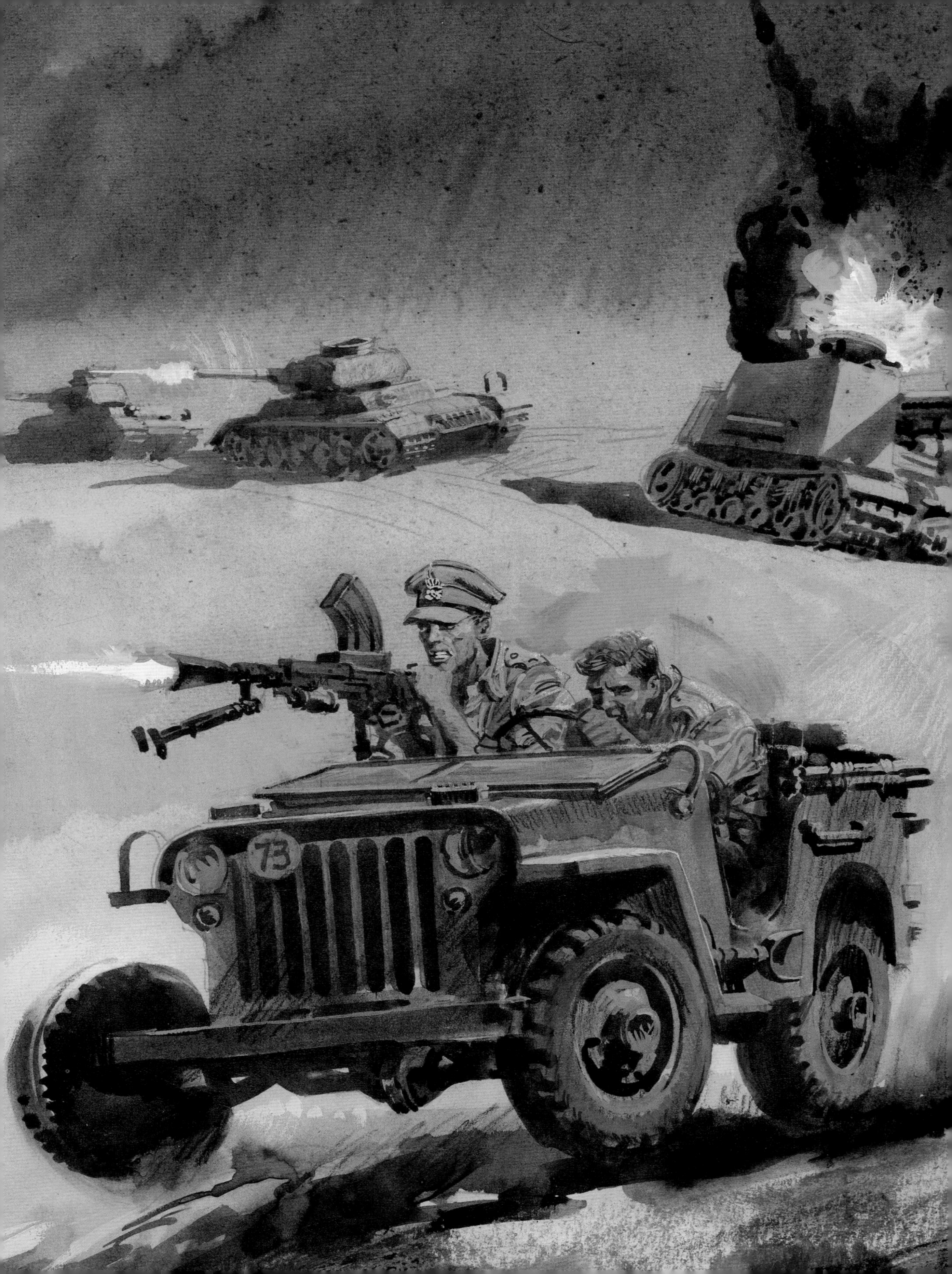
73

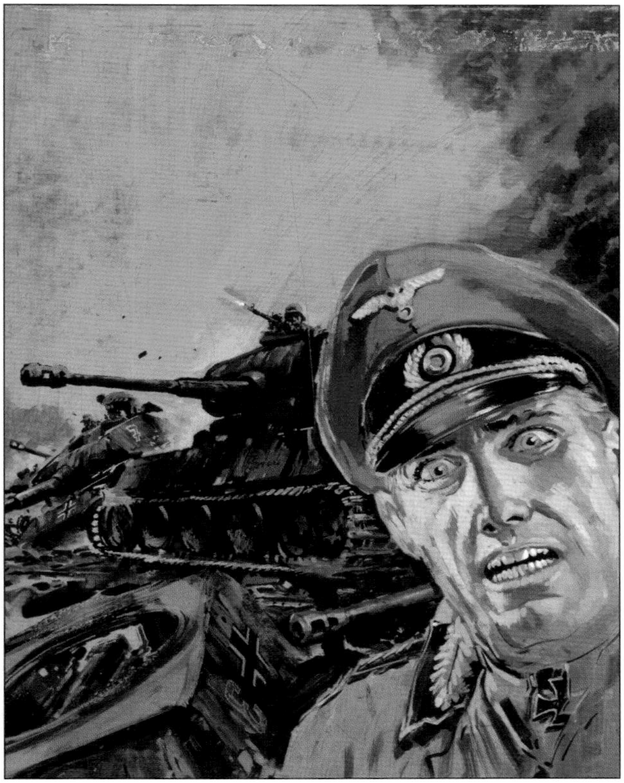

Graham Coton, War 729, February 1972

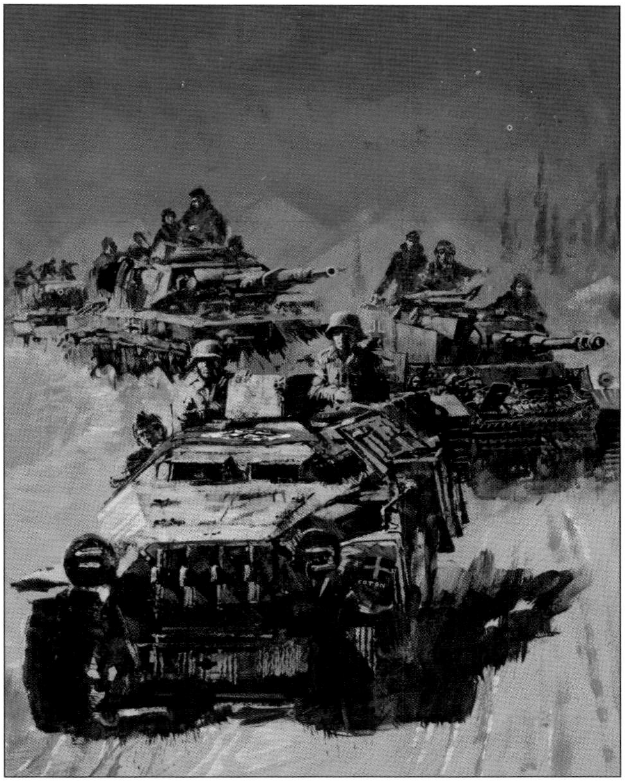

Graham Coton, Battle 1033, September 1976

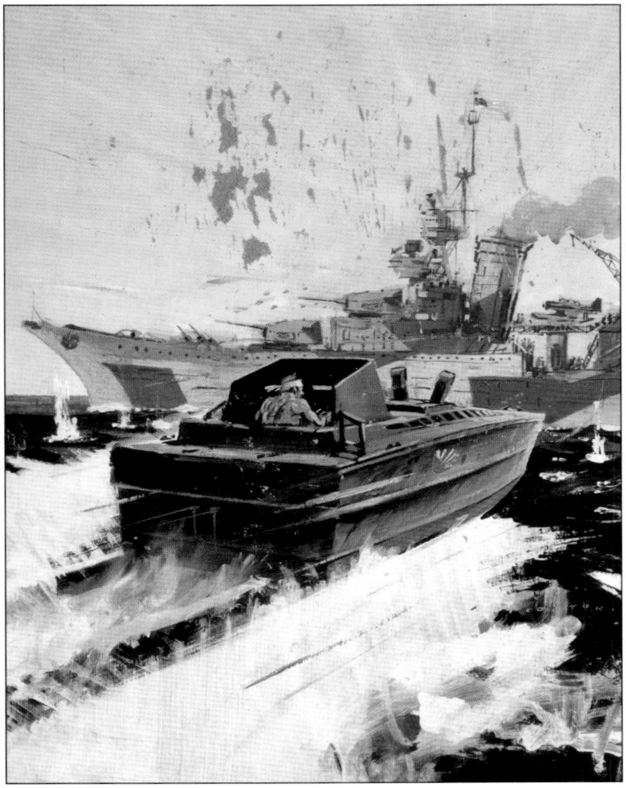

Graham Coton, unknown

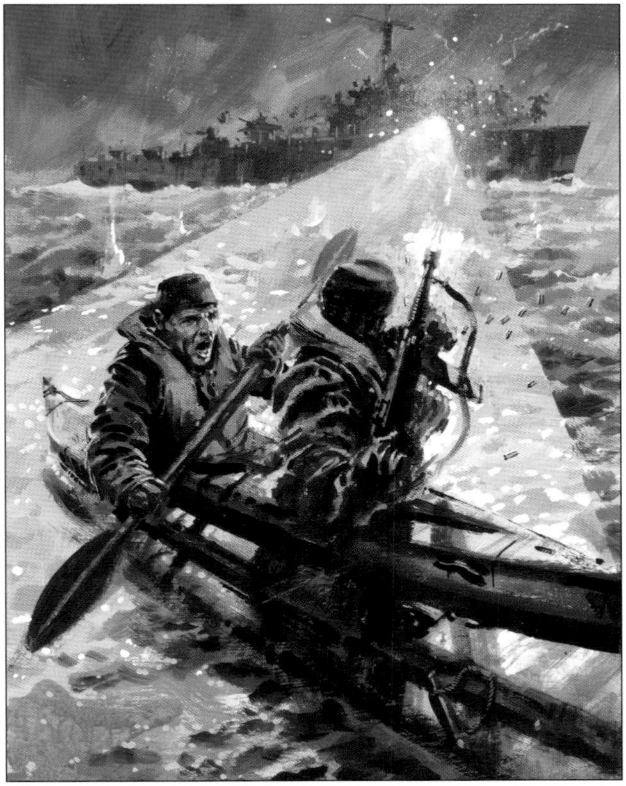

Graham Coton, Battle 1637, November 1983

Opposite: Allessandro Biffignandi, Battle 241, March 1966

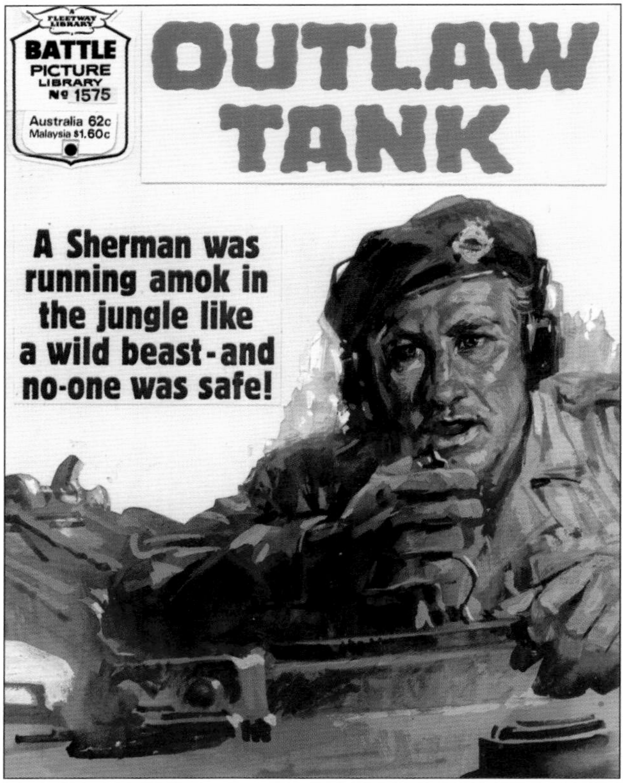
A FLEETWAY LIBRARY
BATTLE PICTURE LIBRARY
Nº 1575
Australia 62c
Malaysia $1.60c
OUTLAW TANK
A Sherman was running amok in the jungle like a wild beast - and no-one was safe!

Pino Dell'Orco, Battle 1575, December 1982

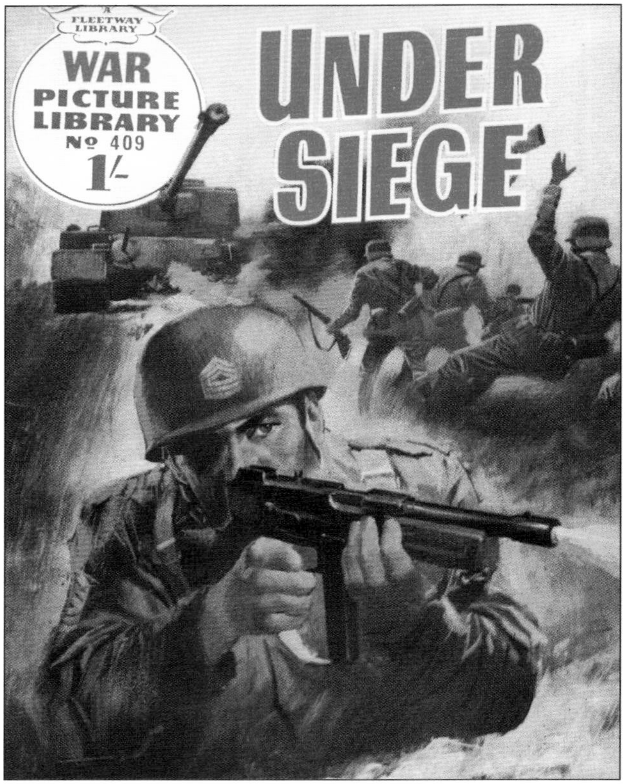
A FLEETWAY LIBRARY
WAR PICTURE LIBRARY
Nº 409
1/-
UNDER SIEGE

Carlo Jacono, War 409, November 1967

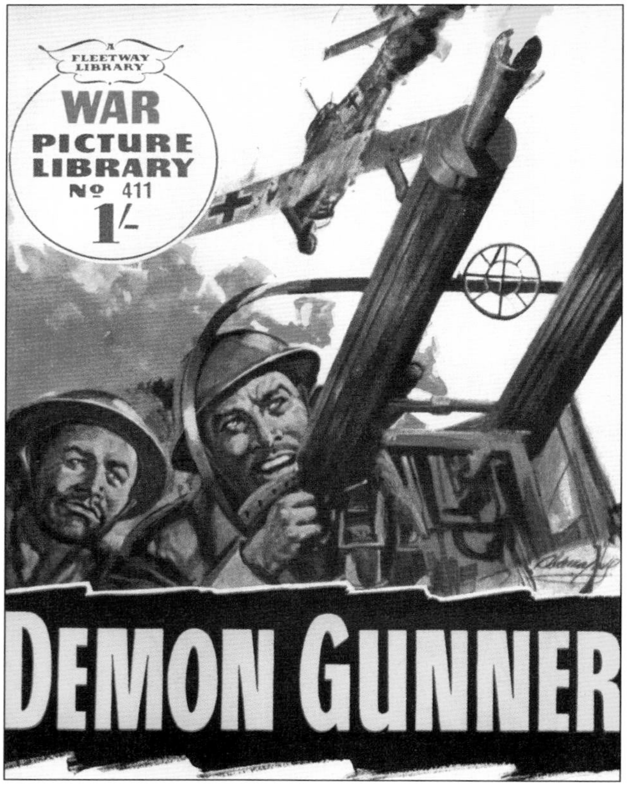
A FLEETWAY LIBRARY
WAR PICTURE LIBRARY
Nº 411
1/-
DEMON GUNNER

Artur Aldoma Puig, War 411, November 1967

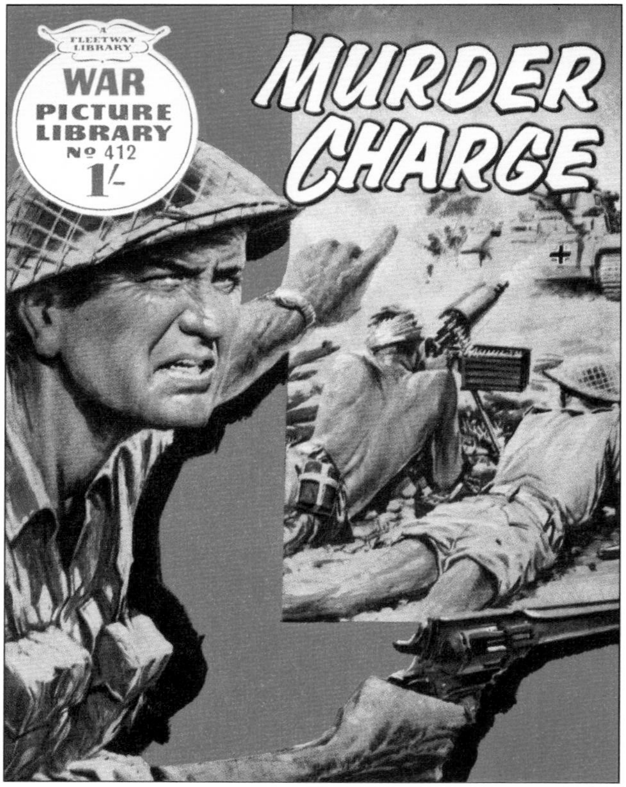
A FLEETWAY LIBRARY
WAR PICTURE LIBRARY
Nº 412
1/-
MURDER CHARGE

Graham Coton, War 412, December 1967

Opposite: Giorgio DeGaspari, Battle 244, March 1966

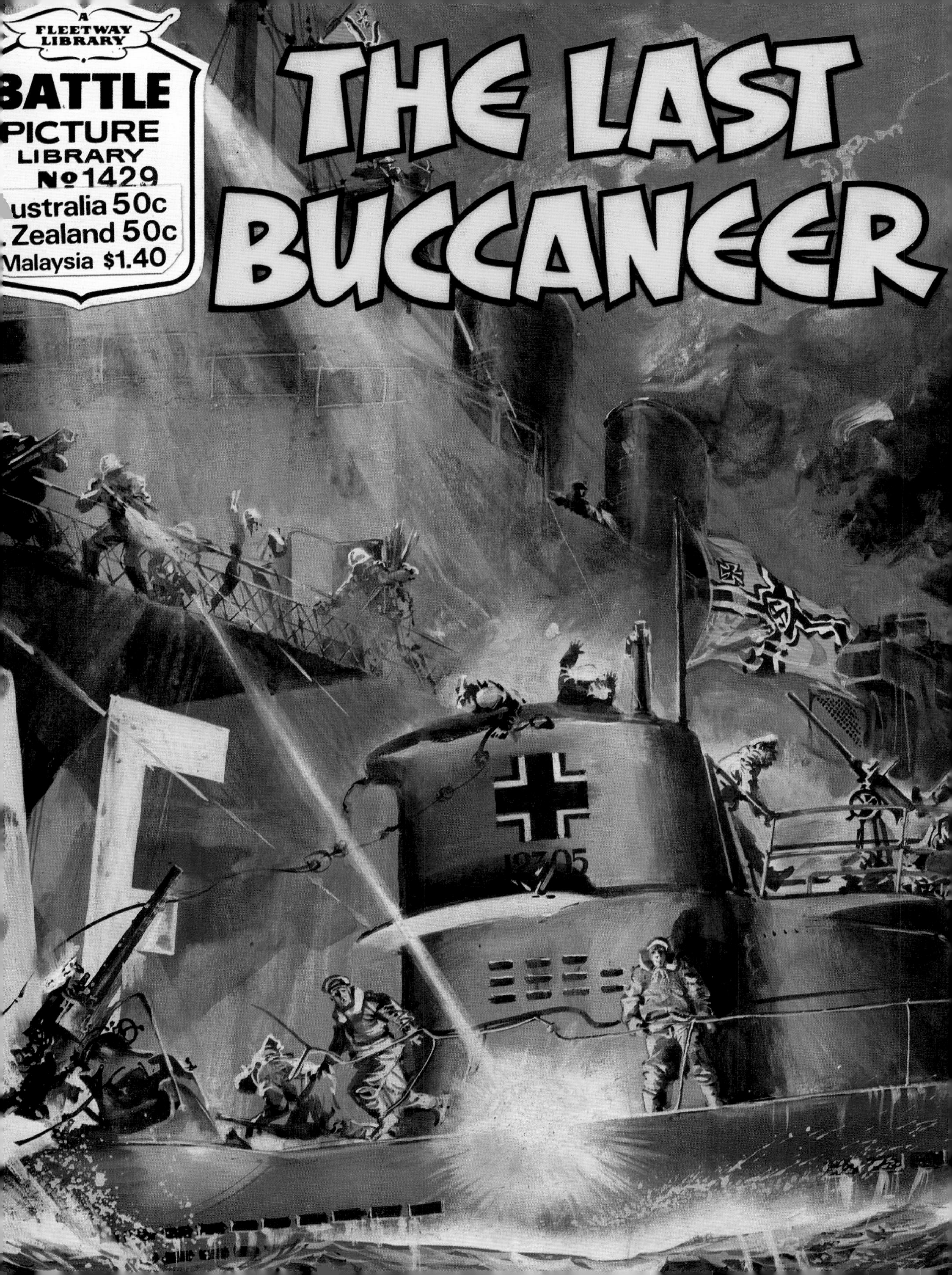
A FLEETWAY LIBRARY
BATTLE PICTURE LIBRARY
No 1429
Australia 50c
N. Zealand 50c
Malaysia $1.40
THE LAST BUCCANEER

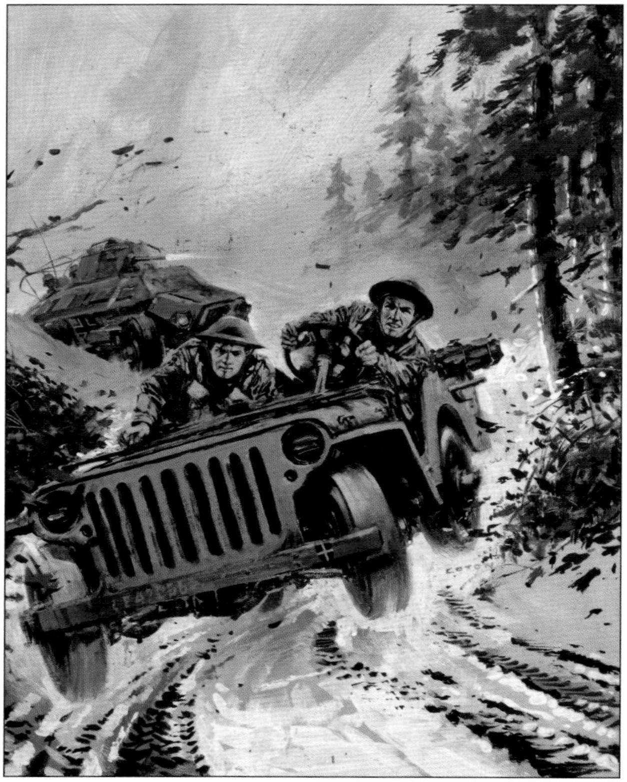

Graham Coton, War 913, January 1974

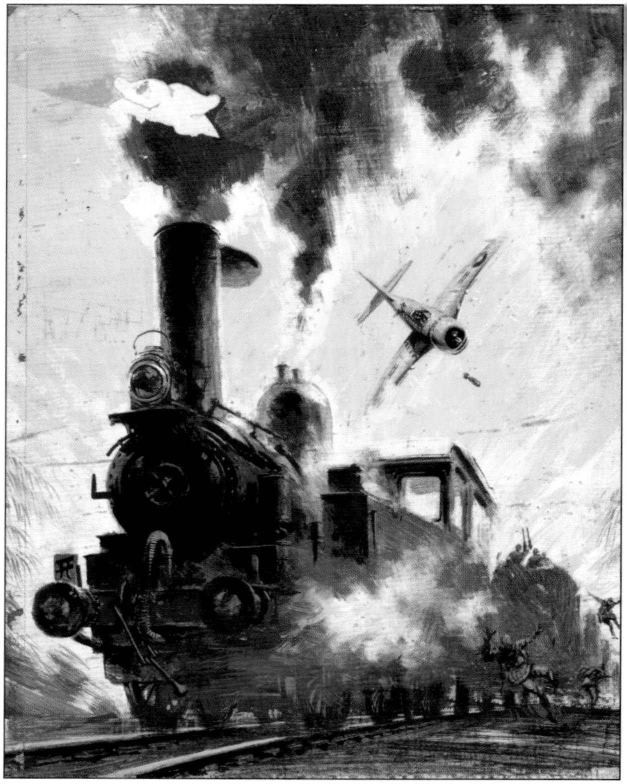

Graham Coton, Air Ace 367, December 1967

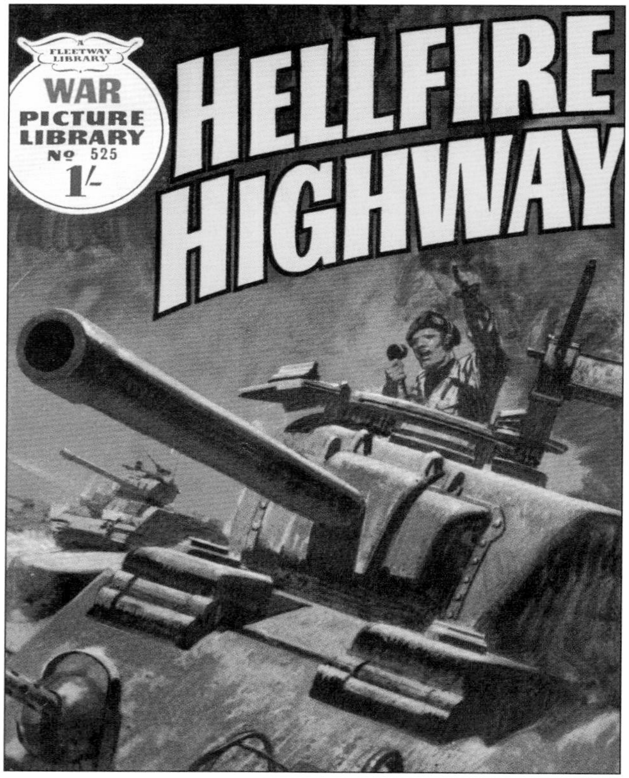
A FLEETWAY LIBRARY
WAR PICTURE LIBRARY
Nº 525
1/-
HELLFIRE HIGHWAY

Allessandro Biffignandi, War 525, July 1969

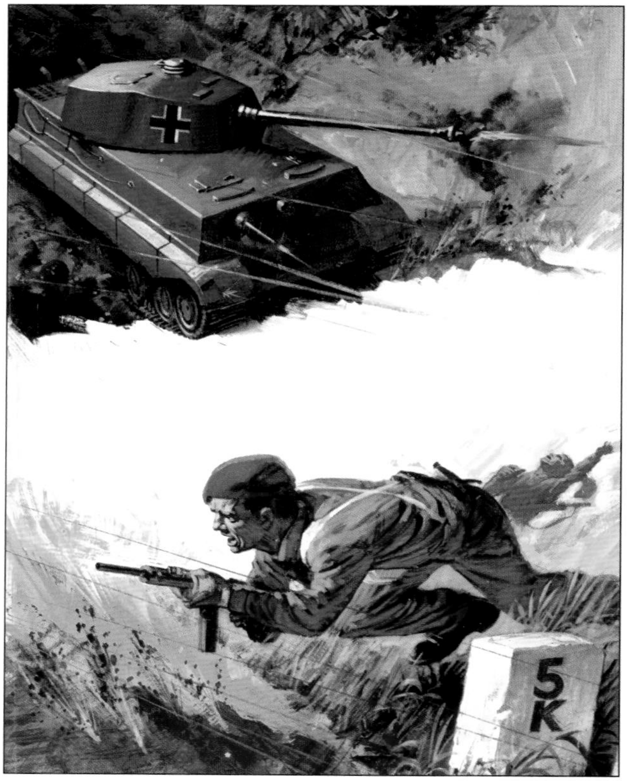
5K

Andrew Howat, Battle 408, July 1969

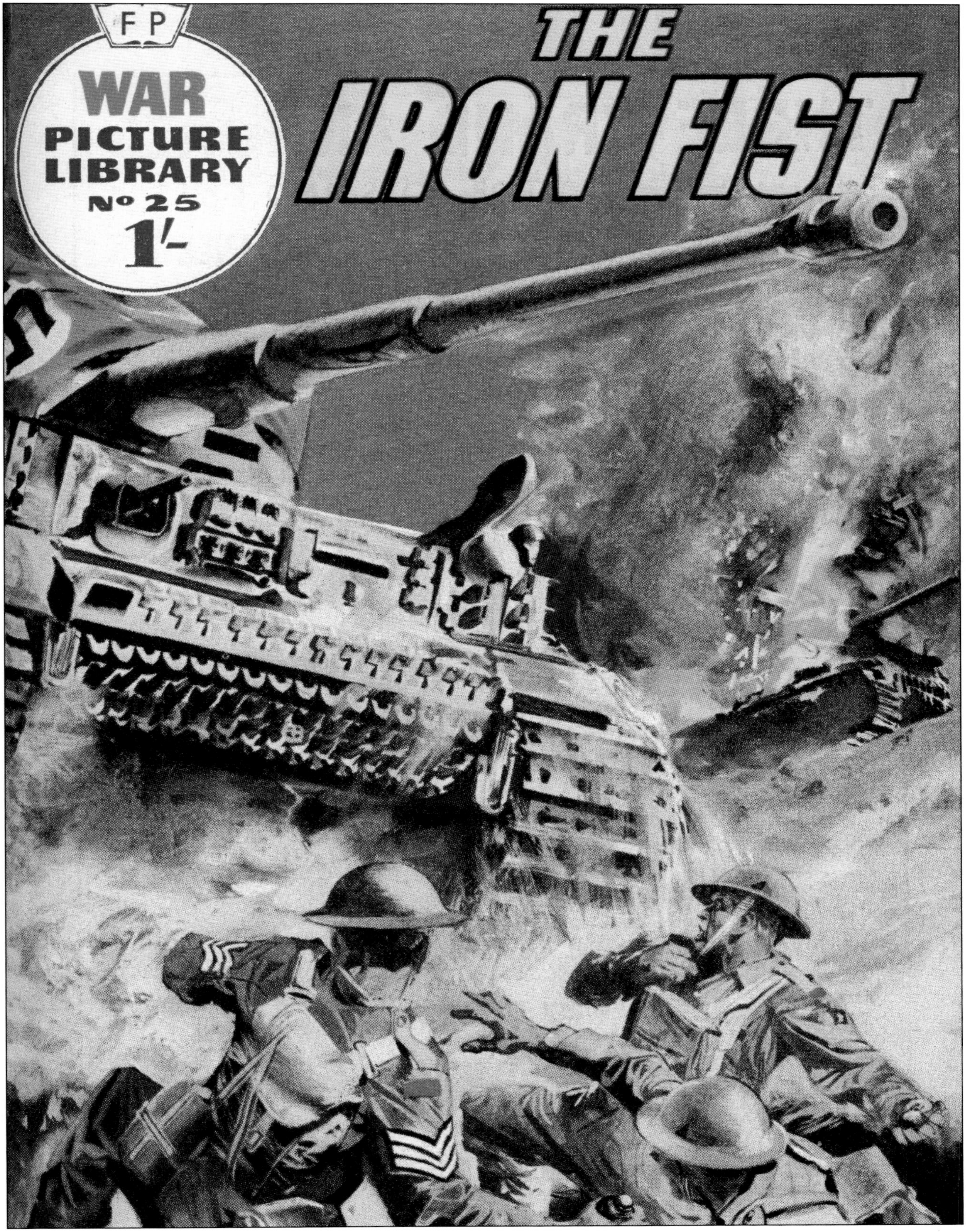
FP
WAR
PICTURE
LIBRARY
Nº 25
1/-
THE
IRON FIST

Giorgio DeGaspari, War 25, September 1959

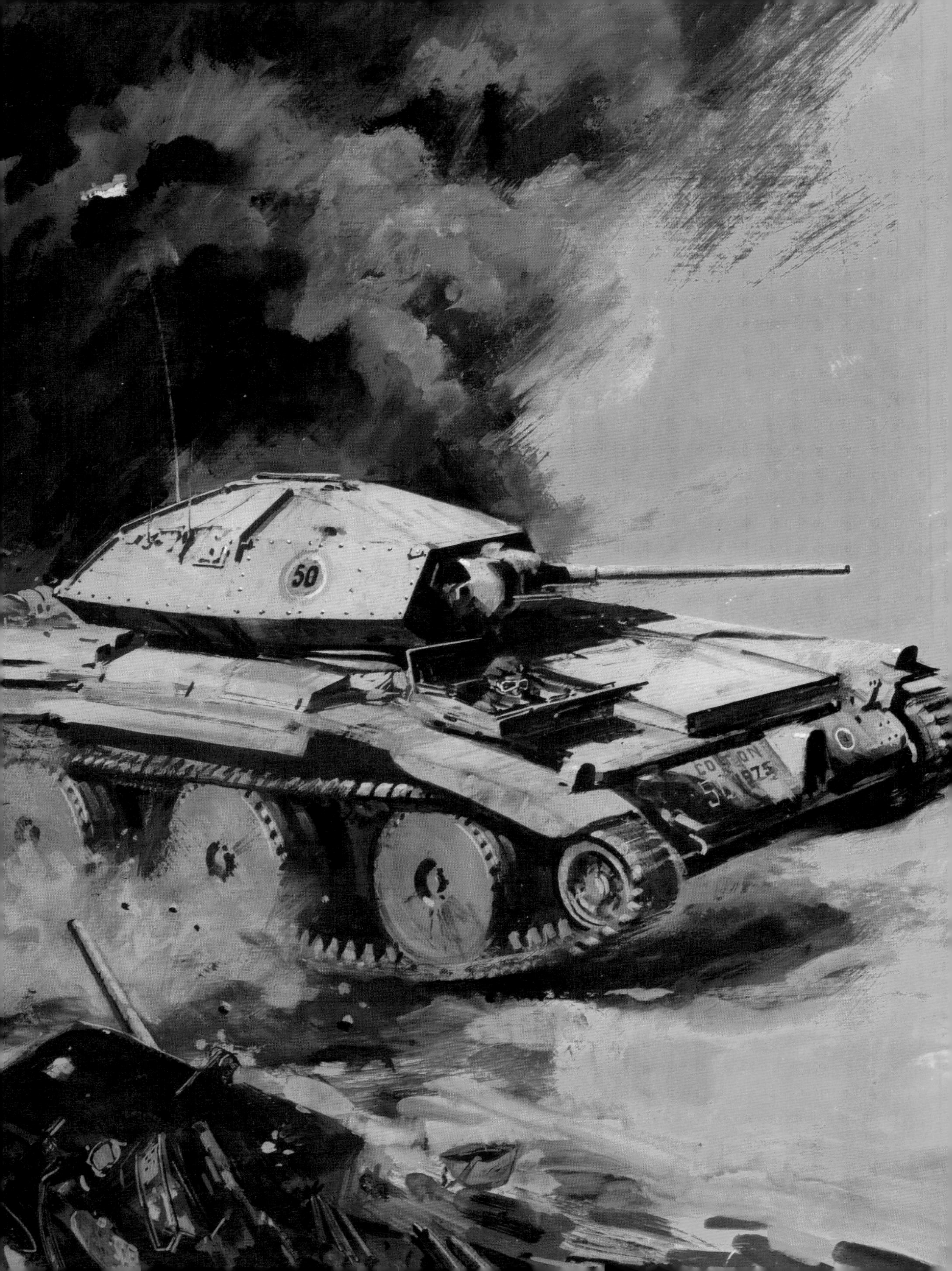
50

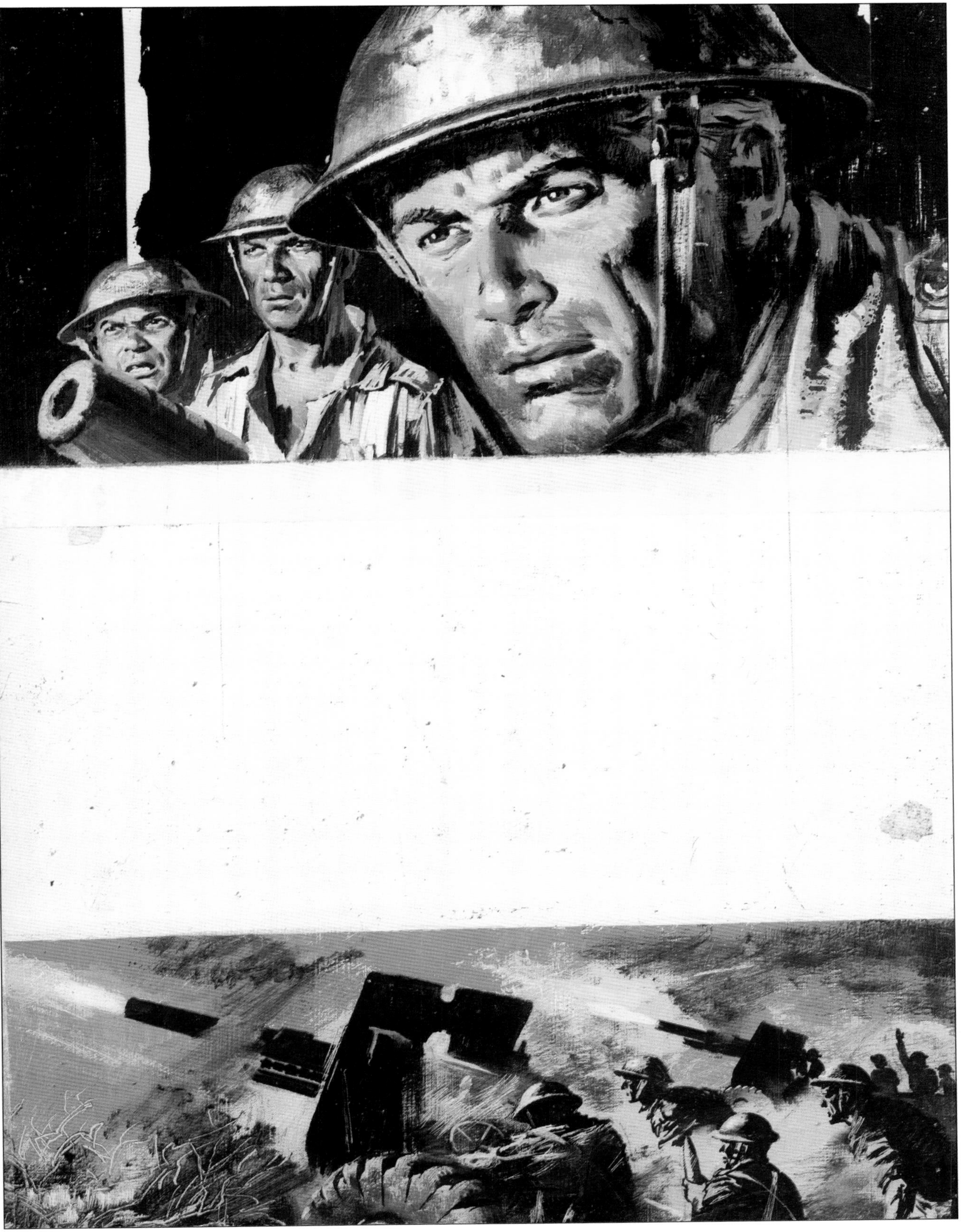

Jordi Penalva, Battle 143, February 1964
Opposite: Graham Coton, War 1086, July 1975

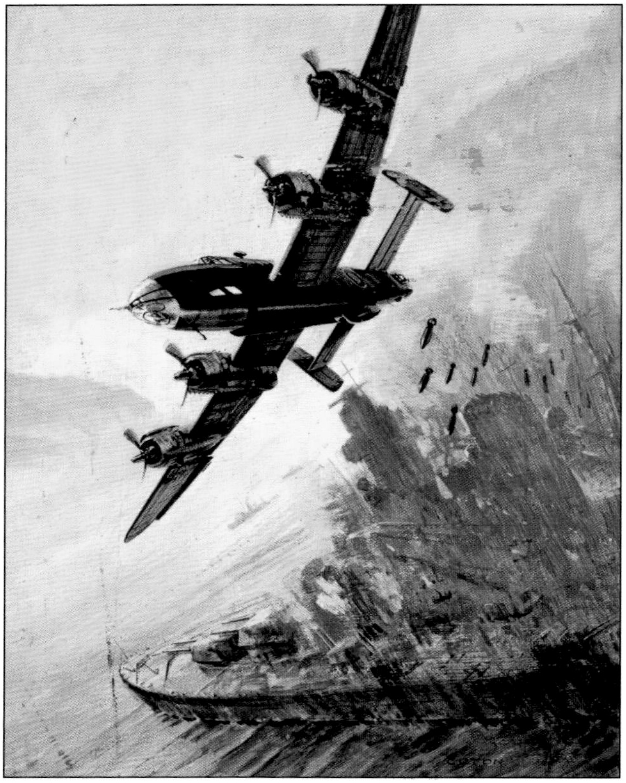

Graham Coton, Air Ace 378, March 68

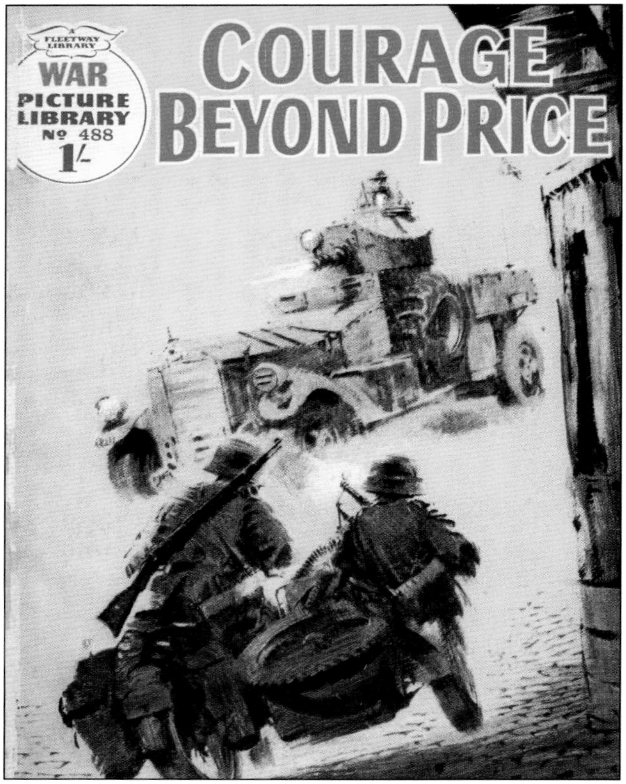
A FLEETWAY LIBRARY
WAR PICTURE LIBRARY
Nº 488
1/-
COURAGE BEYOND PRICE

Graham Coton, War 488, January 1969

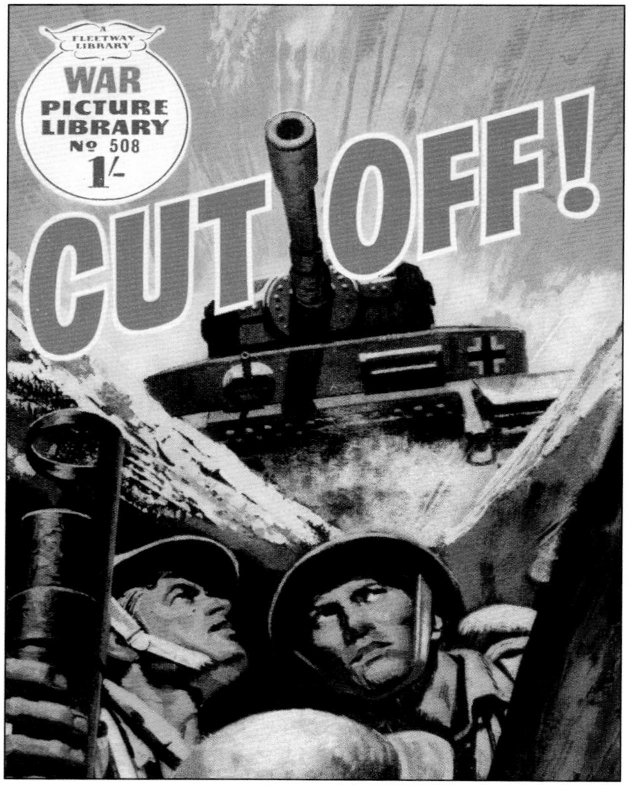
A FLEETWAY LIBRARY
WAR PICTURE LIBRARY
Nº 508
1/-
CUT OFF!

Jordi Penalva, War 508, April 1969

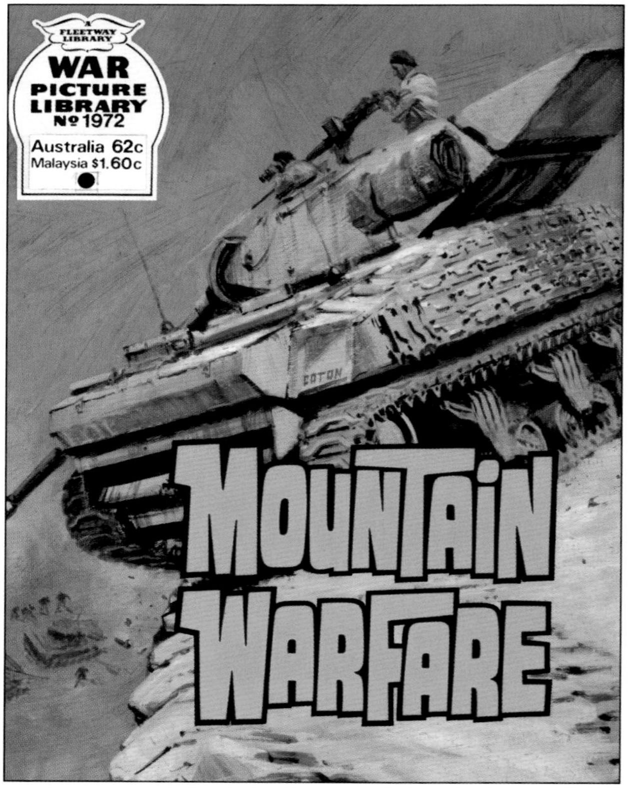
A FLEETWAY LIBRARY
WAR PICTURE LIBRARY
Nº1972
Australia 62c
Malaysia $1.60c
MOUNTAIN WARFARE

Graham Coton, originally War 566, February 1970

Opposite: Graham Coton, War 1374, July 1977

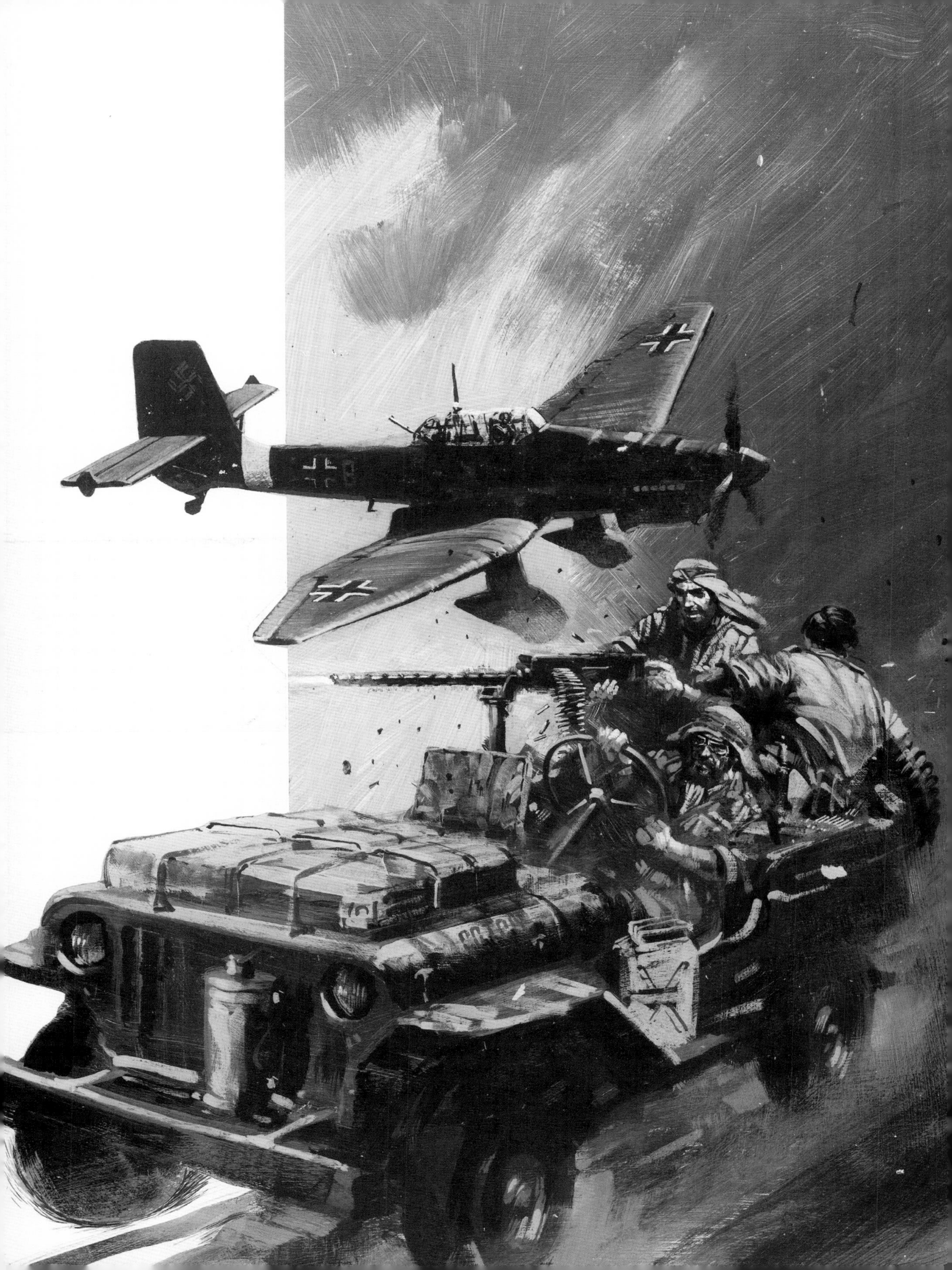

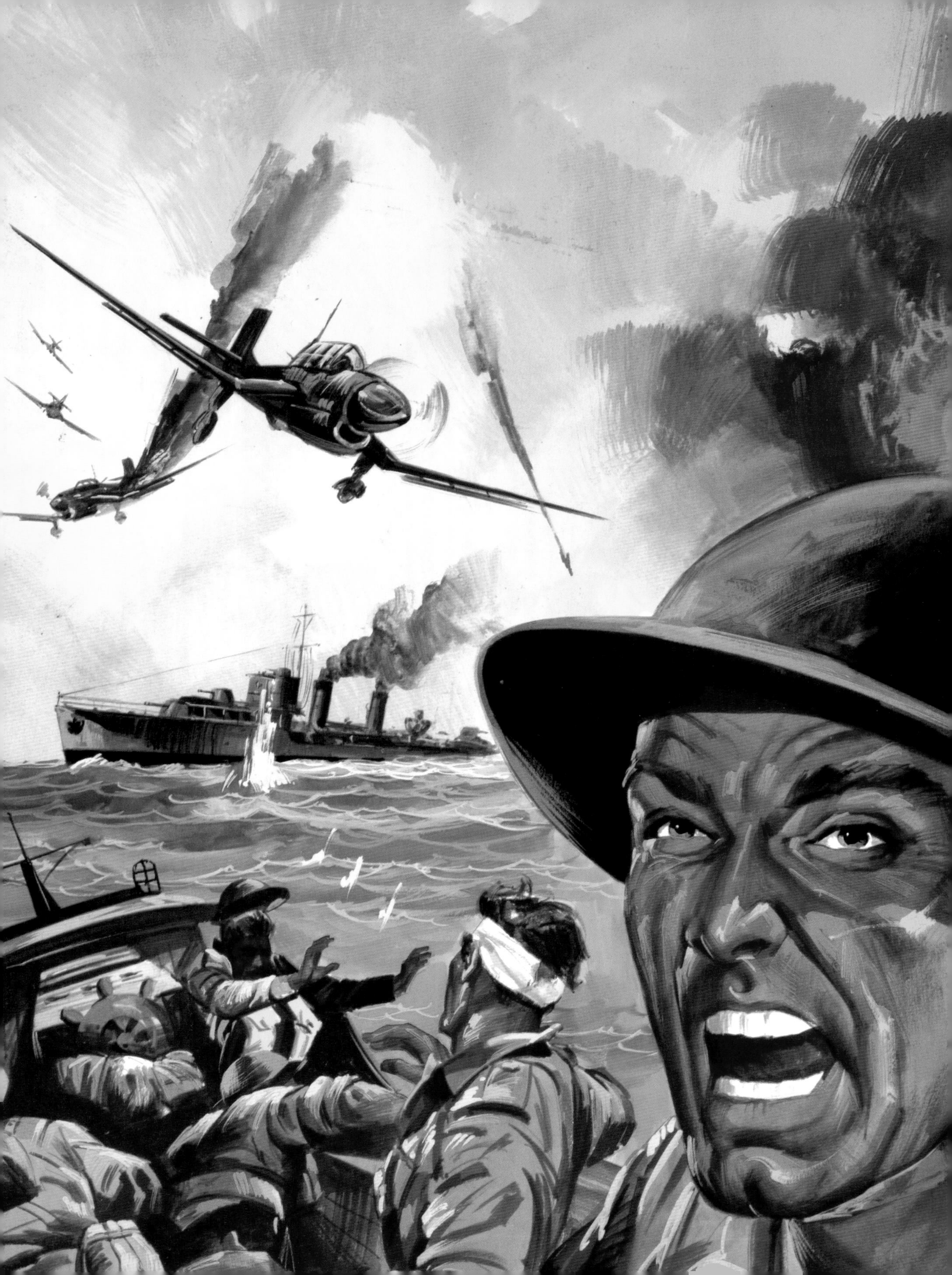

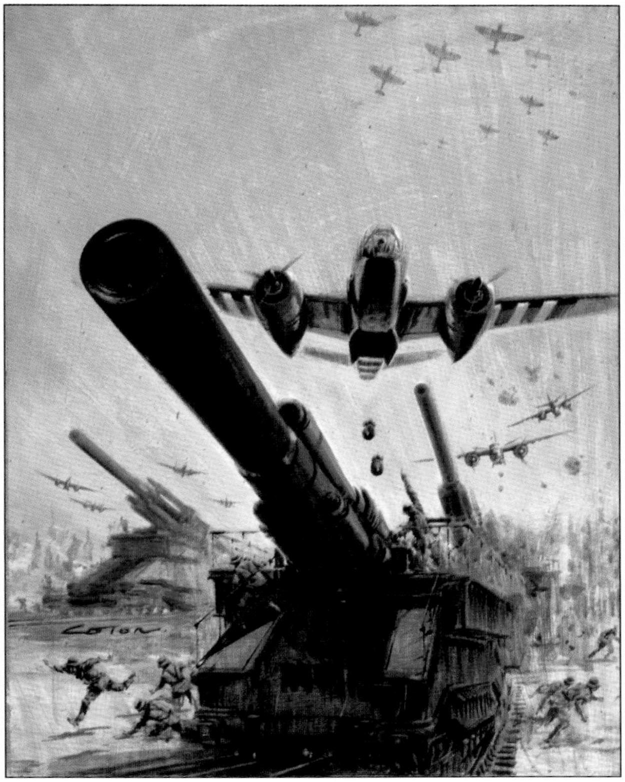

Graham Coton, Air Ace 354, September 1967

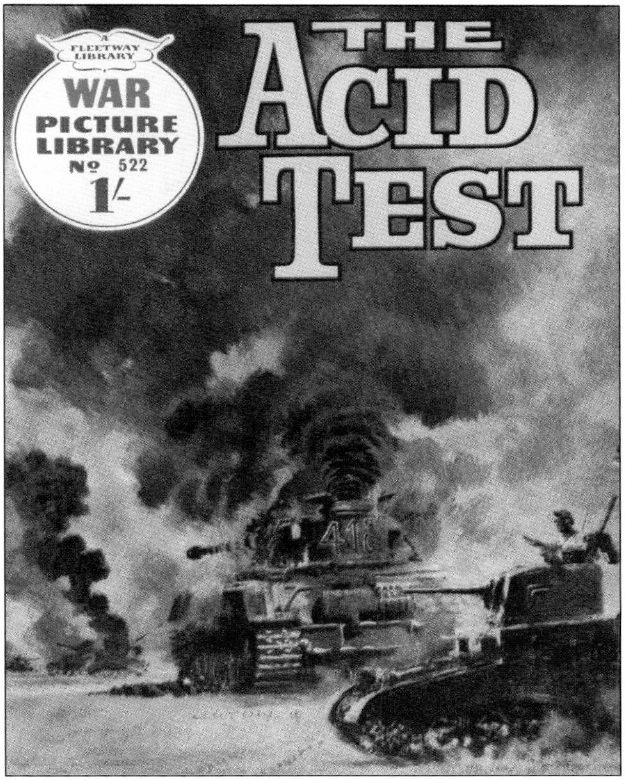
A FLEETWAY LIBRARY
WAR PICTURE LIBRARY
Nº 522
1/-
THE ACID TEST

Graham Coton, War 522, June 1969

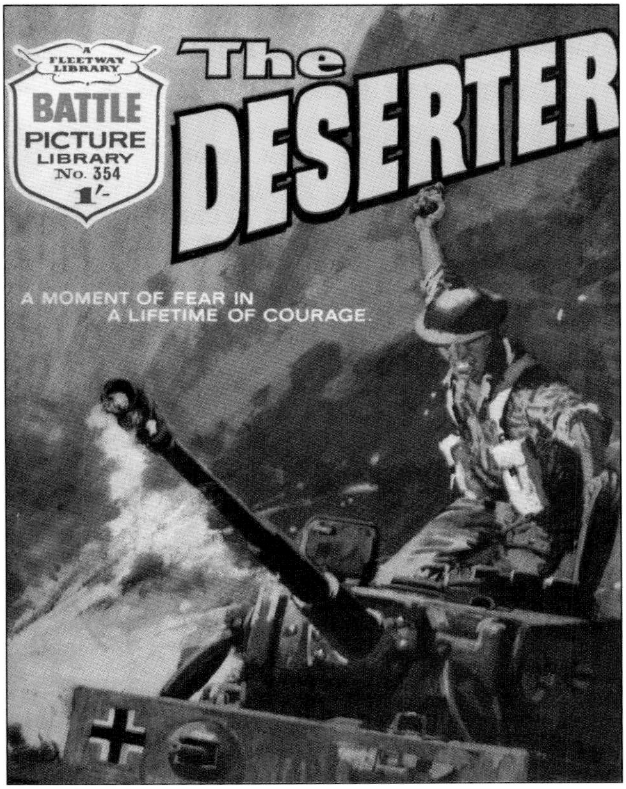
A FLEETWAY LIBRARY
BATTLE PICTURE LIBRARY
No. 354
1/-
The DESERTER
A MOMENT OF FEAR IN A LIFETIME OF COURAGE.

Jordi Longaron, Battle 354, July 1968

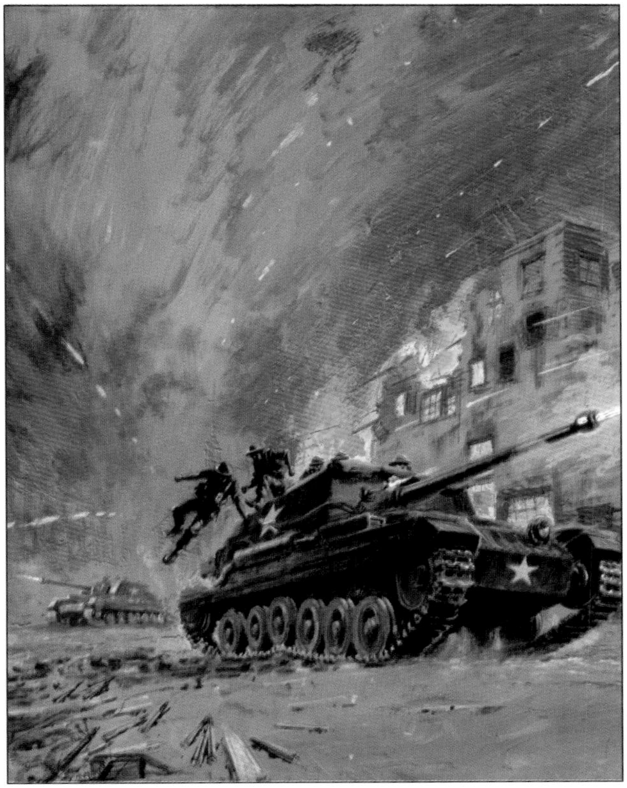

Graham Coton, Battle 284, January 1967

Opposite: Franco Picchioni, War 391, June 1967

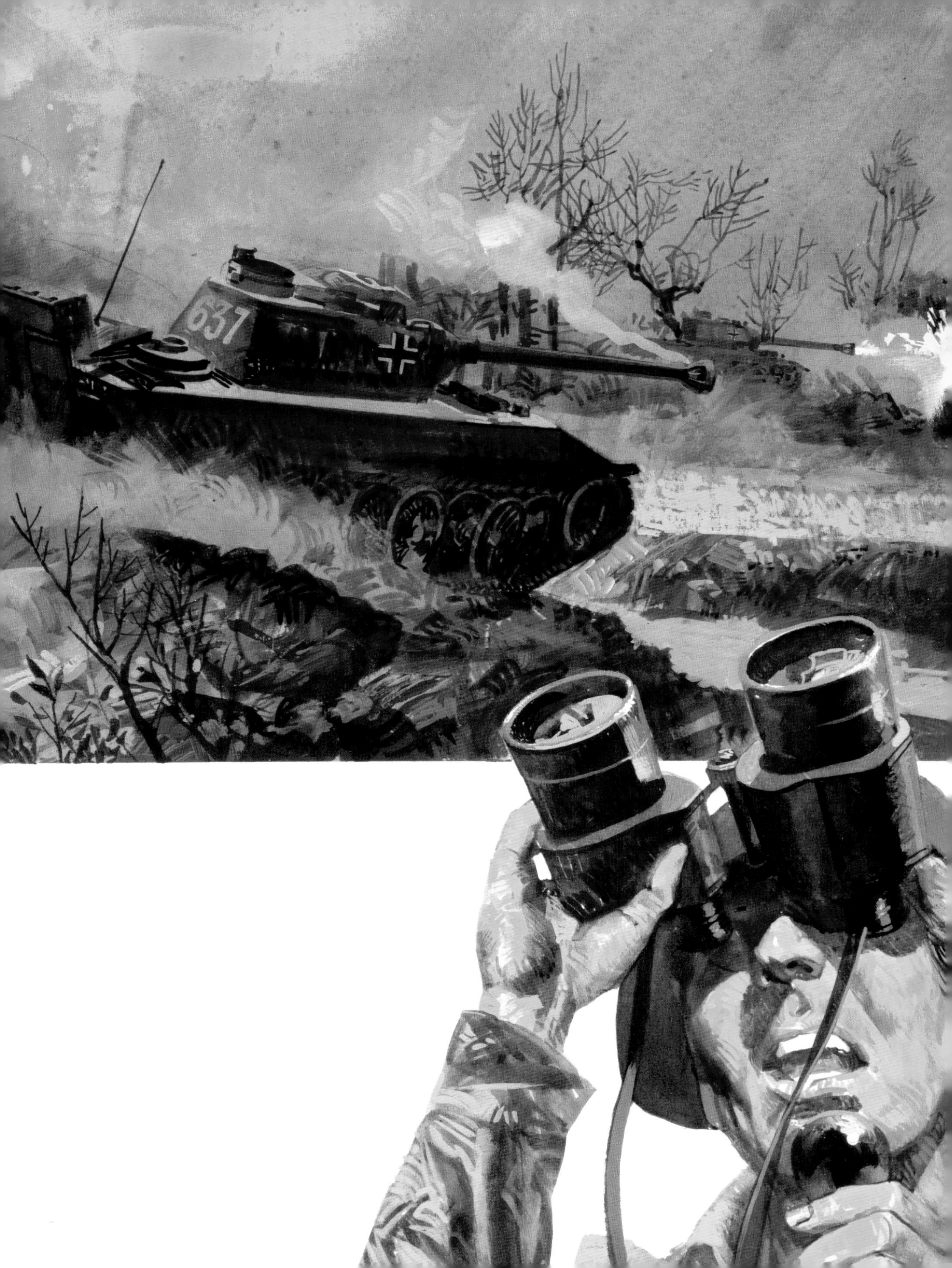
637

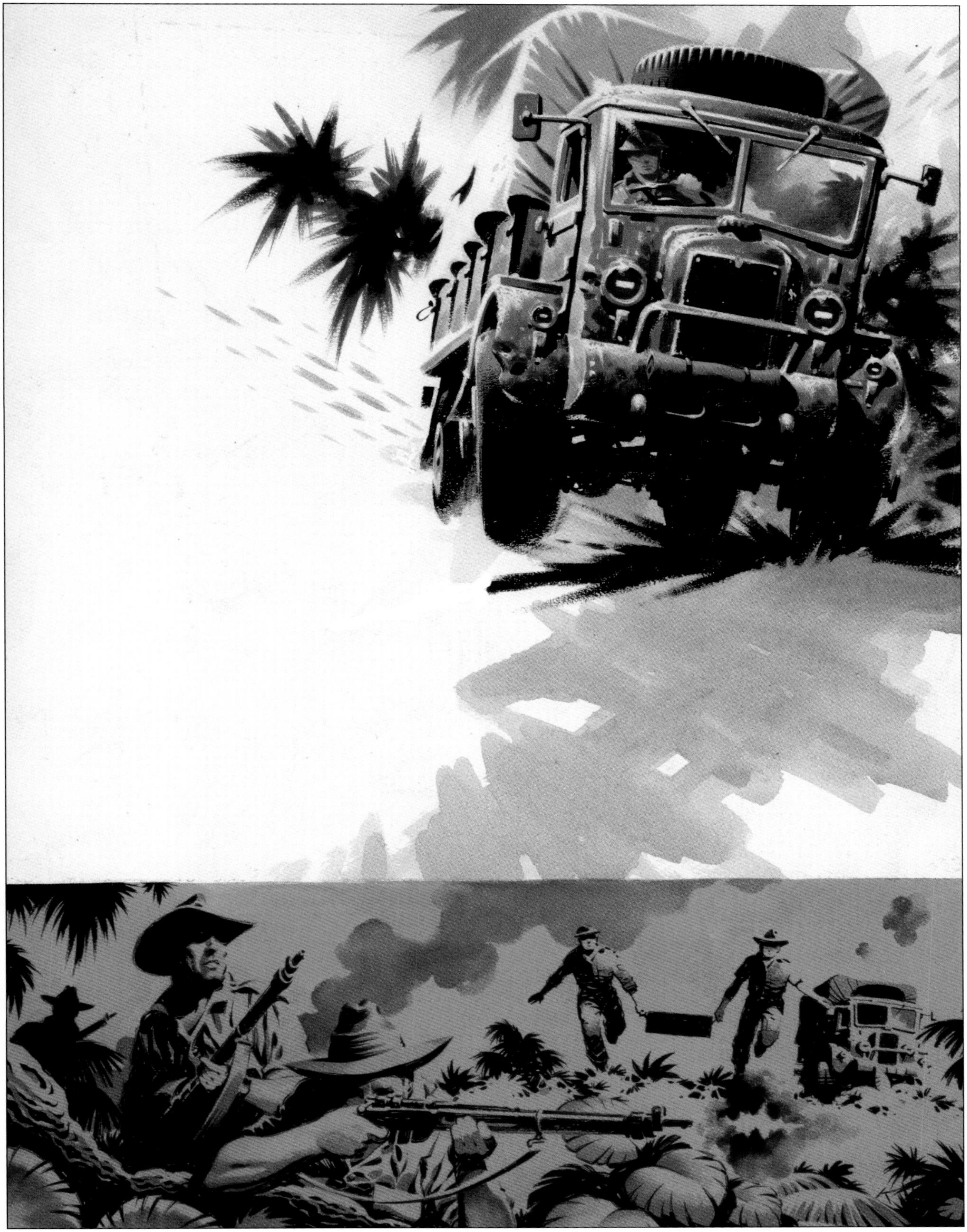

Ian Kennedy, War 417, January 1968
Opposite: Allessandro Biffignandi, War 407, October 1967

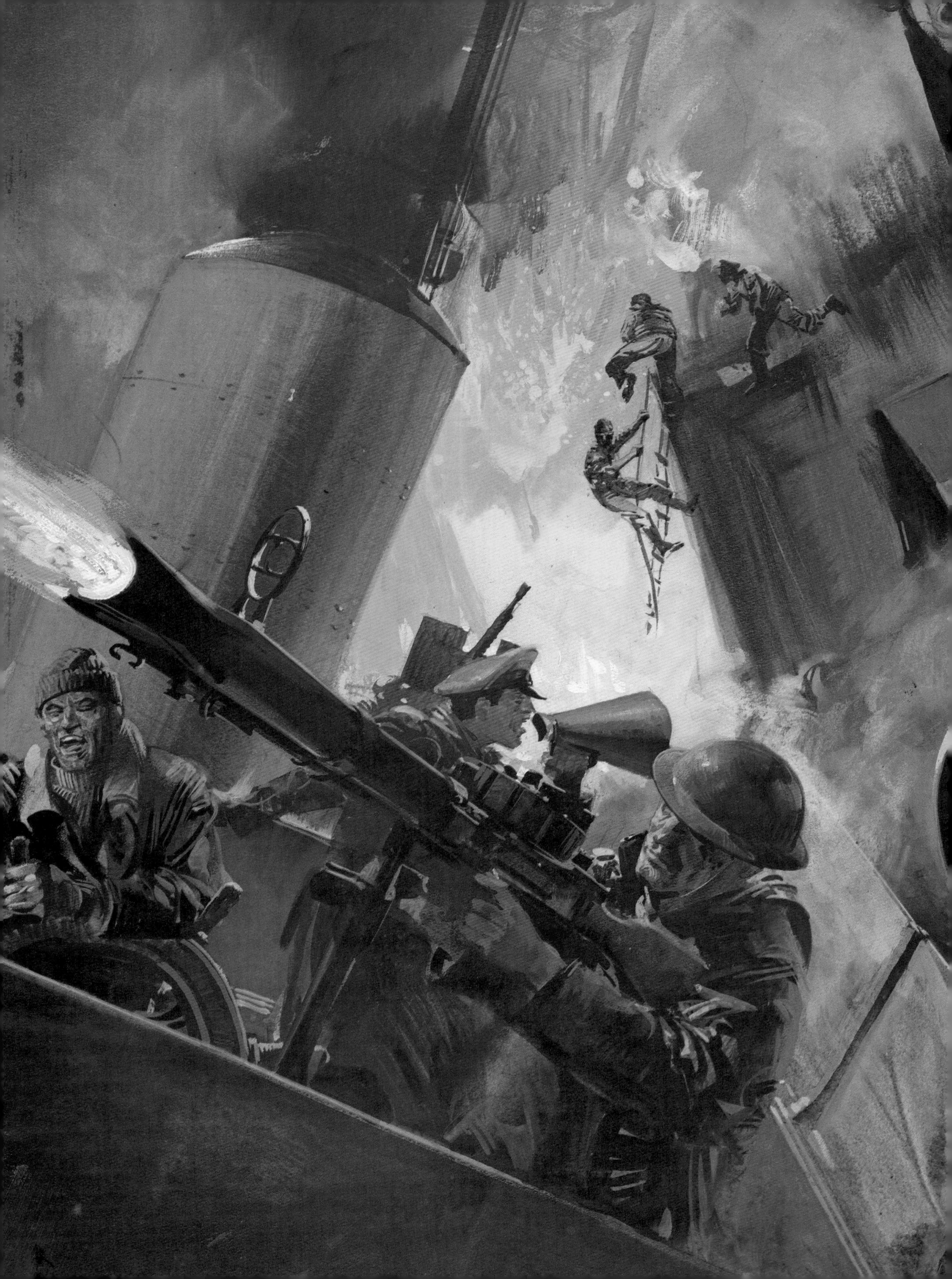

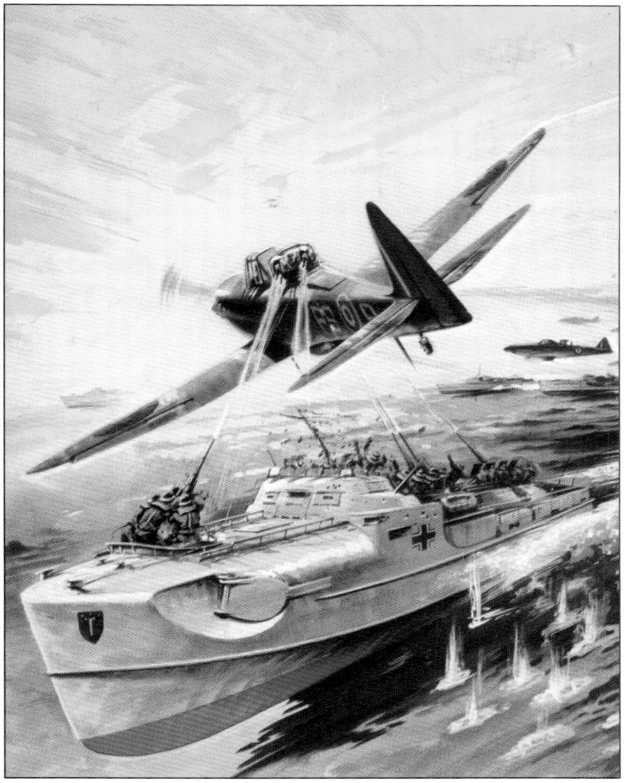

Graham Coton, Air Ace 269, November 1965

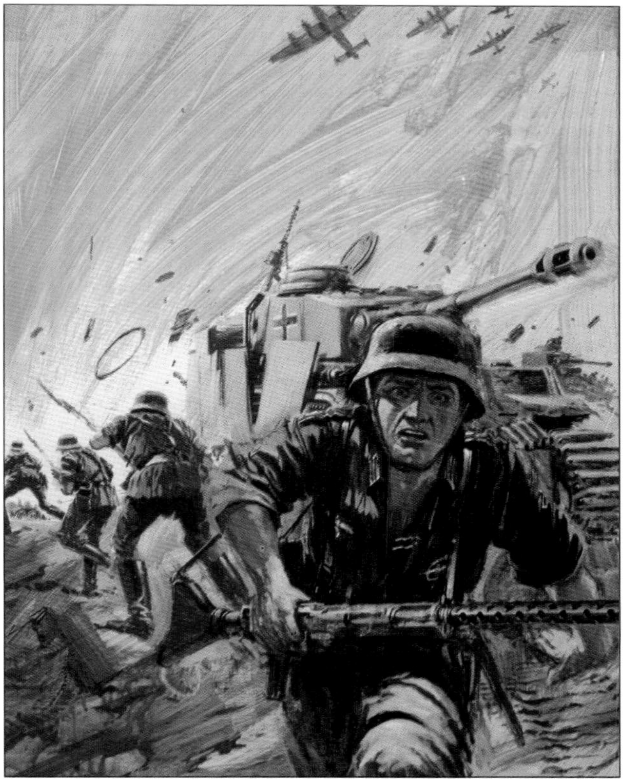

Graham Coton, War 543, October 1969

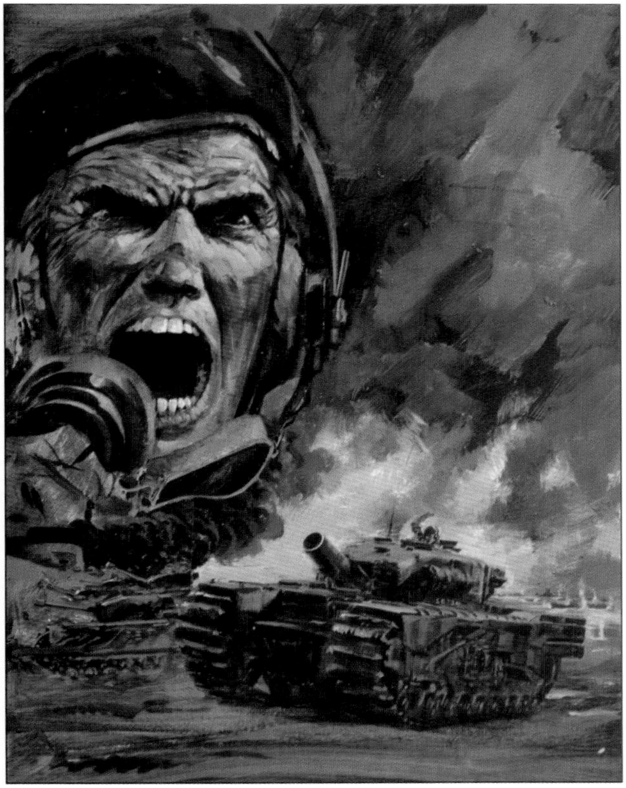

Graham Coton, War 1638, May 1979

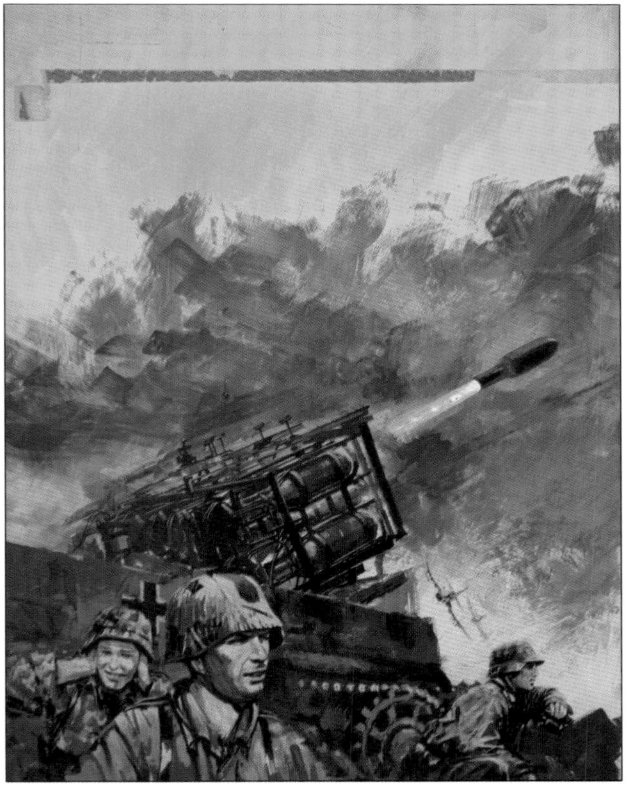

Graham Coton, War 1798, July 1980

Opposite: Allessandro Biffignandi, War 282, March 1965
Overleaf: Pino Dell'Orco, War 147, May 1962

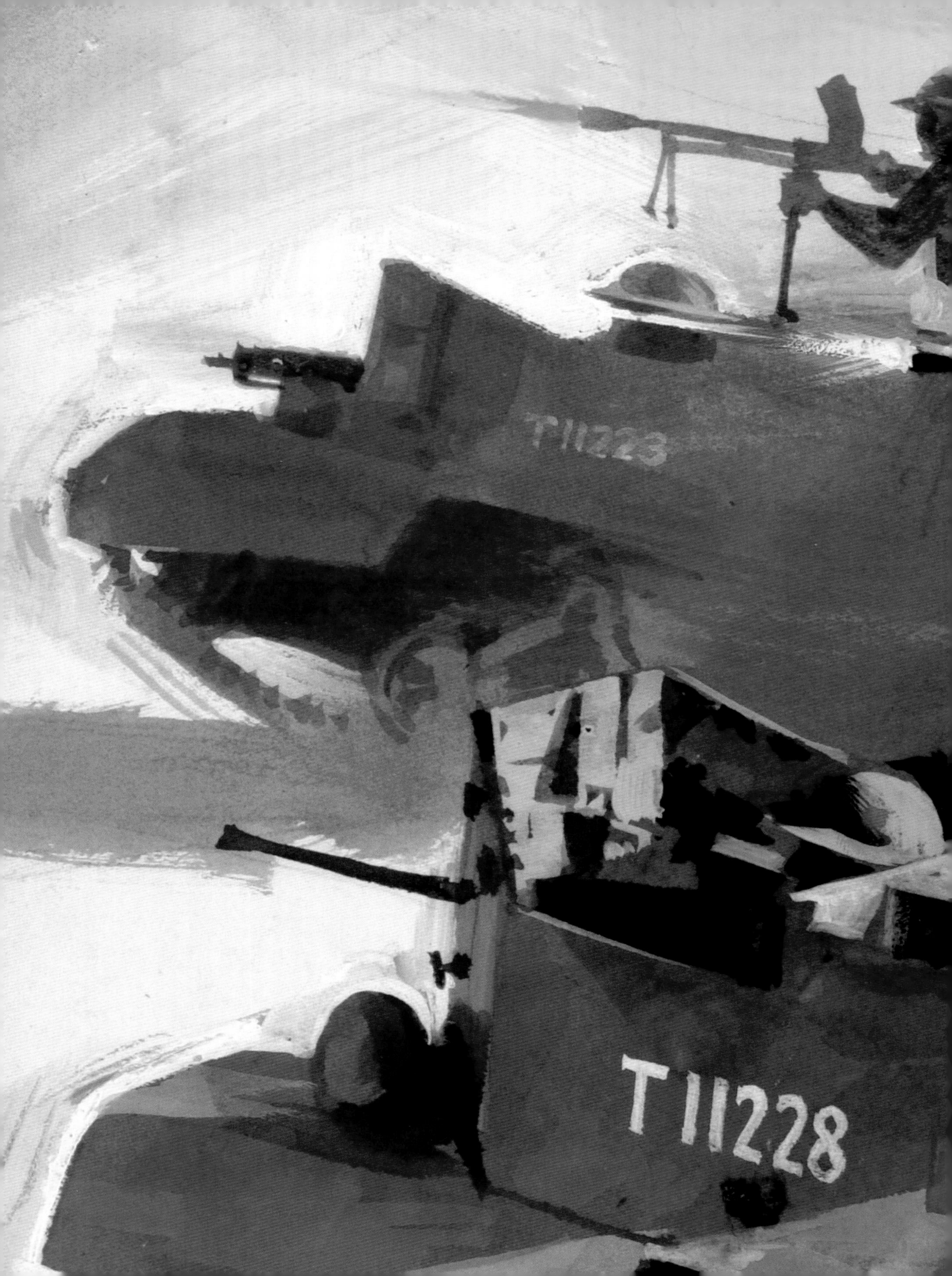
T11223
T11228

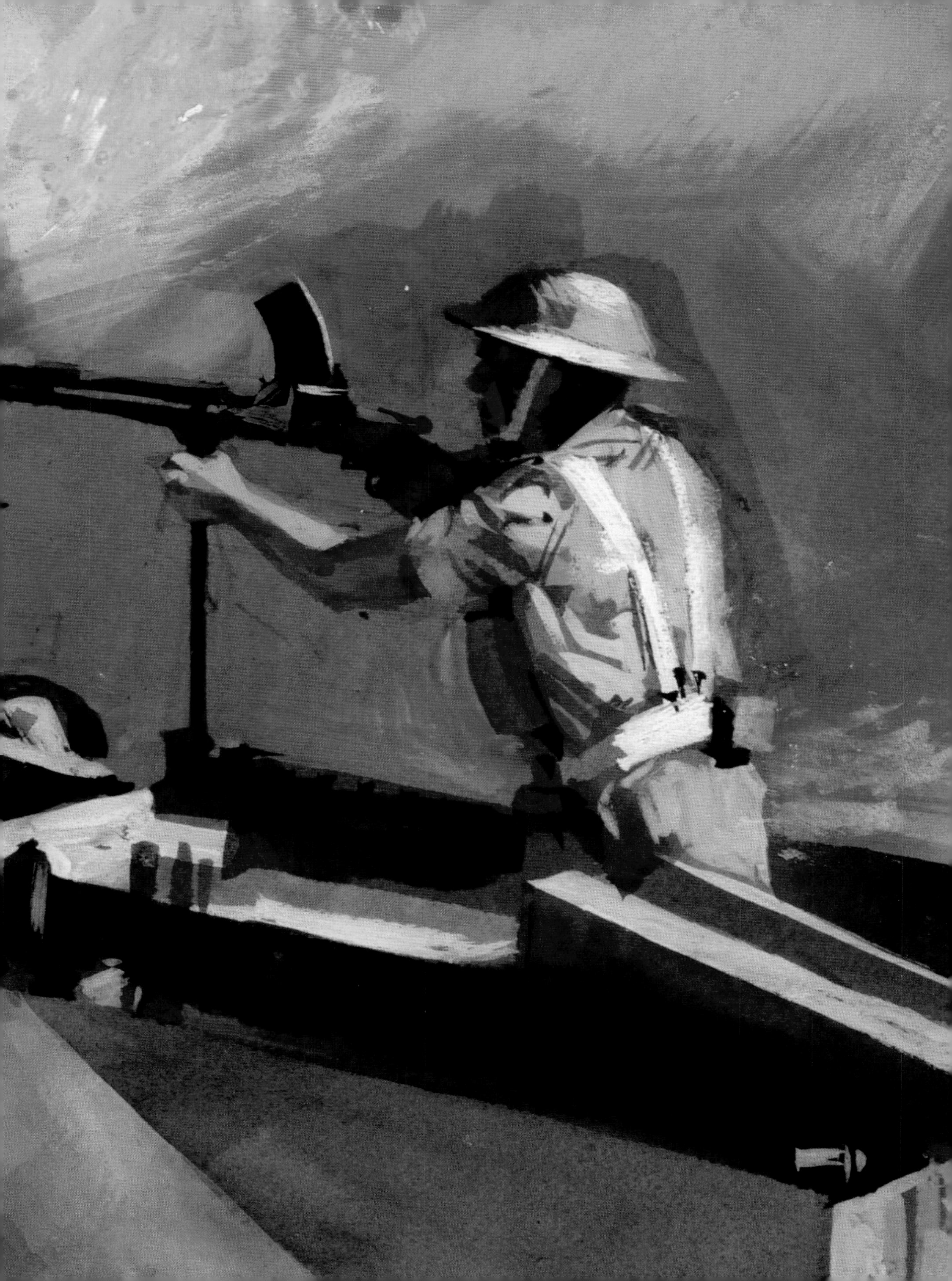

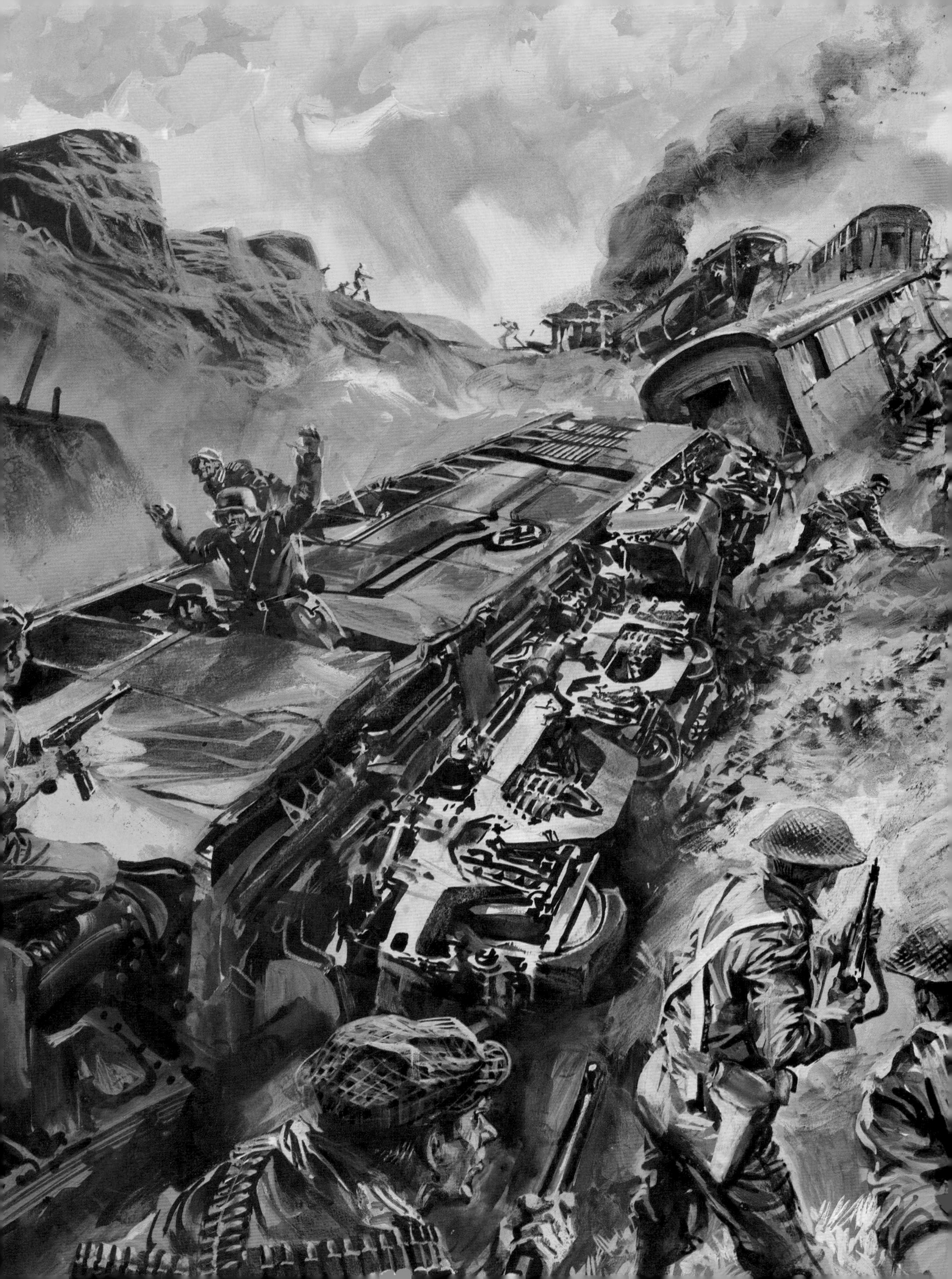

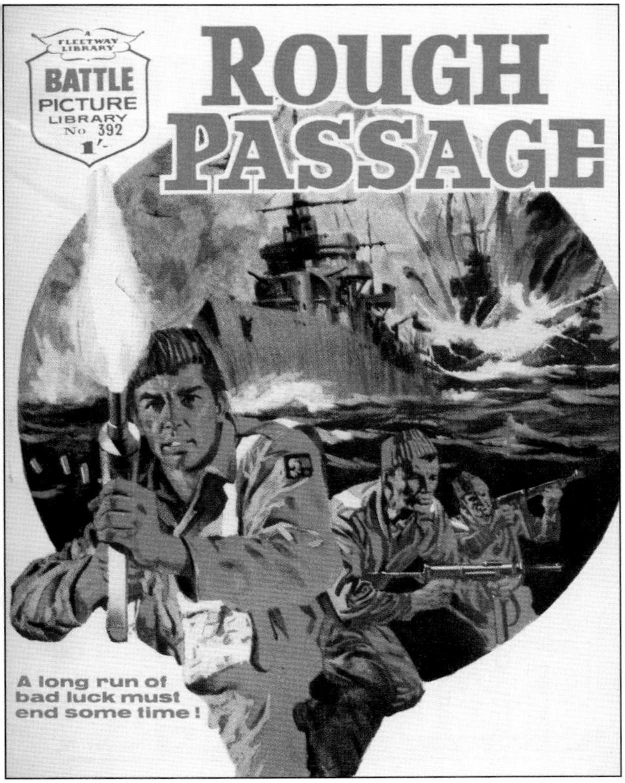
A FLEETWAY LIBRARY
BATTLE PICTURE LIBRARY No 392
1/-
ROUGH PASSAGE
A long run of bad luck must end some time!

Fernando Fernandez, Battle 392, April 1969

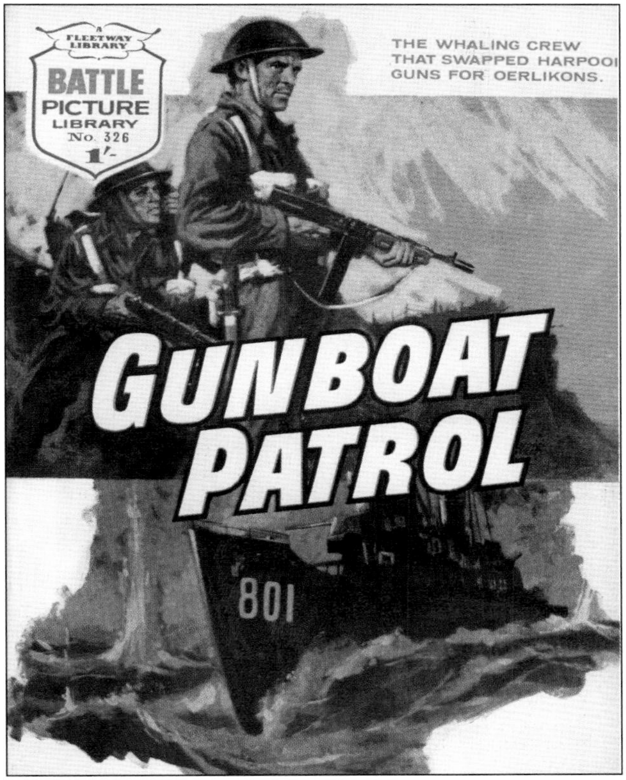
A FLEETWAY LIBRARY
BATTLE PICTURE LIBRARY No. 326
1/-
THE WHALING CREW THAT SWAPPED HARPOO GUNS FOR OERLIKONS.
GUNBOAT PATROL
801

Fernando Fernandez, Batle 326, December 1967

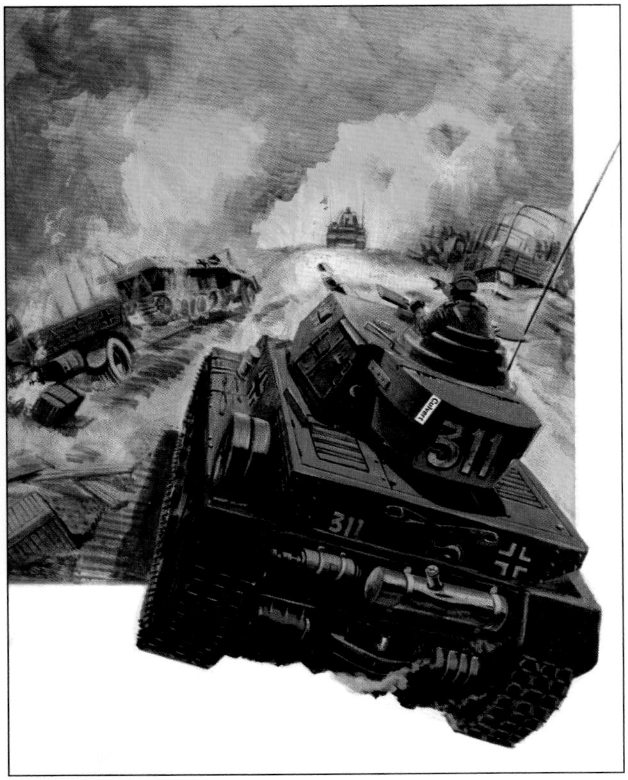
311
311

Graham Coton, Battle 353, July 1968

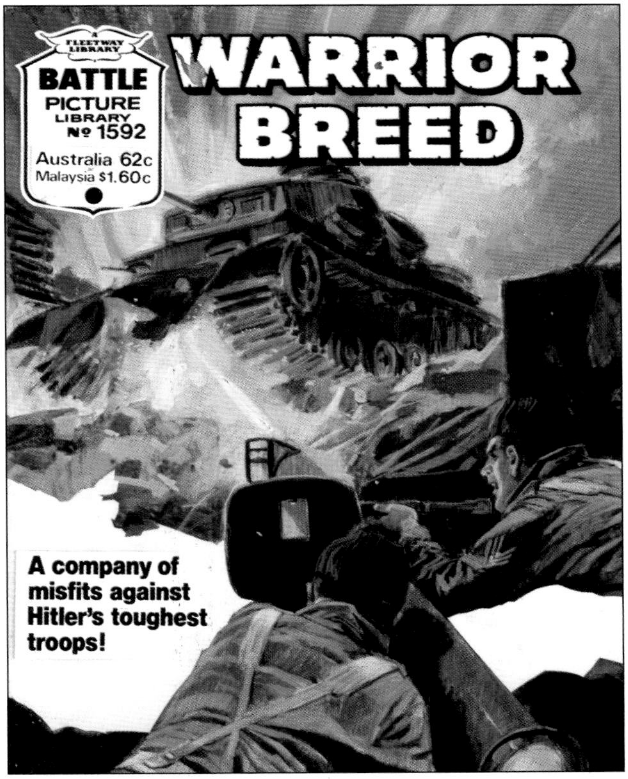
A FLEETWAY LIBRARY
BATTLE PICTURE LIBRARY Nº 1592
Australia 62c
Malaysia $1.60c
WARRIOR BREED
A company of misfits against Hitler's toughest troops!

Jose Luis Macias, Battle 305, July 1967

Opposite: Giorgio DeGaspari, War 45, April 1960

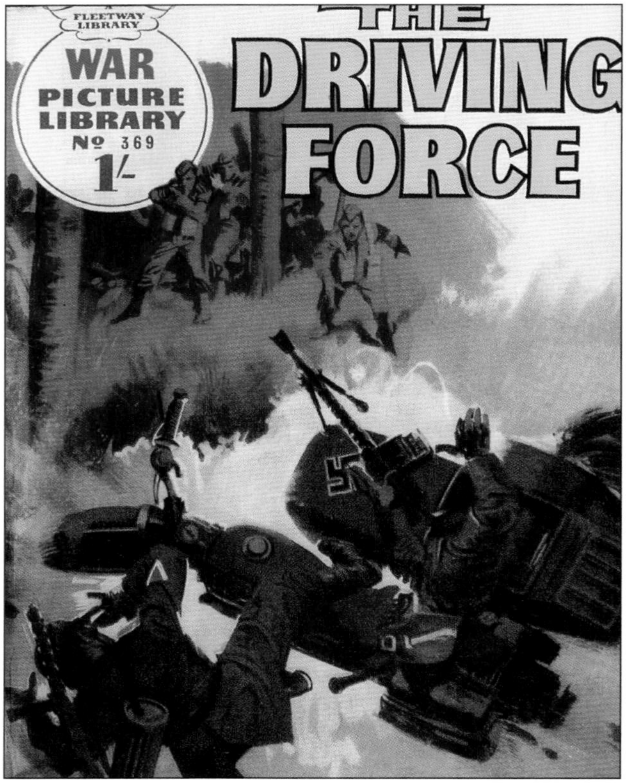
A FLEETWAY LIBRARY
WAR PICTURE LIBRARY
Nº 369
1/-
THE DRIVING FORCE

Allessandro Biffignandi, War 369, January 1967

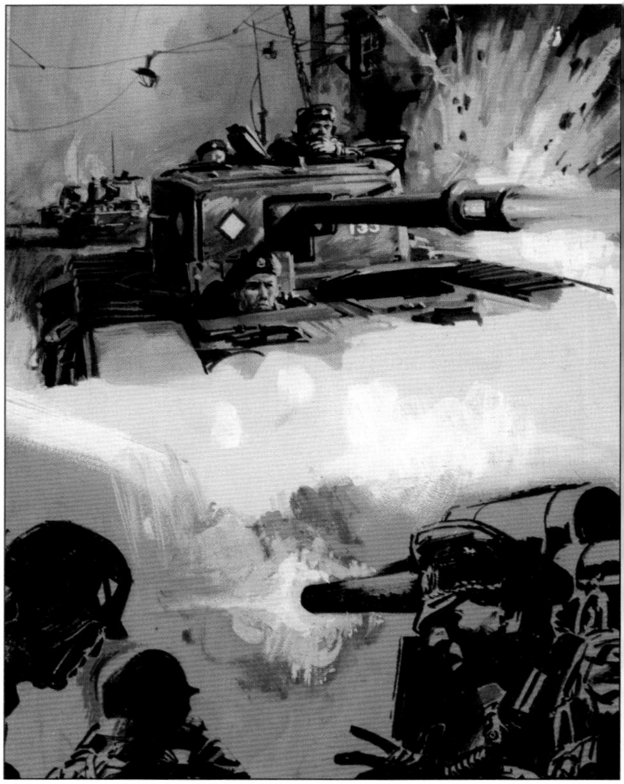

Pino Dell'Orco, War 222, December 1963

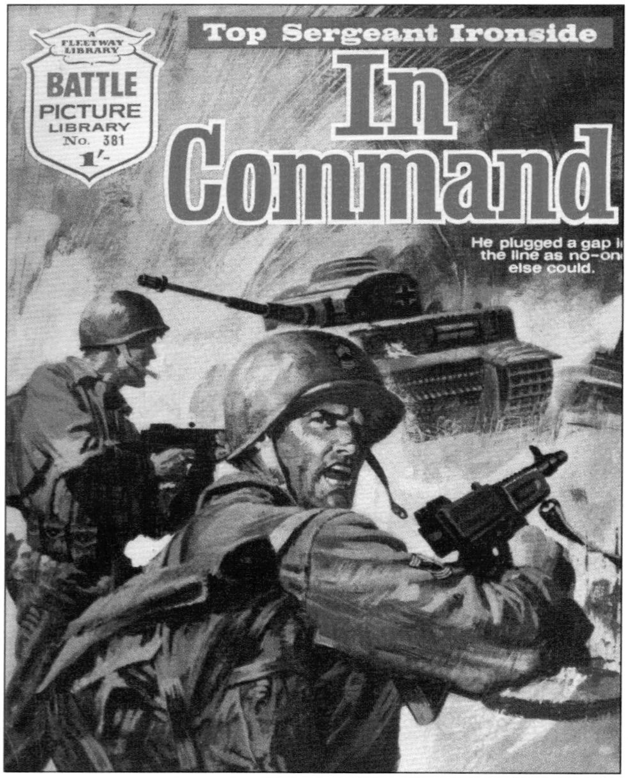
A FLEETWAY LIBRARY
BATTLE PICTURE LIBRARY
No. 381
1/-
Top Sergeant Ironside
In Command
He plugged a gap i
the line as no-on
else could.

Jordi Penalva, Battle 381, February 1969,

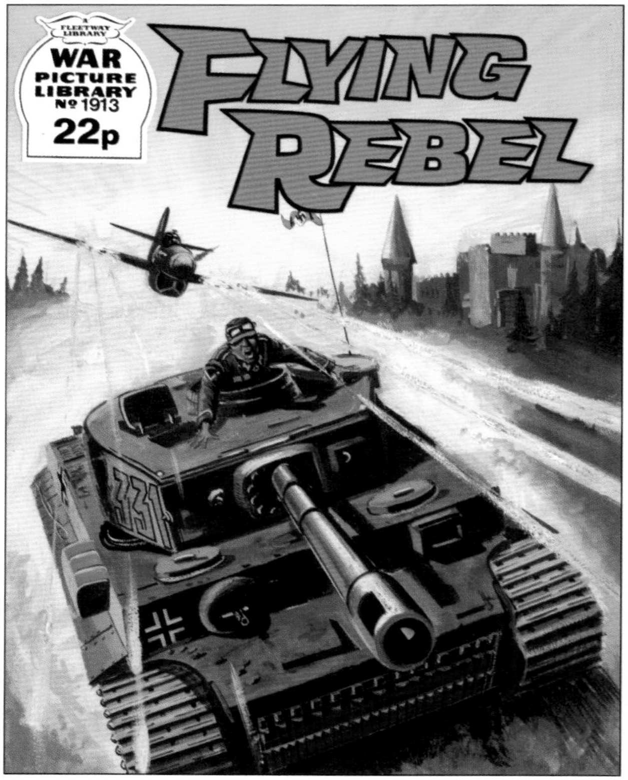
A FLEETWAY LIBRARY
WAR PICTURE LIBRARY
Nº 1913
22p
FLYING REBEL

Alan Willow, Air Ace 253, July 1965

Opposite: Alan Willow, Air Ace 295, June 1966

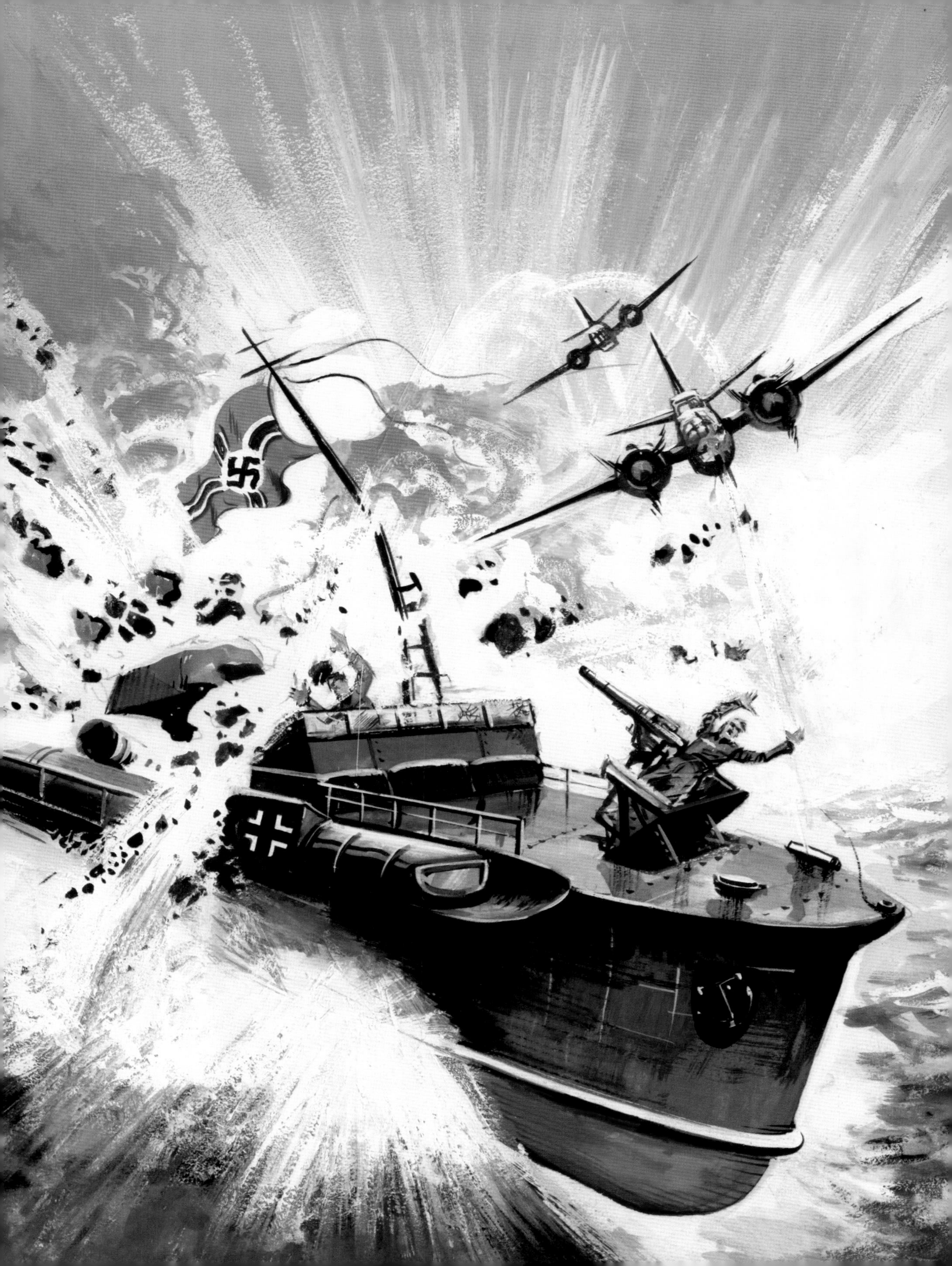

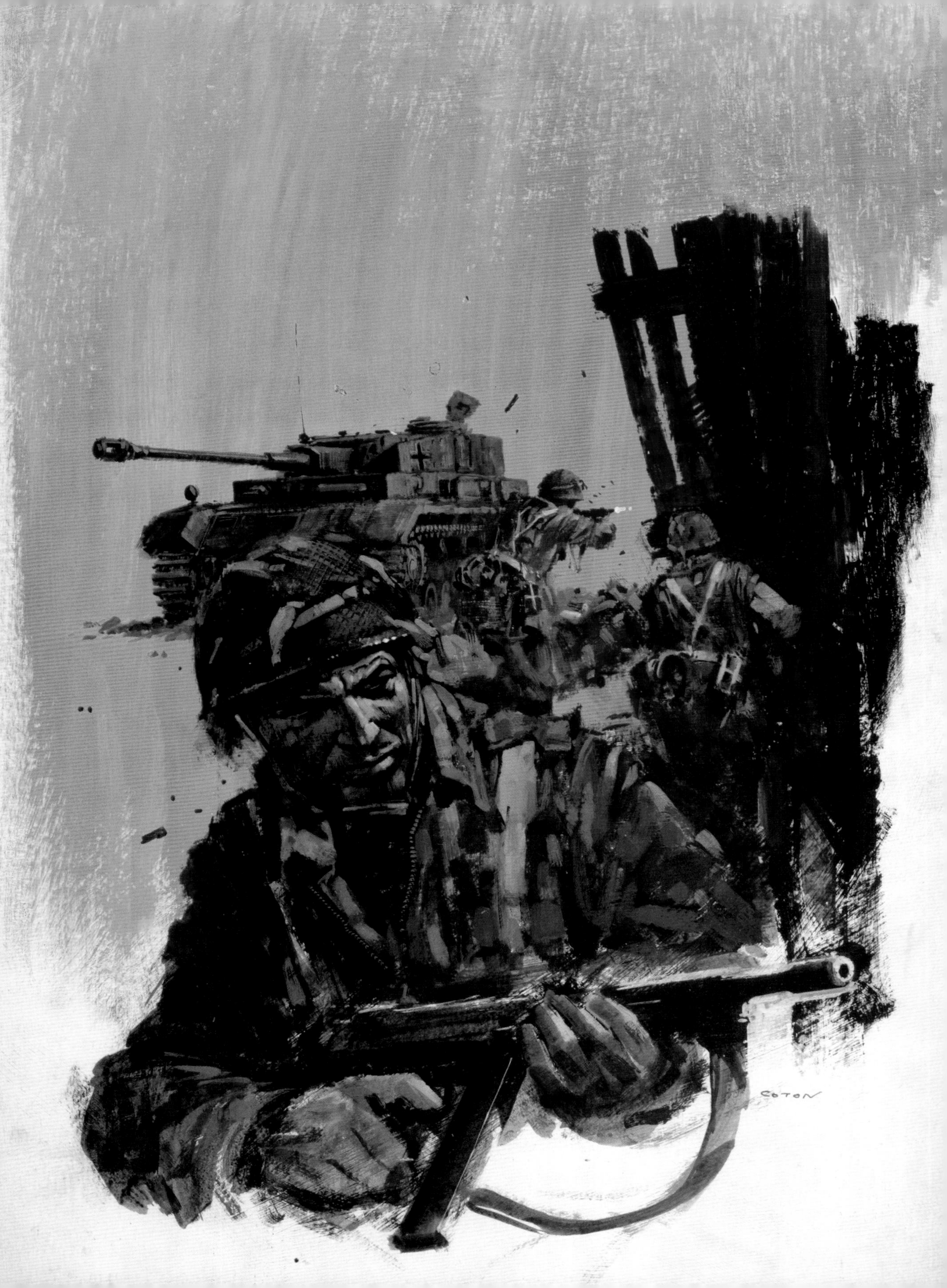
COTON

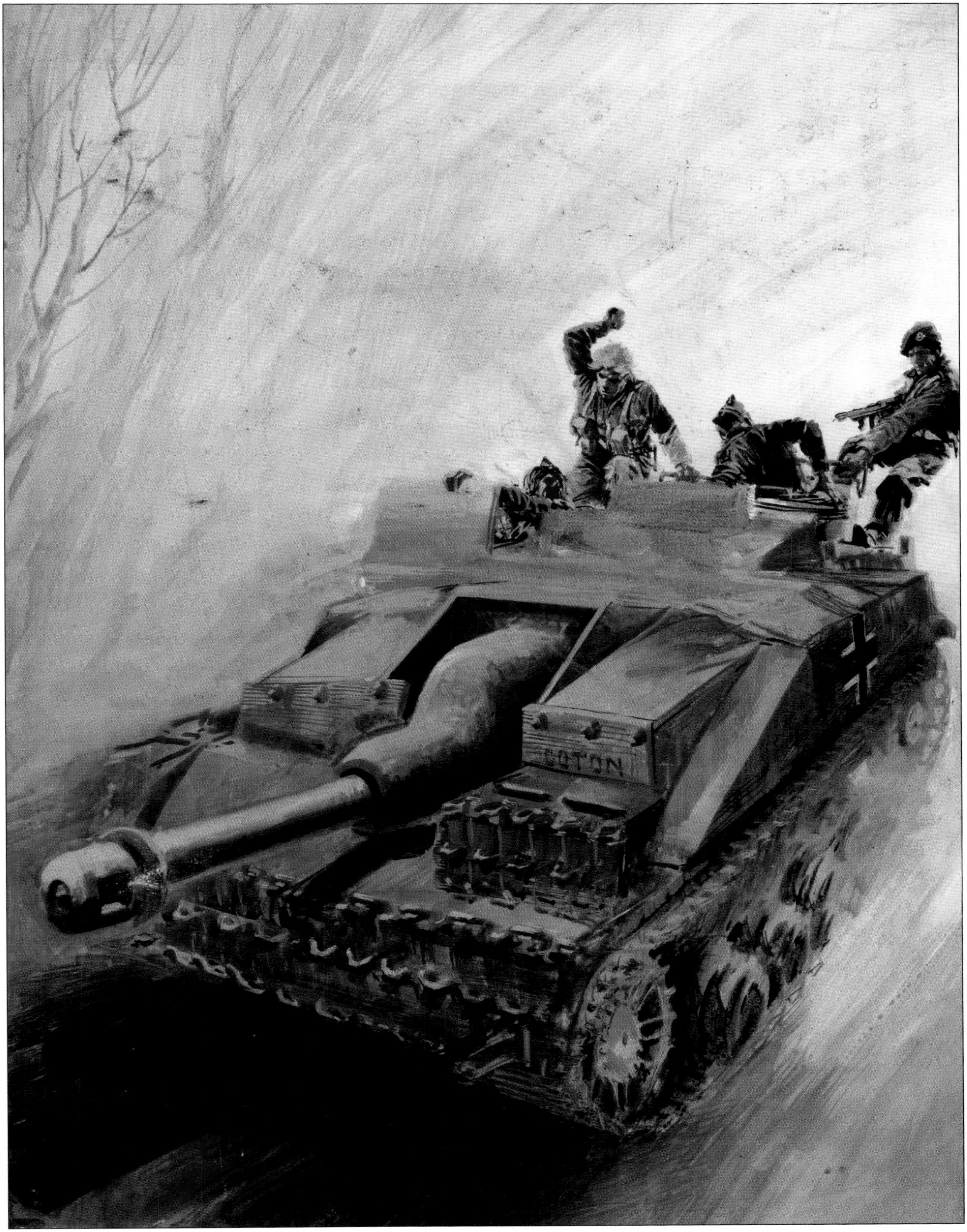
COTON

Graham Coton, War 664, June 1971
Opposite: Graham Coton, War 801, November 1972

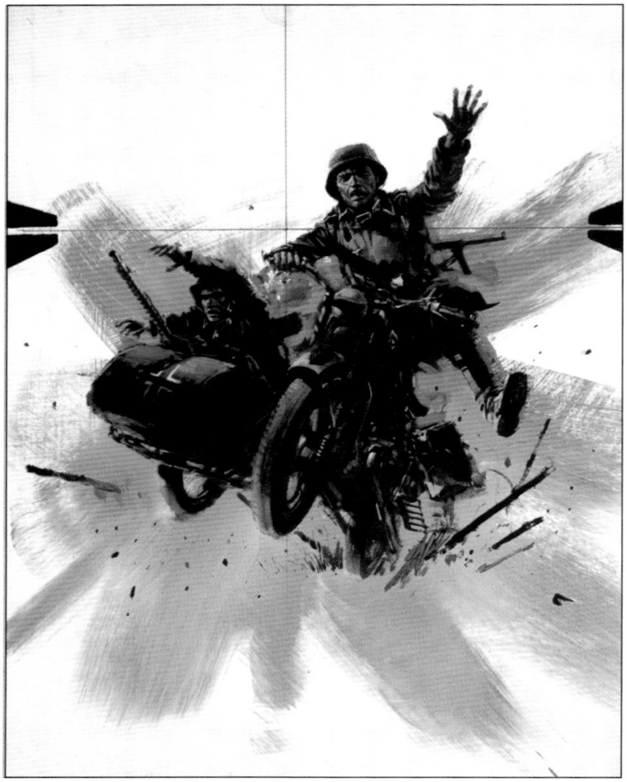

Graham Coton, War 1968, December 1982

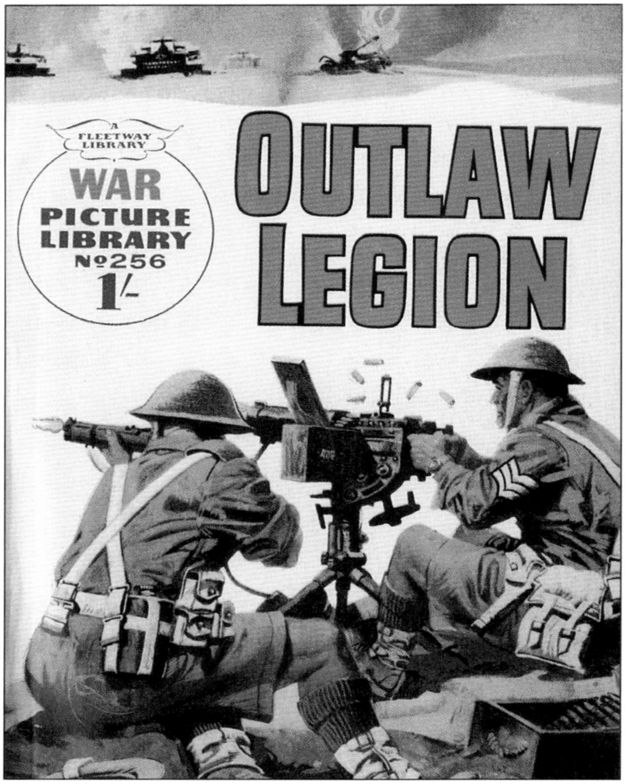
A FLEETWAY LIBRARY
WAR
PICTURE
LIBRARY
Nº256
1/-
OUTLAW
LEGION

Alessandro Biffignandi, War 256, September 1964

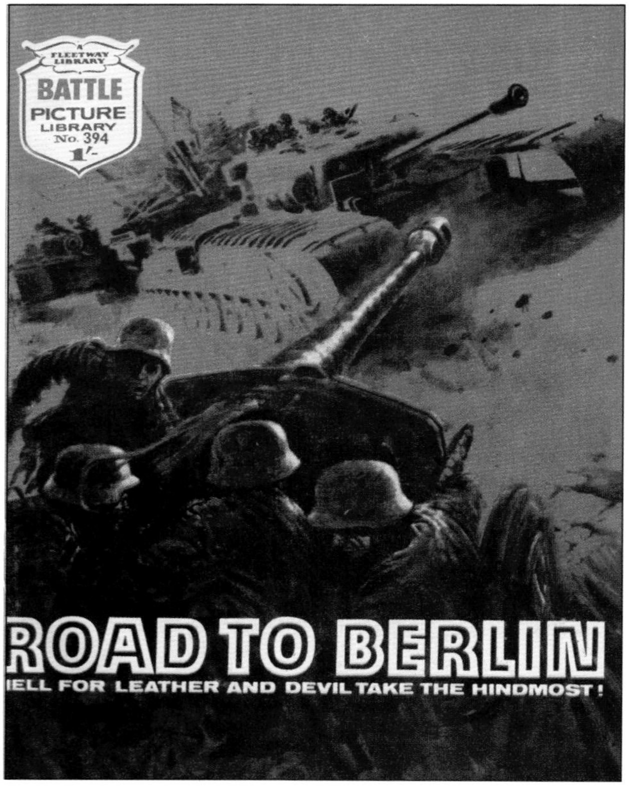
A FLEETWAY LIBRARY
BATTLE
PICTURE
LIBRARY
No. 394
1/-
ROAD TO BERLIN
IELL FOR LEATHER AND DEVIL TAKE THE HINDMOST!

Graham Coton, Battle 394, May 1969

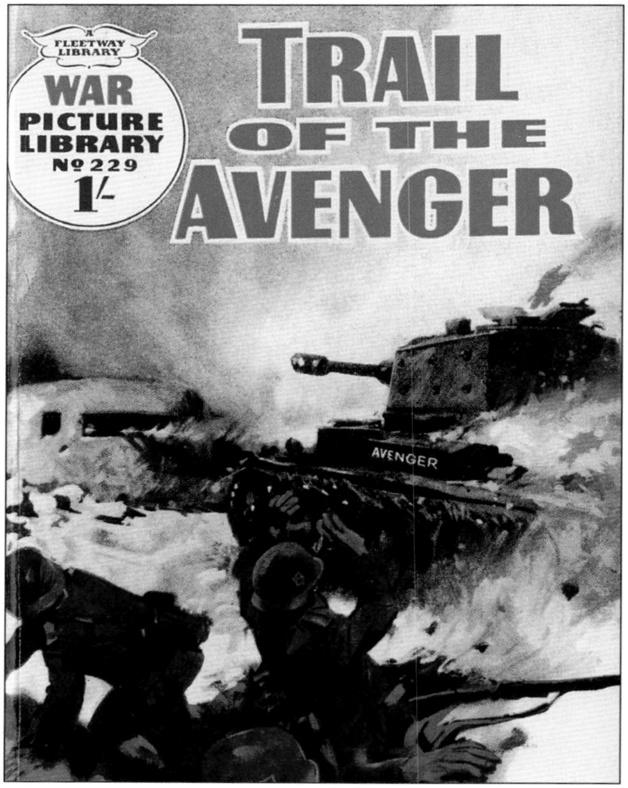
A FLEETWAY LIBRARY
WAR
PICTURE
LIBRARY
Nº229
1/-
TRAIL
OF THE
AVENGER
AVENGER

Pino Dell'Orco, War 229, February 1964

Opposite: Graham Coton, Battle 793, March 1974

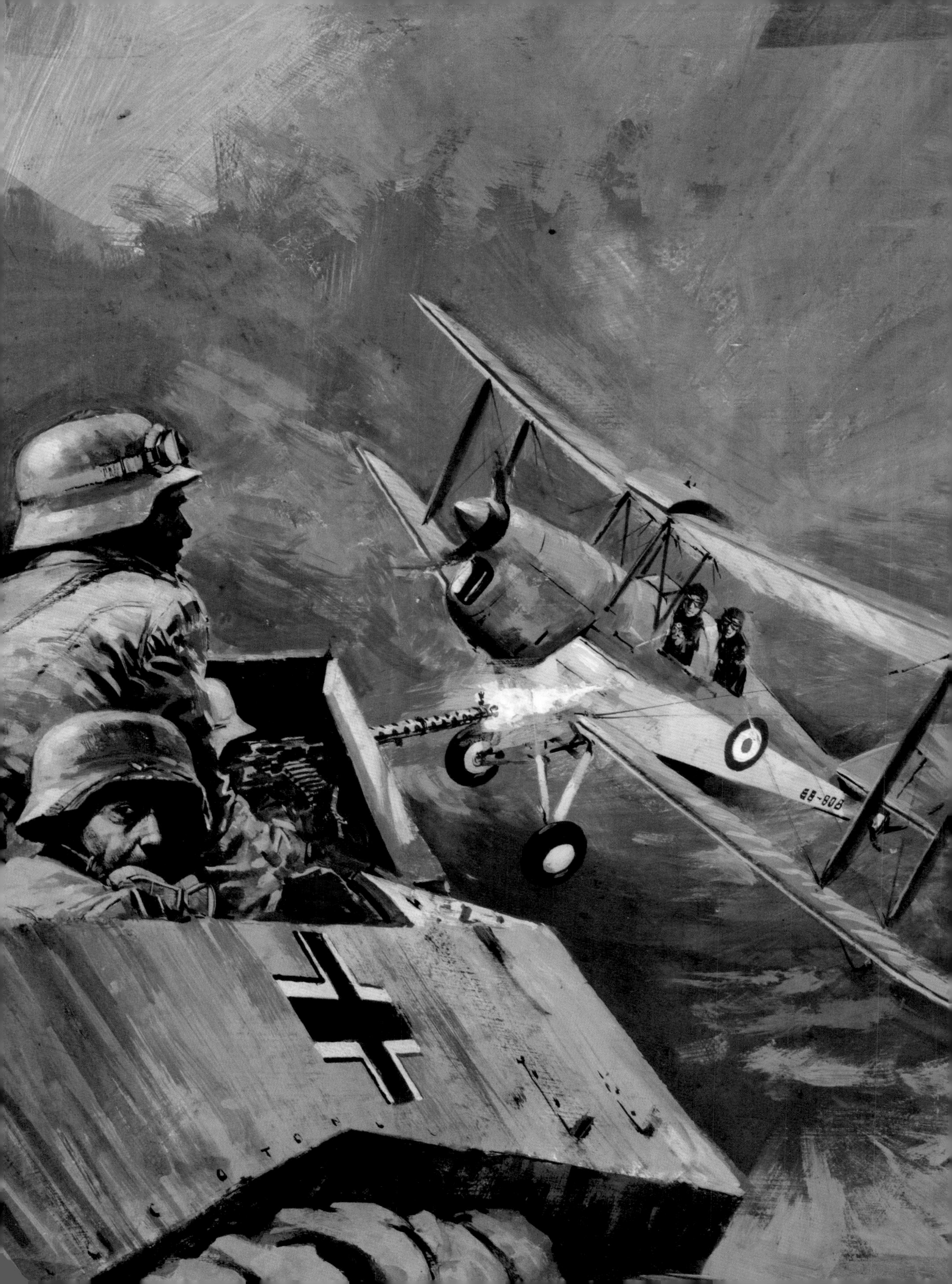

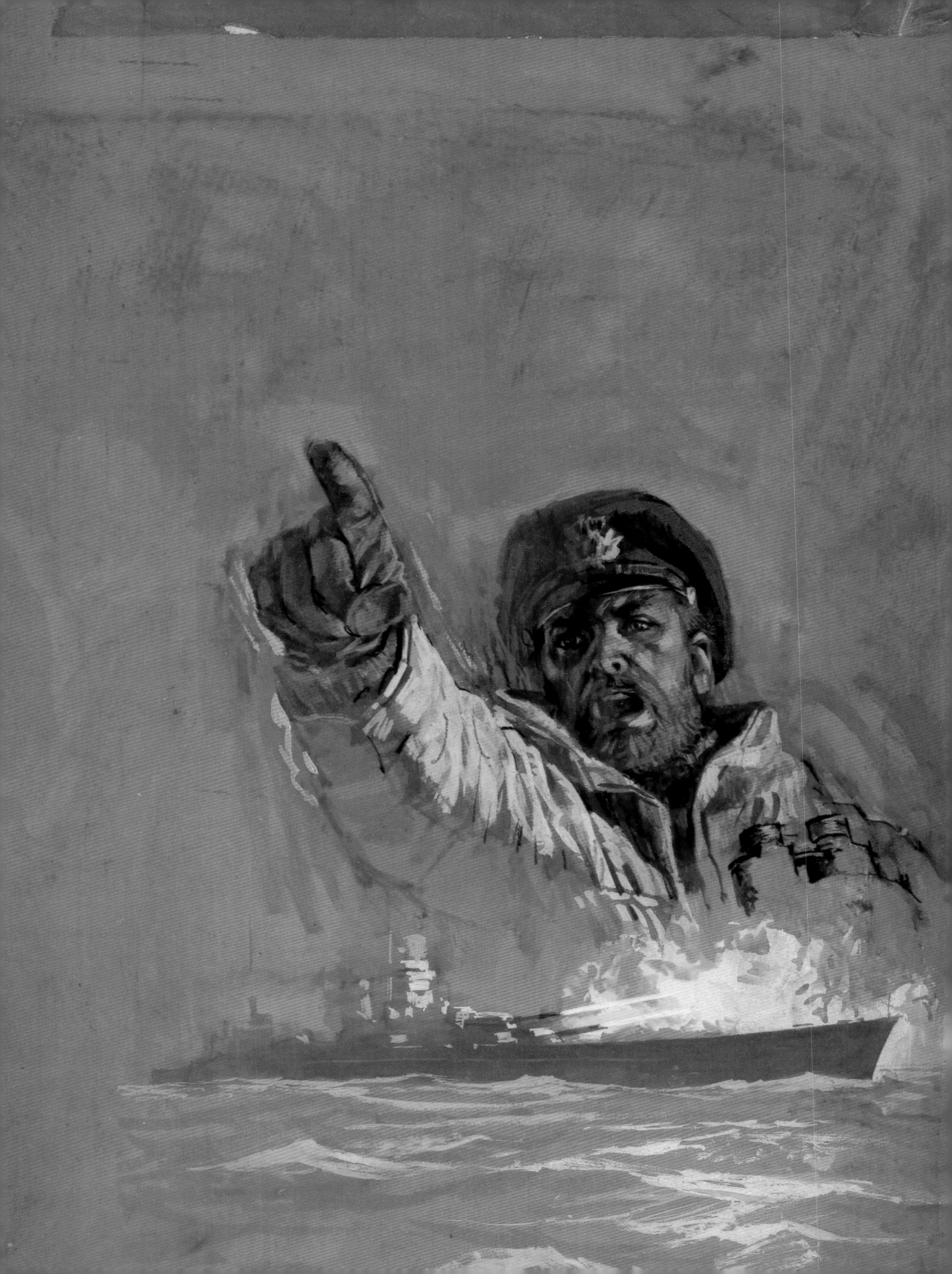

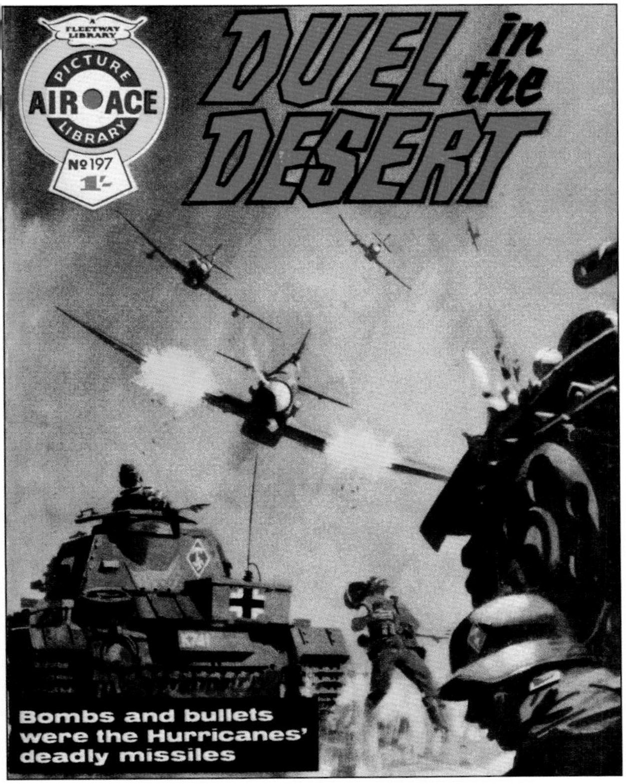
A FLEETWAY LIBRARY
PICTURE
AIR ACE
LIBRARY
№197
1/-
DUEL in the DESERT
Bombs and bullets were the Hurricanes' deadly missiles

Pino Dell'Orco, Air Ace 197, May 1964

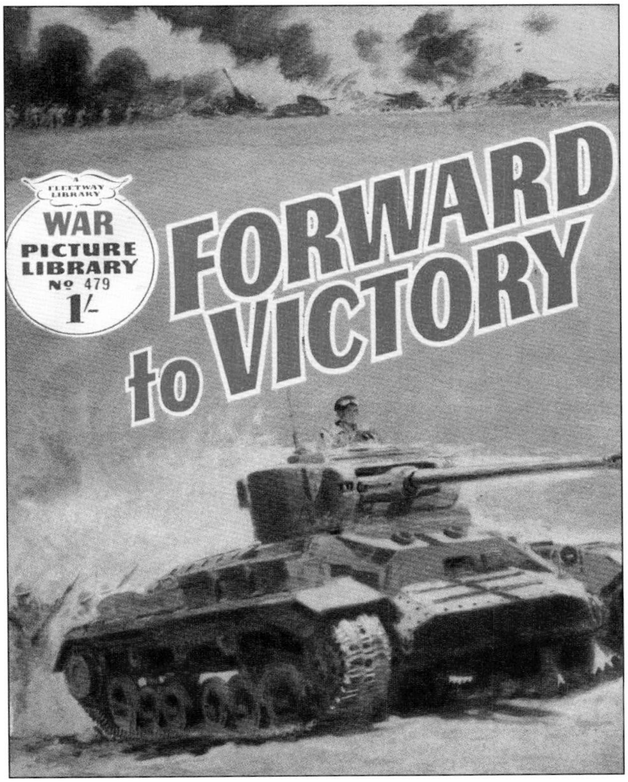
A FLEETWAY LIBRARY
WAR
PICTURE LIBRARY
№ 479
1/-
FORWARD to VICTORY

Graham Coton, War 479, November 1968

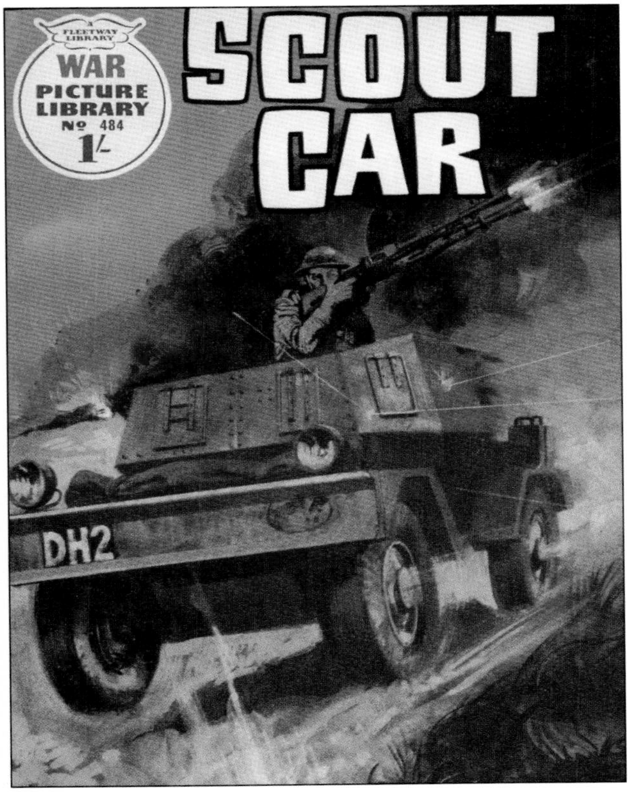
A FLEETWAY LIBRARY
WAR
PICTURE LIBRARY
№ 484
1/-
SCOUT CAR
DH2

Allessandro Biffignandi, War 484, December 1968

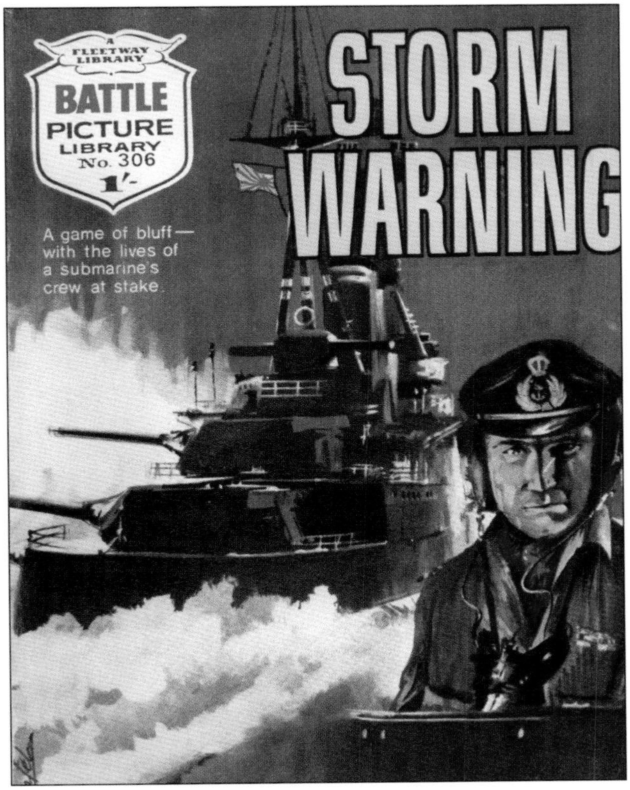
A FLEETWAY LIBRARY
BATTLE
PICTURE LIBRARY
No. 306
1/-
STORM WARNING
A game of bluff— with the lives of a submarine's crew at stake.

Ricardo SanFeliz, Battle 306, July 1967

Opposite: Graham Coton, Battle 611, Apri1972
Overleaf: Graham Coton, War 1962, November 1982

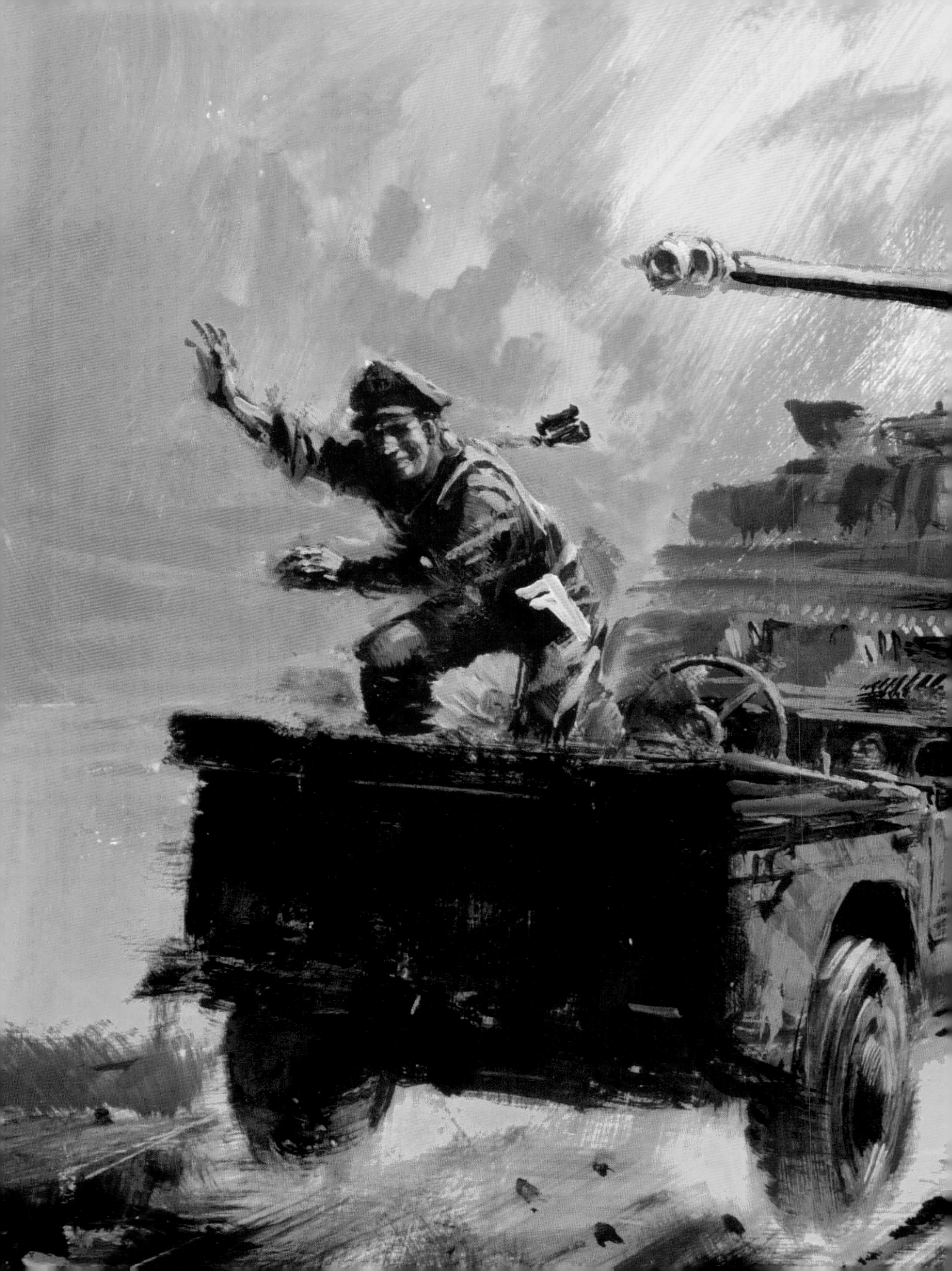

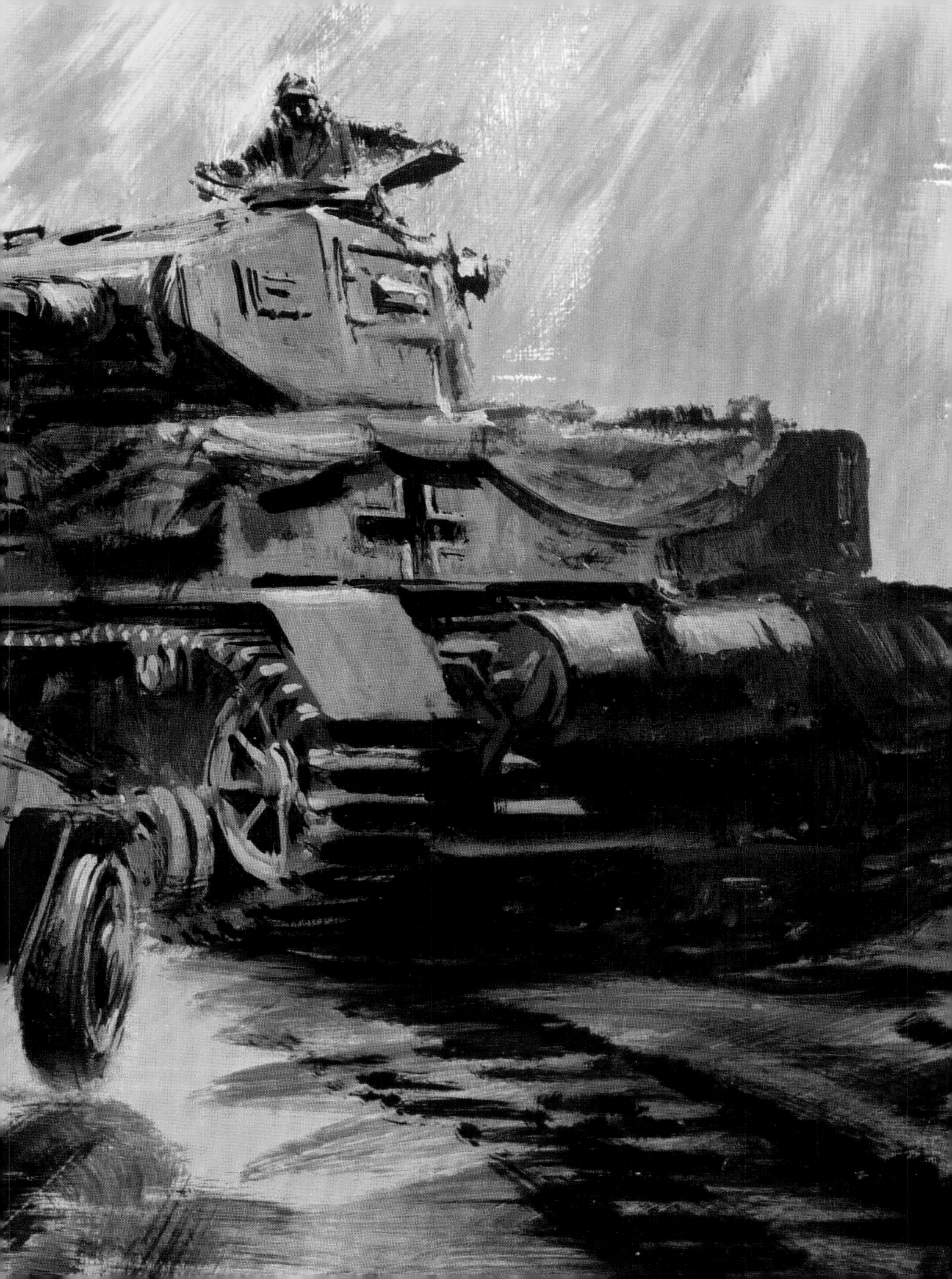

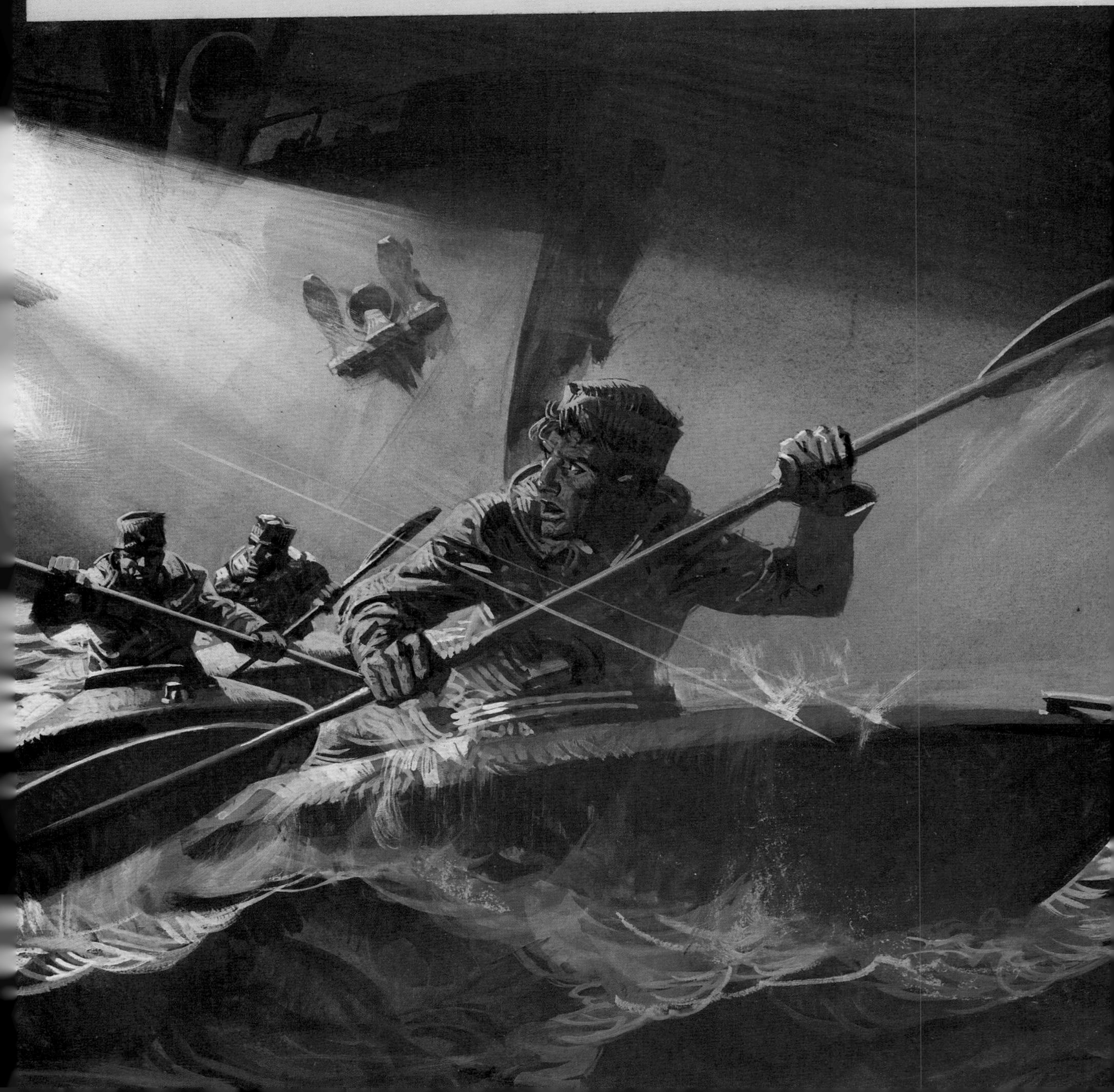

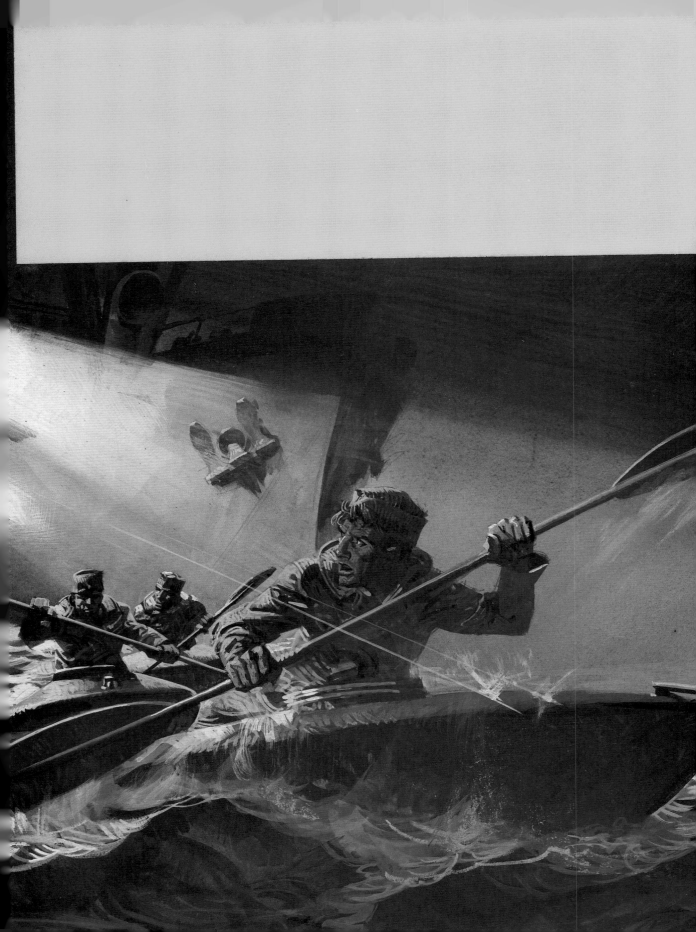

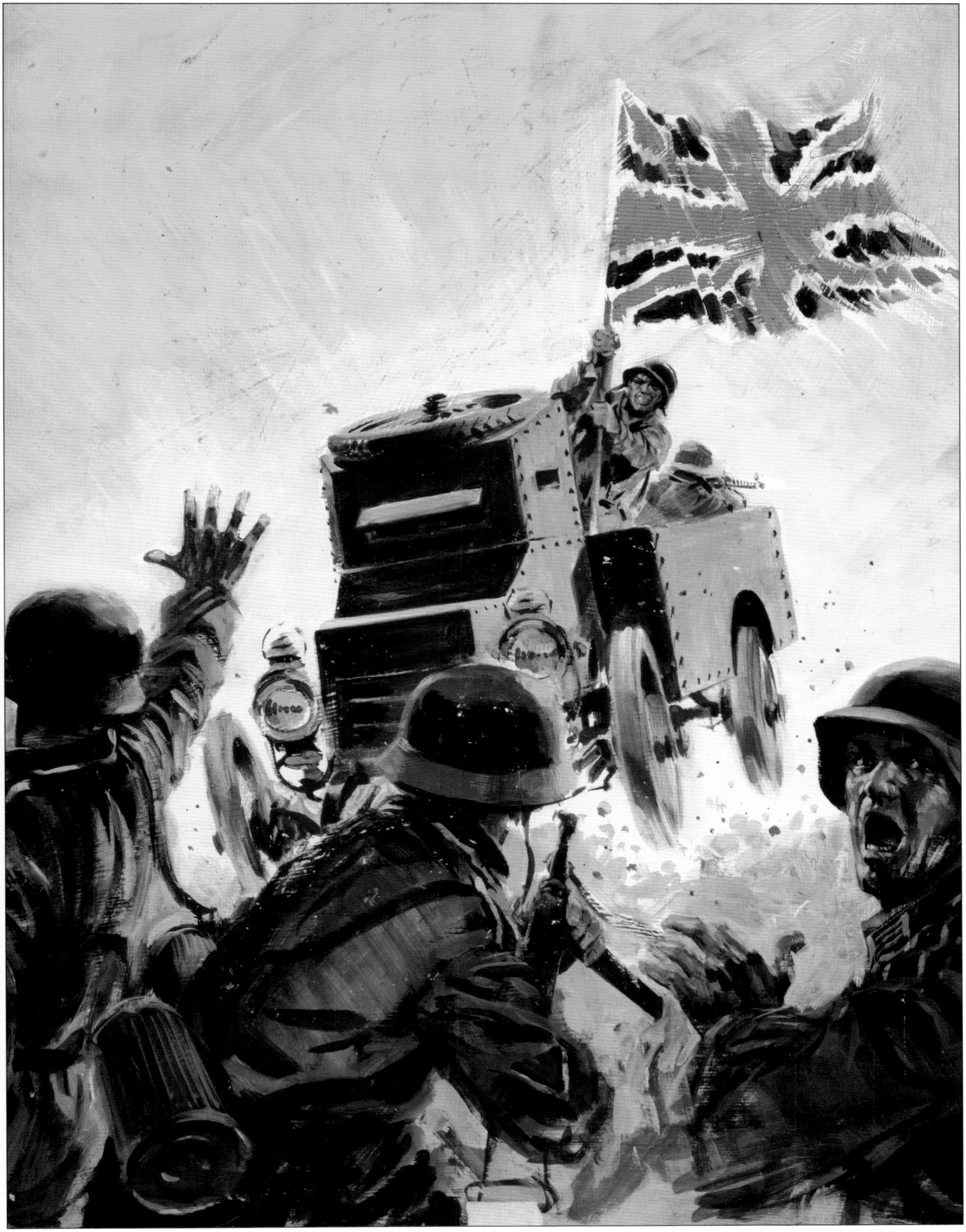

Graham Coton, Battle 1439, February 1981
Opposite: Allessandro Biffignandi, War 410, November 1967

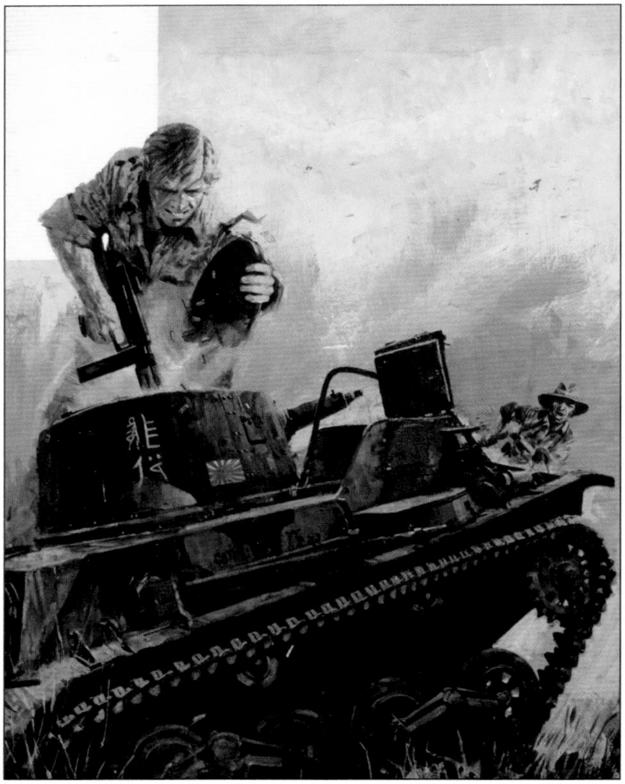

Graham Coton, War 1171, February 1976

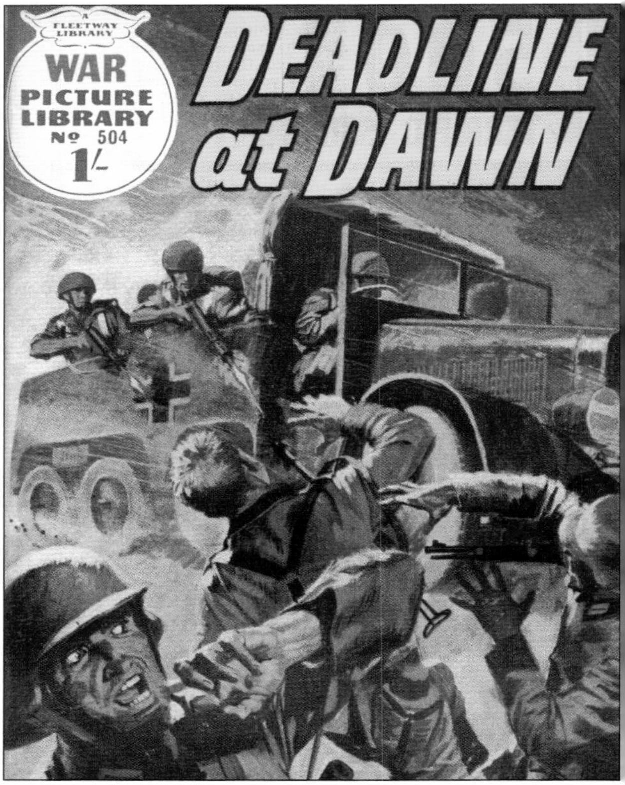
A FLEETWAY LIBRARY
WAR PICTURE LIBRARY
Nº 504
1/-
DEADLINE at DAWN

Jordi Penalva, War 504, March 1968

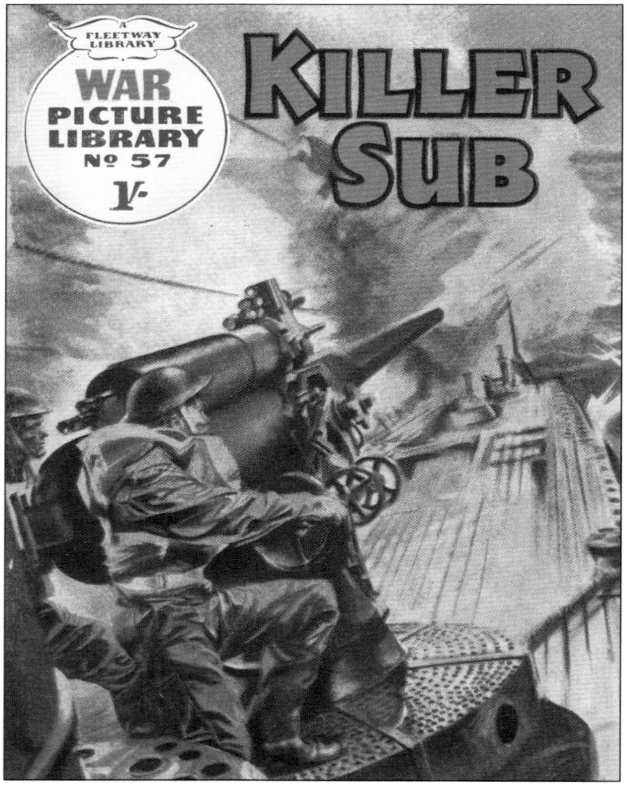
A FLEETWAY LIBRARY
WAR PICTURE LIBRARY
Nº 57
1/-
KILLER SUB

Giorgio DeGaspari, War 57, July 1960

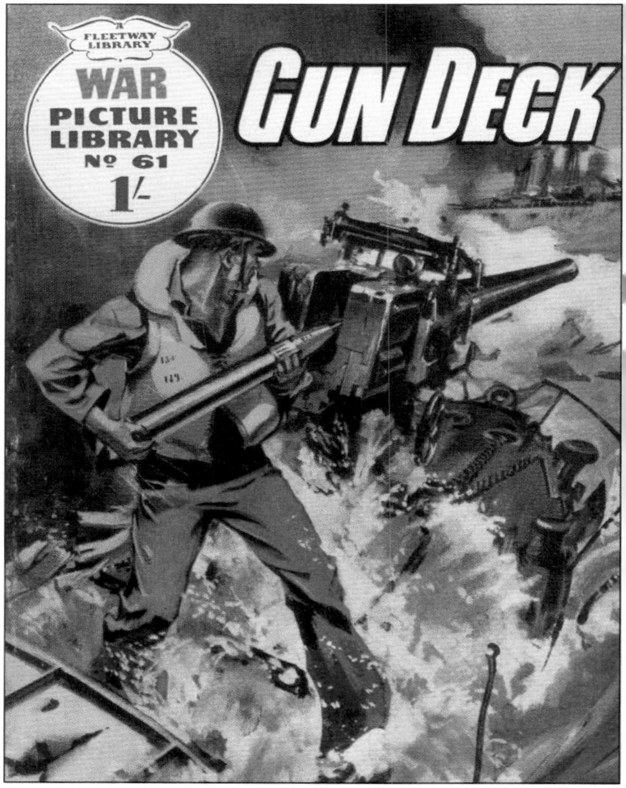
A FLEETWAY LIBRARY
WAR PICTURE LIBRARY
Nº 61
1/-
GUN DECK

Nino Caroselli, War 61, August 1960

Opposite: Graham Coton, War 1410, October 1977

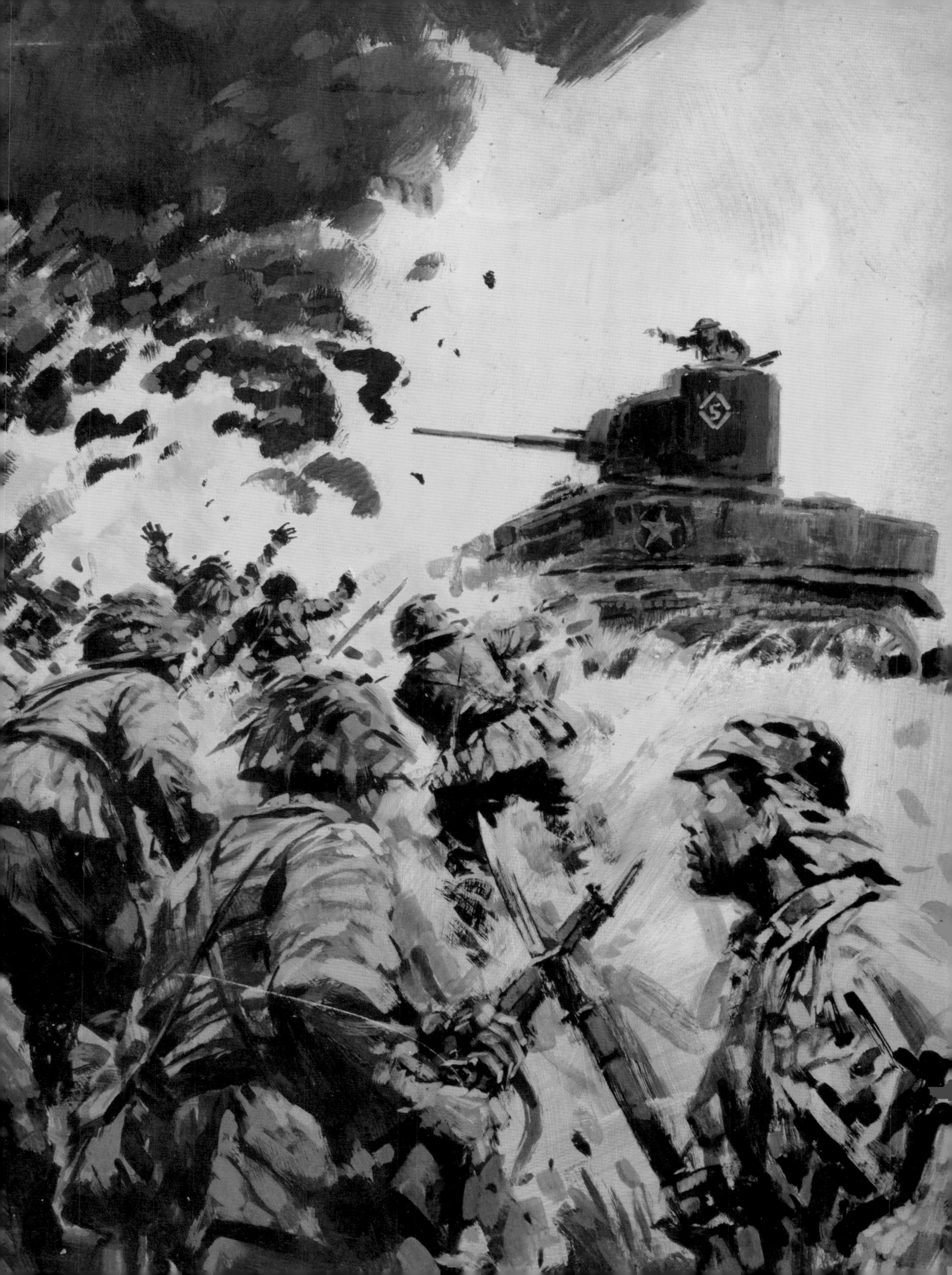

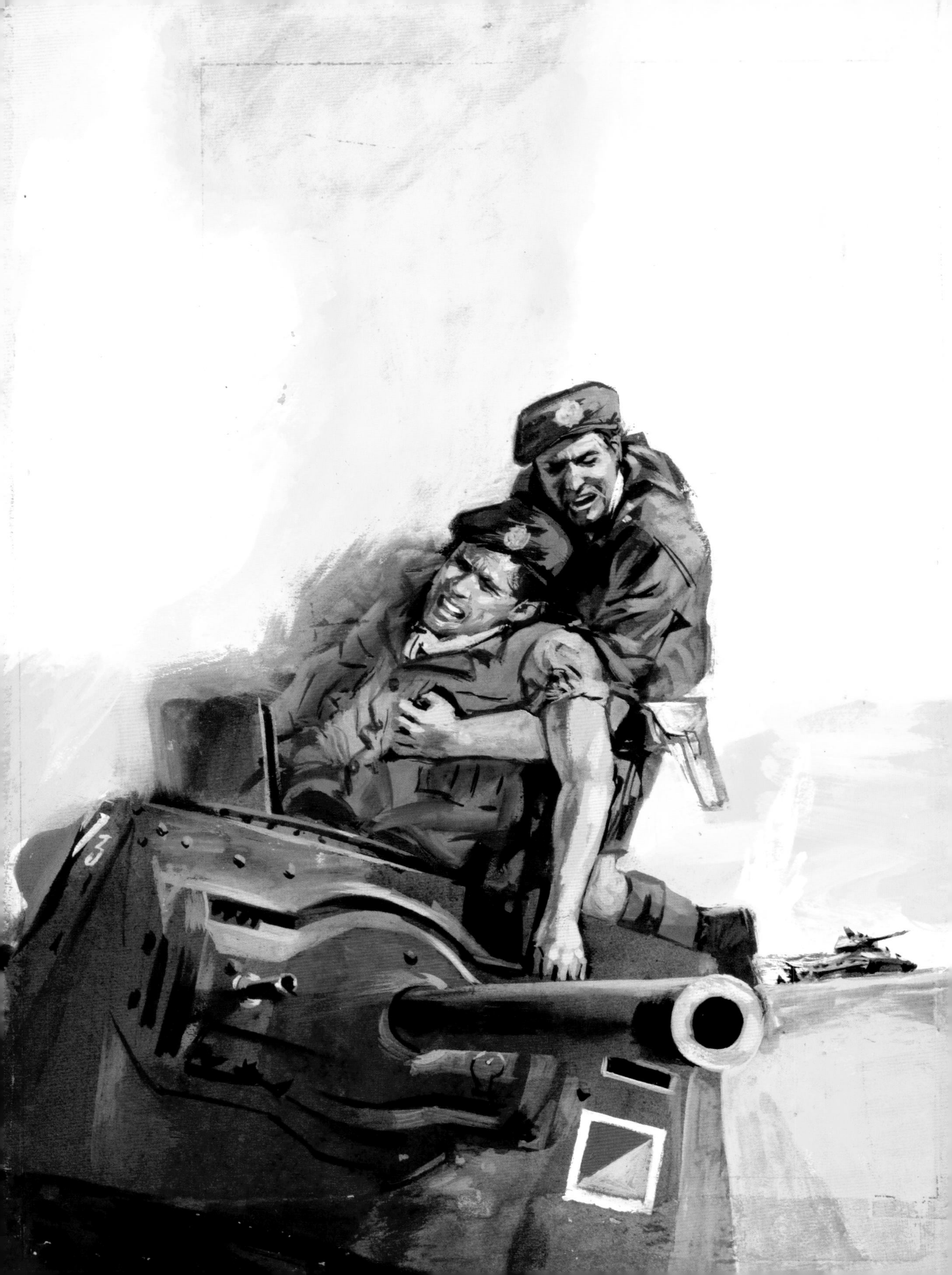
13

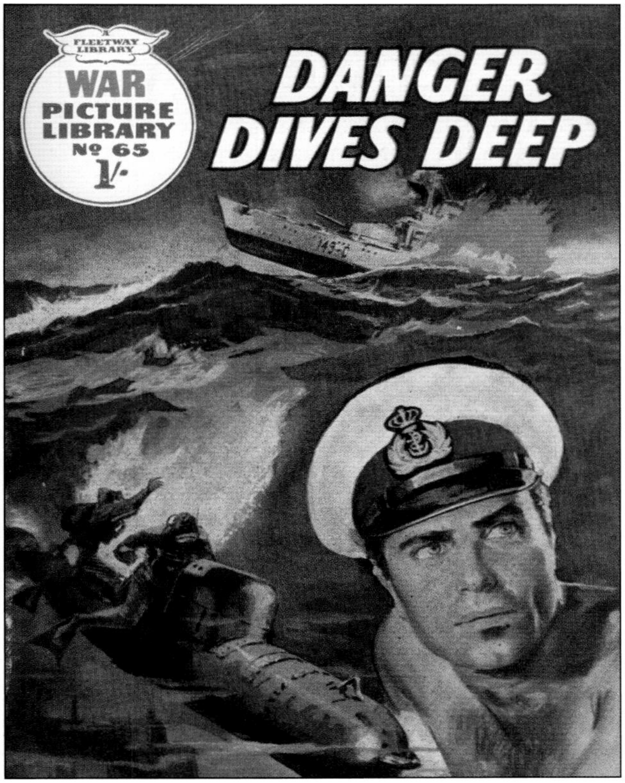
A FLEETWAY LIBRARY
WAR PICTURE LIBRARY Nº 65
1/-
DANGER DIVES DEEP

Allessandro Biffignandi, War 65, September 1960

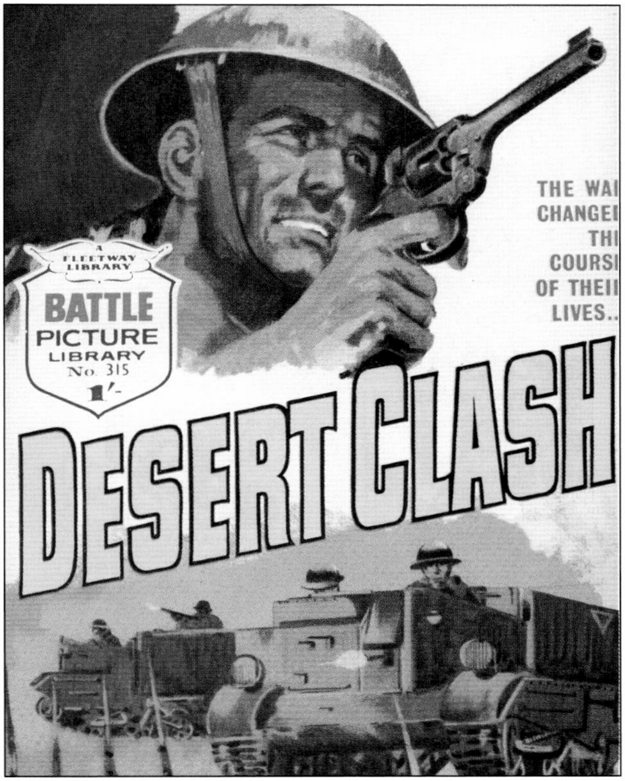
THE WA
CHANGE
TH
COURS
OF THEI
LIVES..
A FLEETWAY LIBRARY
BATTLE PICTURE LIBRARY No. 315
1/-
DESERT CLASH

Carlo Jacono, Battle 315, September 1967

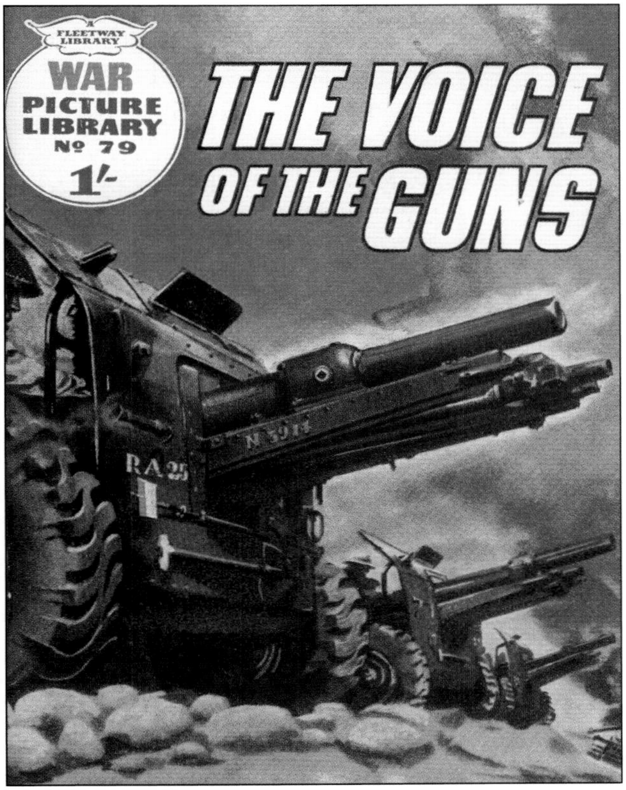
A FLEETWAY LIBRARY
WAR PICTURE LIBRARY Nº 79
1/-
THE VOICE OF THE GUNS
RA 25

Allessandro Biffignandi, War 79, December 1960

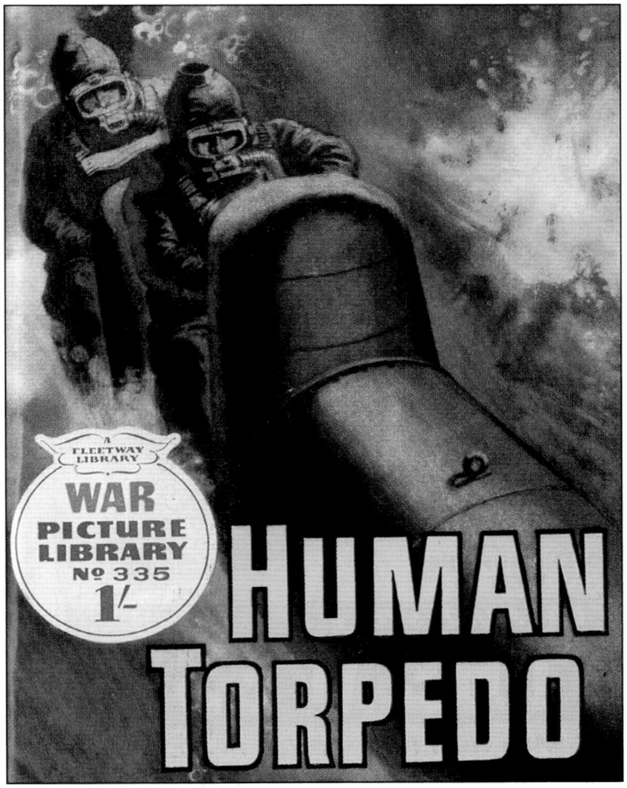
A FLEETWAY LIBRARY
WAR PICTURE LIBRARY Nº 335
1/-
HUMAN TORPEDO

Allessandro Biffignandi, War 335, April 1966

Opposite: Pino Dell'Orco, Battle 40, December 1961
Overleaf: Graham Coton, War 673, July 1971

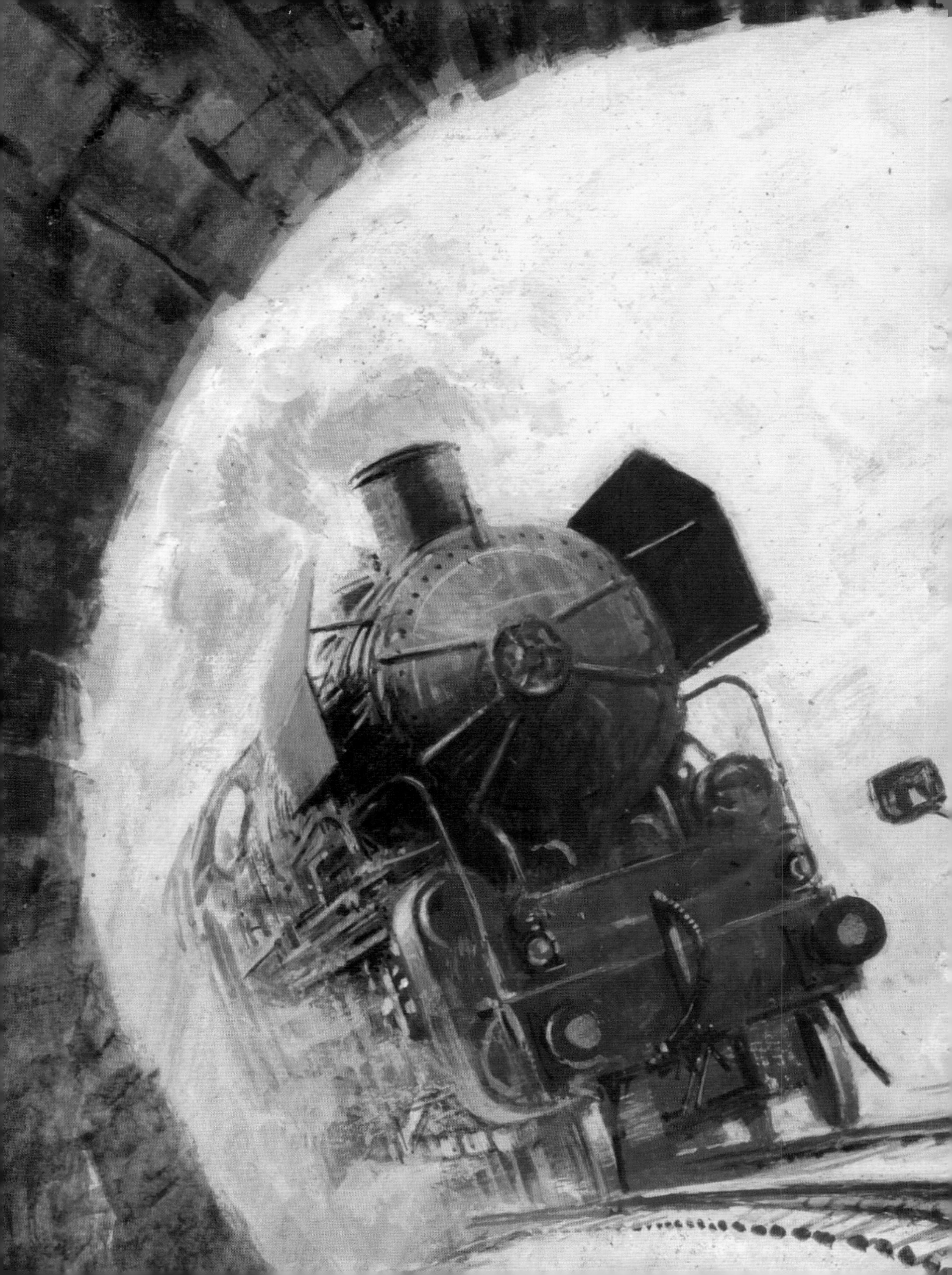

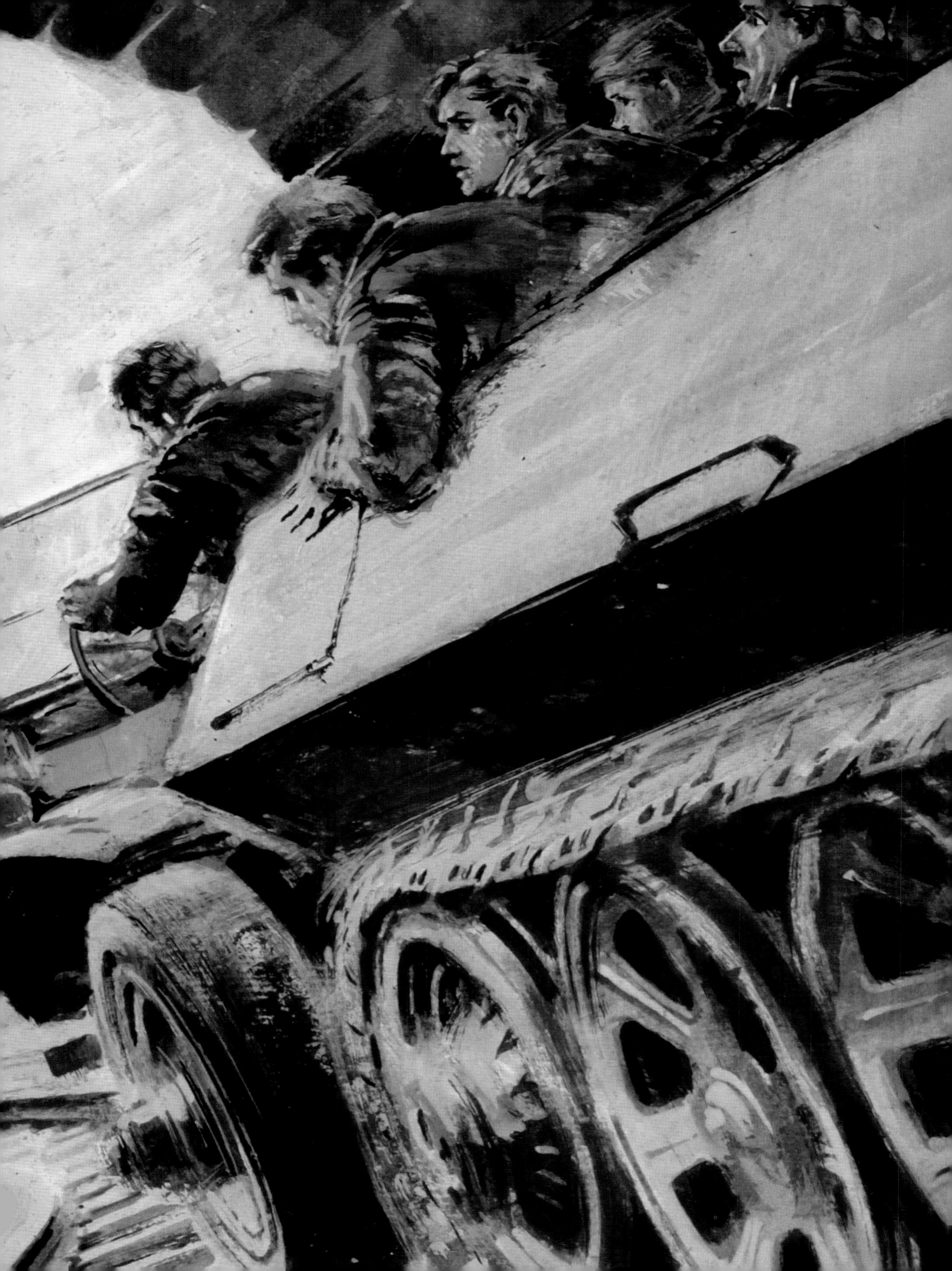

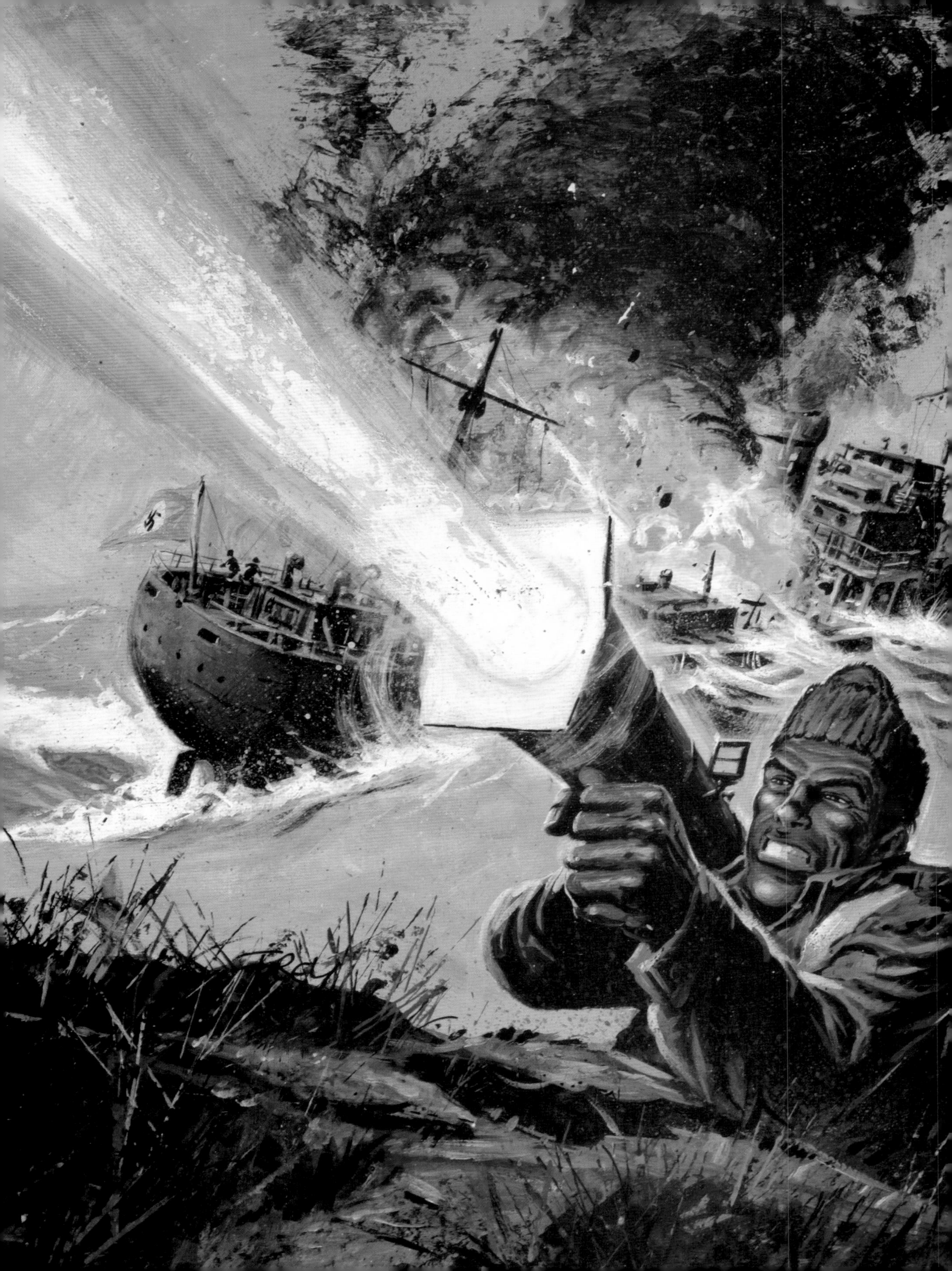

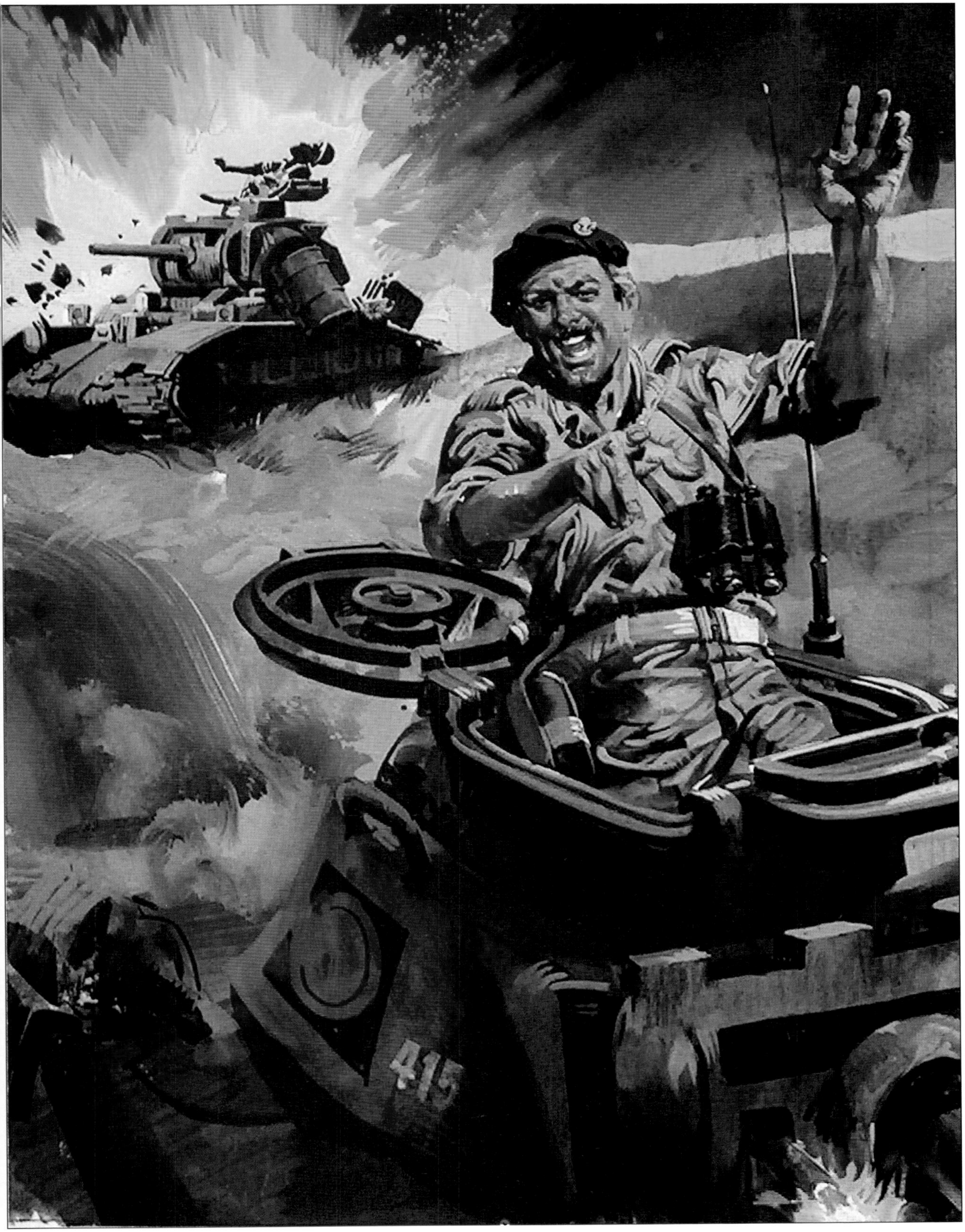
415

Allessandro Biffignandi, unknown
Opposite: Oliver Frey, War 929, March 1974

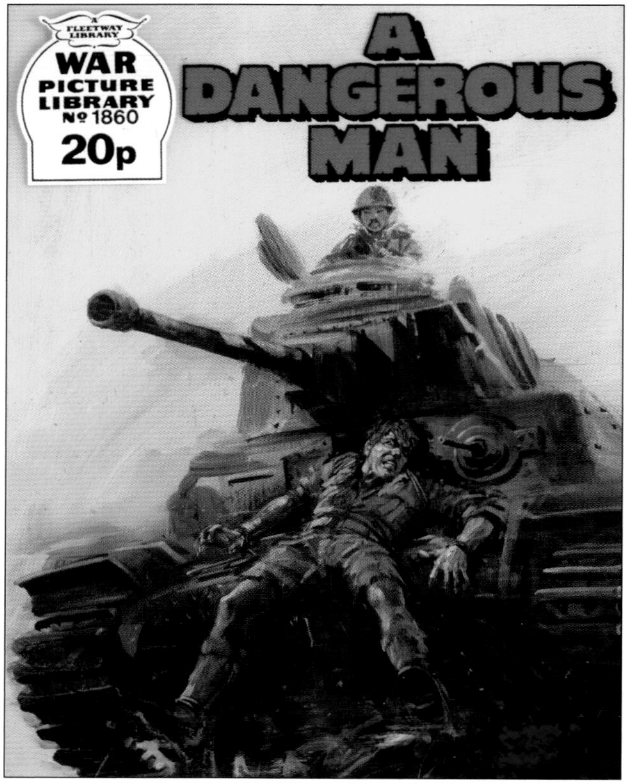
A FLEETWAY LIBRARY
WAR PICTURE LIBRARY
Nº 1860
20p
A DANGEROUS MAN

Graham Coton, War 1860, June 1981

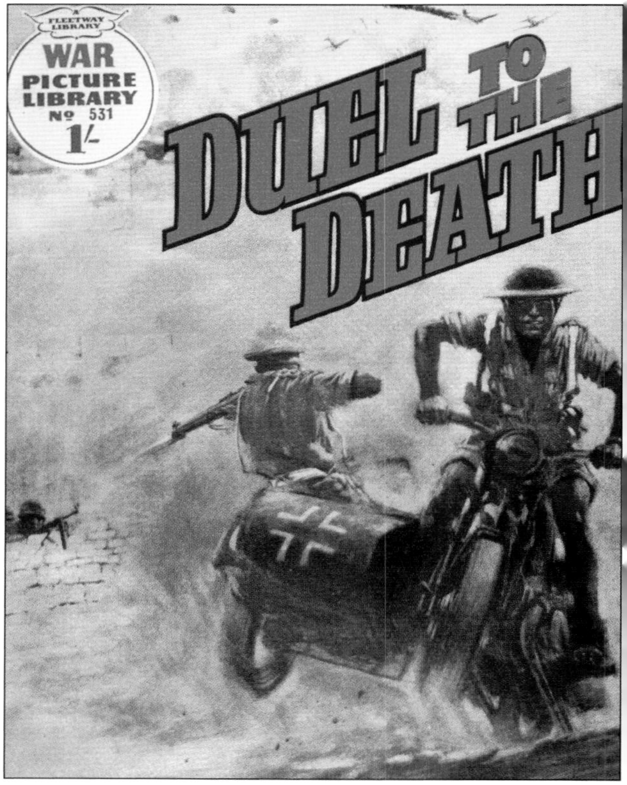
A FLEETWAY LIBRARY
WAR PICTURE LIBRARY
Nº 531
1/-
DUEL TO THE DEATH

Graham Coton, War 531, August 1969

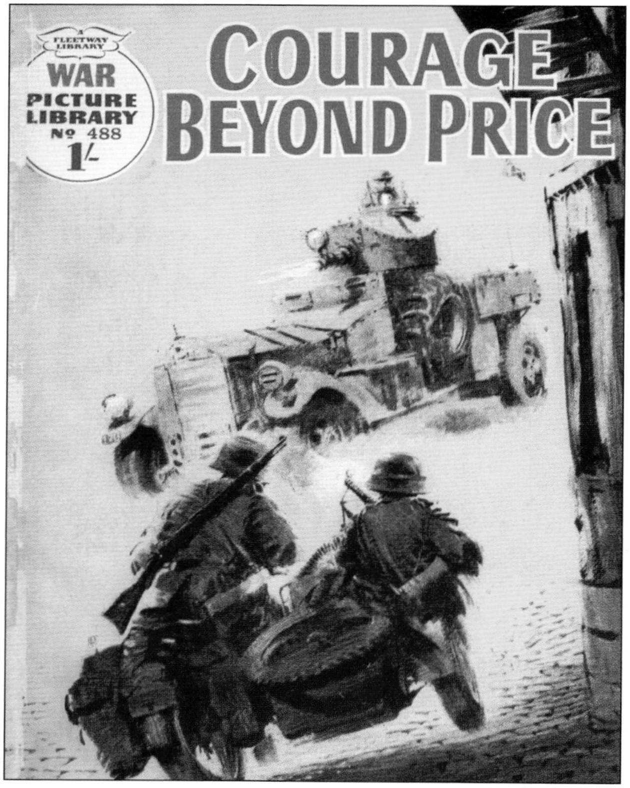
A FLEETWAY LIBRARY
WAR PICTURE LIBRARY
Nº 488
1/-
COURAGE BEYOND PRICE

Graham Coton, War 488, January 1969

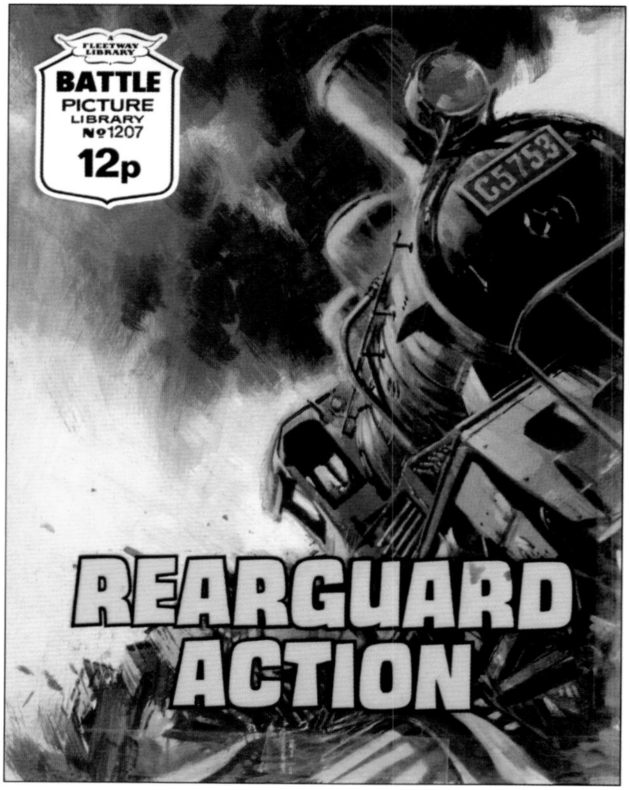
A FLEETWAY LIBRARY
BATTLE PICTURE LIBRARY
Nº1207
12p
C5753
REARGUARD ACTION

Graham Coton, originally War 621, November 1970

Opposite: Graham Coton, War 1411, October 1977

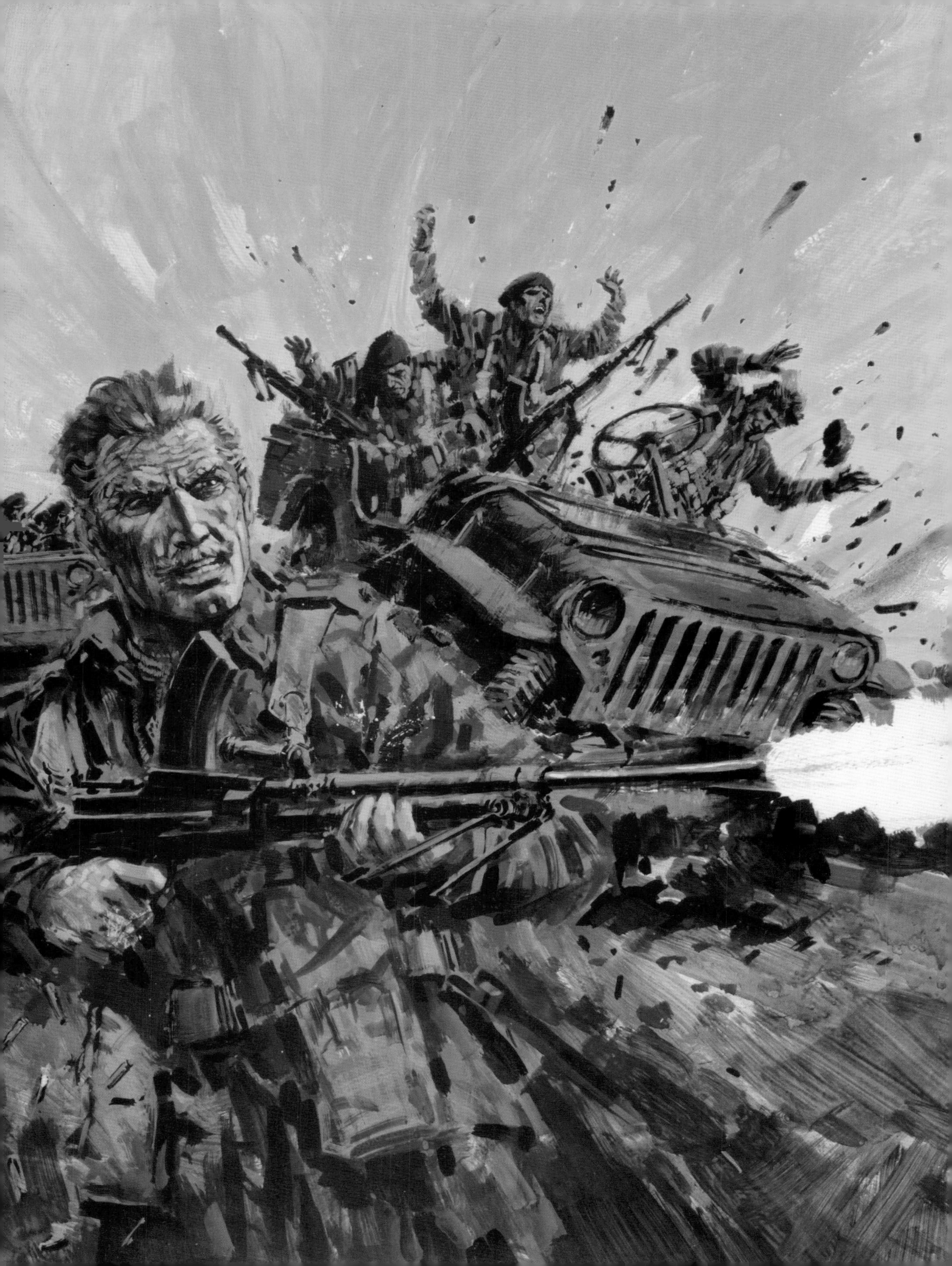

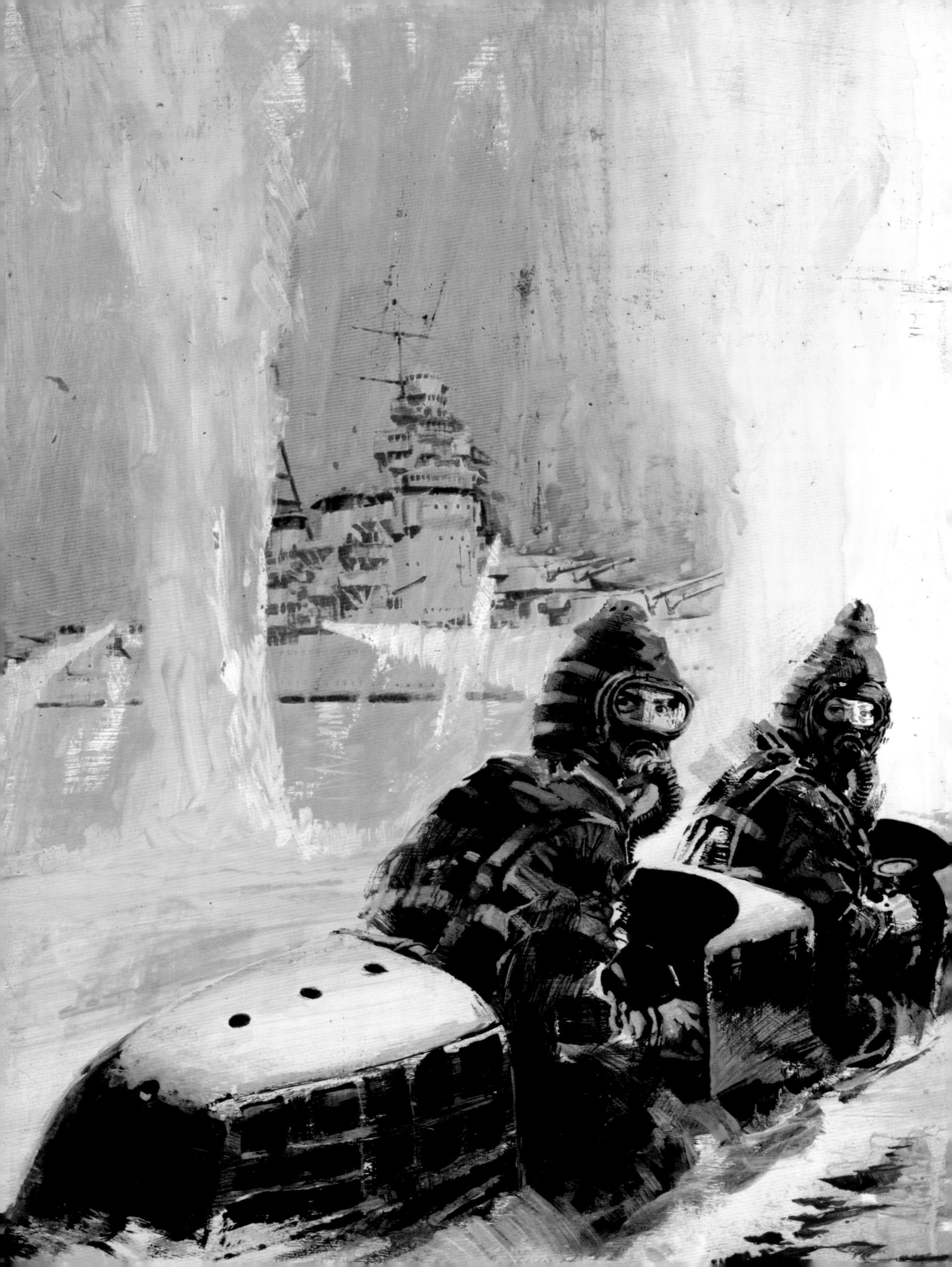

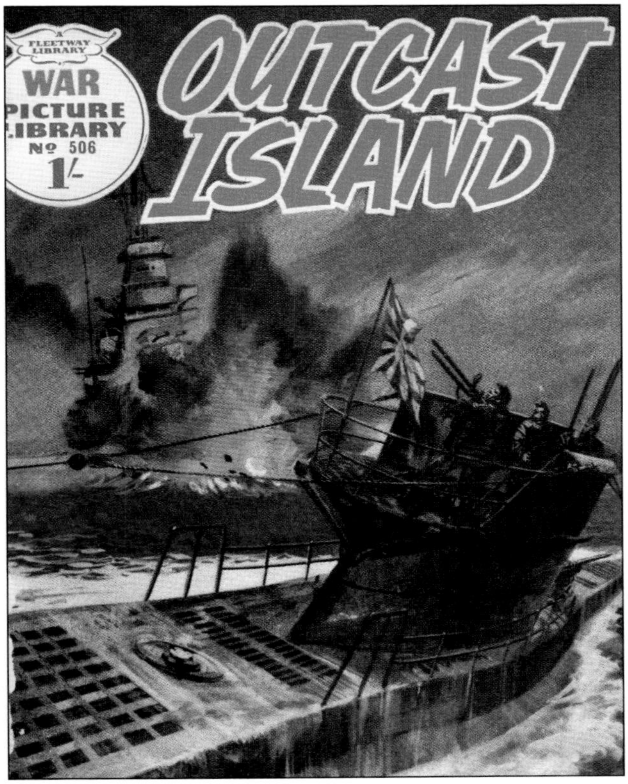
A FLEETWAY LIBRARY
WAR
PICTURE
LIBRARY
Nº 506
1/-
OUTCAST
ISLAND

Allessandro Biffignandi, War 506, April 1969

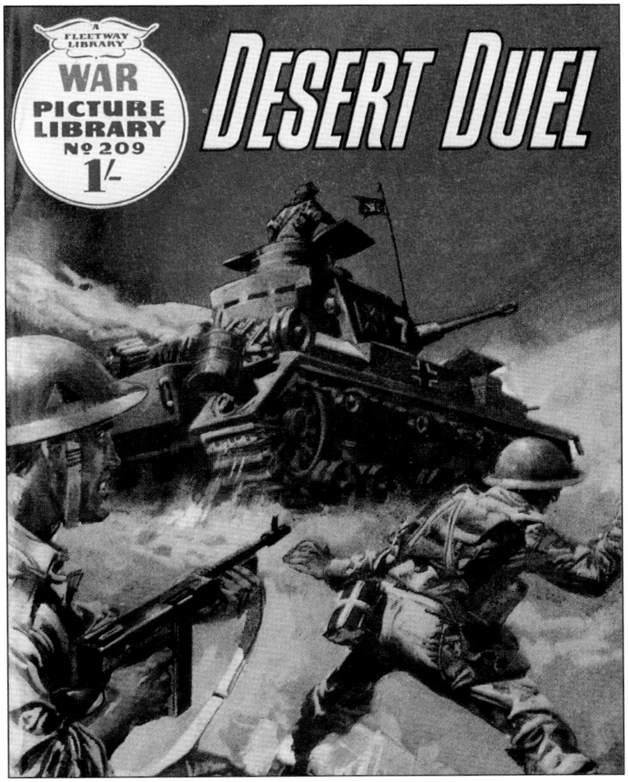
A FLEETWAY LIBRARY
WAR
PICTURE
LIBRARY
Nº 209
1/-
DESERT DUEL

Allessandro Biffignandi, War 209, September 1963

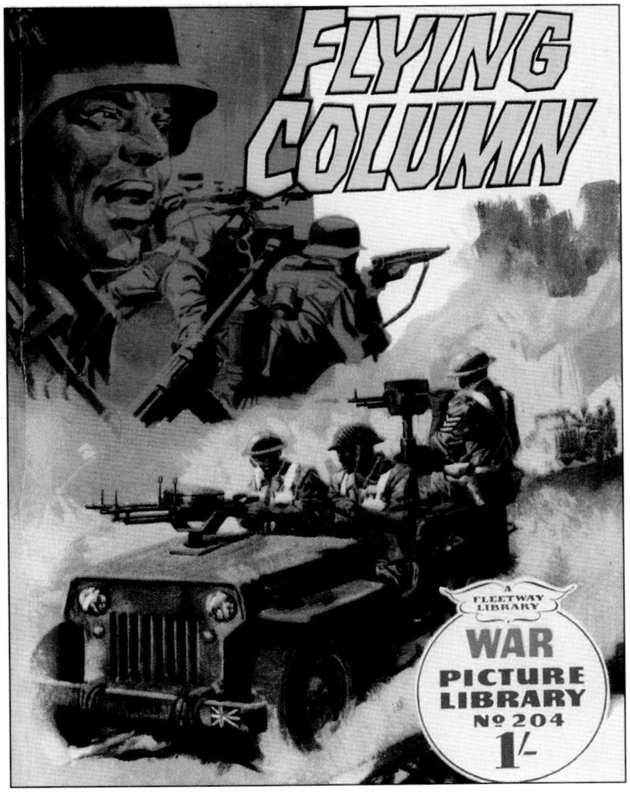
FLYING
COLUMN
A FLEETWAY LIBRARY
WAR
PICTURE
LIBRARY
Nº 204
1/-

Allessandro Biffignandi, War 204, August 1963

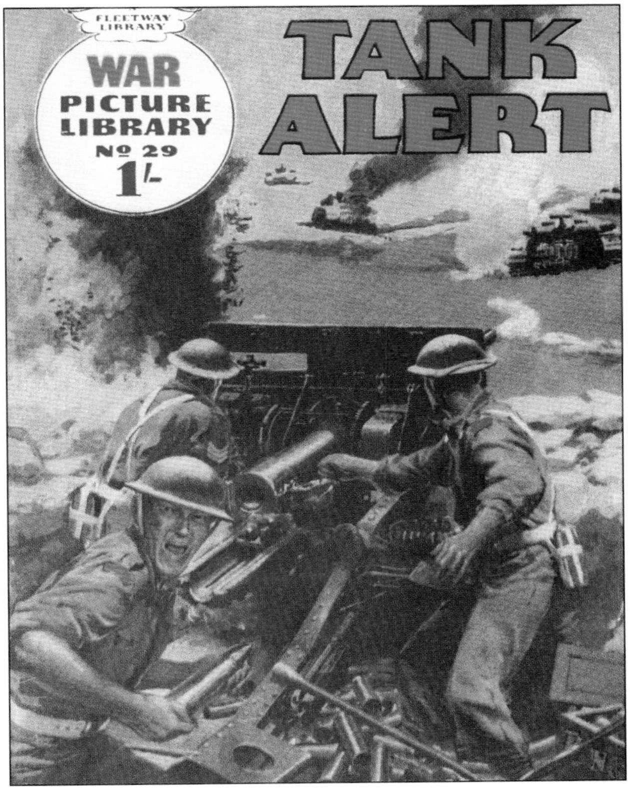
FLEETWAY LIBRARY
WAR
PICTURE
LIBRARY
Nº 29
1/-
TANK
ALERT

Nino Caroselli, War 29, November 1959

Opposite: Graham Coton, War 728, February 1972
Overleaf: Graham Coton, War 656, May 1971

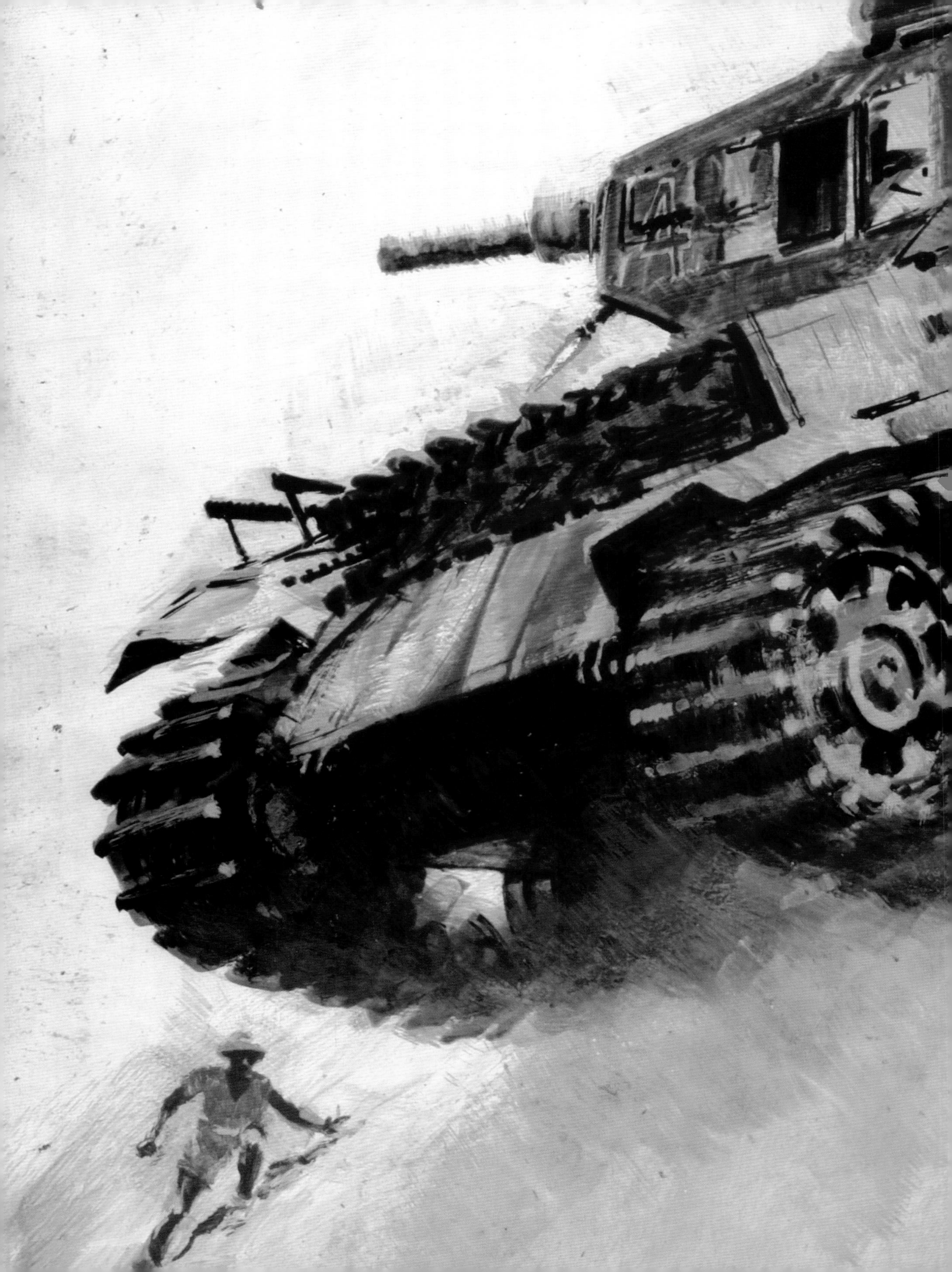

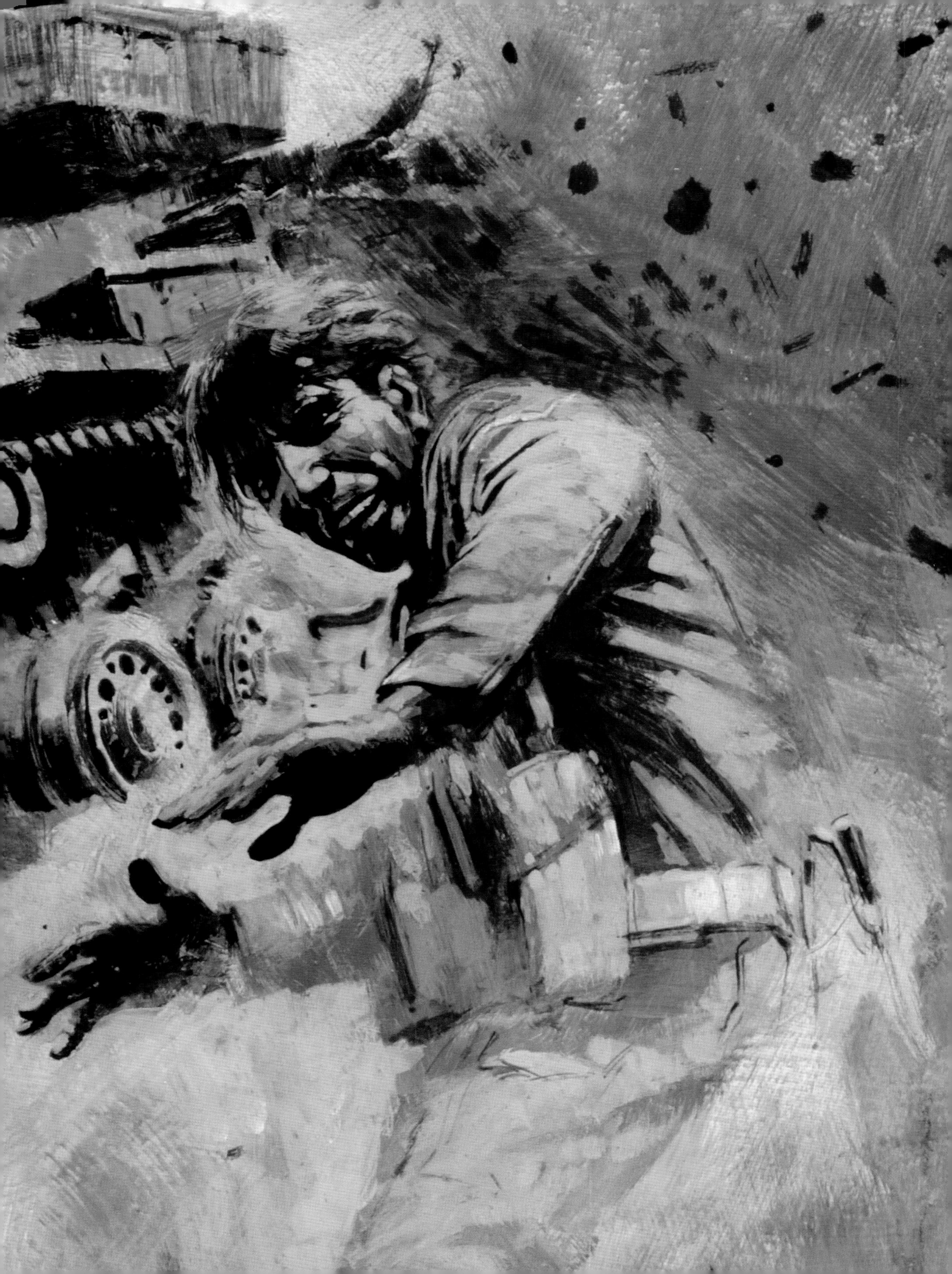

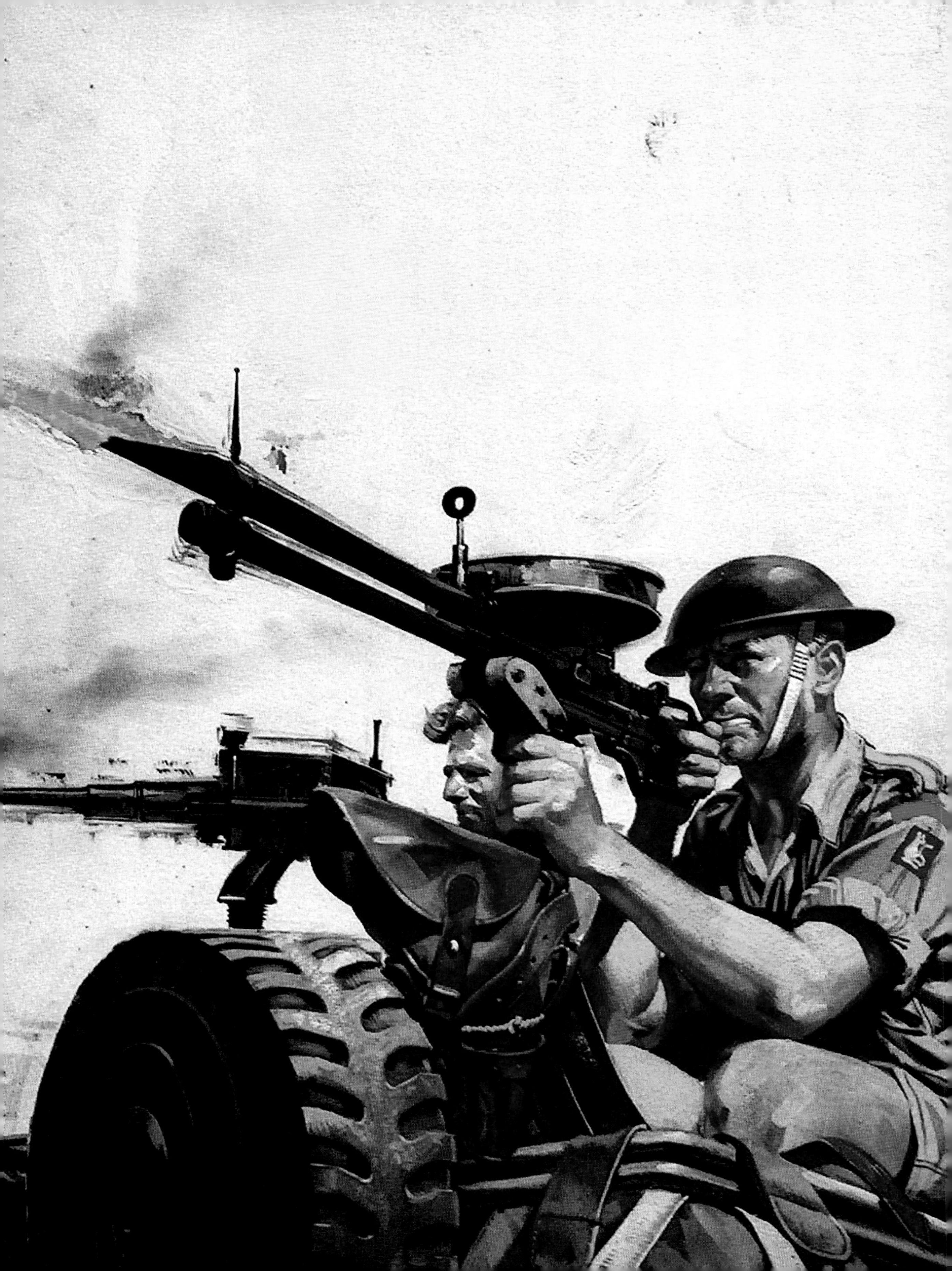

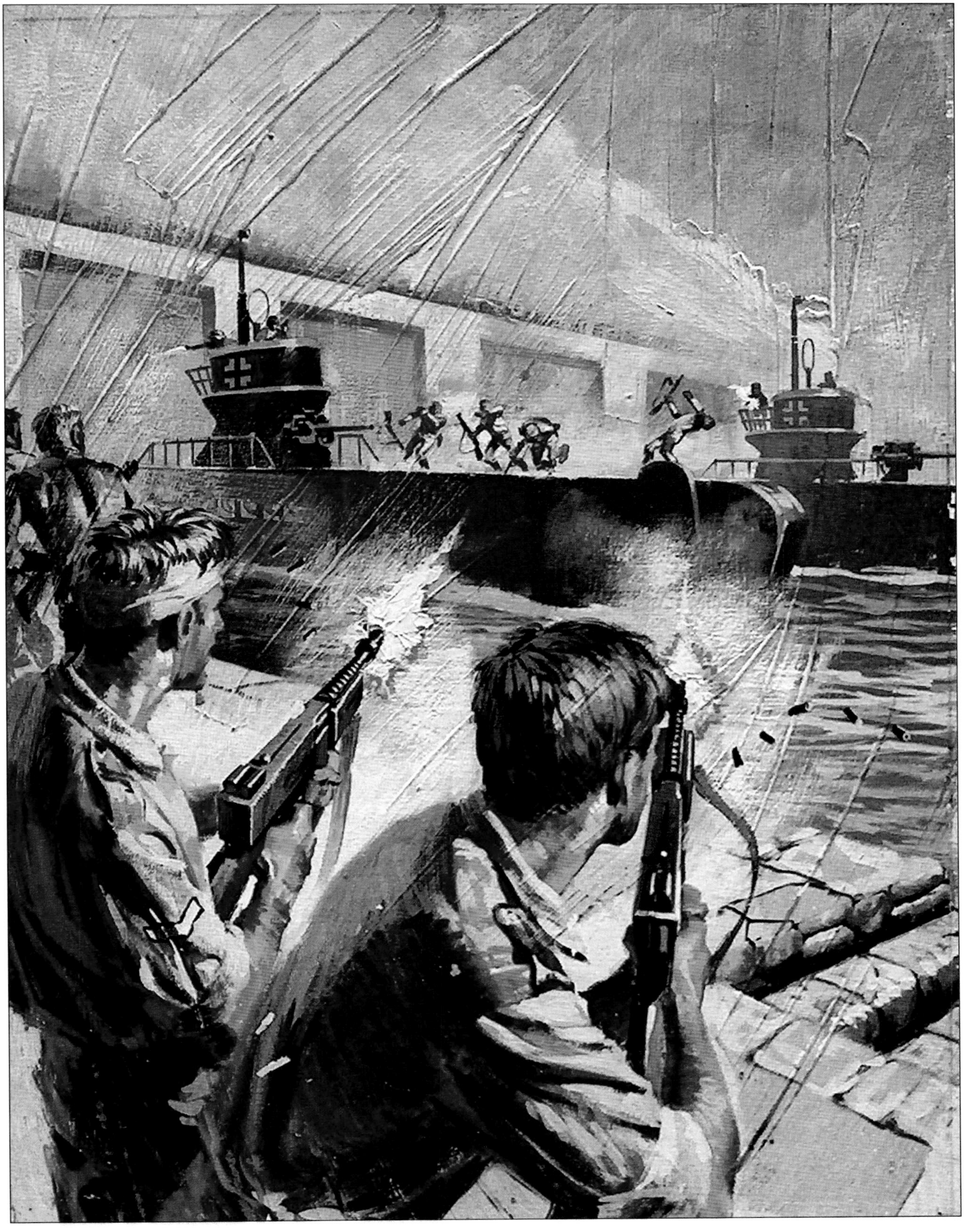

Jordi Penalva, War 496, February 1969
Opposite: Allessandro Biffignandi, Battle 12, May 1961

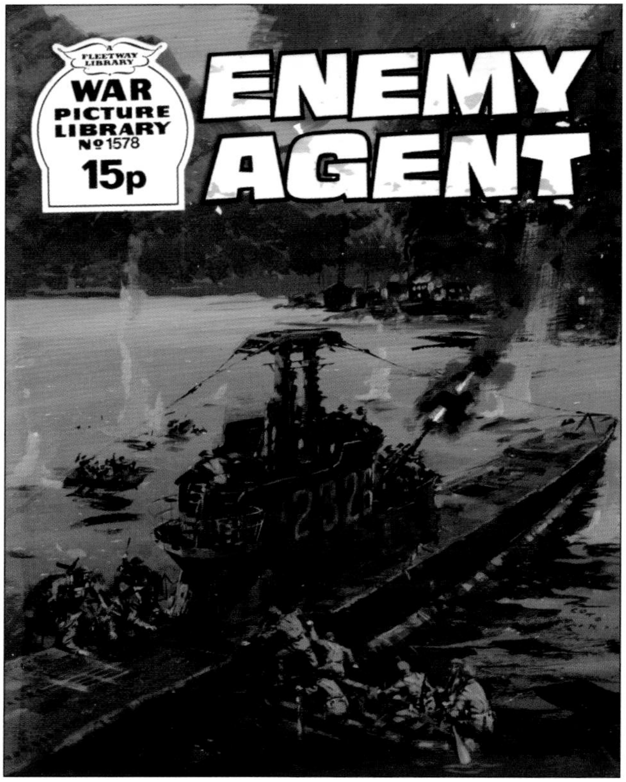
A FLEETWAY LIBRARY
WAR PICTURE LIBRARY
Nº 1578
15p
ENEMY AGENT
Graham Coton, War 1578, December 1978

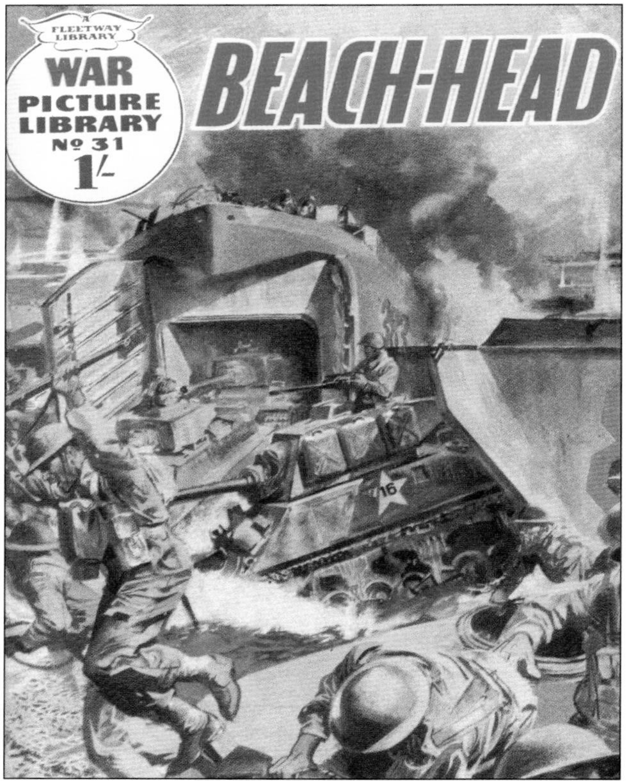
A FLEETWAY LIBRARY
WAR PICTURE LIBRARY
Nº 31
1/-
BEACH-HEAD
Giorgio DeGaspari, War 31, December 1959

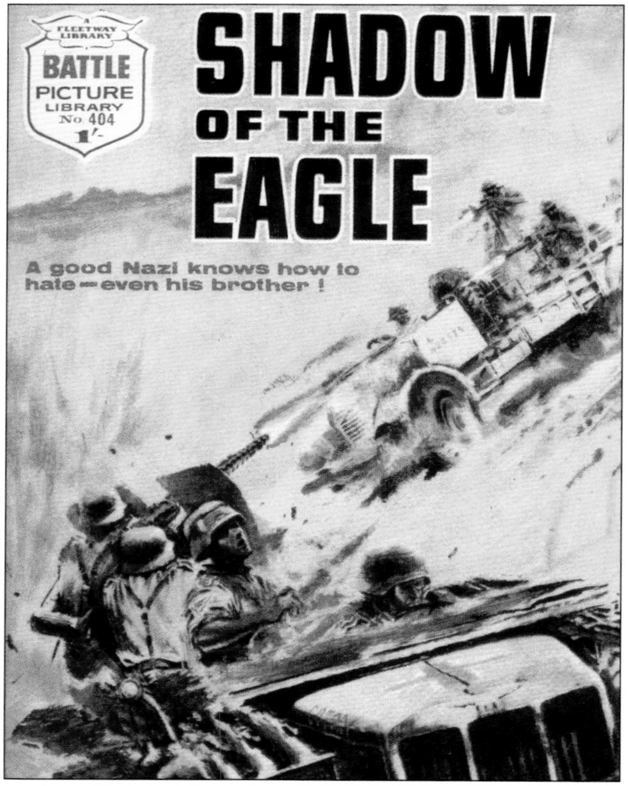
A FLEETWAY LIBRARY
BATTLE PICTURE LIBRARY
No. 404
1/-
SHADOW OF THE EAGLE
A good Nazi knows how to hate—even his brother !
Graham Coton, Battle 404, July 1969

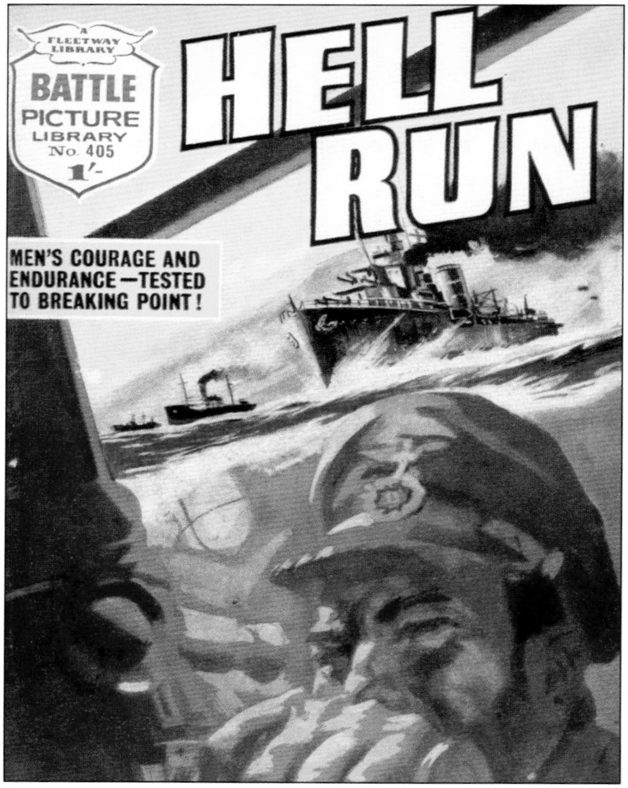
A FLEETWAY LIBRARY
BATTLE PICTURE LIBRARY
No. 405
1/-
HELL RUN
MEN'S COURAGE AND ENDURANCE—TESTED TO BREAKING POINT!
Pino Dell'Orco, originally War At Sea 35, July 1963

Opposite: Graham Coton, Batle 849, October 1974

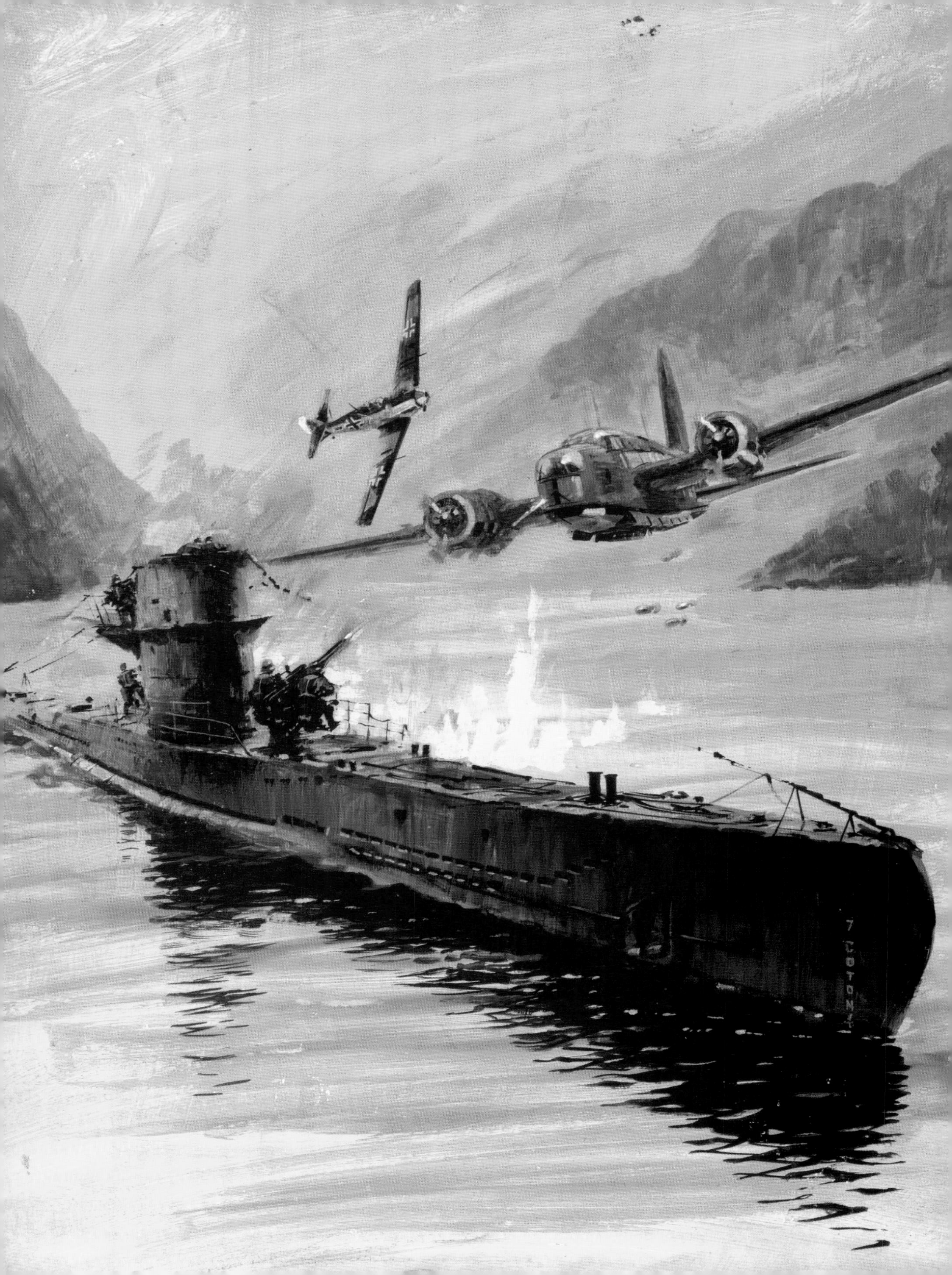

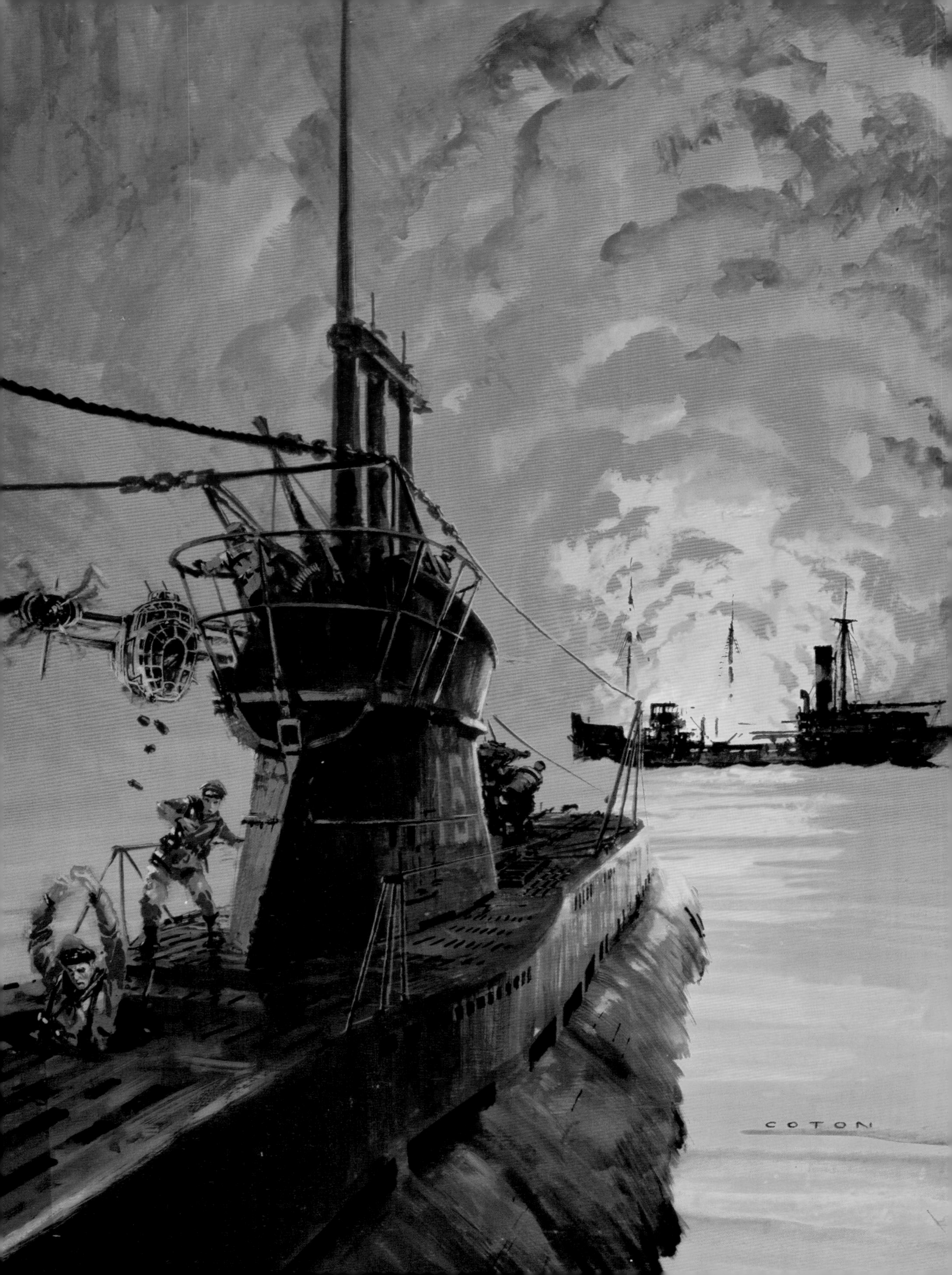
COTON

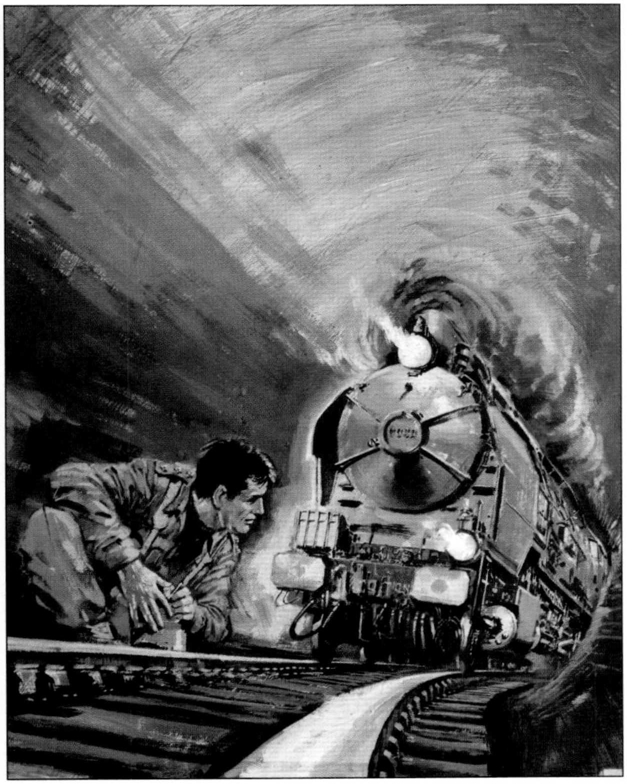

Graham Coton, Battle 873, January 1975

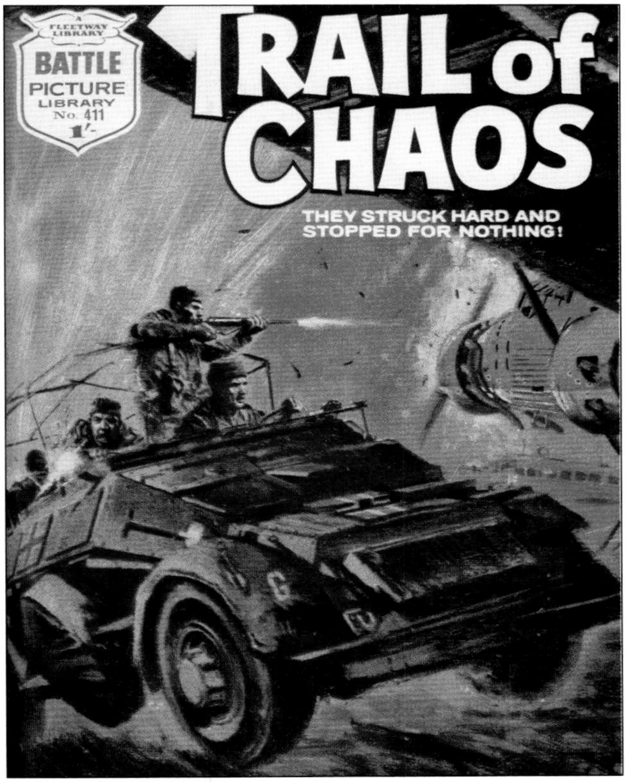
A FLEETWAY LIBRARY
BATTLE
PICTURE
LIBRARY
No. 411
1/-
TRAIL of CHAOS
THEY STRUCK HARD AND
STOPPED FOR NOTHING!

Graham Coton, Battle 411, August 1969

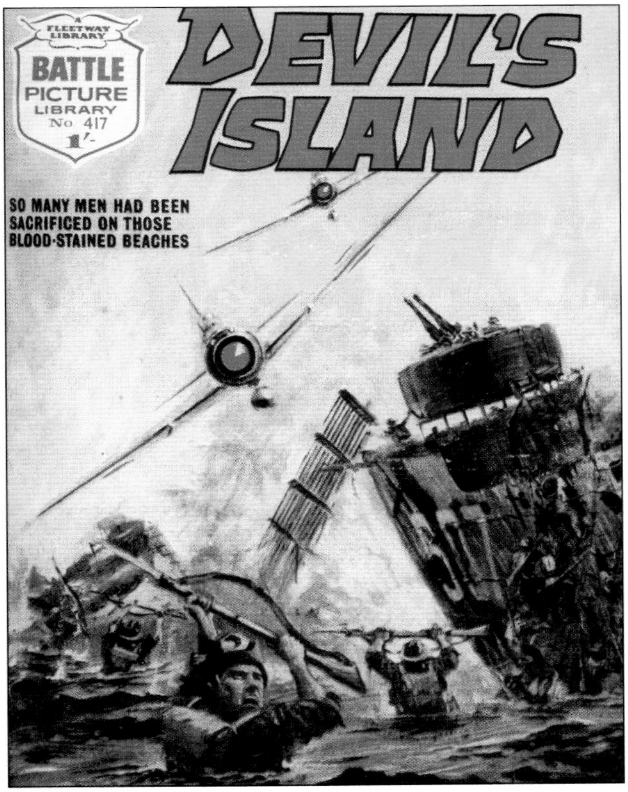
A FLEETWAY LIBRARY
BATTLE
PICTURE
LIBRARY
No. 417
1/-
DEVIL'S ISLAND
SO MANY MEN HAD BEEN
SACRIFICED ON THOSE
BLOOD-STAINED BEACHES

Graham Coton, Battle 417, September 1969

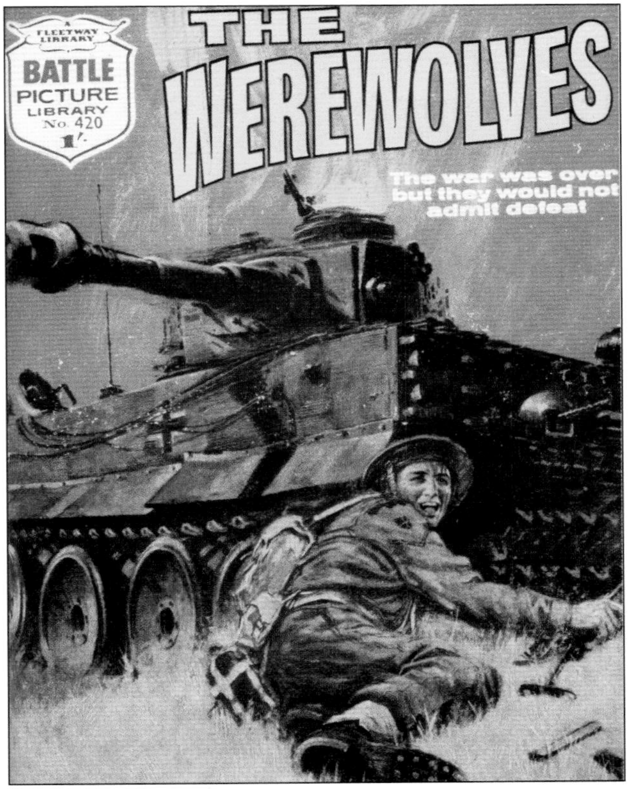
A FLEETWAY LIBRARY
BATTLE
PICTURE
LIBRARY
No. 420
1/-
THE WEREWOLVES
The war was over
but they would not
admit defeat

Graham Coton, Battle 420, September 1969

Opposite: Graham Coton, Battle 763, November 1973
Overleaf: Graham Coton, Battle 691, February 1973

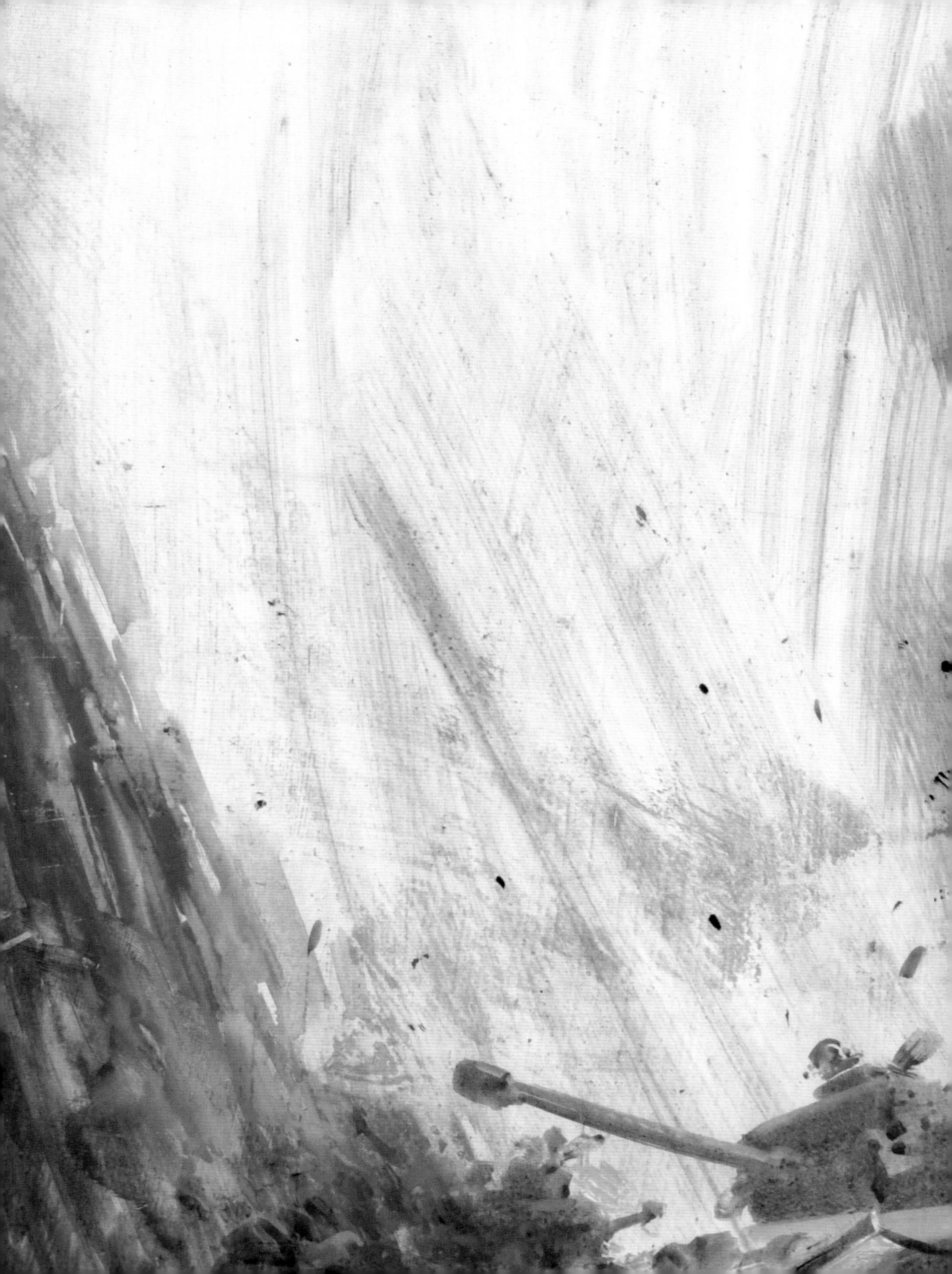

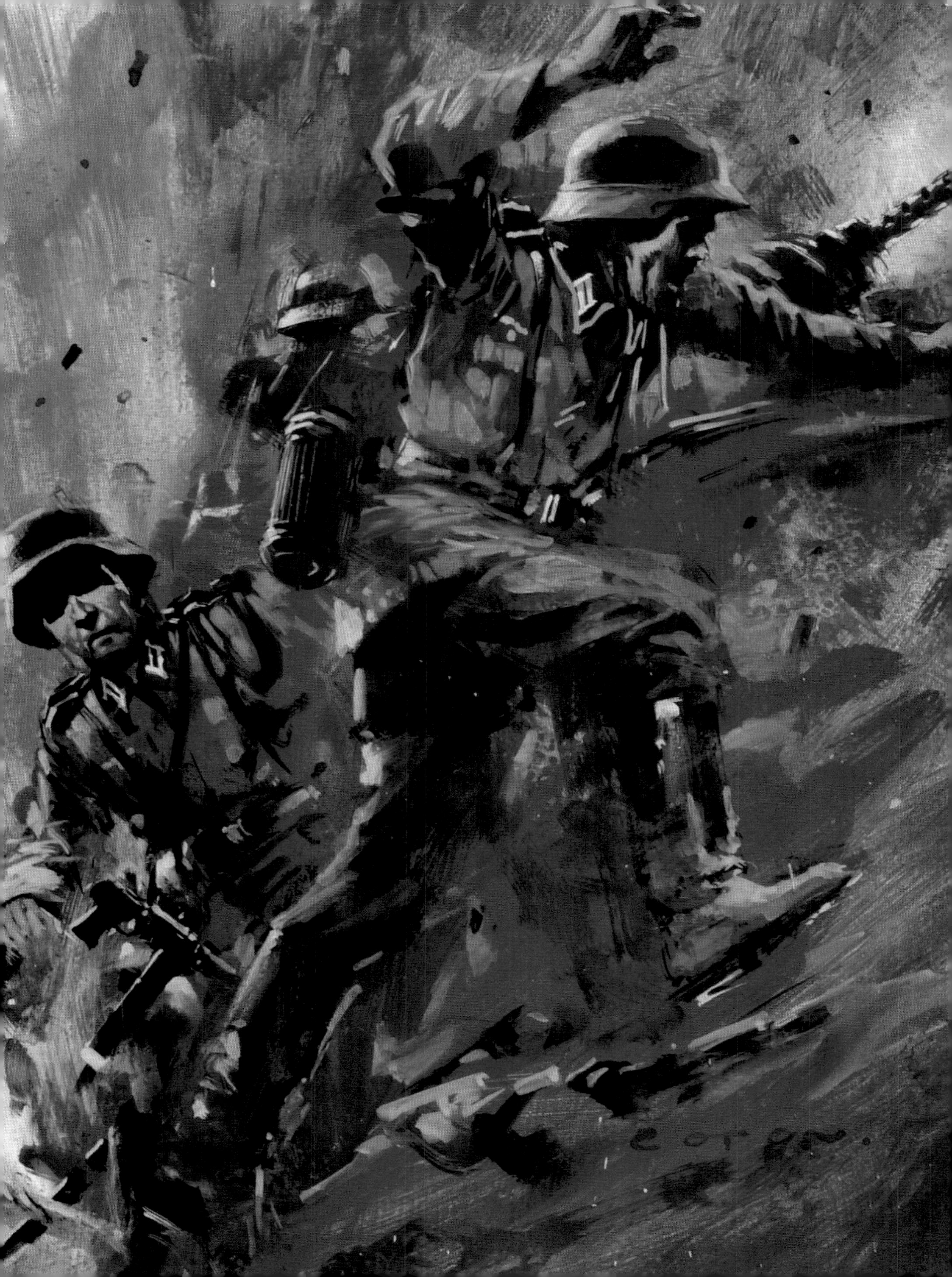

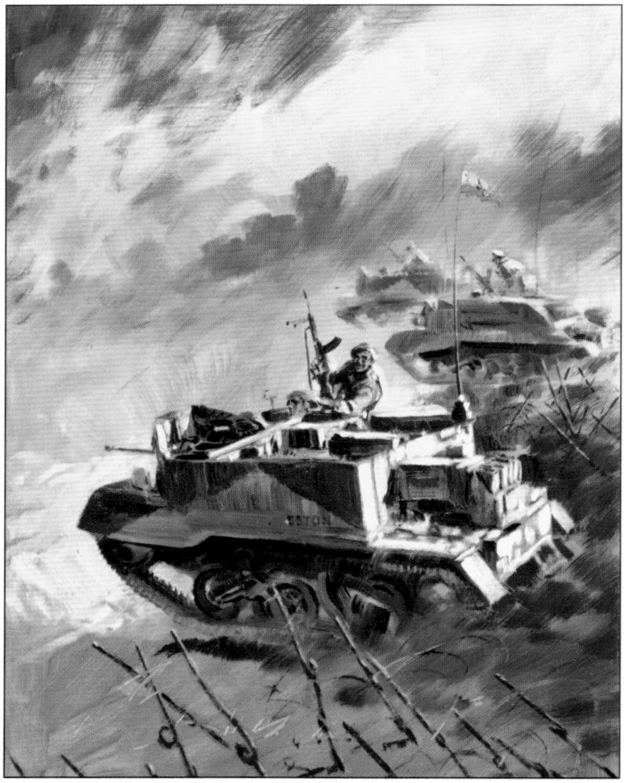

Graham Coton, War 1926, May 1982

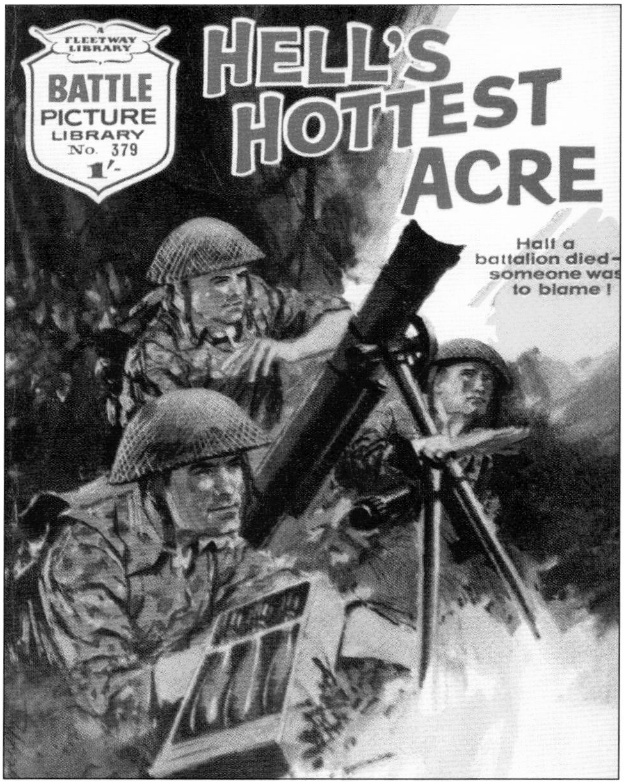
A FLEETWAY LIBRARY
BATTLE PICTURE LIBRARY No. 379 1/-
HELL'S HOTTEST ACRE
Half a battalion died – someone was to blame !

Rafael Lopez Espi, Battle 379, January 1969

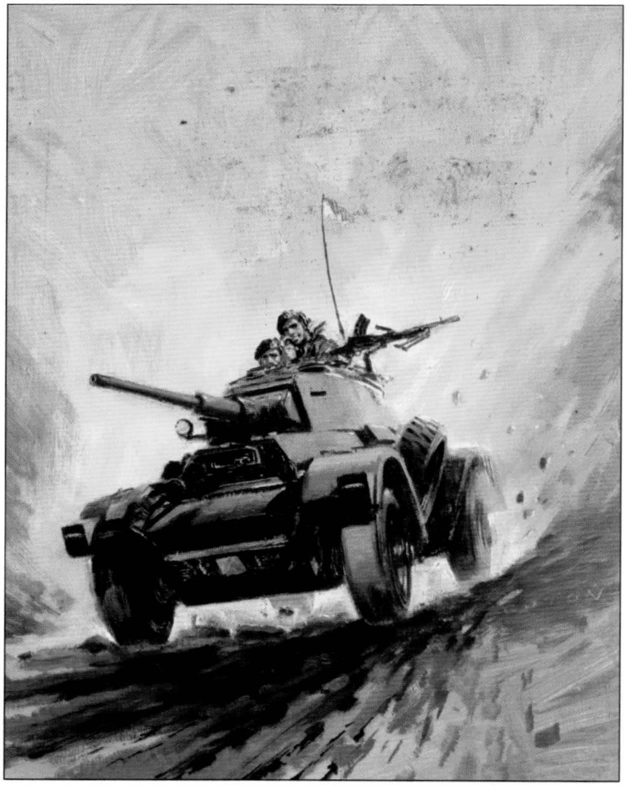

Graham Coton, War 825, February 1973

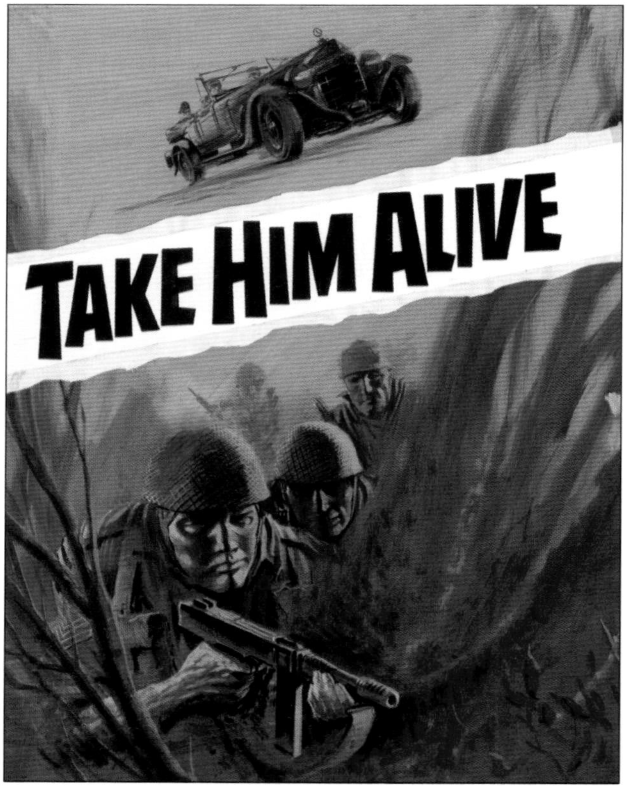
TAKE HIM ALIVE

Graham Coton, Battle 278, December 1966

Opposite: Graham Coton, Battle 615, April 1972

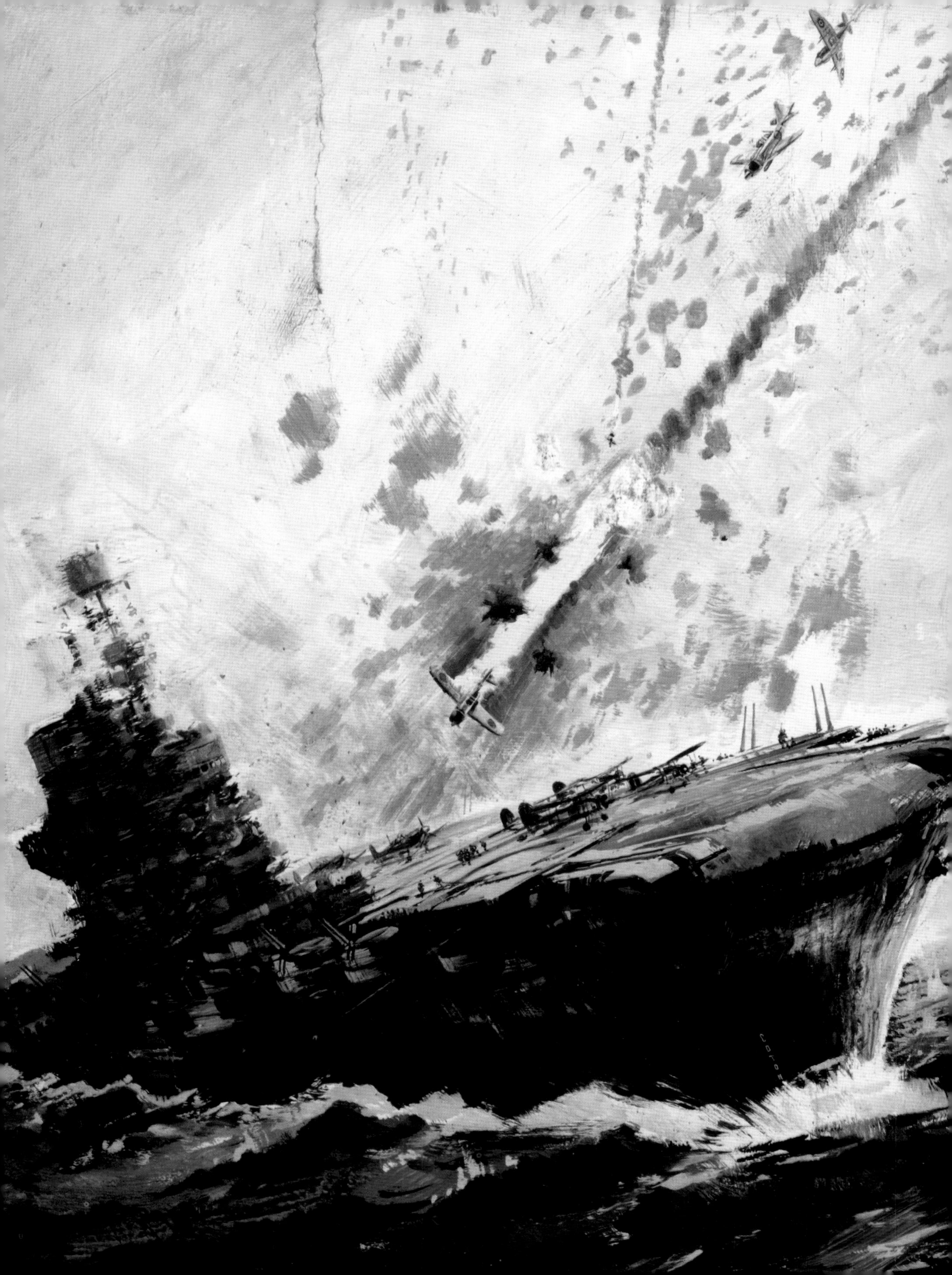

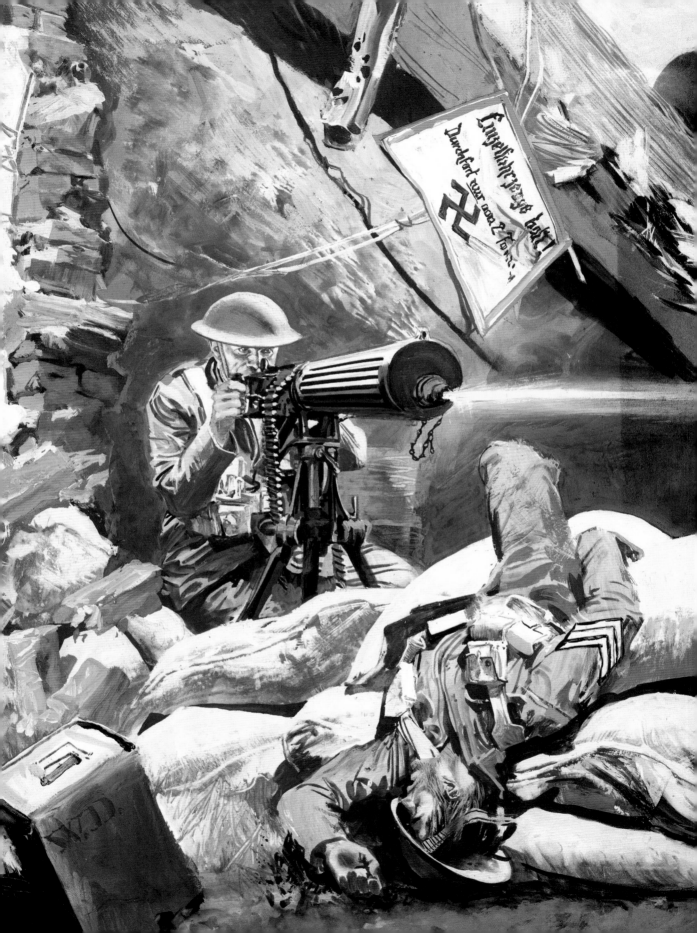

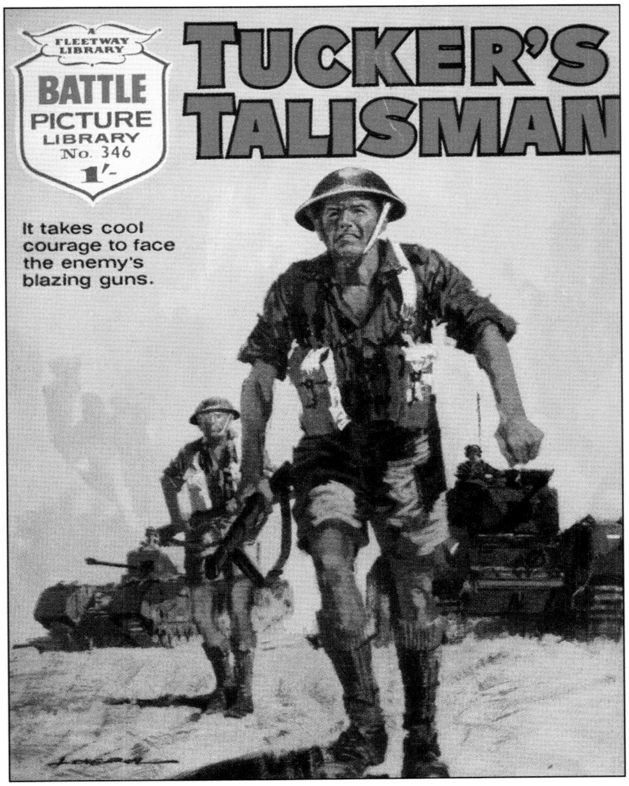
A FLEETWAY LIBRARY
BATTLE PICTURE LIBRARY
No. 346
1/-
TUCKER'S TALISMAN
It takes cool courage to face the enemy's blazing guns.

Jordi Longaron, Battle 346, May 1968

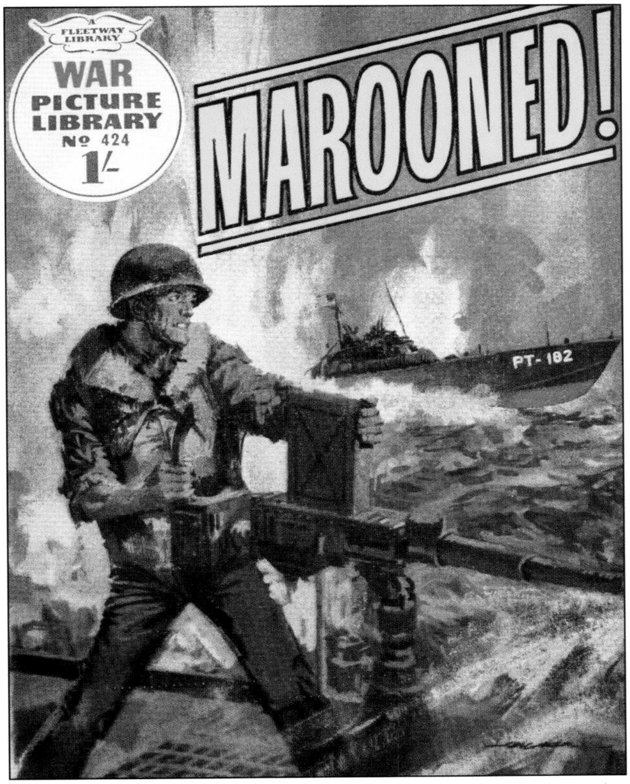
A FLEETWAY LIBRARY
WAR PICTURE LIBRARY
Nº 424
1/-
MAROONED!
PT-182

Jordi Longaron, War 424, February 1968

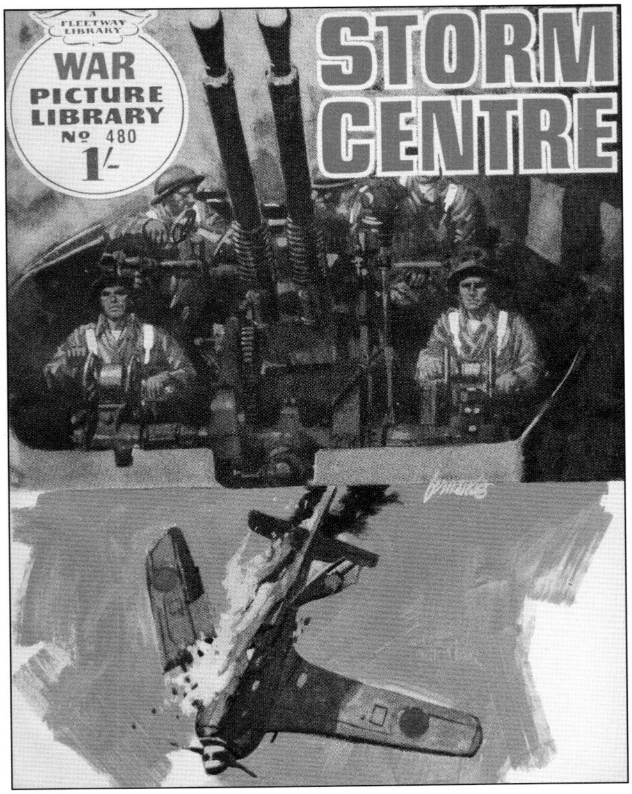
A FLEETWAY LIBRARY
WAR PICTURE LIBRARY
Nº 480
1/-
STORM CENTRE

Fernando Fernandez, War 480, November 1968

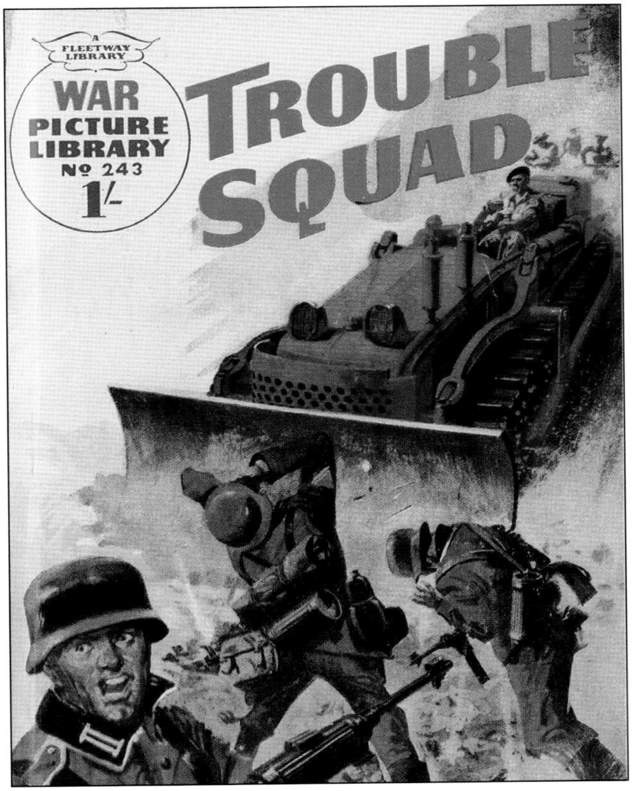
A FLEETWAY LIBRARY
WAR PICTURE LIBRARY
Nº 243
1/-
TROUBLE SQUAD

Allessandro Biffignandi, War 243, May 1964

Opposite: Giorgio DeGaspari, War 42, March 1960

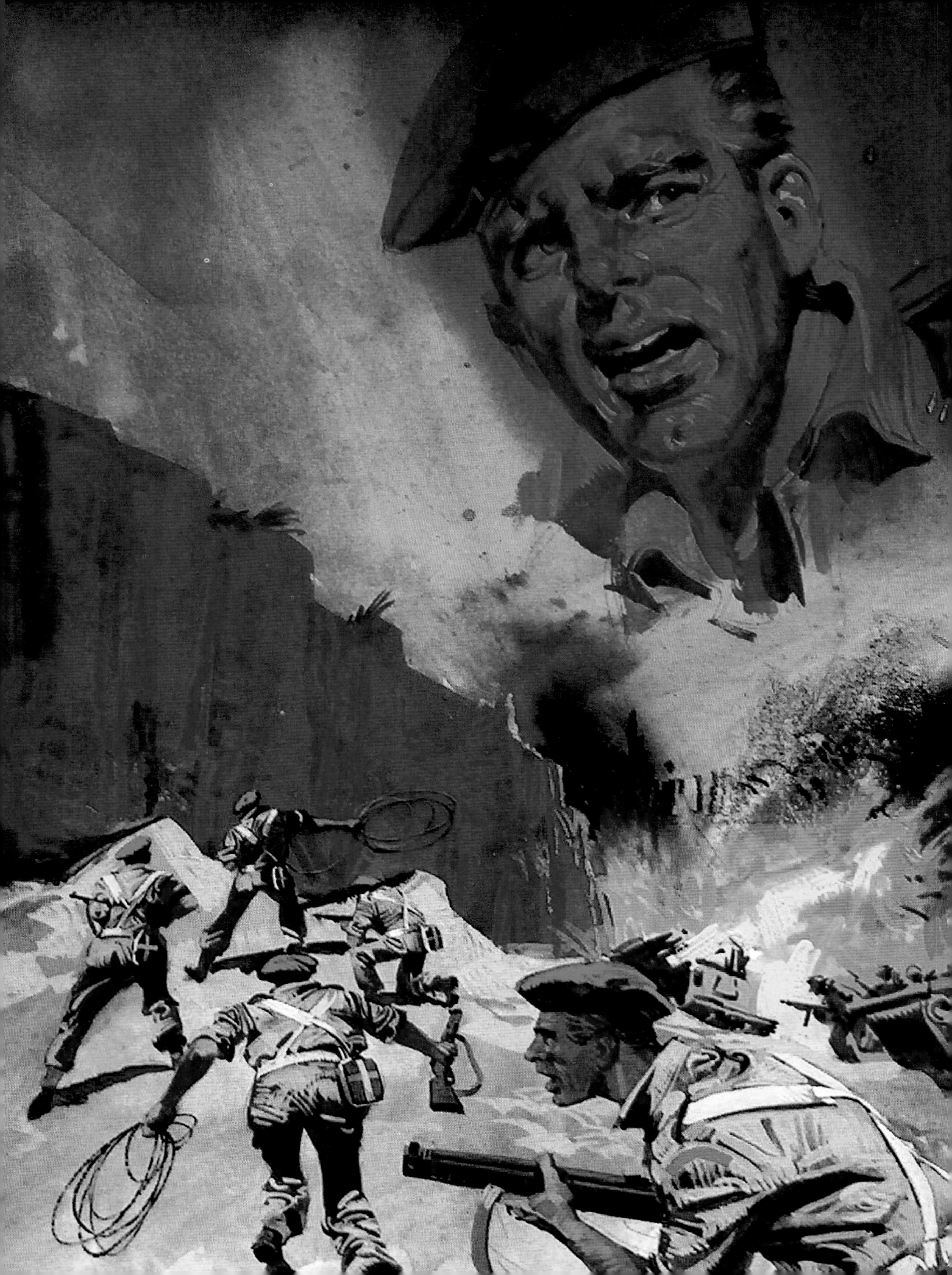

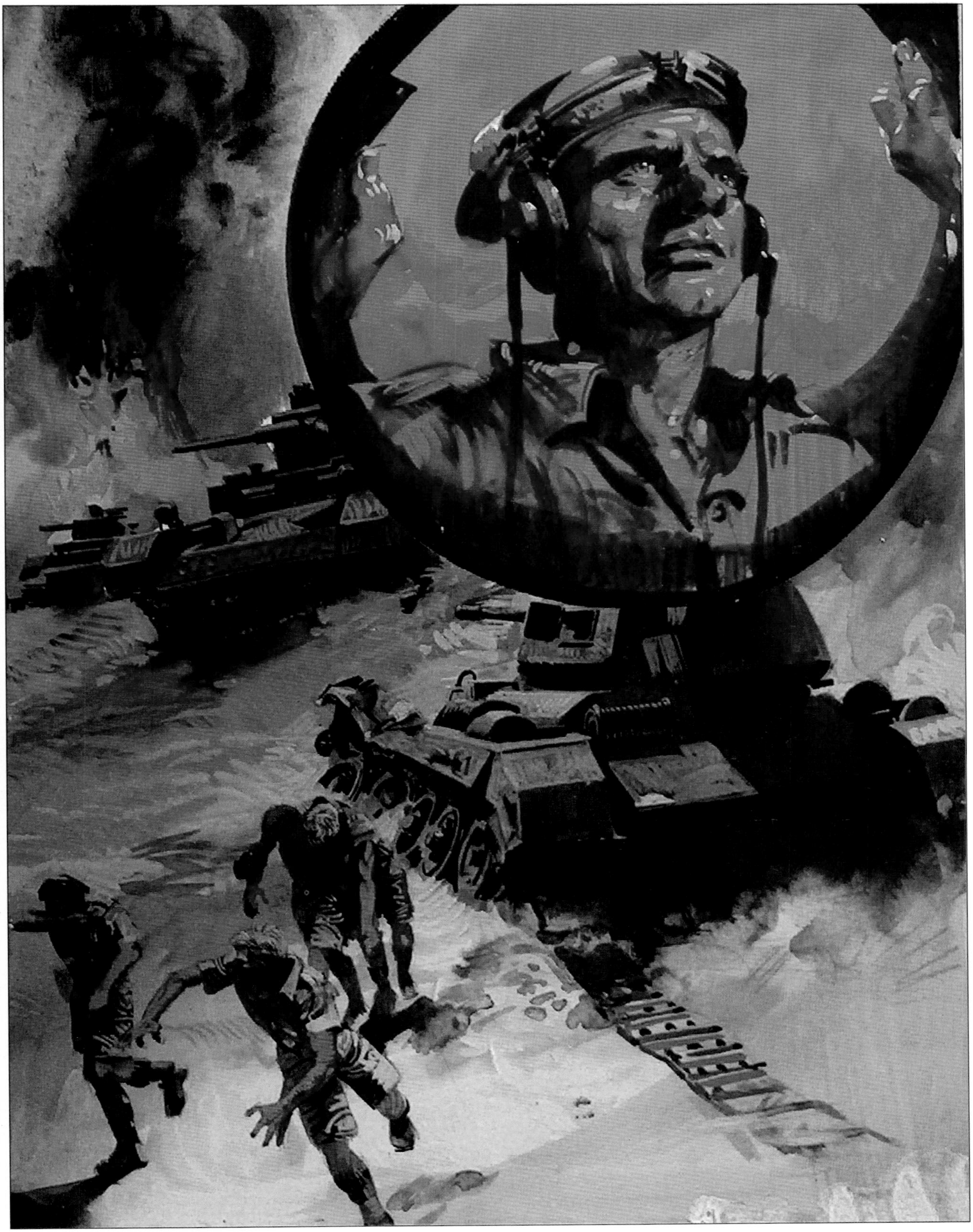

Allessandro Biffignandi, Battle 180, November 1964
Opposite: Allessandro Biffignandi, Battle 181, December 1964

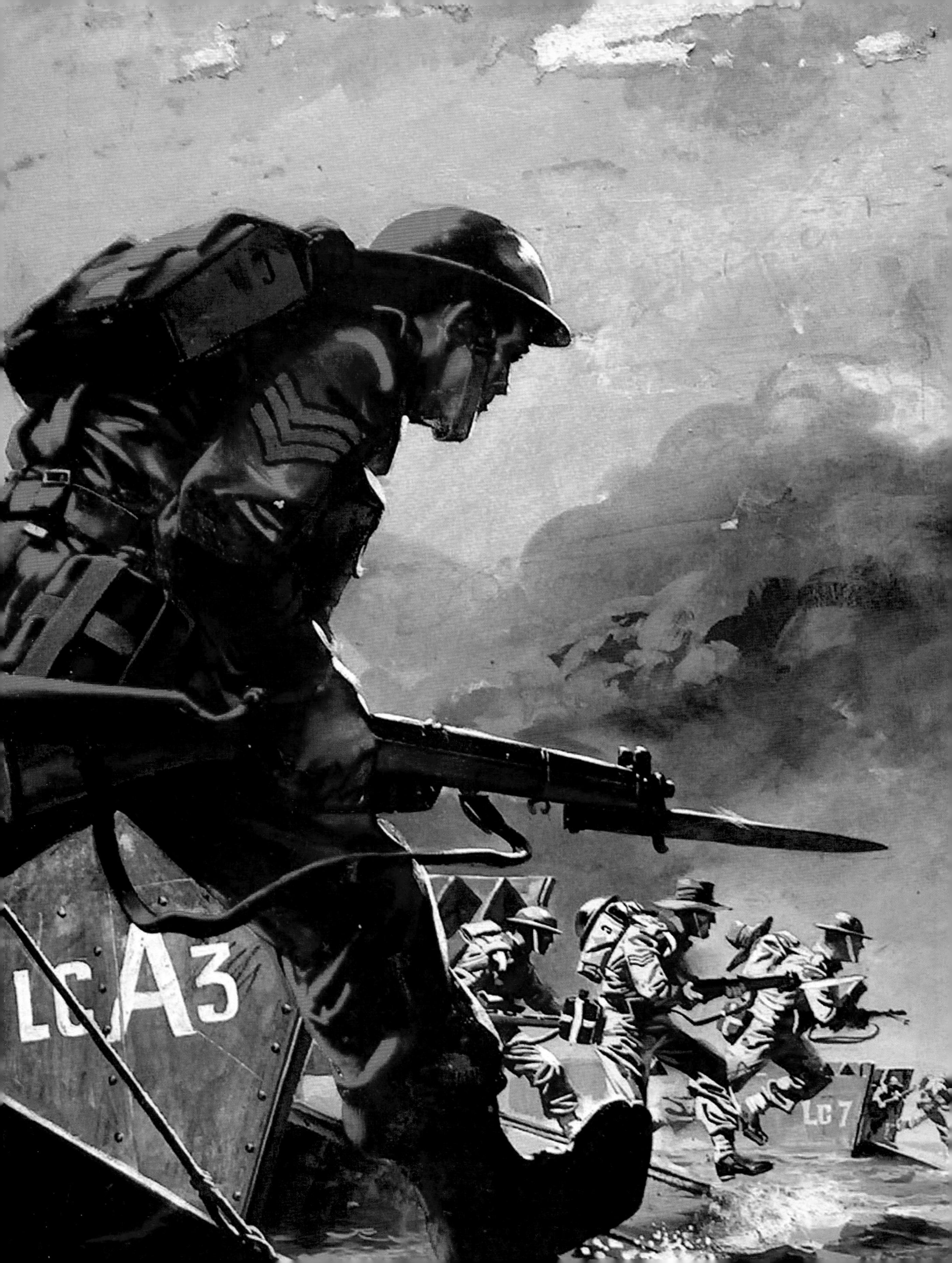
LCA3
LC7

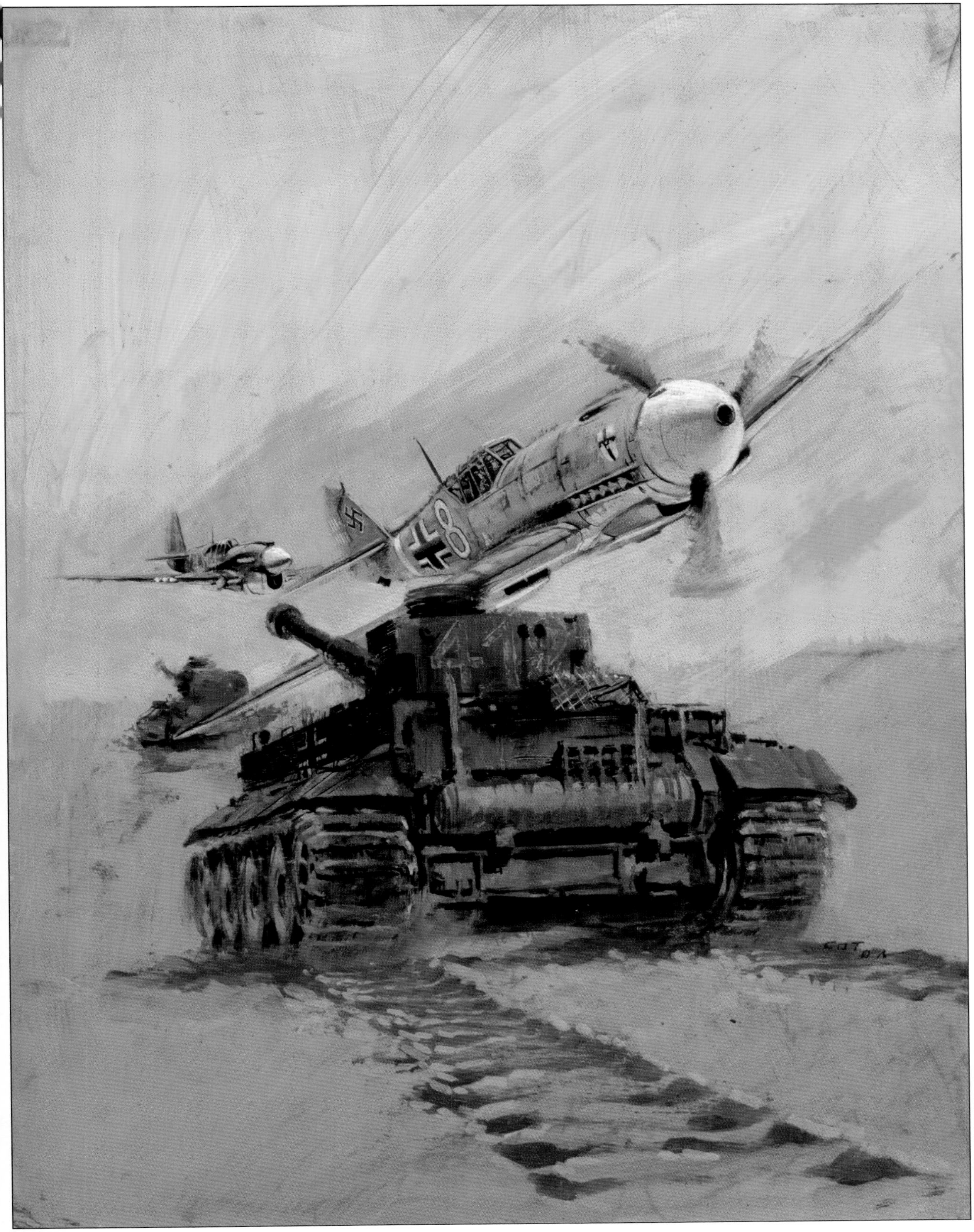

Graham Coton, Battle 629, June 1972
Opposite: Allessandro Biffignandi, War at Sea 9, June 1962

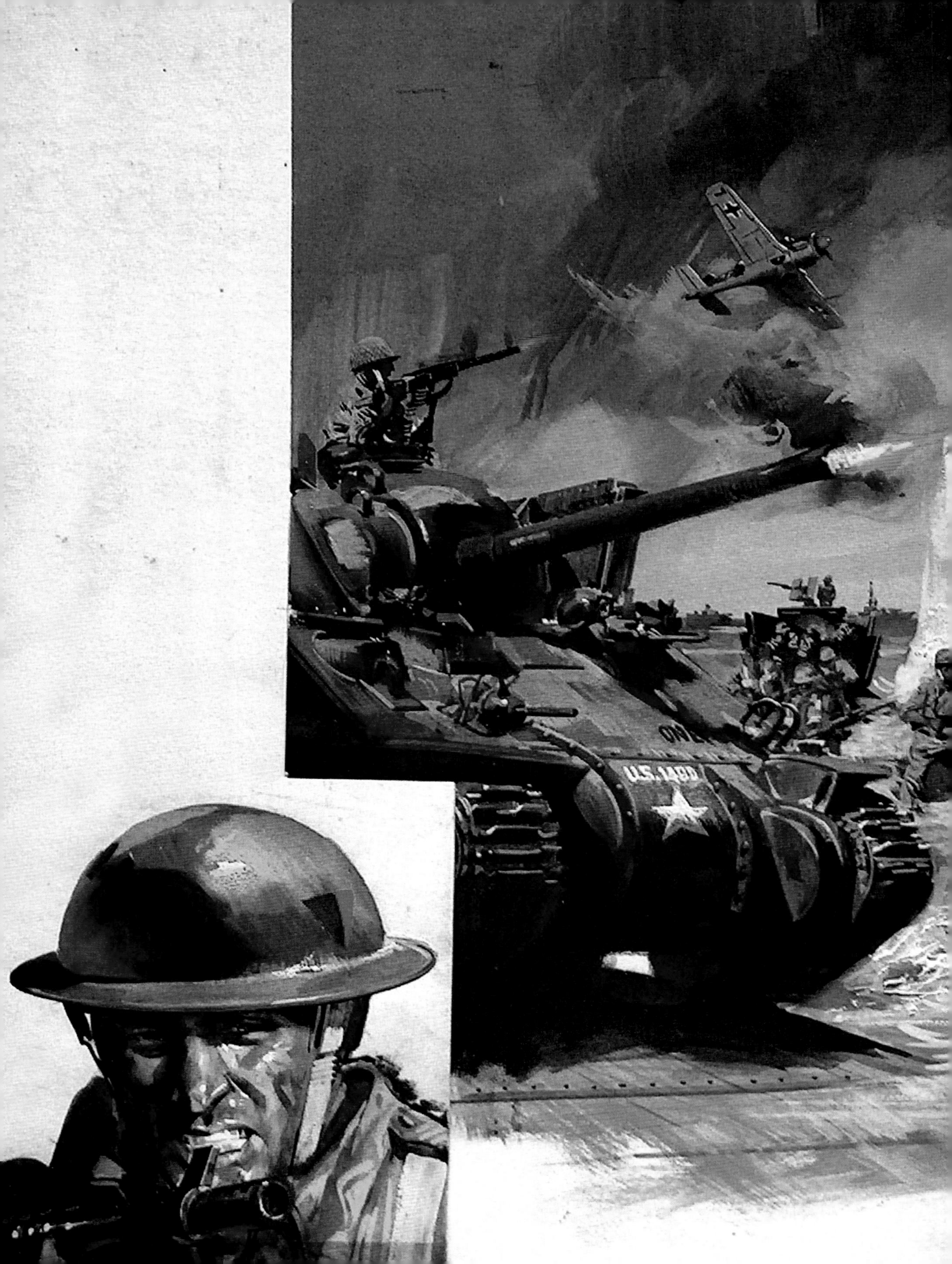

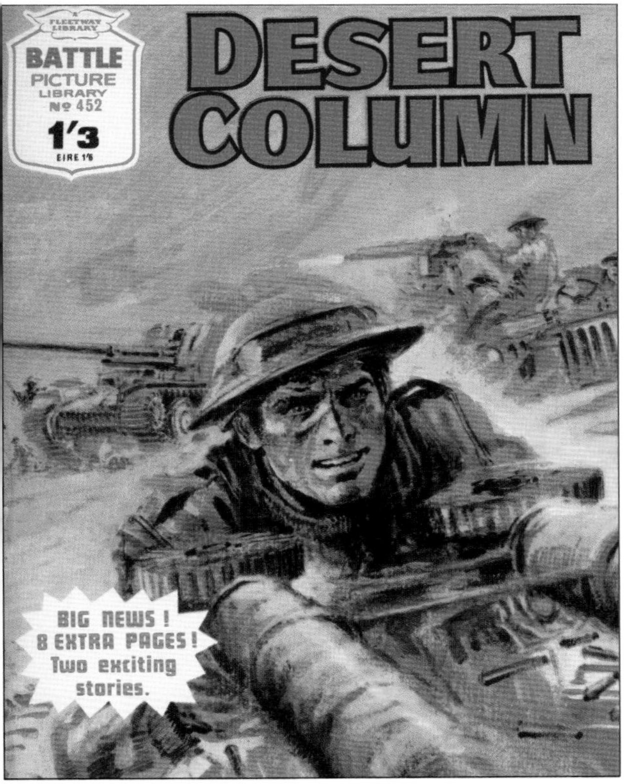
BATTLE PICTURE LIBRARY Nº 452
1'3
EIRE 1'6
DESERT COLUMN
BIG NEWS ! 8 EXTRA PAGES ! Two exciting stories.

Graham Coton, Battle 452, March 1970

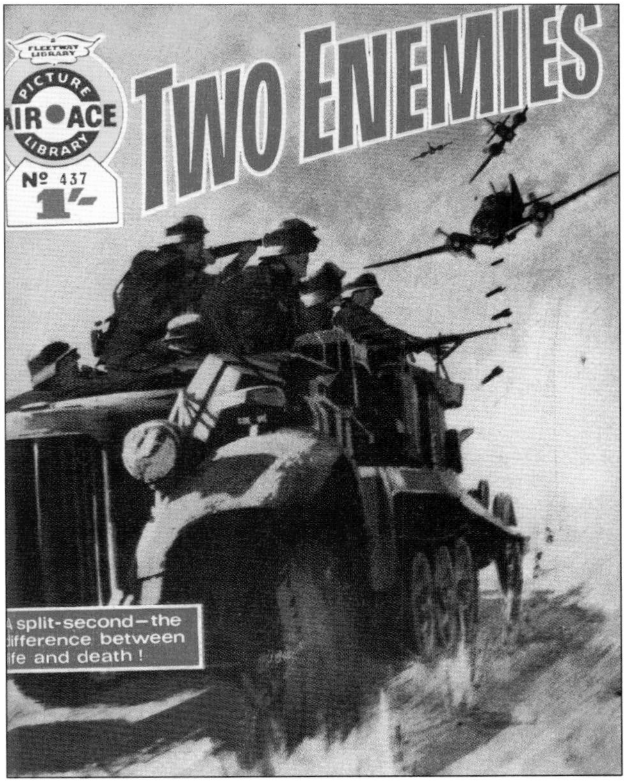
PICTURE AIR ACE LIBRARY
Nº 437
1/-
TWO ENEMIES
A split-second—the
ifference between
fe and death !

Rafael Lopz Espi, Air Ace 437, May 1969

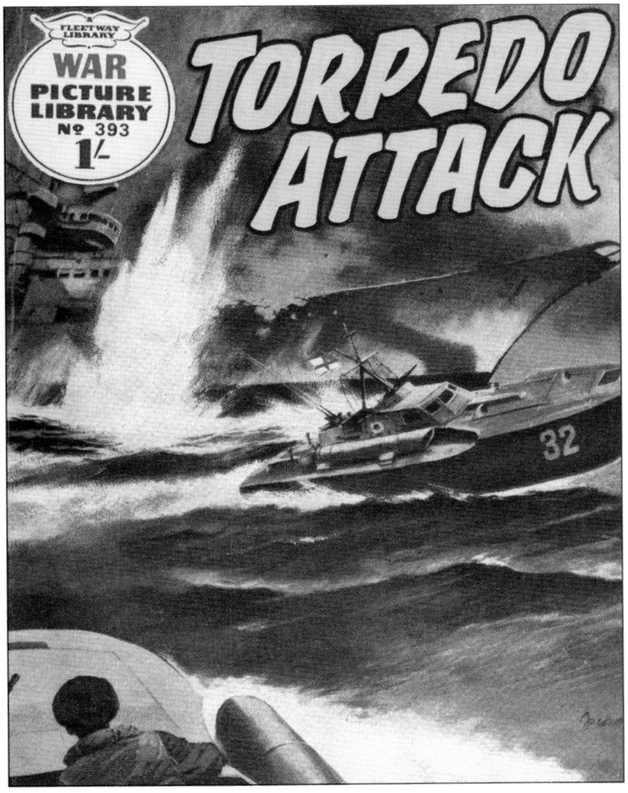
WAR PICTURE LIBRARY Nº 393
1/-
TORPEDO ATTACK
32

Carlo Jacono, War 393, July 1967

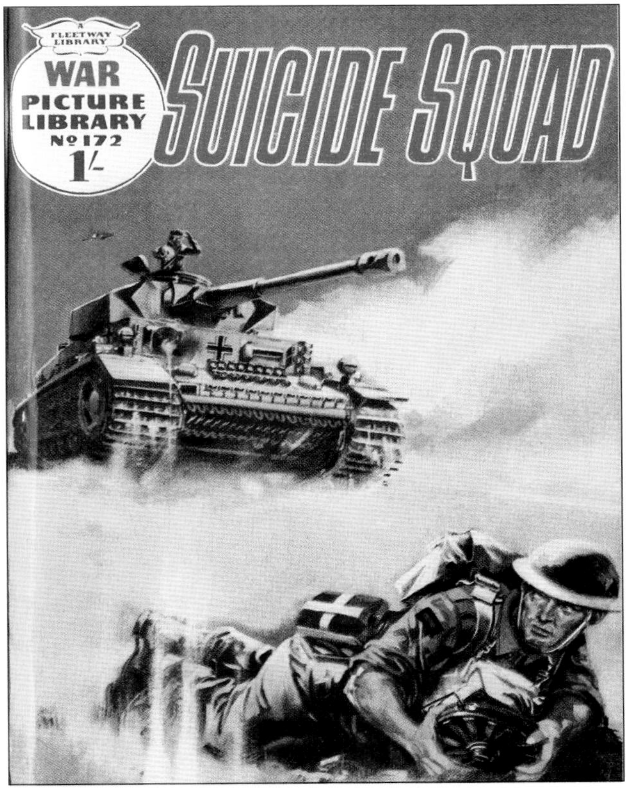
WAR PICTURE LIBRARY Nº 172
1/-
SUICIDE SQUAD

Allessandro Biffignandi, War 172, December 1962

Opposite: Allessandro Biffignandi, War 293, June 1965

BOYS Own HEROES

In a book devoted to the best covers from *War*, *Battle* and *Air Ace* it might seem a little eccentric to dedicate a chapter to strips from other comics, but even a cursory glance here will show that their influence ran far indeed.

Just as the creation of *War Picture Library* was inspired by the success of "Battler Britton" in *Thriller* so in turn *Thriller* was later converted to an out-and-out war comic. In its first incarnation, *Thriller* was conceived as something of a prestige title, mostly adapting classic novels such as *The Three Musketeers*, *Treasure Island* and *Ivanhoe*. With their beautifully painted covers (often by veteran illustrators such as Septimus Scott, J. Millar Watt and James McConnell) and more literate scripts, these early issues were clearly intended to appeal to a slightly older audience than the usual comic fare of *Film Fun*, *Comic Cuts* or *Knockout*. In fact, sister picture library titles *Love Story* and *True Life* were clearly aimed at women in their twenties or older. However, by the mid fifties, *Thriller* had apparently used up its supply of popular classics and was featuring well-crafted, if not exactly cutting edge, fare starring such hardy perennials as *Robin Hood*, *Dick Turpin* and *Wild Bill Hickock*.

In January 1956 the weekly title *Sun* (no relation to the daily newspaper of the same name) had introduced the daredevil fighting ace "Battler Britton" – an RAF pilot in the clean-cut Douglas Bader and Biggles tradition, drawn by A.P.'s top artist, Geoff Campion. "Battler Britton" proved to be immensely popular and new adventures also started to appear in *Thriller* with issue 160 in early 1957. In retrospect, the introduction of a war strip into the picture library format proved to be immensely significant, though at the time no one could have imagined quite how significant. *Thriller* appeared four times a month and very soon one of every four issues starred "Battler Britton" who would go on to appear in 65 issues in all. The strip employed a small army of creators drawn from the cream of British, Italian and Argentinian talent and scripts from the likes of C. F. Thomas, R. Clegg and Val Holding.

For covers, *Thriller*'s editors turned for the first time to the Italian artists of the D'ami studio in what was to be a dry run for the war picture libraries. DeGaspari, Caroselli, Dell'Orco and

Biffignandi all painted their earliest British work for *Thriller,* which in many cases also proved to be among their best. DeGaspari created 16 glorious "Battler Britton" covers, all of them exemplifying his combination of polished realism and taut dynamism. Caroseli followed close behind with 15 paintings, including the iconic cover to issue 353 (on page 355) which is the very embodiment of the British stiff upper lip. In September 1958 (the same month which also saw the release of *War* number one), *Thriller* 242 introduced David Doughty, the secret service legend better known as "Spy-13". Like "Battler Britton" the "Spy-13" stories were set in the Second World War and boasted a similarly disparate creative crew on the inside pages with more covers by the D'ami studio. A year later, the companion title *Super Detective Library* introduced its own Second World War spy, "John Steel" (who would later transfer to *Thriller* and become a fifties film noir-style private eye). Then, in 1960, *Thriller* 307 saw the debut of "Dogfight Dixon".

"Dogfight Dixon" broke the mould of British comics characters by being the first hero from the First World War rather than the Second. At around the same time, in America, DC comics also tackled this period with their "Balloon Buster" and "Enemy Ace" series, although neither those nor "Dogfight" met with much success. It might well have been that the unrelenting horror of trench warfare was simply too much for the readers, despite all three strips starring aviators in an attempt to avoid dealing with this.

"Dogfight Dixon" ended up appearing in only 22 issues of *Thriller* despite some early scripts from legendary science fiction author, Michael Moorcock, and some terrific covers from DeGaspari and Dell'Orco. Perhaps as a consequence of its failure, the other war comics stuck rigidly to their Second World War theme and it was not until the creation of the award-winning "Charley's War" in *Battle Weekly* in the eighties that the period was approached once more .

Thriller itself was cancelled in 1963 and while "Battler Britton" briefly lived on in the weekly comic *Valiant,* he and his fellow heroes soon disappeared from the shelves. However, Fleetway was never a company to let good characters lie fallow for long and throughout the sixties the *Thriller* heroes found themselves reprinted and repackaged in such disparate comics as *Giant War*, *Lion Library*, *Buster Library* and (in the case of "Dogfight Dixon") *Air Ace*. Starting in 1966, *Air Ace* began featuring new "Battler Britton" strips which then transferred over to *Battle,* only finally coming to an end in 1975. While few of these strips were earth-shakingly original, gave Graham Coton an excuse to paint some more wonderful aeroplane covers.

Fleetway, however, was not content to just reprint the same few strips over and over again and in 1967 the company introduced the last of their picture library formats with the *Super Library* series. This comprised three titles; *Fantastic* (renamed *Stupendous* with its third issue), *Secret Agent* and *Front Line*. Each title appeared twice a month and featured 128-page stories of super heroes ("The Spider" and "The Steel Claw" in *Fantastic*), secret agents ("Johnny

Nero" and "Barracuda" in, unsurprisingly, *Secret Agent*) and soldiers ("Sergeant Ironside" and "Maddocks Marrauders" in *Front Line*). "Ironside" was the archetypical grizzled American sarge while "Maddocks Marrauders" were an indomitable platoon of British commandos. Both series featured some grittily effective epics drawn by the best Italian artists. The distinctive yellow-banded covers were almost exclusively painted by Jordi Penalva in full-on action mode, and most featured their stars shooting, running, punching or batting away hand grenades against retina-blinding yellow and orange backgrounds. We will never know precisely why the various *Super Library* series only lasted a year but purchasing three expensive titles simultaneously may just have been too much for cash-strapped young consumers to cope with. Further "Maddocks" and "Ironside" strips appeared in *Battle Picture Library* from 1968 to 1975, not least to satisfy demand from abroad which, by the late sixties, was growing ever stronger.

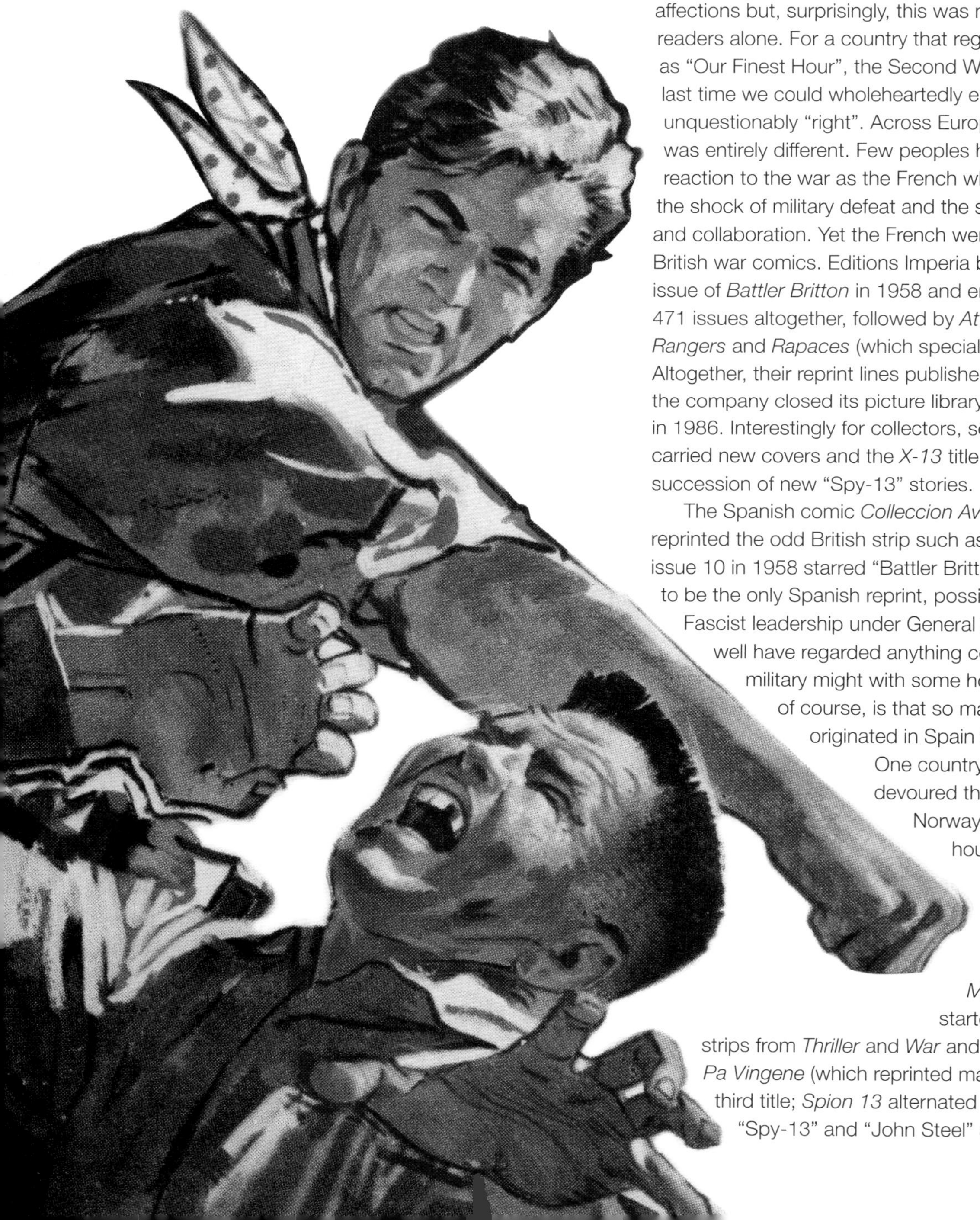

For generations of young (and perhaps not so young) readers, the war comics held a special place in their affections but, surprisingly, this was not restricted to British readers alone. For a country that regarded 1939 to 1945 as "Our Finest Hour", the Second World War was the last time we could wholeheartedly embrace a conflict as unquestionably "right". Across Europe, however, the picture was entirely different. Few peoples have as complicated a reaction to the war as the French who had had to deal with the shock of military defeat and the shame of occupation and collaboration. Yet the French were quick to reprint any British war comics. Editions Imperia brought out the first issue of *Battler Britton* in 1958 and ended up publishing 471 issues altogether, followed by *Attack*, *X-13*, *Panache*, *Rangers* and *Rapaces* (which specialisd in *Air Ace* strips). Altogether, their reprint lines published 2,368 issues until the company closed its picture library comics down in 1986. Interestingly for collectors, some issues carried new covers and the *X-13* title featured a succession of new "Spy-13" stories.

The Spanish comic *Colleccion Aventuras Illustradas* reprinted the odd British strip such as "Buck Jones" and issue 10 in 1958 starred "Battler Britton". This would seem to be the only Spanish reprint, possibly due to their own Fascist leadership under General Franco, which might well have regarded anything connected with British military might with some hostility. The great irony, of course, is that so many of these strips originated in Spain in the first place.

One country that positively devoured the war comics was Norway, whose publishing house SE-Bladene reprinted vast quantities of British war comics. Their first title, *Serie Magasinet*, which started in 1960, reprinted strips from *Thriller* and *War* and was soon followed by *Pa Vingene* (which reprinted material from *Air Ace*). A third title; *Spion 13* alternated between reprints of "Spy-13" and "John Steel" strips and when these ran out some time in the late sixties, the company simply started printing new stories. Their "Spy-13" was given the new name David Holden, though in all other respects he was essentially the same character and it is astonishing to realise that these new adventures ran until 1990, outliving his British counterpart by 27 years. Like the originals, these Norwegian "Spy-13" stories would seem to have been drawn in a different country, Spain in this case, and it is quite possible that they were also published in the French *X-13* comic. In any case, *Thriller* completists who believed there were only 44 "Spy-13" stories published have got an awful lot of comics to hunt down if they want to complete their collections.

As to why the Norwegians should have embraced these strips so enthusiastically, the collector and historian Professor Oystein Sorensen from the University of Oslo has the following theory; "The golden age for these comics in

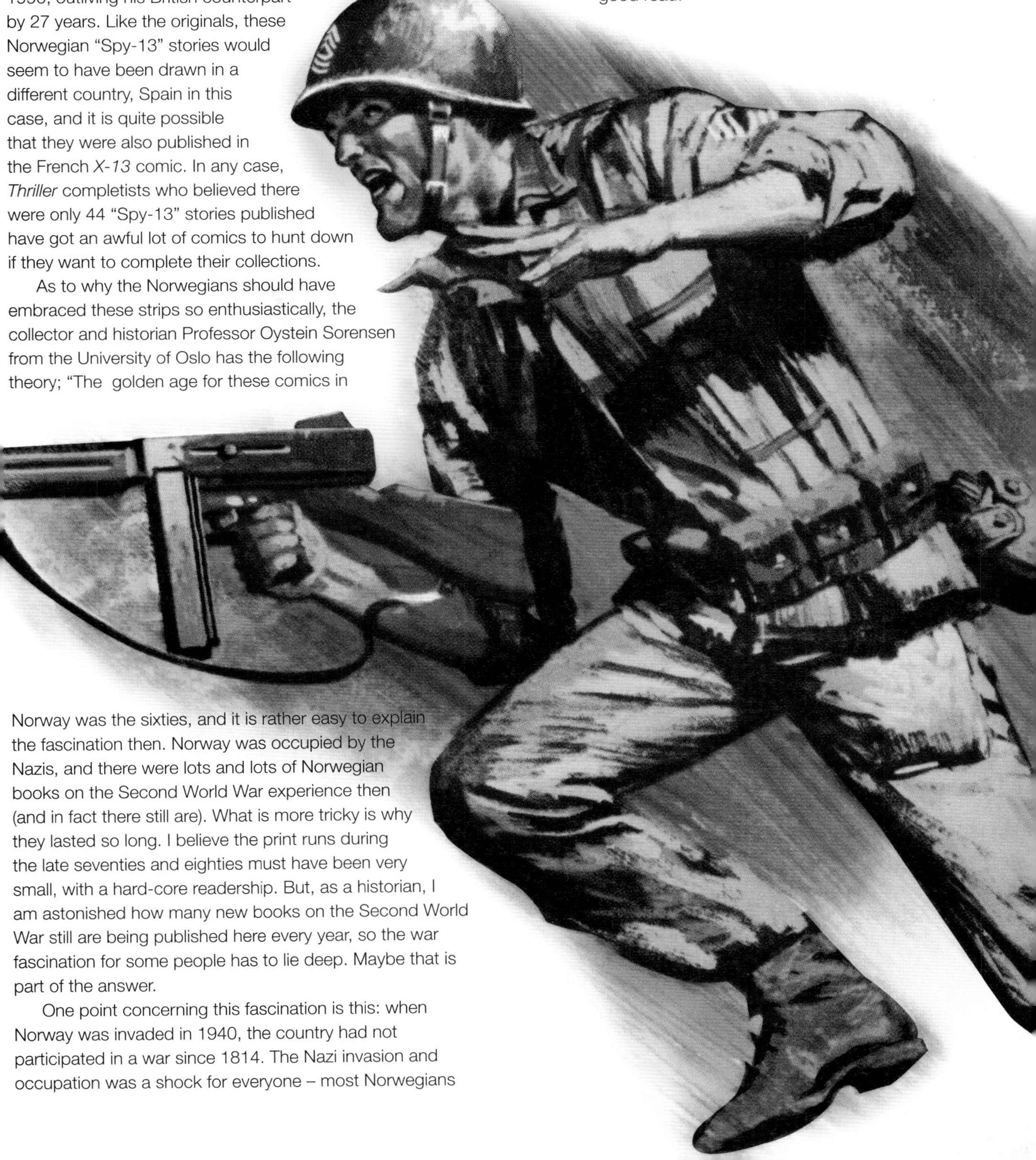

Norway was the sixties, and it is rather easy to explain the fascination then. Norway was occupied by the Nazis, and there were lots and lots of Norwegian books on the Second World War experience then (and in fact there still are). What is more tricky is why they lasted so long. I believe the print runs during the late seventies and eighties must have been very small, with a hard-core readership. But, as a historian, I am astonished how many new books on the Second World War still are being published here every year, so the war fascination for some people has to lie deep. Maybe that is part of the answer.

One point concerning this fascination is this: when Norway was invaded in 1940, the country had not participated in a war since 1814. The Nazi invasion and occupation was a shock for everyone – most Norwegians had probably not considered the possibility at all."

For a country so traumatised by the occupation, these war comics may have been a cathartic experience – one last chance to get back at their oppressors. But then again, maybe they, like the rest of us, just enjoyed a cracking good read.

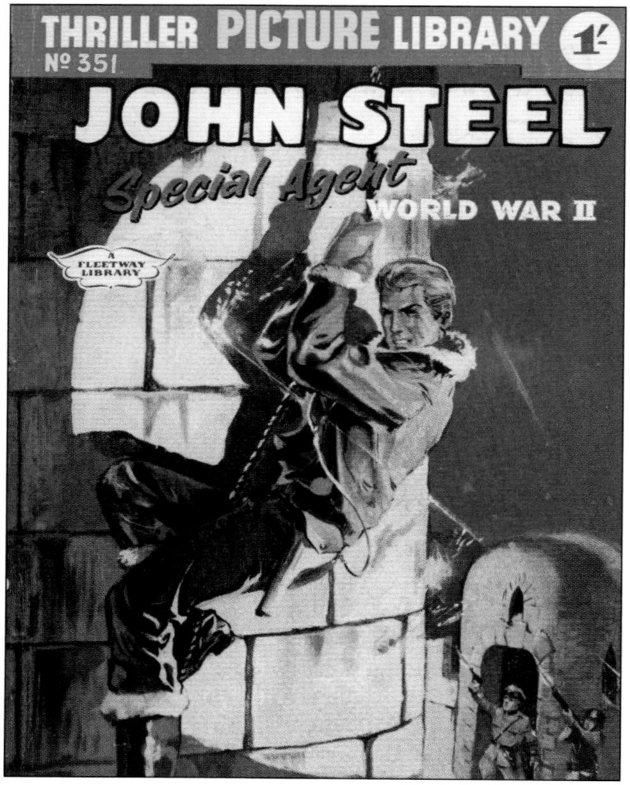
THRILLER PICTURE LIBRARY
1/-
Nº 351
JOHN STEEL
Special Agent
WORLD WAR II
A FLEETWAY LIBRARY

Nino Caroselli, Thriller 351, February 1961

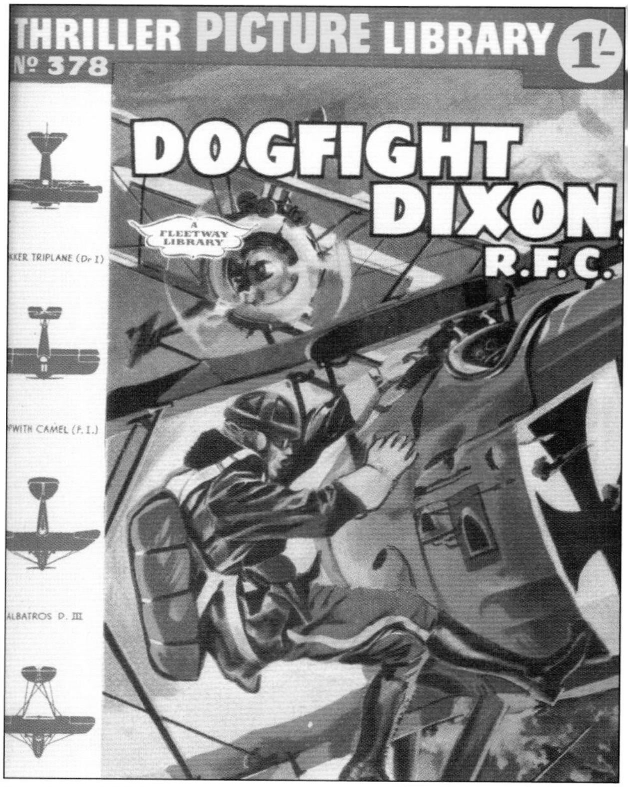
THRILLER PICTURE LIBRARY
1/-
Nº 378
DOGFIGHT DIXON R.F.C.
A FLEETWAY LIBRARY
ALBATROS D. III

Nino Caroselli, Thriller 378, September 1961

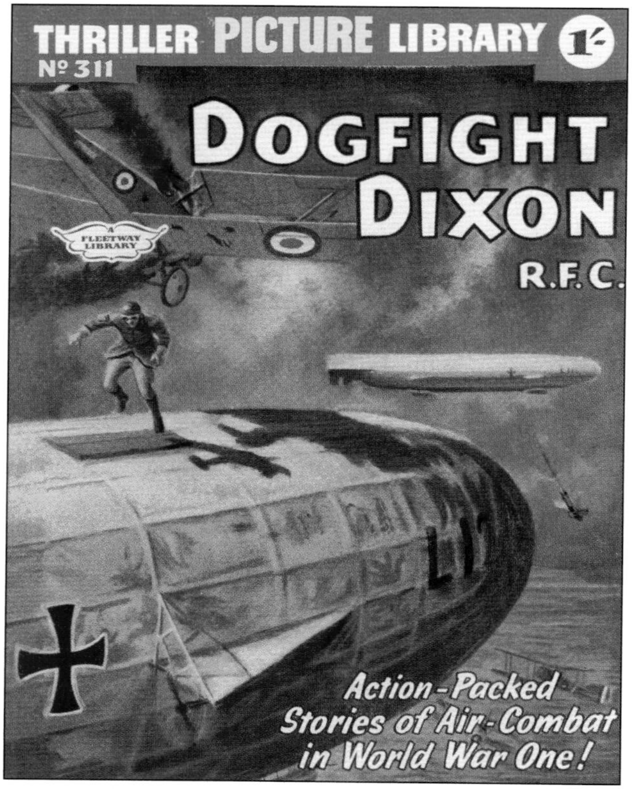
THRILLER PICTURE LIBRARY
1/-
Nº 311
DOGFIGHT DIXON
R.F.C.
A FLEETWAY LIBRARY
Action-Packed Stories of Air-Combat in World War One!

Nino Caroselli, Thriller 311, April 1960

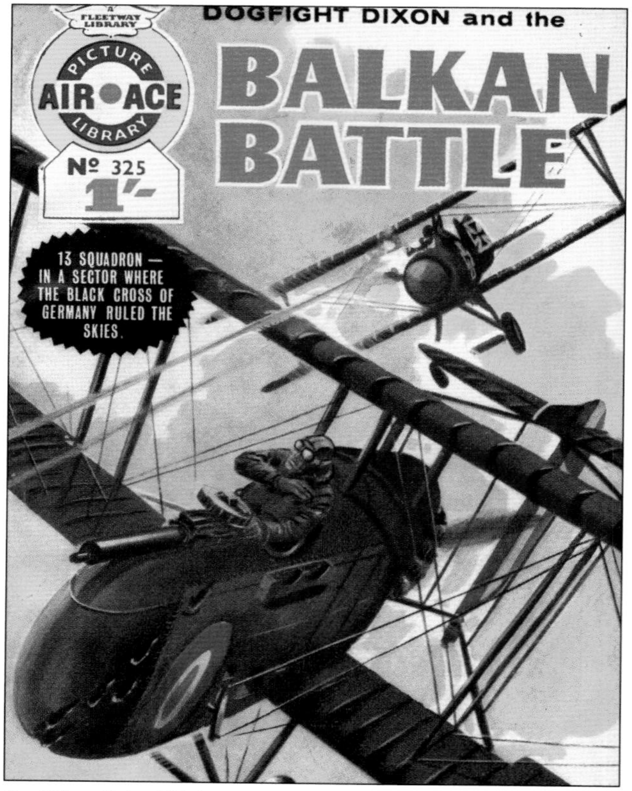
A FLEETWAY LIBRARY
PICTURE
AIR ACE
LIBRARY
Nº 325
1/-
DOGFIGHT DIXON and the
BALKAN BATTLE
13 SQUADRON — IN A SECTOR WHERE THE BLACK CROSS OF GERMANY RULED THE SKIES.

Alan Willow, Air Ace 325, January 1967

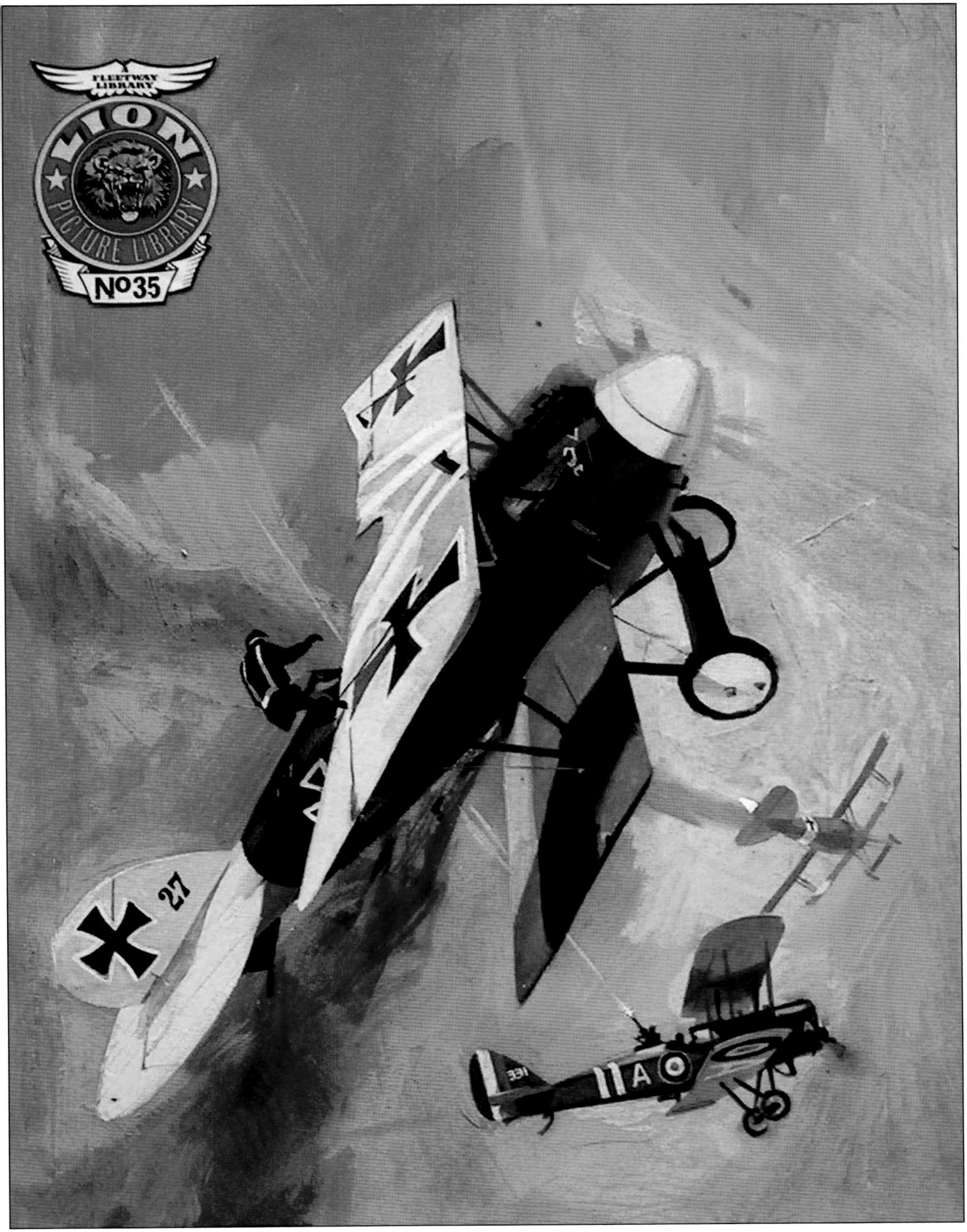
A FLEETWAY LIBRARY
LION
PICTURE LIBRARY
No35
27
A

Pino Dell'Orco, originally Thriller 374, August 1961

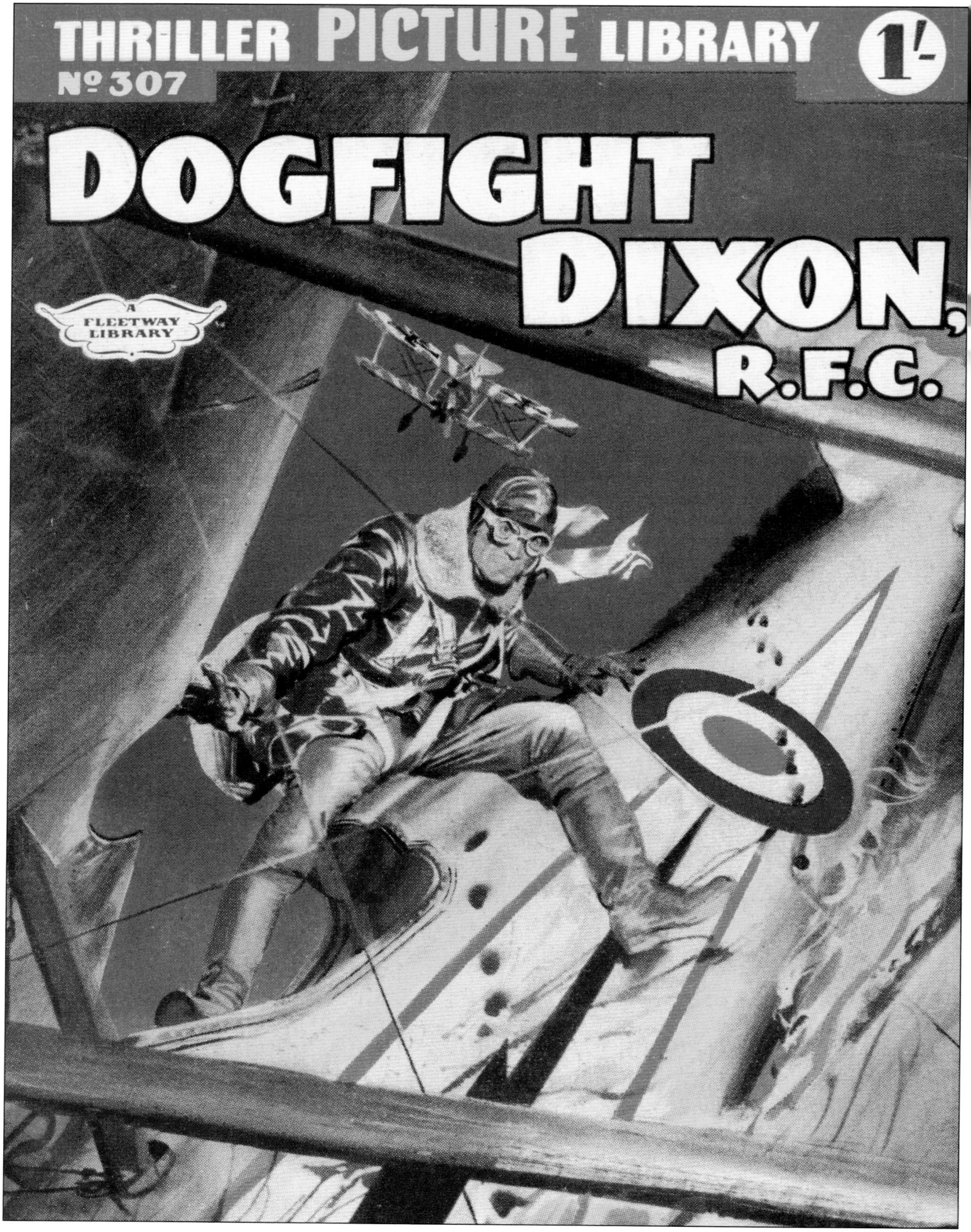
THRILLER PICTURE LIBRARY
Nº 307
1/-
DOGFIGHT DIXON, R.F.C.
A FLEETWAY LIBRARY

Giorgio DeGaspari, Thriller 307, March 1960

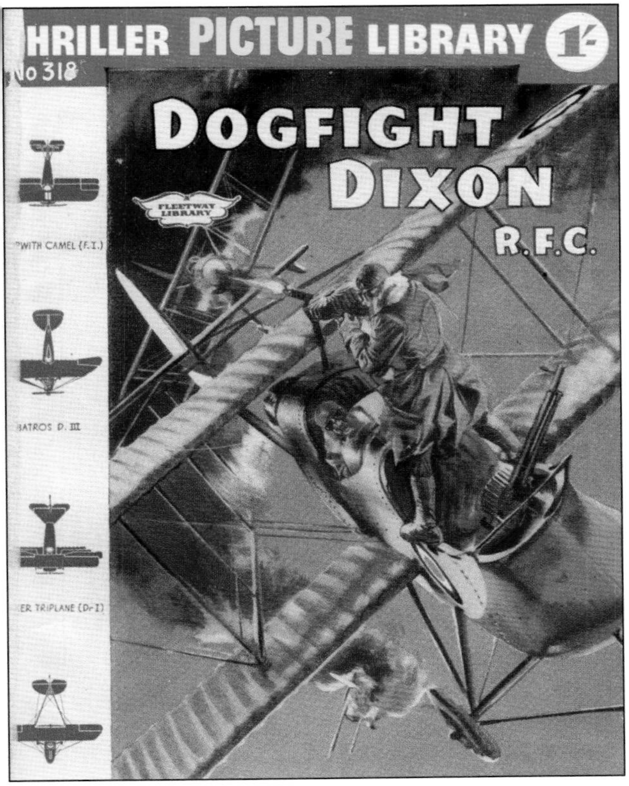
HRILLER PICTURE LIBRARY
1/-
No 318
DOGFIGHT DIXON
R.F.C.
PWITH CAMEL (F.I.)
ATROS D. III
ER TRIPLANE (Dr I)
Giorgio DeGaspari, Thriller 318, May 1960

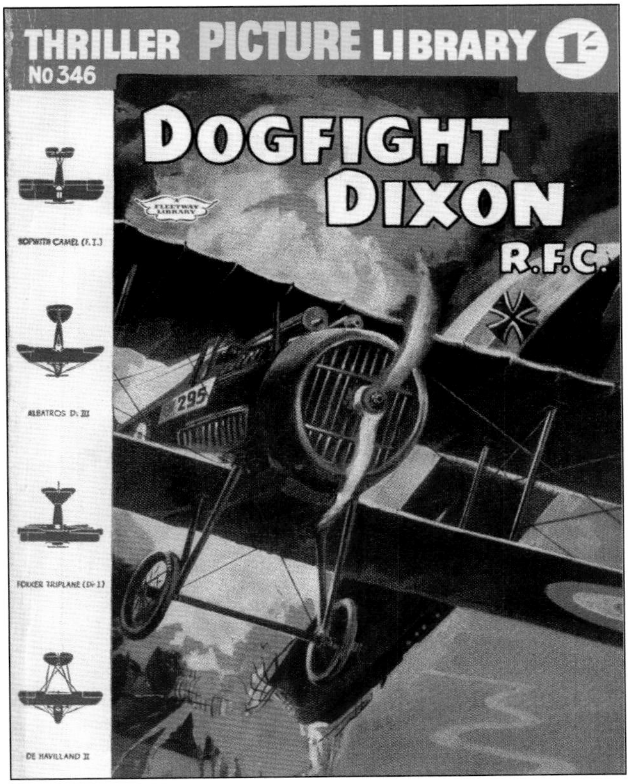
THRILLER PICTURE LIBRARY
1/-
No 346
DOGFIGHT DIXON
R.F.C.
SOPWITH CAMEL (F.I.)
ALBATROS D. III
FOKKER TRIPLANE (Dr I)
DE HAVILLAND II
295
Nino Caroselli, Thriller 346, December 1960

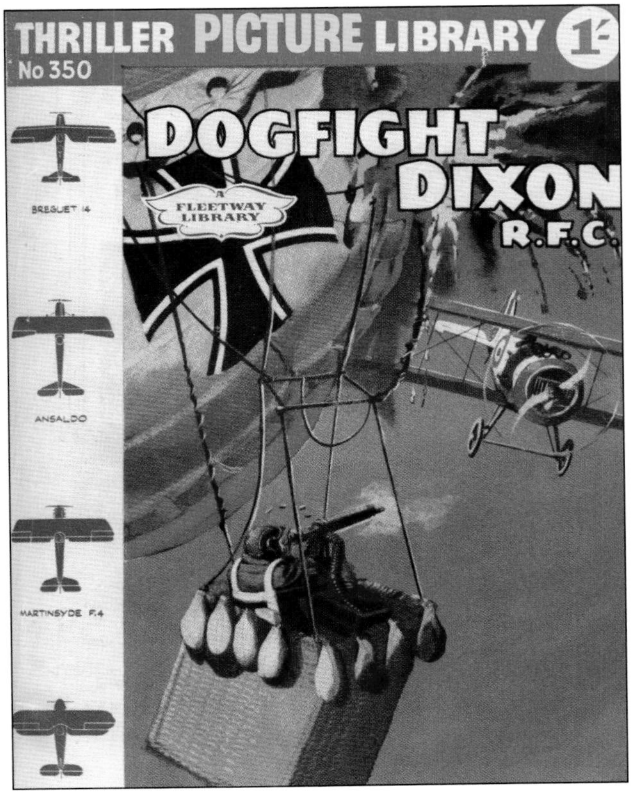
THRILLER PICTURE LIBRARY
1/-
No 350
DOGFIGHT DIXON
R.F.C.
A FLEETWAY LIBRARY
BREGUET 14
ANSALDO
MARTINSYDE F.4
Nino Caroselli, Thriller 350, January 1961

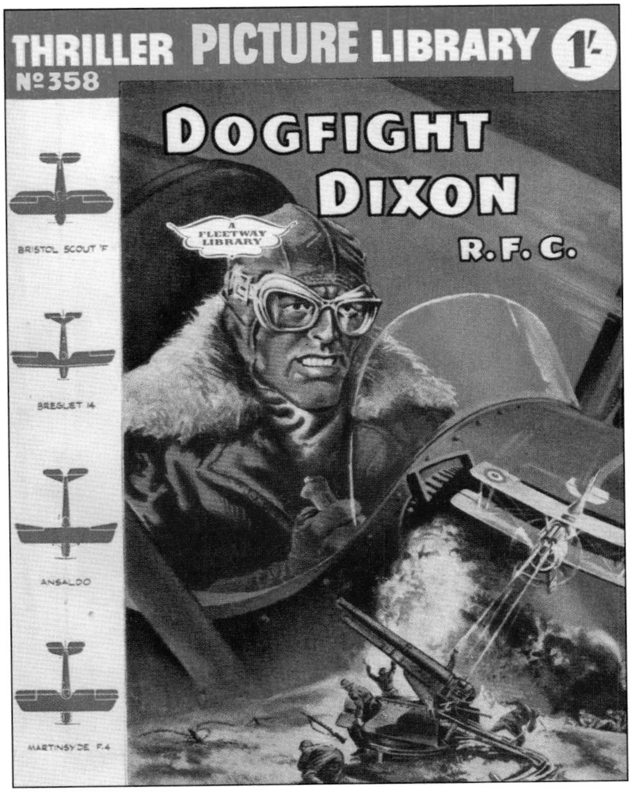
THRILLER PICTURE LIBRARY
1/-
Nº358
DOGFIGHT DIXON
R.F.C.
A FLEETWAY LIBRARY
BRISTOL SCOUT 'F'
BREGUET 14
ANSALDO
MARTINSYDE F.4
Stefan Barany, Thriller 358, March 1961

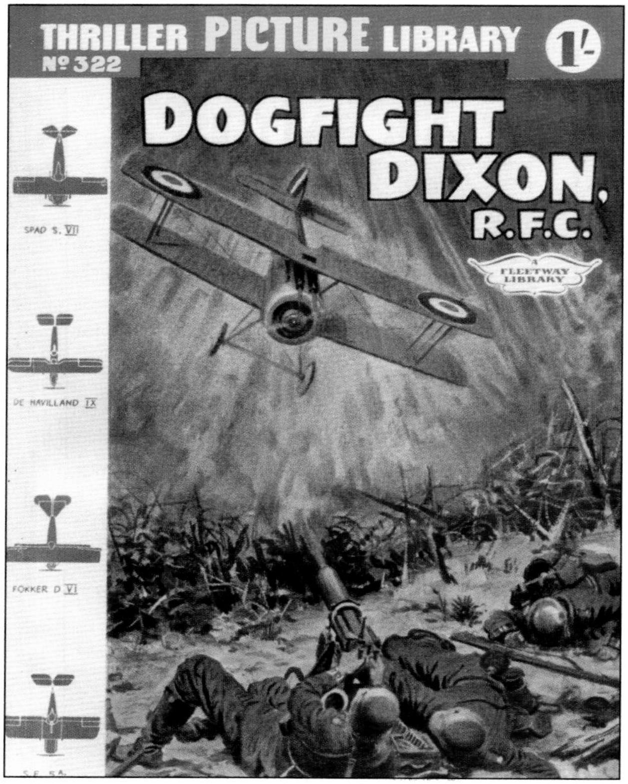
THRILLER PICTURE LIBRARY
1/-
No 322
DOGFIGHT DIXON, R.F.C.
A FLEETWAY LIBRARY
SPAD S. VII
DE HAVILLAND IX
FOKKER D VI
Stefan Barany, Thriller 322, June 1960

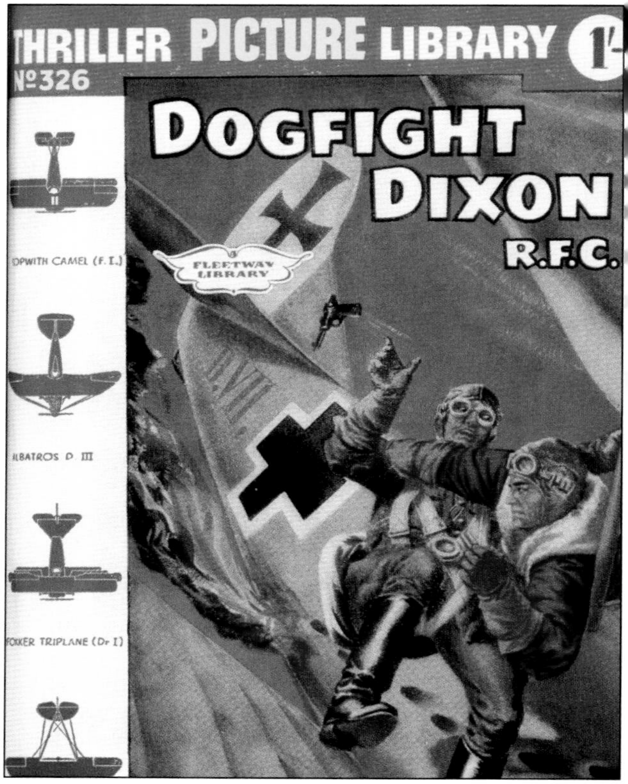
THRILLER PICTURE LIBRARY
1/-
No 326
DOGFIGHT DIXON R.F.C.
FLEETWAY LIBRARY
Stefan Barany, Thriller 326, July 1960

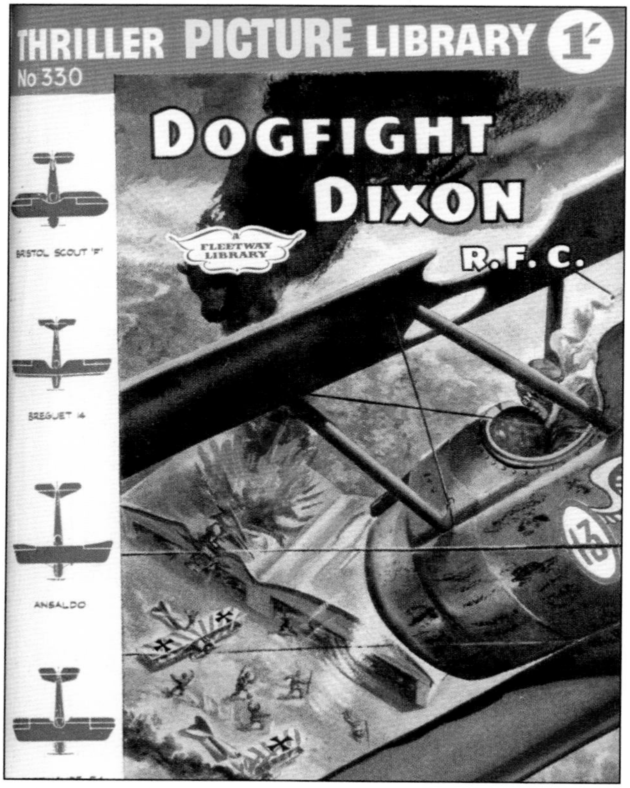
THRILLER PICTURE LIBRARY
1/-
No 330
DOGFIGHT DIXON R.F.C.
A FLEETWAY LIBRARY
BRISTOL SCOUT 'F'
BREGUET 14
ANSALDO
Stefan Barany, Thriller 330, August 1960

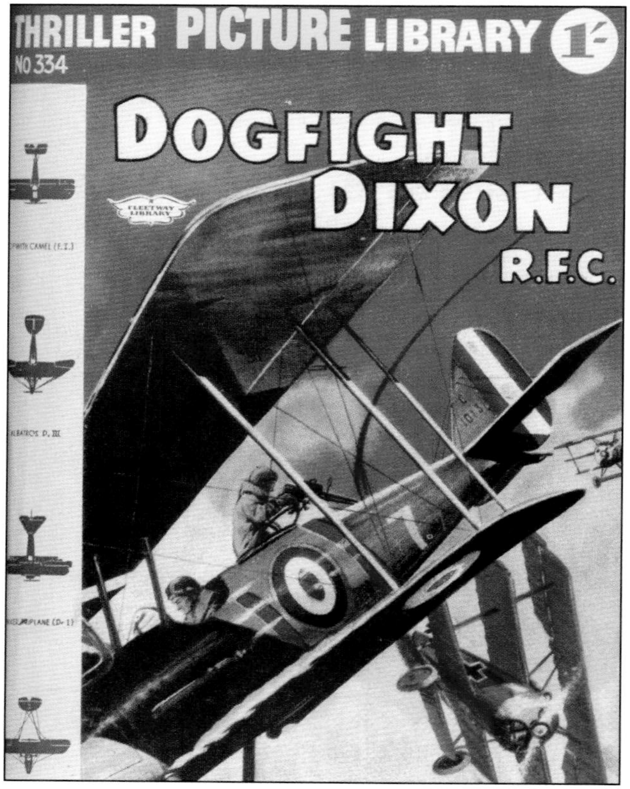
THRILLER PICTURE LIBRARY
1/-
No 334
DOGFIGHT DIXON R.F.C.
S.I. agency, Thriller 334, September 1960

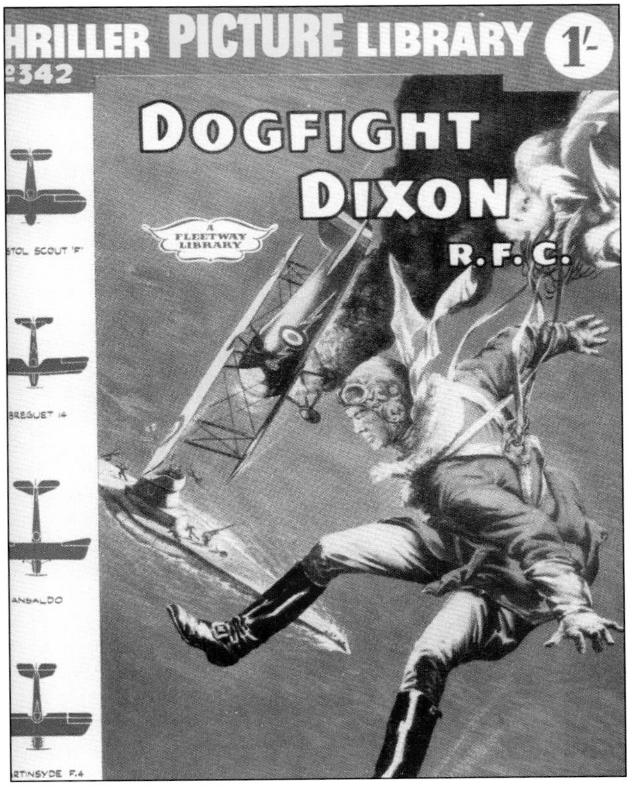
THRILLER PICTURE LIBRARY 1/-
342
DOGFIGHT
DIXON
R.F.C.
A FLEETWAY LIBRARY
BREGUET 14
ANSALDO
Stefan Barany, Thriller 342, November 1960

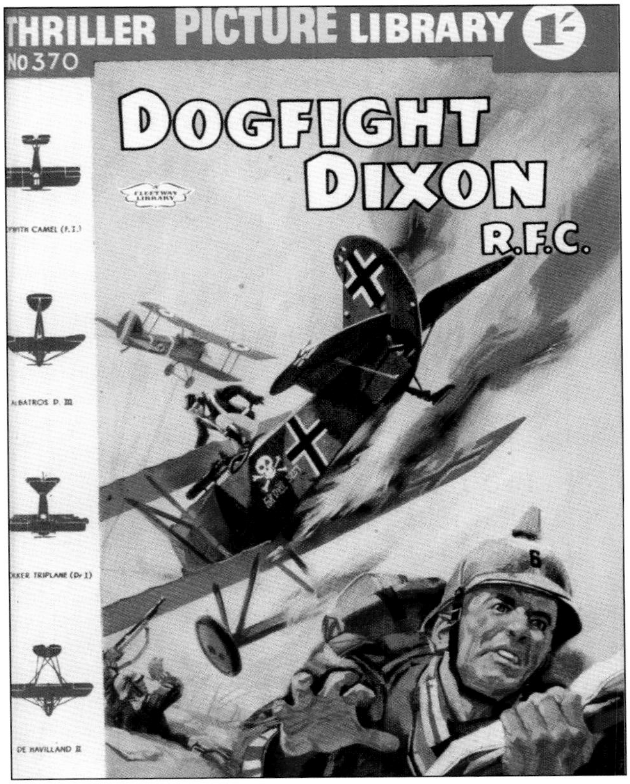
THRILLER PICTURE LIBRARY 1/-
NO 370
DOGFIGHT
DIXON
R.F.C.
A FLEETWAY LIBRARY
ALBATROS D. III
DE HAVILLAND II
Pino Dell'Orco, Thriller 370, July 1961

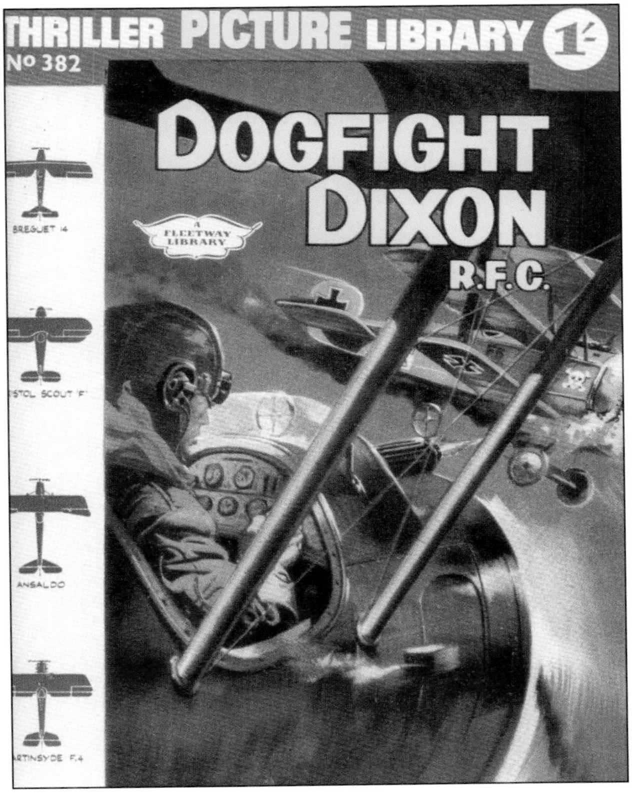
THRILLER PICTURE LIBRARY 1/-
No 382
DOGFIGHT
DIXON
R.F.C.
A FLEETWAY LIBRARY
BREGUET 14
ANSALDO
Allessandro Biffignandi, Thriller 382, October 1961

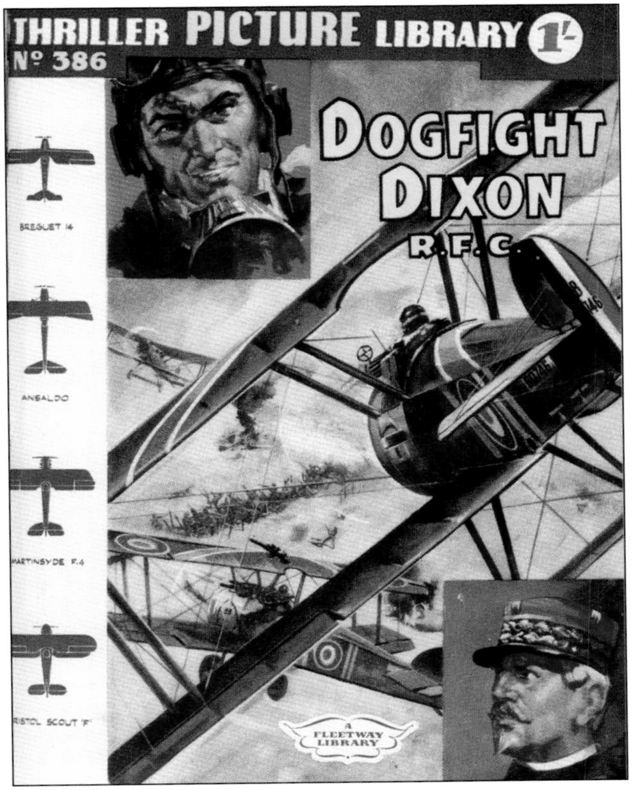
THRILLER PICTURE LIBRARY 1/-
No 386
DOGFIGHT
DIXON
R.F.C.
A FLEETWAY LIBRARY
BREGUET 14
ANSALDO
MARTINSYDE F.4
Allessandro Biffignandi, Thriller 386, November 1961

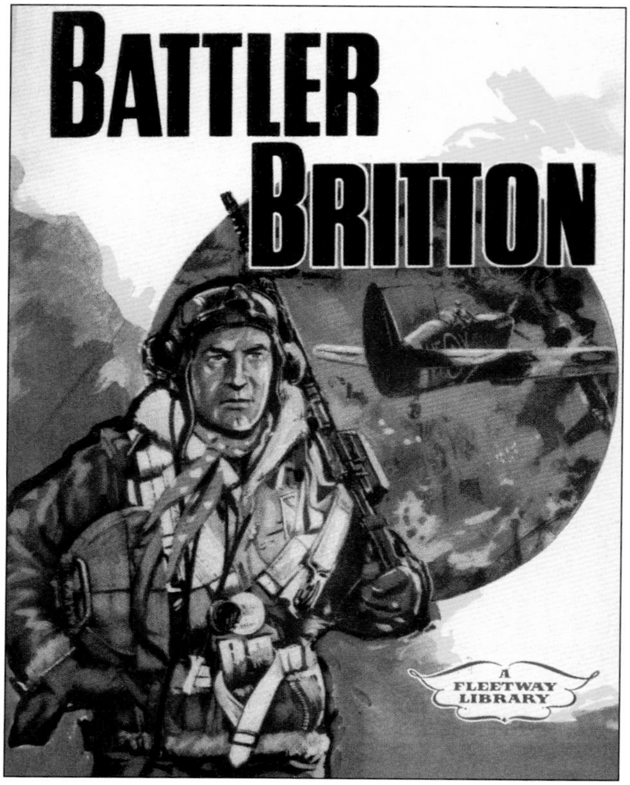
BATTLER
BRITTON
A
FLEETWAY
LIBRARY

Allessandro Biffignandi, Thriller 441, January 1963

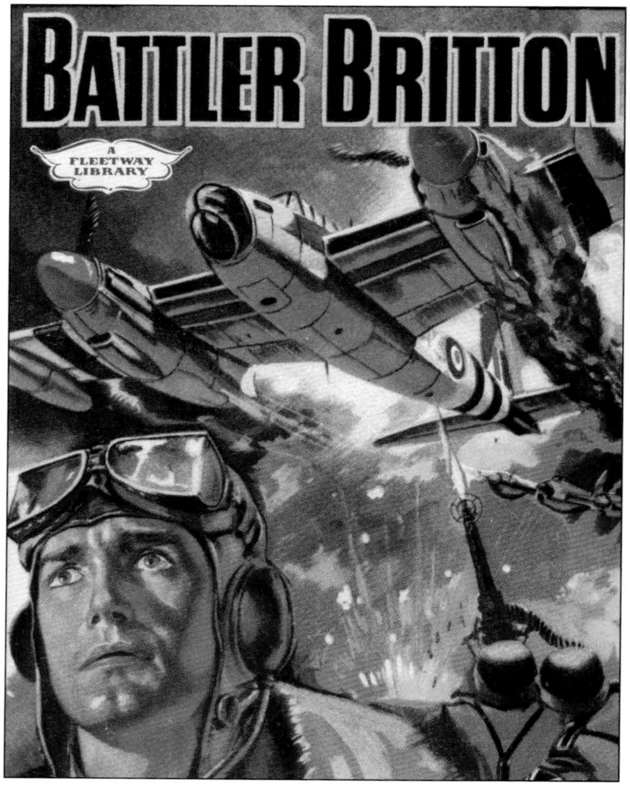
BATTLER BRITTON
A
FLEETWAY
LIBRARY

Nino Caroselli, Thriller 449, March 1963

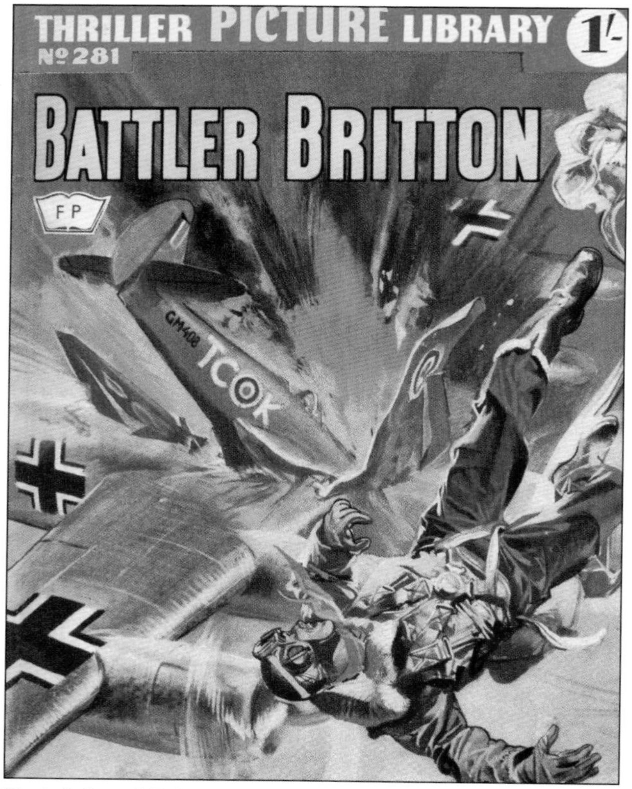
THRILLER PICTURE LIBRARY
1/-
№281
BATTLER BRITTON
FP
TCOK

Giorgio DeGaspari, Thriller 281, July 1959

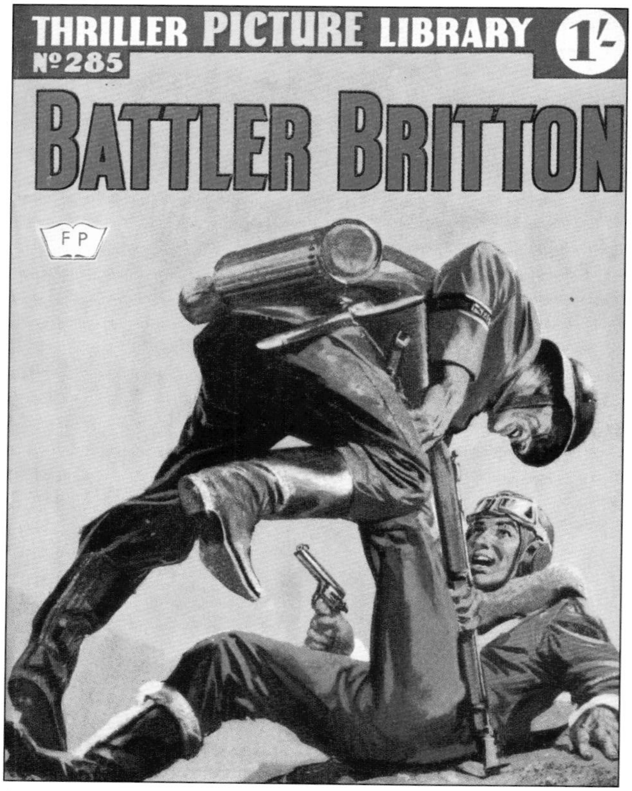
THRILLER PICTURE LIBRARY
1/-
№285
BATTLER BRITTON
FP

Giorgio DeGaspari, Thriller 285, September 1959

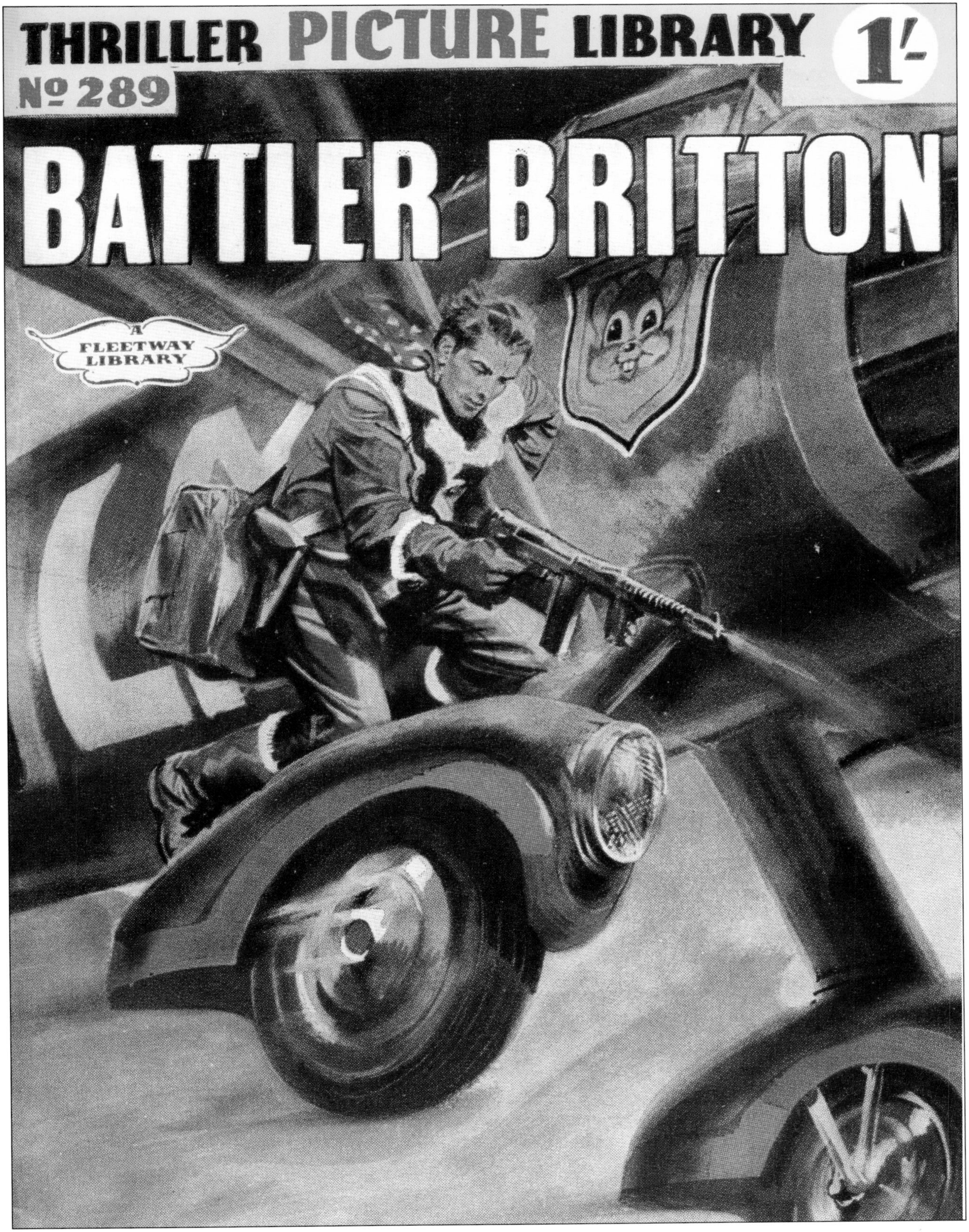
THRILLER PICTURE LIBRARY
1/-
No 289
BATTLER BRITTON
A FLEETWAY LIBRARY

Giorgio DeGaspari, Thriller 289, October 1959

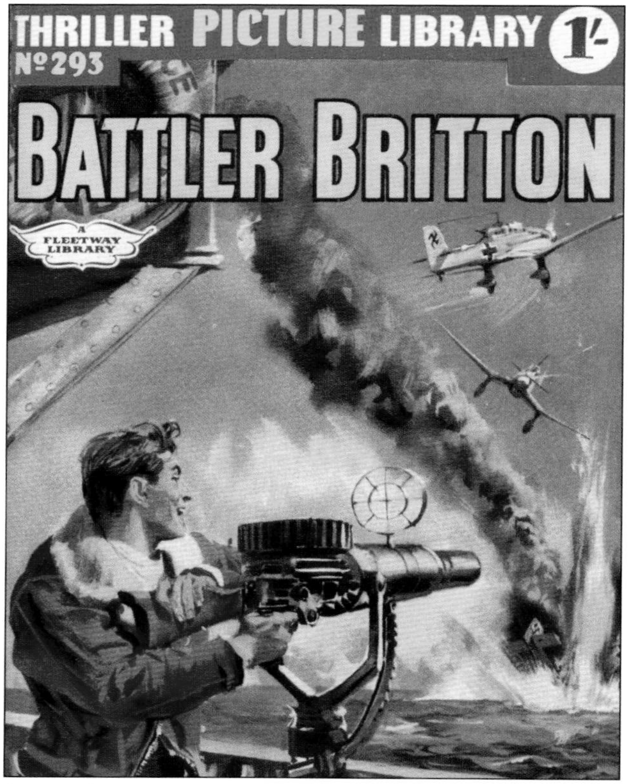
THRILLER PICTURE LIBRARY
1/-
Nº293
BATTLER BRITTON
A FLEETWAY LIBRARY

Giorgio DeGaspari, Thriller 293, November 1959

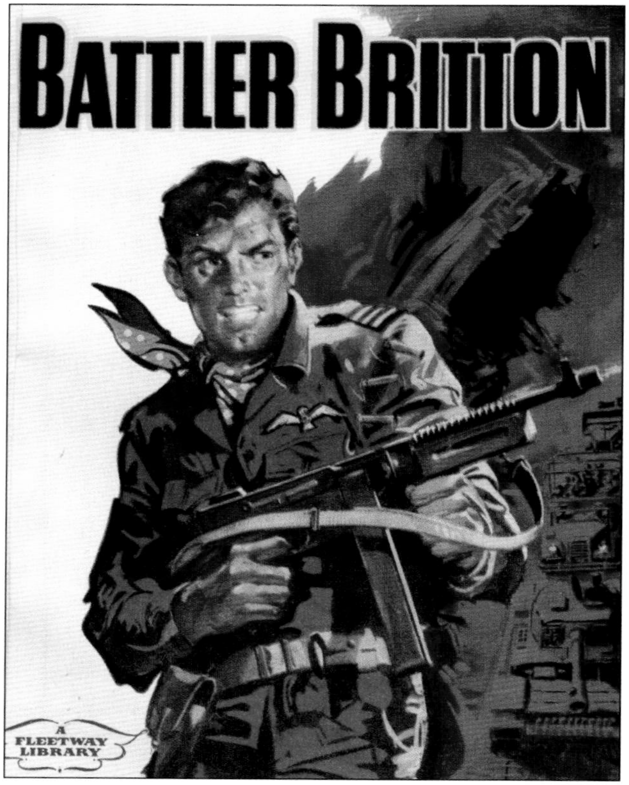
BATTLER BRITTON
A FLEETWAY LIBRARY

Allessandro Biffignandi, Thriller 417, July 1962

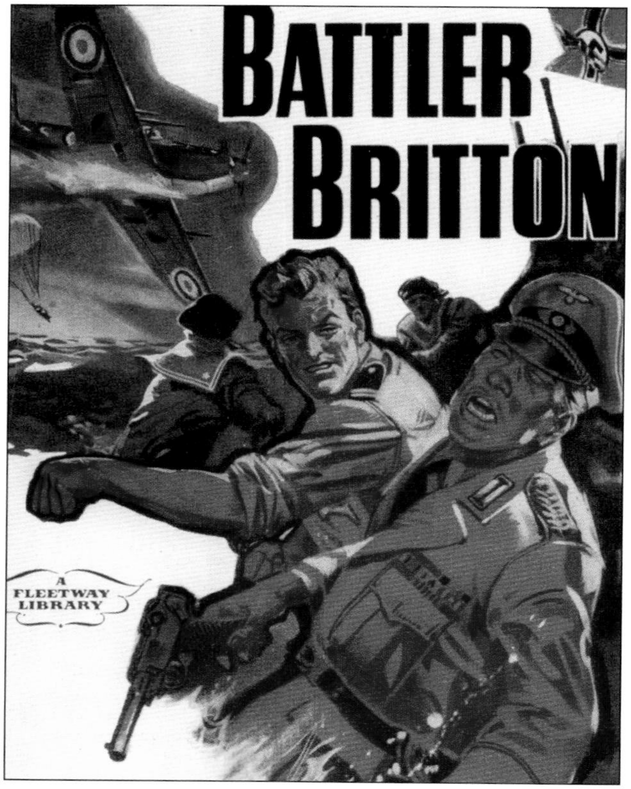
BATTLER BRITTON
A FLEETWAY LIBRARY

Allessandro Biffignandi, Thriller 421, August 1962

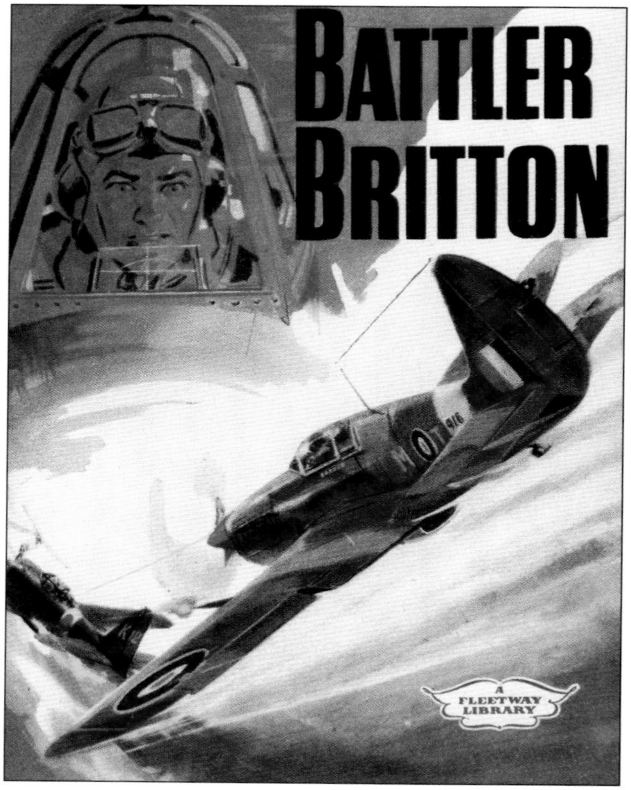
BATTLER BRITTON
A FLEETWAY LIBRARY

Pino Dell'Orco, Thriller 433, November 1962

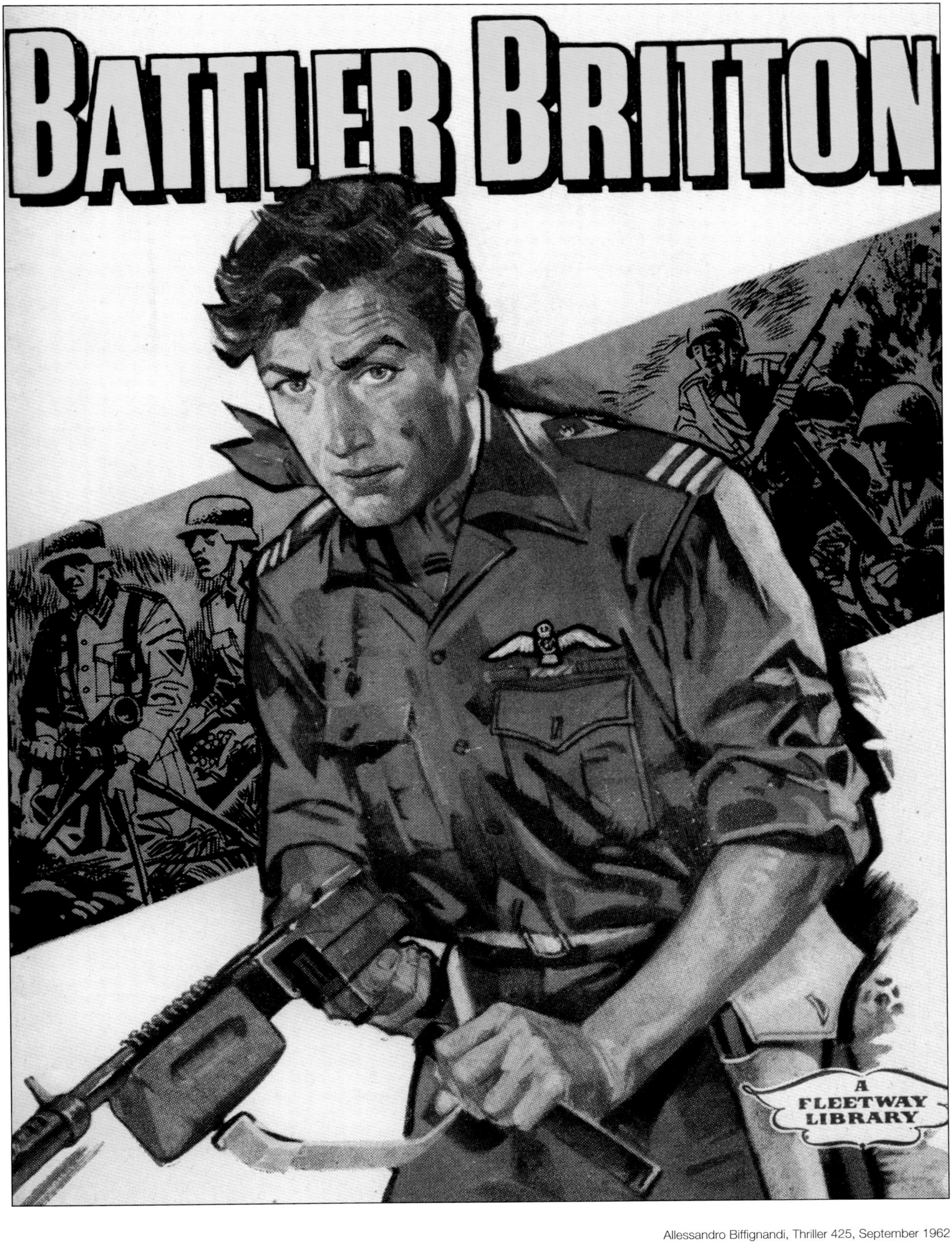
BATTLER BRITTON
A FLEETWAY LIBRARY

Allessandro Biffignandi, Thriller 425, September 1962

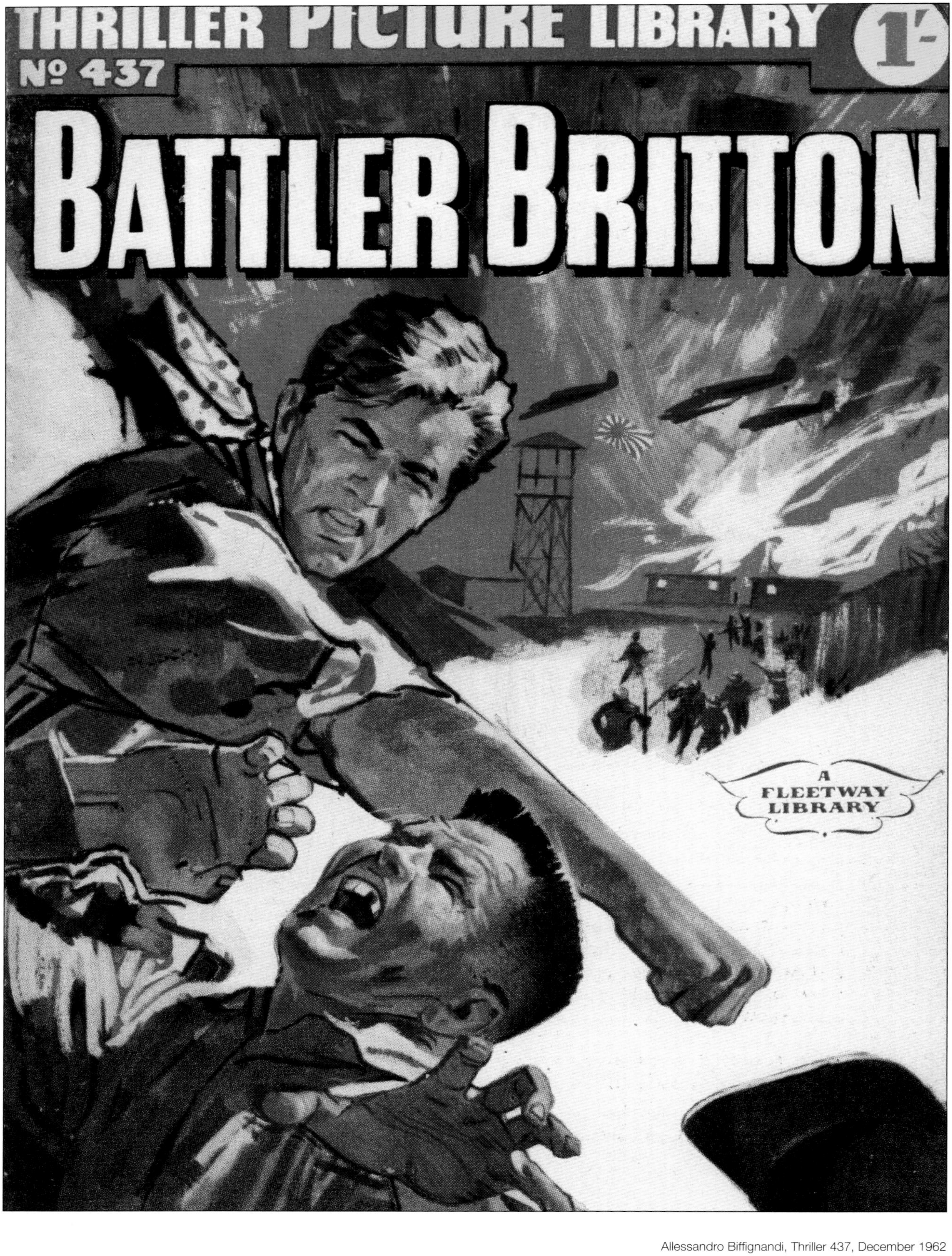
THRILLER PICTURE LIBRARY
1/-
Nº 437
BATTLER BRITTON
A FLEETWAY LIBRARY

Allessandro Biffignandi, Thriller 437, December 1962

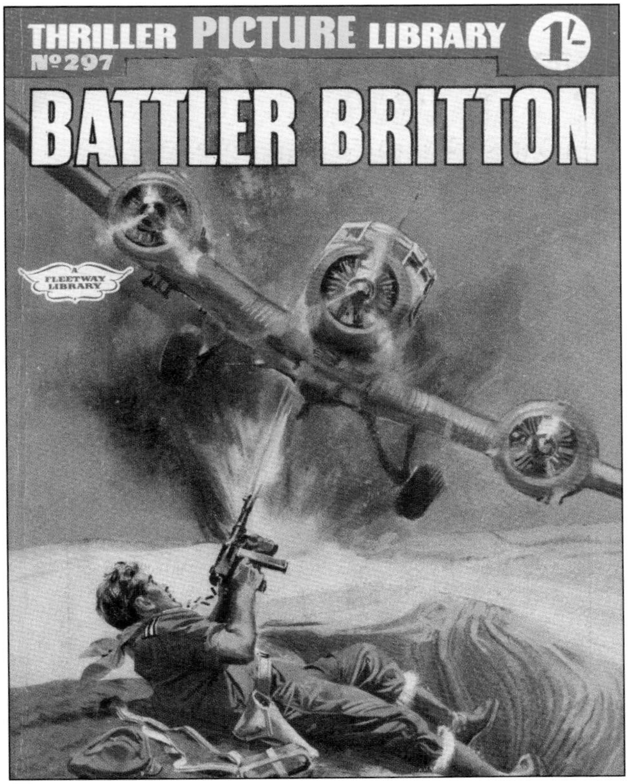
THRILLER PICTURE LIBRARY
1/-
Nº297
BATTLER BRITTON
A FLEETWAY LIBRARY
Giorgio DeGaspari, Thriller 297, December 1959

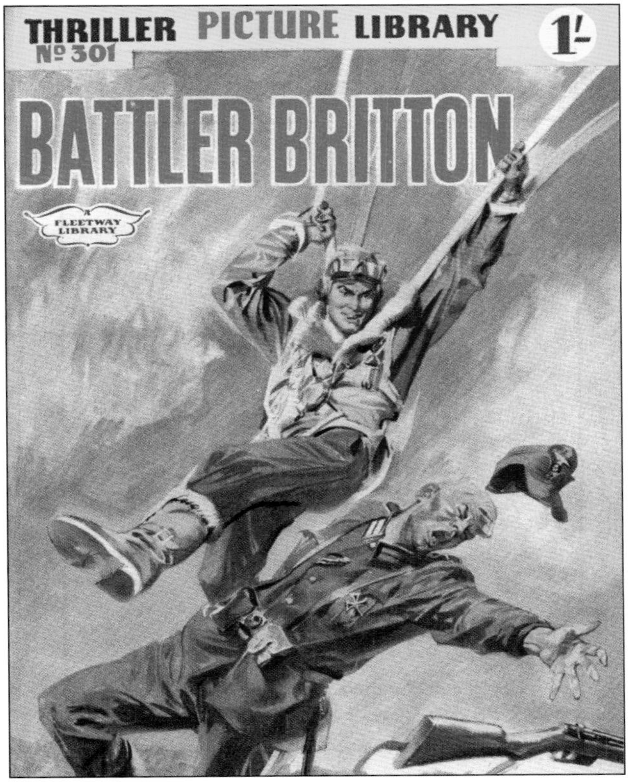
THRILLER PICTURE LIBRARY
1/-
Nº301
BATTLER BRITTON
A FLEETWAY LIBRARY
Giorgio DeGaspari, Thriller 301, January 1960

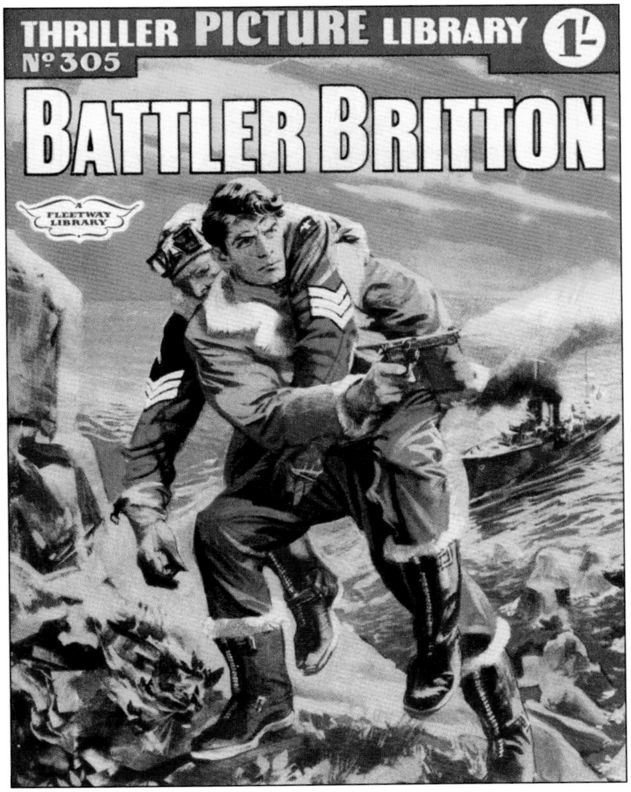
THRILLER PICTURE LIBRARY
1/-
Nº305
BATTLER BRITTON
A FLEETWAY LIBRARY
Giorgio DeGaspari, Thriller 305, February 1960

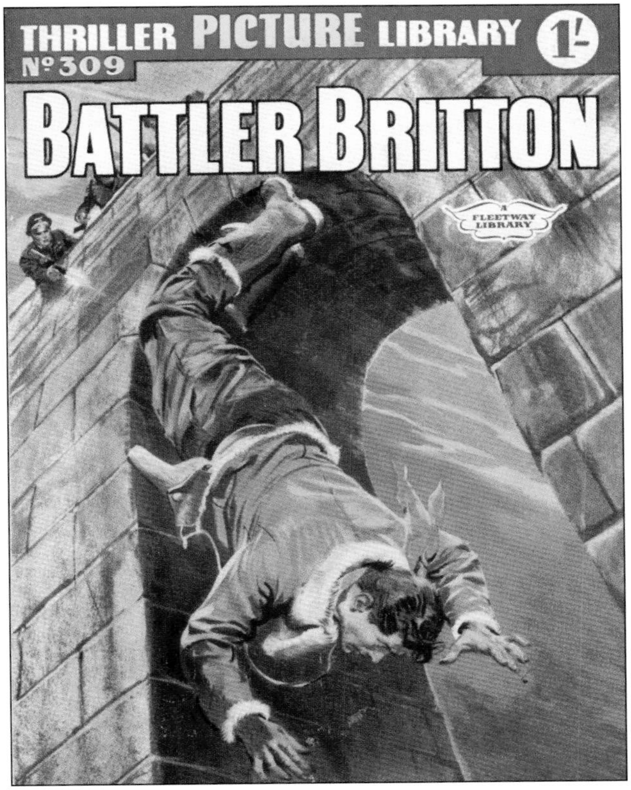
THRILLER PICTURE LIBRARY
1/-
Nº309
BATTLER BRITTON
A FLEETWAY LIBRARY
Giorgio DeGaspari, Thriller 309, March 1960

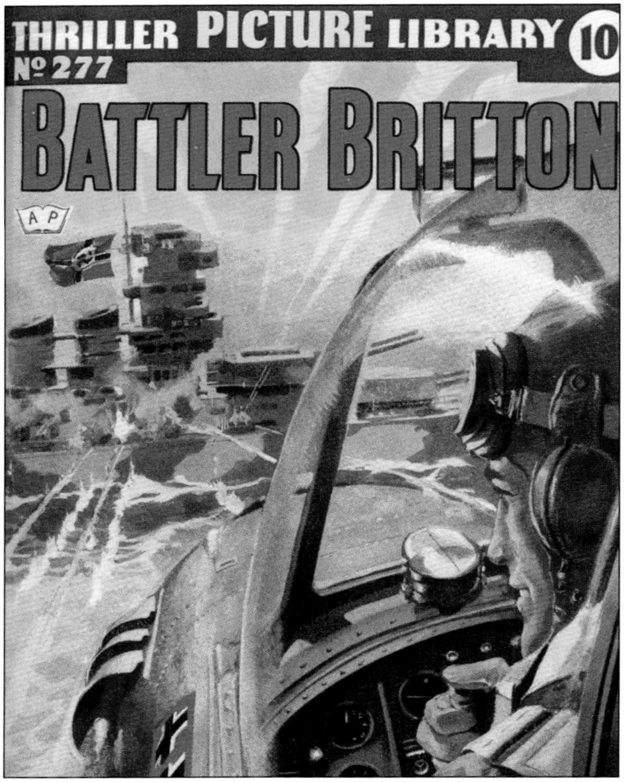
THRILLER PICTURE LIBRARY
10
Nº 277
BATTLER BRITTON
A P

Nino Caroselli, Thriller 277, June 1959

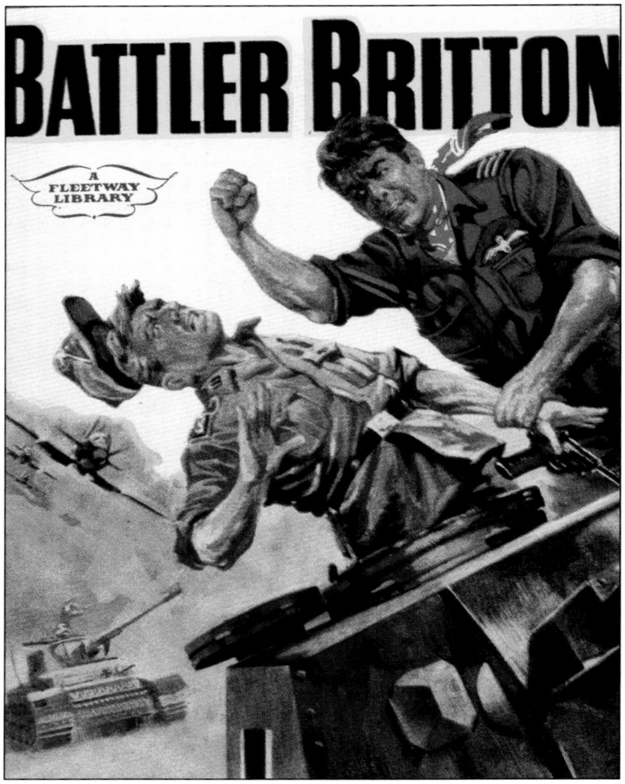
BATTLER BRITTON
A FLEETWAY LIBRARY

Allessandro Biffignandi, Thriller 429, October 1962

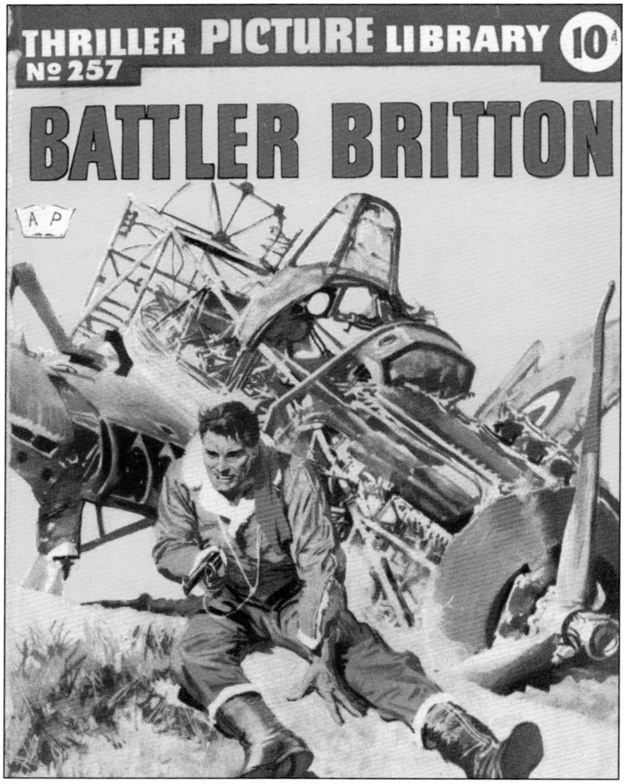
THRILLER PICTURE LIBRARY
10d
Nº 257
BATTLER BRITTON
A P

Giorgio DeGaspari, Thriller 257, January 1959

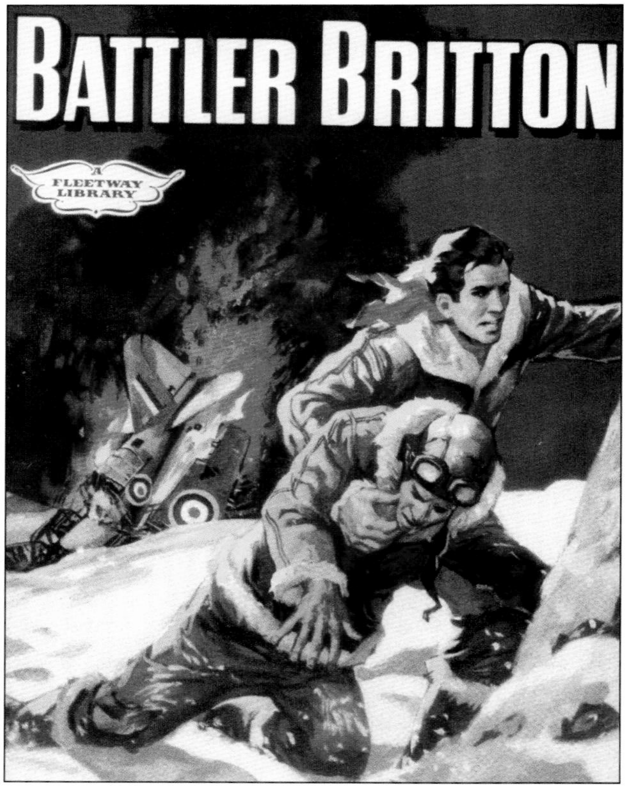
BATTLER BRITTON
A FLEETWAY LIBRARY

Pino Dell'Orco, Thriller 385, November 1961

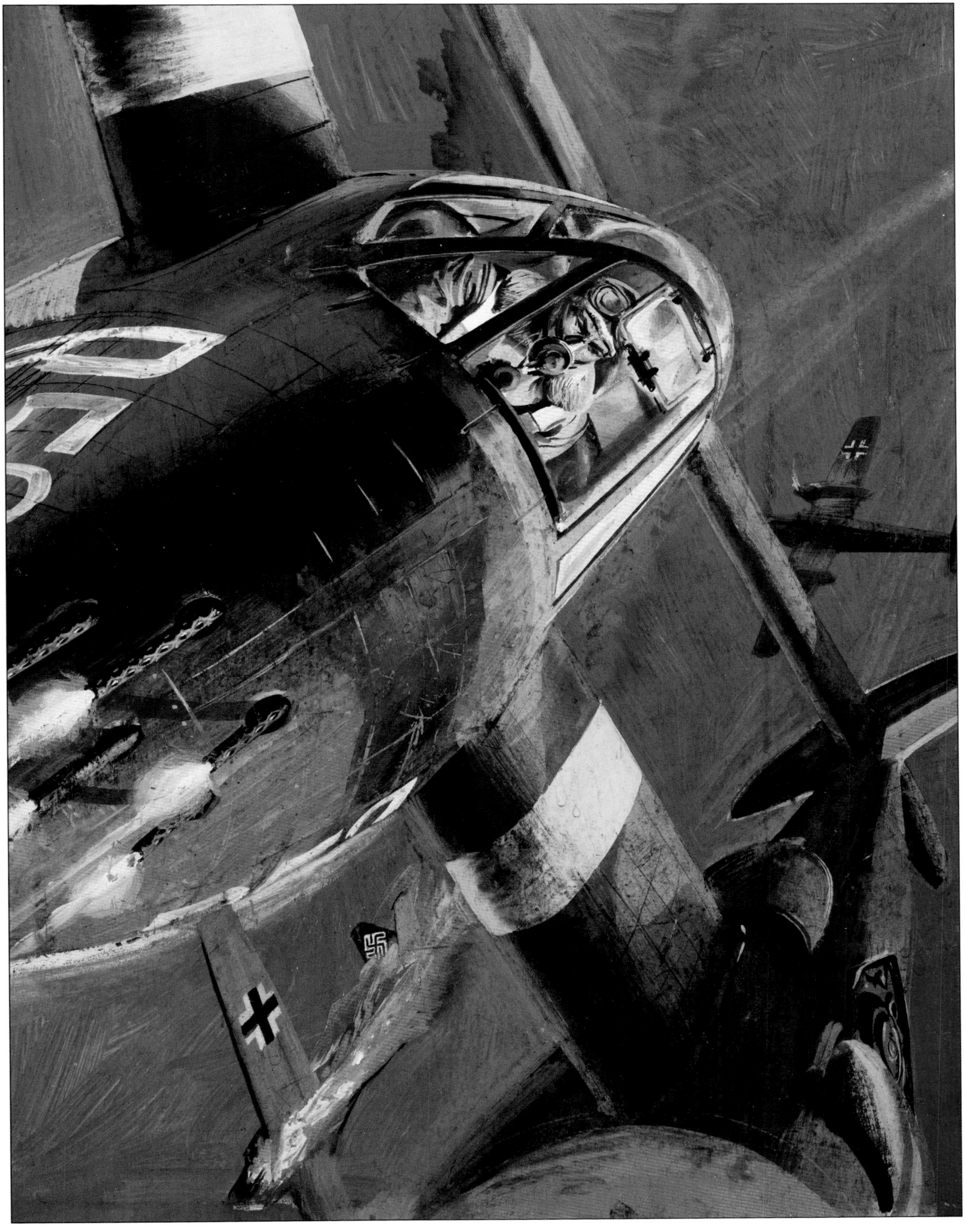

Giorgio DeGaspari, Thriller 261, February 1959

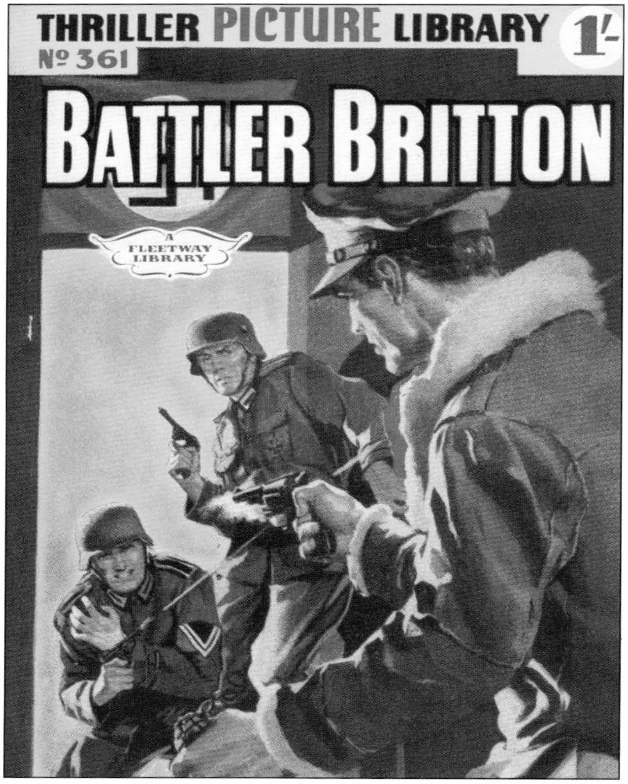
THRILLER PICTURE LIBRARY
1/-
Nº 361
BATTLER BRITTON
A FLEETWAY LIBRARY
Nino Caroselli, Thriller 361, May 1961

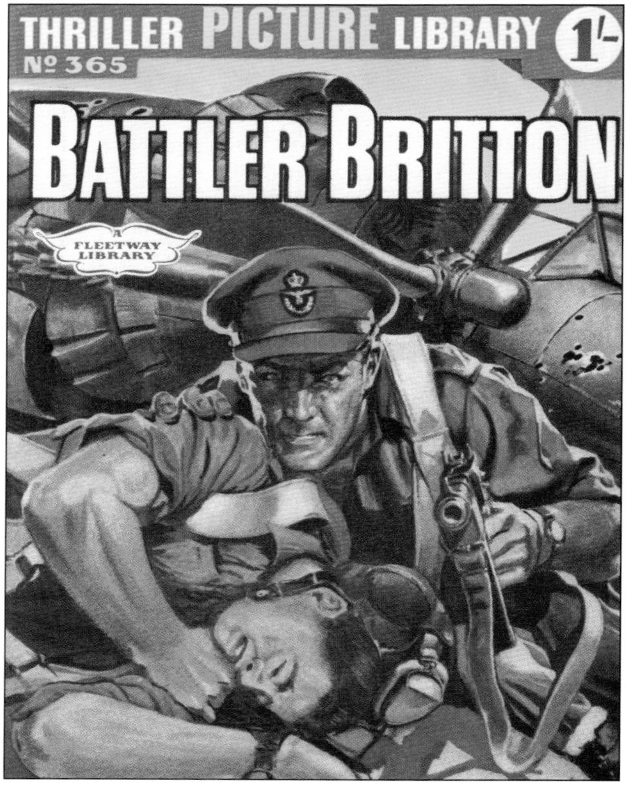
THRILLER PICTURE LIBRARY
1/-
Nº 365
BATTLER BRITTON
A FLEETWAY LIBRARY
Nino Caroselli, Thriller 365, June 1961

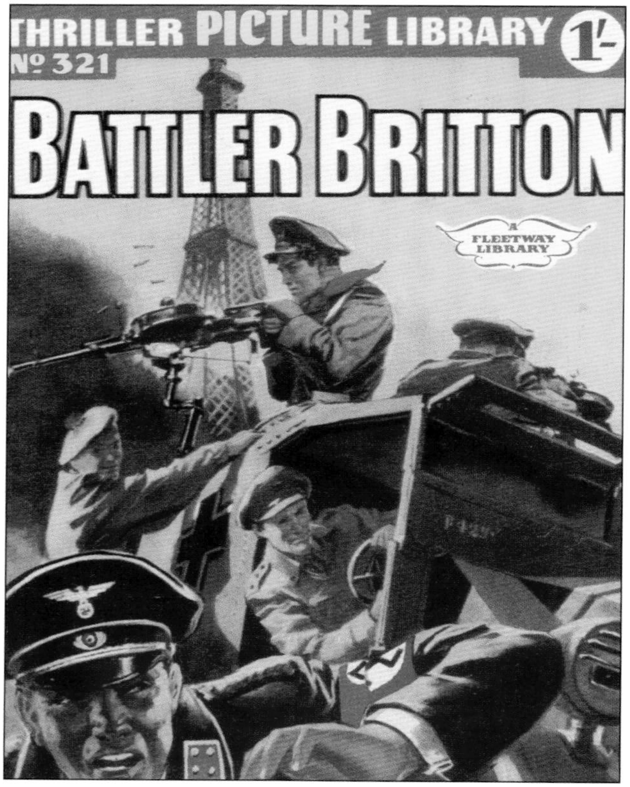
THRILLER PICTURE LIBRARY
1/-
Nº 321
BATTLER BRITTON
A FLEETWAY LIBRARY
Nino Caroselli, Thriller 321, June 1960

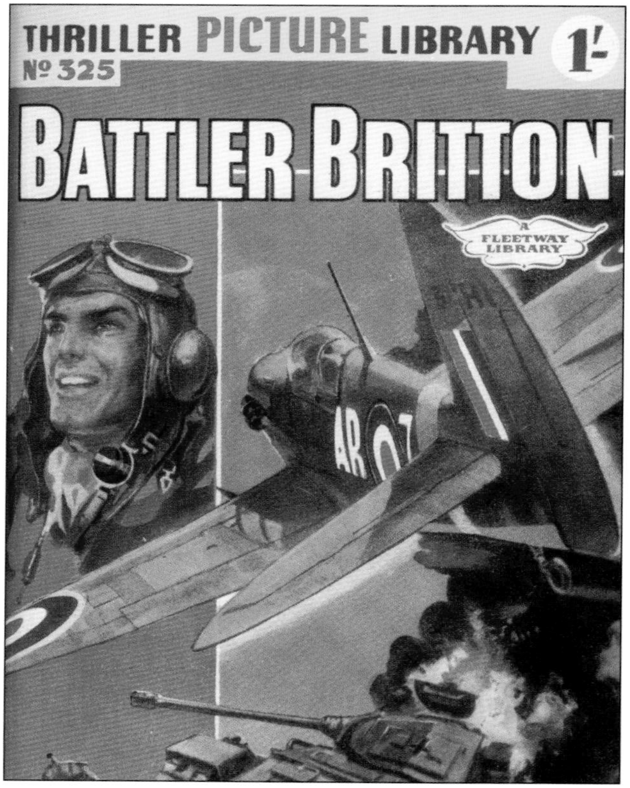
THRILLER PICTURE LIBRARY
1/-
Nº 325
BATTLER BRITTON
A FLEETWAY LIBRARY
Nino Caroselli, Thriller 325, July 1960

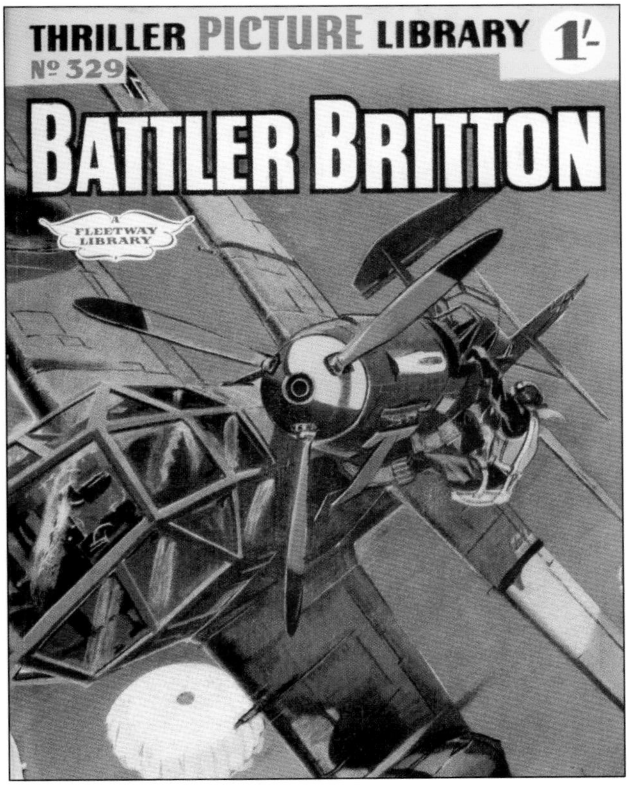
THRILLER PICTURE LIBRARY
1/-
Nº 329
BATTLER BRITTON
A FLEETWAY LIBRARY

Nino Caroselli, Thriller 329, August 1960

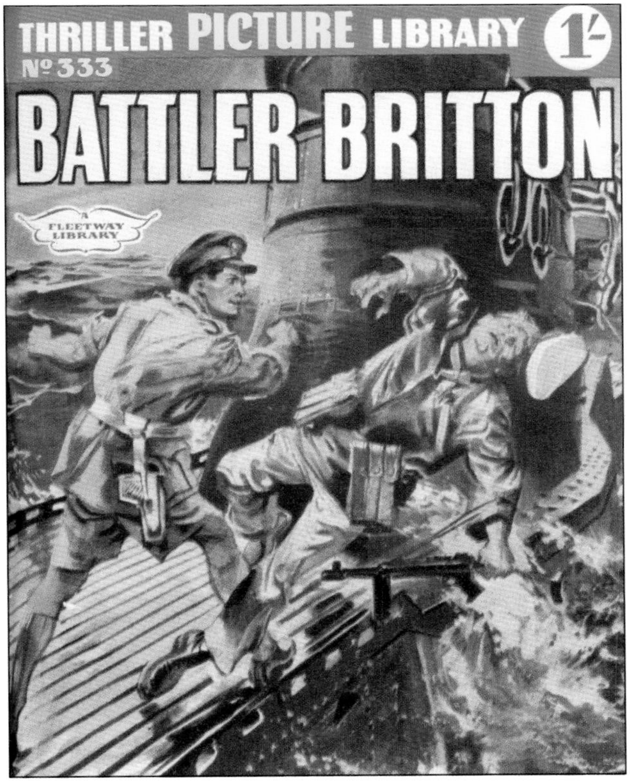
THRILLER PICTURE LIBRARY
1/-
Nº 333
BATTLER BRITTON
A FLEETWAY LIBRARY

Giorgio DeGaspari, Thriller 333, September 1960

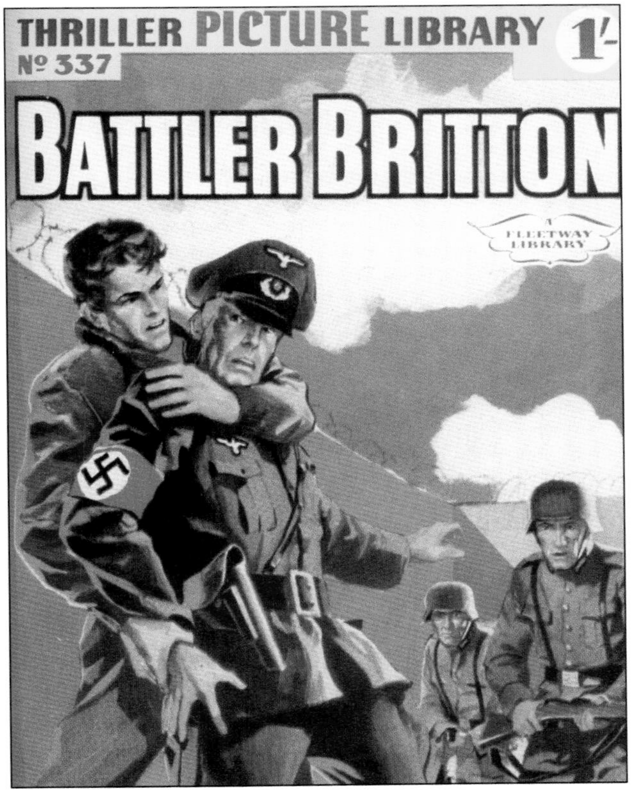
THRILLER PICTURE LIBRARY
1/-
Nº 337
BATTLER BRITTON
A FLEETWAY LIBRARY

Nino Caroselli, Thriller 337, October 1960

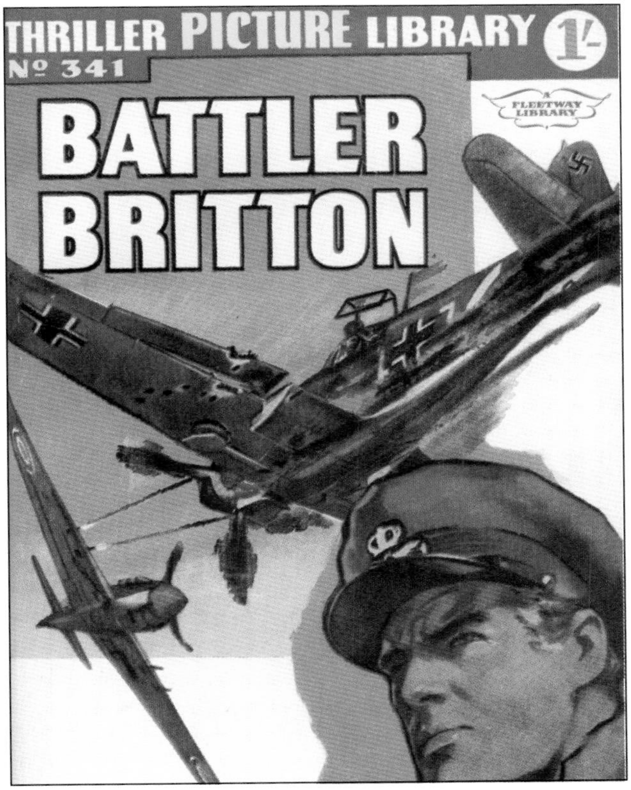
THRILLER PICTURE LIBRARY
1/-
Nº 341
A FLEETWAY LIBRARY
BATTLER
BRITTON

Nino Caroselli, Thriller 341, November 1960

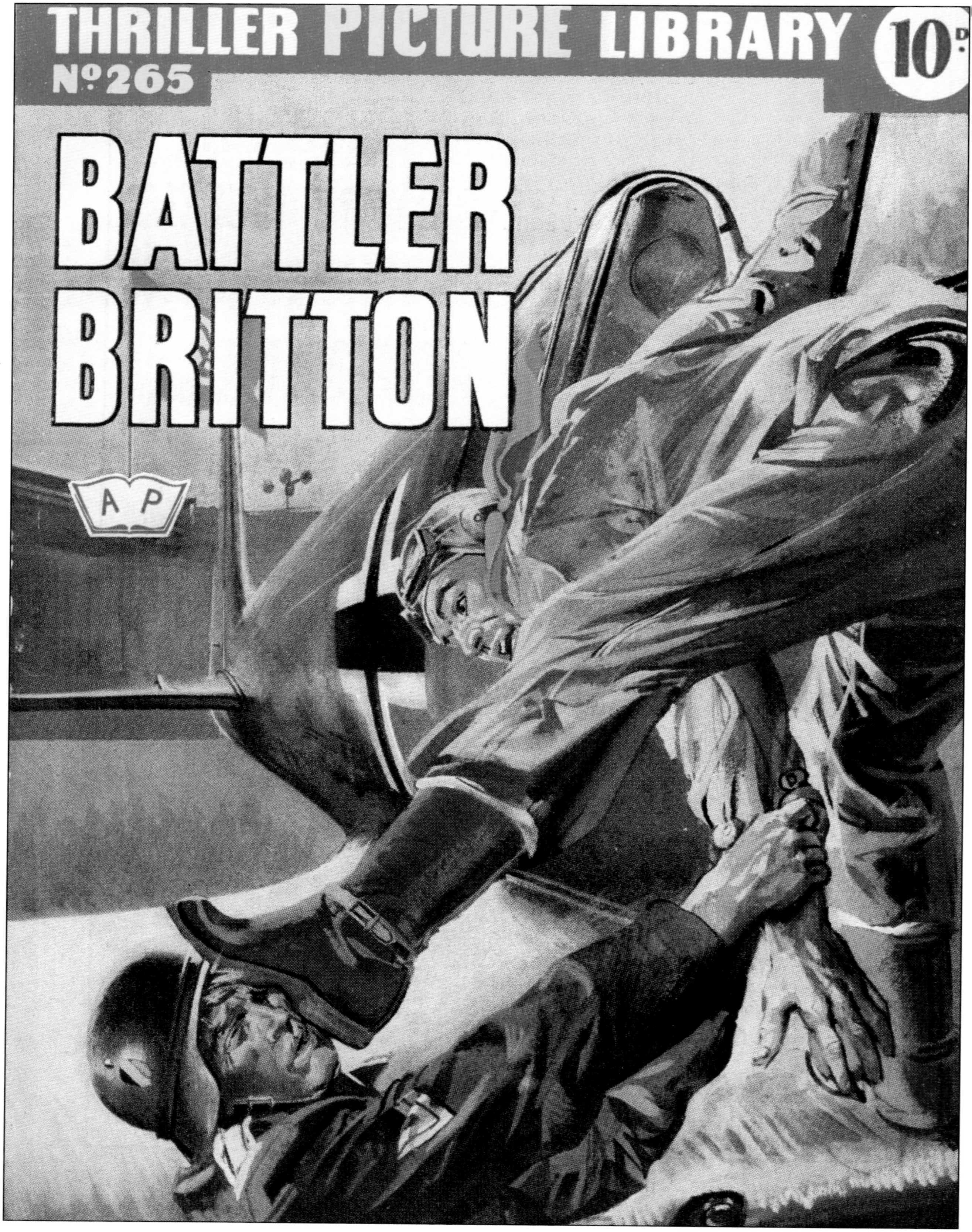
THRILLER PICTURE LIBRARY
Nº265
10D.
BATTLER BRITTON
AP

Giorgio DeGaspari, Thriller 265, March 1959

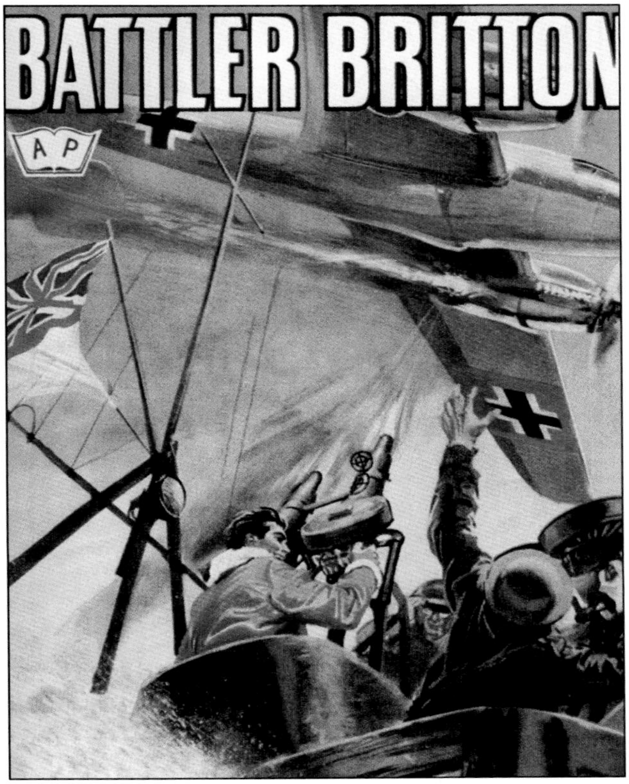
BATTLER BRITTON
A P

Giorgio DeGaspari, Thriller 273, May 1959

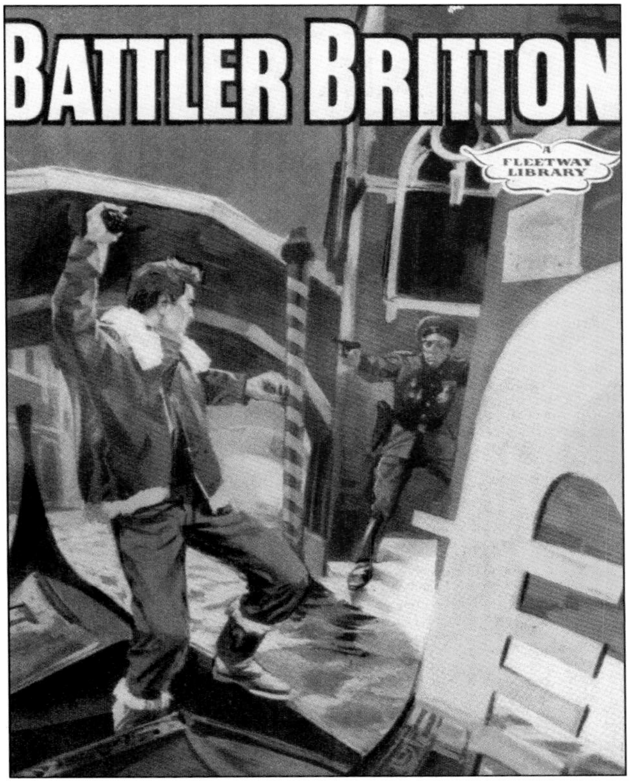
BATTLER BRITTON
A FLEETWAY LIBRARY

Pino Dell'Orco, Thriller 345, December 1960

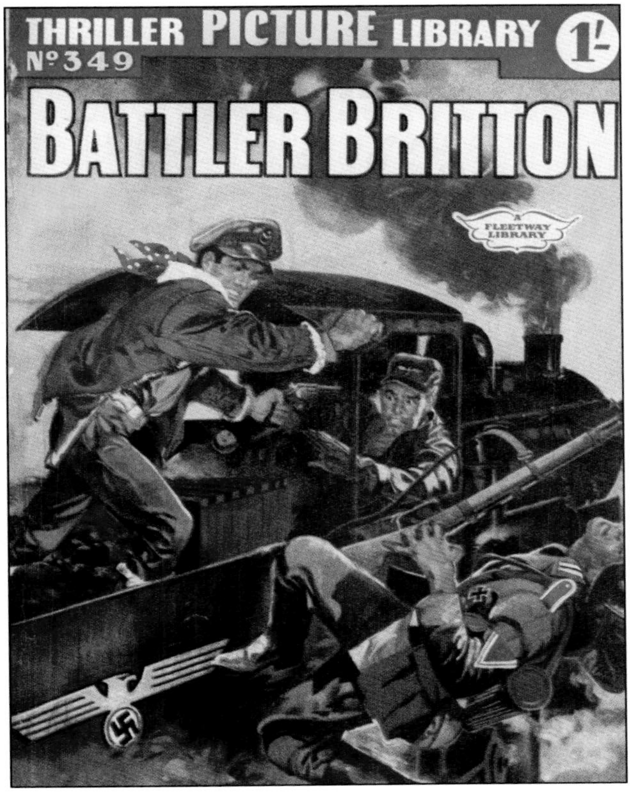
THRILLER PICTURE LIBRARY
Nº349
1/-
BATTLER BRITTON
A FLEETWAY LIBRARY

Stefan Barany, Thriller 349, January 1961

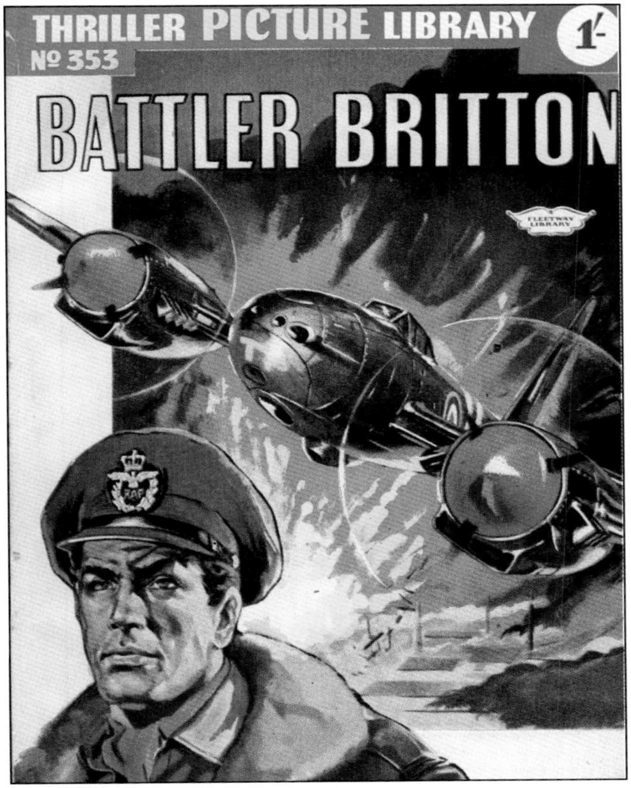
THRILLER PICTURE LIBRARY
Nº353
1/-
BATTLER BRITTON

Nino Caroselli, Thriller 353, February 1961

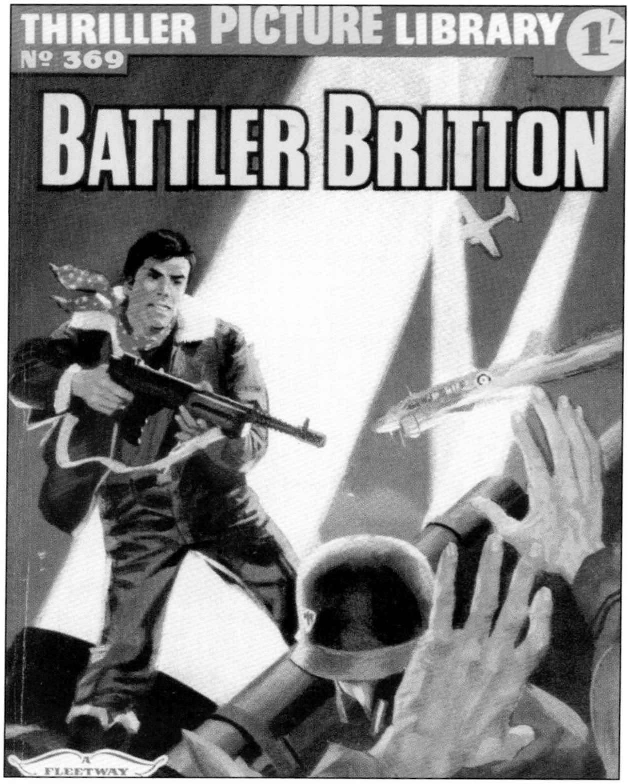
THRILLER PICTURE LIBRARY
1/-
No 369
BATTLER BRITTON
A FLEETWAY

Pino Dell'Orco, Thriller 369, July 1961

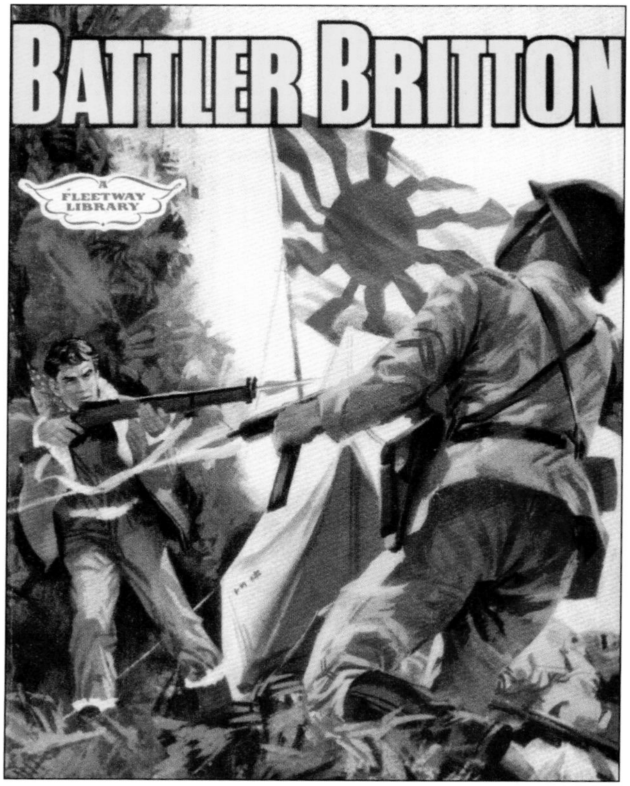
BATTLER BRITTON
A FLEETWAY LIBRARY

Pino Dell'Orco, Thriller 373, August 1961

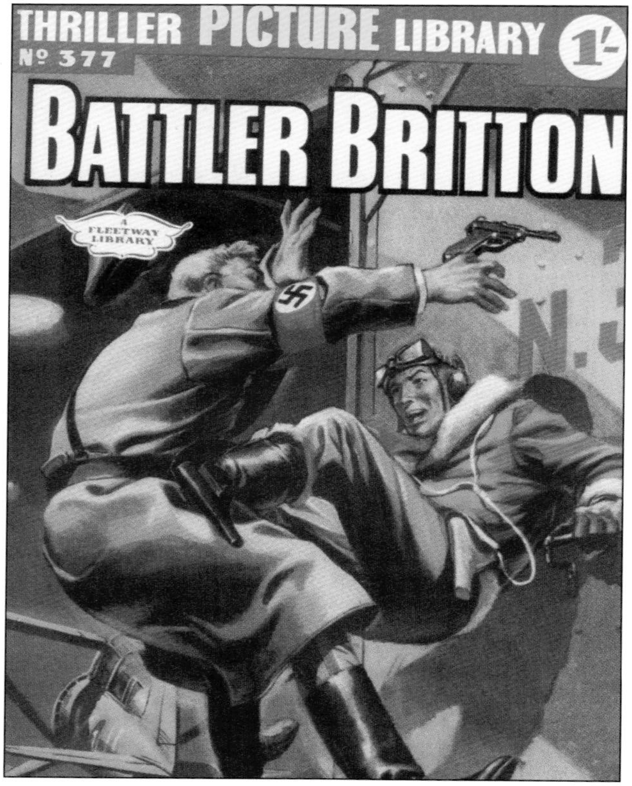
THRILLER PICTURE LIBRARY
1/-
No 377
BATTLER BRITTON
A FLEETWAY LIBRARY

Nino Caroselli, Thriller 377, September 1961

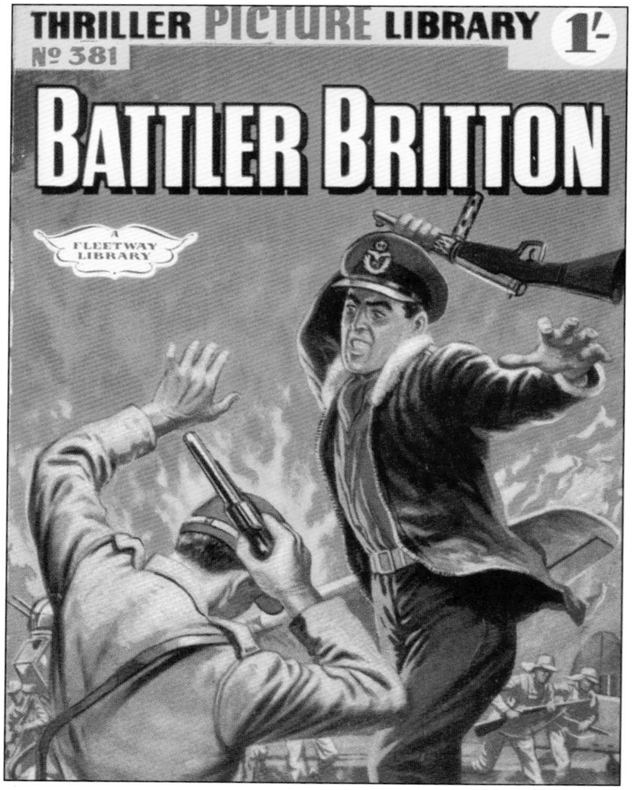
THRILLER PICTURE LIBRARY
1/-
No 381
BATTLER BRITTON
A FLEETWAY LIBRARY

Geoff Campion and Pat Nicolle, Thriller 381, October 1961

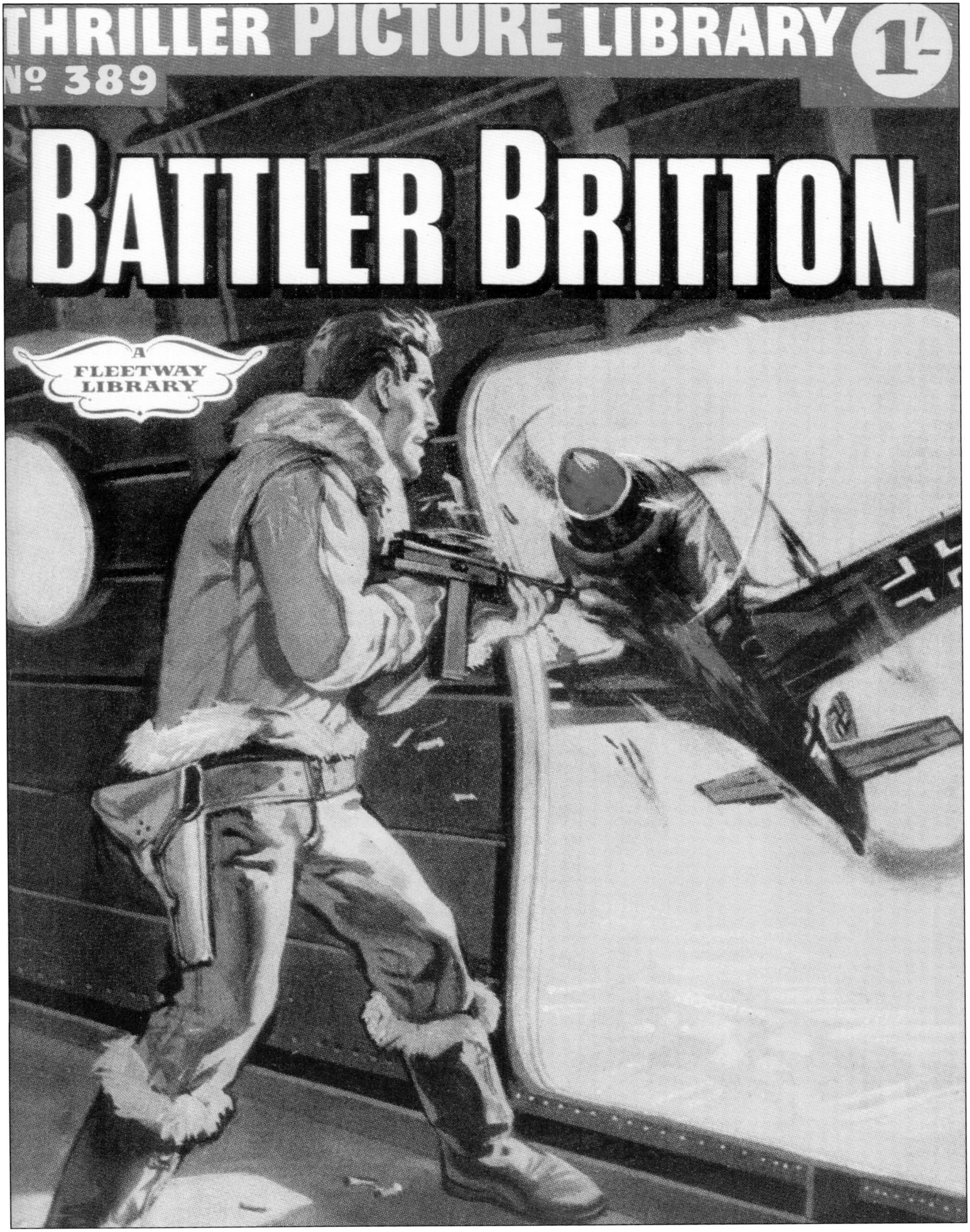
THRILLER PICTURE LIBRARY
1/-
No 389
BATTLER BRITTON
A FLEETWAY LIBRARY

Pino Dell'Orco, Thriller 389, December 1961

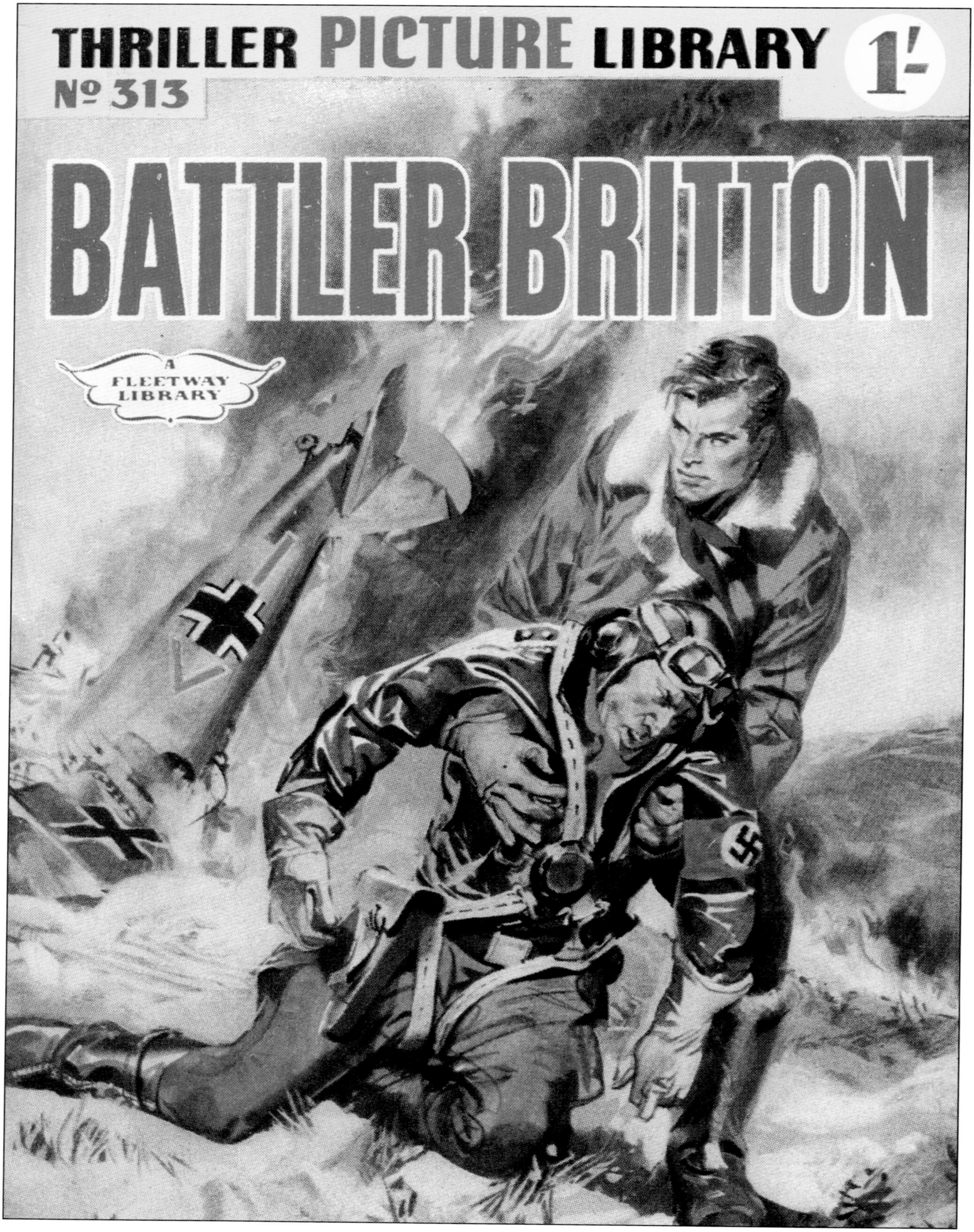
THRILLER PICTURE LIBRARY
1/-
No 313
BATTLER BRITTON
A FLEETWAY LIBRARY

Giorgio DeGaspari, Thriller 313, April 1960

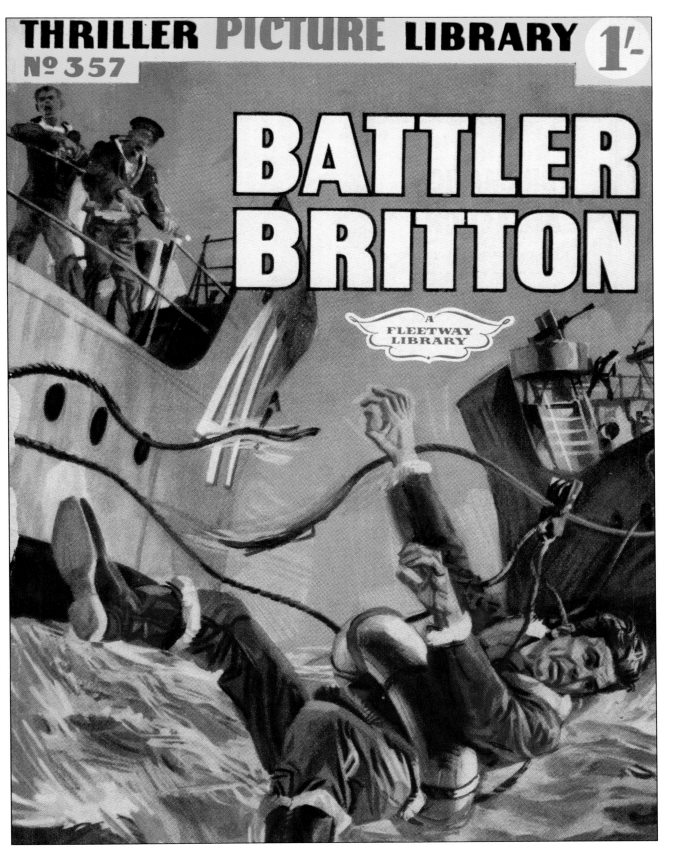

THRILLER PICTURE LIBRARY

Nº 357

1/-

BATTLER BRITTON

A FLEETWAY LIBRARY

Pino Dell'Orco, Thriller 357, March 1961

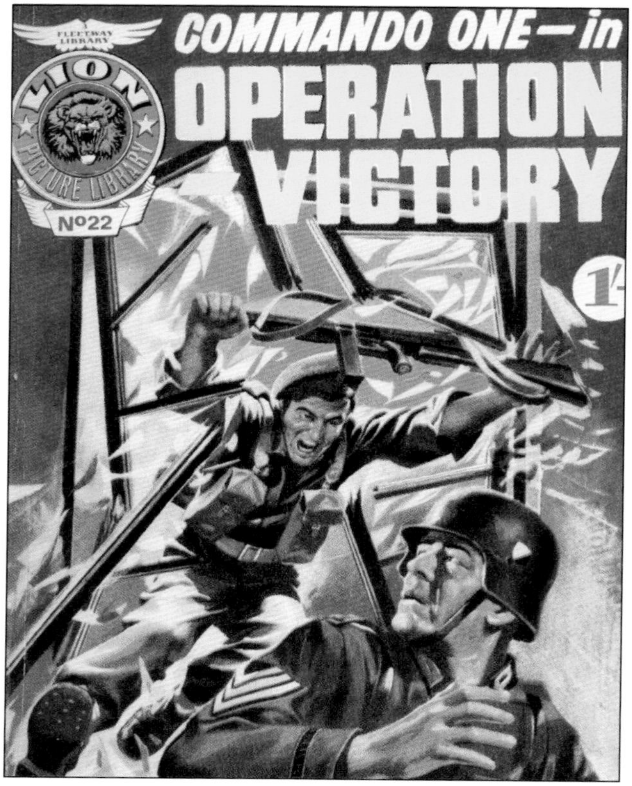
A FLEETWAY LIBRARY
LION PICTURE LIBRARY
Nº22
COMMANDO ONE—in
OPERATION VICTORY
1/-

Unknown, Lion Picture Library 22, August 1964

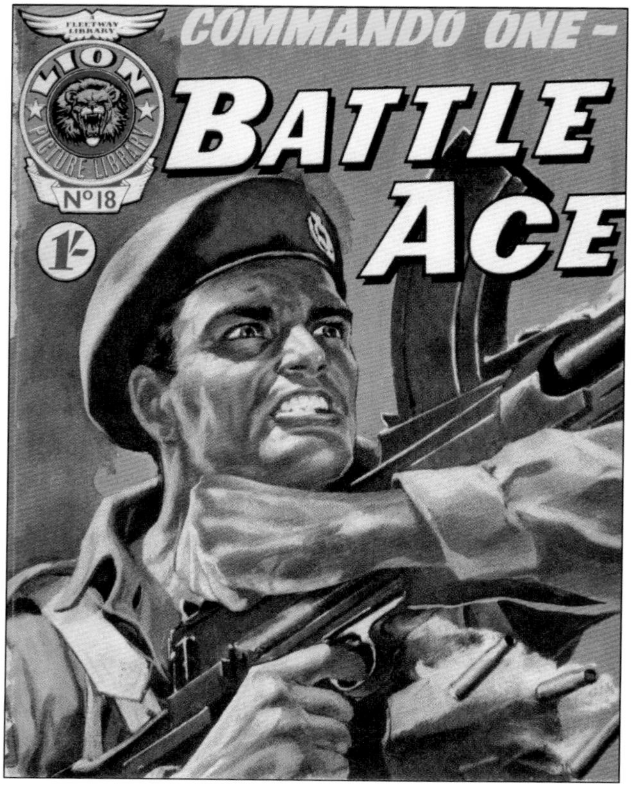
A FLEETWAY LIBRARY
LION PICTURE LIBRARY
Nº18
COMMANDO ONE-
BATTLE ACE
1/-

Giorgio DeGaspari, Lion Picture Library 18, June 1964

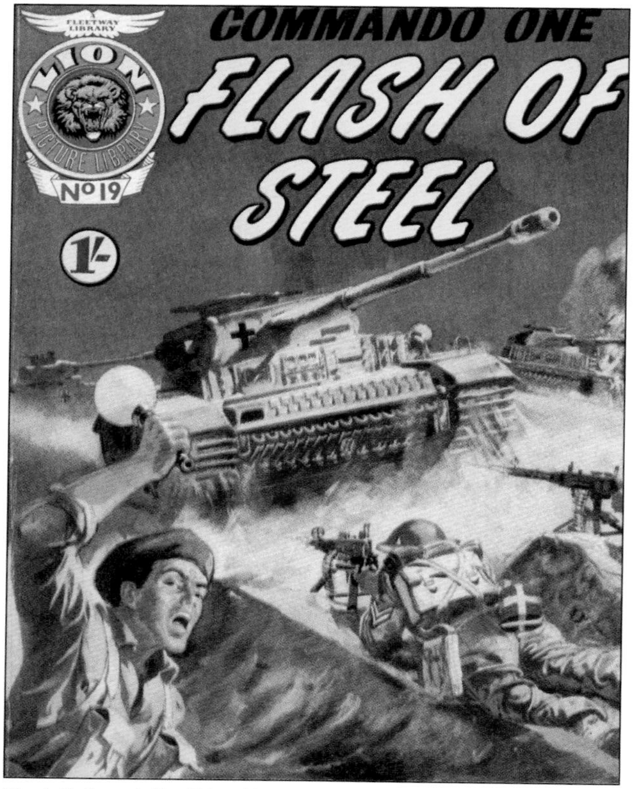
A FLEETWAY LIBRARY
LION PICTURE LIBRARY
Nº19
COMMANDO ONE
FLASH OF STEEL
1/-

Giorgio DeGaspari, Lion Picture Library 19, July 1964

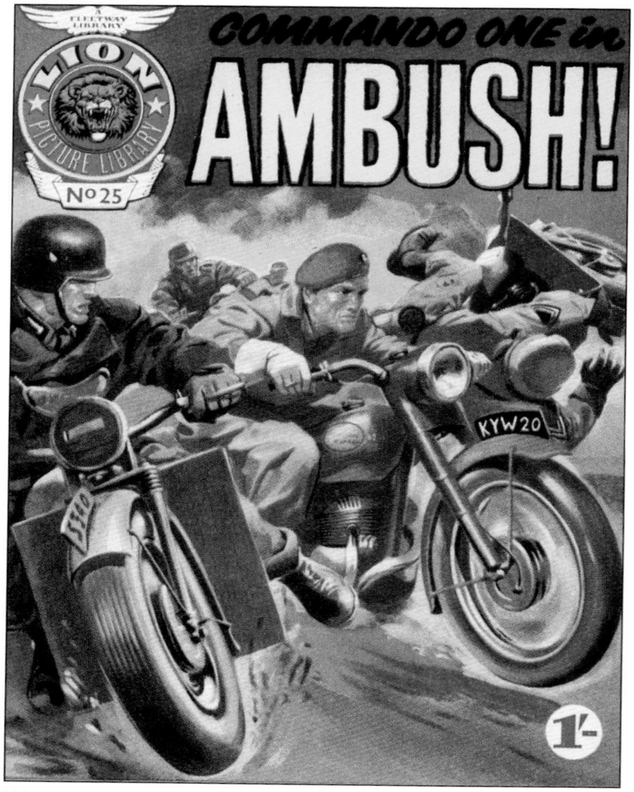
A FLEETWAY LIBRARY
LION PICTURE LIBRARY
Nº25
COMMANDO ONE in
AMBUSH!
KYW 20
1/-

Unknown, Lion Picture Library 25, October 1964

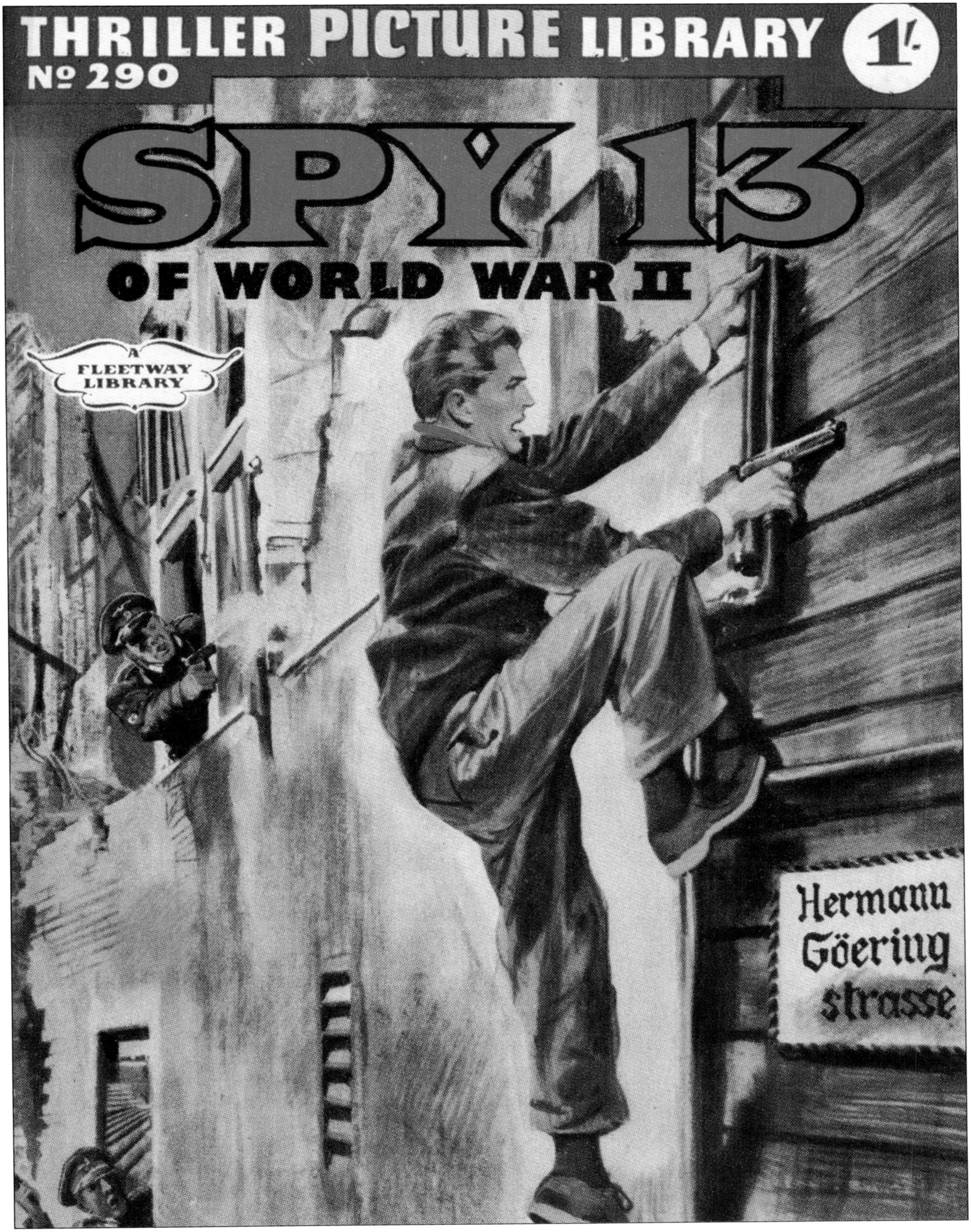
THRILLER PICTURE LIBRARY
Nº 290
1/-
SPY 13
OF WORLD WAR II
A FLEETWAY LIBRARY
Hermann
Göering
strasse

Giorgio DeGaspari, Thriller 290, October 1959

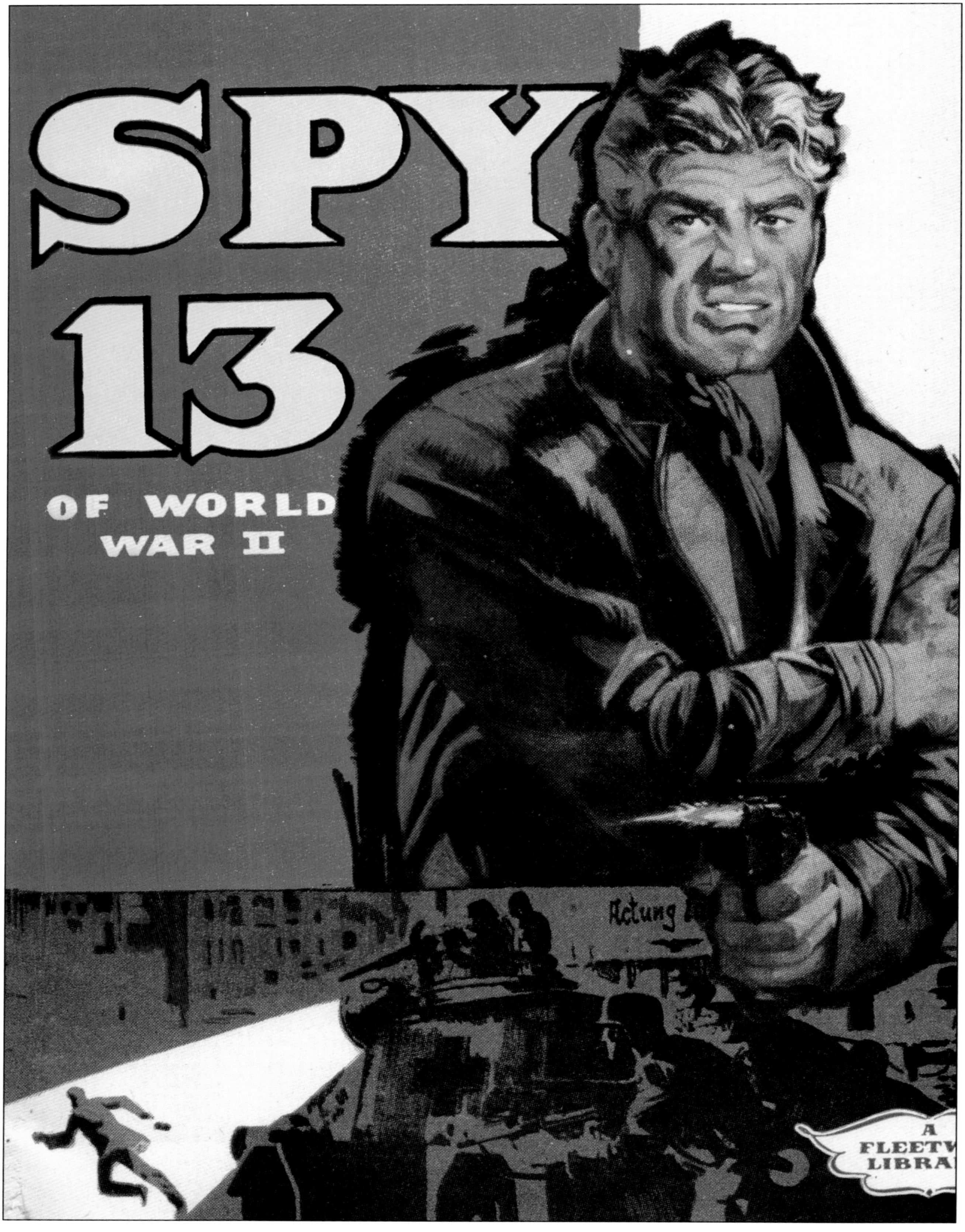
SPY
13
OF WORLD
WAR II
Actung
A
FLEETW
LIBRA

Allessandro Biffignandi, Thriller 420, August 1962

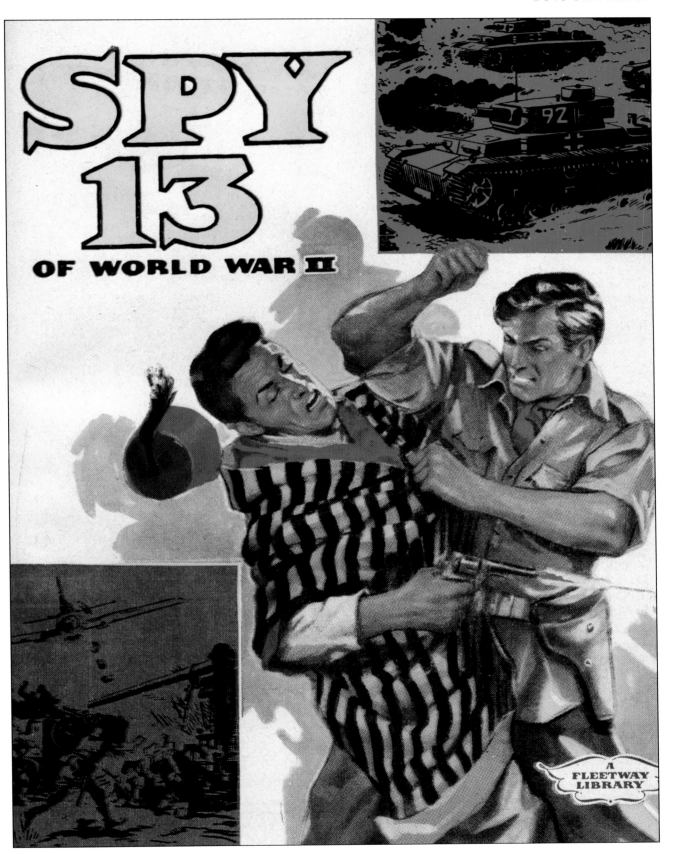

SPY
13
OF WORLD WAR II

A FLEETWAY LIBRARY

Nino Caroselli, Thriller 448, March 1963

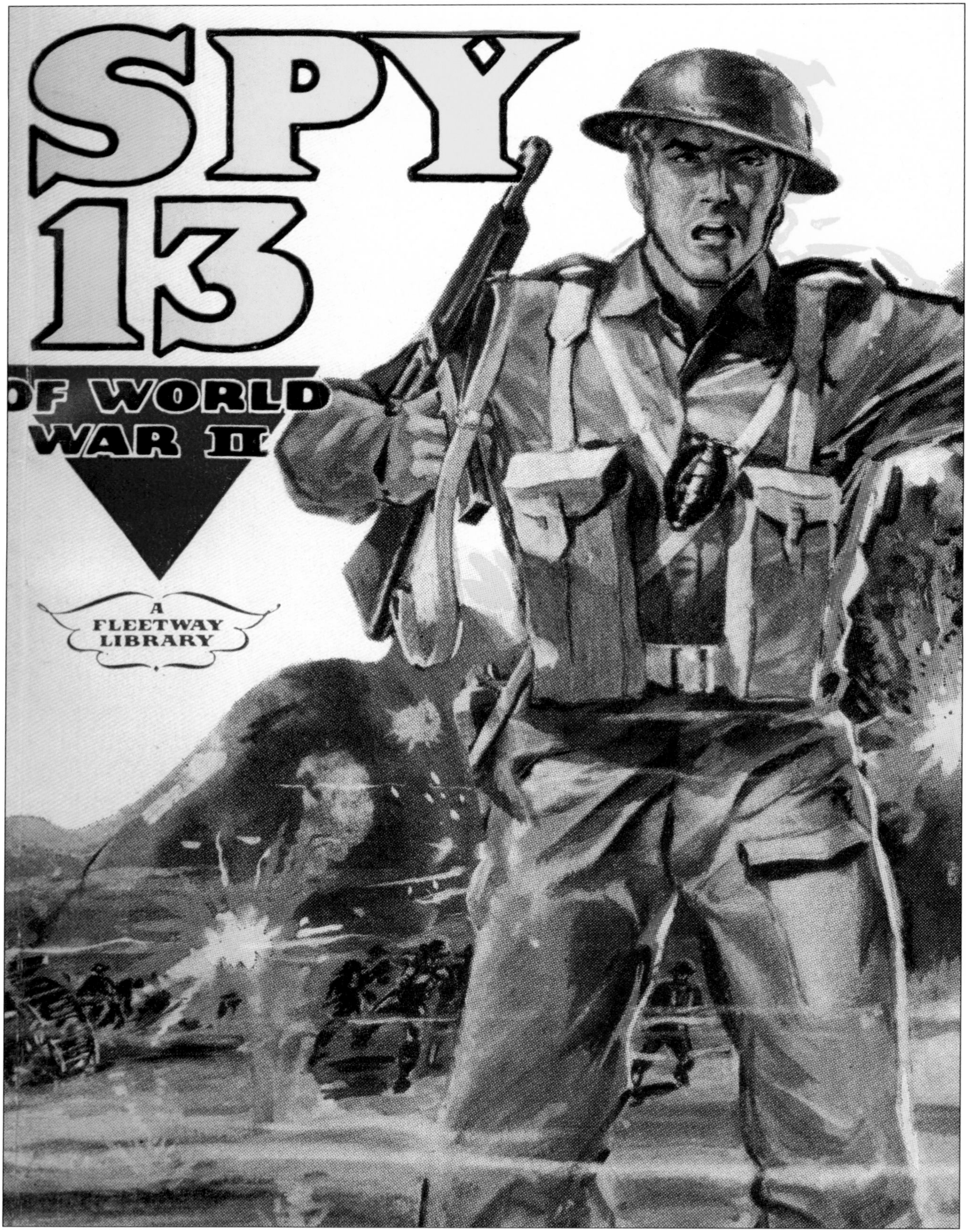
SPY
13
OF WORLD
WAR II
A
FLEETWAY
LIBRARY

Nino Caroselli, Thriller 440, January 1963

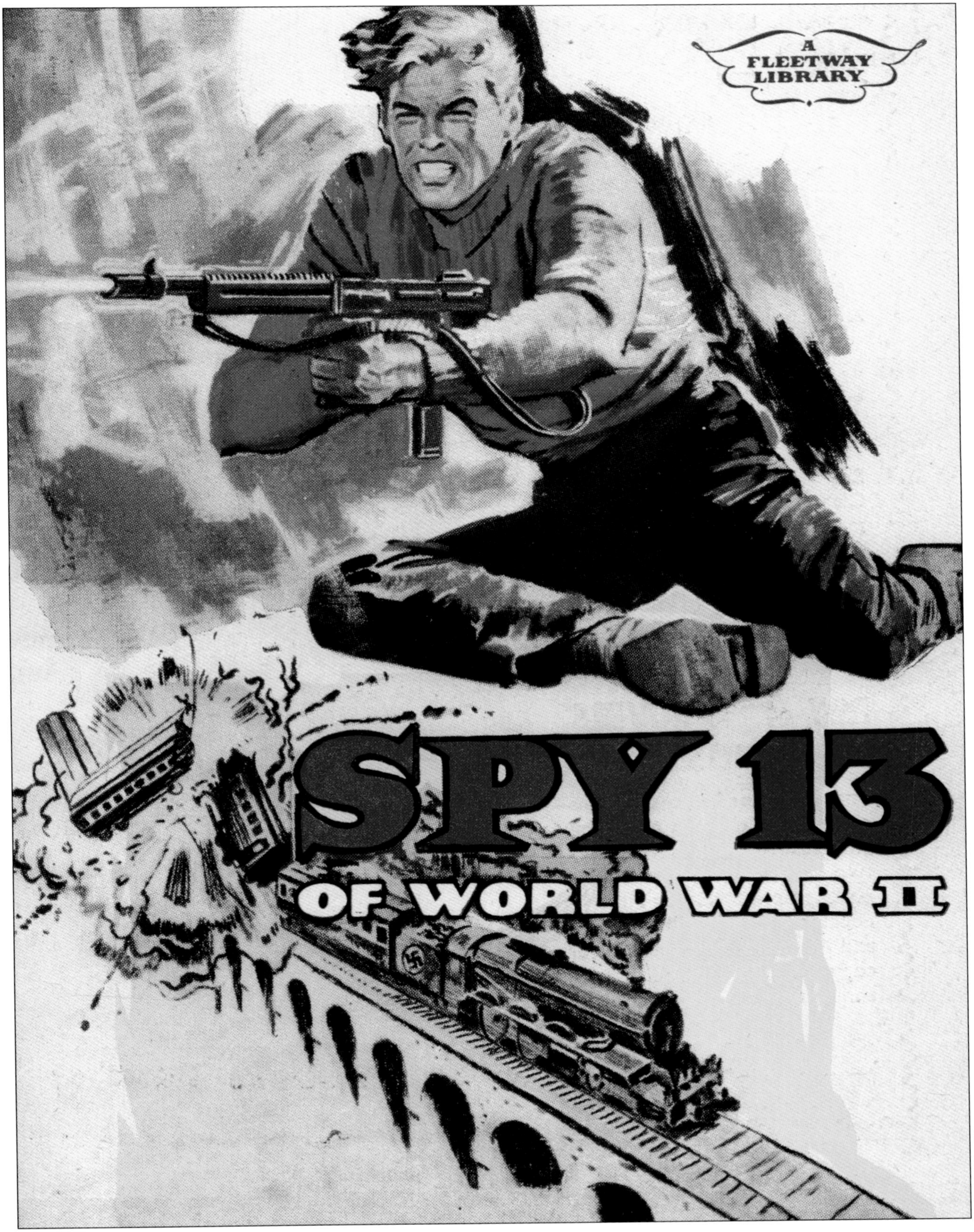
A FLEETWAY LIBRARY
SPY 13
OF WORLD WAR II

Jordi Penalva, Thriller 436, December 1962

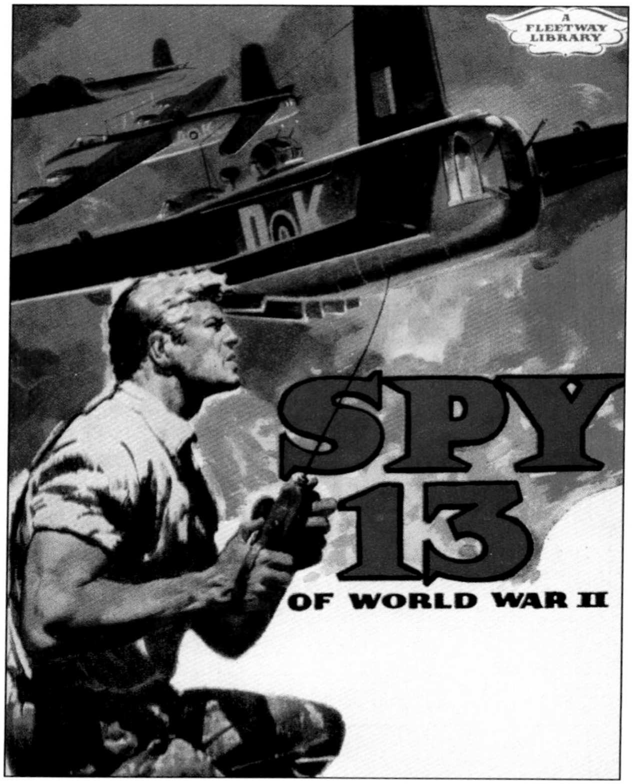
A FLEETWAY LIBRARY
SPY 13
OF WORLD WAR II

Jordi Penalva, Thriller 428, October 1962

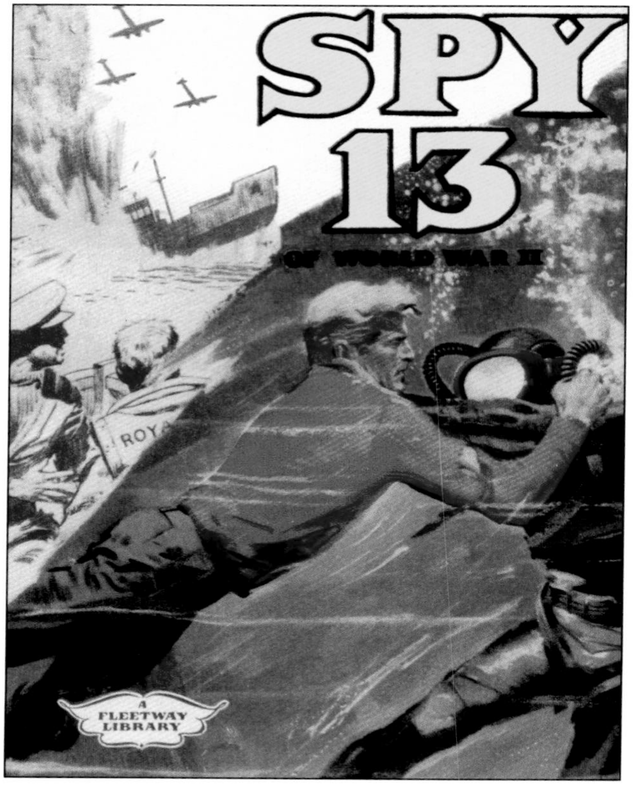
SPY 13
OF WORLD WAR II
A FLEETWAY LIBRARY

Jordi Penalva, Thriller 432, November 1962

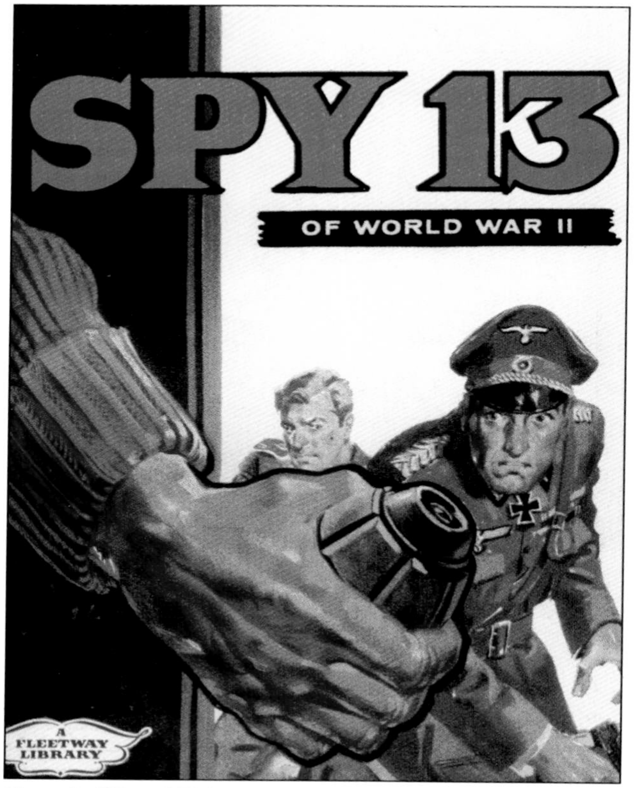
SPY 13
OF WORLD WAR II
A FLEETWAY LIBRARY

Allessandro Biffignandi, Thriller 416, July 1962

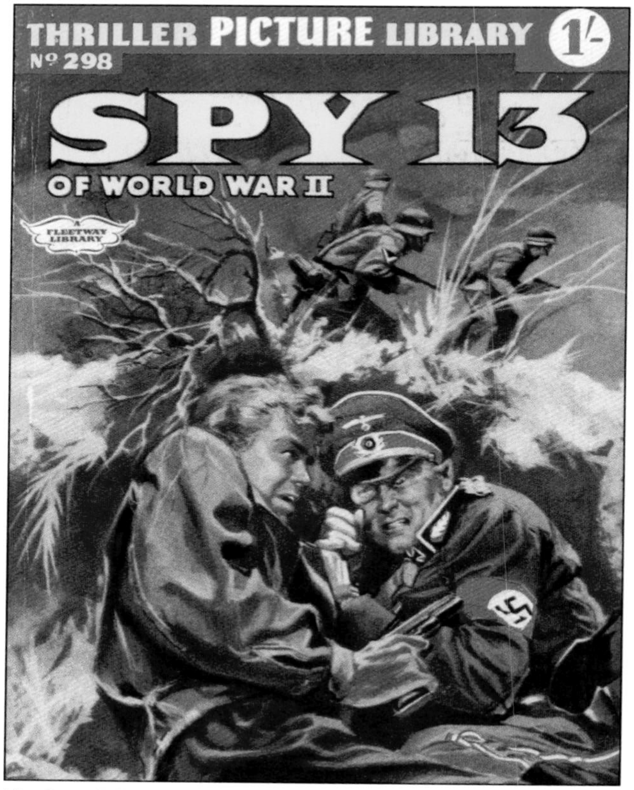
THRILLER PICTURE LIBRARY
1/-
Nº 298
SPY 13
OF WORLD WAR II
A FLEETWAY LIBRARY

Nino Caroselli, Thriller 298, December 1959

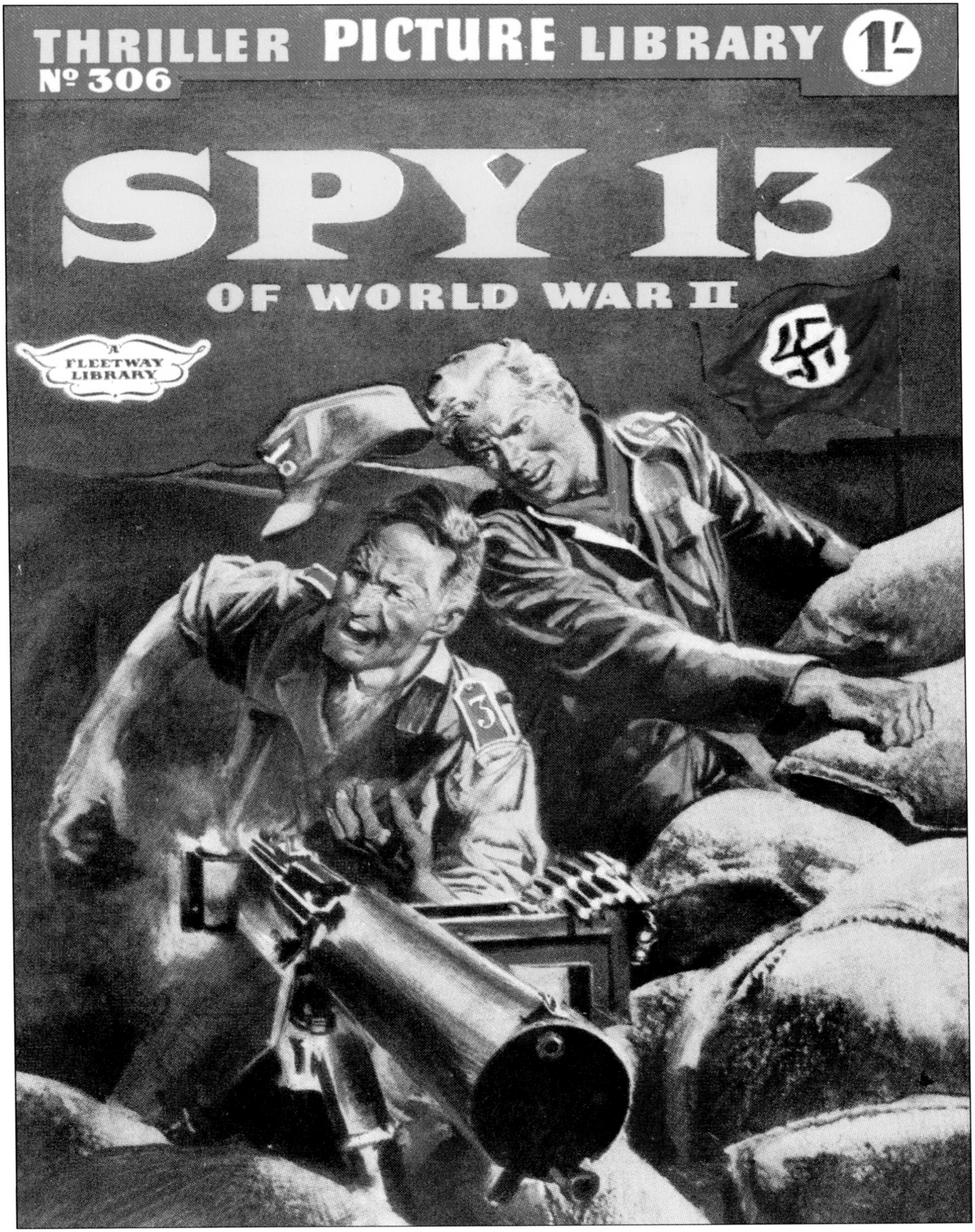
THRILLER PICTURE LIBRARY
Nº 306
1/-
SPY 13
OF WORLD WAR II
A FLEETWAY LIBRARY

Giorgio DeGaspari, Thriller 306, February 1960

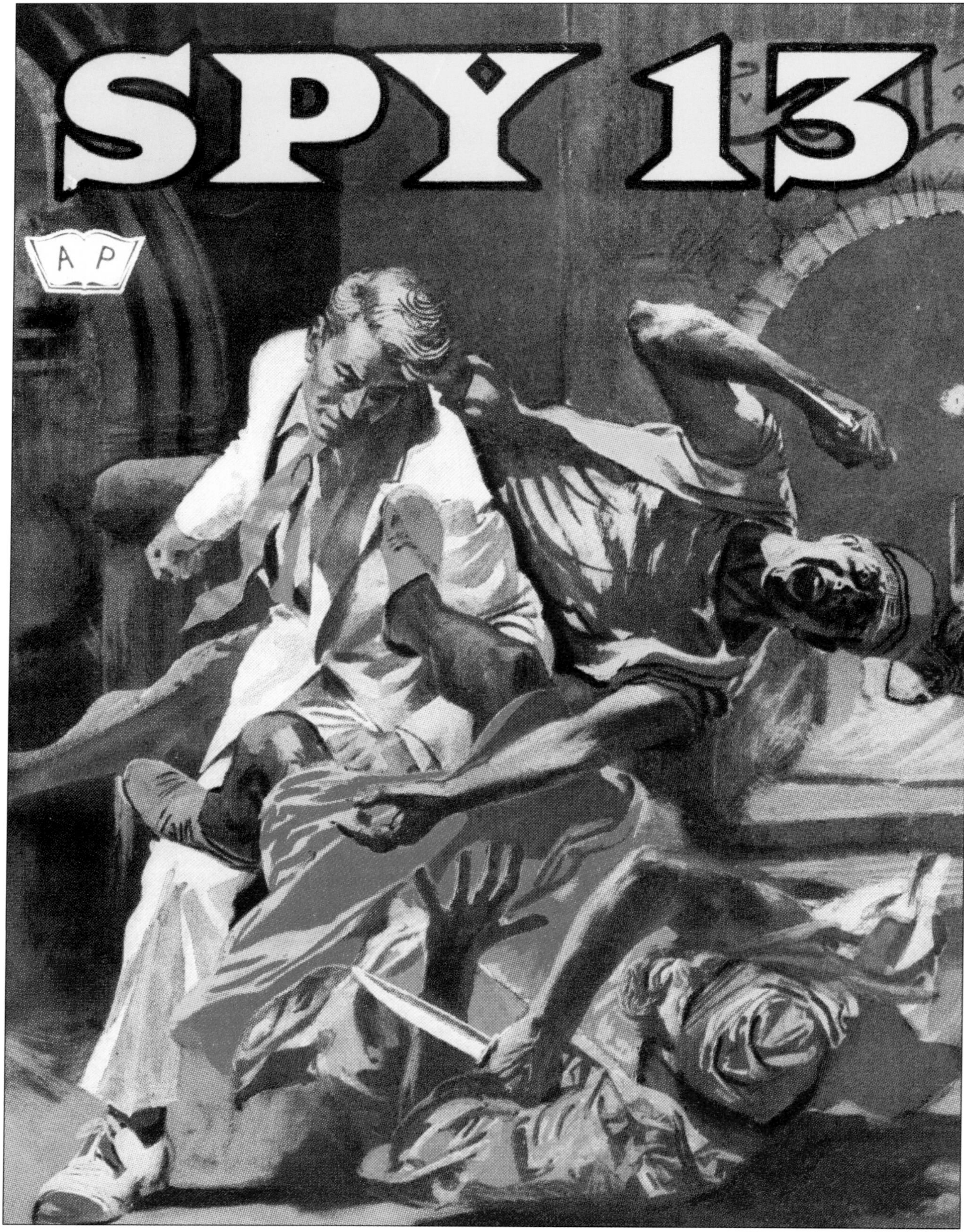
SPY 13
AP

Giorgio DeGaspari, Thriller 258, January 1959

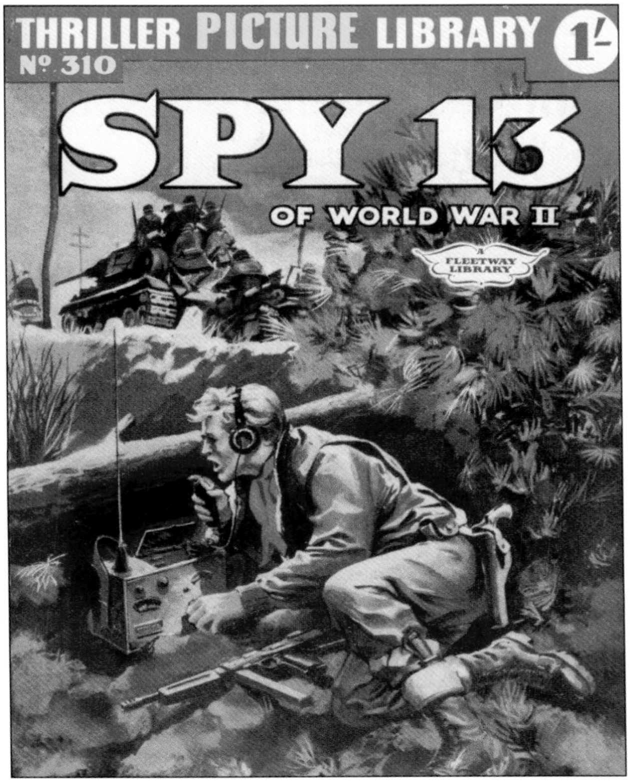
THRILLER PICTURE LIBRARY
1/-
Nº 310
SPY 13
OF WORLD WAR II
A FLEETWAY LIBRARY

Nino Caroselli, Thriller 310, March 1960

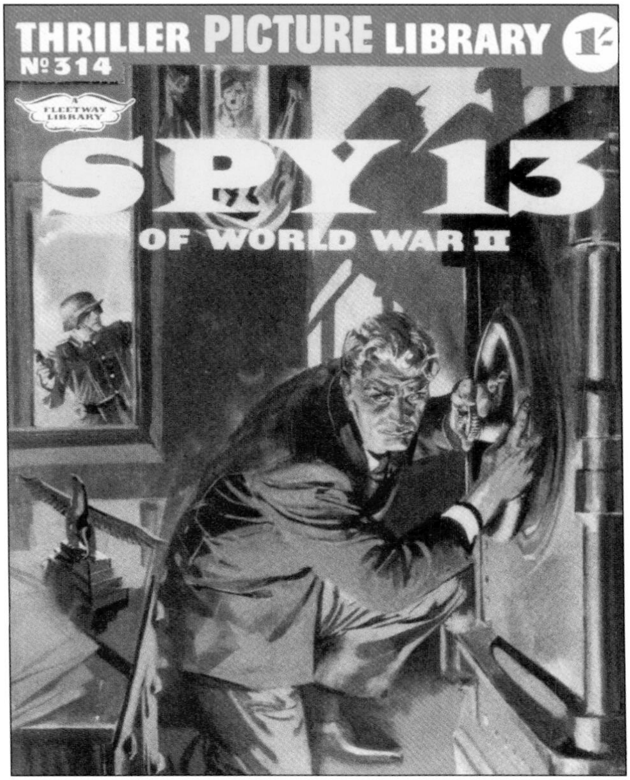
THRILLER PICTURE LIBRARY
1/-
Nº 314
A FLEETWAY LIBRARY
SPY 13
OF WORLD WAR II

Giorgio DeGaspari, Thriller 314, April 1960

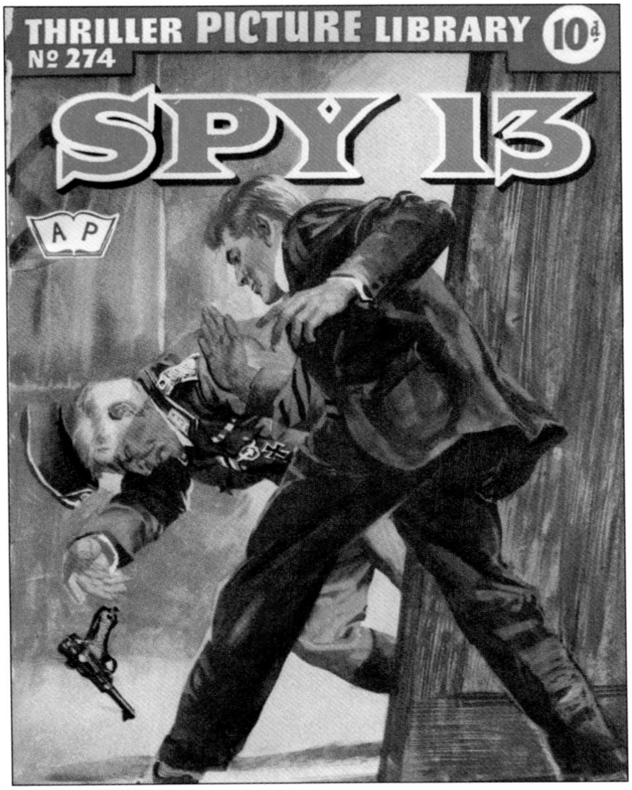
THRILLER PICTURE LIBRARY
10d
Nº 274
SPY 13
AP

Giorgio DeGaspari, Thriller 274, May 1959

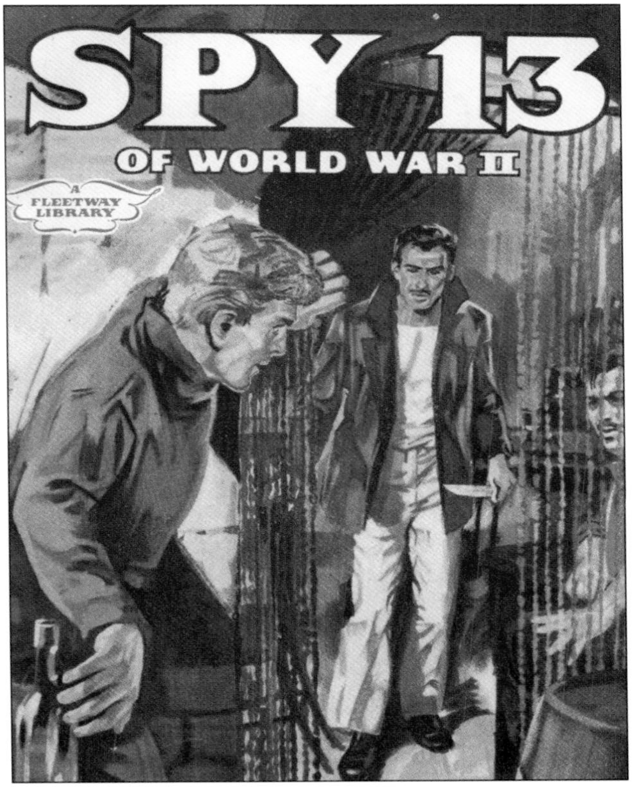
SPY 13
OF WORLD WAR II
A FLEETWAY LIBRARY

Pino Dell'Orco, Thriller 348, January 1961

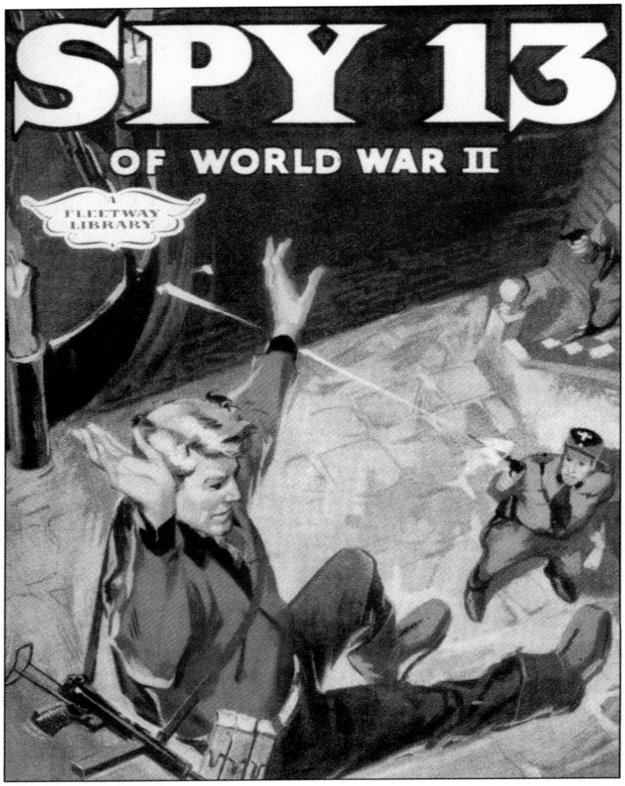
SPY 13
OF WORLD WAR II
A FLEETWAY LIBRARY

Pino Dell'Orco, Thriller 336, March 1961

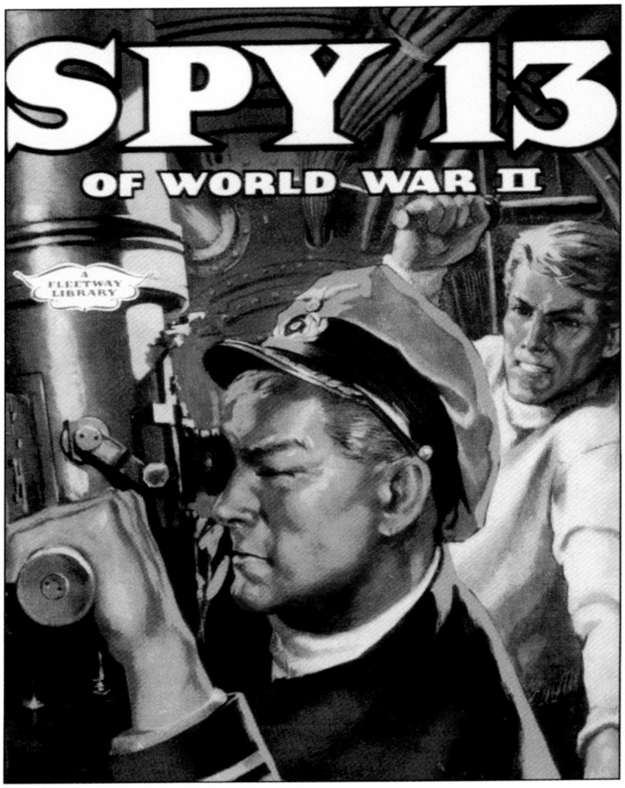
SPY 13
OF WORLD WAR II
A FLEETWAY LIBRARY

Nino Caroselli, Thriller 376, September 1961

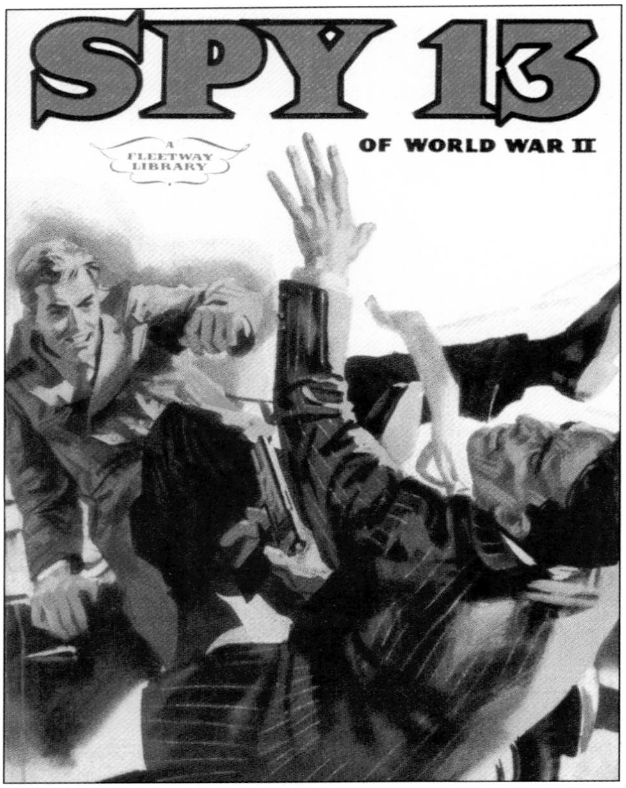
SPY 13
A FLEETWAY LIBRARY
OF WORLD WAR II

Pino Dell'Orco, Thriller 372, August 1961

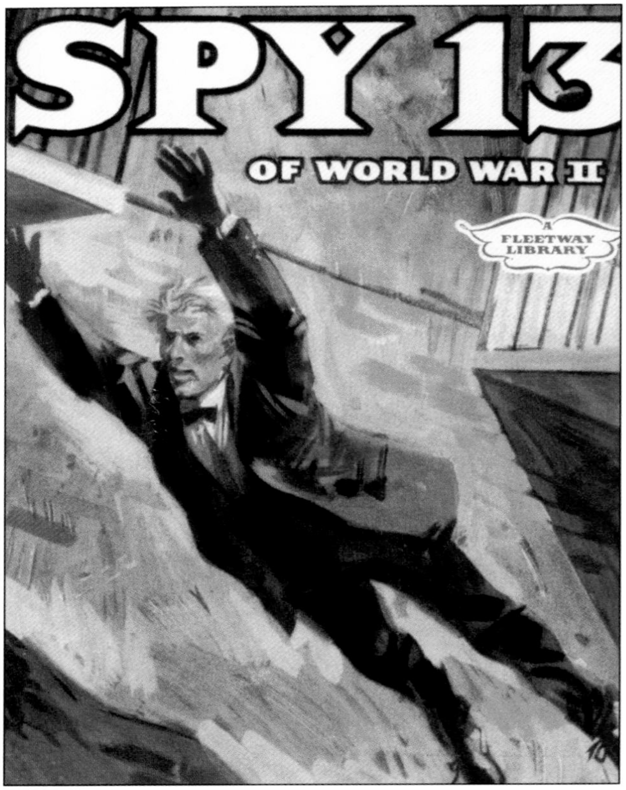
SPY 13
OF WORLD WAR II
A FLEETWAY LIBRARY

Pino Dell'Orco, Thriller 368, July 1961

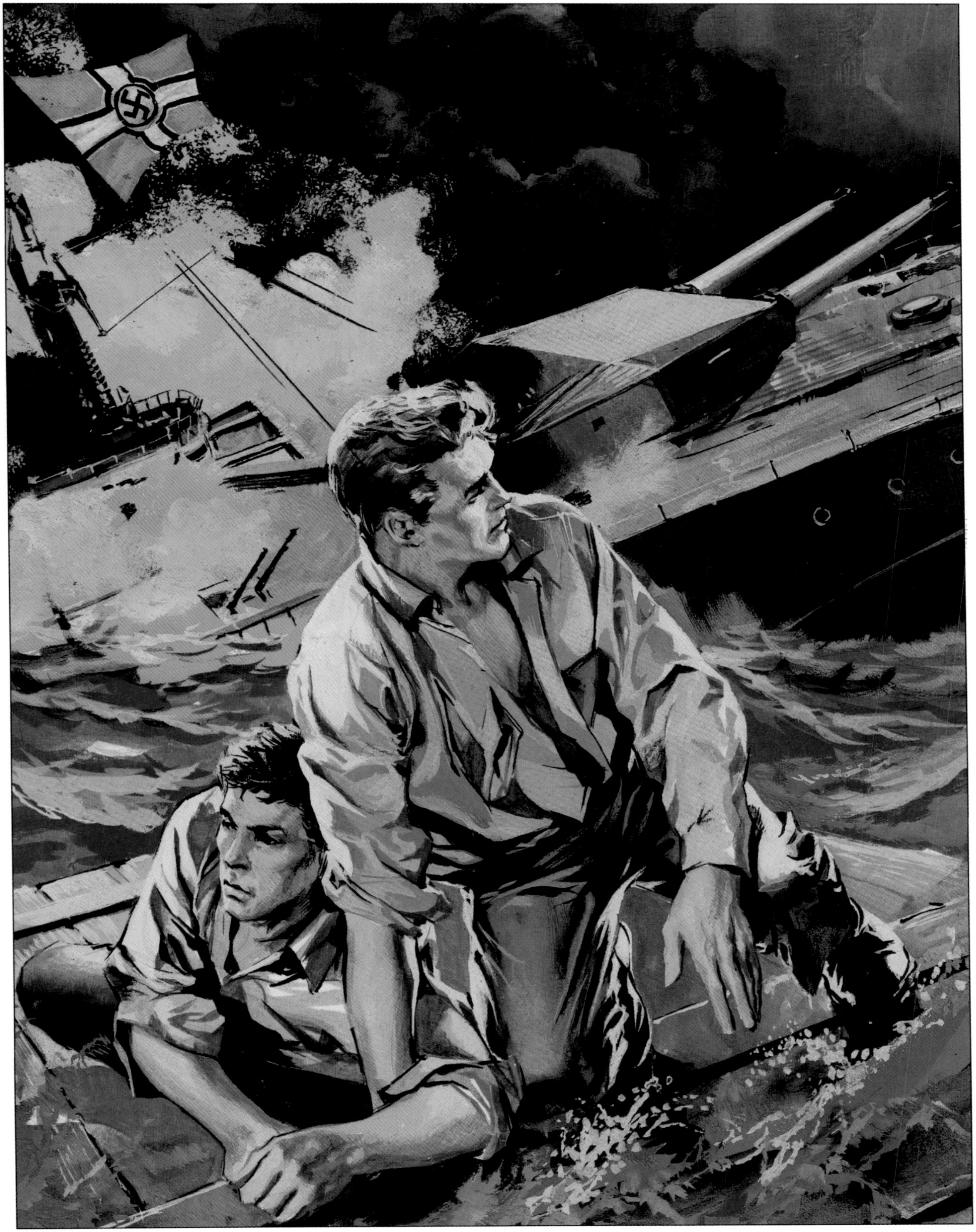

Nino Caroselli, Thriller 340, November 1960

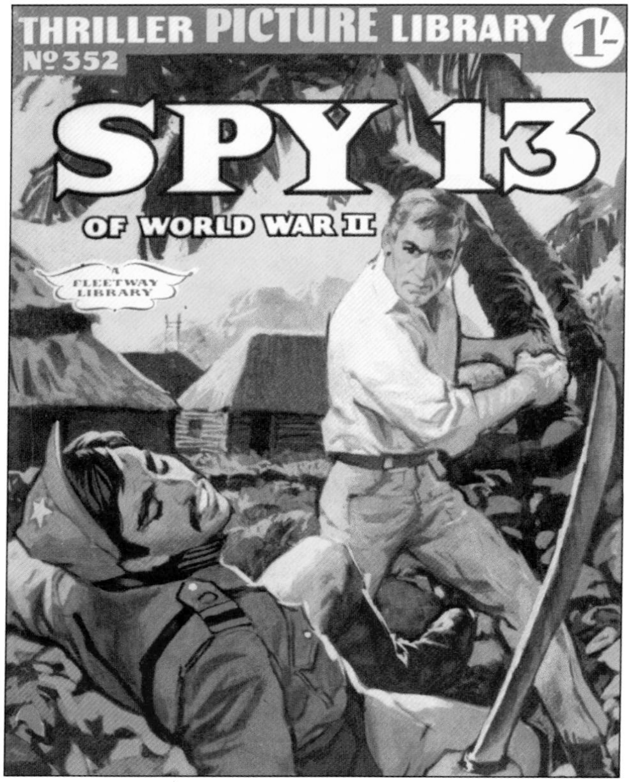
THRILLER PICTURE LIBRARY
1/-
No 352
SPY 13
OF WORLD WAR II
A FLEETWAY LIBRARY
Nino Caroselli, Thriller 352, February 1961

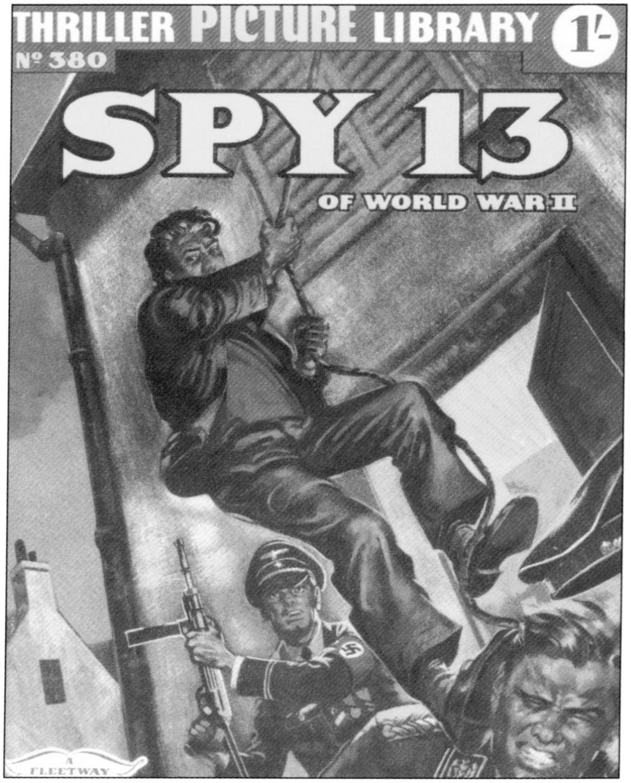
THRILLER PICTURE LIBRARY
1/-
No 380
SPY 13
OF WORLD WAR II
Stefan Barany, Thriller 380, October 1961

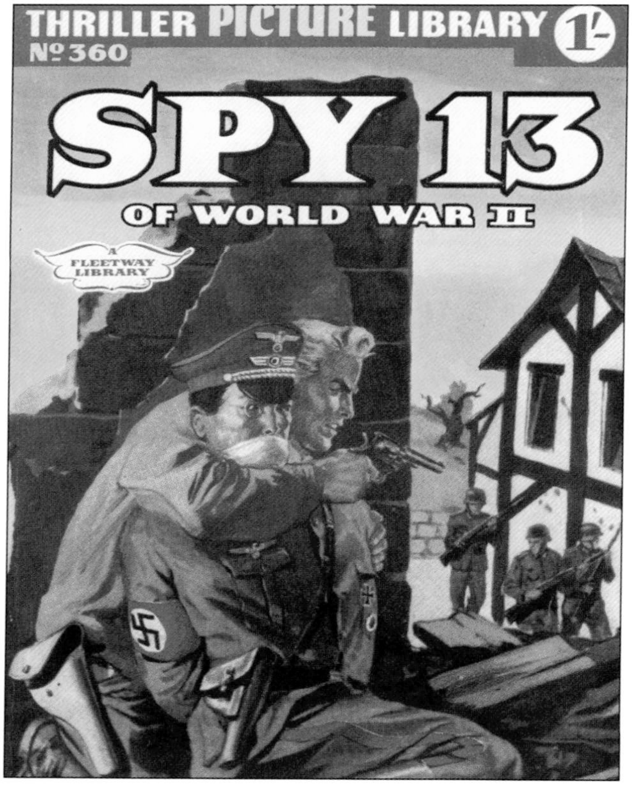
THRILLER PICTURE LIBRARY
1/-
No 360
SPY 13
OF WORLD WAR II
A FLEETWAY LIBRARY
Nino Caroselli, Thriller 360, May 1961

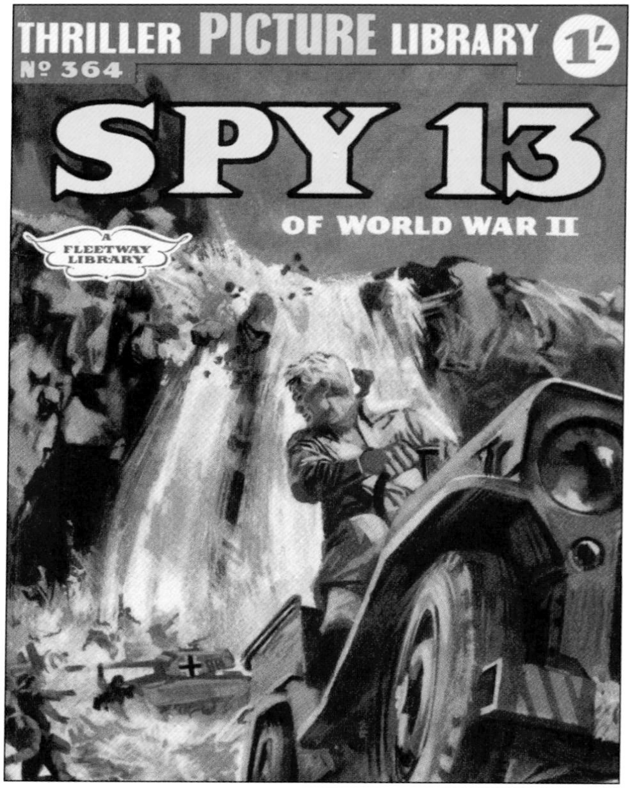
THRILLER PICTURE LIBRARY
1/-
No 364
SPY 13
OF WORLD WAR II
A FLEETWAY LIBRARY
Pino Dell'Orco, Thriller 364, June 1961

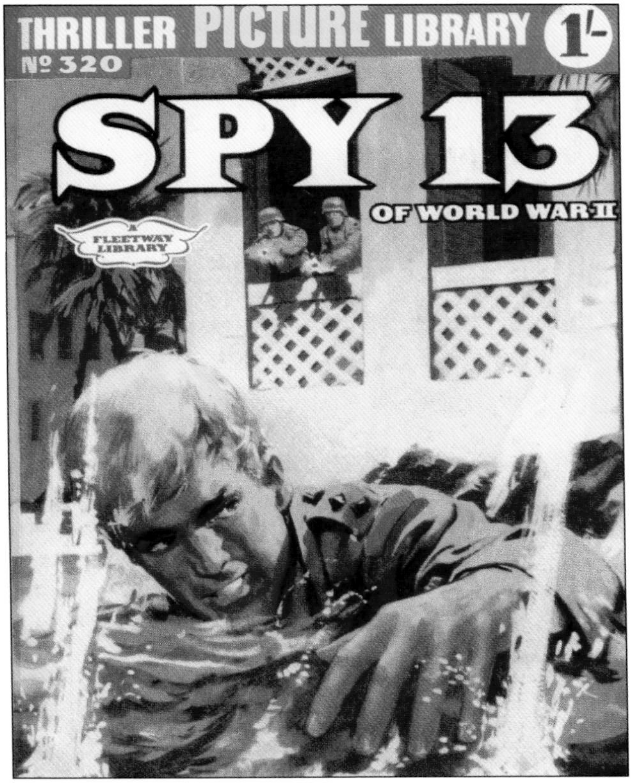
THRILLER PICTURE LIBRARY
1/-
No 320
SPY 13
OF WORLD WAR II
A FLEETWAY LIBRARY
Nino Caroselli, Thriller 320, June 1960

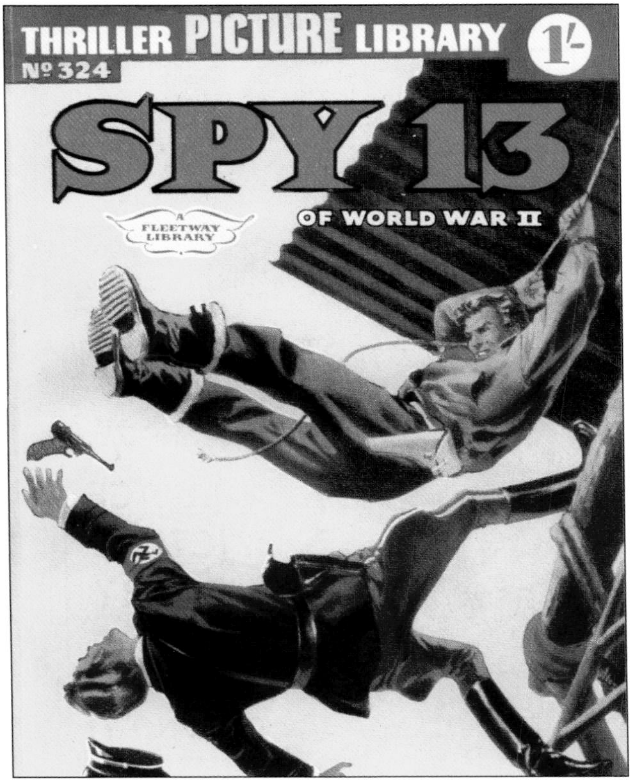
THRILLER PICTURE LIBRARY
1/-
No 324
SPY 13
OF WORLD WAR II
A FLEETWAY LIBRARY
Nino Caroselli, Thriller 324, July 1960

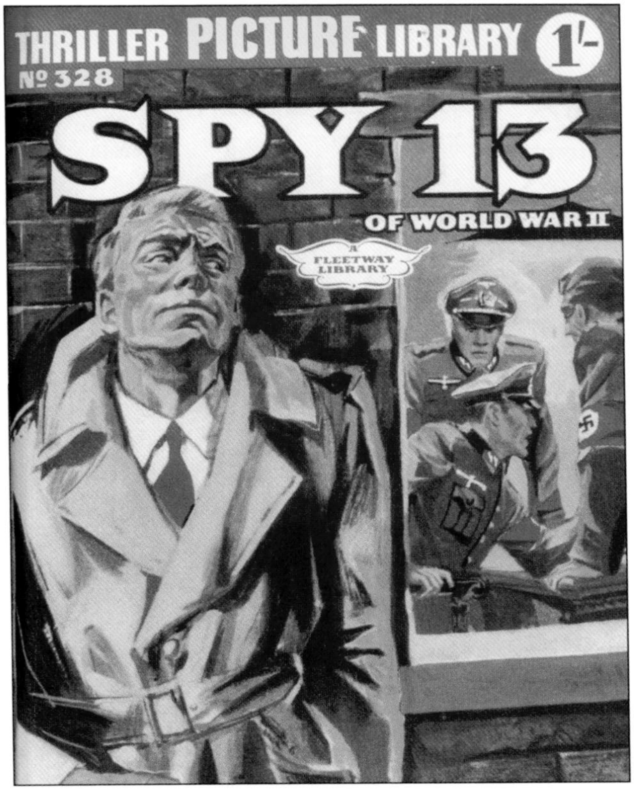
THRILLER PICTURE LIBRARY
1/-
No 328
SPY 13
OF WORLD WAR II
A FLEETWAY LIBRARY
Nino Caroselli, Thriller 328, August 1960

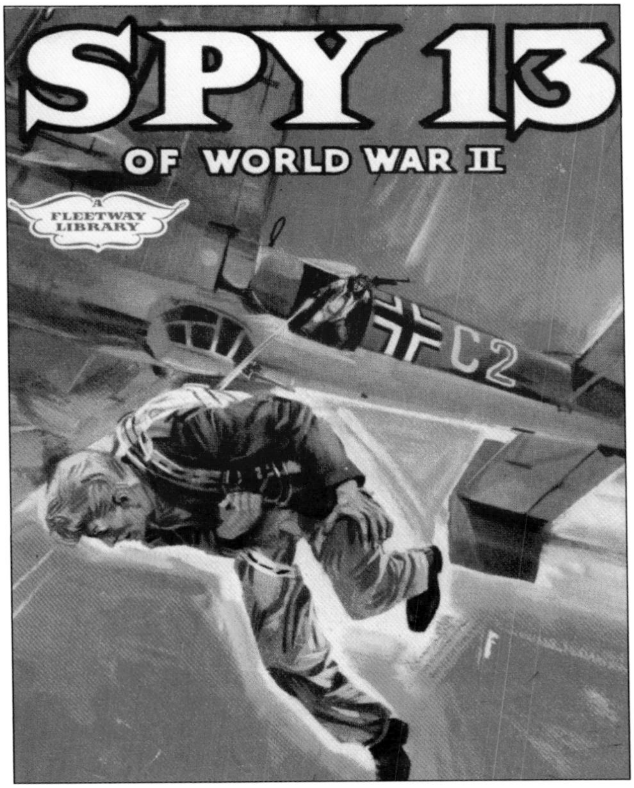
SPY 13
OF WORLD WAR II
A FLEETWAY LIBRARY
C2
Pino Dell'Orco, Thriller 356, March 1961

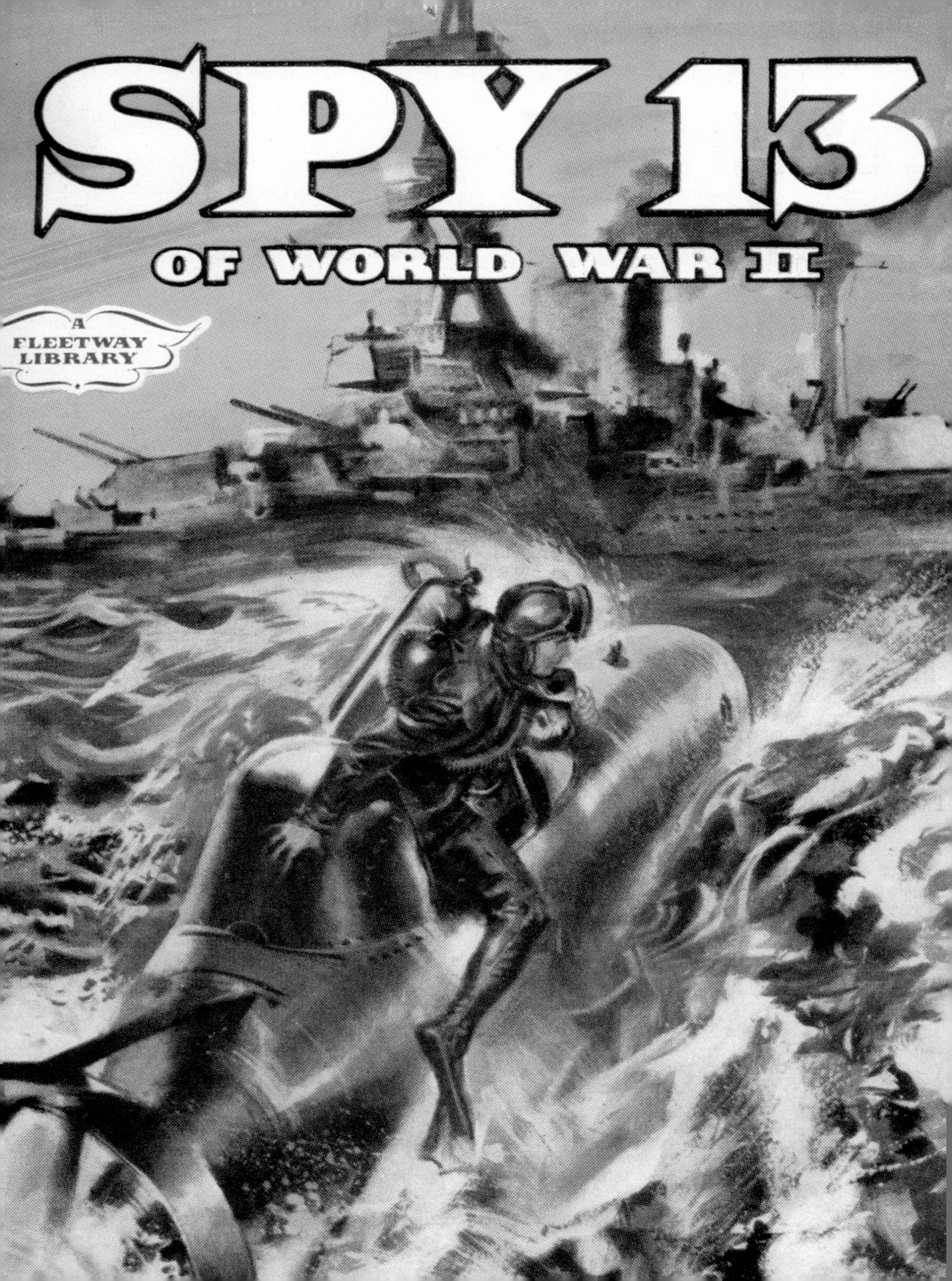
SPY 13
OF WORLD WAR II
A FLEETWAY LIBRARY

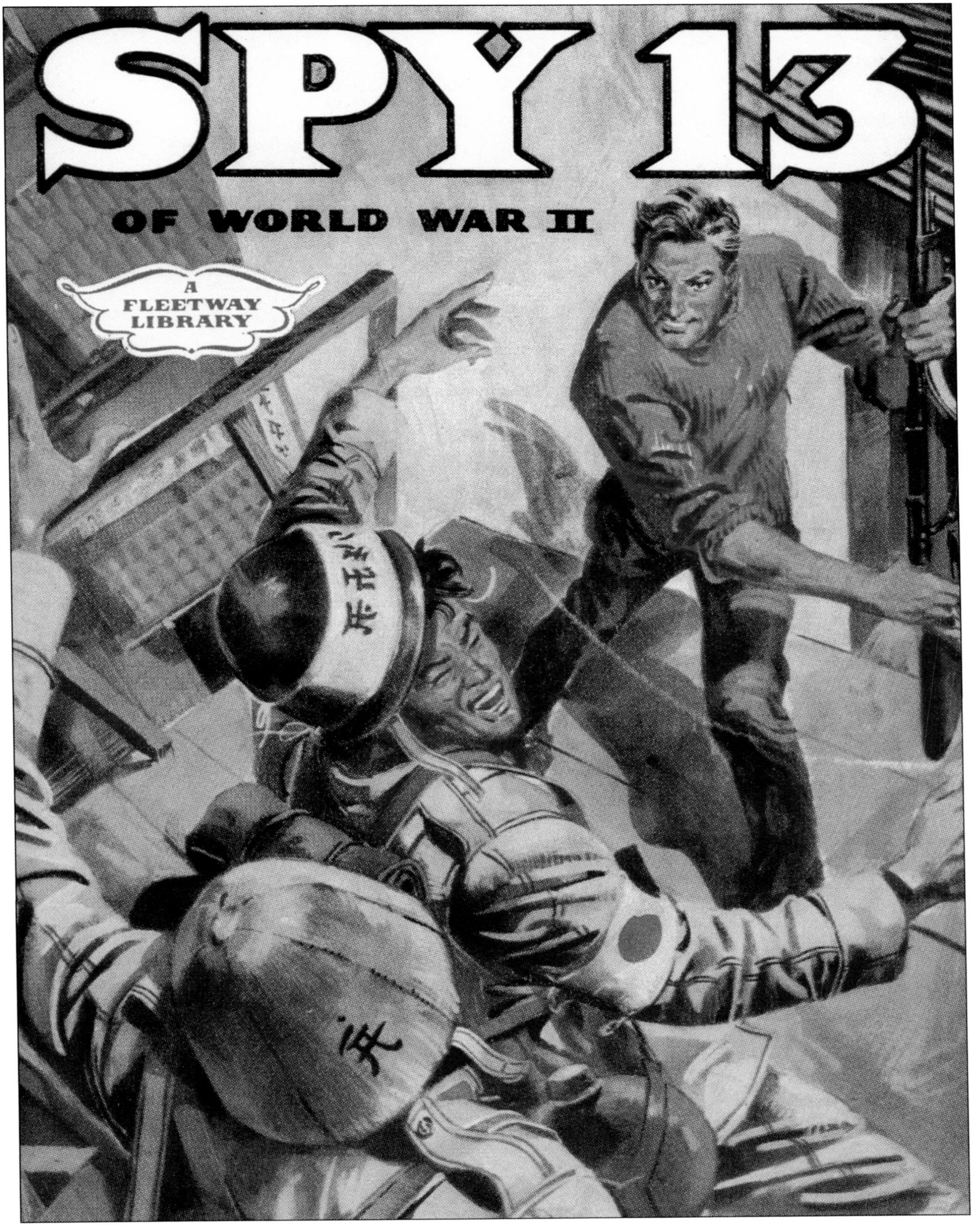
SPY 13
OF WORLD WAR II
A FLEETWAY LIBRARY

Allessandro Biffignandi, Thriller 388, December 1961
Opposite: Giorgio DeGaspari, Thriller 332, September 1960

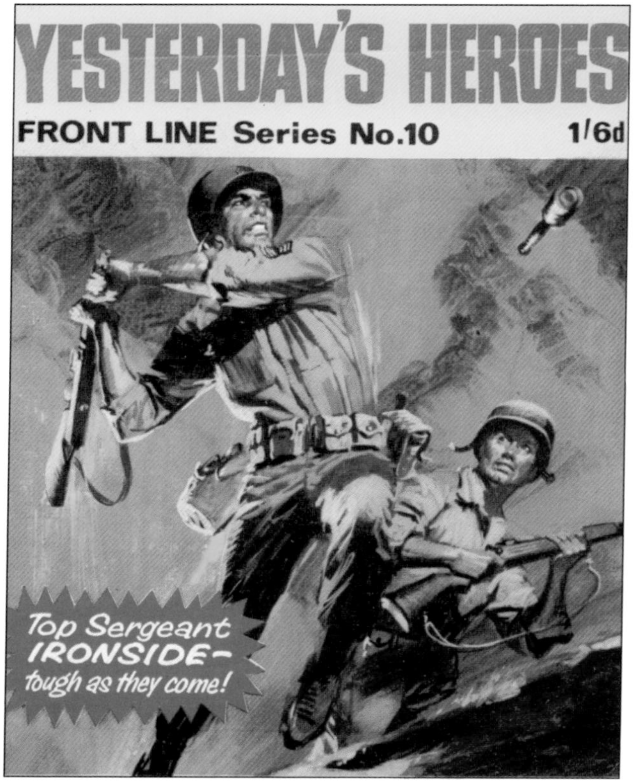
YESTERDAY'S HEROES
FRONT LINE Series No.10
1/6d
Top Sergeant IRONSIDE– tough as they come!

Jordi Penalva, Front Line 10, May 1967

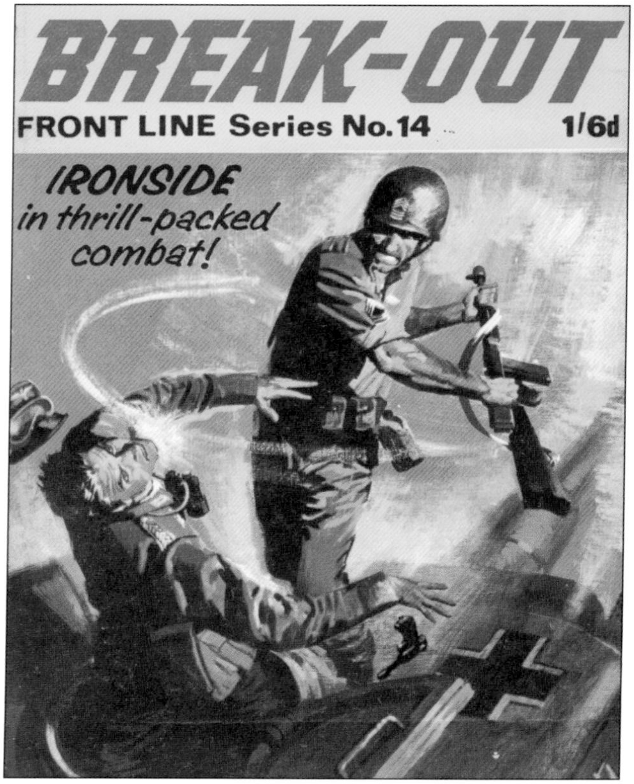
BREAK-OUT
FRONT LINE Series No.14
1/6d
IRONSIDE in thrill-packed combat!

Jordi Penalva, Front Line 14, July 1967

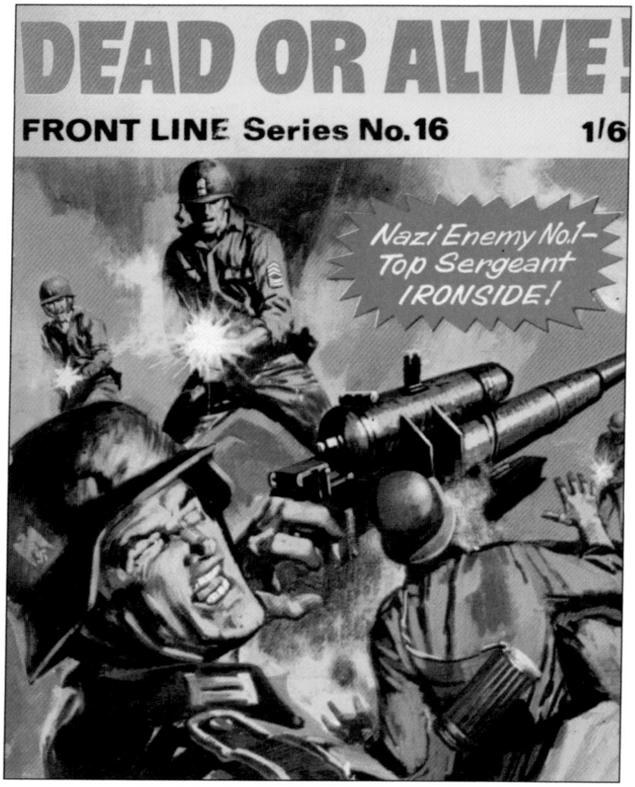
DEAD OR ALIVE!
FRONT LINE Series No.16
Nazi Enemy No.1– Top Sergeant IRONSIDE!

Jordi Penalva, Front Line 16, August 1967

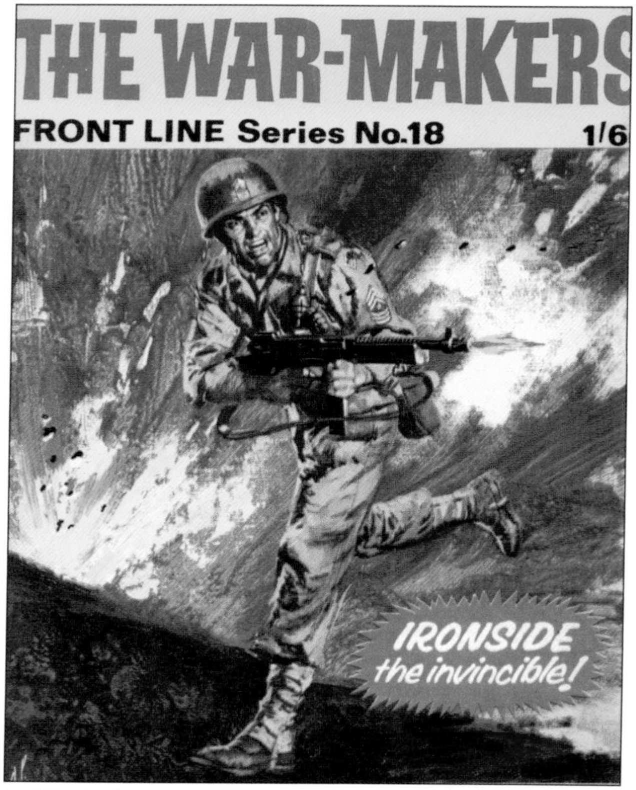
THE WAR-MAKERS
FRONT LINE Series No.18
IRONSIDE the invincible!

Jordi Penalva, Front Line 18, September 1967

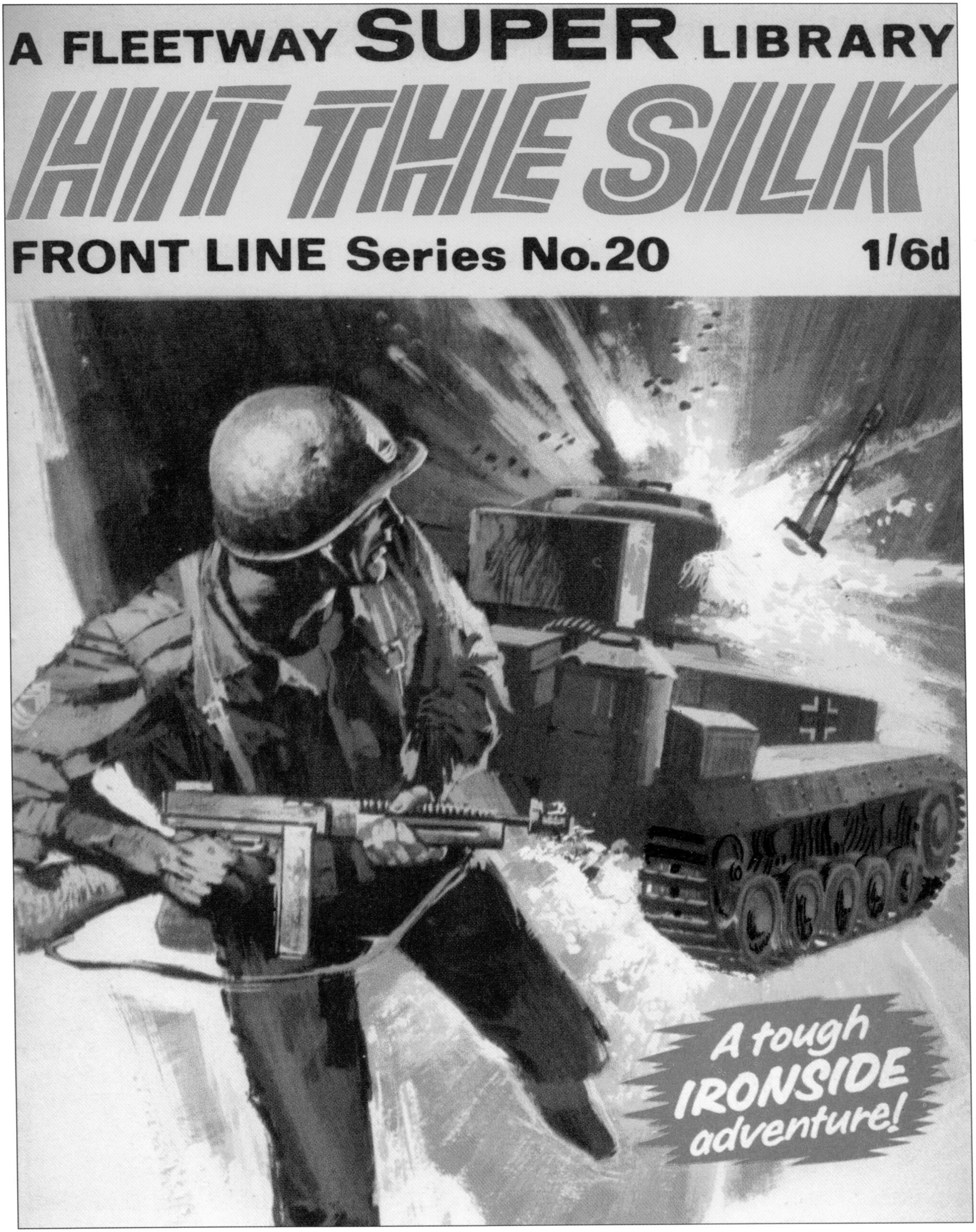
A FLEETWAY SUPER LIBRARY
HIT THE SILK
FRONT LINE Series No.20
1/6d
A tough IRONSIDE adventure!

Jordi Penalva, Front Line 20, October 1967

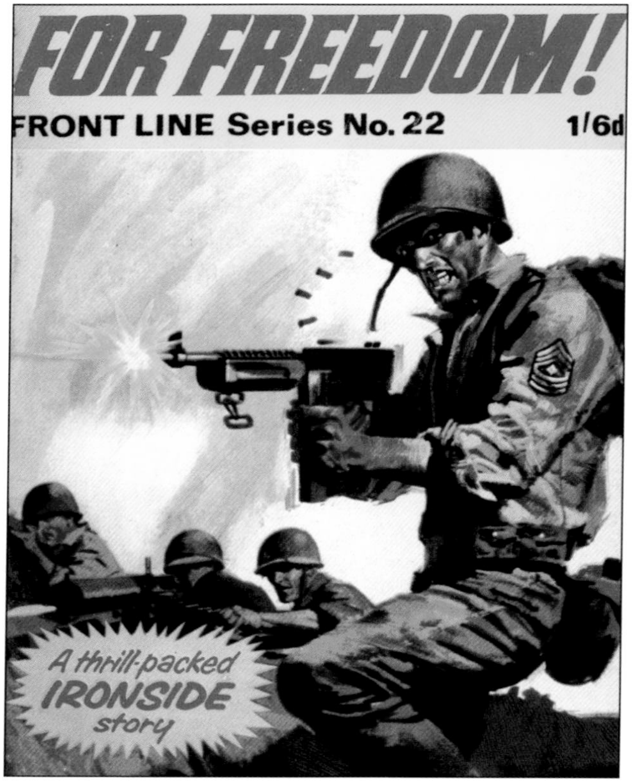
FOR FREEDOM!
FRONT LINE Series No. 22
1/6d
A thrill-packed IRONSIDE story

Jordi Penalva, Front Line 22, November 1967

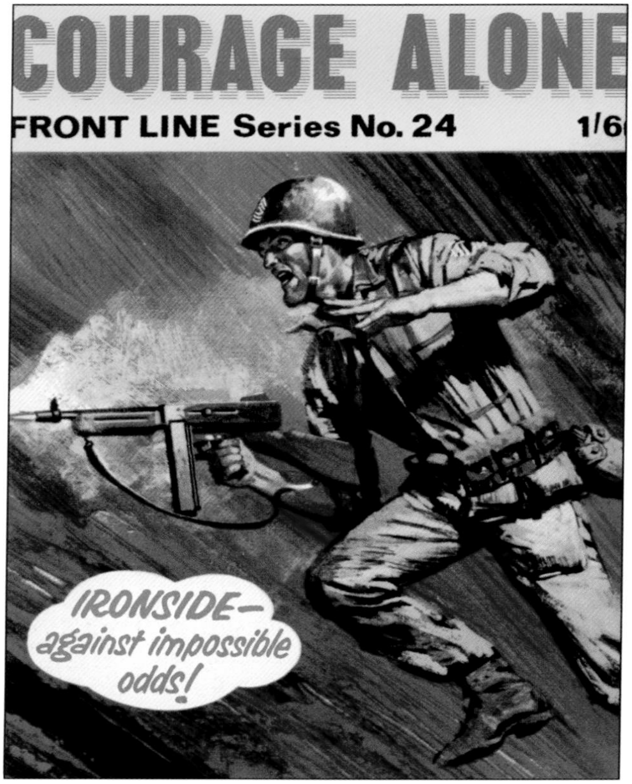
COURAGE ALONE
FRONT LINE Series No. 24
IRONSIDE—against impossible odds!

Jordi Penalva, Front Line 24, December 1967

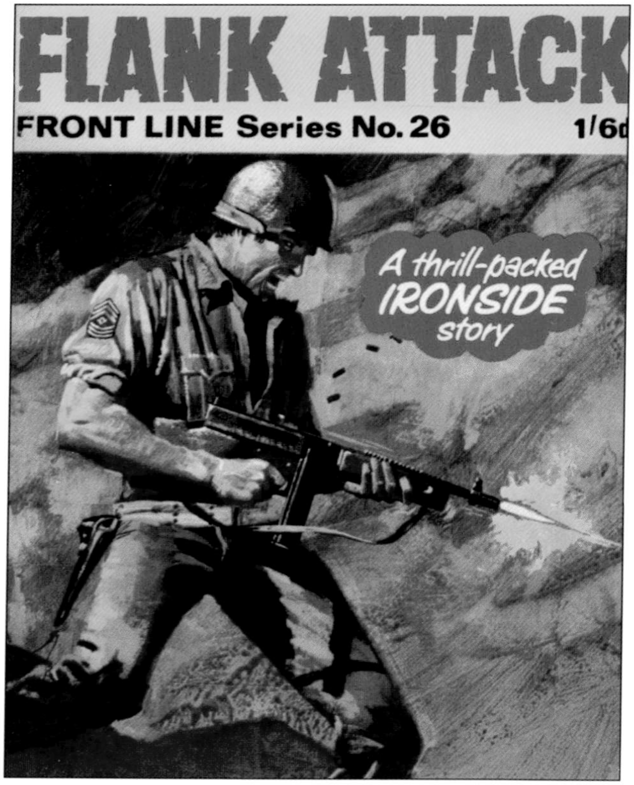
FLANK ATTACK
FRONT LINE Series No. 26
A thrill-packed IRONSIDE story

Jordi Penalva, Front Line 26, January 1968

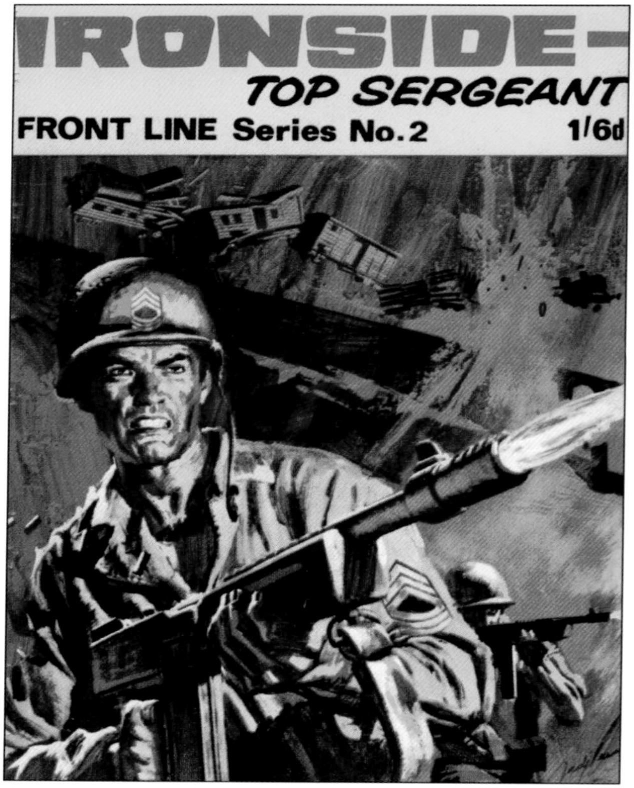
IRONSIDE—
TOP SERGEANT
FRONT LINE Series No. 2
1/6d

Jordi Penalva, Front Line 2, January 1967

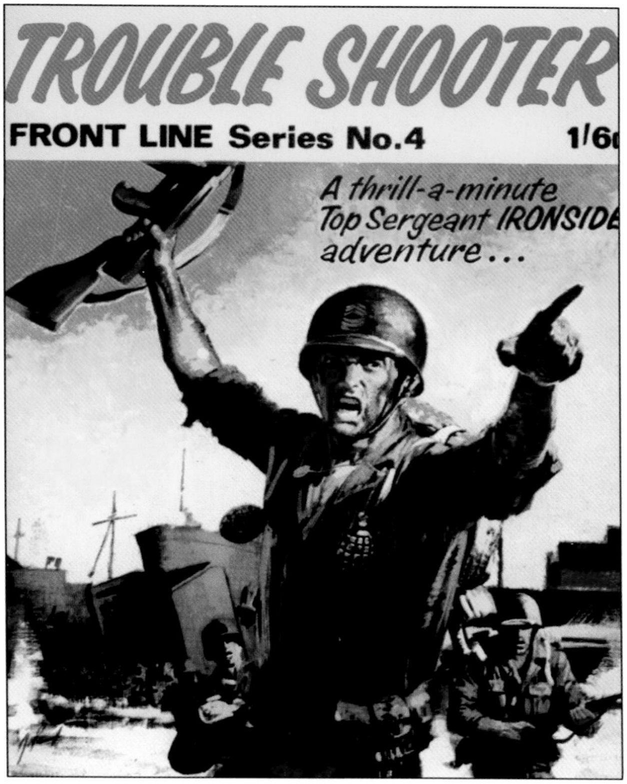
TROUBLE SHOOTER
FRONT LINE Series No.4
1/6d
A thrill-a-minute Top Sergeant IRONSIDE adventure...

Jordi Penalva, Front Line 4, February 1967

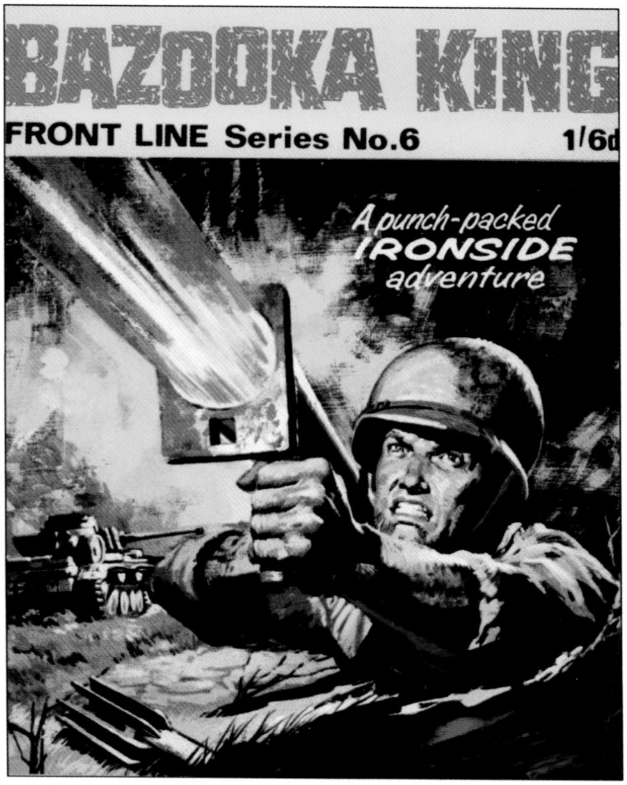
BAZOOKA KING
FRONT LINE Series No.6
1/6d
A punch-packed IRONSIDE adventure

Jordi Penalva, Front Line 6, March 1967

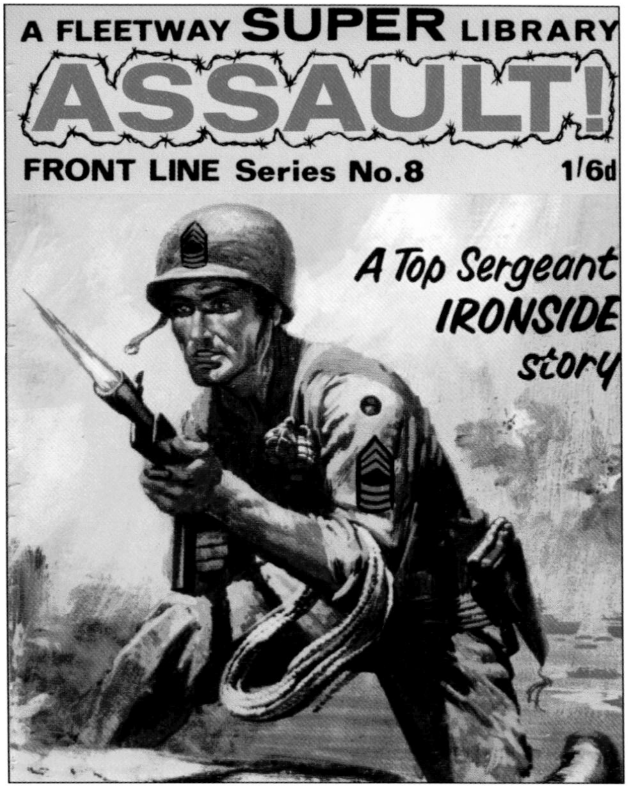
A FLEETWAY SUPER LIBRARY
ASSAULT!
FRONT LINE Series No.8
1/6d
A Top Sergeant IRONSIDE story

Jordi Penalva, Front Line 8, April 1967

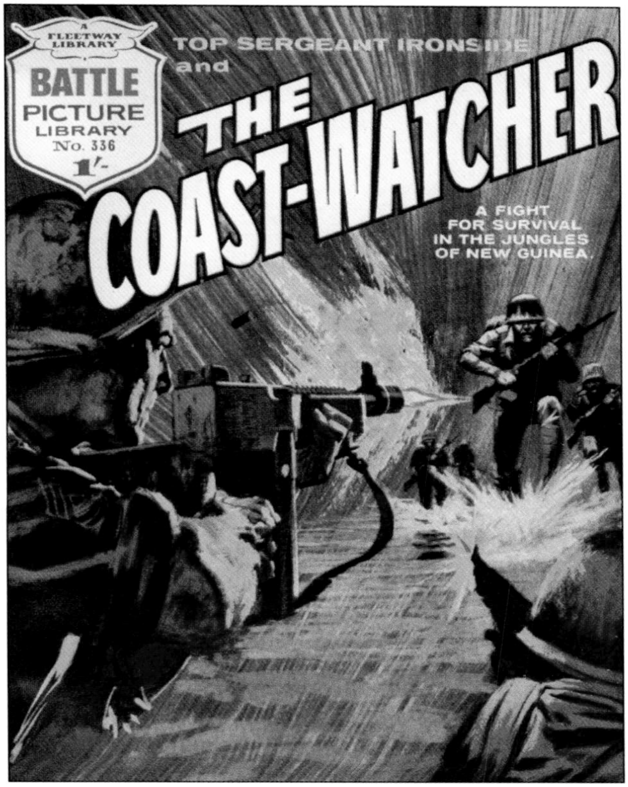
A FLEETWAY LIBRARY
BATTLE PICTURE LIBRARY No. 336
1/-
TOP SERGEANT IRONSIDE and
THE COAST-WATCHER
A FIGHT FOR SURVIVAL IN THE JUNGLES OF NEW GUINEA

Jordi Penalva, Battle 336, February 1968

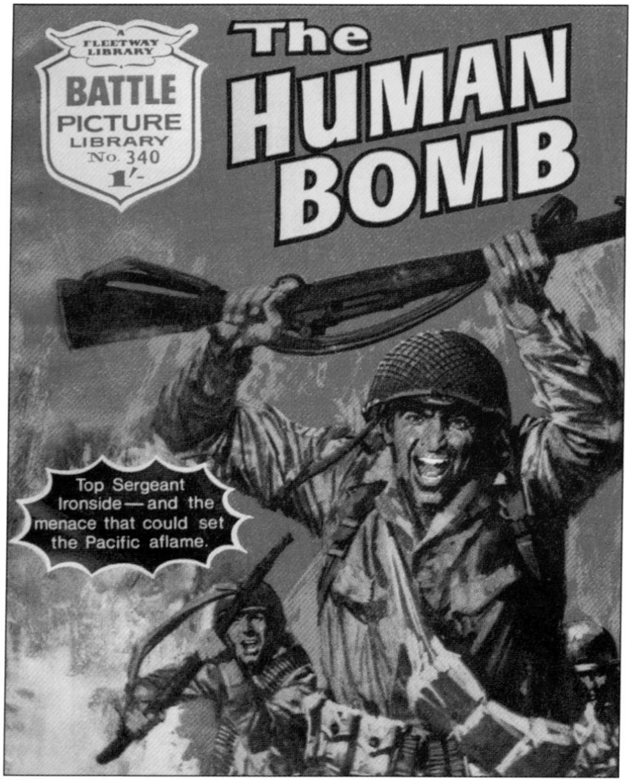
A FLEETWAY LIBRARY
BATTLE PICTURE LIBRARY No. 340 1/-
The HUMAN BOMB
Top Sergeant Ironside—and the menace that could set the Pacific aflame.

Jordi Longaron, Battle 340, March 1968

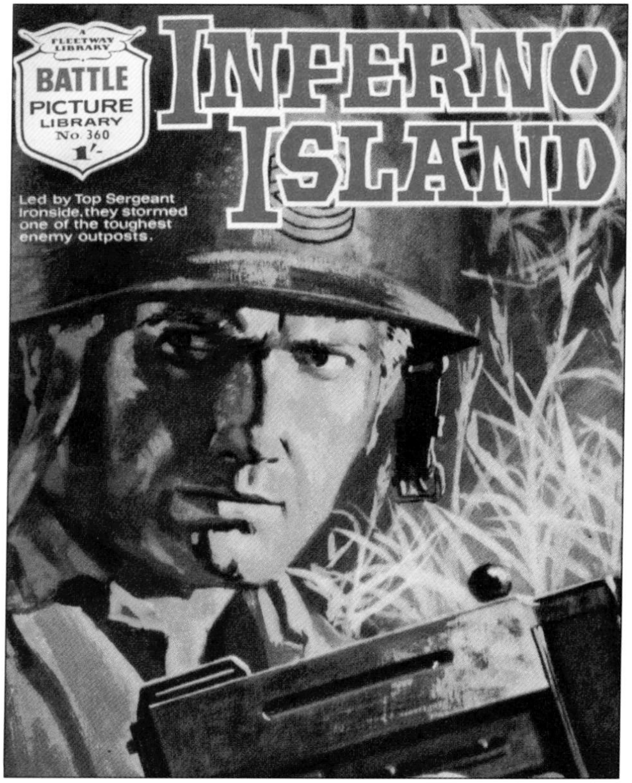
A FLEETWAY LIBRARY
BATTLE PICTURE LIBRARY No 360 1/-
INFERNO ISLAND
Led by Top Sergeant Ironside, they stormed one of the toughest enemy outposts.

Jordi Penalva, Battle 360, August 1968

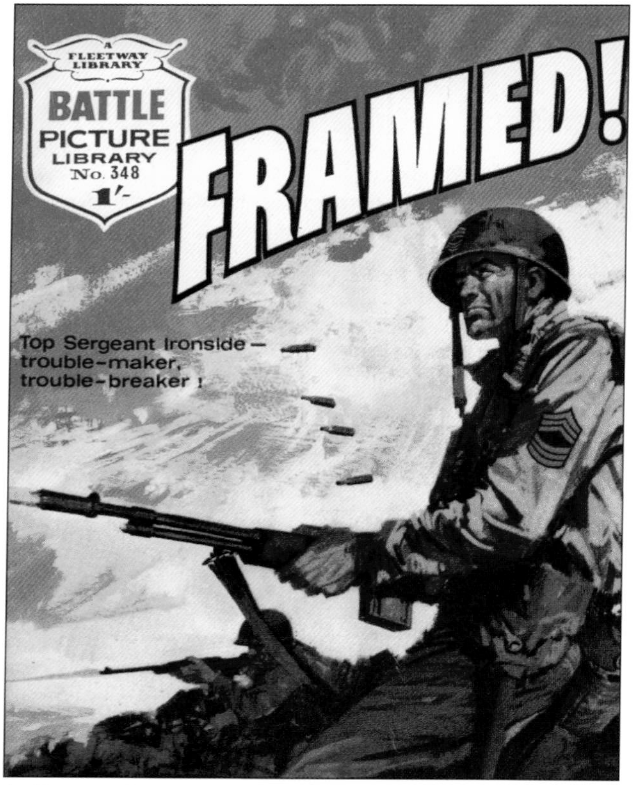
A FLEETWAY LIBRARY
BATTLE PICTURE LIBRARY No. 348 1/-
FRAMED!
Top Sergeant Ironside—trouble-maker, trouble-breaker!

Jordi Longaron, Battle 348, May 1968

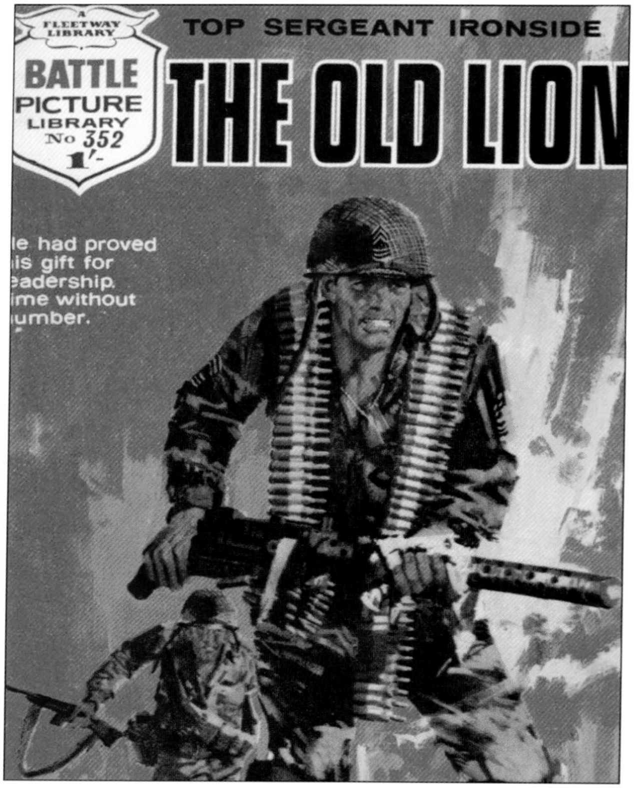
A FLEETWAY LIBRARY
BATTLE PICTURE LIBRARY No 352 1/-
TOP SERGEANT IRONSIDE
THE OLD LION

Jordi Longaron, Battle 352, June 1968

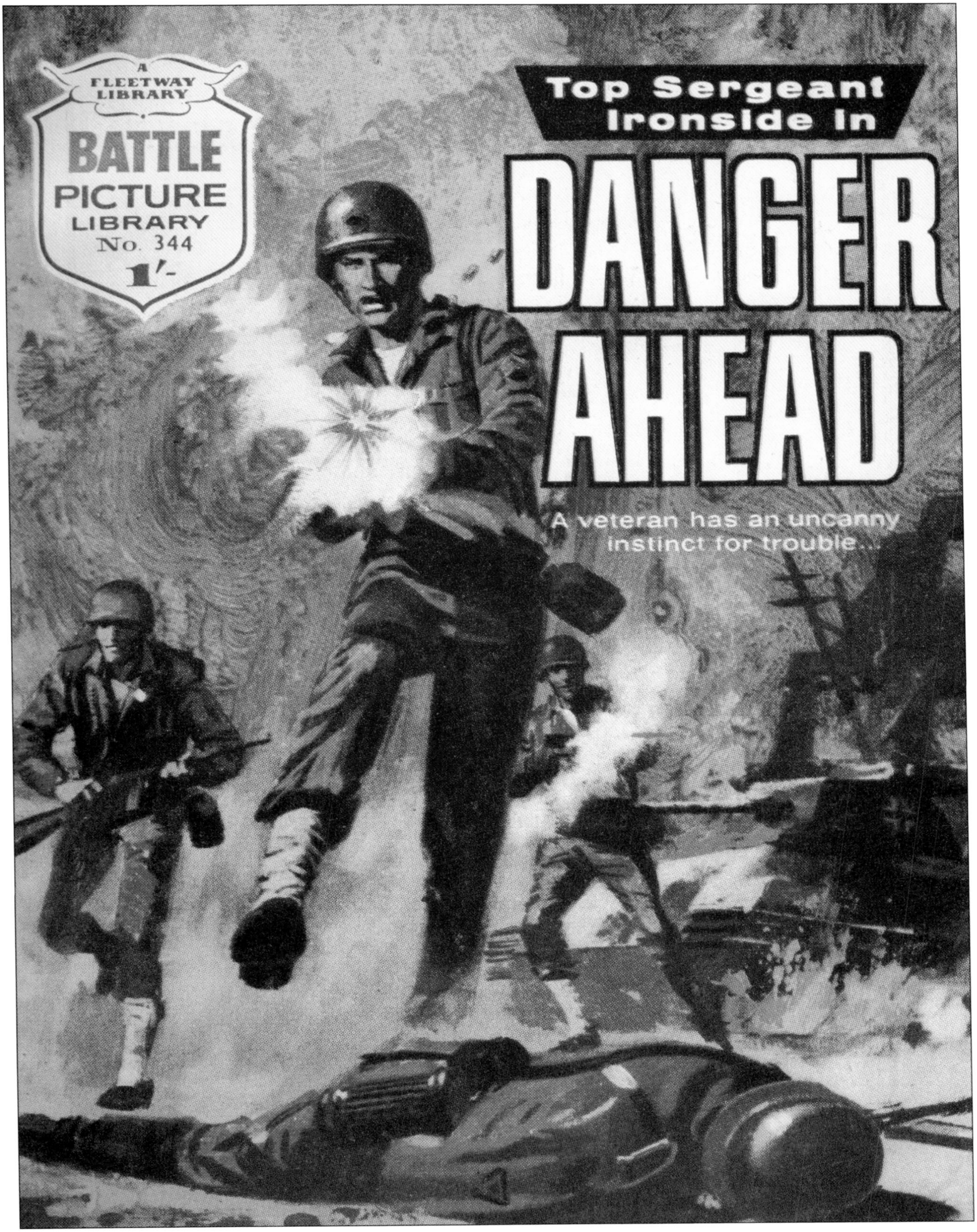
A FLEETWAY LIBRARY
BATTLE PICTURE LIBRARY
No. 344
1/-
Top Sergeant Ironside in
DANGER AHEAD
A veteran has an uncanny instinct for trouble...

Jordi Penalva, Battle 344, April 1968

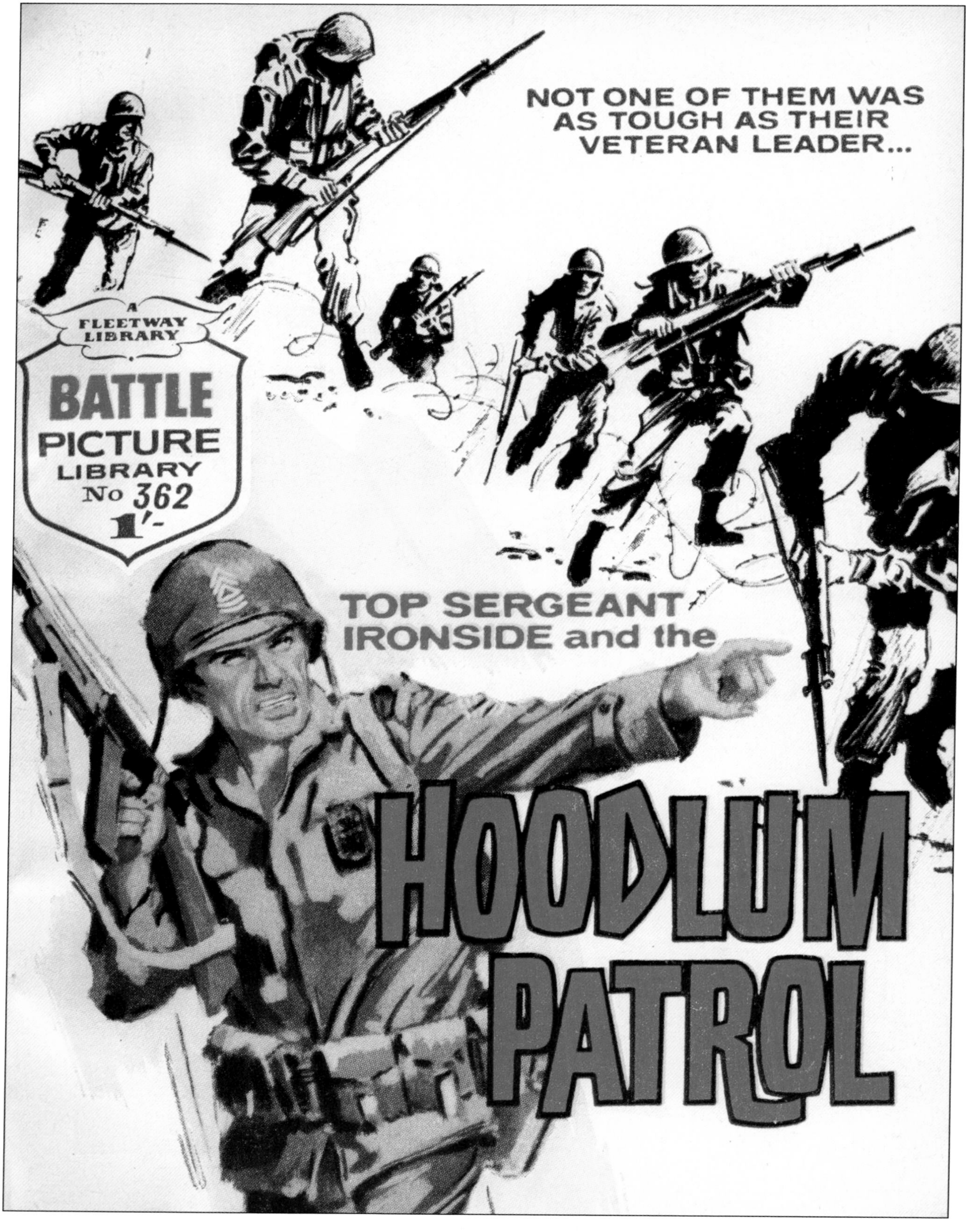
NOT ONE OF THEM WAS AS TOUGH AS THEIR VETERAN LEADER...
A FLEETWAY LIBRARY
BATTLE PICTURE LIBRARY No 362
1/-
TOP SERGEANT IRONSIDE and the
HOODLUM PATROL

Rafael Cortiella, Battle 362, September 1968

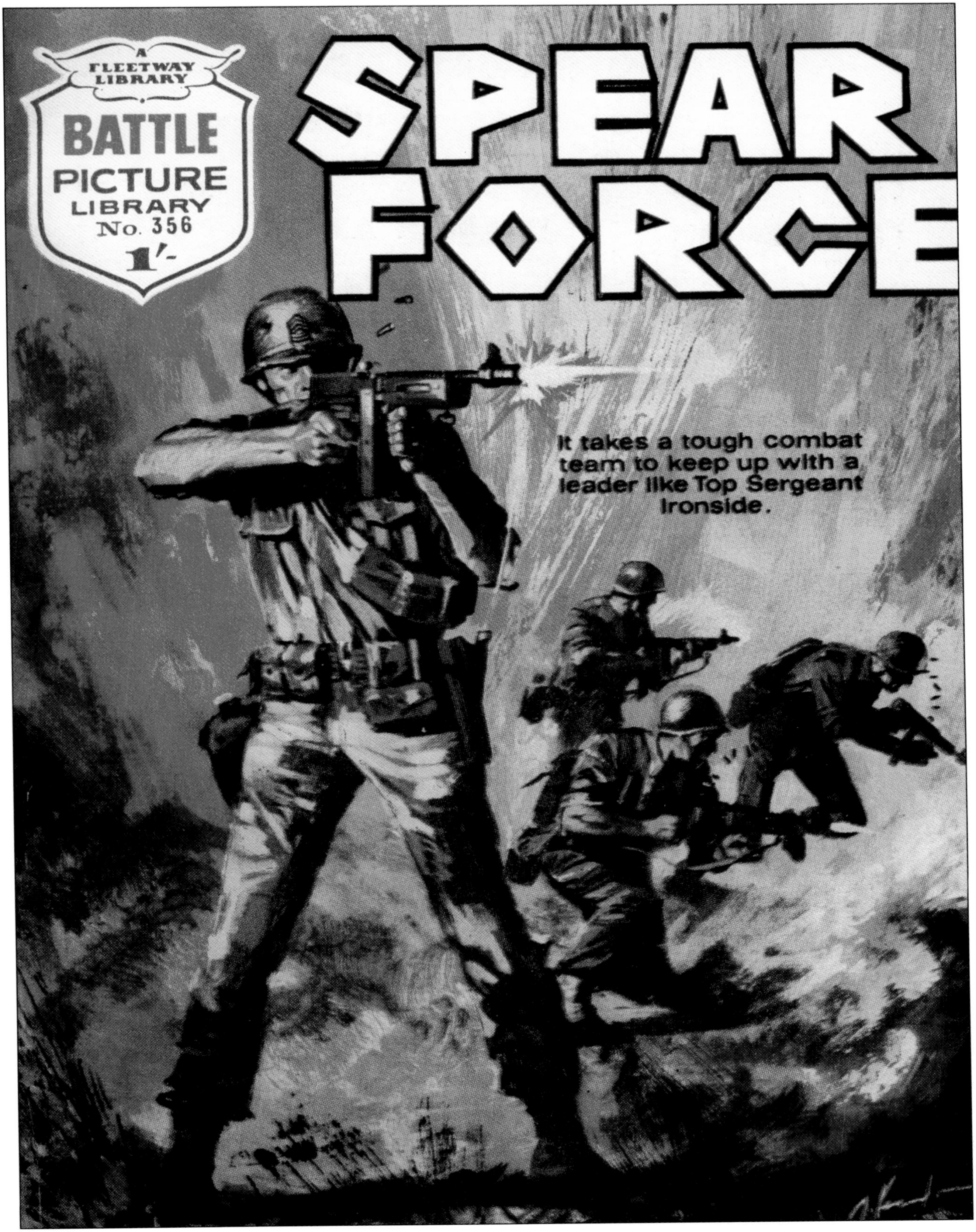
A FLEETWAY LIBRARY
BATTLE
PICTURE
LIBRARY
No. 356
1/-
SPEAR FORCE
It takes a tough combat team to keep up with a leader like Top Sergeant Ironside.

Jordi Penalva, Battle 356, July 1968

Overleaf: Jordi Penalva, Front Line 12, June 1967

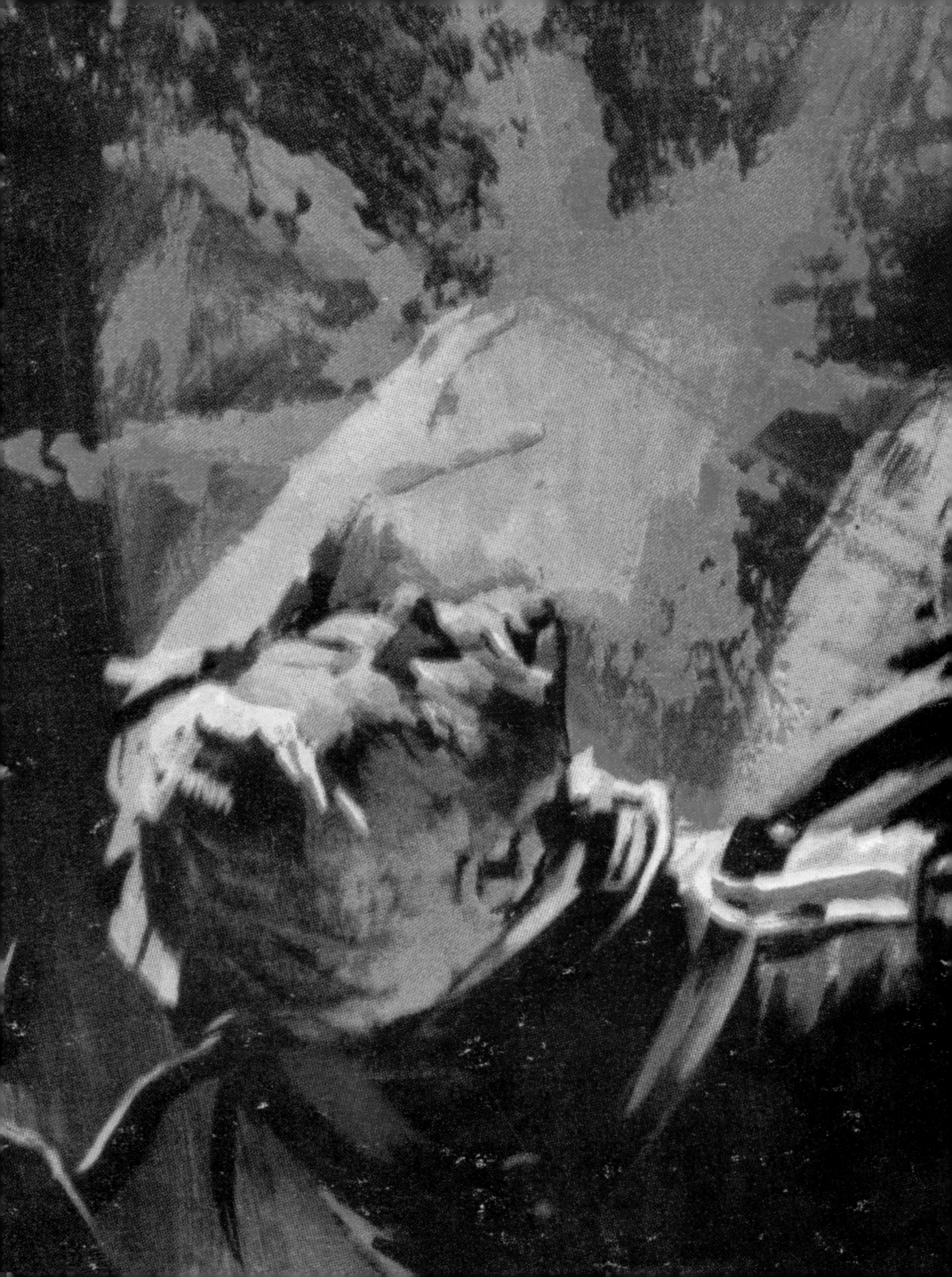

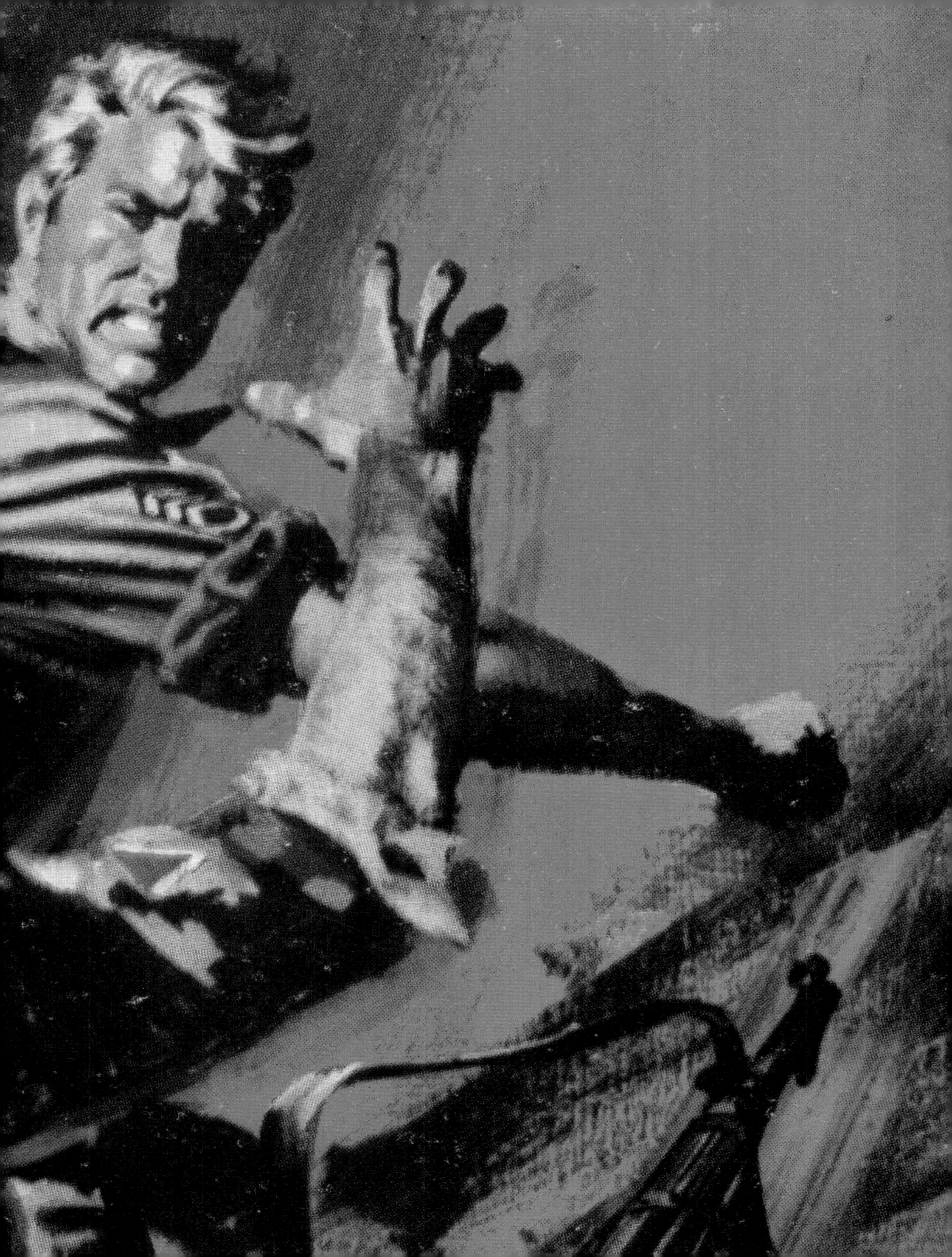

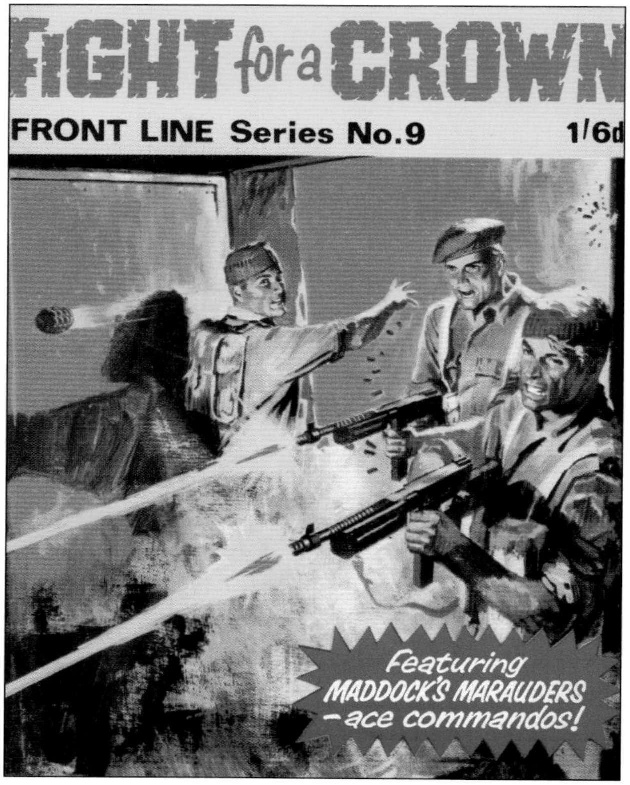
FIGHT for a CROWN
FRONT LINE Series No.9
1/6d
Featuring MADDOCK'S MARAUDERS —ace commandos!

Jordi Penalva, Front Line 9, May 1967

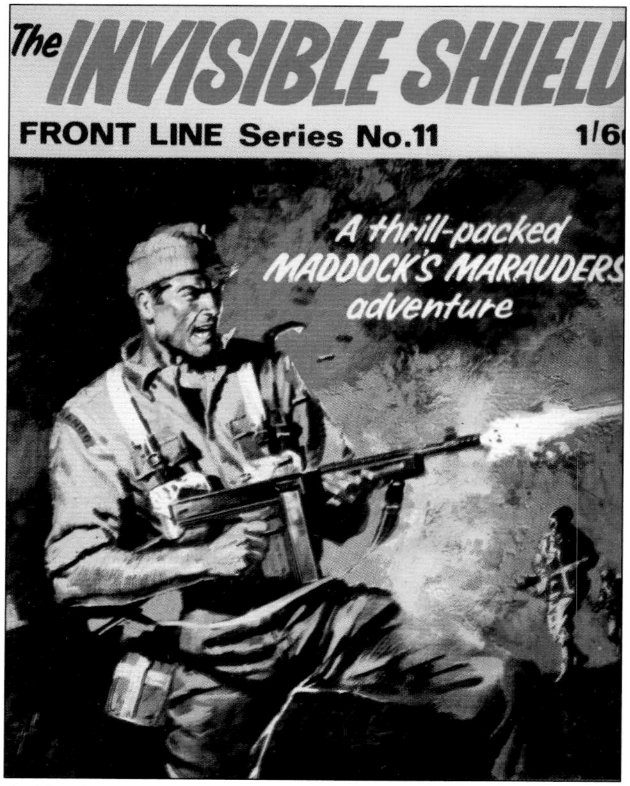
The INVISIBLE SHIELD
FRONT LINE Series No.11
1/6
A thrill-packed MADDOCK'S MARAUDERS adventure

Jordi Penalva, Front Line 11, June 1967

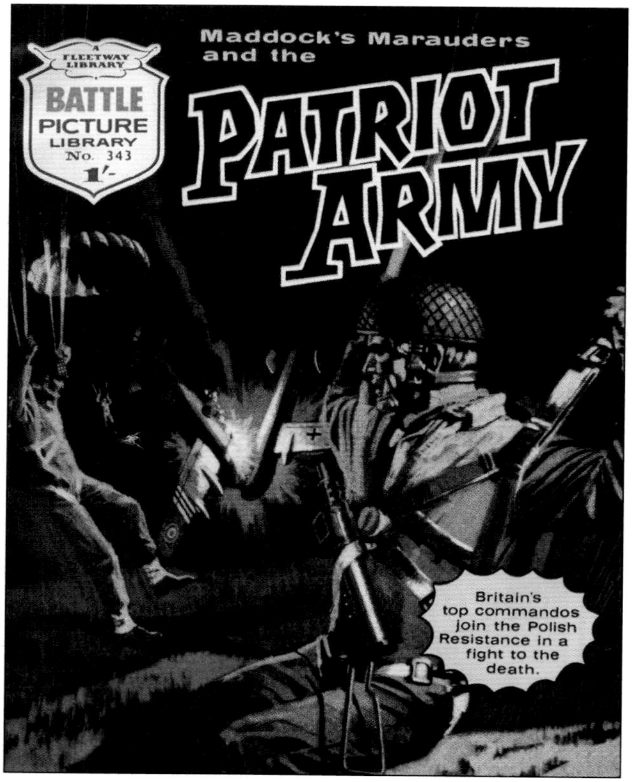
A FLEETWAY LIBRARY
BATTLE PICTURE LIBRARY
No. 343
1/-
Maddock's Marauders and the
PATRIOT ARMY
Britain's top commandos join the Polish Resistance in a fight to the death.

Jordi Penalva, Battle 343, April 1968

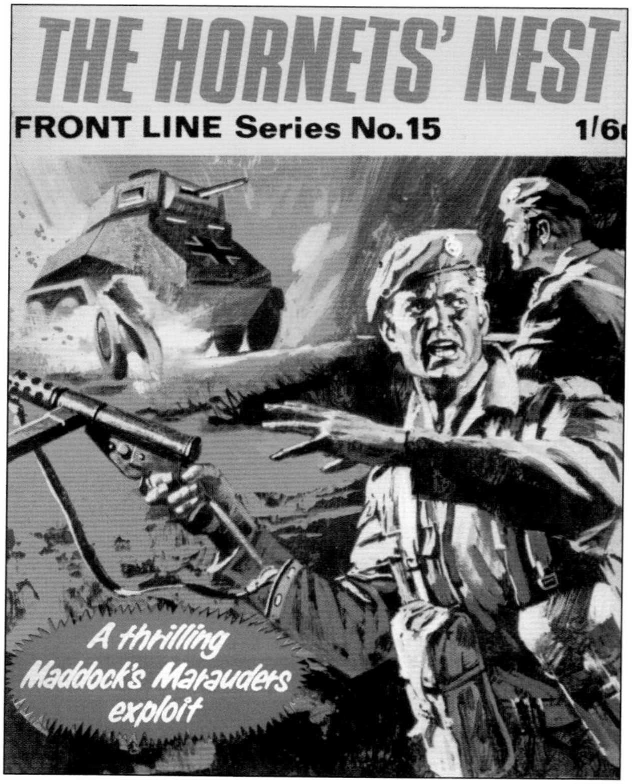
THE HORNETS' NEST
FRONT LINE Series No.15
1/6
A thrilling Maddock's Marauders exploit

Jordi Penalva, Front Line 15, August 1967

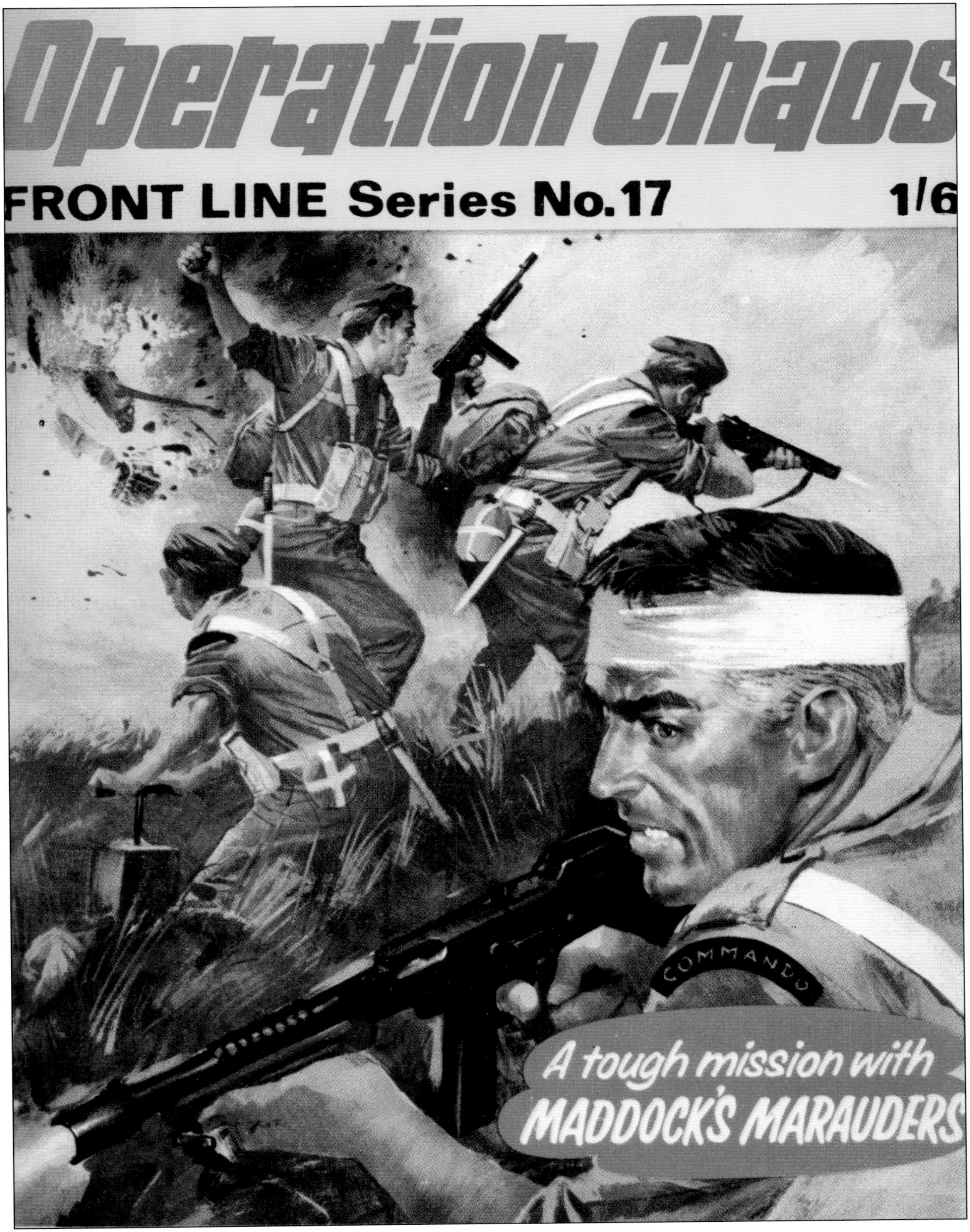
Operation Chaos
FRONT LINE Series No. 17
1/6
COMMANDO
A tough mission with
MADDOCK'S MARAUDERS

Carlo Jacono, Front Line 17, September 1967

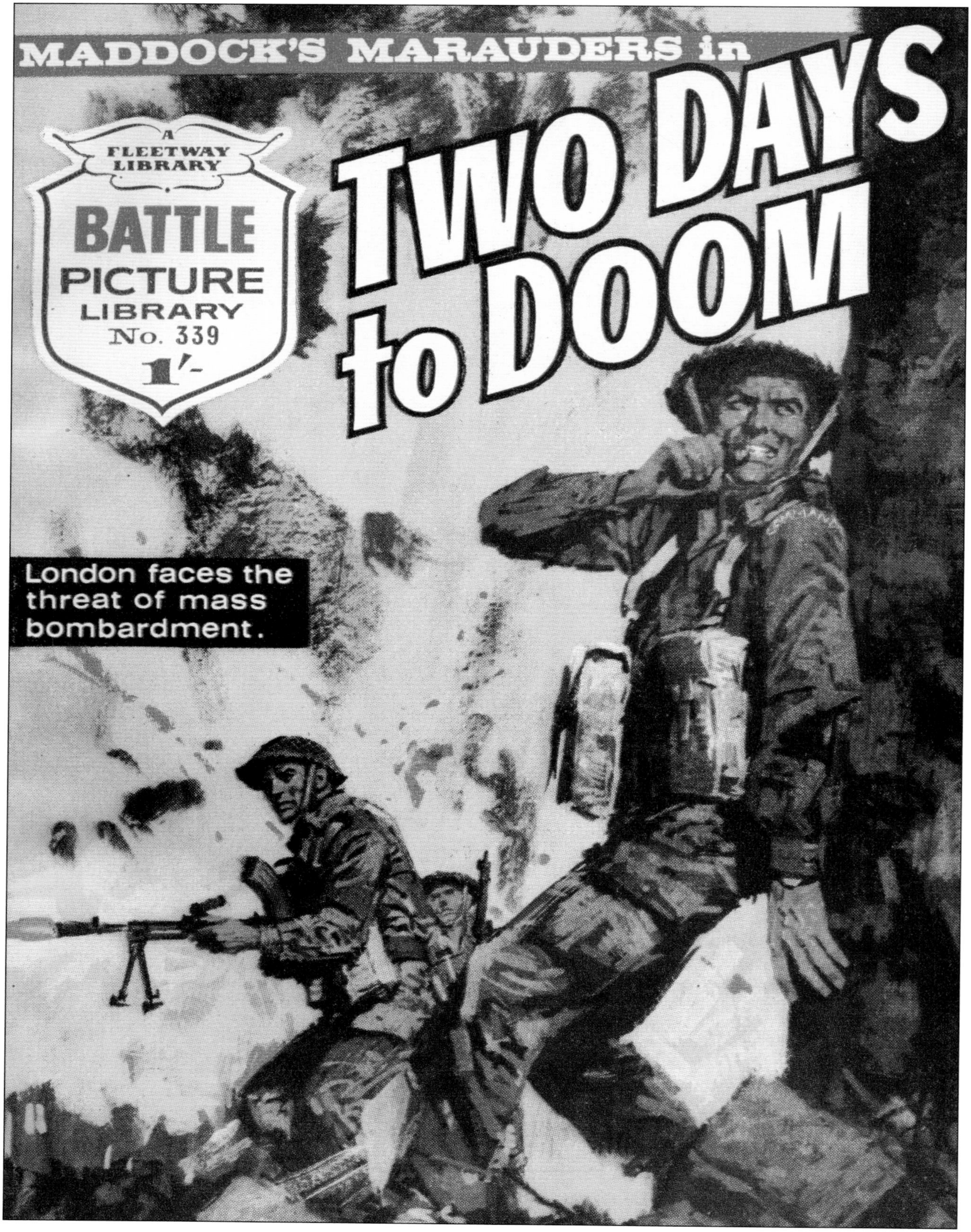
MADDOCK'S MARAUDERS in
A FLEETWAY LIBRARY
BATTLE PICTURE LIBRARY
No. 339
1/-
TWO DAYS to DOOM
London faces the threat of mass bombardment.

Jordi Longaron, Battle 339, March 1968

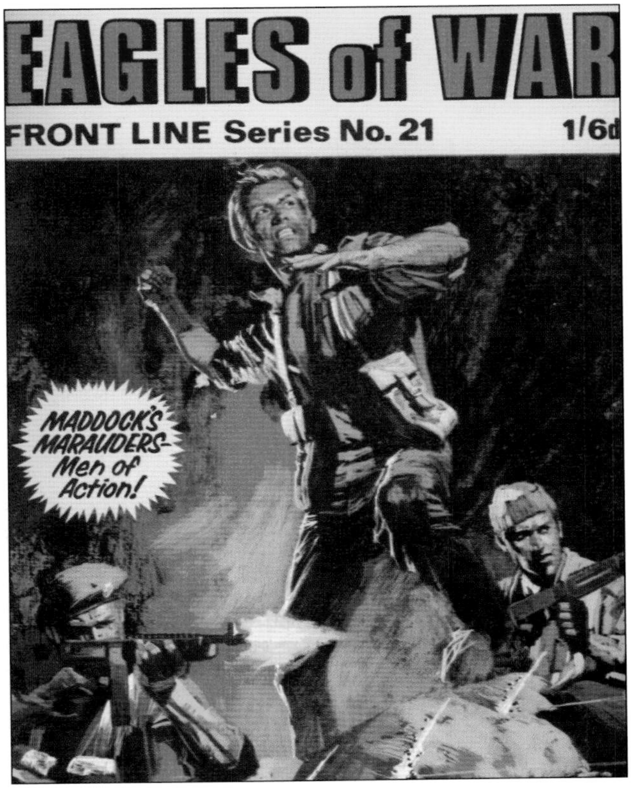
EAGLES of WAR
FRONT LINE Series No. 21
1/6d
MADDOCK'S MARAUDERS- Men of Action!

Jordi Penalva, Front Line 21, November 1967

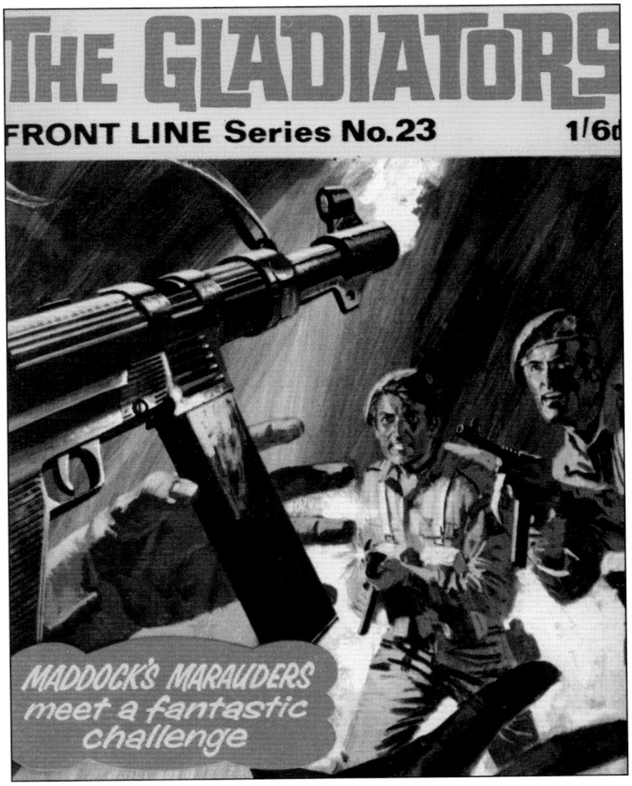
THE GLADIATORS
FRONT LINE Series No.23
1/6d
MADDOCK'S MARAUDERS meet a fantastic challenge

Jordi Penalva, Front Line 23, December 1967

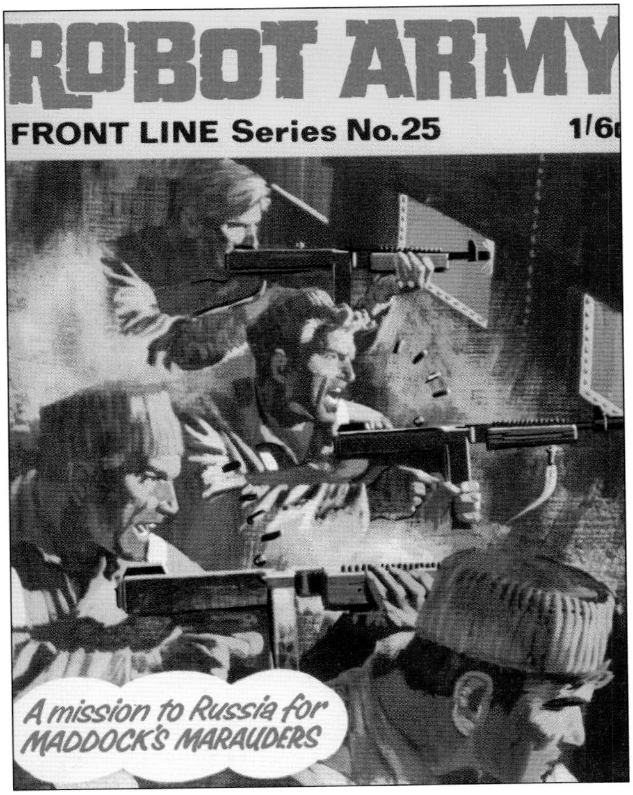
ROBOT ARMY
FRONT LINE Series No.25
1/6d
A mission to Russia for MADDOCK'S MARAUDERS

Jordi Penalva, Front Line 25, January 1968

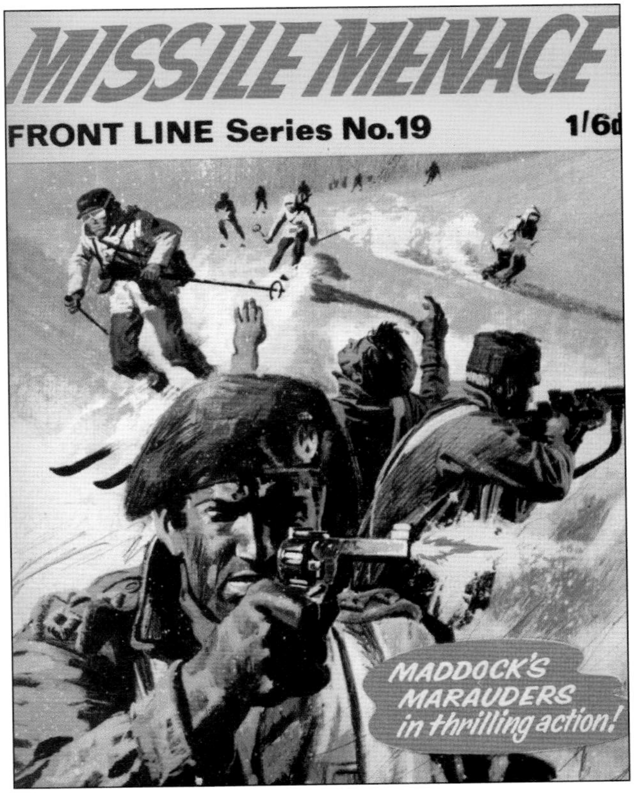
MISSILE MENACE
FRONT LINE Series No.19
1/6d
MADDOCK'S MARAUDERS in thrilling action!

Jordi Penalva, Front Line 19, October 1967

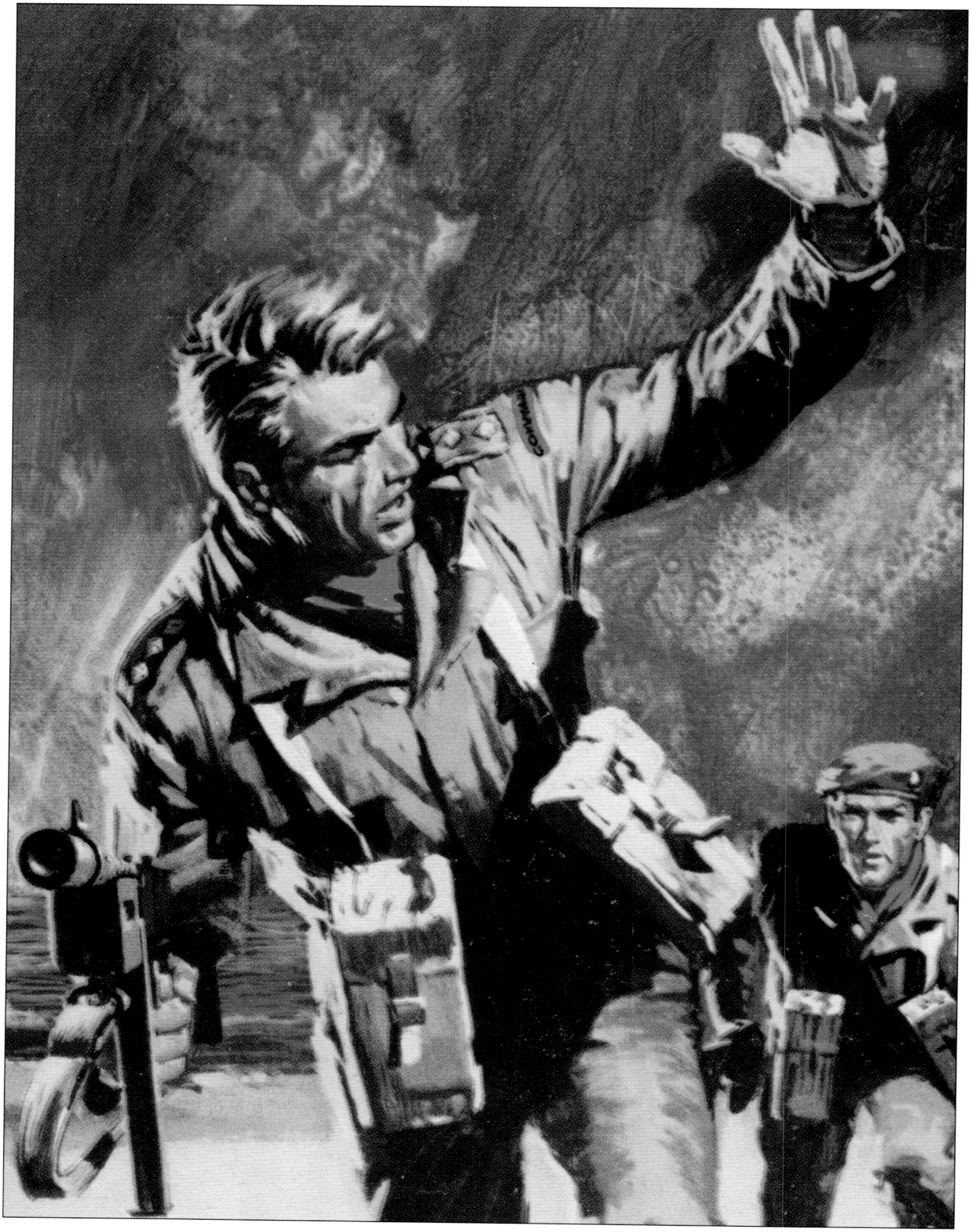

Jordi Penalva, Front Line 1, January 1967

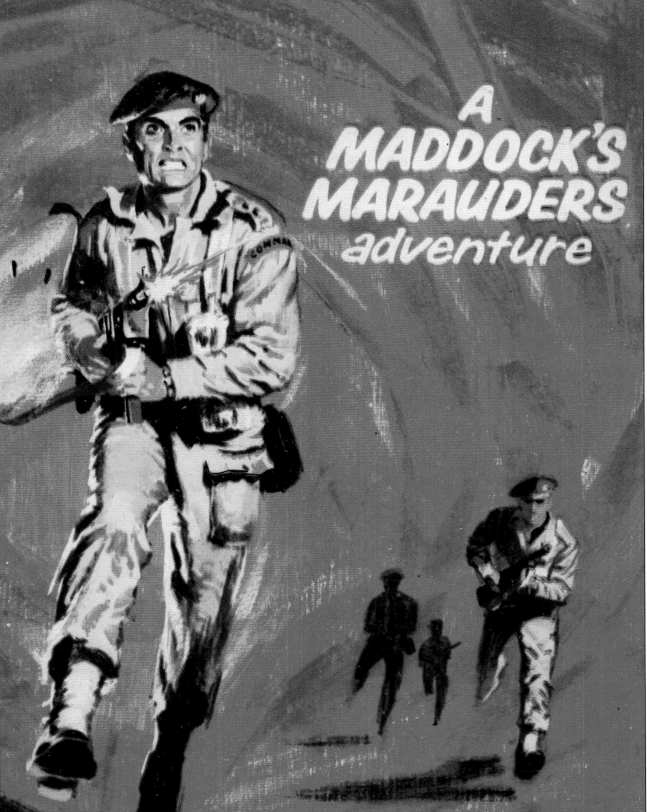

A
MADDOCK'S
MARAUDERS
adventure

Jordi Penalva, Front Line 13, July 1967

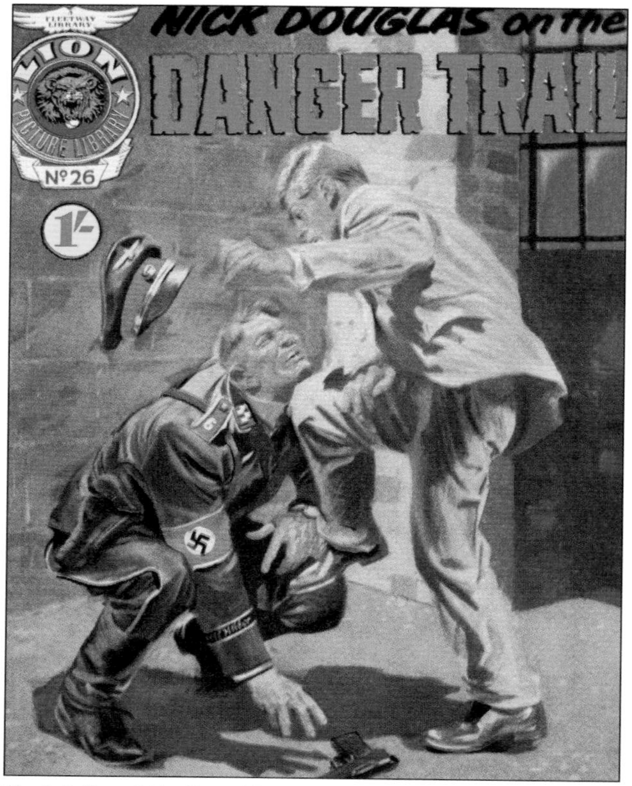
NICK DOUGLAS on the
DANGER TRAIL
LION
PICTURE LIBRARY
Nº26
1/-

Giorgio DeGaspari, Lion Picture Library 26, October 1964

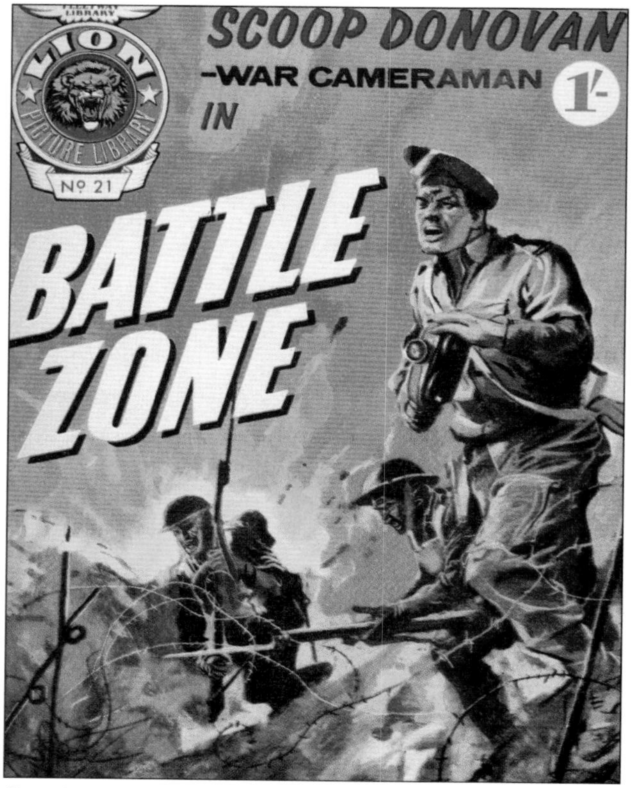
SCOOP DONOVAN
-WAR CAMERAMAN
IN
1/-
LION
PICTURE LIBRARY
Nº 21
BATTLE
ZONE

Giorgio DeGaspari, Lion Picture Library, August 1964

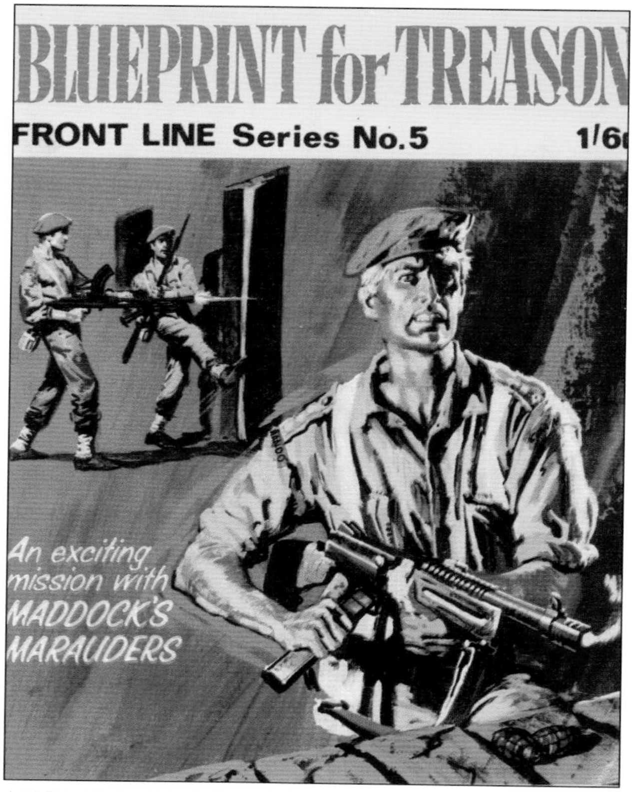
BLUEPRINT for TREASON
FRONT LINE Series No.5
An exciting mission with MADDOCK'S MARAUDERS

Jordi Penalva, Front Line 5, March 1967

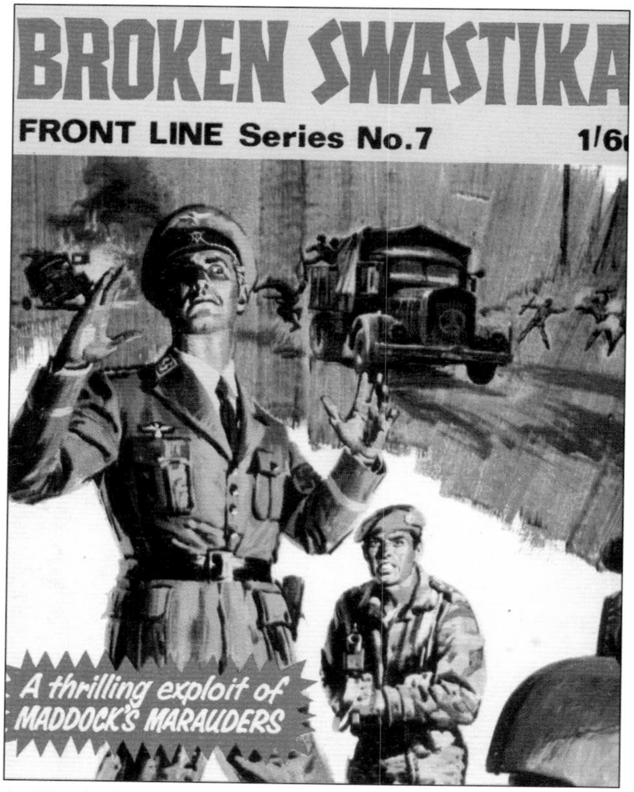
BROKEN SWASTIKA
FRONT LINE Series No.7
A thrilling exploit of MADDOCK'S MARAUDERS

Jordi Penalva, Front Line 7, April 1967

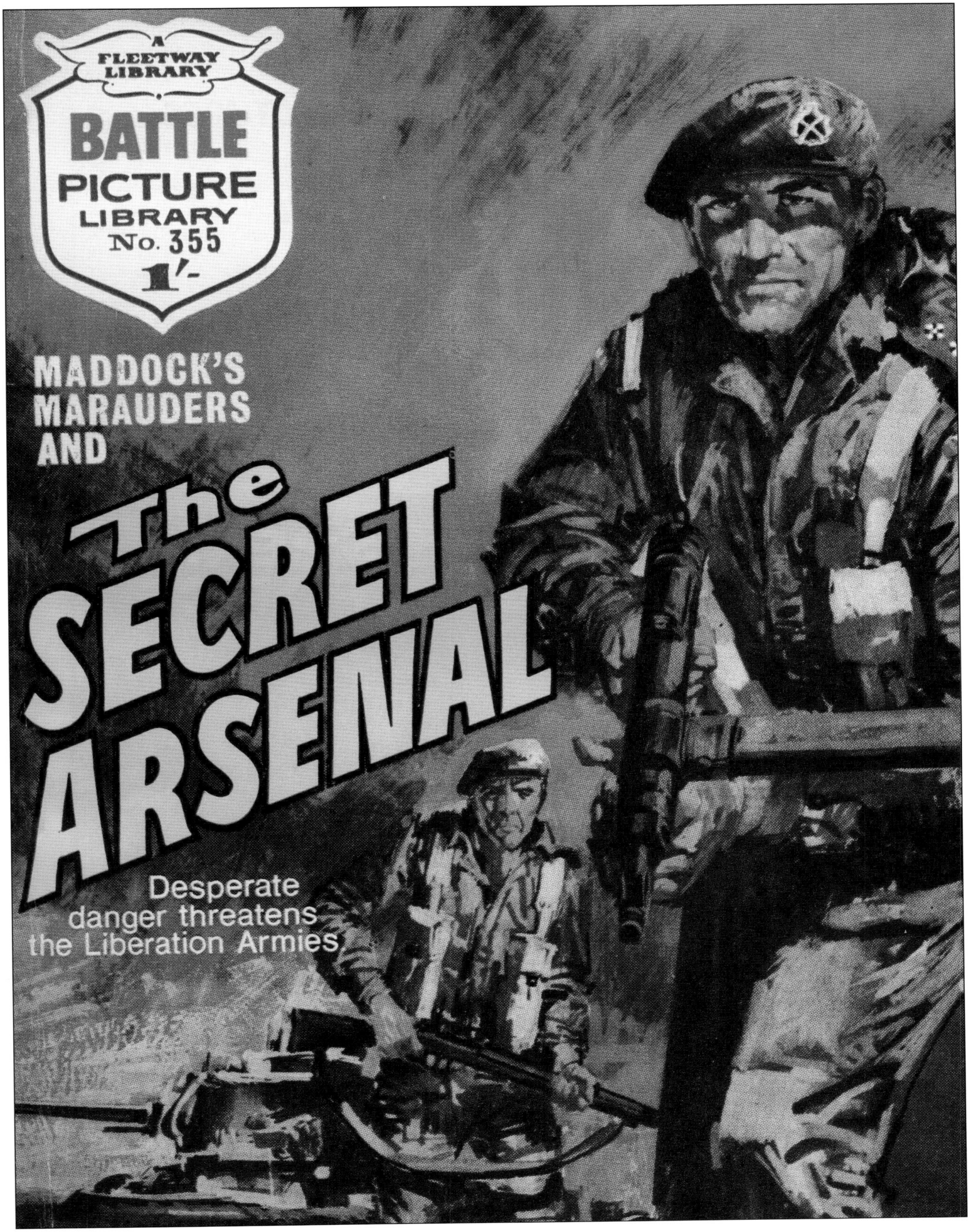
A
FLEETWAY
LIBRARY
BATTLE
PICTURE
LIBRARY
No. 355
1/-
MADDOCK'S
MARAUDERS
AND
The
SECRET
ARSENAL
Desperate
danger threatens
the Liberation Armies

Jordi Longaron, Battle 355, July 1968

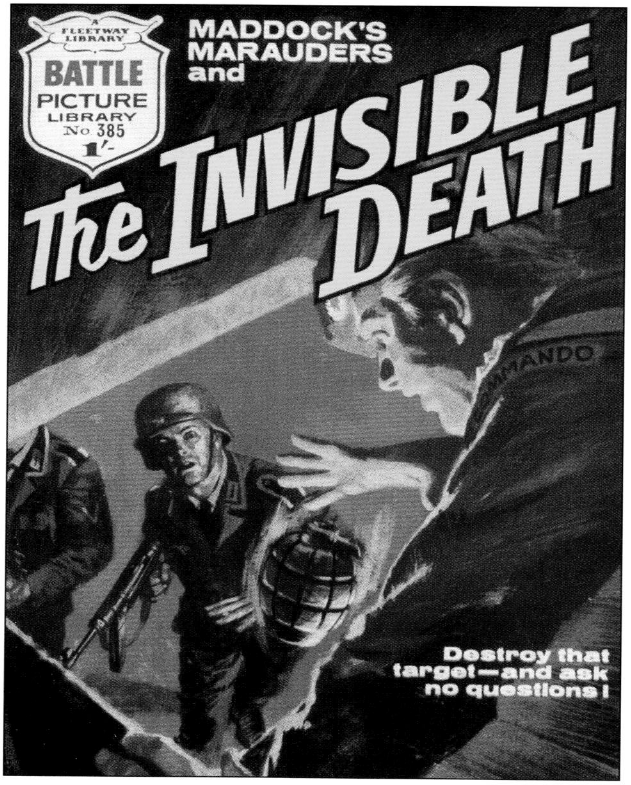
A FLEETWAY LIBRARY
BATTLE
PICTURE
LIBRARY
No 385
1/-
MADDOCK'S
MARAUDERS
and
The INVISIBLE DEATH
COMMANDO
Destroy that
target—and ask
no questions!

Jordi Penalva, Battle 385, March 1969

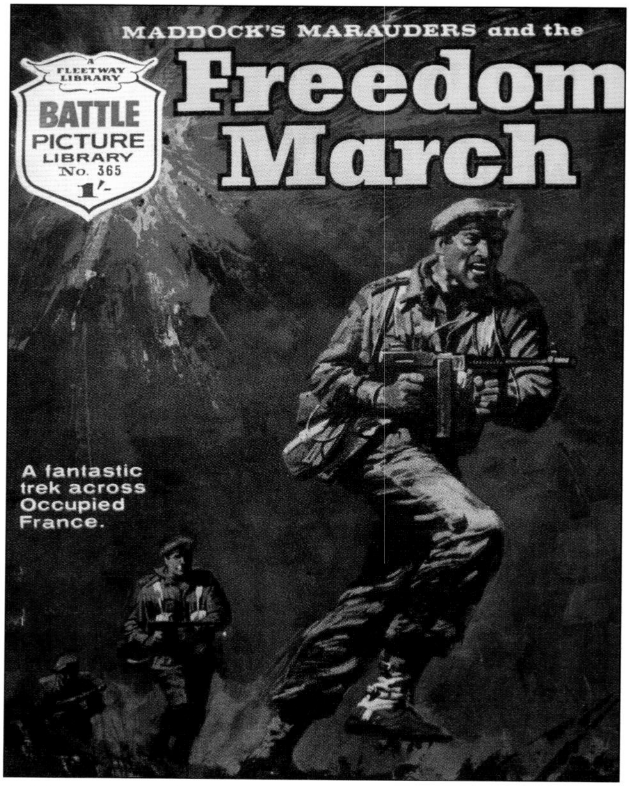
MADDOCK'S MARAUDERS and the
Freedom
March
A FLEETWAY LIBRARY
BATTLE
PICTURE
LIBRARY
No. 365
1/-
A fantastic
trek across
Occupied
France.

Jordi Longaron, Battle 365, October 1968

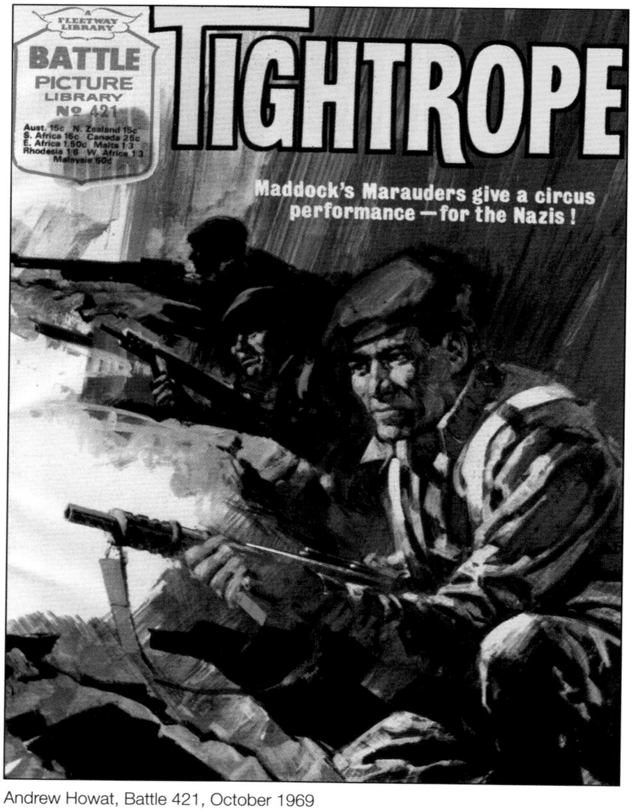
FLEETWAY LIBRARY
BATTLE
PICTURE
LIBRARY
TIGHTROPE
Maddock's Marauders give a circus
performance—for the Nazis!

Andrew Howat, Battle 421, October 1969

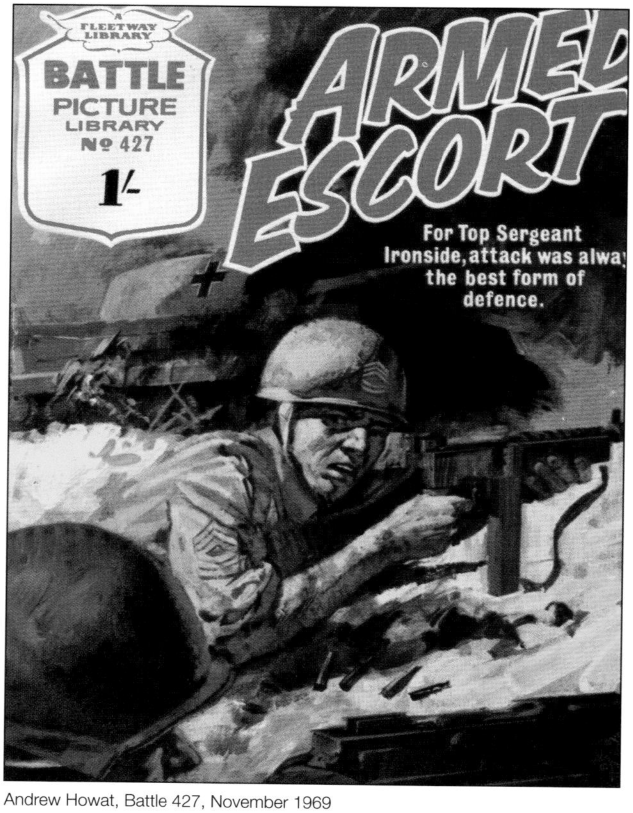
A FLEETWAY LIBRARY
BATTLE
PICTURE
LIBRARY
Nº 427
1/-
ARMED
ESCORT
For Top Sergeant
Ironside, attack was alway
the best form of
defence.

Andrew Howat, Battle 427, November 1969

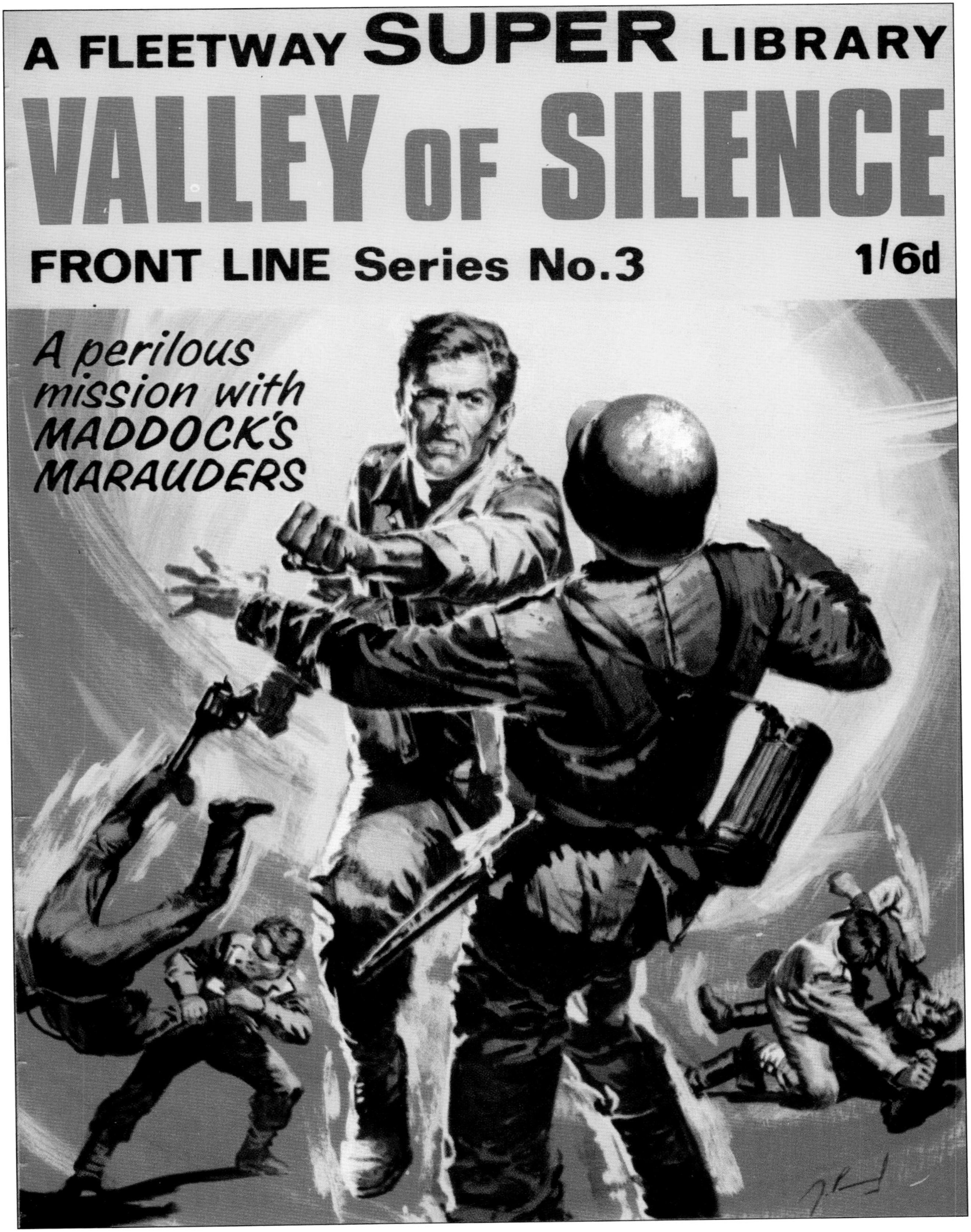
A FLEETWAY SUPER LIBRARY
VALLEY OF SILENCE
FRONT LINE Series No.3
1/6d
A perilous mission with MADDOCK'S MARAUDERS

Jordi Penalva, Front Line 3, February 1967

Front Line
1, 390
2, 378
3, 395
4, 379
5, 392
6, 379
7, 392
8, 379
9, 386
10, 376
11, 386
12, 384-385
13, 391
14, 376
15, 386
16, 376
17, 387
18, 376
19, 389
20, 377
21, 389
22, 378
23, 389
24, 378
25, 389
26, 378

Giant War
unknown, 96

Lion
18, 360
19, 360
21, 392
22, 360
25, 360
26, 392
35, 339

Thriller
250, 122
257, 350
258, 368
261, 351
265, 354
273, 355
274, 369
277, 350
281, 344
285, 344
289, 345
290, 361
293, 346
297, 349
298, 366
301, 349
305, 349
306, 367
307, 340
309, 349
310, 369

311, 338
313, 358
314, 369
318, 341
320, 373
321, 352
322, 342
324. 373
325, 352
326, 342
328, 373
329, 353
330, 342
332, 374
333, 353
334, 342
336, 370
337, 353
340, 371
341, 353
342, 343
345, 355
346, 341
348, 369
349, 355
350, 341
351, 338
353, 372
353, 355
354, 186
356, 373
357, 359
358, 341
360, 372
361, 352
364, 372
365, 352
368, 370
369. 356
370, 343
372, 370
373, 356
374, 339
376, 370
377, 356
378, 338
380, 372
381, 356
382, 343
385, 350
386, 343
388, 375
389, 357
416, 366
417, 346
420, 362
421, 346
425, 347
428, 366
429, 350
432, 366
433, 346

436, 365
437, 348
440, 364
441, 344
448, 363
449, 344

War
9, 117
21, 69
24, 213
57, 302
61, 302
65, 305
25, 275
26, 69
28, 38
29, 313
31, 318
33, 84
34, 99
36, 76
38, 76
39, 193
40, 212
41, 113
42, 326
45, 288
46, 113
48, 118
49, 226
51, 76
55, 77
58, 121
62, 45
63, 94-95
67, 266
71, 82-83
75, 78
78, 118
79, 305
83, 42
84, 199
91, 43
92, 110
94, 59
101, 116
115, 156
121, 40
123, 206
126, 23
128, 34
132, 245
134, 73
146, 44
147, 286-287
157, 70
158, 31
164, 119
172, 333
174, 130
178, 43

187, 153
191, 48
195, 48
197, 48
198, 74
204, 313
207, 140
209, 313
222, 290
229, 294
230, 111
243, 327
256, 294
282, 284
285, 155
293, 332
296, 80
298, 163
300, 99
302, 142
317, 26
318, 143
326, 58
335, 305
354, 135
367, 65
369, 290
371, 148
391, 280
392, 105
393, 333
397, 63
398, 63
399, 63
400, 127
401, 113
402, 105
403, 68
406, 68
407, 282
408, 68
409, 272
410, 300
411, 272
412, 272
417, 283
421, 56
424, 327
426, 59
429, 90
431, 76
470, 110
471, 110
474, 16
475, 146
480, 327
481, 126
482, 19
483, 118
488, 278, 310
491, 87
493, 56

496, 317
499, 24
502, 16
503, 16
504, 302
506, 313
507, 122
508, 278
509, 65
515, 69
517, 89
518, 78
520, 73
522, 281
524, 122
525, 174
526, 86
530, 122
531, 310
533, 127
534, 86
535, 79
536, 87
537, 87
543, 285
544, 75
555, 154
560, 158
562, 77
566, 278
585, 131
589, 166
599, 157
604, 158
614, 248
615, 139
620, 157
621, 310
622, 46
634, 225
650, 200
656, 314-315
664, 293
688, 57
673, 306-307
721, 154
728, 312
729, 271
745, 132-133
768, 154
769, 160-161
785, 57
801, 292
824, 158
825, 324
874, 65
913, 274
921, 242
929, 308
945, 152
970, 150-151
1010, 70

1011, 77
1021, 57
1030, 57
1075, 18
1086, 276
1147, 67
1169, 148 or
165
1183, 138
1195, 250
1206, 154
1243, 106-107
1303, 114-115
1363, 18
1374, 279
1386, 138
1410, 303
1411, 311
1421, 268-269
1458, 65
1506, 56
1507, 56
1518, 163
1546, 66
1578, 318
1579, 202-203
1602, 141
1638, 285
1714, 70
1782, 167
1798, 285
1819, 138
1848, 149
1860, 310
1926, 324
1957, 232
1962, 298-299
1967, 18
1968, 294
1972, 278
1974, 255
1993. 77
2019, 221
2034, 140
2036, 77
2073, 251
2075, 267
2081, 267
2086, 18
2088, 140
2090, 139

War at Sea
9, 330
35, 318

War Holiday Special
1972, 180

Index to COVER ARTISTS

Index to COVER TITLES

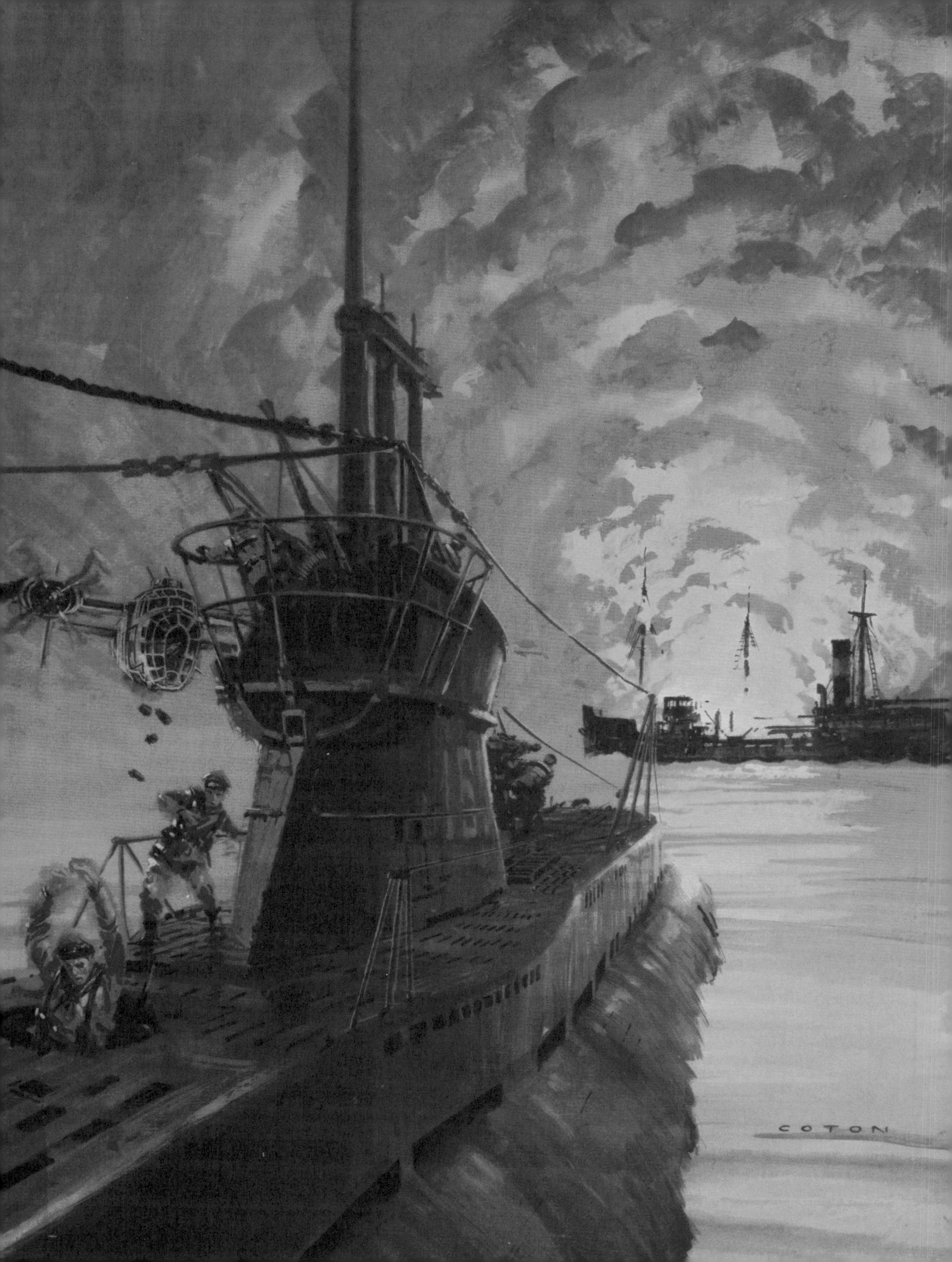
COTON